Academic American Encyclopedia

Academic American Encyclopedia

Grolier Incorporated

Danbury, Connecticut

Library of Congress Cataloging in Publication Data
Main entry under title:

Academic American encyclopedia.

   Includes bibliographies and index.
   Summary: A twenty-one volume encyclopedia with 32,000
entries and more than 16,000 illustrations.
   1. Encyclopedias and dictionaries. [1. Encyclopedias and
dictionaries] I. Grolier Incorporated.
AE5.A23   1985   031   84-215128
ISBN 0-7172-2008-7   (set)

Preface

The *Academic American Encyclopedia,* first published in 1980, is an entirely new reference work, the only completely new general encyclopedia in more than a decade. More than 100 employees, 2,250 scholars and other authorities, plus another 150 consultants, advisors, contributing editors, cartographers, photographers, and illustrators worked for several years to create the 9 million words, 32,000 entries, and more than 16,000 illustrations that select, describe, organize, structure, and interpret a representative portion of the world's corpus of knowledge in a manner that is useful to our readers. For this, the sixth edition, all of the encyclopedia's contents have been thoroughly reviewed and updated as necessary to reflect the most recent developments.

GOALS

The fundamental goal of an encyclopedia is to make accessible to a particular audience definitive information on the broadest possible range of subjects. Depending upon the sophistication and academic preparation of that audience, an encyclopedia should furnish basic information, outline issues and controversies, report judgments, assess importance, and trace influences. Supplemented by creative illustrations and maps, such a work should also reinforce learning, enlarge understanding, and stimulate the imagination. These goals have guided the preparation of this encyclopedia.

PURPOSE

The *Academic American Encyclopedia* has been created for students in junior high school, high school, or college and for the inquisitive adult. Research has determined that such an audience wants an encyclopedia to fulfill four clearly defined objectives:

(1) Students and adults expect an encyclopedia to provide quick access to definitive factual information.

(2) Both audiences also want to find a readily intelligible general overview of a subject that does not compel the reader to grasp intricate subtleties or wade through drawn-out historical analysis.

(3) Among better students, and those who know how to approach a term paper, an encyclopedia is regarded as an excellent starting place for further research if it isolates key concepts, outlines the structure of the subject, and directs the reader to more specialized primary and secondary sources.

(4) Readers at all levels expect a reference work to help them visualize or recognize people, places, objects, and processes by means of maps, photographs, and drawings, many of which should be in full color.

In addition to these objectives, the best reference works today are expected to be comprehensive, current, authoritative, objective, and easy to use.

COMPREHENSIVENESS

A comprehensive general encyclopedia must provide basic information for the nonspecialist reader, coverage of all significant aspects of a subject, and sufficient information placed in a historical or interpretative context.

A comprehensive encyclopedia will contain broad coverage of contemporary events, popular culture, international affairs, and current technology. There must be enough information to take the reader beyond what he or she already knows; dictionary-type definitions will normally be insufficient. Articles should include not only the most interesting or controversial, but all relevant aspects of a topic. Thus the article BRAINWASHING cannot confine itself to that variety practiced in the 1950s by the Chinese Communists. No subject should be excluded on grounds of political or religious belief, social or legal disapproval, or moral prejudice. Unpopular—even notorious—figures and ideas are impartially and systematically discussed. While recognizing a need to be topical, our editors are aware that much contemporary interest is transient, and they have tried to achieve a balance between the timely and the timeless.

The content of the *Academic American Encyclopedia* is not narrowly focused on the United States and its perspectives; articles on ALCOHOL CONSUMPTION, AGRICULTURAL EDUCATION, and LANDSCAPE ARCHITECTURE, for example, grant appropriate recognition to the diversity of practice throughout the world. A sympathetic awareness of non-Western cultures and alternative life-styles, however, need not interfere with an appreciation that a fuller explication of roots and traditions of our audience's dominant culture is appropriate.

The list of entries (and their lengths) reflects the curriculum of American schools and universities, which is to say that there will be few items in any school or college textbook not found as either a subject entry or an index entry in this encyclopedia. Thus science fiction and the literature of American minorities are included not simply because they are artifacts of the times, but because both are currently studied in secondary-school and university programs. This orientation to the curriculum has still left ample space for a myriad of topics of contemporary interest—CLASS ACTION, the history of the MIDDLE EAST, the MX MISSILE, PUBLIC RELATIONS, the SHROUD OF TURIN, and WOMEN IN SOCIETY.

The basic allocation of space among disciplines is as follows:

Humanities and the arts	36 percent

art, architecture, sculpture
history
literature and linguistics
music, theater, dance
religion and philosophy

Science and technology	35 percent

astronomy
chemistry
earth science
life science
mathematics
physics
technology

Social science	14 percent

anthropology and archaeology
business and economics
education
government, politics, and law
psychology
sociology

Geography	13 percent
Sports and contemporary life	2 percent

Thirty-five percent of the entries are biographical, although the percentage of words is much less. The encyclopedia was designed to be comprehensive but not exhaustive; the article CHINA is not book length but furnishes an overview of the physical geography, economy, government, peoples, and educational system. Separate articles are included on Chinese history, archaeology, art and architecture, language, literature, medicine, music, and universities. Readers can therefore seek specific information within the total coverage of Chinese history, peoples, and culture.

CURRENCY

A current encyclopedia must have more than up-to-date information on population, planetary probes, the newest Nobel laureates, and the latest speculations about the origins of the universe. It should also include biographies in the performing arts and popular culture, as well as in the more academic fields. Current biographies are often a highly congenial means of investigating social phenomena or scientific theory. The general reader who inquires into contemporary theories of human behavior and anthropology may well begin by reading about B. F. Skinner and Claude Lévi-Strauss.

All population statistics in these volumes reflect recent census figures or official estimates. The maps and city plans are the most up-to-date of any encyclopedia and reflect current urbanization, new highways and airports, and so on.

The *Academic American Encyclopedia* is revised each year, using the latest computer technology. It is also updated by means of a yearbook, issued annually, that covers the events and developments of the preceding year.

AUTHORITY

The authority of a reference work is evident in the credentials of the people responsible for creating it and, within the articles themselves, in the carefully qualified judgments and an explanatory style that retains the subtlety of a subject while communicating its essence to the nonspecialist. More than 90 percent of the entries have been written by outside scholars and authorities, and 75 percent of the entries are signed. The 2,250 authorities, from all over the world, were selected to write for this encyclopedia on the basis of their specific knowledge and expertise in a particular subject.

The Advisory Board of Editors, consisting of senior scholars and academicians, was involved at virtually every stage, from preparation of the list of entries and the recruitment of other scholars to write for the encyclopedia, to the review of some of the basic or controversial articles.

Many of our editors have advanced degrees, and some are published scholars in their own right. Most have experience on one or more of the major general or technical encyclopedias published in the United States and Europe. A large team of research editors— all specialists in their field—verified every fact, inference, and conclusion against primary and other authoritative sources in several of the world's largest libraries (Princeton, Columbia, New York, and Rutgers universities, as well as the New York Public Library). After this quality-control effort, edited copy had to clear several layers of senior editorial review before it was returned to the author for approval. Every article in the *Academic American Encyclopedia* has been subjected to multiple review to assure objectivity, balance, and accuracy.

OBJECTIVITY

If an encyclopedia is to be reliable, the facts and inferences must be accurate and reflect current scholarship. Scholars may differ among themselves even on questions that do not involve social policy. The aim of the *Academic American Encyclopedia* is to reflect those differences and to consider alternative theories or interpretation as well as opposing points of view, for example, on ABORTION, CENSORSHIP, and INTELLIGENCE. Even though most articles carry the signature of a respected authority in the field, an article cannot represent only a personal point of view, and certainly, large-scale controversies on such things as PREHISTORIC HUMANS, SOCIOBIOLOGY, and STUDENT MOVEMENTS require a balanced treatment that, instead of avoiding all judgments, seeks to incorporate multiple perspectives and to tell who supports what position and why.

A concerted effort has been made to produce an encyclopedia free of sexist language and attitudes, although that task is especially difficult in certain articles in philosophy and religion, where writers before the 20th century commonly used "man" in both a generic and a literal sense.

EASE OF USE

Ease of use means two things: the reader can find what he or she is looking for quickly, and once found, the material can be understood. The *Academic American Encyclopedia* has been designed, written, and edited with both objectives in mind.

The arrangement of entries is alphabetical rather than by topic, and cross-references abound, so if the entry is not where the reader looks first, there is generally a "see" reference that indicates where the subject is covered. The *Academic American Encyclopedia* is a short-entry encyclopedia, with more than half the content in articles of fewer than 500 words in length. Many of the longer articles are further subdivided by smaller boldface topic headings ("history," "people," "economy").

The text of the articles has been carefully edited to be readable; foreign words, abbreviations, detailed etymology, and specialized jargon have been avoided. Technical terms generally are defined in the sentence in which they are used, and readers will be referred to other entries for additional information. Even in the most technical articles no special preparation in higher mathematics is necessary—where the use of some algebra or geometry is of interest to advanced readers, the concepts contained in the article are explained in plain English as well.

Both metric and standard notational systems are used, with meters and kilograms preceding feet and pounds; as appropriate, Celsius and Fahrenheit temperatures, as well as Kelvin, may be used. Nomenclature in the life sciences includes both the Latin and common names, although most subjects are alphabetized by their common name.

The most commonly used information about countries, states and provinces, and U.S. presidents is included in fact boxes at the beginning of the article. The volumes are arranged in letter-units, with entire letters contained wholly within a single volume (except in the cases of A, C, and S, where the number of entries requires two volumes for each).

PHYSICAL ARRANGEMENT
Article headings are set in bold type, with a rule underneath, and ample space is provided between entries to make it easy to pick out any particular article on the page. The paper is specially selected, 60-lb nonglare-surface stock, which provides true color and sharp details. The contemporary typeface (Optima) was selected for its legibility and elegance.

The right-hand margin of each column of type is called "ragged"—that is, variation exists in the length of each line—a modern concept in book design that is more eye-pleasing and less formidable than the traditional solid column.

Guide words at the top of the page enable users to turn quickly to the appropriate page. Page numbers are also prominently displayed in the upper left and right corners of each page spread for rapid access.

ALPHABETICAL ARRANGEMENT
The encyclopedia is arranged alphabetically throughout. The "word-by-word" system is the same as that used in the phone book or in the library card catalog. Entries beginning with a short word appear before entries with the same short word forming the first letters of a longer word. Thus NEW YORK is placed before NEWBERRY LIBRARY, and RADIO GALAXIES before RADIOACTIVITY.

PRONUNCIATION AND ALTERNATE NAMES
Article headings that contain foreign words and other unfamiliar words are provided with pronunciation guides much like the ones used by *Time* Magazine—thus, Kirkcudbright [kur-koo'-bree]. For Chinese names and terms the new Chinese transliteration system, Pinyin, is provided in parentheses in the article title line—CHOU EN-LAI (Zhou Enlai). The traditional Wade-Giles system is otherwise used in the text because most people are more familiar with the form Peking, for example, than Beijing.

CROSS-REFERENCES
There are three kinds of cross-references in the *Academic American Encyclopedia*. A reader who looks first for CIRCADIAN RHYTHM is told to "see BIOLOGICAL CLOCK." Thus, even if one does not know for certain where the information is to be found, the encyclopedia will guide the reader to the proper place with a minimum of hunting and guessing.

The second type of cross-reference is internal, within the text of an article, and appears in small capital letters. In the article GENESIS, BOOK OF, the phrase CREATION ACCOUNTS appears in small capitals, which means that there is a separate article by that title in which additional relevant information is to be found.

The third type of cross-reference appears at the end of many articles. The article ALLOSAURUS (which also contains eight internal cross-references to other dinosaurs) has a note, See also: FOSSIL RECORD; MESOZOIC ERA, after the bibliography. This tells the reader that additional information relevant to allosaurus can be found under those headings.

FACT BOXES, TABLES, AND GRAPHS
For those who are seeking quick answers to many common questions about countries, states, U.S. presidents, and sports records, or for detailed data about even more specific questions, such as the ten leading U.S. government aerospace contractors, the *Academic American Encyclopedia* supplies hundreds of fact boxes, tables, graphs, and glossaries of technical terms throughout.

ILLUSTRATIONS AND MAPS
More than 16,000 photos, maps, and other illustrations, occupying about 33 percent of the available space, appear in the *Academic American Encyclopedia*. A substantial amount

of the total information in this encyclopedia is found in these illustrations and their captions—information that supports, explains, and expands concepts and relationships mentioned in the text. For example, 76 illustrations accompany the BIRD article, detailing anatomy, physiology, the dynamics of wing action in flight, and the structure of different types of feathers. In addition, illustrations of more than 220 separate species appear, many of which show the plumage variations of male and female of the species. The illustrations are always immediately adjacent to the article to which they pertain. In many cases art work rather than photographs is used because of the greater detail and clarity possible in a drawing. Months of research went into some of the illustrations; for the cutaway drawing of the Soviet spaceship SALYUT, some of the key, previously unpublished information was supplied by Eastern European sources. Exploded views, cutaway drawings, and other sophisticated renderings provide a new look and help to explain processes in time and space.

The 1,100 maps, all newly created specially for this encyclopedia by the cartographic experts of Rand McNally, Donnelley Cartographic, and Lothar Roth Associates, are based on the latest research and cover all continents and countries of the world, all U.S. states and Canadian provinces, many historic regions, and cities (including 36 from other countries). In addition to the 235 political reference maps, there are 200 historical and thematic maps and hundreds of locator maps. The map accompanying the article on SLAVERY not only shows the origin and destination of African slaves, but also brings out little-known facts, such as the information that only 11 percent of the slaves taken in Africa were sent to North America. Most political reference maps use longitude and latitude, as well as color-coded isogonics and hypsographic lines to indicate elevation.

BIBLIOGRAPHY

Almost 13,000 entries (about 40 percent of the total) have accompanying bibliographies. The goal is to furnish a well-chosen list of standard and recently published works to which readers may turn for further information or additional development of particular points of view. Leading textbooks, paperbacks, and recordings are included, as well as occasional periodical references. We have not attempted, especially in science, to furnish the most definitive work in the field if, in our opinion, that work would be well beyond the comprehension of our intended reader. No works in foreign languages are cited, and every effort has been made to refer to books currently in print. Where possible, we have attempted to include unusually cogent interpretations or syntheses; thus John Keegan's book *The Face of Battle* is cited in the bibliography for AGINCOURT, BATTLE OF, and Alexander Bickel's *The Morality of Consent* in the article CIVIL DISOBEDIENCE.

INDEX

The 200,000-entry index, in Volume 21, provides quick, helpful, practical, unambiguous guidance to the information in the encyclopedia. The index entries distinguish among identical headings by providing additional information—for example, BACON, FRANCIS (author) and BACON, FRANCIS (painter). The entry supplies the volume, page, and article title in which illustrations and maps are found and also provides additional "See also" references for related information. Complete information on how to use the index is found in the front matter of Volume 21.

ACKNOWLEDGMENTS

A reference work of this scope and depth must acknowledge many debts—to other encyclopedias of this and former generations, to the hundreds of librarians and educators who participated in product and market research, and to the members of the Advisory Board of Editors, whose names are listed on the following page. The 2,250 scholars and authorities who contributed articles did so primarily because of their commitment to the diffusion of knowledge. The most important debt of all, of course, is owed to our staff, whose dedication and professionalism created this work.

Staff

EDITORIAL

Editorial Director
Bernard S. Cayne

Editor in Chief
K. Anne Ranson

Art Directors
Eric E. Akerman
Clare Chapman

Copy Chief
Ronald B. Roth

Managing Editor
Doris E. Lechner

Editors
Donald Cunningham
Saundra France
Carol Mankin
Steven Moll
John F. Robinson
Wesley Strombeck
JoAnn White

Contributing Editors
Alexander Hellemans
Peter Margolin
Beth F. Simon

Associate Editors
Robert S. Anderson
Lynn Augenblick
Daniel J. Domoff
Grace F. Buonocore
David T. Holland
Virginia Quinn McCarthy
Barbara McKinney
Richard N. Morehouse
Jerome Neibrief
Pamela Carley Petersen
Nathan H. Pletcher
Edwin F. Sparn
Linda Triegel
Sharon Wirt
Melvin Wolfson

Editorial Assistant
Catherine Vaughan Bailey

Index
Jill Schuler, *Chief Indexer*
Pauline Sholtys

Production Editor
Cynthia L. Pearson

Photo Research Department
John Schultz, *Director*
Jane H. Carruth
Ann Eriksen
Jane DiMenna
Al Raymond
Elissa G. Spiro
Mickey Austin

MANUFACTURING

Director of Manufacturing
Joseph J. Corlett

Production Manager
Paul M. Smith

Production Manager
Teresa Kluk

Production Assistant
Marilyn Smith

First Edition Staff

EDITORIAL

Editor in Chief
Sal J. Foderaro

Managing Editor
Andrew C. Kimmens

Supervisory Editors
Howard Batchelor
Steven Moll
K. Anne Ranson

Editors
Carol Mankin
Edward McClellan
Francis Pierce
Jerry Ralya
Arthur Biderman
David Buckley
Barbara Cunningham
Steven Dick
Stephen Fleishman
Sarah Fusfeld
Howard Galer
Eleanor Gates
Ronald Goodman
James Greiff
Marjorie Joyce
Pamela H. Long
Jane McArthur
Kathleen Peterson
Edwin Rosenblum
Richard Turner
Craig Waff
Julie Whitaker

Editorial Services
Sandra Purrenhage
Kim Kelly
Krysia Kolodziej
Karlyn Fedosh

Consulting Editors
Stephen P. Elliott
Stanley Schindler

Contributing Editors
Nicholas Acocella
Elizabeth Bartelme
Jim Benagh
Edward Berlin
Robert Bernhard
Alan M. Bernstein
Bruce O. Boston
Marion Bracken
Sarah Bulgatz
Robin Buss
Victor Cassidy
Carol Cleveland
William B. Cummings
G. S. Davis
John Dawkins
Cathy Dubowski
John Elliott
Daniel Flanagan
Deborah Gale
R. M. Goodwin
Ilene Haimowitz
Hallberg Hallmundsson
May Newman Hallmundsson
Florette Henri
Barbara Hillborne
Thomas Hirsch
Manuela Hoelterhoff
Gail Hoffman
Joseph Holub
Donald Wayne Hunt
Lois Krieger
Blanche Krubner
Arthur Latham
Frank Latham
Judith LaVigna
Marian Leighton
Herbert Levine
Michael Levine
Peter Margolin
Maxine Mayewski
Larry B. Miller
Sandra Milliken
Naomi Neft
Mildred Neiman
Lyda Phillips
Jerry Price
Frank Ragland
Harold Rast
Ruby Riemer
Patricia A. Rodriguez
Madelyn Roesch
Carol Rothkopf
Irina Rybacek

Francene Sabin
Lou Sabin
Estelle Silberman
Don Skemer
K. M. Smogorzewski
Charlotte D. Solomon
Barbara Tchabovsky
Heidi Thaens
Karen Tweedy-Holmes
Elsie Weidner
Henry Weinfield
Gail Weiss
Julian Weitzenfeld
Joan Willis

Research Editors
Ira Don Brown, Jr.
Gail Concannon
Roy Crego
Joseph Devlin
Lawrence Fuchsberg
Allan Gilbert
Alfred Harinxma
Richard Hunter
Jean Metzger
Jerome Parchois
Gary Richmond
Thaddeus Tuleja
Susan Vazakas

Caption Writers
Carl Seely
Susan Brown
Arthur Cacella
Joanne Fuccello
Steve Manulkin
Jane Murray

Copy Chief
Ronald B. Roth

Assistant Copy Chief
Jill Lasker

Copy Editors
Roy A. Grisham, Jr.
Stuart Crump, Jr.
George Ellis
Charles Haberstroh
Jenifer McLean
Margaret Roeske
Dena Rogin
Anne Skagen
William W. Van Allen, Jr.

Proofreaders
George J. Cooke, Jr.
Glenn David Hart
Valerie Kambis
David Moreau
Jean F. McFarland

Index
Barbara M. Preschel, *Supervisor*
Catherine Van Orman

Freelance Indexers
Benedict Brooks
Joan C. D'Aoust
Judith B. Katz
Anne M. Pace
Joyce Post
BevAnne Ross
Karen Hegge Simmons
Gwen Sloan
Dorothy Thomas
Mary F. Tomaselli
A. Cynthia Weber
Don Wigal

Bibliographers
Carol Beyer
Doris Murphy

Information Specialist
Lennart Frantzell

Copy Control
Barbara Smith
Laura Willms
Beth Ann Duncan

Secretary to Editor in Chief
Gemma Scherer

GRAPHICS

Art Director
Peter R. Cook

Assistant Art Directors
Frances Gentile
Cheryl Hudson

Design Staff
Dorothy L. Amsden
Nancy Daniels
Joyce Gaval Neubeck
Alexandra Hammond
George Isak
Dilip Kane
Jean Nist

Photo Researchers
Anna Gunn
Sandy Gregg
Anice Hurley
Karla Taylor

Photo Research Consultant
Marion Geisinger

Artwork Consultant
Roger Hyde

Cartographers
Lothar Roth & Associates
Rand McNally and Company
Donnelley Cartographic Services

Illustrators
Norman Barber
Trevor Boyer
Terry Collins
Howard Darden
John Francis
Tony Gibbons
Ed Hanke
Brian Lewis
John Lind
Angus McBride
Kristie McFall
Davis Meltzer
Rebecca Merrilees
John Murphy
Michael O'Reilly
Richard Orr
Allianora Rosse
Eric Rowe
Herman B. Vestal
Brian Watson
Ray Yeldham

Illustration Services
Linden Artists
Mulvey Associates

PRODUCTION

Production Manager
H. Dean Ragland

Margaret Trejo Baldassari
Samuel J. Alu
Cynthia Chorba
Lynn Mendenko
Beverly Cokinos
Janet Kotnarowski
Lorraine Prochazka

Consultants
Robert T. Cobb
Cobb/Dunlop, Inc.

Contributors

Toive Aartolahti
Professor of Geography, University of Helsinki, Helsinki, Finland.

R.L. Abrahamson
Instructor, Rutgers Preparatory School, Somerset, N.J.

Peter Abramoff
Chairman and Wehr Distinguished Professor of Biology, Marquette University, Milwaukee, Wis.

Maria Isabel Abreu
Chairman of Department and Professor of Portuguese, Georgetown University, Washington, D.C.

Andy Adams
Editor and Publisher of *Sumo World,* Nerima-Ku, Tokyo.

Hazard Adams
Professor of English, University of Washington, Seattle, Wash.

Nicholas Adams
Chairman, Department of Fine Arts, Lehigh University, Bethlehem, Pa.

William W. Adams
Professor of Mathematics, University of Maryland, College Park.

Philip J. Adler
Professor of History, East Carolina University, Greenville, N.C.

Alan R. Adolph, M.D.
Head, Neurosciences Laboratory, Eye Research Institute, Retina Foundation, Boston.

James Adshead
Public Affairs Department Manager, DuPont Company, Wilmington, Del.

Charles Affron
Professor of French, New York University, New York City.

Jaakko A. Ahokas
Professor (Acting), Department of Romance Languages, University of Jyvaskyla, Jyvaskyla, Finland.

E. John Ainsworth
Manager, Bevalac Radiobiology-Radiotherapy Program, Division of Biological and Medical Research, Lawrence-Berkeley Laboratory, Berkeley, Calif.

Ernest T. Ajax, M.D.
Chief of Neurology Service, Salt Lake City Veterans Administration Hospital, and Professor of Neurology, University of Utah College of Medicine, Salt Lake City.

S.-I. Akasofu
Professor of Geophysics, Geophysical Institute, University of Alaska, Fairbanks.

Jaime Alazraki
Professor of Romance Languages, Harvard University, Cambridge, Mass.

Claude C. Albritton, Jr.
Senior Scientist, Institute for the Study of Earth and Man, Southern Methodist University, Dallas, Tex.

John Alcock
Associate Professor, Department of Zoology, Arizona State University, Tempe.

Madeleine Alcover
Associate Professor of French, Rice University, Houston, Tex.

James W. Alexander
Chairman, Department of Medieval Studies, University of Georgia, Athens.

Robert J. Alexander
Professor of Economics, Rutgers University, New Brunswick, N.J.

Theron Alexander
Professor of Human Development, Temple University, Philadelphia.

Margaret Alexiou
Senior Lecturer in Byzantine and Modern Greek, University of Birmingham, Birmingham, England.

John Algeo
Chairman, Department of English, University of Georgia, Athens.

Major John I. Alger
Assistant Professor of History, United States Military Academy, West Point, N.Y.

Theodore H. Allegri, Sr.
Professional Engineer and Consultant, McLean, Va.

John L. Allen
Chairman, Department of Geography, University of Connecticut, Storrs.

P. W. Allen
Malaysian Rubber Producers' Research Association, Hertford, England.

Lawrence H. Aller
Professor of Astronomy, University of California, Los Angeles.

Eileen Jorge Allman
Assistant Professor of English, Herbert H. Lehman College, Bronx, N.Y.

David N. Alloway
Professor of Sociology, Montclair State College, Upper Montclair, N.J.

Willard Allphin, P.E., F.I.E.S.
Former Sales Engineer, GTE Sylvania.

Arthur B. Alphin
Assistant Professor, Department of History, United States Military Academy, West Point, N.Y.

Phillip G. Altbach
Professor of Higher Education, State University of New York, Buffalo.

Craig Amerigian
Geologist, Amoco Minerals Co., Chicago.

Harry Ammon
Chairman, Department of History, Southern Illinois University, Carbondale.

Patricia P. Andersen
Director of Communications, International Fabricare Institute, Joliet, Ill.

Edward F. Anderson
Professor of Biology, Whitman College, Walla Walla, Wash.

James M. Anderson
Professor of Linguistics, University of Calgary, Calgary, Alberta.

Lawrence C. Anderson
Professor of Geography, Mankato State University, Mankato, Minn.

Milton W. Anderson, M.D.
Emeritus Professor of Medicine, Mayo Medical School, Rochester, Minn.

Robert T. Anderson
Professor of Anthropology, Mills College, Oakland, Calif.

Steven C. Anderson
Associate Professor of Biology and Environmental Sciences, University of the Pacific, Stockton, Calif.

William S. Anderson
Professor of Classics, University of California, Berkeley.

Johana Gast Anderton
Managing Editor, Athena Publishing Co., North Kansas City, Mo.

Charles F. Andrain
Professor of Political Science, California State University, San Diego.

Klaus Andres
Research Physicist, Bell Telephone Laboratories, Murray Hill, N.J.

Warren Andrew, M.D.
Professor of Anatomy, Indiana University, School of Medicine, Indianapolis.

F. T. Andrews
Professional Engineer, F. T. Andrews, Inc., Fullerton, Calif.

Harry C. Andrews
Director and Associate Professor, Image Processing Institute, Department of Electrical Engineering and Computer Science, University of Southern California, Los Angeles.

Norwood Andrews, Jr.
Professor of Romance Languages, Texas Tech University, Lubbock.

Donald L. Anglin
Automotive and Technical Writer.

Heinz L. Ansbacher
Professor Emeritus of Psychology, University of Vermont, Burlington.

Mary C. Ansbro
Assistant Public Affairs Director, The Soap and Detergent Association, New York City.

Richard A. Anthes
Professor of Meteorology, Pennsylvania State University, University Park.

James Anthony
Professor of Musicology, University of Arizona, Tucson.

Judith Applegate
Assistant Curator, Museum of Fine Arts, Boston.

Milo Don Appleman, F.R.S.M., F.R.S.A.
Professor of Bacteriology, Emeritus, University of Southern California, Los Angeles.

Roy Armes
Senior Lecturer in Film, Television Studies, Middlesex Polytechnic, London.

John B. Armstrong, M.D.
Neurologist, Montreal Children's Hospital, Montreal.

Dale H. Arner
Head of the Department of Wildlife and Fisheries, Mississippi State University, Mississippi State.

Robert D. Arner
Professor of English, University of Cincinnati, Cincinnati, Ohio.

Peter Arnott
Chairman, Department of Drama, Tufts University, Medford, Mass.

Robert F. Arnove
Associate Professor, School of Education, Indiana University, Bloomington.

Arnold Aronson
Assistant Professor, University of Virginia, Charlottesville.

Avner Ash
Ritt Assistant Professor of Mathematics, Columbia University, New York City.

Neil Ashby
Professor of Physics and Astrophysics, University of Colorado, Boulder.

Harry Asher
Former Lecturer, Birmingham University, Birmingham, England

Herbert B. Asher
Professor of Political Science, Ohio State University, Columbus.

Gail M. Ashley
Assistant Professor, Rutgers University, New Brunswick, N.J.

Maurice Ashley
Former Editor of *The Listener.*

Patricia Teague Ashton
Associate Professor, Educational Foundations, University of Florida, Gainesville.

Frank Askin
Professor of Law, Rutgers Law School, Newark, N.J.

Brian Astle
Fellow, Digital Systems Research, RCA Laboratories/David Sarnoff Research Center, Princeton, N.J.

John W. Atkinson
Professor of Pyschology, University of Michigan, Ann Arbor.

R. J. C. Atkinson
Professor of Archaeology, University College, Cardiff, Wales.

George E. Atwood
Associate Professor of Psychology, Rutgers University, New Brunswick, N.J.

John Henry Auran
Senior Editor, *Skiing* Magazine, New York City.

Robert Austerlitz
Professor of Linguistics and Uralic Studies, Columbia University, New York City.

William W. Austin
Goldwin Smith Professor of Musicology, Cornell University, Ithaca, N.Y.

Charlotte J. Avers
Professor of Biology, Rutgers University, New Brunswick, N.J.

Leonid V. Azároff
Director, Institute of Material Science, University of Connecticut, Storrs.

William S. Babcock
Associate Professor of Church History, Perkins School of Theology, Southern Methodist University, Dallas, Tex.

Bernard S. Bachrach
Professor of History, University of Minnesota, Minneapolis.

Walter M. Bacon, Jr.
Assistant Professor of Political Science, University of Nebraska, Omaha.

Lawrence Badash
Associate Professor of History of Science, University of California, Santa Barbara.

Alan Baddeley
MRC Applied Psychology Unit, Cambridge, England.

E. Badian
Professor of History, Harvard University, Cambridge, Mass.

Galal A. Badr
Associate Professorial Lecturer of Sociology, George Washington University, Washington, D.C.

Charles F. Baes, Jr.
Senior Research Scientist, Oak Ridge National Laboratory, Oak Ridge, Tenn.

Howard G. Baetzhold
Professor of English, Butler University, Indianapolis, Ind.

Carolynn Bailey
Director of Music, Trinity Episcopal Church, Fredericksburg, Va.

Roger Bailey
Director of Choral Music, Mary Washington College, Fredericksburg, Va.

Jay W. Baird
Professor of History, Miami University, Oxford, Ohio.

Robert M. Baird
Professor of Philosophy, Baylor University, Waco, Tex.

Carl Jay Bajema
Professor of Biology, College of Arts and Sciences, Grand Valley State Colleges, Allendale, Mich.

Carlos Baker
Woodrow Wilson Professor of Literature, Emeritus, Princeton University, Princeton, N.J.

James R. Baker
Associate Professor of Entomology, North Carolina State University, Raleigh.

John F. Baker
Editor in Chief, *Publishers Weekly,* New York City.

Stuart E. Baker
Assistant Professor, School of Theater, Florida State University, Tallahassee.

V. K. Balakrishnan
Associate Professor of Mathematics, University of Maine, Orono.

David A. Baldwin
John Sloan Dickey Third Century Professor, Department of Government, Dartmouth College, Hanover, N.H.

Tino Balio
Director, Wisconsin Center for Film and Theater Research, Madison.

Kenneth J. Ballard, Pharm. D.
Assistant Clinical Professor of Pharmacy, University of Southern California School of Pharmacy, Los Angeles.

Louis Wayne Ballard
Composer and Former Program Director, Music, Central Office of Education BIA, Department of Interior.

Aurora Garcia Ballesteros
Profesora Adjunta Geografía, Universidad Complutense, Madrid.

Donald E. Ballou
President, Spaulding and Slye Construction Co. Inc., Burlington, Mass.

Enrique Baloyra
Associate Professor of Political Science, University of North Carolina, Chapel Hill.

Bernard J. Bamberger, D.D.
Rabbi Emeritus, Temple Shaaray Tefila, New York City.

H.-G. Bandi
Professor of Prehistory and Paleontology, University of Berne, Berne, Switzerland.

Aaron Bar-Adon
Professor of Linguistics, University of Texas, Austin.

David P. Barash
Professor of Psychology and Zoology, University of Washington, Seattle.

Thomas J. Barbarie
Journalist, National Catholic News Service, Centreville, Va.

Jack Barbash
Professor, Economics and Industrial Relations, University of Wisconsin, Madison.

Thomas K. Barber, D.D.S., M.S.
Chairman, Division of Preventive Dental Sciences and Section on Pediatric Dentistry, School of Dentistry, University of California, Los Angeles.

Eunice B. Bardell
Professor Emeritus, Health Science, University of Wisconsin, Milwaukee.

Jonas A. Barish
Professor of English, University of California, Berkeley.

Col. Arthur James Barker, Retired
Military Historian and Former Infantry Weapons Instructor, Royal Military College of Science, Swindon, England.

Barbara Mackin Barker
Instructor of Dance, University of Texas, Austin.

John W. Barker
Professor of History, University of Wisconsin, Madison.

Lt. Col. Wayne G. Barker, Retired
U.S. Army Signal Corps, Author and Editor.

Melvin L. Barlow
Professor Emeritus, Graduate School of Education, University of California, Los Angeles.

Chester Barnes
English Table Tennis Association.

Frank Barron
Professor of Psychology, University of California, Santa Cruz.

Harold M. Barrow
Professor of Physical Education, Wake Forest University, Winston-Salem, N.C.

Gordon H. Barrows
President, The Barrows Company, Inc., New York City.

Giulia Bartrum
Researcher for the Menil Foundation in the British Museum, London.

David G. Basile
Professor of Geography, University of North Carolina, Chapel Hill.

John V. Basmajian, M.D., F.A.C.A., F.R.C.P. (c)
Director of Rehabilitation Programs, Chedoke Hospitals, and Professor of Medicine, McMaster University School of Medicine, Hamilton, Ontario.

Paul Merritt Bassett
Professor of History of Christianity, Nazarene Theological Seminary, Kansas City, Mo.

Alan Bates
Editor, *ABC Travel Guides.*

Ralph S. Bates
Professor of History, Emeritus, Bridgewater State College, Bridgewater, Mass.

W. Scott Bauman
Professor of Business Administration, The Colgate Darden Graduate School of Business Administration, University of Virginia, Charlottesville.

Nancy Curry Bavor
Curatorial Assistant, Edward Clark Streeter Collection of Weights and Measures, Yale Medical Library, New Haven, Conn.

Tania Bayard
Art Historian.

Stephen Bayley
Lecturer in the History and Theory of Art, University of Kent, Kent, England.

Forrest E. Beck
Director of Technical Services, The Parker Pen Company, Janesville, Wis.

Joseph F. Becker
Professor of Biology, Montclair State College, Montclair, N.J.

Wesley C. Becker
Associate Dean, College of Education, University of Oregon, Eugene.

Robert P. Beckinsale
Fellow, University College, Oxford, England.

Karl Beckson
Professor of English, Brooklyn College, City University of New York, Brooklyn, N.Y.

Richard R. Beeman
Associate Professor of History, University of Pennsylvania, Philadelphia.

Alfred F. L. Beeston
Professor of Arabic, University of Oxford, Oxford, England.

Thomas O. Beidelman
Professor of Anthropology, New York University, New York City.

Hugo Bekker
Professor of German, Ohio State University, Columbus.

Thomas L. Bell
Associate Professor of Geography, University of Tennessee, Knoxville.

Wayne H. Bell
Assistant Professor of Biology, Middlebury College, Middlebury, Vt.

W. L. Bell, C.M.G., M.B.E.
Information Officer, University of Oxford, Oxford, England.

Kenneth Bendiner
Assistant Professor of Art, Wellesley College, Wellesley, Mass.

Michael Les Benedict
Associate Professor of History, Ohio State University, Columbus.

Dwight G. Bennett, D.V.M.
Professor of Equine Medicine, College of Veterinary Medicine, Colorado State University, Ft. Collins.

Geoffrey R. Bennett
Captain, Royal Navy (ret.).

Wm. R. Bennett, Jr., D.Sc.
C. B. Sawyer Professor of Engineering and Applied Science and Professor of Physics, Yale University, New Haven, Conn.

Henry A. Bent
Professor of Chemistry, North Carolina State University, Raleigh.

Martin J. Beran
Member of the Firm of Blum, Kaplan, Friedman, Silberman and Beran, New York City.

W. A. Beresford
Professor of Anatomy, School of Medicine, West Virginia University, Morgantown.

David M. Bergeron
Professor of English, University of Kansas, Lawrence.

J. L. Berggren
Associate Professor of Mathematics, Simon Fraser University, Burnaby, British Columbia.

William A. Berggren
Senior Scientist, Woods Hole Oceanographic Institution, Woods Hole, Mass.

Thomas G. Bergin
Professor of Romance Languages, Yale University, New Haven, Conn.

Bernard Bergonzi
Professor of English and Comparative Literature, University of Warwick, Coventry, England.

Laurence Bergreen
Former Assistant to the President, The Museum of Broadcasting. Author of *Look Now, Pay Later: The Rise of Network Broadcasting.*

Karl Erik Bergsten
Professor of Physical Geography, University of Lund, Lund, Sweden.

Art Berke
Office of the Baseball Commissioner, New York City.

R. N. Berki
Senior Lecturer of Politics, University of Hull, Hull, England.

Edward A. Berlin
Author of *Ragtime: A Musical and Cultural History.*

Bruce Berman
Teaching Assistant in Films, Columbia University, New York City.

Greta Berman
Assistant Professor of Art History, State University of New York, Stony Brook.

Albert Bermel
Professor of Theatre, Herbert H. Lehman College, Graduate Center of the City University of New York, New York City.

Ronald M. Berndt
Foundation Professor of Anthropology, University of Western Australia, Nedlands, Western Australia.

David K. Berninghausen
Professor, Library School, University of Minnesota, Minneapolis.

Charles A. Berry, M.D.
President, National Foundation for Prevention of Disease, Houston, Tex.

William B. N. Berry
Professor of Paleontology and Director of Museum of Paleontology, University of California, Berkeley.

Alan C. G. Best
Associate Professor of Geography, Boston University, Boston.

Catherine T. Best
Professor of Psychology, Michigan State University, East Lansing.

Joel Best
Associate Professor of Sociology, California State University, Fresno.

Jane Colville Betts
Assistant Professor of English, University of Wisconsin, Eau Claire.

R. K. Betts
Research Associate, Brookings Institution, Washington, D.C.

Charles Rowan Beye
Professor of Classics, Boston University, Boston.

Jacquelyn L. Beyer
Professor of Geography and Environmental Studies, University of Colorado, Colorado Springs.

Robert T. Beyer
Professor of Physics, Brown University, Providence, R.I.

Sabyasachi Bhattacharya
James Franck Fellow, James Franck Institute, University of Chicago, Chicago.

Robert Steven Bianchi
Associate Curator, Department of Egyptian and Classical Art, The Brooklyn Museum, Brooklyn, N.Y.

James Biddle
President, National Trust for Historic Preservation, Washington, D.C.

Martin A. Bierbaum
Assistant Professor of Urban Studies, Rutgers University, New Brunswick, N.J.

Julian Bigelow
Institute for Advanced Study, Princeton, N.J.

Willem A. Bijlefeld
Professor of Islamic Studies, The Hartford Seminary Foundation, Hartford, Conn.

George Athan Billias
Professor of American History, Clark University, Worcester, Mass.

Roger E. Bilstein
Professor of History, University of Houston at Clear Lake City, Houston, Tex.

Stephen S. Birdsall
Professor of Geography, University of North Carolina, Chapel Hill.

Donald Birn
Assistant Professor of History, State University of New York, Albany.

Alan C. Birnholz
Associate Professor of Art History, State University of New York, Buffalo.

Adriana Scalamandré Bitter
Executive Vice-President, Scalamandré, Inc., Long Island City, N.Y.

Richard Bjornson
Associate Professor of Comparative Studies, Ohio State University, Columbus.

Robert C. Black
Associate Professor of Biology, Pennsylvania State University, Delaware County Campus, Media.

Robert F. Black
Professor of Geology and Geophysics, University of Connecticut, Storrs.

R. John Blackley
Director, Schola Antiqua, New York City.

John T. Blackmore
Visiting Scholar, History of Philosophy of Science Department, Cambridge University, Cambridge, England.

Wilford A. Bladen
Associate Professor of Geography, University of Kentucky, Lexington.

Peter Blake
Chairman, Boston Architectural Center, Boston.

J. W. Blaker
Professor of Physics, Vassar College, Poughkeepsie, N.Y.

Joseph L. Blau
Professor Emeritus in Religion, Columbia University, New York City.

John P. Blewett
Senior Physicist, Brookhaven National Laboratory, Upton, N.Y.

Charles W. Bodemer
Professor and Chairman, Department of Biomedical History, School of Medicine, University of Washington, Seattle.

Paul Bohannan
Professor of Anthropology, University of California, Santa Barbara.

Albert Boime
Professor of Art History, University of California, Los Angeles.

Larissa Bonfante
Associate Professor of Classics, New York University, New York City.

John Lawrence Boojamra
St. Vladimir's Seminary, Tuckahoe, N.Y.

Jean Boorsch
Professor of French, Emeritus, Yale University, New Haven, Conn.

James A. Booth
Senior Research Engineer, Monsanto Research Corp.

John E. Booty
Professor of Church History, Episcopal Divinity School, Cambridge, Mass.

Richard J. Bord
Associate Professor of Sociology, Pennsylvania State University, University Park.

Jacques Bordaz
Associate Professor of Anthropology, University of Pennsylvania, Philadelphia.

Louise Alpers Bordaz
Assistant Professor of Art History and Archaeology, Columbia University, New York City.

Morton Borden
Professor of History, University of California, Santa Barbara.

Robert F. Borkenstein
Professor of Forensic Studies, Indiana University, Bloomington.

Donald J. Borror
Emeritus Professor of Entomology, Ohio State University, Columbus.

Merle L. Borrowman
Professor of Education, University of California, Berkeley.

Buris R. Boshell, M.D.
Ruth Lawson Hanson Professor of Medicine, University of Alabama, Birmingham.

Thomas Boswell
Assistant Professor of Geography, University of Miami, Miami, Fla.

Issa J. Boullata
Professor of Islamic Studies, McGill University, Montreal.

Cedric G. Boulter
Professor of Classics, University of Cincinnati, Cincinnati, Ohio.

Frank C. Bourne
Kennedy Professor of Latin, Emeritus, Princeton University, Princeton, N.J.

Warren G. Bovée
Professor of Journalism, Marquette University, Milwaukee, Wis.

Henry Warner Bowden
Associate Professor of Religion, Douglass College, Rutgers University, New Brunswick, N.J.

Mary Ellen Bowden
Assistant Dean and Lecturer in History, Goucher College, Towson, Md.

Barbara C. Bowen
Professor of French, University of Illinois, Urbana.

Calvin M. Bower
Professor of Music, University of North Carolina, Chapel Hill.

T. G. R. Bower
Reader in Psychology, University of Edinburgh, Edinburgh.

Fredson Bowers
Emeritus Linden Kent Professor of English, University of Virginia, Charlottesville.

Thadis W. Box
Dean of College of Natural Resources and Professor of Range Management, Utah State University, Logan.

Robert B. Boyd
Power System Consultant.

Paul S. Boyer
Assistant Professor of Geology, Fairleigh Dickinson University, Madison, N.J.

Philip S. Brachman
Director, Epidemiology Program Office, Center for Disease Control, Atlanta, Ga.

Ian Bradley
Superintendent, Research and Development, Vickers-Armstrong Ltd., Wiltshire, England.

Alan E. Branch
Shipping Consultant to British Government, London.

Charles M. Brand
Professor of History, Bryn Mawr College, Bryn Mawr, Pa.

Herbert Brand
Chairman, Transportation Institute, Washington, D.C.

James R. Brandon
Professor, Asian Theatre, University of Hawaii, Honolulu.

E. N. Brandt
Director, Business Communications, Dow Chemical Company, Midland, Mich.

Warwick Bray
Professor of Archaeology, Institute of Archaeology, London University, London.

Francis John Bremer
Professor of English, Millersville State College, Millersville, Pa.

Sara S. Bretsky
Adjunct Associate Professor of Earth and Space Science, State University of New York, Stony Brook.

N. R. Brewer, D.V.M.
Associate Professor of Physiology, University of Chicago, Chicago.

Gert H. Brieger, M.D.
Professor and Chairman, Department of History of Health Sciences, University of California, San Francisco.

Waltraud A. R. Brinkmann
Professor of Geography, University of Wisconsin, Madison.

William M. Brinner
Professor of Near Eastern Studies, University of California, Berkeley.

Wesley E. Brittin
Professor of Physics and Astrophysics, University of Colorado, Boulder.

Michael Broadbent
Wine Auctions Director, Christie's, London.

King Broadrick-Allen
Professor-Director of Honors, University of Illinois, Urbana.

J. J. Brody
Professor of Art and Anthropology, University of New Mexico, and Director of Maxwell Museum of Anthropology, Albuquerque.

Selwyn A. Broitman
Professor of Microbiology and Nutritional Sciences, Boston University School of Medicine, Boston.

Beth Archer Brombert
Lecturer of Romance Languages, Princeton University, Princeton, N.J.

Colette R. Brooks
Yale University School of Drama, New Haven, Conn.

David S. Brose
Curator of Archaeology and Professor of Anthropology, Cleveland Museum of Natural History, Case Western Reserve University, Cleveland, Ohio.

Kenneth N. Brostrom
Assistant Professor of Russian, Wayne State University, Detroit.

C. J. Brown
Professor of Animal Science, University of Arkansas, Fayetteville.

David Alan Brown
Curator of Italian Paintings, National Gallery of Art, Washington, D.C.

David B. Brown, P.E.
Associate Professor of Industrial Engineering, Auburn University, Auburn, Ala.

Douglas M. Brown
Associate Professor of Economics, Georgetown University, Washington, D.C.

Frank Brown
Hockey Editor, The Associated Press, New York City.

Malcolm Hamrick Brown
Professor of Music, Indiana University, Bloomington.

Richard P. Brown
Professor of Theater, University of California, Riverside.

Robert Harold Brown
Professor of Geography, University of Wyoming, Laramie.

Roger Brown
John Lindsley Professor of Psychology, Harvard University, Cambridge, Mass.

Ronald F. Brown
Professor Emeritus of Chemistry, University of Southern California, Laguna Hills.

Ray B. Browne
Director, Center for the Study of Popular Culture, Bowling Green State University, Bowling Green, Ohio.

Charles A. Brownfield
Executive Director, Community Family Guidance Center, Inc., Red Bank, N.J.

Clyde E. Browning
Professor of Geography, University of North Carolina, Chapel Hill.

Robert S. Brumbaugh
Professor of Philosophy, Yale University, New Haven, Conn.

Dieter Brunnschweiler
Professor of Geography, Michigan State University, East Lansing.

Michael H. Bruno
Consultant.

Ruth V. Buckley
Principal Lecturer in Electrical Engineering, Leeds Polytechnic School of Electrical Engineering, Leeds, England.

Louis P. Bucklin
Professor of Business Administration, School of Business Administration, University of California, Berkeley.

Thomas R. Buckman
President, The Foundation Center, New York City.

David N. Buckner
Major, U.S. Marine Corps.

Oscar Büdel
Professor of Italian, University of Michigan, Ann Arbor.

Robert Budny
Professor of Physics, Plasma Physics Laboratory, Princeton, N.J.

Howard A. Buechner, M.D., F.A.C.P., F.C.C.P.
Professor of Medicine, Louisiana State University School of Medicine, New Orleans.

George Buelow
Professor of Musicology, Indiana University, Bloomington.

C. Victor Bunderson
President, Learning Design Laboratories, Wicat Inc., Orem, Utah.

Edmunds V. Bunkse
Assistant Professor of Geography, University of Delaware, Newark.

Amby Burfoot
East Coast Editor, *Runner's World* Magazine.

Fredric D. Burg, M.D.
Professor of Pediatrics, University of Pennsylvania, Philadelphia.

James H. Burke
Executive Director, Back To the City, Inc., New York City.

Marcus B. Burke
Lecturer, The New School, New York City.

Marian Burleigh-Motley
Lecturer, Metropolitan Museum of Art, New York City.

Aubrey F. Burstall
Professor Emeritus of Mechanical Engineering, Devon, England.

Roger V. Burton
Professor and Director of Developmental Psychology Program, State University of New York, Buffalo.

Thomas Buser
Associate Professor, Allen R. Hite Art Institute, University of Louisville, Louisville.

John H. Bushnell
Professor of Environmental, Population, and Organismic Biology, University of Colorado, Boulder.

Edouard Bustin
Professor of Political Science and Research Associate, African Studies Center, Boston University, Boston.

Francelia Butler
Professor of English, University of Connecticut, Storrs.

Patrick H. Butler III
Director, Institute of Museums, History and Secondary Education, North Texas State University, Denton.

Richard Butwell
President and Professor of Political Science, California State University, Dominguez Hills.

Marylou Buyse, M.D.
Assistant Professor of Pediatrics, Tufts University School of Medicine, Boston.

Richard D. Cadle
Scientist, National Center for Atmospheric Research, Boulder, Colo.

John Cady
Professor of History, Ohio University, Athens.

Arno Cahn
Director of Development, Household Products, Lever Brothers Company, Edgewater, N.J.

A. G. Cairns-Smith
Senior Lecturer in Chemistry, University of Glasgow, Glasgow, Scotland.

David K. Caldwell
Research Scientist, Institute for Advanced Study of the Communication Processes of the State University System of Florida, Tallahassee.

Larry D. Caldwell
Professor of Biology, Central Michigan University, Mount Pleasant.

Ronald Calinger
Associate Professor of History, Rensselaer Polytechnic Institute, Troy, N.Y.

Robert G. Calkins
Chairman and Associate Professor, Department of History of Art, Cornell University, Ithaca, N.Y.

James T. Callow
Professor of English, University of Detroit, Detroit.

A. G. W. Cameron
Professor of Astronomy, Harvard University, Cambridge, Mass.

Robert Cammarota
Musicologist, New York City.

Jonathan A. Campbell
Curator of Amphibians and Reptiles, University of Texas, Arlington.

Chas. Cantalupo
Professor of English, Rutgers University, New Brunswick, N.J.

Philip V. Cannistraro
Professor of History, Florida State University, Tallahassee.

Leon Cantrell
Chairman, School of Humanities, Griffith University, Queensland, Australia.

Nicholas Capaldi
Professor of Philosophy, Queens College, Flushing, N.Y.

Roberta Caplan
Mental Health Section, University of Rochester, Rochester, N.Y.

Robert T. Cargo
Professor of Romance Languages, University of Alabama, University.

Richard L. Carlin
Professor of Chemistry, University of Illinois, Chicago Circle.

Robert F. Carline
Fishery Biologist, U.S. Fish and Wildlife Service, Columbus, Ohio.

Eric G. Carlson
Associate Professor of Art History, State University of New York, Purchase.

Marvin A. Carlson
Professor of Theater, Cornell University, Ithaca, N.Y.

F. Paul Carlson
Vice-President, Oregon Graduate Center, Beaverton.

Francis J. Carmody
Professor of French, Emeritus, University of California, Berkeley.

Peter Carstens
Professor of Anthropology, University of Toronto, Toronto.

Dorwin Cartwright
Professor of Psychology, University of Michigan, Ann Arbor.

William M. Casey
Senior Staff Counselor and Psychologist, Psychoendocrinology Clinic, Children's Hospital, Buffalo, N.Y.

David D. Cass
Associate Professor of Botany, University of Alberta, Edmonton.

Eric J. Cassell, M.D., F.A.C.P.
Clinical Professor, Department of Public Health, Cornell Medical Center, New York City.

David Cast
Associate Professor of Art History, Yale University, New Haven, Conn.

Barbara Cavaliere
Art Critic, *Art Magazine.*

Alfred A. Cave
Dean, College of Arts and Sciences, University of Toledo, Toledo, Ohio.

Mary Ann Caws
Professor of Romance Languages and Comparative Literature, Graduate Center of the City University of New York, New York City.

Fred A. Cazel, Jr.
Professor of History, University of Connecticut, Storrs.

Alphonse Cerza
Lawyer, Formerly of John Marshall Law School, Chicago.

Curtis L. Cetrulo, M.D., F.A.C.O.G.
Associate Professor of Obstetrics and Gynecology, Tufts University School of Medicine, Boston.

John Chadwick
Reader in Greek Language, Downing College, University of Cambridge, Cambridge, England.

Robert A. Chadwick
Professor of Geology, Montana State University, Bozeman.

C. K. Chai
Senior Staff Scientist, The Jackson Laboratory, Bar Harbor, Maine.

H. D. Chambliss, Jr.
Vice-President of Public Affairs, Aluminum Association, Inc., Washington, D.C.

T. C. Champion
Lecturer in Archaeology, University of Southampton, Southampton, England.

James Chan
Visiting Professor of Geography, Boston University, Boston.

Stanley A. Changnon, Jr.
Chairman, Atmospheric Sciences Section, Illinois State Water Survey, and Professor of Atmospheric Sciences, University of Illinois, Urbana.

Cornelia Post Channing, M.D.
Professor of Physiology, University of Maryland School of Medicine, Baltimore.

Alphonse Chapanis
Professor of Psychology, The Johns Hopkins University, Baltimore, Md.

C. Richard Chapman
Associate Professor of Anesthesiology, University of Washington School of Medicine, Seattle.

Loren J. Chapman
Professor of Psychology, University of Wisconsin, Madison.

Miles L. Chappell
Chairman and Associate Professor of Fine Arts, College of William and Mary, Williamsburg, Va.

Maurice Charney
Distinguished Professor of English, Rutgers University, New Brunswick, N.J.

Joseph V. Charyk
President, Communications Satellite Corp., Washington, D.C.

Gilbert Chase
Visiting Professor of American Studies, History, and Music, University of Texas, Austin.

Harold W. Chase
Professor of History, University of Minnesota, Minneapolis.

William A. Check
Medical and Scientific Communications, Incorporated, Atlanta, Ga.

Donald Cheney
Professor of English, University of Massachusetts, Amherst.

Eric S. Cheney
Associate Professor of Geology, University of Washington, Seattle.

David A. Chiriboga
Assistant Professor in Residence, University of California, San Francisco.

Robert F. Chirico
Art Historian, Institute of Fine Arts, New York City.

Hong-Yee Chiu
Goddard Space Flight Center, Greenbelt, Md.

Carol T. Christ
Associate Professor of English, University of California, Berkeley.

J. R. Christianson
Professor of History, Luther College, Decorah, Iowa.

Chuen-yan David Lai
Associate Professor of Geography, University of Victoria, Victoria, British Columbia.

Anna M. Cienciala
Professor of History, University of Kansas, Lawrence.

Thomas D. Clareson
Professor of English, The College of Wooster, Wooster, Ohio.

Charles E. Clark
Professor of History, University of New Hampshire, Durham.

E. L. Clark
Consultant, Formerly the Acting Assistant Director for Gasification Development, U.S. Department of Energy.

George A. Clark, Jr.
Associate Professor of Biology, University of Connecticut, Storrs.

John J. Clark
Director of M.B.A. Program in Finance, Drexel University, Philadelphia.

Leslie Clark
Film Scholar and Critic.

N. Brooks Clark
Reporter, *Sports Illustrated*.

Robert Judson Clark
Associate Professor, Department of Art and Archaeology, Princeton University, Princeton, N.J.

Mary H. Clench
Associate Curator of Birds, Carnegie Museum of Natural History, Pittsburgh, Pa.

Christian Clerk
Researcher, Department of Anthropology, University College, London.

James A. Clifton
Professor of Anthropology, University of Wisconsin, Green Bay.

Robert S. Cline
Professor of Insurance, University of North Carolina, Greensboro.

Jerome W. Clinton
Assistant Professor of Near Eastern Studies, Princeton University, Princeton, N.J.

Lawrence M. Clopper
Associate Professor of English, Indiana University, Bloomington.

Stanley W. Cloud
White House Correspondent, *Time* Magazine.

J. L. Cloudsley-Thompson, D.Sc.
Birkbeck College, University of London, London.

Nicholas H. Clulee
Associate Professor of History, Frostburg State College, Frostburg, Md.

Harold Clurman
Adjunct Professor of Theatre, Hunter College, New York City, and Theatre Critic, *The Nation*.

Fergus M. Clydesdale
Professor of Food Science and Nutrition, University of Massachusetts, Amherst.

George W. Coats
Professor of Old Testament, Lexington Theological Seminary, Lexington, Ky.

Robert Cockburn
Chairman, Department of English, University of New Brunswick, Fredericton, New Brunswick.

Carl Cohen
Professor of Philosophy, University of Michigan, Ann Arbor.

Jonathan Cohen
Professor of Orthopedic Surgery, Tufts Medical School, Medford, Mass.

Jan Cohn
Associate Professor of English, Carnegie-Mellon University, Pittsburgh, Pa.

John Colarusso
Professor of Linguistics, McMaster University, Hamilton, Ontario.

Gene L. Colborn
Associate Professor of Anatomy, Director of Medical Gross Anatomy, Medical College of Georgia, Augusta.

Ralph M. Coleman
Professor of Engineering Design Graphics, University of Texas, El Paso.

Marjorie Collins
Assistant Professor of English and Linguistics, Mary Washington College, Fredericksburg, Va.

Robert L. Collison
Professor Emeritus, Library and Information Science, University of California, Los Angeles.

Joel Colton
Director for Humanities, The Rockefeller Foundation, New York City.

Steele Commager
Professor of Greek and Latin, Columbia University, New York City.

Thomas J. Concannon
Project Manager, Gilbert/Commonwealth Engineers & Consultants, Reading, Pa.

Carl W. Condit
Professor of History, Art History, and Urban Affairs, Northwestern University, Evanston, Ill.

Kevin J. Connolly
Professor of Psychology, University of Sheffield, Sheffield, England.

Seymour V. Connor
Professor of History, Texas Tech University, Lubbock.

Douglas M. Considine
Engineer.

Nicholas D. Constan, Jr.
Lecturer, Department of Legal Studies, Wharton School, University of Pennsylvania, Philadelphia.

James A. Constantin
David Ross Boyd Professor of Business Administration, University of Oklahoma, Norman.

Jon R. Conte
Assistant Professor, School of Social Service Administration, University of Chicago.

Donald J. Cook
Chairman, Department of Chemistry, DePauw University, Greencastle, Ind.

J. Patrick Cooney
Lecturer and Curatorial Assistant, The Frick Collection, New York City.

J. R. Cooper
Former Professor of Geography, City of Cardiff Teachers' College, Cardiff, Wales.

Martin Cooper
Former Music Editor, *London Daily Telegram*.

Rita V. Copelman
Publicity Director, Tanners' Council of America, New York City.

Edward P. J. Corbett
Professor of English, Ohio State University, Columbus.

Mary B. Corcoran
Professor of German, Vassar College, Poughkeepsie, N.Y.

Dennis D. Cordell
Assistant Professor of History, Southern Methodist University, Dallas, Tex.

Carl F. Cori
Visiting Professor of Biochemistry, Harvard Medical School, Boston.

Malcolm Cormack
Curator of Paintings, Yale Center for British Art, New Haven, Conn.

Jean Dwyer Cormick
Assistant Professor of English, Rutgers College, New Brunswick, N.J.

Jeffrey M. Cornelius
Associate Dean and Associate Professor of Music, Temple University College of Music, Philadelphia.

Carl M. Corter
Associate Professor of Psychology, Erindale College, University of Toronto, Mississauga, Ontario.

Bard Cosman, M.D.
Professor of Clinical Surgery, Columbia University, New York City, and Attending Plastic Surgeon, Columbia-Presbyterian Hospital, New York City.

Michael C. Cote
Environmental Scientist and President, Environmental Research Association, Inc., New Brunswick, N.J.

Charles H. Cotter
Department of Maritime Studies, University of Wales Institute of Science and Technology, Cardiff, Wales.

William R. Cotton
Associate Professor of Atmospheric Science, Colorado State University, Fort Collins.

Arnold Court
Professor of Climatology, California State University, Northridge.

Gerald Couzens
Author of *A Baseball Album*.

Warren Cowgill
Professor of Linguistics, Yale University, New Haven, Conn.

Alexander Cowie
Emeritus Professor of Mechanical Engineering, Illinois Institute of Technology, Chicago.

Joel Cracraft
Associate Professor of Anatomy, University of Illinois, Chicago.

George B. Craig, Jr.
Clark Professor of Biology, Vector Biology Laboratory, University of Notre Dame, Notre Dame, Ind.

Sam Craver
Professor of Education, Virginia Commonwealth University, Richmond.

John Stephens Crawford
Associate Professor of Art History, University of Delaware, Newark.

Don M. Cregier
Professor of History, University of Prince Edward Island, Charlottetown.

Frederick Crews
Professor of English, University of California, Berkeley.

Howard J. Critchfield
Professor of Geography, Western Washington University, Bellingham.

Melvin Croan
Professor of Political Science, University of Wisconsin, Madison.

Lester G. Crocker
Kenan Professor of French, University of Virginia, Charlottesville.

Lawrence J. Crockett
Professor, Department of Biology, City College, City University of New York, New York City.

Ralph D. Cross
Associate Professor of Geography and Area Development, University of Southern Mississippi, Hattiesburg.

F. Joe Crosswhite
Professor of Mathematics Education, Ohio State University, Columbus.

William H. Crouse
Consulting Editor, Automotive Books, McGraw-Hill Book Company, Naples, Fla.

Richard H. Crowder
Professor Emeritus of English, Purdue University, West Lafayette, Ind.

J. Donald Crowley
Professor of English, University of Missouri, Columbia.

John Cruickshank
Professor of French, University of Sussex, Brighton, England.

Pressley L. Crummy
Emeritus Professor of Anatomy, Kirksville College of Osteopathic Medicine, Kirksville, Mo.

J. A. Cuddon
Author of *A Dictionary of Literary Terms.*

Jonathan Culler
Professor of English and Comparative Literature, Cornell University, Ithaca, N.Y.

Jack Cumbee
Associate Professor of Philosophy, Tuskegee Institute, Tuskegee Institute, Ala.

W. Wilson Cummer III
Associate Professor of Architecture, School of Architecture, Cornell University, Ithaca, N.Y.

William K. Cummings
Project Specialist, Ford Foundation, New York City.

Agnes Cunningham, S.S.C.M.
Associate Professor of Patristic Theology and Early Christianity, Saint Mary of the Lake Seminary, Mundelein, Ill.

H. E. Cunningham
The Aluminum Association Inc., Washington, D.C.

Rick Cunningham
Administrative Assistant, Office of the Baseball Commissioner, New York City.

Nancy A. Curtin
Professor of Physiology, University College London, London, England.

Morton Curtis
W. L. Moody, Jr., Professor of Mathematics, Rice University, Houston, Tex.

William W. Curtis
Associate Professor of Marketing, University of Nebraska, Lincoln.

H. C. Curtiss, Jr.
Professor of Aerospace and Mechanical Sciences, Princeton University, Princeton, N.J.

Frank A. D'Accone
Professor of Music, University of California, Los Angeles.

Magdalena Dabrowski
Curatorial Assistant, Museum of Modern Art, New York City.

Mitchell Dahood
Professor of Ugaritic Language and Literature, Pontifical Biblical Institute, Rome.

D. Martin Dakin
Honorary Member of the Sherlock Holmes Society, London.

Robert T. Daland
Professor of Political Science, University of North Carolina, Chapel Hill.

Lya R. Dams
Prehistoric Archaeologist.

J. M. Anthony Danby
Professor of Mathematics and Physics, North Carolina State University, Raleigh.

Glyn Daniel
Disney Professor of Archaeology, University of Cambridge, Cambridge, England.

Don Daniels
Critic and Dance Historian.

Lawrence Danson
Associate Professor of English, Princeton University, Princeton, N.J.

Michael R. Darby
Professor of Economics, University of California at Los Angeles.

Alan P. Darr
Assistant Curator, European Art Department, Detroit Institute of Arts, Detroit.

Gautam Dasgupta
Publisher and Editor, *Performing Arts Journal.*

Joseph Warren Dauben
Associate Professor of History, Herbert H. Lehman College, City University of New York, New York City.

Abraham A. Davidson
Professor of Art History, Tyler School of Art, Temple University, Ambler, Pa.

Julian M. Davidson
Associate Professor of Physiology, Stanford University, Stanford, Calif.

Hywel Davies, M.D., F.R.C.P., F.A.C.P.
Abdulla Fouad Hospital, Dammam, Saudi Arabia.

Reverend Cyprian Davis, O.S.B.
Associate Professor of Church History, Saint Meinrad School of Technology, Saint Meinrad, Ind.

Dewitt Davis, Jr.
Assistant Professor of Geography, Ohio State University, Colombus.

Edward W. Davis, Jr.
Associate Professor of Computer Science, North Carolina State University, Raleigh.

J. G. Davis, O.B.E.
Dr. J. G. Davis and Partners, Reading, Berkshire, England

Keith F. Davis
International Museum of Photography at George Eastman House, Rochester, N.Y.

Robert Murray Davis
Professor of English, University of Oklahoma, Norman.

Stanley N. Davis
Professor of Hydrology and Water Resources, University of Arizona, Tucson.

Buck Dawson
Executive Director of the International Swimming Hall of Fame, Fort Lauderdale, Fla.

Douglas Day
Chairman, Department of Geography, Saint Mary's University, Halifax, Nova Scotia.

R. J. De Cristoforo
Author of *The Hand Tool Book* and *Carpentry Handbook.*

Peter Dehlinger
Professor of Geophysics, University of Connecticut, Storrs.

Robert J. Delatour, Jr.
Geologist, Environmental Assessment Council, Inc., New Brunswick, N.J.

Charles F. Delzell
Professor of History, Vanderbilt University, Nashville, Tenn.

Robert DeMaria, Jr.
Assistant Professor of English, Vassar College, Poughkeepsie, N.Y.

John G. Dennis
Professor of Geology, California State University, Long Beach.

Paul E. Desautels
Curator, Division of Mineralogy, National Museum of Natural History, Smithsonian Institution, Washington, D.C.

C. D. Deshpande
National Fellow, Jawaharlal Nehru University, New Delhi, India.

Andrée Désilets
Professor of History, University of Sherbrooke, Sherbrooke, Quebec.

Robert W. Desmond
Professor Emeritus of History, University of California, Berkeley.

I. M. Destler
Institute for International Economics, Washington, D.C.

Donald S. Detwiler
Professor of History, Southern Illinois University, Carbondale.

Daniel Deudney
Worldwatch Institute, Washington, D.C.

Joseph A. DeVito
Professor of Communication Arts and Sciences, Queens College of The City University of New York, New York City.

Samuel Devons
Professor of Physics, Columbia University and Director of Barnard-Columbia History of Physics Laboratory, New York City.

Ton DeVos
Professor of Political Science, Trinity University, San Antonio, Tex.

Robert E. Dewar
Assistant Professor of Anthropology, University of Connecticut, Storrs.

Robert S. Dewers
Professor of Forest Science, Texas A&M University, College Station.

Theo D'Haen
Professor of Comparative Literature, University of Massachusetts, Amherst.

Seymour Diamond, M.D.
Director, Diamond Headache Clinic, Ltd., and Clinical Assistant Professor, Chicago Medical School, Chicago.

Jose Luis Diaz, M.D.
Psychopharmacology Research, Instituto de Investigaciones Biomedicas, Universidad de Mexico, Unam, Mexico.

Robert H. Dick
Supervisory Tea Examiner, U.S. Food and Drug Administration, Brooklyn, N.Y.

Steven J. Dick
U.S. Naval Observatory, Washington, D.C.

David Dickason
Professor of Geography, Western Michigan University, Kalamazoo.

Samuel N. Dicken
Emeritus Professor of Geography, University of Oregon, Eugene.

Denis Dickinson
Former Head of Department of Biotechnology, Institute for Industrial Research and Standards, Dublin.

Paul Dickson
Independent Writer.

R. S. Dietz
Professor of Geology, Arizona State University, Tempe.

David Dilks
Chairman, School of History, Leeds University, Leeds, England.

Francis P. Dinneen
Professor of Linguistics, Georgetown University, Washington, D.C.

Jane VanZandt Dingman
Lecturer in Zoology, University of New Hampshire, Durham.

S. Lawrence Dingman
Associate Professor of Water Resources, Institute of Natural and Environmental Resources, University of New Hampshire, Durham.

Anastasia N. Dinsmoor
American School of Classical Studies, Athens.

Joseph R. DiPalma, M.D.
Professor of Pharmacology, Vice-President and Dean, Hahnemann Medical College, Philadelphia.

Mark Dittrick
Writer and Craftsman.

James R. Dixon
Professor of Wildlife Sciences, Texas A&M University, College Station.

J. Michael S. Dixon, M.D., F.R.C.P. (c)
Professor of Bacteriology and Director of Provincial Laboratory, University of Alberta, Edmonton.

Jan E. Dizard
Professor of Sociology, Amherst College, Amherst, Mass.

Frederick J. Dockstader
Indian Art Consultant, Former Director, Museum of the American Indian.

Donald O. Doehring
Associate Professor of Earth Resources, Colorado State University, Fort Collins.

Diran Kavork Dohanian
Professor of Fine Arts, University of Rochester, Rochester, N.Y.

Ralph Dolgoff
Assistant Dean, School of Social Work, Adelphi University, Garden City, N.Y.

Michael W. Dols
Associate Professor of History, California State University, Hayward.

Donald J. Donaldson
Associate Professor of Anatomy, University of Tennessee Center for the Health Sciences, Memphis.

Dave Dooling
Science Writer for *Huntsville Times*, Huntsville, Ala.

Jesse S. Doolittle
Professor Emeritus of Mechanical and Aerospace Engineering, North Carolina State University, Raleigh.

Robert H. Doremus
New York State Professor of Glass and Ceramics, Rensselaer Polytechnic Institute, Troy, N.Y.

Harold Dorn
Professor of the History of Science and Technology, Stevens Institute of Technology, Hoboken, N.J.

Richard M. Dorson
Distinguished Professor of History and Folklore, Indiana University, Bloomington.

Richard G. Doty
Associate Curator of Modern Coins, American Numismatic Society, New York City.

Jack D. Douglas
Professor of Sociology, University of California, San Diego.

Folke Dovring
Professor of Land Economics, University of Illinois, Urbana-Champaign.

Herndon G. Dowling
Professor of Biology, New York University, New York City.

Eric Dowty
Assistant Professor, Department of Geological and Geophysical Sciences, Princeton University, Princeton, N.J.

John P. Doyle
Professor of Philosophy, St. Louis University, St. Louis, Mo.

Milorad M. Drachkovitch
Senior Fellow and Archivist, Hoover Institution on War, Revolution, and Peace, Stanford University, Stanford, Calif.

Frank D. Drake
Director, National Astronomy and Ionosphere Center, Cornell University, Ithaca, N.Y.

Stillman Drake
Former Professor, University of Toronto, Toronto.

Cecelia Hodges Drewry
Assistant Dean of the College, and Department of English, Princeton University, Princeton, N.J.

Henry N. Drewry
Lecturer, Professor in History, Princeton University, Princeton, N.J.

Philip Drucker
Professor Emeritus of Anthropology, University of Kentucky, Lexington.

J. W. Drummond

R. N. Drummond
Professor of Geography, McGill University, Montreal.

Colin G. Drury
Associate Professor of Industrial Engineering, State University of New York, Buffalo.

Roy Dubisch
Professor of Mathematics, University of Washington, Seattle.

G. Dudbridge
Lecturer in Modern Chinese, University of Oxford, Oxford, England.

Alden W. Dudley, Jr., M.D.
Director, Neuropathology Training Program, University of Southern Alabama, Mobile.

John Duffy
Priscilla Alden Burke Professor of History, University of Maryland, College Park.

Joseph W. Duffy
Dean, School of Technology, Central Connecticut State College, New Britain.

Norman V. Duffy
Professor of Chemistry, Kent State University, Kent, Ohio.

Joseph J. Duggan
Professor of French and Comparative Literature, University of California, Berkeley.

J. R. Duhart
Senior Economist, Lloyds Bank International, London.

Charles S. Dunbar, F.C.I.T.
Transport Consultant.

Charles T. Duncan
Professor of Journalism, University of Oregon, Eugene.

Thomas W. Dunfee
Associate Professor of Legal Studies, The Wharton School, University of Pennsylvania, Philadelphia.

Marvin D. Dunnette
Professor of Psychology, University of Minnesota, Minneapolis.

Col. T. N. Dupuy
President and Executive Director, Historical Evaluation and Research Organization, Dunn Loring, Va.

G. H. Dury
Professor of Geography and Geology Emeritus, University of Wisconsin, Madison, Wis.

Ashok K. Dutt
Professor of Geography and of Urban Studies, University of Akron, Akron, Ohio.

Arndt J. Duvall III, M.D.
Professor of Otolaryngology, University of Minnesota, Minneapolis.

Martin Dworkin
Professor of Microbiology, University of Minnesota, Minneapolis.

John M. Dyckman
Clinical Psychologist, Kaiser Foundation Hospital, Vallejo, Calif.

James S. Dyer
Associate Professor, School of Management, University of California, Los Angeles.

Mary Lee Dyer
Former Office Manager and Head Bookkeeper, U.S. Building Packages and Restaurant Construction Services.

Robert F. Dymek
Assistant Professor of Geology, Harvard University, Cambridge, Mass.

John W. Eadie
Professor of History, University of Michigan, Ann Arbor.

Valerie A. Earle
Professor of Government, Georgetown University, Washington, D.C.

Joseph T. Eastman
Assistant Professor of Biology, Brown University, Providence, R.I.

Sir Eric Eastwood, C.B.E., F.R.S.
Former Director of Research, General Electric Co. Limited.

William E. Eaton
Associate Professor of Education, Southern Illinois University, Carbondale.

Jonathan Eberhart
Space Sciences Editor, *Science News.*

John Edwin Ebinger
Professor of Botany, Eastern Illinois University, Charleston.

Kenneth Eble
Professor of English, University of Utah, Salt Lake City.

Garrett Eckbo
Landscape Architect, Garrett Eckbo and Associates, San Francisco.

John A. Eddy
Senior Scientist, High Altitude Observatory, National Center for Atmospheric Research, Boulder, Colo.

Robert I. Ediger
Professor of Biology, California State University, Chico.

I. E. S. Edwards
Former Keeper of Egyptian Antiquities, British Museum, London.

James Don Edwards
J. M. Tull Professor of Accounting, University of Georgia, Athens.

Mary Jane Edwards
Associate Professor of English, Carleton University, Ottawa.

W. Farrell Edwards
Professor of Physics, Utah State University, Logan.

Daniel B. Eisenberg
Professor of Spanish, Florida State University, Tallahassee.

Salah El-Shakhs
Professor and Director, School of Urban and Regional Policy, Rutgers University, New Brunswick, N.J.

Stephen Ellen
Geologist, U.S. Geological Survey, Menlo Park, Calif.

Daniel S. Elliot
Research Assistant, University of Michigan, Ann Arbor.

James E. Ellis
Scientific Director, Colorado State University, Fort Collins.

Keith Ellis
Professor of Spanish, University of Toronto, Toronto.

Robert S. Ellwood, Jr.
Bishop James W. Bashford Professor of Oriental Studies, University of Southern California, Los Angeles.

Betty Elzea
Formerly at Victoria and Albert Museum, London.

Rowland Elzea
Curator, Delaware Art Museum, Wilmington.

Melvin Ember
Professor of Anthropology, Hunter College of the City University of New York, New York City.

R. L. Emerson
Professor of History, University of Western Ontario, London.

Alan R. Emery
Associate Curator, Royal Ontario Museum, Toronto.

Edwin Emery
Professor of Journalism, University of Minnesota, Minneapolis.

Michael Emery
Professor of Journalism, California State University, Northridge.

Suzanne Steiner Emery
Independent Research Specialist, University of Southern California, Los Angeles.

Samuel T. Emory
Professor of Geography, Mary Washington College, Fredricksburg, Va.

A. G. Engelhardt
Staff Member, Los Alamos Scientific Laboratory, University of California, Los Alamos, N.Mex., and Adjunct Professor of Electrical Engineering, Texas Tech University, Lubbock.

Alfred Garvin Engstrom
Alumni Distinguished Professor of French, Emeritus, University of North Carolina, Chapel Hill.

Edmund L. Epstein
Professor of English, Queens College of the City University of New York, Flushing.

Victor Erlich
Bensinger Professor of Russian Literature, Yale University, New Haven, Conn.

Chris W. Eskridge
Assistant Professor, Department of Criminal Justice, University of Nebraska, Lincoln.

Martin Esslin
Professor of Drama, Standard University, Stanford, Calif.

David S. Evans
Professor of Astronomy, University of Texas, Austin.

Rev. Joseph H. Evans
President, United Church of Christ, New York City.

William L. Evans
Professor of Zoology, University of Arkansas, Fayetteville.

David Ewen
Musicologist-Author.

David N. Ewert
Assistant Professor of Biology, Central Michigan University, Mount Pleasant.

Galen Wood Ewing
Professor of Analytical Chemistry, Seton Hall University, South Orange, N.J.

Phyllis Marie Ewy
Department of History, Brandeis University, Waltham, Mass.

Douglas Ezell
Associate Professor of New Testament, Southwestern Baptist Theological Seminary, Fort Worth, Tex.

Brian M. Fagan
Professor of Anthropology, University of California, Santa Barbara.

Maxime A. Faget
Director, Engineering and Development (ret.), Johnson Space Center, Houston, Tex.

Michael A. Fahey, S.J.
Professor of Theology, Concordia University, Montreal, Quebec.

Dianne Fahselt
Associate Professor of Plant Sciences, University of Western Ontario, London.

Michael C. Fairley
Information Services Advisor, Paper and Paper Products Industry Training Board.

Stanley L. Falk
Chief Historian, U.S. Air Force Office of Air Force History, Washington, D.C.

Jacqueline V. Falkenheim
Assistant Professor of the History of Art, Cornell University, Ithaca, N.Y.

Ann Farkas
Professor, New School of Liberal Arts, Brooklyn College, City University of New York, New York City.

Edward L. Farmer
Associate Professor of History, University of Minnesota, Minneapolis.

Louis C. Faron
Professor of Anthropology, State University of New York, Stony Brook.

David M. L. Farr
Professor of History, Carleton University, Ottawa.

Stephen E. Fauer
Terrestrial/Wetlands Ecologist, Environmental Assessment Council, Inc., New Brunswick, N.J.

Gunter Faure
Professor of Geology, Ohio State University, Columbus.

Sylvia F. Fava
Professor of Sociology and Director, Urban Studies Program, Brooklyn College, City University of New York, New York City.

Felix Favorite
National Marine Fisheries Service, Seattle, Wash.

Laurel E. Fay
Assistant Professor of Music, Ohio State University, Columbus.

Joe R. Feagin
Professor of Sociology, University of Texas, Austin.

Olin S. Fearing
Professor of Biology, Trinity University, San Antonio, Tex.

Robert E. Feeney
Professor, Department of Food Science and Technology, University of California, Davis.

Gerald Feinberg
Professor of Physics, Columbia University, New York City.

Ben F. Feingold, M.D.
Chief Emeritus, Department of Allergy, Kaiser-Permanente Medical Center, San Francisco.

S. Norman Feingold
National Director, B'nai B'rith Career and Counseling Services, Bethesda, Md.

John F. Feldhusen
Professor of Education, Purdue University, Lafayette, Ind.

George W. Fellendorf
Executive Director, Alexander Graham Bell Association for the Deaf, Washington, D.C.

John H. Fenton
Commonwealth Professor of Political Science, University of Massachusetts, Amherst.

M. Brock Fenton
Associate Professor of Biology, Carleton University, Ottawa.

John C. Fentress
Professor of Psychology, Dalhousie University, Halifax, Nova Scotia.

Edward A. Fernald
Professor of Geography and Director, Florida Resources and Environmental Analysis Center, Florida State University, Tallahassee.

Jack E. Fernandez
Professor of Chemistry, University of South Florida, Tampa.

Rafael A. Fernandez
Curator of Prints and Drawings, Sterling and Francine Clark Art Institute, Williamstown, Mass.

Robert A. Fernea
Professor of Anthropology and Middle Eastern Studies, University of Texas, Austin.

W. Conard Fernelius
Adjunct Professor of Chemistry, Kent State University, Kent, Ohio.

Robert H. Ferrell
Distinguished Professor of History, Indiana University, Bloomington.

Anne Ferry
Professor of English, Boston College, Chestnut Hill, Mass.

Andrew Field
Professor, Griffith University, Nathan, Brisbane, Queensland, Australia.

G. Wallis Field
Professor of Germanic Languages and Literature, University of Toronto, Toronto.

Kate Fielden
Corpus Christi College, Oxford, England.

Zirka Zaremba Filipczak
Associate Professor of Art History, Williams College, Williamstown, Mass.

Edward R. Finch, Jr.
Finch and Schaefler, New York City.

Donald G. Fink
Executive Director, Retired, Institute of Electrical and Electronics Engineers, New York City.

Ulrich Finke
Senior Lecturer in Art History, University of Manchester, Manchester, England.

K. Thomas Finley
Professor of Chemistry, State University College, Brockport, N.Y.

Bernard S. Finn
Curator, National Museum of History and Technology, Smithsonian Institution, Washington, D.C.

Carl D. Finstad
Associate Professor of Biology, University of Wisconsin, River Falls.

Alfred G. Fischer
Professor of Geology, Princeton University, Princeton, N.J.

Scott K. Fischer

Harold S. Fish, M.D.
Associate Professor of Anatomy, Retired, Chicago Medical School, Chicago.

James S. Fisher
Associate Professor of Geography, University of Georgia, Athens.

Robert C. Fite
Professor and Director, Environmental Extension Project, Oklahoma State University, Stillwater.

Gerald Fitzgerald
Professor of Classical Studies, Monash University, Victoria, Australia.

Joan Fitzpatrick
Research Scientist, Denver Research Institute, University of Denver, Denver, Colo.

Joseph P. Fitzpatrick
Professor of Sociology, Fordham University, Bronx, N.Y.

Kjetil A. Flatin
Assistant Professor of Scandinavian Languages, University of Washington, Seattle.

Seymour L. Flaxman
Professor, City College and the Graduate School, City University of New York, New York City.

Wolfgang B. Fleischmann
Dean, School of Humanities, Montclair State College, Upper Montclair, N.J.

Shirley Fleming
Editor, *Musical America* Magazine.

Barbara Flicker
Associate Director, USC Paralegal Program, and Adjunct Assistant Professor of Paralegal Studies, University of Southern California Law Center, Los Angeles.

Howard H. Flierl
Professor of Geography, State University of New York, Albany.

Steve Flink
World Tennis magazine.

Roy K. Flint
Professor of History, United States Military Academy, West Point, N.Y.

Richard Floberg
Coordinator, Film and Television, Rochester Institute of Technology, Rochester, N.Y.

Marilyn R. Flowers
Assistant Professor of Economics, University of Oklahoma, Norman.

Philip Flynn
Associate Professor of English, University of Delaware, Newark.

Donald E. Foard
Biologist, Comparative Animal Research Laboratory, University of Tennessee, Oak Ridge.

C. L. Foiles
Professor of Physics, Michigan State University, East Lansing.

Bliss Forbush III
Assistant Professor of Physiology, Yale University School of Medicine, New Haven, Conn.

Barbara Brennan Ford
Instructor, Connecticut College, New London.

C. C. Ford
Lecturer in Developmental Biology, University of Sussex, Sussex, England.

Richard Ford

Charles W. Fornara
Professor of Classics and History, Brown University, Providence, R.I.

John C. Forrest
Professor of Animal Sciences, Purdue University, West Lafayette, Ind.

Fred Fortress
Director, Textile and Apparel Research, Philadelphia College of Textiles and Science, Philadelphia.

Edward W. Foss
Professor of Agricultural Engineering, Cornell University, Ithaca, N.Y.

Brian L. Foster
Associate Professor of Anthropology, State University of New York, Binghamton.

Peter V. Foukal
Lecturer in Astronomy, Harvard University, Cambridge, Mass.

Raymond T. Foulds, Jr.
Secretary-Treasurer and Bulletins Editor, Vermont Maple Industry Council, Burlington.

Edward B. Fowler
University of California, Berkeley, Calif.

Gary L. Fowler
Professor of Geography, University of Illinois, Urbana.

Grant R. Fowles
Professor of Physics, University of Utah, Salt Lake City.

Elizabeth Fox-Genovese
Professor of History, Vice Chairperson for Graduate Affairs, State University of New York, Binghamton.

James M. Francis
Principle, James M. Francis & Co., Brooklyn, N.Y.

Marcus Franda
Associate American Universities Field Staff, New Delhi, India.

John A. Franklin
President, Franklin Trow Associates Ltd., Toronto.

F. W. Franz
President, Watch Tower Bible and Tract Society of Pennsylvania, Brooklyn, N.Y.

Hugo F. Franzen
Professor of Chemistry, Iowa State University, Ames.

Derek Fraser
Reader in History, University of Bradford, Bradford, England.

Douglas Fraser
Professor of Art History and Archaeology, Columbia University, New York City.

Michael Frede
Professor of Philosophy, Princeton University, Princeton, N.J.

Aaron D. Freedman, M.D.
Professor of Medicine, Sophie Davis School of Biomedical Education, City College, City University of New York, New York City.

James O. Freedman
Dean and Professor of Law, University of Pennsylvania, Philadelphia.

Richard B. Freeman, M.D.
Associate Professor of Medicine, University of Rochester School of Medicine, Rochester, N.Y.

Thomas Walter Freeman
Emeritus Professor of Geography, University of Manchester, Manchester, England.

Warren French
Professor of English, Indiana University, Indianapolis.

Herbert Frey
Research Associate, Geophysics Branch, Goddard Space Flight Center, University of Maryland, Greenbelt.

H. M. Fried
Professor of Physics, Brown University, Providence, R.I.

Maurice Friedberg
Professor of Russian Literature, and Head, Department of Slavic Languages and Literatures, University of Illinois, Urbana-Champaign.

Robert L. Friedly
Executive Director, Office of Communication, Christian Church (Disciples of Christ), Indianapolis, Ind.

Gerald M. Friedman
Professor of Geology, Rensselaer Polytechnic Institute, Troy, N.Y.

Melvin J. Friedman
Professor of Comparative Literature and English, University of Wisconsin, Milwaukee.

Saul S. Friedman
Associate Professor of History, Youngstown State University, Youngstown, Ohio.

Marilyn Sibley Fries
Assistant Professor of Germanic Languages and Literatures, Yale University, New Haven, Conn.

H. Howard Frisinger II
Professor of Mathematics, Colorado State University, Fort Collins.

Harold C. Fritts
Professor of Dendrochronology, University of Arizona, Tucson.

Steven H. Fritts
Bell Museum of Natural History, University of Minnesota, Minneapolis.

Karlfried Froehlich
Professor of Church History, Princeton Theological Seminary, Princeton, N.J.

J. William Frost
Director, Friends Historical Library, Swarthmore College, Swarthmore, Pa.

William G. Fry
Department of Science, Luton College, Luton, England.

Richard Nelson Frye
Aga Khan Professor of Iranian, Harvard University, Cambridge, Mass.

Armand J. Fulco
Professor of Biological Chemistry, University of California School of Medicine, Los Angeles.

Reginald H. Fuller
Professor, Protestant Episcopal Seminary in Virginia, Alexandria.

J. Z. Fullmer
Professor of History, Ohio State University, Columbus.

Robin Fulton
Førstelektor Rogaland Distriktshøgskole Stavanger, Norway.

Bjarne Furhauge
Lecturer, Emdrupborg College of Education, Copenhagen.

John Furse
The Open University, Milton Keynes, Buckinghamshire, England.

Lilian R. Furst
Professor of Comparative Literature, University of Texas, Dallas.

Ralph W. Gable
Associate Professor of Chemistry, Davidson College, Davidson, N.C.

Warren J. Gadpaille, M.D.
Assistant Clinical Professor, University of Colorado Medical Center, Denver.

Alan M. Gaines
Program Director for Geochemistry, National Science Foundation, Washington, D.C.

Peter Galassi
Columbia University, New York City.

Robert L. Gale
Professor of American Literature, University of Pittsburgh, Pittsburgh, Pa.

Arthur W. Galston
Eaton Professor of Botany, Yale University, New Haven, Conn.

Lewis H. Gann
Senior Fellow, Hoover Institution, Stanford University, Stanford, Calif.

Margaret Ganz
Professor of English, Brooklyn College, City University of New York, New York City.

Paul Gardner
Author of *The Simplest Game: The Intelligent American's Guide to the World of Soccer.*

Wayland D. Gardner
Professor of Economics, Western Michigan University, Kalamazoo.

Sol L. Garfield
Professor of Psychology, Washington University, St. Louis, Mo.

H. B. Garland
Emeritus Professor of German, University of Exeter, Exeter, England.

C. William Garner
Associate Professor of Urban Education, Rutgers University, New Brunswick, N.J.

H. F. Garner
Professor of Geology, Rutgers University, Newark, N.J.

Ronald G. Garst
Assistant Professor of Geography, University of Maryland, College Park.

Roy H. Garstang
Professor of Astrophysics, University of Colorado, Boulder.

Kenneth W. Gatland, F.R.A.S., F.B.I.S.
Past President, The British Interplanetary Society.

William Gaunt
Special Correspondent on Art to *The Times*, London.

Addison Gayle
Professor of English, Bernard Baruch College, City University of New York, New York City.

Charles N. Gaylord
Professor Emeritus of Civil Engineering, University of Virginia, Charlottesville.

Lt. Col. Robert Gayre of Gayre and Nigg
Baron of Lochoreshyre, Editor, *Armorial Who is Who.*

Adelheid M. Gealt
Curator, Indiana University Art Museum, Bloomington.

Ignace J. Gelb
Frank P. Hixon Distinguished Service Professor of Assyriology, The Oriental Institute, University of Chicago, Chicago.

Albert Gelpi
Coe Professor of American Literature, Stanford University, Stanford, Calif.

Frank George
Professor, Brunel University, Uxbridge, Middlesex, England.

William H. Gerdts
Professor of Art History, City University of New York, New York City.

James M. Gerhardt
Associate Professor of Political Science, Southern Methodist University, Dallas, Tex.

Larry R. Gerlach
Professor of History, University of Utah, Salt Lake City.

Daniel Gerould
Professor of Theatre and Comparative Literature, Graduate Center, City University of New York, New York City.

Marvin E. Gettleman
Professor of History, Polytechnic Institute of New York, New York City.

Cecil A. Gibb
Professor of Psychology, Australian National University, Canberra, Australia.

J. Whitfield Gibbons
Research Ecologist, Savannah River Ecology Laboratory, Aiken, S.C.

James Lowell Gibbs, Jr.
Professor of Anthropology, Stanford University, Stanford, Calif.

Walter B. Gibson
Author, *The Complete Illustrated Book of Close-Up Magic, Mastering Magic.*

Frances Carney Gies
Coauthor of *The Ingenious Yankees.*

Joseph C. Gies
Editor of Publications, Association of Governing Boards of Universities and Colleges, Washington, D.C.

Larry A. Giesmann
Associate Professor of Botany, Northern Kentucky University, Highland Heights.

Ray W. Gifford, Jr., M.D.
Head, Department of Hypertension and Nephrology, The Cleveland Clinic Foundation, Cleveland, Ohio.

Perry W. and Claire K. Gilbert
Directors, Mote Marine Laboratory, Sarasota, Fla.

Rex L. Gilbreath
Associate Professor of Animal Sciences, Cook College, New Brunswick, N.J.

Langdon Gilkey
Shailer Mathews Professor of Theology, The Divinity School, University of Chicago, Chicago.

Richard T. Gill
Former Lecturer in Economics, Harvard University, Cambridge, Mass.

B. von Haller Gilmer
Professor of Psychology, Virginia Polytechnic Institute and State University, Blacksburg.

Michael E. Gilpin
Associate Professor of Biology, University of California, San Diego.

Sol Gittleman
Professor of German, Tufts University, Medford, Mass.

Derek C. Gladwell, F.R.S.A., F.H.C.I.M.A.
Head, Department of Hotel and Catering Studies and Home Economics, Sheffield City Polytechnic, Sheffield, England.

Ren Glasser
Author, Playwright.

S. F. Glassman
Professor of Biological Sciences, University of Illinois, Chicago.

Martin I. Glassner
Assistant Professor of Geography, Southern Connecticut State College, New Haven, Conn.

Nahum N. Glatzer
Professor of Religion and of Judaica, Boston University, Boston.

William Glover
Former Theater Critic, The Associated Press.

W. Earl Godfrey
Curator Emeritus of Ornithology, National Museums of Canada, Ottawa.

W. L. Godshalk
Professor of English, University of Cincinnati, Cincinnati, Ohio.

Arnold Goldberg, M.D.
Attending Staff Psychiatrist, Michael Reese Hospital and Medical Center, Clinical Professor, University of Chicago, and Training and Supervisory Analyst, Chicago Institute for Psychoanalysis, Chicago.

Richard B. Goldberg
Assistant Professor of Biology, Temple University, Philadelphia.

Alvin Goldfarb
Assistant Professor of Theatre, Illinois State University, Normal.

Lawrence Goldhirsch
Attorney, Speiser & Krause, New York City.

Frederick Goldin
Professor, City College and the Graduate School, City University of New York, New York City.

David T. Goldman
Associate Director, Long Range Planning, National Measurement Laboratory, National Bureau of Standards, Washington, D.C.

Ralph M. Goldman
Professor of Political Science, San Francisco State University, San Francisco.

Martin G. Goldner, M.D., F.A.C.P.
Emeritus Professor of Medicine, State University of New York, New York City.

William Goldsmith, M.D.
Assistant Clinical Professor of Psychiatry, University of California, and Staff Psychiatrist, Brentwood Veterans Administration Hospital, Los Angeles.

Malcolm Goldstein
Professor of English, Queens College and the Graduate School, City University of New York, Flushing.

Richard P. Goldthwait
Professor Emeritus of Polar Studies, Ohio State University, Columbus.

Danny Gonsalves
Assistant Professor of Geography, Southern Connecticut State College, New Haven.

Roberto González-Echevarría
Associate Professor of Spanish and Portuguese, Yale University, New Haven, Conn.

Erich Goode
Professor of Sociology, State University of New York, Stony Brook.

William Goodman
Professor Emeritus of Political Science, Southern Illinois University, Edwardsville.

Norma L. Goodrich
Professor of French and Comparative Literature, Claremont Colleges, Claremont, Calif.

Alden Rand Gordon
Assistant Professor of Fine Arts, Trinity College, Hartford, Conn.

David S. Gordon
Emory University, School of Medicine, Atlanta, Georgia.

Mel Gordon
Assistant Professor of Drama, New York University, New York City.

Pearl Gordon
Researcher, Museum of Modern Art, New York City.

George Gorin
Professor of Chemistry, Oklahoma State University, Stillwater.

Charles W. Gorodetzky, M.D.
Adjunct Associate Professor of Pharmacology, University of Kentucky College of Medicine, Lexington.

Donald Gotterbarn
Assistant Professor of Philosophy, Albright College, Reading, Pa.

Norman K. Gottwald
Professor of Old Testament and of Biblical Theology and Ethics, Graduate Theological Union, Berkeley, Calif.

William H. Gotwald, Jr.
Professor of Biology, Utica College of Syracuse University, Utica, N.Y.

Lewis L. Gould
Professor of History, University of Texas, Austin.

Philip Gould
Professor of Art History, Sarah Lawrence College, Bronxville, N.Y.

Anthony J. Gow
Research Geologist, U.S. Army Cold Regions, Research and Engineering Laboratory, Hanover, N.H.

Oleg Grabar
Professor of Fine Arts, Harvard University, Cambridge, Mass.

Nelson H. H. Graburn
Professor of Anthropology, University of California, Berkeley.

Otis L. Graham, Jr.
Distinguished University Professor, University of North Carolina, Chapel Hill.

Mark Graubard
Professor Emeritus of Natural Science and History of Science, University of Minnesota, Minneapolis.

Raymond E. C. Graunke
Former Editor and Publisher, *Soundings.*

Donald J. Gray
Professor of English, Indiana University, Bloomington.

Elizabeth A. Gray
Assistant Professor of Celtic Languages and Literatures, Harvard University, Cambridge, Mass.

Alfred de Grazia
Research Professor of Social Theory in Government, New York University, New York City.

Erika Green
Senior Scientist, Hoffmann-La Roche, Inc., Nutley, N.J.

Maurice Green
Professor and Chairman, Institute for Molecular Virology, St. Louis University School of Medicine, Saint Louis, Mo.

Michael E. Green
Associate Professor of Chemistry, City University of New York, New York City.

Tamara M. Green
Assistant Professor of Classics, Hunter College, City University of New York, New York City.

William M. Green, M.D.
Department of Radiology, Medical Center at Princeton, Princeton, N.J.

Fred Greenbaum
Professor of History, Queensborough Community College, City University of New York, New York City.

Bernard Greenberg
Professor of Biological Sciences, University of Illinois, Chicago.

Richard Greenberg
Senior Scientist, Planetary Science Institute, Tucson, Ariz.

David H. Greene
Professor of English, New York University, New York City.

Lee Seifert Greene
Distinguished Professor Emeritus, University of Tennessee, Knoxville.

Charlotte Greenspan
Mellon Post-Doctoral Teaching Fellow in the Humanities, Cornell, University, Ithaca, N.Y.

Edward T. Greenstein, D.V.M.
University Veterinarian, Rutgers University, New Brunswick, N.J.

Roy O. Greep
Professor of Anatomy Emeritus, Harvard Medical School, Boston.

Joel W. Gregory
Professeur agrégé, département de démographie, Université de Montréal, Montréal.

Eamon Grennan
Assistant Professor, Department of English, Vassar College, Poughkeepsie, N.Y.

John A. C. Greppin
Director, Program in Linguistics, Cleveland State University, Cleveland, Ohio.

Robert R. Griffeth
Assistant Professor of History, University of Washington, Seattle.

Dana Griffin III
Associate Professor of Botany, University of Florida, Gainesville, Fla.

James B. Griffin
Senior Research Scientist, Museum of Anthropology, University of Michigan, Ann Arbor.

William S. Griffith
Professor and Chairman, Department of Adult Education, University of British Columbia, Vancouver.

Anthony J. F. Griffiths
Associate Professor of Botany, University of British Columbia, Vancouver.

A. R. G. Griffiths
Senior Lecturer, Flinders University of South Australia, South Australia.

John F. Griffiths
Professor and Texas State Climatologist, Texas A&M University, College Station.

William G. Grigsby
Professor of City and Regional Planning, University of Pennsylvania, Philadelphia.

E. R. Grilly
Staff Member, Los Alamos Scientific Laboratory, University of California, Los Alamos, N.Mex.

Robert E. Grinder
Professor of Educational Psychology, College of Education, Arizona State University, Tempe.

Merilee S. Grindle
Research Associate, Harvard Institute for International Development, Harvard University, Cambridge, Mass.

Larry R. Grisham
Physicist, Princeton University, Plasma Physics Laboratory, Princeton, N.J.

E. E. Grissell
Research Entomologist, Systematic Entomology Laboratory, Washington, D.C.

Daniel P. Griswold, Jr.
Associate Director, Chemotherapy Research, Southern Research Institute, Birmingham, Ala.

Charles F. Gritzner
Associate Professor of Geography, University of Houston, Houston, Tex.

Howard Shea Grob
Professor and Chairman, Department of Biology, Adelphi University, Garden City, N.Y.

Laura V. Grobovsky
Department of Biology, Yale University, New Haven, Conn.

Lawrence Grossman
Associate Professor of Geochemistry, University of Chicago, Chicago.

David I. Grossvogel
Goldwin Smith Professor of Comparative Literature and Romance Studies, Cornell University, Ithaca, N.Y.

Paul A. Groves
Associate Professor of Geography, University of Maryland, College Park.

Lee Guernsey
Professor of Geography, Indiana State University, Terre Haute.

John F. Guilmartin, Jr.
Former Associate Professor of History, U.S. Air Force Academy, USAF Academy, Colo.

Harvey L. Gunderson
Associate Director, State Museum, and Professor of Zoology, University of Nebraska, Lincoln.

Samuel C. Gundy
Assistant Professor of Biology, Kutztown State College, Kutztown, Pa.

Bill Gunston
Assistant Compiler, *Jane's All the World's Aircraft* (annual), and European Editor, *Aircraft.*

Pete A. Y. Gunter
Professor of Philosophy, North Texas State University, Denton.

Maria Teresa Gutiérrez de MacGregor
Doctora en Geografía, Instituto de Geografía, Universidad Nacional Autónoma México, Ciudad Universitaria, Villa Obregón.

Joseph Gutmann
Professor of Art History, Wayne State University, Detroit.

François Haas
Assistant Professor, Department of Physiology, New York University Medical Center, New York City.

John T. Hackett
Associate Professor of Physiology, University of Virginia School of Medicine, Charlottesville.

Elbert H. Hadley
Professor of Chemistry, Southern Illinois University, Carbondale.

Richard L. Haedrich
Associate Scientist, Woods Hole Oceanographic Institution, Woods Hole, Mass.

Kenneth J. Hagan
Associate Professor of History, U.S. Naval Academy, Annapolis, Md.

H. G. Haile
Professor of German, University of Illinois, Urbana.

Franklyn S. Haiman
Professor of Communication Studies, Northwestern University, Evanston, Ill.

Jay L. Halio
Professor of English, University of Delaware, Newark.

A. Rupert Hall
Professor of the History of Science and Technology, Imperial College, London.

Charles V. Hall
Professor of Horticulture, Iowa State University, Ames.

James Hall
Art Historian and Author, *Dictionary of Subjects and Symbols in Art.*

John Whitling Hall
Professor of Geography and Chairman, Department of Social Sciences, Louisiana State University, Shreveport.

Robert B. Hall
Professor of History and Geography, University of Rochester, Rochester, N.Y.

Brig. Gen. William C. Hall, Retired
Executive Director and Editor, The Society of American Military Engineers, Washington, D.C.

Anthony Hallam
Professor of Geological Sciences, University of Birmingham, Birmingham, England.

Richard P. Hallion
Associate Professor, University of Maryland, College Park.

Leslie Halliwell
Film Buyer, ITV Network of Great Britain, and Author, *The Filmgoers Companion, Halliwell's Filmguide.*

Talat Sait Halman
Professor of Near Eastern Studies, Princeton University, Princeton, N.J.

John Halperin
Professor of English, University of Southern California, University Park, Los Angeles.

Arthur M. Halpern
Associate Professor of Chemistry, Northeastern University, Boston.

Richard S. Halsey
Dean, School of Library and Information Science, State University of New York, Albany, and Former Chairman, Reference and Subscription Books Reviews Committee, American Library Association.

Roy Halverson
Associate Professor of Journalism, University of Oregon, Eugene.

Alonzo L. Hamby
Professor of History, Ohio University, Athens.

Jerrold F. Hames
Editor, *Canadian Churchman.*

Stephen Handel
Professor of Psychology, University of Tennessee, Knoxville.

Ted L. Hanes
Professor of Biology, California State University, Fullerton.

Joseph F. Hanlon
Packaging Consultant, Formerly with Hoffmann-La Roche, Inc., Nutley, N.J.

Chad Hansen
Professor of Philosophy, University of Vermont, Burlington.

John W. Harbaugh
Professor of Geology, Stanford University, Stanford, Calif.

William H. Harbold
Professor of Political Science, Whitman College, Walla Walla, Wash.

D. W. Harding
Professor of Archaeology, University of Edinburgh, Edinburgh.

Walter Harding
Secretary, The Thoreau Society, Geneseo, N.Y.

Robert D. Hare
Professor of Psychology, University of British Columbia, Vancouver.

R. P. Hargreaves
Associate Professor of Geography, University of Otago, Dunedin, New Zealand.

Maurice Harmon
Lecturer in Anglo-Irish Literature, University College, Dublin.

Robert A. Harper
Professor and Chairman, Department of Geography, University of Maryland, College Park.

S. C. Harrex
Director, Centre for Research in the New Literatures in English (CRNLE), Flinders University, Bedford Park, South Australia, Australia.

Dale Harris
Professor of Literature, Sarah Lawrence College, Bronxville, N.Y.; College Professor of the Arts, Trinity College, Hartford, Conn.; Adjunct Professor of Art History, Cooper Union for the Advancement of Science and Art, New York City; and Visiting Professor of Dance History, School of the Arts, New York City.

Dudley Arthur Harris
Author of *Hydroponics: Growing without Soil.*

Edward Grant Harris
Professor of Physics and Astronomy, University of Tennessee, Knoxville.

Jessica Harris
Associate Professor of Library and Information Science, St. John's University, Jamaica, N.Y.

Lauren Julius Harris
Professor, Michigan State University, East Lansing.

R. Baine Harris
Eminent Professor of Philosophy, Old Dominion University, Norfolk, Va.

John P. Harrison
Distinguished Professor of History, University of Miami, Coral Gables, Fla.

Donn V. Hart
Professor of Anthropology and Director, Center for Southeast Asian Studies, Northern Illinois University, De Kalb.

James A. Hart
Associate Professor of English, University of British Columbia, Vancouver.

Roy Hartenstein
Professor of Zoology, State University College of Environmental Science and Forestry, Syracuse, N.Y.

Thomas B. Hartmann
Professor of Journalism and Urban Communications, Rutgers University, New Brunswick, N.J.

Joseph H. Hartshorn
Professor of Geology and Geography, University of Massachusetts, Amherst.

Truman Hartshorn
Associate Professor of Geography, Georgia State University, Atlanta.

Donald J. Harvey
Professor of History, Hunter College, City University of New York, New York City.

Van A. Harvey
Professor of Religious Studies, Stanford University, Stanford, Calif.

Dayton Haskin, S.J.
Assistant Professor of English, Boston College, Chestnut Hill, Mass.

Warren W. Hassler, Jr.
Professor of American History, Pennsylvania State University, University Park.

Robert D. Hatcher, Jr.
Professor of Geology, Florida State University, Tallahassee.

Paul G. Hattersley, M.D.
Professor of Internal Medicine and Pathology, School of Medicine, University of California, Davis.

Joseph P. Haughton
Professor of Geography, University of Dublin, Dublin.

William B. Hauser
Assistant Professor of History, University of Rochester, Rochester, N.Y.

B. Austin Haws
Professor of Biology and Entomology, Utah State University, Logan.

Charles H. Haws
Director of the Institute of Scottish Studies, Old Dominion University, Norfolk, Va.

Frank C. Hawthorne
Professor of Earth Sciences, University of Manitoba, Winnipeg.

John Hay
Assistant Professor of Fine Arts, Harvard University, Cambridge, Mass.

Edwin V. Hayden
Christian Minister, Former Editor of the *Christian Standard.*

William Hays
Associate Professor of Organ, Westminster Choir College, Princeton, N.J.

Daniel R. Headrick
Associate Professor of Social Sciences, Roosevelt University, Chicago.

Earl O. Heady
Distinguished Professor and Director of Agriculture, Iowa State University, Ames.

J. R. Healy
Professor of Geography, Hilo College, University of Hawaii, Hilo.

Thomas K. Hearn, Jr.
Professor of Philosophy and Dean, School of Humanities, University of Alabama, Birmingham.

Melvin E. Hecht
Professor of Geography, University of Arizona, Tucson.

J. L. Heilbron
Professor of History of Science and Technology, University of California, Berkeley.

Fred Heilizer
Associate Professor of Psychology, De Paul University, Chicago.

Judith Heilizer
Clinical Psychologist, Private Practice.

Michael Henry Heim
Assistant Professor of Slavic Languages, University of California, Los Angeles.

George E. Hein
Professor, Lesley College Graduate School of Education, Cambridge, Mass.

John F. Heiss
Director, Research and Development, Diamond Crystal Salt Co., Saint Clair, Mich.

Peter Heller
Professor of German and Comparative Literature, State University of New York, Buffalo.

Hal Hellman
Science Writer and Author of *Communications in the World of the Future.*

Jonathan E. Helmreich
Dean of Instruction and Professor of History, Allegheny College, Meadville, Pa.

Paul C. Helmreich
Professor of History, Wheaton College, Norton, Mass.

Randel Helms
Assistant Professor of English, Arizona State University, Tempe.

Janice A. Henderson
Visiting Member, Institute for Advanced Study, Princeton, N.J.

Jeffrey Henderson
Associate Professor of Greek and Latin, University of Michigan, Ann Arbor.

John S. Henderson
Assistant Professor of Anthropology, Cornell University, Ithaca, N.Y.

Ray Henkel
Professor of Geography, University of Arizona, Tempe.

Paul Henkind, M.D.
Professor and Chairman of Department of Ophthalmology, Albert Einstein College of Medicine, Bronx, N.Y.

John Bell Henneman
Professor of History, University of Iowa, Iowa City.

Robert J. Henning, M.D.
Assistant Professor of Medicine, University of Southern California, Los Angeles.

J. David Henry
Biological Consultant, Henry and Associates Co., Waskesiu, Saskatchewan.

Michael K. Herbert
Editor, *Auto Racing Digest,* Century Publishing Co., Evanston, Ill.

Christoph Hering
Professor of German and Comparative Literature, University of Maryland, College Park.

Mary Ann Herman
Co-Director of Folk Dance House and Folk Dance Consultant for Dance Division of Performing Arts Library, New York City.

Robert Herman
Associate Professor of Zoology, Rutgers University, New Brunswick, N.J.

Edwin L. Herr
Professor and Head, Division of Counseling and Educational Psychology, Pennsylvania State University, University Park.

James W. Herrick
Adjunct Professor of Anthropology, State University of New York College of Technology, Utica-Rome.

Robert O. Herrmann
Professor of Agricultural Economics, Pennsylvania State University, University Park.

Martin Hershenson
Contributing and Consulting Editor, *Modern Photography.*

Charles A. Herubin
Associate Professor, Hudson Valley Community College, Troy, N.Y.

Bruce Herzberg
Rutgers University, New Brunswick, N.J.

Robert Hetzron
Professor of Hebrew, University of
California, Santa Barbara.

Robert E. Hicks
Associate Professor of Psychology, State
University of New York, Albany.

Kathryn Hiesinger
Curator of Decorative Arts after 1700,
Philadelphia Museum of Art, Philadelphia.

Ulrich Hiesinger
Art Historian.

Anna Hietanen
Geologist, U.S. Geological Survey, Menlo
Park, Calif.

Don Higginbotham
Professor of History, University of North
Carolina, Chapel Hill.

Larry C. Higgins
Associate Professor of Biology, West Texas
State University, Canyon.

Robert A. Higham
Consultant, Euro-Data Analysts, Ashtead,
Surrey, United Kingdom.

Christopher R. Hill
Director, Centre for Southern African
Studies, University of York, Heslington,
York, England.

Harold C. Hill
Professor of Data Processing, San Diego City
College, San Diego, Calif.

John Walter Hill
Associate Professor of Music, University of
Illinois, Urbana.

Richard Leslie Hills
Director, North Western Museum of
Science and Industry, Manchester, England.

Ronald Hingley
Department of Russian, Oxford University,
Oxford, England.

William M. Hinkle
Professor Emeritus of Art History, Columbia
University, New York City.

Jerry Hirsch
Professor of Psychology and of Ecology,
Ethology, and Evolution, University of
Illinois, Champaign-Urbana.

Richard F. Hirsh
Humanities Center, University of Florida,
Gainesville.

David W. Hirst
Senior Research Historian and Associate
Editor, *The Papers of Woodrow Wilson,*
Princeton University, Princeton, N.J.

Homer W. Hiser
Director, Remote Sensing Laboratory,
University of Miami, Coral Gables, Fla.

Wilbert M. Hite
Consultant, Trucking Industry.

Richard F. Hixson
Professor of Journalism and Urban
Communications, Livingston College,
Rutgers University, New Brunswick, N.J.

Maung Hla Pe
Associate Professor of Physics, Manhattan
College, Riverdale, Bronx, N.Y.

Fred Hobson
Associate Professor of English, University of
Alabama, University.

Julian Hochberg
Professor of Psychology, Columbia
University, New York City.

Paul W. Hodge
Professor of Astronomy, University of
Washington, Seattle.

C. Walter Hodges
Theatre Historian and Designer, Lewes,
Sussex, England.

D. G. Hoffman
Assistant Professor of Mathematics, Auburn
University, Auburn, Ala.

George W. Hoffman
Professor of Geography, University of Texas,
Austin.

Michael J. Hoffman
Professor of English, University of California,
Davis.

Paul Hoffman
Department of Philosophy, Harvard
University, Cambridge, Mass.

Donald F. Hoffmeister
Director, Museum of Natural History and
Professor of Ecology, Ethology, and
Evolution, University of Illinois, Urbana.

Pershing B. Hofslund
Professor of Zoology, University of
Minnesota, Duluth.

Edward Patrick Hogan
Associate Dean of Arts and Sciences, and
Head, Department of Geography, South
Dakota State University, Brookings.

Robert Hogan
Professor of English, University of Delaware,
Newark.

William T. Hogan, S.J.
Professor of Economics and Director,
Industrial Economics Research Institute,
Fordham University, Bronx, N.Y.

Arthur R. Hogue
Professor Emeritus of History, Indiana
University, Bloomington.

Carol J. Rowland Hogue
Chief, Pregnancy Epidemiology Branch,
Division of Reproductive Health, Centers
for Disease Control, Atlanta, Ga.

Arthur I. Holleb, M.D.
Senior Vice-President for Medical Affairs,
American Cancer Society, New York City.

Leo E. Hollister, M.D.
Professor of Medicine, Psychiatry, and
Pharmacology, Stanford University School of
Medicine, Palo Alto, Calif.

W. Eugene Hollon
Ohio Regents Professor of History,
University of Toledo, Toledo, Ohio.

Frederic B. M. Hollyday
Professor of History, Duke University,
Durham, N.C.

George Holmes
St. Catherine's College, Oxford, England.

Jack D. L. Holmes
Director, Louisiana Collection Series of
Books and Documents on Colonial
Louisiana.

R. F. Holmes
Deputy Registrar, University of Cambridge,
Cambridge, England.

James R. Holton
Professor of Atmospheric Sciences,
University of Washington, Seattle.

Seymour Holtzman
Associate Scientist, Medical Department,
Brookhaven National Laboratory, Upton,
N.Y.

Sinclair Hood
Former Director of the British School of
Archaeology at Athens.

William Hood
Assistant Professor of Art, Oberlin College,
Oberlin, Ohio.

Marjorie L. Hoover
Emeritus Professor of German and Russian,
Oberlin College, Oberlin, Ohio.

William E. Hopke
Professor and Head, Department of
Guidance and Personnel Services, North
Carolina State University, Raleigh.

William G. Hopkins
Associate Professor of Plant Sciences,
University of Western Ontario, London.

Peter C. Hoppe
Staff Scientist, Jackson Laboratory, Bar
Harbor, Maine.

David J. Horn
Associate Professor of Entomology, Ohio
State University, Columbus.

Michael H. Horn
Professor of Biology, California State
University, Fullerton.

Roderick H. Horning
Manager, Environmental Affairs, Dyes and
Chemicals Division, Crompton & Knowles
Corp., Reading, Pa.

Franklin E. Horowitz
Associate, American Language Program,
Columbia University, New York City.

A. Doyne Horsley
Assistant Professor of Geography, Southern
Illinois University, Carbondale.

Reginald Horsman
Distinguished Professor of History,
University of Wisconsin, Milwaukee.

Donald D. Howard
Professor of History, Florida State University,
Tallahassee.

Fran P. Hosken
Publisher and Editor, *Women's International
Network News.*

J. R. Houck
Associate Professor of Astronomy, Cornell
University, Ithaca, N.Y.

John G. Houghton
Associate Professor of Geography,
University of Nevada, Reno.

David A. Hounshell
Assistant Professor of History, Harvey Mudd
College, Claremont, Calif.

Charles Howard
Professor of Chemistry, University of Texas,
San Antonio.

Wayne Howard
Former Assistant Professor of Music, Kent
State University, Kent, Ohio.

The Very Reverend Wilbur K. Howard
The United Church of Canada, Ottawa.

Jeffery W. Howe
Assistant Professor of Fine Arts, Boston
College, Chestnut Hill, Mass.

Almonte Howell
Research Professor of Musicology,
University of Georgia, Athens.

John Howell
Contributing Editor, *Performing Arts Journal.*

P. Howse
Department of Biology, University of
Southampton, Southampton, England.

C. T. Hu
Professor of Comparative Education,
Teachers College, Columbia University, New
York City.

William M. Hubbard
Member of Technical Staff, Bell Telephone
Laboratories, Holmdel, N.J.

Robert J. Huckshorn
Professor of Political Science, Florida
Atlantic University, Boca Raton.

Robert V. Hudson
Associate Professor of Journalism, Michigan
State University, East Lansing.

Franklin E. Huffman
Associate Professor of Linguistics and Asian
Studies, Cornell University, Ithaca, N.Y.

William E. Hug
Chairperson, Department of Educational
Media and Librarianship, School of
Education, University of Georgia, Athens.

Charles C. Hughes
Professor of Anthropology, and Family and
Community Medicine, University of Utah,
Salt Lake City.

Jerome Hull, Jr.
Professor and Extension Horticulturalist, Michigan State University, East Lansing.

Chas. B. Hunt
Geologist, Formerly with the U.S. Geological Survey.

Edward E. Hunt, Jr.
Professor of Anthropology and Health Education, Pennsylvania State University, University Park.

George W. Hunt
Instructor-Trainer and Chairman, Chapter First Aid, American Red Cross, Princeton, N.J.

Cornelius S. Hurlbut, Jr.
Professor Emeritus of Mineralogy, Harvard University, Cambridge, Mass.

Farley K. Hutchins
Professor of Music, University of Akron, Akron, Ohio.

Russell J. Hutnik
Professor of Forest Ecology, Pennsylvania State University, University Park.

Corinne Hutt
Reader in Psychology, University of Keele, Keele, Staffordshire, England.

Ray Hyman
Professor of Psychology, University of Oregon, Eugene.

Ernest C. Hynds
Associate Professor of Journalism and Mass Communication, University of Georgia, Athens.

David W. Icenogle
Department of Geography, Auburn University, Auburn, Ala.

Clarence P. Idyll
Chief, Division of International Fisheries Development and Services, National Marine Fisheries Service, National Oceanic and Atmospheric Administration, U.S. Department of Commerce.

Georg G. Iggers
Professor of History, State University of New York, Buffalo.

Aaron J. Ihde
Professor of Chemistry, Integrated Liberal Studies and History of Science, University of Wisconsin, Madison.

J. Rowland Illick
Professor of Geography, Middlebury College, Middlebury, Vt.

Rita J. Immerman
Assistant Professor of Political Science, William Paterson College of New Jersey, Wayne, N.J.

Charles J. Ingardia, M.D.
Director of Maternal/Fetal Medicine Hartford Hospital, Hartford, Conn.

Cynthia E. Irvine
Research Astronomer, Monterey Institute for Research in Astronomy, Monterey, Calif.

David Irwin
Chairman, Department of History of Art, University of Aberdeen, Old Aberdeen, Scotland.

Francis W. Irwin
Emeritus Professor of Psychology, University of Pennsylvania, Philadelphia.

John B. Irwin
Former Associate Professor, Kean College of New Jersey, Union, N.J.

Mark A. Isaacs
Landscape Architect, U.S. Department of Housing and Urban Development, Washington, D.C.

Reginald R. Isaacs
Charles Dyer Norton Professor of Regional Planning, Emeritus, Harvard University, Cambridge, Mass.

Donald W. Ivey
Professor of Music, University of Kentucky, Lexington.

Donald Jackson
Professor Emeritus of History, University of Virginia, Charlottesville.

David Michael Jacobs
Assistant Professor of History, Temple University, Philedelphia.

Jay Jacobs
Food Historian.

Daniel Jacobson
Professor of Geography and Education, Adjunct Professor of Anthropology, Michigan State University, East Lansing.

Martin Jacobson
Supervisory Research Chemist, U.S. Department of Agriculture, Beltsville, Md.

Irma B. Jaffe
Professor of Art History, Fordham University, Bronx, N.Y.

Harold L. James
Former Research Geologist, U.S. Geological Survey.

Jules Janick
Professor of Horticulture, Purdue University, West Lafayette, Ind.

L. B. Jaques
Professor of Physiology, University of Saskatchewan, Saskatoon.

Konrad H. Jarausch
Professor of History, University of Missouri, Columbia.

Raymond Jarvi
Associate Professor of Swedish, North Park College, Chicago.

Alan Jefferson
Former Professor of Vocal Interpretation, Guildhall School of Music and Drama, London.

Graham H. Jeffries, M.D.
Professor of Medicine, Pennsylvania State University, University Park.

Joseph R. Jehl, Jr.
Assistant Director, Hubbs-Sea World Research Institute, San Diego, Calif.

Burgess H. Jennings
Emeritus Professor of Mechanical Engineering, Northwestern University, Evanston, Ill.

R. Bruce Jennings
Assistant Professor of Political Science, Stockton State College, Pomona, N.J.

H. James Jensen
Professor of English, Indiana University, Bloomington.

Wayburn S. Jeter
Professor and Head, Department of Microbiology, University of Arizona, Tucson.

Robert Jewett
Professor of New Testament Interpretation, Garrett-Evangelica Theological Seminary, Evanston, Ill.

J. Michael Jobanek
So-Cal Safety Associates, Reston, Va.

Erwin V. Johanningmeier
Professor, Historical Foundations of Education, University of South Florida, Tampa.

Donald C. Johanson
Curator of Physical Anthropology, Cleveland Museum of Natural History, Cleveland, Ohio.

T. S. K. Johansson
Professor of Biology, Queens College, City University of New York, Flushing.

Bernard John
Professor, Department of Population Biology, Australian National University, Canberra.

B. Edgar Johnson
General Secretary, Church of the Nazarene, Kansas City, Mo.

Curtis D. Johnson
Associate Professor, College of Technology, University of Houston, Houston, Tex.

Douglas Johnson
Associate Professor of Music, University of Virginia, Charlottesville.

Earl Johnson, Jr.
Professor of Law, University of Southern California Law Center, Los Angeles.

Gary E. Johnson
Associate Professor of Geography, University of North Dakota, Grand Forks.

J. Theodore Johnson, Jr.
Professor of French, University of Kansas, Lawrence.

Leonard R. Johnson
Professor of Physiology, University of Texas Medical School, Houston.

Richard A. Johnson
Professor of English, Mount Holyoke College, South Hadley, Mass.

Ronald D. Johnson
Senior Organic Chemist, Eli Lilly and Company, Indianapolis, Ind.

Sherman E. Johnson
Dean and Professor of New Testament, Emeritus, The Church Divinity School of the Pacific, Berkeley, Calif.

Donald H. Johnston
Associate Professor, Graduate School of Journalism, Columbia University, New York City.

S. Paul Johnston
Former Director, National Air and Space Museum, Smithsonian Institution, Washington, D.C.

Clifford Jolly
Professor of Anthropology, New York University, New York City.

Andrew D. Jones, P.E.
Head, Civil Engineering, California Polytechnic State University, San Luis Obispo.

David O. Jones, D.V.M.
Professor, Department of Veterinary Preventive Medicine, Ohio State University, Columbus.

E. L. Jones
Professor of Economics, La Trobe University, Melbourne, Australia.

Leslie Jones
Associate Professor of Art History, Trenton State College, Trenton, N.J.

Lyle V. Jones
Vice-Chancellor and Dean of the Graduate School, University of North Carolina, Chapel Hill.

Oliver W. Jones
Professor of Medicine and Pediatrics, and Director, Division of Medical Genetics, University of California, La Jolla.

Richard C. Jones
Assistant Professor of Geography, University of Texas, San Antonio.

Tom B. Jones
Regents' Professor, Emeritus, University of Minnesota, Minneapolis.

Alan V. Jopling
Professor of Geography, University of Toronto, Toronto.

John E. Jordan
Professor of English, University of California, Berkeley.

Tom Jordan
Assistant Publisher, *Track & Field News.*

Aage Jørgensen
Adjunkt, Cand. art., Langkær Gymnasium, Mundelstrup, Denmark.

Robert A. Joyce, M.D.
Assistant Professor of Medicine, University of Pittsburgh School of Medicine, Pittsburgh, Pa.

Robert W. Jugenheimer
Professor of Plant Genetics and Director of Overseas Projects, Emeritus, University of Illinois, Urbana.

Sidney R. Jumper
Professor and Head, Department of Geography, University of Tennessee, Knoxville.

Jacob Kabakoff
Professor of Hebrew, Lehman College, City University of New York, Bronx.

Adrienne L. Kaeppler
Anthropologist, Bishop Museum, Honolulu, Hawaii.

Alan L. Kagan
Associate Professor of Ethnomusicology, University of Minnesota, Minneapolis.

M. P. Kahl
Author of *Wonders of the Stork World.*

Madlyn Kahr
Acting Professor of Art History and Criticism, University of California, San Diego.

Paul S. Kaiser
National Commander, The Salvation Army National Headquarters, New York City.

Jesse G. Kalin
Associate Professor of Philosophy, Vassar College, Poughkeepsie, N.Y.

Harold Kalter, M.D.
Professor of Research Pediatrics, College of Medicine, University of Cincinnati, Cincinnati, Ohio.

Jonathan Kamin
President and Editor in Chief, Bay Arts Press Service, Oakland, Calif.

Michael Kandel
Freelance Writer.

John F. Kane
Special Librarian, ALCOA, Alcoa Center, Pa.

William B. Kannel, M.D., M.P.H., F.A.C.P., F.A.C.C.
Director, Framingham Heart Study, N.H.L.B.I., U.S. National Institutes of Health, Framingham, Mass.

Bernard Kaplan
Professor of Psychology and Director, Graduate Training Program in Developmental Psychology, Clark University, Worcester, Mass.

Marshall H. Kaplan
Professor of Aerospace Engineering, Pennsylvania State University, University Park.

Ronald A. Kapon
President, Profit Plus Marketing and Merchandising Company, New York City.

Stuart A. Karabenick
Professor of Psychology, Eastern Michigan University, Ypsilanti.

Yehuda Karmon
Professor of Geography, Hebrew University, Jerusalem, Israel.

Michael J. Kasperbauer
Professor of Agronomy, University of Kentucky, Lexington.

Samuel D. Kassow
Assistant Professor of History, Trinity College, Hartford, Conn.

Jack J. Kasulis
Assistant Professor of Business Administration, University of Oklahoma, Norman.

Judith A. Kates
Assistant Professor of English and Comparative Literature, Harvard University, Cambridge, Mass.

Michael Katz
New York Times Sportswriter.

George B. Kauffman
Professor of Chemistry, California State University, Fresno.

Paul A. Kay
Assistant Professor of Geography, University of Utah, Salt Lake City.

Janet Kear
Assistant Director, Wildfowl Trust, and Curator, Martin Mere, Lancashire, England.

Howard Clark Kee
William Goodwin Aurelio Professor of Biblical Studies, Boston University, Boston.

John Keegan
Professor, Royal Military Academy, Sandhurst, England.

Roger M. Keesing
Professor of Anthropology, Australian National University, Canberra.

Noelle L. Kehrberg
Assistant Professor, Foods, Nutrition, and Dietetics, Western Carolina University, Cullowhee, N.C.

Frank S. Kelland
Department of Physics/Geoscience, Montclair State College, Upper Montclair, N.J.

Marylin C. Kelland
Department of Economics, Geography, and Management Science, Kean College of New Jersey, Union.

Philip C. Keller
Professor of Chemistry, University of Arizona, Tucson.

Rev. Dean M. Kelley
Executive for Religious and Civil Liberty, National Council of Churches, New York City.

Robert Kelley
Professor of History, University of California, Santa Barbara.

Andrew J. Kelly
Development Director, Circle in the Square, New York City.

Lawrence C. Kelly
Professor of History, North Texas State University, Denton.

Nora Hickson Kelly
Senior Author of *The Royal Canadian Mounted Police: A Century of History.*

John G. Kelton
Assistant Professor, McMaster Medical Centre, Hamilton, Ontario.

Frederick G. Kempin, Jr.
Professor of Legal Studies, The Wharton School, University of Pennsylvania, Philadelphia.

George Kennedy
Paddison Professor of Classics, University of North Carolina, Chapel Hill.

John S. Kennedy
Professor Emeritus, Imperial College, University of London, London.

Richard S. Kennedy
Professor of English, Temple University, Philadelphia.

Allen Kent
Distinguished Service Professor and Director, Office of Communications Programs, University of Pittsburgh, Pittsburgh, Pa.

J. Alistair Kerr
Senior Lecturer in Chemistry, The University, Birmingham, England.

K. Austin Kerr
Associate Professor of History, Ohio State University, Columbus.

Norman S. Kerr
Professor of Genetics and Cell Biology, University of Minnesota, Minneapolis.

William Kessen
Eugene Higgins Professor of Psychology and Professor of Pediatrics, Yale University, New Haven, Conn.

Ralph Ketcham
Professor of American Studies, Syracuse University, Syracuse, N.Y.

William C. Ketchum, Jr.
Author, Lecturer, and Teacher, New School for Social Research, Hunter College, New York City.

Julia Keydel
Art Historian and Filmmaker.

Nathan Keyfitz
Professor of Sociology and Demography, Harvard University, Cambridge, Mass.

Louis Kibler
Associate Professor of Italian, Wayne State University, Detroit.

Matthew X. Kiernan
Curatorial Assistant, Department of Textiles, Museum of Fine Arts, Boston.

Michael D. Kilian
Columnist, *Chicago Tribune.*

Kenneth W. Kilmer
Executive Project Director, Environmental Assessment Council Inc., New Brunswick, N.J.

Robert Kimbrough
Professor of English, University of Wisconsin, Madison.

Wayne R. Kime
Professor, Fairmont State College, Fairmont, W.Va.

Peter J. King
Associate Professor of History, Carleton University, Ottawa, Ontario.

Keith Kingbay
Cycling Activities Manager, Schwinn Bicycle Company, Chicago.

Douglas Kinnard
Professor of Political Science, University of Vermont, Burlington.

E. T. Kirby
Professor of Theatre, University of Maryland, Baltimore.

F. E. Kirby
Professor of Music, Lake Forest College, Lake Forest, Ill.

Max C. Kirkeberg
Assistant Professor of Geography, San Francisco State University, San Francisco.

James W. Kirkland
Director of Freshman Composition, East Carolina University, Greenville, N.C.

Lyman B. Kirkpatrick, Jr.
Professor of Political Science, Brown University, Providence, R.I.

Edith W. Kirsch
Research Assistant, Institute for Advanced Study, Princeton, N.J.

W. Chandler Kirwin
Professor of Art History, Amherst College, Amherst, Mass.

Joseph M. Kitagawa
Dean of the Divinity School and Professor of History of Religions, University of Chicago, Chicago.

Michael Kitson
Readers in the History of Art, Courtauld Institute of Art, University of London, London.

Gary Klee
Assistant Professor of Environmental Studies, San Jose State University, San Jose, Calif.

Helen Altman Klein
Associate Professor of Psychology, Wright State University, Dayton, Ohio.

Marcus Klein
Professor of English, State University of New York, Buffalo.

Christopher Kleinhenz
Associate Professor of Italian, University of Wisconsin, Madison.

E. D. Klemke
Professor of Philosophy, Iowa State University, Ames.

Glenn C. Klingman
Former Professor, North Carolina State University and Former Scientific Advisor, Eli Lilly and Company.

Jerome Klinkowitz
Professor of English, University of Northern Iowa, Cedar Falls.

Alexander B. Klots
Research Associate in Entomology, American Museum of Natural History and Professor of Biology, Emeritus, City College of New York, New York City.

Bettina L. Knapp
Professor of Romance Languages and Comparative Literatures, Hunter College and the Graduate Center, City University of New York, New York City.

Laurance A. Knecht
Professor of Chemistry, Marietta College, Marietta, Ohio.

Robert J. Knight, Jr.
Research Horticulturist, U.S. Department of Agriculture, Miami, Fla.

Roderic Knight
Assistant Professor of Ethnomusicology, Oberlin College Conservatory of Music, Oberlin, Ohio.

P. F. Knowles
Professor of Agronomy, University of California, Davis, Calif.

William J. Knox
Professor of Physics, University of California, Davis, Calif.

Ronald D. Knutson
Professor of Agricultural Economics, Texas A&M University, College Station, Tex.

A. Robert Koch
Professor of Agricultural Economics, Cook College, Rutgers University, New Brunswick, N.J.

Louis W. Koenig
Professor of Government, New York University, New York City.

H. G. Koenigsberger
Professor of History, University of London, King's College, London.

Gerhard M. Koeppel
Associate Professor of Classical Archaeology, University of North Carolina, Chapel Hill, N.C.

Noretta Koertge
Associate Professor, Department of History and Philosophy of Science, Indiana University, Bloomington, Ind.

Benjamin G. Kohl
Professor of History, Vassar College, Poughkeepsie, N.Y.

Philip L. Kohl
Professor of Anthropology, Wellesley College, Wellesley, Mass.

Alan J. Kohn
Professor of Zoology, University of Washington, Seattle.

Walter B. Kolesnik
Professor of Education, University of Detroit, Detroit.

Willem J. Kolff, M.D.
Distinguished Professor of Surgery and Director, Institute for Biomedical Engineering and Division of Artificial Organs, University of Utah, Salt Lake City.

Paul D. Komar
Professor of Oceanography, Oregon State University, Corvallis.

Victor A. Konrad
Assistant Professor of Geography and Canadian Studies, University of Maine, Orono.

Zdeněk Kopal
Professor of Astronomy, University of Manchester, Manchester, England, and Naval Research Laboratory, Washington, D.C.

Sheldon J. Kopperl
Associate Professor, Grand Valley State Colleges, Allendale, Mich.

Jacob Korg
Professor of English, University of Washington, Seattle.

David H. Kornhauser
Professor of Geography, University of Hawaii at Manoa, Honolulu.

L. A. Kosman
Professor of Philosophy, Haverford College, Haverford, Pa.

Stephen Michael Kosslyn
Associate Professor, Department of Psychology and Social Relations, Harvard University, Cambridge, Mass.

Stephen A. Kowalewski
Assistant Professor of Anthropology, University of Georgia, Athens.

Enno E. Kraehe
William W. Corcoran Professor of History, University of Virginia, Charlottesville.

Konrad B. Krauskopf
Professor of Geochemistry, Emeritus, Stanford University, Stanford, Calif.

Edward V. Krick
Associate Professor of Engineering Science, Lafayette College, Easton, Pa.

M. Kristiansen
P. W. Horn Professor of Electrical Engineering, Texas Tech University, Lubbock.

James Kritzeck
University of Toronto, Toronto.

Sam Kuczun
Professor, School of Journalism, University of Colorado, Boulder.

Albert E. Kudrle
Director of Public Relations, American Hotel and Motel Association, New York City.

Robert G. Kuller
Associate Professor of Mathematics, Northern Illinois University, De Kalb.

Bernhard Kummel
Professor of Geology, Harvard University, Cambridge, Mass.

Armand Kuris
Assistant Professor of Biology, University of California, Santa Barbara.

Diana Kurz
Artist and Former Faculty Member, State University of New York at Stony Brook, Stony Brook.

Patricia Kutzner
Executive Director, World Hunger Education Service, Washington, D.C.

Matti Kuusi
Professor, Emeritus, University of Helsinki, Helsinki, Finland.

Bruce La Rose
Assistant Professor of Geography and Cartography, Pace University, New York City.

Taivo Laevastu
National Marine Fisheries Service, Seattle, Wash.

Lloyd Laing
Senior Lecturer in Medieval Archaeology, Liverpool University, Liverpool.

Kevin Lamb
Sports Writer, Chicago *Sun-Times*.

C. C. Lamberg-Karlovsky
Professor of Anthropology and Director of the Peabody Museum, Harvard University, Cambridge, Mass.

Robert L. Lamborn
Executive Director, Council for American Private Education, Washington, D.C.

Robert Geran Landen
Dean of the College of Liberal Arts and Professor of History, University of Tennessee, Knoxville.

H. C. Robbins Landon
John Bird Professor of Music, University College, Cardiff, Wales.

Larry N. Landrum
Associate Professor of English, Michigan State University, East Lansing.

Fernand Landry
Professor of Physical Education, Université Laval, Québec.

Ronald W. Langacker
Professor of Linguistics, University of California, San Diego.

Paul Langford
Fellow and Tutor in Modern History. Lincoln College, Oxford, England.

Wann Langston, Jr.
Professor of Geology and Research Scientist, Texas Memorial Museum, University of Texas, Austin.

Paul Lansky
Associate Professor, Princeton University, Princeton, N.J.

Alain Larcan
Professor, Université de Médecine, Nancy, France.

Stephen Larson
Astronomer, Lunar and Planetary Laboratory, University of Arizona, Tucson.

Michael C. Latham
Professor of International Nutrition, Cornell University, Ithaca, N.Y.

Abrahim Lavi
Professor of Engineering, Carnegie-Mellon University, Pittsburgh, Pa.

Sister Anna Catherine Lawlor
Professor of Biology, College of Saint Elizabeth, Convent Station, N.J.

George H. M. Lawrence
Director, Emeritus, Hunt Institute for Botanical Documentation, Carnegie-Mellon University, Pittsburgh, Pa.

Robert Lawrence
Artistic Director and Conductor, Friends of French Opera, and Associate Professor of Vocal Studies, Temple University, Philadelphia.

Merlin P. Lawson
Associate Professor of Climatology. University of Nebraska, Lincoln.

Donald L. Layton
Professor of History, Indiana State University, Terre Haute.

Thomas Leabhart
Editor, *Mime Journal* and *Mime, Mask, and Marionette*.

Douglas Edward Leach
Professor of History, Vanderbilt University, Nashville, Tenn.

Peter B. Leavens
Associate Professor of Geology, University of Delaware, Newark.

Alan L. Lebowitz
Associate Professor of English, Tufts University, Medford, Mass.

Charles F. Leck
New Jersey State Ornithologist, Rutgers University, New Brunswick, N.J.

Michael T. Ledbetter
Assistant Professor, Department of Geology, University of Georgia, Athens.

Joseph LeDoux
Postdoctoral Research Fellow, National Institute of Health, New York Hospital-Cornell University Medical Center, New York City.

Kyu Taik Lee, M.D.
Professor of Pathology and Associate Dean for Graduate Studies and Research, Albany Medical College, Albany, N.Y.

Leslie W. Lee
Administrative Director, Laboratories, Orlando Regional Medical Center, Orlando, Fla.

Gerald S. Lefever, M.D.
Assistant Professor of Anesthesia, University of Pennsylvania School of Medicine, Philadelphia.

Winfred P. Lehmann
Ashbel Smith Professor, Linguistics and Germanic Languages, University of Texas, Austin.

Stanford E. Lehmberg
Professor of History, University of Minnesota, Minneapolis.

Henry M. Leicester
Emeritus Professor of Biochemistry, University of the Pacific, Stockton, Calif.

Thomas R. Leinbach
Associate Professor of Geography, University of Kentucky, Lexington.

Harriet Lembeck
Director, Wine/Beverage Program, Forest Hills, N.Y.

Reuel Lemmons
Editor, *Firm Foundation.*

Robert E. Lemon
Department of Biology, McGill University, Montreal.

Marguerite R. Lerner, M.D.
Professor of Dermatology, Yale University School of Medicine, New Haven, Conn.

Michael Lerner
Professor of Dermatology, Yale University School of Medicine, New Haven, Conn.

Laurent LeSage
Professor of Romance Languages, Emeritus, Pennsylvania State University, University Park.

Daniel R. Lesnick
Assistant Professor of History, Hiram College, Hiram, Ohio.

Stephen V. Letcher
Professor of Physics, University of Rhode Island, Kingston.

Rosa Maria Letts
Panel Lecturer, Victoria & Albert Museum, London.

A. Leo Levin
Director, The Federal Judicial Center, and Professor of Law, University of Pennsylvania, Philadelphia.

George L. Levine
Professor of English, Livingston College, Rutgers University, New Brunswick, N.J.

Herbert M. Levine
Professor of Political Science, University of Southwestern Louisiana, Lafayette.

Louis Levine
Professor of Biology, City College, City University of New York, New York City.

Sanford Levinson
Professor of Law, University of Texas Law School, Austin.

Sar A. Levitan
Research Professor of Economics and Director, Center for Social Policy Studies, George Washington University, Washington, D.C.

Milton E. Lewine
Professor of Art History, Columbia University, New York City.

David Levering Lewis
Professor of History, University of the District of Columbia, Washington, D.C.

George K. Lewis
Professor of Geography, Boston University, Boston.

Julian H. Lewis
Department of Biology as Applied to Medicine, Middlesex Hospital Medical School, London.

Peter M. H. Lewis
Aviation Author, Illustrator, and Photographer.

Richard S. Lewis
Freelance Science Writer.

Ronald L. Lewis
Assistant Professor of Black American Studies, University of Delaware, Newark.

Viola G. Lewis
Instructor in Medical Psychology, The Johns Hopkins University School of Medicine and Hospital, Baltimore, Md.

Jay Leyda
Gottesman Professor of Cinema Studies, New York University, New York City.

Ilse Lichtenstadter
Department of Near Eastern Languages and Civilizations, Emerita, Harvard University, Cambridge, Mass.

Lawrence W. Lichty
Professor of Communication Arts, University of Wisconsin, Madison.

Charles T. Lichy
Field Research & Development Specialist, Dow Chemical, USA.

David Lidman
Former News Editor and stamp news columnist, *New York Times.*

David S. Lifson
Professor, Monmouth College, West Long Branch, N.J.

Eric Lincoln
Author of *Backyard Games.*

John R. Lindbeck
Professor of Industrial Education, Western Michigan University, Kalamazoo.

Jerzy Linderski
Professor of History, University of Oregon, Eugene.

Bernth Lindfors
Professor of African and English Literature, University of Texas, Austin.

Robert Lindsay
Professor of Physics, Trinity College, Hartford, Conn.

Howard A. Link
Curator of Asian Art and Keeper of the Ukiyo-e Center, Honolulu Academy of Arts, Honolulu.

Harold A. Linstone
University Professor, Portland State University, Portland, Oreg.

Stephen J. Lippard
Professor of Chemistry, Columbia University, New York City.

Sol Liptzin
Professor Emeritus, City University of New York, New York City.

Howard Liss
Free-lance Sports Writer.

Raymond Lister
Fellow of Wolfson College, University of Cambridge, and President, Royal Society of Miniature Painters, Sculptors, and Gravers, and Chairman of the Board of Governors, Federation of British Artists, Cambridge, England.

Monroe H. Little
Assistant Professor of History, Massachusetts Institute of Technology, Cambridge, Mass.

Richard Stark Little
Associate Professor of Geography, West Virginia University, Morgantown.

C. Scott Littleton
Associate Professor of Anthropology, and Chairman, Department of Sociology and Anthropology, Occidental College, Los Angeles.

John Lloyd
Assistant Professor of Special Education, University of Virginia, Charlottesville.

Phoebe Lloyd
Graduate Center of the City University of New York, New York City.

John Lobell
Associate Professor of Architecture, Pratt Institute, Brooklyn, N.Y.

Richard F. Logan
Professor of Geography, University of California, Los Angeles.

Fred E. Lohrer
Librarian, Archbold Biological Station, Lake Placid, Fla.

Anthony J. Lomando, Jr.
Queens College of CUNY, Flushing, and Lamont-Doherty Geological Observatory, Palisades, N.Y.

Glenn Loney
Professor of Theatre, Graduate Center of the City University of New York, New York City.

Charles H. Long
William Rand Kenan, Jr., Professor of History of Religions, University of North Carolina, Chapel Hill, and Professor of History of Religions, Duke University, Durham, N.C.

John D. Long
Chairperson and Professor of Insurance, School of Business, Indiana University, Bloomington.

Robert Long
Audio-Video Editor, *High Fidelity* magazine.

D. B. Longmore, F.R.C.S.
Consultant Physiologist, National Heart Hospital, London.

R. M. Longyear
Professor of Music, University of Kentucky, Lexington.

O. A. Lorenz
Professor of Vegetable Crops, University of California, Davis.

D. J. Lovell
Professor and Consultant.

Margaretta M. Lovell
Acting Instructor, Department of History of Art, Yale University, New Haven, Conn.

James S. Lovett
Professor and Associate Head of the Department of Biological Sciences, Purdue University, West Lafayette, Ind.

John Lowry
Deputy Keeper, Indian Department, Victoria & Albert Museum, London.

Steven Lubar
Department of History, University of Chicago, Chicago.

John C. Lucchesi
Professor of Zoology and Genetics, University of North Carolina, Chapel Hill.

Georg Luck
Professor of Classics, The Johns Hopkins University, Baltimore, Md.

William A. Lunk
Exhibit Curator and Associate Director, Exhibit Museum, University of Michigan, Ann Arbor.

Gerardo Luzuriaga
Associate Professor of Spanish, University of California, Los Angeles.

James G. Lydon
Professor of History, Duquesne University, Pittsburgh, Pa.

Dorothy Siegert Lyle
Director of Consumer Relations, International Fabricare Institute, Silver Spring, Md.

Donald F. Lynch
Professor of Geography, College of Arts and Sciences, University of Alaska, Fairbanks.

John E. Lynch
Chairman, Department of Canon Law, Catholic University of America, Washington, D.C.

John W. Lyons
Director, National Engineering Laboratory, National Bureau of Standards, Washington, D.C.

John Maass
Information Officer, City of Philadelphia, Philadelphia.

T. T. Macan
Former Naturalist, Freshwater Biological Association, Cambria, England.

Patrick D. McAnany
Associate Professor of Criminal Justice, University of Illinois, Chicago.

Richard P. McBrien
Professor of Theology, Boston College, Chestnut Hill, Mass.

Jeanne McRae McCarthy
Professor of Special Education, University of Arizona, Tucson.

William McCarthy
Associate Professor of English, Iowa State University, Ames.

Stephen P. McCary
Director of Psychological Services, Almeda Clinic, Houston, Tex.

William J. McCauley
Professor of Biology, University of Arizona, Tucson.

J. Forbes McClellan
Associate Professor of Zoology, Colorado State University, Ft. Collins.

James E. McClellan III
Assistant Professor of the History of Science, Stevens Institute of Technology, Hoboken, N.J.

Campbell R. McConnell
Professor of Economics, University of Nebraska, Lincoln.

Jon P. McConnell
Professor, Washington State University, Pullman.

Virginia F. McConnell
Associate Professor, Emeritus, Tulane University, New Orleans, La.

John M. McCorry
Associate Editor, *Backpacking Journal* and *Camping Journal.*

Arthur O. McCoubrey
Associate Director for Measurement Services, National Measurement Laboratory, National Bureau of Standards, Washington, D.C.

James M. McCullough
Senior Specialist in Science and Technology, Science Policy Research Division, Congressional Research Service, Library of Congress, Washington, D.C.

Gail McCutcheon
Assistant Professor, School of Education, University of Virginia, Charlottesville.

W. A. McCutcheon
Director, Ulster Museum, Belfast, Northern Ireland.

Etta Macdonald, M.D.
Associate Professor of Microbiology, University of Texas Medical Branch, Galveston.

Forrest McDonald
Professor of History, University of Alabama, University.

J. Fred MacDonald
Professor of History, Northeastern Illinois University, Chicago.

John E. MacDonald
Foreign Service Officer (ret.).

Micheil MacDonald
Curator, Museum of Scottish Tartans, Comrie, Scotland.

R. Ross Macdonald
Professor of Linguistics, Georgetown University, Washington, D.C.

Jack McDonough
Former Writer-Producer, Sports, WCBS Radio, New York City.

Gerald W. McFarland
Professor of History, University of Massachusetts, Amherst.

James M. McGlathery
Associate Professor of German, University of Illinois, Urbana.

Alice McGrath
Consultant, lecturer of self-defense and co-author of *Self-Defense & Assault Prevention for Girls & Women.*

John C. McGregor
Professor Emeritus of Anthropology, University of Illinois, Urbana.

William J. McGuire
Professor of Psychology, Yale University, New Haven, Conn.

Tibor R. Machan
Senior Editor, *Reason* Magazine and Associate Professor of Philosophy, State University of New York College at Fredonia, Fredonia.

Thomas L. McHaney
Associate Professor of English, Georgia State University, Atlanta.

Ralph McInerny
Michael P. Grace Professor of Medieval Studies, and Director, The Medieval Institute, University of Notre Dame, Notre Dame, Ind.

Donald Macintyre
Captain, Royal Navy (ret.), Kent, England.

Michael McIntyre
Professor of Geography, San Jose State University, San Jose, Calif.

Ross J. MacIntyre
Associate Professor of Genetics, Cornell University, Ithaca, N.Y.

F. Eugene McJunkin
Engineer, Environmental Sciences Corp., Chapel Hill, N.C.

Guy W. McKee
Professor of Agronomy, Pennsylvania State University, University Park.

G. Calvin Mackenzie
Assistant Professor of Government, Colby College, Waterville, Maine.

Ross Mackenzie
Professor of Church History, Union Theological Seminary in Virginia, Richmond.

Tom L. McKnight
Professor of Geography, University of California, Los Angeles.

Peter Mackridge
Lecturer in Modern Greek Language and Literature, University of London, King's College, London.

Ian A. McLaren
Professor, Department of Education, University of Waikato, Hamilton, New Zealand.

Charles A. McLaughlin
Director of Education and General Curator, Zoological Society of San Diego (San Diego Zoo), San Diego, Calif.

Charles Maclean
Author of *The Wolf Children.*

John McLeish
Professor of Psychology, University of Victoria, Victoria, British Columbia.

David S. McLellan
Professor of Political Science, Miami University, Oxford, Ohio.

James McMillan
Political Advisor, *Daily Express,* London.

J. T. McMullan
Energy Study Group, New University of Ulster, Coleraine, Northern Ireland.

Richard M. McMurry
Professor of History, Valdosta State College, Valdosta, Ga.

Bruce McPherson
Boston University, Boston, Mass., and Harvard University, Cambridge, Mass.

John Macquarrie
Lady Margaret Professor of Divinity, University of Oxford, Oxford, England.

Edmund J. McTernan
Professor of Health Sciences and Dean, School of Allied Health Professions, State University of New York, Stony Brook.

Jeffrey McVey
Department of Chemistry, Princeton University, Princeton, N.J.

Eugene W. McWhorter
Engineering Consultant and Writer.

Margaret McWilliams
Professor, California State University, Los Angeles.

Nancy R. McWilliams
Coadjutant Professor of Psychology, Livingston College, Rutgers University, New Brunswick, N.J.

Charles Maechling, Jr.
Senior Fellow, Carnegie Endowment for International Peace, Washington, D.C.

Peter B. Maggs
Professor of Law, University of Illinois, Champaign.

Marcia E. Maguire
Former Professor of Persian, University of Pennsylvania, Philadelphia.

Victor H. Mair
Assistant Professor, University of Pennsylvania, Philadelphia.

Ella A. Malin
Contributing Editor, *The Burns Mantle Theater Yearbook: Best Plays;* Diary Editor, *Dramatists Guild Quarterly.*

V. Standish Mallory
Professor of Geological Science and Chairman and Curator, Division of Geology and Paleontology, Burke Washington State Museum, University of Washington, Seattle.

William P. Malm
Professor of Music, University of Michigan, Ann Arbor.

R. E. Malmstrom
Assistant Professor, University of Wisconsin, Milwaukee.

Joseph L. Malone
Professor of Linguistics, Barnard College and Columbia University, New York City.

William S. Maltby
Associate Professor, University of Missouri, St. Louis.

Leonard Maltin
Member of the Faculty, New School for Social Research, New York City.

Frank Manchel
Associate Dean, College of Arts and Sciences, University of Vermont, Burlington.

Oscar Mandel
Professor, Division of Humanities and Social Sciences, California Institute of Technology, Pasadena.

Michael Mandelbaum
Research and Editorial Director, The Lehrman Institute, New York City.

Gerald L. Mandell, M.D.
Professor of Medicine and Head, Infectious Diseases, University of Virginia School of Medicine, Charlottesville.

John Mandeville
Assistant to the President, American Kennel Club, New York City.

Paul A. Mankin
Professor, Department of French and Italian, University of Massachusetts, Amherst.

Alan Mann
Associate Professor of Anthropology, University of Pennsylvania, Philadelphia.

William E. Mann
Professor of Philosophy, University of Vermont, Burlington.

Peter K. Manning
Professor of Sociology and Psychiatry, Michigan State University, East Lansing.

Robert S. Manthy
Professor of Forestry, Michigan State University, East Lansing.

Roger Manvell
Visiting Professor of Film, Boston University, Boston.

Nina L. Marable
Assistant Professor, Human Nutrition and Foods, Virginia Polytechnic Institute and State University, Blacksburg.

Claudia Marchitiello
Department of Art and Archaeology, Princeton University, Princeton, N.J.

George E. Marcus
Professor of Anthropology, Rice University, Houston, Tex.

Paul Mareth
Consultant, AT&T Bell Laboratories, Business Planning, Product Requirements, and Customer Communications Groups in the Interactive Information Systems Department.

Ronald W. Maris
Professor and Chairman, Department of Sociology, University of South Carolina, Columbia.

Robert Markley
Lecturer in English, Vassar College, Poughkeepsie, N.Y.

William Markowitz
Adjunct Professor of Physics, Nova University, Dania, Fla.

Jonathan Marks
Assistant Professor of Dramatic Literature, Yale School of Drama, New Haven, Conn.

Theresa Marousek
Managing Editor, American College of Hospital Administrators, Chicago.

Bonnie Marranca
Editor, *Performing Arts Journal.*

Michael T. Marsden
Associate Professor, Department of Popular Culture, Bowling Green State University, Bowling Green, Ohio.

Robert C. Marsh
Music Critic, *Chicago Sun-Times.*

Robert L. Marshall
Professor of Music, University of Chicago, Chicago.

Robert T. Marshall
Professor of Food Science & Nutrition, University of Missouri, Columbia.

Alvin R. Martin
Assistant Professor, University of Texas, San Antonio.

Jay Martin
Leo S. Bing Professor of Literature, University of Southern California, Los Angeles.

Samuel P. Martin, M.D.
Professor of Medicine, University of Pennsylvania School of Medicine, Philadelphia.

William H. Martin
Director, Division of Natural Areas, Eastern Kentucky University, Richmond.

Andrew Martindale
Professor of Visual Arts, University of East Anglia, Norwich, England.

Wilson Martins
Professor of Portuguese, New York University, New York City.

John D. Marty III
Professor of Political Science and Associate Director of the Institute of Latin American Studies, University of North Carolina, Chapel Hill.

Martin E. Marty
F. M. Cone Distinguished Service Professor, University of Chicago Divinity School, Chicago.

John D. Martz
Professor of Political Science, Pennsylvania State University, University Park.

James M. Mason
Assistant Professor of Pathology, University of Tennessee Center for the Health Sciences, Memphis.

Gerald Mast
Professor of English, University of Chicago, Chicago.

John R. Mather
Professor, University of Delaware, Newark.

Thomas G. Mathews
Research Professor, University of Puerto Rico, Rio Piedras.

Susan Matisoff
Associate Professor of Japanese, Stanford University, Stanford, Calif.

Myron Matlaw
Professor of English, Queens College, City University of New York, Flushing.

Ralph E. Matlaw
Professor of Russian and Comparative Literature, University of Chicago, Chicago.

J. H. Matthews
Professor of French, Syracuse University, Syracuse, N.Y.

William H. Matthews III
Regent's Professor of Geology, Lamar University, Beaumont, Tex.

Edward L. Mattil
Professor of Art, North Texas State University, Denton.

Thomas P. Mattingly, M.D.
Department of Ophthalmology, University of Florida, Gainesville.

Samuel A. Matz
Vice-President, Research and Development and Regulatory Affairs, Ovaltine Products, Inc., Villa Park, Ill.

Huntington Mavor, M.D.
Associate Professor of Neurology, University of Utah College of Medicine, Salt Lake City.

O. Orland Maxfield
Professor and Chairperson, Department of Geography, University of Arkansas, Fayetteville.

Charles E. May
Professor of English, California State University, Long Beach.

Georges May
Sterling Professor of French, Yale University, New Haven, Conn.

John Guinn May
Department of History and Office for History of Science and Technology, University of California, Berkeley.

Thomas Mayer
Professor of Economics, University of California at Davis, Davis.

Thomas C. Mayer
Professor of Biology, Rider College, Lawrenceville, N.J.

Donald N. Maynard
Professor of Plant Science, University of Massachusetts, Amherst.

Gene F. Mazenko
Assistant Professor of Physics, James Franck Institute, University of Chicago, Chicago.

Jerome Mazzaro
Professor of Comparative Literature and Italian, State University of New York, Buffalo.

Laurence W. Mazzeno, Jr.
Retired Supervisory Chemist, Southern Regional Research Center, Agricultural Research Service, U.S. Department of Agriculture.

Christopher Mead
Department of Art History, University of Pennsylvania, Philadelphia.

John A. Mears
Associate Professor of History, Southern Methodist University, Dallas, Tex.

Beatrice Medicine
Anthropologist, University of Wisconsin, Madison.

Rustem S. Medora
Professor of Pharmacy, University of Montana, Missoula.

Harold A. Meeks
Associate Professor of Geography, University of Vermont, Burlington.

Charles O. Meiburg
Professor of Business Administration, Colgate Darden Graduate School of Business Administration, University of Virginia, Charlottesville.

H. Meijer
Information and Documentation Centre for the Geography of the Netherlands, Utrecht.

R. P. Meijer
Professor of Dutch Languages and Literature, University of London, London.

Geoffrey W. Mellors
Senior Technology Associate, Battery Products Division, Union Carbide Corporation, Parma, Ohio.

William H. Menke
National Science Foundation Fellow, Lamont Doherty Geological Observatory of Columbia University, Palisades, N.Y.

M. Meo
Department of History, University of California, Berkeley, Calif.

Paul Merchant
Lecturer, Department of English and Comparative Literature, University of Warwick, Coventry, Warwickshire, England.

Richard H. Merritt
Professor of Horticulture and Dean of Instruction, Cook College, Rutgers University, New Brunswick, N.J.

Bruce E. Meserve
Professor of Mathematics, University of Vermont, Burlington.

Lisa M. Messinger
Curatorial Assistant, Museum of Modern Art, New York City.

David F. Mettrick
Professor and Chairman, Department of Zoology, University of Toronto, Toronto.

S. Metzger
Assistant Vice-President and Chief Scientist, Communications Satellite Corporation, Washington, D.C.

John Meyendorff
Professor of Church History and Patristics, St. Vladimir's Orthodox Theological Seminary, and Professor of History, Fordham University, New York City.

Albert L. Michaels
Associate Professor of History and Director, Council of International Studies, State University of New York, Buffalo.

John T. Mickel
Curator of Ferns, New York Botanical Garden, Bronx.

Paolo Migliorini
Professor of Economic Geography, University of Rome, Rome.

Vasa D. Mihailovich
Professor, University of North Carolina, Chapel Hill.

David H. Miles
Associate Professor of German, University of Virginia, Charlottesville.

Edwin A. Miles
Professor of History, University of Houston, Houston, Tex.

Anne Millbrooke
Fellow, Smithsonian Institution, Washington, D.C.

Arthur H. Miller
Director, Institute for Social Research, Center for Political Studies, University of Michigan, Ann Arbor.

David Harry Miller
Associate Professor of History, University of Oklahoma, Norman.

David W. Miller
Associate Professor of History, Carnegie-Mellon University, Pittsburgh, Pa.

Douglas T. Miller
Professor of History, Michigan State University, East Lansing.

E. Willard Miller
Associate Dean for Resident Instruction and Professor of Geography, Pennsylvania State University, University Park.

Edwin Haviland Miller
Professor of English, New York University, New York City.

Forrestt A. Miller
Professor of History, Vanderbilt University, Nashville, Tenn.

Henry Knight Miller
Professor of English, Princeton University, Princeton, N.J.

Larry E. Miller
Agricultural Education Program, University of Missouri, Columbia.

Phoebe Ottenberg Miller
Associate Professor of Comparative Sociology, University of Puget Sound, Tacoma, Wash.

Richard B. Miller
Managing Editor, *The Bankers Magazine*.

Richard Gordon Miller
Foresta Institute for Ocean and Mountain Studies, Carson City, Nev.

Robert H. Miller
Professor of Agronomy, Ohio State University, Columbus.

Robert P. Miller
Professor of English, Queens College, City University of New York, Flushing.

Roy Andrew Miller
Professor of Asian Languages and Literature, University of Washington, Seattle.

Victor C. Miller
Professor of Geology, Indiana State University, Terre Haute.

Richard L. Millett
Senior Advisor, Frost & Sullivan Inc., New York City.

Alaric Millington
Lecturer in Mathematics Education, Chelsea College, University of London, London.

Lorus J. Milne
Professor of Zoology, University of New Hampshire, Durham.

Margery Milne
Author and Lecturer, University of New Hampshire, Durham.

Edward J. Milowicki
Associate Professor of English, Mills College, Oakland, Calif.

Kimball A. Milton
Adjunct Assistant Professor of Physics, University of California, Los Angeles.

Forrest M. Mims III
Science Writer.

Eli C. Minkoff
Associate Professor of Biology, Bates College, Lewiston, Maine.

Charles I. Minott
Associate Professor of the History of Art, University of Pennsylvania, Philadelphia.

Richard Minsky
Founder, Center for Book Arts, New York City.

Leigh W. Mintz
Dean of Undergraduate Studies and Professor of Earth Sciences, California State University, Hayward.

Nancy Minugh
Teaching Fellow in Anthropology, University of Pennsylvania, Philadelphia.

William Mishler
Associate Professor of Scandinavian, University of Minnesota, Minneapolis.

John D. Mitchell
Chairman, Newspaper Department, Newhouse School, Syracuse University, Syracuse, N.Y.

Leonel L. Mitchell
Professor of Liturgies, Seabury-Western Theological Seminary, Evanston, Ill.

Charles S. Moffett
Associate Curator, European Paintings, Metropolitan Museum of Art, New York City.

Rabindra N. Mohapatra
Associate Professor, City College, City University of New York, New York City.

Charles Molesworth
Professor, Queens College, City University of New York, Flushing.

John Money
Professor of Medical Psychology and Associate Professor of Pediatrics, The Johns Hopkins University School of Medicine and Hospital, Baltimore, Md.

Karen Monson
Author and former music critic, *Chicago Daily News*.

Ashley Montagu
Former Chairman, Department of Anthropology, Rutgers University, New Brunswick, N.J.

E. William Monter
Professor of History, Northwestern University, Evanston, Ill.

David S. Moore
Professor of Statistics, Purdue University, West Lafayette, Ind.

Harry T. Moore
Research Professor in English, Southern Illinois University, Carterville.

J. N. Moore
Professor of Horticulture, University of Arkansas, Fayetteville.

J. T. Moore
Professor of Philosophy, Phillips University, Enid, Okla.

Thomas Gale Moore
Senior Fellow, Hoover Institution, Stanford University, Stanford, Calif.

A. Lloyd Moote
Professor of History, University of Southern California, Los Angeles.

Marta Morello-Frosch
Professor of Latin American Literature, University of California, Santa Cruz.

Lawrence P. Morin
Assistant Professor of Psychology, Dartmouth College, Hanover, N.H.

J. H. Morley
Director, Royal Pavilion, Art Gallery and Museums, Brighton, East Sussex, England.

Harold J. Morowitz
Professor of Biophysics and Biochemistry, Yale University, New Haven, Conn.

Craig Morris
Associate Curator, American Museum of Natural History, New York City.

John W. Morris
Professor Emeritus of Geography, University of Oklahoma, Norman.

Richard M. Morris
Research and Development Manager, Weir Westgarth, Ltd., Glasgow, Scotland.

Roger B. Morrison
Former Research Geologist, U.S. Geological Survey, and Adjunct Professor, Department of Geosciences, University of Arizona, Tucson.

Irving Morrissett
Executive Director, Social Science Education Consortium, Inc., Boulder, Colo.

Thomas E. Morrissey
Associate Professor of History, State University College, Fredonia, N.Y.

Lester R. Morss
Associate Professor of Chemistry, Rutgers University, New Brunswick, N.J.

Donald E. Morton
Associate Professor of English, Syracuse University, Syracuse, N.Y.

Phillip W. Morton
Manager, Information Department, Alcoa Technical Center, ALCOA, Alcoa Center, Pa.

Jacob E. Mosier
Professor of Veterinary Medicine, Kansas State University, Manhattan.

Victor L. Mote
Associate Professor of Geography, University of Houston, Houston, Tex.

Allen Mottershead
Professor, Physical Science Department, Cypress College, Cypress, Calif.

Benjamin Moulton
Chairman and Professor, Department of Geography and Geology, Indiana State University, Terre Haute.

Timothy L. Mounts
Supervisory Research Chemist, Oilseeds Crops Laboratory, Northern Regional Research Center, U.S. Department of Agriculture, Peoria, Ill.

K. E. Moyer
Professor of Psychology, Carnegie-Mellon University, Pittsburgh, Pa.

Carl R. Mueller
Associate Professor of Theater Arts, University of California, Los Angeles.

Willard F. Mueller
Vilas Research Professor, University of Wisconsin, Madison.

Edward J. Mullen
Professor of Spanish, University of Missouri, Columbia.

Franklin Mullinax, M.D.
Professor of Medicine, Medical College of Virginia, Richmond.

Delmar C. Multhauf
Professor of Geography and Chairman of the Geography and Geology Department, University of Wisconsin, Stevens Point.

Alicia H. Munnell
Assistant Vice-President and Economist, Federal Reserve Bank of Boston, Boston.

Jim L. Munro
Professor of Political Science, University of West Florida, Pensacola.

Pamela Munro
Associate Professor of Linguistics, University of California, Los Angeles.

Hugo Munsterberg
Professor Emeritus, New York State University College at New Paltz.

Kenji Murase
Professor of Social Work, San Francisco State University, San Francisco.

Rhoads Murphey
Professor of Geography, University of Michigan, Ann Arbor.

John F. Murphy
Professor of History and Government, U.S. Coast Guard Academy, New London, Conn.

E. B. Murray
Professor of English, University of Missouri, St. Louis.

Haydn H. Murray
Professor of Geology, Indiana University, Bloomington.

Raymond L. Murray
Professor Emeritus, Department of Nuclear Engineering, North Carolina State University, Raleigh.

Jay C. Musser
Owner and General Manager, Jay C. Musser Consulting Chemist, Mount Joy, Pa.

Thomas A. Mutch
Associate Administrator, NASA, Washington, D.C.

Rodney G. Myatt
Assistant Professor of Biology, San Jose State University, San Jose, Calif.

Joel Myerson
Professor of English, University of South Carolina, Columbia.

Jack Nachbar
Associate Professor of Popular Culture, Bowling Green State University, Bowling Green, Ohio.

Harry S. Nachman
Consulting Engineer, H. S. Nachman & Associates, Inc., Chicago.

Paul S. Nadler
Professor of Business Administration, Rutgers University, New Brunswick, N.J.

Ronald D. Nadler
Developmental Biologist, Yerkes Regional Primate Research Center, Emory University, Atlanta, Ga.

Takesi Nagata
Professor, and Director, National Institute of Polar Research, Tokyo.

Humberto Nagera, M.D.
Professor and Chief, Youth Services, Department of Psychiatry, University of Michigan, Ann Arbor.

Andrew C. Nahm
Professor of History, Western Michigan University, Kalamazoo.

Paul Nash
Professor and Chairman, Department of Humanistic and Behavioral Studies, Boston University, Boston.

Sydney Nathans
Associate Professor of History, Duke University, Durham, N.C.

Mildred Navaretta
Lecturer, Moorpark College, Moorpark, Calif.

John E. Neely
Professor of Machine Technology, Lane Community College, Eugene, Oreg.

Mark E. Neely, Jr.
Director, Louis A. Warren Lincoln Library and Museum, Fort Wayne, Ind.

Lawrence Nees
Assistant Professor of Art History, University of Delaware, Newark.

Bruce C. Nehrling
Assistant Professor of Naval Architecture, United States Naval Academy, Annapolis, Md.

J. Mededith Neil
Arts Writer.

Ulric Neisser
Professor of Psychology, Cornell University, Ithaca, N.Y.

James D. Nelson
Professor of Church History, United Theological Seminary, Dayton, Ohio.

Joseph Schieser Nelson
Professor of Zoology, University of Alberta, Edmonton.

Marion John Nelson
Professor of Art History, University of Minnesota, Minneapolis.

Roy Paul Nelson
Professor of Journalism, University of Oregon, Eugene.

John T. Netterville
Chairman, Department of Chemistry, David Lipscomb College, Nashville, Tenn.

Bruno Nettl
Professor of Music and Anthropology, University of Illinois, Urbana.

Robert M. Neuman
Instructor, School of Art and Art History, University of Iowa, Iowa City.

Alvin L. Neumann
Professor of Animal Science, Emeritus, University of Illinois, Urbana.

Richard Morgan Neumann
Research Scientist, Polymer Science Institute, University of Massachusetts, Amherst.

Jacob Neusner
Professor of Religious Studies, The Ungerleider Distinguished Scholar of Judaic Studies, Brown University, Providence, R.I.

A. C. Neville
Reader in Zoology, University of Bristol, Bristol, England.

Adam Neville
Principal and Vice-Chancellor, University of Dundee, Dundee, Scotland.

Ray L. Newburn, Jr.
Member of the Technical Staff, Jet Propulsion Laboratory, California Institute of Technology, Pasadena.

Richard S. Newell
Professor of History and Asian Studies, University of Northern Iowa, Cedar Falls.

Dika Newlin
Professor of Music, Virginia Commonwealth University, Richmond.

Barbara Newman
Critic, *Dancemagazine* and *Classical Music Weekly.*

Lawrence W. Newman
Assistant Professor, Ohio Wesleyan University, Delaware.

William S. Newman
Alumni Distinguished Professor Emeritus of Music, University of North Carolina, Chapel Hill.

Peter Newmark
Professor and Dean of the School of Languages, Polytechnic of Central London, London.

Brother G. Nicholas
Professor of Biology, La Salle College, Philadelphia.

Robert L. Nichols
Professor Emeritus, Tufts University, Medford, Mass.

Norman L. Nicholson
Professor of Geography, University of Western Ontario, London.

William A. Niering
Professor of Botany, Connecticut College, New London.

Donald L. Niewyk
Associate Professor of History, Southern Methodist University, Dallas, Tex.

Daniel Noin
Professor, University of Paris, Paris.

Kenneth P. Nolan
Attorney, Speiser & Krause, P.C., New York City.

Mark A. Noll
Associate Professor of History, Wheaton College, Wheaton, Ill.

R. Åke Norberg
Department of Zoology, University of Göteborg, Göteborg, Sweden.

Thomas E. Norton
Senior Vice-President, Sotheby Parke Bernet, Inc., New York City.

Frederick A. Norwood
Professor of History of Christianity, Garrett-Evangelical Theological Seminary, Evanston, Ill.

Robert Novak
Research Associate, Vector Biology Laboratory, University of Notre Dame, Notre Dame, Ind.

Martha Craven Nussbaum
Assistant Professor of Philosophy and the Classics, Harvard University, Cambridge, Mass.

Merle C. Nutt
Professor Emeritus of Engineering Sciences, Arizona State University, Tempe.

William H. Nyce
Associate Professor of Chemistry, University of New Haven, West Haven, Conn.

Francis Oakley
Professor of History and Dean of the Faculty, Williams College, Williamstown, Mass.

James E. Oberg
Associate Editor, *Space World* Magazine.

John J. Oberle
Chief Chemist, Benjamin Moore & Co., Newark, N.J.

Joseph F. O'Callaghan
Professor of History, Fordham University, New York City.

David O'Connor
Associate Curator, Egyptian Section, The University Museum, University of Pennsylvania, Philadelphia.

J. Dean O'Donnell, Jr.
Associate Professor, Virginia Polytechnic Institute and State University, Blacksburg.

Jack O'Dwyer
Publisher and Editor, *Jack O'Dwyer's Newsletter.*

William Offenkrantz, M.D.
Professor of Psychiatry, University of Chicago, Chicago.

Daniel Offer, M.D.
Chairman, Department of Psychiatry, Michael Reese Hospital and Medical Center, Chicago.

Daniel T. O'Hara
Department of English, Temple University, Philadelphia.

John Peter Oleson
Associate Professor, University of Victoria, Victoria, British Columbia.

Anita M. Oliva
The Wire Association International, Inc., Guilford, Conn.

L. Jay Oliva
Vice-President for Academic Affairs and Professor of History, New York University, New York City.

Frank J. Oliver
Former Editor, *Electro-Technology* Magazine.

Bertell Ollman
Professor, Department of Politics, New York University, New York City.

James L. Olsen
Head, Division of Pharmaceutics, University of North Carolina, Chapel Hill.

Linda Olsheim
Assistant Director, College and Community Relations, Fashion Institute of Technology, New York City.

John W. O'Malley
Professor, Western School of Theology, Cambridge, Mass.

Elliott I. Organick
Professor of Computer Science, University of Utah, Salt Lake City.

Louis L. Orlin
Professor of Ancient Near Eastern History and Literature, University of Michigan, Ann Arbor.

Martin Orne, M.D.
Professor of Psychiatry, Yale University, New Haven, Conn.

Norman J. Ornstein
Associate Professor, Department of Politics, Catholic University of America, Washington, D.C.

Robert T. Orr
Senior Scientist, California Academy of Sciences, San Francisco.

James M. Ortega
Professor and Head, Department of Mathematics, North Carolina State University, Raleigh.

Stuart Oskamp
Professor of Psychology, Claremont Graduate School, Claremont, Calif.

Donald E. Osterbrock
Director and Professor of Astronomy, Lick Observatory, University of California, Santa Cruz.

R. C. Ostle
Lecturer in Arabic, School of Oriental and African Studies, University of London, London.

John H. Ostrom
Professor of Geology, Yale University, New Haven, Conn.

Donald K. Ourecky
Associate Professor, Department of Pomology and Viticulture, New York State Experiment Station, Geneva.

Roger C. Owen
Professor of Anthropology, Queens College, City University of New York, Flushing.

Susan S. Owicki
Assistant Professor of Electrical Engineering, Stanford University, Stanford, Calif.

David W. Oxtoby
Assistant Professor of Chemistry, University of Chicago, Chicago.

Howard Ozmon
Professor of Education, Virginia Commonwealth University, Richmond.

Sergio Pacifici
Professor of Romance Languages and Comparative Literature, Queens College and Graduate Center, City University of New York, Flushing.

Don. N. Page
Assistant Professor, Department of Physics, Pennsylvania State University, University Park.

Ellis Batten Page
Professor of Educational Psychology, University of Connecticut, Storrs.

Thornton Page
Research Astrophysicist, NASA Johnson Space Center, Houston, Tex.

Angela Jung Palandri
Professor of Chinese, University of Oregon, Eugene.

Nicholas C. Pano
Professor of History, Western Illinois University, Macomb.

S. Victor Papacosma
Associate Professor of History, Kent State University, Kent, Ohio.

Robert J. Paradowski
Assistant Professor of History of Science and Chemistry, Eisenhower College, Seneca Falls, N.Y.

George Park
Professor of Anthropology, Memorial University of Newfoundland, Saint John's.

Franklin Parker
Claude Worthington Benedum Professor of Education, West Virginia University, Morgantown.

Robert L. Parker
Professor of Music, University of Miami, Coral Gables, Fla.

Sandy Parker
Publisher, *Sandy Parker Reports,* and Associate Editor, *Fur Chic* Magazine.

Russell J. Parkinson
Historian, History and Museums Divisions Headquarters, U.S. Marine Corps, Washington, D.C.

Charles Parsons
Professor of Philosophy, Columbia University, New York City.

Melinda B. Parsons
Lecturer, History of Art, Freshman Honors Program, University of Delaware, Newark.

T. R. Parsons
Professor, Institute of Oceanography, University of British Columbia, Vancouver.

William T. Parsons
Director, Pennsylvania Dutch Studies, and Editor, *Pennsylvania Folklife,* Ursinus College, Collegeville, Pa.

J. Francis Paschal
Professor of Law, Duke University, Durham, N.C.

Robert Patch
Instructor in Social Sciences, University of Texas, Dallas.

James T. Patterson
Professor of History, Brown University, Providence, R.I.

Samuel C. Patterson
Professor of Political Science, University of Iowa, Iowa City.

E. Mansell Pattison, M.D.
Chairman and Professor of Psychiatry and Health Behavior, Medical College of Georgia, Augusta.

Phil Patton
Arts Writer for *Artforum, Art in America, Portfolio,* and other magazines.

W. J. Patton
Registered Engineer.

Wendell K. Patton
Professor of Zoology, Ohio Wesleyan University, Delaware.

Erich Robert Paul
Assistant Professor of the History of Science, Dickinson College, Carlisle, Pa.

K. B. Paul
Assistant Professor, Lincoln University, Jefferson City, Mo.

Robert A. Paul
Associate Professor, Graduate Institute of the Liberal Arts, Emory University, Atlanta, Ga.

Frank M. Paulsen
Professor of English, Kuwait University, Kuwait.

David L. Pawson
Curator of Echinoderms, Smithsonian Institution, Washington, D.C.

Leonard A. Pearlman
Professor of Music, Director of Orchestras, University of Arizona, Tucson.

Neal J. Pearson
Associate Professor of Political Science, Texas Tech University, Lubbock.

William S. Pechter
Author, *Twenty-four Times a Second* and *Movies Plus One.*

Michael J. Pelczar, Jr.
President, Council of Graduate Schools in the United States, Washington, D.C.

Marcelino C. Penuelas
Professor of Spanish and Chairman, Department of Romance Languages and Literature, University of Washington, Seattle.

Simon Pepper
Lecturer in Architecture, University of Liverpool, Liverpool.

Don Peretz
Professor of Political Science, State University of New York, Binghamton.

Alfred Perlmutter
Professor of Biology, New York University, New York City.

Laurence Perrine
Frensley Professor of English, Southern Methodist University, Dallas, Tex.

Lawrence A. Pervin
Professor of Psychology, Rutgers University, New Brunswick, N.J.

Jeffrey L. Peters, M.D.
Associate Research Professor of Bioengineering and Assistant Research Professor of Surgery, University of Utah, Salt Lake City.

John Milo Peterson
Professor of Mathematics, Brigham Young University, Provo, Utah.

Martin Severin Peterson
Former General Physical Scientist, U.S. Army, Natick Research and Development Command, Natick, Mass.

Theodore Peterson
Dean, College of Communications, University of Illinois, Urbana.

Peter L. Petrakis
Editor-in-Chief, Life Sciences Editorial Service, Silver Spring, Md.

Terry F. Pettijohn
Assistant Professor of Psychology, Ohio State University, Marion.

David E. Petzal
Managing Editor, *Field & Stream* Magazine.

R. L. Peurifoy
Author and Consulting Engineer, and former Professor of Construction Engineering, Oklahoma State University, Stillwater.

Troy L. Péwé
Professor and Director, Museum of Geology, Arizona State University, Tempe.

Henri Peyre
Distinguished Professor, Graduate Center, City University of New York, New York City.

Carl C. Pfeiffer, M.D.
Director, Brain Bio Center, University of Pennsylvania Medical School, Philadelphia.

Carl J. Pfeiffer
Division of Veterinary Biology and Clinical Studies, College of Veterinary Medicine, Virginia Polytechnic Institute, Blacksburg.

Allan R. Phillips
Guest Research Associate, Autonomous University of Nuevo León, Nuevo León, Mexico.

Jane Philpott
Professor of Botany, Duke University, Durham, N.C.

Martin Picker
Professor of Music, Rutgers University, New Brunswick, N.J.

Calder M. Pickett
Professor of Journalism, University of Kansas, Lawrence.

Roger A. Pielke
Associate Professor of Environmental Science, University of Virginia, Charlottesville.

Robert J. Pierce
Dance Critic, *Soho Weekly News.*

Don Pierson
Sportswriter, *Chicago Tribune.*

John F. Pile
Professor of Design, Pratt Institute, Brooklyn, N.Y.

Edmund L. Pincoffs
Professor of Philosophy, University of Texas, Austin.

David H. Pinkney
Professor of History, University of Washington, Seattle.

Roy Pinney
Former Professor of Journalism, University of Alaska, Fairbanks.

John F. Piper, Jr.
Associate Professor of History, Lycoming College, Williamsport, Pa.

Larry L. Pippin
Professor of Political Science, Elbert Covell College, University of the Pacific, Forest Grove, Oreg.

Hanna Fenichel Pitkin
Professor of Political Science, University of California, Berkeley.

Harvey Pitkin
Professor of Anthropology, Columbia University, New York City.

Henry Pitot, M.D.
Professor of Oncology and Pathology, McArdle Laboratory for Cancer Research, University of Wisconsin, Madison.

David J. Pittman
Professor and Chairman, Department of Sociology, Washington University, Saint Louis, Mo.

Robert Plonsey
Professor and Chairman, Department of Biomedical Engineering, Case Western Reserve University, Cleveland, Ohio.

Henry A. Plotkin
Assistant Professor of Political Science, Livingston College, Rutgers University, New Brunswick, N.J.

Rita M. Plotnicki
Lecturer, Hunter College, New York City.

E. M. Plunkett
Art Historian.

Robert Plutchik
Professor of Psychiatry, Albert Einstein College of Medicine, Bronx, N.Y.

Thomas T. Poleman
Professor of International Food Economics, Cornell University, Ithaca, N.Y.

Richard Polenberg
Professor of American History, Cornell University, Ithaca, N.Y.

John Pollis
President, Museum Marketing Associates, Inc., New York City.

Elizabeth Pollock
Former Assistant for Photography, Department of Prints, Drawings and Photographs, Philadelphia Museum of Art, Philadelphia.

Louis Pomerantz
Former Conservator, Department of Paintings and Sculpture, Art Institute of Chicago, Chicago.

Martin A. Pomerantz
Director, Bartol Research Foundation of The Franklin Institute, University of Delaware, Newark.

Gerald M. Pomper
Chairman and Professor, Department of Political Science, Rutgers University, New Brunswick, N.J.

Joseph R. Pope
United Lodge of Theosophists, New York City.

Richard H. Popkin
Professor of Philosophy, Washington University, Saint Louis, Mo.

John H. Porter
Author.

Donald Posner
Professor of Fine Arts, New York University, New York City.

Stephen E. Posten
Project Manager, Environmental Assessment Council, Inc., New Brunswick, N.J.

Karl H. Potter
Professor of Philosophy, University of Washington, Seattle.

Norman J. G. Pounds
Professor of Geography and History, Indiana University, Bloomington.

Evan Powell
Southeast Editor, *Popular Science.*

James M. Powell
Professor of History, Syracuse University, Syracuse, N.Y.

Robert A. Powers
Director of Technology, Battery Products Division, Union Carbide Corporation, Cleveland, Ohio.

Ivan L. Preston
Professor, School of Journalism and Mass Communication, University of Wisconsin, Madison.

Ronald T. Pretty
Editor, *Jane's Weapon Systems.*

Karl H. Pribram
Professor of Neuroscience, Stanford University, Stanford, Calif.

Steven D. Price
Editorial Director, *The Whole Horse Catalog,* New York City.

Richard K. Priebe
Assistant Professor of English, Virginia Commonwealth University, Richmond.

William H. Pritchard
Editorial Board, *Hudson Review,* and Professor of English, Amherst College, Amherst, Mass.

Roland I. Pritikin, M.D., F.A.C.S., F.I.C.S., F.R.S.H., F.A.C.N.M.
Member of the Faculty, Rockford School of Medicine, University of Illinois Ophthalmology Section, Rockford, and Consultant in Ophthalmology, U.S. Army Health Services Command.

Arthur J. Pulos
President, Pulos Design Associates, Syracuse, N.Y.

Judson D. Purdy
Associate Professor of History of Canadian Education, University of Western Ontario, London.

Carroll Pursell
Professor of History, University of California, Santa Barbara.

Elizabeth Putz
Instructor, California State University, Northridge.

Lewis Pyenson
Professeur Agrégé, Institut d'histoire et de sociopolitique des sciences, Université de Montréal, Montréal.

Peter Quennell, C.B.E.
Author of *Byron: The Years of Fame, Byron in Italy, Alexander Pope: The Education of Genius,* and other works.

Quentin W. Quereau
Assistant Professor of Music, Case Western Reserve University, Cleveland, Ohio.

Dennis E. Quillen
Assistant Professor of Geography, Eastern Kentucky University, Richmond.

Suzanne Rabitz
Research Scientist, Exxon Corporation, Linden, N.J.

Gerald Rabkin
Professor and Director of Livingston College Theater Arts Department, Rutgers University, New Brunswick, N.J.

Howard Rachlin
Professor of Psychology, State University of New York, Stony Brook.

Ramaswami Radhakrishnan
Associate Professor of Linguistics, The University of Calgary, Calgary, Alberta.

Eugene Radwin
Research Associate, Huron Institute, Cambridge, Mass.

John B. Rae
Professor of the History of Technology, Emeritus, Harvey Mudd College, Claremont, Calif.

Marc Raeff
Bakhmeteff Professor of Russian Studies, Columbus University, New York City.

Kristjan T. Ragnarsson, M.D.
Institute of Rehabilitation Medicine, New York University Medical Center, New York City.

Robert J. Raikow
Associate Professor of Biological Sciences, University of Pittsburgh, Pittsburgh, Pa.

Thomas C. Rambo
Associate Professor of Biological Sciences, Northern Kentucky University, Highland Heights.

O. Bertrand Ramsay
Professor of Chemistry, East Michigan University, Ypsilanti.

Harry Rand
Chairman, Department of 20th Century Painting & Sculpture, Smithsonian Institution, Washington, D.C.

John Randolph
Assistant Professor, Environmental and Urban Systems, Virginia Polytechnic Institute and State University, Blacksburg.

Joan A. Range
Associate Professor of Theology, Saint Louis University, Saint Louis, Mo.

Rev. Charles W. Ranson
Former Professor of Theology and Ecumenics, Hartford Seminary Foundation, Hartford, Conn.

Bertram Raphael
Computer Research Center, Hewlett-Packard Laboratories, Palo Alto, Calif.

Carter Ratcliff
Contributing Editor, *Art in America* and Instructor, School of Visual Arts, New York City.

Hugh M. Raup
Charles Bullard Professor of Forestry, Emeritus, Harvard University, Cambridge, Mass.

Stephen L. Rawlins
Research Leader, Physics and Engineering, U.S. Salinity Laboratory, Riverside, Calif.

Philip Rawson
Curator, Gulbenkian Museum of Oriental Art, University of Durham, Durham City, England.

D. Michael Ray
Professor of Geography, Carlton University, Ottawa, Ontario.

Robert W. Read
Associate Curator, Department of Botany, Smithsonian Institution, Washington, D.C.

Reginald Lee Reagan
Major, U.S. Army (ret.), Biologist and Virologist, Laboratory of Toxicology, National Cancer Institute, National Institute of Health, Bethesda, Md.

Gilbert Reaney
Professor of Music, University of California, Los Angeles.

Barbara Straus Reed
Assistant Professor of Journalism, California State University, Los Angeles.

Melvin L. Reed, M.D., F.A.C.P.
Associate Director (Education), Comprehensive Cancer Center of Metropolitan Detroit, and Associate Professor of Oncology, Wayne State University School of Medicine, Detroit.

Robert Reeder
Associate Professor of Mining Engineering, Colorado School of Mines, Golden.

Robert Regan
Professor of English, University of Pennsylvania, Philadelphia.

John B. Rehder
Associate Professor of Geography, University of Tennessee, Knoxville.

Lynn P. Rehm
Professor of Psychology, University of Houston, Houston, Tex.

John J. Reich
Associate Professor of the Classics, Florida State University, Tallahassee.

Michael F. Rein, M.D.
Assistant Professor of Medicine, University of Virginia School of Medicine, Charlottesville.

Stephen Charles Reingold
Research Fellow in Biology, Princeton University, Princeton, N.J.

John F. Reinhard
Professor of Pharmacology Emeritus, Massachusetts College of Pharmacy and Allied Health Sciences, Boston.

Jonathan Reiskind
Associate Professor of Zoology, University of Florida, Gainesville.

W. Michael Reisman
Professor of Law, Yale Law School, New Haven, Conn.

Joseph A. Reiter
Assistant Professor of Modern Languages, Phillips Exeter Academy, Exeter, N.H.

Mostafa Rejai
Professor of Political Science, Miami University, Oxford, Ohio.

John W. Renner
Professor of Science Education, University of Oklahoma, Norman.

Robert P. Renner, D.D.S.
Associate Professor of Prosthodontics, State University of New York, School of Dental Medicine, Stony Brook.

Sarah Rennie
Research Staff Associate, Lamont-Doherty Geological Observatory, Columbia University, New York City.

Franklin V. Reno
Consultant on Physical Problems.

Nicholas Renouf
Assistant Curator, Yale University Collection of Musical Instruments, New Haven, Conn.

Richard Rephann
Director, Yale Collection of Musical Instruments and Associate Professor of Organology, Yale University, New Haven, Conn.

Ronald M. Reuss
Associate Professor of Biology, State University College, Buffalo, N.Y.

Walter Reuther
Professor of Horticulture, University of California, Riverside.

James W. Rhodes
Instructor in Psychology, University of Tennessee, Knoxville.

Edward Ricco
Dance Critic and Writer.

Peter R. Rich
Department of Biochemistry, University of Cambridge, Cambridge, England.

Peter G. Richards
Professor of Politics, University of Southampton, Southampton, England.

Mary Jo Richardson
Research Assistant, Woods Hole Oceanographic Institution, Woods Hole, Mass.

John J. Richetti
Professor of English, Rutgers University, New Brunswick, N.J.

Timothy J. Rickard
Professor of Geography, Central Connecticut State College, New Britain.

David F. Ricks
Professor of Psychology, University of Cincinnati, Cincinnati, Ohio.

Herbert Riehl
Professor Emeritus, Colorado State University, Boulder.

Roderick R. Riewe
Associate Professor of Biology and Zoology, University of Manitoba, Winnipeg.

Ida Katherine Rigby
Assistant Professor of Art History, San Diego State University, San Diego, Calif.

William H. Riker
Wilson Professor of Political Science, University of Rochester, Rochester, N.Y.

Patrick Riley
Professor of Political Science, University of Wisconsin, Madison.

Ingrid Rima
Professor of Economics, Temple University, Philadelphia.

Bernard Rimland
Director, Institute for Child Behavior Research, San Diego, Calif.

John S. Rinehart
Adjoint Professor of Mechanical Engineering, University of Colorado, Boulder.

Arthur J. Riopelle
Boyd Professor of Psychology, Louisiana State University, Baton Rouge.

Guenter B. Risse, M.D.
Professor of the History of Medicine, University of Wisconsin, Madison.

Walter W. Ristow
Formerly Chief, Geography and Map Division, Library of Congress.

J. M. Ritchie
Professor of Germanic Studies, University of Sheffield, Sheffield, England.

S. A. A. Rizvi
Dept. of Asian Civilizations, Australian National University, Canberra.

Robert A. Rizza
Assistant Professor of Medicine, Mayo Medical School, Mayo Foundation, Rochester, Minn.

David C. Roberts
Assistant Professor of Chemistry, Rutgers, The State University of New Jersey, New Brunswick.

J. J. M. Roberts
Associate Professor of Near Eastern Studies, University of Toronto, Toronto, Ontario.

Donald Robertson
Professor, History of Art, Newcomb College, Tulane University, New Orleans, La.

Kenneth C. Robertson
Recording Engineer, CBS/Columbia Records, New York City.

Kenneth R. Robertson
Curator of the Herbarium, Illinois Natural History Survey, Urbana.

Martha Barton Robertson
Library Assistant, Latin American Library, Tulane University, New Orleans, La.

Michael Robertson
Associate Critic, *Dancemagazine*.

Franklin W. Robinson
Associate Professor of Art, Williams College, Williamstown, Mass.

James K. Robinson
Professor of English, University of Cincinnati, Cincinnati, Ohio.

J. Lewis Robinson
Professor of Geography, University of British Columbia, Vancouver.

James W. Robinson
Dean, School of Business, Shippensburg State College, Shippensburg, Pa.

William C. Robison
Geographer, former U.S. Army Engineer, Topographic Laboratories, Fort Belvoir, Va.

Edward T. Roche
Professor of Zoology, California State Polytechnic University, Pomona.

Howard D. Rodee
Associate Professor in Art History, University of New Mexico, Albuquerque.

Harry J. Roedersheimer
Authority on Games.

Delmer D. Rogers
Head, Theory Composition, University of Texas, Austin.

Lt. Col. Lane Rogers, U.S.M.C.
Assistant Chief Historian, History and Museums Division, Headquarters, U.S. Marine Corps, Washington, D.C.

Martha E. Rogers, R.N.
Professor, Division of Nursing, New York University, New York City.

Eldred Rolfe
Associate Professor of Geography, University of Maine, Farmington.

Robert C. Romans
Associate Professor of Biology, Bowling Green State University, Bowling Green, Ohio.

William D. Romey
Professor of Geology, St. Lawrence University, Canton, N.Y.

William S. Romoser
Professor of Zoology, Ohio University, Athens.

Peter A. Rona
Senior Research Geophysicist, Atlantic Oceanographic and Meteorological Laboratories, Miami, Fla.

Gerald C. Roper
Professor of Chemistry, Dickinson College, Carlisle, Pa.

Stephen C. Ropp
Associate Professor of Government, New Mexico State University, Las Cruces.

Theodore Ropp
Professor of History, Duke University, Durham, N.C.

M. Richard Rose
President, Alfred University, Alfred, N.Y.

Peter I. Rose
Sophia Smith Professor of Sociology and Anthropology, Smith College, Northampton, Mass.

Elliot A. Rosen
Professor of History, Rutgers University, Newark, N.J.

Linda J. Rosen
Research Scientist, New York State Drug Abuse Commission, New York City.

Peter D. Rosenberg
Primary Examiner, U.S. Patent & Trademark Office, Washington, D.C.

William G. Rosenberg
Professor of History, University of Michigan, Ann Arbor.

Michael Rosenblum
Associate Professor of English, Indiana University, Bloomington.

Donald Rosenthal
Curator of Collections, Memorial Art Gallery, University of Rochester, Rochester, N.Y.

Erich Rosenthal
Professor of Sociology, Queens College, City University of New York, Flushing.

Sandra B. Rosenthal
Professor of Philosophy, Loyola University, New Orleans, La.

Peter J. Rosenwald
Dance Critic, *Wall Street Journal.*

Mark W. Roskill
Professor, History of Modern Art, University of Massachusetts, Amherst.

Charles A. Ross
Professor of Geology, Western Washington University, Bellingham.

Herbert H. Ross
Professor of Entomology, University of Georgia, Athens.

Thomas B. Ross
Trade Advertising and Public Relations Manager, Oneida Ltd. Silversmiths, Oneida, N.Y.

Jack E. Rossmann
Professor of Psychology, Macalester College, St. Paul, Minn.

Robert I. Rotberg
Professor of History and Political Science, Massachusetts Institute of Technology, Cambridge.

Leland M. Roth
Associate Professor of Art History, University of Oregon, Eugene.

Herbert H. Rowen
Professor of History, Rutgers University, New Brunswick, N.J.

A. L. Rowse
Fellow of the British Academy.

R. R. Roy
Professor of Physics, Arizona State University, Tempe.

Melvin L. Rubin, M.D.
Professor of Ophthalmology, University of Florida College of Medicine, Gainesville.

Darnell Rucker
Professor of Philosophy, Skidmore College, Saratoga Springs, N.Y.

Donald L. Rucknagel, M.D.
Professor of Human Genetics, University of Michigan Medical School, Ann Arbor.

Nancy D. Ruggles
Assistant Director, Statistical Office, United Nations, New York City.

Richard Ruggles
Professor of Economics, Yale University, New Haven, Conn.

George R. Rumney
Professor of Geography, University of Connecticut, Storrs.

Richard H. Runser, M.D.
Department of Clinical Pharmacology, Hoffmann-La Roche, Inc., Nutley, N.J.

Robert C. Runyard
Technical Writer, Kawasaki Motors Corp., Santa Ana, Calif.

Douglas A. Russell
Professor of Drama, Stanford University, Standford, Calif.

Findlay E. Russell, M.D.
Director, Laboratory of Neurological Research, University of Southern California Medical Center, Los Angeles.

Helen Ross Russell
Environmental Education Consultant and Author.

John D. Ryder
Former Professor of Electrical Engineering, Michigan State University, East Lansing.

Mendel Sachs
Professor of Physics and Astronomy, State University of New York, Buffalo.

Richard Saferstein
Chief Forensic Chemist, New Jersey State Police, Forensic Science Bureau, West Trenton.

Constantina Safilios-Rothschild
Professor of Sociology, University of California, Santa Barbara.

Edward Sagarin
Professor of Sociology, City College, City University of New York, New York City.

Arthur Sainer
Drama Critic for *The Village Voice*, and Professor, Wesleyan University, Middletown, Conn.

Peter P. Sakalowsky
Associate Professor of Geography, Southern Connecticut State College, New Haven.

Anthony J. Saldarini
Associate Professor of Biblical Studies, Boston College, Chestnut Hill, Mass.

Henry F. Salerno
Professor of English, State University College, Fredonia, N.Y.

Frank B. Salisbury
Professor of Plant Physiology, Utah State University, Logan.

Neil E. Salisbury
Professor of Geography, University of Oklahoma, Norman.

J. H. M. Salmon
Goodhart Professor of History, Bryn Mawr College, Bryn Mawr, Pa.

P. B. Salmon
Professor of German, University of Edinburgh, Edinburgh, Scotland.

D. K. Salunkhe
Professor, Department of Nutrition and Food Sciences, Utah State University, Logan.

David Sammons
Assistant Professor of Crop Breeding, Department of Agronomy, University of Maryland, College Park.

William F. Sandford
Associate Editor, *The Daily Register*, Shrewsbury, N.J.

Richard A. Santer
Professor of Geography, Ferris State College, Big Rapids, Mich.

Leon Satkowski
Assistant Professor of Architecture, Syracuse University, Syracuse, N.Y.

A. H. Saxon
Editor, The Shoe String Press, Inc., Hamden, Conn.

Paul Schach
Professor of Germanic Languages, University of Nebraska, Lincoln.

Edward L. Schapsmeier
Professor of History, Illinois State University, Normal.

Elaine J. Schechter
Department of Anthropology, Columbia University, New York City.

Carl H. Scheele
Curator, Division of Community Life, Smithsonian Institution, Washington, D.C.

Karl E. Scheibe
Professor of Psychology, Wesleyan University, Middletown, Conn.

Marc N. Scheinman
Assistant Professor of Political Science, Douglass College, Rutgers University, New Brunswick, N.J.

Hilbert Schenck
Professor of Mechanical Engineering, University of Rhode Island, Kingston.

Joseph Scherer
Economist, Federal Reserve Bank of New York, New York City.

James H. Shideler
Professor of History, University of California, Davis.

Lawrence H. Schiffman
Associate Professor of Hebrew and Judaic Studies, New York University, New York City.

Benjamin Schlesinger
Professor of Social Work, University of Toronto, Toronto.

Arthur Schlissel
Associate Professor of Mathematics, John Jay College of Criminal Justice, City University of New York, New York City.

Raymond H. Schmandt
Professor of History, St. Joseph's College, Philadelphia.

Fred Schnaue
Director of Public Relations, American Association of Fund-Raising Counsel, New York City.

Lawrence J. Schneiderman, M.D.
Associate Professor, University of California Medical School, San Diego.

Gary D. Schnell
Associate Professor of Zoology, Curator of Birds, University of Oklahoma, Norman.

C. H. Scholz
Professor of Geology, Columbia University, New York City.

James Morton Schopf
Geologist (ret.), U.S. Geological Survey, Ohio State University, Columbus.

B. Charlotte Schreiber
Professor of Geology, Queens College, City University of New York, Flushing, and Lamont-Doherty Geological Observatory, Palisades, N.Y.

Joanne Schreiber
Columnist, United Media Services, New York City.

Allan M. Schrier
Professor of Psychology, Brown University, Providence, R.I.

Walter A. Schroeder
Instructor of Geography, University of Missouri, Columbia.

A. F. Schuch
Staff Member (ret.), Los Alamos Scientific Laboratory, University of California, Los Alamos, N.Mex.

Jerome L. Schullman
Professor of Microbiology, Mount Sinai School of Medicine, New York City.

Richard Evans Schultes
Paul C. Mangelsdorf Professor of Natural Science and Director, Botanical Museum, Harvard University, Cambridge, Mass.

Max F. Schulz
Professor of English, University of Southern California, Los Angeles.

Ernest L. Schusky
Professor of Anthropology, Southern Illinois University, Edwardsville.

John A. Schuster
University Assistant Lecturer in History of Science, University of Cambridge, and Director of Studies in History and Philosophy of Science, St. John's College, Cambridge, England.

Peter Schwab
Associate Professor of Political Science, State University of New York, Purchase.

Bernard Schwartz
Edwin D. Webb Professor of Law, New York University School of Law, New York City.

Kessel Schwartz
Professor of Foreign Languages, University of Miami, Coral Gables, Fla.

Marvin D. Schwartz
Art Historian.

Richard B. Schwartz
Dean of the Graduate School and Professor of English, Georgetown University, Washington, D.C.

Tony Schwartz
President, Environmental Media Consultants, Inc.

David J. Schwendemann
Chief Taxidermist, American Museum of Natural History, New York City.

Joan M. Scobey
Author of *Rugs and Wallhangings*.

David W. Scott
Planning Consultant, National Gallery of Art, Washington, D.C.

James W. Scott
Chairman, Department of Geography and Regional Planning, and Director, Center for Pacific Northwest Studies, Western Washington University, Bellingham.

John F. Scott
Professor of Art History, Rice University, Houston, Tex.

Peter Scott
Editor, *The Times Higher Education Supplement*, London.

Capt. W. F. Searle, Jr.
U.S. Navy (ret.) and Visiting Professor, Massachusetts Institute of Technology, Cambridge.

Mary Anne Sedney
Associate Professor of Psychology, Providence College, Providence, R.I.

Raymond J. Seeger
National Science Foundation, Retired.

Charles Segal
Professor of Classics and Chairman, Department of Classics, Brown University, Providence, R.I.

Harold B. Segel
Professor of Slavic Literatures, Columbia University, New York City.

Lewis S. Seiden
Professor of Pharmacology and Physiology, University of Chicago, Chicago.

Mitchell A. Seligson
Assistant Professor of Political Science, University of Arizona, Tucson.

Mostafa A. Selim, M.D.
Department of Obstetrics and Gynecology, Cleveland Metropolitan Hospital, Cleveland, Ohio.

Lawrence Senelick
Associate Professor of Drama, Tufts University, Medford, Mass.

Everett E. Sentman
President, Sentman Publishing Enterprises, Lake Forest, Ill.

S. Prakash Sethi
Professor of International Business and Business and Social Policy, University of Texas, Dallas.

Gary S. Settles
Research Staff Member, Mechanical and Aerospace Engineering Department, Princeton University, Princeton, N.J.

David Severn
Technical Information Manager, Amstar Corporation, New York, N.Y.

Martin Seymour-Smith
Formerly Visiting Professor of English, University of Wisconsin, Madison.

Theodore Shabad
Editor, *Soviet Geography* Magazine, New York City.

Sheldon Shaeffer
School of Education, Stanford University, Stanford, Calif.

Lloyd S. Shapley
Senior Mathematician, Rand Corporation.

Don Sharp
Associate Editor, *Motorboat* Magazine, Boston, Mass.

Mitchell R. Sharpe
Historian, Alabama Space and Rocket Center, Huntsville, Ala.

Peter Shaw
Associate Professor, State University of New York, Stony Brook.

Stanford J. Shaw
Professor of Turkish History, University of California, Los Angeles.

Thurstan Shaw
Professor of Archaeology, Cambridge University, Cambridge, England.

Ronald C. Sheck
Associate Professor of Geography, New Mexico State University, Las Cruces.

J. A. Shellenberger
Distinguished Professor of Grain Science and Industries, Kansas State University, Manhattan.

Lillian Overland Sheps
Botanical Consultant, Scientific Engineering Systems, Inc., Reno, Nev.

Robert E. Sheriff
Senior Vice-President, Seiscom Delta Inc., Houston, Tex.

Norman Sherry
Professor of English Literature, University of Lancaster, Lancaster, England.

Ira M. Sheskin
Assistant Professor of Geography, University of Miami, Miami, Fla.

John A. Shimer
Professor of Geology (ret.), Brooklyn College, Brooklyn, N.Y.

Sir Hubert Shirley-Smith, C.B.E.
Past President, Institution of Civil Engineers, Consultant to W. V. Zinn and Associates, Kent, England.

Gerald Shklar, D.D.S.
Charles A. Brackett, Professor of Oral Pathology, Harvard School of Dental Medicine, Cambridge, Mass.

B. M. Shmavonian
Professor and Chief of Medical Psychology and Psychophysiology, Temple University Medical School, Philadelphia.

Diana Sholtz
Faculty, Massachusetts School of Professional Psychology, Newton.

A. Louis Shor
Registrations Coordinator, American Cyanamid Co., Princeton, N.J.

A. H. Short
Senior Lecturer of Physiology and Pharmacology, University of Nottingham Medical School, Nottingham, England.

James R. Shortridge
Associate Professor of Geography, University of Kansas, Lawrence.

Victor W. Sidel, M.D.
Professor and Chairperson, Department of Social Medicine, Montefiore Hospital and Albert Einstein College of Medicine, Bronx, N.Y.

William R. Siebenschuh
Assistant Professor of English, Case Western Reserve University, Cleveland, Ohio.

Joan C. Siegfried
Associate Professor of Art History, Skidmore College, Saratoga Springs, N.Y.

Jay A. Sigler
Professor of Political Science, Rutgers University, New Brunswick, N.J.

Robert H. Silliman
Associate Professor of History, Emory University, Atlanta, Ga.

Burr A. Silver
Professor of Geology and Geophysics, University of Oklahoma, Norman.

George A. Silver, M.D.
Professor of Public Health, Yale University School of Medicine, New Haven, Conn.

Larry A. Silver
Assistant Professor of Art History, University of California, Berkeley.

Philip W. Silver
Professor of Spanish, Columbia University, New York City.

Jean Silverman
Archaeological Institute of America, New York Society, New York City.

Virginia B. Silverstein
Translator and Author.

Dennis Simanaitis
Engineering Editor, *Road and Track*, Newport Beach, Calif.

N. W. Simmonds
Professor, School of Agriculture, Edinburgh University, Edinburgh, Scotland.

Edwin H. Simmons
Brigadier General, U.S. Marine Corps (ret.), Director of Marine Corps History and Museums.

Harold J. Simon, M.D.
Professor of Community Medicine and Associate Dean, School of Medicine, University of California, San Diego.

Norman Sims
Assistant Professor, Journalistic Studies Program, University of Massachusetts, Amherst.

Andrew Sinclair
Author of *Jack: A Biography of Jack London.*
Marcus G. Singer
Professor of Philosophy, University of
Wisconsin, Madison.
Ronald Singer
Professor of Anatomy and Anthropology,
Robert R. Bensley Professor in Biology and
Medical Sciences, University of Chicago,
Chicago.
Donald B. Siniff
Professor of Ecology and Behavioral Biology,
University of Minnesota, Minneapolis.
Guy Sircello
Professor of Philosophy, University of
California, Irvine.
Robert C. Slater
Professor and Director, Department of
Mortuary Science, University of Minnesota,
Minneapolis.
Elizabeth M. Slayter
Former Assistant Professor of Biology and
Biochemistry, Brandeis University, Waltham,
Mass.
Reuben E. Slesinger
Professor of Economics, University of
Pittsburgh, Pittsburgh, Pa.
Mark Slobin
Associate Professor of Music, Wesleyan
University, Middletown, Conn.
Bernice Slote
Professor of English, University of Nebraska,
Lincoln.
Donald Smalley
Professor Emeritus, University of Illinois,
Urbana-Champaign, Urbana.
Larry Smarr
Associate Professor of Astronomy, University
of Illinois, Champaign-Urbana.
George M. Smerk
Professor of Transportation, School of
Business, Indiana University, Bloomington.
Allen R. Smith
Assistant Professor of Geography, Central
Connecticut State College, New Britain.
Charles E. Smith
Professor of Mechanical Engineering,
Oregon State University, Corvallis.
C. Ray Smith
Architecture Critic, Historian, and Author,
*Supermannerism: New Attitudes in Post-
Modern Architecture.*
David S. Smith
Assistant Professor of Anesthesia, University
of Pennsylvania School of Medicine,
Philadelphia.
Elwyn A. Smith
Pastor, Garden Crest United Presbyterian
Church, Saint Petersburg, Fla.
Henry H. Smith
Public Information Officer, Bureau of the
Census, U.S. Department of Commerce.
Howard E. Smith, Jr.
Writer.
J. D. Smith
Professor of Genetics, Plant Sciences
Department, Texas A&M University,
College Station.
Joe K. Smith
Associate Professor of Mathematics,
Northern Kentucky University, Highland
Heights.
P. M. Smith
Lecturer in Botany, University of Edinburgh,
Edinburgh, Scotland.
Richard K. Smith
Aero Historian.
Roger S. U. Smith
Assistant Professor of Geology, University of
Houston, Houston, Tex.

Ronald C. Smith
Southern Alberta Institute of Technology,
Calgary.
Thomas M. Smith
Professor of the History of Science,
University of Oklahoma, Norman.
Warren Thomas Smith
Professor of Church History, The
Interdenominational Theological Center,
Atlanta, Ga.
Whitney Smith
Executive Director, Flag Research Center,
Winchester, Mass.
Howard E. Smither
Professor of Music, Director of Graduate
Studies in Music, University of North
Carolina at Chapel Hill, Chapel Hill.
James N. Snaden
Chairman, Department of Geography,
Central Connecticut State College, New
Britain.
Johan P. Snapper
Queen Beatrix Professor of German and
Dutch, University of California, Berkeley.
Ian N. Sneddon
Professor, University of Glasgow, Glasgow,
Scotland.
Louis L. Snyder
Professor of History, City College, City
University of New York, New York City.
Samuel S. Snyder
Assistant Professor, School of Education,
North Carolina State University, Raleigh.
Dorothy D. Sogn, M.D.
National Institutes of Health.
R. S. Sohal
Associate Professor of Biology, Southern
Methodist University, Dallas, Tex.
Thomas W. Sokolowski
The Institute of Fine Arts, Rome.
Ralph S. Solecki
Professor of Anthropology, Columbia
University, New York City.
Theodore Solis
Assistant Professor of Music, Grinnell
College, Grinnell, Iowa.
George I. Solish, M.D.
Director, Obstetrics and Gynecology,
Downstate Medical Center, State University
of New York, Brooklyn.
Bruce B. Solnick
Associate Professor of History, State
University of New York, Albany.
Robert C. Solomon
Professor of Philosophy, University of Texas,
Austin.
Allen Sommers
Chairman, Sommers/Rosen, Inc., Philadelphia.
Lawrence M. Sommers
Professor of Geography, Michigan State
University, East Lansing.
Waldo Sommers
Professor Emeritus of Public Administration,
George Washington University,
Washington, D.C.
Marian Sotsky
Reading Specialist, Enlarged City School
District of Middletown, N.Y.
Donald Southgate
Reader in Modern Political and
Constitutional History, University of
Dundee, Dundee, Scotland.
Brian Southworth
Head of Publications Group, European
Organization for Nuclear Research.
Suzanne Spain
Assistant for Planning and Institutional
Research, Bryn Mawr College, Bryn Mawr,
Pa., and Assistant Professor, Temple
University, Philadelphia.

Robert D. Sparks, M.D.
Program Director, W. K. Kellogg
Foundation, Battle Creek, Mich.
Eugene Spaziani
Professor of Zoology, University of Iowa,
Iowa City.
Philip J. Spear
Senior Director, Research, National Pest
Control Association.
Richard D. Spear
Chief, Surveillance and Monitoring Branch,
U.S. Environmental Protection Agency.
Stuart M. Speiser
Attorney, Speiser, Krause and Madole, New
York City.
Norman Sperling
Assistant Editor, *Sky & Telescope* Magazine.
Lewis W. Spitz
William R. Kenan Professor of History,
Stanford University, Stanford, Calif.
Bernard Spodek
Professor of Early Childhood Education,
University of Illinois, Urbana-Champaign,
Urbana.
Brian Spooner
Associate Professor of Anthropology,
University of Pennsylvania, Philadelphia.
Frank G. Spreadbury
Senior Member, The Institute of Electrical
and Electronic Engineers, and Associate of
the London College of Music, Paddington
College, London.
Susan Jay Spungin
National Consultant in Education, American
Foundation for the Blind, New York City.
Stephen H. Spurr
Professor of Public Affairs, University of
Texas, Austin.
John F. Stacks
Correspondent, *Time* Magazine.
Ralph W. Stacy
Research Scientist, U.S. Environmental
Protection Agency.
William J. Stadelman
Professor of Animal Sciences, Purdue
University, West Lafayette, Ind.
R. W. Stallman
Professor of English, Emeritus, University of
Connecticut, Storrs.
Hilary Standing
School of African and Asian Studies,
University of Sussex, Sussex, England.
Gordon J. Stang
Editor, *Tuesday* Magazine.
George F. G. Stanley
Emeritus Professor of Canadian Studies,
Mount Allison University, Sackville, New
Brunswick.
Theodore H. Stanley, M.D.
Professor of Anesthesiology, Surgery,
University of Utah Medical Center, Salt Lake
City.
P. Richard Stanley-Baker
Assistant Professor of Art History, University
of Victoria, Victoria, British Columbia.
C. Woodruff Starkweather
Associate Professor of Speech, Temple
University, Philadelphia.
Martin K. Starr
Professor of Management Science,
Columbia University, New York City.
Orestes N. Stavroudis
Professor, Optical Science Center, University
of Arizona, Tucson.
John Montague Steadman
Professor of Law, Georgetown University,
Washington, D.C.
Robert J. Steamer
Vice Chancellor for Academic Affairs and
Provost, University of Massachusetts,
Boston.

Colin Steele
Deputy University Librarian, Australian National University, Canberra.

Merle C. Steelman III
Instructor In Psychology, University of Tennessee, Knoxville.

William C. Steere
President Emeritus, New York Botanical Garden, Bronx.

Carlene E. Stephens
Museum Specialist, National Museum of History and Technology, Smithsonian Institution, Washington, D.C.

Robert M. Stern
Professor of Economics and Public Policy, University of Michigan, Ann Arbor.

Denis W. Stevens
President & Artistic Director, Accademia Monteverdiana Inc., Santa Barbara, Calif.

David B. Stewart
Chief, Branch of Experimental Geochemistry and Mineralogy, U.S. Geological Survey.

James Brewer Stewart
Professor of History, Macalester College, Saint Paul, Minn.

Kenneth M. Stewart
Professor of Anthropology, Arizona State University, Tempe.

Phyllis L. Stewart
Chairperson, Department of Sociology, George Washington University, Washington, D.C.

R. L. Stirrat
School of African and Asian Studies, University of Sussex, Sussex, England.

Noel Stock
Professor of English, University of Toledo, Toledo, Ohio.

Ellwyn R. Stoddard
Professor of Sociology and Anthropology, University of Texas, El Paso.

John G. Stoessinger
Professor of Political Science, Hunter College, City University of New York, New York City.

Robert D. Stolorow
Associate Professor of Psychology, Yeshiva University, New York City.

Joyce Hill Stoner
Paintings Conservator, Winterthur Museum, Winterthur, Del.

William B. Storey
Professor Emeritus of Horticulture, University of California, Riverside.

John F. Stover
Emeritus Professor of History, Purdue University, Lafayette, Ind.

Kaj A. Strand
Former Scientific Director, U.S. Naval Observatory, Washington, D.C.

Herbert L. Strauss
Professor of Chemistry, University of California, Berkeley.

Michael Strauss
Sportswriter, *New York Times.*

Arval L. Streadbeck
Professor of German, University of Utah, Salt Lake City.

Robert E. Street
Professor of Aeronautics and Astronautics, University of Washington, Seattle.

Alan Marc Strizak, M.D.
Consultant, Lenox Hill Hospital, Institute of Sports Medicine and Athletic Traumas, New York City.

John S. Strong
Lecturer in History of Religions, University of Chicago, Chicago.

Sterling Stuckey
Professor of History, Northwestern University, Evanston, Ill.

Jeffrey L. Sturchio
Lecturer in History and Sociology of Science, University of Pennsylvania, Philadelphia.

Charles H. Styer
Department of Botany, University of Maryland, College Park.

Leli Sudler
Assistant to the Chairman, Boston Architectural Center, Boston.

Alan Sugarman
Assistant Professor of Psychiatry, Yale University, New Haven, Conn.

Edward J. Sullivan
Instructor of Art History, New York University, New York City.

Joseph H. Summers
Professor of English, University of Rochester, Rochester, N.Y.

W. F. Summers
Professor, Memorial University of Newfoundland, St. John's.

Eric J. Sundquist
Assistant Professor of English, The Johns Hopkins University, Baltimore, Md.

Ronald Grigor Suny
Alex Manoogian Professor of Modern Armenian History, University of Michigan, Ann Arbor.

Charles Süsskind
Professor of Engineering, University of California, Berkeley.

Herbert L. Sussman
Associate Professor of English, Northeastern University, Boston.

George P. Sutton
Deputy Program Leader, University of California, Livermore.

Myron and Ann Sutton
Authors of *Forests of the World* and *Wild Shores.*

Clifford E. Swartz
Professor of Physics, State University of New York, Stony Brook.

Camm C. Swift
Associate Curator of Fishes, Natural History Museum of Los Angeles County, Los Angeles.

Thomas L. Swihart
Professor of Astronomy, University of Arizona, Tucson.

Richard Switzer
Dean of Humanities, California State College, San Bernardino.

M. J. Sydenham
Professor of History, Carleton University, Ottawa.

Curt Sylvester
Sports Writer, *Detroit Free Press.*

R. D. Sylvester
Professor of Russian, Colgate University, Hamilton, N.Y.

Joseph S. Szyliowicz
Professor of International Studies, University of Denver, Denver, Colo.

Edward Taborsky
Professor of Government, University of Texas, Austin.

Timothy Tackett
Assistant Professor, Marquette University, Milwaukee, Wis.

John L. Tancock
Vice-President, Sotheby Parke-Bernet, New York City.

E. J. Tapp
Associate Professor, University of New England, New South Wales, Australia.

Eric Tappe
Professor Emeritus of Rumanian Studies, University of London, London.

Charles T. Tart
Professor of Psychology, University of California, Davis.

David Tatham
Professor of Fine Arts, Syracuse University, Syracuse, N.Y.

Valèntin Tatransky
Art Critic and Historian.

Ian Tattersall
Associate Curator, American Museum of Natural History, New York City.

M. J. Taussig
Principal Scientific Officer, Arc Institute of Animal Physiology, Babraham, Cambridge, England.

Margaret C. Tavolga
Professor Emeritus of Biology, Fairleigh Dickinson University, Teaneck, N.J., and Research Associate, Department of Animal Behavior, American Museum of Natural History, New York City.

William N. Tavolga
Senior Research Associate, Mote Marine Laboratory, Sarasota, Fla., and Professor Emeritus of Biology and Psychology, City University of New York, New York City.

Ruth Teeter
Associate Professor, Center for Youth Development and Research, University of Minnesota, Saint Paul.

Bruce Tegner
Author of *Bruce Tegner's Complete Book of Self-Defense, . . . Karate,* and *. . . Judo.*

T. Teichmann
Visiting Physicist, Brookhaven National Laboratory, Upton, N.Y.

Werner H. Terjung
Professor, University of California, Los Angeles.

Vincent Terrace
Author of *Complete Encyclopedia of Television Programs.*

Victor Terras
Professor of Slavic Languages, Brown University, Providence, R.I.

Albert Tezla
Professor of English, University of Minnesota, Duluth.

Michael L. Thaller
Associate Professor of Geography, Carroll College, Waukesha, Wis.

H. S. Thayer
Professor of Philosophy, City College, City University of New York, New York City.

Ernst T. Theimer
Consultant, International Flavors and Fragrances, Inc.

George A. Theodorson
Professor of Sociology, Pennsylvania State University, University Park.

Kenneth F. Thibodeau
Archivist, National Archives.

John W. Thieret
Professor of Botany, Northern Kentucky University, Highland Heights.

Alan G. Thomas
Antiquarian Bookseller, London.

Harford Thomas
Journalist, Formerly Deputy Editor, *The Guardian,* London.

F. J. Thorpe
Chief, History Division, National Museum of Man, National Museums of Canada.

William C. Tierson
Director of Wildlife Research, State University of New York, College of Environmental Science and Forestry, Syracuse.

John H. Tietjen
Professor of Biology, City College of New York, New York City.

Helen Tiffin
Lecturer in English, University of Queensland, Queensland, Australia.

Laszlo Tikos
Professor of Russian Language and Literature, University of Massachusetts, Amherst.

Louisa Shen Ting
Lecturer in Art, State University of New York, Stony Brook.

Oswald Tippo
Commonwealth Professor of Botany, University of Massachusetts, Amherst.

Caldwell Titcomb
Professor of Music, Brandeis University, Waltham, Mass.

Tobi Tobias
Associate Editor, *Dancemagazine.*

Janet M. Todd
Associate Professor of English, Douglass College, Rutgers University, New Brunswick, N.J.

Neil B. Todd
Adjunct Professor of Biology, Boston University, Boston.

Maj. Gen. George E. Tomlinson
Former Chief Engineer, Federal Power Commission.

Martin Torodash
Professor of History, Fairleigh Dickinson University, Teaneck, N.J.

Oscar Tosi
Professor, Director, Speech and Hearing Sciences, Michigan State University, East Lansing.

David W. Towle
Associate Professor of Biology, University of Richmond, Richmond, Va.

Terrence J. Toy
Assistant Professor of Geography, University of Denver, Denver, Colo.

Carl J. Tracie
Associate Professor of Geography, University of Saskatchewan, Saskatoon.

Joseph B. Trainer, M.D.
Professor of Medicine, University of Oregon, Portland.

Anne Treisman
Lecturer in Psychology, Oxford University, Oxford, England.

Stanley W. Trimble
Assistant Professor of Geography, University of California, Los Angeles.

Charles L. Trowbridge
Senior Vice-President and Chief Actuary, Bankers Life Company, Des Moines, Iowa.

Christopher G. Trump
Assistant Dean, Columbia University Graduate School of Journalism, New York City.

Jonathan N. Tubb
Research Assistant, British Museum, London.

Arthur O. Tucker
Research Associate, Delaware State College, Dover.

David Tudor
Veterinarian, Cranbury, N.J.

Eleanor Tufts
Professor of Art History, Southern Methodist University, Dallas, Tex.

Jean MacIntosh Turfa
Former Visiting Assistant Professor of Classical Studies, Loyola University of Chicago, Chicago.

Lynn Turgeon
Professor of Economics, Hofstra University, Hempstead, N.Y.

John Turkevich
Eugene Higgins Professor Emeritus of Chemistry, Princeton University, Princeton, N.J.

Martin Turnell
Fellow of the Royal Society of Literature, London.

A. J. Turner
Free-lance Historian, London.

Arthur Campbell Turner
Professor of Political Science, University of California, Riverside, Calif.

Eugene F. Tutt
Eugene F. Tutt and Associates, Architects.

Amos Tversky
Professor of Psychology, Stanford University, Stanford, Calif.

David Tweedie
Associate Professor and Chairman of the Department of Education, Gallaudet College, Washington, D.C.

Dorothy Twohig
Associate Editor, *The Papers of George Washington,* University of Virginia, Charlottesville.

Louise B. Tyrer, M.D.
Vice-President for Medical Affairs, Planned Parenthood Federation of America, New York City.

John Tytell
Professor of English, Queens College, City University of New York, Flushing.

Craig D. Uchida
Assistant Professor, Institute of Criminal Justice and Criminology, University of Maryland, College Park.

Natalie W. Uhl
Senior Research Associate, L. H. Bailey Hortorium, Cornell University, Ithaca, N.Y.

Richard Ulack
Associate Professor of Geography, University of Kentucky, Lexington.

Richard H. Ullman
Editor, *Foreign Policy.*

S. Sidney Ulmer
Alumni Professor, University of Kentucky, Lexington.

Homer Ulrich
Professor Emeritus, University of Maryland, College Park.

Sanford J. Ungar
Managing Editor, *Foreign Policy.*

Robert M. Utley
Deputy Executive Director, Advisory Council on Historic Preservation.

Godfrey Uzoigwe
Professor and Head of Department of History, University of Calabar, Calabar, Nigeria.

Albert Valdman
Professor of French, Italian, and Linguistics, Indiana University, Bloomington.

Elizabeth Kridl Valkenier
Senior Fellow, Russian Institute, Columbia University, New York City.

Pierre L. van den Berghe
Professor of Sociology and Anthropology, University of Washington, Seattle.

Willem van der Bijl
Associate Professor of Meteorology, Naval Postgraduate School, Monterey, Calif.

Frank E. Vandiver
Provost, Vice-President, and Harrison Masterson, Jr., Professor of History, Rice University, Houston, Tex.

Johannes Van Overbeek
Professor Emeritus of Biology, Texas A&M University, College Station.

Pieter van Royen
Chairman, Department of Botany, B. P. Bishop Museum, Honolulu.

Lawrence H. Van Vlack
Professor of Materials Engineering, University of Michigan, Ann Arbor.

Ann Lorenz Van Zanten
Architectural Historian.

Agnes Huszar Vardy
Associate Professor, Robert Morris College, Pittsburgh, Pa.

S. B. Vardy
Professor of History, Duquesne University, Pittsburgh, Pa.

Amy Varin
Adjunct Lecturer in the Humanities, University of Santa Clara, Santa Clara, Calif.

Sir Devendra P. Varma
Professor of English, Dalhousie University, Halifax, Nova Scotia.

David Vaughan
Archivist, Cunningham Dance Foundation, Contributing Editor, *Ballet Review,* and Associate Critic, *Dancemagazine.*

Dame Janet Vaughan, M.D., F.R.C.P.
Bone Research Laboratory, Nuffield Orthopaedic Hospital, Oxford, England.

Terry A. Vaughan
Professor of Zoology, Northern Arizona University, Flagstaff.

Milos Velimirovic
Professor of Music, University of Virginia, Charlottesville.

Bob Verdi
Sportswriter, *Chicago Tribune.*

Charles Verlinden
Professor Emeritus, State University of Ghent, Royal Belgian Academy, Brussels.

Philip E. Vernon
Professor of Educational Psychology, University of Calgary, Calgary, Alberta.

Laurence Veysey
Professor of History, University of California, Santa Cruz.

Walter N. Vickery
Professor of Russian Literature, University of North Carolina, Chapel Hill.

François C. D. Vigier
Professor of City Planning and Urban Design, Harvard University, Cambridge, Mass.

Gennaro F. Vito
Department of Criminal Justice, Temple University, Philadelphia.

Mark S. Vogel, O.D.
Clinical Instructor, State College of Optometry, State University of New York, Stony Brook.

Philip E. Vogel
Chairman, and Professor, Department of Geography, University of Nebraska, Omaha.

Fred W. Voget
Professor of Anthropology, Southern Illinois University, Edwardsville.

Ivan Volgyes
Professor of Political Science, University of Nebraska, Lincoln.

John O. Voll
Associate Professor in History, University of New Hampshire, Durham.

E. Peter Volpe
Professor and Chairman of Biology, Tulane University, New Orleans, La.

Stephanie von Buchau
Performing Arts Editor, *San Francisco Magazine.*

Edward Wagenknecht
Professor of English, Emeritus, Boston University, Boston.

Charles Wagley
Graduate Research Professor of Anthropology, University of Florida, Gainesville.

Linda W. Wagner
Professor of English, Michigan State University, East Lansing.

Thomas K. Wagner
Business Publications Advisor, Former Editor, *Builder* Magazine.

Rev. Dr. Walter D. Wagoner
Senior Minister, Asylum Hill Congregational Church, Hartford, Conn.

P. B. Waite
Professor of History, Dalhousie University, Halifax, Nova Scotia.

Robert Starr Waite
Assistant Professor, Division of Continuing Education, University of Utah, and Assistant Professor of Geography, Brigham Young University, Salt Lake City.

Marvalee H. Wake
Associate Professor of Zoology and Biology, University of California, Berkeley.

Alan M. Wald
Assistant Professor of English, University of Michigan, Ann Arbor.

Benji Wald
Assistant Professor of Linguistics and African Languages, University of California, Los Angeles.

Andrew J. Walker
Botany Department, West of Scotland Agricultural College, Auchincruive, Ayr, Scotland.

Benjamin Walker
Society of Authors, London.

H. J. Walker
Boyd Professor of Geography, Louisiana State University, Baton Rouge.

Ian G. Walker
Professor of Biochemistry, University of Western Ontario, London, Ontario.

William G. Walker
Chief Executive and Principal, Australian Administrative State College, Victoria.

George J. Wallace
Professor Emeritus of Zoology, Michigan State University, East Lansing.

James M. Wallace
Chairman, Department of Education, Lewis and Clark College, Portland, Oreg.

L. Walschot
Conservator, Geological Institute, University of Ghent, Ghent, Belgium.

Barbara Ann Walton
Assistant Professor of Biology, University of Tennessee, Chattanooga.

William S.-Y. Wang
Professor of Linguistics, University of California, Berkeley.

Harold R. Wanless
Assistant Professor of Marine Geology and Geophysics, Rosenstiel School of Marine and Atmospheric Science, University of Miami, Miami, Fla.

Allen Mason Ward
Professor of History, University of Connecticut, Storrs.

John F. Ward
Professor of Physics, University of Michigan, Ann Arbor.

Robert A. Warner
Professor of Music, University of Michigan, Ann Arbor.

Donald R. Warren
Professor and Chairman, College of Education, University of Maryland, College Park.

Edward Wasiolek
Avalon Distinguished Service Professor of Slavic and Comparative Literature, University of Chicago, Chicago.

Jack Wasserman
Wasserman, Orlow, Ginsberg, and Rubin, Washington, D.C.

Alan Watson
Professor of Civil Law, University of Pennsylvania, Philadelphia.

Don A. Watson
Architect.

Fletcher G. Watson
Henry Lee Shattuck Professor of Education, Emeritus, Harvard University, Cambridge, Mass.

Geoffrey S. Watson
Professor of Statistics, Princeton University, Princeton, N.J.

Ronald G. Watt
Assistant Librarian and Archivist, Church of Jesus Christ of Latter-day Saints, Salt Lake City, Utah.

Robert J. Weaver
Professor of Viticulture, University of California, Davis.

S. David Webb
Curator of Fossil Vertebrates and Professor of Zoology, Florida State Museum, University of Florida, Gainesville.

Marjorie K. Webster
Curator, Antique Instrument Collection, Adler Planetarium, Chicago.

Peter J. Webster
Senior Research Scientist, Commonwealth Scientific and Industrial Research Organisation, Aspendale, Victoria, Australia.

Roderick S. Webster
Curator, Antique Instrument Collection, Adler Planetarium, Chicago.

Howard Wechsler
Associate Professor of Asian Studies, University of Illinois, Urbana.

William C. Wees
Associate Professor of English, McGill University, Montreal.

Lilly Wei
Art Instructor, Kingsborough Community College, City University of New York, New York City.

David L. Weide
Assistant Professor of Geography and Geology, University of Nevada, Las Vegas.

Jon Weil
Research Geneticist, University of California, San Francisco.

Max H. Weil, M.D.
Chairman, Division of Critical Care Medicine, and Director, Institute of Critical Care Medicine, University of Southern California, Los Angeles.

Herbert Weiner, M.D.
Professor of Psychiatry and Neuroscience, Albert Einstein College of Medicine, Bronx, N.Y.

Robert S. Weiner
Lecturer in Geography, University of Connecticut, Storrs.

J. Donald Weinrauch
Associate Professor of Business, Tennessee Technological University, Cookeville.

Edwin A. Weinstein
Professor Emeritus of Neurology, Mount Sinai Medical School, New York City.

Thomas R. Weir
Professor Emeritus, University of Manitoba, Winnipeg.

Joseph S. Weisberg
Professor and Chairman, Geoscience Department, Jersey City State College, Jersey City, N.J.

Rev. James A. Weisheipl
Professor of the History of Medieval Science, Pontifical Institute of Mediaeval Studies, and Professor of Medieval Studies, University of Toronto, Toronto.

Richard J. Weiss
Physicist, Materials Research Center, Watertown, Mass.

Herbert Weissbach
Associate Director, Roche Institute of Molecular Biology, Nutley, N.J.

Kenneth F. Welch
Lecturer in English and General Studies (ret.), Oxford College of Further Education, Oxford, England.

Wayne W. Welch
Professor of Educational Psychology, University of Minnesota, Minneapolis.

René Wellek
Sterling Professor Emeritus of Comparative Literature, Yale University, New Haven, Conn.

John M. Weller, M.D.
Professor of Internal Medicine, University of Michigan, Ann Arbor.

Merle Wells
Idaho State Historic Preservation Officer, Idaho State Historical Society, Boise.

William E. Welmers
Professor of Linguistics and African Languages, University of California, Los Angeles.

Gene Weltfish
Professor and Graduate Fellow in Anthropology, New School for Social Research, New York City.

Richard P. Werbner
Senior Lecturer in Social Anthropology, University of Manchester, Manchester, England.

William E. Werner, Jr.
Professor of Biology, Blackburn College, Carlinville, Ill.

Michael Wertheimer
Professor of Psychology, University of Colorado, Boulder.

Robert F. Wesser
Professor of History, State University of New York, Albany.

Bruce West
Columnist and Author, *The Globe and Mail*, Toronto.

Elliott West
Associate Professor of History, University of Texas, Arlington.

Richard F. West
Professor of Forestry, Cook College, Rutgers University, New Brunswick, N.J.

David Westby
Associate Professor of Sociology, Pennsylvania State University, University Park.

B. E. J. Wheeler
Reader In Plant Pathology, Imperial College Field Station, Silwood Park, Sunninghill, Berks, England.

Russell R. Wheeler
Assistant to the Director, Federal Judicial Center, Washington, D.C.

Arthur K. Wheelock, Jr.
Curator of Dutch and Flemish Painting, National Gallery of Art, Washington, D.C.

Dennis F. Whigman
Plant Ecologist, Chesapeake Bay Center for Environmental Studies, Smithsonian Institution, Edgewater, Md.

Lucy A. White
Secretary-Treasurer, American Mobilehome Association, Lakewood, Colo.

Richard E. White
Research Scientist, Systematic Entomology Laboratory, U.S. Department of Agriculture, Beltsville, Md.

Thomas Taylor White, M.D.
Clinical Professor of Surgery, University of Washington School of Medicine, Seattle.

Robert White-Stevens
Chairman, Bureau of Conservation and Environmental Science, Cook College, Rutgers University, New Brunswick, N.J.

John R. Whiting
Former publisher of *Motor Boat and Sailing* magazine.

Robert M. Whiting
Research Associate, The Oriental Institute, University of Chicago, Chicago.

James A. Whitney
Associate Professor of Geology, University of Georgia, Athens.

Ronald Wiedenhoeft
Associate Professor, Graduate School of Architecture, University of Utah, Salt Lake City.

Elwyn A. Wienandt
Associate Dean, School of Music, Baylor University, Waco, Tex.

Eugene P. Wigner
Thomas D. Jones Professor of Mathematical Physics, Retired, Princeton University, Princeton, N.J.

Donald N. Wilber
Author, *Iran, Past and Present.*

E. O. Wiley
Assistant Curator of Fishes, Museum of Natural History, University of Kansas, Lawrence.

Hubert G. H. Wilhelm
Professor of Geography, Ohio University, Athens.

James J. Wilhelm
Professor of Comparative Literature, Rutgers University, New Brunswick, N.J.

Richard Wilkie
Professor of Geology and Geography, University of Massachusetts, Amherst.

B. R. Wilkinson
Senior Lecturer, Department of Wool Science, Lincoln College, Canterbury, New Zealand.

Robert Wilkinson-Latham
British Military Historian.

Clifford M. Will
Assistant Professor of Physics, Stanford University, Stanford, Calif.

David R. Williams, Jr.
Chairman of the Board, Resource Sciences Corporation, Tulsa, Okla.

George Huntston Williams
Professor of Church History, Harvard University Divinity School, Cambridge, Mass.

Martha E. Williams
Coordinated Science Laboratory, University of Illinois, Urbana.

Michael Williams
Associate Professor of Philosophy, University of Maryland, College Park.

Harold F. Williamson
Professor Emeritus of Economics, Northwestern University, Evanston, Ill.

Stephen S. Willoughby
Professor of Mathematics and Mathematics Education, New York University, New York City.

Catherine W. Wilson
Visiting Lecturer, Barnard College, New York City.

Charles L. Wilson
Adjunct Professor, Ohio State University and Ohio Agriculture Research and Development Center, Wooster.

David L. Wilson
Associate Professor of Physiology and Biophysics, University of Miami School of Medicine, Miami, Fla.

Marion B. Wilson
Decorative Arts Expert.

Robert E. Wilson
Associate Professor of Oceanography, Marine Sciences Research Center, State University of New York, Stony Brook.

Calvin H. Wilvert
Assistant Professor of Geography, California Polytechnic State University, San Luis Obispo.

John J. Winberry
Associate Professor of Geography, University of South Carolina, Columbia.

Albert M. Winchester
Professor of Biology, University of Northern Colorado, Greeley.

Brian F. Windley
Lecturer in Geology, University of Leicester, Leicester, England.

Charles L. Winek
Professor of Toxicology, Duquesne University, Pittsburgh, Pa.

Isabel B. Wingate
Professor Emeritus of Retail Management, New York University, New York City.

R. H. Winnick
Co-author of *Robert Frost: The Later Years, 1938–1963.*

David Wistow
Lecturer and Art Historian, Art Gallery of Ontario, Toronto.

William Withington
Associate Professor of Geology and Geography, University of Kentucky, Lexington.

Nancy L. Wityak
Department of Sociology, George Washington University, Washington, D.C.

Richard Wojcik
Assistant Professor, Barnard College, Columbia University, New York City.

William S. M. Wold
Assistant Professor, Institute for Molecular Virology, St. Louis University School of Medicine, St. Louis.

Ernest S. Wolf, M.D.
Training and Supervising Analyst, Chicago Intstitute for Psychoanalysis, Chicago.

Murray Wolfson
Professor of Economics, Oregon State University, Corvallis.

Harry Wollman, M.D.
Robert Dunning Dripps Professor and Chairman, Department of Anesthesia, and Professor of Pharmacology, University of Pennsylvania, School of Medicine, Philadelphia.

Edward A Wolpert, M.D.
Director, Clinical Services, Psychosomatic and Psychiatric Institute, Michael Reese Hospital and Medical Center, Chicago.

Roland E. Wolseley
Professor Emeritus of Journalism, Syracuse University, Syracuse, N.Y.

Robert E. Wolverton
Vice-President for Academic Affairs and Professor of Classics, Mississippi State University, Mississippi State.

William C. Wonders
Professor of Geography, University of Alberta, Edmonton.

George Woodcock
Former Editor, *Canadian Literature.*

Charles Platten Woodhouse
Life-Fellow of the Royal Society of Arts, London.

Paul B. Woodruff
Associate Professor of Philosophy, University of Texas, Austin.

Thomas E. Wren
Associate Professor of Philosophy, Loyola University of Chicago, Chicago.

Conrad Wright
Professor of American Church History, Harvard University, Cambridge, Mass.

David E. Wright
Associate Professor, Lyman Briggs College, Michigan State University, East Lansing.

Marion I. Wright
Professor of Geography, Rhode Island College, Providence, R.I.

Dennis Hume Wrong
Professor of Sociology, New York University, New York City.

William F. Wyatt, Jr.
Professor of Classics, Brown University, Providence, R.I.

Donald Wyman
Horticulturist, Emeritus, Arnold Arboretum, Harvard University, Cambridge, Mass.

Leon Yacher
Assistant Professor of Geography, Southern Connecticut State College, New Haven.

David Yerkes
Assistant Professor of English, Columbia University, New York City.

Arthur E. Yohalem
Editor, *Vending Times.*

T. Leslie Youd
Research Civil Engineer, U.S. Geological Survey.

Bruce A. Young
Professor of Animal Physiology, University of Alberta, Edmonton.

Donald Young
Author, *American Roulette: The History and Dilemma of the Vice Presidency.*

David C. Yu
Professor of History of Religions, Colorado Women's College, Denver.

Hugo Zahnd
Professor Emeritus of Chemistry, Brooklyn College, City University of New York, Brooklyn, N.Y.

Robert L. Zangrando
Associate Professor of History, University of Akron, Akron, Ohio.

Carl A. Zapffe
Professional Engineer, CAZ Lab, Baltimore, Md.

Robert J. Zappalorti
Executive Director, Herpetological Associates, Zoological and Environmental Consultants, Staten Island, N.Y.

John P. Zarling
Professor of Mechanical Engineering, University of Alaska, Fairbanks.

Oscar Zeichner
Professor Emeritus of History, City College, City University of New York, New York City.

David M. Zesmer
Professor of English, Illinois Institute of Technology, Chicago.

Herman E. Zieger
Professor of Chemistry, City University of New York, New York City.

Edward Zigler
Sterling Professor of Psychology, Yale University; Head, Psychology Section, Yale Child Study Center, New Haven, Conn.

Thomas W. Zimmerer
Professor of Industrial Management, Clemson University, Clemson, S.C.

Loretta E. Zimmerman
Associate Professor of History, University of Portland, Portland, Oreg.

Jack Zipes
Professor of German and Comparative Literature, University of Wisconsin, Milwaukee.

Virpi Zuck
Assistant Professor of Scandinavian Studies, University of Oregon, Eugene.

Mark J. Zucker
Assistant Professor of Art History, University of Wisconsin, Milwaukee.

Richard L. Zusi
Curator of Research, National Museum of Natural History, Smithsonian Institution, Washington, D.C.

Academic American Encyclopedia

PHOENICIAN

EARLY HEBREW

EARLY ARAMAIC

EARLY GREEK

CLASSICAL GREEK

Aa

MODERN LATIN

ETRUSCAN **A**

EARLY LATIN **A**

CLASSICAL LATIN **A**

RUSSIAN-CYRILLIC **A**

GERMAN-GOTHIC **A**

A

A/a is the first letter of the English alphabet and of almost all alphabets derived from the ancient Semitic writing system. Both the form of the letter and its position at the beginning of the alphabet are from the Latin alphabet, which derived it from the Greek by way of the Etruscan.

The Greeks call the letter *alpha*. Its name, form, and position were taken by them, along with the rest of the alphabet, from a Semitic writing system—probably Phoenician but possibly Aramaic. In Semitic writing systems, the name of the sign is *aleph*; there, it does not represent a vowel but rather a consonant similar to the glottal stop (a sound produced by closing the gap between the vocal chords) that precedes the emphatic pronunciation of initial vowels in English (*all, in, out, up*).

In English, the letter *a* stands for a number of vowel sounds, as in *bald, father, fat, any, fate,* and *soda,* and occurs in a number of vocalic digraphs (successive vowels that have a single sound), such as *paw, laud, laugh, steady, bear, beacon, moat, aisle, pay,* and *paid*.

The double *a* does not occur in native English words but is found in some words (*aardvark, kraal,* and *Aaron*) taken from languages that have this sequence.

I. J. GELB AND R. M. WHITING

Aachen   [ah'-ken]

Aachen (French: Aix-la-Chapelle) is a city in northwestern West Germany in the state of North Rhine–Westphalia, bordering on Belgium and the Netherlands. It has a population of 242,000 (1976 est.). Aachen is the site of an important engineering school (Technische Hochschule Aachen) and is a rail center of a large coal-mining region. It also has important iron and steel works. Other industries produce textiles, glass, and needles. The mineral spas have operated since Roman times.

Aachen was Charlemagne's northern capital and the center of Carolingian civilization. The German kings from Otto I (936) to Ferdinand I (1531) were crowned here. Aachen remained a free imperial city until occupied by France in 1794. In 1815 it passed to Prussia by an act of the Congress of Vienna. It was occupied by the Allies after World War I until 1930 and was heavily damaged during World War II. Aachen's octagonal cathedral, which Charlemagne founded and which contains his tomb, was modeled after the church of San Vitale in Ravenna, Italy.

Aakjaer, Jeppe   [aw'-kyair, yep'-uh]

Jeppe Aakjaer, b. Sept. 10, 1866, d. Apr. 22, 1930, was one of Denmark's finest social novelists and most popular poets. Such early novels as *Children of Wrath* (1904) deal with the harsh conditions of farm laborers in his native Jutland. His simple, lyric poetry has been set to music and is included in such volumes as *Songs of the Rye* (1906). He also wrote several volumes of memoirs.

Aalborg: see ÅLBORG.

Aalto, Alvar   [ahl'-toh, ahl'-vahr]

Hugo Alvar Henrik Aalto, b. Finland, Feb. 3, 1898, d. May 11, 1976, was one of the major architects of the 20th century and of enormous influence in the development of MODERN ARCHITECTURE. Aalto's greatest contribution was his rare gift for humanizing the technocratic architectural tenets of the BAUHAUS and other exponents of the INTERNATIONAL STYLE. He stated his own credo succinctly: "It is the task of the architect to give life a gentler structure." In all his work, this simple principle is clearly dominant.

Aalto graduated from the Helsinki Polytechnic School in 1921; within a decade he was the acknowledged master of Finnish architecture, which first achieved world renown through his buildings and furniture designs. With his first wife, the architect Aino Marsio, Aalto founded (1935) the Artek firm to produce new household furnishings, many of them in molded and laminated wood.

Aalto established his distinctive style with the Viipuri

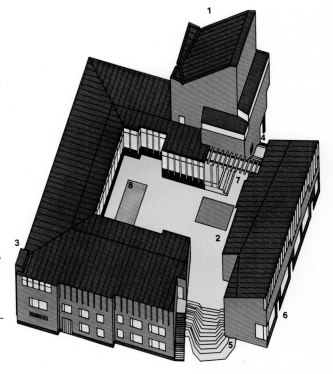

The civic center (1950–52) in Säynätsalo, Finland, was designed by Alvar Aalto. Constructed of red brick with a copper roof, the buildings are grouped around a raised courtyard. Numbers indicate council chamber (1); library (2); municipal offices (3); main staircase (4); garden steps (5); shops (6);) main entrance (7) and pool (8).

Library (1927–35; destroyed 1943)—famous for the undulating acoustic wood ceiling in its lecture hall—and with the Turun Sanomat newspaper building (1927–30), radically innovative then as now for the tapered concrete columns in its press room. The tuberculosis sanatorium in Paimio (1929–33) brought Aalto international fame; the six-story convalescent buildings are screened from the staff quarters and sited for maximum sunlight on their cantilevered balconies. For his industrialist patrons Harry and Mairea Gullichsen, Aalto built Villa Mairea (1938–39). Every element of this airy, elegant country house is fully integrated to achieve luxury without ostentation. Aalto's Finnish pavilions for the Paris Exposition of 1937 and the New York World's Fair of 1939 added to his international stature, augmenting the acclaim for the 1938 exhibition devoted to his work at New York's Museum of Modern Art. For the Massachusetts Institute of Technology in Cambridge, Mass., where he was a visiting professor for six years, Aalto designed Baker House dormitory (1947); its serpentine form affords every room a sweeping view of the Charles River.

The destruction wrought in Finland by the Russo-Finnish War (1940) and World War II necessitated rebuilding and urban planning on a nationwide scale; all of it was designed by a technical office under Aalto's supervision. For the island village of Säynätsalo, Aalto designed a civic center (1950–52) with intimately scaled red-brick structures of various shapes clustered around an elevated grass court that affords vistas of the surrounding lake and forests.

The buildings of Aalto's later years are more austere in appearance, but even the monumental Finlandia House (1967–75), the new cultural center of Helsinki, retains a human scale. The lakeside group of clean geometric shapes in white marble consists of meeting halls, exhibition areas, and an acoustically perfect concert hall. Aalto was deeply sensitive to all the arts, and numbered among his personal friends the artists Jean Arp, Constantin Brancusi, and Fernand Léger, as well as his great compatriot in both homeland and spirit, the composer Jean Sibelius.

Bibliography: Fleig, Karl, ed., *Alvar Aalto* (1975); Gutheim, Frederick, *Alvar Aalto* (1960); Pearson, Paul D., *Alvar Aalto and the International Style* (1978).

See also: ARCHITECTURE; FUNCTIONALISM; FURNITURE; INTERIOR DESIGN; MUSIC AND CONCERT HALLS; SCANDINAVIAN ART AND ARCHITECTURE.

aardvark

The aardvark (or ant bear), *Orycteropus afer*, is the only species in the MAMMAL family Orycteropodidae, order Tubulidentata. Its name is derived from the Afrikaans for "earth pig,"

The aardvark, O. afer, claws soil from a termite mound and uses its long, sticky tongue to capture termites scattering from the mound. Aardvark claws are sometimes kept as good-luck charms.

and this slow, massive animal somewhat resembles a pig. It is brown to yellowish, about 150 cm (5 ft) long, with a 60-cm-long (2-ft) tail, and weighs 45 to 77 kg (100 to 170 lb). It has a narrow head and a long snout. Its ears are large and rabbit-like, and hearing is acute. The short, stout legs, partially webbed feet, and long claws are well suited for burrowing its large sleeping dens and for tearing apart mounds of the ants and termites on which it feeds with its long, sticky tongue.

Aardvarks are found throughout sub-Saharan Africa, usually in open country. They are shy, nocturnal creatures. The female bears one or two young in October or November. Aardvarks live about ten years in captivity. EVERETT SENTMAN

aardwolf

The aardwolf, P. cristatus, has a sloping back and long forelegs as does its larger relative, the hyena. When the aardwolf is excited, it bristles a crest of fur on the back of its neck.

The aardwolf, *Proteles cristatus*, is a CARNIVORE belonging to the family Hyaenidae, order Carnivore. Its name is derived from the Afrikaans for "earth wolf." It is grayish tan with dark stripes, about 76 cm (30 in) long not including a 30-cm-long (12-in) bushy tail, and about 50 cm (20 in) high at the shoulder. The neck is long, with a coarse mane that bristles when attacked. Unlike the hyena, the aardwolf has weak teeth and jaws. It eats termites, insect larvae, and sometimes small mammals. The aardwolf lives on the dry plains of southern and eastern Africa. It is nocturnal in habit. The female produces a litter of two to four young in November and December. EVERETT SENTMAN

Aare River [ah'-ruh]

The Aare River is the longest (295 km/183 mi) river in Switzerland and drains an area of 17,780 km² (6,865 mi²). Rising in the Bernese Alps, it passes by Meiringen, through the Aare Gorge, into Lake Thun, past Bern, and joins the Rhine River at the village of Koblenz.

Aarhus: see ÅRHUS.

Aaron

Brother of MOSES, Aaron was Moses' spokesman before Pharaoh and was his assistant during the Exodus from Egypt. Even though Aaron was involved in constructing the GOLDEN CALF that the Israelites worshiped while Moses was on Mount Sinai, he and his sons were appointed priests, with Aaron as high priest. He was also designated head of the LEVITES, ministers of lower rank, and his authority was miraculously confirmed by a flowering staff (Exod. 28–29, 32; Num. 8, 17–18). Aaron died before his people reached Canaan.

Aaron, Henry

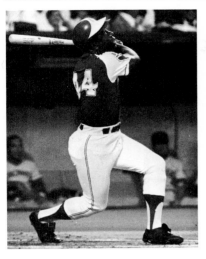

Henry Aaron unleashes the swing that launched the most home runs (755) in the history of American major-league baseball. Aaron, an outfielder, spent most of his 23-year career with the Braves of the National League. He was elected to the Hall of Fame in 1982, his first year of eligibility.

Henry "Hank" Aaron, b. Mobile, Ala., Feb. 5, 1934, is American baseball's all-time champion home-run hitter. Aaron entered the record books on Apr. 8, 1974, by breaking Babe Ruth's record of 714, and he went on to hit a total of 755 homers before completing his 23-year major-league career in 1976. While accumulating a lifetime batting average of .305, Aaron also set major-league career records for games played (3,298), at bats (12,364), and runs batted in (2,297).

Aaron began playing professionally for all-black teams in Mobile, Ala., and Indianapolis, Ind., but he signed with the Milwaukee Braves organization at the age of 18. He reached the Braves major-league team when he was only 20 and in his first year established himself as one of the better hitters and outfielders in baseball. He played for the Braves for almost his entire career, in Milwaukee from 1954 to 1965 and in Atlanta from 1966 to 1974. When he collected his 713th home run at the end of the 1973 season, baseball fans spent the winter anticipating his record-tying and record-breaking homers. He got them in the first and fifth days of the 1974 season. He completed his career by playing with the Milwaukee Brewers in 1975 and 1976.   JIM BENAGH

Bibliography: Aaron, Henry, and Bisher, Furman, *Aaron* (1974).

abacus   [ab'-uh-kuhs]

An abacus is an instrument that helps a person make arithmetic calculations. In its best-known form, as the Chinese *suan p'an*, it is composed of beads strung on parallel wires in a rectangular frame. In ancient times, however, the abacus was composed of a row of grooves in sand into which pebbles were placed. Later, the use of a slate or a board (in Greek, *abax*) made it a portable device; and the pebbles were systematically arranged along parallel lines.

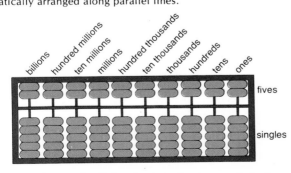

In a Chinese abacus, a bead's location determines its numerical value. Calculations are made by changing the positions of the beads.

The value assigned to each pebble (or bead, shell, or stick) is determined not by its shape but by its position: one pebble on a particular line or one bead on a particular wire has the value of 1; two together have the value of 2. A pebble on the next line, however, might have the value of 10, and a pebble on the third line would have the value of 100. Therefore, three properly placed pebbles—two with values of 1 and one with the value of 10—could signify 12, and the addition of a fourth pebble with the value of 100 could signify 112, using a place-value notational system of multiples of 10.

Thus the abacus works on the principle of place-value notation: the location of the bead determines its value. In this way, relatively few beads are required to depict large numbers. The beads are counted, or given numerical values, by shifting them in one direction. The values are erased (freeing the counters for reuse) by shifting the beads in the other direction. An abacus is used simply as a memory aid by a person making mental calculations. In contrast, ADDING MACHINES, electronic calculators, and computers are used to make physical calculations.   THOMAS M. SMITH

Bibliography: Moon, Parry H., *The Abacus* (1971); Pullan, J. M., *The History of the Abacus* (1969).

Abadan   [ah-bah-dahn']

Abadan (1976 pop., 296,081) is a city on Abadan Island in the Shatt al-Arab, at the head of the Persian Gulf in Khuzestan province, Iran. About 402 km (250 mi) southwest of Isfahan, it is the terminus of pipelines from Iranian oil fields and has one of the world's largest oil-refinery complexes.

Settled as early as 1047, Abadan remained small until oil was discovered there in 1908 and the first refineries were constructed the next year. Abadan's refining facilities, the largest in the world until 1951, processed more than 18 million metric tons (20 million U.S. tons) of crude oil a year before the Iraq-Iran war erupted in 1980. Both Abadan's refinery and its port installations at Ma'shur and Kharg Island were repeatedly attacked and severely damaged during that war. In 1983 an Iraqi attack caused the worst oil spill in Persian Gulf history off Kharg Island.

abalone   [ab-uh-lohn'-ee]

Abalone is the common name applied to any marine GASTROPOD in the MOLLUSK genus *Haliotis*. It is also sometimes applied to other gastropods. Unlike the many gastropods that have highly coiled shells, abalones have a broad, flattened, asymmetrical shell, the shape of which resembles the human ear—hence another common name, ear shell, or sea-ear. This shape minimizes water resistance in the abalones' intertidal habitats. The animals respire and discharge wastes through a row of holes on one side of the shell; old holes fill up and new ones appear as the animals age. Abalones are primitive gastropods along with other members of the order Archaeogastropoda, such as the LIMPET. They are commercially valuable for their large, edible foot and for the mother-of-pearl that lines their shells, which is used to make articles such as buttons.   STEPHEN CHARLES REINGOLD

abandonment

Abandonment, in law, is the voluntary giving up of property or of rights. If a person leaves his or her automobile by the side of a road and does not intend to come back for it, the person has abandoned it. Under the law, abandoned property may be appropriated by the next comer, but the owner's intention to abandon it must be shown.

In divorce law, abandonment occurs when one spouse leaves the other and does not intend to fulfill his or her legal obligations. For example, a man who is legally separated from his wife may be charged with abandonment if he fails to provide the financial support he has promised.

Abbado, Claudio   [ah-bah'-doh]

Claudio Abbado, b. Milan, June 26, 1935, a leading member of the new generation of conductors, comes from a musical family. His father, Michelangelo, was vice-principal of the Milan Conservatory where Claudio and his elder brother, Marcello, studied. He began his career as a pianist, and he studied composition with Bruno Bettinelli and conducting with Hans Swarowsky in Vienna. In 1971 he became permanent conductor of the Vienna Philharmonic Orchestra and in 1973 he became conductor and music director of La Scala Opera House in Milan. He extended La Scala's season and presented Alban Berg's *Wozzeck* in the original German, a considerable innovation for Milan. Subsequently, he received additional appointments as principal conductor of the London Symphony Orchestra (1979) and as principal guest conductor of the Chicago Symphony (1982). Abbado's symphonic repertoire has a wide range, from the traditional to the avant-garde.   ELLA A. MALIN

Abbas I   [ah-bahs']

Abbas I, b. Jan. 27, 1571, d. Jan. 19, 1629, shah of Persia (1588–1629), expanded Persia's boundaries to the Indus in the east and to the Tigris in the west. He created a standing army, the first in Persia, and in 1598 launched an attack on the Uzbeks in the east, defeating them near Herat (now in Afghanistan). From 1602 he campaigned against the Ottoman Turks, capturing Tabriz, Erivan, Shirvan, Baghdad, and Mosul. Abbas also restored internal order, promoted trade and the arts, and made his new capital at Isfahan, one of the most beautiful cities in the world. A member of the Safavid dynasty, he is regarded as one of the greatest Persian rulers.

Bibliography: Arberry, A. J., ed., *The Legacy of Persia* (1953); Frye, Richard, *Persia*, 3d ed. (1969); Savory, Roger, *Iran under the Safavids* (1980).

Abbasids   [ah-bas'-ids]

The Abbasids were the dynasty of caliphs who ruled the Islamic Empire from 750 until the Mongol conquest of the Middle East in 1258. The dynasty takes its name from its ancestor al-Abbas, the uncle of the Prophet Muhammad. In 750 the Abbasids defeated the UMAYYADS and transferred the capital of the CALIPHATE from Damascus to Baghdad, thereby shifting the empire's center from Syria to Iraq.

The regime reasserted the theocratic concept of the caliphate and continuity with orthodox Islam as the basis of unity and authority in the empire. The Abbasid "revolution" also made Islam and the fruits of power accessible to non-Arabs. A strong Persian influence persisted in the government and culture of the Abbasid period, and Hellenistic ideas led to the rapid growth of intellectual life.

The Abbasid period may be divided into two parts. In the period from 750 to 945 the authority of the caliphs gradually declined, while the Turkish military leaders gained increasing influence. The dynasty's power peaked in the reign (786–809) of HARUN AL-RASHID. In the later period, from 945 to 1258, the caliphs generally held no more than nominal suzerainty; real power, even in Baghdad, passed to dynasties of secular sovereigns.   MICHAEL W. DOLS

Bibliography: Ahsan, M. M., *Social Life under the Abbasids* (1979); Hitti, Philip K., *History of the Arabs*, 10th ed. (1970); Mansfield, Peter, *The Arab World: A Comprehensive History* (1976); Shaban, M. A., *The Abbasid Revolution* (1970).

Abbe, Ernst   [ahb'-uh]

The German physicist Ernst Abbe, b. Jan. 23, 1840, d. Jan. 14, 1905, was the principal scientific figure behind the Carl ZEISS Optics Company. A graduate (1861) of Göttingen University, Abbe took a position at Jena University in 1863 and began collaborating with Carl Zeiss. When Zeiss died in 1888, Abbe took over the firm and established the Carl Zeiss Foundation for scientific research and social improvement; in 1896 he reorganized the entire establishment. His innumerable contributions to optics, such as the Abbe REFRACTOMETER and apochromatic lens, led directly to modern phase-contrast microscopy and the ELECTRON MICROSCOPE.   CARL ZAPFFE

Abbevillian   [ab-vil'-ee-uhn]

The Abbevillian, in archaeology, is the earliest stone tool technology of the PALEOLITHIC PERIOD known in western Europe. First identified in the terraces of the Somme River near Abbeville, France, the industry is characterized by few flake tools and by thick, ragged-edged handaxes frequently with unfinished butt ends. Dating from about 500,000 years ago, it precedes the ACHEULEAN.   DAVID S. BROSE

Bibliography: Bordes, François, *The Old Stone Age* (1968); Coles, J. M., and Higgs, E. S., *The Archaeology of Early Man* (1969).

abbey

In the Roman Catholic and Anglican churches an abbey is a monastery, usually belonging to the Benedictine or Cistercian order, governed by an abbot (for communities of men) or an abbess (for communities of women). An abbey is normally an independent institution. Subordinate or less important monasteries are called priories. In Britain the term *abbey* is also used for such churches as WESTMINSTER ABBEY or such country houses as Woburn Abbey, which formerly belonged to monastic institutions.

See also: BENEDICTINES; CISTERCIANS; MONASTICISM; MONASTIC ART AND ARCHITECTURE.

Abbey, Edwin Austin

Edwin Austin Abbey, b. Philadelphia, Apr. 1, 1852, d. Aug. 1, 1911, was an American painter and illustrator. After studying at the Pennsylvania Academy of Fine Arts, he worked as a painter and an illustrator, primarily for *Harper's*, and illustrated works by such authors as Herrick, Goldsmith, and Shakespeare. In 1878, Abbey settled in England, and in 1898 he was elected to the Royal Academy of Art. Abbey dealt with historical and literary themes, as in his mural *The Quest for the Holy Grail* (1901) at the Boston Public Library. In 1902 he was the court portraitist for the coronation of Edward VII.

Abbey Theatre

Ireland's Abbey Theatre opened its doors in December 1904 and quickly became, along with André Antoine's THÉÂTRE LIBRE and Konstantin Stanislavsky's MOSCOW ART THEATRE, one of the seminal producers of modern drama. The Abbey's first directors were W. B. YEATS, Lady GREGORY, and J. M. SYNGE. These writers, along with Padraic COLUM and George FITZMAURICE, discovered a new subject in the Irish peasant. The riots over Synge's *The Playboy of the Western World* (1907) drew attention to the theater as a major exponent of poetic folk drama. Later playwrights, such as Saint John ERVINE, Lennox ROBINSON, and T. C. Murray turned the theater toward realism. However, in Sean O'CASEY's city plays an urban realism was wedded to a kind of earthy poetry, even though Abbey audiences again rioted at his *The Plough and the Stars* (1926). Later Abbey playwrights of world importance have been Brendan BEHAN, Brian FRIEL, and Paul Vincent Carroll. Over the years, dozens of Abbey actors, such as Sara Allgood,

Dublin's Abbey Theatre was founded by the dramatists Lady Gregory, William Butler Yeats, and John Millington Synge. The works of many noted Irish playwrights were first produced there. It was the first theater in an English-speaking nation to receive a government subsidy.

Barry Fitzgerald, and Siobhan McKenna, have made their mark on the stages of London and New York, as well as on the Hollywood screen.   ROBERT HOGAN

Bibliography: Ellis-Fermor, Una, *The Irish Dramatic Movement* (1929); Fay, Gerard, *The Abbey Theatre, Cradle of Genius* (1958); Gregory, Lady, *Our Irish Theatre* (1913); Hogan, Robert, and Kilroy, James, *The Irish Literary Theatre, 1899–1901* (1975), *Laying the Foundations, 1902–1904* (1976), and *The Abbey Theatre, The Years of Synge, 1905–1909* (1978); Kavanagh, Peter, *The Story of the Abbey Theatre* (1950); Robinson, Lennox, *Ireland's Abbey Theatre, a History, 1908–1951* (1951).

See also: IRISH LITERARY RENAISSANCE; PLAYBOY OF THE WESTERN WORLD.

abbot: see ABBEY.

Abbot, Francis Ellingwood

Francis Ellingwood Abbot, b. Boston, Nov. 6, 1836, d. Oct. 23, 1903, was a philosopher and theologian who sought to reconstruct theology in accord with scientific method. As a spokesman for "free religion," he asserted that Christianity, understood as based on the lordship of Christ, is no longer tenable. He rejected all dogma and reliance on Scriptures or creeds, teaching that truth is open to every individual.

Abbot graduated from Harvard University and the Meadville Theological School. He served Unitarian churches in Dover, N.H., and Toledo, Ohio, but left the ministry in 1868 to write, edit, and teach. Abbot's theological position was stated in *Scientific Theism* (1885) and *The Way Out of Agnosticism* (1890). He committed suicide by taking poison at his wife's grave site.   CONRAD WRIGHT

Bibliography: Blau, Joseph L., *Men and Movements in American Philosophy* (1952; repr. 1977); Schneider, H. W., *A History of American Philosophy*, 2d ed. (1963).

Abbott, Bud: see ABBOTT AND COSTELLO.

Abbott, Berenice

The American photographer Berenice Abbott, b. Springfield, Ohio, July 17, 1898, began her career as assistant to the surrealist artist Man Ray. In the 1930s her series of documentary photographs of New York City received wide acclaim. Abbott also rediscovered and brought to public attention the work of the early-20th-century French photographer Eugène ATGET. Her books include *Changing New York* (1939) and *Greenwich Village Today and Yesterday* (1949).

Abbott, George

An American playwright, director, and producer, George Abbott, b. Forestville, N.Y., June 25, 1887, is famous for such farces as *Three Men on a Horse* (1935) and for his fast-paced direction of musical plays, such as *On Your Toes* (1936; 1954; 1983). Among the musicals he coauthored and directed were *The Pajama Game* (1954; film, 1957), *Damn Yankees* (1955; film, 1958), and *Fiorello!* (1959; Pulitzer Prize for drama, 1960). Frequently called in to revive foundering shows, Abbott has a style that often assures success on Broadway. His autobiography, *Mister Abbott*, was published in 1963.

Abbott, Grace

The social worker Grace Abbott, b. Grand Island, Nebr., Nov. 17, 1878, d. June 20, 1939, whose special interests included immigrant and child labor problems, was a pioneer in public welfare administration. In 1908 she joined Jane ADDAMS at Hull House, where she worked with immigrant slum dwellers of Chicago. In 1917 she published *The Immigrant and the Community,* a book instrumental in arousing concern for the problems of recent immigrants from Europe.

Her interest in child welfare led her to join the U.S. Children's Bureau in Washington, D.C., where she helped draft the first Child Labor Act and served as director from 1921 to 1934. She often lectured at the University of Chicago, where her sister Edith (1876–1957) was dean (1924–42) of the School of Social Service Administration.

Abbott, Sir John Joseph Caldwell

Sir John Abbott, b. Mar. 12, 1821, d. Oct. 30, 1893, was prime minister of Canada from 1891 to 1892. A lawyer, he was elected to the Legislative Assembly as a Conservative in 1857. He served there, and later in the Canadian House of Commons, until 1874. Abbott sat in the House again from 1880 to 1887, when he was appointed to the Canadian Senate. He was chosen prime minister on Sir John Macdonald's death in 1891, but poor health forced his resignation after 18 months.

Abbott, Lyman

Lyman Abbott, b. Roxbury, Mass., Dec. 18, 1835, d. Oct. 22, 1922, was an American Congregational minister and editor who popularized liberal theology through his sermons and lectures. In 1876 he joined Henry Ward BEECHER in editing the *Christian Union* (called *Outlook* after 1893); he succeeded Beecher in 1888 as pastor of the Plymouth Congregational Church in Brooklyn. His liberal views about religion and social reform, based on an evolutionary interpretation of doctrine and society, were stated forcibly in his many writings, which included *The Evolution of Christianity* (1892) and *Christianity and Social Problems* (1896).

Bibliography: Brown, Ira, *Lyman Abbott: Christian Evolutionist* (1953; new ed., 1970).

Abbott and Costello

William A. "Bud" Abbott, b. Asbury Park, N.J., Oct. 2, 1895, d. Apr. 24, 1974, and Lou Costello (real name, Louis Francis Cristillo), b. Paterson, N.J., Mar. 6, 1908, d. Mar. 3, 1959, rose from the ranks of burlesque to become one of America's most popular comedy teams. Abbott portrayed a fast-talking con man and Costello a baby-faced patsy. Together they were famous for such rapid-fire dialogue routines as "Who's on First?" Critics called their material old hat, but Abbott and Costello's expert delivery made the oldest jokes seem fresh. They appeared in many films, including *Buck Privates* (1941), *Hold That Ghost* (1941), and *Abbott and Costello Meet Frankenstein* (1948). Their television show was aired from 1952 to 1954.   LEONARD MALTIN

Bibliography: Mulholland, Jim, *The Abbott and Costello Book* (1975); Thomas, Bob, *Bud and Lou* (1977).

ABC: see RADIO AND TELEVISION BROADCASTING.

Abd al-Hamid II, Sultan of the Ottoman Empire [ahb-dul-hah-meed']

Abd al-Hamid II, b. Sept. 21, 1842, d. Feb. 10, 1918, the last major Ottoman sultan (1876–1909), modernized the Ottoman Empire and defended it against foreign attacks and national revolts. Initially he enacted a liberal constitution and frustrated foreign intervention at the Constantinople Conference (1876), turning partial authority over to an elected parliament. Defeats in the Russo-Turkish War of 1877–78 and the parliament's failure to rule efficiently caused him to dissolve it and rule autocratically. The remainder of his reign was disturbed by national revolts in Macedonia and eastern Anatolia as well as by foreign occupation of Cyprus, Tunisia, Egypt, Bosnia and Hercegovina, and East Rumelia.

Abd al-Hamid II stabilized Ottoman administration and finance but drove most intellectuals into exile. The exiled YOUNG TURKS and their Macedonian-army allies finally forced him to restore (1908) the constitution and parliament, but an abortive conservative counterrevolution (Apr. 13, 1909) led to his overthrow and exile.   STANFORD J. SHAW

Bibliography: Haslip, J., *The Sultan: The Life of Abdul Hamid*, 2d ed. (1973); Lewis, B., *The Emergence of Modern Turkey*, 2d ed. (1968).

Abd al-Rahman I, Emir of Córdoba
[ahb-dul-rah-mahn']

Abd al-Rahman I, b. 731, d. Sept. 30, 788, emir of Córdoba (756–88), created an independent Muslim kingdom in Spain.

After the overthrow of his family, the UMAYYADS, who had ruled the Islamic world as successors to Muhammad, he fled to Spain. There he defeated the governor and established his own kingdom. Although faced with numerous rebellions, he maintained his throne and founded a dynasty that lasted until 1031. Charlemagne invaded Spain in 778 and attempted in vain to take Zaragoza. By beginning the construction of the great mosque of Córdoba, Abd al-Rahman laid the basis for the future greatness of the city.   JOSEPH F. O'CALLAGHAN

Bibliography: Hitti, Philip K., *Makers of Arab History* (1968); Watt, W. M., *A History of Islamic Spain* (1965).

Abd el-Krim   [ahb-del-krim']

Abd el-Krim (Muhammed ben Abd al-Karim Khattabi), b. *c.*1882, d. Feb. 5, 1963, led the BERBER tribes of the Rif in Morocco, in revolt against Spanish and French rule. Educated in Spanish schools and a Muslim university, he served as a public official and newspaper editor in Spanish Morocco. Infuriated by corruption and exploitation, he gathered a small rebel force and began attacking Spanish garrisons in 1921. After several major defeats of the Spanish, he advanced into French Morocco in 1925. There he was checked by a Franco-Spanish army under Marshal PÉTAIN in 1926. He was exiled to French Réunion but in 1947 escaped to Egypt, where he fostered Moroccan nationalist efforts.   DONALD J. HARVEY

Bibliography: Woolman, David S., *Rebels in the Rif* (1968).

abdomen

The abdomen, in humans, is the part of the body that lies between the thorax, or chest, and the pelvis. Commonly known as the belly, it does not include the spinal column and the remainder of the back wall; some anatomists include the pelvis, however.

The abdomen is arbitrarily divided into nine regions: the right and left hypochondriacs (derived from the Greek *hypo,* "under," and *chondros,* "cartilage") located uppermost; the right and left inguinals (pertaining to the groin), located lowermost; the right and left laterals, located between the hypochondriacs and inguinals; and the epigastric (meaning above the stomach), umbilical (navel), and pubic or hypogastric (under the stomach) regions.

Present within the abdomen is the abdominal cavity, a space bounded by the abdominal wall in front, the diaphragm above, the lumbosacral wall in back, and the pelvis below. The abdominal cavity is arbitrarily demarcated from the pelvic cavity by an imaginary plane across the top of the hipbones. The abdominal cavity contains the STOMACH, small INTESTINE, most of the large intestine, the LIVER, GALLBLADDER, SPLEEN, PANCREAS, KIDNEYS, and URETERS; the pelvic cavity contains the urinary bladder, sigmoid colon, rectum, and, in the female, the reproductive organs. A serous membrane, the peritoneum, lines the interior of the abdominal wall and the pelvic cavity and extends from the rear wall to cover most of the abdominal organs.

The abdominal wall contains muscles that are arranged in sheets. Together with connective tissue, they protect the delicate abdominal organs.

The term *abdomen* is also applied to the posterior segment of insects, crustaceans, and other arthropods.

ROY HARTENSTEIN

REGIONS OF THE ABDOMEN

liver
diaphragm
pancreas
gall bladder
stomach
spleen
large intestine
small intestine
kidneys
bladder

1. right hypochondriac
2. right lateral
3. right inguinal
4. epigastric
5. umbilical
6. pubic
7. left hypochondriac
8. left lateral
9. left inguinal

The abdominal cavity contains digestive organs as well as the kidneys, spleen, and pancreas. The adrenal glands lie on top of the kidneys. The size and shape of the abdomen can change during respiration and as food passes through the digestive system.

Abdul-Jabbar, Kareem   [ab-dul'-juh-bar', kuh-reem']

Kareem Abdul-Jabbar, b. Ferdinand Lewis Alcindor in New York City, Apr. 16, 1947, has blended height, coordination, and skills to become the "perfect big man" in basketball. Jabbar, 7 ft 2 in (2 m 18 cm) tall, led his New York City high school team, Power Memorial Academy, to 71 consecutive victories. At the University of California, Los Angeles, his team won 3 NCAA titles (1967–69); he was an All-American all 3 years and College Player of the Year twice. As a professional for the Milwaukee Bucks (1969–75) and the Los Angeles Lakers (1976–   ) of the National Basketball Association, he has accumulated, through 1984, 31,527 points (26.9 per game)—breaking Wilt Chamberlain's all-time record—and 15,005 rebounds (12.8 per game)—4th in NBA history. Jabbar was voted the NBA's Most Valuable Player a record 6 times, and his teams have won 3 titles (1971, 1980, 1982).

Bibliography: Haskins, James, *From Lew Alcindor to Kareem Abdul-Jabbar,* rev. ed. (1979).

Abdul Rahman, Tunku   [ahb-dul-rah-mahn', tung'-koo]

Tunku Abdul Rahman, b. Feb. 8, 1903, was the first prime minister of independent Malaya (1957–63) and then (1963–70) of the successor state of Malaysia, incorporating Malaya, the northern Borneo territories of Sabah and Sarawak, and (temporarily) adjacent Singapore.

Receiving his early schooling in Malaya and Thailand, Abdul Rahman later attended Cambridge University and studied law at London's Inner Temple. A founder of the United Malays National Organization (1945), he was chief architect of its alliance with the Malayan Chinese Association (1952) and the Malayan Indian Congress (1955). The resulting Alliance party formed the governments that subsequently ruled Malaya and Malaysia. Abdul Rahman is credited with founding (1961) the Association of Southeast Asia, consisting of Malaya, Thailand, and the Philippines, to resist the claims of SUKARNO of Indonesia. It later became (1967) the Association of Southeast Asian Nations (ASEAN), including Singapore and Indonesia. Domestically, Abdul Rahman attempted to accommodate the large Chinese and Indian minorities in Malaya. Agitation against this policy led to suspension of the constitution in 1969 and Abdul Rahman's retirement in 1970.

RICHARD BUTWELL

Bibliography: Roff, W. R., *The Origins of Malay Nationalism* (1967); Tregonning, K. G., *A History of Modern Malaya* (1964).

Abdullah   [ahb-dul'-ah]

Abdullah (Abd Allah ibn al-Husayn), b. 1882, d. July 20, 1951, was the first ruler of the Hashemite Kingdom of Jordan. A leading Arab nationalist, he occupied Transjordan in 1921 and became its ruler under the British mandate. After independence in 1946 he was crowned king. Abdullah accepted the partition of Palestine and the creation of Israel, but he took part in the 1948 ARAB-ISRAELI WAR, occupying the West Bank of the Jordan River and incorporating a large Palestinian population into Jordan. He was assassinated by a Palestinian nationalist.

Abe Kobo   [ah'-bay koh'-boh]

Abe Kobo, b. Mar. 7, 1924, is a leading experimental Japanese prose writer and dramatist. His best-known works, such as *The Woman in the Dunes* (1962; Eng. trans., 1964; film, 1964), explore in a surrealistic fashion the emptiness and nightmare of urban life.

Influenced by Western avant-garde literature, Abe's novels and short stories have few of the lyrical qualities typical of Japanese literature. His work is often compared to that of Franz KAFKA. His narratives are sparse, elliptical, and normally unresolved. Abe's other works of fiction include *Red Cocoon* (1950; Eng. trans., 1966), *Kabe* (The Wall, 1951), *S. Karuma shi no hanzai* (Mr. S. Karuma's Crime, 1951), and *The Box Man* (1973; Eng. trans., 1974). One of his most widely performed plays is *Friends* (1967; Eng. trans., 1969). Abe has also written plays for radio and screenplays for films and has received numerous Japanese literary awards.   EDWARD B. FOWLER

Bibliography: Abe, Kobo, *Inter Ice Age Four: A Novel of the Future*, trans. by E. D. Saunders (1970); Miyoshi, Masao, *Accomplices of Silence: The Modern Japanese Novel* (1974).

Abel

According to Genesis 4, Abel was the second son of Adam and Eve. A shepherd, he was murdered by his brother CAIN out of envy. His innocence is praised in Matthew 23:35.

Abel, I. W.

Iorwith Wilbur Abel, b. Magnolia, Ohio, Aug. 11, 1908, was president of the UNITED STEELWORKERS OF AMERICA from 1965 to 1977. He began working in a steel mill at the age of 17 and 11 years later he became an organizer for the union. Abel was known for his lack of pretension and for his tolerance of dissent.

Abel, John J.

John Jacob Abel, b. Cleveland, Ohio, May 19, 1857, d. May 26, 1938, was an American physician and physiological chemist who isolated the hormone insulin in crystalline form and also isolated the hormone epinephrine (adrenaline), thus making possible further detailed work on their chemical structures. He studied the chemistry of the endocrine glands and of other animal tissues and fluids.

Abel, Niels Henrik

The Norwegian mathematician Niels Henrik Abel, b. Aug. 5, 1802, d. Apr. 16, 1829, earned wide recognition at the age of 18 with his first paper, in which he proved that the general equation of the fifth degree is insolvable by algebraic procedures. Abel was instrumental in establishing mathematical analysis on a rigorous basis. In his major work, *Recherches sur les fonctions elliptiques* (Investigations on Elliptic Functions, 1827), he revolutionized the understanding of elliptic functions by studying the inverse of these functions.
ARTHUR SCHLISSEL

Bibliography: Ore, Oystein, *Niels Henrik Abel, Mathematician Extraordinary* (1957; repr. 1974).

Abel, Sir Frederick Augustus

An English chemist best known for his invention of cordite, an explosive, Sir Frederick Abel, b. July 17, 1829, d. Sept. 6, 1902, was for many years the British War Department's chief explosives advisor. In 1889 his research into the properties of GUNCOTTON led to the development of cordite, an explosive propellant paste made of guncotton, nitroglycerin, and mineral jelly and named for its cordlike shape. A smokeless, relatively stable substance, it is still in use today. Abel was knighted in 1883, and in 1893 he was created a baronet.

Abelard, Peter   [ab'-uh-lahrd]

Peter Abelard, shown here in a 19th-century engraving, was the most famous of the early scholastics. A brilliant thinker and teacher, he is also known for his tragic love affair with Héloïse. In addition to his theological and philosophical works, Abelard wrote the autobiographical Historia calamitatum mearum *(History of My Adversities). Letters between the lovers, who were secretly married, also survive.*

Peter Abelard, b. *c.*1079, d. Apr. 21, 1142, a French philosopher and theologian, was an early exponent of SCHOLASTICISM. After studying in Paris under WILLIAM OF CHAMPEAUX and ROSCELLIN, he soon became a recognized teacher himself. His brilliant academic career was cut short in 1118–19, however, by the consequences of his love affair with Héloïse (*c.*1098–1164), the young niece of Canon Fulbert of Notre-Dame. Castrated by order of Fulbert and publicly disgraced, Abelard became a Benedictine monk. He continued to devote his vast energies to theological studies and writing, but Saint BERNARD OF CLAIRVAUX, doubting the orthodoxy of Abelard's teaching on the Trinity, instigated the burning of one of his books on the subject at the Council of Soissons (1121).

In 1125, Abelard established a convent called the Paraclete near Troyes; Héloïse became prioress and a famous teacher there. Meanwhile Abelard was unexpectedly elected (1126) abbot of the notoriously immoral monks of Saint-Gildas-de-Rhuis in Brittany. His efforts to reform the monastery ended with his having to flee for his life. Returning to Paris, Abelard resumed his teaching, numbering among his pupils John of Salisbury. At the Council of Sens (1140), however, Saint Bernard again succeeded in having Abelard condemned for heresy. This condemnation was soon confirmed by the pope.

Already a broken man in his sixties, Abelard decided to travel on foot to Rome to appeal his case. He got only as far as Cluny, whose understanding abbot was Peter the Venerable, a personal friend of Bernard and renowned for his moderation in controversy. Through Peter's patient efforts a reconciliation was effected between Abelard and Bernard. Abelard spent the rest of his life at Cluny, dying at the nearby priory of Saint-Marcel-sur-Saône.

In the philosophical controversy over UNIVERSALS, Abelard rejected both the extreme realism of William of Champeaux and the crude nominalism of Roscellin. While denying that universals are real things, he asserted that they are more than mere words since they express factors common to individual, real things; thus universals are tools of logic, the basis for logical predication. This position is essentially Aristotelian, although Abelard had only limited access to the works of Aristotle through the translations of Boethius. Abelard's moderate realism in philosophy, his development of the dialectical method of argument, his familiarity with the Bible and many of the Church Fathers, and his intellectual brilliance—rather than any systematic presentation of Christian theology aided by reason—make him one of the important, although much neglected, pioneers of scholasticism.   JAMES A. WEISHEIPL

Bibliography: Gilson, Étienne, *Héloïse and Abélard,* trans. by L. K. Shook, rev. ed. (1960); Luscombe, D. E., *The School of Peter Abelard* (1969); Moncrieff, C. K. Scott, ed., *The Letters of Abélard and Héloïse* (1925; repr. 1964); Muckle, J. T., ed., *The Story of Abelard's Adversities* (1954); Robertson, D. W., *Abelard and Heloise* (1972); Starnes, Kathleen M., *Peter Abelard* (1981); Whitman, Cedric, *Abelard* (1965); Williams, Paul, *The Moral Philosophy of Peter Abelard* (1980).

Abell, George O.   [aý-buhl]

American astronomer George Ogden Abell, b. Los Angeles, Mar. 1, 1927, d. Oct. 7, 1983, is best known for his work on clusters of galaxies but was also a noted lecturer and author. He published a catalog of 2,712 clusters in 1958 and was preparing a catalog of southern clusters at the time of his death. Studies of these clusters have helped to define the problem of missing mass in the universe that confronts COSMOLOGY today. Abell also determined the relative numbers of galaxies with various absolute magnitudes.

Abell, Kjeld   [ah'-bel, kee-el']

Kjeld Abell, b. Aug. 25, 1901, d. Mar. 5, 1961, is generally considered the most important and innovative Danish playwright of this century. He began his theatrical career as a scene designer and gained recognition as a playwright with *The Melody That Got Lost* (1935; Eng. trans., 1939), an expressionistic tragicomedy that satirizes the dull, unimaginative life of the middle class. *Anne Sophie Hedvig* (1939; Eng. trans., 1944), considered his finest play, condones the use of violence against the evils of nazism. Such postwar plays as *The Blue Pekinese* (1954) and *Skriget* (The Scream, 1961), dealing with the plight of contemporary humankind in an age of conformity, are modern examples of the beast epic. Hans Christian Andersen's influence is most noticeable in the play *Andersen, or the Fairy Tale of His Life* (1955).   KJETIL A. FLATIN

Bibliography: Mitchell, P. M., *A History of Danish Literature,* rev. ed. (1971).

Abercrombie, Lascelles   [las'-ulz]

Lascelles Abercrombie, b. Jan. 9, 1881, d. Oct. 27, 1938, an English poet, critic, and teacher, was called the latter-day Browning. He used the dramatic monologue effectively in his long verse narrative in six acts, *The Sale of St. Thomas* (1911, 1930). Another poetic volume is *Emblems of Love* (1912); notable critical works are *Thomas Hardy* (1912), *The Theory of Poetry* (1924), and *Principles of Literary Criticism* (1932).

Bibliography: Cooper, Jeffrey, *Bibliography and Notes on the Works of Lascelles Abercrombie* (1969); Sastri, C. L., *Abercrombie's Poems: A Critical Study* (1971).

Aberdeen   (city in Scotland)

Aberdeen (1981 pop., 190,200) is the major port and commercial center of northeastern Scotland. Located on the North Sea, it is the center of the Scottish fishing industry and the supply port for the Orkney and Shetland islands. The discovery and development of North Sea oil deposits have brought added growth and prosperity to Aberdeen.

Old Aberdeen developed around the Cathedral of Saint Machar (1424) and King's College (1494), on the Don River. New Aberdeen grew around the superior port on the Dee and around Marischal College (1593). The two colleges combined in 1860 to form the University of Aberdeen, and Old and New Aberdeen merged in 1891. Aberdeen's buildings are distinctive for their use of locally quarried granite.

Aberdeen   (county in Scotland)

Aberdeen, situated on the North Sea, was a civil county in northeastern Scotland until 1975, when it became part of the administrative region of Grampian. The Grampian Mountains cut across the southwestern portion of Aberdeen, and the region is drained by the rivers Dee, Don, Deveron, and Ythan. Along the coast, fishing is a major industry. Inland, farmers raise sheep and cattle; major crops include oats and turnips.

Settled by about 2000 BC, Aberdeen has long been noted for its fertile lowlands. The area was a royalist stronghold during the 17th-century religious wars. Balmoral Castle, the royal residence in Scotland, located in the Dee Valley, was completed in 1856.

Aberdeen, George Hamilton-Gordon, 4th Earl of

Lord Aberdeen, b. Jan. 28, 1784, d. Dec. 14, 1860, was prime minister of Britain (1852–55) through most of the CRIMEAN WAR. Earlier in his long political career he served twice as foreign secretary (1828–30, 1841–46), and his successes included settling of two boundary disputes with the United States by the Webster-Ashburton and Oregon treaties (1842, 1846). As prime minister of a coalition government, Aberdeen allowed a diplomatic drift that led to Britain's entry (1854) into the Crimean War. He was blamed for poor management of the war and was forced to resign.

Bibliography: Conacher, J. B., *The Aberdeen Coalition, 1852–1855* (1968); Jones, Wilbur D., *Lord Aberdeen and the Americas* (1958).

Aberdeen, University of

The University of Aberdeen (enrollment: 5,871; library: about 1,000,000 volumes) was formed by the merger in 1860 of King's College (1494) and Marischal College (1593). Located in Aberdeen, Scotland, it is a coeducational institution and has faculties of arts, science, divinity, law, and medicine. All grant undergraduate and graduate degrees. Associated colleges are Robert Gordon's Institute of Technology and the North of Scotland College of Agriculture.

Aberhart, William   [ay'-bur-hahrt]

The Canadian political leader William Aberhart, b. Dec. 30, 1878, d. May 23, 1943, was the premier of the first Social Credit government (1935–43) in Alberta. A high-school principal and radio evangelist, he adopted Social Credit ideas, which called for a redistribution of wealth, in the early 1930s and won a large following in western Canada. In 1935, Aberhart and his SOCIAL CREDIT PARTY swept to victory in the Alberta provincial elections. His reforms were opposed by the federal government, and many were declared unconstitutional by the courts. Aberhart remained in office, shifting to an increasingly conservative program, until his death.

Bibliography: Irving, John A., *The Social Credit Movement in Alberta* (1959).

Abernathy, Ralph David

Ralph David Abernathy, a Baptist clergyman, has been an active figure in the civil rights movement since 1951. Abernathy helped establish the Southern Christian Leadership Conference (SCLC) and served as its president from 1968 to 1977.

Ralph David Abernathy, b. Linden, Ala., Mar. 11, 1926, is a Baptist minister and black civil rights leader from Alabama. Ordained in 1948, he became the pastor of the First Baptist Church in Montgomery, Ala., in 1951. In 1955 he and the Rev. Martin Luther KING, Jr., organized the Montgomery bus boycott to protest discrimination. Two years later they founded the Southern Christian Leadership Conference (SCLC). Abernathy's home and church were dynamited by white terrorists in retaliation. After Martin Luther King's assassination in 1968, Abernathy served as president of the SCLC until 1977.

aberration, chromatic

Chromatic aberration is a defect in the image-forming property of a simple LENS that results in a colored fringe around an image. The focal length of a lens depends on the curvature of the lens surfaces and the INDEX OF REFRACTION of the lens material. Because the refractive index of any transparent substance varies with the wavelength (or color) of the light (a phenomenon called DISPERSION), a simple lens forms not one but a series of images when white light is used. The result is a colored smearing of the edge of any image. Chromatic aberration can be reduced considerably by a special two-component lens design using glasses with different dispersive properties. Such achromatic lenses are used in better optical instruments.   GRANT R. FOWLES

aberration, spherical

Spherical aberration is a property inherent in any converging LENS or MIRROR that has spherical surfaces, which limits its ability to bring a parallel beam of light into perfect focus. The defect is not caused by any imperfections in the optical surfaces but results entirely from the geometry of the refraction or reflection of the light rays. Specifically, the focal length for rays brought to focus by the central part is different from the focal length for rays focused by the outer portions of the lens. Spherical aberration in a mirror can be corrected by making the surface parabolic rather than spherical, a process called parabolizing. Astronomical reflecting telescopes are generally made with parabolic mirrors. The defect in lenses can be reduced by the use of aspherical surfaces and also by combinations of two or more lenses.   GRANT R. FOWLES

aberration, stellar

The aberration of starlight is the apparent displacement of the path of light from a star caused by the orbital motion of the Earth. James BRADLEY, attempting to measure stellar PARALLAXES, first discovered this effect in 1725, when he observed that all stars seemed to shift their position as much as 20.5 seconds of arc in a period of one year, in a way that could not be accounted for. In the same way that an umbrella must be tilted during a vertical rainfall in proportion to the speed of the pedestrian, so the angle of a telescope pointing at a star must be adjusted for stellar aberration.

Aberystwyth   [ab-ur-ist'-with]

Aberystwyth (1979 est. pop., 12,000) is a municipal borough on Cardigan Bay in the county of Dyfed, Wales. The town grew around a 13th-century Norman castle that was later destroyed. With the establishment of the University College of Wales (1872) and the National Library of Wales (1907), it became a center of Welsh culture.

Abidjan   [ah-bi-jahn']

Abidjan (1975 pop., 685,800) is the capital and chief port of Ivory Coast. Located on the Ébrié Lagoon, Gulf of Guinea, on the coast of West Africa, it is Ivory Coast's largest city. Settled in 1898, Abidjan became a railroad terminus in 1904. It remained a small town until 1950, when the completion of the Vridi Canal opened the lagoon to the sea and made Abidjan an ocean port. Abidjan processes and exports coffee, cacao, timber, manganese, and fruit.

The city is divided into several types of quarters: the commercial and administrative centers, such as the Plateau; the traditional residential and industrial centers of Adjamé and Treichville, a suburb on the island of Petit-Bassam, which is connected to the Plateau area by a bridge; and the modern residential section of Cocody. The climate is humid, and at the outskirts of the city is a tropical rain forest, the Banco National Park. Abidjan has a university (1964) and several cultural buildings, including a museum. The city is served by modern highways, a railroad, and an airport.

Abilene   [ab'-uh-leen]

Abilene (1980 pop., 98,315) is the marketing, shipping, and financial center of west central Texas and the seat of Taylor County. A rapidly growing city with varied industries, it has nevertheless retained its original frontier character. It was founded as a shipping point when the railroad arrived in 1881, and the town was named for Abilene, Kans. Livestock is still a major product of the region served by the city, but agriculture is now supplemented by related industries. Abilene is the site of Hardin-Simmons University, two colleges, and Dyess Air Force Base, a Strategic Air Command unit. The climate is semiarid, with an annual rainfall of 610 mm (24 in).

ablation   [ab-lay'-shuhn]

Ablation collectively describes the processes that decrease the mass of a glacier, iceberg, ice sheet, or snowfield. Melting and evaporation are the most important; calving and removal by wind and by avalanching are less so. In the lower part of a glacier, ablation outpaces accumulation, causing shrinkage. Higher up, the reverse is true, and the glacial mass increases.   ROBERT L. NICHOLS

ABM: see ANTIBALLISTIC MISSILE.

Abnaki   [ab-nah'-kee]

A major group of Algonquian-speaking Indian tribes living along the river valleys of Maine, the Abnaki confederacy was important in American colonial history until the time of the Revolution. The collective name for this confederacy, used by both French and English, means "people of the eastern lands." It included the PASSAMAQUODDY, PENOBSCOT, Sokoki, Malecite, and Etchimin tribes, all of whom were sedentary, horticultural peoples who also depended heavily upon hunting and fishing for subsistence.

The Abnaki began their long association with the French following the visit of Samuel de Champlain in 1607. Threatened by the northward expansion of the English seaboard colonies and aggressive raids of the Five Nations Iroquois, they had become firm allies of New France by the middle of the 17th century. Made vulnerable by their exposed position and weakened by constant wars, the Abnaki began to abandon their homeland in Maine in the 1670s. Most migrated northward to French territory in Quebec and New Brunswick; others moved west to the Great Lakes region. In 1681 a group of Sokoki formed part of the sieur de La Salle's support party during his exploration of the Lake Michigan area, and they settled among the Miami and the Potawatomi there. Other groups of Penobscot, Passamaquoddy, and Malecite remained in Maine after making peace with the English.

In 1972 descendants of the Abnaki brought a suit against the state of Maine for the illegal surrender of their lands in the 1790s. The 1980 settlement gave the Indians about $81 million in federal funds.   JAMES A. CLIFTON

Bibliography: Trigger, Bruce, ed., *Handbook of North American Indians*, vol. 12 (1978); Vetromile, Eugene, *The Abnakis and Their History* (1866; repr. 1977).

abnormal psychology

Abnormal psychology is the study of the nature, causes, and treatment of psychological disorders. Most modern classifications are based on the work of the German psychiatrist Emil KRAEPELIN, who developed (1890s) systematic descriptions of mental illnesses. Although many psychologists do not believe that most problems in thinking, feeling, or behaving are due to organic (bodily) disorder, diagnostic categories are still used as descriptive tools. Persons are classified on the basis of the complaint they bring to the clinician, their behavior, and the results of psychological testing.

The major diagnostic categories are NEUROSIS, PSYCHOSOMATIC DISORDERS, SCHIZOPHRENIA, sexual disorders, affective (feeling emotion) disorders, character disorders, alcohol and drug addiction, and organic brain dysfunction. Each of these includes many identifiable subtypes, such as the paranoid, catatonic, hebephrenic, and simple schizophrenias. Some psychologists reject the notion of diagnostic categories and prefer to focus only on specific behaviors that are maladaptive. Abnormality is defined not only in terms of deviance from the norms of the individual's sociocultural group but also by subjective discomfort.

Treatment varies according to the nature of the disorder and the orientation of the psychotherapist. It may include BEHAVIOR MODIFICATION, individual or GROUP THERAPY, drugs, or milieu therapy. As knowledge increases, specific therapies are being developed for specific problems, such as systematic desensitization for phobias.   JOHN M. DYCKMAN

Bibliography: White, Robert W., and Watt, Norman, *The Abnormal Personality*, 4th ed. (1973); Zax, Melvin, and Cowen, Emory L., *Abnormal Psychology*, 2d ed. (1976).

See also: DEPRESSION; NERVOUS SYSTEM, DISEASES OF THE; PSYCHOPATHOLOGY, TREATMENT OF; PSYCHOSIS; PSYCHOTHERAPY.

abolitionists

In U.S. history, the abolitionists were those who sought to end the institution of black SLAVERY. In the late 18th and early 19th centuries, groups of abolitionists in Britain and France acted vigorously and effectively, protesting slavery in their nations' colonies and exposing the horrors of the African slave trade. Their example was followed in the United States, where abolitionists first achieved prominence during the American Revolution; the opponents of slaveholding included some illustrious Founding Fathers. Certain that slavery violated the ideals of the Declaration of Independence, Benjamin FRANKLIN, Alexander HAMILTON, John JAY, Thomas PAINE, and Benjamin RUSH joined their antislavery efforts with those of the Quakers (Society of FRIENDS) and other religiously inspired Northerners.

By 1804 emancipation on a gradual basis had been enacted by every Northern state legislature. Because, in part, of abolitionists' pressure, measures were also taken on the national level to end U.S. participation in the African slave trade (1808) and to prohibit slavery's expansion in certain Western territories (the MISSOURI COMPROMISE, 1820). Some abolitionists also involved themselves in colonization societies, most notably the AMERICAN COLONIZATION SOCIETY, which sought to resettle freed slaves in Africa. During this era, however, abolitionist efforts proved ineffective in the Southern states, where slaveholding was deeply entrenched. From 1790 to 1830 the advocates of abolition in the South, led by Benjamin LUNDY, spoke mildly and favored gradual emancipation. A disruptive and radical abolitionism, however, had emerged by the early 1830s. Groups of New Englanders had begun branding slavery as a horrible sin and demanding "immediate, complete, and uncompensated emancipation" everywhere in the nation.

These abolitionists constituted one of the most controversial movements in American history. Its leadership included famous blacks and women as well as white males and was typified by editors such as the fiery William Lloyd GARRISON, orators such as Frederick DOUGLASS, Angelina GRIMKÉ, Wendell PHILLIPS, and Theodore WELD, and many other philanthropists, black agitators, and feminists. From the first, their aim was to transform the conscience of each white American, Northerner and Southerner, by preaching against the sin of slavery. They believed that through such agitation it was possible to convince slaveholders to show repentance by releasing their slaves. Abolitionists also called upon each white citizen to cast aside prejudice against blacks and to join the crusade against slavery. In December 1833 the abolitionists formed the American Anti-Slavery Society, hoping to mount a

Abolitionists agitated against slavery with publications such as this almanac, whose cover shows a Northerner freeing a black slave from an angry Southern plantation owner.

national campaign, and by 1835 they had established networks of state and local societies. As they founded abolitionist newspapers (for example, Garrison's *The Liberator*), held rallies, and distributed emancipationist tracts, these reformers also worked to improve conditions for Northern blacks by protesting segregation, founding schools and libraries, and protecting slaves who had escaped from the South. They also petitioned state legislatures and the U.S. Congress, demanding action against slavery. Congress's attempt to stem the flow of petitions by GAG RULES only provoked stronger agitation.

By the early 1840s, however, widespread and often violent opposition to the abolitionists' efforts had caused members of the movement to disagree profoundly about strategies and tactics. Abolitionists had also divided over controversial new issues such as women's rights, black separatism, and opposition to organized religion. They never again formed a united front. In 1840 some of the moderates formed the LIBERTY PARTY, which ran James BIRNEY as its presidential candidate in 1840 and 1844. These advocates of direct political action later supported the FREE-SOIL PARTY and ultimately the REPUBLICAN PARTY.

After the passage of the new FUGITIVE SLAVE LAW in 1850, many abolitionists involved themselves in the UNDERGROUND RAILROAD, by which slaves escaped to the North. That law also provoked Harriet Beecher STOWE to write the abolitionist classic UNCLE TOM'S CABIN (1852). Passage of the KANSAS-NEBRASKA ACT (1854), with its provision that the settlers in these territories decide whether there should be slavery, caused a migration of people dedicated to antislavery. They clashed with proslavery settlers, and a local civil war developed. One such antislavery settler was John BROWN, whose extremism led him to murder five proslavery settlers in Kansas and subsequently (1859) to seize HARPERS FERRY.

During the Civil War, as the organized movement dissolved, many individual abolitionists pushed Abraham Lincoln to issue the EMANCIPATION PROCLAMATION (1863). After the war they still lobbied for constitutional amendments and civil rights laws to protect the newly emancipated slaves. Others raised funds to support black education programs in the old slave states and served in the South as teachers, ministers, and political reformers. The intensity of effort ended, however, with the passage in 1865 of the 13th Amendment abolishing slavery, the goal for which the abolitionists had fought.

JAMES BREWER STEWART

Bibliography: Curry, Richard O., ed., *Abolitionists* (1965); Davis, David B., *The Problem of Slavery in the Age of Revolution* (1975); Hawkins, Hugh, *The Abolitionists: Means, Ends, and Motivations*, 2d ed. (1972); Quarles, Benjamin, *Black Abolitionists* (1969); Stewart, James Brewer, *Holy Warriors: The Abolitionists and American Slavery* (1976); Walters, Ronald G., *The Antislavery Appeal* (1977).

abominable snowman

The abominable snowman, or yeti, is a giant creature believed by Himalayan tribesmen to roam the mountains at night searching for victims. It is described as having an upright stance, a covering of black to reddish hair, and the appearance of a bear, ape, or human. The yeti legend first became known outside the area in 1921, when English explorers found tracks in the snow resembling huge human footprints. Several scientific expeditions failed to find any other evidence of the yeti's existence. Similar creatures are believed to have been sighted elsewhere—such as the Sasquatch, or Bigfoot, of U.S. Pacific Northwest forestland.

Bibliography: Izzard, Ralph, *The Abominable Snowman* (1955); Sanderson, Ivan T., *Abominable Snowmen* (1961).

Aboriginal languages: see OCEANIC LANGUAGES.

Aborigines, Australian   [ab-uh-rij'-uh-neez]

The Australian Aborigines established themselves throughout Australia, including Tasmania, long before Europeans discovered it. By about 40,000 years ago small groups had arrived by sea, probably traveling from Southeast Asia to the north coast of Australia. Aborigines are dark skinned, with numerous regional variations in their anatomical features and hair color. Although they are sometimes classified within the Australasian race, many anthropologists no longer consider Aborigines to be part of a separate racial group. Before the first European settlement of Australia, the Aborigines numbered about 300,000. Their present population is estimated at about 125,000–130,000; about 45,000–50,000 are of homogeneous ancestry, and 70,000–80,000 are mixed Aboriginal and European.

TRADITIONAL ABORIGINAL CULTURE

Australian Aborigines were socioculturally homogeneous only in a general way. Traditionally, about 500 different tribal groups existed, each occupying a particular stretch of country and speaking a different language or dialect. Among the best-known Aboriginal groups are the ARANDA (Arunta), Bidjandjadjara (Pitjantjatjara), Gurindji, Gunwinggu, Kamilaroi, Murngin, Tiwi, Wailbri (Walbiri), Wurora, and Yir-yoront.

As seminomadic HUNTER-GATHERERS, the Aborigines traditionally were restricted to their own territories, but they joined with adjacent groups for certain purposes, among them religious gatherings and trade. They did not have permanent settlements but made small camps near watering places, building windbreaks and huts.

Because the Aborigines needed to be mobile, they had few everyday belongings. Men carried spears, spear-throwers, and various kinds of BOOMERANGS; women, their digging sticks,

Ritually painted Yetibah Aborigines in Arnhem Land perform a ceremonial dance as part of the tribe's puberty rites. Aborigines of unmixed descent, whose forebears were the original inhabitants of Australia, constitute less than 1% of the Australian population.

dishes, and bags or baskets. They usually went naked, but groups in cold southern areas made and wore fur cloaks. Aboriginal society had a well-developed trading economy: goods of various kinds (spears, ochres, implements, pendants) were exchanged and passed from one group to the next—the whole country was crisscrossed with trade routes.

Social Organization and Kinship. Religion and economics played an essential part in the two kinds of social units traditionally found in one form or another throughout the continent. The first, a patrilineal local descent group, owned a specific area of land containing sacred sites of mythototemic significance; its adult male members were responsible for maintaining these sites and for conducting the associated rituals. The second kind of social unit, the mobile residential group, occupied and used available land in a given area. Every person was a member of a specific local descent group but would join with others from the same and from other local descent groups for purposes of food collecting and other activities. The size of such residential groups varied according to the season.

All members of a tribe were linked through kinship, which was expressed in a complex system of genealogical and other types of classification. Every Aboriginal society had its own set of kin terms in its own particular kinship system, but all the societies had some elements in common. Kin terms indicated, among other things, marriage eligibility, responsibilities, and reasons for avoidance of particular individuals. Marriage rules varied, but generally a person had to marry someone who was related to him or her in a specified way. Marriage was seen as a union of individuals and kin groups.

Ritual and Art. In the traditional religious system of the Aborigines, human beings were believed to be a part of nature, intimately associated with other living things. This relationship underlined the concept sometimes called the Dreaming, of which totemism is one aspect. The Dreaming refers to the creative period when mythic spirits were believed to have shaped the land, establishing life. These beings were thought to live on eternally in spirit form and to have left tangible evidence of their presence in the shape of certain prominent land forms considered sacred. Religious ritual was pervasive in traditional Aboriginal life. Although presided over by males, it involved all members of the community. Some rituals, including elaborate funeral customs and initiation rites, served to renew the participants' ties with the Dreaming, considered a continuing stream from which life came.

The Aborigines produced a wide range of ritual objects and emblems. Oral and visual arts were highly developed, including fine bark and cave paintings, rock engravings, and sculptured posts and figures (see OCEANIC ART). Song poetry ranged from the succinct verses of Central Australia and the Western Desert to the elaborate song-cycles of northeastern Arnhem Land, which made use of complex symbolism. Dance and the dramatic arts were also well developed.

ABORIGINAL LIFE AFTER EUROPEAN CONTACT

With the arrival of Europeans in 1788, many Aboriginal societies, caught within the coils of expanding white settlement, were gradually destroyed. Clashes between Aborigines and Europeans were common. Large numbers of Aborigines were killed, others driven into the bush. Epidemics also contributed to their dispersal and depopulation.

Maltreatment and violence gradually declined, but traditional sociocultural life became difficult to maintain. In some areas Aborigines of mixed European and Aboriginal ancestry replaced the traditional population. Over much of the southwestern, southeastern, and mideastern parts of the continent, traditional life ceased to exist. In the central and northern regions it continued in a modified form, especially in Arnhem Land and in the great Central Reserve. Today all Aborigines have had some contact with the Europeans. Those who live in the fringe settlements are rapidly incorporating Australian-European features into their culture.

All Aborigines are now Australian citizens and are no longer subject to restrictive legislation; they are eligible to vote and to receive Social Service benefits. In recent years they have been involved in political protest, which has materially altered their past condition of poverty and deprivation. Issues of paramount importance are land rights, housing and health, and political representation at all levels.

Many Aboriginal communities have their own councils, employ advisors, engage in socioeconomic ventures, and plan and manage many of their affairs. Educational programs include bilingual teaching and special orientation courses in Aboriginal schools and in schools of mixed populations.

RONALD M. BERNDT

Bibliography: Berndt, Catherine and Ronald, *Pioneers and Settlers* (1978), *The First Australians* (1974), and *The World of the First Australians* (1977); Berndt, Ronald, ed., *Aborigines and Change* (1977); Elkin, Adolphus P., *The Australian Aborigines*, 5th ed. (1974); Gale, Fay, ed., *Woman's Role in Aboriginal Society* (1974); Maddock, Kenneth, *The Australian Aborigines: A Portrait of Their Society* (1975); Rowley, Charles D., *The Destruction of Aboriginal Society* (1972); Tindale, Norman B., *Aboriginal Tribes of Australia* (1974).

abortion

An abortion is the termination of a pregnancy before the fetus is viable, or capable of living outside the womb. An abortion may be spontaneous or induced. The term *miscarriage* is sometimes used as a synonym for spontaneous abortion. Voluntary pregnancy termination is an act with ethical and legal ramifications.

Medical Aspects. Spontaneous abortion occurs when the embryo fails to develop, when there is complete or incomplete expulsion of the products of conception—the embryo or fetus, and placenta—or when the fetus dies prior to 20 weeks from the woman's last menstrual period (LMP). If fetal death occurs at 20 weeks or more after the LMP, it is termed a late fetal death or a stillbirth.

Perhaps as many as three-fourths of conceptions are spontaneously aborted, but most of those abortions occur before the woman's pregnancy can be confirmed, prior to 6 weeks after her LMP. Spontaneous abortions constitute about one-fifth of confirmed pregnancies and about one-tenth of all hospitalizations for pregnancy in the United States.

A woman whose pregnancy is spontaneously aborted may experience cramping and blood loss similar to that of a normal menstrual period, heavier cramping or blood loss, or pains closely resembling those of childbirth, depending on the gestational age of the fetus and other factors.

Induced abortion is a procedure intended to terminate a suspected or known pregnancy and to produce a nonviable fetus at any gestational age. Most induced abortions in the United States are performed in the first trimester—within 12 weeks of the LMP. The technique for virtually all first-trimester pregnancy terminations utilizes a procedure called vacuum aspiration or vacuum curettage. The cervix is dilated with a series of graduated, usually tapered dilators or a type of dried seaweed, called laminaria, which expands as it absorbs moisture. After dilation, a hollow plastic tube with a hole near its end is inserted into the uterus. The embryo or fetus and placenta are drawn into the tube through vacuum pressure. For sharp curettage, a procedure seldom used today, a hollow, spoon-shaped knife, or curette, is used instead of the vacuum tube to scrape the uterine walls.

Second-trimester induced abortion involves a more complicated procedure. If the pregnancy has progressed to no more than 16 weeks since the last menstrual period, the most common technique is dilation and evacuation, a method that is similar to vacuum aspiration. The next most common procedure is injection of fluid into the amniotic sac; usually, however, this procedure is postponed until after the 16th week in order to reduce the risk of injection outside the amniotic cavity. Fluid injected into the cavity may be either a saline solution or the hormone PROSTAGLANDINS. Comparative studies of abortion techniques have determined that surgical evacuation techniques, especially up to 17 weeks' gestation, are safer than instillation techniques. Rarely used techniques for second-trimester abortion include hysterotomy (surgical incision of the uterus) and HYSTERECTOMY, used when medically indicated.

Legal Aspects. Although discouraged by most major religions, induced abortion has been practiced in every culture since ancient times. During the 19th century several countries passed laws prohibiting abortion to protect women from the dangerous methods then in use. The USSR legalized abortion in 1920, but in response to a rapid drop in the birthrate, the USSR reinstituted restrictions in 1936. So many complications from illegal abortions occurred, however, that restrictions were withdrawn in 1955. Most Eastern European countries legalized abortion during the next 10 years. Japan liberalized its abortion law in 1948 to decrease its population growth. Scandinavian countries began to liberalize their laws in the 1930s, although most still restrict reasons allowed for the abortion. Great Britain liberalized its abortion statute in 1967. Today most of the world's population live where abortion is either legal or conducted openly.

In the United States legal induced abortion was generally unavailable until 1970, when a few states liberalized their abortion laws. Early in 1973 the U.S. Supreme Court declared most restrictive abortion laws unconstitutional because they violated the woman's right of privacy. Since then abortion has been generally available throughout the United States. The 1973 Supreme Court cases ROE V. WADE AND DOE V. BOLTON left the decision to have a first-trimester abortion to the woman and her physician. States could pass regulations to insure the safety of second-trimester abortions, and they could prohibit third-trimester abortions altogether.

Congress passed the Hyde Amendment in 1976, which severely restricted federal funds for abortions, although many states continue to fund abortions for indigent women. Since 1973 the U.S. Supreme Court has ruled on several local and state regulations, upholding those requiring parental notification for a minor's abortion and parental or judicial consent for an abortion for someone under age 15.

Impact of Legalization. During the 1960s an estimated 200,000 to 1,200,000 illegal abortions were performed each year in the United States. Deaths from illegal abortions amounted to one-fifth of all deaths related to pregnancy and childbirth. Morbidity and mortality from illegal abortions began to decline in the 1960s, but after 1973, mortality and hospitalizations dropped dramatically, in part due to improved training for abortion providers, increased familiarity with treatment of complications, and safer techniques. Legalization stimulated development of more convenient and lower-cost health service. More than 60 percent of abortions were in hospitals in 1973, but more than 70 percent were in freestanding clinics in 1980, about one-half of which were outpatient procedures.

Legalization raised concerns about long-term health consequences of abortion. Studies to date have found that risks of spontaneous abortion, preterm delivery, and low birth weight for a second pregnancy following vacuum aspiration are no greater than risks for a first pregnancy. Other health risks, including a suggested association between abortion of the first pregnancy and breast cancer in later life, have not been adequately studied.

Ethical Aspects. Opponents of legalized induced abortion believe that human life begins at conception and that abortion is the intentional killing of a human being and is thus morally wrong. Members of the "right to life" movement have lobbied for a constitutional amendment on the rights of the unborn. The counterpart to this position is the "pro-choice" stance. Its proponents generally believe that human life begins when the fetus can survive outside the womb. Before then, since the fetus is not a separate human, it is considered morally acceptable to terminate the pregnancy. Supporters of liberalized abortion laws also argue that legal abortion is safer to the woman than illegal abortion and relieves the psychological and social problems associated with bearing an unwanted child.

CAROL HOGUE

Bibliography: Centers for Disease Control, *Abortion Surveillance: Annual Summary 1979–1980* (1983); Hogue, C., et al., "The Effects of Induced Abortion on Subsequent Reproduction," *Epidemiologic Reviews* (1982); Nathanson, B. N., *Aborting America* (1979); Tietze, C., *Induced Abortion: A World Review, 1983,* 5th ed. (1983).

Abraham

Abraham, originally called Abram, was Israel's first great patriarch. He probably lived in the late 3d or early 2d millennium BC, but the earliest source for information on his life is Genesis 11–25, written about 10 centuries later. He was born at Ur in Chaldea, where he married his half-sister SARAH. Under divine inspiration, he went to Haran in Mesopotamia. Later God commanded him to leave his home for a new land; in return God offered Abraham fame, land, and descendants, promising that he would become a blessing to all nations. Abraham obeyed and migrated to Canaan, where he lived as a nomadic chieftain. He soon became wealthy, but he still had no son. Because Sarah was advanced in years, she substituted her Egyptian slave HAGAR, who bore ISHMAEL, Abraham's first son. Later, in accord with a divine promise, Sarah gave birth to ISAAC. Abraham's faith was put to a severe test when God commanded that he sacrifice Isaac, his only son by Sarah. Abraham did not waver and he prepared for the sacrifice, but God spared the boy at the last moment, substituting a ram.

The Bible portrays Abraham as a man struggling to trust God's promises. By his faith Abraham became the father of the Israelite people and is still honored in three different religions. Jewish tradition stresses his monotheism. Christians see him as a model for the man of faith and recognize him as their spiritual ancestor. Muslims accept him as an ancestor of the Arabs through Ishmael. Numerous works of art are based on the story of the sacrifice of Isaac.   J. J. M. ROBERTS

Bibliography: Bright, John, *A History of Israel* (1972); Van Seters, John, *Abraham in History and Tradition* (1975).

Abrahams, Peter

Peter Abrahams, who has used the pseudonym Peter Graham, was born in a township near Johannesburg on Nov. 19, 1919. He was the first black South African writer to gain worldwide recognition and to attract attention to the plight of blacks in that country. In an early novel, *Mine Boy* (1946), in his early short stories in *Dark Testament* (1942), and in his autobiographical novel, *Tell Freedom* (1954), he protests the treatment of blacks under APARTHEID (segregation). He has lived in England and Jamaica for more than 30 years, earning his living as a journalist. Abrahams's later novels include *A Wreath for Udomo* (1956), set in West Africa, and *This Island Now* (1966), set in the Caribbean. Even in his writings set entirely outside Africa, Abrahams remains distinctly African in his outlook.   RICHARD K. PRIEBE

Bibliography: Wade, Michael, *Peter Abrahams* (1971).

Abrams, Creighton

As U.S. commander in the VIETNAM WAR from 1968 to 1972, Creighton Williams Abrams, b. Sept. 15, 1914, d. Sept. 4, 1974, implemented the program of gradual U.S. withdrawal called Vietnamization. A graduate (1936) of West Point, he served in World War II and became army vice chief of staff in 1964. He was later army chief of staff (1972–74).

abrasive

An abrasive is any powdered, granular, or solid substance used to wear off the surface of materials in order to alter their shape or to supply a finish. Common natural abrasives include garnet and emery, used for sandpaper; the quartz grains used in sandblasting stone and metals; and pumice, which is used as a scouring material in soaps and some dental pastes. The most important synthetic abrasives are silicon carbide, known by its trade name CARBORUNDUM, which is used for grinding nonferrous metals and nonmetallic materials; aluminum oxide, a hard, steel-grinding abrasive; and metallic abrasives, such as iron and steel shot, steel wool, and metallic grit. Natural or synthetic diamonds, the hardest of all abrasives, are used in powdered form to grind or machine very hard materials, including solid diamonds.

Abrasives are glued or bonded onto grinding wheels or belts. They are also commonly used as a coating on cutting instruments and as a binder for cement. As a suspension in air, water, or oil, they can be projected against a surface that is to be ground.   JOHN NEELY

See also: MACHINE TOOLS.

Abravanel, Isaac ben Judah   [uh-brah'-vuh-nel]

Isaac Abravanel (or Abrabanel), 1437–1508, was a Jewish biblical scholar, philosopher, and financier. Born in Lisbon, he served the rulers of Portugal (1471–83) and Castile (1484–92) until the Jews were expelled (1492) by Ferdinand and Isabella from Spain. He then served the government of Naples until 1495, when Naples was conquered by the French. He later settled in Venice.

His biblical commentaries on the Pentateuch, Joshua, Judges, Samuel, and 1 and 2 Kings and on both the Major and the Minor Prophets were unusual in introducing comparisons with the social situation of his own time. Abravanel was also one of the earliest Jewish commentators to refer to the contributions of Christian biblical scholars. His acceptance of the historical authenticity of the Bible led him to write a commentary criticizing those chapters of the *Guide for the Perplexed* in which MAIMONIDES had presented a naturalistic view of prophecy. Abravanel also offered philosophic defenses of the traditional messianic expectation that looked forward to the age when the Jews would return to the Holy Land and the MESSIAH would rule the world.
          JOSEPH L. BLAU

Bibliography: Netanyahu, Benzion, *Don Isaac Abravanel*, 2d ed. (1968); Reines, Alvin Jay, *Maimonides and Abrabanel on Prophecy* (1970).

Abravanel, Judah

Judah Abravanel (or Abrabanel), 1460–1523, a Jewish physician and philosopher, wrote *Dialoghi d'Amore* (Dialogues of Love), one of the most widely circulated products of Renaissance NEOPLATONISM. Born in Lisbon, the son of Isaac Abravanel, he fled to Spain in 1483 and then to Naples in 1492 after the expulsion of the Jews. His dialogues, composed by 1502, were first published posthumously in 1535. Probably written initially in Italian, they were later translated into Latin, French, Spanish, and Hebrew; in modern times there have been translations into English (*The Philosophy of Love*, 1937) and German. The central theme of the work, akin to that of the *Symposium* of Plato, is that love is the major creative force in the universe, and that love of God is the ultimate goal of the human soul. Thus a circle of love leads from God's creation in love to man's return to God through love. Abravanel was also a minor poet, but his influence on the poetry of his age was felt more through his dialogues than through his verse.   JOSEPH L. BLAU

Bibliography: Minkin, Jacob S., *Abravanel and the Expulsion of the Jews from Spain* (1938); Netanyahu, Benzion, *Don Isaac Abravanel*, 2d ed. (1968).

Abruzzi   [ah-broot'-see]

A mountainous region of central Italy, Abruzzi has a population of 1,221,900 (1977 est.) and an area of 10,794 km² (4,168 mi²). L'Aquila is the capital city of Abruzzi; its provinces include Chieti, L'Aquila, Pescara, and Teramo. The Adriatic Sea forms the region's eastern border. The average annual temperature is 13° C (55° F), and the rainfall averages 1,015 mm (40 in) in the Apennine Mountains. The Apennines cross the region in three northwest-southeast ranges, reaching a maximum altitude of 2,913 m (9,560 ft) in the Gran Sasso d'Italia group. Abruzzi's chief rivers are the Pescara, the Sangro, and the Tronto. The rugged terrain permits most agriculture of the subsistence variety. The chief crops are grapes, olives, sugar beets, and tobacco. Small amounts of foodstuffs, textiles, and clothing are produced.

Conquered by the Romans in the 4th century BC, Abruzzi later was held by the Lombards (6th–11th centuries), the Normans (12th–13th centuries), and the Kingdom of Naples (13th–19th centuries).   DANIEL R. LESNICK

Abruzzi, Luigi Amedeo, Duca degli
[loo-ee'-jee ah-may-day'-oh]

An Italian explorer, Abruzzi, b. Jan. 29, 1873, d. Mar. 18, 1933, was the son of Amadeus, king of Spain (1870–73), prince of Savoy-Aosta, and a cousin of Victor Emmanuel III, king of Italy. Abruzzi was the first to climb (1897) Mount St. Elias in Alaska and led (1899) a polar expedition that set a new record in the northern latitude reached. He later led mountain-climbing expeditions in the Ruwenzori range of East Africa (1906) and the Himalayas (1909). In World War I, Abruzzi commanded an Italian fleet in the Adriatic Sea and afterward took part in the Italian colonization effort in East Africa.

Absalom   [ab'-suh-luhm]

In the Bible Absalom was a son of King David who led a revolt against his father. He was defeated, and while fleeing was caught by his long hair in a tree; he was then killed by Joab, the commander of David's forces (2 Sam. 15–18).

Absalom, Absalom!

In William FAULKNER's complex, difficult, and innovative novel *Absalom, Absalom!* (1936), racial pride and innocence of human needs and desires destroy the dynastic dreams of Thomas Sutpen. The novel is constructed as a reverie and debate on the meaning of the past, using multiple narrators, including Quentin Compson of *The Sound and the Fury*, and varieties of the stream-of-consciousness technique to speculate on rather than reveal the Sutpen family's mysterious history of aggrandizement, miscegenation, abandonment, and murder. *Absalom, Absalom!*, perhaps Faulkner's most demanding novel, is considered one of his greatest works.

THOMAS L. MCHANEY

Bibliography: Brooks, Cleanth, *William Faulkner: Toward Yoknapatawpha and Beyond* (1978); Pilkington, John, *The Heart of Yoknapatawpha* (1981).

ABSCAM

The ABSCAM (a contraction of "Abdul Scam") investigation conducted by the Federal Bureau of Investigation in 1978–80 resulted in the conviction of seven members of the U.S. Congress and several state and local officials for bribery, conspiracy, and related charges. As revealed early in 1980, FBI agents impersonating an Arab sheikh and his henchmen had offered bribes in return for preferential treatment in gaining entry into the United States, building casinos in Atlantic City, N.J., and other favors. Their encounters were recorded on videotapes, showing public officials and their associates in the act of accepting bribes.

Sen. Harrison Williams and Reps. John Jenrette, Richard Kelly, Raymond Lederer, John Murphy, Michael Myers, and Frank Thompson were the members of Congress convicted. Either already convicted (and, in the case of Myers, expelled from the House—the first expulsion since 1861) or under indictment at the time of the 1980 elections, all the representatives except Lederer lost their bids for reelection. Lederer later resigned. Williams, who was not up for election in 1980, resigned in 1982 to avoid expulsion from the Senate.

Critics of the FBI's methods in the ABSCAM case questioned whether ENTRAPMENT had taken place. Few of the accused based their defense on entrapment, however, because to do so would have required admitting to the acts charged. In the major cases where that defense was offered, the courts ruled that the FBI had not overstepped legal limits.

abscess

An abscess results when bacteria—usually *Streptococcus*—spreading into tissue causes INFLAMMATION. A fibrous wall forms so that the infection is sealed off from other tissue, and pus—yellowish white fluid containing white blood cells, bacteria, and dead tissue—fills the center of the walled-in region. An abscess is painful when the inflamed area becomes congested, causing pressure on nearby nerve endings. In order to

heal, an abscess must be drained and then treated with antibiotic drugs. Common skin abscesses are BOILS and CARBUNCLES, and they can affect such areas as the middle ear (see EAR DISEASE) and the eye (see STY). An abscess of a tooth root can occur if dental decay is advanced (see TEETH), and tuberculosis begins with abscesses in the lungs.

abscisic acid   [ab-sis'-ik]

Abscisic acid, or dormin, is a plant HORMONE that promotes abscission, the process responsible for the fall of leaves, flowers, and fruits. It is produced in response to such stimuli as the changing relative lengths of day and night during autumn. Abscisic acid also counters the growth-stimulating effects of the plant hormones known as AUXINS, GIBBERELLINS, and kinins (see CYTOKININ) and thus induces DORMANCY of buds and inhibits seed germination during winter.

absentee voting

Absentee voting enables voters to cast their ballots in an election without going to the polls. Most democratic countries permit absentee voting for persons who are unable to get to the polls because they are ill or away from their voting districts. Usually ballots are cast by mail. Sometimes voters are permitted to vote ahead of the election date if they are going on a journey. Absentee ballots have been in use for several centuries. During the U.S. Civil War, soldiers in the field were encouraged to vote by absentee ballot. In some Asian and African countries where illiteracy is high, absentee voting is not permitted or is restricted to those who can read and write.

absolute

The word *absolute* is used by philosophers and by theologians to indicate ultimate reality conceived as an all-inclusive whole. This reality is considered to be both the source of and the sum total of everything that exists physically, mentally, and spiritually; it is self-sufficient and unconditional.

The phrase *the absolute* became prominent through the writings of the 18th- and 19th-century German idealists Johann Gottlieb FICHTE, Friedrich W. J. SCHELLING, and especially G. W. F. HEGEL. In Hegelian IDEALISM the absolute is interpreted as rational mind. Hegel, however, emphasized that the absolute can be known and analyzed only as it is manifested in human experience and history. The term is prominent in the writings of the English idealist F. H. BRADLEY and the American philosopher Josiah ROYCE.   ROBERT M. BAIRD

absolute magnitude: see MAGNITUDE.

absolute music

Instrumental music that is abstract, free of literary or pictorial associations, is called absolute music. In contrast with PROGRAM MUSIC it has no titles or story connotations that cause the listener to involve his or her imagination beyond an appreciation of the form and style of the composition or the technical skills of the performers. Attention is focused on the relationship of themes, the formal organization of the musical material, and the beauty of the music itself. Most symphonies, sonatas, concertos, fugues, and chamber music are absolute music.   ELWYN A. WIENANDT

absolute temperature: see KELVIN SCALE.

absolute zero

Absolute zero is the lowest theoretical TEMPERATURE, representing the complete absence of heat. At this temperature matter would possess zero ENTROPY and maximum molecular order, the volume of an ideal gas would vanish, and a thermodynamic heat engine would operate at 100 percent efficiency. Although absolute zero cannot actually be reached, approximations of less than 0.001° C above absolute zero have been created in the laboratory.

Absolute zero is the lowest point of an absolute temperature scale. Such a scale can be established by measuring the pressure of a trapped volume of gas as a function of its temperature in ordinary Celsius or Farenheit degrees. Most gases display a linear relationship between pressure and temperature under conditions not far from ambient; this experimental fact is known as Charles's law. Extrapolating this linear relationship to the point at which the gas pressure becomes zero defines the absolute zero of temperature. The extrapolation is necessary because all gases turn to liquid before absolute zero is reached. The absolute zero thus determined is −273.15° C (−459.67° F). This temperature is the zero point of the absolute Kelvin and Rankine temperature scales. One Celsius degree and one Kelvin are equal in magnitude, as are one Farenheit degree and one Rankine degree, but the absolute Kelvin and Rankine scales assign only positive values to all attainable temperatures.

The fact that absolute zero is unattainable in any real process is known as the Third Law of THERMODYNAMICS. Formulated by Walther Nernst in 1906, this natural law states that no matter how cold an object becomes, it can be made still colder without reaching absolute zero. Thus experiments in low-temperature physics can only approach absolute zero asymptotically.

Absolute zero is an essential concept in low temperature physics, or CRYOGENICS. Attempts to reach cryogenic temperatures began with the liquefaction of air in the late 19th century. James Dewar succeeded in liquefying hydrogen in 1898 and invented the modern vacuum flask that bears his name. Ten years later, helium, the gas with the lowest boiling point, was first liquefied by the Dutch physicist Heike Kamerlingh Onnes. With widespread availability of liquid helium, modern cryogenicists have concentrated on the discovery and investigation of the cryogenic behavior of matter. This field includes SUPERCONDUCTIVITY, the loss of almost all electrical resistance in metals chilled near absolute zero, and a similar effect, the disappearance of viscosity in liquid helium, or SUPERFLUIDITY.

GARY S. SETTLES

Bibliography: Mendelssohn, K., *The Quest for Absolute Zero* (1966).

absolutism

Absolutism is a political system that concentrates power in the hands of one person or a group of persons who have almost unlimited authority. History is replete with tyrants and dictators, but the notion of absolutism became prominent in Europe during the 16th, 17th, and 18th centuries when monarchs were struggling to wrest power from groups such as the church and the nobility and to create national states. The most famous absolutist was Louis XIV of France, who is said to have declared that he himself was the state: "L'état, c'est moi." Others were the Tudor and Stuart rulers of England and Frederick the Great of Prussia.

Bibliography: Beloff, Max, *Age of Absolutism 1660–1815* (1966); Cobban, Alfred, *Dictatorship: Its History and Theory* (1939; repr. 1970).

absorption

In chemistry, absorption is the process by which energy or a material called the absorbate is taken up by some other material, called the absorbent, in such a way that the former is distributed throughout the latter. It is thus differentiated from ADSORPTION, which is a surface phenomenon. This distinction can be made clearly when the absorbent is liquid, but it often becomes blurred in solid absorbents, which are crisscrossed with fine pores, so that taking up of the absorbate on the surface of the pores can result in its dispersion throughout the absorbent. In some instances the absorbent reacts chemically with the absorbate.

A commonplace example of absorption is the action of blotting paper, which is essentially a mat of cellulose fibers; liquids are readily taken up into the interstices between the fibers. In industry, absorption is often used to remove a noxious gas that could cause air pollution, such as the sulfur dioxide produced in the burning of coal. The absorption of light is widely used in quantitative chemical analysis.

In biology, absorption refers to the taking up of substances by the blood or lymph.

GEORGE GORIN

absorption, light

When light is incident on a material, some or all of it may be absorbed, reflected, transmitted, or scattered. Each effect is caused by the interaction of the light with the atoms and molecules of the material; the optical effect that predominates depends on the nature of the material and on the wavelength of the incident light.

Light energy that is absorbed is transformed into internal ENERGY within the material. The most common transformation is to thermal energy, or heat, although changes to other forms such as chemical energy (see PHOTOCHEMISTRY) are possible. Energy that is reradiated at the same wavelength is known as scattered light. FLUORESCENCE and PHOSPHORESCENCE are phenomena in which the incident radiation is reemitted at longer wavelengths.

All transparent substances absorb light to some extent. Small quantities of water may seem completely transparent, but light that traverses large distances through water is diminished, as is obvious at ocean depths. The degree of light absorbance by a substance depends on the wavelength of the incident light. A colorless substance, such as air or quartz crystals, absorbs light uniformly throughout the range of visible wavelengths. In order for a substance to appear colored, it must interact differently with light of various wavelengths. Grass absorbs red light so that the reflected component is seen as green, the complementary COLOR of red.

The absorption characteristics of gases are more easily seen than those of other stages. Gases generally absorb a series of single wavelengths from the spectrum of visible light rather than the broad bands of liquids and solids. The absorption spectrum of each substance enables the spectroscopist to readily determine the structure of the absorbing material.

The absorption of light as it passes through a medium varies linearly with the distance the light travels and with concentration of the absorbing medium. This may be expressed by the simple equation $a = \epsilon c l$ where a is the absorbance, ϵ is a characteristic constant for each material at a given wavelength (known as the extinction coefficient or absorption coefficient), c is concentration, and l is the length of the light path. The relationship is known as Beer's law or Beer-Lambert's law and is used by chemists and physicists to determine the concentration of a component of a solution. The absorption of a given wavelength of light of a solution of unknown concentration is compared with the corresponding absorption of a set of solutions of the same component whose concentrations are precisely known. Using Beer's law, the unknown concentration can be calculated.

Devices that measure light absorption are the colorimeter (usually used only for visible light) and the spectrophotometer (which is able to function at additional wavelengths, including ultraviolet light and infrared radiation). These instruments are common to most laboratories.

D. J. LOVELL

Bibliography: Bragg, W. L., *The Universe of Light* (1969); Ditchburn, R. W., *Light*, 2d ed. (1963); Rublowsky, John, *Light* (1964); Van Heel, A. S. C., and Velzel, C. H. F., *What Is Light?* (1968).

See also: SPECTROSCOPY.

abstract

An abstract, in law, is a summary of a case or a document. Abstracts are often made of titles to real estate, giving the names of past owners and describing liens, easements, or other agreements affecting rights to the property, in order to protect the purchaser against defects in the title.

abstract art

Abstract art is generally taken to mean painting and sculpture by artists for whom the manner and the means are the subject rather than the representation of any object. All art is abstract to some degree; that is, it is removed from the perceived elements of nature. The sculpture of archaic Greece, of Egypt, of primitive tribes, both ancient and modern, use simplified, often geometricized forms, and the frescoes of

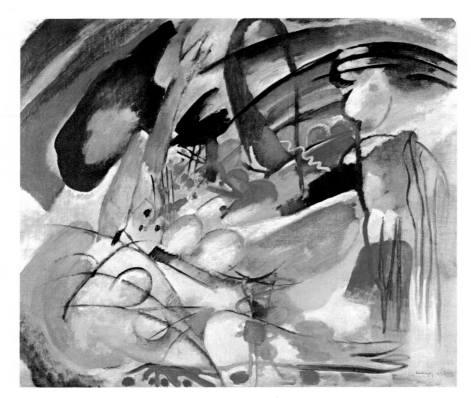

(Left) *In* Improvisation 33 *(1913) Wassily Kandinsky, used the interaction of color, line, and form to express an inner reality or spirituality. One of the principal pioneers of abstract art, Kandinsky considered music be to abstract art in its purest form. (Stedelijk Museum, Amsterdam.)*

(Below) Composition with Red, Yellow, and Blue *(1920) is by the Dutch artist Piet Mondrian. Mondrian restricted his abstract paintings to straight lines and right angles, using only three primary colors and gray, black, and white. Private collection, Amsterdam.)*

GIOTTO DI BONDONE thus honor the two-dimensionality of his medium. The term *abstract art*, however, is best used to signify a main line of development that only began in this century with the profound desire in MODERN ART to express the continuum of inner life in purely pictorial terms. Abstract art's beginnings can be traced to James McNeill WHISTLER's "art for art's sake" theories and to his *Arrangements, Symphonies,* and *Nocturnes,* closely related to the art of music, which, to many abstractionists, is the universal abstract language.

Wassily KANDINSKY, in 1910, made his first consciously abstract watercolor, a composition of swirling, interacting spots of color deeply related to his love of music, the basis of his aesthetic principle. During the same year, Kandinsky began to write *Concerning the Spiritual in Art*, expounding his metaphysically based ideas concerning inner reality. In 1911–12, the Czech artist Frantisek KUPKA painted what is often considered the first totally abstract canvas, *Fugue in Red and Blue* (National Gallery, Prague), whose rhythmic patterns of color were directly inspired by musical correspondences. Pure color as both form and subject was the central idea in the ORPHISM of Robert DELAUNAY and Francis PICABIA, which developed beginning in 1912.

Pure abstraction was, however, carried to its most extreme limits by the Russians, beginning in 1913, who extended the philosophical and geometric elements of CUBISM and developed an architecturally based abstraction completely removed from exterior realms. The most far-reaching experimentation in abstract art as the expression of the reality of the fourth dimension (inner reality) took form in the Rayonism of Natalia GONCHAROVA and Mikhail LARIONOV (begun by Larionov in Moscow in 1911–12); the CONSTRUCTIVISM of Naum GABO, Antoine PEVSNER and Vladimir TATLIN; the nonobjectivism of Aleksandr RODCHENKO; and the SUPREMATISM of Kasimir MALEVICH. The principles established by these artists have had wide significance in successive abstract art movements from the BAUHAUS during the 1920s and '30s to the structures of MINIMAL ART during the 1960s.

Chief among the other innovators of abstract art are Piet MONDRIAN and artists of the DE STIJL movement (such as Theo Van DOESBURG and Bart van der Leck), developed in the Neth-erlands around 1917. In neoplasticism, Mondrian developed his ideas of pure plastic (formative) relationships as the basis for attaining the objective purity and universality of mathematics. In his philosophical reduction of form to the use of the three primary colors (red, yellow, and blue) and the right angle in horizontal-vertical position, Mondrian exerted great influence both on architecture and on painting, from the Bauhaus to the American Abstract Artists (founded in New York in 1936) to the American ABSTRACT EXPRESSIONISTS of the 1940s and '50s.

Abstract art, defined as the expression in pictorial terms of the universal structures and rhythms of inner reality, has continued as the central concern of numerous painters, sculptors, and architects to the present, all of whom have, to some degree, worked from the fundamental contributions of the pioneers in the field.
BARBARA CAVALIERE

Bibliography: Cork, Richard, *Vorticism and Abstract Art in the First Machine Age*, 2 vols. (1976, 1977); Fry, Edward, *Cubism* (1966); Kandinsky, Wassily, *Concerning the Spiritual in Art* (1947; repr. 1976); Malevich, Kasimir, *The Non-Objective World* (1959); Mondrian, Piet, *The New Art: The New Life, The Collected Writings of Piet Mondrian*, ed. by Harry Holtzman (1972); Rickey, George, *Constructivism: Its Origins and Evolution* (1967); Roberts-Jones, Philippe, *Beyond Time and Place: Non-Realist Painting in the Nineteenth Century* (1978); Seuphor, Michel, *Abstract Painting* (1962); Tuchman, Maurice, ed., *The New York School: Abstract Expressionism in the '40s and '50s* (1970); Vallier, Dora, *Abstract Art* (1970).

See also: ARCHITECTURE; ART; PAINTING; SCULPTURE.

abstract expressionism

Abstract expressionism is the collective name for the work of a heterogeneous group of New York artists who produced vivid, emotionally charged nonrepresentational paintings characterized by very bold uses of color and mass. The term *abstract expressionism* was used in 1929 by Alfred H. BARR, Jr., founder of the MUSEUM OF MODERN ART in New York, in reference to the early improvisations of Wassily KANDINSKY. In 1946, Robert Coates, art critic of *The New Yorker* magazine, employed it in relation to a group of paintings done in New York. The term was popularized during a series of discussions that took place in 1952 at the "Club" on Eighth Street in New York City among a number of painters and sculptors; during the sessions, the artists themselves rejected it as an unsatisfactory indicator of their art. Although the term, along with others used to refer to the art that developed in New York during the 1940s—*action painting, the New York school*, and *American-type painting*—is in many ways misleading, it has remained the predominant one in discussion of this art. Abstract expressionism is not a unified artistic style; what the artists who promulgated it had in common was the search for a significant subject in an abstract format. They sought a format that could express their individual personalities and at the same time could lead to the expression, through the process of painting, of a universal, timeless content.

During the 1930s many of these artists had worked on the Federal Art Project under the Works Progress Administration. Some had come in contact with Hans HOFMANN, already an influential teacher of modernist theory in New York City. The majority had been exposed to various modernisms (such as CONSTRUCTIVISM, DADA, SURREALISM and the work of Paul KLEE and Kandinsky) through gallery and museum shows, and most had grappled with CUBISM, specifically in the then overwhelming person of Pablo PICASSO. In 1937, John Graham's influen-

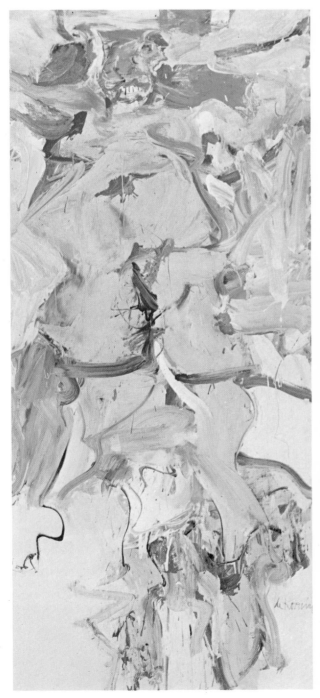

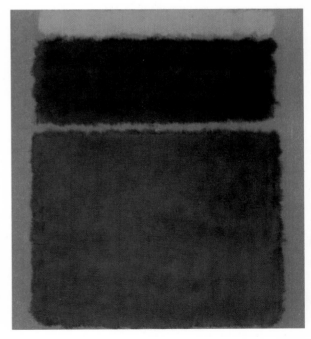

(Above) *Mark Rothko's* Blue, Orange, Red *(1961) is an example of the "color-field" branch of abstract expressionism. In his paintings, Rothko uses the interaction of color relationships to convey such basic human emotions as joy and sorrow.*

(Left) *Willem de Kooning's* Woman, Sag Harbor *(1964) reflects the energetic nature of the "gestural" wing of abstract expressionism. The work is one of a series of paintings entitled* Women. *(Hirshhorn Museum and Sculpture Garden, Washington, D.C.)*

tial book *System and Dialectics of Art* was published, and his ideas on the prominence of the subconscious, based on the theories of Sigmund FREUD and C. G. JUNG, were already becoming an important topic of conversation. Willem DE KOONING and Arshile GORKY, then close friends of Graham, were already showing a shift in style and direction. By the end of the 1930s, a few small groups of painters in New York City were expressing their dissatisfaction with the current, prevalent trends of social realism and geometric abstraction (as exemplified by the group called American Abstract Artists). During the next few years many prominent European modernist artists such as André BRETON, Max ERNST, Fernand LÉGER, André MASSON, and Piet MONDRIAN immigrated to New York to escape the war in Europe. Their arrival reinforced the American artists, who were politically conscious of, as well as schooled in, modernist art theory, Freudian and Jungian psychology, existentialist philosophy, theories of symbolist poetry, and Oriental art and ideas. They also knew the work of Milton AVERY, Arthur DOVE, and the group shown by Alfred STIEGLITZ at his American Place Gallery, the most avant-garde artists of that period in the United States.

During the early 1940s, two important groups of artists were actively meeting and discussing an art that combined mastery of painterly values with psychologically intense content, and thus expressed universal human emotions appropriate to the tragic climate of World War II. In 1941–42 the American artists William BAZIOTES and Robert MOTHERWELL, along with the Chilean surrealist MATTA ECHAURREN, were discussing such ideas; they were soon joined by Jackson POLLOCK and Lee KRASNER. They based their work on surrealism's generative principle of "psychic automatism" but differed from the Europeans in their equal regard for the process of painting, for the plastic qualities of the painterly medium. At the same time, Adolph GOTTLIEB and Mark ROTHKO, soon joined by Barnett NEWMAN and Theodoros STAMOS, were advocating the use of ancient mythology and primitivizing content in their similar efforts to forego current aesthetics. Separately and simultaneously, other artists such as Clyfford STILL, Richard POUSETTE-DART, and Ad REINHARDT were evolving their art of parallel ideas. By the mid-'40s these artists had discovered their unique painting approach, one that placed them at the forefront of abstract painting at midcentury. By the end of the decade, they were moving apart; interrelationships, although intense, were always tentative, largely because of the individualistic nature of their art.

The abstract expressionists are usually divided into two groups: the "gestural" wing inlcudes Gorky, de Kooning, Hofmann, and Pollock; the "color-field" wing, Gottlieb, Newman, Rothko, and Stamos. Any such classification, however, is an oversimplification. Even though the abstract expressionists benefited mutually during their formative years of the 1940s, in the end they must be considered separately, as painters who always work toward the universal via the personal, striving to convey a timeless and deeply emotional human content through abstract form. BARBARA CAVALIERE

Bibliography: Alloway, Lawrence, *Topics In American Art since 1945* (1975); Ashton, Dore, *The New York School: A Cultural Reckoning* (1973); Cavaliere, Barbara, and Hadler, Mona, *William Baziotes: A Retrospective Exhibition* (1978); Doty, Robert, and Waldman, Diane, *Adolph Gottlieb* (1968); Hess, Thomas B., *Willem de Kooning* (1968); Hobbs, Robert Carlton, and Levin, Gail, *Abstract Expressionism: The Formative Years* (1978); O'Connor, Francis V., *Jackson Pollock* (1967); Sandler, Irving, *The Triumph of American Painting: A History of Abstract Expressionism* (1970); Tuchman, Maurice, *Abstract Expressionism in the '40s and '50s* (1971); Wolfe, Tom, *The Painted Word* (1976).

See also: ABSTRACT ART; ART; MODERN ART; PAINTING.

absurdism

Absurdism is an idea commonly associated with EXISTENTIALISM. Beginning in the 19th century, mainly through the influence of Søren KIERKEGAARD, religion was often described as absurd because it could not be justified on rational principles; rather, it was considered as based on what Kierkegaard called "a leap of faith." In their discussions of consciousness, Martin HEIDEGGER and Jean Paul SARTRE have described the human consciousness as facing an apparently absurd world—absurd because it finds itself at the crossroads of Being and Nothingness, baffled by the meaninglessness of the human condition. Sartre's ideas of absurdity, anguish, and disgust are expressed in his plays and novels, especially in *Nausea* (1938; Eng. trans., 1949). A philosophical basis for the modern THEATER OF THE ABSURD has been established by other existentialists, such as Albert CAMUS, Karl JASPERS, and Gabriel MARCEL.
KARL BECKSON

Bibliography: Barrett, William, *What Is Existentialism?* (1963); Esslin, Martin, *The Theatre of the Absurd*, rev. ed. (1973).

See also: ALIENATION.

Abu Bakr [ah'-boo bak'-ur]

Abu Bakr, b. *c.*573, d. Aug. 23, 634, father-in-law of the Prophet MUHAMMAD, was first caliph ("successor") after the Prophet's death in 632.

An early convert and loyal follower of Muhammad, Abu Bakr led the Muslim community from 632 to 634, but his caliphate was contested by ALI, the Prophet's son-in-law. He also faced opposition from unruly tribes and led successful military campaigns across the Arabian peninsula into Syria and Palestine.

Bibliography: Hitti, Philip K., *History of the Arabs*, 8th ed. (1963).

Abu Dhabi [ah'-boo dah'-bee]

Abu Dhabi (1973 est. pop., 50,000) is the capital of the Abu Dhabi sheikhdom on the southeast shore of the Persian Gulf and the capital of the United Arab Emirates. Its climate is arid, with an average annual rainfall of 60 mm (2.4 in). Income from oil production has transformed it from a fishing village in the 1960s into a high-rise city with an international airport and an artificial harbor.

Abu Madi, Iliya [ah'-boo mah'-dee, ee'lee-yah]

Abu Madi, b. 1889, d. 1957, was a Lebanese poet and journalist who immigrated to the United States and collaborated with Kahlil Gibran. He published several collections, of which *The Brooks* (1927) and *The Thickets* (1940) are the most notable. Nostalgia for happiness, philosophical skepticism about the purpose of life, optimism, egalitarianism, and brotherly love among human beings are his main themes.
ISSA J. BOULLATA

Abu Nuwas [ah'-boo noo-wahs']

The Arabic poet Abu Nuwas, Father of the Forelocks, b. *c.*756, d. *c.*810, gained this nickname from two locks of hair that reached to his shoulders. His real name was Hasan ibn Hani. Although he composed a variety of poems in traditional style, such as panegyrics, satires, hunting verses, and elegies—even religious poems—his fame, both in his own time and in posterity, rests on his wine (*khamr*) poetry called *Khamriyat* and on his love poems, which he addressed to young boys in the Persian manner. ILSE LICHTENSTADTER

Abu Simbel [ah'-boo sim'-bul]

Abu Simbel, or Ibsambul, located 282 km (175 mi) south of Aswan, Egypt, on the west bank of the Nile, is the site of two famous rock-hewn temples built during the reign of Ramses II (1304–1237 BC). Four colossal statues of Ramses, measuring about 20 m (65 ft) high, are carved on the facade of the larger temple. Four others, about 10 m (33 ft) high, together with two statues of his principal queen, Nefertari, embellish the facade of the smaller temple.

The inner walls of the larger temple bear painted reliefs of the king performing religious ceremonies and fighting against the Hittites and other foreign foes. At the far end, 55 m (180 ft) from the entrance, are statues of the gods Ptah, Amon-Re, Re-Harakhti, and the deified king, on which the direct rays of the Sun shine at sunrise twice annually, on Feb. 20 and Oct. 20. The smaller temple, also decorated with religious scenes, was dedicated to the goddess Hathor and the deified Nefertari.

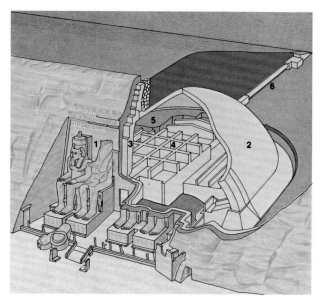

The Great Temple at Abu Simbel, Egypt, was built during the 13th century BC. Guarding its facade (1), which is 36.3 m (122 ft) wide, are four seated colossuses of Ramses II. Each is more than 19 m (63 ft) in height. Inside are two halls, eight adjoining chambers, a vestibule, three apartments, and a sanctuary consecrated to Ramses II and the pantheon of Egyptian gods. The temple was threatened in 1964 by the rising waters of Lake Nasser, an artificial lake created by the newly constructed Aswan High Dam. To save Abu Simbel, UNESCO coordinated a $40 million rescue operation. The project required the disassembling and reconstruction of the temple at a site 61 m (210 ft) higher than the original. Beneath an artificial mountain, an immense concrete dome (2) protects the temple from tons of rock that were piled up to simulate Abu Simbel's original setting. Stepped walls (3) behind the facade serve as reinforcement for the ancient colossuses. A gridlike structure (4) supports the ceiling blocks (5) of the inner chamber, and a pipe at the rear (6) draws fresh air into the shrine.

The construction of the Aswan High Dam and the creation of Lake Nasser made it necessary to move the temples to high ground above the original site. The project was finished in 1968 at a cost of $40 million.   I. E. S. EDWARDS

Bibliography: Desroches-Noblecourt, Christiane, and Gersten, Georg, *The World Saves Abu Simbel* (1968).

abundance

Abundance, or relative abundance, is the percentage of the natural occurrence of an ISOTOPE of an element in the entire population of atoms of that element. The isotope oxygen-16, for example, has an abundance of 99.759% of all oxygen atoms.

Bibliography: Weast, Robert C., ed., *CRC Handbook of Chemistry and Physics* (1977).

Abydos   [uh-by'-duhs]

Abydos, approximately 521 km (324 mi) south of Cairo, is the Greek name for the ancient Egyptian city of Abdu. The shrine of its primeval local god, Khenti-amentiu, became the major sanctuary dedicated to OSIRIS, whose head was traditionally believed to be buried here. Abydos was continuously occupied from the Predynastic to the Roman period. What may be the tombs of kings of the Archaic period were excavated by Sir Flinders PETRIE in the northwest sector of the site. Among the most impressive monuments are the temple of SETI I of the 19th (1320–1200 BC) dynasty, which contains perhaps the finest royal painted relief preserved from ancient Egypt, and the famous Gallery of the List of Kings, on the walls of which appears the chronological succession of most of the Egyptian rulers from Menes to Seti I. To the east of the temple lies the Osireion, also built by Seti I. It is a subterranean complex of chambers dedicated to the cult of Osiris and perhaps symbolizes the emergence of the world from the waters of chaos.
ROBERT S. BIANCHI

Bibliography: Simpson, William K., *The Terrace of the Great God at Abydos* (1974).

abyssal zone   [uh-bis'-ul]

The abyssal zone of the OCEAN is the largest biome, or environmental unit, in the world, with an upper boundary at the 4° C (40° F) ISOTHERM—the water temperature prevalent at depths of about 1,000 to 3,000 m (3,300 to 10,000 ft)—and a lower boundary between about 6,000 and 7,000 m (19,800 and 23,100 ft). Some oceanographers treat the great ocean deeps and trenches as a separate environmental region. The abyssal zone covers more than 75 percent of the total ocean and more than 50 percent of the total area of the Earth.

Temperature and salinity remain nearly constant in a given particular area of this zone, producing a characteristic deep-water fauna that feeds on the rain of organic detritus settling from above. The associated ocean bottom is generally flat in the Atlantic and hilly in the Pacific and is composed mainly of pelagic or partially pelagic muds—that is, open-ocean sediments as contrasted to those deposited near continents by rivers.   HAROLD R. WANLESS

Bibliography: Herring, P. J., and Clarke, M. R., eds., *Deep Oceans* (1971).

See also: BATHYAL ZONE; HADAL ZONE; OOZE, DEEP SEA; SEDIMENT, MARINE.

Abyssinia: see ETHIOPIA.

Abyssinian cat   [ab-uh-sin'-ee-uhn]

The Abyssinian cat, a short-haired breed of domestic cat, is believed to be related to the cats depicted in ancient Egyptian art.

The Abyssinian is a medium-sized cat with a triangular face, large pointed ears, lean body, and long tail. The almond-shaped eyes are hazel to orange, and the fine, short-haired coat ranges from light brown to silver. Each hair is ticked, or banded, with darker brown, gray, or black. The tail and ears are darker toward the tip. The red Abyssinian is a recognized breed.

Despite its name, the Abyssinian probably originated in the upper Nile Valley and may be the closest living relative of the sacred cat of ancient Egypt. It differs from many cats in that it enjoys playing with water.   EVERETT SENTMAN

Abzug, Bella S.   [ab'-zuhg]

Bella Savitzky Abzug, b. July 24, 1920, represented New York's 19th and 20th districts in Congress from 1971 to 1976. A lawyer long active in liberal causes, particularly the civil rights and peace movements, Abzug became nationally prominent

Bella Abzug, whose large floppy hats became a trademark during her congressional terms, has been a prominent figure in the feminist movement. A lawyer by profession, the dynamic Ms. Abzug played a prominent role in the National Women's Political Caucus.

in the early 1970s as an articulate advocate of women's rights and as a leader of the House of Representatives' antiwar group. In 1976, Abzug was unsuccessful in a bid for the U.S. Senate, and she was defeated in 1978 in an attempt to reenter Congress. Prominent in several women's political organizations, she was co-chairwoman of the President's National Advisory Committee on Women from November 1977 to January 1979.

Bibliography: Ziegler, Mel, *Bella! Mrs. Abzug Goes to Washington* (1972).

AC: see ALTERNATING CURRENT.

acacia   [uh-kay'-shuh]

Acacia is the common name for plants of the genus *Acacia* of the legume family, Leguminosae. The genus contains a large number of familiar and useful species. Acacias are known as wattles in Australia, as thorns in eastern Africa, and are sometimes sold by florists as Mimosa in Europe and North America. (The name *wattle* comes from the use of the bark of this plant for temporary "wattle and daub" dwellings in Australia.)

World climatic zones that have a long, dry winter and a

The catlaw acacia, A. greggii, *grows in Mexico and the southwestern United States. It is about 4.5 m (15 ft) tall, with yellow, cylindrical flowers and thin, twisted fruit pods approximately 13 cm (5 in) long.*

short, wet summer often support a shrubby vegetation known as thorn scrub and savanna. Acacia trees constitute much of the vegetation in such climatic regimes. The trees are characterized by their umbrella shape, with basal branching of the stems; the foliage forms a flattened or curved crown. The flowers, usually yellow, grow in crowded, globose heads or cylindrical spikes. Spines are common, and the Central American bull-horn acacia, *A. cornigera*, hosts a pulp-eating ant that hollows out its large spines in search of food and then lives in them. Acacias can tolerate long periods of drought and, because of the thorns, survive heavily grazed areas.

Acacias are used as ornamentals in tropical and subtropical gardens, as shade trees, and as indoor plants. Livestock are fed the leaves of some acacias; in Australia and parts of Africa the seeds or pods of other acacias are used by humans for food.

Australians also use acacia wood for railroads ties, wheels, handles, and furniture. Some pods yield a substance used for washing silk and as a shampoo. Gums derived from various species of African acacias include Sudan, or Kordofan, gum; Senegal, or Berbera, gum; sunt gum; and Suakin, or talha, gum. Wattle gum comes from Australia. "Acacia negra" is the name given to the bark of several acacias used in the tanning industry as a source of tannin. Cutch, a brown or olive vegetable dye, is derived from a stem exudate of acacia.

ROBERT C. ROMANS

academic freedom

Academic freedom traditionally refers to the freedom of scholars, usually at college and university levels, to teach, publish, and engage in research unhindered by others. Those protected by academic freedom, in turn, have the responsibility to conduct research honestly, to report their findings accurately, and to teach without bias. In democratic societies academic freedom is respected as a right. In totalitarian societies, where education is partly directed toward indoctrination, it is rejected.

The modern concept of academic freedom has origins in the 17th- and 18th-century movements for political freedom and freedom of thought and expression developed during the ENLIGHTENMENT. It was further developed by 19th-century German academics who distinguished between, but insisted equally upon, *Lehrfreiheit* ("freedom of teaching") and *Lehrnfreiheit* ("freedom of learning"). *Lehrfreiheit* claimed certain privileges for professors that set them apart from other civil servants; they were not required to submit course plans or articles to higher officials for approval. The academic freedom of students to learn in their own way, *Lehrnfreiheit,* entitled them to move from university to university, to attend lectures or not, and, within generous limits, to live as they pleased, subject only to reckoning of examinations.

As systems of higher education have grown more diverse, it has been necessary to seek common agreement on the principles of academic freedom and to form organizations for their defense. In the United States the American Association of University Professors (AAUP) has generally been accepted as the leader in the movement toward academic freedom for professors. The AAUP's *1940 Statement of Principles on Academic Freedom and Tenure,* adopted jointly with the Association of American Colleges, is now widely accepted as definitive.

Tenure, the practice of assuring professors of continuation in their positions once they have passed successfully through a probationary period and provided they are not later found seriously deficient by a carefully specified procedure, is an important protection of academic freedom. Although academic freedom of untenured professors, and of students, is not formally protected, it is of equal concern in academic communities. Until the STUDENT MOVEMENTS of the 1960s, the United States lagged in recognizing student academic freedom; statements on student academic freedom have now been issued by the AAUP and the American Civil Liberties Union.

The U.S. Supreme Court has given legal status to academic freedom claims as falling under the 1st Amendment in decisions such as *Sweezy* v. *New Hampshire* (1957) and *Perry* v. *Sinderman* (1972).

Despite such actions, challenges to academic freedom regularly occur and have become acute at critical stages in U.S. history. Following World War II, for example, the credentials of academics suspected of Communist-party affiliation were often questioned, and teachers were dismissed as actual or suspected Communists. EDMUND PINCOFFS

Bibliography: Bok, Derek C., *Beyond the Ivory Tower: Social Responsibilities of the Modern University* (1982); Hofstadter, Richard, *Academic Freedom in the Age of the College* (1955); Hook, Sidney, *In Defense of Academic Freedom* (1971); Metzger, Walter P., et al., *Dimensions of Academic Freedom* (1968); Pincoffs, Edmund L., ed., *The Concept of Academic Freedom* (1975).

Académie des Sciences   [ah-kah-day-mee' day see-awns']

Founded in 1666 by Jean Baptiste Colbert and Louis XIV, the Académie des Sciences in Paris quickly became the national center for French science and for the French scientific establishment, as well as the model for similar institutions elsewhere. Until its reform in 1699, the academy numbered a dozen men who worked collectively and anonymously. Enlarged to 50 resident members in various classes and grades, from adjunct to funded pensioner, the academy then formally assumed bureaucratic control over French science and technology.

From 1699 the academy published its famous scientific series *Mémoires*, offered prizes for scientific research, and supported several important scientific expeditions. Buffon, Condorcet, Fontenelle, Laplace, and Lavoisier numbered among its more important members and officers. The academy was closed in 1793 during the French Revolution and reconstituted as part of the INSTITUT DE FRANCE in 1795. It served as an active center for scientific research and debate until the 1830s. Today it continues as the national academy and the premier scientific society in France. JAMES E. McCLELLAN

Bibliography: Hahn, Roger, *The Anatomy of a Scientific Institution: The Paris Academy of Sciences, 1666–1803* (1971).

Académie Française   [ah-kah-day-mee' frawn-sez']

The Académie Française is the most renowned and one of the oldest literary and scientific societies in France. Established by Cardinal Richelieu, the Académie received its charter from Louis XIII in 1635. Besides honoring the foremost scholars, writers, and humanists of the day, Académie members were charged with overseeing the use, growth, and refinement of the French language. This function is still fulfilled today in the Académie's continual revision of the *Dictionnaire*. Eight editions of the work were published from 1694 to 1932, and several volumes of the ninth have been completed. The entries are conservative—words are illustrated with literary citations, and slang and colloquialisms are avoided. A similar conservatism is evident in the Académie's *Grammaire* (1932).

Membership in the Académie today is largely honorary, with writers, professors, theologians, historians, and philosophers filling the 40 chairs to which they are elected for life. Candidates for the Académie file a formal application, stating their qualifications, and elections take place when a chair is vacated. The new *académicien* delivers a discourse thanking the Académie and praising his predecessor.

Since 1914 the Académie has annually bestowed a literary prize, *Le Grand prix du roman de l'Académie Française*, on an author whose work is of "elevated inspiration and style." Laureates have included Georges Bernanos, François Mauriac, and Antoine de Saint-Exupéry. JOSEPH A. REITER

Académie Royale de Danse   [ah-kah-day-mee' rwah-yahl' duh dahns']

The Académie Royale de Danse, established in 1661 by Louis XIV, was the first royally recognized, and therefore officially sanctioned, organization devoted to perfecting the teaching of dance. Its 13 members, all professional dancing masters of the French court, met at the Louvre or informally at a nearby tavern, L'Epée de Bois (The Wooden Sword). In 1672, Louis awarded the supervisory title *maître de ballet* ("ballet master") to the noted choreographer Charles Louis Beauchamps. Guided by Beauchamps and later by Raoul Auger Feuillet and Louis Pécour, the academy began the formal codification of movement through which the *ballet de cour* ("court ballet") evolved into the classical BALLET vocabulary used today. BARBARA NEWMAN

academies of art

Academies of art are generally both art schools and honorary bodies; they provide training for students and, through restricted membership, prestige for recognized professionals. Since such prestige depends on the power and opinion of particular groups, it has varied throughout history, with the academies rising or falling in esteem according to social taste. The aim of art academies is to preserve the Renaissance identification of artistic practice with the ideals of humanism and to perpetuate the craftsmanship that makes this association meaningful.

The term *academy* is derived from the Greek *akademia*, which originally referred to an olive grove situated near Athens and named for Akademus, a local hero. Plato founded his school of philosophy there, and it became known by the same name. Later uses of this term carried all the honorable associations of the philosopher's august assembly. Eventually, it came to mean a higher school or a specialized institution such as a military academy. The term was also used by learned societies that were not schools in the ordinary sense, and it later became attached to honorary groups seeking to cultivate and promote the arts and sciences.

Until recent times, art academies epitomized the highest expression of art for an elite audience and for various government bodies, who relied on academy members to design and decorate royal houses and public monuments. An academy's association with these groups and its tendency to support the status quo predisposed outsiders to label all its products "official art." Modernist ideals in particular have done much to devalue and discredit the historical contribution of art academies. Since 1900 academic art has for many people been associated with "bad art," and the term *academic* is often used as a reproach for hackneyed work. That almost all artists revered in modern times by both specialists and the public attended one form of art academy or another is generally overlooked. Significantly, academic art is being reevaluated as various avant-garde ideals based on tentative experiments ex-

A portraiture class is the subject of Joachim Ferdinand Richardt's Painting Class at the Royal Academy of Fine Arts in Charlottenborg Palace *(1839). Among the artists who studied at the academy in Copenhagen, established in 1754, are Caspar David Friedrich and Phillip Otto Runge. (Thorvalsens Museum, Copenhagen.)*

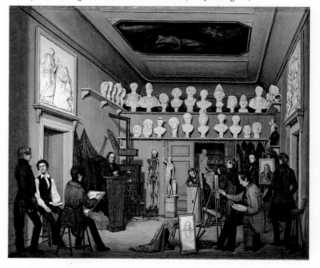

haust themselves and are subject to commercial exploitation. Most of the major academies are still in existence. Society seems to have a need for such institutions, which tend to maintain a balance between tradition and innovation.

The first academies of fine arts were founded in Italy: the Accademia del Disegno (Academy of Design) in Florence in 1563 under the sponsorship of Duke Cosimo I de' MEDICI; and the Accademia di San Luca (St. Luke was the patron saint of artists) in 1593 in Rome. These were primarily associations of artists and patrons that attempted to challenge the powerful and restrictive GUILD system, in which artists were identified with artisans, and to elevate the status of painters and sculptors. Their founders recognized that a permanent break required a drastic revision of the pedagogical system. As against the practical, on-the-job training in the workshops of the guilds, the academies formulated a theoretical component they termed *disegno*—the drawing and design that underlay all artistic activity. This embraced the principles of PERSPECTIVE and ANATOMY. Since Renaissance humanism regarded the human being as the highest expression of the divine ideal, life drawing became the keystone of academic curricula.

The art schools of later academies were divided into two basic sections: one for the study of the antique (plaster casts of ancient Greek and Roman statues and reliefs) and an advanced section for study from live models. Since the academies taught that art should ennoble nature, they claimed that nature itself was an insufficient model for "high" art. The "ideal" works of the ancients compensated for nature's imperfections and were therefore considered a necessary first step in preparation for work with a live model.

The most important academy of modern times was the Académie Royale de Peinture et de Sculpture, founded in 1648 in Paris to overcome restrictions pressed on court painters by the guild. Eventually, this organization was encompassed in the centralized planning of LOUIS XIV and his finance minister Jean Baptiste COLBERT and was subject to their review. They had clear ideas about how art should be used (mainly to glorify the king and to embellish the royal residences), and consequently the Académie Royale systematized its pedagogical procedures. For the first time, problems of technique and composition were explicitly formulated, methods explained, and basic conventions defined. These procedures were in turn handed down to later academies, most notably Madrid's Academia de San Fernando (1752), the Düsseldorf Akademie (1767), London's Royal Academy (1768), the Munich Akademie (1770), and New York's NATIONAL ACADEMY OF DESIGN (1825), founded by the painter-scientist Samuel F. B. MORSE.

Academies burgeoned during the 18th century, often sponsored by the ruling aristocracy since they coveted the implicit commitment to the ENLIGHTENMENT ideals of social progress denoted by academies. Although academies originally obtained support from artists because it gave them improved social and professional status, they proliferated because the dominant classes saw in them an instrument for their own glorification. By also giving the academies a monopoly over art instruction, they could further control the actual images produced. The French Académie Royale instituted a hierarchy of modes that persisted through the 19th century in practice, if not in principle. Subjects for painting were carefully ranked: at the top was history painting and PORTRAITURE, and at the bottom STILL LIFE, LANDSCAPE, and GENRE PAINTING (scenes of everyday life). History painting comprised biblical motifs, events from ancient and contemporary history, especially scenes featuring the king or his ancestors, and allegorical and MYTHOLOGICAL REPRESENTATION.

During the French Revolution, the Académie Royale was suppressed, but it was reconstituted two years later (1795) as part of the Institut de France, with the honorary and pedagogical functions strictly separated. The art school, which eventually became the world-famous ÉCOLE DES BEAUX-ARTS (School of Fine Arts), offered advanced drawing instruction, architectural training, and a series of competitions culminating with the PRIX DE ROME—a special traveling fellowship enabling the gifted pupil to reside at the academy's branch in Rome. Other art academies were established in Rome, for ex-

ample, the American Academy in Rome, founded in 1894 as a school of architecture.

The Royal Academy in London became one of the best regulated in the world under the painter Sir Joshua REYNOLDS, its founder. GEORGE III provided it with "patronage, protection, and support," and he early made his influence felt in selecting as its second president the American expatriate artist Benjamin WEST.

The National Academy of Design in New York is also both a school and a body of professionals. American academies of art such as the National Academy and the PENNSYLVANIA ACADEMY OF THE FINE ARTS, founded in 1805, were unique in admitting women early on, much earlier than the European academies.   ALBERT BOIME

Bibliography: Pevsner, Nicolaus, *Academies of Art, Past and Present* (1940).

academy

An academy is an association dedicated to learning and the arts. It may be a learned society, a professional body, an institution for specialized instruction in a particular subject, or even a high school.

The original Academy was a school founded (c.387 BC) near Athens by PLATO to embody a new educational idea. Plato planned to have a single center for teaching and research that would bring together experts in all branches of learning and that would include younger scholars to give continuity to its work. Mathematics, astronomy, and legislation were three areas in which the Academy became distinguished. The school had a library, a residential building, and a garden. In addition to Plato, the mathematician Eudoxus of Cnidus was a senior member; younger academicians included Aristotle, Xenocrates, and Speusippus. The Academy continued as a center of learning until it was closed by the emperor Justinian in AD 529. It is the direct ancestor of all later Western colleges and universities.

Several academies of poets and artists thrived in France and Italy in the 13th and 14th centuries. The Accademia Platonica, founded in Florence during the 1440s, was the most famous of the Renaissance academies. It stressed the study of Plato's works, the purification of the Italian language, and the study of Dante.

The original Academy, established by the Greek scholar Plato in 387 BC, appears on a mosaic unearthed at Pompeii. The school was named for its location in the grove of Akademe.

The ACADÉMIE FRANÇAISE, chartered in 1635 and still operating today, was established to render the French language "pure, eloquent, and capable of treating the arts and sciences." Other academies, such as the British ROYAL SOCIETY, chartered in 1662, encouraged the growth of experimental science through discussion and occasional sponsorship of scientific projects. Academies of painting and sculpture became common in Europe in the 17th and 18th centuries.

In colonial America, "academies" were established in Pennsylvania, New Jersey, and the Southern states to educate the middle classes in useful skills as well as academic subjects. The word has regained its professional and artistic connotations in modern America without losing the technical overtones of the schools. Perhaps the best-known of the professional institutions is the Academy of Motion Picture Arts and Sciences, which annually gives Academy Awards to outstanding motion pictures, performers, and technicians.

Academy Awards

The Academy Awards are annual awards presented by the Academy of Motion Picture Arts and Sciences for achievement in various categories of filmmaking. Nominees are selected by their colleagues in the movie industry (for example, cinematographers nominate cinematographers and producers nominate producers), and the winners are chosen in secret ballot by a vote of the full academy membership. About two dozen awards are given for American films, of which the most famous are those for best performance by an actor and actress, best director, and best picture. The academy also presents an award for the best foreign film and occasionally presents special awards.

At the awards ceremony, televised each spring, a gold statuette is presented to each winner. This famous symbol of professional success was dubbed "Oscar" in 1931 by a subsequent executive director of the academy, Margaret Herrick, who thought it resembled her uncle of the same name.

The first Academy Awards were presented in 1929, with Paramount's *Wings* (1928) taking the coveted best-picture prize. Since then, Oscars have been awarded to dozens of famous film personalities. M-G-M's 1959 epic *Ben-Hur*, with 11 awards, holds the record for the most prizes won by any one film. Actress Katharine Hepburn and director John Ford hold the most awards given to an individual, 4; 3 awards each have gone to directors Frank Capra, and William Wyler, actress Ingrid Bergman, and actor Walter Brennan.

Bibliography: Michael, Paul, *The Academy Awards, 1927 to 1982* (1982); Osborne, Robert, *The Academy Awards: Years with Oscar* (1977); Sarno, Art, *Academy Awards* (1980).

Academy of Sciences of the USSR

The Academy of Sciences of the USSR oversees the natural and social sciences in the Soviet Union. Organized in 17 scientific, technical, and scholarly departments, including a department for the development of Siberia, the academy supervises more than 260 scientific institutions. Its membership comprises 260 academicians, 412 corresponding and 54 foreign members, and thousands of affiliated scientists. The academy supervises and publishes numerous books and journals yearly and is responsible to the Council of Ministers of the USSR. Founded in 1724 at the request of Peter I (the Great), it was given complete control of Soviet science and technology in 1917. In 1934 its headquarters was transferred to Moscow.   JAMES E. McCLELLAN

Bibliography: Graham, Loren R., *Science and Philosophy in the Soviet Union* (1972); Vucinich, Alexander, *Science in Russian Culture* (1963).

Acadia   [uh-kay'-dee-uh]

Acadia (in French, *Acadie*) is a region of present-day Canada that was a province or colony of NEW FRANCE. Geographically, the term was never clearly defined, but it always referred to at least part of today's Maritime Provinces of Canada (New Brunswick, Nova Scotia, and Prince Edward Island) and to part of Maine.

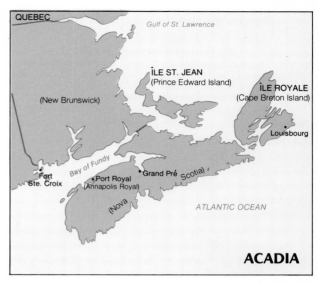

Acadia was a French colony that occupied parts of Canada's present-day Maritime Provinces. Modern place names appear in parentheses.

Throughout the 17th century and until 1713, the colony of Acadia included the mainland of Nova Scotia and some settlements on the Bay of Fundy shore of present-day New Brunswick. The population of the former centered in the settlement of Port Royal (now Annapolis Royal), first founded (1605) by the Sieur de MONTS, and never exceeded 2,100 persons of European descent. Given very little economic support by France and finding itself a pawn in the colonial power struggle among France, Holland, and Britain, the colony was forced to become virtually self-sufficient. It lived off agriculture, fishing, and trade—the last often illicit in the eyes of France.

When the main part of Acadia was ceded to Britain as Nova Scotia in 1713, France retained the rest of the region and tended to refer to all of it, whether under British or French rule, by the traditional name. Some of the French-speaking Acadians moved to Cape Breton and Prince Edward Islands, but most remained in Nova Scotia until they were harshly expelled in 1755 and again in 1758 because they would not swear allegiance to the British crown. Of those among them who survived the resulting severe hardship, many returned later to reestablish themselves in Acadia, or, more commonly, in northern New Brunswick and in pockets of the other Maritimes. Other survivors settled in Louisiana, where their descendants—known as CAJUNS—still preserve a distinct culture. Still others returned to France.   F. J. THORPE

Bibliography: Brebner, J. B., *New England's Outpost: Acadia Before the Conquest of Canada* (1927); Clark, A. H., *Acadia: The Geography of Early Nova Scotia in 1760* (1968).

Acadia National Park   [uh-kay'-dee-uh]

Acadia National Park is a mountainous, forested area along the Atlantic coast of northeastern Maine. The park covers 169 km² (65 mi²) and is primarily on Mount Desert Island, but it also includes several smaller islands and part of Schoodic Peninsula on the mainland. Outstanding features include Cadillac Mountain (466 m/1,530 ft), a fjord called Somes Sound, a 32-km (20-mi) drive that overlooks the ocean, and the Abbe Museum of Stone Age Antiquities. Established as Lafayette National Park in 1919, it was renamed Acadia in 1929. John D. Rockefeller, Jr., donated much of the land.

acanthus   (architecture) [uh-kan'-thuhs]

An acanthus is a leaf-shaped ornament on architectural elements. Based on the leaves of the acanthus plant, the ornament is found especially in the Corinthian and Composite orders in Greek and Roman architecture. Its first known occurrences are on two buildings of the Athenian Acropolis: the Parthenon (447–432 BC), where it is used in acroteria (Pediment plinths); and the Erechtheum (421–405 BC), where it appears on the frieze. Its first use in the Corinthian CAPITAL was attributed (c.425 BC) by Vitruvius to the sculptor CALLIMACHUS of Athens; this may be correct. The style of an acanthus ornament is useful to archaeologists in dating specific monuments.

JOHN STEPHENS CRAWFORD

Bibliography: Dinsmoor, William, *The Architecture of Ancient Greece* (1975); Robertson, D. S., *A Handbook of Greek and Roman Architecture* (1964).

An acanthus, a leafy architectural ornament, adorns this Corinthian capital (right). The decoration, developed in ancient Greece, was patterned after the Mediterranean acanthus (left), or bear's-breech.

acanthus   (plant) [uh-kan'-thuhs]

The acanthus family, Acanthaceae, contains about 250 genera of mainly perennial, thistlelike shrubs native to warmer regions of the world. The name applies most commonly to about 12 species that make up the genus *Acanthus*. Their whitish rose to lilac flowers grow on spikes up to 46 cm (18 in) high, and the leaves are up to 60 cm (24 in) long. The spiny leaves of some species, such as varieties of the Mediterranean acanthus, *A. mollis,* have a hairy, attractive upper surface, and the shrubs are cultivated as border plants. Other genera are also popular, including species of *Ruellia* that are grown in the southern United States.

Acapulco

Acapulco (or in full: Acapulco de Juárez) is a seaport on the Pacific coast of Mexico in the state of Guerrero. It has a population of 462,144 (1979 est.). Located on the bay of Acapulco 305 km (190 mi) south of Mexico City, it is a major resort area and a shipping point for cotton, coffee, and sugar. The rainy season is from June to September, and the average annual temperature is 27.2° C (81° F).

Acapulco was founded (1550) by Spaniards, and until 1815 it was the center for trade with the Philippines and for the transshipment of goods across Mexico to Spain. Fort San Diego was built here in 1616 to protect Spanish shipping. Destroyed by an earthquake (1776) and later rebuilt, Fort San Diego was the site of a Mexican victory over the Spanish in 1821. The climate, atmosphere, deep-sea fishing, and beautiful beaches have made Acapulco an international vacation spot. Many visitors enjoy the cliff divers who leap from the 40-m (140-ft) promontory west of the bay.

Accademia dei Lincei   [ah-kah-day'-meeah day leen-chay'-ee]

Founded in Rome in 1603, the Accademia dei Lincei (Academy of the Linx-eyed) is the oldest extant scientific society in

the world. Derived from Italian literary societies of the Renaissance, the academy flourished until the death of its patron, Duke Federico Cesi, in 1630, when it had 32 members, including Galileo. Sporadically revived in the 18th and 19th centuries, the Accademia Nazionale dei Lincei today serves as Italy's national academy of sciences. It publishes *Atti* (Acts) and *Memorie* (Memoirs).

JAMES E. McCLELLAN

Accademia del Cimento   [ah-kah-day'-meeah del chee-men'-toh]

The *Accademia del Cimento* (Academy of Experiment) in Florence was the first institution devoted solely to scientific experiment. Founded by Leopoldo de'Medici in 1657, the academy consisted of 10 scientists, including G. A. Borelli and Galileo's pupil, Viviani, who performed collective experiments in physics. These were published as the famous *Saggi di naturali esperienze* (1667). The academy ceased functioning in 1667 when Leopoldo de'Medici became a cardinal.

JAMES E. McCLELLAN

Bibliography: Middleton, W. E. Knowles, *The Experimenters: A Study of the Accademia del Cimento* (1971).

acceleration

Acceleration is the rate of change of an object's velocity. The concepts of "speeding up" and "slowing down" actually imply positive and negative accelerations (negative acceleration is commonly called deceleration). For example, if the speed of an automobile traveling in a straight line increases from 15 to 25 meters per second (34 to 55 mph) in 10 seconds, then the auto's average acceleration is 1 m/sec per second (2.1 mph per second). The auto's speed increases every second by an amount equal to 1 m/sec.

Objects falling freely toward the ground experience a uniform acceleration of 9.8 m/sec² (32 ft/sec²) due to gravity.

Types of acceleration other than the uniform linear acceleration described above also occur. Angular acceleration, for example, is the time rate of change of angular velocity. Since velocity is a VECTOR quantity composed of a speed in a given direction, any change in either speed or direction represents an acceleration. An object traveling in a circle has a centripetal acceleration toward the center of the circle because of its constantly changing direction.

GARY S. SETTLES

Bibliography: Halliday, David, and Resnick, Robert, *Fundamentals of Physics* (1974).

See also: FREE FALL; LAWS OF MOTION.

accelerator, particle

A particle accelerator is a device for increasing the energy of electrically charged atomic particles. The particles may be electrons, protons, or charged atomic nuclei. (The particles called neutrons cannot be accelerated individually because they have no charge. They can be given higher energy, however, by accelerating deuterons, the nuclei of heavy hydrogen; the deuteron comprises one proton and one neutron and can be accelerated because the proton carries a charge.) The purpose of increasing the energy of charged particles is to make them useful in studies of nuclear and particle physics, by shooting them at atoms and studying the resulting products with DETECTORS. At very high energies, the charged particles can break up the nuclei of other atoms and interact with other particles, producing transformations that make it possible to study the nature and behavior of the fundamental units of matter. Particle accelerators are also important tools in the effort to develop nuclear fusion devices (see FUSION, NUCLEAR).

The energy of a charged particle is measured in electron volts, where one electron volt is the energy gained by an electron when it passes between electrodes having a potential difference of one volt. Electrons have a negative charge; protons have the same quantity of charge as an electron, but their polarity is positive. Thus, because it includes a proton and an electron, the hydrogen atom is electrically neutral. Other nuclei with several protons in their nuclei have equal numbers of electrons circulating; therefore they too are neutral. If one or more electrons are stripped from an atom, the atom becomes an ion and has a net positive charge equal to the number of electrons removed.

A charged particle can be accelerated only by the application of an electric field, which moves it toward the opposite charge. Beams of particles may be focused by magnets; the effectiveness of the magnets is further enhanced if they are superconducting (see SUPERCONDUCTIVITY). Early machines in nuclear physics used static, or direct, electric fields; but most modern machines, particularly those for the highest particle energies, use alternating fields. The latter are arranged so that particles are exposed to the field only when the field is in the accelerating direction. When the field is reversed and is in a decelerating direction, the particles are shielded from the field by various electrode configurations.

DIRECT VOLTAGE ACCELERATORS

The first accelerator to be used in nuclear physics was the machine designed by J. D. COCKCROFT and E. T. S. WALTON and built in 1932 at the Cavendish Laboratory in Cambridge, England. The machine comprised a high-voltage TRANSFORMER in which the voltage was multiplied by standard engineering techniques to a final value of 700,000 volts (700 kV). An evacuated tube led from the high-voltage terminal to the grounded end of the system. A hydrogen-gas discharge ion source in the terminal was used to direct protons into the tube, where they were accelerated by the high voltage to an energy of 700,000 electron volts (700 keV) to yield the first artificially produced nuclear disintegrations. Cockcroft and Walton received the 1951 Nobel Prize for physics.

Van de Graaff Electrostatic Generator. During the early 1930s another type of direct voltage generator was developed by R. J. VAN DE GRAAFF at Princeton University. In this machine a charge is carried on an insulating belt from a "spray charger," comprising points charged to a relatively high voltage, to a high-voltage terminal where the belt is discharged and the voltage builds up on the terminal. Eventually, if the process is not limited, an electric discharge similar to a lightning bolt will discharge the terminal. With great care, voltages as high as 3 million volts can be achieved. As in the machine built by Cockcroft and Walton, an evacuated tube carries charged particles from an ion source in the terminal to the grounded end of the system, where they are used to disintegrate nuclei.

Later it was shown that much higher voltages are achievable if the machine is enclosed in a tank where a pressure of several atmospheres is maintained. The gas in the tank can be air, or it can be any one of several other gases that seem more suitable for maintaining high voltages. The art of building electrostatic VAN DE GRAAFF GENERATORS continues to advance.

An enormous machine currently being built in Great Britain is expected to be able to maintain 30 million volts on its terminal.

Betatron. Another type of direct-voltage accelerator is the BETATRON, a device in which a varying magnetic field generates the electric field that accelerates a beam of electrons, while the electrons are maintained in a circular orbit by a second magnetic field. The betatron can be thought of as a transformer in which the primary winding excites the magnetic field, and the secondary winding is the accelerating electron beam.

ACCELERATORS USING ALTERNATING ELECTRIC FIELDS

By using alternating electrical fields in the radio frequency (rf) range for acceleration, it becomes possible to accelerate a particle in a number of steps while maintaining the electric fields at manageable levels, thus avoiding problems connected with electrical breakdown.

Linear Accelerator. The simplest rf accelerator is the linear accelerator, or linac. It has different forms, depending on whether the purpose is to accelerate electrons or ions. For the acceleration of ions, an appropriate frequency is 200 million cycles per second (200 MHz) or less. The ions are injected along the axis of a long tank, which is excited by a high-powered rf system in a field pattern that includes an electric field along the axis. While the field is in the decelerating phase, the ions are shielded from it by drift tubes in the tank, which are pipes through which the beam passes. As the particles gain energy and velocity, they travel farther during the deceleration phase; therefore, the drift tubes must be longer toward the end of the tank to match the period of the accelerating field.

The first linear accelerator was built in 1928 by Rolf Wideröe in Norway. Containing three drift tubes, it was used to accelerate sodium and potassium ions. The accelerator was used solely to demonstrate the principle of rf acceleration. During the 1930s further work was done on the ion linear accelerator at the University of California. But the lack of amplifiers for generating high power at high radio frequencies delayed application of the principle until after World War II, at which time rf sources became available through the development of radar. Shortly after the war, Luis Walter ALVAREZ built the first proton linear accelerator in which protons reached an energy of 32 million electron volts (MeV). The power required at a frequency of about 200 MHz was about 2 million watts (megawatts); this very high level limited operation of the machine to pulses less than 1 millisecond long.

Since 1950 several proton and ion linear accelerators have been built, some as injectors for still larger machines and some for use in nuclear physics. The largest accelerator is the 800-MeV machine at the LOS ALAMOS SCIENTIFIC LABORATORY in

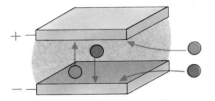

Two means of controlling the motion of a charged particle are an electric field (left) and a magnetic field (right). In an electric field a positive particle (red) is accelerated straight toward the negative electrode and a negative particle (blue) is accelerated toward the positive electrode. In a magnetic field, the moving particles curve toward the south magnetic pole (red) or the north magnetic pole (blue), depending on the charge.

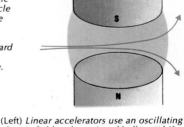

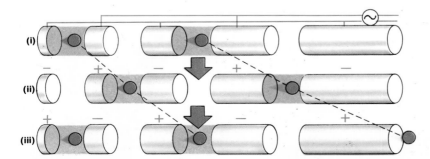

(Left) Linear accelerators use an oscillating electric field and a series of hollow "drift tubes" to accelerate charged particles to high speeds. As positive particles (red) move to the right between tubes, they are pushed by the positively charged tube on their left, and pulled by the negatively charged tube on their right. The electric field on the tubes is reversed only when the particles are within the tubes and shielded from any retarding force. Because the accelerated particles move faster with each alternation of the field (i, ii, iii), it is necessary to lengthen successive drift tubes.

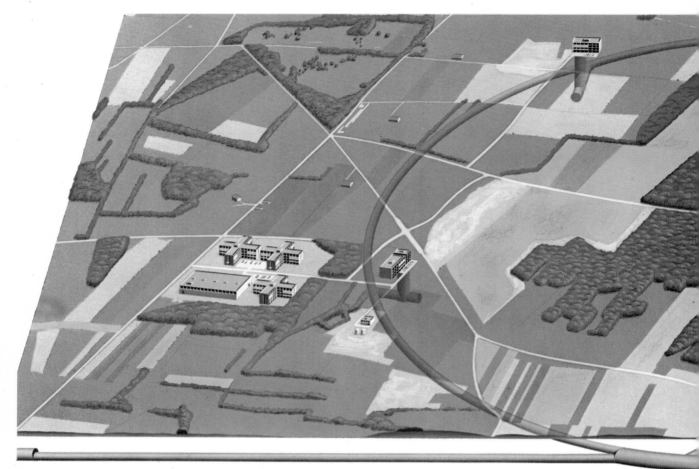

New Mexico. It is used as a meson factory, producing for study the particles of mass that are intermediate between the electron and the proton and that seem to give the force necessary for holding the atomic nucleus together.

Because electrons are much lighter than ions, their velocity at a given energy is significantly higher than that of ions. The velocity of a 1-MeV proton is less than 5 percent that of light, whereas a 1-MeV electron has reached 94 percent of the speed of light. This makes it possible to run electron linacs at much higher frequencies—usually about 3,000 MHz—than those used in ion linacs. The accelerating system for electrons is a few centimeters in diameter, whereas diameters of a few meters are needed for ion linacs. Electron linacs having energies of 10 to 50 MeV are widely used in RADIOGRAPHY as sources of X rays for treating tumors with intense radiation. The largest electron linac in existence today began operation in 1966 at Stanford University. This machine, which is 3.2 km (2 mi) long, yields electrons having energies of more than 20,000 MeV, that is, 20 billion, or giga, electron volts (20 BeV or 20 GeV). It is used as a tool in high-energy physics studies of the fundamental properties of nuclear particles.

Cyclotron. Although the ion linear accelerator evolved slowly, a research report by Wideröe in 1928 was the inspiration for another machine that has proved important: the CYCLOTRON. Ernest LAWRENCE of the University of California read the report the next year and realized that an ion can be deflected in a circle by a magnetic field in such a way that it will return to a gap where it can receive additional acceleration. It was easily shown that, at least at low energies, in a magnetic field the angular velocity of an ion (see MOTION, ROTATIONAL) is independent of its energy. This makes it possible for the ion to return several times to be accelerated again by the same rf field at the same gap. As the energy is increased, the

(Above) *Three underground loops are part of the accelerator facilities of the European Organization for Nuclear Research (CERN) near Geneva, Switzerland. The largest loop is the world's second most powerful proton synchrotron. Its diameter is 2.2 km (1.4 mi) and its area 480 ha (1,190 acres). It can accelerate protons to 500 GeV (a GeV—1,000 million volts—is a measure of particle energy). The smallest loop is a 28 GeV proton synchrotron. The remaining loop is a particle storage, or colliding-beam, ring.*

(Below) *The 200-MeV proton linear accelerator, in operation since 1947 at Brookhaven National Laboratory, Long Island, N.Y., is used to inject high-energy protons into Brookhaven's powerful 33-GeV proton synchrotron. LEBT indicates the "low energy beam transport" at the beginning of the linear accelerator, where the proton beam is injected.*

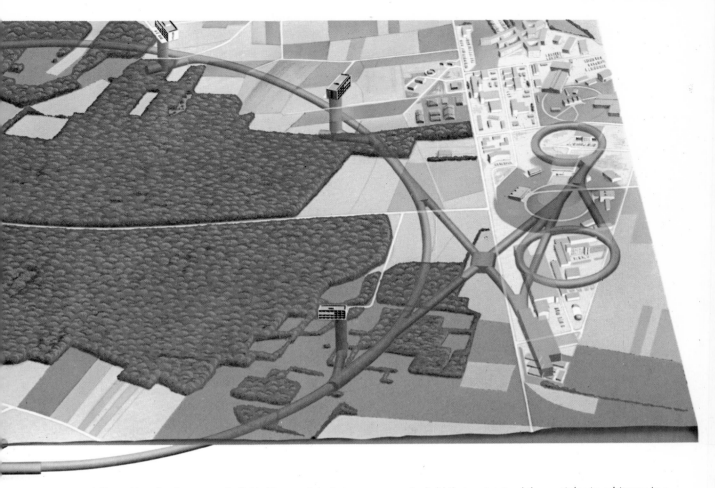

ion is deflected less by the magnetic field. The result is that the ion path is a spiral, beginning near the center of the magnet and eventually emerging with high energy at the edge of the magnet. The linac's drift tubes are replaced by half-pill-boxes (called dees because they are shaped like the letter D), in which the ions are shielded during the deceleration phase of the rf field. With M. S. Livingston, Lawrence built a working cyclotron in 1931. During the 1930s and 1940s larger and larger machines were built at the University of California and elsewhere, primarily for the purpose of accelerating protons and deuterons to energies that reached into the hundreds of MeV.

At energies of a few tens of MeV, relativistic effects begin to appear. Instead of velocity increasing with energy, the ion mass increases. This spoils the operating principle of the cyclotron. In the late 1930s this seemed to set an upper limit on the energy that could be achieved by cyclotrons. In 1945, however, E. M. McMillan in California and V. I. Vekslen in the USSR, working independently, discovered the principle of "phase stability." According to this principle, if the frequency of the accelerating field is changed as the radius of the orbit increases, the energy limit of a cyclotron can be increased indefinitely. Such frequency modulated cyclotrons, also called synchrocyclotrons, were built and soon reached energies of more than 700 MeV.

Synchrotron. At high energies, the magnet required for guiding the particles became massive. Pole diameters approached 6 m (20 ft), which necessitated magnet weights of several thousand tons. To achieve still higher energies, a new device was required. In the machine subsequently developed, which was another result of the principle of phase stability, particles traveled on a roughly circular orbit of constant radius. The

magnetic field that maintained the particles in orbit was increased as a radio-frequency field increased the energy of the particles. Called a SYNCHROTRON in the Western world and a synchrophasotron in the USSR, this machine seemed to have no physical limit on the energy it could attain.

Early synchrotrons were used to accelerate electrons. The first proton synchrotron, Brookhaven National Laboratory's Cosmotron, became operational in 1952. It was the first accelerator capable of producing particle energies above 1 GeV. Several synchrotrons have been built since 1952. Electron synchrotrons, for example, have reached energies of several GeV. The largest machines are for accelerating protons. In the early 1980s the two largest were a 500-GeV accelerator at the CERN Laboratory in Geneva, Switzerland, and a 500-GeV machine at the Fermi National Accelerator Laboratory (Fermilab) in Chicago. By installing superconducting magnets at Fermilab in 1983, the accelerator's energy potential was increased to 1 TeV (1 trillion eV).

Another result of the discovery of phase stability is the microtron, a type of electron cyclotron invented by the Soviet physicist V. I. Veksler. It has been used, primarily in the USSR, to produce energies in the range of a few tens of MeV.

Storage Rings. The most recent development in the accelerator field is the storage ring, in which accelerated beams of particles circulate in opposite directions for periods of several hours. Storage rings are used in studying the collisions of countercirculating beams. Both electron and proton storage rings have been built and put in operation. Construction of the LEP (Large Electron Positron collider), which will accelerate electrons and positrons to energies of 100 GeV, began at CERN in 1983. The still larger Isabelle project at Brookhaven was canceled that same year.

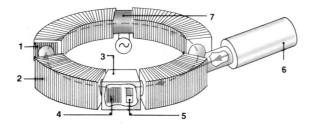

In a synchrotron a beam of charged particles (blue arrows) is made to circulate at a speed near that of light. High-velocity particles are injected into the ring by a linear accelerator (6) and are orbited to near-light speed by an accelerating alternating electric field (7). At such speeds particle mass, and thus outward centrifugal force, increases rapidly with each revolution of the beam. To keep the particles in a fixed circular orbit, this force is offset by steadily increasing the field (1) of the numerous magnetic coils (2). The observation chamber (3) contains a detector such as a spark chamber (4) and the sample (5) to be bombarded by the particles. Recently, synchroton X-ray and UV radiations have also been used to study the atomic structure of materials.

The construction of virtually all types of accelerators was improved by the invention in 1952 of alternating-gradient focusing by E. D. Courant, M. S. Livingston, and H. S. Snyder. This method, which has also lowered the cost of accelerators, involves the alternate focusing and defocusing of particle beams. Used in all synchrotrons and storage rings now being designed or under construction, it drastically reduces the size of magnets needed.   JOHN P. BLEWETT

Bibliography: Bromley, D. A., ed., *Large Electrostatic Accelerators* (1974); Goldsmith, Maurice, and Shaw, Edwin, *Europe's Giant Accelerator: The Story of the CERN 400 GeV Proton Synchroton* (1977); Lapostolle, P. M., and Septier, A. L., eds., *Linear Accelerators* (1970); Livingston, M. Stanley, *Particle Accelerators: A Brief History* (1969); Trefil, J. S., *From Atoms to Quarks* (1980); Wilson, R. R., "The Next Generation of Particle Accelerators," *Scientific American*, January 1980.

See also: FUNDAMENTAL PARTICLES; NUCLEAR PHYSICS.

accelerometer

Accelerometer is a term applied to two classes of test instruments that operate on similar principles but have different purposes: one class measures vibration and shock applied to, or observed on, a structure; the other measures the FORCE required to accelerate or decelerate a body in motion—whether the motion is linear or rotary (see ACCELERATION).

The measurement of vibrations is mainly concerned with the departure of an object from its normal position. Development of linear accelerometers was prompted by the development of guided missiles and space vehicles, because such structures are subject to high vibration and shock conditions on takeoff. Measurement of acceleration is also important in the development of industrial machinery and transportation equipment that are braked automatically.

The basic instrument for measuring vibrations or forces involves a mass suspended from a spring; the mass is mounted within a case attached to the structure under test and filled with some form of fluid. The fluid causes damping, which resists the free vibration of the mass. The period of free oscillation of the spring–mass system is related to the ratio of the stiffness of the spring to the mass and determines whether the instrument will respond as a displacement meter, vibrometer, or linear accelerometer. TRANSDUCERS convert this movement into an electrical signal, which can be recorded on a chart or stored on tape.   FRANK J. OLIVER

accent

Accent is the stress, or vocal emphasis, placed on a certain syllable or syllables in a word. In the word *accent*, the stress is on the first syllable. Rhetorical accent is the stress put on a word because of its function in a line of verse or in a sen-

tence, and metrical accent is the stress pattern established by the meter. If the metrical pattern in a line of verse requires a change in the natural stress, it is called a wrenched accent. A hovering accent occurs when it is not clear whether a syllable should be stressed. (See VERSIFICATION.)

The term *accent* is also applied to the pronunciation and speech patterns of particular regional or other groups. Thus, the English language may be spoken with a Scottish or a midwestern accent, and foreign-language speakers bring distinctive accents to their spoken English.   J. A. CUDDON

accentor

The accentor, any small (13–18 cm/5–7 in) old-world sparrowlike bird of the genus *Prunella*, is found in mountain meadows, scrub vegetation, or forests from Britain across Eurasia to Japan. Both sexes are streaked brownish or reddish, with gray underparts and sometimes a gray head. Of 12 species, the best-known is the sweet-singing European HEDGE SPARROW (*P. modularis*). Accentors feed mainly on insects in summer and on seeds and berries in winter. The cup-shaped nest is built on the ground or in low shrubs, and three or four blue eggs are usually laid. Both sexes feed the young. Accentors constitute the family Prunellidae of the order Passeriformes, suborder Passeres.   ROBERT J. RAIKOW

accessory

An accessory, in criminal law, is one who contributes to or aids in the commission of a crime without participating in the act itself. An accessory before the fact is one who assists or encourages another person to commit a crime; an accessory after the fact is one who, knowing a crime has been committed, helps the criminal escape justice or gives him or her aid or comfort. An accessory during the fact is one who stands by during the crime and does not interfere.

accomplice

An accomplice, in criminal law, is a person who participates knowingly in the commission of a crime. If there is common intent between the person who commits the act and the accomplice, the accomplice is implicated regardless of whether he or she is present. Sometimes the term is used to include accessories after the fact—persons who knowingly gave help to the criminal after the crime was committed. An accused cannot be convicted of a crime on the uncorroborated testimony of an accomplice; in some jurisdictions, accessories have been classed as accomplices to exclude their testimony.

accordion

The accordion is a musical instrument that uses air forced by bellows (center) through tuned reeds to produce its sound. The right hand plays the melody notes on the keyboard, while the left hand plays the harmony by pressing the buttons.

The accordion, a portable reed instrument, produces its sound by means of a bellows suspended between headboards that have studs or buttons for the selection of right-hand pitches and left-hand chords. The horizontal left-hand motion operates the bellows. The instrument was invented (1822) in Germany by Friedrich Buschmann, and was improved (1829) by the Viennese musician Cyril Damian. Popular in folk culture, the accordion became more widely used with the application of a keyboard to the right hand, producing the piano accordion. Concert pieces have been written for it, including a concerto (1946) by the American composer Roy HARRIS. The accordion is the predecessor of the CONCERTINA, invented in England in 1829. ELWYN A. WIENANDT

See also: WIND INSTRUMENTS.

accounting

Accounting is the systematic compilation of financial information for use in making economic decisions. Accountants observe the activities of a business or other organization, and from the welter of events and transactions that take place identify those that are evidence of economic activity. They record the monetary value of these events and transactions. Then they classify and summarize the information and communicate it in the form of financial statements. Finally, accountants interpret financial information by explaining its meaning, uses, and limitations.

BOOKKEEPING is the procedural part of accounting, that is, the day-to-day recording of financial information in a systematic manner. Accounting comprises the rules for determining which events and transactions should be recorded and how they should be measured and classified. Accounting also involves communicating and interpreting the recorded information.

FINANCIAL STATEMENTS

Accounting information is used to make informed decisions. Different users have different needs, but most are concerned with their enterprise's earning power (that is, its ability to generate profits and cash in the future), its resources and obligations, and changes in those resources and obligations. The most commonly used financial statements are the balance sheet, the income or earnings statement (often called a profit and loss statement), a statement of changes in financial position (funds statement), and a statement of retained earnings.

Balance Sheet. A balance sheet presents information about the assets, liabilities, and owners' equity of an enterprise at a particular time. The balance sheet is based on the fundamental accounting equation, according to which a company's assets must equal its liabilities plus the owners' equity. In other words, if the business were sold for the value of its assets, the owners would receive the difference between that value and the amount of liabilities. The balance sheet for an imaginary Apex Corporation is shown at upper right.

The assets of the Apex Corporation, include current assets (relatively short-lived assets such as cash, and assets that are expected to be converted into cash or used in operating the business within a year or so) and property, plant, and equipment. On Dec. 31, 19XX, the Apex Corporation's liabilities included current liabilities of $18,000 and long-term liabilities of $20,000, for a total of $38,000. Its owners' equity, or the difference between assets and liabilities, amounted to $40,000 of common stock (amounts paid by the owners for shares of stock) and $17,000 of retained earnings (earnings not distributed to stockholders).

Earnings Statement. An earnings statement shows the results of a company's operations over a period of time such as a month, a quarter, or a year. An earnings statement for the Apex Corporation is shown at upper right.

In 19XX, the Apex Corporation had net earnings of $49,380. Its sales revenue was $300,000, and its total expenses were $250,620 (obtained by adding $150,000 for the cost of goods it sold to $67,700 for operating expenses and $32,920 for taxes). On the earnings statement, the cost of goods sold is deducted from sales revenue to obtain gross margin. Then other operating expenses are deducted to obtain earnings before taxes. In-

APEX CORPORATION, Balance Sheet
December 31, 19XX

ASSETS

Current Assets:		
Cash	$10,000	
Accounts receivable	20,000	
Inventories	15,000	$45,000
Property, Plant, and Equipment:		
Office equipment, net	$ 5,000	
Store equipment, net	10,000	
Delivery equipment, net	35,000	50,000
Total assets		$95,000

LIABILITIES AND OWNERS' EQUITY

Current Liabilities:		
Accounts payable	$ 8,000	
Notes payable	10,000	$18,000
Long-Term Liabilities:		
Bonds payable		20,000
Owners' Equity:		
Common stock	$40,000	
Retained earnings	17,000	57,000
Total liabilities and owners' equity		$95,000

APEX CORPORATION, Earnings Statement
For the Year Ended December 31, 19XX

Sales revenue		$300,000
Cost of goods sold		150,000
Gross margin		$150,000
Operating expenses:		
Salaries and wages	$50,000	
Rent	9,000	
Advertising	6,000	
Utilities	2,500	
Interest	100	
Miscellaneous	100	67,700
Earnings before taxes		$82,300
Income tax expense		32,920
Net earnings		$49,380

come tax expense is deducted from earnings to obtain net earnings. By observing the trend in earnings and examining the components of earnings, users of financial information can obtain some insight into an enterprise's earning power.

Other Statements. In addition to the balance sheet and earnings statements, accountants prepare numerous other reports. One is the statement of changes in financial position. This explains changes in assets, liabilities, and owners' equity that occur between the beginning and the end of an accounting period. It shows where resources have come from and how they have been used.

Another report is the statement of retained earnings, or earnings not distributed to stockholders through dividends. These are reinvested in the corporation to generate more earnings. Important information is often contained in footnotes and supplementary disclosures explaining items or transactions listed in a financial statement.

ACCOUNTING SPECIALTIES

The discipline of accounting includes the following fields or specialties: financial accounting, managerial accounting, tax accounting, public accounting or auditing, accounting systems, nonprofit accounting, and social accounting.

Financial accounting and managerial accounting are two different approaches to the fundamental accounting task. Financial accounting is concerned with reporting to persons outside the enterprise, such as owners, creditors, and governmental agencies. Financial statements for external users must be prepared in accordance with certain rules known as Generally Accepted Accounting Principles (GAAP), which are established by professional organizations of accountants. Managerial accounting is concerned with reporting to internal management. It furnishes information that will assist management in budgeting and planning and in controlling operations. Managers use managerial accounting information to make decisions about financing, resource allocation, production, and marketing. An important subdivision of managerial accounting is cost accounting, which involves the determination, analysis, and control of costs. Through cost accounting, management can compare the costs of producing each item or service and discover unprofitable activities.

Tax accounting focuses on tax planning and preparing tax returns. Tax accounting for large corporations or wealthy investors is highly complex; tax accountants must be familiar with the tax laws and Internal Revenue Service regulations that affect their clients, and also with a stream of administrative rulings and court decisions.

Auditing is a review of a company's books by outside accountants. Firms hire auditors in order to assure investors and the public that their accounts are fairly presented. To satisfy auditors, financial statements must be prepared in accordance with Generally Accepted Accounting Principles. Auditors must satisfy the public that they are independent and reliable.

Accounting systems is the field of accounting that concerns the design and installation of procedures for collecting and reporting financial information. A good system makes necessary information available when it is needed. Such information may include the accounts receivable balance of each customer, the data needed to pay each employee and to satisfy government regulations for reporting payrolls and deductions, and inventory reports. The system should meet the requirements of accountants and auditors and operate efficiently, effectively, and accurately.

Nonprofit accounting is accounting for nonprofit organizations such as government agencies, schools, churches, foundations, and charitable organizations.

Social accounting, the newest field of accounting, is still in its early stages. It is concerned with measuring the costs and benefits of public programs or corporation activities that affect the public well-being (see COST-BENEFIT ANALYSIS).

CAREERS IN ACCOUNTING

Careers in accounting fall into three general categories: (1) public accounting, (2) private or industrial accounting, and (3) nonprofit accounting. The last category encompasses accounting work for government agencies, churches, charities, educational institutions, and other nonprofit enterprises.

Public Accounting. Public accountants offer their services to the general public for a fee. Those who wish to practice public accounting must pass a rigorous examination prepared by the American Institute of Certified Public Accountants—the accounting profession equivalent of the American Medical Association or the American Bar Association. The CPA examination generally contains four sections: Accounting Practice, Accounting Theory, Auditing, and Business Law. In addition, a candidate must meet certain experience and education requirements that are prescribed by the state.

A principal activity of CPAs is auditing the accounts of business clients. A company's financial statement is more readily accepted by investors and other interested parties if it is accompanied by the favorable report of an auditor. The report customarily takes the following form:

We have examined the balance sheets of Apex Corporation as of Dec. 31, 19XX, and the related statements of income, retained earnings, and changes in financial position for the year then ended. Our examinations were made in accordance with generally accepted auditing standards and, accordingly, included such tests of the accounting records and such other auditing procedures as we considered necessary in the circumstances.

In our opinion, the financial statements referred to above present fairly the financial position of Apex Corporation as of Dec. 31, 19XX, and the results of its operations and the changes in its financial position for the year then ended, in conformity with Generally Accepted Accounting Principles applied on a basis consistent with that of the preceding year.

Certified public accountants prepare tax returns and perform other tax and management advisory services. They also advise clients on the design and installation of accounting systems, budgeting, inventory control, and financial planning.

Private Accounting. Most accountants work as salaried employees in private industry. They prepare general-purpose financial statements and financial reports required by various government agencies; design and install accounting systems; prepare budgets and performance reports; accumulate, analyze, and help control costs; and undertake special cost studies. The person primarily responsible for the accounting function in a business firm is usually given the title of controller.

Large business firms also employ internal auditors who independently review the work of other accountants. Internal auditors also offer recommendations for improving efficiency and internal control.

Internal auditors can obtain a Certified Internal Auditor (CIA) designation by demonstrating professional competence in the field of internal auditing. They must have three years of experience as internal auditors and pass a 12-hour examination given by the Institute of Internal Auditors.

Management accountants can obtain a Certificate in Management Accounting (CMA) if they have two years of experience in management accounting and pass the CMA examination given by the Institute of Management Accounting.

DEVELOPMENT OF ACCOUNTING

Systems of record keeping existed as early as 3600 BC; priests in ancient Babylonia kept accounts of their temple receipts on clay tablets. Modern accounting methods stem from 14th-century Italy, when merchants in trading centers such as Genoa used a double-entry bookkeeping system to account for what they owned (assets) and what they owed (liabilities). The first printed work on accounting was written by Luca Pacioli, a Franciscan monk, mathematician, and tutor to the children of a prince. His *Summa de arithmetica, geometria, proportioni, et proportionalità* (1494) contained a chapter on accounting that described double-entry bookkeeping.

In the 16th and 17th centuries the Italian method of bookkeeping spread to other commercial centers in Europe. It was introduced in London about 1550 but did not become well known for another century. Public accounting developed in England, Scotland, and Ireland. By the middle of the 19th century, companies regulated by Parliament were required to have audits. Public accountants were also employed in bankruptcies, receiverships, and business consulting.

Just as common law and commercial practice came to the United States from England and Scotland, so did the practice of accountancy. The earliest reference to men performing the functions of public accountants in North America is dated 1748. In the 19th century, foreign shareholders and bondholders in large enterprises such as railroads desired that the accounts be audited, and they sent auditors from England to perform the task. This led English and Scottish auditors to open offices in the United States.

The profession grew rapidly in the 20th century with the passage of income tax laws. By 1923 all states had enacted CPA legislation. The responsibilities of accountants were further enlarged in the 1930s with the enactment of laws regulating the sale of corporate securities. World War II brought additional demands on the profession with the introduction of government cost-plus contracts for defense industries. The number of Certified Public Accountants grew from fewer than 250 at the turn of the century to more than 100,000 in the 1970s. Accountants often move into high executive positions in business. Among presidents of large U.S. corporations, accountants are more numerous than persons of any other background. Professional schools of accountancy are developing that may someday parallel schools of law, medicine, and engineering.

JAMES DON EDWARDS

Bibliography: Briloff, Abraham, J., *Unaccountable Accounting* (1972); Brock, Horace, et al., *Accounting: Basic Principles*, 3d ed. (1974); Chatfield, Michael, *A History of Accounting Thought* (1977); Dierkes, Meinolf, and Bauer, Raymond A., eds., *Corporate Social Accounting* (1973); Woolf, Arthur H., *A Short History of Accountants and Accountancy* (1976).

Accra [uh-krah']

Accra, a manufacturing center, is the capital and largest city of GHANA. Situated on the coastal Accra Plains on the Gulf of Guinea, it has a population of 700,000 (1974 est.). The landscape is primarily flat, with the exception of some notable hills, including Legon, where the University of Ghana is located. The main streets of the city radiate from the center and are connected by Ring Road. The temperature varies little from the annual mean of 29° C (84° F); rainfall averages 735 mm (29 in) a year, considerably less than the rest of the west African coast. The economy is based upon the busy port and the manufacturing of processed foods, timber and plywood, and clothing.

The population is primarily of the GA ethnic group, although it consists of substantial numbers of AKAN and EWE. Nearly two-thirds are Christian; most of the remainder adhere to Islam or traditional African religions.

The site of modern Accra has been occupied for centuries by Ga villages. Between 1650 and 1680 European activity began with the construction of a castle and two fortified trading posts near the site of present-day Accra. The city of Accra traces its formation to 1877, when the capital of the British Gold Coast colony was transferred from Cape Coast to Osu, which is one of the Ga villages in the area. In 1898 the Accra Municipal Council was formed to carry out local government functions. Today Accra is a federal area separate from the regions of Ghana. RONALD D. GARST

See also: AFRICA; AFRICA, HISTORY OF.

accreditation of schools and colleges

Accreditation is the practice of certifying schools and universities to ensure that their educational programs and practices meet generally recognized standards. This procedure is usually performed by national governments, but in the United States, which has a long tradition of locally controlled education, it is done by six private regional organizations. These organizations were established between 1885 and 1924, as increases in public education and geographical mobility made it necessary for students, educators, parents, and universities to be able to judge schools with which they were personally unfamiliar. The six regional accreditation associations in the United States, in the order of their founding, are the New England Association of Colleges and Secondary Schools (1885), the Middle States Association of Colleges and Secondary Schools (1887), the North Central Association of Colleges and Secondary Schools (1895), the Southern Association of Colleges and Schools (1895), the Northwest Association of Secondary and Higher Schools (1917), and the Western Association of Schools and Colleges (1924). The Southern Association is the only accrediting body that accredits elementary as well as secondary schools and colleges. In the other regions, the state education department evaluates the performance of elementary schools. Evaluations take into account credentials of the teachers, the courses offered in the school, the amount of money spent on each student in the school, and physical facilities such as the number of library books and the laboratory facilities for science courses. DALE KOCH

acculturation

In anthropology, acculturation is the influence of one society or ethnic group on another as a result of continuous face-to-face contact. Acculturation, or culture contact as it is also called, is a form of DIFFUSION of culture traits and institutions. It differs from other forms of diffusion, however, in that it involves direct interaction between groups.

Although acculturation involves changes in both of the societies and cultures in contact, the term generally is used to refer to changes that occur in a nonindustrial society under the influence of a complex Western society. An example of this is the influence of American culture on the native tribes of North America. Anthropologists often study acculturation resulting from the effect of colonialism and of modern national cultures on nonindustrial peoples.

Acculturation became a strong interest of social and cultural anthropologists in the 1930s. In 1935, the Social Science Research Council formed a committee of three noted anthropologists, Melville HERSKOVITS, Ralph LINTON, and Robert REDFIELD, to define the nature and scope of the acculturation process. Since then others have refined and extended such studies. Recently acculturation brought about by governmental programs or agencies has been called "directed culture change." CHARLES WAGLEY

Bibliography: Bredy, Ivan A., and Isaac, Barry L., *A Reader in Culture Change* (1975); Cohen, Yehudi A., *Man in Adaptation*, 2d ed. (1974); Herskovits, Melville J., *Acculturation: The Study of Culture Contact* (1938); Malinowski, Bronislaw, *The Dynamics of Culture Change* (1961; repr. 1976); Teske, R. H. C., and Nelson, B. H., "Acculturation and Assimilation: A Clarification," in *American Ethnologist*, vol. 1 (1974).

Acetabularia [as'-uh-tab-yoo-lair'-ee-uh]

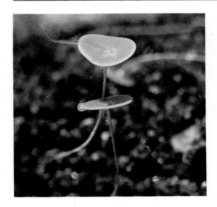

Acetabularia mediterranea, a green algae, has a delicately shaped ridged disk attached to a slender stalk. This species, as well as A. crenulata, is used to study the role of the nucleus of a cell during reproduction.

Acetabularia is a genus of unicellular green ALGAE with a unique umbrellalike shape and a height of up to several centimeters (1-3 in). This curious organism, with its single cell differentiated into a long stalk, a cap, and a rootlike base that contains the cell nucleus, has played a key role in the history of BIOLOGY. Some of the best evidence that hereditary information is transmitted by the cell nucleus comes from experiments with *Acetabularia* conducted by the German embryologist Joachim Hämmerling in the 1930s. Hämmerling found that when he cut one of these algae in fragments, those fragments containing at least some nucleus material could develop into complete new, fertile algae, whereas those without nucleus material might also grow awhile but remained sterile.

Bibliography: Bold, Harold C., and Wynne, M. J., *Introduction to the Algae* (1978).

acetaldehyde [as-uht-al'-duh-hide]

Acetaldehyde, CH_3CHO, also known as ethanal and as acetic aldehyde, is an organic compound belonging to the ALDEHYDE group. It is a colorless liquid with a fruity odor and boils at 20.8° C. Acetaldehyde is produced in industrial quantities by the hydration of acetylene or by the oxidation of ethyl alcohol. Acetaldehyde is widely used as a starting material for the synthesis of many organic compounds.

acetaminophen [uh-seet-uh-min'-uh-fin]

Acetaminophen is a drug often used as a substitute for ASPIRIN to relieve pain and reduce fever. As a pain-reliever, or ANALGESIC, acetaminophen relieves moderate pain of HEADACHES and muscle or peripheral nerve disorders, but not intense pain or the pain caused by spasms of smooth muscles (such as the muscles lining the digestive or urinary tracts). Its virtue as an aspirin substitute is that it does not upset the stomach, as aspirin sometimes does. However, it does not have the anti-inflammatory and antirheumatic properties of aspirin. Acetaminophen's fever-reducing, or antipyretic, properties result from its chemical similarity to the antipyretic drug phenacetin, which is a more toxic chemical.

acetate   [as'-uh-tayt]

In organic chemistry, acetates are the salts or esters derived from acetic acid, CH_3COOH. The salts, such as sodium acetate, CH_3COONa, are obtained by the reaction of acetic acid with bases; the esters, such as ethyl acetate, $CH_3COOC_2H_5$, by the reaction of acetic acid with alcohols. The name *acetate* is used commercially for cellulose acetate, which is used as a synthetic fiber and obtained by the reaction of acetic acid with CELLULOSE.

acetic acid   [uh-see'-tik]

Acetic acid, CH_3COOH, is a weak organic acid and the sour constituent of VINEGAR. The latter is obtained by the enzymatic oxidation of the ethyl alcohol in wine or cider by the bacterium *Mycoderma aceti*; concentrations of 3%–6% acid are reached. In industry, acetic acid is produced by the destructive distillation of wood and by the catalytic oxidation of acetaldehyde. The pure acid is called glacial acetic acid and is a corrosive, colorless liquid with a pungent smell. It solidifies at 16.63° C. Acetic acid reacts with alcohols to form ACETATES that are widely used as solvents. It reacts with cellulose to form cellulose acetate, which is the starting material for rayon and other artificial fibers and for photographic film.

Acetobacter   [uh-see'-toh-bak'-tur]

Acetobacter is a genus of rod-shaped BACTERIA that are found on fruits and vegetables, in souring fruit juices, in vinegar, and in alcoholic beverages. They are commonly called acetic-acid bacteria because of their ability to convert ethyl alcohol to acetic acid (vinegar) and are used industrially for this purpose.   WAYBURN S. JETER

acetone   [as'-uh-tohn]

Acetone, CH_3COCH_3, or 2-propanone, or dimethylketone, is a fragrant, colorless, and flammable liquid that boils at 56.2° C and solidifies at −34.8° C. Acetone is mainly produced by the dehydrogenation of isopropyl alcohol, which is obtained from propylene. Small amounts of acetone are present in blood and urine, but some diabetic patients show larger than normal concentrations. Diabetics evacuate this excess in urine (acetonuria) and through their lungs; its presence in the exhaled air causes an odor known as "acetone breath." In industry, acetone is an important solvent for cellulose nitrate and cellulose acetate and is also used in the production of explosives.

See also: RAYON.

acetyl group   [uh-see'-tul]

The acetyl group is a common constituent of organic molecules; it has the structure CH_3CO. The acetyl group takes its name from acetic acid, which consists of an acetyl group combined with a hydroxyl group, OH. Other simple compounds containing the acetyl group include ACETALDEHYDE, ACETONE, and acetophenone.

acetylcholine   [uh-see'-tul-koh'-leen]

Acetylcholine is a neurotransmitter, an organic chemical that promotes the transmission of electrical impulses from one nerve cell to the next in the autonomic nervous system. When an electrical impulse reaches the tip of a nerve cell's axon, it causes acetylcholine to be released into the space, or synapse, lying between that cell's axon and the dendrites of the next cell. The chemical diffuses across the synapse and binds to receptors on the other side. It reverses the polarity of the receiving membrane, causing the impulse to be transmitted. Acetylcholine is also involved in the transmission of impulses from nerve cells to smooth and cardiac muscles and to certain glands, and from motor nerve cells to skeletal muscles.

See also: BIOPOTENTIAL; NEUROPHYSIOLOGY.

acetylene   [uh-set'-uh-leen]

Acetylene, or ethyne, C_2H_2, is a colorless and flammable gas with a characteristic odor. It sublimes at −84° C at normal pressure. Most acetylene is manufactured by the reaction of water with calcium carbide: $CaC_2 + 2H_2O \rightarrow Ca(OH)_2 + C_2H_2$. This reaction also occurs in carbide lamps, where a steady gas flow is obtained from water dripping on a carbide tablet. Acetylene is also produced by cracking methane obtained from natural gas: $2CH_4 \rightarrow C_2H_2 + 3H_2$. This reaction takes place only at temperatures above 1,200° C, for example, in an electric arc or in special burners that operate with a deficiency of oxygen. Only a part of the gas mixture in these burners is consumed; the unburned gas is cracked by the combustion heat, and acetylene is formed.

The structure of acetylene is $CH{\equiv}CH$. Because of its triple bond, acetylene easily undergoes addition reactions. Vinyl chloride is manufactured from acetylene by the addition of hydrogen chloride: $CH{\equiv}CH + HCl \rightarrow CH_2{=}CHCl$. Similar additions with acetic acid, CH_3COOH, and with hydrogen cyanide, HCN, yield vinyl acetate, $CH_3COOCH{=}CH_2$, and acrylonitrile, $CH_2{=}CHCN$. Both compounds are important in the production of artificial fibers and plastics. Acetylene gas is used in metal cutting and welding because of its high combustive temperature.

See also: ALKYNES.

Achad ha-Am   [ah-kahd' hah-ahm']

Achad ha-Am, b. Aug. 18, 1856, d. Jan. 2, 1927, was a Jewish scholar and Zionist leader originally named Asher Ginzberg. He was born in the Ukraine and adopted the name Achad ha-Am (One of the People) with his first published article, *Lo Zeh ha-Derech* (This is Not the Way, 1889). In that article, he disagreed with those advocating mass settlement in Palestine (see ZIONISM). Like his compatriots Sholem Aleichem and Hayyim Bialik and others in the pacifist *Choveve Zion* movement, Achad ha-Am saw the need for a cultural and spiritual revival of Jews. What was needed was not the Jewish state proposed by Theodor Herzl ("a state of Germans or Frenchmen of the Jewish race"), but a center where "the creative faculties of the nation" and "a system of Jewish education" would radiate outward to imbue ghetto Jews with pride. After World War I, Achad ha-Am emigrated to Palestine, where he worked to achieve the cultural hub he thought so essential to the rebirth of the Jewish people, without impinging on the rights of the Arabs.   SAUL S. FRIEDMAN

Achaea   [uh-kee'-uh]

Achaea was an area of ancient Greece in the northern Peloponnesus and southeastern Thessaly, settled by a people known since the 14th–13th centuries BC as the Achaeans. Probably of Mycenaean origin, the Achaeans by the 4th century BC had formed a confederation of small cities, the first of two Achaean leagues, as a defense against pirates. A more powerful second league was formed in 280 BC, liberating Sicyon (251 BC), and later CORINTH, from Macedonian domination. CLEOMENES III of Sparta warred with the confederacy (228 BC), which first allied itself with Rome and Macedonia and then in 146 BC opposed Rome in a battle at Corinth that resulted in the dissolution of the league. Modern Achaea (Akhaia), a Greek department, roughly corresponds to the Peloponnesian portion of the ancient region.

Bibliography: Larsen, F. A. O., *Greek Federal States* (1968).

Achaemenids   [uh-kee'-meh-nidz]

The Achaemenids were Persian kings who ruled over a vast empire extending from the Aegean Sea to the Indus River from 549 to 330 BC. They were named after an eponymous ancestor, Achaemenes. This was the first world empire of antiquity, and many civil institutions first appeared under the Achaemenids' rule. Universal law (the king's law), the postal system, coinage, and other institutions were used, and ZOROASTRIANISM became widespread in this period. The first Achaemenid ruler was CYRUS THE GREAT, but DARIUS I was the real architect of the empire; DARIUS III, its last monarch, was defeated and succeeded by Alexander the Great. RICHARD N. FRYE

Bibliography: Frye, R. N., *Heritage of Persia* (1962; repr. 1976); Huot, J. L., *Persia: From Its Origins to the Achaemenids*, trans. by H. S. Harrison (1965); Olmstead, A. T. E., *History of the Persian Empire* (1948; repr. 1959).

Achebe, Chinua   [uh-chay'-bay, chin'-wah]

The Nigerian Chinua Achebe, b. Nov. 16, 1930, is perhaps the best-known of contemporary African novelists. His works, written in English, give a sharply realistic view of Ibo society from the late 19th century, when European missionaries first arrived, through the 1960s. Achebe's first and most famous novel, *Things Fall Apart* (1958), was followed by *No Longer at Ease* (1960), *Arrow of God* (1964), and *A Man of the People* (1966).

By focusing on an aspect of African society that was largely unknown to Westerners, Achebe made it possible for other writers whose work was shaped by distinctly African experience to gain world recognition.

Achebe grew up in a small, traditional Ibo community where his father taught in a mission school. He graduated (1953) from Ibadan University and worked for the Nigerian Broadcasting Company. During the Biafran secession from Nigeria (1967–70) he served Biafra as a diplomat. Subsequently, he taught at several universities in the United States and Nigeria. RICHARD K. PRIEBE

Bibliography: Killam, G. D., *The Novels of Chinua Achebe* (1969); Ravenscroft, Arthur, *Chinua Achebe* (1969).

Achernar: see STAR.

Acheson, Dean   [ach'-uh-suhn]

Dean Gooderham Acheson, b. Middletown, Conn., Apr. 11, 1893, d. Oct. 12, 1971, was a U.S. secretary of state (1949–53) and a major architect of the nation's foreign policy after World War II. Acheson graduated from Yale (1915) and Harvard Law School (1918) and was private secretary to U.S. Supreme Court Justice Louis D. Brandeis before joining (1921) a prominent Washington law firm. In 1933, President Frank-

lin D. Roosevelt appointed him undersecretary of the treasury. Except for several brief periods with his law firm, Acheson worked for the State Department from 1941 to 1953.

Acheson helped formulate an active role for the United States in the postwar world, reversing earlier isolationist policies. As undersecretary of state to George C. Marshall, he helped to develop a policy of containment toward communism and to secure aid for Greece and Turkey against Communist-backed insurgents in 1947. He also helped draft the MARSHALL PLAN to rebuild Western Europe.

Appointed secretary of state by President Harry S. Truman, Acheson continued the containment policy by supporting the formation of the NORTH ATLANTIC TREATY ORGANIZATION in 1949. In Asia he attempted to disentangle the United States from the Chinese Nationalist regime on Taiwan while rejecting recognition of the Communist regime on the mainland. In 1950, Acheson used the Soviet boycott of the United Nations Security Council to secure UN support for U.S. intervention in the Korean War. The war also enabled Acheson to push for expansion of U.S. and NATO forces and for West German rearmament. By signing a peace treaty with Japan and supporting France in Indochina, Acheson extended containment to include East Asia.

While in office, Acheson received much criticism. Despite his strong anti-Communist stand, he was accused of having permitted the Communist victory on mainland China, and the military setbacks in Korea brought additional criticism. Senator Joseph R. McCarthy even accused Acheson of harboring known Communists in the State Department. Acheson, however, remained in office until the end of Truman's administration and afterward continued to advise succeeding presidents.

Among Acheson's published writings his autobiographical *Present at the Creation* (1969) won a Pulitzer Prize.
Reviewed by DAVID S. MCLELLAN

Bibliography: McLellan, David S., *Dean Acheson: The State Department Years* (1976); Smith, Gaddis, *Dean Acheson* (1972).

Acheulean   [uh-shoo'-lee-uhn]

The Acheulean, in archaeology, is an Old Stone Age tool industry first identified at Saint Acheul along the Somme River in northern France. Acheulean industries are now recognized as a major Lower Paleolithic tool tradition that existed from about 1,000,000 to 125,000 years ago throughout Africa, Europe, and Western Asia. Essentially a continuation of the CHELLEAN tradition, the Acheulean is characterized by numerous varieties of oval, pointed, and cleaver-edged hand axes with broad, shallow flake scars. Associated forms include a large series of flake tools, including scrapers, side scrapers, borers, and backed knives, and many notched and denticulate tools. Numerous functional differences occur among Acheulean artifacts found at sites in western Europe, north and sub-Saharan Africa, the Near East, and India. The LEVALLOISIAN technique is often associated with Acheulean industries in European assemblages. The Acheulean is associated with *Homo erectus* in lower Bed II at Olduvai Gorge in Tanzania and with *Homo erectus* fossils of somewhat later date at Swanscombe in England. DAVID S. BROSE

Bibliography: Bordes, François, *The Old Stone Age*, trans. by J. E. Anderson (1968); Coles, J. M., and Higgs, E. S., *The Archaeology of Early Man* (1976); Leakey, Mary, *Olduvai Gorge*, vol. 3 (1971).

achievement motivation

Achievement MOTIVATION is the tendency to strive to excel when one knows that performance will be evaluated in relation to a standard. That standard may be an ideal, the performance of others, or one's own past performance. Those who are encouraged to be independent, responsible, and competent in childhood are likely to become more motivated to achieve than others.

When too strong, achievement motivation can produce overexcitement that interferes with efficient performance. This often happens in the opening plays of a football game or when students take an important test. The same strong moti-

Dean Acheson, who was U.S. secretary of state (1949–53) under President Truman, helped establish the North Atlantic Treaty Organization (NATO) as part of the policy of containment of Communist expansion throughout the world.

vation will produce greater investment of time in achievement-related activities, such as schoolwork or a career.

The interest in achievement expressed in the literature of different societies throughout history serves as a gauge of the economic development (and decline) of those societies. The strength of achievement motivation (as distinct from leadership) in men reaches a peak in their thirties and then declines. Research begun in 1968 indicates that women may have a stronger fear of success than do men, which may interfere with achievement motivation in a career. Although this theory attracted much initial support, its conclusions remain unsubstantiated. Subsequent research has focused on the process of achievement (not the consequences) for both men and women.   J. W. ATKINSON

Bibliography: Atkinson, John, and Birch, David, *An Introduction to Motivation*, rev. ed. (1978); Fyans, Leslie J., ed., *Achievement Motivation* (1980); McClelland, David C., et al., *The Achievement Motive* (1976); Stewart, Abigail J., ed., *Motivation and Society* (1982).

Achilles   [uh-kil'-eez]

In Greek mythology Achilles was the strongest, swiftest, and most competent of the Greek heroes who fought in the TROJAN WAR. He was the son of the nymph THETIS, who dipped him as an infant into the River Styx and thus made every part of his body invulnerable—except the heel by which she held him. Knowing that Achilles would die at Troy, Thetis sought to prevent his going by hiding him among the women of the court of King Lycomedes. He was found there by Odysseus, however, and persuaded to join the Greek army before Troy.

According to Homer's ILIAD, in the tenth year of the Trojan War, Achilles withdrew from the fighting after Agamemnon seized Briseis, his favorite slave girl. He sulked in his tent until the death of his close friend Patroclus stirred him to return to battle. The smith-god Hephaestus forged him a fine set of arms, including a famous shield on which was depicted the whole range of the human condition. Thus equipped, he avenged Patroclus's death in a celebrated duel with the great Trojan hero HECTOR. After dragging Hector's body seven times around the walls of Troy behind his chariot, Achilles was persuaded to allow the slain Trojan hero a proper funeral. According to other traditions, Achilles died shortly after when wounded in his heel—his one vulnerable spot—by an arrow fired by Paris or Apollo. His armor was awarded to Odysseus.

Achilles, the great warrior of the Greek army that fought against Troy in Homer's Iliad, *is shown in this vase painting after he had been slain. His body is carried by his comrade-in-arms Ajax.*

achondrite   [ay-kahn'-dryt]

An achondrite is a stony meteorite (see METEOR AND METEORITE) that contains no chondrules (small rounded bodies of chiefly silicate minerals) and only traces of metallic nickel-iron. Achondrites are breccias containing broken fragments whose mineralogy and texture resemble those of a variety of basaltic igneous rocks. Like lunar breccias, achondrites probably formed when basaltic rocks were fragmented and rewelded during meteorite impacts on the surfaces of their parent bodies. In most cases, their constituent igneous rocks crystallized 4.6 billion years ago, but some achondrites were recrystallized much more recently.   LAWRENCE GROSSMAN

acid rain

Acid rain is a common term for pollution caused when sulfur and nitrogen dioxides combine with atmospheric moisture to produce a rain, snow, or hail of sulfuric and nitric acids. Such pollution may also be suspended in a fog, or the pollutants may be deposited in dry form. In recent decades researchers in northern Europe and in North America have reported environmental damage from acid rain, which is sometimes as acidic as vinegar. Acid precipitation has destroyed animal life in some freshwater lakes, damaged forests and crops, eroded structures, and contaminated drinking water with toxic metals that the acid leached from the soil or that were borne along with the other pollutants.

Environmental studies suggest that the pollutants are produced to a large degree by the combustion of oil and coal with a high sulfur content, and by exhaust from gasoline engines. Winds can carry the pollutants from tall smokestacks to sites thousands of kilometers from their source. Studies of the northeastern United States and Canada, for example, contend that acid rain in these regions is caused by the heavy use of coal as fuel in power plants of the midwestern United States. Industrialists, however, suuggest that it could be caused by such natural phenomena as volcanic gas and ash. In 1983, government-sponsored studies definitely placed much of the blame on industrial sources, indicated that affected areas are increasing, and called for control measures even though much more research is still needed.

The most direct action would be to cut off the pollution at its source. Regulations of the Environmental Protection Agency (EPA) require that new coal-burning plants must install expensive scrubbers in their smokestacks to remove most of the dioxides (see POLLUTION CONTROL). Other possible measures include burning only low-sulfur oil or crushing coal with high sulfur content and removing the sulfur. The question of the cost of these measures as compared to the undetermined degree of actual industrial responsibility remains controversial.

Bibliography: Howard, Ross, and Perley, Michael, *Acid Rain* (1982); Ostmann, Robert, Jr., *Acid Rain: A Plague upon the Waters* (1982); Record, Frank, et al., *Acid Rain Information Book* (1982); Rhodes, S.L., and Middleton, P., "The Complex Challenge of Controlling Acid Rain," *Environment*, May 1983.

acidosis   [as-i-doh'-sis]

Acidosis, the presence of excess acids in body fluids, depresses the nervous system and, in severe cases, may lead to coma and death. Acidosis may accompany kidney and liver diseases, diabetes mellitus, or lung disorders that cause too much carbon dioxide to be retained in the body. It can also result from ingesting too many acid salts and from severe diarrhea or dehydration. The opposite disorder is ALKALOSIS.

acids and bases

Acids and bases, and the SALTS produced by the reaction between acids and bases, are principal classifications of chemical substances. These categories were established long before their physical nature or the reasons for their characteristic properties were understood (see CHEMISTRY, HISTORY OF). Acids were recognized originally by their sour taste in water and because they could attack and dissolve some metals. The word *acid* is derived from the Latin *acetum*, "vinegar". Bases were substances that were usually soapy to the touch and that could react with acids in water to form salts.

Definition. Attempts to define acids and bases more precisely began in 1777 when the French chemist Antoine Laurent Lavoisier suggested that acids were compounds that contained oxygen. It was then discovered that hydrochloric acid (HCl) contained no oxygen. The English chemist Sir Humphry Davy proposed in 1810 that hydrogen rather than oxygen was the necessary element in acids. In 1838 the German chemist Justus von Liebig offered the first really useful definition of an acid, namely, a compound (HA) containing hydrogen that can react with a metal (M) to produce hydrogen gas according to the following reaction:

$$HA + M \rightarrow MA + \frac{1}{2}H_2$$

About 50 years later another German chemist, Wilhelm Ostwald, and the Swedish chemist Svante August Arrhenius realized that when acids, bases, and salts are dissolved in water they are separated (dissociated) either partially or completely into charged particles called IONS, that is, positively charged CATIONS and negatively charged ANIONS. Because solutions of ions are good electrical conductors, the substances that produce them are called ELECTROLYTES. By this definition acids were considered electrolytes that produced the hydrogen ion (H^+), and bases as electrolytes that produced the hydroxide ion (OH^-).

Brønsted-Lowry Theory. Although extremely useful, the hydrogen ion-hydroxide ion definition of acids and bases was confined by its nature to solutions that contained water, not organic solvents. In 1923 the Danish chemist Johannes Nicolaus Brønsted and the English chemist Thomas Martin Lowry independently formulated a more general definition. They proposed that an acid was any species that could give up a proton, and a base was any species that could accept a proton. The term *species* includes ions and molecules, and the proton denotes a hydrogen atom that has lost an electron.

Although the definition of an acid was not greatly changed by this theory, that of a base became more general. Any acid, by definition, produces a (conjugate) base by loss of a proton. Thus, for the reaction $HCl + NH_3 \rightleftharpoons NH_4^+ + Cl^-$ the anion Cl^- is the conjugate base of the acid HCl. Because some acids can yield two or more protons by stepwise dissociation, certain species produced can act as both acids and bases; that is, they are AMPHOTERIC COMPOUNDS. For example, the stepwise dissociation of phosphoric acid (H_3PO_4) produces three species, $H_2PO_4^-$, HPO_4^{2-}, and PO_4^{3-}, the first two of which are amphoteric.

Lewis Acids. In 1923 the American chemist Gilbert Newton Lewis defined acids and bases in terms of electron rather than proton transfer. By his theory an acid is a species that can accept electrons from a base to form a chemical bond. The Lewis definition has proved useful, especially in describing systems that do not contain hydrogen. It has not been as widely accepted, however, as the Brønsted-Lowry definition, perhaps because it does not recognize the special role of the hydrogen ion. Therefore, the term *Lewis acid* is generally reserved for reagents that function by accepting electrons from donor molecules without the participation of hydrogen or hydroxide ions.

Acid Strength. The strength of an acid in water is indicated by the extent of its DISSOCIATION. Dissociation is the separation of an acid, HA, into the hydrogen ion, H^+, and its conjugate base, A^-. Similarly, a base MOH can dissociate into the hydroxide ion, OH^-, and a metal ion, M^+. Strong acids and bases are highly dissociated in water; weak acids and bases may be dissociated to the extent of only a few percent, and often considerably less than 1 percent.

The strength of a solution of an acid or base is designated by its pH on a scale of 0 to 14. A pH of 7 is defined as neutral; solutions with a lower pH are acidic, and those with a higher pH are basic, or alkaline. The pH scale is related to the concentration of hydrogen ions in solution so that a tenfold increase or reduction in the hydrogen-ion concentration reduces or increases the pH of the solution by 1 pH unit.

Neutralization. Acids and bases can react with each other to produce a neutral salt solution. As an example, when the same number of molecules of sodium hydroxide (NaOH) and hydrochloric acid (HCl) are mixed, the hydrogen ions (H^+) and hydroxide ions (OH^-) react to form water (HOH, or H_2O), leaving only the sodium ions (Na^+) and chloride ions (Cl^-) in solution. Evaporation of the solution yields NaCl, or table salt.

Inorganic Acids and Bases. Inorganic acids and bases are those made from such minerals as sulfur, phosphorus, and nitrogen. The inorganic acid sulfuric acid (H_2SO_4) is by far the largest single product of the chemical industry. It is used in the manufacture of fertilizer, the refining of petroleum, and the pickling of metals. Nitric acid (HNO_3) is used in the manufacture of explosives and dyestuffs. Of the bases, the hydroxides of sodium (NaOH) and potassium (KOH) are used in soap, and ammonia (NH_3) is used in fertilizer.

Organic Acids and Bases. The several classes of organic acids have characteristic acid groups that are attached to one or more hydrocarbon (R) groups. Thus CARBOXYLIC ACIDS have the general formula RCOOH, and sulfonic acids, the formula RSO_2OH. AMINES (R_nNH_{3-n}) are an important class of organic bases. They form their conjugate acids by attaching an additional proton to the nitrogen atom.   C. F. BAES, JR.

Bibliography: Bates, R. G., *Determination of pH: Theory and Practice*, 2d ed. (1973); Brown, Theodore L., and LeMay, H. E., *Chemistry* (1977); Drago, Russell S., and Matwiyoff, Nicholas A., *Acids and Bases* (1968); Hamm, D. I., *Chemistry: An Introduction to Matter and Energy* (1965).

See also: BUFFER; TITRATION.

acmeists   [ak'-mee-ists]

The acmeists were a group of Russian poets, including Anna AKHMATOVA and Osip MANDELSTAM, who were active between 1912 and 1922. Their concreteness of imagery and coherent expression were a reaction to the mystical vagueness of the Russian symbolists. Their name is derived from the Greek *acme*, "highest point," or "perfection."

Bibliography: Strakhovsky, Leonid I., *Craftsmen of the Word: Three Modern Poets of Russia: Gumilyov, Akhmatova, Mandelstam* (1949).

acne   [ak'-nee]

Acne is a disorder of the sebaceous glands of the skin. Sebaceous glands secrete through pores and hair follicles—which are most abundant on the face and scalp—a fatty lubricant known as sebum. Acne occurs when the pores become clogged with sebum. Blackheads—external plugs formed of sebum and dead cells—may be invaded by bacteria, which cause pus-filled inflammations, or pimples. The overlying skin may become stretched to the point of rupture, resulting in lesions and, in prolonged severe cases, eventual scarring. Adolescents are most prone to acquiring a case of acne.

The exact cause of acne is not known but is believed to be related both to genetic predisposition and to the increased hormonal activity that occurs during puberty. Poor skin hygiene and lack of sunlight or exercise can often aggravate acne. In a reaction comparable to allergy, certain foods may increase irritation in susceptible persons.

A physician may evacuate the contents of blackheads and pimples under aseptic conditions, thus lessening the possibility of scarring. Astringent lotions are sometimes used to counteract the oiliness of the skin, and therapeutic creams are considered useful in releasing blackheads. Antibiotics, particularly tetracycline, are prescribed in more severe cases of acne to reduce infection from bacteria and prevent the appearance of new lesions. Long-term use of antibiotics, however, can result in bacterial resistance. A drug related to vitamin A is currently being tested as a promising means of treating acne. The appearance of scarred skin may be improved by a surgical procedure called dermabrasion.

PETER L. PETRAKIS

Acoma   [ak'-oh-maw]

Acoma, a pueblo founded about AD 1100, is possibly the oldest continuously inhabited settlement in the United States. It is located 135 km (84 mi) west of Albuquerque, N.Mex. Perched atop a sandstone mesa that rises 109 m (357 ft) above the valley floor, it stands at an elevation of 2,130 m (about 7,000 ft). Since prehistoric times, a PUEBLO Indian people who speak a Western Keresan language have lived at Acoma in three-storied homes made of flat stones plastered with adobe and supported with wooden beams. Their irrigated fields of maize, beans, and squash are located below the mesa approximately 19 km (12 mi) away at Acomita. Acoman legend refers to ancestors pushing their way up from the worlds below to the present world. Their mother-creator, Latiku, is credited with establishing the religious and social order of the Acomans, who are organized into matrilineal clans with animal and plant names. The male head of the Antelope clan, traditionally considered the father of the KACHINAS (spirits who bring rain for the crops), was also the religious and political head of the village.

Spaniards led by Francisco Vázquez de Coronado contacted the Acoma people in 1540; in 1599, Juan de Oñate brought about their conquest. The missionary father Juan Ramírez arrived in 1629 and began construction of a church dedicated to Saint Stephen, who later became patron saint of the Acomans. A proud and independent people, they supported the Pueblo Revolt of 1680; only after intense fighting did they again submit to colonial rule in 1699. The aboriginal population of Acoma at the time of European contact was probably about 3,000. In 1760, 1,052 villagers were reported; in the 1920s their numbers had declined to fewer than 1,000. Their population in 1980 was 2,940. Although a majority of the Acoma people are Catholic, a number of social and religious traditions of village life are maintained.   FRED W. VOGET

Bibliography: James, Harold L., *Acoma: The People of the White Rock* (1970); Minge, Ward A., *Acoma: Pueblo in the Sky* (1976); White, Leslie, *The Acoma Indians* (1932; repr. 1973).

Aconcagua   [ah-kohn-kah'-gwah]

Mount Aconcagua is a peak in the Andes Mountains in Argentina near the Chilean border and about 88 km (55 mi) north-northeast of Santiago. It is the highest peak in the Western Hemisphere, rising 6,960 m (22,834 ft) above sea level and a total of 12,954 m (42,500 ft) above the deep ocean trench off the nearby coast of Chile. The peak was first reached in 1897 by Mattias Zurbriggen.

Aconcagua's west and northwest sides are gently sloped, windswept, and covered with loose rock. The steeper south and southwest sides are mainly clear of snow and ice except for a glacier flanked by mountain spurs. The mountain is located in a region of frequent earthquakes. Its treacherous climate, with temperatures as low as −25° C (−13° F) and strong winds, makes it difficult to climb.

acorn worm: see HEMICHORDATE.

acoustics: see SOUND AND ACOUSTICS.

Acre   (Brazil)   [ah'-kray]

Acre is a state in western Brazil, bordered by Peru on the west and south and Bolivia on the east. It covers an area of 152,590 km² (58,915 mi²) and has a population of 288,100 (1980 est.). The capital is Rio Branco. Located in the rain-forest zone, Acre is a major producer of rubber and brazil nuts, and coffee, rice, and sugar are grown. Acre was ceded to Bolivia by Brazil in 1867, but it was settled in the late 19th century by Brazilian rubber gatherers who declared Acre an independent nation in 1899. Acre was reannexed to Brazil as a territory in 1903, and it became a state in 1962.

Acre   (Israel)   [ahk'-ur]

Acre (Hebrew: Akko) is a coastal city of Israel, on the Bay of Haifa, 19 km (12 mi) north of Haifa. It has a population of 38,700 (1980 est.). Although its once thriving port has filled with sand, its beaches are popular with vacationers. A fortified harbor and old crusader capital, Acre has been besieged repeatedly over the centuries by Romans, Arabs, Crusaders,

Turks, and British. The Crusaders called it Saint Jean d'Acre. In 1922, Acre became part of the British mandate of Palestine, and in 1948, part of Israel. The ancient section of the city includes the Crypt of Saint John, dating from the 13th century, and old Arab inns. The Mosque of Jazzar Pasha and other elaborate buildings were constructed in the 18th century. The British citadel prison in Acre was the scene of fierce Jewish resistance fighting in 1948.

acrobat: see CIRCUS.

acrophobia: see PHOBIA.

Acropolis   [uh-krahp'-uh-lis]

The term *acropolis* (Greek, "uppermost city") refers to the highest and most defensible part of an ancient Greek city. In classical Greece every important settlement had an acropolis, on which were placed temples, treasuries, and other important civic buildings. In times of attack the acropolis became the last bastion of defense.

The best-known acropolis is that of Athens, upon which the ancient Greeks built one of the finest groups of temples in the ancient world. The Athenian Acropolis rises from the plain of Attica to 152 m (500 ft) above sea level. First settled in Neolithic times, by the Bronze Age (c.3000 BC) the plateau was occupied by houses and a royal palace. The buildings that survive date from an extensive building program initiated by the 5th-century BC statesman PERICLES. The major monuments, in the order in which they were built, are the temple of Athena Parthenos (the Parthenon), 447–432 BC; the Propylaea (gateway), 437–432 BC; the temple of Athena Nike, 427–424 BC; and the temple of Erechtheus (the Erechtheum), 421–405 BC. Sizable portions of these structures are still standing, but little remains of the other buildings and enclosures that filled the Athenian Acropolis.

Parthenon. The largest building atop the Athenian Acropolis is the Parthenon, a temple dedicated to Athena Parthenos (Athena the Warrior Maiden). It is a Doric building, made entirely of white pentelic marble and surrounded by free-standing columns. It was designed by ICTINUS and CALLICRATES, with sculpture by PHIDIAS. The sculpture was composed of a giant ivory and gold figure of Athena, a continuous frieze band inside the colonnade depicting the Panathenaic procession, and metope panels depicting, among other scenes, the Battle of the Lapiths and the Centaurs. The temple was unusual in that it had two rooms within its cella, the enclosed space inside the colonnade. The smaller room, dedicated to the maiden goddess (parthenon), eventually lent its name to the whole building. The larger chamber housed the huge image of Athena by Phidias, which much later was removed by the Crusaders to Constantinople and there destroyed.

The Parthenon later served in succession as a Byzantine church, a Roman Catholic church, a Turkish harem, and a Turkish powder magazine. On Sept. 16, 1687, a direct hit by Venetian artillery caused the powder in the Parthenon to explode, scattering debris across the Acropolis. The remaining sculpture rapidly began to disappear. A few pieces were taken to France by the duc de Choiseul, but most of it was sent to Britain in 1802–03 by the 7th earl of ELGIN. In 1922–23 the Greek archaeologist Nicolas Balanos collected the remaining fragments of the temple and restored a number of columns and parts of the entablature that they carried.

Propylaea. The Propylaea, located at the west end of the hill, is the gateway into the Acropolis. Although never completed, the present structure was worked on in 437–432 BC by the architect Mnesicles. His gate was intended to replace an earlier one built under the administration of Peisistratus in c.530 BC. The inner and outer colonnades are Doric, recalling those of the Parthenon although they are much more severe. Inside are more slender Ionic columns. Flanking the central gate-hall are two chambers. One was used as a *pinakotheke* ("painting gallery"); the other, although never completed, was probably intended as a *glyptotheke* ("sculpture gallery").

Temple of Athena Nike. The diminutive temple of Athena

1. The Parthenon
2. The Propylaea
3. The Temple of Athena Nike
4. The Erechtheum
5. Bronze statue of Athena Promachos

The early Greeks often chose an easily defended hill, or acropolis, as the central feature of their cities. The most famous of these, the Acropolis of Athens, contains some of the finest surviving classical structures. This complex of temples was built during the 5th century BC.

Nike (Athena of Victory), which measures only 5.64 by 8.34 m (18.5 by 27 ft), stands southwest of the Propylaea, on a rebuilt Mycenaean fortification. The only wholly Ionic building on the Acropolis, it was designed by the architect Callicrates in a delicate style, with four columns on the front and on the rear porches. The Nike temple remained intact until 1686, when the Turks dismantled the building to use the blocks in fortifications. It was reassembled hastily in 1836 and then more carefully reerected by Balanos and A. K. Orlandos in 1935–40.

Erechtheum. The temple of Erechtheus, or *Erechtheum*, was the last, the most complex, and the most richly embellished of the Periclean buildings. The unorthodox two-level plan adopted by the architect (perhaps MNESICLES) served to accommodate several sites long held sacred by the Athenians. The upper portion of the temple, facing east, contained a sanctuary dedicated to Athena Polias (Athena Protectress of the City); on a lower level at the west end were three smaller chambers dedicated to local gods and to Poseidon. The large porch opening to the north, enclosed by elegantly proportioned Ionic columns, protected a stone believed to have been struck by Poseidon's trident.

The Erechtheum is best known for its caryatid porch on the south side, facing the Parthenon. The six caryatids, or columns in the form of female figures, have basketlike capitals on the women's heads. Like the Parthenon, the building was variously used as a church and later as a Turkish harem.

LELAND M. ROTH

Bibliography: Bruno, V. J., ed., *The Parthenon* (1974); Carpenter, Rhys, *The Architects of the Parthenon* (1970); Hopper, R. J., *The Acropolis* (1971); Travlos, John, *Pictorial Dictionary of Ancient Athens* (1971).

See also: GREEK ARCHITECTURE.

acrostic [uh-kraws'-tik]

An acrostic is formed when the words of a poem or other composition·are so ordered that the first, last, or middle letters (sometimes syllables) of successive lines make a word or phrase when read vertically or diagonally. Acrostics are found in the Old Testament and were especially popular among the early Christians. Two of history's better-known examples are plays on the name Jesus Christ. The initial Greek letters in the words making up the phrase "Jesus Christ, Son of God, Savior" spell out ΙΧΘΥΕ ("fish"), a symbol with which Jesus and his followers were associated. A Latin verse was triply acrostic in spelling out Jesus, IESVS in Latin, with the center IESVS bisecting a horizontal IESVS to form a Greek cross. Acrostics, motivated by the delight in wordplay, were also a characteristic feature of Renaissance poetry.

Acrostics is also a word-building game. A word of at least three letters is written vertically down the left side of a sheet of paper and also, with the letters reversed, down the right side. The space between the columns is filled with the same number of words as there are letters in the key word, starting and ending with the letter at either side. The winner is either the first person to fill in all the words, or the player with the longest or most original words.

acrylonitrile

Acrylonitrile is a colorless, flammable, toxic liquid with a boiling point of 77° C. An organic molecule with formula $CH_2CH\ CN$, acrylonitrile is slightly soluble in water and completely soluble in most organic solvents. Because acrylonitrile readily undergoes POLYMERIZATION, it is a valuable precursor to such common acrylic fibers as Orlon and Acrilan. It is also used in the making of surface coatings, adhesives, and beverage and food containers. In 1977, studies found acrylonitrile to be a potential carcinogen. The United States government set standards for exposure in processing plants in 1978. A 1977 order, later overturned, banned its use in beverage containers because of fear that the molecule could migrate into the liquid contents.

act: see NARRATIVE AND DRAMATIC DEVICES.

act of God

An act of God is the legal term for a natural event of overwhelming force, an accident or disaster not resulting from human action and that no amount of prudence or foresight could have prevented. Under the law of negligence, a party cannot be held responsible for resulting damages or injuries.

ACT Tests: see EDUCATIONAL MEASUREMENT.

Actaeon   [ak'-tee-uhn]

In Greek mythology, Actaeon was a hunter, the son of Aristaeus. When he unintentionally surprised the goddess Artemis bathing naked in the woods, she changed him into a stag, and his dogs killed him.

ACTH: see ADRENOCORTICOTROPIC HORMONE.

acting

Acting is the practice of performing a role so that an audience may participate in the illusion that it is observing and reacting to a character rather than the actor. No simple definition can fully cover what the actor does to create this illusion. Over the centuries many differing opinions have been held about what acting is and how it is achieved. But most theorists agree that a strong link exists between acting and the imaginative structures created in childhood, in everyday social interaction, and in religious rituals. Many cultures have been able to touch deep and fundamental truths about life through the disciplined and structured playing out of events.

THEORIES
Acting theory began with the effort to discover how actors might induce a creative state that would free them from extreme variations of performance. Foremost among the 20th-century theorists of Western theatrical traditions who sought to create a practical system for disciplined creativity was Konstantin STANISLAVSKY, founder (1898) and director of the MOSCOW ART THEATER. Stanislavsky approached acting by dividing it into two parts: work on the self and work on the role. In the first area he stressed the need for freeing spontaneous impulses, for responding to imaginative stimuli, for concentrating attention, and for using personal experience as the basis for portraying character. Work on the role stressed a full understanding of the world of the character within the play. The character's needs, wants, and habits were to be communicated by a system of physical actions.

Most modern theories of acting have taken Stanislavsky's work as their starting point, even if their major thrust is not the direct emotional involvement of the realistic theater. Bertolt BRECHT, whose work with the Berliner Ensemble in a style he called epic realism aimed at putting the audience in a judicial frame of mind, owed much to Stanislavsky (see EPIC THEATER). Jerzy GROTOWSKI, director of the POLISH LABORATORY THEATER, stresses the need for a rigorous physical and spiritual discipline, but even he claims that his almost acrobatic performance mode is aimed at the revelation of inner truth.

Controversy arises over the question whether acting is an internal or external process or a blend of the two, but many actors and theorists doubt whether the distinction is useful. Those who favor a holistic approach note that almost all external behavior has its roots in the workings of the inner life. The French actor François Joseph TALMA put it this way about 200 years ago: "To form a great actor, the union of sensibility and intelligence is required."

TRAINING
Whether in a college or in a professional conservatory, actor training seeks to achieve the union of which Talma spoke. Professionally oriented programs usually include study in script analysis and scene studies, ensemble techniques, improvisation, and sensory and imaginative awareness training, as well as the development of physical, voice, and speech skills. Fencing, dance, martial arts, and circus techniques are often taught. Some courses include specialized camera work.

HISTORY
Acting in a formal sense probably began in Greece in the 5th century BC, growing out of the celebration of religious festivals. The Greek THESPIS, standing apart from the chorus to de-

(Below) *The comic role of the slave, as portrayed by this Greek ceramic figure (2d century BC), was popular in Greek plays.*

(Above) *Molière* (far left), *a famous 17th-century French playwright and actor, introduces the presentation of a farce by his theatrical company, the Comédie Française. Acting of this era was highly stylized because of the lingering influence of theories about classical Greek tragedy.*

(Left) *Sir Henry Irving, the first British actor to achieve knighthood, appears in the title role of Hamlet in 1874. Like many actors before and since, Irving established his career by his interpretation of characters from the plays of Shakespeare.*

Will KEMP, who created many great comic roles such as Falstaff, and Richard BURBAGE, who first played most of the major tragic roles. Female roles were played by boys, since women were not allowed on the public stage until the Restoration of the Stuarts in the middle of the 17th century.

In France, between 1658 and 1673, Molière also combined the functions of actor and playwright. Building on the *commedia dell'arte* tradition, Molière wrote and played in a number of comedies. The acting company that he founded eventually became the COMÉDIE FRANÇAISE, which continues today.

In the late 17th century, actors emerged as powerful figures in their own right. By the 18th century many of Shakespeare's plays had been rewritten to suit the tastes of the leading English actors and their audiences. A florid and artificial style of acting held the stage until David Garrick appeared in 1741 and introduced a style that was, by the standards of his day, extremely realistic, using simplified movement and gesture and a diction closer to the everyday manner of speech.

At about the same time, America's first significant acting company was established. Lewis Hallam opened his performance schedule in Williamsburg, Va., in 1752 and then toured from the Carolinas to New England.

The 19th century was a golden age for actors in the United States. English stars such as Edmund KEAN, Fanny and Charles

liver a separate solo text, is the first recorded actor. Later, Aeschylus added a second actor to his tragedies, making dialogue and play structure possible. Sophocles introduced a third actor to the cast, increasing complexity. Euripides gave drama greater potential by diminishing the use of the chorus.

Acting under the Romans grew increasingly bawdy and further removed from its Greek origins. Performances were stopped by the Christian church in the 6th century. For several centuries actors were denied access to the rites of the church and were reduced to the status of jugglers and mountebanks. During the Middle Ages acting was revived, although mostly on an amateur and church-related level. Simple plays based on the Bible and the lives of the saints were performed by members of trade guilds and by priests.

It was not until the Renaissance that acting became a profession once again. Versions of Greek and Roman plays were performed throughout Italy in elaborate theaters at the great courts of the princes. Troupes of actors meanwhile traveled around playing pieces that were essentially improvisations built on traditional characters and situations, developing a style called COMMEDIA DELL'ARTE. These plays and players inspired playwrights such as MOLIÈRE and GOLDONI to incorporate their free spirit and traditional characters into more formal plays.

In Elizabethan England, theatrical companies played in a simple style to audiences that represented a cross section of the community. Like many playwrights of his time, William SHAKESPEARE was himself an actor, taking such roles as the ghost in *Hamlet*. Prominent in Shakespeare's company were

(Above) *Beggars congregate in a dank basement in Konstantin Stanislavsky's 1902 production of Gorky's* The Lower Depths. *His insistence on a more natural style of expression led to the technique known today as "method acting."*

(Left) *Sir Laurence Olivier, one of the greatest contemporary British actors, appears in the 1956 screen adaptation of Richard III. Since 1930, Olivier has made several films of Shakespeare's plays, including* Henry V *(1944) and, more recently, The* Merchant of Venice *(1974).*

KEMBLE, and William Charles MACREADY toured the nation. American stars such as Edwin Forrest and Edwin Booth had devoted followers. Joseph Jefferson, playing in *Rip Van Winkle*, was among the most popular comedy stars.

The stars' domination of the theater began to diminish when George II, duke of SAXE-MEININGEN, formed a company in Germany devoted to the notion that all members of the ensemble were of equal importance. Between 1874 and 1890 his troupe toured widely and greatly influenced André ANTOINE, proponent of naturalism who founded the THÉÂTRE LIBRE in Paris in 1887.

Realistic ensemble acting came to dominate early 20th-century theater. The style was exemplified by the work of Stanislavsky and the Moscow Art Theater, especially in their productions of the plays of Anton CHEKHOV. In the United States, Stanislavsky's work was taken up by the GROUP THE-ATER, which included, among others, Lee STRASBERG, a founder of the ACTORS STUDIO. Stanislavsky's system came to be called The Method in popular discussion. Such teachers as Uta HA-GEN, Stella Adler, Herbert Berghof, and Sandford Meisner have contributed to the widespread use of Stanislavsky's system.

The Method inspired other groups that have grown in individualistic ways. For example, the POLISH LABORATORY THE-ATER has influenced many groups. In the United States, the profound influence of Viola Spolin, who created a systematic approach to theater improvisation, can be seen in the work of The Second City Company and Paul Sills's Story Theater. Stanislavsky's emphasis on inner truth has not been overthrown, but it has been interpreted and adapted to a number of different ends. In recent years American directors such as Joseph CHAIKIN, Richard SCHECHNER, and Andre Gregory have founded acting companies that perform in a style grounded in human reality. They incorporate both the improvisational thrust of Spolin and the physical activity characteristic of Grotowski. Today, productions everywhere blend elements of realistic and nonrealistic acting styles to produce what they consider truthful human characters.   RICHARD P. BROWN

Bibliography: Billington, Michael, *The Modern Actor* (1973); Chaikin, Joseph, *The Presence of the Actor* (1972); Cole, Toby, and Chinoy, H. K., eds., *Actors on Acting* (1970); Grotowski, Jerzy, *Towards a Poor Theatre* (1968); Hagen, Uta, with Frankel, Haskel, *Respect for Acting* (1973); Spolin, Viola, *Improvisation for the Theatre* (1963); Stanislavsky, Konstantin, *Stanislavsky on the Art of the Stage*, trans. and ed. by David Magarshack (1961); Willet, John, trans., *Brecht on Theatre* (1964).

See also: COSTUME AND MAKEUP, THEATRICAL; MIME AND PANTOMIME; THE-ATER, HISTORY OF THE.

actinide series   [ak'-tuh-nyd]

The actinide elements are the 14 chemical elements that follow ACTINIUM in the PERIODIC TABLE. Because of some chemical similarities, actinium is usually included in the series. All of the actinides are radioactive, because their nuclei are so large that they are unstable and release great amounts of energy when they undergo spontaneous FISSION. Most of the actinides are not found in nature but are artificially produced in the laboratory.

Actinides Found in Nature. Two of the actinides have isotopes with such a long HALF-LIFE that they have not completely decayed since the Earth was formed. One isotope of thorium, Th-232, has a half-life of 14 billion years and has an abundance of 12 parts per million in the Earth's crust. It is a principal constituent of some minerals, notably thorite and monazite (a mixture of rare earth phosphates and thorium oxide). Three isotopes of uranium are found in nature. Their isotopic abundances and half-lives are U-234, 0.006%, 230,000 years; U-235, 0.72%, 696 million years; and U-238, 99.27%, 4.51 billion years.

The overall abundance of uranium in the Earth's crust is about 4 parts per million, and it is concentrated in many minerals, principally pitchblende, autunite, torbernite, and carnotite. Deposits of uranium minerals large enough to be profitably mined are found principally in parts of Africa and in Canada, the Soviet Union, and the southwestern United States.

Actinium and protactinium, as well as some isotopes of thorium and uranium, are found in nature as decay products of Th-232, U-235, or U-238. All of the heavier actinide elements, the TRANSURANIUM ELEMENTS, as well as some isotopes of the lighter actinides, have been synthesized since 1940. Small amounts of neptunium-239 and plutonium-239 have been found in uranium ores; they are produced by the absorption of neutrons generated by the spontaneous fission of U-238.

THE ACTINIDE ELEMENTS

Atomic Number	Name	Symbol	Melting Point, °C	Most Stable Isotope	Half-life
89	Actinium	Ac	1,050	^{227}Ac	21.8 yr
90	Thorium	Th	1,750	^{232}Th	1.4×10^{10} yr
91	Protactinium	Pa	1,570	^{231}Pa	32,800 yr
92	Uranium	U	1,132	^{238}U	4.51×10^{9} yr
93	Neptunium	Np	639	^{237}Np	2.14×10^{6} yr
94	Plutonium	Pu	640	^{244}Pu	7.6×10^{7} yr
95	Americium	Am	995	^{243}Am	7,400 yr
96	Curium	Cm	1,350	^{247}Cm	1.6×10^{7} yr
97	Berkelium	Bk	986	^{247}Bk	1,400 yr
98	Californium	Cf	900	^{251}Cf	800 yr
99	Einsteinium	Es		^{254}Es	276 day
100	Fermium	Fm		^{257}Fm	80 day
101	Mendelevium	Md		^{258}Md	56 day
102	Nobelium	No		^{259}No	1.5 hr
103	Lawrencium	Lr		^{256}Lr	35 sec

Discovery of Actinide Series. Many chemists at first considered actinium to be chemically similar to lanthanum, thorium to hafnium, protactinium to tantalum, and uranium to tungsten. Neils Bohr suggested in 1923, however, that actinium might begin a series of elements similar to the series of rare earth elements and filling the 5f subshell, parallel to the LAN-THANIDE SERIES, which fills the 4f subshell. In 1944 Glenn Seaborg and co-workers hypothesized that the elements following uranium would indeed parallel the lanthanides. These predictions were correct, and many of the actinides are in fact chemically similar to the lanthanides—for example, the chemistry of curium is much like that of gadolinium.

Characteristics. All of the actinide elements are shiny, hard metals that tarnish in air and are so electropositive that they are difficult to reduce from their compounds. Oxides have been prepared for all the elements through einsteinium; the elements thorium through berkelium have stable dioxides. Thorium, uranium, and plutonium dioxides are used in nuclear reactors. Because U-235 and Pu-239 undergo nuclear fission when they absorb neutrons, they are used in nuclear reactors and in nuclear weapons. The actinide elements are among the most prevalent of radioactive waste products from nuclear reactors. Many compounds of the actinides have been studied, often using only a few micrograms because of the elements' scarcity and intense radioactivity.

LESTER R. MORSS

Bibliography: Bagnall, K. W., *The Actinide Elements* (1972); Katz, Joseph J., and Seaborg, G. T., *The Chemistry of the Actinide Elements* (1957).

actinium   [ak-tin'-ee-uhm]

The chemical element actinium is a radioactive metal, the first member of the ACTINIDE SERIES. Its symbol is Ac, its atomic number 89, and its atomic weight 227 (stablest isotope). Actinium was discovered in 1899 by A. Debierne, who found it in pitchblende residues. Many radioactive isotopes of actinium are known, one of which, ^{227}Ac, has a HALF-LIFE of 21.6 years and is present in natural uranium. The other isotopes have half-lives of 10 days to less than 5 seconds.

actinolite: see AMPHIBOLE.

actinometer   [ak-tih-nahm'-uh-tur]

An actinometer is an instrument for measuring the ability of ELECTROMAGNETIC RADIATION coming from the Sun or an artificial light source to produce chemical changes. Such an ability is called an actinic property. Actinic rays range from the ultraviolet to infrared. Actinometers are primarily used in PHOTOGRAPHY, to measure the light intensity, and hence they are called light meters or exposure meters. The first actinometer was devised in 1840 by J. B. F. Soleil. In their study of sensitive emulsions, Ferdinand HURTER and V. C. Driffield used an actinometer in the form of a gas thermometer that registered the amount of light in terms of the heat it produced.

The modern form of actinometer is the photoelectric exposure meter. The original Weston type used a selenium barrier-layer PHOTOELECTRIC CELL that produced an electric current proportional to the flux density of radiation. The present type of exposure meter typically uses a cadmium sulfide photoconductive cell, which changes resistance and hence causes a change in the current produced by a miniature battery, in response to changes in light intensity.　　　FRANK J. OLIVER

Actinomyces　[ak-ti-noh-my'-seez]

Actinomyces is a genus of rod-shaped BACTERIA that microscopically show occasional branching. The natural habitat of these organisms is the soil, but two species, *A. bovis* and *A. israelii,* cause the disease actinomycosis in cattle and in humans. *A. israelii* can be isolated from most human tonsils, gums, and teeth. ·　　　WAYBURN S. JETER

actinosphaerium　[ak-ti-noh-sfir'-ee-uhm]

An actinosphaerium is any member of the genus of freshwater PROTOZOA belonging to the order Heliozoa. Actinosphaeria are famous as the "sun animalcules" described by early Victorian microscopists. The spherical, one-celled heliozoans are closely related to the planktonic RADIOLARIANS and, like them, usually have silica-containing skeletons. The actinosphaeria, however, are naked, with no stiffening skeleton. Like all heliozoans, actinosphaeria reproduce by binary fission; they may also reproduce sexually. They obtain food by extending axopodia (footlike projections that are stiffened with axial filaments) and then drawing the food back into the cell body.

Bibliography: Grell, Karl G., *Protozoology,* 2d rev. ed. (1973).

ACTION

ACTION is an independent U.S. government agency that aims to encourage Americans to participate in voluntary programs within the United States and in foreign countries. It administers several voluntary programs, including Volunteers in Service to America (VISTA). The Peace Corps is an autonomous agency within ACTION.

The Peace Corps. The Peace Corps was created in 1961 by President John F. Kennedy for the purpose of sending American volunteers with technical skills to countries that request them. It helps other countries meet their needs for trained workers and gives Americans and other peoples an opportunity to meet and understand one another.

Volunteers are given about 3 months' training in the language and customs of the locality in which they are to serve. During a 2-year term of foreign service, they receive allowances for food, clothing, housing, and incidental expenses as well as a small salary. Nearly 5,000 volunteers were serving in 61 countries of Latin America, Africa, the Middle East, and the Pacific in 1981. They worked primarily in agriculture, rural development, health, and education.

Volunteers in Service to America (VISTA). VISTA was established in 1964 to recruit volunteers for work in needy communities in the United States. It was conceived as a domestic counterpart of the Peace Corps. VISTA volunteers come from all age and occupational groups; they work in the inner cities, in small towns, in rural areas, among Indians and migrant workers, and in institutions for the mentally ill.

Other ACTION Programs. ACTION has enlisted many low-income elderly persons to work in their own communities in schools, parks, libraries, hospitals, and day-care centers. Its Senior Companion Program puts older persons to work

among the handicapped and others needing individual care. The Foster Grandparent Program provides retarded, disturbed, and handicapped children with personal attention.

Other ACTION programs are designed for young people. The National Center for Service Learning encourages student community-service learning programs. The center administers the University Year for Action, which enables students to spend a year off campus working in poor communities. Academic credit is granted. The Youth Challenge Program organizes young people 14 to 21 years of age for volunteer service in local communities.

Bibliography: ACTION, *Domestic Programs Factbook* (annual); Balzano, Michael P., *Reorganizing the Federal Bureaucracy* (1977); Carey, Robert G., *The Peace Corps* (1970); Crook, William, and Thomas, Ross, *Warriors for the Poor: The Story of VISTA* (1969); Hapgood, David, and Bennett, Meridan, *Agents of Change: Close Look at the Peace Corps* (1968); U.S. General Accounting Office, *ACTION's Progress toward Meeting the Goals of Its Establishment; Report to the Congress* (1976).

Action Française　[ahk-see-ohn' frawn-sez']

The Action Française was a right-wing political movement in France active from 1899 to 1944. Founded by Charles Maurras (1868–1952), it espoused royalism, authoritarianism, nationalism, and anti-Semitism. Through its newspaper, *L'Action Française,* and its student groups, called Camelots du Roi, the movement attacked the democratic institutions of the Third Republic. In 1926, Pope Pius XI banned Roman Catholic participation in the movement, and in 1936 it was officially dissolved by the French government for complicity in a physical attack on Léon BLUM. Surviving clandestinely, the Action Française contributed to the ideology of the VICHY GOVERNMENT during World War II. It disintegrated in 1944 when France was liberated and Maurras was imprisoned for collaboration.　　　DONALD J. HARVEY

Bibliography: Weber, Eugen, *Action Française: Royalism and Reaction in Twentieth Century France* (1962).

Actium, Battle of　[ak'-tee-uhm or ak'-shee-uhm]

The battle of Actium, which resulted in the decisive defeat of Mark Antony by Octavian (later the Roman emperor Augustus), took place at sea on Sept. 2, 31 BC, outside the Gulf of Arta in western Greece.

active transport

Active transport is the process by which dissolved substances (solutes) are moved across biological membranes and accumulated against concentration gradients at the expense of metabolic energy. This process contrasts sharply with passive diffusion, whereby a dissolved substance becomes evenly distributed on both sides of a membrane that is permeable (allowing passage) to it. The membranes of cells and the special structures, or organelles, within them are impermeable to most water-soluble substances. The contents of cells and organelles are controlled by transport proteins embedded in the membranes and designed for the movement of particular solutes across them. This movement occurs against concentration gradients, that is, in the direction of the greater existing concentration. Without this control system, life would be impossible because cells and their organelles would simply not contain the necessary materials for metabolism and other life activities. For example, specific concentrations of ions (charged atoms) of certain chemical elements are essential to enzyme function, muscle contraction, protection of cells from osmotic swelling (see OSMOSIS), and the conduction of nerve impulses (see NEUROPHYSIOLOGY).

Primary active transport directly uses metabolic energy in the form of adenosine triphosphate (ATP), which contains a high-energy phosphate bond, to move small ions across membranes. The transport proteins are termed *ion pumps* or transport "ATPases." These include the sodium pump, which transports sodium ions (Na^+) outward and potassium ions (K^+) inward across animal cell membranes, and the calcium pump, which moves calcium ions (Ca^{2+}) back into the sarcoplasmic reticulum (a completely intracellular membrane system for calcium storage) following MUSCLE CONTRACTION.

Other small molecules, such as sugars and amino acids, are accumulated by secondary active transport, in which a transport protein couples the movement of two different solutes across a membrane. In such a case, an ionic concentration gradient established by primary active transport provides the energy for moving the second solute.

Recent advances in the study of active transport have used X-ray diffraction, electron microscopy, and high-speed centrifugation to analyze the structure of ion pumps. Radioactive tracers have been employed to follow solute movement using intact membranes and isolated pumps that have been reconstituted into artificial membranes. Other sophisticated techniques have been applied to the detection of changes in pump shape. Although the detailed molecular mechanism is still a mystery, it is now known that transport proteins are too large to shuttle back and forth across the membrane in the manner of a ferry. Rather, they appear to operate as restricted pores, with a binding site accessible to one and then the other side of the membrane. Energy enters the cycle when the transport protein reacts with ATP. The high-energy phosphate bond of ATP breaks, and a phosphate group becomes bonded to the transport protein, causing a change in the shape of the protein that alters the position of the binding site. Investigation of this very basic process continues.   BLISS FORBUSH III

Bibliography: Andreoli, T. E., Hoffman, J. F., and Fanestil, Darrel D., *Membrane Physiology* (1978); Weissmann, Gerald, and Claiborne, Robert, *Cell Membranes, Biochemistry, Cell Biology, and Pathology* (1975).

activity

In physical chemistry the concept of activity is used to modify thermodynamic calculations to allow for the nonideal behavior of SOLUTIONS. The activity of a component in a solution is a measure of its tendency to take part in a given reaction and depends on the pressure and temperature. The activity coefficient is a ratio of the activity and the actual concentration of the component. These terms were introduced by the American chemist Gilbert N. LEWIS in 1907.

An ideal solution is one in which the solution's components display certain physical or chemical behavior depending on their concentrations. Some solutions, however, are nonideal—the components behave as though their concentrations were greater or less than they actually are. The activity can express how much a nonideal solution differs from an ideal one and often replaces the concentration value in thermodynamic equations for greater accuracy. For example, chemical equilibrium constants usually are expressed in terms of concentrations, as though the solutions were ideal. For a more exact treatment in equilibrium constants of nonideal solutions, however, activities are used. A similar concept, fugacity, allows for the nonideal behavior of gases.

                                    GERALD C. ROPER

Bibliography: Bailar, John C., Jr., et al., *Chemistry* (1978).

Acton, John Emerich Edward Dalberg Acton, 1st Baron

The historian John Emerich Edward Dalberg Acton, b. Jan. 10, 1834, d. June 19, 1902, was one of the greatest spokesmen of English liberalism. He served in the House of Commons from 1859 to 1865 and was created 1st Baron Acton in 1869.

Acton edited *The Rambler,* a Roman Catholic monthly, from 1859 to 1864, when he resigned because of church limitations on its independence. Although he remained a devoted member of his church, he opposed such measures as the Syllabus of Errors issued by Pope Pius IX and the declaration on papal infallibility at the First Vatican Council.

Lord Acton espoused the rigorous methods of the new scientific school of history and set out to write the definitive history of liberty. He never completed this book, but he set forth his ideas in two lectures delivered in 1877—"The History of

Freedom in Antiquity" and "The History of Freedom in Christianity." In 1886, Acton became a founder of the *English Historical Review,* and in 1895 he was named regius professor of modern history at Cambridge. In 1899 he also became the editor of the *Cambridge Modern History,* which under his direction became a model of careful scholarship.   JOEL COLTON

Bibliography: Himmelfarb, Gertrude, *Lord Acton: A Study in Conscience and Politics* (1952); Schuettinger, Robert L., *Lord Acton: Historian of Liberty* (1977).

Actors' Equity Association

Actors' Equity Association, founded in 1913, is the union encompassing all professional performers who work in the legitimate theater in the United States. It affiliated with the American Federation of Labor in 1919 and is now part of the AFL-CIO. The union determines the minimum pay scales for Broadway and Off Broadway performers, provides for arbitration arising out of members' contracts, and regulates the importation of foreign actors and the use of nonunion performers. Any actor who has worked within Equity's jurisdiction or who has a bona fide offer from an Equity producer is qualified to join. The union had 30,000 members in 1983, of which 80 percent were unemployed at any one time.

Actors Studio

The Actors Studio is an actors' workshop founded in New York City in 1947 by Cheryl Crawford, Elia Kazan, and Robert Lewis and joined in 1948 by Lee STRASBERG, who was its artistic director until his death in 1982. Later, performers Ellen Burstyn and Al Pacino became codirectors. The studio is known for its controversial "method" approach to acting, an adaptation of the acting system first developed by the Russian director Konstantin STANISLAVSKY. In such training the actor works by improvisation and emotional exercises.

During the 1950s the Actors Studio had a profound influence on American theater, training for the stage and screen such leading actors as Marlon Brando, Montgomery Clift, Julie Harris, Paul Newman, and Geraldine Page. Although its influence has declined, the studio still trains actors at its principal centers in New York City and Los Angeles. In 1957 the studio added a Playwrights Unit, in 1960 a Directors Unit, and in 1962 a Production Unit.

Bibliography: Edwards, Christine, *The Stanislavsky Heritage* (1965); Strasberg, Lee, *Strasberg at the Actors Studio* (1965).

Acts of the Apostles

The Acts of the Apostles is the fifth book of the New Testament, written between AD 70 and 90 by the author of the Gospel according to LUKE. Acts is an account of the early preaching about Jesus Christ, the growth of the primitive Christian community, and the spread of the Christian message. It covers the period from the Ascension of Christ (chapter 1) and the Pentecost to the visit of Saint PAUL to Rome, where he was placed under house arrest.

The early chapters of Acts contain an idyllic portrait of the Jerusalem community praying together, practicing common ownership of property, and preaching. The author attributes the vitality and activity of Christianity to the Holy Spirit, which plays a prominent part in Acts. Speeches constitute one-third of the book, and the early sermons of PETER summarize the message as understood by the author of Acts. Three of the key ideas are that Christ fulfills the promises of the Old Testament, that salvation comes through him, and that the Christian community is the new chosen people.

After chapter 10, the emphasis shifts to the spread of Christianity to the Gentiles through the missionary work of Saint Paul. In contrast to earlier New Testament documents, such as, 1 Thessalonians, written by Paul about AD 51, the end of the world is not considered imminent but has receded into the vaguely distant future. The very composition of Acts focuses attention on the present and on spreading Christianity "to the ends of the earth" (1:8). Thus Acts is a fairly detailed account of early Christianity in its progress from Jerusalem to Rome. ANTHONY J. SALDARINI

Bibliography: Haenchen, Ernst, *The Acts of the Apostles: A Commentary* (1971).

actuary [ak'-chuh-wair-ee]

An actuary estimates risks and determines premiums for insurance companies. For example, an actuary may calculate the likelihood of fires causing losses for a particular group of property owners, basing the projection on their past rate of fires. The profession requires intensive training in mathematics, statistics, accounting, and insurance probabilities.

acupuncture

Acupuncture is a form of medical therapy (see MEDICINE) that involves inserting thin, solid needles into selective sites on the surface of the body. It has been part of CHINESE MEDICINE since ancient times. Acupuncture was long in use in immigrant Chinese communities, but Western interest in it did not become widespread until the 1970s, when physicians in the People's Republic of China demonstrated that it could be used to control surgical pain.

The early Chinese postulated a system of energy circulation that predated by many centuries current understanding of blood circulation and the nervous system. They thought that vital life energy flows through a series of pathways, or meridians, 12 of which were on each side of the body. Meridians were said to course through the deep tissues of the body, surfacing occasionally. The areas where the meridians touch the surface were considered useful treatment points for diseases, which were thought to be caused by imbalances in the energy flow. Inserting a needle into certain points could increase energy flow, and the needles also were used to drain away excessive pressure or to break down blocks or dams in energy flow. Meridians were variously related to the heart, the lungs, the colon, the gallbladder, the liver, and the other organs. The flow of energy in each meridian was read by taking the pulse associated with it at the wrist. Therapy was aimed at restoring normal energy flow so that perfect equilibrium existed throughout the body.

The use of acupuncture for controlling surgical pain is a recent development in China, and it does not strictly reflect the ancient medical philosophy. Classical Chinese medicine concerned itself with restoring normal function as opposed to creating abnormal conditions, such as total pain reduction. To control surgical pain in contemporary China, needles are inserted into various parts of the body, and the patient is stimulated by electrical current delivered through the needles or by the more traditional manual twirling of the needles. Practitioners may also inject various solutions at these body sites or use ultrasonic probes instead of needles. After about 20 minutes of stimulation, the surgery can begin. If acupuncture treatment has been effective, the patient will be wide awake, alert, and aware of all the major surgical procedures but will experience little or no pain (see ANESTHETICS).

The mechanisms by which Chinese patients are able to tolerate surgery during acupunctural stimulation are still unknown. Some scientists speculate that large sensory fibers are activated, which inhibits transmission of impulses from the small fibers carrying the sensory input of pain. Other scientists speculate that naturally produced morphinelike substances—endorphins and enkephalins—may be released within the brain in response to acupuncture. When these substances bind to OPIATE RECEPTOR cells, a pain-inhibition system is activated. More research is needed before mechanisms of acupuncture pain-control can be specified, and almost certainly psychological factors will be shown to play a crucial role.

Acupuncture pain-control for surgery may well be more a scientific curiosity than a practical innovation in the West. It cannot compete with conventional anesthesia and nerve-block anesthesia because these procedures are safe, fast, and virtually 100 percent reliable. Acupuncture is time-consuming and significantly less reliable, although Chinese researchers

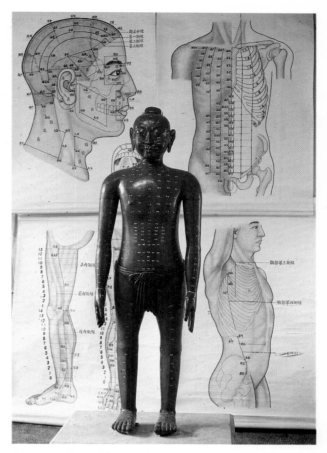

Diagrams and a model are used to study acupuncture meridian points. Needles inserted into specific meridian points supposedly affect energy flow and relieve pain in corresponding body organs.

assert that besides reducing pain, it also reduces the possibility of shock and infection. It holds some promise for treating such chronic-pain states as backache, headache, and abdominal pain. Acupuncture is highly effective in giving short-term relief to patients suffering from such pain, but it is less impressive in the long-term rate of cure. Nevertheless, it offers hope to many patients who, having explored all conventional alternatives, have no place to turn. A small percentage of American physicians are adding acupuncture to their therapeutic methods because it is safe, it works well for certain problems, and it is an alternative to treatment by medications that have undesirable side effects. C. RICHARD CHAPMAN

Bibliography: *A Barefoot Doctor's Manual, the American Translation* (1977); Duke, Marc, *Acupuncture* (1972); Manaka, Yoshio, and Urquhart, I. A., *The Layman's Guide to Acupuncture* (1975); Mann, Felix, *Acupuncture,* rev. ed. (1978); Omura, Yoshiaki, *Acupuncture Medicine* (1981).

Ada

Ada is a high-level COMPUTER LANGUAGE commissioned in the late 1970s by the U.S. Department of Defense and designed by a team at the French company CII-Honeywell Bull. It is named for Ada Lovelace (1815–52), Lord Byron's only legitimate daughter and a friend and commentator on the work of Charles BABBAGE, who anticipated many of the principles of the modern computer. Based on PASCAL, Ada is a general-purpose language designed to be readable and easily maintained, and to reconcile the separate requirements of machine efficiency and ease of use. It is intended to become a standard language to replace the many specialized languages now in use. BRIAN ASTLE

Adam

According to the Bible, Adam was the first man. His name, which means "man" in Hebrew, is probably derived from the Hebrew word for "earth." The first three chapters of Genesis relate that God created Adam from dust, breathed life into him, and placed him in the Garden of EDEN, where he lived with his wife, EVE, until they ate the forbidden fruit from the tree of knowledge of good and evil (see ORIGINAL SIN). The biblical account is similar to Egyptian and Mesopotamian accounts, in which the first man was made from clay, infused with life by a divine being, and placed in a paradise of delight.

Adam, Adolphe

Adolphe Charles Adam, b. July 24, 1803, d. May 3, 1856, was a French composer who is today best known for his score to the ballet *Giselle* (1841). After overcoming parental opposition, he studied music at the Paris Conservatory. Adam composed music for 13 ballets and 20 comic operas, of which the most successful was *Le Postillon de Longjumeau* (1836).

Adam, Robert

Robert Adam, one of the major English architects of the second half of the 18th century, was a leader in international neoclassicism (see NEOCLASSICISM, art) and the creator of the Adam style in interior design.

Adam was born in Kirkcaldy, Scotland, on July 3, 1728. He was trained by his wealthy architect father, William Adam, and began his architectural career in Scotland with his oldest brother, John. From 1754 to 1758 he undertook an extensive tour of Italy (considered obligatory for educated Britons of the period), which was to change the course of his career. He was much inspired by the widespread renewed interest in antiquity and by personal acquaintances with such influential contemporaries as the French interior designer Charles Louis Clérisseau and the Italian artist and antiquarian Giovanni Battista Piranesi. The presence in Italy of numerous well-traveled English noblemen (and potential clients) led Adam to establish himself in London on his return home early in 1758. He was later joined there by his younger brother, James.

Robert Adam began to attract patrons immediately. By the early 1760s he had a great many commissions and had been appointed joint architect to the King's Works, along with Sir William Chambers, who was to be his principal rival for leadership in English architecture. The publication of Adam's *Ruins of the Palace of the Emperor Diocletian at Spalatro in Dalmatia* (1764) firmly established his version of neoclassical style in England. The Adam style replaced the Burlingtonian Palladian style—derived from the much-published work of the Italian architect Andrea Palladio—which was heavier and closer to its Greek and Roman sources. Adam used the same elements but with far more freedom and imagination.

Adam's work in the late 1750s and '60s included a series of major remodelings of country houses and completion of houses begun by others, as well as a few houses built from the ground up; his finest accomplishments were to be in the planning and decoration of interiors, always to the smallest details. Among his principal commissions of this type were Syon House, Middlesex (*c.*1760–1769); Kedleston Hall, Derbyshire (*c.*1759–1771); Kenwood, London (1767–69); Harewood House, Yorkshire (*c.*1758–1771); Nostell Priory, Yorkshire (1766–76); and Osterly Park, Middlesex (1761–80). Adam also began work on a number of London town houses, such as Lansdowne House (*c.*1760–1768; partially demolished; dining room in Metropolitan Museum of Art, New York City), but was even more active in the 1770s, as at Wynn House (1772–74), Derby House (1773–74; destroyed), and Home House (1775–77; now the Courtauld Institute of Art).

Adam was also responsible for a number of town-planning schemes, such as the Adelphi (1768–72; destroyed), Portland Place (1776–*c.*1780), and Fitzroy Square (*c.*1790–1800) in London and Charlotte Square in Edinburgh (1791–1807). The Adelphi scheme, a group of sumptuous town houses on the

The Roman anteroom of Syon House, located in Middlesex, England, is an important example of Robert Adam's rich neoclassical decoration. Designed about 1760–69, Syon House represented a new freedom in the use of Roman classical elements.

River Thames, bankrupted Adam and may have been responsible for occasional lapses of quality in his output after 1775. His public buildings include the Admiralty Screen, London (1759–60); the Register House, Edinburgh (*c.*1774–1792); and Edinburgh University (begun 1789–93). Although Adam was less active in the early 1780s, during the last years of his life he received a number of commissions, many for large Gothic Revival castles, especially in Scotland. He died on Mar. 3, 1792, and is buried in Westminster Abbey.

Adam exerted an enormous influence, clearly seen in the work of such other English architects as George Dance, James Wyatt, and the young Sir John Soane, who in 1833 bought most of Adam's drawings, now in the Soane Museum, London. In the architectural pattern books of the day, the Adam style predominates. Adam's influence reached as far as the new United States, as in the buildings of Charles Bulfinch and Benjamin Latrobe, and the Russia of Catherine II, in the palaces of the Scottish architect Charles Cameron.

Bibliography: Adam, Robert and James, *The Works in Architecture of Robert and James Adam,* 3 vols. (1773–1822; repr. 1975); Fleming, John, *Robert Adam and His Circle* (1962); Harris, Eileen, *The Furniture of Robert Adam* (1963); Stillman, Damie, *The Decorative Work of Robert Adam* (1966); Yarwood, Doreen, *Robert Adam* (1970).

Adam Bede   [beed]

Adam Bede (1859), George ELIOT's first full-length novel, takes up the theme of moral growth through suffering. Set in late 18th-century England, the novel depicts a stable, rural society of farmers, artisans, and gentry. Adam Bede, a talented and intelligent carpenter, loves Hetty Sorrel, a young woman with nothing more than looks to recommend her. After Hetty is seduced by Arthur Donnithorne, a young village squire, she becomes pregnant, runs off, and is eventually charged with murdering her child. Donnithorne, who is sympathetically portrayed, and Hetty grow into greater moral awareness, while Adam, by observing them, comes to realize that his self-righteousness is a form of pride. The novel idealizes the values of work and social stability.   CHARLOTTE D. SOLOMON

Bibliography: Hardy, Barbara, *The Novels of George Eliot* (1959).

Adam de la Halle [duh lah ahl]

Adam de la Halle, known as Adam le Bossu (Adam the Hunchback), c.1250–c.1288, was a French poet and musician who wrote lyrics of courtly love and two popular plays, *Le Jeu de la Feuillée* (The Play of the Greensward, 1276) and *Le Jeu de Robin et Marion* (c.1283). The former, a satirical comedy, presents an early form of the harlequin, later a stock character of the Italian commedia dell'arte. Adam's second drama is a pastoral set to music that anticipates the style of comic opera. He is regarded as the originator of French secular drama.

Adamic, Louis [ad'-uh-mik]

Louis Adamic, b. Slovenia (now part of Yugoslavia), Mar. 23, 1899, d. Sept. 4, 1951, emigrated to the United States in 1913 and eventually wrote books about both countries. After achieving considerable success with *The Native's Return* (1934), a novel about his homeland, Adamic wrote novels about American immigrant life, such as *Grandsons* (1935), and an autobiographical volume called *My America* (1938). His death was apparently a suicide. A biography of Marshal Tito, *The Eagle and the Roots* (1952), was published posthumously.

Bibliography: Christian, H. A., ed., *Louis Adamic: A Checklist* (1971).

Adamov, Arthur [ad-uh-mawf']

Arthur Adamov, b. Aug. 23, 1908, d. Mar. 16, 1970, was a Russian-born French dramatist whose early plays are surrealist fantasies of a nonsensical world whose cruelty and uncertainty recalls the work of Franz Kafka and Eugène Ionesco. His first play, *La Parodie* (1947), was performed in Paris in 1952. In *Ping Pong* (1955; Eng. trans., 1962), a satire on business and politics, Adamov adopted a realistic style. His later works, such as *Les Petits Bourgeois* (1959) and *Les Âmes mortes* (Dead Souls, 1960), adapted from Maksim Gorky and Nikolai Gogol respectively, were influenced by the theater of Bertolt Brecht.

Bibliography: Esslin, Martin, *The Theatre of the Absurd* (1968).

Adams, Abigail

Abigail Adams, wife of U.S. president John Adams, was one of history's most famous letter writers. Her written plea to her husband that Congress should "Remember the Ladies" was an early proposal that the new American government guarantee women's rights. (Courtesy National Gallery of Art, Washington, D.C. Gift of Mrs. Robert Homans, 1954.)

Abigail Adams, b. Weymouth, Mass., Nov. 11, 1744, d. Oct. 28, 1818, was the wife of John Adams, the second president of the United States, and the mother of John Quincy Adams, sixth president. Originally named Abigail Smith, she was the daughter of a clergyman in Weymouth.

Educated at home by her grandmother, she displayed a lively intelligence and expressed her strong opinions in a straightforward manner. She is credited with having had a notable influence on the long and distinguished career of her husband, accompanying him on his diplomatic missions to Europe and advising him by letter when she remained in Massachusetts managing family affairs. As First Lady, she was a skillful political hostess, although she offended some by her strong Federalist views.

Abigail Adams was a prodigious letter writer, and many editions of her letters have been published. Her grandson Charles Francis Adams (1807–86) published the most nearly complete edition in 1841 and 1876.

Bibliography: Butterfield, L. H., et al., eds., *The Book of Abigail and John: Selected Letters of the Adams Family, 1762–84* (1975); Withey, Lynne, *Dearest Friend: A Life of Abigail Adams* (1981).

Adams, Ansel

The American photographer Ansel Adams, b. San Francisco, Feb. 20, 1902, d. Apr. 22, 1984, became a recognized leader of modern photography through his sharp and poetic landscape photographs of the American West. Trained as a pianist, he divided his time between music and photography until 1930, when, impressed by the work of Paul Strand, he decided to concentrate fully on photography. In 1932 he had his first solo show in a major museum and, with Imogen Cunningham, Edward Weston, and others, founded the influential Group F/64. In 1937, Adams moved to Yosemite, Calif., and after 1940 he photographed extensively in the country's national parks. His sharply defined prints are in marked contrast with the evocative work of earlier pictorialists and even surpass the realistic detail of 19th-century landscape photographs. Working exclusively in black and white, Adams used brilliant light to produce intense images. His collections include *My Camera in Yosemite Valley* (1949); *Portfolio Two: The National Parks* (1950); *This Is the American Earth* (1960); *Ansel Adams, Images 1923–1974* (1975); and *The Portfolios of Ansel Adams* (1977). ELIZABETH POLLOCK

Bibliography: Newhall, Nancy, *Ansel Adams: The Eloquent Light* (1963).

Adams, Brooks

Brooks Adams, b. Quincy, Mass., June 24, 1848, d. Feb. 13, 1927, the fourth son of Charles Francis Adams (1807–86), was an American historian who applied laws of science to the study of the development of civilizations. In *The Emancipation of Massachusetts* (1887) he employed the concept of survival of the fittest. Adams utilized the principles of energy in propounding a cyclical interpretation of history in *The Law of Civilization and Decay* (1895).

Adams, Charles Francis

Charles Francis Adams, b. Boston, Aug. 18, 1807, d. Nov. 21, 1886, was an American historian and diplomat. The son of President John Quincy Adams, he spent his early years managing the family property in Massachusetts, writing historical articles, and editing the letters of his grandmother Abigail Adams and writings of his grandfather John Adams. Holding antislavery views, he was the vice-presidential candidate of the Free-Soil party in 1848.

Elected to Congress in 1858 as a Republican, Adams was appointed minister to Great Britain in 1861. His major task was to prevent British recognition of the Confederate States. In this he was successful despite the open sympathy of the British ruling classes for the South. Personally well-liked and an adroit and tactful diplomat, he was able to prevent a rupture over the delicate TRENT AFFAIR. The success of his mission was a vitally important contribution to the Northern victory.

After his return to the United States in 1868, except for membership in the Alabama Claims Commission, Adams retired from public life. In 1874 he began the publication in 12 volumes of his father's diary. HARRY AMMON

Bibliography: Duberman, Martin B., *Charles Francis Adams, 1807–1886* (1961).

Adams, Charles Francis, Jr.

Charles Francis Adams, Jr., b. Boston, May 27, 1835, d. Mar. 20, 1915, the third son of Charles Francis Adams, was a railroad expert whose interest turned to writing New England history. After fighting in the Civil War, he wrote *Chapters of Erie* (1871), in which he exposed the stock manipulations of the directors of the Erie Railroad. He became chairman of the Massachusetts Board of Railroad Commissioners (1872-79) and then president (1884-90). His works include *Richard Henry Dana: A Biography* (1890), *Massachusetts: Its Historians and History* (1893), and a biography (1900) of his father.

Bibliography: Kirkland, Edward Chase, *Charles Francis Adams, Jr., 1835-1915* (1965).

Adams, Franklin Pierce

The American humorist and journalist Franklin Pierce Adams, b. Nov. 15, 1881, d. Mar. 23, 1960, informed and entertained millions through his newspaper column "The Conning Tower," started in 1914, and his work on the "Information Please" radio program (1938-48). Adams's humor, epigrams, and poetry made the column a popular feature first in the *New York Tribune* and subsequently in the *World, Herald Tribune,* and *Post.* His puns, quips, and overall knowledge helped make "Information Please" one of radio's top shows.

ERNEST C. HYNDS

Adams, Henry

Henry Brooks Adams, b. Feb. 16, 1838, d. Mar. 27, 1918, an American historian, was the son of Charles Francis ADAMS and the descendant of two presidents, but he gradually abandoned his family's involvement in politics to pursue the study of history. After completing his studies at Harvard, he traveled abroad as the secretary of his father, a diplomat. In 1870 he began teaching history at Harvard and became the editor of the *North American Review,* a reform journal that focused attention on corruption and advocated civil service reforms. From 1877 to 1879 he edited the papers and wrote a biography of Albert GALLATIN. A decade later his research in this period of American history culminated in his 9-volume *History of the United States* (1889-91).

In the meantime, Adams's disillusionment with politics surfaced in a satirical novel, *Democracy,* which he published anonymously in 1880. In 1885 his wife's suicide drove him to search for new meaning in life and history. Adams recorded this spiritual odyssey in two important works that went far beyond the narrow political approach of his earlier work: in *Mont Saint Michel and Chartres* (1913) he expressed his admiration for the medieval church, and in his autobiography, *The Education of Henry Adams* (1918), he gave a moving account of one man's struggle to understand change.   JOEL COLTON

Bibliography: Adams, James Truslow, *The Adams Family* (1930); Levenson, J. C., *The Mind and Art of Henry Adams* (1957); Samuels, Ernest, *The Life of Henry Adams,* 3 vols. (1948-64).

Adams, Herbert Baxter

Herbert Baxter Adams, b. Apr. 16, 1850, d. July 30, 1901, was an American historian who, as a professor (1876-1901) at Johns Hopkins University, shaped U.S. graduate studies in history and political science. Receiving his doctorate in 1876 from the University of Heidelberg, he introduced the German seminar-teaching method at Johns Hopkins and trained many prominent scholars. In monographs written in 1882 and 1883, Adams argued for the Germanic origins of New England towns. He was a founder (1884) of the American Historical Association.

Bibliography: Holt, W. S., ed., *Historical Scholarship in the United States, 1876-1901, as Revealed in the Correspondence of Herbert B. Adams* (1938).

Adams, James Truslow

James Truslow Adams, b. Oct. 18, 1878, d. May 18, 1949, was a popular American historian who wrote primarily about New England. After working from 1900 to 1912 for a New York Stock Exchange firm, he turned to historical writing. *The Founding of New England* (1921), in which he stressed social history and was critical of Puritanism, won a Pulitzer Prize.

Adams continued this story with *Revolutionary New England, 1691-1776* (1923) and *New England in the Republic, 1776-1850* (1926). *The Epic of America* (1931), a sweeping historical survey, won acclaim in the United States and abroad. Adams's other works include studies of the Adams family of Massachusetts (to which he was not related) and of the British Empire. He was editor in chief of the *Dictionary of American History* (6 vols., 1940).

Bibliography: Nevins, Allan, *James Truslow Adams: Historian of the American Dream* (1968).

Adams, John

In three remarkable careers—as a foe of British oppression and champion of Independence (1761-77), as an American diplomat in Europe (1778-88), and as the first vice-president (1789-97) and then the second president (1797-1801) of the United States—John Adams was a founder of the United States. Perhaps equally important, however, was the life of his mind and spirit; in a pungent diary, vivid letters, learned tracts, and patriotic speeches he revealed himself as a quintessential Puritan, patriarch of an illustrious family, tough-minded philosopher of the republic, sage, and sometimes a vain, stubborn, and vitriolic partisan.

John Adams was born in Braintree (now Quincy), Mass., on Oct. 30, 1735, in a small saltbox house still standing and open to visitors. His father, John Adams, a deacon and a fifth-generation Massachusetts farmer, and his mother, the former Suzanna Boylston, were, their son wrote, "both fond of reading"; so they resolved to give bookishly inclined John a good education. He became the first of his family to go to college when he entered Harvard in 1751. There, and in six further years of intensive reading while he taught school and studied law in Worcester and Boston, he mastered the technicalities of his profession and the literature and learning of his day. By 1762, when he began 14 years of increasingly successful legal practice, he was well informed, ambitious, and public spirited. His most notable good fortune, however, occurred in 1764 when he married Abigail Smith. John Adams's marriage of 54 years to this wise, learned, strong-willed, passionate, and patriotic woman began the brilliant phase of Adams family history that produced their son John Quincy, his son Charles Francis, his sons Henry and Brooks, and numerous other distinguished progeny.

In 1761, John Adams began to think and write and act against British measures that he believed infringed on colonial liberties and the right of Massachusetts and the other colonies to self-government. A pamphlet entitled *A Dissertation on the Canon and the Feudal Law* and town instructions denouncing the STAMP ACT (1765) marked him as a vigorous, patriotic penman, and, holding various local offices, he soon became a leader among Massachusetts radicals. Although he never wavered in his devotion to colonial rights and early committed himself to independence as an unwelcome last resort, Adams's innate conservatism made him determined in 1770 that the British soldiers accused of the BOSTON MASSACRE receive a fair hearing. He defended the soldiers at their trial. He also spoke out repeatedly against mob violence and other signs of social disintegration.

In 1774-76, Adams was a Massachusetts delegate to the CONTINENTAL CONGRESS in Philadelphia. His speeches and writings (especially a newspaper series signed "Novanglus" in 1775) articulating the colonial cause and his brilliant championing of American rights in Congress caused Thomas JEFFERSON to call him the "Colossus of Independence." Adams helped draft the DECLARATION OF INDEPENDENCE, secured its unanimous adoption in Congress, and wrote his wife on July 3, 1776, that "the most memorable Epoch in the History of America has begun."

After 18 months of toil in committee and on the floor of Congress managing the AMERICAN REVOLUTION, Adams crossed the Atlantic to be an American commissioner to France. The termination of this mission after less than a year in Paris allowed him to return home long enough to take a leading role in drafting the new Massachusetts constitution. He sailed

to Britain, Adams presented his credentials to George III in 1785, noting his pride in "having the distinguished honor to be the first [ex-colonial subject] to stand in your Majesty's royal presence·in a diplomatic character." The king, aware of the poignancy of the occasion, returned Adams's compliments and hoped that the "language, religion, and blood" shared by the two nations would "have their natural and full effect," but the British ministry obstructed Adams's efforts to restore equitable commerce between the two nations.

When he returned to the United States in 1788, Adams was greeted by his countrymen as one of the heroes of independence and was promptly elected vice-president under the new Constitution. This post, regarded by Adams as "the most insignificant office that ever the invention of man contrived or his imagination conceived," left him time to work out his increasingly sober views of republican government. In Europe he had been impressed with both the unsuitability of self-government for masses of destitute, ignorant people, and the usefulness, in evoking patriotism and in maintaining order, of the pomp and ceremony of monarchy. He was thus appalled, but not suprised, at the riotous French Revolution and emphasized the need for dignity, ritual, and authority in a republic like the United States. He also supported the efforts of George WASHINGTON to give the presidency an almost regal quality and to extend executive power, and he agreed with Alexander HAMILTON on most of the latter's fiscal plans. He never accepted, however, the "high" Federalist biases toward commercial growth and government by "the rich, the well-born, and the able."

Although his own presidency (1797–1801) was a troubled one, Adams made uniquely important contributions during his term as chief executive. He managed orderly transitions of power at both the beginning and the end of his administration, and he gave the government stability by continuing most of the practices established under Washington. The major crisis he faced, however, arose from strained relations with revolutionary France. When, in the so-called XYZ AFFAIR (1797–98), American peace commissioners returned from Paris with lurid stories of deceit and bribery, Adams called for an assertion of national pride, built up the armed forces, and even accepted the ALIEN AND SEDITION ACTS as emergency national security measures. With his opponents (led by Jefferson) charging oppression and some of his own FEDERALIST PARTY (led by Hamilton) urging war and conquest, Adams kept his nerve and, when the opportunity arose, dispatched another peace commission to France. This defused the crisis and led in 1800 to an agreement with France that ended the so-called Quasi-War. Nonetheless, deserted by Hamilton and other Federalists who disapproved of his independent course, and attacked by the Jeffersonian Republicans as a vain monarchist, Adams was forced out of office after one term.

When he and Abigail returned to Massachusetts, they moved into a comfortable but unpretentious house in Quincy (it is known today and open to visitors as the Adams National Historic Site) they had bought 12 years before. There, tending to his fields, visiting with neighbors, and enjoying his family, John Adams lived for 25 years as a sage and national patriarch. Of his numerous correspondences, the cherished 14-year (1812–26) one with Jefferson became a literary legacy to the nation. Although the debilitations of old age and the death of his beloved Abigail in 1818 troubled his last years, his mind remained sharp and his spirit buoyant until the end. Like Jefferson, he died on July 4, 1826, the 50th anniversary of the Declaration of Independence. Ninety years old at his death, Adams was revered by his countrymen not only as one of the founding fathers but also as a plain, honest man who personified the best of what the nation could hope of its citizens and leaders.

RALPH KETCHAM

JOHN ADAMS
2d President of the United States (1797–1801)

Nickname: "Atlas of Independence"
Born: Oct. 30, 1735, Braintree (now Quincy), Mass.
Education: Harvard College (graduated 1755)
Profession: Lawyer
Religious Affiliation: Unitarian
Marriage: Oct. 25, 1764, to Abigail Smith (1744–1818)
Children: Abigail Amelia Adams (1765–1813); John Quincy Adams (1767–1848); Susanna Adams (1768–70); Charles Adams (1770–1800); Thomas Boylston Adams (1772–1832)
Political Affiliation: Federalist
Writings: *The Life and Works of John Adams* (10 vols., 1856); *The Adams' Papers* (13 vols., 1961–77)
Died: July 4, 1826, Quincy, Mass.
Buried: First Unitarian Church, Quincy, Mass.

Vice-President and Cabinet Members
Vice-President: Thomas Jefferson
Secretary of State: Timothy Pickering (1797–1800); John Marshall (1800–01)
Secretary of the Treasury: Oliver Wolcott, Jr. (1797–1801); Samuel Dexter (1801)
Secretary of War: James McHenry (1797–1800); Samuel Dexter (1800–1801)
Attorney General: Charles Lee
Secretary of the Navy: Benjamin Stoddert

again for Europe, accompanied by two of his sons, in November 1779 as a commissioner to seek peace with Britain. After quarrels in Paris with Benjamin FRANKLIN and French officials, he left for the Netherlands, where he secured Dutch recognition of American independence and a substantial loan as well. He returned to Paris in October 1782 to insist on American rights (especially to fish on the Grand Banks of Newfoundland) in the negotiations that led to Britain's recognition of the independence of the United States in the Treaty of Paris of Sept. 3, 1783.

For two more years Adams helped Franklin and Jefferson negotiate treaties of friendship and commerce with numerous foreign powers. Then, appointed the first American minister

Bibliography: Adams, John, *The Adams Papers*, 13 vols., ed. by Lyman H. Butterfield et al. (1961–77); Handler, Edward, *America and Europe in the Political Thought of John Adams* (1964); Howe, John R., *Changing Political Thought of John Adams* (1966); Kurtz, Stephen G., *The Presidency of John Adams* (1957); Peterson, Merrill D., *Adams and Jefferson: A Revolutionary Dialogue* (1976); Shaw, Peter, *The Character of John Adams* (1976); Smith, Page, *John Adams,* 2 vols. (1962).

Adams, John Couch

John Couch Adams, b. June 5, 1819, d. Jan. 21, 1892, was an English astronomer and mathematician who, at the age of 24, was the first person to predict the position of a planetary mass beyond Uranus. He subsequently became the subject of a famous priority dispute with the French astronomer Urbain LEVERRIER, whose later prediction was published before Adams's and led directly to the discovery of NEPTUNE ON Sept. 23, 1846. Adams was educated at Cambridge and became a fellow, tutor, and professor of astronomy and geometry before being named director of Cambridge Observatory in 1861. Adams's many other astronomical contributions, notably his studies of the Leonid meteor shower and of the motion of the Moon, have been overshadowed by his role as the codiscoverer of Neptune.

Adams, John Quincy

John Quincy Adams, the sixth president of the United States, was a child of American independence, the primary architect of the first century of the nation's foreign policy, and an implacable foe of slavery.

Adams was born in Braintree (now Quincy), Mass., on July 11, 1767, the first son of the brilliant, patriotic, and strong-willed Abigail Smith Adams and her husband, John Adams, then a little-known country lawyer. When John Quincy was seven years old, his father, who was in Philadelphia attending the First Continental Congress, wrote to his wife of her duty to "mould the minds and manners of our children. Let us teach them not only to do virtuously, but to excell. To excell they must be taught to be steady, active, and industrious." A year later, mother and son watched the smoke and heard the cannons from the Battle of Bunker Hill. The letter, and the close, frightening, but also exhilarating event, set the boy's life on its course.

John Quincy Adams began 70 years of public service when in 1778, at the age of 11, he acted as his father's secretary during a diplomatic mission to France. In 1780 he again went to Europe with his father, this time as an official secretary, and a year later he served as secretary and interpreter to Francis Dana on the first American mission to the Russian court at St. Petersburg. Returning to western Europe via Sweden, Denmark, and Germany in early 1783, Adams lived for the next two years in The Hague, London, and Paris, where he pursued his formal education. When he came back to America in 1785 to enter Harvard College, he knew five or six modern languages as well as Latin and Greek, had traveled throughout northern and western Europe, had been under the close tutelage of his father for seven years, and had taken part in much of the diplomacy of the American Revolution.

Adams graduated from Harvard in 1787 and two years later finished his legal apprenticeship. Without enthusiasm he began to practice law in Boston in 1790. He was soon easily distracted into writing a notable series of newspaper articles attacking the ideas of Thomas Paine's *The Rights of Man*, and in 1794 he eagerly accepted President Washington's appointment of him as American minister to Holland. He subsequently served as minister to Prussia from 1797 to 1801. His letters to American officials contained by far the most perceptive and influential news coming back across the Atlantic during the crucial years of Napoleon's rise to dominance. During a mission to London in 1796–97 he married Louisa Catherine Johnson, the daughter of a Maryland merchant serving as U.S. consul in London. Their marriage produced three children and lasted until his death 51 years later.

Home again in 1801, Adams served briefly in the Massachusetts Senate and then in the U.S. Senate from 1803 to 1808. Although nominally in the FEDERALIST PARTY, he had no use for that party's increasingly regional posture and instead supported most of the policies of Thomas Jefferson's administration, including the EMBARGO ACT of 1807. His refusal to bow to heavy pressure from the Massachusetts legislature to repudiate that measure led to his resignation from the Senate—and, 150 years later, to his inclusion in John F. Kennedy's *Profiles in Courage*.

JOHN QUINCY ADAMS
6th President of the United States (1825–29)

Nickname: "Old Man Eloquent"
Born: July 11, 1767, Braintree (now Quincy), Mass.
Education: Harvard College (graduated 1787)
Profession: Lawyer
Religious Affiliation: Unitarian
Marriage: July 26, 1797, to Louisa Catherine Johnson (1775–1852)
Children: George Washington Adams (1801–29); John Adams (1803–34); Charles Francis Adams (1807–86); Louisa Catherine Adams (1811–12)
Political Affiliation: Federalist; Democratic-Republican; Whig
Writings: *Memoirs* (12 vols., 1874–77); *Writings of John Quincy Adams* (7 vols., 1913–17).
Died: Feb. 23, 1848, Washington, D.C.
Buried: First Unitarian Church, Quincy, Mass.

Vice-President and Cabinet Members
Vice-President: John C. Calhoun
Secretary of State: Henry Clay
Secretary of the Treasury: Richard Rush
Secretary of War: James Barbour (1825–28); Peter B. Porter (1828)
Attorney General: William Wirt
Secretary of the Navy: Samuel L. Southard

President James Madison then appointed Adams minister to Russia, and he sailed—this time with members of his own young family—for St. Petersburg, arriving just before ice closed the Baltic in December 1809. He lived there for four years and gained the confidence of Russian officials, who began negotiations leading to the end of the War of 1812. Adams traveled about northern Europe for 18 months pursuing these negotiations. As chief American commissioner, he signed the Treaty of Ghent on Christmas Eve, 1814. Madison promptly appointed him the first postwar American minister to Britain. Like his father before him and his son, Charles Francis Adams, after him, he stood proudly before the king of the former mother country as the representative of his independent nation.

As secretary of state during the administration (1817–25) of James MONROE, Adams took a leading role in all its deliberations and earned his standing as perhaps the most successful secretary of state in American history. He concluded negotiations he had begun in London to demilitarize the American border with Canada (1818), purchased Florida (1819), demarked a long southern boundary with Spanish Mexico that for the first time recognized American claims extending to the Pacific Ocean (1819), and set forth the principles of Anglo-American reconciliation and New World independence from the Old, known ever since as the MONROE DOCTRINE (1823).

Increasingly bitter political strife, however, puzzled and eventually infuriated Adams. He felt, justly, that he was entirely qualified—indeed that it was his due—to become president in 1825; yet he had only contempt for the selfish machinations and public circus apparently necessary for electoral success. His ambition triumphed, however. Although no candidate won a majority of the electoral vote in 1824, Adams accepted the support of Henry CLAY to secure his final selection—over Andrew JACKSON and William H. CRAWFORD—by the House of Representatives. Although inaugurated as a "minority president," he nonetheless submitted a broad, national program to an increasingly factional and sectionally oriented Congress and public. He called in 1825 for recognition of the new Latin American republics, support of canals and other internal improvements, establishment of a national university, support for scientific explorations, and in general for Congress "to give efficacy to the means committed to us for the common good." Congress ignored these grand programs and instead increasingly responded to the rising tide of laissez-faire expansionism and frontier individualism that swept Adams out and Andrew Jackson into the White House in 1829.

Retired permanently—he thought—to his books and to his farm in Massachusetts, Adams nevertheless responded dutifully when his neighbors elected him to the House of Representatives in 1830 and kept him there for nine consecutive terms. There, as "Old Man Eloquent," again and again speaking his conscience and calling the nation to respond to its highest impulses, he lived out his last and perhaps most remarkable career. In his relentless, eventually successful opposition to the so-called GAG RULES, which stifled antislavery petitions, Adams dramatized for the nation the repressive character of slavery. When fatally stricken in the House in 1848, almost 70 years to the day after he had first sailed for Europe with his father, he had just voted against a resolution thanking the American generals of the MEXICAN WAR, a conflict he had opposed.

When Adams died on Feb. 23, 1848, he was not only the last surviving statesman of the American Revolution but also the first national leader to have dramatized the moral issue that precipitated the Civil War. He thus nearly encompassed in his public career the "four score and seven years" of which Abraham Lincoln was soon to speak; he had also defined the foreign and domestic purposes that in his view undergirded the nation that his father had helped to found and his son would help to preserve. Although he was at times rigid, demanding, self-righteous, and even quaint, John Quincy Adams possessed the personal integrity, devotion to principle, intellectual intensity, and strong will that have made his name and his family a national resource. RALPH KETCHAM

Bibliography: Adams, John Q., *Memoirs*, 12 vols., ed. by C. F. Adams (1874–77; repr. 1970); Bemis, Samuel F., *John Quincy Adams and the Foundations of American Foreign Policy* (1949; repr. 1973); Ford, W. C., ed., *The Writings of John Quincy Adams*, 7 vols. (1913–17); Hecht, Marie B., *John Quincy Adams* (1972); Seward, William H., *The Life and Public Services of John Quincy Adams* (1849; repr. 1971).

Adams, Maude

Maude Adams, b. Nov. 11, 1872, d. July 17, 1953, an American actress of both intellect and pixielike charm, is best remembered for her performance in the title role of Sir James M. Barrie's *Peter Pan* (1905–07). A successful child actress (she

Maude Adams, a star of the American stage during the early 20th century, was noted for the delicacy of her acting style. She received enthusiastic reviews in 1906 as the lead in J. M. Barrie's Peter Pan.

first appeared on stage at the age of nine months), she made her New York debut in 1888 and became famous playing threatened heroines of melodrama. Producer Charles Frohman made her a star, and Barrie wrote her most successful parts, in such plays as *The Little Minister* (1897–98), *Quality Street* (1902), and *What Every Woman Knows* (1908–09). After Frohman's death in 1915 her career declined, and she retired in 1918. ANDREW KELLY

Bibliography: Davies, Acton, *Maude Adams* (1901); Patterson, Ada, *Maude Adams* (1907; repr. 1971); Robbins, Phyllis, *The Young Maude Adams* (1959).

Adams, Robert McCormick

Robert McCormick Adams, b. July 23, 1926, is an American anthropologist and archaeologist who is best known for his studies of the development of ancient cities and states, based on his excavations in Mesopotamia. He has proposed that these complex societies developed not as a result of a single condition, such as technological or scientific growth, but as a product of numerous interrelated conditions, particularly social organization and craft specialization. His best-known book is *The Evolution of Urban Society* (1966). Adams has been a professor at the University of Chicago since 1955.

Adams, Samuel

Samuel Adams, as a revolutionary spokesman and writer, profoundly swayed public opinion in favor of American independence. The artist John Singleton Copley portrayed Adams pointing to the Massachusetts Charter. (Courtesy Museum of Fine Arts, Boston. Deposited by the City of Boston.)

Samuel Adams, b. Boston, Sept. 17, 1722, d. Oct. 2, 1803, was a major leader in the American Revolution. The son of a wealthy brewer, he inherited one-third of the family property but lost most of it through poor management. After attending Harvard, he became active in colonial politics and enjoyed a popular following through his activities in the Boston political clubs, such as the Caucus Club, which was influential in nominating candidates for local office. He was an effective spokesman for the popular party opposed to the entrenched circle around the royal governor.

Adams organized the protest against the STAMP ACT (1765) and was a founder of the SONS OF LIBERTY. Undoubtedly the most influential member of the lower house of the Massachusetts legislature (1765–74), he drafted most of the major protest documents, including the Circular Letter (1768) against the TOWNSHEND ACTS. He also wrote frequently for the press in defense of colonial rights. Adams formed close ties with John HANCOCK, whose connections with the Boston merchants made him useful in the revolutionary cause. After 1770 he was the focal point in the creation of intercolonial committees of correspondence to sustain the spirit of resistance. He was a principal organizer of the BOSTON TEA PARTY (1773).

Because of the intemperate language of his essays for the press (Lt. Gov. Thomas Hutchinson called him the greatest "incendiary" in the empire) and his early advocacy of independence, Adams was regarded as a radical. At the First Continental Congress he worked closely with John Adams, his second cousin. Their influence was crucial in the rejection of the plan of union presented by Joseph GALLOWAY and in the adoption of a compulsory nonimportation agreement (in effect a boycott of British goods). Samuel Adams remained in Congress until 1781, participating in the drafting of the Articles of Confederation. After the Revolution his influence in Massachusetts was never as great, although he continued to be active in state politics, serving as lieutenant governor (1789–93) and as governor (1794–97). A more conservative figure in later years, he condemned the farmers' actions during SHAYS'S REBELLION and endorsed ratification of the federal Constitution.   HARRY AMMON

Bibliography: Cushing, Harry A., ed., *The Writings of Samuel Adams*, 3 vols. (1904–08; repr. 1968); Galvin, John B., *Three Men of Boston* (1976); Gerson, Noel B., *Grand Incendiary: A Biography of Samuel Adams* (1973); Harlow, Ralph V., *Samuel Adams, Promoter of the American Revolution* (1972); Hosmer, James, *Samuel Adams* (1898; repr. 1972); Miller, John C., *Sam Adams, Pioneer in Propaganda* (1936; repr. 1960).

Adams, Samuel Hopkins

Samuel Hopkins Adams, b. Jan. 26, 1871, d. Nov. 15, 1958, was an American journalist and novelist whose muckraking articles on public health and medicine printed in *McClure's* and *Collier's* magazines helped bring about the Pure Food and Drug Act of 1906. He also wrote both a fictional account, *Revelry* (1926), and a factual one, *Incredible Era* (1939), of the scandal-ridden Harding administration.

Adams, Walter Sydney

The research of the American astrophysicist Walter Sydney Adams, b. Kessab, Syria, Dec. 20, 1876, d. May 11, 1956, ranged from the study of planetary atmospheres to his greatest achievement, the discovery of a fundamentally new method for determining stellar distances. A graduate of Dartmouth College and the University of Chicago, Adams excelled first at Yerkes Observatory in Wisconsin (1901–04) and then at Mount Wilson in California (1904–46), where, under his direction from 1923 to 1946, the observatory attained a position of worldwide preeminence. His early work on sunspot spectra furnished clues that were crucial to the development of the method of spectroscopic parallax, whereby stellar luminosities, and thereby distances, can be determined from the intensities of certain sensitive spectral lines.

Adam's Peak

Adam's Peak (also known as Samanala or Sri Padastanaya) is a cone-shaped mountain in south central Sri Lanka about 72 km (45 mi) east of Colombo. It is 2,243 m (7,360 ft) high and is considered a sacred mountain by Buddhists, Hindus, and Muslims because of a 1.5-m-long (5-ft) depression of its summit resembling a footprint, variously believed to be that of Buddha, Shiva, or Adam.

Adamson, Robert: see HILL, D. O., AND ADAMSON, ROBERT.

Adana   [ah-dah-nah']

Adana (1978 est. pop., 562,200) is the capital city of Adana province on the southern coast of Turkey. Located on the banks of the Seyhan River, 52 km (32 mi) north of the Mediterranean, it is Turkey's fourth largest city. The climate is hot and semiarid, with summer temperatures above 29° C (84° F) and average yearly rainfall of 619 mm (24.4 in). Adana is the center of the Turkish cotton industry.

Possibly an ancient Hittite city, Adana was later a Roman military station. It became a Turkish city during the 16th century. Notable buildings in the city include 16th-century mosques and the ancient covered market Kapali Carsi.

adaptation, biological: see ADAPTIVE RADIATION; EVOLUTION.

adaptive radiation

Adaptive radiation is the EVOLUTION of a species into many diverse species, each adapted to a different habitat. Differentiation and complexity of the species are increased, with the resulting decrease in competition. As a result, the species is able to make use of all available niches in the habitat so that more populations flourish. Adaptive radiation occurs most rapidly when a species colonizes a new environment in which many ecological niches are unoccupied. The results are a population increase and multiple divergence. After a species radiates and diverges, dominant forms eventually prevail. When environmental conditions change, those forms of the species which cannot readapt may become extinct.

DARWIN'S FINCHES (see also DARWIN, CHARLES) are a classic example of adaptive radiation. All 14 species living on the Galápagos Islands are derived from a single species of finch— a ground-dwelling seedeater—that migrated to those islands. Because the ecological niches on the isolated islands were unoccupied, the finch differentiated into 14 diverse species. Some remained ground-dwelling seedeaters, and others lived on cactus or insects and dwelled in trees.

Addams, Charles

The American cartoonist Charles Samuel Addams, b. Westfield, N.J., Jan. 7, 1912, is an undisputed master of macabre humor in which humanoid monsters are shown in everyday situations. His cartoons have appeared in the *New Yorker* magazine since 1935. One depicts his favorite character, a haggard vamp, knocking at the door of an old crone and asking, "May I borrow a cup of cyanide?" His cartoons have been published in 11 anthologies, including *Drawn and Quartered* (1942) and *My Crowd* (1970), and were the basis for a television series, "The Addams Family" (1964–66).
                                    CHRISTOPHER G. TRUMP

Addams, Jane

Jane Laura Addams, b. Cedarville, Ill., Sept. 6, 1860, d. May 21, 1935, was an American social reformer, pacifist, and women's rights advocate. In 1889, influenced by British precedents, she founded Hull House, an institution in Chicago where she and other social reformers lived and worked to improve conditions in the city's slums. Hull House became a model for many other settlement houses in the United States. Jane Addams became president of the Women's International League for Peace and Freedom in 1919. Together with Nicholas Murray Butler, she received the Nobel Peace Prize in 1931. Her books include *Democracy and Social Ethics* (1902) and *Twenty Years at Hull House* (1910).   JOHN ROBINSON

Jane Addams, an American social worker, was awarded the 1931 Nobel Peace Prize. She supported investigations that resulted in child labor reform, an 8-hour working day for women, and better housing. Hull House, the settlement house in Chicago that was the center of her work, furnished such services as day-care for working mothers.

Bibliography: Addams, Jane, *The Social Thought of Jane Addams*, ed. by Christopher Lasch (1965); Davis, Allen F., *American Heroine: The Life and Legend of Jane Addams* (1973); Farrell, John C., *Beloved Lady: A History of Jane Addams's Ideas on Reform and Peace* (1967).

addax [ad'-aks]

The addax, *Addax nasomaculatus*, is the single species of addax among many antelope species in the family Bovidae of the order Artiodactyla. It is found only in the Sahara, where it was once widespread. The plump, short-legged addax is more than 1.8 m (6 ft) long and about 1 m (39 in) tall at the shoulders, and it weighs up to 120 kg (265 lb). Both sexes have long horns that are ringed and screw-shaped. The coat is gray to white, with a black skullcap and facial markings. The broad hooves are an adaptation for travel on desert sands. Addaxes usually get water only from the plants they eat, but in captivity they drink large amounts. Unable to flee hunters as speedily as some other antelopes do, the addax is an endangered species.   EVERETT SENTMAN

The addax, A. nasomaculatus, *an endangered species of antelope, is hunted for its flesh and hide. Both male and female addaxes have curved, spiraled horns.*

adder

An adder is any of several venomous snakes of the viper family, Viperidae. The name is also applied to several other kinds of snakes, some nonpoisonous. The species best known simply as "adder" is the common adder, or European viper, *Vipera berus*, found throughout Europe and northern Asia. Its stocky body—typical of vipers, which ambush and strike their prey and wait for them to die, rather than actively pursue them—reaches a length of about 60 cm (2 ft) and is usually brownish, with a black zigzag stripe down the back. The snake feeds on lizards and small mammals, and its bite is rarely fatal to humans. It is ovoviviparous; the eggs reach full development within the female and the young are born live or hatch immediately upon laying.   PETER L. PETRAKIS

Bibliography: Minton, Sherman A., and Madge R., *Venomous Reptiles* (1969).

The common adder, V. berus, *is a venomous snake of Europe and Asia. It feeds on rodents and birds and may hibernate during winter. The adder's venom is seldom fatal to human beings.*

adder's-tongue

Adder's-tongue is any of about 25 species constituting the herb genus *Erythronium* of the lily family, Liliaceae. Other common names are dog's-tooth violet, fawn lily, and trout lily. The plants are 15–60 cm (6–24 in) high, and their two broad leaves are richly mottled, and the graceful flowers may be a variety of colors, making them attractive plants for rock gardens. They are native to North America, with one species in Eurasia. Adder's-tongue fern is the common name for the fern genus *Ophioglossum*, which is widely dispersed in temperate and tropical regions.   CHARLES WILSON

addiction: see DRUG ABUSE.

adding machine

The adding machine is a mechanical device that adds numbers. The forerunners of such devices were prehistoric and may have been scratches in rock, notches in wood, knots in a strip of hide, or pebbles grouped together. The regularly spaced knots in a ship's line that were added to tell the depth of the water, or an array of stone counters shifted on a board in ancient and medieval times, were used to perform some of the functions of an adding machine, as were the beads-on-wires of the medieval Chinese *suan p'an*, called ABACUS today (from Greek *abax*, meaning "counting board"). All these early devices required their operators to know how to count, and they demonstrated that physical objects could be placed and moved to represent numbers and sums.

MECHANICAL DEVICES

Knowledge of these devices was used to design the earliest-known machine that itself added numbers by moving and shifting physical objects without requiring a human operator to know how to add. The physical objects were gear wheels and worm gears, meshed to form a train of gears. Described in a treatise by Hero of Alexandria that dates from the 2d century AD, this machine could add up the *stades* (kilometers or miles) that a carriage traveled.

The principle of its operation, based on the rotation of the pegged or single-tooth wheel, is still found today in water meters, gas meters, and bicycle and automobile ODOMETERS. If a one-tooth gear, driven by a wheel of the carriage, engages its single tooth with the ten-teeth gear once every time it revolves, the result will be that it must make ten revolutions in order to rotate the ten-teeth gear once. If the ten-teeth gear has on its axle a second one-tooth gear that engages a second ten-teeth gear, then the second ten-teeth gear will revolve once for every 100 revolutions of the original single-tooth gear.

If the vehicle travels 0.01 km every time the first single-tooth gear revolves once, then the second ten-teeth gear will revolve once per kilometer. If the ten numbers 0 through 9 are evenly spaced around the rim of the second ten-teeth gear wheel, then as each number appears behind a tiny window in front of the rim, 1 km is registered. For every matched pair of one- and ten-teeth gears added to the train thereafter, another window may be added. Thus, two windows read up to 99 km, and four windows up to 9,999 km.

In the 17th century the French mathematician Blaise Pascal converted this mechanical arrangement of the odometer into an adding machine that a clerk could operate. He made each ten-teeth wheel accessible to be turned directly by a person's hand (later inventors added keys and a crank), with the result that when the wheels were turned in the proper sequences, a series of numbers was entered and a cumulative sum was obtained. The gear train supplied a mechanical answer equal to the answer that is obtained by using arithmetic.

In the same century the German mathematician and philosopher Gottfried Wilhelm von Leibniz extended the adding ability of Pascal's machine to produce a multiplying calculator that achieved results by adding. Thus, the answer to 14 x 5 was obtained by adding 14 five times. The mechanical principles of the adding machine were extended and incorporated in hand-cranked calculators during the 18th and 19th centuries and in electrically operated calculators during the 20th century.

ELECTRONIC DEVICES

By the middle of the 20th century, the electronic circuitry of the COMPUTER began to replace the electromechanical adding operations of business office machines, and by the last quarter of the century microminiaturization of circuits made handheld CALCULATORS possible. The startlingly rich and varied logical capacities of these devices virtually eclipsed their still-retained ability to function as adding machines. Thus, although the familiar adding machine of the 19th and early 20th centuries became obsolete in the face of technological progress, human exploitation of the fundamental capacity of machines to "add" by physical operations persists.   THOMAS M. SMITH

Bibliography: Merchant, Ronald, *Adding Machines and Calculators* (1974); Walker, A. L., et al., *How to Use Adding and Calculating Machines*, 3d ed. (1967).

Addis Ababa   [ad'-is ah'-buh-buh]

Addis Ababa ("New Flower") is the capital of Ethiopia and has a population of 1,277,159 (1980 est.). It is located in the Entoto Mountains of Shewa province in the northwestern region of the African high plateau. At an elevation of 2,400 m (8,000 ft), the city has a pleasant temperature range of 15°–18° C (60°–65° F). The rainy season, with cooler temperatures, lasts from mid-June to mid-September. The average yearly rainfall is 1,120 mm (44.1 in).

Addis Ababa was established in 1887 by Emperor Menelik II. Amharas predominate, but other ethnic groups are also represented. In addition, an international community of approximately 50,000 is concentrated around the Organization of African Unity (OAU) and the UN Economic Commission for Africa, both of which have headquarters in the city.

The architectural pattern reflects the mixed population. The upper section of the city includes traditional living areas, shanty towns, the central market, and Addis Ababa University. The newer and lower section contains government buildings, international offices (such as the OAU's Africa Hall), the Jubilee Palace, and other palaces of former emperors. The growth of the city has been sporadic and unplanned, however.

Addis Ababa is the site of Addis Ababa University (1950), and numerous churches. Many artists, most of whom paint church scenes on animal skins or canvas, reside in the city. Jewelry, rugs, and baskets are also produced. Many industrial establishments, such as cement factories, beer and tobacco plants, and textile mills, are located in the city.

PETER SCHWAB

Addison, Joseph

Joseph Addison, an 18th-century English essayist, appears in this portrait by Michael Dahl. Addison's importance to English prose is summarized by Samuel Johnson, who claimed, "Whoever wishes to attain an English style, familiar but not coarse, and elegant but not ostentatious, must give up his days and nights to the volumes of Addison."

Joseph Addison, b. May 1, 1672, d. June 17, 1719, an English poet and essayist, was coauthor with Sir Richard STEELE of the great series of periodical essays *The Tatler* and *The Spectator*. He is ranked among the minor masters of English prose style and credited with raising the general cultural level of the English middle classes.

Political Career. Addison, educated at Oxford, had his first poem published in 1693. He was politically ambitious, and much of his literary effort was an adjunct to his ambition. His early poems paid court to important Whig leaders; he first achieved celebrity with *The Campaign* (1704), a poem commemorating the Battle of Blenheim. Later he wrote two series of essays, *The Whig Examiner* (1710) and *The Freeholder* (1715–16), in defense of his party. So closely was he identified with the Whigs that when he produced his only play, *Cato* (1713), a tragedy whose hero is the Roman patriot, it enjoyed great success as an allegory of contemporary politics.

These efforts proved effective: Addison was appointed undersecretary of state (1706), secretary to the lord lieutenant in Ireland (1709), and secretary to the Regency following the death of Queen Anne (1714). His highest office was secretary of state (1717–18), from which he retired with a generous pension. His personal conduct had always been sober; on his deathbed he is said to have summoned his stepson to his side so that he might see "in what peace a Christian can die."

Writings. Addison had been schoolboy friends with Steele, to whose *Tatler* (1709–11) he became chief contributor. In *The Spectator* (1711–12) their positions were reversed: of 555 essays, Addison wrote 274. Addison adopted Steele's purpose from *The Tatler*, "to enliven Morality with Wit, and to temper Wit with Morality," and added a further purpose: to introduce his middle-class public to recent developments in philosophy and literature and thus to educate their taste. Thus Addison helped to popularize the philosophy of John Locke; he devoted a series of *Spectator* essays to criticism of John Milton's *Paradise Lost;* and he inculcated principles of good judgment in the arts. He did this with the urbanity of a man about town, and in prose that remains a model of intelligent, graceful simplicity.

He also continued from *The Tatler* the practice of inventing fictional characters who represented different walks of life and whose adventures entertained readers. The most popular of these was Sir Roger de Coverley, a country gentleman of charming eccentricity, good sense, and kindness. To later generations this character embodied a sentimental ideal of the English country squire.   WILLIAM McCARTHY

Bibliography: Allen, Robert J., *Addison and Steele: Selections from "The Tatler" and "The Spectator"* (1957); Smithers, Peter, *The Life of Joseph Addison*, 2d ed. (1968).

Addison's disease

Addison's disease is caused by insufficient production of hormones by the cortex of the ADRENAL GLANDS, usually resulting from damage by tuberculosis or by fungal infections. The disease is named for Thomas Addison, the English physician who first described it in 1855. Symptoms are weakness, anemia, weight loss, gastrointestinal problems, low blood pressure, tanning of the skin, and sometimes nervousness and irritability. Although the disease was once nearly always fatal, patients treated with synthetic cortical hormones may now expect to recover completely. PETER L. PETRAKIS

addition: see ARITHMETIC.

Ade, George [ayd]

The journalist, humorist, and playwright George Ade, b. Kentland, Ind., Feb. 9, 1866, d. May 16, 1944, mastered a midwestern idiom of homespun phrases and incongruous moralisms best illustrated in *Fables in Slang* (1899). His parables of naiveté and pomposity first appeared in his *Chicago Record* newspaper column. Ten of his plays appeared on Broadway, including *The County Chairman* (1903) and *The College Widow* (1904).

Bibliography: Shepherd, Jean, *The America of George Ade* (1961).

Adelaide

Adelaide is the capital city of South Australia and Australia's fourth largest city, with a population of 899,300 (1975 est.). Located in the southeastern part of Australia, it is on the Torrens River approximately 8 km (5 mi) inland from the Gulf of St. Vincent on an alluvial plain between the coast and the Mount Lofty Range. It is about 11 km (7 mi) from its port city, Port Adelaide. The average annual temperature is 17.7° C (64° F), with mild winters and summer temperatures often above 37.7° C (100° F).

Adelaide, founded in 1836, was named for Queen Adelaide, consort of William IV. It is a planned and uncongested city, whose center is divided by the Torrens into two areas, the northern, residential area and the southern business area. A parkland belt runs along the river, and a green belt surrounds the central city.

Adelaide is a major industrial city; most heavy industry— automobile plants, tire plants, steel works, chemical plants, oil refineries, and sugar refineries—is located along the rail link between Adelaide and Port Adelaide. An oil refinery is also located at Hallett Cove, approximately 32 km (20 mi) south of

the city. Dairy farming and apple orchards flourish in the fertile areas around the city.

Adelaide is the home of the University of Adelaide (1874) and the biennial Adelaide Festival of Arts. Two museums, The Institute of Art and the Adelaide Museum, are located here.

Adelaide, University of: see AUSTRALIAN UNIVERSITIES.

Aden [ay'-den or ah'-den]

Aden (1973 est. pop., 264,000) is the capital of the People's Democratic Republic of Yemen (formerly Aden Crown Colony and Aden Protectorate). Located on the northwest shore of the Gulf of Aden, about 160 km (100 mi) east of the Bab el-Mandeb, it is the country's principal port. Aden, a drab city, is hot and extremely dry. The average temperature is 29° C (84° F), and the average annual rainfall is 39 mm (1.54 in). Oil is the most important product, and extensive oil bunkerage facilities have been built in the harbor. Salt, tiles, bricks, textiles, coal, and hides are also produced.

The city is made up of several separate areas. Crater, or the old city, is on a small peninsula and within the walls of an ancient volcano. The Crescent, or new city, includes the port and commercial area on the western peninsula. The oil refinery is on the mainland at Little Aden. The University of Aden was founded here in 1975.

Settled as early as the 3d century BC, Aden was a Roman trading port. It was captured by the Turks in 1538 and controlled by Yemen (Sana) until 1728. From 1839 to 1967 it was controlled by Great Britain. The port was used as an important station on the route from the Eastern Mediterranean to India.

Aden, Gulf of

The Gulf of Aden is the sea link between the Red Sea and the Arabian Sea extending between the Arabian Peninsula and the Horn of Africa. It is bordered on the north by Yemen (Aden), on the west by Djibouti, and on the south by Somalia. In the northwest it is connected with the Red Sea by the strait of Bab el-Mandeb; on the east it opens to the Arabian Sea. The gulf was heavily used by oil tankers heading south toward the Cape of Good Hope and north through the Suez Canal, but such traffic has declined in recent years. It is of strategic importance for oil-consuming states. The main ports on the gulf are Aden, Djibouti, and Berbera. PETER SCHWAB

Adelaide's columned Parliament House serves as the legislative center of South Australia. Important for its industry and manufacturing potential, Adelaide experienced rapid growth at the turn of the century after the discovery of iron ore deposits nearby.

Adenauer, Konrad   [ah'-duh-now-ur]

Konrad Adenauer, b. Jan. 5, 1876, d. Apr. 19, 1967, was the first chancellor of the Federal Republic of Germany. The son of a court clerk in Cologne, he became a lawyer, entered politics, and was mayor of his native city from the last year of World War I until his expulsion by the National Socialists in 1933. He was a leader of the catholic Center party; he also served (1920–33) as chairman of the Prussian upper house, the Council of State, during the Weimar Republic and twice was seriously considered for the chancellorship.

Relatively undisturbed during the Third Reich until, late in 1944, the Gestapo imprisoned him for two months, Adenauer was reinstated as mayor when U.S. forces took Cologne in spring 1945. He then became cofounder and leader of the postwar Christian Democratic Union, president of the assembly that drafted the constitution of the Federal Republic of Germany being formed from the U.S., British, and French zones of occupation, and, in 1949, the republic's first chancellor. He retired from this office in 1963 at the age of 87, but he remained in the West German parliament until his death four years later.

A stern patriarch and shrewd politician, Adenauer was deeply committed to the traditional values of Western Christendom that Adolf Hitler and many of his followers had repudiated. But he was no less opposed than Hitler to communism and therefore pursued throughout his long chancellorship a single-mindedly Western-oriented foreign policy, with the result that West Germany became not only a major economic and political power in Western Europe but also a pillar of NATO.

DONALD S. DETWILER

Konrad Adenauer, as West German chancellor (1949-63), was a staunch foe of the Communist East German regime, which erected the Berlin Wall in 1961 to stem the flow of refugees to the West. Here Adenauer has just inspected the wall, which is immediately behind him in front of the Brandenburg Gate.

Bibliography: Adenauer, Konrad, *Memoirs*, 4 vols., trans. by Beate von Oppen (1966–70); Heidenheimer, Arnold J., *Adenauer and the CDU: the Rise of the Leader and the Integration of the Party* (1960); Hiscocks, Richard, *The Adenauer Era* (1966); Prittie, Terence, *Konrad Adenauer, 1876–1967* (1971); Ryder, A. J., *Twentieth-Century Germany* (1973).

adenoids   [ad'-uhn-oidz]

Adenoids are tonsillike folds of lymphoid tissue in the nasopharynx, the passage leading from the nose to the throat. They are correctly called pharyngeal tonsils; the term *adenoids* is applied when the tissues are enlarged and inflamed. Their function is not known exactly, but they tend to atrophy

as a child grows up. The adenoids can become infected, however, in which case they cause earaches and interfere with breathing. The infection may spread to the tonsils or to the eustachian tubes. The standard treatment of infected pharyngeal tissues is to remove them surgically.   PETER L. PETRAKIS

See also: TONSILS.

adenoma   [ad-uh-noh'-muh]

An adenoma is a nonmalignant tumor of glandular tissue. It can occur in mucous glands of the gastrointestinal and respiratory tracts and in endocrine glands. Although adenomas are not likely to become malignant, they can cause medical problems. For example, adenoma in the stomach is associated with vague stomach pain, lack of stomach hydrochloric acid, and pernicious anemia. Bronchial adenoma is associated with the coughing up of blood and with repeated pulmonary infections. Adenoma in the endocrine glands can result in excessive secretion of endocrine hormones by these glands, which affects numerous body organs.

PETER L. PETRAKIS

adhesion

In physics, adhesion is the attraction of two different substances, one of which is usually a liquid and the other a solid. Adhesion results from intermolecular forces between the substances and is distinct from cohesion, which involves only intermolecular attractive forces within a single substance. The forces in both adhesion and cohesion are chiefly van der Waals forces. The competition of adhesive and cohesive forces results in CAPILLARITY, in which a liquid either rises or falls in a fine tube.

Bibliography: Weber, Robert, et al., *College Physics* (1974).

See also: SURFACE TENSION.

adhesive

An adhesive is a substance capable of holding two surfaces together in a strong, often permanent bond. Adhesives may be classified as natural or synthetic; or they may be classified by their reaction to heat (thermoplastic and thermosetting adhesives) or by their ability to remain rigid or to stretch (ELASTOMER adhesives).

In the 20th century, natural adhesives—primarily organic and of animal or vegetable origin—have been replaced or modified by synthetics, either used alone or added to natural adhesives. Most synthetics are polymers—composed of huge molecules formed by the union of many simple molecules—and supply great strength and flexibility. Thermoplastic resin adhesives, such as vinyl resins and cellulose derivatives that can be softened by heating, are used for the manufacture of safety glass and for the bonding of wood, rubber, metal, and paper products. Some thermoplastics, such as the polyamides, ROSIN derivatives, polyethylene, and polyvinyl acetate, are used as hot-melt adhesives: they are applied in the molten state to form a rigid bond on cooling. Thermosetting adhesives, which include a large number of synthetic resins, are converted by heat or a catalyst into insoluble and infusible materials. Tough, strong EPOXY RESINS shrink little as they harden. They are applied in two parts; the resin itself is cured or set by the addition of a catalyst, and the mixture usually hardens rapidly at room temperature to form a permanent bond. Elastomeric adhesives include natural and synthetic rubber cements and are used for bonding flexible materials such as paper, textiles, and leather.

See also: PLASTICS; RESIN.

adiabatic process   [ad-ee-uh-bat'-ik]

Adiabatic compression and expansion are thermodynamic processes in which the pressure of a gas is increased or decreased without any exchange of heat energy with the surroundings. In fact, any process that occurs without heat transfer is called an adiabatic process. (See HEAT AND HEAT TRANSFER.)

The adiabatic compression or expansion of a gas can occur if the gas is insulated from its surroundings or if the process takes place quickly enough to prevent any significant heat transfer. This is essentially the case in a number of important devices, including air compressors, rockets, and internal combustion engines. The propagation of sound through the atmosphere also takes place due to a series of adiabatic compression and expansion waves.

An adiabatic expansion is usually accompanied by a decrease in the gas temperature. This can be observed in the case of a common aerosol can, which becomes cold after a quantity of gas has been released. The reason for the temperature drop is that the gas is released too quickly to absorb any significant heat energy from its surroundings. Thus, the work performed in expanding the released gas drains some of the internal energy of the gas still in the can, making it colder. Once the can itself becomes cold to the touch, however, the process is no longer adiabatic.

In a similar fashion, adiabatic compression usually increases the temperature of a gas, since work is done on the system by the surroundings. For example, when air is pumped into an automobile tire, the air's temperature rises as a result of compression.

Adiabatic compression and expansion also occur in liquids and solids. Liquid and solid matter, however, compress and expand to a much smaller degree than matter in the gaseous state.

GARY S. SETTLES

Bibliography: Resnick, R., and Halliday, D., *Physics for Students of Science and Engineering, Part I* (1960).

See also: CARNOT CYCLE; GAS LAWS; THERMODYNAMICS.

Adige River   [ah-dee'-jay]

Located in northern Italy, the Adige River rises in Alpine lakes and runs 410 km (255 mi) past Bolzano and the Val Lagarina, near Verona, to enter the Adriatic Sea about 24 km (15 mi) south of Venice. It has a drainage area of 12,200 km² (4,710 mi²). The Adige supplies hydroelectric power in the Alps and irrigates portions of the Veneto.

Adirondack Mountains

The Adirondack Mountains are a group of rounded, forested peaks in northeastern New York covering about 12,950 km² (5,000 mi²). Forty-five summits exceed 1,200 m (4,000 ft) in height; the tallest is Mount Marcy (1,629 m/5,344 ft). Ancient Precambrian rocks (over 1 billion years old) underlie the mountains. Lake George, Lake Placid, and the Upper, Lower, and Middle Saranac lakes are among the many lakes created by glaciation. The Hudson River rises near the top of Mount Marcy. Other river systems draining the region are the Sacandaga, the Black, and the Oswegatchie.

Almost two-thirds of the region is included in the wilderness Adirondack State Park, created by the state, and although winter temperatures of −36° C (−35° F) are registered, it is a year-round recreation resort. Some iron ore deposits are mined. The Indians never settled permanently here, and the area remains sparsely populated. The name is derived from the Indian for "they of the Great Rocks."

Adivar, Halide Edib: see HALIDE EDIB ADIVAR.

adjective: see PARTS OF SPEECH.

Adler, Alfred

Alfred Adler, b. Feb. 7, 1870, d. May 28, 1937, was an Austrian physician and psychologist who created a socially oriented personality theory and system of psychotherapy called individual psychology. According to this theory, people are guided by values and goals of which they may be aware, not driven by unconscious instincts. A younger contemporary of Sigmund FREUD, Adler attended Freud's circle from 1902 to 1911, leading Freud to claim him as a disciple who later defected. Adler rejected the label of disciple, conceding only, "I

Alfred Adler, Viennese physician, was an early follower of Sigmund Freud but split with him over differences in their approach to psychology. Adler is remembered as the founder of individual psychology, a school of thought stressing the influence of inferiority feelings on human behavior.

learned from his mistakes." Adler pioneered in preventive psychiatry by establishing more than 30 child-guidance centers in Vienna and by countless speaking engagements to large audiences. From 1926 until his death he lectured extensively in the United States, where he settled in 1935. Adler presented his system in *The Neurotic Constitution* (1912; Eng. trans., 1917), *Practice and Theory* (1920; Eng. trans., 1925), *Understanding Human Nature* (1927; Eng. trans., 1927), *Social Interest* (1933; Eng. trans., 1938), and other works.

In individual psychology, the person is seen as moving away from situations that make him or her feel inferior and toward goals of success and superiority. Adler accepted the phrase *inferiority complex* to denote extreme feelings of inadequacy. How one sees oneself and the world, one's goals, and one's manner of striving for these goals constitute one's *lifestyle*. It is manifested in all one does, including one's dreams and early recollections. An individual is part of larger systems: physical; social, ranging from the family to all humanity; and biological, including the male-female system. These create the problems of work, friendship, and sexual love. Their solution requires development of the human capacity for *social interest*. This coordinates one's striving with that of one's fellow humans. All forms of maladjustment, failure in life, are striving for socially useless goals. In Adler's psychotherapy the patients' self-esteem is boosted and they are made aware of mistakes in life-style so that they may correct them.

By emphasizing the whole person as an active agent relating to the surrounding world, Adler anticipated recent trends, and his psychology is increasingly popular.

H. L. ANSBACHER

Bibliography: Adler, Alfred, *Superiority and Social Interest: A Collection of Later Writings*, ed. by H. L. and R. R. Ansbacher, 3d rev. ed. (1979), *The Individual Psychology of Alfred Adler*, ed. by H. L. and R. R. Ansbacher (1956), and *What Life Should Mean to You* (1931); Bottome, Phyllis, *Alfred Adler: Apostle of Freedom*, rev. ed. (1957); Orgler, Hertha, *Alfred Adler: The Man and His Work* (1939; 3d ed., 1963); Sperber, Manès, *Masks of Loneliness: Alfred Adler in Perspective* (1974).

Adler, Cyrus

Cyrus Adler, b. Van Buren, Ark., Sept. 13, 1863, d. Apr. 7, 1940, was an American educator and spokesman for Jewish rights. After graduating from the University of Pennsylvania and Johns Hopkins University, he taught Semitic languages at the latter from 1884 to 1893. Other positions followed at the National Museum, the Smithsonian Institution, Dropsie College, and Jewish Theological Seminary, where he was president from 1915 to 1940. A regular contributor to publications of the American Jewish Historical Society, Adler helped to establish the Jewish Publication Society of America. He also edited the articles on postbiblical antiquities and American Jews in the *Jewish Encyclopedia* (1905). Adler reacted publicly against anti-Semitic excesses in Kishinev (1903), Poland (1917), the Ukraine (1919), and Palestine (1929). As president of the American Jewish Committee (1929–40), he spearheaded relief to Jews during the early years of Adolf Hitler.

SAUL S. FRIEDMAN

Bibliography: Adler, Cyrus, *Jews in the Diplomatic Correspondence of the United States* (1906); Neumann, A. A., *Cyrus Adler* (1942).

Adler, Dankmar

The German-born American architect Dankmar Adler, b. July 3, 1844, d. Apr. 16, 1900, was a member of the CHICAGO SCHOOL of architects that greatly influenced modern architecture in the United States. Adler gained his training by working for various architectural firms after immigrating to Detroit in 1854. He moved to Chicago about 1865, and there he formed a partnership with Louis SULLIVAN that lasted from 1881 until 1895. In the partnership Adler was engineering designer and administrator, and Sullivan was planner and artist for the buildings their firm constructed. Adler's mastery of acoustics, first evident in his plans for the Central Music Hall in Chicago (completed in 1879), achieved its zenith in the theater (now restored) of the AUDITORIUM BUILDING (built 1887–89). The son of a liberal rabbi, Adler took part in the design and construction of a series of synagogues in Chicago, including Kehillath Anshe Ma'ariv for his father's congregation and, most notably, Isaiah Temple (1899).   J. MEREDITH NEIL

Bibliography: Morrison, Hugh Sinclair, *Louis Sullivan: Prophet of Modern Architecture*, rev. ed. (1971); Mumford, Lewis, ed., *Roots of Contemporary American Architecture* (1952).

Adler, Felix

Felix Adler, b. Aug. 13, 1851, d. Apr. 24, 1933, was an American educator and founder of the ETHICAL CULTURE movement. He studied at Columbia College and at the universities of Berlin and Heidelberg. After two years as professor of Hebrew and Oriental literature at Cornell, Adler founded (1876) the New York Society for Ethical Culture. The Ethical Culture society welcomed people from all backgrounds and taught that an ethical reality existed independently of the existence of a personal God. Under Adler, the society was active in child welfare, medical care for the poor, slum improvement, labor relations, and city politics.

Adler also pioneered in education, advocating progressive education, free kindergartens, and vocational training schools. He was professor of political and social ethics at Columbia from 1902 to 1918. His books include *Creed and Deed: A Series of Discourses* (1877).

Adler, Jacob, Stella, and Luther

The Russian-born actor **Jacob P. Adler**, b. Jan. 1, 1855, d. Mar. 31, 1926, is widely considered to have been one of the greatest dramatic actors of the Yiddish stage. While the YIDDISH THEATER was in its infancy, the 24-year-old Adler joined a professional troupe that toured Russia, presenting popular operettas. Although not a gifted singer, he excelled in romantic parts. Following the 1882 tsarist ban on Yiddish theater, Adler immigrated to London, and four years later he went to the United States. Unsuccessful, he soon went back to Europe, but he returned to New York in 1890. His first production there failed, but his second offering, *Soldier Moishele*, was enthusiastically received. Overnight, he became the idol of the Yiddish stage, a position he held for the rest of his life. One famous role was as Shakespeare's Shylock, which he played (1893) in Yiddish with an English-speaking cast. He also adapted Shakespeare's *Hamlet* and *King Lear* for the Yiddish theater and often directed the productions in which he appeared.

Adler (reverently referred to as the "Great Eagle") always starred in his own productions. He had commanding stage presence, enhanced by a fiery temperament, a striking physique, and a rich, sonorous voice. He was at his best when playing highly dramatic or tragic roles. Adler was also instrumental in introducing the plays of Jacob GORDIN, the most celebrated Yiddish playwright of his time. Adler's 1891 presentation of *Siberia*, the first Gordin play ever produced, inaugurated the "golden epoch" of the Yiddish theater.

Two of Adler's children distinguished themselves in the American theater. **Luther Adler**, b. May 4, 1903, was a prominent actor in both New York and London and also appeared in movies. **Stella Adler**, b. Feb. 10, 1902, was one of the original members of the Group Theater and later opened her own acting studio, establishing herself as one of the foremost American interpreters of the Stanislavsky acting method.

EDNA NAHSHON

Bibliography: Rosenfeld, Lulla, *Bright Star of Exile: Jacob Adler and the Yiddish Theatre* (1977).

Adler, Mortimer J.

The American professor and editor Mortimer Jerome Adler, b. New York City, Dec. 28, 1902, is best known for conceiving large publishing ventures, including the 54-volume *Great Books of the Western World*. Adler received his doctorate at Columbia University. For 22 years he taught philosophy of law at the University of Chicago, becoming associated with Robert M. Hutchins in the revision of the university's curriculum.

Adler believed that a liberal education could be derived from reading great works. With Hutchins, he arranged the publication, in 1952, of the Great Books series, to which he appended a 2-volume index, the *Synopticon*.

Adler became director of the Institute for Philosophical Research in 1952. For Encylopaedia Britannica, Inc., he edited a 10-volume *Gateway to the Great Books* (with Hutchins) and a 20-volume *Annals of America*. He then served as director of planning of the 15th edition of the *Encyclopaedia Britannica*. Adler also wrote the best-selling *How to Read a Book* (1940).

Bibliography: Adler, Mortimer, *Philosopher at Large: An Intellectual Autobiography* (1977).

Adler, Renata

Renata Adler, b. Oct. 19, 1938, is an American writer known for her sharp, witty essays and inventive fiction. After studying at the Sorbonne and Harvard, Adler became a staff writer (1962) for *The New Yorker*. Her essays in *Toward a Radical Middle* (1970) covered a variety of political and cultural topics; her film reviews (1968–69) for *The New York Times* were collected in *A Year in the Dark* (1970). Her novel *Speedboat* (1976), an artistically detached and fragmented work of dry humor, was received with excited but mixed critical reaction.

administrative law

Administrative law is the branch of law that governs and limits the exercise of decision-making authority by governmental agencies and officials. It consists of policies and procedures designed to prevent bureaucratic arbitrariness, to ensure that administrative officials adhere to legislative mandates, to guarantee a fair hearing to individuals when significant interests may be affected by governmental action, and to subject administrative authority to judicial control.

THE DEVELOPMENT OF ADMINISTRATIVE AGENCIES

Administrative law is a response to the growth of the governmental administrative process in the United States. As the nation expanded, and as it became increasingly industrialized and urbanized, it faced economic and social problems that required responses more technologically expert, more institutionally flexible, and more procedurally expeditious than either Congress or the courts could provide. Administrative agencies—now numbering in the scores in the federal government and in the thousands in the state governments—were created to remedy institutional deficiencies in formulating and administering public policy.

As a result, the administrative process has become a fourth branch of government, comparable in the scope of its authority to the three traditional branches—the executive, the legislative, and the judicial. In fact, the decisions of administrative agencies probably affect the lives of ordinary citizens more pervasively and more intimately than the decisions of the federal courts. Administrative law—the governing of the fourth branch of government—takes on importance because of its capacity to subject the decisions of administrative agencies to procedural fairness and democratic accountability.

The modern administrative process dates from the establishment of the Interstate Commerce Commission in 1887. Among the most prominent federal administrative agencies are the FEDERAL COMMUNICATIONS COMMISSION (1934), the NATIONAL LABOR RELATIONS BOARD (1935), the SECURITIES AND EXCHANGE COMMISSION (1934), the Equal Employment Opportunity Commission (1965), and the Environmental Protection Agency (1970). State governments generally rely on administrative agencies to regulate public utilities, to administer workers' compensation and public assistance programs, to collect taxes, and to supervise land use and zoning.

The gradual growth in the number and influence of the federal administrative agencies has required that new principles of law be developed to govern administrative agencies because they differ so significantly in structure and function from the legislature and the courts. For example, the members of an administrative agency are appointed by the president and confirmed by the Senate for limited terms of office, rather than being elected directly by the people as legislators are. In addition, the members of an administrative agency, unlike other officials of government, are permitted to combine the inconsistent functions of investigating, prosecuting, and adjudicating—despite the risks of bias that such a combination of functions introduces—in order to enhance their decision-making capabilities. Finally, administrative agencies, unlike other government institutions, are authorized to develop policy by a coordinated reliance on trial-type adjudicative proceedings characteristic of courts and on rule-making proceedings similar to legislative hearings.

PRINCIPLES OF ADMINISTRATIVE LAW

The principles of administrative law are rooted in the U.S. Constitution, the Administrative Procedure Act (a comprehensive federal statute enacted in 1946), federal legislation creating the individual administrative agencies, the rules and procedures adopted by the agencies for the conduct of their responsibilities, and court decisions.

The Nondelegation Doctrine. A fundamental principle of administrative law prohibits Congress from delegating legislative power to administrative agencies without providing statutory standards to guide the exercise of the delegated power. The nondelegation doctrine requires Congress to provide statutory standards in order to ensure that important public-policy issues are decided, at least in broad outline, in legislative forums that more closely reflect popular political sentiments. The Supreme Court, however, has almost invariably sustained the constitutionality of statutes delegating legislative power, even when the standards have been vague and indefinite. A typical formulation directs an agency to serve "the public interest, convenience, and necessity." Therefore, many commentators believe that the nondelegation doctrine has been ineffective in preventing the unrestricted transfer of legislative power to administrative agencies.

The Right to a Hearing. Another fundamental principle of administrative law requires an administrative agency to grant a hearing to those whose interests are likely to be affected significantly by the agency's proposed action. This requirement reflects the historic judgment that the right to a hearing is an important protection for the individual against precipitate, possibly erroneous, governmental action. Administrative law, however, intentionally departs from the traditional judicial practice of trial-type hearings. It permits agencies considerable flexibility in designing hearing procedures that are specifically adapted to the task at hand. Thus, the procedures by which an agency conducts its hearings may be ADVERSARY in nature if factual issues are in dispute or legislative in nature if policy choices are involved. Sometimes they are an intermediate blend of trial-type and legislative procedures when factual and policy issues are intertwined. Whatever procedures an agency chooses, it must comply with the DUE PROCESS clause of the Constitution and grant the affected individual an opportunity to be heard at a meaningful time and in a meaningful manner.

Judicial Review. Still another fundamental principle of administrative law requires that decisions of administrative agencies typically be subject to review by the courts. Judicial review of administrative action vindicates the rule of law, under which courts have always been the ultimate guarantors of the legality of governmental action. It also ensures that administrative agencies, which may sometimes act with excessive zeal, pursue their mandate within the limits of their legislative authority and with a proper respect for individual rights. Nevertheless, much administrative decision making remains beyond effective judicial control. No system can hope to review the vast number of informal decisions that every agency makes regularly. JAMES O. FREEDMAN

Bibliography: Davis, Kenneth C., *Administrative Law of the Seventies* (1976) and *Administrative Law Treatise*, 2d ed. (1977); Freedman, James O., *Crisis and Legitimacy: The Administrative Process and American Government* (1978); Lorch, R. S., *Democratic Process and Administrative Law* (1969; repr. 1973); Schwartz, Bernard, *Administrative Law* (1976); Wade, H. W., *Administrative Law*, 4th ed. (1978).

See also: GOVERNMENT REGULATION, SCOPE OF.

administrator

An administrator, in law, is a person given the authority to manage the ESTATE of a deceased person. An administrator differs from an EXECUTOR in being appointed by a court rather than being named in the will of the deceased person.

Admiral's Men

The Admiral's Men, a major Elizabethan acting company, was formed in 1594 as a successor to Lord Strange's Men and the Earl of Derby's Men. It was the chief rival of Shakespeare's CHAMBERLAIN'S MEN. After 1603 it became Prince Henry's Men. The company's principal actor was Edward ALLEYN, featured in the tragedies of its leading playwright, Christopher MARLOWE: DOCTOR FAUSTUS, TAMBURLAINE THE GREAT, and *The Jew of Malta*. Also in its repertoire were plays by George CHAPMAN, Thomas DEKKER, Ben JONSON, and Thomas KYD. DAVID M. ZESMER

Bibliography: Chambers, E. K., *The Elizabethan Stage*, 4 vols. (1923).

admiralty: see MARITIME LAW.

Admiralty Islands

The Admiralty Islands, in the Bismarck Archipelago, lie in the Pacific between the equator and New Guinea. They have a population of 27,600 (1974 est.). The daily mean temperature is 27° C (81° F); average annual rainfall is 2,030–2,540 mm (80–100 in). Manus Island makes up about three-fourths of their 2,070 km² (800 mi²). The Dutch mariner Willem Schouten sighted the islands in 1616.

About 16 islands are volcanic, and two dozen are coral. Heavily forested mountains on Manus reach an elevation of 718 m (2,356 ft). Lorengau, the main port, is also the administrative center. The people, mostly members of Melanesian tribes, farm and fish. Commercial products include shells, pearls, and copra.

Japan occupied Manus during World War II, after which the Admiralties became part of a UN trust territory administered by Australia (1946). They are now part of Papua New Guinea, which gained independence in 1975.

adobe [uh-doh'-bee]

Adobe is sun-dried brick made of clay mixed with vegetable matter. It is believed to be African in origin, the word being derived from the Arabic for "brick." Adobe dwellings are common in the southwestern United States and in Mexico, and the ruins of early pueblos reflect such construction.

An ideal building material for areas having little rainfall, adobe is made by kneading clay with a vegetable fiber such as straw, which acts as a binder and reduces shrinkage during the curing process. Water is added to make a stiff plastic compound that is forced by hand into a wooden mold. The brick is placed outside to bake in the hot sun for several weeks and then set with moist adobe as a cementing mortar. The finished building is also called an adobe. Inexpensive, fireproof, and an excellent insulating material, adobe is still used wherever the climate and the native clay are suitable.

adolescence

Adolescence is the developmental stage between childhood and adulthood; it generally refers to a period ranging from age 12 or 13 through age 19 or 21. Although its beginning is often equated with the onset of puberty, adolescence is characterized by psychological and social stages as well as by biological changes.

Adolescence can be prolonged, brief, or virtually nonexistent, depending on the type of culture in which it occurs. In technologically simple societies, for example, the transition from childhood to adulthood tends to be rapid and is marked by traditionally prescribed PASSAGE RITES. By contrast, in American and European society the transition period for young people has been steadily lengthening over the past 100 years, giving rise to an adolescent subculture and to a variety of problems and concerns specifically associated with this age group. Psychologists single out four areas that especially touch upon adolescent behavior and development: physiological change and growth; cognitive, or mental development; identity, or personality formation; and parent-adolescent relations.

PHYSIOLOGICAL CHANGE
Between the ages of 9 and 15, almost all young people undergo a rapid series of physiological changes, known as the adolescent growth spurt. Beginning in the pituitary gland, these hormonal changes include an acceleration in the body's growth rate; the development of pubic hair; the appearance of axillary, or armpit, hair about two years later; changes in the structure and functioning of the reproductive organs (see REPRODUCTIVE SYSTEM); the mammary glands in girls; and development of the sweat glands, which often leads to an outbreak of ACNE. In both sexes, these physiological changes occur at different times in different cultures, generally earlier in southern climates and later in northern climates.

Girls typically begin the growth spurt shortly after age 10, reach a peak at about age 12, and decelerate markedly by age 14. The spurt occurs almost two years later in boys; thus, girls are typically taller and heavier than boys from about ages 10½ to 13.

In girls, the enlargement of the breasts is usually the first external sign of impending puberty. Actual puberty is marked by the beginning of MENSTRUATION, or menarche. In the United States, 80 percent of all girls reach menarche between the ages of 11½ and 14½, 50 percent between 12 and 14, and 33 percent at or before age 11. The average age at which menstruation begins for American girls has been dropping about six months every decade, and today contrasts greatly with the average age of a century ago, between 15 and 17.

Boys typically begin their rapid increase in growth at about 12½ years of age, reach a peak slightly after 14, and slow down sharply by age 16. This period is marked by the enlargement of the testes, scrotum, and penis; the development of the prostate gland; darkening of the scrotal skin; the growth of pubic hair and pigmented hair on the legs, arms, and chest; and the enlargement of the larynx, containing the vocal cords, which leads to a deepening of the voice following a transitional period in which the voice "cracks."

COGNITIVE DEVELOPMENT
Current views on the intellectual changes that take place during adolescence have been heavily influenced by the work of the Swiss psychologist Jean PIAGET, who sees the mental capability of adolescents as both qualitatively and quantitatively superior to that of younger children. According to Piaget and the developmentalist school of psychology, the thinking capacity of young people automatically increases in complexity

as a function of age. Developmentalists find distinct differences between younger and older adolescents in ability to generalize, to handle abstract ideas, to infer appropriate connections between cause and effect, and to reason logically and consistently.

Whether these changes in cognitive ability should be attributed primarily to a new and invariant developmental stage, as Piaget suggests, or should be considered the result of accumulating knowledge that allows for new mental and moral perspectives, an enlarged capacity for making distinctions, and a greater awareness of and sensitivity to others, is a question on which psychologists continue to disagree. Behaviorists such as Harvard's B. F. SKINNER, for instance, do not believe intellectual development can be divided into distinct stages. Rather, they emphasize the influence of conditioning experiences on behavior, that is, of a continuous flow of punishments and rewards. Thus, to the extent that intellectual ability in adolescence differs from that of earlier years, they see it as the result of learning, or the acquisition of more appropriate responses brought about by conditioning. Other investigators have found a strong association between certain socioeconomic characteristics and adolescent intellectual achievement. Findings suggest that well-educated, economically secure, small-sized families provide the kind of environment—including parental encouragement, books and other cultural tools, individual attention, and an extended vocabulary—in which intellectual development among adolescents is most apt to flourish. Test scores, however, seem to be more related to the verbal ability than to the performance aspects of adolescents' intelligence.

IDENTITY FORMATION
Psychologists also disagree about the causes and significance of the emotional and personality changes that occur during adolescence. Many Freudian psychologists believe that the overt sexual awakening of adolescents is an inevitable cause of emotional strain, sometimes leading to neurosis. Psychologists following other schools of thought place less emphasis on the specifically sexual aspects of adolescence, considering sex as only one of many adjustments young people must make in their search for a stable identity.

The effects of physical change, the development of sexual impulses, increased intellectual capacity, and social pressure to achieve independence all contribute to molding a new self-definition. The dynamics of identity formation are linked to the adolescent's self-image. This is especially affected by the opinions of people who are important in the lives of adolescents and interact with them. Gradually, the emotional dependency of childhood yields to an emotional commitment to meet the expectations of others—parents, peers, teachers, employers. If adolescents fail to meet the goals set for them by the important people in their lives, they usually feel obliged to reevaluate their motives, attitudes, or activities. The ensuing censure or approval to which they are subjected in this learning cycle help determine both their later commitment to responsible behavior and their sense of social competence throughout life.

The peer group also provides a standard by which individuals can measure themselves during the process of identity formation. Within the peer group, a young person can try out a variety of roles—leader or follower, deviant or conformist. The values and norms of the group permit adolescents to acquire a perspective on their own values and attitudes. A peer group can also help them to make the transition from reliance on the family to relative independence. The common language, clothing, music, and customs adopted by their generation allow them to express a distinct identity that in turn eases the anxiety of separation from past sources of reference and identity.

A prime source of identity for adolescents is the type of work chosen or envisioned. The vocational decision can lead to an "identity crisis" before a specific career is finally chosen. Adolescent girls who either marry early or make no career plans beyond the prospect of marriage and children often experience a sense of identity diffusion, an incomplete sense of identity.

PARENT-ADOLESCENT RELATIONS

The FAMILY has traditionally provided a set of values and the milieu where young people can observe and begin to learn adult ways of behavior. The extended family of previous generations, which often included grandparents and relatives as distant as nieces and nephews, has in many Western countries given way to the nuclear family unit, consisting of parents and one or two children. In modern industrial societies, however, the nuclear family has come to seem relatively unstable, as divorce grows increasingly common and many children reach adolescence with only one parent. In addition, rapid social changes have weakened the continuity of life experience and values between the generations, and adolescents may often view their parents as having little capacity to guide them in their adjustment to the larger world. The conflict that sometimes results from differing parent-adolescent perceptions is called the "generation gap." Such conflict is by no means inevitable and is less likely to characterize families in which both adolescents and parents have been exposed to the same new ideas and values.

Other parental characteristics likely to influence adolescents include social class, the pattern of equality or dominance between mother and father, and the consistency with which parental control is exercised. Young people with parents whose guidance is firm, consistent, and rational tend to possess greater self-confidence than those whose parents are either overly permissive or authoritarian.

CONCLUSION

Adolescence is often looked upon as a period of stormy and stressful transition. Margaret MEAD, in her extensive study of Samoan culture, however, found no evidence of tension in the transition from childhood to adulthood in Samoa. In part, this was because the Samoans made no rigid demarcation between childhood and adulthood. Children of all ages participated in the activities of the community. At puberty no basic change occurred in the way young people were treated. Parental control remained the same, and avoidance of conflict was stressed. By contrast, as life in industrialized societies becomes increasingly complex, adolescents are more and more cut off from the economic and social activities of their elders, leaving most young people with education as their sole occupation. Inevitably, this has isolated many of them from the adult world and has prolonged their adolescence.

ROBERT E. GRINDER AND THERON ALEXANDER

Bibliography: Conger, John J., *Adolescence: Generation under Pressure* (1980); Matteson, David R., *Adolescence Today: Sex Roles and the Search for Identity* (1975); Mead, Margaret, *Coming of Age in Samoa* (1928; repr. 1971); Sebald, Hans, *Adolescence: A Social Psychological Analysis*, 2d ed. (1977).

See also: DEVELOPMENTAL PSYCHOLOGY; YOUNG PEOPLE.

Adonais   [ad-uh-nay'-is]

In his poem "Adonais" (1821) Percy Bysshe SHELLEY recast a Greek pastoral elegy into a formal lament for the poet John Keats, whose death (1821) Shelley felt had been hastened by the critics blamed in the poem. Its concluding 18 Spenserian stanzas are a magnificently sustained exposition of the variant forms of immortality that Shelley not only accorded Keats but shared with him through the intensity of his poetic inspiration. "Adonais" ranks with John Milton's "Lycidas" as the greatest of English elegies.   E. B. MURRAY

Adonis   (mythology)

In Greek mythology, Adonis was a handsome young shepherd loved by APHRODITE. The offspring of a love affair between King Cinyras of Cyprus and his daughter Myrrha, Adonis was born from the trunk of the myrrh tree into which his mother had been changed by the gods. Aphrodite left the infant Adonis in the care of PERSEPHONE, the queen of the underworld, who also fell in love with him. While hunting, Adonis wounded a wild boar, which turned on him and killed him. Aphrodite pleaded that he be restored to her, but Zeus decided that both goddesses should share him for eternity:

Adonis would spend the spring and summer with Aphrodite and the rest of the year with Persephone in the underworld. The anemone, the wild flower that each year blooms briefly and then dies, is said to have sprung from his blood. Adonis, imported probably from the Phoenicians, came to be revered as a dying-and-rising god. Athenians held Adonia, a yearly festival representing his death and resurrection, in midsummer.   ROBERT E. WOLVERTON

adoption and foster care

Adoption is the legal proceeding whereby a court declares a person who is not a child's natural parent to be the child's legal parent and the relationship to be permanent. Adopted children have all the rights and duties of natural parents. Foster care, on the other hand, is a temporary arrangement, usually made by a state or municipal child-welfare agency, that places a child from a broken, abusive, or poverty-stricken home in the care of a foster family until such time as the circumstances of the child's natural family can be corrected.

Adoptions are often arranged through public or private agencies who investigate both the child's parentage and the suitability of the adoptive family. Most U.S. states require the sealing of agency records to the adoptive family, the child, and the natural parents. Many adopted children have pressed for legislation to open these records, feeling that they have the right to know their "true" identities. In Great Britain a 1975 act gave adopted children over the age of 18 access to their birth records. Only about 2 percent of British adoptees have used the act, but since its passage the number of children offered for adoption has been reduced by almost 50 percent.

In the past most babies put up for adoption were the children of unwed mothers. In recent years, however, the availability of abortion has reduced the proportion of illegitimate births. Moreover, because illegitimacy itself has lost much of its stigma, the majority of unwed mothers have chosen to keep their babies. The number of available adoptees has thus shrunk dramatically. Many U.S. families have been forced to seek their adoptive children outside the United States. Latin America and Southeast Asia, particularly Vietnam in the late 1970s, have been important sources for young adoptive children. Many U.S. babies are also adopted outside the usual agency channels, through black-market arrangements made between the natural mother and the prospective parents with the aid of a doctor or lawyer, often for a very high fee.

In 1980 the U.S. Congress passed legislation designed to encourage the adoption of children in foster care by providing foster families with maintenance payments and Medicaid when they adopt. (Under previous regulations, if the foster family adopted, maintenance payments were cut off.) This legislation recognized the essential failure of the foster-care system, which since the 1960s has provided federal subsidies for placing children with foster families, while neglecting to subsidize attempts either to rehabilitate natural families or to find some means by which children can remain with one set of foster parents rather than being shifted from family to family. There were some 500,000 U.S. children in foster care in 1980, about one-fifth of whom had been in the system for more than six years. It is estimated that about 100,000 of all children in foster care are adoptable, although many are older, handicapped, or nonwhite.

Bibliography: Fanschel, David, and Shinn, Eugene, *Children in Foster Care* (1978); Hubbell, Ruth, *Foster Care and Families* (1981); Wishard, Laurie and William R., *Adoption: The Grafted Tree* (1979).

adoptionism

Adoptionism, or adoptianism, was a Christian heresy that Jesus Christ was simply a human being who was possessed by the divine spirit after his birth and was thereby adopted by God as his son. Early church teaching on the divinity of Christ was in opposition to this doctrine, first prevalent among the EBIONITES and later among followers of MONARCHIANISM and NESTORIANISM. The heresy arose again in 8th-century Spain and was condemned under Leo III (795–816).

Adorno, Theodor W.

Adorno, b. Sept. 11, 1903, d. Aug. 6, 1969, was a German sociologist, philosopher, and musicologist. He is perhaps best known as coauthor (with Else Frenkel-Brunswik and others) of *The Authoritarian Personality* (1950), a survey of Fascist mental attitudes. He also wrote *The Dialectic of Enlightenment* (1947; Eng. trans., 1972), with Max Horkheimer; *Philosophy of Modern Music* (1949; Eng. trans., 1971); studies of Hegel and Kierkegaard; and several other works. He spent the Nazi years in England and in the United States. Strongly influenced by Marx and Hegel, Adorno was an intellectual leader of West Germany's New Left movement in the 1960s.

JOHN ROBINSON

adrenal gland   [uh-dreen'-ul]

The adrenal glands are major endocrine glands anatomically associated with the kidneys. Each adrenal gland consists of two parts, an inner portion called the medulla and an outer portion called the cortex. Both parts secrete into the bloodstream important HORMONES that regulate the functions of other organs and systems.

The adrenal medulla secretes only two hormones, ADRENALINE (or epinephrine) and NORADRENALINE (or norepinephrine), which have similar actions. The medulla is not essential to life and can be removed without causing much disturbance to body functioning, since its hormones are also secreted by portions of the nervous system. Adrenaline and noradrenaline regulate activity in the sympathetic nervous system, the involuntary part of the nervous system that controls automatic functions such as blood vessel constriction, heart rate, gastrointestinal movements, pupil dilation, and glucose METABOLISM. Thus, when secretion by the adrenal medulla is increased, blood vessels constrict, the heart accelerates, gastrointestinal movements diminish, and glucose is released into the bloodstream. These events occur in emergencies and are adaptations that help the individual survive.

The adrenal cortex secretes a variety of hormones called corticosteroid hormones. In contrast with the adrenal medulla, the cortex is essential to life. The steroid hormones secreted by the cortex regulate many important body functions, including salt and water metabolism; carbohydrate, fat, and protein metabolism; neuromuscular function; sexual function; resistance to infection and other stresses; and the action of other endocrine glands. Death after removal of the adrenal glands is the result of the loss of cortical hormones and is usually due to disturbances in water and salt metabolism or to circulatory collapse.

The most important corticosteroid hormone is 17-hydroxycorticosterone, since it regulates the greatest number of physiologic activities. It can be administered to maintain life in an animal that has had its adrenals removed or to a patient with Addison's disease, a disease of the ENDOCRINE SYSTEM in which hormone secretion by the cortex is impaired.

In some persons, the adrenal cortex may produce excessive quantities of hormones, including the hormones that regulate sexual function. This can cause precocious sexual development in very young male children or masculinization in women.

PETER L. PETRAKIS

Bibliography: Williams, Robert H., ed., *Textbook of Endocrinology*, 5th ed. (1974).

adrenaline   [uh-dren'-uh-lin]

Adrenaline is another name for epinephrine, the HORMONE produced in the ADRENAL GLAND that is vital in enabling an individual to meet sudden dangers and emergencies. In states of alarm, adrenaline pours into the bloodstream, from which it affects other parts of the body. Carbohydrate reserves are mobilized; muscle strength is increased; pupils are dilated, letting in more light; and peripheral blood vessels contract, causing increased blood pressure. Adrenaline is synthesized for use as a drug to check the hemorrhaging of wounds, to relieve asthma, and to counteract the effects of hypoglycemia.

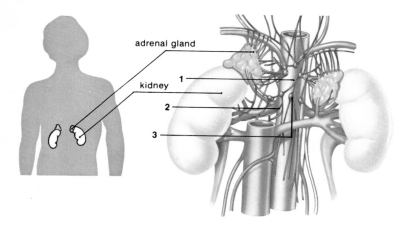

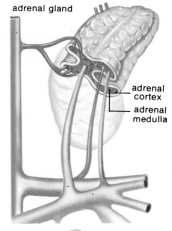

The adrenal glands, located on top of the kidneys, manufacture hormones that affect a person's reaction to stress, emergencies, and infection. Blood flows from the aorta (1) and renal arteries (2) into the extensive network of vessels, supplying the adrenal glands with nourishment and oxygen. Veins leaving these glands transport adrenal hormones throughout the body. The brain sends nervous impulses to the adrenal glands by means of nerves (3) of the sympathetic system. The two basic tissues of the adrenal glands, the cortex and the medulla, act as two different organs. The outer cortex, which is essential to life, comprises three layers of cells, each of which secrete several hormones that affect body metabolism. The inner medulla secretes epinephrine and norepinephrine, both of which prepare the body for "fight or flight" in reaction to emergencies. During stress, these two hormones mobilize energy reserves, increase heart action, and direct the blood flow to muscles of the arms and legs.

adrenocorticotropic hormone

Adrenocorticotropic hormone (ACTH) is one of several hormones secreted into the bloodstream by the pituitary gland, an endocrine gland located below the brain, when the gland is stimulated by substances from the area of the brain called the hypothalamus. The hormone, in turn, stimulates the outer layer, or cortex, of the ADRENAL GLAND—another endocrine gland—to secrete several of its hormones into the bloodstream. Such hormones include CORTICOSTERONE and CORTISOL. Thus all body functions regulated by these hormones are indirectly controlled by the pituitary gland through the action of ACTH. The functions include metabolism of salt, water, carbohydrate, fat, and protein; neuromuscular function; sexual function; resistance to infection and other stresses; and the actions of other endocrine glands. If ACTH is absent, the adrenal cortex may continue to secrete hormones, but at a lower level than normal. Because ACTH secretion increases in response to stress and various external stimuli, the resulting increase in secretion of adrenal cortical hormones accounts for some of the disturbances seen when the body is under stress. ACTH has been synthesized and is used in treating asthma, arthritis, and several other disorders.

PETER L. PETRAKIS

Bibliography: Turner, C. D., and Bagnara, J. T., *General Endocrinology* (1976); Williams, R. H., ed., *Textbook of Endocrinology*, 5th ed. (1974).

Adrian, Edgar Douglas

Edgar Douglas Adrian, b. Nov. 30, 1889, d. Aug. 4, 1977, was an English physiologist who, along with Charles Scott Sherrington, was awarded the 1932 Nobel Prize for physiology and medicine for his work on the function of nerve cells. Adrian demonstrated that the speed and strength of a nerve impulse does not diminish but travels along the nerve fiber at a steady rate once stimulus threshold is reached. Now known as the all-or-none law, this finding was an important step in understanding nerve function.

Bibliography: Singer, C., and Underwood, E. A., *A Short History of Medicine* (1962).

Adrian I, Pope

Adrian I, b. c.720, d. Dec. 25, 795, was pope from 772 to 795. He allied the PAPACY with the Frankish king CHARLEMAGNE who, at Adrian's behest, deposed the Lombard king Desiderius and returned to Adrian papal territories that had been annexed by Desiderius. This alliance limited Adrian's independence, but his personal relations with Charlemagne were amicable. Adrian opposed ICONOCLASM and ADOPTIONISM, worked for uniformity in LITURGY and CANON LAW, and sponsored extensive building and fortification projects in Rome.

Bibliography: John, Eric, *The Popes* (1964).

Adrian IV, Pope

Adrian IV, b. c.1115, d. Sept. 1, 1159, has been the only Englishman elected (Dec. 4, 1154) pope. His original name was Nicholas Breakspear. As pope, he was involved in the continuing reform of the papal financial administration and in the reclaiming of lands that had been usurped by the Italian nobility. Throughout his pontificate he was embroiled in serious difficulties with Frederick I of Germany concerning the conflicting claims of the German monarchy and the papacy to political and ecclesiastical overlordship in north and central Italy. He was once believed to have issued the bull *Laudabiliter*, giving Henry II of England the right to seize Ireland, but this document is now assumed to be a forgery.

DAVID HARRY MILLER

Adrian VI, Pope

Adrian VI, b. Mar. 2, 1459, d. Sept. 14, 1523, was pope from 1522 to 1523. A Dutchman whose name was Adrian Florensz Dedal, he was the first pope to respond to the Protestant REFORMATION by attempting to reform the Roman Catholic church. After teaching theology at the University of Louvain, he succeeded LEO X. Adrian VI was the last non-Italian to be elected to the PAPACY before JOHN PAUL II.

Adrianople, Treaty of   [ay-dree-uh-noh'-pul]

The Treaty of Adrianople (Sept. 14, 1829) ended the RUSSO-TURKISH WAR of 1828–29. By its terms Russia gained control of the mouth of the Danube and navigational rights through the Dardanelles and Bosporus. The Ottoman Empire, or Turkey, was required to pay an indemnity to Russia, to grant autonomy to Greece, and to reconfirm the autonomy of Moldavia, Walachia, and Serbia.

Adrianople: see EDIRNE.

Adriatic Sea

The Adriatic Sea is an arm of the Mediterranean Sea extending about 800 km (500 mi) northwest from the Strait of Otranto between Italy and the Balkan Peninsula. Its average width is 160 km (100 mi). In the Middle Ages the Adriatic served as the major shipping route between Europe and the Orient. Venice, located at its head, never regained commercial vitality after the fall of Constantinople in 1453 and the subsequent development of alternate sea routes around Africa.

The sea was named for the town of Adria, possibly an ancient Etruscan settlement and later a Roman port; now, because of siltage from the Po River, Adria is located 21 km (13 mi) inland. The Italian coast of the Adriatic is generally low and straight; much of it is sandy, with marshy northern headlands. The shores of Yugoslavia are steep and rocky, fretted with numerous islands and inlets. The sea bottom reflects this configuration, with shallow waters near the Italian shore and deeper waters off Yugoslavia. The average depth is 444 m (1,457 ft).

Accessible to northern Europe and noted for its mild climate (surface water temperature in August is 24° C / 76° F), the Adriatic coast, particularly Yugoslavia, has become popular with tourists. Fishing is locally important, but the sea is somewhat deficient in nutrients and marine life. Northeast squalls, called *bora*, are a danger to winter navigation.

adsorption

Adsorption is the process by which a solid, liquid, or gas (the adsorbate) is held at the surface of some other material (the adsorbent). The adsorbent is usually a solid but may also be a liquid. The process results from molecular interaction at surfaces. Activated charcoal is widely used for its exceptional adsorbing powers. In water purification, for example, it adsorbs a wide range of dissolved organic impurities.

The method of separating the components of a mixture by CHROMATOGRAPHY depends on adsorption. The basis of the technique is that the forces binding each component to an adsorbent can differ greatly, and each component can be released sequentially by changes in the chemical environment.

Adsorption phenomena are usually studied quantitatively by measuring the amount of adsorbate per unit of surface. A related phenomenon, chemisorption, is essentially adsorption in which the adsorbate is held strongly to the adsorbent (binding energy greater than about 60 kilojoules per mole of adsorbate).

GEORGE GORIN

Bibliography: Adamson, A., *Physical Chemistry of Surfaces* (1976).

See also: ABSORPTION; QUANTITATIVE ANALYSIS.

adult education

Adult education involves a variety of programs aimed at improving the skills, knowledge, or sensitivity of men and women after their formal schooling is completed. Public and private educational institutions, especially COMMUNITY AND JUNIOR COLLEGES, and religious and professional groups sponsor adult education, which includes elementary, secondary, and higher education programs as well as nondegree continuing education. Evening and weekend sessions make this form of education more convenient for many. Other forms of adult education include on-the-job training and self-education programs. Less formally, adult education is provided by such institutions as libraries and museums, by community organizations, and through such media as television and radio.

OBJECTIVES

Adult education has traditionally been justified as serving a socially desirable purpose. The first known book on adult schools, published by Thomas Pole in 1814, praised them in its lengthy subtitle: ''An Account of Some of the Beneficial Effects already Produced on the Moral Character of the Laboring Poor (and) Considerations of the Important Advantages likely to be productive to Society at Large.''

Programs have frequently been funded on the premise that they would alleviate some major problem of concern to the society. From time to time adult education has been promoted through the use of slogans such as ''Open a school and close a jail,'' as though education were guaranteed to reduce crime. In times of high unemployment, adult education may be funded ostensibly as a solution, in the belief that the lack of some given level of educational attainment is the condition that produces the unemployment.

In Western countries, adult education is being used to prepare women for jobs that have traditionally been considered suitable only for men, to assist segments of society that historically have been underprivileged, and to retrain workers for new industries. In Third World countries, adult education is an important part of modernization and industrialization, where goals cannot be met without increasing the literacy rate (see LITERACY AND ILLITERACY). Other campaigns are directed at preventing disease, raising agricultural production, and increasing the use of family planning.

In all countries, adult education is used to bring about a more equitable distribution of the opportunities of the society. It has traditionally emphasized the practical rather than the academic, the applied rather than the theoretical, the acquisition of skills rather than knowledge of facts; but many adults take courses because they simply want to broaden their knowledge. On the whole, persons who are relatively secure economically and who have some postsecondary education show interest in college credits, certificates, diplomas, and degrees.

BARRIERS TO ADULT EDUCATION

One obstacle to adult education is the misconception that adults do not learn as well as younger people. A major study called *Adult Learning* (1928), by Edward L. THORNDIKE and others, demonstrated that adults can learn well until at least the age of 70. Subsequent studies by educators on several continents demonstrated that adults 90 years old and older can learn foreign languages and master other difficult subjects. In recent years many colleges and universities have established special programs for older persons.

Several studies have shown that the primary obstacle to full-time adult education for Americans is cost. About half the adults who say they are interested but not involved in systematic learning cite the financial barrier. The second most important obstacle is lack of time.

In the Western democracies, the most persistent problem facing adult education is the lack of participation by the least-educated groups in the society. Illiterate adults do not perceive education as a means of improving their lives; so they generally do not enroll. If enrolled, they often do not attend the classes designed for them.

ADULT BASIC EDUCATION IN THE UNITED STATES

Adult basic education (ABE) programs to improve basic reading, writing, and computation skills are designed to enable undereducated adults to function more effectively in the workplace, at home, and in the community. ABE was given impetus when economic opportunity legislation passed in the 1960s granted funds to the individual states for adult basic education programs.

In the early 1980s more than 21 million people were enrolled in some form of adult education program in the United States. Of these, 54% were enrolled in programs sponsored by educational institutions, 14% were in programs sponsored by business and industry, 8% in community sponsored programs, 8% in government sponsored programs, and 5% in programs sponsored by labor or professional organizations.

WILLIAM S. GRIFFITH

Bibliography: Cross, K. Patricia, *Adults as Learners* (1981); Darkenwald, Gordon G., and Merriam, Sharan B., *Adult Education: Foundations of Practice* (1982); Harrington, Fred, *The Future of Adult Education* (1977); Knowles, Malcolm, *The Adult Education Movement in the U.S.* (1962; repr. 1976) and *Modern Practice of Adult Education*, rev. ed. (1980); Knox, Alan, *Adult Development and Learning* (1977).

See also: CHAUTAUQUA; CORRESPONDENCE SCHOOL.

adultery

Adultery is usually defined as voluntary sexual relations between a married person and someone other than his or her spouse. Most religions place strong taboos on adultery. Throughout history, social and religious sanctions against adultery have ranged from death by stoning to furnishing sufficient legal grounds for divorce, though men have usually been treated more leniently than women.

Advanced Placement Program

The Advanced Placement Program, established in 1955 by the College Entrance Examination Board, helps secondary schools offer college-level courses for advanced students. It sets, administers, and grades examinations and sends the grading documents to colleges, as well as providing consulting services to the schools. The program is administered by the Educational Testing Service in Princeton, N.J.

advection

Advection is the process by which one or more physical properties or components of the atmosphere—such as temperature, moisture, or a pollutant—are affected by horizontal (and sometimes vertical) air movements. Thus cold advection occurs when cold air moves toward the equator from polar regions, and moisture advection occurs when oceanic air blows toward a dry continent. The term also applies to the effects of ocean currents.

RICHARD A. ANTHES

Bibliography: Anthes, Richard A., et al., *The Atmosphere* (1978).

Advent

A Christian liturgical season, Advent is the period of preparation for both Christmas and the Second Coming of Christ. It extends over the four Sundays preceding Christmas. Festivities are discouraged, and the solemn character of the period is demonstrated by the use of purple vestments. Fasting was formerly prescribed. The first Sunday of Advent marks the beginning of the church year.

Adventists

Adventists are members of various Christian groups who believe that the SECOND COMING OF CHRIST is imminent. Their millennial hopes (see MILLENARIANISM) were aroused by the preaching of William MILLER (1782-1849). On the basis of a detailed examination of the Bible, especially the books of Daniel and Revelation, Miller predicted that Mar. 21, 1844, and later that Oct. 22, 1844, would be the day when Christ would return in glory and the Earth would be cleansed by fire, ushering in the millennium—a 1,000-year reign of righteousness and peace before the Last Judgment. When the time passed without event, many believers drifted away.

The faithful remnant of Millerites coalesced into several religious bodies, the most important of which are the Seventh-Day Adventists and the Advent Christian Church. Leaders of the former group had been influenced by Sabbatarian Baptists; thus, in that denomination, Saturday rather than Sunday is kept as the Sabbath. The most important early leader of the Seventh-Day Adventists was Ellen G. White (1827-1915). She was interested in health reform, and Seventh-Day Adventists continue to be noted for their medical missionaries, sanitoriums, and concern for sound health practices, as well as for their millennialism and Sabbatarianism.

In 1981 the Seventh-Day Adventists (headquarters in Washington, D.C.) had 3,668,000 members in 184 countries, and the Advent Christian Church (headquarters in Charlotte, N.C.) had 29,800 members in 9 countries.   CONRAD WRIGHT

Bibliography: Damsteegt, P. Gerard, *Foundations of the Seventh-Day Adventists: Message and Mission* (1977); Gaustad, Edwin S., ed., *The Rise of Adventism* (1975); Hoekema, Anthony A., *Seventh Day Adventism* (1974); Sandeen, Ernest, *The Roots of Fundamentalism: British and American Millenarianism, 1800-1930* (1970).

Adventures of Augie March, The

With his picaresque novel *The Adventures of Augie March* (1953), Saul BELLOW won both a National Book Award and his first popular success. The first-person story of a young Chicagoan from a lower-class Jewish background, it follows Augie through a series of jobs, locales, and relationships—both comic and serious—that constitute the "hero's" education in life. Augie's refusal to follow the opportunistic path to success taken by his older brother Simon, his insistence on maintaining his freedom and an integrity of sorts, and, above all, his inextinguishable spontaneity and optimism lead him (and the reader) by the novel's end to recognize that freedom resides in admitting that one's fate is one's character.

JEROME KLINKOWITZ

adverb: see PARTS OF SPEECH.

adversary procedure

Adversary procedure, in law, is the form of trial procedure used in the United States, England, and other COMMON LAW countries. The defense and prosecution both offer evidence, examine witnesses, and present their respective sides of the case as persuasively as possible. The judge or jury must then decide between the adversaries. In the inquisitorial procedure, used in countries with CIVIL LAW systems, the court—as well as the prosecution and defense—investigates the case before it. The court staff and the judge gather evidence and conduct interrogations, and the judge's decision of guilt or innocence is based on the investigation.

advertising

An advertisement is a message—printed in a newspaper or magazine, broadcast on radio or television, sent to individuals through the mails, or disseminated in some other fashion—that attempts to persuade readers or listeners to buy a particular product, favor a particular organization, or agree with a particular idea. It is paid for by the advertiser and may be prepared either by the advertiser or, more commonly, by a professional advertising agency.

National advertising, which promotes the products or the identity of a firm that markets nationwide, is the dominant form of advertising. Retail and other local business advertising is second in importance. Other types include trade advertising, which addresses retailers, asking them to stock and promote the advertised brand; industrial advertising, which sells goods from one producer to another; and professional advertising, from producers to professionals, such as doctors, who influence consumer purchases.

Supplementing the print and broadcast media of mass communication, direct mail is used by advertisers to mail advertisements to the persons appearing on lists of names that are chosen for particular characteristics, such as age or income.

The Advertising Industry. Essentially, the industry is a triad consisting of advertisers, the media, and the advertising agen-

In a prize-winning series of television commercials, Brother Dominic praises the miraculous capacities of such Xerox products as the home computer shown in this scene. The cost of these sophisticated machines has plummeted as manufacturers sell thousands to the mass market reached by television.

(Left) *Posters, like the handbills on a London wall in 1835, traditionally have been an effective advertising medium.* (Below) *An "Uncle Sam" poster recruited Americans for Army service through two wars.*

cies who create and place most national and many retail ads. In 1981 an estimated $60 billion was spent in the United States by about 250,000 national advertisers and 1,750,000 local advertisers. About 25 percent of the total was spent by the 100 top national advertisers, led by Procter and Gamble (whose advertising budget was about $700 million) and followed by Sears Roebuck, General Foods, Philip Morris, K Mart, General Motors, R. J. Reynolds, Ford, AT&T, and Warner-Lambert.

Of about 4,000 agencies in the United States, the 10 largest handled ("billed") 14 percent of the $60 billion spent on advertising. Large U.S. agencies also participate in advertising abroad, and many have offices overseas. Foreign agencies are also active in world billings, particularly in Japan, which has 10 of the 50 largest agencies worldwide, including the world's largest, Dentsu, with a 1981 gross income of $428 million.

The nations with the largest advertising expenditures are the United States, Japan, Great Britain, West Germany, and France. Advertising in the Communist nations, while having grown substantially in recent years, is still relatively small.

The Advertising Agency. Agencies serve their clients with a variety of experts. The account executive acts as liaison between advertiser-client and agency, meeting with the client to determine objectives and budgets. The agency's copywriters and art directors take their assignments from the account executive, who brings their work back to the client for approval or modification. When decisions on content are completed, often after research studies to determine consumer re-

sponse, the production department prepares the finished ads, with the aid of typographers, engravers, printers, and radio or television commercial production companies. The media department, in the meantime, has prepared a comprehensive media plan that will involve the purchase of space in a newspaper or magazine or time on radio or television. After the completed printing plates, tapes, or films are shipped to the appropriate media, the account executive checks media performance for proper scheduling and adequate reproduction.

Closely related MARKETING activities, such as PUBLIC RELATIONS and sales promotion, are handled by the agency, by other outside organizations, or by the advertiser. Advertising must be coordinated with these other activities and with the company's overall objectives.

The Advertising Media. A magazine, television program, or any other advertising medium is judged by an advertiser according to "exposure opportunity," the number of people who might see the ad, and "message opportunity," the way in which a particular medium allows the ad to communicate.

In considering exposure, advertisers speak of "reach"—the number of people who see the ad at least once—and "frequency"—the average number of times each person is reached. An ad's total impact is indicated by its number of gross impressions: reach × frequency. A further aspect of exposure is cost, usually stated as cost per thousand gross impressions (CPM). Another is target reach, the number of people within a specific audience who have seen the ad. Often advertisers want to reach only women, only teenagers, or Presbyterians, or residents of Chicago, and so on.

The media vary in these characteristics. Television provides high exposure and low CPM nationwide but is not efficient for specific targets. Newspapers have much lower absolute exposure but reach a higher percentage of the areas they cover; they are excellent for geographic targeting. Radio is good for targeting to various geographic, age, and interest groups; its CPM is very low. Magazines provide less exposure nationally than television but are highly selective on audience interests. Direct mail is not cheap but is the most selective of all, because the advertiser uses mailing lists containing only persons within the selected audience.

Because television supplies sound, pictures, and movement, it offers the most complete message opportunity; it cannot distribute coupons as can print, however. Television and radio messages disappear after running, but print can be saved for future reference. Radio, offering nothing but sound, is the most limited medium. Magazines can reproduce more attrac-

TEN LARGEST U.S. ADVERTISING AGENCIES

Agency	1981 Gross Income	
	World	United States
Young & Rubicam	$353,000,000	$222,800,000
J. Walter Thompson	331,700,000	153,700,000
Ogilvy & Mather	286,500,000	157,500,000
McCann-Erickson	277,300,000	75,800,000
Ted Bates	236,700,000	129,100,000
BBDO	205,000,000	127,900,000
Leo Burnett	198,600,000	124,000,000
SSC&B	176,400,000	41,700,000
Foote, Cone & Belding	170,300,000	116,500,000
Doyle Dane Bernbach	165,000,000	115,000,000

SOURCE: *Advertising Age*, Mar. 24, 1982. Reprinted with permission. Copyright, 1982, by Crain Communications, Inc.

These three advertisements were created for different media by Doyle Dane Bernbach, an American advertising agency. (Left) The subway card for Levy's bread, from a series of ethnically inspired ads, helped to widen the appeal of a specialized product. (Center) The Avis magazine advertisement set a trend in comparison advertising with its allusion to a larger, but less caring, competitor. (Right) The Volkswagen newspaper ad visually conveys its message to the economy-conscious motorist to whom the ad is directed.

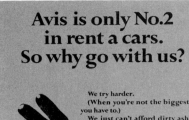

tively than newspapers, but newspapers are printed more often. Direct mail can offer lengthy messages but may be discarded without being examined.

Newspapers earn the highest proportion of total advertising expenditures, 29 percent of the total (of which 85 percent comes from local advertisers). Television earns 21 percent (74 percent supplied by national advertisers); direct mail, 14 percent; magazines, 9 percent; and radio, 7 percent.

Advertising Goals. The most common advertising goal is to influence consumer choice of a particular brand. Marketing, or motivation, research can determine which types of consumers are most likely to buy the advertised product, and it can also test the features, benefits, images, or other appeals to which consumers might respond. The advertising will then associate the brand with those appeals.

Different ads focus on different immediate goals. A sign at a bar advertising a beer is aimed at producing immediate purchase, but it may not be effective without previous ads that produce public familiarity with the name, associate appeals with the brand, and create favorable beliefs and attitudes.

Restraints on Advertising. The U.S. government and most states prohibit deceptive or unfair ads. The criterion is whether the consumer is harmed, not whether the ad is technically false. Some true claims may deceive by omitting important facts. For example, "This catfood contains more phosphorous" may be a true statement, but cats do not need phosphorous. On the other hand, some false claims may be unharmful because they are obviously false ("You'll feel like you're flying in brandname auto!"). Violators are ordered to "cease and desist" from running harmful ads. There are no fines or other criminal penalties for violations unless the advertiser persists beyond the order date.

Although in the early 1980s regulatory pressures were decreasing, many developments from the 1960s and 1970s remain. In addition to withdrawing their ads, advertisers may be asked to run "corrective advertising," in which they restate earlier claims accurately, or to offer substantiation for their claims.

U.S. advertisers are also controlled by their own self-regulatory body, the National Advertising Review Board, as well as by the media, which often refuse ads they consider unfit in their editorial or programming context. Advertisers have also felt compelled to respond to organized public pressure, as when Action for Children's Television attacked the advertising aimed at children that was presented by Captain Kangaroo and other hosts of children's programs.

Economic Effects of Advertising. Critics claim that advertising costs consumers money; advertisers assert that it saves consumers money. Certainly, a low CPM makes advertising more efficient than the personal selling it replaces and allows it to supply most efficiently the consumer information that can create a mass market, with its associated economies of scale.

Much of today's advertising, however, wastes money because competitors cancel out each other's efforts. If two companies producing similar soft drinks spend great sums to increase their market shares, with the result that neither gains, then that money has been spent with no benefit to either producers or consumers. If neither company advertised it could avoid such waste, but no company can stop while its competition continues, for fear of losing market share. Thus the money must be spent, and the extra expense will be passed on to consumers. Nor do consumers receive any informational benefit, because the product category is an established, familiar one, and the information conveyed by advertising amounts only to artificial brand distinctions based on images.

Even when advertising reduces marketing costs, producers may refrain from passing the savings on to consumers and may actually raise prices when the artificial brand distinctions produced by advertising lead to consumer brand loyalty and a willingness to pay more. Thus a mass market may be created for a product category, but if advertising channels much of the market share to one particular brand, the result may be lower producer costs and higher consumer prices simultaneously.

The Social Impact of Advertising. Advertising has been accused of ruining everything from the environment (billboards blocking scenic views) to the English language ("Nobody doesn't like Sara Lee"). It has been charged with making people buy things they do not really need or want, often by invoking negative motivations such as guilt, anxiety, or fears of inferiority. It is said to encourage people to regard purchasing and consuming as the major activities of their lives and to create false images—depicting the average citizen, for instance, as young, attractive, wealthy, and leisured. There have been strong criticisms of the stereotypical images of women and minorities in many advertisements.

In defense, advertisers argue that consumers are well able to make up their own minds and will not buy things they do not want. The public, they claim, is very tolerant of mass persuasion and has generally not raised serious objections to advertising content.

In recent years advertisers have created new social impacts by the heavy use of advocacy ads, which persuade the public not about products but about public issues over which companies wish to influence opinion. Mobil's ad series in the late 1970s and early '80s, which presented its version of the role of the oil companies in the energy shortage, is a famous example. Critics say that such ads are unfairly one-sided; advertisers say that the mass media have been equally one-sided in failing to report company views.

Another important social impact stems from advertising's financial support of the mass media: it provides about two-thirds of print revenue and virtually all broadcast revenue. Media operators thus see the public not as their primary audience, but as mere bait for attracting advertisers; media content, by and large, is designed to attract those citizens whose spending power is greatest.

Advertising and Politics. Perhaps the most controversial of advertising's effects is in politics, where heavy media campaigns have been common since the 1952 presidential candidacy of Dwight D. Eisenhower. Unlike competing brands, political candidates are not usually similar, yet their campaign ads often hide important differences behind smokescreens of smiles and empty slogans. Political claims are not subject to regulation as are product claims. Opponents' complaints and public pressures on occasion have resulted in the withdrawal of objectionable messages, but no law prohibits even the most blatant political lies.

Another source of complaint is that wealthy candidates can gain an unfair advantage in buying extensive advertising campaigns and that third-party candidates have no chance to match the campaign funds available to nominees of the two major parties. Under Federal Elections Commission rules, major candidates may use federal funds for campaigning, up to a limit ($29,440,000 in 1980), but only if they accept no additional funds from elsewhere. The rules also provide, however, that groups and individuals may do their own advertising for candidates, without a spending limit, so long as they have no contact with the candidates or their organizations.

In 1980 that provision resulted in a sizable inequality, with most of the independent expenditures aiding Republican Ronald Reagan. A direct-mail specialist, Richard Viguerie, is credited with producing several million dollars of these additional funds through his expertise in identifying Reagan's target audiences. Because of his success, there probably will be a greater emphasis on such advertising in the future.

IVAN L. PRESTON

Bibliography: *Advertising Age* (periodical); Berman, Richard, *Advertising and Social Change* (1981); Bovee, Courtland L., and Arens, William F., *Contemporary Advertising* (1982); Fine, Seymour, *The Marketing of Ideas and Social Issues* (1981); Ogilvy, David, *Blood, Brains, and Beer* (1978); Polykoff, Shirley, *Does She or Doesn't She? And How She Did It!* (1975); Preston, Ivan L., *The Great American Blow-Up* (1975).

advocate

In law, an advocate is one who represents another person in court. In the United States, any lawyer may act as an advocate. In England, a BARRISTER represents the client in court, but a solicitor prepares the case.

Ady, Endre   [ah'-dee, en'-dreh]

Endre Ady, b. Nov. 22, 1877, d. Jan. 27, 1919, is generally considered the greatest Hungarian poet of the 20th century. His innovative poems, influenced by French symbolism, countered the earlier poetic tradition of János Arany and Sándor Petőfi.

Ady left the study of law to become a journalist. After he met Adele Brull, called "Leda" in many of his poems, he followed her to Paris, where he came in contact with new literary fashions. When he returned to Hungary, his unconventional beliefs and attacks on the Hungarian aristocracy made him a controversial figure. His break with poetic and social traditions came with *Uj versek* (New Poems, 1906) and continued in nine subsequent volumes. Beginning about 1909 he contributed poetry and prose to *Nyugat* (West), a leading lit-

erary and social journal. Ady's lyrical and religious verse draws on colloquial and biblical sources and explores suffering and death in a world that has lost God.   ALBERT TEZLA

Bibliography: Ady, Endre, *Poems of Endre Ady*, trans. by Anton N. Nyerges (1969).

adz   [adz]

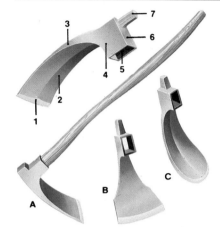

An adz tool (top) . comprises a cutting edge (1), blade (2), shoulder (3), head (4), eye (5), and poll (6), which may have a projecting pin (7). Different heads still presently in use include a carpenter's adz (A), a shipbuilder's adz (B), and a curved-blade adz (C), used to cut small hollows, as in making wooden bowls.

An adz, or adze, is a woodworking tool with a wide, thin, slightly curved blade placed at right angles to a long handle. A finishing tool, it is used to shape wood and to give the wood surface a distinctive texture, ranging from uniformly rippled to flat and almost smooth. Various types of blade have been designed to meet the specific requirements of such operations as carpentry, shipbuilding, and wood carving. The gutter adz has a concave blade for forming a troughlike shape. Some adzes are made with a poll, a projection opposite the blade's cutting edge that is used to drive down nails so that the blade will not be nicked. Most have removable heads so that they can be sharpened on a grindstone. Generally, the tool's application falls between that of the ax, which leaves a rough surface, and the plane, which leaves the smoothest surface of all. In use, the tool is swung so that its handle is the radius of an arc formed by the blade.

R. J. DE CRISTOFORO

Æ: see RUSSELL, GEORGE WILLIAM.

Aeacus   [ee'-uh-kuhs]

In Greek mythology, Aeacus was a just king who in life ruled the island of Aegina but in the afterlife was a judge of the dead in Hades. He was the son of the nymph Aegina and of Zeus, ruler of heaven. When Hera, Zeus's wife, discovered her husband's infidelity, she took revenge by visiting a deadly plague on the island whose misfortune it was to be called Aegina, the name of her rival.

Aegean civilization   [ee-jee'-uhn]

Aegean civilization is the name given to the highly developed BRONZE AGE culture in existence between 3000 and 1000 BC in the area that corresponds to modern Greece. The main geographical divisions of this area are the island of Crete, the Cycladic islands to the north, and the Greek mainland.

The location and fertile character of Crete gave it importance in early times. The first high civilization on European soil arose here during the 3d millennium BC. The impetus for this may have been the introduction of the working of copper and bronze by emigrants from Anatolia or Syria.

Sir Arthur EVANS named the Cretan Bronze Age civilization Minoan, after MINOS, the legendary king of KNOSSOS, which was the chief Bronze Age center of the island. The Bronze Age of the Cyclades is known as Cycladic; and that of the

AEGEAN CIVILIZATION

▨	Areas under Minoan control c. 1700-1450 B.C.	Areas under Mycenaen control c. 1450-1250 B.C.

The Aegean Bronze Age, which flourished from the 20th century BC until the 12th century BC, was dominated first by Minoans of the island of Crete and later by Mycenaeans of mainland Greece. Minoan and Mycenaean influence expanded through colonization and trade.

Greek mainland, as Helladic, from Hellas, the ancient name of Greece. The developmental sequences in these areas are divided into Early, Middle, and Late phases, based upon changes of fashion distinguishable chiefly in pottery styles. The term *Mycenaean*, after the site of MYCENAE on the mainland, is often used for the Late Bronze Age there, and sometimes for that of the whole Aegean.

The three main phases of the Aegean Bronze Age correspond roughly in time with the Old, Middle, and New Kingdoms in ancient Egypt. Approximate dates for the Aegean Bronze Age are based upon connections with Egypt, supplemented by scientific methods of age determination.

SOURCES OF KNOWLEDGE

Later Greeks were aware of a previous age when iron was unknown and weapons were of bronze, as described by Homer. Their legends preserved some names and vague traditions from this age. Massive Bronze Age defensive walls, such as those at Mycenae and TIRYNS, were thought to be the work of giant CYCLOPES, but factual information about this Bronze Age has only come from excavations in the past hundred years.

In 1876, Heinrich SCHLIEMANN found unplundered royal shaft graves with spectacular gold treasures at Mycenae. Work there and at Tiryns and elsewhere in the PELOPONNESUS, the southernmost region of the mainland, revealed much about the Mycenaean civilization of the Late Bronze Age, with its palaces and impressive corbel-vaulted beehive tombs, or *tholoi*. In the 1890s the Cyclades were explored, and a complete Bronze Age town was cleared at Phylakopi on Melos.

From 1900 onward attention shifted to Crete, where Sir Arthur Evans exposed the great palace of Minos at Knossos, and a Minoan civilization was revealed, older than the Mycenaean and ancestral to it. Between the wars further work was begun on the mainland, where Carl Blegen discovered (1939) the well-preserved Mycenaean palace of Nestor at PYLOS. In recent years Nicolas Platon uncovered a Minoan palace at Zakros in eastern Crete, and Spyridon Marinatos identified a rich Minoan settlement buried under ash at Akrotiri on the volcanic island of THERA (Thíra), also called Santorini.

EARLY AEGEAN PEOPLES

Bands of primitive hunters roamed the Greek mainland during Paleolithic (Old Stone Age) times. At the beginning of the 6th millennium BC or earlier, groups of people still using stone tools but with knowledge of agriculture reached the Aegean from Anatolia or farther east and settled in parts of the mainland and in Crete.

Other emigrants from the east may have entered the Aegean at the beginning of the Bronze Age about 3000 BC. Early Bronze Age settlements in the Aegean were usually small but situated in defensible positions and surrounded by strong walls. This type of settlement suggests the existence of many tiny independent states ruled by chieftains inhabiting small palaces. Conditions were probably similar to those after the end of the Bronze Age from about 1000 BC, when the Aegean was divided among small communities engaged in constant warfare.

Names of centers like Knossos and Tiryns appear to be non–Indo-European and evidently date back to Early Bronze Age times or earlier. The early Aegean peoples may have spo-

(Above) *Excavation of the Minoan palace at Knossos revealed a sophisticated multistoried structure with broad terraces, ceremonial staircases, and indoor plumbing. (Right) A terra-cotta statue (c.1600 BC), believed to represent a snake goddess, was found in a temple at Knossos. It typifies the Minoan women's mode of dress, which included a tightly fitting bodice that exposed the breasts, an embroidered apron, and a flounced skirt.*

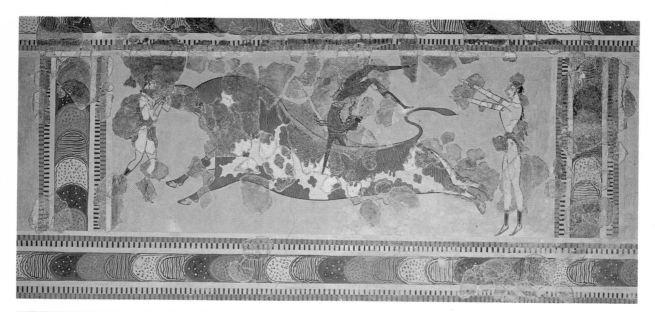

(Above) *In this fresco (c.1500 BC) from the Palace at Knossos, a youth vaults over a bull in a dangerous sport that possibly had religious significance to Minoans. The vigorous, lively style used to paint the fresco characterizes Minoan art, which utilized bright colors and curving lines.*

(Left) *A fresco of a fisherboy was discovered in a house on Thera, one of the Cycladic islands. A tremendous volcanic eruption there about 1500 BC buried towns in ash. Excavations have revealed many wall paintings and other artifacts.*

ken a common language, or related languages, akin to the earliest languages known in Anatolia. The same types of bronze tools and weapons were used, and similar fashions were followed in gold and silver jewelry throughout the Aegean area. But considerable local differences existed, notably in pottery and in burial customs. Thus the remarkable corbel-vaulted circular tombs were built in some parts of Crete to house the dead of a whole clan over many generations; smaller family vaults were more usual on the mainland. In the Cyclades, individual slab-lined cist-graves were prevalent.

EMERGENCE OF MINOAN CIVILIZATION

From about 2500 BC Crete began to take the lead in the emergence of a civilization marked by an extensive use of sealstones and the development of writing. Seal usage and perhaps even writing were also known in the Cyclades and on the mainland, notably at Lerna. But further progress there was inhibited for a time by an influx of relatively barbarous peoples from the east and from the north.

Invaders from various parts of Anatolia occupied many of the Cycladic islands about 2200 BC and settled at Lerna and other sites in the eastern Peloponnesus. A few centuries later, invaders coming from the Balkans appear to have reached the Peloponnesus and left traces at Lerna. These northerners may have spoken an Indo-European language, perhaps an early form of Greek.

Crete does not appear to have suffered invasion at this time. The Minoan civilization continued to develop, and great palaces were eventually built at PHAISTOS, Knossos, Mallia, and Zakros. The early palaces at Knossos and Phaistos were destroyed by fire about 1700 BC, perhaps in warfare between the Cretan states. But in the time of the second palaces, from about 1700 to 1450 BC, Minoan civilization reached its height in terms of artistic achievement, which may have been matched by political expansion. A Cretan colony was established well before 2000 BC at Kastri on the island of Kythera, between Crete and the Peloponnesus. After 1700 BC, Cretan settlers appeared alongside the native inhabitants on many other Cycladic islands, notably at Akrotiri on Thera, Phylakopi on Melos, and Hagia Irene (Ayia Iríni) on Kea.

The Cyclades and some parts of the mainland may by this time have become tributary to Crete, as suggested by legends about sons of Minos ruling the islands and by the legend of THESEUS and the tribute of young men and women imposed on Athens. The 16th-century BC shaft graves at Mycenae, with their lavish funerary articles, also date from this period. Many of the finest treasures found in the graves—magnificent swords, inlaid daggers, and gold signet rings engraved with scenes of warfare and hunting—may have been made by Cretan artists.

EMERGENCE OF MYCENAEAN CIVILIZATION

The settlements on the island of Thera were buried by a volcanic eruption about 1500 BC. At a later time, about 1450 BC, Crete was overrun by invaders from the Greek mainland, perhaps from the region of Mycenae. People from the mainland also occupied the Cyclades and built a small palace on the site of an earlier one at Phylakopi on Melos, where they surrounded the town with massive defensive walls.

Mainland palaces like that at Phylakopi differed from those of Minoan Crete. They centered around a great hall with a large central hearth and an entrance porch, developed from the long house standard in the Middle Bronze Age on the mainland. This hall is called the *megaron* in Homer's *Odyssey*, in which comparable palaces are described. In front of its porch was a courtyard, with various rooms and offices clus-

(Left) *A death mask of beaten gold, found over the face of a mummified king in the royal tombs at Mycenae, dates from the 16th century BC. The mask portrays a man wearing a full beard and mustache, a Mycenaean fashion. (National Museum, Athens.)*

tered around it. In contrast to this, a Minoan palace was built around a spacious rectangular court, which was given a north-south orientation, perhaps for ritual reasons. The Mycenaean invaders of Crete destroyed the palaces at Phaistos, Mallia, and Zakros, but spared and adapted that at Knossos. At Hagia Triada (Aýia Tríadha) near Phaistos, they appear to have constructed a palace of the mainland type on the ruins of a small Minoan one.

New burial customs and changes in pottery reflect the presence of mainland conquerors after about 1450 BC at centers like Knossos. A different system of writing, called LINEAR B to distinguish it from the Linear A script used in Crete before the conquest, appeared at Knossos, where many clay tablets with inscriptions have been recovered. In 1952 the language of the tablets was deciphered by Michael VENTRIS as Greek. His decipherment, if accepted, implies that the Mycenaean conquerors of Crete spoke Greek and were ancestors of the non-Dorian Greeks of later times.

The Aegean, under Mycenaean domination from about 1450 BC onward, became the scene of a uniform civilization, although local differences can be distinguished, especially in the style of pottery decoration. Palaces at centers like Mycenae, Tiryns, Pylos, and Thebes on the mainland, or Knossos in Crete, indicate the existence of several relatively large independent states. Some of these states were probably absorbed by others before the end of the Bronze Age. The palace at Knossos in particular may have been destroyed for the last time in the 14th century BC.

In the 13th century BC, Mycenae, with the largest of the circular vaulted *tholoi* for royal burials (including the so-called Treasury of Atreus) may have been the capital of a miniature empire controlling most of the Aegean. *Ahhiyava*, which occurs in contemporary texts of the Hittite empire of Anatolia, appears to be the same word as *Achaioi*, Homer's name for the Greeks besieging Troy, and may refer to such a Mycenaean empire or to some lesser state. Mycenaeans were now in control of places on the western coast of Anatolia such as MILETUS, which Minoans had colonized before them.

DECLINE OF AEGEAN CIVILIZATION
Warfare between the Mycenaean states may have led to the dissipation of wealth and military resources. In the years around 1200 BC the palaces on the mainland were destroyed and never rebuilt. But sites such as Mycenae and Tiryns, or Knossos in Crete, continued to be occupied, although in much reduced fashion.

Scholars have proposed several theories concerning the destruction of the palaces and the eventual disappearance of the Mycenaean civilization. In one view, the Mycenaens were

(Above) *The Lion's Gate is the western entrance through a wall built about 1250 BC around Mycenae, a citadel that was a major center of Mycenaean culture. The entrance and wall are composed of massive stones fitted together without mortar. The two lions, which are now headless, stand 3 m (10 ft) tall.*

(Right) *A Mycenaean soldier is depicted wearing a boar's-tusk helmet and armor that were found in a Mycenaean tomb (1400–1200 BC). His shield, of ox hide, was constructed in a figure-eight pattern.*

overwhelmed by the first wave of Greeks to invade from the north and settle in their lands; but this is incompatible with a belief that the language of the Linear B script is Greek. Other possible agents of destruction were the DORIANS, the last wave of Greeks to enter the Peloponnesus; but they seem to have come later. Alternatively, raiders such as the SEA PEOPLES, who attacked Egypt during this period, might, with concomitant drought and consequent famine, have created a vacuum that the Dorians afterward filled. Wars between the Mycenaean states have also been suggested as a reason for the destructions.

In the wake of the destructions, Mycenaean refugees from the Peloponneseus migrated to the Cyclades and to Crete, and even as far afield as Cyprus. Evidence indicates that at the same time barbarous peoples from beyond the northern frontiers of the Mycenaean world began to settle in the southern parts of Greece after about 1200 BC, introducing new burial customs and fashions in dress. These newcomers evidently mixed with remnants of the indigenous population and adopted some of the Mycenaean civilization, which continued in an adulterated form with many local variations until the end of the Bronze Age. Then, about the middle of the 11th century BC, this hybrid evolved in some areas, notably ATTICA, into what is recognizably the ancestor of the civilization of classical Greece.

What brought about the downfall of the Mycenaean world is the most obscure and difficult question confronting scholars of the Aegean civilization. Much also remains to be learned about the beginnings of the Bronze Age in Crete and other parts of the Aegean. Meanwhile, excavations continue in Greek lands with spectacular results, notably at Akrotiri on Thera and at such long-established centers as Mycenae, Tiryns, and Knossos.   SINCLAIR HOOD

Bibliography: Branigan, Keith, *The Foundations of Palatial Crete* (1970); Chadwick, John, *The Mycenaean World* (1976); Hood, Sinclair, *The Minoans: The Story of Bronze Age Crete* (1971); Sandars, N. K., *The Sea Peoples* (1978); Vermeule, Emily, *Greece in the Bronze Age* (1964); Warren, Peter, *The Aegean Civilization* (1975).

See also: GREECE, ANCIENT; MINOAN ART.

Aegean Sea   [ee-jee'-uhn]

The Aegean Sea is a branch of the MEDITERRANEAN extending northward between Greece and Turkey. It covers an area of about 214,000 km² (82,625 mi²) and is studded with islands. Its southern entrance is partially blocked by the islands of CRETE and RHODES. The Aegean extends about 640 km (400 mi) from Crete northward to the coast of Thrace, and its width ranges from 195 to 400 km (120 to 250 mi).

The coast of the Aegean is mountainous, and only in Macedonia and Thrace in the north are there extensive coastal plains. Few large rivers discharge into the sea. In the north, the Vardar (Axiós), Struma (Strimón), and Maritsa (Evrós) enter from the Balkan Peninsula, and the Menderes enters from Anatolia. Most others are small, and in many the flow is seasonal. The narrow waterway known as the DARDANELLES enters the Aegean from the northeast and carries the discharge from the Black Sea. It gives access through the Sea of Marmara and the Bosporus to Soviet and Danubian ports.

The Aegean Basin consists of a submerged block of the Earth's crust, across which long belts of folded rocks extend from the mountains of Greece to the mountains of Turkey. On the seafloor these belts form submarine ridges, separated by deep basins. The ridges, clearly traceable on the seafloor, are the foundation of most of the Aegean islands. In the north the islands of Límnos and Imroz lie between the Khalkidhiki Peninsula in Greece and northwestern Turkey. To the south, the Sporades group, Psará, and Chios (Khíos), form another such island chain. From Attica and the island of EUBOEA (Évvoia), the CYCLADES (Kikládhes) stretch southeastward toward the promontories of southwest Anatolia. Last, Crete, Rhodes, Kithera, and Karpathos stretch from southern Greece toward the Taurus Mountains of Turkey and enclose the Aegean Sea on the south. Recently, volcanoes have been active in the more southerly islands. The greatest depth, about 2,010 m (6,600 ft), is north of Crete.

Several important ports ring the Aegean littoral, among them PIRAEUS and SALONIKA in Greece and IZMIR (Smyrna) in Turkey. Bulgaria has long sought access to the sea and held the port of Kavalla at various times from 1912 to 1944.

A major feature of the Aegean is that no ship can be out of sight of land for long. In classical times, this encouraged navigation and facilitated movement between its shores; the sea was a link between the Greek cities that lay around it. Thus, a cultural unity within the Aegean Basin lasted with few interruptions from the 2d millennium BC until the Turkish conquest of Anatolia in the 11th century. The Turks never destroyed the Greek character of the Aegean Sea, and not until the exchange of population of the 1920s were Greek settlements eliminated along the Turkish shore. Most of the islands remain politically and culturally Greek.

NORMAN J. G. POUNDS

Aegina   [ee-jy'-nuh]

Aegina (Greek: Aíyina) is an island of Greece in the Saronic Gulf of the Aegean Sea, 23 km (14 mi) south of Athens. Triangular in shape, it has an area of 83 km² (32 mi²) and a population of 5,704 (1971). The main seaport town, Aegina, is located on the northwestern coast, where olives, figs, nuts, and grapes are cultivated. Inland gorges and coastal cliffs of volcanic rock render most of the rest of the island unproductive. Tourism, sponge fishing, and ceramics aid the economy.

Named for the mythological nymph Aegina, the island has been settled since Late Neolithic times. There is evidence of Mycenaean occupation before about 1500 BC, followed by Dorian Greek conquest (c.1100 BC). During the Archaic Period, Aegina was noted for its powerful navy and merchant marine and was an important artistic center. Aeginetan coinage appeared in the 7th century, and the island flourished commercially until defeated by its rival, Athens, in the 5th century. Of several ancient towns and sanctuaries, the most important site is the shrine of the native goddess Aphaia. It consists of a monumental gateway, altar, priests' quarters, and a partially reconstructed Doric temple (c.500 BC). Its pediment contained the famous Aeginetan marbles (now in the Glyptothek, Munich), sculptures of Athena and heroes in combat.

JEAN MACINTOSH TURFA

aegirine: see PYROXENE.

aegis   [ee'-jis]

In Greek mythology, the aegis was a shield associated with ZEUS, who was called "the aegis bearer," and with the goddess ATHENA. HOMER described the aegis as a shaggy breastplate bordered with serpents. The tasseled aegis of Athena, constructed of goatskin, was set with the fearful head of MEDUSA, the gorgon.

Aegyptopithecus   [ee-jip'-toh-pith'-uh-kuhs]

Aegyptopithecus ("Egyptian ape") is a genus of fossil apes found in the Fayum desert region of Egypt. Fossil bones belonging to this extinct PRIMATE, first identified in 1964, were recovered from sediments deposited about 33–36 million years ago, during the Oligocene Epoch. Certain features of the teeth and skull suggest that *Aegyptopithecus* may have been ancestral to the Miocene ape DRYOPITHECUS, which is believed to be the direct ancestor of the modern chimpanzee and gorilla. Unlike these more recent primates, however, *Aegyptopithecus* was a relatively small-brained animal with a tail and a large snout, indicating that, unlike its descendants, the sense of smell was still of considerable importance.   ALAN MANN AND NANCY MINUGH

Ælfric   [al'-frik or al'-fritch]

Ælfric, 955–1020, was one of the most prolific writers in Old English. A Benedictine monk, he was a respected scholar and educator of his time. His *Homilies* and other works, including translations from Latin, were designed to give instruction in Roman Catholic doctrine. He also wrote biographies, a Latin grammar, and a series of dialogues in Latin called the *Colloquium*, which gives a vivid picture of Anglo-Saxon life and society.   ROBIN BUSS

Bibliography: Greenfield, Stanley B., *A Critical History of Old English Literature* (1965); Hurt, James, *Aelfric* (1972).

Aelian   [ee'-lee-uhn]

Aelian, or Claudius Aelianus, 170–235, was a literary historian and teacher of rhetoric in Rome. His two main works, written in Greek, are *De natura animalium* (On the Nature of Animals) and *Varia historia* (Miscellany). The first is a collection of animal tales with moralizing lessons. The second is a collection of curious lore about men and manners.

Bibliography: *De natura animalium* and *Rustic Letters*, ed. and trans. by A. F. Scholfield, 2 vols. (1958–59).

Aeneas   [i-nee'-uhs]

In the *Aeneid* of VERGIL, Aeneas was the Trojan hero whose descendants founded Rome. When the Greeks destroyed Troy, many survivors fled the burning city. Among the refugees were Aeneas, his wife and small son, and his aged father, ANCHISES. His wife was lost in the confusion, but Aeneas, leading his son and carrying his aged father on his back, made his way to safety. With a band of fugitives Aeneas set sail to find a new beginning but was shipwrecked at Carthage, where he stayed with Queen DIDO. The *Aeneid* describes the wanderings of the Trojans who after many adventures finally reached the shores of Italy.

Aeneid   [i-nee'-id]

VERGIL's epic masterpiece, the *Aeneid*, written between 30 BC and 19 BC, was to Augustan Rome what Homer's *Iliad* and *Odyssey* had been to the classical Greeks—an explanation of their origins and heroic past. The poem, in 12 books, treats of the founding of Roman civilization by the Trojan AENEAS. It traces his career from his escape from the ruins of Troy, through his extended wanderings westward and his tragic love affair with DIDO, queen of Carthage, to his establishment in Italy after long years of bitter conflict with the indigenous Latins and Rutulians.

The poem is cast in the heroic mold, with its characters and events modeled after their Homeric predecessors; Vergil thereby appears to be glorifying the ideals of Rome and its first emperor, Augustus. However, by a judicious use of symbol, image, and analogy, Vergil's critical emphasis falls on the cost in sacrifice and loss of humanity inherent in such ideals. Accordingly, the tradition of Vergil as the "emperor's poet" has been challenged by recent critics.   GERALD FITZGERALD

Bibliography: *The Aeneid*, trans. by W. F. Jackson Knight (1956); Camps, W. A., *Introduction to Virgil's Aeneid* (1969); Highet, Gilbert, *The Speeches in Vergil's Aeneid* (1972); Poeschl, Viktor, *The Art of Virgil: Image and Symbol in the Aeneid*, trans. by Gerda Seligson (1962); Putnam, Michael C., *Poetry of the Aeneid* (1965); Quinn, Kenneth, *Virgil's Aeneid: A Critical Description* (1968).

aeolian harp   [ee-oh'-lee-uhn]

The aeolian harp is a shallow box ZITHER about 1–1.5 m (3–5 ft) long, strung with multiple strings of the same length but of different thicknesses and tuned in unison. The harp is suspended where the wind will set the strings in motion; the wind force and the different diameters of the strings cause the eddies of air immediately downwind to vary considerably, which in turn causes variations in tone. Thus, the harp produces strange, ghostly sequences of harmonies, swelling and diminishing with the strength of the wind. Named for AEOLUS, god of the winds, the aeolian harp originated in the 17th century and achieved its greatest popularity in the romantic era.
                                                    ROBERT A. WARNER

Bibliography: Marcuse, Sybil, *Dictionary of Musical Instruments*, 2d ed. (1975); Richardson, E. G., *Sound*, 4th ed. (1947); Sachs, Curt, *History of Musical Instruments* (1940).

See also: HARP.

Aeolus   [ee'-oh-luhs]

In Greek mythology, Aeolus was the god of the winds and ruler of the Aeolian Islands. According to HOMER, he gave ODYSSEUS favorable winds for his homeward voyage and a bag in which the contrary winds were confined.

aerial photography

Photographs of land areas taken by CAMERAS mounted in aircraft or satellites are, like maps, extremely useful in interpretation of the Earth's surface features, both natural and manmade. Geologists, agricultural and economic geographers, soil scientists, foresters, civil engineers, students of urban and rural studies, hydrologists, and archaeologists all make extensive use of aerial photographs.

Air cameras are typically rigid fixed-focus instruments designed for electrically powered operation using roll FILM. Formats generally range from 18 by 18 cm (7 by 7 in) to 23 by 23 cm (9 by 9 in). Film, usually fast panchromatic emulsions, is carried in interchangeable magazines holding lengths of up to 300 m (1,000 ft).

Although often erroneously referred to as photomaps, aerial photographs are unlike maps in one important way. A map has a uniform or controlled variable scale—the latter dependent on choice of map projection. The aerial photograph, on the other hand, does not have a constant or uniformly changing scale. Hypothetically, if a photograph of a perfectly flat horizontal ground surface is exposed at an instant when the camera is pointing downward exactly at a right angle to that surface and is taken with a camera whose lens is distortion-free, the photograph will have a uniform scale. In actuality, these conditions are never met.

Scale is defined as the ratio between (1) the length of a ground distance shown on a map and (2) the actual ground distance. For example, if a 5-cm line on a map represents a ground distance of 1.5 km, the scale is computed as follows:

$$\frac{5 \text{ cm}}{1.5 \text{ km}} = \frac{5 \text{ cm}}{150,000 \text{ cm}} = \frac{1}{30,000}$$

Although the measurements are made in units of length (centimeters and kilometers), the scale itself is dimensionless. Thus, an inch on the map in the example above would equal 30,000 inches (2,500 ft, or 0.473 mi) on the ground. The same principle applies to the ideal photograph. The scale of the photograph (ratio of image length to ground distance) is equal to the ratio between focal length and camera height (aircraft altitude). A photograph taken at an altitude of 1,000 m by a camera with a focal length of 10 cm would thus have a scale of

An aerial photograph of the Rajang River in Malaysia makes use of a mosaic—a combined series of individual, overlapping pictures. Such mosaics can be used to make better, more detailed geographical maps of particularly remote areas quickly and inexpensively.

$$\frac{10 \text{ cm}}{1,000 \text{ m}} = \frac{10 \text{ cm}}{100,000 \text{ cm}} = \frac{1}{10,000}$$

or 10 cm = 1 km (about 6 in. per mi).

Aside from lens imperfections, which for all practical purposes—except when utmost precision is demanded—may be considered negligible, the two major factors responsible for variations in the scale of a photograph are topographic relief (land, no matter how flat, is never quite horizontal) and the tilt of the optical axis of the camera. The optical axis is the line along which the camera points, through the center of the lens, perpendicular to the film. When the axis is perpendicular to the land surface, a vertical photograph is produced; when it is inclined, an oblique photograph is produced. When a vertical photograph is taken of a nonhorizontal surface, distances that are of equal length on the ground will appear unequal on film because of topographic irregularities. Topographically higher distances (nearer the camera) will appear longer than those that are topographically lower.

Aerial photographs have two primary uses: mapmaking and interpretation. Numerous photogrammetric instruments are used in making maps from aerial photographs: simple and complex, small and large, inexpensive and extremely costly. One of the functions of many of these instruments is to remove distortion (scale variability) resulting from axial tilt. Perhaps the most important characteristic of aerial photographs is that they can be viewed stereoscopically, or in three dimensions. This is true whether they are black-and-white, color, infrared, or any other special type, and whether used by the photogrammetrist or the photo interpreter. When an area is photographed from two positions in space, the two photographs that are produced are not geometrically identical. The brain, however, transforms the two distinct images into a three-dimensional mental image of the irregular ground surface. The stereoscopic effect enables photo interpreters to extract many kinds of useful information from aerial photographs. Military applications, for example, include tasks such as identifying military installations, selecting targets, and estimating bomb damage. Using aerial photographs, the geologist can identify rock types, determine geologic structure, and obtain information that will assist in the search for petroleum and mineral deposits. In the fields of GEOMORPHOLOGY and hydrology, aerial photographs find application in watershed studies, flood control, and evaluation of water pollution and shoreline changes. Geographers and agronomists use the photographs to chart crop distribution, to plan blight-control programs, and to monitor land use and changes in urban characteristics and industrial development and for soil mapping. In forestry, the photographs are extensively used for species identification and distribution mapping, to map forest reserves, and for implementing disease control. From aerial photographs engineers gather data necessary for highway, dam, and pipeline construction, for detecting slope instability, and for locating deposits of natural construction materials such as sand and gravel.   VICTOR C. MILLER

Bibliography: American Society of Photogrammetry, *Manual of Photographic Interpretation* (1960) and *Manual of Color Aerial Photography* (1968); Miller, Victor C., *Photogeology* (1961).

See also: REMOTE SENSING; SATELLITE, ARTIFICIAL.

Color differences in this infrared aerial photograph of the downtown area of Washington, D.C., reveal congested housing, industrial areas, unused land, waterways, roads, and bridges. Photographs of this type are used by geographers and urban planners to study land use, industrial growth, and the spread of urban areas.

aerial sports

Aviation has been a popular sport almost from the moment the airplane was invented. The Fédération Aéronautique Internationale (FAI), which oversees all international aerial competition and certifies all official aviation and space records, was founded in 1905, just two years after the WRIGHT brothers' famous first flight.

In its first full decade, aviation was considered nothing more than a sport, a pastime for daredevils. Its military possibilities were not fully realized until well into World War I, and commercial aviation did not begin to prosper until the 1930s.

Most of the early FAI-sanctioned competitions were for power-driven AIRCRAFT, but some competitions were held for ballooning and GLIDER flying (soaring). Since World War II, such pursuits as parachuting (skydiving), hang gliding, and model-airplane flying have been included as aerial sports. The FAI lists speed records for feats as obscure as a flight between Capetown, South Africa, and Auckland, New Zealand, via the South Pole at a speed of 860.09 km/h (534.43 mph) in a Pan American Airways 747 SP. It even considers the American-Soviet space race to be a kind of aerial competition.

POWERED FLIGHT

The first official FAI-sanctioned air race, involving 38 primitive power-driven airplanes, was held at Reims, France, in 1909.

A glider, or sailplane, soars in silence after being launched by a powered aircraft. Competitive gliding, popular among affluent sports enthusiasts, is judged by distance, altitude, and duration of flight.

Most of the entrants crashed before completing the contest. By the 1920s, competition for such air-racing trophies as the Bennett, Schneider, and Bendix cups was avidly followed and keenly waged as a matter of national honor. Speeds as high as 708 km/h (440 mph) were attained as early as 1933.

Since World War II, the fastest planes have been military aircraft costing millions of dollars, and therefore impractical for civilian use. Most of the planes used in continuing events, such as the U.S. National Air Races, are remodeled P-51 Mustangs and other World War II–era aircraft.

The first records for speed and for distance over a measured course—41.292 km/h (25 mph) and slightly more than 180 m (200 yd)—were certified by the FAI in 1906. More recent speed and altitude records—3,529.56 km/h (2,193.16 mph) by an American in 1976 and 37,650 m (123,524 ft) by a Russian in 1977—illustrate how far powered aviation has advanced.

Long-distance events such as the Powder Puff Derby in the United States for women, employing conventional pleasure aircraft and testing navigational skills and fuel economy, remain popular.

Precision aerobatics is another popular and spectacular powered-aircraft competition. Pilots must perform intricate maneuvers within specified altitude limits. An outgrowth of the barnstorming and dogfighting days, it has fostered the manufacture of an entirely new line of high-performance aircraft.

Competitions are organized for antique aircraft, such as the still numerous World War II–era Steerman biplane, and for experimental aircraft, including many bizarre designs powered by small automobile engines.

The holder of the most individual records for powered flight is Jacqueline Cochran, with more than 250 for speed, distance, altitude, and innovator flights.

POWERLESS FLIGHT

Gliding. Gliding or soaring is considered the most beautiful of the aerial sports. It has enjoyed a phenomenal popularity in recent times. Towed aloft by powered aircraft (usually to about 600 m/2,000 ft) or launched by an automobile or winch tow, gliders fly by using air currents and updrafts in the atmosphere for lift. Their slender, fragile design and long wingspan permit them to travel as much as 12 meters forward for every meter they drop.

Although gliders were used by such aviation pioneers as

Spectators look over the streamlined racing planes at the Reno Air Races. Before World War II, many of the major advances in aircraft design resulted from these popular competitions.

(Left) Hang gliding, a sport popularized in the 1970s, borrows designs and technology from the ancient pastime of kite flying. The pilot, who is suspended by a harness within a triangular frame, steers the hang glider by shifting his weight. (Right) Balloon racing, the oldest aerial sport, originated in 18th-century France. Following a series of 20th-century dirigible explosions, interest in lighter-than-air craft waned. The transatlantic flight by an American team of balloonists in August 1978, however, rekindled enthusiasm for the sport.

the Wright brothers and their predecessor, Otto Lilienthal, in the late 1890s, the first FAI glider meet was not held until 1922. World soaring championships are now held every 2 years, for both open and standard classes. American, German, and Australian pilots are usually the most successful.

Soaring's elite are the "diamond badge" pilots who must achieve a 4,000-m (13,123-ft) or more altitude gain, fly 500 km (310.7 mi) or more cross-country, and also fly 300 km (186.4 mi) or more to a specific goal to qualify for the honor. The long-distance record for a glider is 1,460 km (907 mi), achieved by Hans Grosse of West Germany on Apr. 25, 1972.

Hang Gliding. Hang gliding, in which fliers suspend themselves from what is little more than a rudimentary, kitelike wing and work the updrafts along cliffs and bluffs, was once considered only a dangerous novelty but is now accorded full FAI status. World hang-gliding championships have been established, and a world-record distance of 153 km (95 mi) has been flown. In the United States alone, it is estimated that there are about 50,000 devotees of the sport.

Ballooning. Ballooning, the oldest aerial sport, was invented by France's famous MONTGOLFIER BROTHERS in 1782. BALLOON flights were commonplace throughout the 19th century, and observation balloons were used widely in the U.S. Civil War and in World War I.

Balloon competition includes cross-country races, won by the balloon pilot who travels the farthest and fastest, and hare-and-hound races, in which a group of balloons chase a balloon that has been given a head start. The balloon that comes the closest to the "hare" wins.

Even the most sophisticated balloon is at the mercy of the prevailing winds and can be steered only by seeking different winds at different altitudes. More than 15 attempts have been made to cross the Atlantic Ocean in a balloon since 1873, and some have been fatal. Finally, in 1978, a three-man team (Ben Abruzzo, Maxie Anderson, and Larry Newman) from Albuquerque, N.Mex., succeeded. They remained aloft for 173 hr, 3 min on *Double Eagle II* in a flight from Presque Isle, Maine, to Miserey, France. In doing so, the Americans set a distance record of 5,020 km (3,120 mi). In 1980, Anderson made headlines again when he and his son, Kris, completed the first nonstop transcontinental flight in the *Kitty Hawk*. The voyage, which began near San Francisco and ended on Canada's Gaspé Peninsula, covered more than 5,000 km

(3,100 mi), a record for overland balloon flights.

Parachuting. Sport parachuting, or skydiving, was not developed until the 1950s. The jumper falls several thousand feet at the rate of 193 km/h (120 mph) before opening the chute. Competitions are judged on style (maneuvers or group formations achieved during the free-fall) or accuracy (how close a jumper can land to a 15-cm/6-in disk on the ground). In a recent competition an American parachuting team was able to achieve a box formation of 40 jumpers linking hands in a free-fall. A German precision jumper has been able to hit the disk dead center 50 consecutive times.   MICHAEL D. KILIAN

Bibliography: Carrier, Rick, *Fly: The Complete Book of Safe and Successful Sky Sailing*, new ed. (1976); Halacy, D. S., Jr., *Complete Book of Hang Gliding* (1975); Sellick, Bud, *Parachutes and Parachuting* (1971); Underwood, John W., *Acrobatics in the Sky* (1972).

See also: FLIGHT, HUMAN-POWERED.

Aerobee

Aerobee, one of the most successful SOUNDING ROCKETS developed in the United States, was designed in 1946 to explore the upper atmosphere. In its original form it weighed a little more than 453 kg (1,000 lb) and had an overall length of 5.73 m (18.8 ft) and a diameter of 0.38 m (1.25 ft). The rocket was launched with the assistance of a high–thrust, solid-propellant booster and ultimately reached a velocity of 4,489 km/h (2,790 mph) and an altitude of about 28,956 m (95,000 ft).

Following the first successful launching (1947), summit altitudes of more than 112 km (70 mi) were regularly achieved. A typical payload comprised a magnetometer, Geiger-Mueller counters, and a cosmic-ray telescope. One of the world's first experiments to test the reactions of space flight on small mammals was made by the U.S. Air Force in 1952 using an Aerobee launched from Holloman Air Force Base. Two monkeys and two mice, rocketed to an altitude of about 60,960 m (200,000 ft), were recovered by parachute in the Aerobee nose cone.

Later, much-improved models have included Aerobee-Hi, Aerobee 200, and Aerobee 350, produced by Aerojet Liquid Rocket Company. The Aerobee 350, 15.2 m (50 ft) long and 0.55 m (1.8 ft) in diameter, can carry a 272-kg (600-lb) payload to a height of 325 km (202 mi).

See also: ROCKETS AND MISSILES.   KENNETH GATLAND

aerodynamics

Aerodynamics is the study of the flow of air and other gases and of the forces acting on bodies moving through the gases. It is a branch of fluid mechanics, in which the same principles are also applied to the study of liquids. Aerodynamics is mainly employed to study the flight of heavier-than-air craft, and is so discussed here. It is also used to describe the motion of lighter-than-air craft such as dirigibles and blimps and to determine the aerodynamic forces acting on bridges, buildings, and other structures. WIND TUNNELS are basic tools of aerodynamic research.

Underlying aerodynamics and all other branches of theoretical mechanics are the laws of motion developed by Isaac NEWTON in the 17th century. These laws state the effects of forces acting on bodies in motion or at rest. Newton also developed the concept of fluid friction, or viscosity—the resistance of air or any other fluid to motion, whether its own or that of a body moving through it. A younger contemporary, Daniel BERNOULLI, applied Newton's laws of motion to the study of fluids in particular. He developed the principle that the velocity of a fluid is related to the pressure within it: the faster the fluid flow, the lower the pressure. (See BERNOULLI'S LAW.) These concepts formed the basis for future studies.

Airplane Flight. Such concepts were essential before humans could realize the ancient dream of being able to fly through the air. As early as the 16th century, Leonardo da Vinci had sketched devices resembling the modern helicopter, but without understanding the aerodynamic forces involved in flight, practical attempts were doomed to failure.

Four main forces act on an aircraft: thrust, gravity, and the aerodynamic forces of drag and lift. Thrust and drag work against each other, as do gravity and lift.

An aircraft moves forward because of the thrust supplied by its propellers or jet engines. Forward motion continues as long as the thrust forces are greater than the drag forces, which result from the viscosity of air. Aircraft are therefore designed to reduce as much as possible the drag forces acting on different parts of the craft.

In order to overcome the Earth's gravity and rise into the air, an aircraft must be acted on by a lift force. This is supplied mainly by the craft's wings. A wing or other surface designed to produce a desired effect when acted on by flowing air is called an airfoil. Bernoulli's law forms the basis for the theory of the lift exerted on an airfoil such as a wing. The cross section of a wing is designed so that the angle at which the wing meets the air causes the air to flow more rapidly past the upper surface of the wing than the lower surface. As a result, air pressure is lower above the wing than below it, resulting in lift.

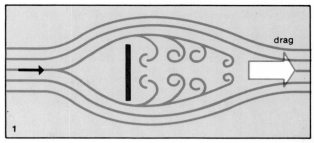

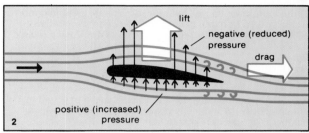

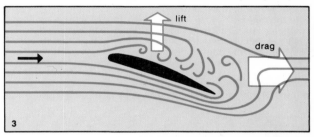

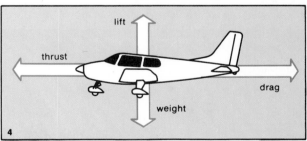

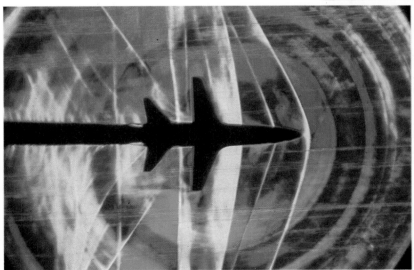

(Above) *Turbulent airflow behind a vertical plate (1) results in high drag and no lift. A properly designed airfoil, or wing (2), generates lift by reducing air pressure above the wing. Decreased air friction and turbulence minimize drag. Increasing the angle at which the wing meets oncoming air increases lift to a point. Beyond a critical angle airflow becomes turbulent (3), increasing drag and decreasing lift. Four forces act on an aircraft in flight (4). Thrust, a forward-driving force, is opposed by air friction, or drag. Lift is an upward force that keeps the vehicle airborne. Weight, resulting from Earth's gravitational pull, must be overcome by the lift for flight to occur.*

(Left) *This photo reveals the airflow pattern over an early model of the space shuttle orbiter in simulated motion near the speed of sound. The shock-wave pattern (visible in the bowed lines) results from air compression on the fuselage and on the control surfaces of the model being tested.*

Modern Aerodynamic Design. In making an aerodynamic analysis of an aircraft, it is necessary to consider the component parts of the vehicle and to calculate the airflow about each part separately. The results are combined to obtain the forces acting on the vehicle as a whole. Thus, the wing and tail are analyzed, and then the passage of air around the fuselage is included as a disturbance of the flow about the first two. In modern aerodynamic design, the availability of computers has made it possible to study the complete wing, body, and tail configuration.

Designers of high-speed aircraft must also take into account other aerodynamic concepts such as the boundary layer. This is the layer of air nearest the skin of the craft where the effects of the turbulence caused by air resistance are exhibited most strongly. It is desirable to keep turbulence to a minimum, so aircraft are designed to keep the stream of air flowing around the craft as undisturbed as possible—hence the term *streamlining*.

Supersonic Flight. Such considerations become especially important at very high speeds. High aircraft speeds are described in terms of Mach numbers, this number being the ratio of the speed of a given aircraft to the speed of sound in air of that density. When the two speeds are equal, the Mach number is 1. Speeds less than Mach 1 are called subsonic, those above Mach 1 are supersonic, and those above about Mach 5 are called hypersonic.

In the region of Mach 1 and above, special aerodynamic problems arise. At lower speeds, the air flowing around a craft can be considered an incompressible fluid, that is, a fluid whose density does not change. At high speeds, however, the density of the air increases sharply, as does its pressure and temperature. To offset this effect, supersonic aircraft fly at a considerably higher altitude than subsonic craft, to pass through thinner air. As the aircraft approaches the speed of

A space shuttle orbiter model undergoes simulated flight tests in the Ames Research Center wind tunnel installation in California. Such tests furnish data that enable prediction of expected flight performance. If any problems are found, design modifications can be made to ensure that the actual shuttle will work properly.

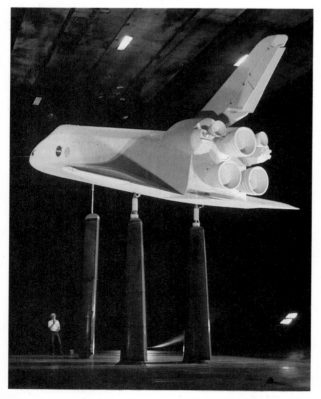

sound, shock waves form on its body wherever the local Mach number exceeds 1. As the speed of the craft increases further, these shock waves become more intense, producing a sonic boom.

The increase in speed from just below to just above the speed of sound is called the transonic speed range. Fighter pilots of World War II referred to it as "breaking the sound barrier" when, in flight, their craft entered this transonic region, developing shock waves that buffeted the craft. This buffeting was brought about by the unsteadiness of the shock waves at local spots on the wings in transonic flow. At supersonic speeds the shock waves become steady and remain firmly attached to the entire aircraft.

The swept-back wing was designed to delay the formation of shock waves on all aircraft made to fly at high subsonic speeds. For flying at higher, supersonic speeds, the sweep-back is further increased to form a delta wing. Such a wing is seen on the *Concorde*, which flies at a Mach number of about 2. Only experimental craft have been designed to fly at still higher speeds, in the hypersonic region. For example, the SPACE SHUTTLE will pass through this flight region as it reenters the Earth's atmosphere from orbit, slows down, and makes a conventional landing. Space vehicles that have returned from outer space thus far have not been flown in but have simply made a so-called ballistic landing. (See BALLISTICS.)

A characteristic feature of all supersonic flight, and a phenomenon even more characteristic of hypersonic flight, is the generation of intense heat. This is caused by friction between the vehicle and the atmosphere. All the kinetic energy of these fast-moving bodies is converted into heat, which in turn is dissipated into the atmosphere. To prevent returning spacecraft from burning up as meteors do when they enter the atmosphere, heat shields have been developed. These shields are insulated and coated with special material that melts and burns off at a carefully controlled rate.

Aerodynamic Testing. Aerodynamic testing is performed extensively, in conjunction with theoretical research, in order to gain a better understanding of aerodynamic problems. Most testing is done in wind tunnels; about 400 exist in the world, about half of them in the United States. Some wind tunnels are highly specialized; they can generate airflows of short duration or in an intermittent way, such as in large shock-tubes.

Wind tunnels are usually classified as subsonic, transonic, supersonic, or hypersonic, according to their Mach number capability. It is important to simulate the air friction of the full-size flight vehicle, but this is often difficult and extremely expensive. It requires a very large tunnel and correspondingly large models, or a pressurized tunnel to attain low air-friction. A few tunnels in the subsonic region can do this, but no tunnel has been built to operate at low-friction flow in the supersonic region. Wind tunnels are also used to test design models of bridges and other structures.   R. E. STREET

Bibliography: Allen, John E., *Aerodynamics: The Science of Air in Motion* (1982); Clancy, L. J., *Aerodynamics* (1975).

aerolite: see CHONDRITE.

aeronautics: see AERODYNAMICS; AEROSPACE INDUSTRY; AIRCRAFT.

aerosol

An aerosol is a relatively stable suspension of liquid or solid particles in a gas, especially air. Smoke, fog, and mist are aerosols. Sometimes the term is incorrectly applied to the familiar particles alone.

Aerosols are ubiquitous in the Earth's ATMOSPHERE, which can properly be considered one huge aerosol, and these naturally occurring aerosol particles can have major effects on the Earth's CLIMATE. Aerosols can also be prepared by any of a large number of artificial methods; these usually involve either the dispersion of a liquid or powder or the condensation of a vapor. Aerosols in which the particles are nearly the same size (monodisperse) are often prepared for research purposes. The various properties of aerosols—particle concentra-

280 billion kg · 1,250 billion kg

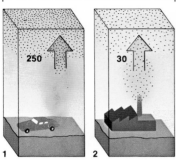

Aerosol particles entering the atmosphere originate mainly in natural sources, but an increasing proportion stems from industrial processes. Each year, industrial sources account for 280 billion kg (616 billion lb) and natural sources for 1,250 billion kg (2,750 billion lb) of pollutants. Industrial sources include pollutants, such as nitrogen oxides, sulfur oxides, and hydrocarbons from automobile exhausts (1), as well as smoke from factories (2). Natural sources include salt spray from the ocean (3); windblown dust from arid areas, such as deserts (4); emanation of gaseous compounds, such as hydrocarbons, from plants and trees (5); smoke from forest fires (6); and emission from volcanoes (7). A large proportion of these particles begin as gases, which are converted to solids by chemical changes that occur in the atmosphere.

tions, the rates of sedimentation and coagulation, light-scattering properties, and the degree of penetration of the particles into the lungs—are often measured.

The term *aerosol* has recently been used to refer to a package with the capability of converting its contents to a spray, foam, paste, or cream. The walls of the package may be of metal, plastic, or glass, and the interior is pressurized so that the contents are expelled through a nozzle when a valve is opened. Among the large number of products packaged in this manner are deodorants, hair sprays, paints, pesticides, dessert toppings, shoe polish, and window cleaners.

The propellants that furnish the pressurization may be either liquid or gaseous at room temperature. They serve the dual purposes of forcing the contents from the chamber and helping to produce a spray or foam. Chlorofluorocarbons have been used extensively as propellants because of their vapor

An aerosol can comprises a plunger cap (A) that is pressed to allow a high-pressure mixture of liquefied gas and product (D) to flow through a plastic tube (E) and out of an exit orifice (C). A fine mist (B) of product results as the liquefied gas vaporizes at atmospheric pressure. The base (F) is domed at the bottom to withstand pressure.

pressure, lack of toxicity, inflammability, and chemical inertness. However, because they lead to the destruction of stratospheric OZONE, they are being replaced by hydrocarbons and other substances. In 1979, Sweden banned the use of most aerosol sprays. RICHARD D. CADLE

Bibliography: Davies, C. N., ed., *Aerosol Science* (1966); Hidy, G. M., ed., *Aerosols and Atmospheric Chemistry* (1972).

See also: ENVIRONMENTAL POLLUTION.

aerospace industry

The aerospace industry encompasses a worldwide complex of manufacturers who produce airplanes, helicopters, military aircraft, missiles, rockets, spacecraft, and satellites. These manufacturers employ a vast number of supplier firms who make a variety of products ranging from avionics and hydraulic systems to rubber gaskets and adhesives.

History. From its beginnings—from the Wright brothers' primitive wind tunnel—aerospace has depended on scientific research for the knowledge that could be translated into airborne and space-going machinery. The National Advisory Committee for Aeronautics (NACA; established 1915) began the first important programs in aeronautic research in the United States. Work done by NACA, and in the laboratories of aircraft manufacturers, culminated in the 1930s in a new generation of efficient and reliable metal airliners. The now classic DC-3, with its wing flaps, retractable gear, and controllable pitch propellers, set the standard for air travel for many years. On the eve of World War II, American manufacturers had already produced pressurized, four-engine airliners whose availability in the early postwar era lengthened the U.S. lead in the field of transport design.

World War II forced the urgent development of many technologies that would characterize the aerospace industry of the postwar years. Rocketry, for example, grew dramatically (see ROCKETS AND MISSILES), along with advanced electronic technologies, such as RADAR, a British invention, and jet-powered aircraft, which were first used during the war by both Great Britain and Germany (see JET PROPULSION). In order to mass-produce such highly complex aircraft as the B-29, the United States developed systems for coordinating the work of thousands of independent contractors and suppliers. Moreover, these systems, which grew into the fields of SYSTEMS ENGINEERING and OPERATIONS RESEARCH, became essential for manufacturing the complex and interdependent products that would soon be required of the industry.

Research and development continued in the postwar era not only within NACA and in many aerospace firms, but also in research facilities established by the military services. Universities also conducted research under contract. Entities such as the Jet Propulsion Laboratory of the California Institute of Technology were almost entirely funded by government contracts.

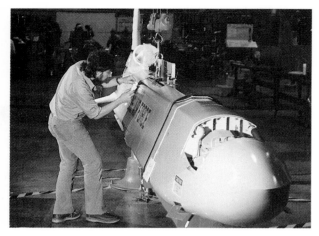

A technician inserts a component into the shell of an Air-Launched Cruise Missile (ACLM). The production line at the Boeing Space Center, near Seattle, Wash., produces 40 of these weapons a month.

In 1958, NACA became the NATIONAL AERONAUTICS AND SPACE ADMINISTRATION, underscoring the interrelated aspects of the growing aerospace field, which now included SPACE EXPLORATION vehicles and the development of long-range BALLISTIC MISSILES. New generations of civilian jet transports not only utilized advanced electronic instrumentation, but also created new demands for navigational equipment and air-traffic control; new systems were evolved using advanced electronic techniques. Jet fighters and bombers, now flying at supersonic speeds, were equipped with increasingly sophisticated electronics, becoming integrated weapons systems.

The technological advances that fueled the growth of the U.S. industry contributed to its development in Europe and the USSR as well. By the 1970s, smaller nations, such as Israel and Italy, had also become significant aerospace manufacturers.

The Industry Today. The United States and the USSR are the world's leading aerospace producers. Details of the Soviet Union's industry are sketchy; experts believe that although it may equal the United States in production capacity, it trails in technological capability. Several European nations, however, possess technological skills equal to those in the United States in many areas.

During 1983, analysts anticipated that sales in the non-Communist bloc would reach $100 billion for the first time, with the United States accounting for 70% of the total. In 1982 the U.S. industry generated sales of $62 billion, of which $14.6 billion was sold abroad: $21 billion for military aircraft; $7.6 billion for missiles; $7.5 billion for space; $7.3 billion for commercial transports; $2.0 billion for general aviation; $10 billion in nonaerospace sales. The remainder, about $7 billion, represents miscellaneous avionics, spares, and ground-support equipment.

The British aerospace industry reported $10 billion in sales for 1982, of which $5.1 billion represented exports. France's industry had $8.5 billion in sales, including exports of $6.3 billion.

The Role of Governments in Aerospace. Of the principal government agencies involved in U.S. aerospace activities, NASA plans, directs, and conducts nonmilitary research and development in the design, construction, and navigation of aircraft and spacecraft. NASA also has a special relationship with the Department of Defense in regard to space activities and aeronautical research that might apply to military aircraft. At its eight major installations, NASA engages in extensive research and development. Although production of NASA projects, such as the SPACE SHUTTLE, is accomplished by contractors and their subcontractors across the country, the principal management decisions are coordinated by NASA personnel at the lead center for each project. Johnson Space Center in Texas, for example, is responsible for the Orbiter of

the Space Shuttle; the prime contractor is Rockwell International. The large solid-propellant boosters and the liquid propellant tank are the responsibility of the Marshall Space Flight Center in Alabama, and the prime contractors are the Thiokol Chemical Corporation and Martin Marietta Aerospace. NASA headquarters in Washington, D.C., carries out overall planning.

Very similar arrangements are made by the Department of Defense and other government agencies. Defense, in addition to the acquisition of missiles and military aircraft, also funds a number of research and development projects for communications and surveillance satellites and for related technologies, including launch vehicles. The Department of Commerce operates weather and environmental satellites. The Department of Energy has been involved in nuclear-powered electric generators for NASA and Defense missions, as well as studies for solar-energy satellites. The Department of the Interior manages a variety of satellite data systems for resource management and cartography. The Federal Aviation Administration engages in extensive aeronautical research. It should be noted that the International Civil Aviation Organization, operating under the authority of the United Nations, establishes worldwide guidelines for aircraft navigational and communications procedures, and thus influences the development of certain types of equipment, such as the new microwave landing system coming into use at major commercial airports during the early to mid-1980s.

Partly in an effort to compete with the United States in aerospace, the British, French, and Italians in the 1970s established nationalized industries (British Aerospace Corp., Aerospatiale, Aeritalia), which have assumed a primary role in aerospace development. Western Europe has also begun to develop consortia, the largest of which, the 11-member EUROPEAN SPACE AGENCY (ESA), has built the 3-stage ARIANE launch vehicle. By agreement with NASA, ESA has also produced the SPACELAB, a laboratory module to be carried into orbit aboard the Space Shuttle. ESA also produces other payloads and hardware.

The extensive aerospace industry in the USSR has separate ministries for astronautics and aeronautics. Aeronautics design work is carried out in a number of bureaus named for their founders (Ilyushin, Yakovlev, and so on). Manufacture takes place at plants run by a separate production ministry.

Research and Development. The evolution of most aerospace products relies heavily on applied research. In the case of an aircraft, designers use computers to generate mathematical models that are then used to simulate hundreds of different flight patterns. When a successful design has emerged from this process, extensive wind-tunnel research, using scale models of the plane and its components, verifies the final configuration. A full-scale vehicle is then fabricated. Its wings, fuselage, landing gear, movable surfaces, and other assemblies are subjected to simulated flight loads and operational requirements. The findings of the simulated flights are incorporated into one or more operational aircraft, which undergo flight testing. For large airliners, testing may take several months. A complex military aircraft may require several years. When the aircraft finally enters production, the prime contractor assembles it from components and subsystems supplied by hundreds of contractors.

Specifications relating to the function of the aircraft also play a large role in its design. For a military fighter, designers must consider the types of targets to be attacked, the desired speed, fuel capacity, and range of the vehicle, and its weaponry, which will differ in planes intended for high- or low-altitude combat. A low-level combat plane will generally carry heavier armor plate, more specialized weapon-control systems, and equipment to reduce the threat of ground-based heat-seeking missiles. The manufacturer of the craft must also consider the man-hours required to supply and maintain the vehicle, as well as the training required for maintenance crews.

Maintenance costs and training are also considerations in the design of civil aircraft, in addition to the other requirements peculiar to airline operations. The length of runways and their load-bearing weight may influence the proposed gross weight of the plane, the design of its wings, and the configuration of its landing gear. Allowances must be made for different seating patterns for high-density and low-density routes. Performance requirements will vary for operations from airports in hot climates at sea level or cold climates above 1,500 m (5,000 ft).

The Internationalization of the Industry. Because of the immense costs of developing and producing aircraft, risk-sharing agreements have become increasingly common. The acquisition of a foreign partner can be vital, because the U.S. market, in itself, may not produce enough sales to insure profitability. For foreign partners such investment means new jobs, visibility in a high-technology field, and the acquisition of advanced aerospace technologies, in addition to the potential for profits.

Boeing's new twinjet wide-body airliner, the 767, demonstrates current risk-sharing practice. In 1978, Boeing signed risk-sharing agreements with two foreign partners, making them major participants in the development and production of the 767. Italy's Aeritalia designed and manufactured the mov-

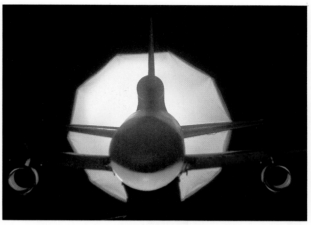

(Above) *Scale models of future jet-plane designs are tested in wind tunnels under simulated flight conditions to verify their expected flight performance. Changes in design are made if the data obtained indicate problems.*

(Left) *Assembling and testing of a wide-bodied L-1011 Tristar jet is done in a Lockheed plant, using components built by many subcontractors. Experienced workers follow a strict set of procedures in the assembly and checking of the jet before delivery.*

ing surfaces for the 767's wings and tail, as well as the vertical fin and the nose radome, using advanced composites incorporating graphite and kevlar. A consortium of Japanese manufacturers produced the 767's body panels. (An additional 1,300 firms in 26 U.S. states and 7 countries also contributed to the 767, not including "second-tier suppliers" who provided parts to the subcontractors.)

Several other major aerospace firms in the United States have entered into substantial collaborative ventures. In the mid-1970s General Dynamics concluded arrangements with the governments of Belgium, Denmark, Norway, and the Netherlands for coproduction of the advanced F-16 fighter. In this case the plane was completely designed in the United States, but the Europeans built large numbers in their own factories.

The European aircraft sector itself is becoming increasingly multinational. Airbus Industrie, a European consortium embracing France, Germany, Great Britain, the Netherlands, and Spain, has produced the A300 and A310 wide-body transports and has proved a formidable competitor in international markets. Japan's versatile aerospace industry produces U.S. aircraft under license and works with U.S. firms in the development of launch vehicles and satellites. In Canada, a nationalized organization, Canadair, produces aircraft and aerospace components. Israel's aerospace firms market both military and civil aircraft as well as electronic equipment. In South Ameri-

ca, Brazil has successfully marketed a twin-engine commuter transport.

Aerospace Contributions to Other Technologies. Artificial satellites (see SATELLITES, ARTIFICIAL) have had a profound impact on earth science, agriculture, and communications. The spread of materials—paints, adhesives, fabrics, fasteners, and alloys—that were first developed in space research can be traced throughout almost every major manufacturing area. NASA's research has broadened to include such projects as electricity generation through giant windmills and more economical fuel-burning and electrically powered automobiles. NASA experiments with ferrofluids (magnetic liquids) have led to advances in the fabrication of semiconductor chips and other industrial applications.

COSMIC, the Computer Software Management and Information System, represents a comprehensive library of computer programs developed by NASA and other federal agencies with high-technology activities. COSMIC's programs are available to industry at a fraction of their original cost and have been used in the design of hydroelectric equipment, valves for nuclear generators, oil-refinery turbines, and other advanced machinery.

Other spinoffs from the aerospace industry include a wide range of devices for monitoring or controlling complex processes in physiology, astronomy, and materials science.

ROGER E. BILSTEIN

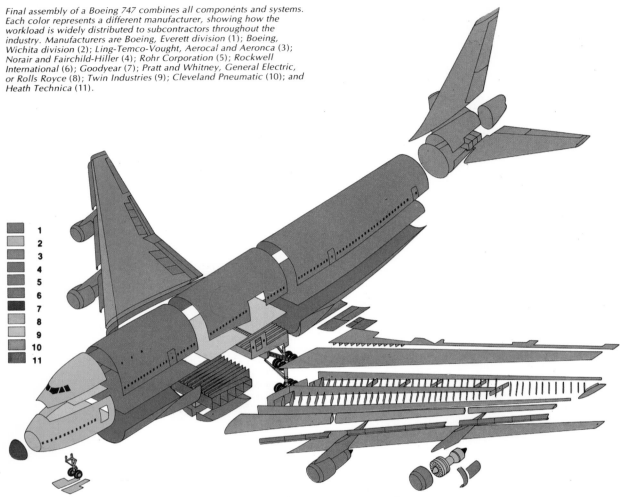

Final assembly of a Boeing 747 combines all components and systems. Each color represents a different manufacturer, showing how the workload is widely distributed to subcontractors throughout the industry. Manufacturers are Boeing, Everett division (1); Boeing, Wichita division (2); Ling-Temco-Vought, Aerocal and Aeronca (3); Norair and Fairchild-Hiller (4); Rohr Corporation (5); Rockwell International (6); Goodyear (7); Pratt and Whitney, General Electric, or Rolls Royce (8); Twin Industries (9); Cleveland Pneumatic (10); and Heath Technica (11).

MAJOR U.S. GOVERNMENT AEROSPACE CONTRACTORS

Company	Defense Contracts*	NASA Contracts*	Total
General Dynamics Corp.	5,891	114	6,005
McDonnell Douglas Corp.	5,630	220	5,850
United Technologies Corp.	4,208	90	4,298
Rockwell International Corp.	2,691	1,564	4,255
General Electric Co.	3,654	97	3,751
Lockheed Corp.	3,499	159	3,658
Boeing Corp.	3,239	123	3,362
Hughes Aircraft Co.	3,141	40	3,181
Martin Marietta Corp.	2,008	310	2,318
Raytheon Co.	2,262	20	2,282
Grumman Corp.	1,900	—	1,900
Northrop Corp.	1,598	25	1,623
Westinghouse Electric Corp.	1,492	—	1,492
FMC Corp.	1,371	—	1,371
Litton Industries, Inc.	1,317	—	1,317

SOURCE: Adapted from *Aerospace Facts and Figures*, 1983–84.
*In millions (FY 1982).

Bibliography: Aerospace Industries Association, *Aerospace Facts and Figures* (annual); *Aviation Week & Space Technology* (special annual issue, "Aerospace Forecast and Inventory"); Bilstein, Roger, *Flight in America: From the Wright Brothers to the Astronauts* (1984); Gidwitz, Betsy, *The Politics of International Air Transport* (1980); Miller, Ronald, and Sawers, David, *The Technical Development of Modern Aviation* (1970); National Aeronautics and Space Administration, *Aeronautics and Space Report of the President* (annual) and *Spinoff* (annual).

aerospace law: see SPACE LAW.

Aeschines [es'-kuh-neez]

Aeschines, *c.*390–*c.*322 BC, was a fine Athenian orator who is primarily known as the political enemy of DEMOSTHENES. Their point of contention was Athenian public policy with regard to PHILIP II of Macedonia. Although Aeschines initially favored resistance to Philip's expansionism, he came to advocate a negotiated peace. This was achieved in 346, after two diplomatic missions in which both Aeschines and Demosthenes participated. However, Demosthenes accused Aeschines first of accepting Macedonian bribes and then (343) of treason. Aeschines successfully defended himself against the latter charge in his speech *On the False Embassy*.

Perhaps encouraged by his victory, in 336 he attacked Demosthenes by accusing Demosthenes' friend Ctesiphon of illegally proposing a state honor for his friend. The case was not heard until 330. Demosthenes, speaking in Ctesiphon's defense, so successfully defended his own career that Aeschines lost the suit and was required to pay a fine. Discredited, he left Athens for Anatolia and apparently died there.

CHARLES W. FORNARA

Bibliography: Pickard-Cambridge, A. W., *Cambridge Ancient History*, vol. 6 (1953).

Aeschylus [es'-kuh-luhs]

Aeschylus, the Greek dramatist who wrote the earliest surviving Greek tragedies, was born about 525 BC at Eleusis in Attica and died in 456 BC at Gela, Sicily. The PERSIAN WARS, in which he fought at Marathon (490) and Salamis (480), together with the consolidation of Athenian democracy and the spread of Athens' empire, strongly influenced his work. In his hands, early drama took on a high religious purpose, serving as a forum for resolving profound moral conflicts and expressing a grandeur of thought and language.

Aeschylus wrote between 80 and 90 plays. Of these, 7 tragedies are preserved intact, along with substantial fragments of a SATYR PLAY and smaller bits of other works. In all, he won 13 victories at the Greater Dionysia, the annual dramatic festival held in Athens. A special law allowed his plays to be performed after his death.

Of Aeschylus's early life little is known. He began to submit plays in the opening decade of the 5th century and won his first victory in 484. Although associated with Athens, Aeschylus spent much of his life in Syracuse, in Sicily, which he initially visited about 475 and where he presented *The Women of Ætna* to celebrate the tyrant Hieron's founding (476) of the city of Aetna. From at least 468 to 458, he was back in Athens, but then returned to Sicily, allegedly dissatisfied with the Athenian public. He died in Gela (according to a comic legend, a tortoise shell dropped by an eagle struck his bald head). The Geloans honored him with a splendid tomb and an epigram—possibly composed by the poet—commemorating his valor at Marathon but saying nothing of the many plays he created.

CONTRIBUTIONS TO THE DEVELOPMENT OF DRAMA

Inheriting a primitive form of drama from his predecessors and contemporaries—THESPIS, Choerilus, Pratinas—Aeschylus added a second actor, reduced the role of the chorus, and gave greater prominence to dialogue. The ancient anonymous *Life of Aeschylus* also credits him with introducing a third actor, but Aristotle assigned this innovation to SOPHOCLES. Aeschylus, however, effectively utilized the third actor at dramatic moments in the *Oresteia* (the Cassandra and Pylades scenes) and possibly in the *Prometheus*. A true showman, he staged his own plays as spectacles with striking visual effects: exotic robes, painted scenery, daring costumes and masks,

The painting on a Greek vase portrays the judgment of Orestes in a scene from Aeschylus's Eumenides, *the final play of the* Oresteia *trilogy. Aeschylus, who lived in Athens during the 5th century BC, is known as the father of classical Greek tragedy.*

high boots (*kothornoi*) that magnified the height of the actors, and elaborate machinery to shock his audience. The *Life* reports that at the appearance of the FURIES in the *Eumenides*, "boys fainted and women miscarried."

In his earliest preserved play, the *Persians* (472 BC), which recounts Athens' naval victory over Persia at Salamis, Aeschylus exhibited remarkable sympathy for the defeated invaders: the audience sees Atossa, the Persian queen, experiencing the blow of her son's defeat, while XERXES' initial pride in conquest degenerates into mere vengeful destructiveness toward his subjects' lives and property. The catastrophe attendant upon dynastic ambition is a recurrent theme in Aeschylus's work.

Seven Against Thebes (467 BC) is the last play of a trilogy about the destruction of the House of OEDIPUS. It focuses on the decision of Eteocles, the son of Oedipus and the ruler of Thebes, to meet his brother in battle, where each kills the other.

Because of its archaic structure, the *Suppliant Women* was long thought to be the poet's earliest work, but recent evidence based on a papyrus introducing the play suggests a date about 463. The first play in a trilogy, it dramatizes the decision of the king of Argos to shelter the Danaids, 50 Egyptian women fleeing marriage to their cousins.

The *Oresteia* (458 BC), the only surviving trilogy from ancient times, dramatizes the curse on the House of Atreus from the time of AGAMEMNON's return and murder to Orestes' matricide and purification. Inspired by confidence in Athens' democratic institutions, Aeschylus here celebrated the evolution of justice from primitive blood vengeance to civic law.

Prometheus Bound (*c*.460–56 BC), like the *Oresteia*, concerns divine justice and the cosmic order: ZEUS, a harsh god, punishes the Titan PROMETHEUS for giving fire to mortals. The lost plays of the trilogy presented Prometheus's liberation and perhaps his reconciliation with Zeus. Because of its intellectual, Sophistic vocabulary, some have doubted its Aeschylean origins.

AESCHYLEAN CHARACTERISTICS

Apart from the *Persians*, the surviving plays date from the last decade of Aeschylus's life and form parts of connected trilogies, possibly a late development in his work. His tragedies are generally more formal than those of Sophocles or EURIPIDES, less concerned with character development, and more stylized in the use of ritual elements such as responsive prayer or chant. His heroes, for instance, rather than being three-dimensional individuals, are bearers of tragic conflicts often rooted in the acts of a past generation. They are usually larger than life. His plots involve the rebellion of Titans, the downfall of aristocratic houses, and the capriciousness of the gods. The Aeschylean hero must make tragic choices between alternatives that both involve suffering. The hero's personal choice is the arena in which the issue of cosmic justice is worked out. In the connected trilogy, justice is accomplished over the course of several generations or even, as in the *Prometheus* trilogy, over thousands of years.

Aeschylus used bold metaphors, vivid images, flamboyantly poetic words, and magnificent geographical description. His religious grandeur is probably unequaled in classical literature. In ARISTOPHANES' satire *The Frogs* (405 BC), Aeschylus defeats Euripides in a literary contest and embodies the original vitality of tragedy: its martial, public spirit, democratic energy, and nobility of language and ideas.

Recent scholarship has stressed the range and boldness of Aeschylus's religious conceptions, the depth and intensity of his presentation of tragic conflict, and the coherence and psychological incisiveness of his mythic and poetic imagery.

CHARLES SEGAL

Bibliography: Finley, John H., *Pindar and Aeschylus* (1955); Gagarin, Michael, *Aeschylean Drama* (1976); Golden, Leon, *In Praise of Prometheus: Humanism and Rationalism in Aeschylean Thought* (1966); McCall, Marsh, ed., *Aeschylus, A Collection of Critical Essays* (1972); Murray, Gilbert, *Aeschylus, the Creator of Tragedy* (1940); Podlecki, Anthony J., *The Political Background of Aeschylean Tragedy* (1966); Smyth, Herbert W., *Aeschylean Tragedy* (1924; repr. 1969).

See also: GREEK LITERATURE, ANCIENT; ORESTEIA; TRAGEDY.

Aesop

An early engraving illustrates "The Fox and the Lion," a fable by Aesop, the Greek storyteller. Like most of Aesop's tales, it reveals some aspect of human foibles through the use of an amusing animal story.

Aesop, a Greek folk hero who is supposed to have lived in the 6th century BC, acquired a great reputation as a teller of animal FABLES. According to one tradition, he was born in Thrace, lived for a while as a slave on the island of Samos, was freed and traveled widely, and was murdered while visiting Delphi.

Aristotle describes (330 BC) how Aesop defended a corrupt politician by telling the story of the fox and the hedgehog. A fox, Aesop said, was troubled by fleas, and a hedgehog asked if he could help remove them. The fox replied: "No, these fleas are full and no longer suck much blood. If you take them away, new, hungry fleas will come." "So, gentlemen of the jury," Aesop is supposed to have said, "if you put my client to death, others will come along who are not rich and will rob you completely."

No evidence indicates that Aesop wrote down his fables or published them. Collections of fables, authentic or imitative, were made as early as the 4th century BC. The two oldest surviving collections date from the 1st century AD; they were written by Phaedrus in Latin and by Babrius in Greek. Aesop's fables later served as a springboard for the verse satires of the 17th-century French writer Jean de LA FONTAINE.

Because Aesop's fables are short, simply expressed, and entertaining to children, they have been used since classical times as texts in elementary schools. The most popular English version is probably that by Samuel Croxall, originally published in 1722 and widely read throughout the 18th and 19th centuries in Britain and North America. Croxall saw a political meaning in the fables and accompanied each with an "application," or moral.   GEORGE KENNEDY

Bibliography: Aesop, *Fables*, trans. by S. A. Handford (1964) and *Fables*, trans. by John Warrington (1961); Jacobs, Joseph, ed., *History of the Aesopic Fable* (1889; repr. 1970), vol. 1 in *The Fables of Aesop*; Perry, Ben Edwin, *Aesopica* (1952).

aestheticism

Aestheticism was a literary and artistic movement that flourished in England and France toward the end of the 19th century. It was based on the theory that the intense perception of beauty ("art for art's sake") is the highest good and, as such, is independent of social, political, or ethical considerations. For the so-called aesthete, life itself must be lived as a work of art.

The basic concept of aestheticism was derived from the writers and philosophers of German ROMANTICISM, particularly KANT. In France, Benjamin CONSTANT is believed to have coined the phrase *l'art pour l'art* ("art for art's sake") in 1804, and Théophile GAUTIER further articulated the concepts of aestheticism in the preface to his novel *Mademoiselle de Maupin* (1835). The works of the American writer Edgar Allan POE also influenced the French movement. The notion was

central to the poetry of Charles BAUDELAIRE, particularly in his *Les Fleurs du mal* (*The Flowers of Evil*, 1857), and influenced the later writers and painters of French SYMBOLISM.

Aestheticism in England can be traced to the poetry of KEATS, the criticism of John RUSKIN and Walter PATER, and the paintings and poetry of such PRE-RAPHAELITES as Dante Gabriel ROSSETTI. Pater concluded in his *Studies in the History of the Renaissance* (1873) that, in a world without God, value lies in moments of intense sensation. He urged his readers "to burn always with this hard gem-like flame" and embrace "the love of art for art's sake." Pater's ideas particularly influenced Oscar WILDE and the poets of the Rhymers Club, founded by W. B. YEATS. Such painters as James McNeill WHISTLER rapidly moved away from representationalism and toward an abstract art of pure form and color. During the 1890s the elevated sentiments of aestheticism were gradually superseded by the more perverse and flamboyant style called DECADENCE.

HERBERT SUSSMAN

Bibliography: Hough, Graham, *The Last Romantics* (1949); Spencer, Charles, ed., *Aesthetic Movement: 1869–1890* (1973); Spencer, Robin, *Aesthetic Movement* (1972).

aesthetics

Aesthetics is the branch of philosophy that aims to establish the general principles of art and beauty. It can be divided into the philosophy of art and the philosophy of beauty. Although some philosophers have considered one of these a subdivision of the other, the philosophies of art and beauty are essentially different. The philosophy of beauty recognizes aesthetic phenomena outside of art, as in nature or in nonartistic cultural phenomena such as morality, science, or mathematics; it is concerned with art only insofar as art is beautiful. The history of the arts in the West, however, has made it increasingly clear that there is much more to art than beauty and that art often has little or nothing to do with beauty. Until the 18th century, the philosophy of beauty was generally given more attention than the philosophy of art. Since that time, aestheticians have devoted more energy to the philosophy of art.

PHILOSOPHY OF ART

Metaphysics of Art. Aestheticians ask two main questions about the metaphysics of art: (1) What is the ontological status of works of art, or what kind of entity is a work of art? (2) What access, if any, does art give the viewer or hearer to reality, or what kind of knowledge, if any, does art yield? The first question arises, in part, because some works of art, such as SCULPTURES, are much like ordinary physical objects; others, such as PAINTINGS, have aspects that suggest that not all works of art can be merely physical objects. A painting, for example, is typically flat, but it can represent spatial depth; and what the painting represents often seems more relevant aesthetically than its physical dimensions. To some aestheticians, the representational character seems to be what is essential to a painting as a work of art. Some philosophers have therefore concluded that works of art are mental entities of some sort, because it is mental entities, such as visions and dreams, that are typically representational. Other philosophers, who have noticed that artists can and do express some of their own attitudes, emotions, and personality traits in their art, have concluded that art works belong in a category with NONVERBAL COMMUNICATIONS rather than with physical objects.

A different line of thought suggests that works of art are not like objects even on a first impression. For example, the score of a SYMPHONY is not the same as the symphony. The score is a set of directions for playing the music, but the musical work can exist even if no one ever plays the score. Considerations such as these have led many philosophers to say that works of art exist only in the minds of their creators and of their hearers, viewers, or readers.

The question whether art can provide knowledge of, or insight into, reality is as old as philosophy itself. Plato argued in *The Republic* that art has the power to represent only the appearances of reality. According to this theory, a painter reproduces (imitates) a subject on canvas. The counterposition, that art can yield insight into the real, is common among modern philosophers, artists, and critics. Many, in fact, allege that art offers a special, nondiscursive, and intuitive knowledge of reality that science and philosophy cannot achieve.

Experience of Art. Modern discussions about how art is experienced have been dominated by theories devised in the 18th century to describe the experience of beauty. As a consequence, many philosophers still think of the typical experience of art as distanced, disinterested, or contemplative. This experience is supposed to be different from everyday affairs and concerns. A few modern aestheticians, especially John DEWEY, have stressed the continuity between aesthetic and everyday experience and have claimed for the experience of art a psychological integrative function.

Judgments and Interpretations. The study of critics' judgments and interpretations of art tries to specify the kind of reasoning involved in such opinions. One question is whether evaluative judgments can be backed by strictly deductive reasoning based on premises descriptive of the artwork. A radical answer is that evaluative judgments are merely expressions of preference and thus cannot be considered either true or false. With respect to critical interpretations of a work, as distinct from evaluations, a basic question is whether conflicts over interpretations of a work can be definitively settled by facts about the work, or whether several incompatible but reasonable interpretations are possible. A related concern is what the criteria of relevance are for justifying an interpretation or evaluation. Some aestheticians in this century, for example, have argued that appeals to the artist's intentions about a work are irrelevant.

Production of Art. Philosophical speculation about the production of art centers primarily on the following questions: What is the role of genius, or innate ability, in artistic production? What is the meaning of creativity? How do the conditions for producing fine art differ from those for producing crafts? On the last issue, ancient and medieval philosophers assumed the same model for producing fine art and crafts; they had no conception that the two are distinct. The present distinction between the two emerged in Western culture after the Renaissance.

Definition of Art. Attempts to define art generally aim at establishing a set of characteristics applicable to all fine arts as well as the differences that set them apart. By the middle of the 20th century, aestheticians had not agreed on a definition of art, and a skeptical position became popular, holding that it is impossible in principle to define art.

PHILOSOPHY OF BEAUTY

A comparable skepticism about the possibility of defining beauty had arisen in the 18th century, culminating in the *Critique of Judgment* (1790), Immanuel Kant's contribution to aesthetics. In that work, Kant analyzed the "judgment of taste," that is, the judgment that a thing is beautiful. He asserted that the judgment of beauty is subjective. Before Kant, the common assumption was that "beauty" designated some objective feature of things. Most earlier theories of beauty had held that beauty was a complex relation between parts of a whole. Some philosophers called this relation "harmony." From the time of the Greeks, a common assumption was that beauty applied not only, or primarily, to art, but that it manifested itself in cultural institutions and moral character as well as in natural and artificial objects. By the end of the 18th century, however, the range of accepted beautiful things was becoming more and more restricted to natural things and artworks.

Whereas theorists of beauty had generally admitted that the perception of beauty always gives pleasure to the perceiver, Kant turned the pleasure into the criterion of beauty. According to Kant, people can judge a thing beautiful only if they take pleasure in experiencing it. George SANTAYANA took this subjectivism a step further by declaring that beauty is the same as pleasure—but pleasure then can be seen as "objectified" in things. Santayana's *The Sense of Beauty* (1896) marked the virtual end, until recently, of aestheticians' serious theoretical interest in beauty.   GUY SIRCELLO

Bibliography: Beardsley, Monroe, *Aesthetics: Problems in the Philosophy of Criticism* (1958); Collingwood, R. G., *The Principles of Art* (1938); Croce, Benedetto, *Aesthetic,* trans. by Douglas Ainslie (1909); Dewey, John, *Art as Experience* (1934); Langer, Susanne K., *Feeling and Form* (1953); Sircello, Guy, *A New Theory of Beauty* (1975); Tartarkiewicz, W., *History of Aesthetics,* 3 vols. (1970, 1974).

Æthelbert, King of Kent   [ath'-uhl-burt]

Æthelbert, 552–616, king of Kent from 560, was the first Christian Anglo-Saxon ruler in England. He married Bertha, a Christian Frankish princess, and in 597, Æthelbert himself was converted by the missionary Saint Augustine of Canterbury. Æthelbert issued a code of laws (*c*.600) that is the oldest surviving document in Old English.

Æthelflæd   [ath'-uhl-flad]

Æthelflæd, d. 918, daughter of King Alfred of Wessex, ruled the semiautonomous Anglo-Saxon kingdom of Mercia, first with Æthelred, ealdorman of Mercia, whom she married *c*.880, and then on her own during the illness that preceded his death (911) and thereafter until her own death. Known as the Lady of the Mercians, she built fortresses and helped recover areas held by the Danes—victories that facilitated the ascendancy of her brother EDWARD THE ELDER. After Æthelflæd's death, Edward incorporated English Mercia into Wessex.

Æthelred II, King of England   (Æthelred the Unready)   [ath'-uhl-red]

Æthelred II, 968–1016, king of England (978–1016), lost his kingdom to Danish conquerers. His nickname, "the Unready," is derived from the Old English *unrede,* meaning that he lacked advice. Beginning his reign under suspicion of murdering his half-brother, King Edward the Martyr, Æthelred proved a weak ruler. In 980 the Danes renewed their raids on England after a 25-year truce. Unable to mount effective resistance, Æthelred began payment (991) of the Danegeld, a form of tribute, to buy off the raiders. In 1013, however, the Danes under SWEYN overran the entire country, and Æthelred fled to Normandy. Although he returned in 1014, the Danish king CANUTE completed the Danish conquest of England in 1016, shortly after Æthelred's death.

Bibliography: Stenton, F. M., *Anglo-Saxon England,* 3d ed. (1971).

Aetius, Flavius   [ee'-shuhs, flay'-vee-uhs]

Flavius Aetius, AD 396–454, was a Roman general who, winning favor with Valentinian III, became virtual ruler of the western empire. He was first given command in Gaul. There, after the death (432) of the powerful rival general Boniface, he (433) crushed the rebels and destroyed the Burgundian kingdom. Allying his forces with the Visigoths in 451, Aetius defeated ATTILA and the Huns in the Battle of Châlons. Aetius had been made consul three times, and his power threatened Valentinian, who had him assassinated.

Aetolia   [ee-toh'-lee-uh]

Aetolia was a district of ancient Greece that lay north of the Gulf of Corinth and was bordered on the east by Mount Oxya and on the west by the Achelous River. The Aetolians had several coastal towns, but most of the area was cut off from the sea by mountains. The people pursued an agrarian economy, farming their rich interior plains. They maintained an important shrine to Apollo at Thermum and to Artemis at Calydon.

The Aetolian League was formed in the 4th century BC. A strong confederacy, it seized Delphi about 300 and became a major opponent of the Achaean League and Macedonia. The league allied with the Romans to defeat PHILIP V of Macedonia in 197, but it later sided with ANTIOCHUS III against Rome, and with his downfall (189 BC) the Aetolians were forced to become subject allies of Rome. Although the league survived, its influence was destroyed.

Afanasiev, Aleksandr Nikolayevich [uh-fuh-nah'-see-ev, ul-yik-sahn'-dur nik-ul-ly'-uh-vich]

The Russian writer Aleksandr Nikolayevich Afanasiev, b. July 11 (N.S.), 1826, d. Oct. 23 (N.S.), 1871, was an outstanding collector of folktales, literary historian, and bibliographer. His *Russian Folk Tales* (8 vols., 1855–64; Eng. trans., 1945) was, when published, the most extensive compilation of these stories and had a considerable influence on Russian literature.

RALPH E. MATLAW

Afars and Issas, Territory of the:

see DJIBOUTI (country).

affenpinscher [ah'-fen-pin-shur]

The affenpinscher is a toy dog that is native to Europe. Its name derives from German for "monkey dog" and refers to the appearance of the affenpinscher's head. The Brussels griffin was bred from the affenpinscher.

The affenpinscher is a toy breed that resembles the terriers. It has bushy eyebrows that hang down over large black eyes, a mustache, and a slightly protruding lower jaw that bears a hair-tuft. Its stiff, wiry coat is usually black but may have tan, gray, or red markings. The tail is usually docked. The affenpinscher stands about 25 cm (10 in) high at the shoulder and weighs up to 3.6 kg (8 lb). It was recognized as a separate species as long ago as the 17th century in Europe.

affidavit

An affidavit is a sworn statement made before a notary or other person authorized to administer an oath; it is used in court to advise the court of certain facts. It differs from a DEPOSITION in that the person making the affidavit may not be cross-examined. An affidavit of merits states that a defendant in a legal action has a meritorious defense and informs the court of the facts on which the defense is based.

affirmative action

Affirmative action is a formal effort to provide increased employment opportunities for women and ethnic minorities, to overcome past patterns of discrimination (see EQUAL OPPORTUNITY). Under the Equal Employment Opportunity Act of 1972, most federal contractors and subcontractors, all state governments and institutions (including universities), and most local governments must initiate plans to increase the proportions of their female and minority employees until they are equal to the proportions existing in the available labor market. The measures employers and institutions should take to demonstrate their compliance with the law have been the subject of controversy. Affirmative action plans that establish racial quotas were declared unconstitutional by the Supreme Court in UNIVERSITY OF CALIFORNIA V. BAKKE (1978) but upheld in the case of private businesses and unions in UNITED STEELWORKERS OF AMERICA V. WEBER (1979). In (Memphis) *Firefighters* v. *Stotts* (1984) the Court reaffirmed the position that seniority outweighs race in determining layoffs. The ruling itself had fairly narrow application, but it rekindled the debate over affirmative action.

Bibliography: Walker, M.A., and Block, W., eds., *Discrimination, Affirmative Action, and Equal Opportunity* (1982).

Afghan hound

The Afghan hound, a hunting dog and pet, originated in ancient Egypt but developed its present traits in mountainous Afghanistan. With wide-set prominent hipbones, it can run easily over rocky and hilly terrain with powerful leaps and quick turns. A large and slender dog, the Afghan hound measures 61 to 71 cm (24 to 28 in) high at the shoulder and weighs 22 to 27 kg (50 to 60 lb). It is one of the few hounds that hunts by sight rather than scent. Long silky hair, which may be of any color, grows in a topknot on its head and also covers its body, legs, and long, drooping ears. The comparatively hairless tail is held in a high, tight curve.

Bibliography: Miller, Constance, and Gilbert, Edward, *The Complete Afghan Hound.* 3d ed. (1975).

The Afghan hound is a hunting dog that originated in ancient Egypt. It is much admired for its regal stance and fluid, graceful movements.

Afghanistan

The Democratic Republic of Afghanistan (DRA) is a country situated between the Indian subcontinent, Soviet Central Asia, and the nations of the Middle East. Although it has no access to the sea, its location was central to the wars, migrations, and trade that dominated inner Asia until early modern times. It is bordered by Pakistan on the east and south, the USSR on the north, Iran on the west, and China in the extreme northeast. The USSR occupied the country in 1979 on behalf of its Marxist government, which had seized power in a violent coup the previous year. Since then, Afghanistan has been in a state of civil war.

LAND AND RESOURCES

Afghanistan is dominated by rugged mountains and arid plains. Its central and eastern regions are covered by high mountain ranges centering on the HINDU KUSH. The system spurs off from the Himalayas; many peaks in the extreme northeast reach more than 6,100 m (20,000 ft). Barren plains flank the mountain core to the north, west, and south. In the southwest the plains become deserts.

Climate. Afghanistan's dry, continental climate produces sharp contrasts in temperatures by day, by season, and by elevation. Winters bring snow followed by early spring rains. Summers are hot and dry. Falls are moderate and also dry. Average annual rainfall is about 180 mm (7 in) and is rarely more than 380 mm (15 in) anywhere in the country.

Drainage. Afghanistan's major internal rivers rise in the central mountain core and flow outward generally in the four cardinal directions. Only the Kabul River, flowing east to join the Indus in Pakistan, reaches the sea. The largest is the Helmand, which runs south-southwest past KANDAHAR to the swamps of Sistan on the Iranian border. The Hari Rud flows west past Herat, and the Kunduz north to meet the AMU DARYA (Oxus), which forms the northern border. After a heavy spring flow, the runoff of the rivers is irregular and low.

Vegetable and Animal Life. Thin soil and a harsh climate limit natural life to the sturdiest strains. Tree cover is concentrated in the east where pine forests are common. Pistachio grows wild on the slopes of the hills of the north and northwest. Thin grasses briefly provide mountain grazing for nomadic herds in the spring and summer. Wildlife includes wolves, hyenas, foxes, leopards, gazelles, bears, ibex, and wild Marco Polo sheep.

Resources. Incompletely surveyed and only marginally exploited, Afghanistan's mineral resources offer considerable potential for development. There are major deposits of iron, chrome, copper, natural gas, and possibly of uranium. Soft coal is available at numerous sites, and recent surveys suggest that the country may have exploitable oil reserves. Lapis lazuli continues to be taken from ancient mines in the northeast. Timber harvest is restricted to the eastern mountains. There is considerable hydroelectric potential in the flow of the rivers.

PEOPLE

Afghan society is a composite of primary family, village, and tribal units scattered within a mosaic of ethnic, linguistic, and regional communities. Millennia of conquests and folk movements have left remnants of all the peoples who have roamed inner Asia.

The PATHAN (Pashtun) people form the dominant ethnic and linguistic community, accounting for perhaps half the population. Tribally organized, the Pathan are concentrated in the east and the south. As they gained control over the rest of the country in the 19th century, however, many of them settled in other areas too. The Dari- (Persian-) speaking TADZHIK (Tajik) are the second largest community, accounting for approximately one-third the population. They are strongly identified with sedentary farming and town life, mostly in the fertile eastern valleys north and south of the Hindu Kush. Some 10% of the population are Turkic, mostly UZBEK and TURKMEN, who live in the northern plains as farmers and herders. The central mountains yield a meager living to some 1 million Hazaras, a Mongoloid people who mostly speak Persian. There are many

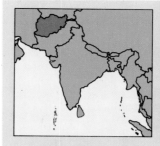

DEMOCRATIC REPUBLIC OF AFGHANISTAN

LAND. Area: 647,500 km² (250,000 mi²). Capital and largest city: Kabul (1979 pop., 913,164).

PEOPLE. Population (1984 est.): 14,400,000. Density (1984 est.): 22.2 persons per km² (57.6 per mi²). Distribution (1984 est.): 16% urban, 84% rural. Annual growth (1978): 2.4%. Official languages: Pushtu, Dari (Persian). Major religion: Islam.

EDUCATION AND HEALTH. Literacy (1984 est.): 10% of adult population. Universities (1984): 2. Hospital beds (1976): 2,914. Physicians (1976): 719. Life expectancy (1984): 40. Infant mortality: 182 per 1,000 live births.

ECONOMY. GNP (1979): $2.8 billion; $225 per capita. Labor distribution (1980 est.): agriculture—67.8%; industry—10.2%; services—7.7%; other —14.3%. Foreign trade (1980): imports—$839 million; exports—$7.05 billion; principal trade partner—USSR. Currency: 1 afghani = 100 puls.

GOVERNMENT. Type: one-party communist state. Legislature: Revolutionary Council acts as legislature. Political subdivisions: 29 provinces.

COMMUNICATIONS. Railroads (1982): 9.2 km (5.7 mi) total. Roads (1982): 3,000 km (1,864 mi) paved; 18,000 km (11,185 mi) unpaved. Major ports: none. Airfields (major, 1982): 6.

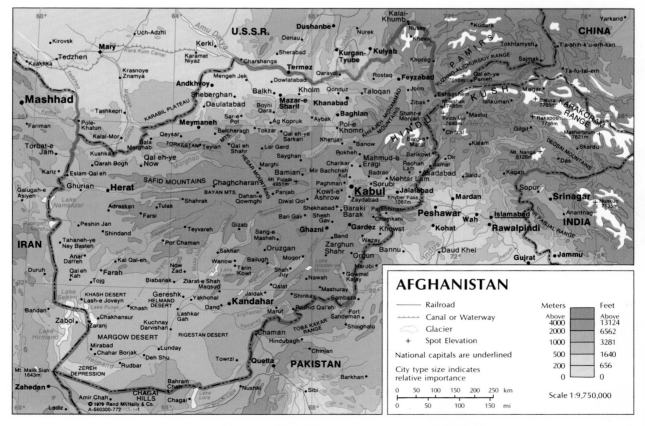

AFGHANISTAN

	Meters	Feet
———— Railroad	Above 4000	Above 13124
Canal or Waterway	2000	6562
Glacier	1000	3281
+ Spot Elevation	500	1640
National capitals are underlined	200	656
City type size indicates relative importance	0	0

0   50   100   150   200   250 km
0   50   100   150 mi

Scale 1:9,750,000

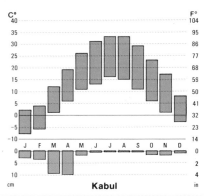

(Left) *Kabul, situated on a plain dominated by the Hindu Kush Mountains, is the capital and largest city of Afghanistan.*

(Right) *Bars indicate monthly ranges of temperatures (red) and precipitation (blue) of Kabul, which has a steppe climate typical of the country as a whole.*

Kabul

Pashtun herders shear karakul sheep in their summer camp in the Hindu Kush; the wool will be used to make felt and carpet thread. The nomadic way of life in Afghanistan is rapidly disappearing. Since 1979, many nomads have crossed the mountains into Pakistan and Iran.

smaller communities, the most important of which are the Nuristanis of the high mountains of the east and the BALUCH of the desert south.

Virtually all Afghans are Muslim, four-fifths of them Sunni. A few thousand Hindus and Sikhs live as traders in the cities.

Demography. Population data are imprecise and incomplete; there has never been a census. The pre-1980 population of perhaps 15 million was at least 90% rural. Most farmers lived in settled villages in the best watered valleys where the major rivers intersect the plains. Various forms of nomadic herding are practiced by as much as 20% of the population. The warfare that has disrupted the country since the Soviet occupation has forced more than 4 million Afghans to become international refugees, mostly in Pakistan and Iran. Large tracts of the best agricultural land have been systematically depopulated, and about 250,000 Afghans have been killed. By 1983 the major cities were swollen with internal refugees fleeing from the fighting in the countryside. It is estimated that Kabul, the capital, has recently doubled in size. The other major cities—Kandahar, Herat, Mazar-e-Sharif, Jalalabad, and Kunduz—have also experienced sudden increases.

Health. Whereas such endemic diseases as malaria and cholera have been recently brought under control, effective medical care and public health services have been largely limited to the cities. The situation has been aggravated by warfare and the breakdown of central government control. The population has been growing slowly, its high birthrate offset by very high infant and child mortality.

Education. Great expansion in education was accomplished between 1950 and 1973. Primary schools became accessible to more than half the school-age children, and secondary schools were functioning in nearly all provincial towns. Facilities for female education lagged far behind those for males but were expanding rapidly. The national university at Kabul offered increasingly sophisticated graduate-level programs in professional, scientific, and technical fields. Despite this progress, made possible largely by assistance from many countries, 90% of the population remained illiterate.

Education, especially in the rural areas, has been devastated by the war; government schools and teachers are principal targets of the anti-Soviet resistance. In the cities education is being Sovietized in curriculum and organization, with many younger students being sent to the USSR for education and indoctrination.

THE ARTS

Afghanistan has been a center of Persian, Indo-Greek, Buddhist, and Islamic cultures. Numerous archaeological sites of great potential significance await excavation. Among the architectural remains that have been excavated are the Buddhist monasteries at BAMIAN and Hadda, the Ghaznavid palace complexes at Ghazni, and the Greek city at ai-Khanum. Herat was a major center of Persian culture from the 11th to the 16th centuries, renowned especially for the exquisite miniature painting patronized by the TIMURIDS in the late 15th century. Carpet making remains the primary folk art, especially among the Turkmen of the northwest.

ECONOMIC ACTIVITY

Modern economic change began in Afghanistan early in the 20th century with superficial efforts to expand trade, begin manufacture, improve transportation, and generate greater government revenue. Substantial commercial progress came in the 1930s through the promotion of traditional fruit, fur, and carpet exports in return for manufactured imports, mostly from India. Wide-ranging development efforts, however, became possible only in the 1950s, mostly through foreign assistance at first mainly from the United States and the USSR, and later from Iran and the oil-rich Persian Gulf states. Since 1979 war has destroyed or dispersed much of the physical and human resources created by a generation of rapid development. Evidence suggests that the Soviets are interested in Afghanistan as a source of valuable metals and natural gas.

Agriculture. Afghanistan's economy is essentially agrarian; the livelihood of more than 80% of the population is directly dependent on farming or herding. Wheat, the primary food-grain, is grown mostly as an irrigated winter crop. Recently, cotton has become an important cash crop. Fruits, especially grapes and melons, are important seasonally; their famed quality has made them major exports to the subcontinent and the USSR. Skins, hides, and the fur of the karakul lamb are also important exports. Large multipurpose irrigation and reclamation schemes have been developed in the Helmand and Hari Rud valleys and in the Parwan and Jalalabad areas.

Industry and Transportation. Industrial development remains rudimentary; there are less than 50,000 factory workers, mostly engaged in agricultural processing. The greatest progress made was in building an infrastructure base in transportation and energy. All-weather paved roads now connect all major cities and the principal border points, and a network of airports connects nearly all of the provinces. Power production near Kabul has outrun industrial needs but remains in short supply throughout the rest of the country. Natural gas is exported to the USSR and also used for fertilizer production.

GOVERNMENT

Afghanistan is formally governed as a democratic republic on the Soviet Marxist pattern. Power is officially held by the Revolutionary Committee of the People's Democratic party of Afghanistan (PDPA). It controls the cabinet, which ostensibly runs the government. Babrak KARMAL serves as chairman of the committee and president of the republic. Soviet advisors play critical roles in every major government agency. This establishment is challenged by a diverse resistance movement.

HISTORY

Afghanistan's crossroads position in Central Asia has subjected it to constant invasion and conquest throughout its long recorded history. The parade of conquerors in historic times includes Darius I of Persia in the 6th century BC; Alexander the Great in 328 BC; the Sakas (Scythians), Parthians, and the Buddhist Kushans in the 2d and 1st centuries BC; and the Hephthalites, or White Huns, in the 5th and 6th centuries AD. The Arabs introduced Islam in the 7th century, and the Turks under MAHMUD OF GHAZNI briefly made Afghanistan the center of Islamic power and civilization at the beginning of the 11th century. The Mongols invaded Afghanistan early in the 13th century, and TIMUR added it to his empire at the end of the 14th century. In the early 16th century, Timur's descendant BABUR, first of the MOGULS, founded an empire in India from his base at Kabul. During the 16th and 17th centuries some parts of the country owed allegiance to the Moguls, and others to the Safavids of Persia.

In 1747 the Pathan, having thrown off the Persian yoke, established a dynasty of their own under Ahmad Shah Sadozai, the leader of a tribal confederation. Pathan strength was consolidated by Dost Muhammad Khan (r. 1826–63), who founded a second dynasty early in the 19th century. Effective physical control over all of the country, however, was first achieved by Dost Muhammad's grandson, Abdur Rahman Khan (r. 1880–1901); Abdur Rahman's diplomacy also prevented either the British or the Russian empires from gaining internal control over Afghanistan. Frustrated by their failure to subdue the country in the Anglo-Afghan wars of 1839–42 and 1878–80, the British agreed to subsidize an Afghan ruler strong enough to serve as a buffer between the empires.

Abdur Rahman's grandson, Amanullah Shah (r. 1919–29), ended (1921) British involvement in Afghan affairs. He also initiated a series of ambitious efforts at social and political modernization, but tribal opposition forced him to flee the country. Zahir Shah ruled Afghanistan from 1933 to 1973. In 1964 he sponsored a serious attempt at liberal, Islamic constitutionalism including free elections and partial parliamentary democracy. When the experiment foundered, the king's cousin Mohammad Daud Khan seized power in a nearly bloodless coup and ruled as a republican president from 1973 to 1978.

Daud was killed in a Marxist coup in April 1978. This brought the semiclandestine PDPA to sudden power under Nur Mohammad Taraki. Its brutal methods and impractically radical reforms in education and land and family law fomented a popular backlash, especially in the rural areas. Despite growing Soviet support, the regime was increasingly threatened by general revolt late in 1979. Its link with Moscow was weakened in September when Taraki was removed (and later killed) by his lieutenant, Hafizullah Amin.

The USSR intervened militarily in December 1979. Amin was executed and replaced by Babrak Karmal, who had been a long-time Marxist rival of Taraki and Amin. Karmal's government has since attempted to establish control over the country with the help of Soviet air and land forces and several thousand Soviet civilian advisors.

After the Soviet intervention, popular opposition became a national resistance movement active throughout the whole of Afghanistan. The movement has remained politically divided between rival claimants to leadership based in Pakistan. Operationally, the resistance is separated into regionally and locally organized groups carrying out guerrilla warfare within the country. After more than four years of fighting, the poorly equipped *mujahidin* (Islamic warriors) have denied control of most of the countryside and the population to the Soviet forces. The stalemated war continued into the mid-1980s with no visible prospect of a victory by either side, or of a political settlement.

RICHARD S. NEWELL

Bibliography: Bradsher, Henry, *Afghanistan and the Soviet Union* (1983); Dupress, Louis, *Afghanistan* (1973); Fraser-Tyler, W. K., *Afghanistan* (1967); Gregorian, Vartan, *The Emergence of Modern Afghanistan* (1969); Newell, Nancy and Richard S., *The Struggle for Afghanistan* (1981); Poullada, Leon, *Reform and Rebellion in Afghanistan, 1919–1929* (1973).

AFL-CIO: see AMERICAN FEDERATION OF LABOR AND CONGRESS OF INDUSTRIAL ORGANIZATIONS.

Afonso: for Portuguese kings of this name see ALFONSO.

Africa

Africa is the second largest continent after Asia. It is separated from Asia by the Suez Canal, the Gulf of Suez, and the Red Sea, and from Europe by the Straits of Gibraltar and Mediterranean Sea. It is bounded by the Atlantic Ocean on the west and the Indian Ocean on the east. Offshore islands considered part of Africa include, in the Indian Ocean, MADAGASCAR, MAURITIUS, RÉUNION, ZANZIBAR, PEMBA, the SEYCHELLES, and the COMOROS. In the North Atlantic Ocean are the CANARY ISLANDS, CAPE VERDE ISLANDS, and MADEIRA ISLANDS; in the South Atlantic are ASCENSION ISLAND and SAINT HELENA; and in the Gulf of Guinea (see GUINEA, GULF OF) are Pagalu, Bioko, São Tomé, and Príncipe.

The earliest known protohuman fossils have been found in Africa, primarily in Kenya and Tanzania. The continent was also the home of one of the world's oldest civilizations, that of ancient Egypt. Egyptian influence spread south up the Nile into present Sudan by the 1st millennium BC, at the same time as the Phoenicians were founding Carthage and other city states along the Mediterranean coast north of the Atlas Mountains. North Africa came under European influence during the period of Roman rule (1st century BC—7th century AD). Beginning in the 7th century, Arab culture and the Muslim faith spread across the Sahara following trade routes between the north

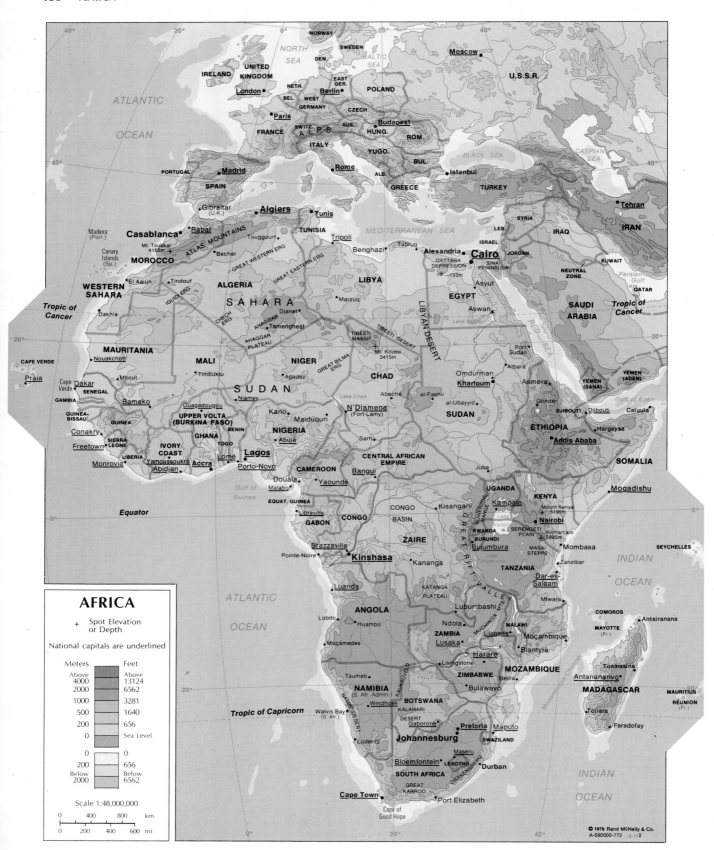

AFRICA

+ Spot Elevation
  or Depth

National capitals are underlined

Meters	Feet
Above 4000	Above 13124
2000	6562
1000	3281
500	1640
200	656
0	Sea Level
0	0
200	656
Below 2000	Below 6562

Scale 1:48,000,000

| 0 | 400 | 800 | km |
| 0 | 200 | 400 | 600 | mi |

© 1979 Rand McNally & Co.
A-580000-772 -2-:-2

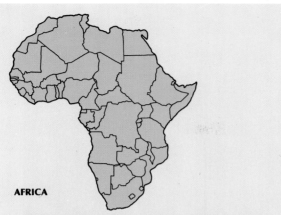

AFRICA

   Area: 30,330,000 km² (11,710,500 mi²); 22% of the world's land area.
   Population: 530,000,000 (1984 est.); 11% of the total world population. *Density*—16 persons per km² (41 per mi²). *Annual rate of increase* (1982–83), 3.0%.
   Coastline: 30,500 km (18,950 mi).
   Elevation: *Highest*—Mount Kilimanjaro, 5,895 m (19,340 ft); *lowest*—Lake Assal, 155 m (510 ft) below sea level.
   Northernmost Point: Cape Ben Sekka, Tunisia, 77°46′N.
   Southernmost Point: Cape Agulhas, South Africa, 34°52′S.
   Easternmost Point: Cape Hafun, Somalia, 51°26′E.
   Westernmost Point: Cape Almadies, Senegal, 17°32′W.
   Principal Rivers: Nile, Congo (Zaire), Niger, Zambezi, Orange, Volta.
   Principal Lakes: Victoria, Tanganyika, Nyasa (Malawi), Nasser, Kariba, Chad, Rudolf (Turkana).
   Principal Mountain Ranges: Atlas, Ruwenzori, Drakensberg, Cameroon.
   Principal Deserts: Sahara, Kalahari, Namib.
   Political Divisions: 52 independent countries; Namibia (South West Africa) and Western Sahara (former Spanish Sahara), the status of which are in dispute; 4 homelands declared independent by the Republic of South Africa; 2 Spanish exclaves; several island dependencies.
   Largest City: Cairo (1981 est. pop., 5,650,000).
   Busiest Ports: Durban, Lagos, Alexandria, Dar es Salaam.
   Most Populous Country: Nigeria (1982 est. pop., 89,118,000).

coast and towns along the Sahara's southern border region. There a number of powerful African kingdoms, including Ghana, Mali, KANEM-BORNU, and SONGHAI, flourished during the Middle Ages. Further south in the rainforests the kingdoms of ASHANTI, BENIN, KONGO, Oyo, and Dahomey emerged after the 14th century and lasted until the colonial partition of Africa. East-central Africa was occupied by the kingdoms of Ankole, Buganda, Bunyoro, Luba, and Lunda.

The modern European colonization of Africa was begun by the Portuguese, who established trading stations on the coasts in the 15th and 16th centuries, but the interior of what Europeans called "the Dark Continent" was not explored or colonized until the 19th century. By the early 20th century nearly all of Africa had been subjected to European rule. Since World War II, 46 nations have gained their independence, but the colonial experience left Africa with arbitrarily defined boundaries, a diversity of political systems and problems, and economies dependent upon the industrial world. (The Republic of South Africa, though independent, is controlled by descendants of European settlers; its black African majority is not represented in the government.) Africa's peoples remain divided by race, language, religion, and politics in a complex cultural mosaic. In the mid-1980s Africa contained about 11% of the world's population and was the second most populous continent after Asia.

LAND AND RESOURCES

Africa has a number of outstanding natural features that have influenced its history and development. The northern coastal area is separated from the rest of the continent by the SAHARA, the largest desert in the world. The coastlines are remarkably straight with few large bays, estuaries, and protected indentations that can serve as harbors. Most major rivers have waterfalls and rapids close to the coast, which hindered colonial penetration and still limit navigation. In Subsaharan Africa a narrow coastal plain, often swampy along the Gulf of Guinea, arid from Angola south to Cape Town, and swampy, forested, or arid northward along the east coast to the Red Sea, is backed by steep escarpments and mountain ranges that form the edge of the African high plateau.

Africa lacks a major mountain system like the Andes of South America or the Himalayas of Asia. Several small ranges, however, break the monotony of the flat to gently rolling plateaus that constitute the bulk of Africa. The ATLAS MOUNTAINS of northwest Africa extend from east to west across Tunisia,

A camel caravan winds its way across a stretch of the Sahara in southern Algeria. The world's largest desert, the Sahara dominates the topography of northern Africa. It spans the continent from the Atlantic Ocean to the Red Sea and covers more than 8 million km² (20.7 million mi²).

(Above) *Kilimanjaro, Africa's tallest mountain, rises to a height of 5,895 m (19,340 ft) above the grasslands, or savannas, of Kenya's Amboseli Park. The sub-Saharan savannas, which host a great variety of wildlife, cover an estimated 40 percent of Africa's land area.*

(Below) *The beauty of a waterfall is enhanced by the lush vegetation that lines the banks of the Blue Nile, the Nile's major tributary, in the highlands of western Ethiopia. The enormous energy potential of Africa's water resources has barely been tapped.*

The contrast between semiarid, mountainous northern Africa and wet, tropical central Africa is striking. The road to Marrakesh winds along the Tizi n'Test Pass (top) at 2,100 m (6,900 ft) in the High Atlas Mountains of Morocco. A rain forest (bottom) in equatorial Africa spreads a living canopy over the terrain. With the exception of slight seasonal variations, the climate of the rain forest is hot and humid.

Algeria, and Morocco, reaching their highest elevation, 4,166 m (13,668 ft), at Mount Toubkal, Morocco. The DRAKENSBERG, rising above 3,000 m (10,000 ft), extends through eastern South Africa and Lesotho. The high plateau of Africa stretches from Ethiopia southwest to Angola and Namibia and includes the Ethiopian Massif, the East African Plateau, the RUWENZORI (Mountains of the Moon), the Munchinga Mountains of Zambia, and the Bihe of Angola. Rising above this plateau are Mount KILIMANJARO (5,895 m/19,340 ft), a semi-active volcano and Africa's highest peak, Mount Kenya (5,199 m/17,085 ft), and Mount Elgon (4,321 m/14,178 ft), also of volcanic origin. The Sahara is interrupted by the TIBESTI MASSIF and the Ahaggar and Air mountains. The Cameroon Mountains, a volcanic chain extending northeast through Cameroon, are the highest mountains in western Africa. The Futa Jallon of Guinea and Liberia contains the headwaters of the NIGER (Djouf) RIVER and the SENEGAL RIVER, West Africa's largest. Between these highland zones are a series of shallow sedimentary basins usually associated with rivers. They include the basins of the Niger, Chad, and Sudd rivers on the southern margins of the Sahara, the CONGO (Zaire) RIVER of central equatorial Africa, and the KALAHARI DESERT in southern Africa.

One of Africa's most distinct topographical features is the GREAT RIFT VALLEY. This is a giant trough that cuts into the high plateaus and extends from the Dead Sea in the Middle East southward to Mozambique and Swaziland, a distance of almost 6,900 km (4,300 mi). The northern section is filled by the Red Sea between Africa and Arabia. The central section cuts through Ethiopia and divides near Lake Rudolf, or Turkana (see RUDOLF, LAKE), into two branches: the western rift arcs through Uganda to Lake NYASA (Lake Malawi) and is occupied by Lakes Albert (Mobuto Sese Seko), Edward (Idi Amin), Kivu, and Tanganyika (see ALBERT, LAKE; EDWARD, LAKE; KIVU, LAKE; TANGANYIKA, LAKE); the eastern rift cuts through Kenya and Tanzania and joins the western rift near Lake Nyasa. In places the rift-valley walls rise more than 3,200 m (10,500 ft) above the flat and sometimes drowned valley floor. (See also EAST AFRICAN RIFT SYSTEM.)

Geology. Africa is a massive crystalline platform of ancient granites, schists, and gneisses, the oldest of which are more than 3.2 billion years old. They contain rich and varied minerals including copper, zinc, lead, gold, uranium, diamonds, and many rare metals. Present-day Africa was once part of the supercontinent known as GONDWANALAND, which also included Australia, Antarctica, South America, Madagascar, and the Indian subcontinent. During the Late Jurassic and Early Cretaceous periods these land masses drifted apart, but compared with the other continents, Africa remained relatively stable. South America was separated from Africa about 80 million years ago. Arabia split off about 20 million years ago.

As Gondwanaland fractured and drifted, Africa acquired its scarp-dominated coastline, interior seas that occupied shallow depressions emptied, and rivers carved steep gorges and formed new courses. Volcanic outpourings covered vast areas of east and southern Africa. As the Cretaceous Period came to an end, the sedimentary rocks of northwestern Africa were severely folded and uplifted in a series of orogenic phases to form the Atlas Mountains, which geologically are part of Europe's alpine system. Epicontinental seas extended across North Africa linking the present Mediterranean with the Gulf of Guinea, which in their wake left extensive deposits of limestone and sandstone. Gigantic meridian fractures occurred in the African shield producing the Great Rift Valley. As tensional forces wrenched the land apart, some land blocks sank while others rose and tilted, allowing volcanic materials to break the surface. Mount Kilimanjaro and Mount Cameroon were formed this way.

During Gondwana's last 100 million years of existence, southern Africa was covered by the Dwyka ice field, which scoured the crystalline surface and deposited tillites hundreds of meters thick. Following the glacial age, southern Africa became progressively drier, and a lengthy period of sedimentary accumulation began in the Kalahari and Karroo basins. These sediments in turn were covered by outpourings of basalt as much as 7,600 m (25,000 ft) thick.

Climate. The climates of Africa are predominantly tropical. Limited areas of subtropical and temperate climates are found only at the northern and southern extremities and in the high altitudes of Ethiopia and East Africa. The cold ocean currents that parallel the western Sahara (Canaries Current) and Nami-

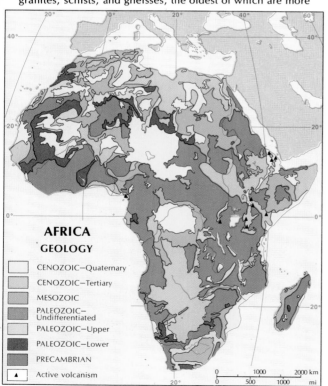

AFRICA
GEOLOGY

- CENOZOIC–Quaternary
- CENOZOIC–Tertiary
- MESOZOIC
- PALEOZOIC–Undifferentiated
- PALEOZOIC–Upper
- PALEOZOIC–Lower
- PRECAMBRIAN
- ▲ Active volcanism

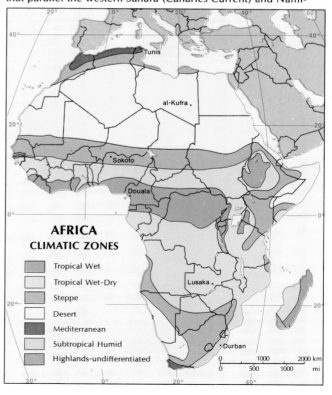

AFRICA
CLIMATIC ZONES

- Tropical Wet
- Tropical Wet-Dry
- Steppe
- Desert
- Mediterranean
- Subtropical Humid
- Highlands-undifferentiated

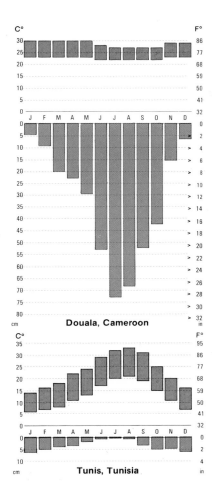

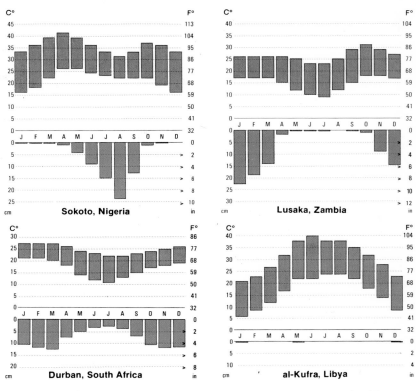

Annual climate charts for six localities in Africa illustrate the distinct climate zones of the continent. Bars indicate monthly ranges of temperatures (red) and precipitation (blue). Douala, Cameroon, on the Bight of Biafra, has a tropical wet climate; Sokoto, a commercial center in northwestern Nigeria, a steppe climate; Lusaka, the centrally located capital of Zambia, a tropical wet-dry climate; Tunis, Tunisia, a port city in northern Africa, a Mediterranean climate; Durban, South Africa, a resort city on the Indian Ocean, a subtropical humid climate; and al-Kufra, Libya, a cluster of Saharan oases, a desert climate.

bia (Benguela Current) modify the temperatures of the adjoining coastal lowlands. The absence of lengthy high mountains and other weather divides permits a free circulation of tropical air over the continent so that changes in climate occur very gradually. Rainfall is heaviest along the coast of the Gulf of Guinea, in the equatorial lowlands facing the Atlantic, in scattered mountain locations, and in eastern Madagascar. There the average annual rainfall exceeds 2,032 mm (80 in). Africa's wettest place is in western Cameroon (10,160 mm/400 in). Rainfall decreases poleward from the equator to the Sahara, Kalahari, and NAMIB deserts, regions that generally receive less than 150 mm (6 in) of rain in the average year. Rainfall rather than temperature is the most variable element of climate effecting distribution of soils, vegetation, and populations. There is increasing evidence that much of Africa is becoming progressively drier.

Six major climate types prevail and are arranged in a series of parallel zones ordered around the equator. The tropical wet climate is characterized by uniformly hot temperatures, a heavy and evenly distributed rainfall, and year-round high humidity. This climatic region is bounded by the tropical wet-dry, or savanna, climate, which is distinguished by its long dry season (coincidental with the period of low Sun) and by a short, wet summer. The savanna gives way to tropical steppes where rainfall is light and highly variable from year to year, and prolonged droughts are common. The steppes of West Africa are called the SAHEL, literally the "border" of the desert.

The tropical deserts have the least rainfall and the greatest temperature range of any African climate. Diurnal temperature ranges may exceed 10°C (50°F). Africa's highest temperature (57.8°C/136°F) was recorded in the Libyan desert. Small areas of Mediterranean climate occupy coastal Morocco, Al-

geria, Tunisia, and South Africa's Cape of Good Hope region. A narrow zone of humid subtropical climate, similar to that of the southeastern United States, is located along South Africa's Natal coast.

Drainage. Africa's major rivers have cut deep gorges in their upper courses and through the coastal rimlands before emptying into the oceans. Waterfalls, rapids, and irregular flows due to seasonal variations in rainfall all make river navigation difficult. Only a small percentage of the continent's vast waterpower potential is used to generate electricity. The Congo River alone has 13% of the world's hydroelectric power potential.

The NILE, the world's longest river (6,650 km/4,132 mi), rises in Burundi and Uganda in equatorial east Africa. From Lake Victoria it flows north through the swampy Sudd of Sudan and over six cataracts before entering the Mediterranean, where it has built a 25,000-km² (9,653-mi²) delta. Its major tributary, the Blue Nile, rises in the headwaters of Lake Tana (see TANA, LAKE), Ethiopia, and joins the White Nile at Khartoum. The ASWAN DAM and Lake Nasser now regulate the flow of water downstream to the densely settled farmlands of lower Egypt. The Congo, Africa's second longest river (4,670 km/2,900 mi), drains an area larger than the Nile. Fed by many tributaries including the UBANGI, Kasai, and Kwango, it sweeps around the Congo Basin and cuts through the Crystal Mountains to empty into the Atlantic. Africa's third longest river, the Niger (4,185 km/2,600 mi), rises in the Futa Jallon of West Africa, flows northeast through the Djouf Basin of Mali, and then southeastward to Nigeria to form a delta on the Gulf of Guinea. The ZAMBEZI (about 2,650 km/1,650 mi) rises in south central Africa and flows east over the VICTORIA FALLS and through a narrow gorge between Zimbabwe and Zambia to the Indian

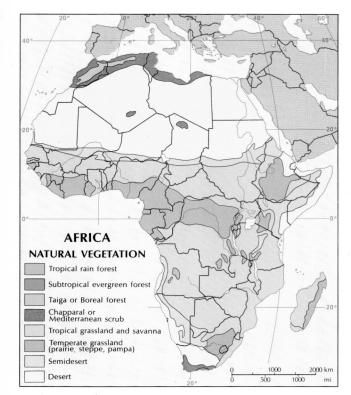

AFRICA
NATURAL VEGETATION

Tropical rain forest

Subtropical evergreen forest

Taiga or Boreal forest

Chapparal or
Mediterranean scrub

Tropical grassland and savanna

Temperate grassland
(prairie, steppe, pampa)

Semidesert

Desert

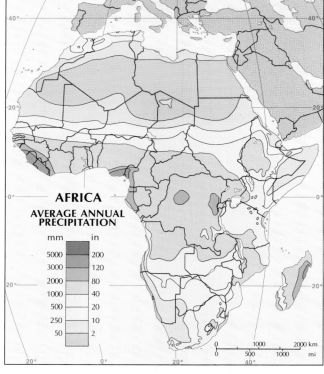

AFRICA
AVERAGE ANNUAL PRECIPITATION

mm	in
5000	200
3000	120
2000	80
1000	40
500	20
250	10
50	2

Ocean in central Mozambique. The ORANGE RIVER (2,100 km/ 1,300 mi) rises in the Drakensberg and flows west through South Africa to the Atlantic.

Africa's largest and deepest lakes are found in East Africa, generally associated with the rift valley. They include, from north to south, Lakes Albert (Mobuto Sese Seko), Edward (Idi Amin), Kivu, Tanganyika, and Nyasa in the western rift, and Lakes Rudolf (Turkana), Natron, and Eyasi in the eastern rift. Lake Tanganyika is the world's second deepest lake (1,436 m/ 4,710 ft). Between the two limbs of the rift valley lies Lake Victoria, Africa's largest (69,481 km²/26,827 mi²). Lake Chad (see CHAD, LAKE), between Nigeria and Chad, is extremely shallow, and its boundaries vary greatly with rainfall.

Soils. Few areas of Africa possess fertile soils. In the humid tropics, lime, potash, phosphorus, and humus material are washed out of the soil's top layers while high temperatures accelerate bacterial activity. What remains is a soil high in iron and aluminum that forms a hardpan through which roots penetrate with difficulty and that facilitates runoff and the loss of surface water. In the dry regions the soils are thin, stony, high in calcium, and low in humus. The richest soils are associated with Africa's rivers. Among the richest, most extensive, and most productive alluvial soils are those along the Senegal, the central reaches of the Niger, and the lower Juba, those at the confluence of the White and Blue Niles in central Sudan, and those in the Nile delta. There, large-scale irrigation projects have been developed. Nonalluvial soils of good quality, often associated with volcanic materials, are found on the high veld of South Africa and in parts of Kenya and Cameroon. Inappropriate technology, such as the utilization of heavy farm machinery, and overuse have destroyed millions of hectares of marginal soil in several climatic regions.

Vegetation. Africa has little natural vegetation that has not been modified by humans and their livestock. Overgrazing in the Sahel has destroyed the short grassland ecology and hastened desert encroachment. The forests and grasslands have been cut and burned to provide building materials, agricultural land, and pastures. The tropical forest of the west equatorial belt produces mahogany, teak, ebony, rubber, oil palm, and silk-cotton trees. Mangrove swamps clog many estuaries.

North and south of the rainforests stretch the tropical grasslands or savannas with their characteristic acacia trees and baobabs. As rainfall decreases, the savannas give way to scrubby grasslands, thorn bush, and eventually to the deserts that are virtually devoid of vegetation other than such widely scattered xerophytic plants as the stipa grass, tamarisk, and date palm. In the Mediterranean climatic zone, stands of pine, juniper, cork, cedar, and olive are common.

Fauna. Animal life in Africa is remarkable for its great diversity, vast numbers, and the presence of both primitive and more advanced forms of life. This is due to the continent's general climatic stability and land connections with Asia. Animals such as the elephant evolved in Africa and spread to Asia across the Suez land bridge. Asia's elephants, monkeys, great apes, and certain bird groups such as the hornbills exhibit close relations with those in tropical Africa. Among the truly indigenous African animals are the aardvark, the secretary bird, and the whale-headed stork of the Nilotic marshes.

Africa's rainforests contain gorillas, chimpanzees, monkeys, wild pigs, and bongos. The tropical rivers, lakes, and swamps are populated by crocodiles, hippopotamuses, lizards, snakes, and an abundance of bird life including flamingos, pelicans, herons, storks, and kingfishers. The grasslands of the east and south contain some of the world's largest herds of elephant, rhinoceros, wildebeeste, giraffe, zebra, buffalo, and antelope as well as the carnivores that prey upon them, such as lions, leopards, cheetahs, hyenas, and jackals. The grasslands also support a great diversity of birds including the bustard, falcon, hornbill, and ostrich. Uncontrolled hunting and poaching have severely reduced the animal populations, especially the elephant and rhinoceros, which are killed for their ivory tusks.

Africa's insects and other invertebrates are as varied as the larger animals. The tsetse fly, which carries sleeping sickness (see TRYPANOSOMIASIS), and the malaria-bearing mosquito limit the amount of land that humans and livestock may occupy. Common snakes include the cobra, python, and mamba.

Among Africa's largest game reserves are Tanzania's SERENGETI NATIONAL PARK, Kenya's Tsavo Park and Amboseli Game Reserve, and South Africa's Kruger National Park.

Water Resources. Africa has approximately 40% of the world's hydroelectric potential, about half of it in Zaire. Most countries have chosen to build a few large facilities rather than several small dams. Africa's largest hydroelectric facilities are Egypt's Aswan High Dam (which produces 10 billion kW h annually), Mozambique's Cabora Bassa (which can generate 18 billion kW h), Zaire's Inga Dam, Ghana's Akosombo Dam, Nigeria's Kainji and Jos projects, and Cameroon's Edea project. A few projects, including the Aswan Dam, the Kariba Dam (shared by Zambia and Zimbabwe), and South Africa's Orange River Project, provide not only power but water for irrigation, fishing, and soil-conservation purposes.

Mineral Resources. African mineral resources are plentiful but only partially explored and exploited. Mining became an important and highly profitable activity during the colonial period, and today the bulk of prospecting and exploitation remains in the hands of multinational corporations. With few exceptions, Africa's minerals and fuels are exported and have not given rise to local industry and general economic prosperity. Minerals provide the bulk of foreign revenues in several states including Angola, Algeria, Libya, and Nigeria (petroleum); Liberia and Mauritania (iron ore); and Zambia (copper). South Africa has the greatest variety, total reserves, and current output of minerals in Africa. It has the world's largest

(Right) A shaduf, an implement used by the ancient Egyptians, draws water from a well in the Algerian Sahara. This primitive device, which operates as a lever counterbalanced by a stone weight, is also used extensively along the waterways of northern Africa for irrigation.

(Below) The Kariba Dam restrains the fast-flowing Zambezi River downstream from Victoria Falls. The lake formed behind the dam (Kariba Lake) is one of the world's largest artificial bodies of water. Zimbabwe (Rhodesia) and Zambia each derive a share of the hydroelectric power generated by the project.

known reserves of manganese, platinum, chromium, vanadium, gold, and aluminum ore and is the largest producer of chromium, antimony, and manganese.

The major oil and natural gas reserves are located in Algeria, Libya, Egypt, and in the coastal areas of Nigeria, Gabon, and Angola. Africa has limited coal reserves, especially coking coal for steel manufacture. The largest reserves are found in South Africa, Zimbabwe, Mozambique, and Nigeria. Uranium is widely distributed, but significant deposits occur in South Africa, Niger, Namibia, and Gabon. The largest iron ore deposits are found in South Africa, Liberia, Mauritania, Angola, and Algeria. The major copper producers are Zambia, Zaire, and South Africa. Africa has the largest known reserves of chromium, antimony, and manganese, as well as significant amounts of bauxite (Guinea), diamonds (South Africa, Botswana), cobalt, and zinc.

PEOPLE

Africa contains a complex mosaic of peoples, languages, and cultures. Few of its states are ethnically homogeneous, and few have developed a strong sense of national unity. For cen-

(Above) *A young Masai tribesman from Kenya displays a colorful, feathered headdress. The egalitarian, nomadic Masai, livestock-raisers of Nilotic descent, have proved extremely resistant to cultural changes.* (Below) *Residents of Kano, Nigeria, pay homage to their emir, until recently the traditional feudal ruler, as his procession passes through the streets. Kano, a state capital, was once the center of a powerful, independent polity.*

The peoples of the African continent include (left to right) the Berber, who inhabit Morocco and other North African countries and who retain a distinct cultural identity; the Afrikaner, of European descent, who settled the Cape of Good Hope during the mid-17th century; and the San, or Bushman, whose ancestors are thought to have been the original inhabitants of southern Africa.

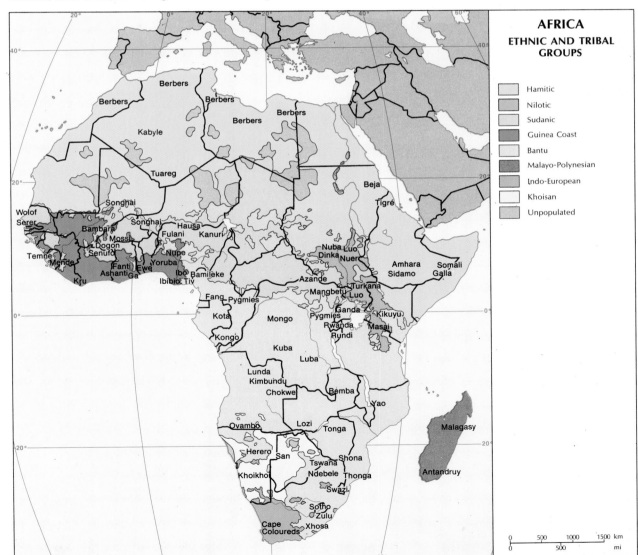

AFRICA
ETHNIC AND TRIBAL GROUPS

- Hamitic
- Nilotic
- Sudanic
- Guinea Coast
- Bantu
- Malayo-Polynesian
- Indo-European
- Khoisan
- Unpopulated

Berbers
Berbers
Berbers
Berbers
Berbers
Kabyle
Tuareg
Wolof
Serer
Songhai
Songhai
Bambara
Mossi
Dogon
Senufo
Temne
Mende
Fanti Ewe
Ashanti Ga
Kru
Ibibio Tiv
Hausa
Fulani
Nupe
Yoruba
Ibo Bamileke
Kanuri
Beja
Tigré
Nuba Luo
Dinka Nuer
Azande
Amhara
Sidamo
Somali
Galla
Fang Pygmies
Mangbetu
Turkana
Luo
Kota
Mongo
Pygmies
Ganda
Kikuyu
Kongo
Rwanda
Rundi
Masai
Kuba
Luba
Lunda
Kimbundu
Chokwe
Bemba
Yao
Ovambo
Lozi
Tonga
Malagasy
Herero
San
Shona
Antandruy
Khoikhoi
Tswana
Ndebele Thonga
Swazi
Sotho
Zulu
Cape
Coloureds Xhosa

0   500   1000   1500 km
0   500   mi

turies traditional values prevailed. Africans identified first and foremost with members of their own tribe or nation and avoided or competed with those who spoke a different language and were of a different culture. The imposition of colonial boundaries without regard for the indigenous cultural mosaic further divided the African people.

Population is unevenly distributed. Highest densities occur along the coast of the Gulf of Guinea, in the lower reaches of the Nile, in the highlands of East Africa and Madagascar, along the northern coast, and in the urban and mining areas

Children in Togo attend an outdoor primary school. In this West African nation, about 55% of children between the ages of 7 and 14 are enrolled in educational institutions, approximately half of which are operated by religious missions.

of South Africa, Zimbabwe, and Zaire. Lowest densities are found in the deserts, high mountains, and thick forests where economic opportunities are poor.

In the Saharan states the dominant groups are ARABS, BERBERS, and TUAREGS. Beyond the cities the Berbers are agriculturists, and the Tuaregs are pastoral nomads. The Sahara forms an effective divide between these peoples and the predominantly Negroid peoples of the south. In the Sahelian zone sedentary farmers are interspersed with pastoralists, the major groups being the HAUSA, FULANI, BAMBARA, and WOLOF. In the Horn of Africa (Somalia and eastern Ethiopia), the pastoral SOMALI and GALLA are dominant, while the Dinka and Nuer prevail in the upper Nile. The densely settled coast of the Gulf of Guinea is home for literally hundreds of different ethnic groups, each with its own language, territory, culture, and values. Among the numerically strongest are the YORUBA and IBO of Nigeria, the ASHANTI and GA of Ghana, and the KRU of Ivory Coast and Liberia. The sparsely populated forests of equatorial Africa are home to FANG, Bateke, PYGMY, and others. In the east African savannas, the pastoral people, including the MASAI, KIKUYU, and KAMBA, have historically competed for grazing land and watering places. The LUO and Baganda occupy densely settled farms along the north shore of Lake Victoria.

Ethnic diversity and population density tend to be less south of Zaire, except in the urban areas of South Africa, Zambia, and Zimbabwe. South Africa has ten indigenous groups, the largest being the ZULU in Natal and the XHOSA of the eastern Cape; South Africa's AFRIKANERS are a people of Dutch and French descent. Swaziland, Lesotho, and Botswana are rare examples of ethnically homogeneous states and are populated by the SWAZI, SOTHO, and TSWANA respectively. Arid Namibia's population includes the SAN (Bushmen), who are hunters and gatherers, and the HERERO, Damara, and OVAMBO. Other major groups in southern Africa are the SHONA and NDEBELE of Zimbabwe, the BEMBA of Zambia, the Makonde and Makua of Mozambique, the YAO of Malawi, and the Ovimbundu of Angola. Madagascar is populated by the Betsimisaraka and by the Merina and Betsileo, whose ancestors came from Southeast Asia some 2,000 years ago.

The nonindigenous peoples of Africa include Europeans and South Asians in southern and eastern Africa, especially South Africa and Kenya; Europeans in most capital cities; and a few Syrians and Lebanese who live primarily as traders in the urban areas of the coast along the Gulf of Guinea.

Languages. The number of languages spoken in Africa has been variously estimated at between 800 and 1,700. Five major stocks are generally recognized. Afroasiatic languages, dominant in North Africa and the Horn, include Berber, Kushitic, Semitic, Chad, and Coptic languages. Click languages, so named because of their characteristic implosive "click" sounds, include Khoisan, which is spoken by the Khoikhoi of southern Africa. The Niger-Congo languages cover almost all of West Africa south of the Sahara and most of the Congo Basin and southern Africa and include Hausa, Peul, and Wolof in West Africa and SWAHILI, Tsonga, and Bemba east and south of Zaire. Sudanic languages include Kanuri, Songhai, Turkana, and Masai. The MALAYO-POLYNESIAN LANGUAGES of Madagascar were introduced from Southeast Asia about 2,000 years ago. (See AFRICAN LANGUAGES; AFROASIATIC LANGUAGES.)

Superimposed on this linguistic mosaic are English, French, Italian, Portuguese, German, and languages of the Indian subcontinent. English is the official language, or one of the two official languages, in all ex-British colonies, excluding Tanzania, where Swahili has been adopted. French is the official language of most former French possessions south of the Sahara. Arabic is the official language of seven Saharan states. Numerous lingua franca, such as Lingala in Zaire and Mandingo in West Africa, are used for commerce and in mixed-language areas. The multilinguistic nature of most states has hindered nationalism and perpetuates tribal and local identities.

(Left) The modern campus of Kumasi's University of Science and Technology serves almost 2,000 students in Ghana's Ashanti region. The university is one of 12 Ghanian institutions of higher education.

Religion. The dominant religion of northern Africa is Islam, which replaced Christianity in the 7th century and spread west and south across the Sahara and into the equatorial zones. With an estimated 155 million believers, Islam is the fastest-growing faith in Africa.

The Christian churches claim a membership of some 140 million Africans of whom 55% are Protestants. Many denominations are present, including a number of indigenous churches. Christianity's earliest hold in Africa was in Egypt and Ethiopia, home of the COPTIC CHURCH. European missionaries introduced Christianity into sub-Saharan Africa during the 19th century. Approximately two-fifths of the African population follows traditional religions and animism.

Education. Educational standards, facilities, and programs vary considerably and reflect differences in class, ethnicity, sex, and location. In all countries literacy rates for women are lower than those for men, more males than females attend primary school, and urban education is superior to rural. The richest countries invest more in education than the poorest, and in most states, secondary school enrollments are less than half the primary school enrollments. Only a small fraction of Africa's young people attend universities. Adult literacy rates range from 6% in Niger and 10% in Mali to approximately 70% in South Africa and Tanzania. Because of the lack of prestigious universities in Africa, many qualified students receive their training in U.S. and European universities.

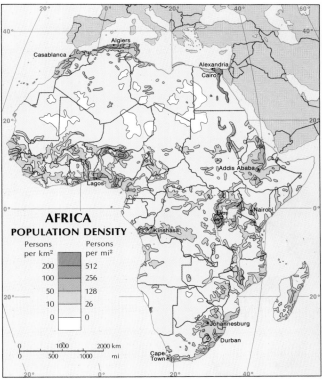

AFRICA POPULATION DENSITY

Persons per km²	Persons per mi²
200	512
100	256
50	128
10	26
0	0

(Above) *Conical, straw roofs and earthen walls are characteristic features of Mande dwellings and grain storage bins. The Mande, a group of agricultural tribes speaking related languages, live in the savanna region of West Africa.*

(Right) *Dar-es-Salaam, which means "haven of peace" in Arabic, is a seaport on the Indian Ocean. The modern city is Tanzania's capital and serves as headquarters of several pan-African organizations.*

(Below) *A crew of fellahin, or agricultural laborers, perform the arduous task of tilling by hand on a cooperative farm at Kom Ombo, in southern Egypt. Kom Ombo, which draws water for irrigation from the Nile, grew rapidly during the late 1960s, when the area served as a relocation center for Egyptians displaced by the construction of the Aswan High Dam. Because more than 90% of the nation's population are crowded into the Nile River valley, the government has instituted agrarian reforms and a land-reclamation project.*

(Above) *Farm laborers plant potatoes on an experimental farm in Gabon, where food production has traditionally failed to meet the nation's demands. The establishment of modern agriculture in Africa's tropics is hindered by poor soils that have had essential nutrients leached by heavy rains.*

Health. There is an urgent need to improve general health and nutritional standards in Africa. A significant number of persons in every country suffers from chronic malnutrition due to poverty, ignorance, and poor agricultural practices. On a per capita basis, malnutrition rates in Africa are the highest in the world. In several countries of the Sahel, Guinea Coast, and equatorial Africa, as much as 40% of the population are malnourished and suffer from such diseases as malaria, dysentery, schistosomiasis, and yaws. Other common ailments include influenza, tuberculosis, river blindness, and a host of parasitic disorders associated with unsanitary living conditions.

Most of the doctors and general hospitals are situated in the capitals and towns, whereas the more populated rural areas have few health facilities and high incidences of disease, malnutrition, and infant mortality. Since World War II, national and international efforts to control mosquitoes, locusts, tsetse flies, and other pests have increased. The Sahelian states from Senegal to Somalia recorded exceptionally high rates of death and malnutrition during the severe droughts of 1968–74, and again in the early 1980s.

Demography. Africa's population numbered some 530 million in the mid-1980s. The most populous states are Nigeria, Egypt, Ethiopia, Zaire, and South Africa. If Africa's population continues to increase at its present rate, it will double by the first decade of the 21st century. Improved diets and sanitary conditions and improved medical technologies and insecticides have lowered death rates considerably since 1960, but infant mortality rates remain the highest in the world. Life expectancy at birth is about 50 years, compared with more than 70 years in the United States. Birthrates will remain high unless the general desire for large families changes and more Africans accept family planning. Africa has the highest fertility rates in the world, and nearly half its population are under 15 years of age.

Africa is the most rural and least urbanized of the continents. Less than a third of the population live in cities, but several countries, including South Africa, Egypt, Nigeria, and Morocco, have large urban-industrial areas. In most countries the largest city is the capital, which is often also the only city of significant size. Urban-population growth rates exceed rural growth rates as more and more Africans migrate to the cities in search of jobs, education, and security. Slums are growing and urban living conditions are deteriorating in most countries.

In the 1970s and '80s civil strife and political upheaval displaced millions of people in Ethiopia, Somalia, Sudan, Uganda, Angola, and other areas. Few countries have been willing or able to accommodate the refugees despite United Nations assistance.

ECONOMY

Despite Africa's great natural resources and energy potentials, industrialization is in its infancy. Africa contributes only 1% of worldwide industrial production. South Africa is the only modern industrial state, although manufacturing is becoming increasingly strong in Zimbabwe, Nigeria, Egypt, and Algeria. Handicaps to rapid industrialization are weak agricultural economies, inadequate and poorly integrated transport facilities, insufficient capital technology, political instability, a poorly trained work force, a small purchasing power, and economic policies and practices determined outside of Africa.

Since gaining independence, most African countries have promoted import substitution industries to reduce their dependence on European and American manufactured goods. Light industries, including textiles, clothing, pharmaceuticals, food processing, and beverages, are the most common and account for 70% of industrial employment. Heavy industry, including the manufacture of petrochemicals, iron and steel, rubber products, and cement, is concentrated in South Africa, which supplies a higher percentage of its industrial needs than any other African state. Industry tends to be concentrated in capital cities, is generally small scale, and is capital- rather than labor-intensive despite the cheap labor.

Agriculture. Agriculture accounts for about one-third of the continent's total economic output and more than half its export earnings; agriculture also employs 75% of the work force. Two distinct agricultural systems operate side by side: a traditional subsistence sector and a modern commercial sector. The traditional sector employs the majority of Africa's rural population and is characterized by small and frequently fragmented farms, little use of technology or fertilizer, high reliance on human labor, low yields, infrequent surpluses, and an emphasis on staple crops such as corn, millet, rice, cassava, sweet potatoes, peanuts, and other high-starch foods. Work on the farms is increasingly being left to women, children, and the aged as men migrate to the cities. Traditional slash-and-burn practices are being restricted as population increases and land-ownership systems change.

The modern commercial sector is the economic backbone of many countries and the principal source of their foreign-exchange earnings. Coffee, for example, is a major export for Burundi, cocoa for Ghana, and peanuts for Gambia. Other major cash crops include cotton, sugar, bananas, tea, oil palm, tobacco, and citrus fruits. These are produced on large estates and plantations that are frequently owned by expatriates, urban elites, the state, and multinational corporations, and depend on cheap, abundant, and often seasonal labor. They tend to have much higher inputs of fertilizer, insecticides, and capital in the form of machinery, processing, and storage facilities than the traditional sector.

(Right) *At the open-air market of Arusha, in northern Tanzania, farm women sell produce to Masai herdsmen. The scene illustrates the continuation of the traditional economic system of rural East Africa.*

(Below) *A drover urges his zebus along a dusty path on the island of Madagascar. African cattle raisers favor this ancient breed of oxen for its tolerance of heat and resistance to a variety of tropical diseases.*

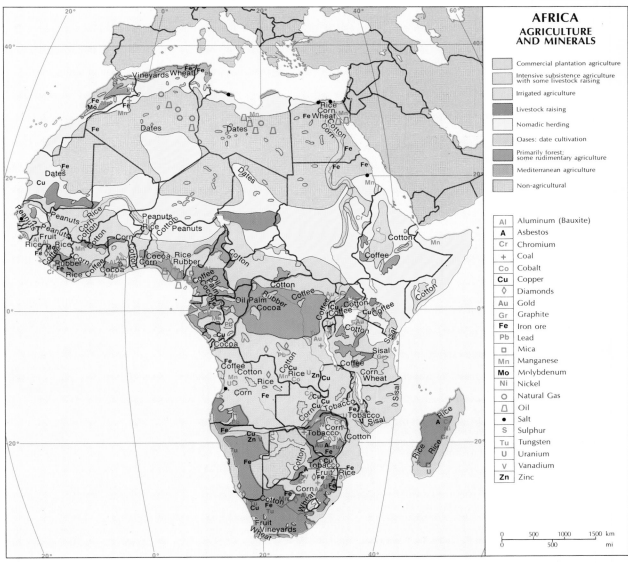

AFRICA
AGRICULTURE AND MINERALS

- Commercial plantation agriculture
- Intensive subsistence agriculture with some livestock raising
- Irrigated agriculture
- Livestock raising
- Nomadic herding
- Oases: date cultivation
- Primarily forest; some rudimentary agriculture
- Mediterranean agriculture
- Non-agricultural

Al	Aluminum (Bauxite)
A	Asbestos
Cr	Chromium
+	Coal
Co	Cobalt
Cu	Copper
◇	Diamonds
Au	Gold
Gr	Graphite
Fe	Iron ore
Pb	Lead
□	Mica
Mn	Manganese
Mo	Molybdenum
Ni	Nickel
O	Natural Gas
◁	Oil
●	Salt
S	Sulphur
Tu	Tungsten
U	Uranium
V	Vanadium
Zn	Zinc

0   500   1000   1500 km
0   500   mi

The copper mines of Shaba province, formerly known as Katanga, provide steady income and employment for the developing nation of Zaire. One of Africa's most mineral-rich regions, Shaba also contains the world's principal reserves of cobalt.

The raising of cattle, goats, and sheep is very important in much of the savanna and steppe lands. Africans are only gradually improving the quality of their herds, decreasing the traditional emphasis on herd size and the social importance attached to cattle ownership, and commercializing this activity. Commercial cattle farming is most advanced in areas of European settlement such as South Africa, Kenya, and Zimbabwe. Africa possesses about 14% of the world's cattle population.

In the 1970s food production for subsistence and local markets failed to keep pace with population growth and rising demands, especially in the urban areas. Famine conditions, which first appeared in the Sahel and Ethiopia during the droughts of 1972, later worsened and became more general. Low prices for farm products, rising costs of fertilizer, fuel, and seed, poor farm management, soil deterioration, and the common practice of using land for export crops rather than staple foods, have all contributed to the shortage of food. On a per-capita basis, less food is produced today than in 1970, and food imports are rising.

Forestry and Fishing. Although forests cover about 25% of Africa's land surface, the forest industry in general is not developed. High costs of clearing the forests, poor and costly transport, and a limited amount of usable forest have hindered profitable exploitation. Cameroon, Congo, Gabon, and Ivory Coast are the main producers; mahogany, ebony, and okoume are the major commercial woods.

Ocean commercial fishing is economically more important than freshwater fishing. The major fishing grounds are off South Africa, Namibia, and Angola; the West African coast from Morocco to Liberia; and in the Mediterranean Sea. Much of the catch from southern Africa is exported as fish oil, fish meal, and fertilizer. Fresh and dried fish are important as food in certain areas of Ghana, Sierra Leone, and Zaire, but in general fish plays a minor role in the diet, despite government promotion efforts. Tilapia is the most widely consumed fish.

Transportation and Communications. Africa's transportation systems were developed during the colonial era to move minerals and other raw materials to seaports for export. Roads and railroads were used by the Europeans mainly to facilitate control over their African possessions. As a consequence, neighboring colonies were rarely linked, and even today the countries of Africa are poorly interconnected by road, rail, and air. Africa has the lowest railroad density in the world, and 13 countries (including landlocked Niger, Chad, and Burundi) have no railroads. South Africa has more than one-third of the continent's railroad tracks and the most modern railroad facilities.

Railroads continue to convey the bulk of Africa's minerals. The Great Uhuru (or Tan-Zam) Railway, built with help from China and completed in 1976, connects the copper mines of

Zambia with Tanzania's Indian Ocean port of Dar es Salaam. The Benguela Railway carries copper from Zaire's Shaba province across Angola to the Atlantic port of Benguela. Zimbabwe's mineral areas are linked by rail with ports in Mozambique and South Africa.

Africa has the least developed road system in the world. Less than 100,000 km (62,000 mi) of the 1,350,000 km (837,000 mi) of roads are paved. The greatest densities of well-maintained roads occur in South Africa and the Mediterranean states. All countries need additional feeder roads to link the rural populations and agricultural projects with the towns, cities, and railroads. Isolation, particularly severe during the rainy season when unpaved roads may become impassable, is a major handicap to develop.

River transport is handicapped by waterfalls and rapids and in many areas by irregular stream flow due to seasonal rainfall. Countries dependent on rivers to supplement their road and rail systems include Zaire, Congo, Nigeria, and Sudan. Lengthy unnavigable stretches of the Congo River are bypassed by railroads that carry copper and other exports to the coast.

Air transport is of growing importance in Africa. Since independence, many countries have established national airlines and extended their international routes. Few are profitable. In remote areas air travel is often the only practical means of transportation.

Africa's telecommunications systems are underdeveloped but expanding. Radio, television, and telephone systems are concentrated in the urban areas, however, and rural districts are poorly served.

Trade. Africa's principal trade is with Europe and North America. In most cases, an African country's leading trade partner is the colonial power with which it was formerly connected. Since independence, however, trade contacts have diversified and increased, especially with the United States and the Soviet Union. Under the Lomé Convention, first signed in 1975, 63 African, Caribbean, and Pacific (APC) countries have preferred trade and economic-aid agreements with the European Economic Community (EEC). The African members of APC send about half their exports, mainly agricultural and mineral products, to the EEC and receive about half their imports, mainly manufactured goods, from the EEC.

Trade between African nations is very limited, but mechanisms exist to promote it. West Africa has two regional trade groups: the 16-nation Economic Community of West African States (ECOWAS) and the smaller, French-speaking *Communauté Economique de l'Afrique de l'Ouest* (CEAO), whose six members also belong to ECOWAS. In southern Africa, South Africa, Botswana, Lesotho, and Swaziland are joined together in the South African Customs Union.

RECENT DEVELOPMENTS

Since independence the primary concerns of African governments have been economic development, the reduction of poverty, greater political stability, and increased politico-economic cooperation with other African countries. One of the most persistent problems in inter-African relations is the antagonism between white-dominated South Africa and the other African states, which regard South Africa as an oppressive relic of colonialism. All of the African nations except South Africa belong to the ORGANIZATION OF AFRICAN UNITY, which was founded in 1963 to foster pan-African cooperation.

Economic development did not come with political independence, and the difficulties of improving Africa's economy were exacerbated by the rising cost of imported oil during the 1970s. Initially, most governments concentrated their efforts in the manufacturing sector, especially in promoting import substitution industries. However, only South Africa has achieved a high order of industrial self-sufficiency, and most industries are merely final-stage assembly operations.

The majority of governments have recognized the failure of industry to alleviate poverty and are now promoting agriculture. Tanzania's approach to development has been through the *ujamaa* program of village cooperatives; Ghana and Guinea introduced state farms; Kenya, Zimbabwe, and others have undertaken major rural reform programs aimed at land redistribution and changing land ownership; Senegal, Kenya, and others have introduced high-yielding cereals and modern farm methods. Despite these and other efforts, food production declined in the 1970s, giving rise to increased malnutrition and poverty. Prolonged droughts in the early 1980s were attended by widespread famines in southern and eastern Africa.

High population growth continues to be a major constraint on development. Some progress was made in the 1970s in introducing the concept of family planning. Some 20 countries have some form of government-sponsored program.

On the political front, Africa continues to be plagued by instability and corruption. No other continent recorded so many coups, countercoups, military takeovers, insurgency movements, and boundary disputes as Africa did in the 1960s and 1970s. Most African countries are one-party states.

In 1980, Zimbabwe gained its independence after more than a decade of civil war. Libyan forces invaded Chad in 1983, and South African forces have attacked insurgents in Namibia, Mozambique, and Angola. In the early 1980s Cuban forces supported the South West African Peoples Organization (SWAPO) in their armed struggle to bring independence in Namibia. There is a general consensus among African leaders that African-based regional organizations such as ECOWAS and the OAU must play a more active role in solving the common problems of poverty, underdevelopment, and political instability.

ALAN C. G. BEST

Bibliography:
GENERAL: Best, Alan C. G., and deBlij, Harm J., *African Survey* (1977); Bohannan, Paul, *Africa and Africans* (1971); Davidson, Basil, *Africa: History of a Continent* (1966); Europa Publications, *Africa South of the Sahara* (annual); Legum, Colin, *Africa Contemporary Record* (1984) and *Africa in the 1980s: A Continent in Crisis* (1979).
GEOGRAPHY: Boateng, E. A., *A Political Geography of Africa* (1978); Brown, Leslie, *Africa: A Natural History* (1963); Hance, W. A., *The Geography of Modern Africa* (1975); Thompson, B. W., *The Climates of Africa* (1965).
ECONOMICS AND POLITICS: Austin, Dennis, *Politics in Africa* (1978); Economic Intelligence Unit (London), *A Study on the African Economies* (1981); Gutkind, Peter C. W., and Wallerstein, I., eds., *The Political Economy of Contemporary Africa* (1976); Mazrui, Ali A., *The African Condition: A Political Diagnosis* (1980); Organization of African Unity, *Famine in Africa* (1982); Odetola, T. O., *Military Regimes and Development* (1982); Offiong, D. A., *Imperialism and Dependency* (1982); Young, Crawford, *Ideology and Development in Africa* (1982).
PEOPLES AND CULTURES: Economic Commission for Africa, *Demographic Handbook for Africa* (1975); Hance, W. A., *Population, Migration and Urbanization in Africa* (1970); Mojekwu, C. C., and Uchendu, V. C., eds., *African Society, Culture and Politics* (1977); Mortimer, D. M., *Population Problems in Africa* (1973).
PLANT AND ANIMAL LIFE: Carr, Archie, *The Land and Wildlife of Africa* (1964); Dorst, J. and D., *A Field Guide to the Larger Mammals of Africa* (1970); Moreau, R. E., *The Bird Faunas of Africa and Its Islands* (1966).

Africa, history of

Although the oldest dated bones of human beings have been found in eastern Africa, little else is known of the 3 or 4 million years from the days of these ancestors to the earliest substantial accounts of peoples inhabiting Africa. This article will highlight the history of these peoples, generally in sub-Saharan Africa. For accounts of archaeological findings in Africa and the ancient civilizations of North Africa, see the following articles: AFRICAN PREHISTORY; CARTHAGE; CYRENE; EGYPT, ANCIENT.

EARLY AFRICA

Aksum and the Eastern City-States. CUSH, with its Egyptianlike civilization on the Nile, and the flourishing, irrigation-based culture of SHEBA (or Saba, modern north Yemen) together contributed in about the 2d century AD to the rise of the kingdom of Aksum (Axum). This kingdom was located in the highlands above the Red Sea in and around what is now the Tigre region of northern Ethiopia. Originally a colony of emigrants from Yemen, Aksum had begun trading with Greece, Rome, Cush, and Egypt. Local farmers grew spices and gum arabic, which Aksum exchanged—together with tortoise shell collected along the Red Sea and ivory and gold obtained in Cush—for Egyptian cloth, linen, articles of flint, glass, brass, sheets of soft copper, iron ingots, wine, olive oil, and gold and silver.

The army of this young kingdom made its force felt along and across the Red Sea and beyond the Nile. In the 3d century Aksum conquered Yemen. During the 4th century, Aksum's finest, the famed king Ezana unified his African holdings and converted himself and his kingdom to Christianity.

To the south a profitable commerce had begun to develop between the peoples of the coastal towns and seafaring merchants from Arabia, Persia, and other Asian centers. Some of the visitors, especially the ARABS, settled and intermarried with indigenous residents. Their descendants formed the nuclei for a series of impressive East African city-states that

The colored lines on the map indicate the centuries in which selected African kingdoms achieved their maximum territorial extent.

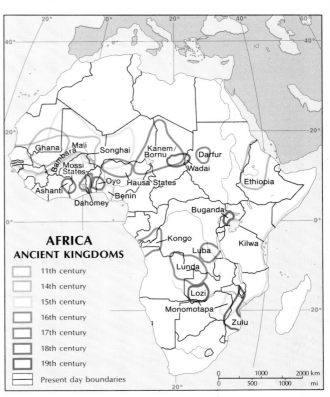

AFRICA
ANCIENT KINGDOMS

- 11th century
- 14th century
- 15th century
- 16th century
- 17th century
- 18th century
- 19th century
- Present day boundaries

flourished until the arrival of the more powerful Portuguese in the 16th century.

Interior Migrations. During the centuries of the ascent of Aksum and the city-states, the pattern of life of innumerable interior Africans began to alter drastically. Agriculturists, endowed with new crops and new tools and weapons of iron, began to effect a major change in the preexisting arrangements of African life across a great belt of Africa from Nigeria in the west to Kenya in the east. The change included or was generated by a population explosion. This in turn propelled at least one set of agriculturists from their original base in eastern Nigeria southeastward toward the border of Zaire and Zambia; this group then traveled westward, southward, and northeastward until it met a southern- and western-moving flank of peoples involved in pastoral pursuits.

The descendants of the first group now inhabit nearly all of Africa south of an imaginary line across central Kenya, southern Uganda, northern Zaire, and southern Nigeria. The second, linguistically less numerous and markedly different from the first in the features of its members, includes the cattle herders of Kenya, Uganda, Ethiopia, the Sudan, and northern Nigeria. Yet both migrated (and were migrating until the colonial incursions of the 19th century) in large numbers, and both may well have owed their newfound mobility to the adaptation of new crops and new techniques from Asia.

Whatever the impetus, a demographic and political revolution resulted from the dramatic movement of agriculturists and pastoralists from opposite directions and their final clash in the interior, possibly as late as the 8th century.

West African Kingdoms. For West Africa the pattern seems strikingly different, at least insofar as it emerges from the Arabic writings of early travelers and geographers. These writ-

Both Christianity and Islam have long histories in many parts of Africa. The subterranean church of Saint George (top) at Lalibela, Ethiopia, was carved from solid rock in the 13th century; the Sankore mosque (bottom) at Timbuktu, Mali, dates from the 14th century.

ings, which date back to the 8th century, contain much information about the powerful empires and other significant states that succeeded one another in western Africa (from the Senegal River to Lake Chad) from that period to the 19th century.

The main theme of early West African history was the rise and fall of imperial fortunes along the great rivers that thread through the sub-Saharan dry zones—rather than in the crowded preurban environment of Nigeria's forests. From the earliest years small, tightly knit, and fiercely autonomous states existed side by side, were created and destroyed, and fought to avoid being swallowed up by the major empires that sprang periodically from the ambitions, economic circumstances, or martial abilities of a particular emerging state. Although some peoples of eastern and southern Africa lived, and still live, without chiefs or other hierarchically arranged organizations, West Africans experienced the government of single chiefs (sometimes men accorded divine rights and powers), the government of chiefs and their councils, and—rarely—the government of councils of equals.

Alluvial gold was the first of the important raw materials that the states monopolized in order to supply the markets of northern Africa and southern Europe; a second was salt mined near oases in the southern Sahara. Slaves captured in raids and war grew in importance as a commodity after about the 10th century. Kola nuts and other agricultural products were also important, as were the dyestuffs of northern Nigeria. All these goods were highly prized in and around the Mediterranean basin, and West Africans traveled across the vast desert in mighty caravans to the markets of Fez and Marrakesh in Morocco, Tunis in Tunisia, Tripoli in Libya, and Cairo in Egypt. In exchange the traders of the north brought cloth, horses, glass and metal ware, swords and armor, and—in time—muskets and other equipment of early modern warfare. The caravans from the north also brought ISLAM and its scriptures and written language.

GHANA was the earliest of the great empires. From a capital in the southeastern corner of what is now Mauritania, near the Malian border and not far from the Senegal River, it flourished during the 9th, 10th, and 11th centuries.

Ghana's fall may have contributed to the development, from a series of smaller states in the old Ghana, of the nucleus of what became the empire of MALI. Its center was east of Ghana, in the comparatively fertile plateau region between the upper reaches of the Senegal and Niger rivers. Mali's elite was influenced by Islam at least as early as the 12th century, and its 14th-century ruler MANSA MUSA made the ritual pilgrimage to Mecca. In the 14th century, Mali stretched from the highlands of modern Ghana to the great bend of the Niger and from the upper reaches of the Volta rivers to the southernmost market towns of the western Sahara. The rulers of Mali, a mercantile state much more sophisticated than Ghana, held splendid court, but they maintained traditional rituals and observed the integrity of local chiefs. They set the governmental tone for succeeding empires and for the smaller states that somehow managed to maintain their autonomy within or on the borders of the larger entities.

In northern Nigeria several city-states existed between Mali and its successor SONGHAI to the west and KANEM-BORNU, the growing empire to the east. Bornu dominated the Lake Chad region throughout the 16th and 17th centuries and until the onset of colonialism.

Songhai succeeded Mali as the major empire of the sub-Saharan region. Its capital, Gao, was on the Niger River far to the east of Mali and on the frontier of the very different forest zone to the south. After the reign of its king, Sonni Ali, in the mid-15th century, the might of Songhai encompassed the semidesert regions once ruled by Ghana, the northern sections of today's Upper Volta and Dahomey, and all the lands in between on either side of the Niger River.

Early European Contacts. With the coming of the Europeans and, after about 1550, an increasing demand for slaves to open up America, first Portugal and Spain and then England, France, and others began trading along the coasts of Senegal and Guinea and, later, in the Gulf of Guinea. They even es-

European contact with equatorial Africa, established by 15th-century explorers, brought a succession of colonial invaders. (Left) A bronze Benin sculpture (16th or 17th century) depicts a Portuguese musketeer. British and French penetration came later. (Below) A pair of 19th-century British explorers are borne aloft by servants as they embark on an expedition.

tablished fortified warehouses along the Gold Coast (Ghana)—the first toeholds of colonialism. At these warehouses and on ships, floating warehouses, along the eastern Nigerian coast, goods of the interior—eventually mostly slaves—began to be traded for the copper, cloth, and guns of Europe. The guns in turn gave the forest kingdoms new power over their neighbors and assisted the rise to power of BENIN (see BENIN, KINGDOM OF) and Oyo in western Nigeria; Dahomey, Akwamu, and Ashanti along the Gold Coast; and smaller states to the west and north along the Atlantic. Westernization followed this trade.

Seeking a sea route around Africa to the Orient, Portuguese sailors began sailing down the unknown west coast of Africa in 1418. They reached the coast of sub-Saharan Africa in 1441, crossed the equator and reached the mouth of the Congo River in 1482, rounded the Cape of Good Hope in 1487, and sailed past the city-states of eastern Africa in 1498.

The discovery of America quickened Europe's demand for slaves. On the islands of the Caribbean, at first indigenous Indians were enslaved to work plantations and dive for pearls. Similarly, on the mainland, Indians were for a short time used in the gold and silver mines. The Indians soon died, however, and Africans were thus sought as replacements by the Portuguese and Spanish colonists in the Americas. Even so, the trade from Africa grew only gradually until the last decades of the 16th century, when the American demand suddenly began to outstrip the available supply. Thereafter, the slaves were taken out of Africa in increasing numbers from all along the coast, but more and more from the lands in and around what is now Senegal, Ghana, Nigeria, and Angola.

Portugal and Spain were the original merchants of the Atlantic slave trade, but the profits of the trade were sufficiently enticing to attract competition. In the 17th century the Dutch entered African commerce in earnest, to be followed in the middle of the century by Swedish, Danish, German, French, and English syndicates. Each established trading posts and forts wherever it could along the coast of West Africa. From these, they shipped slaves, gold, and agricultural produce to their colonies in the New World and sometimes home to Europe. Despite their activity and the profits involved, they were dependent throughout upon the cooperation and toleration of African entrepreneurs.

These early colonial ventures were ineffectual. Except in Mozambique and the Congo, the merchants of Europe knew nothing of most of Africa and, aside from providing markets for slaves and thus the thrust of Africa's commercial energies, influenced the evolution of inner Africa little until about 1700. There rivalries between pastoralists and agriculturists for available arable lands continued. Masses of people moved out of the central African heartland eastward and westward into Malawi, Zambia, and Angola, out of the upper Nile region into Uganda and Kenya, and across the sub-Saharan zone of western Africa from the Atlantic highlands toward and into northern Nigeria. These migrations of peoples and cultures—and the effect each had on the face of Africa—were more important, until the 19th century, than the activities of Europeans and, in most respects, more than the trade in slaves that the Europeans had intensified.

AFRICA IN MODERN TIMES

Two Africas. During the 17th century two Africas emerged. One focused inward on the kinds of problems of statecraft and economic self-sufficiency that had long engendered inter-ethnic conflict, migration of peoples, and the wholesale transformation of regions from one religious and cultural persuasion to another. Around the central African lakes, centralized, highly stratified kingdoms began to replace the egalitarian, clan-based societies of an earlier era. A similar growth in centralization was occurring in the grasslands of the Cameroons and, with an intensity and success peculiar to its locale, in and around the Gold Coast. In the basin of the Congo and on the high plateau along its rim this process would occupy the 18th century as well, with many preexisting agricultural peoples being absorbed into larger collectivities ruled by groups of innovative migrants.

In religion too it was a time of elaboration and differentiation. Economically, it was a period of expanding horizons, of the intensification of long-distance trade involving astonishing journeys from the center of the continent to either coast, and of the development of markets, especially in the west and the north but also in the east and central regions. Parts of Africa that had not yet fully entered the Iron Age began to use the metal, thus enhancing their abilities to cultivate and hunt—and also their propensity for wars. The stakes of war had grown higher too, making conflict everywhere more frequent and costly.

The first Africa merged into the second Africa in and because of the clash of armies. The second Africa was, from the 17th century, thoroughly involved with the wider world. European contacts increased everywhere and were felt in a special way in the south after the settlement of the Dutch Boers (see AFRIKANERS) at the Cape of Good Hope in the mid-17th century; contact also grew with the Arabs in the east. The predominant form of involvement was the enslavement and sale of men and women. Wars supplied captives, and, as the

Africans are driven toward the coast for sale to European traders in the west or Arab traders in the east. Most of the African slaves were shipped across the Atlantic to labor in the mines and plantations established in the New World colonies.

needs of the Americas increased, so the frontier of European and Arab influence—but at this point not of European and Arab settlement—expanded.

The underlying cause of this process was the growing demand for, and increased production of, sugar. Only in the 17th century did sugar begin to be cultivated successfully and extensively in the West Indies. The production of sugar demands backbreaking labor, especially during the cane-cutting season. Without ready supplies of African labor, it would have proved costly—perhaps impossible—to grow cane successfully in the West Indies and Brazil.

The Slave Trade. Fueled by this foreign demand, the slave trade enveloped Africa throughout the 17th and 18th and a large part of the 19th centuries. The apparatus necessary for obtaining slaves, walking them to the marshaling yards at the coast, fattening and feeding them there, and selling them—individual by individual—to ship captains for transport overseas demanded entrepreneurial initiative and managerial competence of a high and complex order. As the enlightenment of the 18th century superseded the mercantilism of the 17th, it presumably also required a strong stomach and a hard heart on the part of Europeans and Africans alike. Certainly the treatment of slaves in the African ports was degrading. Even more inhumane was the shackling and cramming of anxious, potentially rebellious slaves into ships and their transport across occasionally windless and often stormy seas to auction yards in the Americas. If enslavement was an abomination—even by the standards of the day—the sea voyage, the so-called Middle Passage of six to ten weeks, was totally destructive.

Approximately 10 million Africans were forcibly removed from Africa. A large number must have died during the Middle Passage, others as a result of abortive rebellions or the original opposition to capture. Nevertheless, some of the areas well known for their slaves—eastern Nigeria, the Gold Coast, western Angola, and others—flourished demographically as well as economically during the centuries of the slave trade. As cruel as enslavement was for individuals, the societies of Africa may themselves have suffered far less than has

often been supposed. For individuals fortunate enough to remain behind, the trade in slaves brought new sources of capital for development, markets for commodities in addition to slaves, the transfer of technology from the West to Africa, and an outlet—however perverse—for the talents of certain groups within the coastal and forest states. The rise of ASHANTI, Dahomey, Oyo, and many less well-known peoples in the Congo basin and the hinterlands of Angola stem directly from their important roles in taking advantage of new, slave-centered terms of trade.

When pressure from humanitarians in Europe was brought to bear on the iniquities of the slave trade in the late 18th century, the merchants of Africa were naturally among the loudest in defending their livelihood. After slavery's abolition (1807) by Britain, and Britain's effective persuasion of France, Portugal, and Spain—and later Zanzibar in the east—to follow suit, Africans complained ever more bitterly and sought to frustrate the activities of Britain's antislave patrol in the Atlantic. Yet as they protested, many of these Africans found that their commercial talents could be put to good use supplying industrializing Europe with palm oil—for soap and industrial lubricants—and other crops.

The effects of the slave trade and its abolition were felt increasingly in the inland regions as well as in areas nearer the coast. The quest for slaves naturally involved peoples farther and farther afield. In the mid-19th century, for example, Arabo-Swahili caravan leaders from ZANZIBAR were scouring the lands within the distant Congo basin for slaves to supply the developing markets of Arabia and the Indian Ocean islands, where sugar was being grown, as well as the clove plantations of Zanzibar itself. Earlier the hinterlands of Malawi and Zambia had been crisscrossed innumerable times for slaves and ivory, and virtually no part of Africa was unacquainted with the horrors of enforced enslavement.

Areas Resistant to the Slave Trade. Some peoples, however, erected effective barriers against the traders. Those who were warlike and aggressive, like the MASAI and their herding cousins the TURKANA and the Karamojong, all in East Africa, were never molested. Also, where there were centralized kingdoms like RWANDA and Buganda on the great lakes, Africans moved freely and feared the slave trade little.

In Buganda, the nucleus of modern Uganda, a kabaka, or king, ruled autocratically with the assistance of a complex bureaucratic apparatus. Throughout the middle of the 19th century, successive rulers of Buganda increased their personal power by curbing the religious authority of the indigenous priests, phasing out the autonomy of clans and clan leadership by installing regional subordinates in their place, and enlisting an army responsible to themselves. By breaking the old societal bonds, the kabakas of Buganda created a society remarkably fluid and achievement oriented (as was the IBO society of eastern Nigeria); commoners could obtain advancement and prestige more easily than they could elsewhere in Africa. As a result, the people of Buganda were receptive to Islam and Christianity when both arrived toward the end of the century.

Zulu Nation and Nguni Dispersal. The rise of Buganda was paralleled in time by the rise of other aggressive new states. Each was stimulated by a set of local circumstances—by a shift in ecological fortunes or the nature of trade, or by the rise of a great leader. Each, in one way or another was the end product of a chain of reactions set off by the increasing activity and encroachment of Europeans. Among the more dramatic and far-reaching of these developments, which set off a series of chain reactions of its own, was the forcible integration of a number of Nguni-speaking clan units of southeastern Africa (what is now NATAL) into the great ZULU nation. Under SHAKA (c.1787–1828), a charismatic leader who modernized methods of warfare and introduced new, superior weapons, the Zulu, unified for the first time, presented a solid front to the British and Boers, or Afrikaners (descendants of Dutch and Protestant French who settled the Cape of Good Hope during the 17th and 18th centuries). Shaka was a tyrant who came to power behind an assegai (a powerful stabbing spear) and left a legacy of autocratic centralization.

Yet Shaka could not gain the obedience of all Zulu. After their defeat by his armies, several clans set in motion a far-ranging diaspora that, before the mid-19th century, engulfed virtually the whole of southern and central Africa. Three Zulu groups conquered their way northward, creating havoc and ending the independence of numerous peoples across whose territories they marched. In nearby Rhodesia, the NDEBELE offshoot established a major state that ruled south of the Zambezi River until the coming of the Europeans. The Kololo offshoot gained control for a time and thus linguistically and materially influenced the kingdom of the Lozi on the upper reaches of the Zambezi River.

A larger detachment of Nguni smashed its way northward through Mozambique, eastern Rhodesia, and modern Zambia until, in about 1839, it too suffered from internal rivalry. Fission resulted, with one Nguni group carving out a niche for itself in western Tanzania, another in southwestern Tanzania; a third began to dominate eastern Zambia; a fourth similarly ruled northern Malawi; and two others held sway in southern Malawi. In addition, a separate segment gained control of southern Mozambique. Taken as a whole, the Nguni diaspora profoundly altered the nature of government and society in most of central and southern Africa. By laying waste to the territories through which they passed and thoroughly cowing the agricultural peoples whom they encountered, the Nguni made conditions easier for slavers and, ultimately, for the conquest of the area by Europeans.

Islamic Revolutions. This cataclysm in the east had its counterpart in the west. However, where the Nguni were thoroughly traditional in their culture and religion, in their delight in cattle, and in their willingness to absorb the conquered into their new states, in the west—as later in the north—the significant upheavals in large part received their legitimacy by promising religious purification. Without the support of the doctrines of fundamentalist Islam, the leaders of what was a religious revival might not have been able to stimulate a war between believers and traditionalists throughout the breadth of Hausaland—now northern Nigeria.

Most believers were also immigrants, largely FULANI from the west, who, like so many minorities, felt themselves disadvantaged under the various rulers of the separate HAUSA city-states. USMAN DAN FODIO, a Fulani leader who had studied with Muslim theologians, was in the forefront of this movement of reform. He particularly wanted to reintroduce into Hausaland a spirit of religious orthodoxy that was in keeping with the literal teachings of the Koran and that would help foster the ideal society of an earlier golden age.

Usman's followers overran Hausaland; the cities of Kano, Katsina, and Zaria fell like duckpins. By 1810 the victory had been won, and Usman ruled about 460,000 km² (180,000 mi²) and 15 city-states. His revolution integrated an enormous area that remained intact until its conquest, early in the 20th century, by the British and its subsequent incorporation into the mammoth state of Nigeria.

Three other Islamic revolutions transformed sub-Saharan Africa on the eve of colonial rule. Ahmadu bin Hammadi Boubou, a Fulani who had studied under Usman, in 1818 led Muslims in the Maçina region of the upper Niger River against their BAMBARA overlords. By 1827, his state reached to the northern extremities of the Volta rivers in the south and to TIMBUKTU in the north. Over its five emirates, Ahmadu ruled as the head of an intolerant theocracy. Beer, tobacco, and dancing were banned, and even foreigners were compelled to order their daily lives according to the dictates of the new government.

In the 1850s al-Hajj UMAR, another religious reformer who had studied with the descendants of Usman, led a further revival along the upper reaches of the Niger River. His armies won victories against the Bambara and against peoples to the west in what is now Senegal. They even battled the French,

(Below) *Shaka, who ruled the Zulu during the early 1800s, transformed his small tribe into a powerful military nation. Shaka brandishes a broad-bladed spear and large shield, weapons he developed that gave the Zulu a strategic advantage in warfare with their neighbors. (Right) Three Zulu warriors display the tribe's ornate battle regalia. The variations in their garb reflect memberships in different regiments.*

who were approaching from the west. Toward the east, al-Hajj Umar conquered Ahmadu's empire, proclaiming a holy war against it, although it had earlier been created by the same process. These victories were short-lived, however, as Umar died soon after, and the French destroyed his state a decade later.

A Muslim holy war of even greater consequence took place in the SUDAN during the twilight years of African independence. By 1880 the Sudan had been controlled for 60 years by the Turkish-speaking administration of Egypt. During these years trade in slaves had provided its economic lifeblood. The more powerful of these slavers even came to rule vast regions in the south and southwestern portions of the territory. In the 1860s and 1870s, however, the rulers of Egypt attempted to curtail the slave trade, employing foreigners to manage the campaign. Muhammad Ahmad ibn Abdallah took advantage of these dissatisfactions by uniting the proslavers, the anticorruptionists, and the anti-Egyptians in a brilliantly arranged revolution that engulfed the Sudan in the 1880s.

Proclaimed the MAHDI, or Savior, this learned Islamic fundamentalist declared a holy war against backsliding infidels—who happened to be the rulers of the Sudan. In a series of decisive battles, his fanatical warriors conquered the Egyptian army and captured Khartoum (1885). For the next 13 years the puritanical followers of the Mahdi reigned supreme throughout virtually all of the Sudan. It took a major British assault to subordinate the Sudan in 1898. By then, however, most of the rest of Africa had also fallen to one or another of the European powers.

Colonial Partition. The European conquest of Africa began with the slave trade and the subsequent establishment of commodity exchange centers along the coasts. It was fueled by the exciting explorations of Mungo PARK, David LIVINGSTONE, Henry Morton STANLEY, Sir Richard BURTON, and Joseph THOMSON, who provided a collective prelude to the partition of Africa. Equally important were the activities of Roman Catholic and Protestant missionaries, who intrepidly entered the interior in the wake of the explorers, developed systems for writing the indigenous languages, and then expounded their beliefs on why and how Western influence would benefit Africa.

Commercial interests were also important, especially in West Africa where, during the 19th century, the early outposts became enclaves ruled by Europeans with the collaboration

(Above) *The Mahdi, a religious mystic, led a bloody revolt against Anglo-Egyptian rule in the Sudan in the 1880s. The death of the British hero Charles George Gordon at the hands of the Mahdi's warriors is portrayed in this painting of the fall of Khartoum in 1885.*

(Below) *During the Zulu War of 1878–79, Zulu warriors destroyed a British column at Isandhlawana. They were routed at Ginginhlovo (shown here) and Ulundi, however, and their power was broken.*

This engraving from the Illustrated London News was based on Henry Morton Stanley's personal description of his rendezvous with Dr. Livingstone. David Livingstone, a British explorer who had previously discovered and named the Victoria Falls, set out in 1866 to discover the headwaters of the Nile. No word of his whereabouts had been heard for several years when Stanley, a journalist, embarked on an expedition to find the missing explorer. After an 8-month search, Stanley found Livingstone in 1871 at Ujiji, a village near Lake Tanganyika.

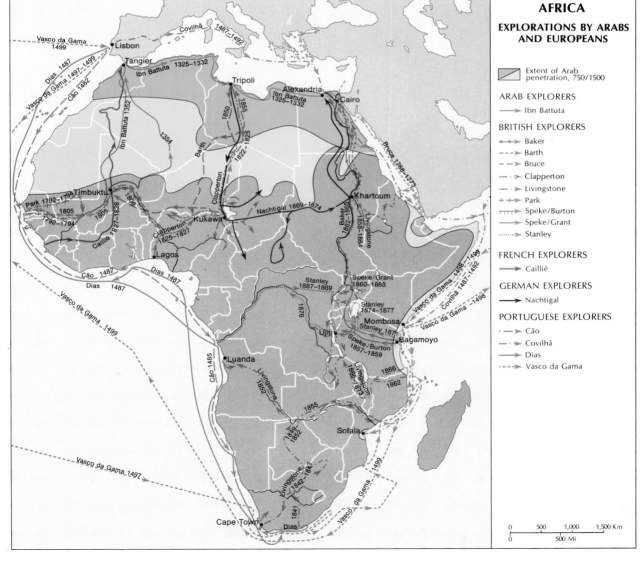

AFRICA

EXPLORATIONS BY ARABS AND EUROPEANS

Extent of Arab penetration, 750/1500

ARAB EXPLORERS
→ Ibn Battuta

BRITISH EXPLORERS
Baker
Barth
Bruce
Clapperton
Livingstone
Park
Speke/Burton
Speke/Grant
Stanley

FRENCH EXPLORERS
→ Caillié

GERMAN EXPLORERS
→ Nachtigal

PORTUGUESE EXPLORERS
Cão
Covilhã
Dias
Vasco da Gama

0   500   1,000   1,500 Km
0   500 Mi

of Africans. Minor wars led to the gradual, unanticipated growth of these outposts. In South Africa, too, animosity between English- and Afrikaans-speaking whites led to wars with Africans, the expansion of the frontier there, and the occupation by European powers of all of southern and central Africa. Everywhere the actions of a few commercial promoters were important.

Above all, it was the political rivalries of the new Europe that accelerated the decisive carving up of the continent. Throughout the late 19th century, France, Germany, and Britain each attempted to gain a competitive edge over the others by controlling sources of raw materials overseas—in East and South Asia and in the Pacific Islands, among other places. A war in Europe to end competition seemed an undesirable alternative; so instead they exploited Africa to satisfy their strategic and economic needs.

Between 1880 and 1914, Europe systematically occupied Africa. Persuading Africans to sign treaties requesting protection, or using machine guns to silence opposition when treaties were disdained, Europeans annexed one region after another. Because the Europeans had superior weapons and ready access to ammunition and other supplies, there was surprisingly little resistance. Most important, Africans were rarely united, and many welcomed whites for protection

against more powerful Africans, such as the Nguni.

Nevertheless, there were bitter battles in opposition. The Ashanti resisted British conquest from the 1820s to 1902, and the French had to overcome the armies of Ahmadu and Umar as well as those of a late 19th-century mercenary state created by Samori of Guinea. Along the coast opposite Zanzibar, Arabo-Swahili warriors resisted the Germans for two years in the late 1880s. Up-country, Hehe warriors were subdued only after long, costly battles. In South Africa the Zulu twice defeated the British and the Afrikaners before being humbled by bigger and better guns. In Rhodesia the Ndebele fought to retain their power. There were innumerable rearguard actions too where isolated clans or tribes burned European camps and for years continued to attack European soldiers before finally being worn down.

In ETHIOPIA, King MENELIK II was able in 1896, at Adwa near the capital of much earlier Aksum, totally to oust a large army of invading Italians, as he had sufficient guns of European manufacture and a large, well-trained army. As a result Ethiopia remained undominated by outsiders until 1936, when the Italians avenged their previous defeat, then governing the empire until 1941.

Colonial Rule. Racial prejudice and segregation accompanied colonial rule, preeminently in the settler colonies of southern

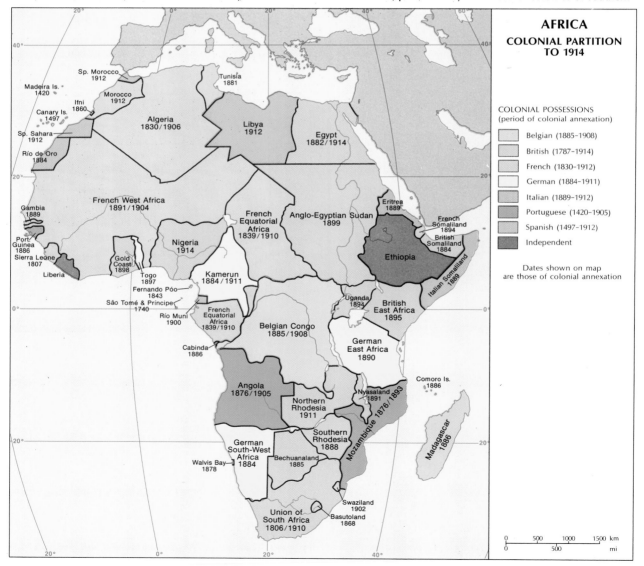

(Left) *Sékou Touré was Guinea's leader from 1958, when the country gained its independence, until his death in 1984.* (Center) *Zimbabwe's prime minister Robert Mugabe is shown here at a press conference following his party's victory at the polls in February 1980.* (Right) *Julius Nyerere has been Tanzania's president since 1964, when Tanganyika and Zanzibar merged to form that nation.*

and eastern Africa, but their collective taint poisoned the atmosphere everywhere. Legal segregation and denial of voting and other rights, the hated pass, or identification certificate, that everyone with black skin had to carry, the taking of African-owned land without compensation, and the effective denial of any remedy in the courts were standard practices across the entire swath of Africa from the Cape of Good Hope to the northern borders of Kenya. These measures themselves, and more particularly the attitudes that accompanied them, effectively stymied African creativity and initiative and fostered a strong, deep-seated resentment of whites as well as their colonial regimes. The actions of missionaries did little to counter this reaction; Africans heard them preaching equality as they heard the administrators talking about trusteeship and protection. Nevertheless, when it came to their own advance, however limited, toward the distant objective of home rule, Africans could never achieve satisfaction.

When whites of the day even understood this complaint, they often pointed to their economic, educational, and medical achievements. According to their justification, the powers of Europe had brought the progressive ideas of their civilization to Africa. They opened schools and hospitals, introduced mercantile concepts, built roads and railways, erected impressive buildings, extracted minerals, and harvested profitable crops. Everywhere they advanced the cause of materialsm and launched Africa on the road toward modernity.

Resistance to Colonial Rule. It is hardly surprising that colonial rule, with its coercive demands and regulations, its racism, and its unfulfilled promises of personal growth and national evolution, encouraged a hostile response. This response took many forms. Some protest was manifested religiously, with Africans taking refuge in millennialistic flights from the reality of foreign rule. Many Africans, most commonly but not always those from a traditional, rural background, were less patient.

When foreign rulers attempted to exact the last ounce of flesh, Africans rebelled violently. In 1896–97 the Ndebele and SHONA almost succeeded in ending settler control of Rhodesia. In 1898, Bai Bureh led a revolt against taxation in SIERRA LEONE that undercut British rule. For three years in the first decade of the 20th century German rule in East Africa was threatened by the success of the conglomerate of ethnic groups that was called Maji Maji. In 1915 in Nyasaland (now Malawi) an abortive uprising was led by John CHILEMBWE, a Christian preacher educated in the United States. Although few lives were lost, Chilembwe's followers might have overrun

the colony had their preparations been more complete.

The most recent of these violent outbursts against colonial rule was the MAU MAU rebellion in KENYA. From 1951 to 1956 whites farming in the rural areas lived in terror. So did Africans, mostly KIKUYU, who refused to pledge their loyalty to the forces of Mau Mau. In no case, not even the last, did Africans succeed in overthrowing white rule by force. Their actions may, however, occasionally have changed policies for the better.

Achievement of Independence. For the most part Africa won its independence peacefully. There were no struggles of the Indonesian, Indochinese, or Algerian duration or intensity. Nevertheless, there was always the threat of violence. The colonial powers also were influenced in their decisions to relinquish colonies by the changing climate of world opinion, the altered circumstances of their own economic fortunes, and a lessening interest in colonies in an age of hydrogen bombs and conquests of outer space.

The participation of Africans in the Allied effort in World War II, the liberationist rhetoric of that war, and the altered fortunes of France and Britain after the war all contributed to the rise of nationalism and the drive toward freedom. The first political parties were formed in Nigeria and Nyasaland during the war; both evolved from a search by the elite for ways to bring pressure to bear on overseas administrators. Shortly thereafter similar parties were established on the model of the Congress party of India in the Gold Coast (now Ghana), Kenya, Northern Rhodesia (now Zambia), and Uganda. In the French colonies branches of metropolitan French parties had always existed. After the war leaders of these branches formed their own party, uniting the political movements of all the colonies in Africa; however, it soon fractured again into separate territorial organizations.

Most of these incipient nationalist movements (the Belgian, Italian, and Portuguese colonies stifled such activity) drew upon the older, Westernized elites and the traditional leadership of chiefs. Some, however, began to broaden their bases of support to include the laboring classes and the school dropouts of the towns. In this respect, as in so many others, the Gold Coast showed the way. Kwame NKRUMAH, another American-educated leader, molded this new ferment into a cohesive social and political attack on British rule. Employing little real violence, but cleverly manipulating the electoral and constitutional formulas established by Britain, he gained self-government for the Gold Coast in 1954 and independence in 1957. This example, the fear of another Mau Mau episode, the failure of European intervention at Suez in 1956, and France's losing war in Algeria thereafter hurried the transfer of power in one colony after another.

All of France's colonies but Somaliland (now DJIBOUTI) and the Comoro Islands were free by 1960. With the exception of GUINEA, all maintained close relations with France, receiving substantial economic aid. All adopted strong presidential forms of government, and although some have been subject to repeated coups and unrest, others—for example, SENEGAL, IVORY COAST, and Guinea—experienced long periods of rule by their original presidents.

In 1960, Belgium rapidly disengaged from a Congo (now ZAIRE) that had no preparation, no new class capable of ruling, and only bad Belgian examples to copy. The so-called CONGO CRISIS ensued, in which the mineral-rich province of Katanga (now SHABA) seceded but was forced back (1963) into the Congo by United Nations intervention. Fifteen years later (1978), Zaire was shaken by another revolt in Shaba, suppressed with the aid of Moroccan and French troops.

In 1960 the former British colony of Nigeria, still split into the three regions that reflected the process of its conquest, was declared independent as a federation. Unresolved ethnic and political tensions subsequently brought about a series of coups in 1966, the secession (1967) of the eastern region, BIAFRA, and a bitterly fought civil war. This ended with a federal victory in 1970. During this period Ghana also experienced a series of new regimes following the overthrow of Nkrumah in 1966.

The settler-dominated colonies in East and Central Africa and the small British-run protectorates in and around South Africa were the last African dependencies to be set free by Britain from 1962 to 1966. The East African Community, a common market formed in 1967, largely disintegrated because of the political divergencies between the pro-Western Kenya

The Organization of African Unity, headquartered in Addis Ababa, Ethiopia, was founded in 1963 to promote unity among African states and to eradicate colonialism. The OAU includes every independent nation in Africa except South Africa and Zimbabwe (Rhodesia).

under Jomo KENYATTA and TANZANIA (a union of Tanganyika and Zanzibar) under Julius NYERERE, the chief proponent of "African socialism." Uganda, the third partner, began to follow its own erratic path under the arbitrary and ruthless rule of Idi AMIN DADA.

The position of the central African states of ZAMBIA (formerly Northern Rhodesia) and MALAWI (formerly Nyasaland) was complicated by their preindependence ties with Rhodesia (formerly Southern Rhodesia), ruled by the white-supremacist regime of Ian SMITH. Like South Africa, which after the Boer defeat by the British in the SOUTH AFRICAN WAR (1899–1902) was granted self-rule in 1910, white Rhodesians had enjoyed self-government since 1923. After the breakdown of the Rhodesian Federation, which linked Southern Rhodesia with Northern Rhodesia and Nyasaland from 1953 to 1963, and the institution of majority (black) rule in Zambia and Malawi, the white Rhodesians declared unilateral independence in 1965 to forestall a similar development there. Forced into close dependence on South Africa, whose APARTHEID policies it closely imitated, Rhodesia held out against international pressure and increasing nationalist attacks until the late 1970s. In 1980, Rhodesia, renamed ZIMBABWE, became legally independent under black majority rule.

A major reason for the white Rhodesian acquiescence was the final withdrawal of Portugal from its former African colonies—including MOZAMBIQUE, which provided landlocked Rhodesia with its access to the sea—in 1974–75. In ANGOLA, the other principal Portuguese holding, civil war followed independence, bringing also an international confrontation between the Soviet and Western power blocs. Cuban troops, who helped secure victory for the People's Republic of Angola, remained in Africa after the conclusion of the war (1976) and thus introduced a new element in the jockeying for influence between East and West among the African countries. This international contest, the ethnic animosities that beset many African countries, the continuing white domination of South Africa, and the attempt to find a common voice in such organizations as the ORGANIZATION OF AFRICAN UNITY are among the main themes of contemporary African affairs.   ROBERT I. ROTBERG

Bibliography: Collins, Robert, *African History* (1971); Davidson, Basil, *Africa in History* (1968); Fage, J. D., *History of Africa* (1978); Hallett, Robin, *Africa to 1875* (1970) and *Africa since 1875* (1974); Oliver, Roland, and Atmore, Anthony, *Africa since 1800* (1967); Oliver, Roland, and Fage, John, *A Short History of Africa* (1962); Rotberg, Robert I., *A Political History of Tropical Africa* (1965).

See also: COLONIALISM; IMPERIALISM; SLAVERY.

African archaeology: see AFRICAN PREHISTORY.

African art

The traditional art of Africa consists principally of masks and figures of magico-religious significance, decorative objects used for personal adornment, and implements and insignia of rank or prestige. Most of these objects are in some way allied to ceremonial and other structured activities (such as singing, dancing, drumming, and storytelling), without which the visual arts could not function in traditional African society.

The forms and functions of traditional African art are strikingly diverse. Certain patterns of form and meaning can be discerned, however, by both a regional and a more general scrutiny. Sculpture is generally considered Africa's greatest achievement in the visual arts, but, although sculpture is found in many parts of Africa, this medium of expression occurs with the greatest frequency in western and central Africa. The majority of sculptures are of wood, but objects are also made in metal, stone, terra-cotta, mud, beadwork, ivory, and other materials.

In southern and eastern Africa are found ancient rock paintings attributed to the SAN (Bushman) people. The only other major rock art tradition in Africa is that of Algeria, Libya, and Chad, the work of the prehistoric inhabitants of the Sahara (see PREHISTORIC ART). Islamic influence is seen throughout the west African savanna and the east African

(Below) *The prehistoric Bushman rock painting is from a cave near Omaruru, Namibia. Such paintings, found throughout southern Africa, often represent hunting scenes. (Right) The wooden Bambara dance headdress from Mali is used in the agricultural rites of the Tyiwara society. Made in the form of an antelope, it is attached to a basketry cap worn by dancers who imitate the movements of this animal. (Nationalmuseet, Copenhagen.)*

coast; populations of both areas have been involved with Islamic culture for at least a thousand years. Some groups like the YORUBA of Nigeria carve a great variety of objects; others like the nomadic Pakot of Kenya rejoice in writing poetry about their cattle. Thus, one cannot generalize about African societies and their art forms merely because the people live on the same continent.

GENERAL CHARACTERISTICS

At least three basic themes occur again and again in traditional African art: (1) the distinction between bush and village, (2) the problematic relationships between the sexes, and (3) the struggle to control various forces, natural as well as supernatural, to achieve desired ends.

The dualism of bush and village is pervasive in Africa, although the forms by which it is expressed vary from place to place. The underlying notion is that the world consists of two complementary spheres: one a wild, chaotic, uncontrolled, exuberant region (or nature); the other an ordered, controlled, measured, predictable domain (or culture), the human world of the village. The IBO of Nigeria express this dualism by means of masks and headdresses: the male symbolizes the elephant, most powerful of all bush creatures; the female symbolizes culture and is delicately coiffed to express refinement and civilization.

Among the Yaka and other Congolese groups, masks that police the initiation rites are made of rough bush materials and have relatively abstract features; those worn at the conclusion of the rites—when the boys have been symbolically brought from nature into culture—are made of wood, are more naturalistic, and are used to make fun of human foibles. For the DOGON of Mali, the distinction is embodied in the contrast between spirals (nature) and rectangular forms (culture).

To deal with problems and issues surrounding the relations between the sexes, various African societies employ art as a therapeutic device. The Baule of Ivory Coast, for example, carve images supposed to represent one's spirit lover because it is believed that these beings, if jealous, can cause the living unending problems with their spouses.

Africans are by no means passive in the face of powerful natural or supernatural forces. Indeed, the principal function of art in traditional African society has been to help manipulate the forces that affect people's lives. These forces are not seen as preternaturally good or evil as they are in Western society; rather, natural and supernatural powers are perceived as malleable and subject to influence and manipulation, provided the proper techniques are used. Thus, the Yoruba of southwestern Nigeria perform elaborate masked ceremonies known as *Gelede* to please and honor witches; behind this lies an anthropomorphizing outlook which assumes that if flattery works on ordinary people it will on witches too.

Deliberately hideous masks intended to expel witches, such as the SENUFO "firespitter" of Ivory Coast and many related savanna forms, constitute a violent counterattack on witchcraft that literally fights fire with fire. The same is true of FETISHES—magically constructed and empowered objects found throughout Africa. These assemblages are specific prescriptions aimed at bringing about a desired end, whether the breaking of a bad habit, the improvement of one's love life, the destruction of a human enemy, or the warding off of a supernatural threat. In short, traditional African art is essentially functional and optimistic. Its aims are primarily positive and are intended, through elaboration and vigorous expression, to enhance the human condition.

REGIONAL STYLES

Western Sudanic Region. This area includes Upper Volta, western Mali, and northern Ivory Coast. Among its most famous art-producing peoples are the Dogon, Bambara, Bwa, and Senufo. The fertility of crops is of basic importance in this dry area, as is the placation of the ancestors and the indoctrination of the young in the ancient traditions of each society. To these ends, masks and figures representing legendary ancestors dance or receive sacrifices. Forms in the western Sudan tend to be relatively stylized, austere, and angular.

Central Sudanic Region. Centered in northern Nigeria, the central Sudan is dominated by the Muslim HAUSA and FULANI peoples, who have developed numerous city-states. Central Sudanic art is mostly nonrepresentational and includes mud architecture, sometimes with molded, low-relief decoration; embroidered textiles; elaborate coiffure; metal and beadwork jewelry; and leatherwork decorated with geometric appliqué. In addition, terra-cotta sculptures dating from about 500 BC to AD 200, associated with the so-called Nok culture, have been unearthed over a 480-km (300-mi) stretch of uplands in the

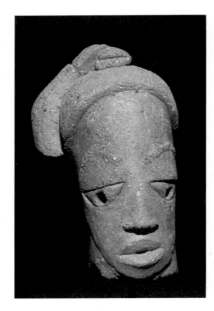

The terra-cotta Nok sculptures from northern Nigeria, dating from about 600 BC to AD 200, are the oldest known sculptures of sub-Saharan Africa. This example shows the cylindrical head and elaborate headdress typical of the Iron Age Nok culture.

A bronze plaque from the court of Benin in Nigeria represents a king and his kneeling attendants. Dating from about 1550–1680, the plaque was produced by the lost-wax process. (Courtesy British Museum, London.)

southern part of the region. The Nok tradition represents the earliest known sculpture yet found in sub-Saharan Africa and seems to have paved the way for the tradition of superb portrait terra cottas and bronzes that later developed at the holy city of IFE in western Nigeria. Some modern peoples in the central Sudanic region such as the TIV, Goemai, Montol, Mama, Waja, Jukun, Mumuye, Chamba, and Afo carve masks or figures; these objects show a striking similarity to the art of the western Sudanic peoples. This suggests ancient linkages across the savanna belt that have been disrupted only within approximately the past 1,000 years by the Islamic incursions.

West Guinea Coast Region. This region consists of Guinea-Bissau, Sierra Leone, Liberia, and the densely forested coastal portion of Guinea and southwestern Ivory Coast. Characteristic masks and figures from the area are made by such peoples as the MENDE, Baga, Gola, and Dan. Forms in the west Guinea Coast are generally softer, shinier, and more rounded than in the neighboring western Sudanic region. Carved wood masks are the dominant art form in the region, where they perform a great variety of functions. Masks are used to police ceremonies, punish wrongdoers, settle land disputes, and start and end wars. An apt expression for the traditional west Guinea Coast way of life is "government by mask."

Central Guinea Coast Region. The Central Guinea Coast extends from southeastern Ivory Coast, southern Ghana, Togo, Benin, and southern Nigeria to the lower Niger River with an offshoot in the Cameroons grasslands. Central Guinea Coast art is the richest and the most complex of any area in Africa. Such well-known societies as the AKAN (ASHANTI), FON,

YORUBA, and Benin inhabit this region. Traditionally, these groups were courtly in character with divine kingship and other centralizing institutions; their art employs aristocratic materials including gold, silver, bronze, brass, beadwork, silk, and ivory. Specialized guilds of artists attached to the courts produced intricately crafted art forms mainly for the benefit of the leaders. Guinea Coast art forms include stools, drums, elaborately decorated cloth, pottery, terra-cotta figurines, ornamental swords, miniature masks, combs, mirrors, staffs, pipes, containers, and carved musical instruments. The affluence and accompanying artistic wealth of this region was in part the result of the lucrative trade with European ships that began to visit the west African coast beginning in the late 15th century.

East Guinea Coast Region. The lower Niger marks the approximate boundary between the aristocratic centralized societies of the central Guinea Coast and the more loosely organized peoples of southwestern Nigeria. Here, in the absence of kings and paramount chiefs, one finds elaborately developed masquerades and plays, sometimes staged by SECRET SOCIETIES, sometimes by graded title societies. These performances serve to maintain law and order in groups that vest leadership in their elders. Characteristic of the east Guinea Coast area is a dazzling array of masks, puppets, headdresses, and other theatrical devices. Prominent groups in the area include the IBO, IBIBIO, Idoma, Ijo, Ejagham (Ekoi), and Ogoni.

Equatorial Forest Region. Among the best-known peoples of the equatorial forest, which extends across Gabon and northern Zaire, are the FANG, Kota, Kwele, Ngbaka, Mbole, and Lega. This region, which is covered with dense rain forest ex-

A Kota funerary figure from Gabon is made of wood covered with copper. Representing the spirit of the dead, it was used in ancestor-cult rituals. (Collection of Princess Gourielli, New York.)

This wooden fetish figure was fashioned by the Yaka tribe of Zaire. A fetish sculpture is believed to be endowed with magical properties that protect its owner. (Ethnographical Museum of Berlin.)

cept where trees have been cleared for agriculture, still includes Pygmies, the original inhabitants, who are hunters and gatherers. The art-producing agricultural peoples began moving into this region from southern Nigeria some 2,000 years ago, in what is frequently called the Bantu Expansion. Their art forms include numerous masks, figures, beautifully designed weapons, divination objects and carved fetishes, wall paintings, musical instruments, and practical implements. One widespread visual motif is the so-called heart-shaped face, a method of rendering the face as a concavity from the eye sockets to the vicinity of the mouth. This motif may well have been brought by Bantu migrants from Nigeria, where it is also used.

Lower Congo Region. The styles that developed in the general vicinity of the mouth of the Congo River were influenced about 1500 by the Portuguese, who converted the king (the *Mani-kongo*) and many of his courtiers to Christianity. During the next three centuries, Portuguese influence introduced a number of Christian themes. Following the Portuguese withdrawal, many of these borrowed symbols acquired pagan meanings; crucifixes, for example, became symbols of chiefly power. Christian origins have also been suggested for other Lower Congo art forms, including stone mortuary statues, mother-and-child figures, and fetishes with nails driven into them.

Southern Savanna Region. In the broad upland belt of central

Africa are numerous Bantu peoples such as the CHOKWE, LUBA, Songye, Yaka, Pende, and Kuba and related groups such as the MBUNDU and Makonde. Perhaps the prime generators of art in these groups are the initiation rites that mark the passage of boys from adolescence to manhood. Masks, figures, costumes, and spectacular theatrical effects are part of these initiations, functioning often as didactic devices to instruct the boys in their culture and in proper manly behavior. The Kuba of central Zaire, in addition to complex initiation rites, have elaborate courtly art forms, including royal portrait statues, elegant cups, drums, containers, dolls, and numerous regalia for persons of high rank.

Eastern Sudanic Region. The artistic production of most of the peoples in this area is restricted to decorative art, but a few groups in the southern Republic of the Sudan and southwest Ethiopia, including the Bongo, Konso, and Borana, carve wood figures to commemorate ancestors. This tradition probably relates more to the ancient pagan art still discernible in a broad arc across southern Asia than to the majority of African styles. Similarly distinct is Ethiopian art, which shows strong links with Egyptian COPTIC ART and BYZANTINE ART.

East and Southern African Region and Madagascar. Apart from Bushman paintings and engravings, eastern and southern Africa have only a limited number of distinctive figural styles. The predominant arts in this region are architecture and architectural decorations, including the boldly patterned

(Above) *The Ndebele people of southern Africa are known for the mural paintings that adorn the clay walls of their houses and enclosures. This example, from a village near Pretoria in the Transvaal, demonstrates the rich variety of colors and geometric patterns.*

(Below) *A wood and fiber initiation mask was made by the Yaka tribe of Zaire. The elaborately painted and sculpted headdress is worn by a young man during a circumcision ceremony and dance exhibition. (Collection of Karl-Ferdinand Schadler, Munich.)*

wall paintings of the NDEBELE in the Transvaal, and personal ornaments, especially beadwork. Madagascar, the only large island lying off Africa's coast, was first settled not from Africa but from Indonesia, perhaps early in the Christian Era. Conspicuous here is the commemorative ancestor figure notable also in the eastern Sudanic region and typical of Indonesia. Certain raffia textiles made by the *ikat* process find their closest parallels in Indonesia.

Influence in the West. From the 16th century, European travelers acquired objects of African art, particularly bronzes and ivories from the Benin court. Collections of African art were being formed in Europe by the 19th century. Early in the 20th century, African sculpture had an impact on the work of such modern artists as Georges BRAQUE, Henri MATISSE, Amedeo MODIGLIANI, and Pablo PICASSO, who were attracted by the aesthetic values they perceived in African art forms.

DOUGLAS FRASER

Bibliography: Bascom, William, *African Art in Cultural Perspective: An Introduction* (1973); Delange, Jacqueline, *The Art and Peoples of Black Africa*, trans. by Carol F. Jopling (1974); Fagg, William, *African Tribal Images* (1968); Fraser, Douglas, and Cole, Herbert M., eds., *African Art and Leadership* (1972); Laude, Jean, *The Arts of Black Africa* (1971); Leiris, Michel, and Delange, Jacqueline, *African Art* (1968); Leuzinger, Elsy, *Africa: The Art of the Negro Peoples*, 2d ed. (1967) and *The Art of Black Africa* (1972); Wassing, René S., *African Art: Its Background and Traditions* (1968); Willett, Frank, *African Art: An Introduction* (1971).

See also: AFRICAN MUSIC.

African hunting dog

The African hunting dog, *Lycaon pictus*, is a wild CARNIVORE in the DOG family, Canidae, order Carnivora. It may be 104 cm (41 in) long and weigh 23 kg (50 lb). Sparse, mottled hair covers a dark-pigmented skin. The animal has a musky odor. It is found south and east of the Sahara and kills more prey than it eats.

EVERETT SENTMAN

African hunting dogs, Lycaon pictus, *attack a zebra exhausted from a long chase. The frantic zebra futilely kicks its powerful hind legs in an attempt to ward off the dogs, while one attacker clings to the zebra's lip to avoid the hooves. The zebra will finally fall from loss of blood. These dogs are among the most feared predators of Africa.*

African languages

More than 1,700 distinct languages are spoken on the African continent, and they constitute about 30 percent of all world languages. The exact number is impossible to ascertain, because not enough information is available about many of them to determine whether different names refer to distinct languages or merely to mutually intelligible dialects of larger languages. Groups of people who speak a distinct African language range in size from several million down to a thousand or even fewer. Apart from North Africa, only a few African countries, for example, Somalia, Rwanda, and Burundi, have a single or a dominant language. As a result, official languages are usually English, French, or Portuguese.

HISTORY

The study of African languages began before 1600 and was the task of early Christian missionaries. Few works of lasting importance, however, were produced before 1850. Missionaries and some governmental administrators and agencies, in the colonial era and in the present time of independent African nations, have always been the primary contributors to research in African languages. Their goals have been largely practical: literacy, evangelization, and education. Strictly scholarly interest in African languages, centered in university programs, dates back to about 1850 in South Africa, the late 1920s in Europe, 1959 in the United States, and about 1960 in a number of other African institutions. At present, no more than ten American universities offer serious programs in African languages. Since 1970 annual academic conferences on African linguistics have been held in the United States. The survey of the classification of African languages in the last section of this article is, with a few minor refinements, that proposed by Joseph H. Greenberg in 1963. Recently, some revisions in the subclassification of the Niger-Congo languages have been suggested, but these are only tentatively accepted at present. Edgar Gregerson has recently theorized that the Nilo-Saharan and Niger-Kordofanian language families may have been related in the extremely distant past as members of an even older "Kongo-Saharan" superfamily.

CHARACTERISTICS OF AFRICAN LANGUAGES

Because of the variety and number of African languages, they possess a number of distinct phonetic and grammatical features, as well as marked similarities within families.

Phonetic Characteristics. Although the Khoisan languages, spoken by some hunting and gathering or cattle-raising peoples in southern Africa, make up only a fraction of the languages of Africa, they are of special interest because of their unique use of "click" consonants. This click is similar to the sound one makes when saying "tsk, tsk" or that one uses to spur on a horse or to imitate the sound of a cork popping out of a bottle. But clicks function as the following consonants do in the Roman alphabet: *p, t,* and *k.* In most Khoisan languages, almost every noun, verb, and adjective begins with such a click. The use of clicks has spread into some neighboring Bantu languages, notably IsiXhosa; they are generally represented in the written language by the letters *c, x,* and *q,* which are not needed to represent other sounds.

Languages of the Niger–Kordofanian and Nilo–Saharan families, spoken by the majority of Saharan and sub-Saharan peoples, generally do not permit consonant sequences like those in such English words as *struts* or *prints.* Consonants followed by "glides," such as the *w* and *y* sounds, however, are common. Examples are the Igbo word *ákwà* ("cloth") and the Nupe word *kyàkyá* ("bicycle"). Common consonantal sequences are a nasal followed by an oral consonant: *mb, nd,* and *ng* and also *mp, nt, nk,* and other combinations. These may function as unit consonants; some well-known names, for example, are properly syllabified as Ta-nza-ni-a, U-ga-nda, and Zi-mba-bwe. In some languages, however, nasals may be syllables in their own right; they are just hummed, without a preceding or following vowel. An example is the Igbo word *ńtà* ("small"). Many languages permit only a few different syllable-final consonants or none at all.

Almost all languages of sub-Saharan Africa are tone languages; the northern West Atlantic languages, Swahili, and a few others are not. In a tone language, distinctions in pitch are as important in the makeup of words as are distinctions in consonants or vowels. In Igbo, for example, *ákwà* (high-low) means "cloth"; *àkwà* (low-low) means "bed"; and *àkwá* (low-high) means "egg." Every word has its own tone or tone sequence, which may, however, undergo definable changes in some contexts. Tone may also signal grammatical differences. For example, in Kpelle *è pìlì* (low-low-low) means "he jumped," but *é pílí* (high-high-high) means "he should jump." Some languages have two to four distinct tone levels ("discrete level" systems). Others have two, sometimes three levels, plus a slight lowering of nonlow tones ("downstep"), as much as six or seven times in a phrase or sentence ("terraced level" systems).

Grammatical Characteristics. A striking grammatical feature of most African languages is that modifiers come after, rather than before, the noun. For example, the translation of the Swahili sentence *kisu kikubwa kimoja kile changu* ("that one big knife of mine") is literally "knife big one that my." The order of grammatical elements in a sentence must also be noted. In some languages, like English, an object follows a verb. This is the rule in Igbo: *ó zùrù m̀mà* ("he stole a knife"). The order of the Igbo words is the same as that of the English translation. However, in Kpelle the verb follows the object: *è kâli yà* (literally, "he a hoe bought").

At least some languages in every branch of the Niger-Kordofanian family, except Mande, have noun classes and agreement, or concord. This characteristic is most easily illustrated in a Bantu language such as Swahili. Personal nouns in Swahili have a singular prefix *m-* and a plural prefix *wa-*, for example, *mtu* ("a person") and *watu* ("people"). Terms for trees and many other items have a singular prefix *m-* and a plural prefix *mi-*, for example, *mti* ("a tree") and *miti* ("trees"). Many other nouns have a singular prefix *ki-* and a plural prefix *vi-*, for example, *kisu* ("a knife") and *visu* ("knives").

Other singular-plural pairs are used as well as a "liquid mass" class with the prefix *ma-*, for example, *maji* ("water") and *mafuta* ("oil"). Each prefix determines an appropriate concord prefix for noun modifiers as well as for verbal subject and object markers. Concord prefixes for a modifier meaning "that" are shown in the following examples: *mtu yule* ("that person"), *watu wale* ("those people"); *mti ule* ("that tree"), *miti ile* ("those trees"); *kisu kile* ("that knife"), *visu vile* ("those knives"); *maji yale* ("that water"). Such systems vary from language to language, including the use of class-marking suffixes, rather than prefixes, but recognizable similarities pervade the Niger-Kordofanian languages. Many Kwa languages have no singular-plural contrast in nouns at all and yet show remnants of noun classification in what must once have been prefixes, for example, Igbo *m̀pì* ("horn [of an animal]"), but *òpì* ("musical horn, flute").

CLASSIFICATION

Four main language families—groups of languages presumably descended from distinct ancestral languages—are recognized in Africa: Afroasiatic, Nilo-Saharan, Niger-Kordofanian, and Khoisan.

Afroasiatic. The AFROASIATIC family is considered a distinct language grouping. Its various languages are spoken primarily in northern Africa and in Ethiopia and Somalia, as well as outside the African continent. The branch called Chadic is spoken in northern Nigeria and adjacent territories. Hausa is the most widely spoken of the Chadic languages and, after Swahili, the second most widely spoken language of sub-Saharan Africa. Between 10 and 15 million people are native Hausa speakers, and many others use it as a second language.

Nilo-Saharan. Languages in the Nilo-Saharan family are spoken in and just south of the Sahara, from Mali in the west to the Nile basin, and southward into Uganda, Kenya, and northern Tanzania. The Songhai branch of Nilo-Saharan is spoken by the 500,000 or so people who live along the great bend of the Niger from Mali to northwestern Nigeria. It consists of Songhai, Dyerma, and Dendi, all closely related and possibly mutually intelligible. The Saharan branch, primarily Kanuri and Teda, is spoken by more than 2.5 million people who live from northeastern Nigeria north through Niger and Chad to the Libyan border. Maban, Fur, and Koman are three small branches; each comprises one or only a few languages. The remaining branch of the Nilo-Saharan family is Chari-

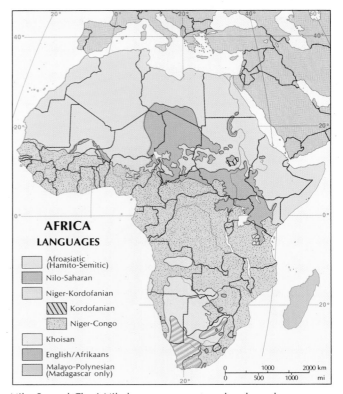

AFRICA LANGUAGES

- Afroasiatic (Hamito-Semitic)
- Nilo-Saharan
- Niger-Kordofanian
- Kordofanian
- Niger-Congo
- Khoisan
- English/Afrikaans
- Malayo-Polynesian (Madagascar only)

Nile. Several Chari-Nile languages, most spoken by only a small number of people, form the Central Sudanic group of languages, which are spoken by people scattered from the vicinity of Lake Chad to the Nile basin. An Eastern Sudanic group primarily includes the Nilotic languages: Dinka, which is spoken by 1 to 2 million people; Nuer and Shilluk in southern Sudan; Achooli and Lwo in Uganda; Nandi and Suk in Kenya; and Masai in northern Tanzania. Each of the Eastern Sudanic languages is spoken by a few hundred thousand people. Two small isolated languages, Berta and Kunama, complete the Chari–Nile branch.

Niger-Kordofanian. The third African language family is the Niger-Kordofanian, the languages of which are spoken in nearly all the areas from Senegal to Kenya, and south to South Africa. Niger-Kordofanian is divided into two subfamilies. The first, Kordofanian, is small and encompasses five branches: Koalib, Teqali, Talodi, Tumtum, and Katla. All are spoken in southern Sudan. None, however, are well known, nor are they spoken by any sizable number of people. The Niger-Congo subfamily, on the other hand, includes a majority of all the languages of Africa.

The Niger-Congo subfamily comprises seven or perhaps eight branches. The Mande branch was apparently the first to diverge from the parent Niger-Congo stock, possibly 6,000 years ago. Mande languages are spoken in a large area of West Africa, from Senegal and Mali to Liberia and Ivory Coast, but they are not spoken along the Atlantic coast, except in Liberia, where about 40,000 people speak Vai. Isolated Mande languages are spoken in eastern Ivory Coast and western Ghana, in Upper Volta, and in Benin and Nigeria. Mandekan is the most widely spoken and most important Mande language. It is better known by the names of its major dialects—Bambara, Maninka or Malinke, and Dyula—and several million people use it. Other important Mande languages are Mende in Sierra Leone and Kpelle in Liberia.

A second branch of Niger-Congo is West Atlantic, which may include two relatively distinct branches of the subfamily—northern and southern; the latter is also called Mel. The major Mel language is Temne, which is spoken by perhaps as many as 500,000 people in Sierra Leone. The northern

West Atlantic languages of the Niger-Congo subfamily include Wolof, which is spoken by about 700,000 people and is the major language of Senegal and its capital city Dakar. Much more widely spoken, however, is Fula (also known as Fulani, Fulfulde, Peuhl), which is used by perhaps 4 to 5 million people. A major Fula concentration is found in northern Guinea. Some 2,400 km (1,500 mi) to the east, in northeastern Nigeria and Cameroon, is another large concentration of Fula speakers. Between these extremes are other permanent Fula settlements, and a great many more Fula speakers are semi-nomadic cattle herdsmen. Several West Atlantic languages are spoken by small groups of people along or near the Atlantic coast from Senegal to Liberia.

The Kru branch of the Niger-Congo subfamily consists of about 30 languages that are spoken in southeastern Liberia and southwestern Ivory Coast. Probably the most widely used is the language known as Krahn in Liberia and as Gueré in Ivory Coast; about 350,000 people use this language. Better known are Bassa, Kru, and Grebo in Liberia, and Bete in Ivory Coast.

The Gur, or Voltaic, branch of Niger-Congo is spoken in interior parts of West Africa, from eastern Mali and northern Ivory Coast through northern Benin. The most widely used Gur language, spoken by about 2 million people, is Mooré in Upper Volta.

Languages of the Kwa branch of Niger-Congo are spoken along the south-facing Atlantic coast from central Ivory Coast to Cameroon, and generally for a few hundred miles inland. Some major Kwa languages are Baule in Ivory Coast; Akan, including Fante, Twi, and Ashanti, in Ghana; Ewe in Ghana, and Togo along with Fon in Benin (the two perhaps constitute a single language); Yoruba, Igbo, and Efik in Nigeria. Yoruba and Igbo are the most widely spoken of these; between 6 and 10 million people speak each.

Languages of the Adamawa-Eastern branch are spoken from northeastern Nigeria east to Sudan, north almost to the Sahara, and south to extreme northern Zaire. In most of this area, these languages are interspersed with Chari-Nile languages of the Nilo-Saharan family; in the extreme west, Chadic languages of the Afroasiatic family are also spoken. Most of the Adamawa–Eastern languages are spoken by a relatively small number of people, and the status of many as distinct languages has not been determined. Zande is spoken by some 700,000 people in northern Zaire and adjacent parts of Sudan and the Central African Empire. Sango, a derivative of Ngbandi in northern Zaire, has become a widespread language of trade and government in the Central African Empire and, to some extent, in Chad.

The Benue-Congo branch of Niger-Congo includes a number of groups of languages in northern and eastern Nigeria, most not widely spoken, and almost all languages of the great southern projection of Africa from Nigeria to northern Kenya to Capetown. The latter are the well-known Bantu languages. Apart from Bantu, the most widely used Benue-Congo language is Tiv in Nigeria; it is spoken by perhaps 1.4 million people. The Bantu languages were long thought to be an independent language family, partly because of the vast area in which they are spoken, the large number of languages that can be considered Bantu, and the large number of their speakers. More than one-third of the most widely used languages in Africa are Bantu languages. In terms of linguistic relationships, however, the Bantu languages are only an enormously overgrown subgroup within the Benue–Congo branch.

Most Bantu language names, as used by their own speakers, consist of a prefix and a stem. What is widely known as "Swahili," for example, is properly KiSwahili; in written references, the stem -Swahili is capitalized, since non-Africans commonly use the stem alone. According to this convention, the following Bantu languages, each spoken by a million or more people, may be distinguished: KiKongo and LiNgala (Zaire); Umbundu (Angola); IsiZulu and IsiXhosa, which are largely mutually intelligible (South Africa); SeSotho, SePedi, Setswana, which are largely mutually intelligible (Lesotho, Botswana, South Africa); ChiShona (Zimbabwe); ChiBemba (Zambia and Zaire); ChiNyanja (Malawi); ShiTswa (Mozam-

bique); KinyaRwanda and KiRundi, which are mutually intelligible (BURUNDI and Rwanda); LuGanda (Uganda); GiKikuyu (Kenya); KiSwahili (Tanzania, Kenya, and, to some extent, Uganda and Zaire). Of these languages, KiSwahili is the most widely spoken; however, for a vast majority of its 20 to 30 million speakers, Swahili is a second language, although they may speak it fluently.

Khoisan. The fourth and smallest language family of Africa is the Khoisan. Most Khoisan languages are spoken by the so-called Bushmen and Hottentots of southern Africa. These peoples include a few cattle-raising groups such as the Nama, totaling perhaps 50,000 speakers, and hunting and gathering groups in the Kalahari Desert of Botswana and Namibia. Many of these are bands of fewer than a hundred speakers of distinct languages. Also included in the Khoisan language family are two languages in northern Tanzania: Sandawe, which is spoken by perhaps 25,000 people, and Hatza, which is spoken by only a few hundred people. The study of language relationships reveals the dramatic and pathetic absorption, dispersion, and isolation of peoples such as most of the Khoisan speakers. Many of the PYGMY groups found in Zaire and Cameroon are thought to be Khoisan peoples who have adopted their neighbors' Niger-Congo languages.

WILLIAM E. WELMERS

Bibliography: Bryan, Margaret A., *The Languages of West Africa* (1952); Greenberg, Joseph H., *The Languages of Africa*, 3d ed. (1970) and *Studies in African Linguistic Classification* (1955); Guthrie, Malcolm, *Comparative Bantu*, 4 vols. (1967–70); International African Institute, *Handbook of African Languages* (1975–   ); Murphy, John D., and Goff, Harry, *A Bibliography of African Languages and Linguistics* (1969); Sebook, Thomas A., ed., *Linguistics in Sub-Saharan Africa* (1971), vol. 7 in *Current Trends in Linguistics*; Tucker, Archibald N., and Bryan, Margaret A., *The Non-Bantu Languages of North-Eastern Africa* (1956); Welmers, William E., *African Language Structures* (1971); Westermann, Diedrich, and Ward, I. C., *Practical Phonetics for Students of African Languages* (1933).

African literature

African literature comprises the oral and written works of the continent, composed in either AFRICAN LANGUAGES or foreign ones. Most formal African literature is still developing distinctive styles. The widespread African oral tradition, however, is rich in folktales, myths, riddles, and proverbs that not only convey an imaginative view of the world but also serve a religious, social, and educational function. The oral tradition has had a significant effect on the written literature. Although some African poetry was written more than a thousand years ago, the majority of African literary works have only been produced in the 20th century, most of them after World War II. Unlike Europe, the Middle East, and parts of Asia, black Africa has no ancient traditions of written literature. The earliest examples are Muslim-inspired religious writings from North Africa. Much of sub-Saharan Africa was illiterate until Christian missionaries arrived in the 19th century. Therefore, little African literature has existed for more than a hundred years; the major exceptions are an Arabic literature in the western Sudan, Swahili literature on the East African coast, and Ge'ez literature in Ethiopia.

AFRICAN LANGUAGE LITERATURES

Linguists estimate that more than a thousand languages and dialects are spoken in Africa. Written, creative literature—novels, short stories, plays, and poetry—has been produced in about 50 of these languages. Because most early works were published by missionary presses, they are heavily imbued with Christian didacticism. The first full-length narratives in Sesotho, Yoruba, and Ibo were modeled on John BUNYAN's 17th-century allegory PILGRIM'S PROGRESS. The first written literature in several other African languages consisted of translated church hymns and retold biblical stories. Later, as more of the population became literate and government agencies began to publish books, newspapers, and magazines in local languages, a secular literature emerged, much of it focusing on problems of personal adjustment to Western ways or modern institutions. Today diverse themes are treated in some African language literature, but topics such as sex and politics are seldom explored, possibly because publication is still strictly censored and controlled by the church and by the state.

The strongest traditions in African-language literatures have developed in southern Africa and those parts of West and East Africa colonized by the British. English colonial policy, which emphasized indirect rule, encouraged Africans to retain some of their institutions and traditions, and looked favorably upon the use of indigenous languages for instructional purposes in elementary schools. The French and Portuguese, by contrast, aimed at assimilating the Africans in their colonies by giving them a Western education and, therefore, did not allow the use of local languages in their schools. As a result, hardly any African-language literature has developed in countries formerly ruled by France and Portugal.

The most important African literary languages are Sesotho, Xhosa, Zulu, and Northern Sotho in southern Africa; Nyanja, Bemba, and Shona in Central Africa; Swahili and Luganda in East Africa; and Yoruba, Asante-Twi, Akuampem-Twi, and Ewe in West Africa. The best-known works from these literatures are Thomas MOFOLO's legendary romance *Chaka the Zulu* (1925; Eng. trans., 1931) and D. O. Fagunwa's folkloric *The Forest of a Thousand Daemons* (1938; Eng. trans., 1968).

AFRICAN LITERATURE IN EUROPEAN LANGUAGES

African literature written in European languages—notably French (Francophone), English (Anglophone), and Portuguese (Lusophone)—is better known outside Africa than are translated works.

French. French-African writing first attracted international attention in the 1930s, when African and Caribbean students in Paris launched a literary and philosophical movement known as NEGRITUDE, which gathered great momentum after World War II. By the late 1940s one of the founders of the movement, the Senegalese poet and statesman Léopold Sédar SENGHOR, had published his first volumes of verse, edited an influential anthology of Negritude poetry, and helped to establish (1947) *Présence Africaine* as the most important literary journal in the black world. As a movement, Negritude was greatly influenced by such European political and artistic movements as MARXISM and SURREALISM and by the Afro-American cultural awakening known as the HARLEM RENAISSANCE. Major figures in the movement include Aimé CÉSAIRE and Léon DAMAS.

The poetry written by advocates of Negritude fused anticolonial political ideas with romantic evocations of an idyllic African past expressed in vivid surrealist images. In the 1950s, as African nations prepared for independence, these highly charged poetic images, which emphasized the humanity of black peoples, gave way to prose that satirized the colonizer and the colonized. Since independence, French-African writers have reexamined the past from a new perspective and have focused on the social and political problems of the present. Negritude is not entirely dead in French-African writing, but most young authors now regard it as passé. Other influential French-African writers include Mongo BETI, CAMARA LAYE, Birago DIOP, David DIOP, Ferdinand OYONO, Jean Joseph RABEARIVELO, and Tchicaya U Tam'si.

English. The English-African literary movement emerged later than the French, but in recent years has become as mature. The first major works in West Africa appeared in the 1950s at the end of the colonial era and were primarily concerned with reinterpreting African history from an indigenous point of view that stressed the dignity of the African past. Chinua ACHEBE's novel *Things Fall Apart* (1958) documents the disintegration of a rural community under the impact of Westernization and is a classic statement of this archetypal theme. Another celebrated classic is Amos TUTUOLA's *The Palm-Wine Drunkard* (1952). After independence, the literary emphasis in West Africa changed from a preoccupation with the past to a confrontation with the present. Wole SOYINKA, Achebe, and Ayi Kwei Armah wrote bitter satires aimed at contemporary evils in their own societies, and in recent years Nigerian poets, novelists, and dramatists have described the horrors of the Nigerian-Biafran war. The distant past is no longer a major concern.

Writers in Anglophone East Africa followed those of Anglophone West Africa in first producing anticolonial fiction and then self-critical, satirical fiction and drama. The early works of Kenya's leading novelist, NGUGIWA Thiong'o, express nationalistic enthusiasm, but his later fiction is characterized by deep postindependence disillusionment. The East African literary scene is distinguished from that of West Africa by its poetry, particularly the style of comic singing introduced by OKOT P'BITEK in *Song of Lawino* (1966). P'Bitek and his followers have used a popular, humorous idiom to express serious social and political ideas.

In South Africa, creative writing in English by blacks and by Coloureds (racially mixed South Africans) has been impeded by racial oppression and censorship. The novelist Peter ABRAHAMS found conditions so repressive that he left South Africa in 1939 at the age of 20 and has lived ever since in England and Jamaica. In the 1950s the emergence of magazines designed for nonwhite readers led to a spurt of short-story writing, which practically ceased when the harsh Publications and Entertainments Act of 1963, the first of many such censorship laws, severely limited popular and political publications alike. The most talented African writers left South Africa in the mid-1960s and turned to writing autobiographies, fiction, and poetry. A promising poetry movement began in South Africa in 1971 with the publication of Oswald Mtshali's obliquely militant *Sounds from a Cowhide Drum*, but by the mid-1970s even poetry was being banned in South Africa. Many poets have been imprisoned, and many others have left the country. Although the literary attempts of South African blacks, Coloureds, and other nonwhites have been severely thwarted, those of white South Africans writing in English and Afrikaans have met with more success. Among the best known of these authors are Roy CAMPBELL, Athol FUGARD, Nadine GORDIMER, Alan PATON, and Olive Schreiner.

Portuguese. Portuguese-African literature appeared earlier than the African literature written in French and English, but it is not as well known outside Africa. Poetry has been the favorite literary form in Portuguese-speaking areas of Africa since the 19th century, but strong short-story movements emerged in Angola and Mozambique in the 1950s. Anticolonial political themes dominated much recent literary work until the mid-1970s, when Angola, Mozambique, and Guinea-Bissau achieved independence. Now writers in Lusophone Africa, like their counterparts in Francophone and Anglophone Africa, are no longer concerned with white European models but base their work on indigenous African themes.

BERNTH LINDFORS

Bibliography: Blair, Dorothy, *African Literature in French* (1976); Dathorne, O. R., *African Literature in the Twentieth Century* (1976) and *The Black Mind: A History of African Literature* (1974); Gérard, Albert S., *Four African Literatures: Xhosa, Sotho, Zulu, Amharic* (1971); Hamilton, Russell G., *Voices from an Empire: A History of Afro-Portuguese Literature* (1975); Jahn, Janheinz, *A History of Neo-African Literature*, trans. by Oliver Coburn and Ursulu Lehrburger (1968); Kariara, Jonathan, and Kitonga, Ellen, eds., *An Introduction to East African Poetry* (1977); Roscoe, Adrian A., *Mother is Gold: A Study in West African Literature* (1971) and *Uhuru's Fire: African Literature East to South* (1977); Wauthier, Claude, *The Literature and Thought of Modern Africa: A Survey*, trans. by Shirley Kay (1975); Wright, Edgar, ed., *The Critical Evaluation of African Literature* (1977).

See also: AFRICAN LANGUAGES; AFROASIATIC LANGUAGES.

African music

The many music cultures of Africa may be broadly classified as North African and sub-Saharan. This article discusses only traditional music of the dominant population south of the Sahara, as North African culture is essentially Islamic or Arabic. The diversity of this population is reflected both in the number of languages spoken—about 800 to 1,000—and in the wide variety of music traditions cultivated. Fortunately, these traditions have many traits in common, permitting a discussion of them in general terms.

MUSICAL INSTRUMENTS

Africa probably has the largest variety of drums to be found in any continent, but virtually every other type of musical

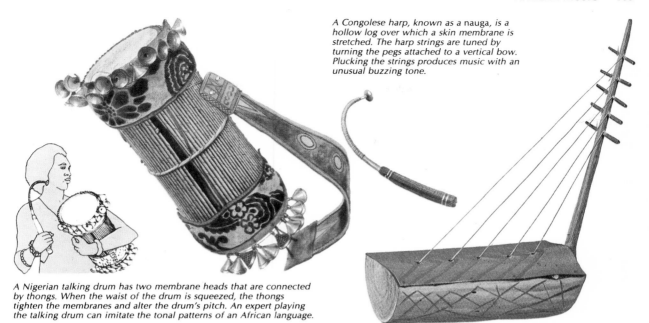

A Congolese harp, known as a nauga, is a hollow log over which a skin membrane is stretched. The harp strings are tuned by turning the pegs attached to a vertical bow. Plucking the strings produces music with an unusual buzzing tone.

A Nigerian talking drum has two membrane heads that are connected by thongs. When the waist of the drum is squeezed, the thongs tighten the membranes and alter the drum's pitch. An expert playing the talking drum can imitate the tonal patterns of an African language.

instrument is also represented throughout Africa.

Some distinctively African instruments, however, are unique to the continent. Of the drums, the most characteristically African are those known as "talking drums" because they can reproduce the tonal inflections and rhythms of African languages. Their musical potential is also fully realized. The western African hourglass drum is the most versatile talking drum. Squeezing the lacing between the two heads produces PITCHES that can vary more than an octave. Another is the slit drum, made from a hollowed log on which two tones are produced by striking on either side of a longitudinal slot.

Of the myriad types of rattle, the western African net rattle, made of a handle gourd encased in a beaded net, is unique. The Yoruba *shekere* of Nigeria has a tight net, and the loose net on the Mende *shegbule* of Sierra Leone is held taut by the player. Because of the external beads, precise rhythms can be played on both these versions of the net rattle.

XYLOPHONES, widespread in Africa, are of two basic types. The frame xylophone, such as those played by the MANDÉ and Lobi of West Africa, the FANG of Cameroon, and the Chopi of Mozambique, has gourd resonators hung beneath each key. The loose-key xylophone, such as the Ganda *amadinda* of Uganda, is left unassembled when not in use; when played, the keys are laid across two banana stems.

As widespread as the xylophone, and unique to African and African-derived cultures, is the *mbira*, which consists of flat iron strips mounted on a board or box with one end of each strip left free to be plucked by the thumbs or thumbs and forefingers.

The simplest of the many stringed instruments found throughout Africa is the musical BOW, resonated with a gourd or with the mouth of the player. ZITHERS and HARPS are common in eastern and central Africa, and the LYRE, which has a hemispherical or rectangular body and two arms extending to a crossbar where the strings are attached, is played in Ethiopia and Uganda.

In western Africa the most common stringed instrument is the skin-covered LUTE, either boat-shaped with two to five plucked strings or hemispherical with one bowed string.

Three stringed instruments unique to Africa are the bridge harp (or harp lute), the harp zither, and the bow lute. The best-known form of the bridge harp is the 21-string Manding *kora* of western Africa. It is held facing the player, who plucks two planes of strings mounted in notches on either side of a high bridge. The harp zither, best known as the Fang *mvet* of

Cameroon, also has a notched bridge that is mounted in the center of its long tubular body. The bow lute, such as the Bambara *ndang*, is plucked and has an individual curved neck for each string.

The FLUTES of Africa are of every type except the RECORDER. In eastern, central, and southern Africa, groups of musicians play sets of single-note vertical pipes, each person contributing a single note to create a complex polyphonic texture. Panpipes are also played in this area. Of the various reed instruments of Africa, the most notable is the Hausa *algaita* of Nigeria, a short conical-bore double reed. African TRUMPETS include the *kakaki*, a straight herald trumpet of tin associated with Hausa aristocracy, but the most typical African trumpets are made of natural animal horns, ivory, or hollowed wood and are played in sets in the same manner as the single-note vertical pipes.

MUSICIANS

Music is closely integrated into everyday activities in Africa. Vocal music, instrumental music, and dance are often inseparable, and the emphasis is on participation rather than on performance before an audience. Even in traditions where professionalism or virtuosity does result in a distinction between performer and audience, the audience often dances to show its appreciation.

The role and status of a musician in Africa vary widely and are determined in part by the social and political structure of the community. In egalitarian societies that are organized into small political units and that are composed of individuals generally involved in the same activities such as hunting, herding, or farming, a musician has no special status. Still, particularly talented instrumentalists or persons who are adept at leading vocal ensembles will become known for their abilities and will be called upon to perform at all musical occasions.

In those societies in which a high degree of political organization exists, in which royal courts once flourished, and in which craft specialization has developed, the role of the musician is more clearly defined and distinct. For example, in the West African savanna, complex hierarchical societies grew hand in hand with the great empires of the 10th to 20th centuries, and musicianship and such related skills as oratory, historical narrative, genealogy, and stylized praise developed into a hereditary profession.

Today, descendants of these empires still largely regard music and related activities as the exclusive province of particu-

Members of a Hausa instrumental ensemble from northern Nigeria play the duma (1), the obodo (2), the gangi (3), the goge (4), the shantu (5), the sarewa (6), and the silver flute (7). The duma is a spherical drum made from a hollow gourd over which a skin is stretched. The musician beats the drum with one hand and a slightly bent stick. The obodo is a talking drum that has a wide tonal range. It is played with a narrow, curved stick. The gangi is a drum made from a calabash gourd. It is held against the musician's chest and beaten with two sticks. The goge is a lute-type instrument played with a bow. The soundboard is made of a calabash gourd and crocodile skin. The shantu, a horn instrument, is made from various sizes of gourds that are joined together with cow skin. When it is blown, a buzzing sound is produced. The sarewa is a flute made of bamboo and a cow's horn. A silver flute has a chain hanging from its bell, which affects the resonance.

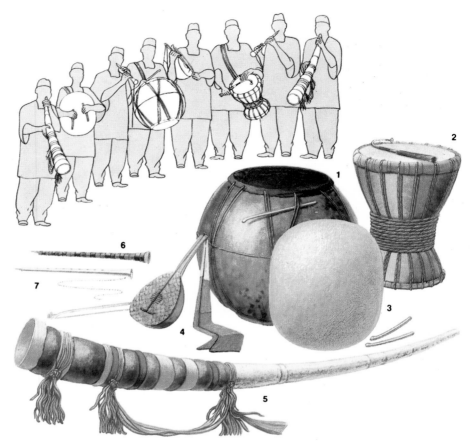

lar families. Although present-day musicians (known as *griots*) in these societies no longer perform at the courts of kings, they still direct much of their attention to the wealthy and influential, encouraging historical awareness through their commemorative songs. Their role is important, and their status is similar to that of professional experts anywhere. These musicians are highly respected for their knowledge and abilities and are valued for their role in ceremonies and festivities. At the same time, they are regarded with a degree of caution, because of the potential power of their words and actions. The privileges afforded members of the profession often include the right to criticize or make moral judgments.

FUNCTION AND PERFORMANCE

As in all parts of the world today, the live performance of music in Africa is threatened by the ever-increasing popularity of transistor radios, cassette tape recorders, and other sources of recorded sound. Still, the participatory nature of most African music and its close association with dance assure the continuance of live performances for many occasions.

The music for these occasions may be broadly classified as either daily or festive. Daily music includes all types of children's songs and game music, lullabies, songs to accompany tedious chores or to synchronize work, songs for personal enjoyment, and many types of music designed primarily for mass entertainment, such as social dances or dramatic performances staged by traveling troupes. Festive music is closely linked to special events in the human life cycle, such as births, initiations, weddings, and funerals, and to special national, religious, and agricultural events. The elaborate and spectacular masked dances for which Africa is famous are usually associated with such festivities.

In some societies another category of festive music is associated with particular individuals rather than with events. The festivity is generated by the mere presence of the musician,

usually a professional, who sings songs of commemoration and praise for a given patron. These praise songs serve to verify the claim to greatness of various leaders and heroes, both past and present. In the hierarchical societies this genre of song is still important as it serves to establish and maintain the necessary rapport between leaders and populace.

Allied to the praise song are the historical song and its extension, the epic narrative. Both are common in various parts of Africa, and in both a story is told with musical accompaniment. Songs are incorporated at appropriate points in the story to depict particular scenes. A more popular version of this type is the story-song, in which the content is not necessarily true but often incorporates a well-known FABLE or other entertaining story. The story-song is a vehicle for moral teaching and entertainment.

Whether daily or festive, almost all African music plays a strong socializing role. Annoyances and jealousies are often vented in extemporized, obliquely stated song texts, which, if sung within hearing of the offender, can achieve the desired effect. Work-synchronizing songs promote efficiency and together with those calendrical events in which everyone takes part, contribute to a feeling of group solidarity. Music and instruments associated with royalty or leadership command respect. In the past, some societies even regarded royal instruments as the seat of the king's power; if they were captured by enemies, it marked the downfall of the kingdom.

STYLISTIC TRAITS

In general, the sound of African music may be characterized as polyphonic (see POLYPHONY). Vocal-instrumental combinations are as common as purely instrumental music, and in all types of music a predilection for the combination of melodic and rhythmic sounds is apparent.

Nearly all melodic instruments of Africa (including many drums) have a device that provides a percussive rhythmic accompaniment.

The stylistic trait for which African music is most famous is rhythmic organization. Although individual parts in some performances may be extremely complex rhythmically, in most instances rhythmic complexity is created by the manner in which the relatively simple rhythms of individual parts are combined. This combination is often effected in such a way that the accent patterns of each part run counter to each other, creating a composite rhythm or melody that no single part can play alone (see musical example).

African melodies are built on scales of five, six, and seven tones, and the intervals used are sufficiently close to Western scales to sound familiar and appealing. In addition, multipart music often employs the harmonic intervals of thirds, fourths, and fifths. The melodic style of instrumental music is based on a short repeated phrase (ostinato) that is subjected to minute but continuous VARIATION with occasional breaks for longer improvised passages. Vocal lines may also be short but are often extremely long and complex. A descending melodic line is common, reflecting the tonal nature of many African languages (see musical example).

The formal structure of most African music is based on the ostinato. In some performances several different ostinatos may be repeated in various sequences at the discretion of the performer.

The ostinato form is used in vocal music as well, but it is usually modified by the addition of a solo part inserted between repetitions of the unchanging chorus part. The potentials for variation of this basic form are exploited to the fullest throughout the continent. An overriding stylistic trait of African music is its ability to generate an engaging mood and active involvement in the performance.   RODERIC KNIGHT

Bibliography: Berliner, Paul, *The Soul of Mbira* (1979); Blacking, John, *Venda Children's Songs* (1967); *Essays for a Humanist: An Offering to Klaus Wachsmann* (1977); Brandel, Rose, *The Music of Central Africa* (1961); Knight, Roderic, "Music in Africa: The Manding Contexts," in *Performance Practice: Ethnomusicological Perspectives* (in press); Nketia, J. H. Kwabena, *The Music of Africa* (1974); Wachsmann, Klaus, ed., *Essays on Music and History in Africa* (1971); Warren, Fred, *The Music of Africa* (1970); Waterman, Richard, "African Influence on the Music of the Americas," in *Mother Wit from the Laughing Barrel*, ed. by Alan Dundes (1973).

See also: AFRICAN ART; AMERICAN MUSIC; ARABIAN MUSIC; JAZZ; PERCUSSION INSTRUMENTS; PIPE AND TABOR; POLYPHONY; SONG; STRINGED INSTRUMENTS; WIND INSTRUMENTS.

African prehistory

African prehistory encompasses the vast span of time before the practice of making written records began in Africa. The greater part of the continent's history lies within the realm of prehistory and can only be ascertained through ARCHAEOLOGY, HISTORICAL LINGUISTICS and related disciplines, and oral traditions (as far as they will reach back in time and only to the point where they are reliable).

The field of African prehistory is of special importance because more than 90 percent of the evidence concerning human origins has thus far come from Africa. Consequently, during the past 20 years archaeological research in Africa has been part of a massive, fast-moving investigative campaign that has involved many disciplines and research tools and a large, dedicated body of scientists.

PREHISTORIC ARCHAEOLOGY IN AFRICA

The acquisition of an abnormally large number of finds from a particular area may merely reflect an extremely thorough investigation. On the other hand, it may reflect a genuine pattern from the past. Grounds now exist for believing that it was in eastern Africa from Ethiopia to the Transvaal, where more early hominid fossils have been found than anywhere

The Mandinka song (top), written in a recitative style with a long vocal line, demonstrates the descending profile common to much African music. The Mandinka drum rhythm (bottom) illustrates the complexity that results from an integration of two separate drum melodies.

A Mandinka song in recitative style

A Mandinka drum rhythm combination

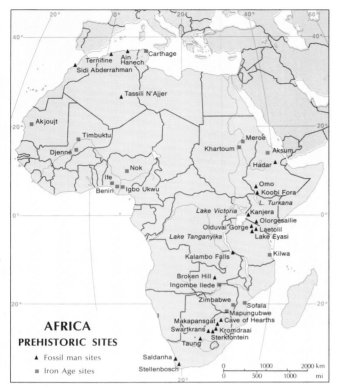

AFRICA
PREHISTORIC SITES

▲ Fossil man sites
■ Iron Age sites

(Above) *The locator map of prehistoric Africa indicates sites where fossilized hominid remains and major centers of Iron Age culture have been unearthed. Because of the continent's favorable conditions for the preservation of archaeological materials, considerable evidence relating to human origins and culture comes from these excavations.*

else in the world, that early MAN evolved out of the common ancestry he shares with the apes.

Apparently, Old World apes and monkeys evolved in Africa during a time when the continent was an island. Then, about 20–15 million years ago, CONTINENTAL DRIFT joined it to Asia in its northeastern part, and apes and monkeys appeared in southern Asia for the first time. The extinct genus DRYOPITHE-CUS ranged over the tropical regions of Africa and Asia, which were then more widely forested than today. With the final shrinking of the Tethys Sea that lay between the two continents, many of these forested areas became savanna or grassland. About 14 million years ago, a new type of ape appeared, RAMAPITHECUS, better adapted to such conditions although still associated with forest.

The Fossil Record. A number of archaeologists consider Ramapithecus the earliest known ancestor of man. Specimens have been found in Europe and East Africa, but the greatest number are from southern Asia. It now appears that this area was the locus of man's most important evolutionary developments. The fossil record between 8 and 5 million years ago is incomplete, but apparently bipedalism, the ability to walk upright, was developed during this period. By about 3 million years ago the changed environmental conditions sparked a burst of evolutionary activity, and in eastern Africa remains have been found of a number of bipedal hominids adapted to open country. Important finds have been made in the Afar and the OMO Valley in Ethiopia, on the shores of Lake Turkana in Kenya, in OLDUVAI GORGE and LAETOLIL in Tanzania, and in South Africa at MAKAPANSGAT, STERKFONTEIN, TAUNG, Kromdraai, and Swartkrans.

These upright-moving hominids included two species of AUSTRALOPITHECUS—*Australopithecus robustus* and *Australopithecus africanus*—and the creature called HOMO HABILIS. *Australopithecus robustus*, as well as being larger and more massive than the slender, gracile *A. africanus*, had enormous molar teeth adapted to a hard, coarse vegetable diet; the dentition of both *A. africanus* and *H. habilis* seems to have been better adapted to an omnivorous diet. The separate taxonomic status of *Homo habilis* and the question whether *A. africanus* could have been in the direct line of human ances-

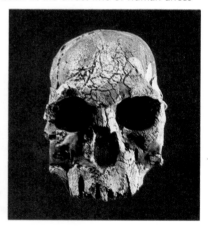

(Above) *Skull 1470, believed to be the oldest "complete" hominid skull in existence, was discovered in 1972 by a fossil-hunting team near Lake Turkana, in Kenya. Dating by the potassium-argon method indicates an age of more than 2.6 million years.*

(Left) *Famed British anthropologists Louis and Mary Leakey gaze out over Olduvai Gorge in northern Tanzania, the site of their discovery of 1.8 million-year-old Homo habilis, or "tool-using man." The Leakeys' excavations of fossilized hominid remains in the region have advanced the idea that the earliest ancestors of the human species evolved on the African continent.*

try have been subjects of unresolved debate.

It is also not clear which of these creatures were toolmakers and tool users. More than one type of hominid has been found in the deposits yielding the earliest recognizable stone artifacts, dating from around 2 million years ago. The sites of the deposits are at East Turkana, in the Shungura Formation of the Lower Omo Valley, and in Bed I at Olduvai Gorge.

Homo habilis is considered by a number of archaeologists as probably the earliest toolmaker. The earliest stone tools, rough choppers, are called OLDOWAN after Olduvai Gorge. Although there is some overlap, they were succeeded, about 1 million years ago, by tools of a more developed type, characterized by their bifacial manufacture—oval or pointed-oval stones carefully chipped over both faces to a regular pattern.

Some bifaces, also called handaxes, have a straight chisel-like cutting edge at one end and are known as cleavers. Such collections of stone tools are called ACHEULEAN (after St. Acheul in France, where they were first recognized). Acheulean tools are commonly associated with a more advanced type of hominid, HOMO ERECTUS. This hominid species succeeded in "breaking out" of East Africa and spreading Acheulean tools over southern Eurasia, as well as other parts of Africa. In some areas, however, *Homo erectus* seems to have maintained the chopping-tool tradition.

Homo erectus had a brain about twice the size of the australopithecines but only two-thirds that of modern man. Sites in Africa associated with *H. erectus* remains or early Acheulean tools include Sidi Abderrahman in Morocco; Ternifine in Algeria; Melka Kontoure in Ethiopia; Peninj in Kenya; and Swartkrans, Vereeniging, Sterkfontein, and Stellenbosch in South Africa. Later Acheulean sites are widespread in Africa, including parts of what is now the Sahara but was then not a desert. Important sites have been investigated at AÏN HANECH in Algeria, OLORGESAILIE and Olduvai Gorge in Kenya, KALAMBO FALLS in Zambia, Kamoa in Zaire, and the Cave of Hearths in South Africa.

Middle Stone Age in Africa. The Acheulean tool industry persisted for a long time, until 100,000 to 50,000 years ago, but thereafter an increasing regionalized specialization occurred, first into the industries called Fauresmith in southern Africa and Sangoan in central and western Africa, and later into those of the African Middle Stone Age. The human type in Africa was then comparable to that of the NEANDERTHALERS of Europe and western Asia and includes the fossils of BROKEN HILL MAN in Zambia and Saldanha man in South Africa.

Much greater regional diversity began to occur in the Middle Stone Age. More and more specialized tool industries developed as different groups of the growing population adapted their way of life to a greater variety of ecological niches. Hunting, fishing, and gathering remained the basic way of life, but a greater variety of strategies was employed in exploiting the resources of different environments. The Acheuleans had a wooden thrusting spear, which later was made more lethal with a stone point, and many of the Middle Stone Age peoples had a light stone-tipped throwing spear. *Homo sapiens sapiens* (modern man) was now the human type throughout Africa, and by the beginning of the late Stone Age used the bow and arrow and made composite tools of wood, stone, and bone.

Late Stone Age in Africa. In northwest Africa, the Aterian (c.40,000–25,000 BC), an advanced tool industry of the Middle Stone Age, was succeeded by the Oranian (c.14,000–8,000 BC) and Capsian (c.7,000–4,000 BC) tool cultures. South of the Sahara the Late Stone Age seems to have begun at dates ranging from 40,000 to 10,000 BC in different areas. Small shaped-stone artifacts, known as microliths—some of which were slotted into arrow shafts to make the points and barbs—indicate that in these communities hunting was an important economic activity. Gathering the products of the wild was also important, although it usually leaves less obvious traces in the archaeological record.

As population increased, different communities exploited an even greater range of environments and devised more specialized techniques for dealing with them. Seasonal movement was often involved, and in Nubia and in areas near the

| ■ Mainly stone-axe industries | — Living sites |
| ■ Pebble tool industries | |

(Above) *A cutaway drawing of Olduvai Gorge, the site of celebrated archaeological excavations, reveals the levels at which habitation sites of early humanlike creatures have been discovered. The gorge, in northern Tanzania, cuts through numerous layers of lake and volcanic sediment. Anthropological studies of these layers have yielded a wealth of information regarding human evolution.*

Oldowan tools, named for the archaeological finds at Olduvai Gorge, are little more than chipped stone. The hominids who fashioned these crude implements lived more than a million years ago.

Nile Valley in Egypt, evidence indicates that wild grain was extensively collected. Nubian cemeteries dating from 10,000 BC contain bodies pierced by stone arrow-points, which suggests intercommunity warfare.

From the 6th to the 4th millennium BC, the southern Sahara and the Sahel were considerably wetter than at present and supported communities that depended on fish from lakes and rivers for a considerable part of their diet. This way of life extended into the north part of the Great Lakes area of East Africa. Dependence on such aquatic resources would seem to imply at least a semisedentary type of existence.

Animal and Plant Domestication. The central Sahara was also wetter than at present, and the highlands in particular supported large numbers of cattle pastoralists. The cattle, widely portrayed in prehistoric rock art, may have been derived from an indigenous domestication of the wild North African ox or from cattle introduced via Tunisia or Egypt. The culture of these pastoralists and fishing peoples is sometimes referred to as the Saharan Neolithic.

By the 5th millennium BC, people in the lower Nile Valley adopted cereal agriculture, using the Nile floodwaters to irrigate their crops of wheat and barley. In sub-Saharan Africa, which lies in the summer rainfall area, it is impossible to grow wheat and barley by dry-farming methods. Therefore, local wild grasses had to be domesticated to form the African tropical cereals known today: the millets (Guinea corn, or sorghum; pearl, or bulrush; millet; finger millet); African rice; fonio; chindumba; and the tiny Ethiopian grain called teff. These were domesticated in different areas of a broad zone stretching south of the Sahara from Senegal to Ethiopia and down into the northern Great Lakes area of East Africa.

From the beginning of the 3d millennium BC the Sahara began to dry up. The fishing populations must have found that the stands of wild grasses that they also depended on became thinner and harder to find, which probably stimulated the process of cereal domestication. Whatever the reason, domestication first occurred in the zone across Africa where they lived. Goats, sheep, and pigs must have been introduced into the rest of Africa from its northeast corner.

BRONZE AGE AND IRON AGE AFRICA

Most of sub-Saharan Africa missed out on a BRONZE AGE and passed directly, at different times in different areas, from the Stone Age into the IRON AGE. Apparently only in Nubia and in the extreme west, in Mauritania, was there a period during which copper was exploited for tools and weapons before the advent of an iron technology. At Akjoujt, Mauritania, copper ores were exploited in the 5th century BC, and numerous copper arrowheads and other weapons and tools have been found in the surrounding area. It is not known whether the metallurgy practiced at Akjoujt gave rise to an iron technology or whether this knowledge was introduced to sub-Saharan West Africa from the area of North Africa influenced by CARTHAGE on the northeast coast or from the Nubian kingdom of MEROË on the Nile.

The city of Carthage was founded at the end of the 9th century BC by settlers from the Levant. Iron was commonly used for tools and weapons in this area before it was so used (after 600 BC) in Egypt. In Meroë, an African kingdom independent from but much influenced by Egypt, iron smelting was practiced on a large scale by the 4th century BC. Iron-smelting furnaces of about the same date in central Nigeria are associated with the Nok people, who produced the remarkable terra-cotta heads for which the Nok culture is famous. By the early 2d century AD, Meroë had been surpassed in importance by the newly emergent power of AKSUM. This kingdom was founded farther to the east in the highlands of present-day Ethiopia by Semitic-speakers who had earlier come from southern Arabia.

By this time there were long-established farming communities throughout the savanna lands. In the forests of the eastern part of West Africa food production had also been established, presumably based on yams, tuberous crops, and oil-palm products. In the central parts of eastern Nigeria and in Cameroon, people speaking a language ancestral to the BANTU group of languages apparently began to move eastward through the savanna lands and northern forest margins of what is today the Central African Empire. In their migration they reached the northeast angle of the equatorial rain forest, where they turned southward. What generated this movement is not yet known; data are insufficient to demonstrate a population explosion as the stimulus, although this is the most commonly offered explanation.

Another group from the same homeland area in southern Cameroon apparently reached the savanna lands south of the equatorial forest, either by traveling along the coast or along Zaire River tributaries, at a somewhat later date. These eastern and western streams of Bantu interacted and dispersed in complex ways over the rest of southern Africa as far as a line from Windhoek to Port Alfred. Much of this area had been inhabited by hunter-gatherer Khoisan-speaking peoples, among them the SAN (Bushmen). In some places the Khoisan-speakers survived and were able to maintain their way of life alongside the Bantu-speaking farmers; in others they were driven out or absorbed. In West Africa, a similar stone technology appears to have remained in use for more than a thousand years after iron was first used in other places.

Where a population of settled peasants remains over a long period, towns and other kinds of centralized institutions tend to become established. The stimulus for this development is not the same in all areas. A number of potentially conducive circumstances sometimes work together and sometimes work in isolation, and historical or geographical accident may determine the pace. Two situations in sub-Saharan Africa combined to delay centralization. First, Africa's indigenous cereal grains had to be domesticated. Unlike Egypt and Europe, Africa could not, for climatic reasons, accommodate the grain grasses that were domesticated in southwest Asia. Second, just when the urban arts were being developed in Egypt, the desiccation of the 3d millennium BC changed the Sahara from a broad grassland corridor into a desert barrier.

Nevertheless, towns did emerge in a number of widely separated places. With the Arab conquest of North Africa in the 7th century, long-distance trading was injected into localized exchange networks south of the Sahara. This development further stimulated both the growth of urbanized communities and the centralization of political power.

The ancient kingdom of GHANA prospered as middleman in the gold trade between the West African forests and the Islamic world and was succeeded by the kingdoms of MALI and SONGHAI. The state Bono Manso was based on the same trade

(Below) *A bronze head produced by the lost-wax method illustrates the high quality of metalwork in 13th-century Ife, Nigeria.*

(Above) *Prehistoric rock paintings at Tassili n' Ajjer, in the Algerian Sahara, are believed to have been made about 3000 BC. Animals and agricultural activities portrayed in the artworks indicate that the region had a wetter climate before the Sahara Desert expanded southward.*

with Begho as the collecting point for gold on the way to the great market center of Djenné. The center of political power later moved into the forest itself when the ASHANTI established power. BENIN, IFE, and Igbo-Ukwu were other important West African centers of wealth and remarkable artistic achievement.

Another route by which the Islamic and Indian world obtained the tropical African products they desired, above all ivory, was by sea from the East African coast. Beginning about the 9th century, voyagers from the Persian Gulf, and later from northwest India, were able to take advantage of the monsoon winds in the Indian Ocean and establish a string of entrepôts from the Somali coast as far south as Sofala, of which the most important and the best investigated is KILWA. The great fortified center of ZIMBABWE prospered in the 14th century as a result of its middleman position in this trade.

THURSTAN SHAW

Bibliography: Clark, J. Desmond, ed., *Atlas of African Prehistory* (1967) and *The Prehistory of Africa* (1970); Davidson, Basil, *Africa,* rev. ed. (1972); Leakey, Louis S., *Progress and Evolution of Man in Africa* (1961) and *Stone Age Africa* (1936); Oliver, Roland A., and Fagan, Brian M., *Africa in the Iron Age* (1975); Phillipson, D. W., *The Later Prehistory of Eastern and Southern Africa* (1977); Shaw, Thurstan, "The Prehistory of West Africa," in *History of West Africa,* ed. by J. F. Ade Ajayi and Michael Crowder (1976).

See also: AFRICA, HISTORY OF.

African universities

University education in Africa was extremely limited before World War II. With the exceptions of South Africa, a few centers of Islamic studies in North Africa, and Egypt (discussed in MIDDLE EASTERN UNIVERSITIES), only a few specialized postsecondary schools existed to train civil servants, ministers, or physicians. Most African universities were founded between 1945 and 1970, and few became full-scale universities until their countries gained independence from colonial rulers.

In general, a version of the French educational model prevails in the former French colonies of West Africa, and a British model has been the most common point of departure in East Africa. These models have been modified in various ways since independence, and both tend to be state systems with advancement based on competitive examinations.

Countries such as Zaire (the former Belgian Congo) or Ethi-

(Above) *A royal burial at 9th-century Igbo-Ukwu, near the Niger River delta, is re-created in an artist's rendering. The seated corpse was decorated with intricate copper ornaments and flanked by bronze artifacts. The deceased nobleman's slaves were then buried atop the sealed sepulcher.*

(Right) *The fortress of Great Zimbabwe, in southern Zimbabwe (Rhodesia), was the center of the 15th-century empire of Mwanamutapa. The site, one of several scattered throughout southern Africa, is built of granite slabs and covers 20 h (60 acres). At the height of its influence, Zimbabwe was a major center of the east African gold trade.*

AFRICAN UNIVERSITIES*

University and Location (Language of Instruction)	Date Founded	Enrollment	University and Location (Language of Instruction)	Date Founded	Enrollment
Algeria			University of Jos (English)	1975	3,700
University of Algiers (Arabic, French)	1879	17,000	University of Lagos (English)	1962	8,000
University of Sciences and Technology of Algiers (Arabic, French)	1974	8,500	University of Nigeria, Nsukka (English)	1960	9,900
			University of Port Harcourt (English)	1975	2,000
University of Constantine (Arabic, French)	1961	8,500	**Senegal**		
University of Oran (Arabic, French)	1965	9,000	University of Dakar, Dakar-Fann (French)	1949	11,700
University of Setif (Arabic, French)	1978	1,400	**Sierra Leone**		
Angola			University of Sierra Leone, Freetown (English)	1967	2,300
University of Angola, Launda (Portuguese)	1962	3,100	**Somalia**		
Benin			Somalia National University, Mogadishu (Somali, Italian, English, Arabic)	1954	3,700
National University of Benin, Cotonou (French)	1970	2,600	**South Africa†**		
Cameroon			University of Cape Town[1] (English)	1829	11,000
University of Yaoundé (English, French)	1962	10,000	University of Fort Hare,[2] Ciskei (English)	1916	2,400
People's Republic of the Congo			University of Durban-Westville,[3] Durban (English)	1960	4,900
University of Marien-Ngouabi, Brazzaville (French)	1961	7,400	University of Natal,[1] Durban and Pietermaritzburg (English)	1910	9,000
Ethiopia			University of the North,[4] Pietersburg (Afrikaans, English)	1959	2,200
University of Addis Ababa (English)	1950	11,200	University of the Orange Free State,[1] Bloemfontein (Afrikaans)	1855	8,300
Ghana			University of Port Elizabeth[1] (Afrikaans, English)	1964	3,000
University of Ghana, Legon (English)	1948	3,700	Potchefstroom University for Christian Higher Education[1] (Afrikaans)	1869	6,700
University of Science and Technology, Kumasi (English)	1951	3,100	University of Pretoria[1] (Afrikaans)	1908	16,700
University of Cape Coast (English)	1962	1,500	Rand Afrikaans University,[1] Johannesburg (Afrikaans)	1966	5,200
Ivory Coast			Rhodes University,[1] Grahamstown (English)	1904	2,900
National University of the Ivory Coast, Abidjan (French)	1958	12,800	University of South Africa,[5] Pretoria (Afrikaans, English)	1873	56,000
Kenya			University of Stellenbosch[1] (Afrikaans)	1881	12,100
University of Nairobi (English)	1956	6,800	University of the Western Cape,[6] Belleville (Afrikaans, English)	1960	3,500
Liberia			University of the Witwatersrand,[1] Johannesburg (English)	1921	14,200
University of Liberia, Monrovia (English)	1862	3,200	University of Zululand,[7] Natal (English)	1960	2,500
Libya			**Tanzania**		
University of Garyounis, Benghazi (Arabic, English)	1955	9,400	University of Dar es Salaam (English)	1961	2,700
Alfateh University, Tripoli (Arabic, English)	1973	7,500	**Togo**		
Malawi			University of Benin, Lomé (French)	1965	3,700
University of Malawi, Zomba (English)	1964	1,700	**Tunisia**		
Morocco			University of Tunis (Arabic, French)	1960	29,600
Hassan II University, Casablanca (Arabic, French)	1976	11,600	**Uganda**		
Mohammed Ben Abdellah University, Fez (Arabic, French)	1973	9,900	Makerere University, Kampala (English)	1922	4,800
Mohammed V University, Rabat (Arabic, French)	1957	39,000	**Zaire**		
Quaraouyine University, Fez (Arabic, French)	859	1,600	National University of Zaire, Kinshasa (French)	1954	‡
Nigeria			**Zambia**		
Ahmadu Bello University, Zaria (English)	1962	15,700	University of Zambia, Lusaka (English)	1965	3,200
Bayero University, Kano (English)	1975	2,500	**Zimbabwe**		
University of Benin, Benin City (English)	1970	4,000	University of Zimbabwe, Harare (English)	1955	2,500
University of Calabar (English)	1975	2,800			
University of Ibadan (English)	1948	8,500			
University of Ife, Ile-Ife (English)	1961	8,700			
University of Ilorin (English)	1976	2,100			

*Only institutions with more than 1,000 students are listed. Enrollment figures are approximate and from the early 1980s. Dates of foundation are the original ones, although there may have been subsequent changes of status or name.

†In accordance with its official policy of apartheid, South Africa maintains a racially segregated educational system. University admission is restricted on the following bases: [1]Whites only; [2]Xhosa peoples; [3]Indians and Whites only; [4]Sotho, Tsonga, Tswana, and Venda peoples; [5]multiracial correspondence and examining institution; [6]Coloureds (mixed descent) only; [7]Zulu and Swazi peoples.

‡The National University has 28,000 students on campuses in Kinshasa, Kisangani, and Lubumbashi, and is growing as it takes over private colleges in Zaire.

opia (briefly an Italian colony) have tended to follow the educational patterns prevailing in neighboring countries, although they have developed their own variations. African universities have, for the most part, native-born faculties and administrators, many of whom earned their degrees in American, British, or continental European universities.

BRITISH AND FRENCH TRADITIONS

Two characteristics of the French colonial educational system have proved useful to the universities of West Africa and have enabled them to meet the educational needs of their popula-

tions more effectively than the former British colonies. The French introduced central planning of enrollment and programs, and they used French as the language of instruction in all grades. These seemingly authoritarian practices prepared the countries of West Africa to deal with some difficult educational decisions of the postindependence period without the political pressure East African leaders faced from a population unaccustomed to firm governmental policies.

The French tradition of centralized planning emphasized controlled enrollments in advanced programs to ensure jobs for university graduates in their chosen fields. The use of controlled enrollments enabled the French colonial authorities to increase vocational training by channeling unsuccessful university applicants into vocational schools.

Political leaders in East Africa, working from a British tradition that placed more emphasis on free choice of academic fields, have been unable to resist popular pressure for expansion of prestigious degree programs. They have thus wasted effort and resources in training more persons than could be employed in some professional areas and have suffered shortages in critical vocational skills.

The imposition of French as the language of education in West Africa has also been useful, since it has helped unify the countries that retained it as their official language. In East Africa, the indecision of Uganda, Kenya, and Tanzania about the language of instruction retarded educational progress.

In recent years, however, African countries have increased their emphasis on vocational and agricultural education. Many have placed less stress on university education, believing that literacy, industrialization, and increased agricultural production must take precedence.

SOUTH AFRICA

Since the University Apartheid Act (1959), South African universities have been divided into three systems: white Afrikaans-speaking, white English-speaking, and nonwhite. Government permission was required for a nonwhite student to be admitted to a white university until the passage of the Universities Amendment Act of 1983, which empowered the minister of national education to impose, when necessary, a quota for nonwhite students at white universities. The act, however, retained the requirement for ministerial approval for nonwhite students wishing to study medical and health sciences, agriculture, and surveying at white universities.

The oldest English and Afrikaans universities were established in the 19th century. The newest universities are those for black South Africans and the one for South Africans of Indian descent. These universities are still small. The English-language universities at one time led such opposition to apartheid as existed. Research is restricted by the establishment of apartheid as an official doctrine. South African universities now suffer from increasing isolation as many academics in other parts of the world tend to avoid contact with them.

DALE KOCH

Bibliography: Ashby, Eric, *African Universities and the Western Tradition* (1964); Brown, Godfrey N., and Hiskett, Mervyn, *Conflict and Harmony in Education in Tropical Africa* (1976); Fafunwa, A. B., and Aisku, J. U., eds., *Education in Africa: A Comparative Study* (1982); Furley, O. W., and Watson, Tom, *A History of Education in East Africa* (1978); Thompson, A. R., *Education and Development in Africa* (1981).

Ivory Coast students work in the language laboratory of the Abidjan Secondary School Teacher Training Institute. In addition to training and retraining teachers, the institute engages in educational research under a UNESCO program providing equipment and expertise.

African violet

The African violet, S. ionantha, a plant originally from eastern Africa, has velvety, oval leaves crowned by long-lasting flowers. Many hybrids and varieties have been developed, offering a wide range of colors and of petal shapes and numbers.

African violet is the common name for about 24 species of small evergreen plants, native to Tanzania and Kenya, that make up the genus *Saintpaulia* in the family Gesneriaceae, which also contains the gloxinia. Since its discovery in the late 19th century, *S. ionantha* has become a popular house and greenhouse plant; other species are also cultivated. The wild *S. ionantha* has five-petaled, violet flowers and densely baired, dark green leaves that may be purplish below.

Afrikaners

The Afrikaners are a South African people of Dutch or French Huguenot descent. Formerly also known as Boers (from the Dutch word for farmer), Afrikaners make up about 60 percent of South Africa's white population of 4,528,000 (1980). Their language is Afrikaans, a derivative of Dutch.

History. The first Afrikaners were Dutch pioneers who settled (1652) in what is now Cape Province. During the 18th and 19th centuries, Afrikaans-speaking settlers pushed into the interior, fighting both their Bantu neighbors and the British (see GREAT TREK). They established two independent states, the South African Republic (1852; later the Transvaal) and the Orange Free State (1854). After the Afrikaner defeat in the Second SOUTH AFRICAN WAR (1899–1902), these territories were annexed by the British and the Union of South Africa was formed. Politically, the Afrikaners played a secondary role to the English-speaking South Africans until 1948, when the electoral victory of the Afrikaner National party solidified the Afrikaners' political supremacy in South Africa.

Originally a rural people for the most part, the Afrikaners began to migrate to the towns at the end of World War I. (Today more than 70 percent live in cities.) Until relatively recently they were the least prosperous of the white groups, employed mainly in farming or in laboring jobs. During the 1930s, South Africa's "poor whites"—mainly Afrikaners—accounted for nearly half the white population. After World War II, however, Afrikaners began to rise rapidly in the socioeconomic scale. Today they hold key positions in the South African government and in industries that were formerly largely controlled by English-speaking whites.

Religion. The overwhelming majority of Afrikaners are Calvinists and belong to the three Dutch Reformed churches, which have been a powerful integrating force since the first years of settlement. Urbanization, however, has somewhat diminished the hold of the churches, as it has also weakened the power of the traditional Afrikaner family.

Language. Afrikaans is the most widely spoken language in South Africa. It is the native tongue not only of the Afrikaners but also of the majority of South Africa's COLOUREDS, a people of mixed Euro-African background. Together with English, Afrikaans is the official language of the Republic of South Africa. Afrikaans has shed many of the inflections that characterize its mother language, Dutch, and has been enriched by

The South African Voortrekker Monument, near Pretoria, commemorates the Great Trek of the 1830s and '40s. Traveling in ox-wagon trains, some 14,000 Afrikaner farmers and their families migrated from the Cape Colony into the interior, to escape British rule and to find more and better lands to farm.

loan words from other languages including English, German, and Khoisan.

Once a rural patois spoken mainly by poor people (Dutch was the language of the well educated), Afrikaans began to be accepted as the national language only in the 19th century. The exertions of the Gennootskap van Regte Afrikaners, an Afrikaner nationalist organization, led to the publication of the first Afrikaans grammar (1876), and to increasing commitment to Afrikaans as the Afrikaners' national tongue. The South African War intensified linguistic and cultural—as well as political—nationalism. In 1925, Afrikaans officially superseded Dutch. In 1933 the first Afrikaans translation of the Bible was published. Concern with Afrikaans has always formed an essential component of Afrikaaner nationalism, and various Afrikaner groups have tried to promote Afrikaans culture in a manner that has found no parallel within the English-speaking community, whose language operates in an international context and whose members never experienced the Afrikaners ever-present sense of cultural jeopardy.

Literature. At the same time that Afrikaans was winning acceptance as their national language, the Afrikaners were developing a striking literature. In its 19th-century beginnings, its focus was essentially rural and religious. Eugene Marais (1871–1936) wrote what is considered the first important poem in Afrikaans, "Winternag" (1905), and produced a body of work—both verse and prose—in a homespun Afrikaans that is still ranked as exemplary in the literary use of the language. The South African War provided new intellectual dimensions for such writers as Totius (J. D. Du Toit, 1877–1953), a poet and biblical translator whose By die monument (1908) was the first volume of poems by a single writer published in Afrikaans. C. J. Langenhoven (1873–1932), a champion of the Afrikaans language, was an essayist, novelist, and journalist whose prolific writings served his stated purpose: to teach his people to read in their own language. The physician C. Louis Leipoldt (1880–1947), who had been a newspaper reporter during the Boer War, produced several volumes of highly regarded war poems. The novelist Jochem Van Bruggen (1881–1957) wrote humorous, naturalistic fiction about the lives of rural "poor whites."

The Dertigers (Men of the '30s) were a group of talented poets who emerged during the 1930s. W. E. G. van Wyk Louw (1913–) wrote Die ryke dwaas (The Rich Fool, 1934), breaking new ground in his treatment of love, youth, and religion. His elder brother N. P. van Wyk Louw (1906–70) began his celebrated career with an epic poem (Raku, 1941) and a

dramatic monologue (Die Hond von God, 1942), both still unsurpassed in Afrikaans literature. Uys Krige (1910–), noted novelist, playwright, and translator, published his first novel, Kentering, in 1935.

In the 1940s and '50s, World War II and the increasing industrialization of South Africa broadened the scope of Afrikaans writing. Poets D. J. Opperman (1914–) and S. J. Pretorius (1917–) both wrote about the chaos created by urbanization. Opperman, especially, revealed new possibilities in Afrikaans as a poetic language. The Sestigers, men of the '60s, introduced a new and more radical note into Afrikaans literature. Two Coloured poets, P. J. Philander (1921–) and Adam Small (1936–), published notable work in Afrikaans. The novelist Andre Brink (1935–), who writes in English as well as Afrikaans, produced the first Afrikaans work to confront the issue of apartheid (Looking on Darkness, 1973; Eng. trans., 1974), which was the first work in that language to be banned by the South African authorities. Etienne Leroux (1922–), ranked as the most important contemporary Afrikaans prose writer, published his most significant novel, Sewe dae by die Silbersteins (Seven Days at the Silbersteins, 1967), in 1962. That novel and his later Magersfontein, O Magersfontein (1976) both won South Africa's most prestigious literary award, the Hertzog Prize.   L. H. GANN

Bibliography: Davenport, T. R. H., South Africa: A Modern History (1977); Fisher, John, The Afrikaners (1969); Harrison, David, The White Tribe of Africa (1981); Munger, Edwin S., Afrikaner and African Nationalism (1967); Villet, Barbara, Blood River (1982); Wilson, Monica H., and Thompson, Leonard M., eds., The Oxford History of South Africa, 2 vols. (1969–71).

Afro-American cults

Afro-American cults are religions of African origin now practiced in the Caribbean islands and parts of South America; they often include elements derived from Christianity. Known as VOODOO in Haiti, Macumba or Candomblé in Brazil, Shango in Trinidad, Santería in Cuba, and Kumina or Pocomania in Jamaica, these cults are devoted to West African deities or spirits of the dead, which in Roman Catholic countries are identified with various Christian saints. They typically emphasize magical practices designed to bring good luck to the devotees or to work harm on their enemies. Cult ceremonies, in which participants experience ecstatic states and are believed to be possessed by spirits, usually involve singing and dancing and sometimes animal sacrifices. In Jamaica, possession by spirits is known as myal, and their invocation for harmful purposes is called obeah. In Brazil there is no clear distinction between folk Catholicism and the Macumba sects, which have flourished despite past governments' efforts to suppress them.

Afro-American literature: see BLACK AMERICAN LITERATURE.

Afroasiatic languages

Also known as Hamito-Semitic languages, Afroasiatic languages are spoken by 175 million persons representing a wide range of cultures through most of the Middle East, the Horn of Africa, North Africa, and large portions of West Africa. The languages include Arabic and Hebrew. Afroasiatic is commonly divided into five main branches based on ancient roots: Egyptian, Semitic, Cushitic, Berber, and Chad. Omotic, formerly called West Cushitic, has recently been suggested as constituting a sixth branch. These languages differ in their particulars, and the exact relationship among the branches has not yet been established. Scholars postulate, however, that all are derived from an unknown ancestor language that was probably spoken in northeast Africa or the Sahara about the 6th millennium BC.

EGYPTIAN

Egyptian is the oldest attested language of the family, and it has the longest known continuous history. As a written language it proceeded in five distinct stages. The first three—Old Egyptian (c.3000 to c.2200 BC), Middle Egyptian (c.2200 to *c.*1200 BC), and Late or Neo-Egyptian (*c.*1300 to *c.*700 BC)—were all written in HIEROGLYPHICS. Demotic (*c.*700 BC to AD *c.*300) was written in a simplified cursive script based on hieroglyphics and spoken by early Christians. Coptic (from AD 300), written in an alphabet based on Greek and comprising many dialects, was still widely spoken in the 16th century and in some places possibly as late as the 19th century. One Coptic dialect, Bohairic, is now the liturgical language of the Christian Monophysite Coptic Church.

SEMITIC

Semitic was originally confined to the Near East but gradually spread to the Horn of Africa and then throughout North Africa. It comprises two major groups, which in turn comprise many smaller affinity groups. Semitic embraces the languages used by a number of cultures prominent in ancient times, including the people of the BIBLE, as well as modern Arabic and Hebrew.

East Semitic includes Akkadian, the language of the Assyro-Babylonians that was spoken in Mesopotamia from *c.*3000 to *c.*400 BC. It was written, usually from left to right, in a cuneiform script. West Semitic can be further divided into central and southern branches and embraces the Hebrew, Aramaic, Arabic, South Arabian, and Ethiopian languages. Most languages in this group were or still are written from right to left in a consonantal script without marked vowels. As Hebrew, Syriac, and Arabic further developed, users added diacritical vowel symbols or "points," which are now optional. The main branches of Central Semitic are Aramaic, Arabic, and Canaanite.

Aramaic. One of the branches of Central Semitic, Aramaic was once the colloquial language of the Near East after the decline of Akkadian. It was the native tongue of Jesus Christ and the language of the Jewish Talmud. Syriac, one of its eastern branches, was used to transmit early Christian culture up to the 13th century. Today eastern Aramaic is still spoken by about 100,000 persons—many of whom are Jacobite and Nestorian Christians—in northeast Iran and neighboring areas of Iraq and the USSR, as well as by Jews from the same region who have immigrated to Israel. Mandaic, the language of a Gnostic sect, is also still spoken in the region.

Arabic. As a literary language, Arabic dates back to the 7th century AD. It is the language of the KORAN, the holy book of ISLAM, and thus assumed tremendous importance because it was adopted by most of the peoples conquered and converted by Muslim Arabs. Arabic has also been spoken by the Christian and Jewish minorities of the Islamic world. A North African branch, spoken by Christians and written in Roman characters, is the official language of Malta. A modernized version of classical Arabic, Modern Literary Arabic, is used in education, literature, and mass communication by about 100 million persons.

Canaanite. Canaanite comprises Hebrew and such ancient languages as Phoenician-Punic, Moabite, and Ugaritic. Hebrew, attested from the 10th century BC to the present, is the language of Judaism and the Old Testament Bible. Its original domain included what is now Israel and nearby areas. Biblical Hebrew is found in texts dating from *c.*1000 to 400 BC. Mishnaic (Rabbinical) Hebrew (AD *c.*200) is the language of the MISHNAH, the first great legal document of Judaism, and shows the influence of vernacular Aramaic.

Medieval Hebrew (6th to 13th century) was the written language of religious literature and poetry of Arabic-speaking Jews, notably in Spain. Early modern Hebrew developed in the 18th century and became the vehicle for a secular literature and for correspondence between Jews, mainly in Eastern Europe. The Zionist settlers of Palestine (Israel) also adopted it as a colloquial language, as a result of the systemization of modern Hebrew by Eliezer BEN-YEHUDAH early in this century. Today, Israeli Hebrew is spoken by about 3 million persons in Israel.

Phoenician-Punic was spoken in what is today Lebanon, from the 10th century BC to the beginning of the Christian era. Phoenicians brought their language to the colonies that they established around the Mediterranean, the most famous of which was CARTHAGE.

Moabite, which was related to biblical Hebrew, died out long ago, as did Ugaritic. Written in a cuneiform consonantal script, Ugaritic was the language of the city of UGARIT up to the 14th century BC. Its affiliations, as well as those of Amorite and of the recently discovered language of Ibla, remain disputed.

South Semitic. South Semitic is represented by three branches whose exact relationship has not yet been discerned. The original language of the southern half of the Arabian peninsula was South Arabian and not Arabic. Epigraphic South Arabian is known only from short inscriptions dating from the 9th century BC to the 6th century AD. Its main varieties were Sabaean (Sheba), Minean, Awsani, Qatabani, and Hadramauti.

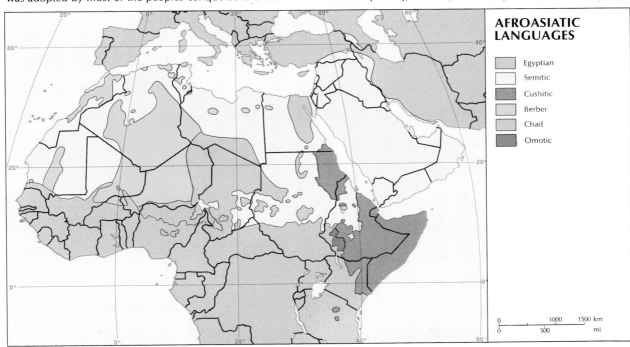

AFROASIATIC LANGUAGES

- Egyptian
- Semitic
- Cushitic
- Berber
- Chad
- Omotic

Modern South Arabian is not descendant from the former. These languages are spoken by about 25,000 people in the Dhofar and on the island of Socotra (Soqotri).

Ethiopian. Spoken in Ethiopia and Sudan in the Horn of Africa, Ethiopian languages were transplanted to the area from South Arabia, possibly around 2000 BC. They were greatly transformed by the indigenous populations that adopted them. The script, written from left to right, is a continuation of the South Arabian consonantal script. Here, however, a character stands for a consonant-vowel group, and the vowel is marked by a modification of the basic shape of the consonantal letter.

Ethiopian languages comprise northern and southern branches. In the North Ethiopic group—Ge'ez, Tigrinya, and Tigre—Ge'ez was the language of civilization centering on Aksum. First attested in inscriptions from the 4th century AD, it died out as a spoken language in the 9th century but continued to be used as a literary language and as the liturgical language of the Ethiopian Coptic Church. Tigrinya has about 3.5 million speakers in Eritrea and the Governate-General of Tigre, while Tigre has about 350,000 Muslim speakers.

The South Ethiopic group comprises two branches: Transversal South Ethiopic and Outer South Ethiopic. Transversal South Ethiopic includes Amharic, the official language of Ethiopia, with more than 8 million, mainly Christian, speakers; the almost extinct Argobba: Harari, the language of the Muslim city of Harar; and East Gurage. Outer South Ethiopic includes the recently extinct Gafat and the rest of the so-called Gurage languages (Soddo, Chaha, and others).

CUSHITIC

Cushitic is the most heterogeneous of the Afroasiatic languages. It comprises about 40 different languages spoken by 15 million persons in the Horn of Africa and surrounding areas. Beja or Bedauye, spoken in eastern Sudan and northern Ethiopia by about 100,000 Muslims, has been classified as North Cushitic but may be an independent branch of Afroasiatic. Central Cushitic, comprising the Agau languages, is spoken within enclaves of predominantly Semitic Ethiopia. East Cushitic, the largest member of the group, with about 2 million speakers in South Central Ethiopia, comprises Highland East Cushitic (Burji, Sidamo, Hadiyya, and others) and Lowland East Cushitic, which is the most widespread. Its northern branch comprises the Afar-Saho or Dankali dialect cluster, with about 500,000 speakers located in south Eritrea and the Republic of Jibuti.

The other branch contains the widest diversity. Somali, with about 4 million speakers, is the official language of Somalia and is also spoken in the Republic of Jibuti, in the Ogaden area of Ethiopia, and in the northwestern territory of Kenya. It is written in Roman script, although Arabic and an indigenous script have also been used. Its closest relatives are Boni and Rendille in Kenya.

The most widely spoken Cushitic language is Oromo, or Galla, with about 8 million speakers. It is spoken in the southern half of Ethiopia and in the adjacent areas of Kenya. It is written in the Ethiopian script and is grouped with the Konso cluster. South Cushitic comprises Dahalo or Sanye, Ma'a or Mbugu (a mixture of Cushitic and Bantu), both of which are spoken in Kenya. Iraqw, Asax, and Quadza are spoken in Tanzania.

OMOTIC

About 30 Omotic languages are spoken in the Omo valley in southern Ethiopia by about 1.3 million people. Once considered to constitute West Cushitic, the Omotic languages are so different from the other Afroasiatic languages that their inclusion in the family has been questioned. The most important of these languages is Walamo, followed by Gonga (Kafa) and Janjero.

BERBER

The Berber languages (formerly Numidian and Libyan) at one time dominated the whole of North Africa, west of Egypt. Today the separate Berber languages are spoken in Arabic-speaking territories across North Africa by perhaps 10 million speakers. Tuareg is spoken in southern Algeria, Niger, and

Mali. Morocco has the largest concentration of Berber speakers—with 6 million speakers of the Tamazight, Tashelhit, and Tarifit dialects—followed by Algeria, with 2.5 million Kabyles, Chowiya, and other Berber tribes. These dialects are written in Arabic script, although the consonantal writing of Libyan inscriptions still survives. (See BERBERS.)

CHAD

The Chadic languages are spoken in west central Africa in the area around Lake Chad. Hausa, with 15 million speakers, is the most widely spoken, mainly in northwestern Nigeria, Niger, Chad, and northern Ghana. It is written in Roman script, although Arabic script is also used. The other Chadic languages, between 100 and 200 with a total of 7 million speakers, are located in areas east of the Hausa territory. Chadic languages comprise West Chadic (including Hausa, Bole, Kanakuru, Angas, Ron, Bade, Ngizim, Wanji), Biu-Mandara (including Tera, Margi, Higi, Mandara, Bata, Kotoko, Musgu), East Chadic (including Somrai, Dangla, Mubi, and Sokoro), and Masa as a separate branch.

CHARACTERISTICS OF AFROASIATIC

Despite grammatical differences, the kinship among the various branches of Afroasiatic can be seen through basic similarities in their structures and vocabularies. For example, all branches except Egyptian have a set of emphatic consonants in addition to voiced and voiceless consonants. Lateral consonants (for example, *tl, dl*) are found in some languages. The Cushitic, Omotic, and Chadic languages also have tones.

All branches of the family have masculine and feminine gender distinction, usually characterized by the feminine marker *t* (Arabic: *kalb/kalbat,* "dog/bitch"); gender distinction in the plural, however, has disappeared in many of the languages. Ancient Egyptian and classical Semitic had not only singular and plural forms but a grammatical distinction for "two" or "double."

Egyptian, Semitic, Berber, and, in remnants only, Cushitic use a system in which a root comprising two, three, or four consonants is used to create different words; this is done by superimposing on it a pattern comprising vowels, and often of further consonants. Thus, in Arabic, the root *k-t-b*, meaning "write," is used in various combinations to form allied words, such as "writer" (*ka:tib-*) or "written" (*maktu:b-*). This root-and-pattern system is particularly important in the verbal system: an original root *m-w-t* produces in Arabic the words *ma:ta/yamu:tu* to express "he died/dies."

In Semitic, Berber, and, to a limited extent, Cushitic, basic verbal conjugations are characterized by the addition of prefixes and suffixes. Root vocalization marks tense. Egyptian, by contrast, has no prefix conjugation; its verbal system is of nominal origin—of the type "I am on/in/to doing," "is done by me," "I am a doer of" for various tenses and aspects of "I do." In Chadic, a typical conjugation comprises a preposition containing a subject marker and a tense-and-aspect marker, followed by one of the major stem forms of the verb. Verbal derivation is quite rich in all these languages. A passive formation in *t* and a causative in *s* or its developments; a reduplication of the verb, of a syllable, or of a consonant for repeated actions; and other methods of word formation are attested everywhere. In many languages, the verb has special negative forms. Likewise, different verbal forms for main and subordinate clauses are found in several branches.

In the Cushitic and Omotic languages, the verb typically occupies the final position in the sentence, and subordinate clauses precede the main one. Ethiopian Semitic has adopted the same order of elements. In old Egyptian, Berber, and classical Semitic, the verb is at the beginning of a sentence. Akkadian, an exception, placed the verb in the final position. Coptic, modern Arabic dialects, Aramaic, and Hebrew now use a subject-verb-object order, as do almost all the Chadic languages.

In Hebrew and Arabic, adjectives follow the noun and agree with it in gender, number, and definiteness. Case marking is prepositional in Chadic, Berber, Egyptian, and Semitic, though classical Semitic has some residual suffixal cases; Cushitic and Omotic use suffixes, but Somali expresses most case relations by means of preverbal particles.

Similarity of numerals occurs only between Semitic and Berber. In both branches, nouns following smaller numerals are in the plural, but after large numbers they are in the singular. In Semitic, numerals having a feminine ending occur with masculine nouns and vice versa.

LINGUISTIC INVESTIGATION

The formal study of Hebrew and Arabic has an extensive history. Motivated by the study of Judaism and Islam, it spread widely among scholars with the influence of the two religions. Geez and Amharic were first studied in the 17th century. Investigation into most of the other Afroasiatic languages grew from contact between indigenous speakers and Europeans—first travelers, then missionaries and colonial administrators, and ultimately scholars whose motives were purely intellectual.

The extinct languages—Egyptian, Libyan, and those of the Semitic group—were preserved in inscriptions that were copied and, with the help of bilingual inscriptions or of known related scripts, deciphered by scholars mainly during the past 100 years (see WRITING SYSTEMS, EVOLUTION OF). In recent years an upsurge has occurred in the study of Cushitic and Chadic languages in particular. Modern advances in general linguistic theory have greatly stimulated the investigation of all branches. Two periodicals are devoted exclusively to the Afroasiatic language family: the *Comptes Rendus* of the Groupe Linguistique d'Études Chamito-Sémitiques (Paris), founded in 1931; and *Afroasiatic Linguistics* (Malibu, Calif., 1974–   ). The *Afroasiatic Dialects* series (Malibu, Calif.) publishes introductory grammars of these languages. Every 4 years an International Hamito-Semitic Congress is held.   ROBERT HETZRON

Bibliography: Bender, Marvin L., ed., *The Non-Semitic Languages of Ethiopia* (1976); Bynon, James and Theodora, eds., *Hamito-Semitica* (1975); Diakonoff, Igor M., *Semito-Hamitic Languages* (1965); Gardiner, Alan N., *Egyptian Grammar* (1950); Gesenius, Wilhelm, *Hebrew Grammar*, ed. by E. Kautzsch (1963); Greenberg, Joseph H., *The Languages of Africa* (1966); Hodge, Carleton T., ed., *Afroasiatic, a Survey* (1971); Moscati, Sabatino, et al., *An Introduction to the Comparative Grammar of Semitic Languages* (1964); Newman, P. and R. M., eds., *Papers in Chadic Linguistics* (1977); Wright, William, *A Grammar of the Arabic Languages* (1967).

afterimages

Afterimages are experienced when a prolonged or intense visual stimulus ceases. Because afterimages result from fatigue in portions of the retina, the visual afterimage seems to move with the eye, unlike external objects that normally appear stationary despite eye movements. When one looks at a gray or white surface, the resulting negative afterimage that is seen is close to the complementary color of the original stimulus. After blue, a gray patch looks yellow; after green, it looks red. Positive afterimages (of the same color as the original stimulus) are briefly seen, especially after short exposures or in a dark postexposure field. Afterimages mix to affect appearances of colored postexposure fields, enhancing the color saturation of the fields when the afterimage and the postexposure field are of the same color.   JULIAN HOCHBERG

Afternoon of a Faun, The

The orchestral music for the *Prelude to the Afternoon of a Faun* (*Prélude à l'Après-midi d'un Faune*, 1894) by Claude DEBUSSY is one of the finest works of musical impressionism. Debussy's composition was inspired by the poem *L'Après-midi d'un faune* (1876) by his friend the French symbolist poet Stéphane MALLARMÉ.

The poem describes a faun who, while playing his flute on a hot afternoon, encounters two nymphs who are on their way to bathe. He becomes enamored of one of them, who escapes his advances, leaving him playing with her scarf.

Debussy, in musically illustrating the dreamy eroticism of the poem's text, used several devices: chromaticism, whole-tone scales and modes, dissonance, parallel chords, subdued dynamics, and subtle rhythm and meter changes. The wood-wind solos, harp glissandi, and muted horns all suggest an idyllic dream. Composed in three continuous sections, the tone poem conveys constant, flowing motion.

The Afternoon of a Faun was first performed as a ballet in Paris in 1912 by the Ballet Russes de Serge Diaghilev and caused a scandal. Vaslav NIJINSKY, who choreographed the ballet and danced the part of the faun, eventually won acclaim for the work. In 1953 the American choreographer Jerome ROBBINS presented a contemporary interpretation of the work, which has since become a staple of the New York City Ballet's repertory.

Bibliography: Kirstein, Lincoln, *Movement and Metaphor* (1970); Lockspeiser, Edward, *Debussy*, 4th ed. (1972); Palmer, Christopher, *Impressionism in Music* (1974).

Afzelius, Arvid August   [ahf-zay'-lee-us, ahr'-veed ow'-goost]

Arvid August Afzelius, b. May 6, 1785, d. Sept. 25, 1871, was a Swedish folklorist, poet, and historian. After studying theology at Uppsala University, he became bishop of Enköping, but he is best known for his translations of Icelandic sagas and collections of early Swedish ballads and folktales. These influenced Swedish poetry and stimulated the study of Nordic mythology.

Aga Khan   [ah'-guh kahn]

The Aga Khan is the spiritual leader, or imam, of the ISMAILI sect of Shiite Muslims. The hereditary title was first granted by the Persian court to **Hasan Ali Shah**, 1800–81, a supposed descendant of Ali, son-in-law of the Prophet Muhammad. He revolted against the shah, however, and fled to India in 1840. His grandson **Aga Khan III** (Sultan Sir Mohammed Shah), b. Nov. 2, 1877, d. July 11, 1957, was a founder (1906) of the All-India Muslim League and took part in the London conferences on Indian constitutional reform in 1930–32. In 1937 he was president of the League of Nations Assembly. He was succeeded on his death by his grandson Karim al-Hussain Shah, **Aga Khan IV**, b. Dec. 13, 1936. The present Aga Khan is known primarily for his business interests, which include a Thoroughbred-horse-breeding enterprise begun by his grandfather. He has promoted development projects among the Ismailis and sponsored a major study of Islamic architecture.

Agadir   [ah-guh-deer']

Agadir (1971 pop., 61,192) is a seaport in Agadir province of southwestern Morocco. It is located on the Atlantic coast, at the mouth of the Oued Sous, about 220 km (135 mi) southwest of Marrakech. Agadir is Morocco's main fishing port, noted for its sardine catch. Founded by the Portuguese in the 16th century, Agadir was the scene of confrontation between Germany and France in 1911 (see MOROCCAN CRISES). It was largely destroyed by earthquakes in 1960; a modern city was built around the port facilities.

Agam, Yaacov   [ah-gahm', yah'-kawf]

Yaacov Agam, b. May 11, 1928, is a leading Israeli painter, sculptor, and kinetic artist. After studying in Jerusalem, Zurich, and Paris, Agam mounted his first one-man show in Paris in 1953. His painting and sculptural style is derived in part from the geometric severities of the Dutch modernist Piet Mondrian and the tradition of neoplasticism (the rules of abstract composition formulated by the movement called DE STIJL), into which Agam injects a characteristic liveliness and visual wit.   CARTER RATCLIFF

agama   [ag'-uh-muh]

Agamas are about 60 species of Old World lizards in the genus *Agama*, family Agamidae, order Squamata. These rough-scaled lizards have more or less flattened, robust bodies, well-developed limbs, and moderately long tails. They feed on insects and other small animals; some also consume vegetation. Most small species are ground-living. The large species often live on rocky cliffs or in trees. They are found in southeastern Europe and in the jungles, steppes, savannas, and desert regions of Africa, Arabia, and Southwest and Central Asia.

STEVEN C. ANDERSON

Bibliography: Carr, A. F., *The Reptiles* (1963); Schmidt, Karl P., and Inger, R. F., *Living Reptiles of the World* (1957; repr. 1975).

See also: LIZARD; REPTILE.

Agamemnon   [ag-uh-mem'-nahn]

In Greek mythology, Agamemnon, a son of ATREUS, was the commander in chief of the Greeks in the TROJAN WAR. He was the king of Mycenae and a brother of MENELAUS, whose kidnapped wife, HELEN OF TROY, was the immediate cause of the conflict. On his way to Troy, Agamemnon agreed to sacrifice his daughter IPHIGENIA in order to ensure a fair wind for his ships. Upon Agamemnon's return from the war, his wife CLYTEMNESTRA, who had betrayed him with Aegisthus, resolved to avenge her daughter's sacrifice. When her husband was at ease in the bath, she and her lover murdered him. Agamemnon's death was later avenged by his son ORESTES. These tragic events are the subject of a trilogy, the ORESTEIA, written by the 5th-century BC dramatist AESCHYLUS.

C. SCOTT LITTLETON

Agana   [ah-gahn'-ah]

Agana (1970 pop., 2,119) is the capital of Guam, a U.S. unincorporated territory in the western Pacific. Situated on the west coast of the island, the town was destroyed in World War II and has been gradually rebuilt since then.

Aganippe   [ag'-uh-nip-ee]

In Greek mythology, Aganippe, daughter of the river-god Permessus, was a NYMPH. Her fountain on the slopes of Mount Helicon was sacred to the MUSES. It was believed that mortals who drank of its waters would receive poetic powers.

Agar   [ah'-gahr]

Agar is a substance prepared from a mixture of red algae, such as *Gelidium*, for laboratory or industrial use. It is made mainly in the Far East—the name *agar*, or *agar-agar*, is a Malay word for a type of seaweed common in the area—and in California. The algae are washed and dried, and the agar, part of the cell wall, is extracted with boiling water, forming a gel as it cools. The gel is a complex mixture of several sugar compounds.

Agar is the substance most commonly used in laboratories for making media in which to grow microorganisms. It is nontoxic, dissolves poorly in water, and is relatively unaffected by the salts and nutrients in the media or by the organisms themselves. Agar is used to stabilize and thicken emulsions such as ice creams, jellies, soups, and sauces. It is also used to size, or fill the pores of, textiles and paper and in treating some intestinal disorders.   CHARLES L. WILSON

Bibliography: Stewart, Joyce, *Methods of Media Preparation for the Biological Sciences* (1974).

Agassiz, Lake: see LAKE, GLACIAL.

Agassiz, Louis Rodolphe   [ag'-uh-see]

One of the most influential scientists of the 19th century, the Swiss-born American naturalist Jean Louis Rodolphe Agassiz, b. May 28, 1807, d. Dec. 14, 1873, is known for his pioneering work on fossil fish and as the originator of the concept of ICE AGES.

A graduate in philosophy and medicine of the universities of Munich and Erlangen (1829, 1830), Agassiz worked in Paris with Georges CUVIER, the founder of the discipline of comparative anatomy, and in 1832 became professor of natural history at the College of Neuchâtel, Switzerland. Here he undertook the research that resulted in his 5-volume work *Récherches sur les poissons fossiles* (Studies on Fossil Fish,

Louis Agassiz, a Swiss-born American, was one of the 19th century's leading naturalists. Agassiz developed and popularized the concept of an Ice Age and was noted for his efforts to promote the study of natural sciences in the United States.

1833–44), which, using the principles of comparative anatomy, describes more than 1,700 species.

In the late 1830s Agassiz began his study of glaciers, charting their movement and asserting on the basis of geological evidence that ice had once covered much of the European continent. His view of this catastrophic event opposed the famous doctrine of the Scottish geologist Sir Charles LYELL that only uniform and gradual changes occur in the Earth's history. But geological formations, as well as the scratched surfaces of rocks in certain areas, supported Agassiz's theory.

In 1846 Agassiz went to the United States to deliver a series of lectures but remained for 25 years, teaching at Harvard. Renowned for his teaching abilities, Agassiz trained an entire generation of naturalists. He enthusiastically explored the United States both east and west of the Mississippi and applied his theory of ice ages to North America. He established (1859) the Museum of Comparative Zoology at Harvard and played an important role in founding (1863) the National Academy of Sciences. He was the most important scientist in the United States to oppose Darwin's theory of evolution.

Bibliography: Agassiz, Elizabeth Cary, ed., *Louis Agassiz, His Life and Correspondence*, 2 vols. (1885); Cooper, Lane, *Louis Agassiz as a Teacher*, rev. ed. (1945); Lurie, Edward, *Louis Agassiz: A Life in Science* (1960) and *Nature and the American Mind: Louis Agassiz and the Culture of Science* (1974); Marcou, Jules, *Life, Letters, and Work of Louis Agassiz*, 2 vols. (1896).

agate   [ag'-uht]

The common, widespread SILICA MINERAL (SiO_2) agate often occurs in bands of varying color and transparency. A semiprecious variety of CHALCEDONY, it has long been used as a GEM and as an ornamental material. Agate is identical with QUARTZ

Agate is a semiprecious variety of transparent to translucent quartz arranged in curved or circular bands of different colors. Long used for jewelry, it is now mainly used to make such ornamental objects as ashtrays and umbrella handles. Because the mineral is relatively porous, such objects are often dyed with metal salts to furnish a greater variety of colors.

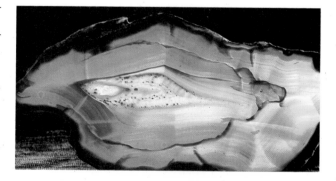

in composition and physical properties. Composed of silicon dioxide, it has a HARDNESS of 7, a glassy LUSTER, a conchoidal fracture, and a SPECIFIC GRAVITY of 2.60. The colored bands are iron hydroxide impurities added during formation.

Agate forms when gas bubbles trapped in solidifying LAVA become filled with alkali and silica-bearing waters, which co-agulate into a GEL. The alkali attacks the iron in the surrounding lava, and bands of the resulting iron hydroxide are created in the gel, which loses water and crystallizes, leaving the bands intact. Many agates, when cut in cross-section, reveal forms that resemble familiar objects, giving rise to names such as eye or ring agate, fortification agate, moss agate, and landscape agate. Agate that has alternating, parallel bands of cloudy and colored material is called ONYX.

According to ancient superstition, wearing agate made one agreeable, persuasive, prudent, and bold. It brought God's favor and bestowed the power to vanquish enemies and acquire riches. White agate supposedly cured insomnia.

Ider and Oberstein, West Germany, once famous agate localities, have been superseded as a source of the stones by the Rio Grande de Sul region of Brazil and Uruguay.

JOHN B. WHEELER

agave [uh-gah'-vay]

Agave, *Agave*, is any of several plants with handsome foliage belonging to the agave family, Agavaceae. They form long, stiff evergreen leaves in clumps, or rosettes, from which tall, bare flower stems arise. Agave plants are native to warm arid and semiarid regions of North and South America. They are used as HOUSEPLANTS and, in the South, as landscape plants.

The century plant, *A. americana*, erroneously received its name because it was believed to bloom only when 100 years old. It has leaves up to 1.8 m (6 ft) long and a flower stalk up to 12 m (40 ft) in height. It generally blooms after it is 10 years old; thereafter it dies back but suckers sprout again from the base to form new plants. This is the most popular species for landscaping and potting.

Some common agaves have commercial value. Pulque agave, *A. atrovirens*, is used in Mexico to produce pulque, and tequila is fermented from other Mexican species. Fibers derived from henequen, *A. fourcroydes*, and sisal, *A. sisalana*, are used to make rope. The pulp of other species is used to produce soap and food.

CHARLES L. WILSON

age: see AGING; LIFE SPAN.

age of consent

The age of consent is the age at which a person is legally competent to give consent, as in making a contract or agreeing to marriage or to nonmarital sexual relations. It varies for different purposes and may be lower for women than men.

age determination: see RADIOMETRIC AGE-DATING.

Agee, James [ay'-jee]

An American writer, James Agee, b. Nov. 27, 1909, d. May 16, 1955, won distinction in a variety of literary forms. His volume of poems *Permit Me Voyage* (1934) was included in the Yale Series of Younger Poets. His nonfictional LET US NOW PRAISE FAMOUS MEN (1941), illustrated with Walker EVANS's photographs of sharecroppers, is an evocative view of the DEPRESSION OF THE 1930s. As film reviewer for the magazines TIME and the NATION in the 1930s and 1940s, he brought unusual rigor and insight to film criticism; his reviews were later collected in two volumes, *Agee on Film* (1958, 1960). His autobiographical novel *A Death in the Family* (1957; film, 1963) won the 1958 Pulitzer Prize for literature for its poignant and honest treatment of the effect of a man's death on his 6-year-old son. Agee's credits as a screenwriter include *The Night of the Hunter* (1955) and the classic *The African Queen* (1951).

Bibliography: Agee, James, *Letters of James Agee to Father Flye*, 2d ed., ed. by James H. Flye (1971); Kramer, Victor, *James Agee* (1975).

Agena (astronomy): see STAR.

Agena (rocket) [uh-jee'-nuh]

The Agena system is an upper rocket stage that employs a restartable rocket engine. It can operate as a satellite in its own right or it can be used to launch satellites and space probes in conjunction with more powerful lower rocket stages. Typical first-stage boosters were THOR and ATLAS.

Agena B, built by Lockheed Aircraft Corporation, was used in a number of early U.S. Air Force satellite projects, including DISCOVERER, SAMOS, MIDAS, and VELA, and a variety of NASA projects, including ECHO, MARINER, NIMBUS, and RANGER. Agena stages also were used as docking targets in the GEMINI manned space program. Dimensions of the stage depended on the mission. A typical Agena B stage used in the U.S. Air Force programs of the 1960s was 8 m (26.5 ft) long and 1.5 m (5 ft) in diameter. The stage had a fueled weight of about 7,167 kg (15,800 lb). The PROPELLANTS were IRFNA and UDMH, and the Bell 8096 rocket engine developed a thrust of 7,257 kg (16,000 lb).

Agena D, the vehicle in current use, has a length, excluding payload, of 7 m (23.25 ft) and carries more propellant than its predecessors. Basic vehicles include TITAN 3B, Atlas SLV-3A, and Thor.

KENNETH GATLAND

See also: ROCKETS AND MISSILES.

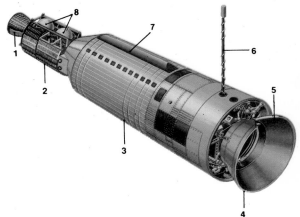

The Lockheed Agena target vehicle was part of the first manned space docking maneuver (Mar. 16, 1966) during the U.S. Gemini 8 mission. The Agena was composed of a (1) 7,260-kg-thrust (16,000-lb) restartable rocket engine; (2) secondary propulsion system composed of two 91-kg (200-lb) rockets and two 7.3-kg (16-lb) rockets; (3) mainstage propellant tanks; (4) docking cone; (5) 'V' notch, to facilitate vehicle linkup; (6) L-band antenna, used during docking; (7) external conduit; and (8) attitude-control nitrogen-pressure bottles.

Agency for International Development

The Agency for International Development (AID) is an agency of the U.S. Department of State, established by the Foreign Assistance Act of 1961 to assist other countries in developing their economies and improving the quality of life for their inhabitants. AID makes loans and grants to less developed countries for economic improvement programs and for programs relating to population growth. It also administers famine and disaster relief assistance. In cooperation with the Department of Agriculture, it distributes farm commodities under the Food for Peace program.

Bibliography: Tendler, Judith, *Inside Foreign Aid* (1977).

agent

In law, an agent is a person authorized by another to act for him or her, particularly to transact business or to manage certain affairs. A large body of law deals with the relationship among agents, the persons for whom they act (principal), and the persons with whom they deal (third party). The law of agency is important in business relationships, in that employees are agents for their employers, and brokers or lawyers are agents for their clients. The manager of a business firm who has complete control of all its operations is given broad powers under the law. Agents hired to manage investments, on the other hand, are expected to exercise prudence in their dealings. Attorneys have the duty to advance their clients' interests, but they cannot sign away their clients' rights except when authorized—even though it may benefit the client.

Agent Orange: see POLLUTANTS, CHEMICAL.

ageratum   [aj-ur-ay'-tuhm]

The ageratum A. houstonianum has clusters of tiny flowers and heart-shaped leaves. Wild ageratum grows in damp woodlands and along streams.

Ageratum, a member of the aster (Compositae) family, is an annual plant native to central and tropical South America. Commonly called flossflowers, they have clusters of small blue, white, or pink flowers with a pleasant odor. Because they flower for long periods, they are used as border plants in gardens and as summer bedding plants in temperate climates. One species, *Ageratum conyzoides*, contains hydrocyanic acid, coumarin, and an alkaloid and is poisonous to animals.
ROBERT C. ROMAN

Agesilaus II, King of Sparta   [uh-jes-i-lay'-uhs]

Agesilaus II, c.444-360 BC, succeeded his half brother Agis II as one of the two Spartan kings in 399. In Anatolia from 396, he defeated the Persian satrap TISSAPHERNES but was driven back by the powerful Persian navy. On his return (394) to Greece he defeated the Thebans and their allies at Coronea, but his losses were so heavy that he was forced to withdraw to the Peloponnesus. When a Sparto-Persian alliance forced Athens and Thebes to abandon the Greek cities in Anatolia to Persian domination (the Peace of Antalcidas, 386), the Thebans and Athenians renewed war against Sparta. At peace talks in 371, Agesilaus refused to recognize the Theban general EPAMINONDAS as the representative of all Boeotia. The Spartans soon invaded Boeotia and were overwhelmingly defeated by the Thebans at Leuctra. Sparta never regained its military strength. Agesilaus later tried to increase the state's revenues by leading Spartan mercenaries in Anatolia and in Egypt.

Bibliography: Bury, J. B., and Meiggs, Russell, *A History of Greece*, 4th rev. ed. (1975); Hammond, N. G. L., *A History of Greece to 322 B.C.*, 2d ed. (1967); Jones, A. H. M., *Sparta* (1967); Laistner, M. L. W., *A History of the Greek World from 479 to 323 B.C.*, 3d rev. ed. (1957).

aggregation

Aggregation is the process by which particles come together and grow to form an entity with its own characteristic properties. Often the term refers to processes involving the elementary constituents of matter—molecules and ions—but larger particles may also be involved. Gases, liquids, and solids represent different states of aggregation of molecules. In gases at low pressure, the molecules are separate; in liquids the molecules are in contact but can move past one another; in solids the forces of attraction hold the molecules in fixed positions. In substances that are liquid or solid at room temperature the intermolecular attraction is stronger than it is in gases.

The causes of intermolecular attraction are not completely understood, but it is believed that they have an electrical nature. Many solid substances are made up of ions that have a permanent charge; in other cases, the interaction is between two dipoles or between two charges that are transient.

The shape of the molecules also has an effect on the attractive force because it determines how closely they can be packed. Spherical particles occupy a space about two times larger than their volume, but they may be packed more closely if they are elongated or flattened.

Aggregation is involved in the formation of some colloids and in their behavior. Some proteins and other macromolecules aggregate spontaneously to form complex biological structures; examples include antigen-antibody complexes, some viruses, and ribosomes.
GEORGE GORIN

aggression

Aggression is attacking behavior that may be either self-protective and self-assertive or hostile toward others or toward oneself. Aggressive behavior ranges from mere self-assertion to the infliction of injury to the total destruction of others. It has two main aspects: the intent of the act and the act itself. Acts that appear to be hostile may in fact not involve an intention to inflict injury but merely the intention to establish a dominant position in relation to another. Threat rather than actual aggression is the usual means of establishing dominance, and the greater part of seemingly aggressive behavior in animals is of this type.

By far the most common forms of aggressive behavior among animals involve neither fighting, violence, injury, nor physical contact. Aggression is ritualized and involves withdrawal or flight as well as threat. Ritualization, behavior that consists of social signals that are recognized and elicit an appropriate response, obviates the need for fighting.

Observers distinguish 13 kinds of aggression according to the stimuli that elicit them: (1) Predatory aggression is evoked by the presence of a natural object of prey. (2) Antipredatory aggression is elicited by the presence of a predator. (3) Territorial aggression is elicited by an intruder invading the animal's domain. (4) Dominance aggression is elicited by a challenge to the animal's rank or desire for an object. (5) Maternal aggression is elicited by the proximity of some threatening agent to the young of a particular female. (6) Weaning aggression is elicited by the increased independence of the young, when the parents will threaten or even (with restraint) attack their offspring. (7) Parental disciplinary aggression is elicited by a variety of stimuli, such as unwelcome suckling, rough or overextended play, wandering, and the like. (8) Sexual aggression is elicited by females for the purpose of mating or the establishment of a prolonged union. (9) Sex-related aggression is elicited by the same stimuli that produce sexual behavior. (10) Intermale aggression is elicited by the presence of a male competitor of the same species. (11) Fear-induced aggression is elicited by confinement or cornering or by the presence of some threatening agent. (12) Irritable aggression is elicited by the presence of any organism or object with characteristics (such as color or darting movement) that stimulate an attack response. (13) Instrumental aggression includes any change in the environment as a consequence of the above types of aggression that increases the probability that aggressive behavior will recur in similar situations.

None of these types of aggression is mutually exclusive. Each, however, has different underlying neural and endocrine bases. Nor do all these forms apply equally to humans and animals. Clearly, then, aggressive behavior is not a single phenomenon, but something to be understood at many different levels. Predatory behavior among animals, for example, is found not to be aggressive behavior at all but rather a search for food that does not involve hostility.

Psychologists and animal behaviorists are finding that, in most higher animals, especially human beings, learning plays a role in the development of aggressive behavior. This is hopeful evidence, for it counters the theory (argued by Konrad LORENZ) that humans have inherited murderous tendencies from their animal past and the contention of Sigmund FREUD that human aggression springs from basic drives.

ASHLEY MONTAGU

Bibliography: Bandura, Albert, *Aggression: A Social Learning Analysis* (1973); Fromm, Erich, *The Anatomy of Human Destructiveness*, rev. ed. (1973); Johnson, Roger N., *Aggression in Man and Animals* (1972); Lorenz, Konrad, *On Aggression*, trans. by Marjorie K. Wilson (1966); Montagu, Ashley, *The Nature of Human Aggression* (1976); Otten, Charlotte M., ed., *Aggression and Evolution* (1973).

Agincourt, Battle of   [aj'-in-kort or ah-zhin-koor']

The English victory over the French at Agincourt in northwest France on Oct. 25, 1415, was one of the most significant battles in the HUNDRED YEARS' WAR. A triumph for the English bowmen, it is celebrated in Shakespeare's play *Henry V*.

Bibliography: Keegan, John, *The Face of Battle: A Study of Agincourt, Waterloo, and the Somme* (1976).

aging

Aging, or senescence, is a widespread biological phenomenon that occurs in all higher organisms and in many of the lower ones. Its signs usually are a decrease in such functional capacities as the metabolic rate, the ability to sense and respond to stimuli, and the ability to move and also to reproduce. Aging organisms also have an increased susceptibility to disease, injury, and predators. In contrast, protoplasm—the living substance that makes up both the cytoplasm and nuclei of cells—appears to be potentially immortal.

Chronological age refers to the passage of time; generally, when the question is asked how old a person or an animal is, the answer is given in units of time. Physiological age means the condition of the organism in relation to aging. A mouse of 3 years is a "very old" mouse, but a dog is not "very old" until about 15 years, nor a human being until 80 (see OLD AGE). Knowing the chronological age of an animal is almost meaningless unless the LIFE SPAN of that animal's species is known as well.

THE PROCESS OF AGING

The decline of metabolic rate (see METABOLISM) is an important index of the progress of aging. This decline, however, is more complex than appears at first sight. The oxygen uptake in human beings, for example, does not decrease with advancing age; the mean resting heart rate, on the other hand, continues to decline throughout fetal and postnatal life.

The organism ages primarily because the cells of the body, especially those which cannot replace themselves, undergo changes that result in decreased function, degeneration, and death. The different kinds of cells vary markedly in their ability to replace themselves. Such surface layers of cells (epithelia) as those which form the outermost skin and the lining of the digestive and other tracts are able to replace themselves rapidly. Red blood cells are constantly generated in red bone marrow, as are white blood cells in such lymphoid tissues as the lymph nodes, the thymus, and the spleen. The nervous system, conversely, has generally irreplaceable cells known as neurons. As a consequence, with the loss of neurons the brain, the spinal cord, and the ganglia age. Cells of the heart, the voluntary muscles, and certain parts of the immune and endocrine systems also cannot be easily replaced.

Among mammals the size of the body is limited (determinate growth), and when growth ceases certain changes set in. With increasing age come changes in the genetic components of a certain number of somatic (body) cells. These changes may be marked aberrations in the size and shape of the cell nuclei and nucleoli, abnormalities of chromosomes, and the occurrence of irregular cell division. The nucleic acid DNA may incur permanent lesions, especially in the liver.

Immunological changes with age are those which involve the defense mechanisms, especially those against bacteria, viruses, and other foreign substances. The cellular defenses consist of the white blood cells, including some phagocytes that devour bacteria and others that produce antibodies. During the aging process in certain mammals, marked changes—including decrease in size—occur in the lymph nodes, spleen, and bone marrow where these cells are produced. Macrophages—large phagocytic cells in the tissues—become clogged with pigment accumulation. Certain immune functions decrease with age while the incidence of cancer, of immune diseases, and of infections increases.

The steps leading to the death of cells of the nervous system include a decrease or disappearance of the Nissl substance, which is a basophilic material rich in ribosomes that is located in the cytoplasm. Lipofuscin, a yellow green pigment, begins to accumulate in the cytoplasm, and cell nucleoli and nuclei degenerate. These changes are known to occur in such mammals as mice, rats, guinea pigs, dogs, and apes. Changes in human neurons, and the loss of these cells, occur in all parts of the human brain. Although the disorder atherosclerosis may greatly increase the rate and severity of neuronal changes, such changes occur independently as part of the aging process.

Hormonal changes (see HORMONES) profoundly affect the functioning of the body. The most apparent change in humans is the decreased production of sex hormones, producing the onset of MENOPAUSE in women and certain changes in men. Among other changes, lowered levels of insulin occur, causing increased risk of diabetes mellitus. In plants, certain hormones serve to delay senescence, including auxins, cytokinins, and giberrelins.

The stage in which changes occur in the functioning of the nervous system, especially of its higher centers, is termed SENILITY. It is difficult to differentiate senility from senescence. Changes in gait, for example, may be due to changes in the nervous system or to changes in joints, ligaments, or muscles. Senility is probably a distinctive condition, not just an acceleration of the normal aging process. Personality changes are common in senility, as are the onset of paranoid tendencies and fits of irritation or depression.

DIFFERENCES AMONG VARIOUS LIFE FORMS

Vast structural differences exist among classes and phyla of animals, making difficult any comparisons of change of structure with age. Some such comparisons have been detailed.

Plants. Because of the nature of the life processes in plants, their photosynthetic capacity, and their long-continued ability to grow, any statement about aging in plants is complicated. Plants nevertheless share with animals the general properties of LIFE. As knowledge of the ultrastructural features of cells increases, more and more similarities of plant cells to those of animals have been discovered, including similarities between the organelles—mitochondria, endoplasmic reticulum, and Golgi apparatus—of plant and animal cells.

Even in natural conditions the life span of different kinds of plants varies from a few days or hours—as in single-celled plants that reproduce continuously by cell division—to plants that flower annually or perenially to such giant trees as the redwoods that live thousands of years. The actual living part of such trees is relatively small in amount, consisting chiefly of the green cambium layer just beneath the bark.

Certain morphological changes mark the aging process in plants. As a plant passes from youth to old age, the size of the area of the leaf that is enclosed by the smallest branches of the fibrovascular bundles—areas known as leaf islets—becomes smaller and smaller. Propagation by asexual means does not reverse or change this trend; offspring grown from seed, on the other hand, have larger islets. Leaves and fruits of higher plants show signs of senescence and eventual death. Such functional traits as respiratory intensity in leaves decrease with aging.

Invertebrates. Within the phylum Protozoa—organisms that consist of a single cell—are numerous species that reproduce by fission and in which some investigators have observed a real or potential immortality. Other kinds of Protozoa produce offspring within the body of a mother. In such species the adult body shows definite changes of senescence. Clones of certain Protozoa begin to show age changes in their individual members after a certain number of generations.

In other invertebrate phyla, such as the Rotifera, a more typical relation to aging exists. In rotifers, the older the mother from which an egg is produced, the shorter the life and the more rapid the aging process of the individual derived from the egg. In higher phyla of the invertebrates, such as Mollusca, Annelida, and Arthropoda, a decrease in reproductivity capacity occurs with age, and senile changes occur in tissues and cells, especially in the nervous system.

Vertebrates. The five classes of vertebrates differ considerably in the length of the growth period, in the duration of reproductive processes, and in the aging process. Many fishes exhibit such characteristics as indefinite growth, no evidence of declining vigor, and no definite life span. Conversely, accelerated aging occurs in migratory salmon, whereby they pass from vigorous sexual maturity to death in a period of a few weeks, with extensive aging of tissues throughout the body.

Many species of Amphibia have a definite growth period and an absolute adult size, but some species of salamanders and frogs do not. Among vertebrates, reptiles show the greatest longevity. Individuals of at least five species of turtles have lived to more than 100 years of age in captivity. Evidence of a decline in reproductive capacity with age is scanty for snakes, but many species do grow to a specific size at a relatively early age. In birds, the small and fast-breeding species are shorter-lived than the larger and more slowly breeding ones. Anatomical changes with age have been described in both domestic and wild birds.

In the mammals, determinate growth, definite adult size, and rather well-defined life span are the predominant traits. Changes during aging in tissues and organs occur at about the same time in individual species. The major changes with age in humans are graying of the hair; wrinkling of the skin; formation of the arcus senilis, a light-colored ring at the edge of the iris of the eye; bowing of the back; and atrophy of the muscles. The internal organs similarly display certain characteristics of aging.

THEORIES ON AGING

Various theories of the aging process have been proposed. Among these are the environmental theory, the metabolic theory, the genetic theory, and the immunological theory.

The environmental theory of aging stresses the importance of the changes with age in the environment of the living cells. For instance, such deposits as collagen and calcium salts may accumulate, and in a number of organs—including the thyroid gland, the gonads, and the muscles—the number of fibers and the bulk of fibrous tissue may increase. As a result, the epithelial cells often are living in a different and less favorable environment in old than in young individuals.

The metabolic theory of aging is actually a more scientific version of the old "wear and tear" theory, which says that the body of an organism—like many of the machines produced by humans—has a life span limited by the amount of daily use. According to this concept, a life of stress and overexertion, with inadequate time for rest and recuperation, is a deterrent to longevity. Also, each individual supposedly has a particular amount of metabolic energy, and the rate of expenditure of this energy will determine the organism's life span.

Animal longevity is almost always species-specific, which indicates to some investigators that a genetic basis for life span exists. The genetic, or gene-mutation, theory of aging stresses that during the life of an animal spontaneous mutations occur that lead, with advancing age, to malfunctions of tissues and organs and finally to senescence.

The immunological, or autoimmune, theory states that every cell in an individual organism is immunologically similar to every other cell in that organism. If cells undergo change from their genetic pattern, as occurs in mutation, the immunological character of those cells may change. Both nuclei and cytoplasm of such cells may produce substances known as autoantigens. Other cells react to autoantigens by rejecting and killing such cells or by walling them off by deposits.

PREMATURE AGING

An interesting phenomenon known as premature aging (progeria) is a condition observed only in humans. It is distinguished partly by the age of onset. Infantile progeria occurs in childhood, usually after an apparently normal infancy. Retarded growth, dwarfism, and progressively increasing physical abnormalities appear. The skin atrophies, and hypertension occurs. Mental development is often precocious in individuals so afflicted, and they generally die of coronary disease before the age of 30. Cataract and other phenomena of old age often have developed before death.

Adult progeria, or Werner's syndrome, usually occurs after growth has been largely or wholly completed. Persons affected often are short and of unusual appearance. In the third or fourth decade graying of hair and sometimes baldness occur, and the skin atrophies. Hypogonadism, calcification of the arteries, and a tendency to diabetes also are evident. Some of the changes in progeria, especially progeria of the adult form, may prove useful in elucidating the mechanisms of change in normal senescence.

WARREN ANDREW

Bibliography: Barash, David P., *Aging: An Exploration* (1983); Comfort, A., *The Biology of Senescence* (1979); Cox, Harold, ed., *Aging*, 2d ed. (1980); March, James, and McGaugh, James, eds., *Aging* (1981); Strehler, B. L., *Time, Cells, and Aging* (1977).

See also: ALZHEIMER'S DISEASE; GERIATRICS.

Aglipay, Gregorio   [ah-glee-py']

Gregorio Aglipay, 1860–1940, was the first bishop of the Philippine Independent Church. A Roman Catholic priest in Manila, he became chaplain to the forces of Emilio Aguinaldo in the revolution (1898) against Spanish rule. He was appointed vicar-general by Aguinaldo and was excommunicated as a result. Aglipay and his followers then formed (1902) the Philippine Independent Church, which, although divided into trinitarian and unitarian factions, continues in existence today with a membership of 1.4 million (3.9 percent of the Philippine population). In 1935, Aglipay unsuccessfully sought election to the presidency of the Philippines as a militantly nationalist candidate.

Agnatha   [ag'-nuh-thuh]

The Agnatha (superclass Agnatha) are primitive vertebrate fishes that lack true jaws, vertebrae, and pelvic fins. Living species have long eel-like bodies. Two living groups, the HAGFISHES and the LAMPREYS, diverged almost 500 million years ago. The hagfishes, family Myxinidae, are marine scavengers with fingerlike whiskers around the mouth. The lampreys, family Petromyzontidae, inhabit both fresh and marine habitats. All lampreys breed in freshwater streams, where the young go through a larval stage and are called the ammocoete larva. Some species are parasitic and grow into adults that prey on other fish. In nonparasitic species the adults live only long enough to breed.

EDWARD O. WILEY

Agnew, Spiro T.

Spiro Theodore Agnew, b. Baltimore, Md., Nov. 9, 1918, is a former U.S. vice-president and governor of Maryland. Agnew studied law at the University of Baltimore and was admitted to the bar in 1949. He served as Baltimore County executive from 1962 to 1966, when he was elected Republican governor.

As Richard Nixon's vice-president (1969–73), Agnew became known for his colorful speeches attacking dissidents and the news media. Charged with accepting bribes while governor and vice-president, he resigned on Oct. 10, 1973. He pleaded no contest to one count of income tax evasion and was sentenced to 3 years probation and fined $10,000. In 1983, as a result of a civil suit, he paid Maryland $270,000 as reimbursement for kickbacks he allegedly received. He has written a novel, *The Canfield Decision* (1976).

Bibliography: Cohen, Richard M., *A Heartbeat Away: The Investigation and Resignation of Vice-President Spiro T. Agnew* (1974); Lippman, Theo, *Spiro Agnew's America* (1972); Marsh, Robert, *Agnew: The Unexamined Man: A Political Profile* (1971).

Agnon, S. Y.   [ahg'-nohn]

Shmuel Yosef Agnon, b. July 17, 1888, d. Feb. 17, 1970, earned his reputation as a master craftsman of the Hebrew novel and short-story form. The acknowledged dean of Hebrew letters, he received international recognition when he was awarded the Nobel Prize for literature in 1966.

Fully rooted in the traditions of his people, Agnon depicted the spiritual richness of East European Jewish life and its sad decline in the 1930s, as well as the struggles of the early Jewish settlers in Palestine. He wrote realistic, psychological fiction and highly symbolic tales. In expressionistic dreamlike stories, he portrayed human helplessness in a manner reminiscent of Franz KAFKA, the European writer to whom he has most often been compared. His unique style is derived from classical Hebrew sources and marks a departure from contemporary usage.

Agnon's family name was originally Czaczkes. He was born in Galicia (now in Poland), immigrated to Palestine in 1908 and, except for 11 years in Germany, lived in Jerusalem for most of his adult life. His first major novel, *The Bridal Canopy* (1930; rev. Eng. trans., 1967), offered a panoramic view of Jewish life in late 18th- and early 19th-century Galicia. *In the Heart of the Seas* (1933; rev. Eng. trans., 1967) is a folk tale about the pilgrimage of pious 19th-century Jews to Palestine. In his autobiographical work *A Guest for the Night* (1939; Eng. trans., 1968), Agnon revisits his hometown and views its postwar decline. The collection of tales titled *Twenty-one Stories* (1970) reveals the author's modernity. Many critics look upon *Temol Shilshom* (The Day Before Yesterday, 1945), which concerns the problems of the westernized Jew, as Agnon's greatest novel.   JACOB KABAKOFF

Bibliography: Fisch, Harold, *S. Y. Agnon* (1975); Hochman, Baruch, *The Fiction of S. Y. Agnon* (1970).

agnosticism   [ag-nahs'-tuh-sizm]

Agnosticism is the philosophical position that it is impossible to know about the nature or existence of GOD. The term was coined in 1869 by Thomas H. HUXLEY from the Greek *agnōstos* ("unknowable") to refer to his own conviction that knowledge is impossible on many matters covered by religious doctrines. Agnosticism is therefore concerned with questions of EPISTEMOLOGY, the examination of human knowledge; it considers valid only knowledge that comes from ordinary and immediate experience. Agnosticism is distinct from ATHEISM on the one hand and SKEPTICISM on the other. Atheists reject belief in the existence of God. Skeptics hold the strong suspicion or probabilistic estimate that God does not exist. Agnostics refuse to make such judgments.

The agnostic position is as old as philosophy and can be traced to the pre-Socratics and to the Skeptics of ancient Greece. In modern times, agnosticism became prevalent during the 18th and 19th centuries, mainly because of the growing mass of scientific data that seemed to contradict the biblical position and because of the disagreement of theologians and church authorities over the use of textual and historical criticism in the interpretation of the BIBLE. Many of the best-known philosophers have been agnostics. Among them are Auguste COMTE, William JAMES, Immanuel KANT, George SANTAYANA, and Herbert SPENCER.   THOMAS E. WREN

Bibliography: Armstrong, Richard A., *Agnosticism and Theism in the Nineteenth Century* (1977); Budd, Susan, *Varieties of Unbelief: Atheists and Agnostics in English Society, 1850-1960* (1977); Burtt, E. A., *Types of Religious Philosophy* (1951); Collins, James, *God in Modern Philosophy* (1959); Huxley, Thomas H., "Agnosticism" and "Agnosticism and Christianity," in *Collected Essays*, vol. 5 (1902; repr. 1969); Mavrodes, George, *Belief in God* (1970); Russell, Bertrand, *Why I Am Not a Christian* (1957).

agon: see NARRATIVE AND DRAMATIC DEVICES.

agora   [ag'-uh-ruh]

In ancient Greece, an agora was a public area or marketplace, usually located in the middle of the city or near a harbor.

Generally square in shape, it was always surrounded by a colonnade of single or double ranges of columns. In early Greek times public assemblies were held in the agora. Later it functioned primarily as the center of commercial life in the city; markets were held here, and it was the site of transactions of all kinds.

In later Greek times the agora also became a religious center and contained temples, altars, commemorative statues, and sometimes even the tombs of important personages. The porticoes were often decorated with murals. The Roman FORUM was essentially an adaptation of the ancient Greek agora.   LELAND ROTH

See also: GREEK ARCHITECTURE.

agoraphobia   [ag-uh-ruh-foh'-bee-uh]

Agoraphobia is an intense, irrational fear of being in or crossing through a wide-open space; see PHOBIA.

Agostino di Duccio   [ah-goh-stee'-noh dee doo'-choh]

Agostino di Duccio, b. 1418, d. c.1481, was a Florentine sculptor of the RENAISSANCE whose contribution comes from important works done outside Florence. Influenced by DONATELLO at an early stage, he developed a highly individual style, involving swirling linear surface play of a particularly lyrical quality. His most important works are relief panels (1447-54) in the Tempio Malatestiano, RIMINI, and at the Oratory of San Bernardino (1457-61), PERUGIA. He also worked in Venice, Bologna, and Modena. In 1463 he completed the first (now lost) of two commissions for colossal statues for the Duomo, the Cathedral of Florence. The second statue remained incomplete, and the huge marble block was used 40 years later by MICHELANGELO for his statue of DAVID (1501-04; Accademia, Florence).   GIULIA BARTRUM

Bibliography: Hartt, F., *History of Italian Renaissance Art* (1969); Keller, H., *The Renaissance in Italy* (1969); Pope-Hennessy, J., *Italian Renaissance Sculpture* (1958); Stokes, A., *The Stones of Rimini* (1969).

See also: ALBERTI, LEON BATTISTA; ITALIAN ART AND ARCHITECTURE; SCULPTURE.

agouti   [uh-goo'-tee]

The orange-rumped agouti, D. agouti, tames easily and is sometimes kept as a pet. In the wild, the agouti burrows among boulders, under trees, and into riverbanks.

The agouti, genus *Dasyprocta*, is a RODENT belonging to the family Dasyproctidae, order Rodentia. About 24 species exist. Agoutis are about 61 cm (24 in) long, have short tails (10-35 mm/$\frac{2}{5}$-1$\frac{2}{5}$ in), and weigh up to 3 kg (7lb). The coarse, glossy coat ranges from pale orange to shades of brown and near-black; the underparts are whitish. The body is slender with a high, muscular rump well adapted for running. The front paws have five claws and the hind have three that are hooflike.

Agoutis live from southern Mexico to southern Brazil. They flourish in cool, damp lowland forests, grasslands, and brush, and feed on leaves, fruit, nuts, and roots. They dig burrows in which they raise litters of two to four.   EVERETT SENTMAN

Bibliography: Hanney, Peter W., *Rodents: Their Lives and Habits* (1975).

Agra   [ah'-gruh]

Agra, a city in north central India on the right bank of the Yamuna River, is the administrative headquarters of the Agra district in Uttar Pradesh state. The population is 591,917

(1971). The average annual temperature is 26° C (78° F), and rainfall averages 765 mm (30 in) annually. Although Agra has a rich Muslim heritage, the majority of its present population is Hindu. Agra was developed as a trading post and strategic capital site. Today it is a center for light industry, and tourism is significant. Agra University was founded in 1927.

Babur, founder of the Mogul Empire (1526), informally established Agra as the administrative seat of his rule. In 1566, Akbar, grandson of Babur, formally made the city the imperial capital. Agra is famous for its fine examples of Mogul architecture. These include Agra Fort, a red sandstone fortress complex, the mausoleum of Itimad-ud-daulah, and the world-renowned TAJ MAHAL, constructed of white marble by Shah Jahan as a sepulcher for his empress Mumtaz Mahal.

ASHOK K. DUTT

agranulocytosis

Agranulocytosis is a disorder of the blood in which the number of white cells is markedly reduced, usually resulting in the development of infected ulcers on the skin and in the throat, intestinal tract, and other mucous membranes. The condition is usually caused by interference with the production and release of white cells in the bone marrow. This may result from damage to the bone marrow by ionizing radiation or by drugs used to treat cancer and leukemia, as well as by certain antibiotics, tranquilizers, antidepressants, antithyroid agents, anti-inflammatory drugs, insecticides, and solvents. The condition may also be caused by certain hereditary disorders affecting the bone marrow by a deficiency of folic acid and vitamin B$_{12}$.

Acute cases are characterized by chills, fever, and prostration. Because white blood cells are an important defense against invading microorganisms, agranulocytosis may cause a bacterial infection to become life-threatening.

PETER L. PETRAKIS

Agrarians: see FUGITIVES AND AGRARIANS.

agribusiness

Agribusiness is the name for the sector of the economy that purchases and processes agricultural commodities—and often produces them—and fabricates and sells agricultural production materials and equipment.

The agribusiness sector is much larger than the farming industry. Of each dollar spent by consumers on food, only 38 percent goes to farms; 62 percent is absorbed by the transportation, processing, packaging, refrigerating, storage, marketing, and retailing of foods transformed from farm commodities. In addition, the agribusiness sector processes the fertilizers, insecticides, herbicides, veterinary supplies, feed, and feed additives for growing or raising food. It also supplies improved seed varieties, machinery and equipment, automotive vehicles, and many other requirements of modern farming.

The growth of agribusiness parallels the rapid rise in capital-intensive industry during the past half century and is largely responsible for the industrialization of the food system in America. Today, tractors, machines, and other equipment have replaced most farm labor. Advances in the sciences have resulted in chemical fertilizers, pesticides, and other materials that greatly increase farm yields. Sophisticated food technology, combined with massive advertising expenditures, has created consumer acceptance of highly processed packaged foods, instant cereals, frozen vegetables, protein concentrates in the form of breakfast bars, and so on. The rapid growth of the fast-food industry is an extension of this trend.

Another result of the growth of agribusiness has been the vertical integration of portions of the food industry. A case in point is broiler chicken production: a firm will furnish the baby chicks and feed to a farmer, who supplies the labor to produce market-weight broilers. These are then purchased, processed, shipped, and marketed by the firm. Some large supermarkets reach back through the food chain to contract directly with farmers for their output.

Whereas most farmers remain relatively free in making de-

cisions, the various phases of the food chain are becoming more interdependent.

EARL O. HEADY

Bibliography: Ritson, Christopher, *Agricultural Economics: Principles and Policy* (1977); Roy, Ewell P., *Exploring Agribusiness*, 2d ed. (1975); Weyant, J. Thomas, et al., *Introduction to Agriculture Business and Industry* (1971); Wills, Walter J., *An Introduction to Agri-Business Management* (1973).

See also: FOOD INDUSTRY; FOOD TECHNOLOGY.

Agricola, Georgius   [uh-grik′-oh-luh, jor′-jee-uhs]

The German educator, city official, and physician Georgius Agricola (Latinized form of Georg Bauer), b. Mar. 24, 1494, d. Nov. 21, 1555, is best known as the author of *De re metallica* (1556), a treatise on mining and metallurgy. The treatise was translated into English in 1912 by Herbert Hoover and his wife, Lou Henry Hoover. Agricola studied medicine at Leipzig University. He became a devoted follower of Erasmus, who wrote a foreword to Agricola's first book on mining and metallurgy (1530). While town physician of Joachimsthal (now Jáchymov, Czechoslovakia), he became intensely interested in all aspects of the mining and metallurgy industry by which the town thrived and began a 25-year study of the subject, which culminated in his posthumously published masterpiece. The 12-chapter treatise included 292 woodcut illustrations carefully executed by Blasius Weffring. Agricola also wrote a number of works on medicine, geology, mineralogy, politics, and economics.

DAVID HOUNSHELL

Bibliography: Agricola, Georgius, *De re metallica*, trans. by Herbert Clark Hoover and Lou Henry Hoover (1912; repr. 1950); Dibner, Brian, *Agricola on Metals* (1958).

Agricola, Gnaeus Julius   [uh′-grik′-oh-luh, gnay′-uhs]

Gnaeus Julius Agricola, b. June 13, AD 37, d. Aug. 23, 93, was a Roman general who served ably as a conqueror and governor (78–84) of Britain. He subdued North Wales and expanded Roman rule north into Scotland, defeating the Caledonians at Mons Graupius (location unknown) in 83. Agricola Romanized Britain in a shrewd and gradual fashion, fostering urbanization and partial self-rule in the south. His son-in-law TACITUS left an account of his enlightened rule.

Bibliography: Burn, A., *Agricola and Roman Britain* (1953; repr. 1965).

Agricultural Adjustment Administration

Created by the U.S. Congress under the Agricultural Adjustment Act of May 1933, the Agricultural Adjustment Administration (AAA) was the most important early NEW DEAL effort to combat the effects of the DEPRESSION OF THE 1930s on the nation's farms. The AAA attempted to raise farm prices by restricting agricultural output. Under the Domestic Allotment Plan, which affected such staple crops as wheat, cotton, corn, and tobacco, benefits were paid for lowered crop production. This plan helped raise commodity prices, but land-owning farmers benefited most; tenant farmers and sharecroppers often faced eviction when production was curtailed.

In January 1936 the U.S. Supreme Court, in *U.S.* v. *Butler*, declared the Domestic Allotment Plan unconstitutional on the grounds that subsidies imposed an unacceptable system of regulation. Congress responded by passing the Soil Conservation and Domestic Allotment Act (1936), which allowed the AAA to pay benefits to farmers who planted soil-enriching instead of staple crops, and the Agricultural Adjustment Act (1938), which allowed the AAA to fix acreages for staple export crops and grant loans on the basis of stored surplus crops. The AAA continued to function, with reduced authority, until 1945, when it was absorbed by the Production and Marketing Administration.

RICHARD POLENBERG

Bibliography: Conrad, David, *The Forgotten Farmers* (1965); Mitchell, Broadus, *Depression Decade* (1947; repr. 1977); Nourse, Edwin G., et al., *Three Years of Agricultural Adjustment Administration* (1937; repr. 1971); Perkins, Van L., *Crisis in Agriculture: Agricultural Adjustment and the New Deal, 1933* (1969); Shannon, David A., ed., *The Great Depression* (1960).

agricultural education

Agricultural education, as a field of formal study, instructs in the sciences and the arts of farming and in the processing and distribution of foods and other agricultural products. One of the newer major branches of education, it extends through the high school, college, and graduate levels. Continuing education—often referred to as AGRICULTURAL EXTENSION SERVICES—is extensive; constantly revised best practices of production and management are provided to farmers and others already formally educated.

Agricultural education in the United States began in the late 18th century with societies for the advancement of agriculture; these societies encouraged agricultural instruction in the public schools and often published their own teaching materials. Agricultural schools began to flourish after the Morrill Act of 1862 established LAND-GRANT COLLEGES. In the United States and other developed nations the emphasis has shifted from technical instruction to management during the latter half of the 20th century.

Agricultural education is far less available in the developing countries, but national governments and international organizations have recognized the need to invest in schools that modernize farming. Since 1964 the World Bank has been lending funds for agricultural education, mostly for buildings and equipment. Many Asian countries emphasize the building of vocational agriculture schools at the high school level. In 1970, 214,000 students were enrolled in 19 Asian countries, but only about 27,000 students were graduating annually at this level. Enrollments decreased as young people chose general education programs suitable for city jobs. Japan has 315 vocational agriculture schools, and India has 92 universities offering specialized agricultural instruction. Laos, Nepal, Afghanistan, Burma, Sri Lanka, and Malaysia have one agricultural school each. Enrollments for agricultural study are increasing at the university level in Asia, except in Japan and Korea, the countries of the region that are industrializing the fastest. Graduates often go into technical jobs related to agriculture, rather than directly into farming.

The bureaucratic organization of agricultural education and extension has often been cumbersome. In former British and French colonies in Asia and Africa the difficulties have been compounded by the overlapping and conflicting roles of ministries of agriculture and ministries of education. In many countries the small number of highly trained educators cannot adequately instruct an enormous farm population not previously reached by agricultural educators or extension workers. Such countries as India, however, have produced enough agricultural graduates to enable these countries to place many of them at the village level. Educational methods needed to communicate agricultural knowledge to peasant farmers vary according to the levels of poverty and illiteracy in individual countries (see AGRICULTURE AND THE FOOD SUPPLY). Broadcasting, for instance, reached huge populations untouched by agricultural instruction in any previous generation. In Egypt, for example, each of 4,000 village cooperatives now has a television set receiving a 4-hour farming program every week.

E. L. JONES

Bibliography: Axinn, George Harold, and Thorat, Sudhakar, *Modernizing World Agriculture: A Comparative Study of Agricultural Extension Education Systems* (1972); FAO, *World Conference on Agricultural Education and Training, Copenhagen, 1970 Report*, 2 vols. (1971); Scott, Roy V., *The Reluctant Farmer* (1970); UNESCO, *Agricultural Education in Asia* (1971); Williams, D. B., *Agricultural Extension: Farm Extension Services in Australia, Britain and the U.S.A.* (1968).

agricultural extension service

Agricultural extension services worldwide provide education on farming techniques and management skills on a local or regional level (see AGRICULTURE AND THE FOOD SUPPLY). The Cooperative Extension Service of the U.S. Department of Agriculture was established in 1914 to apply the results of agricultural research done in U.S. land-grant colleges. Operating through state and county extension agents, it helps U.S. farmers to learn and use new agricultural techniques. Home-demonstration agents supply information and advice on food-preserving and cooking techniques and on farm economics and financing. The 4-H PROGRAMS train young people in agricultural, food-processing, and management techniques.

agriculture, history of

Agriculture involves raising deliberately bred crops and livestock (see ANIMAL HUSBANDRY) for food, fiber, and other materials. Although thousands of plant and animal species exist, only 200 plant and about 50 animal species have been domesticated. About 12 or 13 plant crops are important staples, and almost all of these are GRAINS—especially wheat, rice, and maize (corn)—that were domesticated from wild GRASSES by deliberate cultivation of their seeds.

During the PALEOLITHIC PERIOD—from at least 2.5 million years ago to about 8000 BC—people hunted, fished, or gathered their food (see PREHISTORIC HUMANS). From about 11,000 to 8000 BC, flint-edged wooden sickles were used to gather wild grains, which were stored in caves; about 9000 BC, sheep were domesticated in the Near East. From approximately 8300 to 6500 BC, during the MESOLITHIC PERIOD, groups of people began to practice natural plant husbandry by simply broadcasting seeds and waiting for the harvest. The only crude tool needed was a haft of bone, wood, or antler fitted with a microlith—a small, sharp blade of stone—for reaping grain.

Models of an Egyptian hoe (left) and plow (right), from a 4,000-year-old tomb, illustrate the rudimentary state of agricultural technology. Both tools are of wood, but the plow uses ox-power, allowing the farmer to cultivate a far greater area than he could plow by himself.

Dogs were the first animals to be tamed, usually to help in hunting. In the Near East such herd animals as goats, sheep, and cattle were domesticated.

The practice of cultivating plants became established in the Near East and Europe about 6500–3500 BC, in southeast Asia about 6800–4000 BC, and in Mesoamerica and Peru about 2500 BC. Most areas where cultivation began were located in river valleys having semiarid climates. The process of cultivation in the Old World (see NEOLITHIC PERIOD) involved preparing soil by harrowing—breaking down and smoothing with a tree branch—and sowing choice seeds with a stick plow. In Mesoamerica, where no species of draft animal existed and where the chief grain—maize—required individual planting, a plowless form of cultivation developed, whereby a digging stick was used to make holes into which the seeds were dropped.

Early Agriculture in the Old World. The evolution from nomadic HUNTER-GATHERERS to cultivators allowed people to establish permanent villages because they had a reliable food supply close at hand. More people were freed from providing food and were able to develop technologies and services that led to the shift from farming communities to towns; eventually, agriculture-based civilizations were formed.

In MESOPOTAMIA, the region between the Tigris and Euphrates rivers in present-day Iraq (see FERTILE CRESCENT), cultivation began in the 9th millennium BC. The wheel was invented, pulleys were used to draw water from artificial canals, and complex IRRIGATION systems were constructed. Mesopotamians raised wheat and other cereal grains; were skilled in gardening; and domesticated the camel, donkey, and horse.

Relying on the water and fertile silt of the Nile, Egyptians (see EGYPT, ANCIENT) irrigated land to ensure large crops of wheat and barley, which, along with flax, provided the basis for their agriculture. Several types of palm trees were cultivated, and wild papyrus was harvested to make paper. In addition to oxen and horses, the Egyptians kept poultry, sheep, goats, swine, and cattle.

The INDUS CIVILIZATION of northern India, which existed from about 2300 to 1750 BC, raised wheat, barley, and rice. These people grew such plants as cotton, sesame, tea, and sugarcane. Chickens were domesticated from Indian jungle fowl, and the water buffalo and zebu cattle were used as draft animals. Farmers used plows, designed effective irrigation systems, and built large granaries. Among the river valleys of China, people learned how to cultivate soybeans, oranges, peaches, pears, hemp, and tea. They kept livestock, practiced intensive gardening, and excelled at flower horticulture.

Agriculture in Pre-Columbian America. In Mesoamerica—what is now Mexico and Central America—gourds, peppers, avocados, and a grain, amaranth, were domesticated from 7000 to 5000 BC. The people of Mesoamerica were nomadic hunters and semiagriculturists, however, until 2500 BC, when maize was domesticated. The Maya-Toltec-Aztec civilization flourished in Mexico and Central America from AD 250 to

1600 (see AZTEC; MAYA). These people hybridized corn to increase yields and also cultivated beans, squash, chili peppers, avocados, and potatoes. They grew tobacco and several species of cotton. They built irrigation canals and made artificial gardens that floated on water, such as those seen at XOCHIMILCO. Dry farming—cultivation of nonirrigated lands by moisture-retaining tillage—was practiced.

At about AD 1200 the INCA were carving out an empire in the Andes amid a harsh environment. They used stone hoes and digging sticks with a foot rest for pushing the end into the soil. Terraces, irrigation, and drainage systems were constructed skillfully; land was fertilized, and stone storehouses were built to preserve food. The Inca cultivated such foods as corn, white and sweet potatoes, and squash. They domesticated the llama as a beast of burden and kept alpacas for wool.

Early Greece and Rome. From 2000 BC on, the Greeks cultivated cereal grains—chiefly barley—raised olive and fig trees, and kept vineyards and livestock. The Greeks are credited with inventing a water wheel equipped with buckets to raise water to a higher level. Farmers used wooden implements primarily, including a threshing sledge with rocks for teeth.

The Romans advanced farm technology in the Mediterranean world by making tools, including the plow, reaper, hoe, and sickle, that had iron parts. They cultivated wheat, barley, and millet; kept vineyards; and raised livestock. Before 200 BC, Roman farmers were independent, each owning about 1.8 to 6.1 ha (4 to 15 acres). During the next 200 years the wealthy acquired publicly owned lands until they each controlled hundreds or thousands of hectares, which were worked by slaves. Throughout this period a series of agrarian laws were enacted to divide land held by the wealthy and distribute it to small farmers. These attempts at land reform eventually failed, and by AD 200 many farmers were tenants on estates. By AD 400 the rights of these tenants were reduced until they became serfs, bound to the land.

Medieval Europe. Farmers who did own small holdings divided their land among their sons. The subsequent small holdings ensured poverty among independent farmers, and especially after the Roman Empire collapsed in AD 476, small farmers were forced to surrender their lands to powerful nobles in return for protection. This arrangement evolved during the High MIDDLE AGES (AD 1000–1300) into MANORIALISM, especially in England, France, and Germany.

Under manorialism, serfs lived in villages near the lord's manor and farmed their own plots in open, commonly held fields as well as laboring on the lord's land, or demesne. Each serf farmed 5 to 12 ha (12 to 30 acres), which were divided into 0.4-ha (1-acre) strips and scattered throughout three fields among the holdings of other serfs. One field remained fallow for a year in order to rejuvenate its fertility. Such crops as wheat, barley, beans, oats, and rye were planted in the other fields. Similar manorial systems developed in China, Japan, and India.

Enclosure and the Agricultural Revolution. During the 15th century the owners of English landed estates began to en-

Three illustrations from a Peruvian manuscript reveal Inca methods of farming. A man opens ground with a digging stick (left) while one woman scatters corn seeds and another holds a seed basket. A reservoir tank (center) supplies water to irrigation channels that crisscross fields. Bags of corn (right) are transported by llamas to a granary.

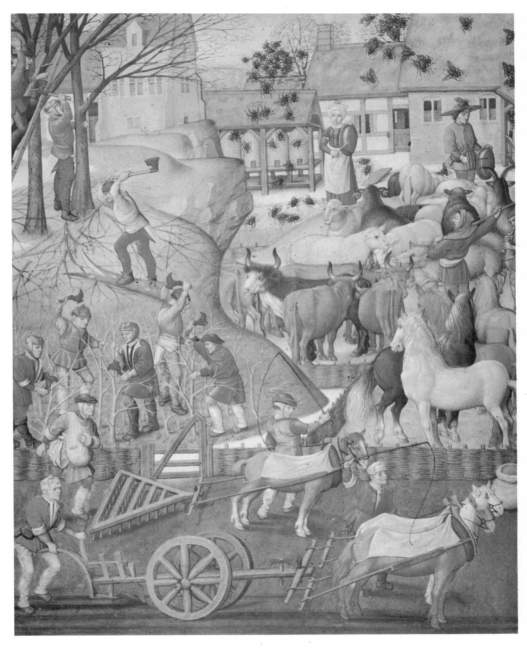

A 15th-century Flemish miniature of farming activities includes (at top right) the persuading of swarming bees into their hives—the four round structures sheltered by a thatched roof—by beating sticks on metal dishes. Oxen, sheep, horses, and a boar are herded together in unusual proximity (center right) to the music of a recorder. A field (foreground) is plowed and harrowed with ironwrought implements, and a laborer broadcasts seed. Five men (center left) with iron billhooks prune young trees in an orchard. To their rear, workers use axes to chop wood at the edge of a forest. By the Middle Ages in Europe, horses had replaced oxen as the principal draft animals. One of the greatest contributions to agriculture of this period in European history was the invention of the horse collar, which subsequently remained unchanged in design for centuries.

close their lands with hedges (see ENCLOSURE). The first enclosure movement (1485–1603) converted arable land to pasture for sheep. Enclosure movements of the 1600s and especially from 1750 to 1831 permitted holders to cultivate large sections of land with the same crop. This procedure was more efficient than farming strips, eliminated the practice of letting land lie fallow, and allowed farmers to experiment with crop rotation and other agricultural technologies. Enclosure of lands, however, served to displace farmers, who either became tenants or landless farm laborers or migrated into the growing cities (see INDUSTRIAL REVOLUTION). Other European countries slowly began to enclose lands after 1800.

The invention of mechanical farm implements during the 17th and 18th centuries created an agricultural revolution in England. The inventions included Joseph Boyce's REAPER (1799) and Jethro TULL's horse-drawn drill (1701). Charles, 2d Viscount TOWNSHEND, of Norfolk introduced crop rotation of clover, wheat, turnips, and barley—an alternation of grain crops with nitrogen-fixing legumes and grasses that put nutrients back into the soil. Such FERTILIZERS as guano, lime, gypsum, and sandy clay, known as marl, were used to improve the soil. The first agricultural society (founded 1793) included Arthur Young (1741–1820), an educator who spread English agricultural innovations to the rest of Europe and the United States. In France during this period (1756–70) a group of men called PHYSIOCRATS—notably François Quesnay and Pierre Samuel du Pont de Nemours (see DU PONT family)—began to outline agricultural economics.

With the age of colonialism, the European powers established plantations throughout Africa, Asia, the Pacific, the Caribbean, and Latin America. On these large land holdings, such cash crops as coffee, tea, bananas, and rubber were introduced, and indigenous people worked as wage laborers.

Colonial America. Throughout the coastal colonies settlers

(Above) A steel plow patented by John Deere in 1837 was the first implement capable of breaking sod in the U.S. prairies. Unlike cast-iron plows, the steel plow could cut through the deeply rooted prairie grass, and the heavy soil did not stick to the blade. The availability of the steel plow made it possible for U.S. prairie land to become one of the vital grain-providing regions of the world.

(Right) A combine harvester is pulled through an Oregon wheat field in this 1880s photo. Horse-drawn combines, which both cut and threshed wheat, weighed up to 14 metric tons (15 U.S. tons) and used teams of 30 or more horses. In the late 1800s the wide, flat wheat fields of the western and midwestern United States easily accommodated these huge machines.

were taught by native Americans how to plant corn and other indigenous crops. In Canada during the 1700s mainly fur trappers and only a few farmers in Quebec occupied the land. Farmsteads along the St. Lawrence River were laid out in long strips, with one edge along the river and the farm building along a road; agriculture was on a subsistence level because the land was relatively infertile and the growing season short. New England farms were small subsistence farms, yielding rye, corn, barley, oats, and apples. Livestock was allowed to forage in woodlands. The larger farms of the middle colonies—New Jersey and Pennsylvania, for instance—originally grew New World crops because they were easier to plant and yielded more per hectare than Old World crops. These larger farms later introduced wheat, however, a crop that could be sold to the European market and that allowed farmers to become more commercial. Southern plantations—which used slave labor—covered hundreds of hectares and usually grew one crop intensively for commerce, particularly tobacco (introduced in 1614), rice (1696), indigo (mid-1700s), and cotton (1780s). Eli WHITNEY invented (1794) the cotton gin, which spurred Southern states to intensive cotton planting.

18th- and 19th-Century America. After the American Revolution the U.S. federal government began to develop land policies that would promote settlement of the West quickly and at low cost. The Land Ordnance of 1785 stipulated that land be surveyed in square blocks; the Northwest Ordnance (see NORTHWEST TERRITORY) encouraged free exchange of land. Federal expansion policies continued in the 1800s following the Louisiana Purchase (1803), the acquisition of Texas as a state (1845), the Oregon settlement (1846), and the Mexican Cession (1848).

Such improved transportation as canals (see ERIE CANAL), steamboats, and railroads allowed commercial crops to be shipped more easily and quickly to market. Wars in Europe increased the demand for cotton, tobacco, and food. Such inventions as Cyrus McCORMICK's reaper (1831) and John DEERE's steel plow (1837) allowed the heavy, rich soils of the prairie to be tilled, opening new regions for the cultivation of wheat. The invention of barbed wire and the steel windmill made farming possible in what had been open range for Texas longhorn cattle. Food-processing techniques, such as canning, improved flour milling, and refrigeration, were developed during the 1840s. Refrigeration was especially important in making it possible for such distant countries as Argentina (beef) and New Zealand (mutton, milk, butter, and

cheese) to export food to Europe.

In 1862, Abraham Lincoln signed the HOMESTEAD ACT, which allowed a settler 160 acres (64.7 ha) free after working it for 5 years. The U.S. Department of Agriculture was formed in 1862, which year also saw the passage into law of the MORRILL ACT, which granted land to states for the establishment of agricultural colleges (see LAND-GRANT COLLEGES). In 1867 the National GRANGE, an organization for the alleviation of poverty among farmers, was created.

During the 1870s wheat farmers and cattle ranchers flourished in the prairies. A specific variety of wheat—Turkey Red—adapted particularly well to prairie soil, and wheat economy improved. Ranchers began to feed cattle grain, which resulted in better-quality beef sold to urban markets. The development of steam power resulted in mechanized COMBINES, TRACTORS, and threshers, which further improved wheat farming.

Although Canada's expansion policies did not open up prairie land until the 1870s, Thomas Douglas, 5th earl of SELKIRK, attempted to establish an experimental colony in Manitoba in 1812. He had received a land grant from the Hudson's Bay Company for the site where present-day Winnepeg exists and brought Scotch and Irish settlers to work the land. Despite crop failure, the agricultural inexperience of the farmers, and hostilities of the neighboring métis (people of mixed French and Indian ancestry), this RED RIVER SETTLEMENT eventually succeeded, especially after the introduction of an iron plow in 1824. Further colonization was minimal until legislation to section off land in squares and a homesteading act in 1870 encouraged immigration.

In 1887 the HATCH ACT, in the United States, ensured federal funding to land-grant colleges in order to set up agricultural experiment stations. During this time the agricultural scientist George Washington CARVER developed soybean flour, 118 products from sweet potatoes, and 300 products from peanuts at his research station at Tuskegee Institute, Alabama, in an effort to spur economic growth in the South by developing new crop potentials.

20th-Century United States. By the 1890s the gasoline tractor had been invented, providing power to do in minutes what took horses and farmers days. Gregor Johann MENDEL's theories of HEREDITY came to light in the early 1900s, after which PLANT BREEDING became a science. By 1910 most of the arable land in the United States had been settled, and with the foresight of the conservationist Gifford PINCHOT, methods for

(Above) *The Case steam engine, patented in 1886, replaced horses in pulling plows and combines. Modeled on early railway engines, this tractor was used for a short time until the invention of gasoline-powered engines.*

(Left) *A machine, following the contours of the land, harvests wheat on a large farm in the state of Washington. Farming has been mechanized in the United States and other developed countries to such an extent that almost all work formerly performed by hand is now done by machine.*

prevention of soil erosion began to be developed (see CONSERVATION). In 1914 the SMITH-LEVER ACT provided funding for extension work (see AGRICULTURAL EXTENSION SERVICE), which involves educators' traveling to instruct farmers and their families in farm management and home economics.

U.S. and Canadian farmers mobilized to provide food for Europe during World War I. As a result of European postwar poverty and U.S. overproduction, however, farmers experienced a depression lasting from 1922 to 1927. Nevertheless, Clarence BIRDSEYE perfected (1920s) a method for freezing foods, and supermarkets were springing up, both of which spurred farming of produce previously too perishable to be of commercial value. The Cooper-Volstead Act (1922) allowed farmers to join COOPERATIVE organizations that controlled the marketing of their commodities, resulting in greater profits. Despite the progress, farmers' incomes were lower than the national level; therefore, legislative efforts to alleviate the disparity in income began (see PARITY, economics).

In the early 1930s DROUGHTS and dust storms caused by poor tillage practices devastated farms and ranches of the Great Plains (see DUST BOWL). Franklin D. Roosevelt's NEW DEAL sought to satisfy the demands of striking farmers by a series of acts that included the Agricultural Adjustment Act (1933; see AGRICULTURAL ADJUSTMENT ADMINISTRATION)—by which the secretary of agriculture could control crop production and reduce unfair practices toward farmers—and acts to improve rural roads and introduce electricity and telephone service. The Agricultural Marketing Act (1937) improved prices for producers of perishables and allowed the federal government to buy surpluses, which were then donated to the poor and used in school-meal and food-stamp programs. During the 1930s more-powerful tractors were built, and harvesters for root and vegetable crops were invented. Hybrid corn was planted, and the Santa Gertrudis and American Brahman cattle, which could tolerate hot weather, were bred.

By the 1960s farmers required a huge outlay of capital and demanding marketing skills to deal with suppliers and food distributors in a network known as AGRIBUSINESS. High-powered machinery, feed, fertilizers, and pesticides began to be used, and poultry was raised in completely controlled environments (see FACTORY FARMING and EGG PRODUCTION). At the same time, lobbies of migrant laborers, environmental groups, and consumers began to affect agricultural policy. Some farmers initiated organic farming—using nonpolluting, nontoxic methods of cropping and animal breeding. The

GREEN REVOLUTION of the 1960s, spearheaded by the plant geneticist Norman Ernest BORLAUG, was developed as a crop improvement program for small farmers of developing nations (see AGRICULTURE AND THE FOOD SUPPLY). Technologies of the 1970s included a machine that used air flow to distribute seeds during planting and the use of LANDSAT satellites to remotely sense crop growth, yields, insect and disease occurrence, and soil and water conditions. Such crops as soybeans, sunflowers, and sorghum have been increasingly important, as well as such arid plants as jojoba—which yields an oil similar to that of the sperm whale—and guayule, a rubber substitute. In 1981 researchers at the International Center for Tropical Agriculture in Colombia were developing crops that need little fertilizer and irrigation. These crops include beans, cassava, and rice, all of which, it is hoped, will benefit small farmers.

Bibliography: Baker, Herbert G., *Plants and Civilization*, 3d ed. (1978); Bender, Barbara, *Farming in Prehistory* (1975); Grigg, D. B., *Agricultural Systems of the World* (1974); Harlan, Jack R., *Crops and Man* (1975); Hutchinson, Joseph, et al., *The Early History of Agriculture* (1977); Killingray, Margaret, *Agricultural Revolution* (1980); King, Russell, *Land Reform: A World Survey* (1978); Mingay, G. E., *Enclosure and the Small Farmer in the Age of the Industrial Revolution* (1968); Rasmussen, Wayne, ed., *Agriculture in the United States*, 3 vols. (1979); Simmonds, N. W., ed., *Evolution of Crop Plants* (1979); Struever, Stuart, ed., *Prehistoric Agriculture* (1971).

Agriculture, U.S. Department of

One of the largest departments of the federal government, the U.S. Department of Agriculture administers programs and services concerned with farmers and consumers. These include farm price-supports, food stamps for low-income citizens, loans to farmers, soil conservation, biological research, the grading and inspection of meat and other products, crop forecasting, crop insurance, and negotiations with foreign governments for trade in agricultural products.

Established in 1862, the department was given cabinet status in 1889. In 1981 the department was composed of about 20 agencies, with a staff of 106,000 and a budget of $4 billion. The Forest Service manages 154 national forests and 19 national grasslands. The Agricultural Stabilization and Conservation Service works to stabilize farm prices for wheat, feed grains, cotton, rice, and other commodities by making loans, establishing acreage allotments, and purchasing surplus crops. The Foreign Agricultural Service promotes export sales of farm products and analyzes and reports on agricultural production and trade in more than 100 countries. The Food and Nutrition Service makes low-cost food available to people who need it through such channels as the FOOD STAMP PROGRAM, the National School Lunch Program, and the Food Distribution Program. The Science and Education Administration works to improve research, extension, and teaching in the food and agricultural sciences. It conducts research programs in animal and plant production and human nutrition. It also administers federal grant funds for research and cooperates with state governments in the Cooperative Extension Service, which assists in such areas as agricultural production, marketing, natural resources, home economics, food and nutrition, 4-H development, and community and rural development.

Bibliography: Gaus, John M., and Wolcott, Leon O., *Public Administration and the Department of Agriculture* (1975); United States Department of Agriculture, *A Century of Service: The First One Hundred Years of the Department of Agriculture* (1963).

agriculture and the food supply

The supply of food depends on three factors: how much has been produced by agriculture and fishing (see FISHING INDUSTRY); how much has been consumed; and how much has been preserved by safe processing and storage (see FOOD TECHNOLOGY). The most important agricultural products for the world's food supply are cereals (GRAINS), pulses, and, to a lesser extent, livestock (see ANIMAL HUSBANDRY). Cereals, such as wheat, rice, maize (corn), millet, and sorghum, provide nearly all the food energy (calories) and up to 90% of all protein consumed by the world's people. Pigs are the chief meat animal worldwide, followed by poultry, beef cattle, and sheep. Pulses—the seed parts of such legumes as dried beans, soybeans, and peanuts (groundnuts)—are important sources of protein in the world food supply. Except for sugar and bananas, few of the other crops that are prominent in the world agriculture trade have nutritional significance in the food supply. Many fruits, grains, and vegetables that are often unfamiliar to Western agricultural scientists, however, serve as important local food supplies.

Supply and Population. About 90% of all grain produced is consumed in the countries where it is grown. The 10% that enters world trade comes from the few countries—the United States, Canada, Australia, and Argentina—where the grain produced far exceeds domestic needs. Most countries

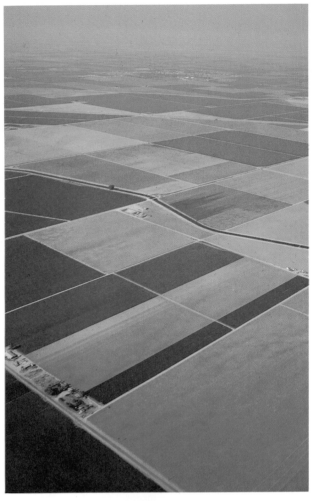

(Above) *Commercial farmers in the United States have used agricultural technology— irrigation, fertilizers, pesticides, and large machinery—to yield crops from large expanses of otherwise uncultivable land, thus meeting the increasing demand for adequate food supplies.*

(Left) *The Ifugao tribe of the Philippines cuts terraces into steep, fertile mountain slopes. The heavy rainfalls caught by these terraces supply the water necessary for rice cultivation. The construction of terraces is one of many ways that farmers of various regions in the world adapt land to meet agricultural needs.*

depend to some extent—and developing countries tend to depend heavily—on cereal imports to augment their own crops.

Some authorities predict that POPULATION growth will eventually surpass world food production and that massive FAMINE will result—a theory first proposed by the British social philosopher Thomas MALTHUS. Other authorities, who point to a recent decrease of population growth rates as well as to dramatic gains in agricultural production, insist that such a tragedy can be prevented by a combination of appropriate governmental policies and appropriate research and technology.

Effective Demand. Both high population growth and the effects of a minority of the world's people having the money to consume more than they need can cause stresses in the food supply. Persistent POVERTY, however, is the underlying cause of the world's hunger problem because in many places the ability to obtain food is determined by income and purchasing power no matter how large the supply may be. People or governments without enough purchasing power lack what is called *effective demand* for food in the marketplace.

Many governments find it necessary, therefore, to protect the nutritional needs of their own low-income populations, and sometimes those of others, with special programs. The most extensive food-aid program undertaken is the Food for Peace program conducted since 1954 by the U.S. government. Through this program, U.S. surplus grain either can be sold to developing countries at normal market prices with the aid of low-interest loans or can be distributed at no charge by such organizations as Catholic Relief Services or Cooperative for American Relief Everywhere (see CARE) to developing countries faced with food emergencies. Efforts have also been made to avoid harming agricultural development in countries that receive food aid.

Sometimes the laws of effective demand hurt the poor in unexpected ways when traditional agriculture in developing countries is modernized and brought into the international market system. When India's farmers, for example, began to find wheat and rice production more profitable than before the green revolution, they lost interest in traditional pulse production. As pulses became less plentiful in the local markets, their prices rose. Malnutrition increased because the poorest could no longer afford to balance their incomplete grain-protein diet with pulses.

FACTORS AFFECTING FOOD SUPPLY

Basic farming practices (see FARMS AND FARMING)—planting, harvesting, and storage of crops—are generally similar everywhere, but various systems of farming exist. In many developing nations much of the cropland is currently devoted to subsistence agriculture, a food-production system characterized by minimal mechanization, high reliance on human labor, and mostly on-farm consumption of what is grown. About 60% of the world's cropland is estimated to be in subsistence agriculture. Another form of food production, particularly in North America, Europe, Central America, and Oceania, is commercial agriculture, which is large-scale, highly mechanized, and entirely market-oriented (see AGRIBUSINESS). A third important system is that characteristic of centrally planned, or socialist, nations. These systems include state farms and COLLECTIVE FARMS, as in the USSR, and communes, as in China. In general, these systems are designed to provide food for the workers on the farms in return for their labor and also to provide food for the nation as a whole according to a national plan.

Arable Land. Agriculture depends ultimately on arable land—land that has the potential to produce a crop. About 3.2 billion ha (7.9 billion acres) of arable land exist worldwide, which is about 24% of the total ice-free land. Currently, less than half of the Earth's arable land is actually under cultivation. The largest reserves of unused arable land are located in Africa, where 72% of the arable land is not used for crops. Huge investments would be necessary to do the clearing, leveling, disease control, and irrigating required for much of this land to become fully productive. Consequently, many concerned authorities believe that efforts to improve agricultural production should focus on currently cropped land.

As demand for food has increased, land and SOIL mismanagement has occurred with alarming frequency. In the past 100 years in parts of the American Midwest, more than 50% of the topsoil has been lost to wind and water EROSION through improper cropping and tillage practices. About 1 million ha (2.5 million acres) of cropland are lost each year in the developing nations, due mostly to poor land management. Overgrazing and deforestation of land has occurred in such areas as Mexico, Malaysia, and the Sahel. Arable land may be turned to DESERT by the combined effects of destroyed vegetation and erosion.

Arable land in urban and suburban areas worldwide has also been lost by conversion for housing and business purposes. Such loss of prime agricultural land in North America—more than 600,000 ha (1,482,600 acres) a year—is espe-

(Above) *The cultivation of rice, as by these farmers in Thailand, traditionally has required intensive hand labor. All the people of a village may be engaged in the field during the planting and harvesting seasons. Although rice thrives in a limited geographical zone, it is a basic food source for more than half the world's population.*

(Right) *A machine for harvesting tomatoes—a perishable vegetable—moves through a large commercial field in California. Vegetable-harvesting machines, used mainly on large farms, displace hundreds of laborers.*

cially serious, and this land can only be replaced by bringing less productive, or more erosion-prone, land under cultivation. Efforts are now being made by a number of states in the United States and also by governments of other wealthy nations to preserve their best remaining agricultural land.

Water Supply. Many experts now believe that in the remaining years of the 20th century lack of water (see WATER RESOURCES) rather than lack of arable land will be the major obstacle to expanded worldwide food production. As with land, the amount of water available for agricultural use cannot easily be increased, but it can be better used. The total volume of all water on Earth is estimated to be 1.46 billion km³ (350.3 million mi³), but of this only 0.004% of all water is present in the soil and subsoil, only a fraction of which is currently cultivated. An additional 0.32% of the Earth's water is present in groundwater reserves and freshwater lakes, which can make a contribution to agricultural demands. The remainder is either too salty for agricultural use or is permanently frozen and inaccessible, and these resources are not evenly distributed. Research is now being done in the areas of IRRIGATION, seawater DESALINATION, and WEATHER MODIFICATION to improve water availability and thus increase the amount of land that can be farmed.

Climate and Weather. Climate, the long-term atmospheric conditions of a region, determines the cropping possibilities in an area. Rice grows in a wet, tropical climate, for instance, and corn grows in a humid subtropical or temperate climate. Weather is the daily expression of climate and can change greatly from day to day or seasonally. Weather patterns may occasionally set limits on agricultural productivity, even in generally favorable climates. Recent famines in India and China can be traced to such erratic weather patterns as high (causing floods) and low (causing DROUGHTS) precipitation in climate zones that otherwise would be expected to produce successful crop yields. Climates, although relatively stable, also change. In the Northern Hemisphere, for example, climatic patterns appear to be becoming more extreme, which

may cause serious agricultural disruption.

Fertilizer. Because soils often lack the right kind and amount of plant nutrients for the best crop results, the farmer must supply such missing nutrients. In many parts of the world, fertility needs are met by the use of inorganic chemical FERTILIZER. For developing nations, however, the cost of such fertilizer is often too high. Less than 20% of the world's inorganic fertilizer supply is used in these countries. Organic sources of plant nutrients are widely used to increase soil fertility in subsistence farming in the developing nations where inorganic chemical fertilizers are scarce or too costly. Even the efficient use of these materials, however, fails to substitute fully for the boost in crop productivity yielded by chemical fertilizer.

Pests. Once a crop has been established, the farmer is immediately threatened with crop losses from a variety of pests. Annual losses due to pests amount to 20%–40% of potential production, and the crops destroyed by pests each year are worth about $30–80 billion worldwide. In developed nations, pests have been controlled by chemical PESTICIDES—particularly HERBICIDES, for weed control—and insecticides. Chemical pesticides, however, can cause ecological damage and present hazards to human health. Increasingly, chemical pesticides and their hazardous potential are being introduced into developing regions of the world. Appropriate pest-control strategies, however, are able to replace the exclusive use of chemicals and include a combination of crop breeding for genetic resistance to specific pest problems and other management practices that create environments unfavorable to pests.

Energy. Increased food productivity is related to increased use of energy. In the developing world the major source of power for agriculture continues to be human labor and animal power. In developed nations, power is supplied by agricultural machinery that is fueled largely by petroleum. Much energy is also consumed in irrigation, transportation, food processing, and the manufacture of agricultural chemicals

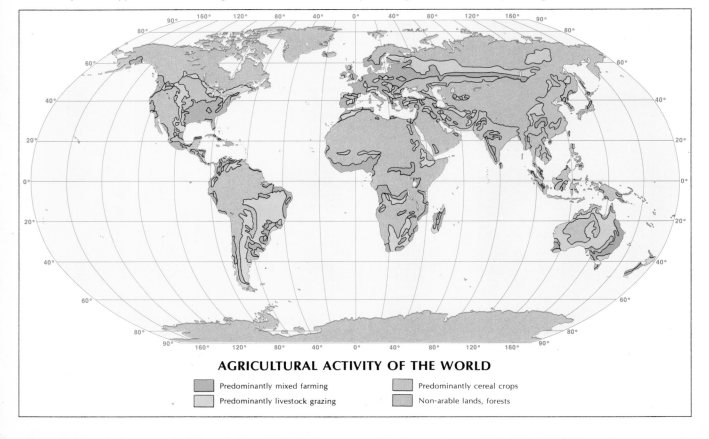

AGRICULTURAL ACTIVITY OF THE WORLD

▓ Predominantly mixed farming	▓ Predominantly cereal crops
░ Predominantly livestock grazing	▒ Non-arable lands, forests

FOOD PRODUCTION—SELECTED AREAS, CROPS, AND YEARS
(in 1,000 metric tons)

	North America		Western Europe		Africa (excluding South Africa)	
	1961–65	1981	1961–65	1981	1961–65	1981
Cereals	97,287	384,005	109,364	165,307	36,211	47,271
Root crops	15,133	18,266	72,461	48,169	56,612	82,552
Pulses	1,169	1,826	2,594	1,569	3,278	4,561
Vegetables and melons	20,356	26,630	41,675	48,811	7,514	13,778
Fruits	17,740	26,544	53,799	56,856	18,524	26,749
Nuts	244	709	1,032	1,027	316	313
Meat	20,098	27,449	16,380	28,969	2,803	4,734
Milk	65,355	68,186	111,160	143,078	5,171	8,166

	Latin America		Far East*		USSR and Eastern Europe	
	1961–65	1981	1961–65	1981	1961–65	1981
Cereals	53,189	105,193	163,279	292,119	172,159	247,355
Root crops	7,300	46,807	30,327	61,010	148,036	135,249
Pulses	3,788	5,577	13,413	13,346	8,562	5,859
Vegetables and melons	9,650	16,973	36,109	62,316	40,615	43,263
Fruits	33,086	58,521	23,260	41,329	13,592	25,783
Nuts	82	180	188	297	262	194
Meat	8,395	14,820	2,701	5,341	14,664	25,071
Milk	19,615	34,365	26,344	44,614	94,262	128,249

SOURCE: *Food and Agricultural Organization Yearbook,* 1981. *Excluding China, Japan, Kampuchea, Mongolia, North Korea, and Vietnam.

and fertilizers. One effect of such modernization is that fewer people can produce greater quantities of food. A point of diminishing returns can be reached, however, where adding more energy to agricultural processes becomes an inefficient use of that energy. In mechanized agricultural systems, as much as 10 times more energy is used to produce food than is returned to society as food for consumption. In many developing nations, however, energy invested in agricultural production generally returns up to 20 times more in food products than is expended during production. Nevertheless, developing nations, in order to most fully utilize their food potential, will have to apply much more energy than previously to agriculture, especially in the areas of improved tillage, more fertilizer, and timely harvesting.

Alternative energy resources are drawing increased attention as fuel from conventional sources becomes more costly and less available. One alternative is to manufacture gasohol, which is a combination of gasoline and alcohol from plant materials, particularly grain. The use of grain as fuel is controversial because that grain could be used as food. Some peo-

(Left) *Norman Borlaug received the 1970 Nobel Peace Prize for his contributions to the green revolution, an effort to meet world food needs through the development of improved strains of basic crops. He developed short-stemmed, vigorous wheat that, unlike taller varieties, could tolerate the intensive use of fertilizer to increase the yield.*

(Above) *In a California desert, dry dunes (background) are transformed into agricultural fields (foreground) with irrigation. The water required is supplied by the Colorado River.*

(Right) *Crop-dusting planes spread pesticide over an Arizona cotton field. To prevent the pesticide from drifting into residential or business sites, dusting can be carried out only in windless weather.*

ple conclude that strong efforts at petroleum conservation would better meet the demand for energy security than the use of such costly and untested synthetic fuels as gasohol.

INCREASING FOOD PRODUCTION

As world population grows, the productivity of the world's cropland must increase rapidly to maintain the minimal supplies currently available in many developing nations. If standards of living in developing countries are to be raised beyond subsistence level, the increase in food production must exceed population growth in those countries.

Land Reform. In many parts of the world—particularly in Latin America—the distribution of land is grossly inequitable, with small minorities of wealthy landowners controlling major portions of the best agricultural land. Often these landowners focus on the production of cash crops for the export market. Poor subsistence farmers are forced to farm small plots of marginally productive land to provide for their own needs. The need for reform of land-tenure patterns is apparent in these situations, but land reform is a political issue; often those with the power to direct such land-reform policies are the very people who stand to lose land. Consequently, land-tenure patterns tend to change slowly.

Governments of several nations—notably Bolivia, Chile, China, Cuba, Egypt, Iran, Kenya, Mexico, and Taiwan—have experienced some success with land-reform programs. Generally, these programs provide poor farmers with secure access to agricultural land through such policies as rent control for tenant farmers or direct expropriation and redistribution of large land holdings. Increased employment opportunities in the rural sector of the economy, increased land productivity, and a rise in the standard of living have resulted but are dependent on the small farmers' access to credit, education, and other government support services coupled with land reform itself.

Use of Machinery. In the more affluent nations, large-scale mechanization of agriculture has increased the amount of food that can be produced by each worker in agriculture and thus has reduced the need for labor and the number of on-the-farm jobs. In developing nations, where labor is plentiful and incomes are often desperately low, mechanization of agriculture must not reduce employment opportunities but should be designed to reduce the drudgery of specific operations and improve the quality and efficiency of human labor. It should also be scaled to the small farm size typical in these regions.

Genetic Technology. PLANT BREEDING is modification of a plant's genetic makeup in a purposeful way. The general goal of plant breeding is to assemble into single varieties the best possible combination of genes that control desirable traits. The traits of importance include yield, local environmental adaptation, uniformity, quality, disease or insect resistance, and early maturity. Numerous plant-breeding methodologies can be used worldwide, but actual testing of experimental varieties must be done in the regions in which they are planned for use in order to ensure suitability. Because the raw material for plant breeding is genetic diversity, GENE BANKS—which have collections of seeds of wild relatives and unimproved and improved varieties of crops—have been organized to preserve the genetic resources of major food crops for future use by plant breeders.

Efforts of agricultural research in the 1960s to find ways for farmers in developing countries to produce far more food on the same amount of land led to early successes popularly called the GREEN REVOLUTION, initiated by a plant scientist, Dr. Norman BORLAUG. Eleven crop and livestock research centers, located in Asia, Africa, and Latin America, conduct applied research on subsistence food crops and livestock problems of regional importance. The best-known centers are the International Rice Research Institute in the Philippines—which developed hardy, short-stemmed rice—and the International Center for the Improvement of Corn and Wheat in Mexico, which developed high-protein corn and wheat adaptable to subtropical regions. Nearly 50% of the world's wheat land was sown in the new wheats, and more than a quarter of all rice land was sown in the new rice by the mid-1970s.

SELECTED POPULATIONS ENGAGED IN AGRICULTURE, 1981

Country	Percentage	Country	Percentage
More Developed		**Less Developed**	
United Kingdom	2.0	Jordan	25.0
United States	2.1	Peru	36.6
Germany, West	3.8	Iraq	39.6
Canada	4.8	Philippines	45.3
Australia	5.6	Algeria	48.7
Israel	6.6	Nigeria	52.3
Germany, East	9.3	Indonesia	58.1
Japan	10.4	China and Taiwan	58.9
Argentina	12.7	Albania	59.7
USSR	15.8	India	62.4
South Africa	28.1	Haiti	65.8
Poland	29.5	Laos	73.2

SOURCE: *Food and Agricultural Organization Yearbook,* 1981.

Enthusiasm for the early success of the international research centers has been tempered by a growing realization that agricultural change is much more complex than had originally been anticipated, and that high production levels with the new seeds require a costly package that includes, for instance, chemical fertilizers and pesticides that are often unavailable to small farmers. Among other unforeseen side effects, the emphasis on cereals has been related to a decline in the production of pulses, the important, protein-rich legume crops of poor nations.

Agricultural Education. New information and technology that can help farmers increase their production must be communicated effectively if it is to achieve its purpose (see AGRICULTURAL EDUCATION). Physical constraints, such as a poor road system or underdeveloped mass communications system, can handicap the spread of information, but various cultural constraints—including verbal or scientific illiteracy among farmers or the communication gap between farmers and agricultural researchers and technicians created by such differences as economic class and cultural assumptions—may present an even greater challenge.

Effective communications with small farmers varies in approach according to circumstances. In parts of Africa, for example, radios and puppet shows have been used to spread agricultural information quickly and effectively. In the Philippines, specially trained agricultural agents provide assistance to farmers and spread information by demonstrating it in the farmers' fields. In China, agricultural communes often have one of their members responsible for spreading information about improved practices to the commune workers. In each instance, the approach, although carried out by some institution, operates outside the formal educational channels.

INCREASING FOOD AVAILABILITY

Efforts to meet the need of agricultural assistance and adequate food supply include the FOOD AND AGRICULTURE ORGANIZATION; the WORLD BANK, 30% of whose loans has been for agricultural development; and the United Nations Development Program, 30% of whose technical assistance goes to developing irrigation systems, controlling erosion, and creating effective storage, transportation, and marketing systems. The UNITED NATIONS CHILDREN'S FUND has among its many programs one in which women of developing nations are given assistance in producing and processing food at the village level.

In 1974, at the height of an international food crisis, participants of the World Food Conference, called by the United Nations, resolved to increase food production in developing nations by means of increased investment, more earnings from foreign trade, and foreign aid for agricultural development. The conference also urged all nations to establish a system of both national and international grain reserves and asked that a minimum international food-aid commitment of 10 million metric tons annually be established among those nations which are able to provide for countries having food shortages. Before the World Food Conference, all grain-exporting countries and some other nations had signed a Food

Aid Convention (renewed five times since 1968) that pledges them to a minimum amount of food aid each year in wheat and other grains. The United States has pledged 4.47 million metric tons of grain annually under the recent terms of this treaty. The total of all pledges, however, falls short of the 10 million metric tons recommended by the World Food Conference. The World Food Council, which annually reviews problems and policy issues affecting the world food situation, was created as a result of this conference.

Relatively little consideration has been given by governments to the politics or sociology of agriculture and economic development—how to redistribute national income or to increase the income of the poor so that they can participate fully in the market for food, or how to give small farmers more incentives to produce for the market through land ownership, credit on reasonable terms, or farming necessities at fair prices. A growing international consensus, however, is that food should be economically available to people having low income and that small farmers of developing nations need aid to produce more food in ways that fit their circumstances. The underlying problem, according to this consensus, is not a lack of food supply, but rather the lack of enough political will to resolve food problems with the knowledge and resources that are available.

PATRICIA KUTZNER AND DAVID SAMMONS

Bibliography: Cox, G. W., and Atkins, M. D., *Agricultural Ecology* (1979); Hall, Alan, et al., "The Second Green Revolution," *Business Week*, Aug. 25, 1980; Harwood, R., *Small Farm Development* (1979); Kutzner, Patricia L., *Who's Involved with Hunger*, rev. ed. (1976); Lappe, Frances Moore, and Collins, Joseph, *Food First* (1979); National Research Council of the National Academy of Sciences, *World Food and Nutrition Study: The Potential Contributions of Research* (1977); Pimentel, David and Marcia, *Food, Energy, and Society* (1979); Presidential Commission on World Hunger, *Overcoming World Hunger: The Challenge Ahead* (1980); Walinsky, Louis J., ed., *Agrarian Reform as Unfinished Business* (1977); Wortman, S., and Cummings, R. W., Jr., *To Feed This World—The Challenge and the Strategy* (1978).

Agrigento   [ah-gree-jen'-toh]

Agrigento is the capital of Agrigento province in southwestern Sicily, Italy. It has a population of 50,000 (1976 est.), and the economy centers on agriculture, tourism, and sulfur and potash mining. Founded by Greeks about 580 BC as the colony of Akragas, it became one of the largest and richest Greek cities of the classical world. In 480 BC an alliance between Akragas and SYRACUSE brought about a decisive victory over the Carthaginians and put most of Sicily under Greek control for 70 years. This period of economic expansion—reflected in a prolific output of silver coinage—saw the rapid construction of at least ten temples, including the huge (113 by 56 m/372 by 184 ft) temple of Zeus, one of the largest in the Greek world, and the organization of a grid of streets for a population of about 150,000 at its peak.

Akragas was destroyed by CARTHAGE in 406 BC and refounded by Syracuse after 338, but it suffered badly during the PUNIC WARS, falling to Rome in 210 BC. Called Agrigentum by the Romans, the city was colonized by Saracens in 828 and was captured by the Norman rulers of Sicily in 1086. The ancient site, which has been partially excavated, includes a row of well-preserved 5th-century BC temples. Agrigento is also the site of early Christian CATACOMBS and two medieval churches. The city's most notable modern son was the playwright Luigi PIRANDELLO.   JOHN P. OLESON

agrimony   [ag'-ruh-moh-nee]

The common name *agrimony* is used for two different plants in two different families. One plant, the genus *Agrimonia* in the rose family, Rosaceae, is a widely distributed genus of perennial herbs that includes agrimony, cocklebur, and harvest-lice.

A. eupatoria, bearing slender clusters of yellow flowers in the fall, has long been used as a mild astringent and to treat diarrhea and liver ailments. The plant contains a compound that causes human skin to become light-sensitive, resulting in a sunburnlike rash after contact with the plant followed by exposure to sunlight. A yellow dye is produced from the leaves of agrimony.

The other plant, a perennial herb known as hemp agrimony (*Eupatorium cannabinum*, in the Compositae family), is found in wet areas throughout Europe, northern Africa, and west and central Asia.   ROBERT C. ROMANS

Agrippa, Marcus Vipsanius   [uh-grip'-uh, vip-say'-nee-uhs]

Marcus Vipsanius Agrippa, c.63–12 BC, was a Roman general and trusted friend of Octavius (later Emperor AUGUSTUS). As consul he organized (37 BC) a fleet for Octavius that won decisive victories over Sextus Pompeius at Mylae and Naulochus. Subsequently, his masterful deployment of the fleet in the Battle of ACTIUM (31 BC) was the principal cause of Mark ANTONY'S defeat. During Augustus' rule, Agrippa consolidated Roman power in the east, in Gaul, and in Spain. He spent much of his personal fortune on public works for Rome, building the Pantheon and the first public baths. His third wife was Julia, Augustus' daughter.

Bibliography: Reinhold, Meyer, *Marcus Agrippa* (1933); Syme, Sir Ronald, *The Roman Revolution* (1939).

Agrippina II   [ag-ruh-pee'-nuh]

The Roman matron Julia Agrippina, b. AD 15, was the daughter of GERMANICUS CAESAR and Agrippina I and mother (by her first husband Ahenobarbus) of NERO. She held power during the reign of her brother CALIGULA but was banished after plotting against him. Her uncle CLAUDIUS I recalled her to Rome and married her in 49. He allowed her ambitions full scope and favored Nero over his own son, Britannicus. Agrippina is thought to have poisoned Claudius to make Nero emperor. Ruling with Nero for a time, she abused her power and quarreled with his supporters. In 59 he ordered her put to death.

agronomy: see AGRICULTURE AND THE FOOD SUPPLY; FARMS AND FARMING.

Aguascalientes   (city)   [ah'-gwahs-kahl-yayn'-tays]

Aguascalientes is the capital of Aguascalientes state in central Mexico. The population is 257,179 (1979 est.). The city lies at an altitude of about 1,890 m (6,200 ft) in a mountainous area about 420 km (260 mi) northwest of Mexico City. Its mild climate and hot mineral springs have made Aguascalientes a popular health resort. The city is noted for its plazas, parks, and colonial architecture. It is also a textile center and is famous for breeding fighting bulls.

The city was founded in 1575 as a fortified Spanish outpost on the trail from silver mines to Mexico City. In 1914 the Convention of Aguascalientes—an unsuccessful meeting of the revolutionary leaders Emiliano Zapata, Pancho Villa, and Venustiano Carranza—was held here. Underneath the city are extensive tunnels, apparently built by an ancient Indian civilization.

Aguascalientes   (state)

Aguascalientes (1980 provisional pop., 504,300) is a state in central Mexico on the Anahuac plateau, 900 to 3,050 m (3,000 to 10,000 ft) above sea level. The capital city is Aguascalientes. Climate is moderated by the high elevation, and numerous thermal springs are in the region, whose Spanish name means "hot waters." Aguascalientes is a fertile agricultural region, much of which is irrigated. Crops include fruit, maize, and grapes (for wine). Livestock raising is important, and zinc, silver, and gold are mined. First explored by the Spanish in the 16th century, Aguascalientes was the scene of heavy fighting during the revolution of 1910–20.

Aguinaldo, Emilio   [ah-gee-nahl'-doh]

Emilio Aguinaldo, b. Mar. 25, 1869, d. Feb. 6, 1964, was a leader of the revolution to end Spanish rule of the Philippines. Becoming mayor (1895) of Kawit in his native province of Cavite, he subsequently directed attacks against the Spanish military presence in Cavite, making it a focal point in the nationalist revolt and earning himself the title of general from his followers.

In 1897 he was elected president of the revolutionary assembly at Tejeros, Cavite. Exiled to Hong Kong when the insurrection faltered, Aguinaldo was encouraged to return by the United States when the SPANISH-AMERICAN WAR that erupted in the Caribbean was extended to the Philippines. Declaring the independence of his country from Spain on June 12, 1898, he became president of the first Philippine Republic on Jan. 23, 1899. The American defeat of Spain was followed in 1899 by war between the previously allied Filipinos and the United States. Aguinaldo was captured in 1901, and when war ended (1901), he swore allegiance to the United States, which annexed the Philippines, and retired from public life. After World War II, he was charged with cooperating with the Japanese but was never tried. The Philippines finally became independent in 1946.   RICHARD BUTWELL

Bibliography: Aguinaldo, Emilio, and Pacis, Vincente A., *A Second Look at America* (1957); Grunder, Garel A., and Livezey, William E., *The Philippines and the United States* (1951); Quirino, Carlos, *The Young Aguinaldo* (1969).

Aguirre, Lope de   [ah-geer'-ray, loh'-pay day]

Lope de Aguirre, b. c.1518, d. Oct. 27, 1561, was a Spanish adventurer in South America. An infamous and treacherous explorer, he joined the expedition (1560) of Pedro de URSÚA to find Eldorado at the headwaters of the Amazon River in Brazil. He mutinied, killing Ursúa and many others in the party. He was captured in Venezuela, after murdering his daughter and several priests, and was executed by the Spanish.

Agulhas, Cape   [uh-gul'-uhs]

Cape Agulhas is the extreme southern point of the African continent. Located in the Cape Province of South Africa, it is on the dividing line between the Atlantic and Indian oceans. Early sailors erroneously believed the tip of Africa to be the Cape of GOOD HOPE, about 145 km (90 mi) to the northwest.

Agulhas Current   [uh-gul'-uhs]

The Agulhas Current is a warm (20° C/68° F) surface current that forms part of the large-scale counterclockwise circulation in the Indian Ocean. It flows westward with the Indian South EQUATORIAL CURRENT, breaks southward along the east coast of Africa, and then turns eastward to join the West Wind Drift. About 100 km (60 mi) wide, it flows at 20–60 cm/sec (8–24 in/sec). Salinity is approximately 35 parts per 1,000.
                                                        JOHN B. WHEELER

See also: OCEAN CURRENTS.

Ahab, King of Israel   [ay'-hab]

Ahab was a king of Israel, the northern kingdom of the Jews, in the 9th century BC. Under his leadership, Israel experienced constant warfare with neighboring Aram (Syria) and also accomplished great building programs in such cities as Jericho. Ahab is perhaps best known for his political marriage to the Sidonian JEZEBEL. Her zealous worship of BAAL, and its influence on Ahab, clashed with the Israelite concept of worshiping the one God Yahweh (1 Kings 17–19).

Ahad ha-Am: see ACHAD HA-AM.

Ahaz, King of Judah   [ay'-haz]

Ahaz was king (r. c.735–20 BC) of JUDAH, the southern kingdom of the Jews. He is described in 2 Kings 16 as worshiping BAAL and even sacrificing his own sons. When Judah was threatened by Aram (Syria) and the northern kingdom of ISRAEL, Ahaz appealed to the Assyrian king, over the objections of the prophet ISAIAH. The Assyrians conquered the entire area and exercised a decisive political and religious influence. The altar at the Assyrian headquarters in Damascus so impressed Ahaz that he copied it in Jerusalem. Ahaz's reputation sharply contrasts with the reform achieved under his son, King HEZEKIAH.

Ahithophel   [uh-hith'-oh-fel]

Ahithophel was a counselor of King DAVID who joined Absalom, David's son, in a revolt against the king. When the revolt failed, Ahithophel hanged himself (2 Sam. 15–17). The story was used by John DRYDEN in his poem *Absalom and Achitophel* (1681).

Ahlin, Lars

Lars Ahlin, b. Apr. 4, 1915, is an award-winning Swedish storyteller, aesthetician, and novelist. His unstable youth, including a mystical experience at the age of 18, resulted in two unpublished novels before his novel *Tåbb with the Manifesto* (1943) and his first story collection, *No Eyes Await Me* (1944), won acceptance. His work suggests both the social consciousness tradition in the proletarian novel and fervent Christian idealism. Critics have compared him with both Fyodor Dostoyevsky and Thomas Mann. Among Ahlin's dozen other novels are *If* (1946), *The Great Amnesia* (1954), and *Bark and Leaves* (1961).

Ahmadabad   [ah'-mah-dah-bahd']

Ahmadabad, a city in Gujarat state of western India, was founded in 1411 by a Gujarati king, Ahmad Shah. It is an industrial and cultural center lying 445 km (280 mi) north of Bombay and has a population of 1,950,000 (1976 est.). The average annual temperature is 28° C (82° F), and rainfall is moderate, 521 mm (32 in). Ahmadabad is India's most important center for cotton textile manufacture. The city is also known for its dyeing and printing industries, handicrafts, and brass articles.

The old city, situated on the left bank of the Sabarmati River, formerly had encircling walls; only fragments still remain. The old city is crowded and interspersed with busy shopping districts. The area on the right bank of the river is better planned and more functional. Gandhi Ashram, located on a bluff of the river, is where Mahatma GANDHI spent a considerable part of his political career. Although 93% of the city's population adhere to the Muslim or Hindu faith, the proportion of adherents of JAINISM is significantly high compared to the national average. Historic mosques and tombs represent a fusion of Islamic, Hindu, and Jain traditions: Jami Masjid (Great Mosque), built in 1423, is one example. Hathi Singh Jain temple was built in 1848.   ASHOK K. DUTT

Ahmed III, Sultan of the Ottoman Empire

Ahmed (or Ahmad) III, 1673–1736, ruled the Ottoman Empire from 1703 to 1730, when he was overthrown in a revolt of the JANISSARIES. After giving asylum to CHARLES XII of Sweden in 1709, Ahmed became embroiled in war with Russia (1710–11). The Russians were defeated, however, and by the Treaty of Pruth (1711) gave up Azov to Turkey. Turkish seizure (1715) of the Peloponnesus from Venice provoked Austrian intervention. After numerous defeats by EUGENE OF SAVOY, the Turks concluded the Treaty of Passarowitz (1718), by which they lost northern Serbia and Little Walachia to the Austrians. Ahmed was also involved in an unsuccessful war against NADER SHAH of Persia, who drove the Turks out of Transcaucasia in 1730.

Bibliography: Shaw, S. J., *History of the Ottoman Empire and Modern Turkey*, 2 vols. (1976; 1977).

See also: RUSSO-TURKISH WARS.

Ahmet Haşim

Ahmet Hasim, b. 1884, d. June 4, 1933, was an influential Turkish poet. His early work was written in classical Ottoman style, but after studying Baudelaire, Mallarmé, and Rimbaud, he championed the cause of symbolism, introducing into Turkish poetry the lush images, obscurity, and extreme moods characteristic of the French movement. He visited Paris twice, where in an article on Turkish literature for the *Mercure de France* (1924), he defined poetry as an ''intermediate language'' between music and speech. This notion is evident in his collection *Göl saatleri* (The Hours of the Lake, 1921).

Ahmose I, King of Egypt [ah'-mos]

Ahmose I, king of Egypt (r. *c.*1570–1546 BC), was the founder of the 18th dynasty, one of the most outstanding in the history of ancient Egypt. His principal achievement was to weaken the HYKSOS, who had dominated Egypt for some 300 years, by taking Avaris, their citadel in the north.

Ahmose II, King of Egypt

Ahmose II was king of Egypt from about 570 to 526 BC, in the 26th dynasty. He came to power with the help of mercenary soldiers, overthrowing King Apries who had been blamed for the failure of an attack on Libya. According to the Greek historian Herodotus, Ahmose II's reign was prosperous: he left many architectural monuments, developed relations with Greece, and married Ladice of Cyrene, a Greek. He may also have conquered Cyprus. A few months after his death, however, his son Psammetichus III was deposed when the Persians under King CAMBYSES II invaded Egypt.

Ahura Mazda: see ZOROASTRIANISM.

Aïda [ah-ee'-duh]

Giuseppe VERDI's (1813–1901) *Aïda* received its world premiere at Cairo, Egypt, on Dec. 24, 1871. Negotiations with the composer had begun in 1869, initiated by the Khedive of Egypt in connection with the opening of the Suez Canal and the building of a modern opera house in Cairo, the nation's capital. Verdi at first demurred, but he was spurred by receipt of a prose sketch based on an incident in Egypt's past, the work of a noted historian, Auguste MARIETTE. Verdi invited the French librettist Camille du Locle to expand this sketch and summoned the poet Antonio Ghislanzoni to supply the necessary Italian verses, a project in which Verdi himself shared. The opera represents the composer in full creative maturity.

The plot, set in ancient THEBES, concerns a young Egyptian warrior, Radames, chosen to lead his country's army against the enemy, Ethopia. Secretly, Radames loves Aïda, an Ethiopian slave, and is loved in turn by the jealous Princess Amneris, the pharaoh's daughter. Radames returns victorious but is tricked into betraying military secrets to Aïda's father, Amonasro, the defeated king of Ethiopia, who has been taken captive while in disguise. About to flee with Aïda, Radames is caught and sentenced to die in a sealed tomb beneath the Temple of Ptah. Somehow Aïda manages to join him there, and as both bid farewell to Earth, Amneris implores peace for their souls in the temple above.   ROBERT LAWRENCE

Bibliography: Osborne, Charles, *The Complete Operas of Verdi* (1977); Weaver, William, *Verdi: A Documentary Study* (1977).

AIDS

AIDS, or Acquired Immune Deficiency Syndrome, was first reported in New York City in 1979 and has since reached epidemic proportions. By mid-1984 more than 4,000 cases had been identified in the United States, and numerous cases had been reported from more than 20 other countries. The fatality rate is at least 50% thus far. Most AIDS patients are male homosexuals, along with intravenous-drug abusers and a small number of hemophiliacs. Victims who do not fit these categories have been identified, however, and in countries such as Zaire about half of them are women.

AIDS attacks the body's immune system (see IMMUNITY). The mode of transmission appears to be primarily through sexual or other intimate contact with body secretions, through tainted hypodermic needles, and through blood products and transfusions. (Blood donors are not at risk.) The immune system of AIDS victims breaks down, particularly the function of T lymphocytes, leaving the individual prone to a wide range of disorders. Among those most frequently observed are

Kaposi's sarcoma, a rare form of cancer; an unusual form of pneumonia; neurological complications, such as encephalitis and meningitis; and other infections, such as toxoplasmosis and herpes. The response to treatment of AIDS patients with Kaposi's sarcoma may be better than those with severe infections.

The agent that transmits AIDS has not been established, but current studies strongly indicate it to be a virus. In 1983 and 1984, respectively, French and U.S. research teams announced identification of viruses found in a large percentage of AIDS victims. Research is now under way to determine whether the two viruses are identical; both are other forms of the retrovirus associated in 1980 with human T-cell lymphoma, a form of cancer. Even if the viruses do not prove to be the actual agent of AIDS, they are likely to be of value in the effort to develop a prognostic marker for the disease.

DAVID S. GORDON, M.D.

Bibliography: Check, William A., *The Truth about AIDS* (1984).

Aiken, Conrad [ay'-ken]

Conrad Aiken, a 20th-century American poet, won the 1930 Pulitzer Prize for his Selected Poems (1929). His works include short stories, novels, and critical essays.

Conrad Potter Aiken, b. Savannah, Ga., Aug. 5, 1889, d. Aug. 17, 1973, was an American poet, prose fiction writer, and critic who is best known for the musical quality of his poetry. He sought to divest verse of its intellectual content and to achieve ''absolute'' poetry, in which the poet's intention is to employ emotion with the same detachment as a composer uses notes or chords. In some of Aiken's poetry, however, and much of his prose, he is concerned with metaphysical matters and psychoanalytic insights. This tendency was probably fostered in part by finding, at the age of 10, that his father had fatally shot his mother and then committed suicide.

Aiken's early poetry, which shows the influence of T. S. Eliot (who was his classmate at Harvard), John Masefield, Edgar Lee Masters, Edgar Allan Poe, and the imagists, is largely narrative verse, but these poems foreshadow the mature Aiken in the role of poet as musician. This musicality is evident in his best-known lyric, ''Morning Song from Senlin,'' contained in *The Charnel Rose* (1918). His *Selected Poems* (1929), which won the Pulitzer Prize for poetry, reflects both Aiken's attempt to create musical structure with words and his exploration of the psyche. Similar emphasis appears in *Collected Poems* (1953) and throughout his often moody and dreamlike short stories and novels. Most of his stories date from the '20s and '30s and were published as collections in 1950 and 1964.

As a critic, Aiken helped to establish Emily Dickinson's reputation by editing and writing an introduction for her *Selected Poems* (1924). His reviews were published as *Collected Criticism* in 1958. He held the chair in poetry at the Library of Congress from 1950 to 1952 and received, among other prizes, the National Medal for Literature in 1969. *Ushant: an Essay* (1952; repr. 1971), Aiken's autobiography, is unique in that chronology and the true identities of the characters are purposely obscured.   JAMES HART

Bibliography: Aiken, Conrad, *Collected Poems*, 2d ed. (1970), *Collected Short Stories*, ed. by Mark Shorer (1960), and *Selected Letters of Conrad Aiken*, ed. by Joseph Killorin (1978); Barrett, Gerald R., and Erskine, Thomas L., *From Fiction to Film: Conrad Aiken's "Silent Snow, Secret Snow"* (1972); Hoffman, Frederick J., *Conrad Aiken* (1962); Lerner, Arthur, *Psychoanalytically Oriented Criticism of Three American Poets: Poe, Whitman, and Aiken* (1970); Martin, Jay, *Conrad Aiken* (1962).

Aiken, George David

George David Aiken, b. Dummerston, Vt., Aug. 20, 1892, was a U.S. senator from Vermont (1940–75). A progressive Republican, he opposed the policies of Sen. Joseph MCCARTHY in the 1950s, and in the 1960s advocated U.S. withdrawal from Vietnam. He was governor of Vermont and held several other state offices before being elected to the Senate.

Bibliography: Aiken, George David, *Aiken* (1976).

Aiken, Howard Hathaway

Howard Hathaway Aiken, b. Mar. 8, 1900, d. Mar. 14, 1973, was an American engineer who invented the first large-scale automatic COMPUTER. He also trained many persons who became outstanding in the field. After earning a B.S. degree in electrical engineering in 1923, he worked for several years in private industry. He resumed his education at Harvard University in 1935, where he studied physics and received an M.A. degree in 1937 and a Ph.D. degree in 1939.

By 1937 Aiken had developed the basic plan for a programmable mechanical computer, the Mark I. This computer was built by International Business Machines (IBM) between 1939 and 1944. Aiken designed three more computers, each more advanced than its predecessor. The last, the Mark IV, was completed in 1952. Aiken taught at Harvard from 1939 to 1961. He founded the Harvard Computation Laboratory in 1947 and directed it until his retirement, after which he founded Aiken Industries.   KENNETH THIBODEAU

Aiken, Joan

Joan Delano Aiken, b., Sept. 4, 1924, the daughter of the American writer Conrad AIKEN, is a prolific writer of fiction, poetry, and plays for children and young adults. Two of her books, *The Whispering Mountain* (1968) and *Night Fall* (1969), have won awards in the field of children's literature. She specializes in suspense and historical thrillers, romance, and fantasy, and, in the view of some critics, she possesses wit and stylistic talent surpassing the skills of a mere genre specialist.

aikido: see MARTIAL ARTS.

ailanthus   [ay-lan'-thuhs]

The ailanthus is a handsome tree of southeastern Asia and northern Australia. It has been naturalized in temperate climates, where it is valued as a shade tree in cities and parks for its high tolerance of air pollution. Because its seeds sprout rapidly in hot weather and cut-back trees may form thickets hard to destroy even with herbicides, the tree can be a pest. Male flowers have an unpleasant odor. The ailanthus has spreading limbs and can grow as high as 20 m (65 ft) or more—hence its name, a Moluccan word meaning "tree of heaven." The leaves, up to 1 m (3 ft) long, are composed of from 11 to 35 oval, pointed leaflets with glands on the largest notches of their margins. The small, greenish flowers grow in clusters on upper branches. In autumn the female flowers ripen into reddish-orange samara (winged fruit) that drop to the ground and are spread by winds. *Ailanthus* is a genus of the quassia family, Simaroubaceae. The most common species is *A. altissima*.

The *ailanthus*, A. altissima, *is a tree that spreads quickly, even in smoggy cities. Its male flowers emit a lingering, unpleasant odor.*

Ailey, Alvin   [ay'-lee]

Alvin Ailey, b. Rogers, Texas, Jan. 5, 1931, is America's foremost black choreographer and is generally considered the first modern dancer to have choreographed for a ballet company (*Feast of Ashes*, for the JOFFREY BALLET, 1962). His own troupe, the Alvin Ailey American Dance Theater, is America's most successful nonclassical repertory company.

Ailey's dances are often drawn from his black heritage and experience. His most consistently popular work, *Revelations* (1960), for example, "explores motivations and emotions of American Negro religious music." Ailey's dances are highly theatrical and energetic and are an effective blend of styles derived from African ethnic dance, MODERN DANCE—particularly the techniques of Lester HORTON and Martha GRAHAM—BALLET, JAZZ, and gestures and attitudes of American black vernacular movement. Since the mid-1970s, however, his dances have become more abstract and balletic.

Ailey began dancing with the Horton Dance Theatre in Los Angeles in 1953, appeared as a dancer on Broadway and in films, and formed his own company in 1958.

ROBERT J. PIERCE

The choreographer Alvin Ailey uses techniques of modern dance, ballet, jazz, and black African dance. His works, such as Revelations (1960), often involve themes relating to his black heritage. Ailey founded his own dance company in 1958, the Alvin Ailey American Dance Theater, which has made many appearances abroad.

Bibliography: Mazo, Joseph H., *Prime Movers: The Makers of Modern Dance in America* (1977); McDonagh, Don, *Complete Guide to Modern Dance* (1976); Philip, R., "Twenty Years Later: The Alvin Ailey American Dance Theater," *Dance Magazine* 52 (October 1978).

See also: DANCE.

Ailly, Pierre d' [dy-ee']

The French philosopher and theologian Pierre d'Ailly, b. 1350, d. Aug. 9, 1420, became prominent in public life as a vigorous promoter of church unity and reform. He dominated the early sessions of the Council of Constance (1414–18), which brought to an end the Great Schism, the period between 1378 and 1417 when Western Christendom was divided by the creation of antipopes. Educated at the University of Paris, he became successively its chancellor, bishop of Cambrai (1397), and cardinal (1411). Of his numerous writings, the most famous was the geographical treatise *Imago mundi,* which Christopher Columbus read and annotated before embarking on his historic voyage.   FRANCIS OAKLEY

Bibliography: Loomis, Louise R., *The Council of Constance: The Unification of the Church* (1961); McGowan, John P., *Pierre d'Ailly and the Council of Constance* (1936); Oakley, Francis, *Political Thought of Pierre d'Ailly* (1964).

AIM: see AMERICAN INDIAN MOVEMENT.

Aïn Hanech [ine hah-nek']

Aïn Hanech is an important Lower Pleistocene site in Tunisia. It has been investigated by a number of French archaeologists, among them the paleontologist Charles Arambourg. The site consists of a series of streambeds of gravel and sand in which tools were found associated with numerous fossil animal bones. The fossil fauna is of the characteristic Lower Pleistocene type known as the Villafranchian, with distinctive extinct mammal forms, including a five-toed horse. This helps assign the site to a period between 1.5 and 3 million years ago; a more precise date has not yet been obtained.

The Aïn Hanech artifacts consist of crudely flaked pebbles and rocks shaped into polyhedral artifacts and simple choppers. These artifacts bear some resemblance to early human artifacts of the OLDOWAN type found at Olduvai Gorge in Tanzania and elsewhere. The site expands the distribution of the earliest human culture into northern Africa.
                                                                    BRIAN M. FAGAN

Bibliography: Clark, J. Desmond, *Prehistory of Africa* (1970).

Ainu

The Ainu are an aboriginal people of the northern Pacific, who live principally on Hokkaido, the northernmost island of Japan, and in the southern part of the Soviet island of Sakhalin. Until recently, they also occupied the Soviet Kuril Islands, where their population is now extinct. The Ainu population is rapidly dwindling as a result of intermarriage and cultural assimilation by the Japanese. Only a small percentage of the estimated 12,000 Ainu on Hokkaido and 600 on Sakhalin are of unmixed descent.

Unlike other East Asian peoples, Ainu possess wavy brunette hair, light-skinned complexions, and abundant body hair. They also lack the epicanthic fold of skin over the upper eyelids, a Mongoloid racial characteristic. Their language is unrelated to any known Asian linguistic family.

The Ainu, a hunting and gathering people, formerly lived throughout the Japanese archipelago but were gradually pushed north to their present location by the invading Japanese. The men used the bow and arrow to hunt bear, deer, fox, otter, and other land animals during the winter; in summer they fished the sea and rivers. The women gathered such wild foods as roots, berries, mushrooms, and nuts and also engaged in small-scale agriculture based on crop rotation.

Traditionally, the Ainu traced their genealogical descent through both parents, and the family was the most important social and economic unit. The men were skilled woodcarvers; women were experts in embroidering and weaving. They had

An Ainu chief and his wife wear traditional ceremonial costumes. The intricate, striking embroidery on the robes is an art that is highly developed among the Ainu. The man wears a woven hat adorned with a wooden carving of a bear, and the woman has tattooed lips.

many songs, games, epic tales, and riddles, and their chief musical instruments were the drum and flute. Their highly animistic religious beliefs included many gods of the mountains, land, sky, and sea. Most important was the bear cult, which each year culminated in an elaborate ritual sacrifice of a captive bear raised from a cub in the Ainu community.
                                                                    DONN V. HART

Bibliography: Hilger, M. Inez, *Together with the Ainu: A Vanishing People* (1971); Munro, Neil Gordon, *Ainu Creed and Cult* (1962); Ohnuki-Tierney, Emiko, *The Ainu of the Northwest Coast of Southern Sakhalin* (1974); Takakura, Shin'ichiro, *The Ainu of Northern Japan,* trans. by John A. Harrison (1960).

air

Air, a gas composed principally of nitrogen and oxygen (78% and 21%, by volume), surrounds the Earth with a stable mass of about 1 kg/cm² (14 lb/in²) of Earth surface. Some of the other planets are thought to have had atmospheres that they lost because of weak gravitational fields. Atmospheres that are not accelerated to more than 20% of escape velocity (the velocity that must be reached to escape a planet's gravitational pull) are considered stable. On Earth, where escape velocity is 11 km/sec (7 mi/sec), no such accelerations occur, even during volcanic explosions.

The atmosphere is mixed as far as the STRATOSPHERE, with argon (0.93%) and carbon dioxide (0.03%) in addition to the principal gases as constituents of dry air. Water vapor is present in variable amounts, mostly in the lower half of the atmosphere. It can make up from near zero to 4% of the mass of air; however, total precipitable water content (the amount of water vapor in an air column) seldom exceeds 1 or 2 cm (about 0.5 in) at low temperatures and 6 cm (2.5 in) in a warm, humid atmosphere. Although the principal gases are nearly transparent to radiation, the tiny amounts of water vapor and carbon dioxide absorb and emit long-wave radiation, resulting in the GREENHOUSE EFFECT. Hence the gradual increase of carbon dioxide observed in the air in recent years might affect CLIMATE. Ozone in the stratosphere, a trace gas measured in fractions of parts per million, absorbs a large amount of ultraviolet light from the Sun, thus heating the stratosphere and protecting life on Earth from lethal SOLAR RADIATION. Because air is highly compressible, it is impossible to define a distinct upper boundary for the atmosphere. Pressure decreases by a factor of 10 over an altitude of 16 km (10 mi); for example, pressure at sea level is 1 atmosphere, but it is only 0.1 atm at an altitude of 16 km and 0.01 atm at 32 km (20 mi). Density varies mostly with pressure over large vertical distances; at constant height, pressure variation with temperature becomes important. In the low atmosphere, air is heavy, with a stable mass of roughly one kilogram per cubic meter (1 oz/ft³). A room of 500 m³ (650 yd³) thus contains 0.05 metric ton of air. At an altitude of 3 km (2 mi), however, density is 30% less than at sea level, causing initial breathing difficulties for many people from lowlands. The world's highest permanent settlements are at altitudes of nearly 4 km (3 mi), and mountaineers climbing the highest peaks (up to 8,800 m/5 mi) carry oxygen.   HERBERT RIEHL

air conditioning

Air conditioning is the process of supplying clean air at the proper temperature and humidity to maintain a space at a desirable comfort level. To do this, the air supply must be heated, cooled, filtered, and delivered to the conditioned area. The basic components of the most common type of air conditioning are the following: a compressor, which pressurizes a refrigerant such as FREON; a condenser, which liquefies the hot gaseous refrigerant by removing the heat from compression; an expansion valve, which allows the liquid to expand back to a gas; an evaporator, in which the air supply is cooled by giving up some of its heat to the refrigerant; an air distribution system to deliver the cool air by fan through ducts and diffusers into the conditioned space; and a control system to regulate the temperature and humidity for the comfort of the room's occupants.

Air conditioning systems are usually classified by the method of heating or cooling, by refrigerant, by equipment, by the method of air distribution, or by the system of temperature control. For example, heating may be supplied by steam or hot water. Cooling may be accomplished by expanding the refrigerant in an evaporator or by circulating chilled water.

The refrigeration cycle of an air conditioning system is often described by the kind of equipment used to achieve the cooling effect. For example, the compressor may be of the reciprocating, centrifugal, or screw type. Alternatively, a gas absorption machine, which uses a chemical principle to create a cooling effect, may be employed.

Air distribution systems fall into many different types. Simple, common duct systems use a one supply-air and return-duct system. Double duct systems supply hot and cold air through two separate ducts. A control system consisting of electric, pneumatic, or solid-state thermostats and appurtenances regulates the temperature of the air in the conditioned space.

Air conditioners take in warm room air, then blow it over cooling coils and back into the room. The heat removed is discharged outdoors.

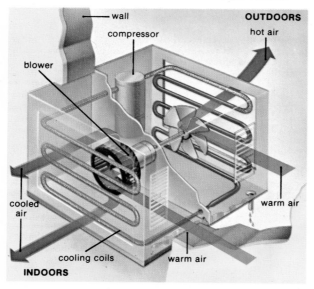

A more basic method of classification is based on how and where the system is used. Under this concept, air conditioners fall into three general categories: residential, commercial, and industrial.

Residential air conditioning systems are employed in homes. Such systems are predominantly packaged equipment in which all the components are placed in one or two pieces of equipment. In the case of split systems, one piece contains the cooling and heating equipment and the other the air distribution equipment.

Commercial systems employ bigger units in large buildings. They are characterized by centralized boilers and refrigeration equipment, usually centrifugal compressors with separate cooling towers. Hot and chilled water is piped to remotely located air-handling equipment, which conditions the air supplied to rooms to achieve a desirable comfort level.

Industrial systems are used in manufacturing plants that have a specific humidity or temperature requirement, or both. A candy factory, for example, often must maintain a specific temperature and humidity level while the candy is being made or packed so that it will not spoil. An electronics plant usually requires close temperature and humidity control as well as extremely clean air in its white rooms, where electronic devices are made and assembled.

Although air conditioning originated in the 19th century, it remained a curiosity until the turn of the 20th century, when Willis Carrier designed (1911) the first practical air conditioning system. It was not until 1930, however, that air conditioning systems began to be installed in office buildings, hospitals, apartments, trains, and buses. World War II halted progress temporarily. Air conditioning became firmly established about 1950, and today few large buildings are constructed without it.   F. T. ANDREWS

Bibliography: Ebeling, Alvin M., and Schweitzer, G., *Basic Air Conditioning*, 2 vols. (1971).

air-cushion vehicle

The air-cushion vehicle (ACV), also known as a ground-effect machine and often popularly called a Hovercraft, is a conveyance that rides on a cushion of air at a pressure slightly above atmospheric. The difference between atmospheric and air-cushion pressure is so small that a large ACV can be safely driven over a person lying prone. Air must be constantly pumped into the cushion, and this consumes at least as much power as is needed to propel the vehicle. A great advantage of the ACV, however, is its versatility; it can be routed over water, ice, mud, quicksand, marsh, and many other surfaces that are inaccessible to traditional vehicles.

The basic idea of an air-cushion vehicle is a century old, but the modern ACV stems from work done in the 1950s by the British electronics engineer Sir Christopher Cockerell. He constructed a model from two coffee tins and a hair dryer and measured its lift with kitchen scales. He obtained a patent in 1955, and in 1959 the first full-scale ACV, the SR.N1, was successfully tested at Cowes, England.

The largest of today's ACVs is the SR.N4, a class of vehicle that is used for ferry service across the English Channel. When originally built, the N4 class carried 34 cars and 174 passengers; the Super 4 type, with an extra section amidships, can transport 60 cars and 416 passengers. Powered by four 3,800 horsepower gas-turbine engines that drive four lift fans and four swiveling air propellers, these big craft cruise smoothly at up to 77 knots, making them the fastest class of seaworthy water vehicles in the world.

Some purely marine ACVs have rigid sidewalls extending down into the water along each side to help contain the air cushion. This reduces the power needed to keep the cushion inflated but increases drag (resistance to motion) because part of the vehicle is immersed in the water. Most ACVs have a flexible skirt of tough, rubberized fabric around the underside. Ducts direct air inward and downward, which helps to contain the air cushion and replace air that escapes from the cushion. The lower part of the skirt is especially flexible, enabling the vehicle to move smoothly over waves. In the

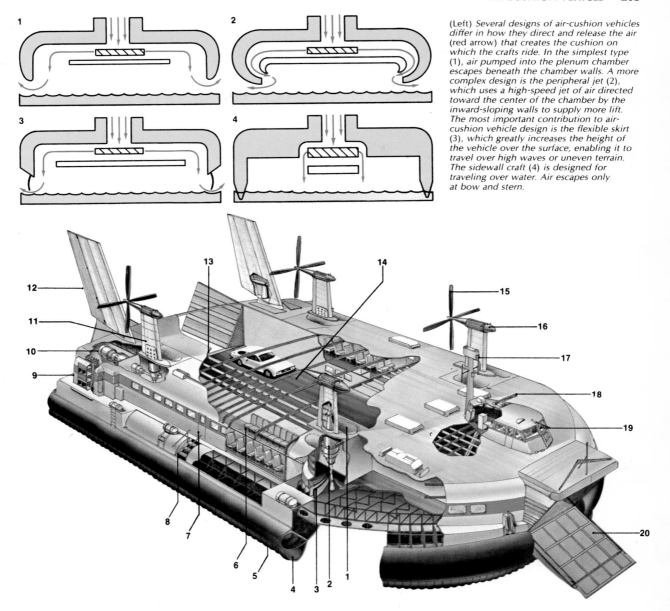

(Left) *Several designs of air-cushion vehicles differ in how they direct and release the air (red arrow) that creates the cushion on which the crafts ride. In the simplest type (1), air pumped into the plenum chamber escapes beneath the chamber walls. A more complex design is the peripheral jet (2), which uses a high-speed jet of air directed toward the center of the chamber by the inward-sloping walls to supply more lift. The most important contribution to air-cushion vehicle design is the flexible skirt (3), which greatly increases the height of the vehicle over the surface, enabling it to travel over high waves or uneven terrain. The sidewall craft (4) is designed for traveling over water. Air escapes only at bow and stern.*

The British Hovercraft Corporation's SR.N4, one of the largest air-cushion vehicles (about 200 tons), carries 30 percent of the English-French cross-Channel auto and passenger traffic. Some of its parts are: *lift-fan air intakes* (1); *main bevel drive gearbox* (2); *12-blade lift-fan* (3); *skirt fingers* (4); *flexible skirt* (5); *main passenger cabin* (6); *entrance to passenger cabins* (7); *extensible stairs* (8); *engine air intakes* (9); *gas turbine* (10); *pylon* (11); *fin* (12); *rear car ramp* (13); *car deck* (14); *propeller for drive and dynamics* (15); *propeller gearbox* (16); *radio antenna* (17); *radar scanner* (18); *control deck* (19); and *forward car ramp* (20).

SR.N4, the cushion height is 2.75 m (9 ft) so that the craft can pass over a projecting obstacle of that height. The skirted ACV is, in theory, fully amphibious; but the N4, with its beam of 28 m (92 ft), is too wide to be driven over land areas containing obstructions, although it can cross deserts or ice floes.

Many ACVs are used by the military. They can be armed with missiles, guns, antisubmarine weapons, and other special equipment. In Vietnam, British ACVs developed further by Bell Aerospace were used for patrolling various rivers and estuaries. Since they ride above the water, they are less vulnerable to torpedoes and undetectable by sonar. Many countries use small ACVs as high-speed frontier or customs enforcement vehicles, and thousands are used as amphibious, sporting runabouts.

A special class of ACV is the tracked ACV (TACV), or hov-

ertrain, which was pioneered in France. One experimental version called the Aérotrain is the holder of the "railroad" speed record of 375 km/h (233 mph), set in 1967. The cars of the Aérotrain are supported by an air cushion on a track of inverted T form.

A novel form of propulsion that is also under consideration is the linear induction MOTOR. This is a form of electric motor in which the coils, and hence the attached vehicle, are propelled forward by a magnetic force, with no physical contact between the motor and the ground surface. If perfected, such a system would make possible noiseless travel at more than 480 km/h (300 mph).   BILL GUNSTON

Bibliography: Gunston, William T., *Hydrofoils and Hovercraft* (1969); McLeavy, Roy, and Wood, John W., *Hovercraft and Hydrofoils* (1977); *Jane's Surface Skimmers* (annual).

(Left) The three paintings on this page by aviation artist Keith Ferris illustrate specific incidents in the history of the United States Air Force. (Left) Lt. Benjamin D. Foulois, a former balloonist, pilots his Wright Type A biplane to a height of 31 m (100 ft) over Fort Sam Houston in San Antonio, Tex. The flight, which took place on Mar. 2, 1910, was one of the first undertaken by a military aviator in a government-owned plane. (Courtesy National Bank of Fort Sam Houston.)

(Right) Fortresses Under Fire depicts a flight of B-17 Flying Fortresses under attack by German planes over Wiesbaden, Germany, in 1944. The Flying Fortress, armed with 2,727 kg (6,000 lb) of bombs and 13 machine guns to fight off enemy aircraft, was one of the principal U.S. strategic bombers of World War II. (Courtesy National Air and Space Museum, Smithsonian Institution.)

(Left) An American F-105 Thunderchief pulls into a steep climb to evade SAMs (surface-to-air missiles) and antiaircraft shells after a successful strike on the Paul Doumer Bridge in Hanoi, the capital of North Vietnam. The F-105, a single-seat fighter-bomber, achieved speeds of more than twice the speed of sound in combat. Early in the Vietnam War, F-105s flew more than 75 percent of all air missions over North Vietnam. (Courtesy U.S. Air Force Art Collection/Fairchild Republic Company.)

(Right) *American military flight dress evolved over four distinct periods. U.S. aviators in World War I relied on the superior flight gear of the European allies. During World War II, the Army Air Corps introduced the oxygen mask, an innovation required by high-altitude flight. In Korea, the Air Force drew on research and flight experience in developing the rigid helmets and electrically heated suits worn in jet combat. Modern flight equipment has been further refined through the use of light, strong, Space Age materials.*

World War I

Korean War

World War II

Vietnam War

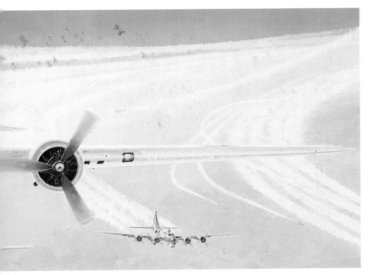

air force

An air force is the branch of a nation's armed forces that uses aircraft and missiles as its chief weapons. In peacetime, its primary mission is to deter or guard against an enemy attack. In wartime, it tries to destroy or neutralize hostile forces and to defend friendly forces or territories. It seeks to gain and maintain general and local air supremacy, to destroy enemy targets or interdict supply lines, to support friendly ground and sea forces in battle and provide them with supplies and transportation, and to carry out reconnaissance, rescue, and other aerial missions. In order to do these things, the air force organizes, trains, and equips combat and support units; develops, tests, and produces AIRCRAFT, missiles, and associated weapons and communications systems; and establishes, maintains, and defends air bases and installations.

The United States and the USSR maintain the world's largest air forces. They are the only nations capable of carrying out intercontinental air and space warfare with powerful, long-range bombers and missiles. They also boast strong tactical and air-defense forces. Great Britain, France, and the People's Republic of China maintain shorter-range strategic forces as well as tactical air units. Countries such as Vietnam, Cuba, North and South Korea, the Communist states of East-

ern Europe, West Germany, Japan, Israel, and some other Middle Eastern nations have strong tactical air forces but little or no strategic capability. The United States is the only country still possessing a strong naval air force, although the USSR may be moving in that direction.

DEVELOPMENT OF AIR FORCES

Modern military aviation began with the development of the BALLOON at the end of the 18th century. Successful balloon flights in France led to the establishment (1794) of what can be regarded as the world's first air force: the Aerostatic Corps, which briefly conducted aerial reconnaissance for the armies of revolutionary France.

In the American Civil War, the Balloon Corps of the Army of the Potomac constituted, in effect, the first American air force, although it did not outlast the war. In the decades that followed, several European armies developed balloon corps, but not until 1892 was a balloon section established as part of the U.S. Army Signal Corps.

The introduction of powered flight by means of the dirigible, a cylindrical balloon driven by propellers, and more important, by the first primitive airplanes gave impetus to the development of military air forces. In 1907, four years after the first flight of the Wright brothers, the U.S. Army established a small aeronautical division that in 1914 became the much larger aviation section, still within the Signal Corps. Military aviation was finally removed from the Signal Corps in 1918 with the creation of the Army Air Service.

First Air Fleets. The infant U.S. air organization saw only brief service on the Mexican border in 1916, but organized military aviation came into its own in Europe during WORLD WAR I (1914–18). All the major participants had small air forces when the war began, but these were used at first primarily for reconnaissance missions. As the war went on, opposing flyers began to shoot at each other with hand weapons and machine guns, and the development of a MACHINE GUN synchronized to fire through a plane's propeller opened the way for large-scale aerial combat. Large air fleets soon appeared over the battlefields, employing elaborate aerial tactics. The air units not only fought each other in ambitious efforts to gain control of the skies but also bombed and strafed troops, equipment, and installations on the ground. German air attacks on London, using both planes and dirigibles, constituted the first attempts at strategic bombing, although they were largely ineffectual.

The still relatively primitive state of World War I aircraft restricted the air forces to short-range and somewhat unreliable auxiliary maneuvers, but the possibilities of air power were apparent to some military leaders, primarily airmen, who saw in the new aerial weapons the key to future victory in war.

The emerging theories of airpower, characterized by the views of Giulio Douhet, an Italian, called for the establishment of separate air forces that by their own independent actions could bring about the defeat of an enemy. Freed of the necessity to support ground and sea forces, air units would first drive hostile aircraft from the skies and then penetrate deep into rear areas to bomb at will, until the enemy was forced to surrender. Americans such as William ("Billy") MITCHELL, Benjamin D. Foulois, and Henry ("Hap") ARNOLD were passionate supporters of these views, as were England's Hugh M. Trenchard and other European airmen.

Separate Air Forces. Despite strong opposition—and a persistent skepticism about the feasibility and value of strategic bombing—the idea of a separate air force slowly took hold. England established (1918) a separate Royal Air Force (RAF), coequal with the army and navy, and Canada and Australia quickly followed suit. Italy created a separate air force in 1923, France in 1934, and Germany in 1935; but the missions of the Regia Aeronautica, Armée de l'Air, and Luftwaffe were primarily tactical support of ground forces rather than strategic bombardment, and their independence was in many ways more apparent than real. By the eve of World War II, only three major powers—the United States, the USSR, and Japan—lacked separate air forces.

In the United States the interwar years had seen a good deal of progress toward an independent air force. In 1926, as a means of "strengthening the conception of military aviation as an offensive, striking arm rather than an auxiliary service," Congress had replaced the Air Service with the Army Air Corps. Initial hopes of expansion had been frustrated by budgetary restrictions, but creation of the General Headquarters Air Force in 1935 to provide centralized command of combat air units gave the Air Corps increased autonomy. At the same time, the development of a heavy bomber and of a strategic doctrine for its use lent additional weight to the arguments for a separate air force. Finally, on June 20, 1941, all army air elements were combined into the Army Air Forces (AAF), with Gen. Henry Arnold as commander. Nominally a part of the army, the AAF soon gained equal status with the ground forces, and Arnold became a full and equal member of the newly created Joint Chiefs of Staff.

The United States and Great Britain fought World War II with essentially separate air forces. The navies of both countries, however, maintained their own air arms, and U.S. naval aircraft carriers played a major role in the war in the Pacific. Other major air forces were closely tied to support of ground or naval forces. The German Luftwaffe failed in its effort to mount a strategic bombing campaign against England largely because of its prewar concentration on tactical operations, and only the United States and Great Britain had the organizational and technical means to carry out sustained long-range bombing attacks.

The dominant role of air power in World War II, enhanced by the introduction of nuclear weapons, made postwar organizational changes almost inevitable. On September 18, 1947, the U.S. Air Force became a fully independent military force. Gen. Carl Spaatz, an outstanding wartime leader, became its first chief. Although the U.S. Navy continued to maintain its own air arm, the Air Force quickly assumed responsibility for strategic bombing as well as tactical and logistical support of the ground forces. With the advent of long-range missiles, the Air Force also became responsible for the development and operation of land-based strategic missiles.

In Great Britain, the Royal Air Force retained its independent status, while the USSR, the only other nation to remain a major air power, maintained an air force fragmented but nonetheless autonomous in many respects. Elsewhere in the world, most nations followed the American example, although the independent status of many air forces remained somewhat weakened by their primary responsibility to support the ground forces.

THE U.S. AIR FORCE

The U.S. Air Force is one of three military departments, under civilian secretaries, within the Department of Defense. The Air Force is headed by a chief of staff, a four-star general who

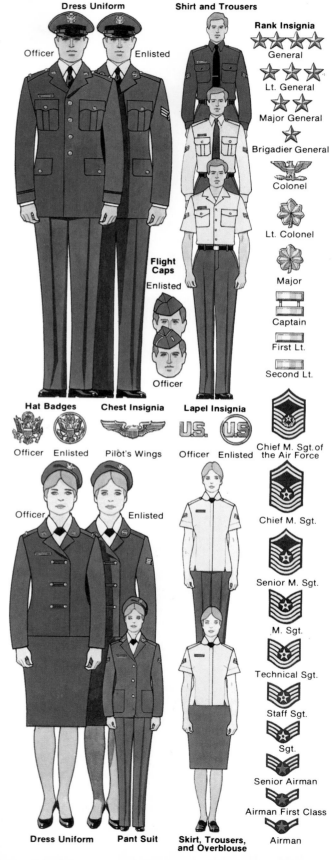

Dress Uniform

Officer — Enlisted

Shirt and Trousers

Rank Insignia

General

Lt. General

Major General

Brigadier General

Colonel

Lt. Colonel

Major

Captain

First Lt.

Second Lt.

Flight Caps

Enlisted

Officer

Hat Badges

Officer — Enlisted

Chest Insignia

Pilot's Wings

Lapel Insignia

Officer — Enlisted

Chief M. Sgt. of the Air Force

Chief M. Sgt.

Senior M. Sgt.

M. Sgt.

Technical Sgt.

Staff Sgt.

Sgt.

Senior Airman

Airman First Class

Airman

Officer — Enlisted

Dress Uniform — Pant Suit

Skirt, Trousers, and Overblouse

(Opposite page) *In the United States Air Force, officers and enlisted personnel (known as "airmen" regardless of gender) wear uniforms of identical design. Rank is indicated only in hat emblems and through rank insignias, which are affixed to sleeves, collars, or epaulets. Wing decorations, worn on the chest, indicate specific flight assignments, for example, gunner, bombardier, command pilot, or navigator.*

reports to the secretary of the Air Force. The Air Force chief of staff also serves as a member of the Joint Chiefs of Staff, together with the Army and Navy chiefs.

Under the chief of staff, the Air Force includes an Air Staff, 13 major commands, and 15 separate operating agencies. Among the major commands are the following: the Strategic Air Command (Offut Air Force Base, Nebr.), comprising the nation's long-range striking force of bombers and missiles; the Military Airlift Command (Scott AFB, Ill.), furnishing worldwide aerial transportation and supply to the entire defense establishment; the Tactical Air Command (Langley AFB, Va.), responsible for tactical air support of U.S. combat forces; the Air Force Systems Command (Andrews AFB, Washington, D.C.), which manages scientific and technical resources and the acquisition of new aerospace systems; the Air Force Logistics Command (Wright-Patterson AFB, Ohio), responsible for procurement, maintenance, and distribution of equipment and supplies; and the United States Air Forces in Europe (Lindsey Air Station, Wiesbaden, Germany), which constitutes the U.S. air forces of the North Atlantic Treaty Organization.

Other major commands include the Alaskan Air Command (Elmendorf AFB, Alaska), Air Force Communications Service (Scott AFB, Ill.), Pacific Air Forces (Hickham AFB, Hawaii), USAF Security Service (San Antonio, Tex.), Air Training Command (Randolph AFB, Tex.), and the Air University Space Command (Maxwell AFB, Ala.). The separate operating agencies include the Air Force Accounting and Finance Center (Denver, Colo.), the Air Force Intelligence Service (Washington, D.C.), the Air Force Manpower and Personnel Center (Randolph AFB, Tex.), and the Air Force Test and Evaluation Center (Kirtland AFB, N.Mex.). Behind the Air Force stand the Air Force Reserve and the Air National Guard.

The U.S. Air Force employs a wide variety of aircraft and missiles. It has more than 1,000 intercontinental ballistic missiles, such as the Titan and the Minuteman. It also has many air-to-air and air-to-surface missiles of varying ranges and capabilities. Approximately 400 B-52s and FB-111s constitute the strategic bomber force. They are supported by about the same number of KC-135 and KC-10 tankers, which also supply aerial refueling. Fighters and fighter-bombers in the Air Force inventory include such aircraft as the F-4, F-15, F-16, F-106, and F-111. Transports such as the C-5, C-130, and C-141 supply airlift; A-7s and A-10s fly close ground-support missions; and a variety of other aircraft carry out reconnaissance, communication, rescue, and other special tasks. In 1983 the U.S. Air Force had about 7,000 aircraft, including helicopters. The Air National Guard and Air Force Reserve had roughly another 2,000 planes.

Air Force active and reserve forces are stationed at approximately 135 major Air Force bases and nearly 2,600 smaller installations throughout the United States and overseas. These range in size from huge complexes near major cities to tiny radio relay stations on isolated mountaintops or ice caps.

Approximately 591,000 men and women were in the active Air Force in 1983 and approximately 236,000 in the reserve forces. A broad recruiting and reenlistment program serves to maintain the force of enlisted personnel, and the Air Force Academy and the Reserve Officers Training Corps are the primary sources for officers. Some 2,000 pilots and 850 navigators are trained each year, and the Air Force also maintains a wide-ranging educational and training system for recruits and career personnel. Promotional opportunities are tied closely to educational advances and increased professional skills in an effort to develop effective career patterns. Nearly 100 career fields are available to personnel in the Air Force. More enlisted men are assigned to the aircraft maintenance field than to any other, and more officers are assigned to the pilot field. (See also DEFENSE, NATIONAL.) STANLEY L. FALK

Bibliography: Anderton, David A., *Strategic Air Command* (1976); Craven, Wesley F., and Cate, James L., eds., *The Army Air Forces in World War II*, 7 vols. (1948–58); Emme, Eugene, ed., *The Impact of Air Power: National Security and World Politics* (1959); Glines, Carroll V., Jr., *The Compact History of the United States Air Force* (1979); Hewish, Mark, et al., *Air Forces of the World* (1979); Higham, Robin, *Air Power: A Concise History* (1972); International Institute for Strategic Studies, *The Military Balance* (annual); Polmar, Norman, *Strategic Air Command* (1979).

air law

Air law is the body of laws, regulations, and international agreements that apply to civil aviation. Each country has its own air laws and can choose to prevent foreign aircraft from entering, as the United States did in 1976 with the French and British CONCORDE. The United States acted in conformance with the basic principle of international air law—first affirmed in 1919 at the Paris Convention on the Regulation of Aerial Navigation—that gives every state sovereignty over the airspace above its territory. Subsequent to the Paris Convention other international meetings—principally, the Chicago Convention on International Civil Aviation (1944)—established agreements covering such matters as liability for damage to passengers and cargo on international flights, AIRPLANE HIJACKING, and sabotage. The Chicago Convention also established the International Civil Aviation Organization (ICAO, 1947), which is affiliated with the United Nations and is concerned with problems of air law and with the improvement of navigation facilities. Membership in the ICAO includes every country whose planes fly internationally.

A national airspace is prohibited to another nation's military aircraft, and the shooting down of a United States U-2 reconnaissance plane by the USSR in 1960 was not considered a violation of international air law. Where civil aircraft are involved in unannounced intrusions, however, the issues become far less clear. A Korean passenger liner strayed into Soviet airspace over Siberia in 1978, and was forced to land in the USSR. In 1983 a Korean passenger plane was shot down in the same area. The USSR claimed that it had "used every opportunity under international rules" to force the plane to land before shooting. At the United Nations the incident was denounced as an act of violence that posed a threat to the safety of international civil aviation.

Bibliography: Taneja, Nawal K., *International Aviation Policy* (1980); Wassenbergh, H. A., *Public International Air Transportation Law in a New Era* (1976).

air lock: see CAISSON.

air mass

An air mass is a body of air with fairly uniform temperature and moisture over an area of at least 1,000 km² (400 mi²). The principal distinction in temperature is between tropical and polar air masses; the latter are formed mainly in central Canada and Siberia. The terms *maritime* and *continental* distinguish between high and low moisture. The four principal air masses are the continental polar, maritime polar, continental tropical, and maritime tropical. Polar and tropical air masses are also distinguished by temperature in the upper ATMOSPHERE. HERBERT RIEHL

air pollution: see POLLUTION, ENVIRONMENTAL.

air rights

Air rights are the rights to build in the space above a tract of land, most commonly over railroad tracks or above another building. The owner of the land has the legal right to lease or sell the airspace above the property. In New York City, large buildings have been erected in the space above the New York Central Railroad tracks. In Chicago, the Merchandise Mart, one of the world's largest office buildings, makes use of airspace belonging to the Chicago and North Western Railroad, and the 41-story Prudential Building stands above the tracks of the Illinois Central Gulf Railroad.

airborne troops

Airborne troops are soldiers trained and equipped to go into battle from the air, particularly by parachute. Units in which all members must be parachutists ("jump qualified," in American military parlance) are generally considered airborne regardless of how they are deployed. Infantry units that conduct helicopter assaults are usually termed air assault units or air cavalry; units intended to be carried into action by powered transport aircraft are normally termed air landing or air transportable units.

The heavy opening-shock and landing-impact of early parachutes severely restricted the paratrooper's load. In addition, the small doors of early transport aircraft forced the troopers to jump in file, one at a time, resulting in considerable dispersion on the drop zones. Gliders partly solved these problems and were used extensively in World War II. Subsequent developments in parachutes and in techniques for air-dropping heavy loads rendered them obsolete.

The main advantages of airborne operations are surprise, the ability to bypass ground defenses, and speed of movement from assembly areas to distant targets. Helicopter operations share all but the last of these advantages, being limited by relatively short range and slow speed. All airborne units, however, are handicapped by the fact that the equipment they use in an assault—and afterward, until conventional resupply is established—must be light and small enough to be dropped by parachute.

Germany perfected the first airborne striking force, which it employed with great effect during the invasion of the Low Countries in 1940. It subsequently captured Crete in its only all-airborne campaign; following heavy losses there, the Germans abandoned large-scale airborne operations. British and American airborne forces were successfully used later in the war, particularly in the Normandy invasion. The French used parachute assault extensively in Indochina in 1946–54, although mainly in relatively small, battalion-sized drops. U.S. forces mounted only one mass drop in Korea. During their involvement in Vietnam (1964–73), where they had large numbers of helicopters, the Americans avoided large airborne operations.

In recent years airborne troops have increasingly become an elite force of shock infantry. The mystique attached to voluntary acceptance of the danger and rigors of parachute training sets paratroopers apart from their nonairborne colleagues.   JOHN F. GUILMARTIN, JR.

Bibliography: Clark, Alan, *The Fall of Crete* (1962); Galvin, John, *Air Assault: The Development of Airmobile Warfare* (1969); Marshall, S. L. A., *Night Drop* (1962).

Airborne Warning and Control System

The Airborne Warning and Control System (AWACS) is a high-speed U.S. Air Force plane designed to monitor all air and sea activities over a large area. AWACS is a greatly modified Boeing 707 heavily outfitted with electronic equipment. The plane's most distinguishing feature is a 9-m (30-ft) rotating radome, resembling a giant mushroom, that houses its special antennae. The radars, sensors, computers, and high-speed communications equipment that make up the AWACS payload can detect, identify, and track planes, missiles, and ships within its surveillance range during any kind of weather and over every kind of terrain, as well as over water. Among the most expensive aircraft ever built for the U.S. Air Force, the AWACS is considered the ultimate battlefield management center. The air force plans an eventual fleet of 34 AWACS, and 18 more are to be acquired by NATO. The USSR has at least 10 TU-126 turboprops, modified to carry AWACS equipment.   PAUL DICKSON

airbrush

The airbrush is a device for applying liquid as a fine spray. It is commonly used by commercial artists to facilitate drawing, shading, and retouching artwork. It can also be used to retouch photographs. An industrial type is used to apply various surface finishes, most commonly paint, but also ink, varnish, enamel, and lacquer. The liquid is fed into the nozzle of the airbrush by gravity or suction, or under pressure. A flow of compressed air atomizes the liquid (breaks up the particles into a fine mist), which is then carried along with the airstream coming out of the nozzle. A paint spray gun is essentially an airbrush. The principle is similar to that of the common perfume atomizer and the automobile carburetor.

The airbrush is designed so that normally only the supply of liquid is adjusted; the air supply and consequently the air flow from the nozzle remain constant. This design minimizes the spattering and dribbling of the pigment.   IAN BRADLEY

Bibliography: Dember, Sol, *Complete Airbrush Techniques for Commercial, Technical, and Industrial Applications* (1974); Maurello, S. Ralph, *Complete Airbrush Book* (1954).

aircraft

The development of the airplane and other heavier-than-air craft has had the most far-reaching effects of any 20th-century invention. Although many scientific disciplines are involved in the rapid advances in aviation technology, none is as important as the aircraft itself. In this article the anatomy of an airplane is examined along with recent developments in such unconventional aircraft as helicopters. Basic principles of flight can be found in AERODYNAMICS; the history of airplane development and a description of contemporary air transportation are the subjects of AVIATION and AIRPORT. Lighter-than-air craft are discussed in AIRSHIP.

The first powered, controllable aircraft, the Orville and Wilbur WRIGHT's flying machine, demonstrated in its structure the same basic principles of flight as do today's high-flying jets. The wings, or airfoils, of the original 1903 Wright *Flyer* resembled a box kite. A small pair of wings, called a canard, was located forward of the main wings and provided control about the pitch axis, allowing the aircraft to climb or descend. The canard performed the same function as the elevators that are attached to the horizontal stabilizers on most modern aircraft (and the device is increasingly used again today on small, experimental aircraft). Controlled, coordinated turns in the air were achieved through a method called "wing warping," which deflected the rear, or trailing, edges of the wing and rudder. With no cockpit, the pilot lay prone over the wing in a cradle arrangement and moved his body from side to side to actuate the controls that effected wing warping and changed the plane's direction.

The Wright *Flyer* was an extremely difficult aircraft to fly because it was statically unstable: it could not "fly by itself" but had to be constantly controlled by the pilot. European inventors believed that an aircraft should be inherently stable, and they soon improved upon the Wright brothers' design by developing dynamically stable and controllable aircraft that were safer and easier to fly. The concept of static stability has carried over to virtually all aircraft designs—although recent developments in fighter aircraft, such as the General Dynamics F-16, show that aerodynamically unstable aircraft have some advantages in maneuverability.

The success of any one of the thousands of different craft made since the Wright brothers' first flying machine depended on the quality of research, design, engineering, and manufacturing used to produce it. By the time World War II began, the aviation industry had accumulated enough experience in aerodynamics, materials, and structures to ensure uniformity in aircraft development. As a result, most modern aircraft exhibit many structural similarities. They are almost always monoplanes—single- rather than double-winged. They are made of metal, are powered by one to four jet or reciprocating engines, and are supported on the ground by retractable landing gear.

ANATOMY OF THE AIRPLANE
The main structural components of modern aircraft are the fuselage; wings; empennage, or tail surfaces; power plant; and landing gear, or undercarriage.

Fuselage. The fuselage is the main body structure to which the wings, tail, landing gear, and power plants are attached. It contains the cockpit of flight deck, passenger compartment, cargo compartment, and—in the case of fighter aircraft—the engines and fuel tanks.

Wings. The wing is the most important lift-producing element of an aircraft. Wing designs vary, depending on the type and purpose of the aircraft. Propeller-driven aircraft normally have an all-metal straight wing with a thick camber, or curvature. Jet transports have swept-back wings of medium camber that lower aerodynamic drag and improve performance at high airspeeds. Both straight- and swept-wing aircraft normally have ailerons attached to the outermost trailing edges of the wing. These ailerons raise and lower in opposition to one another, to increase or decrease lift on their respective wing in order to facilitate turning the aircraft. The wing also has flaps along the trailing edge, inboard of the ailerons. Flaps increase aerodynamic lift and drag and are used during takeoff and landing to increase lift at low speeds. Modern swept-wing transport aircraft have, additionally, high lift devices called leading-edge slats, which extend in conjunction with the flaps to fur-

(Above) *Otto Lilienthal, a German aviation pioneer, conducted glider flights from an artificially made hill near Berlin. On Aug. 9, 1896, he crashed while attempting to extend the length of his flight beyond 320 m (1,050 ft) and died the next day.*

(Left) *The first controlled airplane flight, lasting 12 seconds, was made by the Wright brothers on Dec. 17, 1903, at Kitty Hawk, N.C. Orville piloted the craft. Wilbur is seen at the right.*

ther increase the lifting capability of the wing.

An aircraft flies when the lift, or upward force generated by the wing, increases to a value larger than the aircraft's total weight. The most critical element in a wing's ability to produce lift is its cross-sectional shape. Early aerodynamic research on kites and gliders indicated that a flat plate would produce lift, but even more lift could be produced if the plate was inclined slightly into the wind. If the leading edge of the flat plate was rounded and the trailing edge tapered to streamline the wing, drag could be reduced. By increasing the camber of the top surface of the wing, while flattening the lower surface, lift could be dramatically improved. Wind tunnels, used extensively in airfoil research, have facilitated the compilation of a large amount of data on airfoil types and design.

Tail Surfaces. The tail, or empennage, provides stability and control for the aircraft and is mounted on the aft portion of the fuselage. It consists of two main parts: the vertical stabilizer, or fin, to which the rudder is attached; and the horizontal stabilizer, to which the elevator is connected. The rudder is used in conjunction with the ailerons to make coordinated turns, while the elevator is used to climb or descend. The horizontal stabilizer is sometimes mounted high on the vertical stabilizer, as is the case with the DC-9 and Boeing 727. The new Boeing 757 and 767 have the horizontal stabilizer attached to the rear section of the fuselage.

Propulsion Systems. The many aircraft propulsion systems include those which drive a PROPELLER, primarily reciprocating and turbine (turboprop) engines; and propellerless systems that use the energy of rapidly expanding gases as a propulsive force (see JET PROPULSION). The turbojet and the turbofan—a turbojet modification—are the most widely used commercial jet engines, and the reciprocating engine is still used extensively in light general aviation aircraft. Jet engines are normally attached to the wing or aft fuselage on pylons, but occasionally they are imbedded in the wing root next to the fuselage. On many fighter-bomber aircraft they are mounted in the fuselage in order to reduce aerodynamic drag and improve performance.

Engine-propeller combinations on single-engine aircraft are usually located in the nose, or forward-most, section of the fuselage and pull the aircraft through the air. When two or more engine-propeller combinations are used, they are mounted on the wing, but forward of the leading edge. "Pusher"-type aircraft have the engine mounted in the rear section of the fuselage. Several aircraft designs utilize two engines, one pushing and one pulling.

With respect to performance, turbojet engines operate most efficiently at high altitudes (above 7,600 m/25,000 ft); turboprops at mid altitudes (4,5–7,600 m/15–25,000 ft); and reciprocating engines at low altitudes (0–4,500 m/15,000 ft).

Landing Gear. Fixed gear consists of a simple design of struts, wheels, and brakes that is not retractable into the wings or fuselage. It is usually found on light aircraft of simple design. The static nature of fixed gear reduces the probability of landing gear problems, but it creates increased drag on a plane in flight. Retractable gear is used on more complex aircraft. Since it reduces drag, it increases range significantly.

Flying Controls. The relatively simple controls on a light, general aviation airplane govern the speed of the craft and its direction, both on the ground and in the air. The control wheel at which the pilot sits may be pushed forward or pulled back to move the tail elevators; pushing forward causes the plane to nose down. The control wheel also alters the position of the ailerons. The movements of the rudder are controlled from foot pedals in front of the pilot's seat; the pedals activate the wheel brakes when the plane is on the ground. Wing flap controls are usually powered, either hydraulically or by electric motors. Engine thrust, and thus airplane speed, is controlled by a throttle.

UNCONVENTIONAL AIRCRAFT

Many of today's new craft are heralded as innovations, although some are old, reliable concepts wrapped in new packaging. Hang gliders, for example, operate on the same principles as the early gliders developed by such 19th-century aerodynamicists as Sir George Caley and Otto LILIENTHAL. The wood frames and heavy fabric coverings of the original gliders have been replaced by lightweight aluminum, fiberglass, and synthetic fibers. Design of the modern hang glider was evolved from research at the National Aeronautics and Space Administration (NASA) into spacecraft reentry.

The GLIDER, or sailplane, has the same basic structure as other "heavier than air" machines but does not use a power plant. Instead, it is towed into the air by another aircraft and released at an altitude that permits it to soar along the "thermals," the columns of warm air that help keep it aloft. Gliders normally have a thin fuselage and very long wings with a narrow width, or chord. Many of the aerodynamic characteristics of the glider have been incorporated into high-altitude reconnaissance aircraft, such as the U-2 and the RB-57 operated by the U.S. Air Force. Research into glider aerodynamics continues today at NASA and military test-flying programs.

STOL Aircraft. Short takeoff and landing aircraft (see STOL) have gained popularity in recent years as air transportation has changed its emphasis from speed to efficiency. De Havilland Aircraft of Canada has developed the DHC-7, a four-engine STOL aircraft that requires only a very short runway for takeoff and landing. It utilizes advanced lightweight structural materials, new improved engines, and high lift devices to give it its STOL capability. An economical airplane to operate, it is used by many small commuter and local service airlines around the world.

VTOL and V-STOL Aircraft. Vertical takeoff and landing aircraft (see VTOL), which include HELICOPTERS, are still being developed for commercial and military use. For many years the military has utilized helicopters with great success on a variety of missions: medical evacuation, supply, troop transport, reconnaissance, attack. Industrial helicopters transport materials and personnel to and from areas where no landing strip is available to accommodate a fixed-wing aircraft. Some aircraft combine vertical and short takeoff and landing (V/STOL) capabilities. The propellers, the craft's power plants, or the wings themselves can tilt upward for takeoff and landing, but reverse to a horizontal position for flight. The Harrier, a British fighter plane, achieves vertical takeoff by rotating the exhaust nozzles of its jet engines downward in what is called a deflected thrust.

Airships, or Blimps. The high price of aircraft fuel has inspired a new interest in lighter-than-air AIRSHIPS, which use relatively little fuel and offer the promise of great economy. Some analysts feel that 10 to 15 small, effective airships could be built for the price of one jumbo jet. One of these craft might be capable of airlifting 1,000 tons of cargo or a passenger load greater than that of a jumbo jet, at speeds of up to 200 miles per hour. It could operate at one-third the cost of a passenger liner and would not require a large airport for take-off and landings. In addition, the airship is a quiet craft, and—unlike the jet—its exhausts are comparatively nonpolluting. The U.S. Coast Guard is presently testing airships at the Naval Air Test Center in Maryland.

Supersonic and Hypersonic Planes. Supersonic transports, or SSTs, aircraft that can fly faster than the speed of sound, have been used by the military for many years. Commercial supersonic flight has been limited to the CONCORDE, built by the British and French in 1976, which has proved to be a commercial failure in large part because of the vast amounts of fuel it consumes. The Russians have also built an SST, the TU-144, but it was not a successful design and was withdrawn from service after several disastrous crashes.

Occasionally, aviation futurists speak of developing a hypersonic transport that would travel beyond the stratosphere at speeds in excess of 8,000 km/h (5,000 mph); given the price of fuel, however, it is doubtful that this type of aircraft will be developed in the near future.

Ultralight Aircraft. Small aircraft made from ultralight, superstrong materials are increasing the range of present-day aeronautics. The current interest in ultralight planes began with the surge in popularity of the hang glider; a hang glider equipped with a small golf-cart engine and a propeller (1976) was the first member of this new generation of aircraft. The enthusiasm for ultralights came originally from a few engineers who manufactured make-it-yourself kits for home builders, and from the kit buyers who found that they could make their own planes for a cost as low as a few thousand dollars.

Some of the new ultralights resemble the earliest experimental aircraft. Others incorporate the most advanced aerodynamic shapes—achieved by computer modeling—and the newest materials: carbon fiber, kevlar, fiberglass-and-epoxy laminates, plastic foams. Design innovations include the rebirth of the Wright brothers' canard, which now takes the form of a second wing and acts to maintain lift; "winglets," vertical fins on the wing ends that increase wing efficiency; and rear-mounted, or tail, propellers that provide greater speed and stability. Ultralights range in cruising speed from 50 to upward of 320 km/h (30 to 200 mph). Some can reach altitudes of 4,300 m (14,000 feet).

AIRCRAFT NAVIGATION

Map reading and "dead reckoning"—manual speed and distance calculations—were the principal methods of navigation during the pioneer days of aviation, when a sudden change in weather combined with inadequate charts or maps could result in a forced landing or crash. One of the first reliable radio navigation aids was the Non-Directional Beacon, a radio signal that could be picked up by a cockpit device and used as a checkpoint to verify that the aircraft was on course. VOR (Very High Frequency Omni Directional Range) and TACAN (Tactical Air Navigation) were developed by the military and combined into the present-day VORTAC system that provides the majority of checkpoints that mark today's airway system, although increased airway congestion will necessitate a modernization of these facilities.

Among the new navigation technologies that are or will soon be used by commercial aviation, Area-Navigation, or R-Nav, is an on-plane system using computers, dopplers, and inertial navigation to produce a self-contained navigational system that needs no ground-based signals as reference points. Omega, developed originally for ships, uses Very Low Frequency radio beams sent out by eight ground-based stations located across the globe. The signals can be picked up by any plane equipped with Omega receivers. The Global Positioning Satellite system uses a number of earth-orbiting satellites to provide two- or three-dimensional fixes (including altitude). Although confined to military planes at present, GPS will be operational for civilian use in the near future and will allow pinpoint navigational accuracy at any location in the sky.

All of these new systems permit the pilot to do his or her own navigation, so that navigation officers are no longer needed for most commercial and military flights

Fifty percent of all fatal air accidents occur during the approach and landing phase of flight, and it is imperative that

The basic structure of an airplane comprises an airframe (fuselage, wing, tail assembly, and landing gear) and an engine. The ailerons, elevators, flaps, trim tabs, and rudder all serve to control the plane's flight. This light aircraft is a Piper Cherokee, 7 m (23 ft) long.

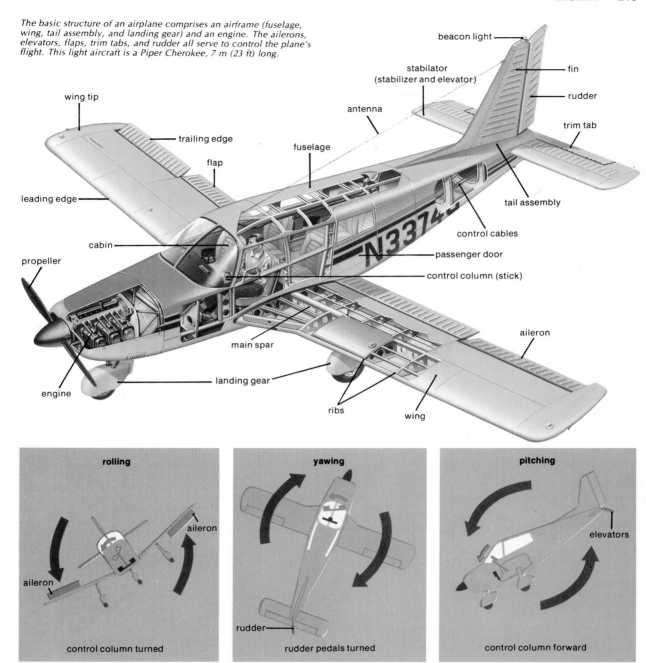

Three rotational motions are possible for an airplane. Rolling, or rotating an aircraft about a longitudinal axis from nose to tail, is accomplished by turning the control column so that one aileron is pulled up and the other aileron is pulled down. Yawing, or rotation about a vertical axis, utilizes the vertical rudder on the tail, which is controlled by the rudder pedals. Pitching, or rotation about an axis from one wing tip to the other, depends on the elevators and is achieved by moving the control forward (to dive) or backward (to climb).

the most precise navigational aids be utilized during this critical period. The ILS, or Instrument Landing System, is the best navigational aid available. An airport ILS transmits several electronic signals to the pilot of an approaching plane. These define the approach course and glide slope—the angle of descent that must be used. The MLS, or Microwave Landing System now being installed at many airports, is similar to the ILS but allows curved approaches to be flown to the runway, alleviating the noise and congestion problems that plague the modern jet airport.

RADAR is used by an airport's Air Traffic Control to separate

aircraft and vector them to the airport for landing. Aircraft may utilize radar as a navigation aid, and new radars now being used on some commercial aircraft also have the capability of detecting turbulence.

AIRCRAFT INSTRUMENTATION

Power, performance, and navigational instruments are used by the pilot to evaluate the well-being of the aircraft and to check its course. The power instruments check engine performance, power output, and airspeed. The TACHOMETER is the basic power-indicating instrument. Jet aircraft use engine-pressure ratio gauges to determine thrust output. On piston-powered aircraft manifold pressure gauges measure the pressure under which the fuel-air mixture is supplied to the engine. Turboprop aircraft measure power output on a torque gauge that monitors the power available at the prop shaft. All aircraft have instruments that check oil temperature and pressure and fuel flow. The electrical and hydraulic systems are also monitored with gauges and caution lights.

Performance instruments show how well and at what altitude the aircraft is flying. They include the artificial horizon, a gyroscope-mounted device that shows the pilot the plane's relation to the real horizon; the altimeter and vertical velocity gauges, which indicate height above mean sea level and the rate of climb or descent; and the airspeed indicator. A turn-and-bank indicator and an accelerometer, or G meter, keep the pilot informed as to the direction of turn and the loading, or strain, on the aircraft. (On some military aircraft, accelerometers are also used in inertial guidance systems to detect flight-course deviations.)

The location of all these instruments in the cockpit is vital to the pilot's ability to assess craft conditions quickly and accurately. Instrument design and location is a science in itself and is constantly undergoing study. The "electronic cockpit," or EFIS (Electronic Flight Information System), a computerized instrumentation array that includes the presentation of flight information via television screens, is revolutionizing the way flight instruments are used. Its introduction has caused some difficulty because it requires a change in habit patterns; in the long run, however, it will simplify cockpit design and enable the pilot to make better decisions in critical situations involving mechanical failure, weather avoidance, or navigational problems. The new Boeing 757, the 767, and the European Airbus A-310 are all being equipped with the EFIS.

J. MICHAEL JOBANEK

Bibliography: Anderson, John D., Jr., *Introduction to Flight: Its Engineering and History* (1978); Jerram, M., *Classic Aircraft* (1981); Markowski, Michael A., *Ultralight Aircraft* (1981); Nayler, J. L., *Aviation: Its Technical Development* (1965); Stinton, Darrol, *The Anatomy of the Aeroplane* (1980); Swanborough, Gordon, *Civil Aircraft of the World*, rev. ed. (1980); Taylor, J. W. R., ed., *Jane's All the World's Aircraft* (annual).

aircraft, military

The importance of aircraft designed specifically for use by the military was recognized within a decade of the initial controlled, power-driven airplane flights achieved by Orville and Wilbur Wright on Dec. 17, 1903. Although zeppelins had been flown since 1900—and more than 100 were built by Germany for use in World War I (see AIRSHIP)—the smaller, faster, more maneuverable airplane quickly proved superior for warfare, and it is today the principal weapon of military attack and defense. (See AIRCRAFT and AVIATION for the technology and development of planes. For the development of independent military air units, see AIR FORCE.)

TYPES OF MILITARY AIRCRAFT

The military aircraft's original function was large-scale reconnaissance. A scout plane equipped with bombs proved to be a weapon of unprecedented destructive potential; inevitably, the use of bomber aircraft led to the development of the fighter, an airplane capable of intercepting and destroying bombers. In addition to its use above the battlefield, the fighter was used extensively against enemy aircraft for home defense, as a protective escort for bombers, and as a strike plane against such objectives as enemy airports and railroads.

The introduction of the airplane provided a TORPEDO-launching device with several advantages over ships, particularly in speed of approach to a target. Torpedo-dropping experiments commenced early in the development of aircraft and were soon followed by the production of specialized torpedo-bombers.

Mine-laying aircraft were used to inhibit enemy ship movements, and during World War II the airplane was also adapted to counter the magnetic mine by exploding it electronically in the water after locating it.

Between the wars increasing attention was paid to the development of transport aircraft, in particular for the landing of

(Opposite page) Fighter aircraft have improved greatly in performance—speed, armament, range, ceiling, and load-carrying capacity—since World War I. The Fokker D-VII, Germany's most important World War I fighter, was about 7 m (23 ft) long, and had a maximum speed of about 187 km/h (117 mph) and a ceiling of about 6,100 m (20,000 ft). It had two forward-mounted machine guns. The North American P-51D Mustang, of which there were about 15,000 built by the Allies during World War II, mounted six machine guns and flew at about 700 km/h (437 mph). The North American F-86 Sabre jet fighter, in use during the Korean War, had a range of about 1,600 km (1,000 mi) and a speed of about 1,080 km/h (675 mph). The Soviet MiG 21FL jet fighter, a version of the MiG 21 series introduced in 1956, flew at Mach 2 (twice the speed of sound) and carried two air-to-air missiles and automatic cannons. The U.S. F-15A Eagle twin turbofan fighter, 19.4 m (63.8 ft) in length, flies at Mach 2.5 and has a ceiling of about 30,500 m (100,000 ft). (At upper left is a scale drawing showing relative sizes of the fighters.)

troops and equipment and for the deployment of both soldiers and arms by PARACHUTE (see AIRBORNE TROOPS). For a short time during World War II, GLIDERS were also used extensively. They were towed to their destination and then released to land with their cargoes. Since 1945, development has been concentrated on the HELICOPTER as a transport vehicle, because it can take off and land vertically and can hover to provide support for ground troops. As early as 1942 the helicopter was also being tested as a combat craft, and it has now been developed into a strike aircraft heavily armed with cannon, machine guns, rockets, torpedoes, and a variety of powerful missiles. It can be equipped to operate as an antisubmarine weapon as well.

The outstanding success of the fighter in strike missions during World War II was responsible for the production after the war of an entirely new class of airplane, the attack aircraft, designed specifically for close support and strike functions but also able to intercept. Emphasis in an attack aircraft is on flexibility and on bomb transport and targeting capacity, coupled with the ability to fly at low altitudes to evade RADAR detection, ground fire, and ground-to-air missiles.

The counterinsurgency (COIN) aircraft has emerged as a distinct class of warplane since World War II, serving as a comparatively lightweight, low-cost, and simple strike plane for close support of ground forces in relatively elementary tactical operations. In many cases obsolescent strike and trainer planes have been adapted to serve as COIN aircraft.

The serious threat to a nation's shipping posed by fleets of advanced nuclear submarines requires the maintenance of strong maritime patrol forces and antisubmarine aircraft. With long ranges and advanced equipment and weapons, these types of aircraft have assumed a role of the utmost significance since 1945.

The need for immediate warning of approaching hostile aircraft has led to the development of extremely sophisticated airplanes capable of extended patrol missions. A plane equipped with an AIRBORNE WARNING AND CONTROL SYSTEM (AWACS) is vastly more effective, and has much greater range, than a similar system based on the ground or at sea.

Training aircraft have also assumed a vital role, and specialized airplanes have been developed to train crews for all categories of operational aircraft. Many of these training planes can be converted quickly into warplanes.

HISTORY

The U.S. Army was the first armed service to acquire an airplane. On Dec. 23, 1907, Brig. Gen. James Allen, the chief signal officer, issued a specification for a military aircraft, and a contract was placed with the Wright brothers on Feb. 10, 1908. Italy was the first country to use an airplane in war. On Oct. 23, 1911, during the Italo-Turkish War in North Africa, a plane was employed for reconnaissance. Soon after, Italian airplanes dropped bombs and propaganda leaflets and photographed enemy positions.

World War I. By the beginning of World War I, little progress had been made by the belligerents in formulating distinct policies for the use of aircraft. Military airplanes were unarmed and were used primarily for visual and photographic reconnaissance over enemy lines. The opposing sides were quick to develop armament to protect their scouting aircraft from ground fire, and such armed aircraft were soon developed

Fokker D.VII

P-51D Mustang

F-86 Sabre

MIG 21

F-15A Eagle

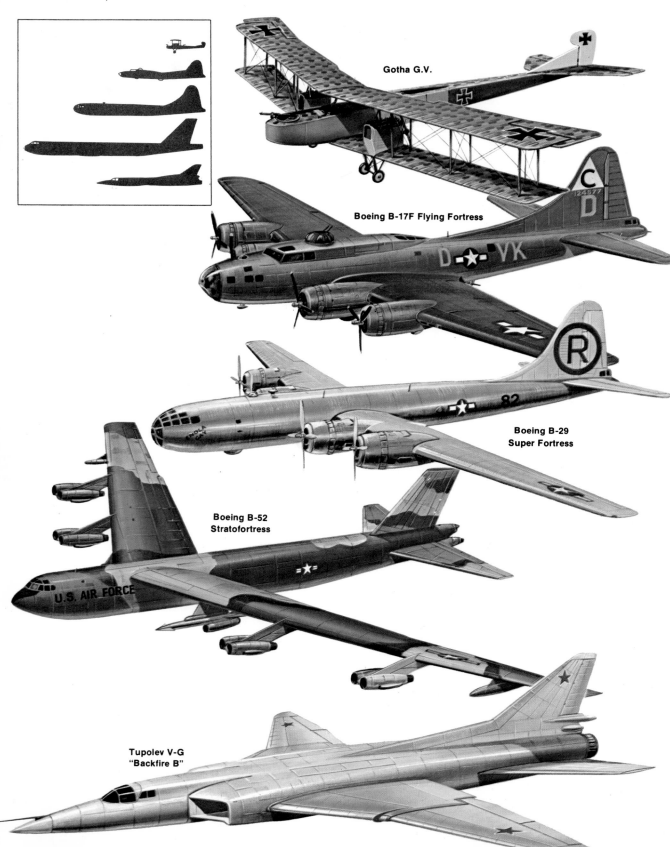

Gotha G.V.

Boeing B-17F Flying Fortress

Boeing B-29
Super Fortress

Boeing B-52
Stratofortress

U.S. AIR FORCE

Tupolev V-G
"Backfire B"

(Opposite page) *Bombers have always been the foundation of airpower. The German World War I Gotha G. V., with a range of more than 800 km (500 mi) and speed less than 160 km/h (100 mph), carried six 50-kg (110-lb) bombs. The U.S. World War II B-17F Flying Fortress, about 21 m (70 ft) long, flew almost 480 km/h (300 mph). It more than doubled the range of the Gotha and carried a 2,720-kg (6,000-lb) bombload. The B-29 Superfortress, of which almost 4,000 were built during World War II, flew at more than 560 km/h (350 mph). It had a range of almost 5,200 km (3,250 mi) and a bombload of about 9,080 kg (20,000 lb). The B-52, introduced in the late 1950s and used in the Vietnam War, is the primary U.S. global nuclear bomber. Flying at almost the speed of sound (1,060 km/h; 660 mph), it has a range of nearly half the Earth's circumference (20,000 km; 12,500 mi) and a huge armament-carrying capability of 27,000 kg (60,000 lb)—almost 100 times more than the Gotha. The B-52 is slightly less than 49 m (160 ft) long. The Soviet swingwing Tupolev V-G (called Backfire B by NATO), the only operational (since 1975) supersonic bomber, has a range of 5,745 km (3,570 mi). (The bombers are drawn to scale at upper left.)*

into fighter planes that could be used to intercept roving reconnaissance planes. The latter, in turn, acquired escort fighters for their own protection. Combat between fighters began, and it continued with formations of increasing size until the Armistice. Early in the war, bombing raids were made against the bases that sheltered German zeppelins, which had been used in bomb attacks against Britain; specialized bombing airplanes were developed subsequently.

By 1915 the value of the airplane in war had been recognized fully, and design, development, and production of aircraft were given the highest priority. The wood-and-fabric biplane predominated, but military forces also developed monoplanes and triplanes, with single, twin, and multiple engines of rotary, radial, and in-line types, both air-cooled and water-cooled. The synchronization of machine-gun fire through the propeller arc without hitting the blades and the evolution of bombsights proved of extreme importance, and many technical advances were made in airplanes themselves. Particular emphasis was laid on increasing speed, height, range, and load-carrying capacity, and during World War I the airplane evolved into a highly effective weapon. Its potential was confirmed on Apr. 1, 1918, with the formation of Britain's Royal Air Force (RAF), the world's first independent air service. On June 6, 1918, the Independent Force was constituted within the RAF for the strategic bombing of the German munitions industry.

Between the Wars. Although the Armistice on Nov. 11, 1918, brought immediate disarmament and attendant financial constraint, the war had been a strong stimulus to the development of military and naval aircraft. Nations able to retain air services encouraged their designers of airplanes, engines, and armaments to produce improved equipment. Three prominent advocates of air power were the U.S. brigadier general Billy MITCHELL, the British general Hugh Montague Trenchard, and the Italian general Giulio Douhet, whose *Command of the Air* (1921) set forth theories—held in common by all three—that were to form the basis for the future development of military airpower. Essentially, these theorists believed that the first function of an air force was to carry the attack beyond the battlefield into the heart of enemy country, to destroy the industries that support the opposing armies, and to sap the will of the civilian population.

The biplane remained dominant for naval use until the 1930s. U.S. government sponsorship of monoplane designs, however, exerted such a great influence on airframe design and related engine, propeller, and fuel developments that the monoplane eventually became the only type able to meet the incessant demand for increased aircraft performance. Significant innovations adopted during this period included retractable landing gear, flaps, the variable-pitch propeller, and the supercharger. The wars in Ethiopia, Spain, and China during the 1930s enabled the Germans, Italians, Russians, and Japanese to evaluate their new warplanes under battle conditions.

World War II. Before the outbreak of World War II, each belligerent had equipped and trained its air arms to fulfill specific, clearly defined functions. In accordance with the prophetic doctrines of Mitchell, Trenchard, and Douhet, the United States, Great Britain, and Italy had concentrated particularly

on developing the long-range strategic bomber. Germany, the USSR, and Japan, however, had built air forces designed expressly to support army operations. Additionally, the United States and Japan had supplied their navies with airplanes of the dive-bombing type. Being an island power, Japan had stressed the requirement that its navy be adequately equipped with torpedo bombers for action against enemy ships.

During the action in Europe, the British Isles served as the main base for Allied strategic bombing operations against the Axis, with the U.S. Army Air Force engaged primarily in daylight attacks and the RAF conducting night raids. The AIRCRAFT CARRIER demonstrated its worth in highly specialized actions in the war in the Pacific. Radar quickly assumed a role of paramount importance in detecting approaching raiders and as a navigational and bombing aid. Newly developed airplanes were equipped with advanced armament and weapons, including new types of bombs, heavy-caliber cannon, and rocket projectiles. Rocket-propelled fighters were introduced by the Germans, and the Japanese used Kamikaze (suicide) aircraft in attacking Allied ships. Two innovations, however, transcended all others: the turbojet engine and the ATOMIC BOMB. On July 12, 1944, the RAF became the first in the world to utilize JET PROPULSION for aircraft in operational service. About a year later, atomic bombs were dropped by the U.S. Army Air Force on Hiroshima (Aug. 6, 1945) and on Nagasaki (Aug. 9, 1945), bringing World War II to an end on Aug. 14, 1945.

After World War II. A new generation of advanced bombers with unprecedented range and speed was developed to serve as vehicles for nuclear bombs, for conventional bombs, and for missiles. (Much of the engineering for this new generation of bombers was based on highly advanced German research carried out during World War II.) The jet engine and rocket propulsion were developed further, along with numerous exterior design innovations, notably delta and swept-back wings. To enable airplanes to remain airborne for extended periods, refueling in flight from tanker aircraft evolved.

The development of all categories of airplanes and associated weapons was accelerated by the Berlin Airlift and by the outbreak of wars in the Middle East, Korea, and Vietnam. Supersonic flight was achieved and eventually became a necessity in the performance of fighters and bombers. The high speed of jet aircraft necessitated the development of a high-speed method of abandoning a plane in an emergency. The ejection seat, first tried in 1946, uses an explosive charge to catapult the entire seat unit clear of the plane. A parachute then opens automatically, floating the crew member to a safe landing.

A significant advance in fixed-wing aircraft design was the vertical takeoff and landing craft (see VTOL), a British accomplishment that produced a fighter aircraft with reconnaissance and strike functions. In armament, the machine gun and cannon were augmented by the rapid-fire multibarrel cannon and an extensive array of guided MISSILES. The dramatic increase in performance engendered by the jet engine was made possible by the concurrent development of a wide range of new materials for airframe construction, including light metal alloys, plastics, fiberglass, and carbon-fiber.

NEW TECHNOLOGIES

The most significant recent advances in military aviation technology have been made in the area of flight guidance and control—both of the planes themselves and their weaponry. The pilotless plane, or drone, is a prime example. One of the first drones, the Firebee (originally produced in 1959), is launched and controlled from the ground or a plane; or, when fitted with a computer, it is capable of following a preset course and returning. The present-day Firebee can fly at altitudes of up to 18,250 m (60,000 ft) at speeds approaching 800 km/h (500 mph). It is usually equipped with radar and camera systems and functions as a reconnaissance craft. The U.S. Army is currently developing a 68-kg (150-lb) drone, the Aquila, that in addition to performing reconnaissance duties will also be capable of directing laser-guided missiles.

The technologies used in advanced drones—sophisticated radar systems that are capable of ground mapping, laser iner-

REPRESENTATIVE MILITARY AND NAVAL AIRCRAFT

Name	Country	Year	Maximum Speed km/h (mph)	Wingspan	Length	Comments
Bombers						
Caproni	Italy	1915	161 (100)	39.7 m (130'0")	14.6 m (48'0")	5-seat triplane
Handley Page 0/400	Britain	1916	156 (97)	30.5 m (100'0")	19.2 m (62'10")	Heavy night biplane bomber
Voisin 13	France	1916	146 (91)	30.0 m (98'5")	17.5 m (57'5")	4-engine night bomber
Gotha G.IV	Germany	1917	140 (87)	23.7 m (77'8")	12.5 m (41'0")	Twin "pusher"-engine biplane bomber
Vickers F.B.27 Vimy	Britain	1917	145 (90)	20.5 m (67'2")	13.3 m (43'7")	Heavy bomber
Fairey Swordfish Mk.I	Britain	1935	224 (139)	13.9 m (45'6")	11.1 m (36'4")	Fleet Air Arm carrier-borne biplane
Junkers Ju87B-1 Stuka	Germany	1938	373 (232)	13.8 m (45'3")	11.1 m (36'5")	Single-engine inverted gull wing dive bomber
Junkers Ju88A-1	Germany	1939	460 (286)	18.3 m (59'11")	14.4 m (47'1")	High-speed medium bomber
Consolidated B-24D Liberator	U.S.	1940	488 (303)	33.5 m (110'0")	20.2 m (66'4")	4-engine monoplane
Vickers Wellington B.Mk.1C	Britain	1940	378 (235)	26.3 m (86'2")	19.7 m (64'7")	Long-range Bomber Command monoplane
Heinkel He 111K5a	Germany	1940	416 (258)	22.6 m (74'1")	16.6 m (54'5")	Low-wing monoplane
Dornier Do17z	Germany	1941	440 (273)	18.0 m (59'0")	16.3 m (53'6")	Advanced monoplane
Boeing B-17D Flying Fortress	U.S.	1941	523 (325)	31.6 m (103'9")	20.7 m (67'11")	Heavily armed 4-engine bomber
Handley Page Halifax B.Mk.II Ser.I	Britain	1941	426 (265)	30.1 m (98'10")	21.4 m (70'1")	Night bomber
de Havilland D.H. 98 Mosquito B.Mk.IV	Britain	1941	612 (380)	16.5 m (54'2")	12.4 m (40'10")	Fast, unarmed, all-wood twin-engine bomber
Avro Lancaster B.Mk.I	Britain	1941	462 (287)	31.1 m (102'0")	21.2 m (69'6")	Night bomber
Boeing B-29 Superfortress	U.S.	1943	576 (358)	43.1 m (141'3")	30.2 m (99'0")	Dropped atomic bombs
Boeing B-47B Statojet	U.S.	1951	1,014 (630)	35.4 m (116'0")	32.7 m (107'2")	Swept-wing jet aircraft
Tupolev Tu-95 Bear	USSR	1955	869 (540)	51.1 m (167'8")	54.1 m (177'6")	Heavy bomber
Boeing B-52G/H Stratofortress	U.S.	1958	1,062 (660)	56.4 m (185'0")	48.0 m (157'7")	SAC bomber for delivery of nuclear bombs
English Electric Canberra B(I) Mk.8	Britain	1958	832 (517)	19.5 m (64'0")	20.0 m (65'6")	RAF's first jet bomber
Tupolev Tu V-G Backfire	USSR	1969	Mach 2.5			Advanced supersonic bomber
General Dynamics FB-111A	U.S.	1969	Mach 2.5	21.4 m (70'0")	22.4 m (73'6")	2-seat tactical fighter-bomber
Rockwell International B-1	U.S.	1974	Mach 2.0	41.7 m (136'8")	45.8 m (150'2")	Supersonic bomber (under development)
Fighters						
Nieuport XVII	France	1916	175 (109)	8.2 m (26'10")	6.0 m (19'7")	Single-engine biplane
Sopwith F.I. Camel	Britain	1917	185 (115)	8.5 m (28'0")	5.7 m (18'9")	Single-engine biplane
SPAD XIII	France	1917	224 (139)	8.1 m (26'6")	6.2 m (20'4")	Single-seat biplane
Fokker D-VII	Germany	1918	188 (117)	8.9 m (29'3")	7.0 m (23'0")	Single-engine biplane
Boeing P-26A	U.S.	1933	377 (234)	8.5 m (28'0")	7.3 m (23'10")	First all-metal single-engine monoplane
Hawker Hurricane Mk.I	Britain	1937	539 (335)	12.2 m (40'0")	9.6 m (31'5")	Single-engine monoplane
Supermarine Spitfire F.Mk.I	Britain	1937	591 (367)	11.3 m (36'10")	9.1 m (29'11")	Single-engine monoplane
Messerschmitt Bf 109E-1	Germany	1939	570 (354)	9.9 m (32'4")	8.6 m (28'4")	Single-engine monoplane
Messerschmitt Bf 110C-4	Germany	1939	562 (349)	16.3 m (53'5")	12.1 m (39'9")	Twin-engine long-range aircraft

REPRESENTATIVE MILITARY AND NAVAL AIRCRAFT (continued)

Name	Country	Year	Maximum Speed km/h (mph)	Wingspan	Length	Comments
Ilyushin I1-2 Shturmovik	USSR	1940	423 (263)	14.6 m (47'11")	11.6 m (38'1")	Single-engine ground-attack monoplane
Mitsubishi A6M2 Model 21 Zero-Sen	Japan	1940	533 (331)	12.0 m (39'4")	9.1 m (29'9")	Single-engine interceptor and Kamikaze aircraft
Focke-Wulf Fw 190A-2	Germany	1941	626 (389)	10.5 m (34'6")	8.8 m (28'11")	Single-engine monoplane
Curtiss P40E Warhawk	U.S.	1941	570 (354)	11.4 m (37'4")	9.6 m (31'4")	Single-engine monoplane
Lockheed P-38	U.S.	1941	628 (390)	15.9 m (52'0")	11.5 m (37'10")	Long-range twin-engine escort aircraft
Mikoyan-Gurevich MiG-3	USSR	1941	576 (357)	11.4 m (37'5")	9.5 m (31'3")	Single-seat fighter-bomber
Grumman F6F-3 Hellcat	U.S.	1942	603 (375)	13.1 m (42'10")	12.2 m (33'7")	Carrier-borne single-engine monoplane
Gloster Meteor F.Mk.I	Britain	1944	660 (410)	13.1 m (43'0")	12.6 m (41'4")	RAF's first jet aircraft
Messerschmitt Me 262A-Ia Schwalbe	Germany	1944	863 (536)	12.5 m (41'0")	10.6 m (34'9")	Twin-engine jet aircraft
North American F-86A Sabre	U.S.	1948	1,086 (675)	11.3 m (37'1")	11.4 m (37'6")	First USAF single-seat swept-wing interceptor
Mikoyan-Gurevich MiG-15	USSR	1949	1,101 (684)	10.1 m (33'1")	11.1 m (36'3")	Early single-engine jet aircraft
Mikoyan-Gurevich MiG-21F	USSR	1956	Mach 2.0	7.6 m (24'11")	16.8 m (55'1")	Widely used single-seat multirole aircraft
North American F-100D Super Sabre	U.S.	1956	1,390 (864)	11.8 m (38'9")	14.3 m (47'0")	Single-engine supersonic fighter
McDonnell F4B Phantom	U.S.	1961	Mach 2.6	11.7 m (38'5")	17.8 m (58'3")	Twin-engine long-range all-weather interceptor
Mikoyan-Gurevich MiG 25 Foxbat	USSR	1967	Mach 3.2	12.2 m (40'0")	21.0 m (68'11")	Advanced fighter-interceptor
Dassault Mirage 5	France	1967	Mach 2.2	8.2 m (27'0")	15.6 m (51'0")	Widely used ground-attack aircraft
Hawker Siddeley Harrier G.R.Mk.1	Britain	1969	1,186 (737)	9.1 m (29'8")	13.9 m (45'6")	V/STOL tactical strike aircraft
McDonnell-Douglas F15A Eagle	U.S.	1974	Mach 2.5	13.1 m (42'10")	19.4 m (63'9")	Advanced single-seat fighter
Fairchild A-10, Thunderbolt	U.S.	1975	722 (449)	17.5 m (57'5")	16.2 m (53'1")	Close-support fighter
General Dynamics F-16	U.S.	1976	Mach 2+	9.4 m (31'0")	14.5 m (47'7")	Lightweight supersonic fighter
Transports and Others Junkers Ju-52	Germany	1934	270 (168)	29.3 m (96'0")	18.9 m (62'0")	Major Luftwaffe transport
Lockheed U2A	U.S.	1955	795 (494)	24.4 m (80'0")	15.1 m (49'7")	High-altitude reconnaissance and research aircraft
Boeing KC-135A Stratotanker	U.S.	1957	857 (532)	39.9 m (130'10")	41.6 m (136'3")	Jet-powered fuel carrier for midair refueling
Mil Mi-8 (V-8)	USSR	1961	250 (155)	21.3 m (69'10") (rotor)	25.3 m (82'11")	Turbine-powered transport helicopter
Lockheed C-130E Hercules	U.S.	1962	555 (345)	9.9 m (32'7")	29.8 m (97'9")	Heavy transport
Lockheed SR-71	U.S.	1964	Mach 3	16.9 m (55'7")	32.7 m (107'0")	Supersonic reconnaissance aircraft
Bell AH-1G HueyCobra	U.S.	1967	353 (219)	13.4 m (44'0") (rotor)	16.2 m (53'0")	Armed utility helicopter used in Vietnam
Antonov An-22	USSR	1967	741 (460)	64.5 m (211'4")	57.8 m (189'7")	Heavy transport
McDonnell KC10-A	U.S.	1980	908 (564)	50.4 m (165'4")	55.3 m (181'7")	Tanker/cargo transport

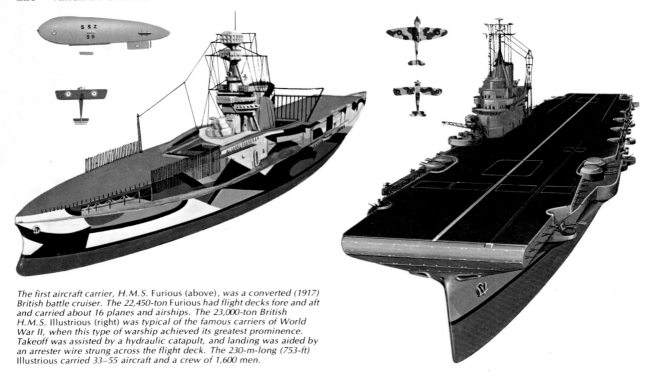

The first aircraft carrier, H.M.S. Furious (above), was a converted (1917) British battle cruiser. The 22,450-ton Furious had flight decks fore and aft and carried about 16 planes and airships. The 23,000-ton British H.M.S. Illustrious (right) was typical of the famous carriers of World War II, when this type of warship achieved its greatest prominence. Takeoff was assisted by a hydraulic catapult, and landing was aided by an arrester wire strung across the flight deck. The 230-m-long (753-ft) Illustrious carried 33–55 aircraft and a crew of 1,600 men.

tial navigation, computers that can control and target weapons systems—are also used in piloted military aircraft, which supplement these systems with sophisticated electronic display panels.

Another major development is the V/STOL plane, which is capable of taking off and landing either vertically or on very short runways. Some new craft are hybrid mixtures of helicopters and conventional airplanes, whose wings carry large-bladed propellers that can be rotated parallel to the wing to lift the vehicle, or moved forward to allow it to cruise like a plane.   PETER M. H. LEWIS

Bibliography: Bruce, J. M., *War Planes of the First World War*, 5 vols. (1969–72); Green, William, *Warplanes of the Third Reich* (1970); Jackson, Robert, *World Military Aircraft since 1945* (1980); *Jane's All the World's Aircraft* (annual); Lewis, Peter, *The British Fighter since 1912* (1974) and *The British Bomber since 1914* (1974); Munson, Kenneth, *Aircraft of World War II*, rev. ed. (1972); Polmar, Norman, and Kennedy, Floyd, *Military Helicopters of the World* (1981); Wagner, William, *Lightning Bugs and Other Reconnaissance Drones* (1982); Walters, Andrew W., *All the United States Air Force's Airplanes, 1907–80* (1982).

See also: B-1 BOMBER; B-17 FLYING FORTRESS; B-24 LIBERATOR; B-29 SUPERFORTRESS; B-52 STRATOFORTRESS; CORSAIR; F-16 FLYING FALCON; F-86 SABRE; FOKKER D-VII; GOTHA (aircraft); GRUMMAN TBF-1 AVENGER; HURRICANE; MESSERSCHMITT BF-109; MIG; MIRAGE; MOSQUITO; MUSTANG; P-38 LIGHTNING; P-40; SOPWITH CAMEL; SPAD; SPITFIRE; STUKA; U-2; ZERO.

aircraft carrier

An aircraft carrier is a warship that contains a flight deck for launching and recovering AIRCRAFT and associated hangaring and support facilities. It is usually distinguished by a full-length flight deck and arresting gear to halt landing aircraft in the limited space available. Recent years, however, have seen the development of cruiser-carrier hybrids, notably the Soviet navy's *Kiev*, that carry a mixed complement of HELICOPTERS and VTOL (vertical takeoff and landing) fighters. Specialized amphibious assault ships, or commando carriers that carry only helicopters, are operated by several navies, but these are distinct from true aircraft carriers.

Shipboard air operations are complicated and difficult. Aircraft are catapulted off the deck and land over the stern, using the carrier's forward velocity to reduce the speed of approach

to the carrier; the aircraft also use tailhooks to engage arresting cables stretched across the flight deck. Large elevators are set into the flight deck and along its sides to transfer aircraft to and from the hangar deck below. Because the amount of space on a carrier is limited, aircraft must have folding wings and tails, and helicopters are equipped with folding rotors.

High standards of teamwork, precision, and flying skill are required to operate aircraft safely from shipboard, particularly at night and in bad weather. Simply moving aircraft from the hangar deck to the catapults and from the arresting cables to the correct spot below is an intricate and dangerous maneuver.

The aircraft carrier is basically a British, American, and Japanese development. Eugene Ely, an American aviator, pioneered shipboard takeoffs and landings from improvised platforms in 1910–11. Britain converted the cruiser *Furious* into the first carrier in 1917; the *Argus*, which was the first carrier with a true flight deck, soon followed. The first American carrier, the converted collier (coal cargo-ship) *Langley*, became operational in 1922, the year in which Japan's *Hosho*, the first ship specifically designed as a carrier, was launched.

By the onset of World War II, both Japan and the United States had powerful carrier forces. Following the Japanese attack on Pearl Harbor by carrier-based aircraft, carriers dominated fleet engagements in the Pacific. British carrier deployment was more limited, but still had major impact. The attack on Taranto by carrier-based torpedo bombers in November 1940 crippled the Italian fleet, and the German battleship *Bismarck* was put out of action by carrier-based aircraft. British and American escort carriers played a major role in defeating German SUBMARINES.

After World War II, Britain pioneered the technical developments that made jet carrier operations practical—the steam catapult, visual approach aids, and the angled deck. The last refers to a deck that has the landing section laid out at an angle to the takeoff section so that a plane approaching poorly can fly off the deck and make another attempt without danger of running into other planes.

American carriers were used effectively in both Korea and in Vietnam, and the U.S. Navy, with 14 carriers, is the main exponent of carrier aviation today. The first nuclear carrier, the U.S.S. *Enterprise,* was launched in 1960. It was followed

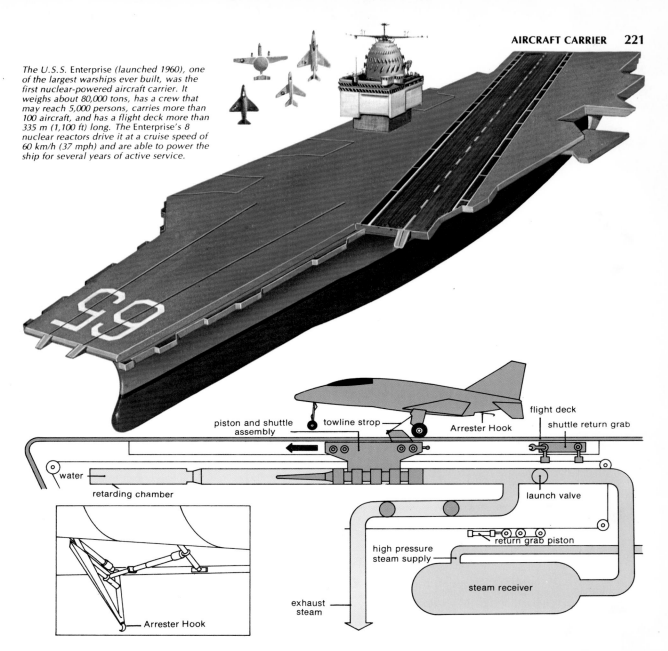

The U.S.S. Enterprise (launched 1960), one of the largest warships ever built, was the first nuclear-powered aircraft carrier. It weighs about 80,000 tons, has a crew that may reach 5,000 persons, carries more than 100 aircraft, and has a flight deck more than 335 m (1,100 ft) long. The Enterprise's 8 nuclear reactors drive it at a cruise speed of 60 km/h (37 mph) and are able to power the ship for several years of active service.

piston and shuttle assembly — towline strop — Arrester Hook — flight deck — shuttle return grab

water — retarding chamber — launch valve — return grab piston — high pressure steam supply — exhaust steam — steam receiver

Arrester Hook

A steam catapult on the U.S.S. Enterprise aids in launching aircraft from the carrier deck. Four such catapults are in operation aboard the vessel. Powered by high-pressure steam from the ship's eight nuclear reactors, each catapult can launch four aircraft a minute. A 36-ton aircraft can be accelerated to a speed of 260 km/h (161 mph) in a little more than 2 seconds with the use of only 76 m (250 ft) of flight deck. The arrester hook (inset) of a landing plane engages a wire strung across the ship's flight deck, stopping the craft within a few meters.

in 1972 by the Nimitz, the first in a class that has since become the U.S. standard for aircraft carriers.

Slightly smaller and slower than the Enterprise, the Nimitz has only two nuclear reactors (the Enterprise has eight) and can operate—at a speed of 30 or more knots (55.5 km/h; 34.5 mph)—for up to one million miles between refuelings. With a crew of 3,300 and an additional 3,000 personnel attached to its air wing, the carrier is capable of storing, fueling, and launching over 90 aircraft. It is equipped both for attack (it carries three missile launchers) and for antisubmarine warfare. The U.S. Navy now operates three Nimitz-class carriers, which are ranked as the most powerful surface warships afloat. A fourth, the Theodore Roosevelt, is scheduled for launching in 1985.

Recent criticism of the aircraft carrier has been widespread, however, and has centered on its high cost and its vulnerabili-

ty to missile attack. The Theodore Roosevelt, with its complement of aircraft and protective escort ships, will cost an estimated $17 billion. Many strategists have now come to favor smaller, less expensive carriers, such as the three-carrier fleet that Britain is building to replace its aging carrier Hermes, which served in the 1982 Falklands war with Argentina. Nevertheless, both the USSR and France are planning to build nuclear carriers. Argentina, Brazil, and India operate World War II carriers bought from Great Britain, and Australia also has a one-carrier fleet of the same vintage.

JOHN F. GUILMARTIN, JR.

Bibliography: Bryan, Joseph, III, Aircraft Carrier (1982); Clark, J. J., and Reynolds, Clark, Carrier Admiral (1967); Friedman, Norman, Carrier Air Power (1981); Moore, John, ed., Jane's Fighting Ships (annual); Roberts, John, Aircraft Carrier Intrepid (1982); Sullivan, George, The Supercarriers (1980).

Airedale terrier   [air'-dayl]

The Airedale terrier, the largest member of the terrier group, is an intelligent breed and a vigilant watchdog.

The Airedale terrier, the largest of the terriers, is a wiry-coated black-and-tan dog that has a muscular, compact body and a docked tail. It has a square muzzle, upright but folded ears, and keen, intelligent eyes. It is classified a long-legged terrier, measures 57–59 cm (22–24 in) high at the shoulder, and weighs 17–22 kg (38–50 lb). It is a good swimmer and runner.

Dog breeders of Aire Valley, northern England, developed the Airedale terrier in the mid-19th century from the otterhound and a now extinct breed of English fox terrier. During World War II, Airedale terriers were trained to carry messages between troops; now they are used as guard dogs and for hunting big game in India and in Africa.

Bibliography: Edwards, Gladys, *The New Complete Airedale*, 3d ed. (1978).

airglow

Airglow is a luminosity of the Earth's upper atmosphere that occurs globally day and night. Like the AURORAS, airglow derives from interactions of the Earth's MAGNETOSPHERE with the SOLAR WIND. Night airglow, which is twice as bright as all starlight, originates at altitudes of 100–190 km (62–118 mi). The light is emitted by atoms and molecules excited by ultraviolet radiation and X rays or by collision with charged particles in the upper atmosphere. Airglow hampers ground-based astronomical observation of faint celestial objects. In itself, however, airglow is of interest to scientists because of the exotic chemical reactions taking place in the upper atmosphere, including reactions of excited atoms and molecules of oxygen and nitrogen that cannot be observed in ground-based laboratories. Such studies are important for understanding the processes affecting the atmosphere's ozone layer, which protects the Earth's surface from excessive ultraviolet radiation, and for learning more about the ways in which solar radiation changes affect climate.

Bibliography: Lin, Leslie Y., "Aurorae and Airglow," *The Research News* (University of Michigan), November–December 1982; McCormac, B. M., *Aurora and Airglow* (1967); Roach, Franklin E., and Gordon, Janet L., *The Light of the Night Sky* (1973).

Airlangga   [air-lahn'-gah]

Airlangga, c.1001-49, a ruler who reunited the empire of eastern Java, is a national hero of Indonesia. Airlangga was the son-in-law of Dharmavamsa, whose Javanese kingdom was dismembered by the SRIVIJAYA EMPIRE at the beginning of the 11th century. As Srivijaya was weakened by the attacks of the Indian Cholas, Airlangga was able to reestablish the eastern Javanese empire, with his capital near modern Surabaya. He divided his kingdom between his sons and retired to a monastery c.1041. During Airlangga's reign the Javanese writer Mpu Kanwa composed the *Arjunavivaha,* an adaptation of the Indian epic *Mahabharata* that marks the beginning of a national literature.

airliner: see   AIRCRAFT; AVIATION.

airmail

Airmail is the delivery of letters and other postal material by aircraft. Before World War I, experimental airmail flights were made in both England and the United States, but the world's first regularly scheduled airmail service began in the United States on May 15, 1918, when the War Department started routes between New York, Philadelphia, and Washington, D.C. The Post Office Department continued airmail service after the war and in 1920 developed a coast-to-coast route in conjunction with the railroads, which carried mail sacks during the nighttime segments. Four years later, a string of flashing beacons and emergency landing fields was established across the country to permit around-the-clock operations, providing a 32-hour coast-to-coast airmail delivery that was at the time three days faster than railroad service.

Under the terms of the Air Mail Act of 1925 (the Kelly Bill), the Post Office Department contracted for service with privately owned airlines. These early mail routes became the basis for major companies that currently serve the United States. Air express also began in the later 1920s, gradually developing into a significant aspect of modern air transport. By the late 1930s, transoceanic routes carried passengers, freight, and mail across the Caribbean, Pacific, and Atlantic, completing the pattern of today's global air network. Depending on the distance involved, almost all domestic first-class mail is currently delivered by air.   ROGER E. BILSTEIN

Bibliography: Davies, R. E. G., *Airlines of the United States since 1914* (1972); Shamburger, Page, *Tracks across the Sky: The Story of the Pioneers of the U.S. Air Mail* (1964).

See also: POSTAL SERVICES.

airplane: see AIRCRAFT.

airplane hijacking

Airplane hijacking is the forcible seizure of a commercial aircraft in flight and the holding of its crew and passengers hostage against the acceptance of the hijackers' demands. Between 1948 and 1960 some 32 hijackings took place; almost all were attempts by Eastern Europeans to escape from Communist countries to the West. In 1959 several planes carrying escapees from the Cuban Revolution were forcibly diverted to the United States and were welcomed by U.S. authorities. The violence inherent in the act of hijacking became apparent to much of the world only in the early 1960s when U.S. jetliners were detoured at gunpoint to Cuba, by Cubans seeking to return or by people with ideological or criminal motives. Arab terrorists used hijacking from the late 1960s to attempt to enforce political demands.

To counter the threat of hijacking, X-ray and other machines have been used to screen passengers and baggage at airports. The Hague Convention of 1970 required its signers to prosecute or extradite hijackers who landed in their countries. Several of the nations that had offered a safe haven to hijackers did not sign the Convention; but since 1980—during a period of resurgence in U.S. hijack attempts—Cuba has jailed or returned hijackers almost as soon as they land, and hijackers headed for Libya or Algeria can no longer assume a welcome there. Nevertheless, the crime has spread throughout most of the world, and even China experienced several hijack attempts in the early 1980s.

Bibliography: Joyner, Nancy D., *Aerial Hijacking as an International Crime* (1974).

John F. Kennedy International Airport (JFK), in Queens, New York City, is among the world's busiest. The central terminal area shown here consists of ten airline terminals surrounding five large auto parking lots. Runways and taxiing and parking areas for aircraft form the spokes to the central hub of the terminal area. A major highway enters the terminal area from bottom right. JFK is one of four airports serving metropolitan New York–New Jersey. The others are La Guardia, which handles domestic flights, Newark International, and Teterboro, a smaller airport for general aviation aircraft. Together the four airports handle the largest number of scheduled and chartered flights in the world—about 10,000 domestic and 2,000 overseas flights weekly.

airport

An airport is a facility for handling the arrival and departure of AIRCRAFT, passengers, and freight. Today's modern passenger airports, which are the nuclei of the world's most extensive and heavily used travel network, are shaped by certain exacting requirements: sufficient space to accommodate the long runway needs of jumbo jets, as well as the hangars, terminals, parking lots, and cargo and accessory buildings necessary for efficient airport operation; sufficient highways and public transportation to allow passengers access; and sufficient distance from residential areas so that adjacent neighborhoods will not be subjected to aircraft noise. (See also AVIATION.)

HISTORY

Before World War I any spot large and level enough for a pilot to take off and land was considered an airport. The brothers Orville and Wilbur WRIGHT made do with a level cow pasture. The first experimental flights in Canada were made from the frozen surface of a lake. An old barn to house tools, a workshop, and some storage space were all that was required for early experiments in aviation.

Between 1909 and 1914 the airplane swiftly gained popularity. Well-publicized world records for speed, altitude, and distance of flights were continually surpassed, and a number of national and international races were organized. Newspapers and other organizations put up substantial cash prizes for special events, which were usually staged on racetracks with large, level fields for takeoffs and landings.

Europe. The big bombers used in World War I had demonstrated a capability for carrying considerable loads and for operating at night, thus proving that air passenger service was theoretically feasible. Shortly after the war, a few former British military pilots acquired some surplus warplanes and refitted them for passengers. By 1919 the first London-to-Paris passenger services were inaugurated, and within the year scheduled passenger flights were offered to Amsterdam and to other cities on the Continent. By about 1928, scheduled commercial air routes crisscrossed all of Europe, and most cities had adequate airports.

United States. In the years after World War I, manufacturers left with large inventories of airplane parts from canceled war contracts began to produce planes for peacetime use. Small, short-hop airlines came into existence and vanished quickly; few people were willing to risk a journey in the tiny, fragile planes of the time. Charles LINDBERGH's transatlantic flight of 1927, however, triggered a great upsurge in public interest and generated programs in aeronautical education and research that eventually established the airplane as an effective means of mass transportation.

A string of small airports and emergency fields had been established from coast to coast to service AIRMAIL planes. During the early 1930s the first transcontinental operations were inaugurated. The first long-distance airline schedules were begun in conjunction with the existing railroad systems. Airports were sited adjacent to railroad stations, and passengers flew by day and traveled in railroad sleeping cars at night. Coast-to-coast travel time was about 48 hr by combined rail and flight. By 1932, light BEACONS and radio communication had been installed along the airways, making it possible for planes to fly through the night. Travel time became about 33 hr, with 12 to 15 stops for fuel and food.

Overseas Flights. In the late 1930s commercial overseas services to South America and Europe were started. The plane most widely used over water was the flying boat (a large four-engine vehicle with a watertight body that acted as a hull, allowing the plane to float), operating out of harbors on the east and west coasts (see SEAPLANE). It was anticipated that the flying boat would be the eventual solution for worldwide air commerce. By the end of World War II, however, further development and plans for future use of flying boats were totally abandoned, and today airport-seaport combinations are not in commercial use.

TYPES OF AIRPORTS IN THE UNITED STATES

Three types of airports are now in common use: government airports, operated mostly for the military; public and private airports, primarily to serve general aviation; and commercial airports, including those for domestic and foreign airline operations. Federal regulations govern their operational methods and set safety standards.

Government Airports. Government airports serve the U.S. Air Force, Navy, and Marine Corps, as well as NASA and various installations for research and development. They also support such special activities as the landing and recovery of space vehicles on 8-km (5-mi) desert runways. They furnish long-range jets and short-haul helicopters for presidents and foreign dignitaries. General-aviation and commercial planes are usually prohibited from using U.S. government airports, except in emergencies or when a government facility is designated a ''joint use'' airport.

General-Aviation Airports. General-aviation activities—including private flying for recreation, instruction, and business—account for 80 percent of the air-hours flown, and it is anticipated that by the 1990s the number of privately owned planes will double. Of more than 12,000 airports listed in the U.S. directories, the majority are available for general use, subject to FEDERAL AVIATION ADMINISTRATION (FAA) rules and regulations. General-aviation airports are often privately owned and are usually located near small cities and towns that are not along the routes of commercial airlines. In addition, most commercial airports designate specific areas for general aviation use and require all planes to be subject to the same traffic control and regulations that are imposed on commercial airline traffic.

Commercial Airports. Commercial airports are usually publicly owned, and operated by municipal, county, or other government agencies. The location of many modern urban airports was originally determined largely on the basis of available real estate and local politics. Before World War II, airfields in such major cities as London and New York often occupied less than 202 ha (500 acres). (By contrast, the Dallas/Fort Worth Airport in Texas has an area of more than 7,080 ha/17,500 acres; and Montreal's Mirabel Airport has more than 35,600 ha/88,000 acres in reserve, although at present it uses only about one-fifth of its total area.) As airline traffic increased in the 1950s and '60s, airports enlarged to accommodate it; the most important single change in aviation, however, was the introduction (1958) of jet planes, which made unprecedented demands on the length and strength of runways, taxiways, and ground facilities of every kind. As a result, cities with major airports enlarged them greatly or moved them into nearby rural areas.

Despite the enlarging of airport facilities, many hub airports—those in large cities which serve as major transfer points—find themselves increasingly short of space. Their

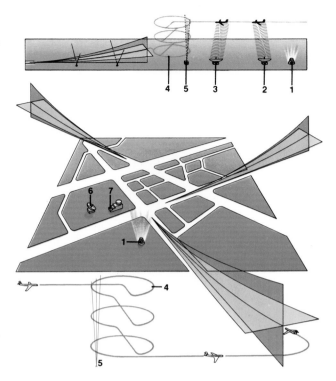

Air traffic arriving at airports often follows airways the way an auto follows a street map. Navigation aids (top), such as very-high-frequency omnirange (VOR) beacons (1) at intersections, give bearings and distances. At the destination, traffic plotted by primary radar (2) will be followed by secondary surveillance radar (3) and individually identified and guided to a holding stack (4) and around to a radio beacon (5), where inbound aircraft fly circular patterns at successively lower levels. From the bottom of the stack each aircraft captures the sloping glide-path of the landing runway and is guided by it to a landing. Airport surveillance radar (6) follows all aircraft, and the aircraft control center (7) coordinates all their movements.

problems are exacerbated by the growth of the suburban areas that were relatively empty when the airports were first located there. In their search for space, airports now look to ''reliever'' airports, smaller nearby facilities that could absorb some of the pressure during periods of heavy airline traffic. In addition, airports are investigating the possibility of increased joint use of military air bases.

AIRPORT FACILITIES
The modern airport consists of facilities for handling airplanes: runways and taxiing areas; hangars and machine shops for plane maintenance, repair, and fueling; and traffic control towers, whose personnel track aircraft and guide them through landings and takeoffs. Passengers are received in the terminal buildings, which are connected to nearby highways and to parking facilities by access roads and which contain airline ticket counters and reception desks, baggage-handling facilities, plane-boarding gates, security-inspection devices, and such ancillary services as restaurants. In addition, airports provide special buildings and services for air freight, a business that has grown substantially in recent years.

Traffic Control. The most conspicuous and important structure at any airport is the TRAFFIC CONTROL tower. Located approximately in the center of the runway complex, it is high enough to permit a clear view of landing, takeoff, and loading areas. It contains a complex of communications and electronic surveillance gear by which the airport controllers monitor and direct all plane movements on or near the field.

All commercial airlines, the military, and most general-aviation flights operate according to flight plans. Prepared by pilots before their departure, flight plans are filed with the

WORLD'S BUSIEST COMMERCIAL AIRPORTS (1981)

Airport and Location	Total Passengers (millions)	Total Operations (All Takeoffs and Landings)
O'Hare; Chicago	37.9	645,500
Hartsfield; Atlanta, Ga.	37.6	601,000
Los Angeles Int'l	37.7	503,000
Heathrow; London	27.5	287,500
Kennedy Int'l; New York City	25.7	285,900
Dallas/Ft. Worth; Texas	25.5	471,900
Stapleton Int'l; Denver, Colo.	22.6	479,700
Haneda; Tokyo	21.2	144,700
Miami Int'l; Florida	19.8	350,900
San Francisco Int'l; California	19.8	319,500
La Guardia; New York City	18.1	308,200
Osaka; Japan	17.0	129,100
Orly; Paris	17.0	181,600
Frankfurt/Main; West Germany	16.9	236,700
Logan Int'l; Boston	14.8	284,000

SOURCE: Airport Operators Council International.

originating airport and transmitted to the airport of destination. Flights follow predetermined routes, and reports on their progress are made from checkpoints along the airways. Control towers are advised of the estimated time of arrival (ETA) for all aircraft in their approach areas. The pilots are then given detailed landing instructions: approach routes to be followed, rate of descent, proximity of other aircraft, weather conditions, and designated landing runways. For departures, procedures are reversed. Pilots are advised what taxiways to use, what runways are available, the traffic conditions on and around the field, and the procedures to follow to reach their designated flight path at the predetermined altitude. This is particularly necessary in bad weather or at night, but such procedures are followed at all times, in the interest of maximum flight safety.

In 1981 the Professional Air Traffic Controllers Organization (PATCO), the union representing all nonmilitary air traffic controllers, called a strike over issues of pay and working conditions. President Reagan declared the strike illegal and fired 11,500 controllers, replacing some of them with controllers borrowed from military airfields. As a result of the strike, the FAA reduced both commercial and general air traffic into most airports, while it recruited trainees for a new generation of traffic controllers. At the same time, the agency began working on plans for reducing air-traffic facilities in the future by relying more heavily on new computer capabilities, new plane-borne radar signaling devices, and new automated control systems. If its plans are carried through by the year 2000, the number of major air-traffic control centers will be reduced from 20 to 16, and of smaller flight service stations from nearly 300 to about 60.

Noise. Aircraft noise became a major issue in the early 1960s, when commercial jet aircraft first came into wide use. Al-

The airport's air-traffic control center tracks airplane movements by radar within a radius of 20–50 km (12–30 mi). A computer digests the data from the radar and displays it on a screen. Air controllers use such screens to guide pilots to safe takeoffs and landings.

though those who live and work near large airports have long complained of the extraordinary burden of noise they bear, the first widely publicized controversy developed over the landing of the CONCORDE, the Anglo-French supersonic transport, at Kennedy International Airport in New York City on Oct. 19, 1977. Strenuous protests led to court hearings, delays, and, for a time, restricted experimental service. Today Concorde landings are limited to a few airports, and the plane is not allowed to exceed the speed of sound when it flies over the continental United States.

In suits brought against airports by nearby towns or citizens' groups, the courts have generally found airport operators primarily responsible for controlling noise. Since 1976 the FAA has funded noise studies at most large airports and has issued guidelines for reducing airport noise—in addition to the existing regulations that limit the noise produced by aircraft. These guidelines recommend restrictions on airport acquisition of land and on the utilization of runways whose flight paths are over residential areas. Compliance with the FAA regulations has proven costly in terms of both money and available space. Nevertheless, airport operators will in the future have to adjust their plans to conform to more stringent noise-control requirements.

Security. Since the 1960s, the threat of AIRPLANE HIJACKING and of terrorist attacks on the ground and in the air has forced many airports to adopt special security measures. All passengers are required to pass through electronic gates just before boarding their planes, in order to ensure that no weapons are being carried. Armed security guards are stationed throughout the public areas to watch for any suspicious activity. In spite of these precautions, however, the threat of violence remains.

The Effects of Airline Deregulation on Airports. The Airline Deregulation Act of 1978 removed route-regulating authority from the Civil Aeronautics Board (CAB), leaving each airline free to choose whatever routes seemed to promise the most success and to set its own fares independent of the CAB. The years since deregulation have seen several new airlines come into existence and flourish because they offered cheaper fares or regular schedules to certain areas that had not been well served by the older, established airlines. Some older airlines have faltered, however; Braniff, which extended its routes and its capital investment too far, declared bankruptcy in 1982. The effect of deregulation on U.S. airports has not been altogether beneficial. In their scramble for the most popular routes, the airlines have overloaded the major airports—already laboring under the limitations produced by the PATCO strike—while leaving many secondary airports, once on mandatory CAB routes, without regular airline service. The federal government provides incentive subsidies for such service, but they are being gradually removed.

At the present time a hub airport may be unable to provide "slots" (landing rights) for every airline planning to use its facilities. Some airports have been embroiled in legal actions when they attempted to restrict airport use. The use of congested hub airports by increasing numbers of private planes is also coming under question.

The initial few years of deregulation have been a difficult period for airport operators, who must deal with new laws regulating noise and other environmental issues, as well as with the problems that deregulation and the PATCO strike have created. In the coming years, air traffic inevitably will increase, and the problems of noise and lack of runway and terminal space will grow more pressing. In addition to the more obvious solutions, such as increasing the size of airports, operators have suggested improved Instrument Flight Rule (IFR) systems to permit reduced spacing between parallel runways and shorter distances between arriving or departing aircraft, and the construction of separate, shorter runways for commuter and business aircraft.   S. PAUL JOHNSTON

Bibliography: Allen, Roy, *Major Airports of the World* (1979); Amann, Dick, *Airports: Today's Small Field, Tomorrow's Neighborhood Nightmare* (1981); Horonjeff, Robert, *The Planning and Design of Airports*, 2d ed. (1975); Nelkin, Dorothy, *Jetport: The Boston Airport Controversy* (1974); Stratford, Alan H., *Airports and the Environment* (1974).

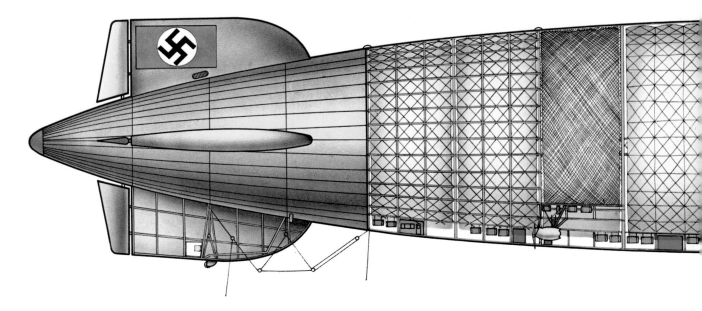

The airship, or dirigible, marked the climax of travel in lighter-than-air aircraft. The longest airship ever built was the German Hindenburg, (above) which was 245 m (804 ft) long. It carried 200,000 m³ (7 million ft³) of hydrogen in envelope bags, housed within an aluminum framework covered with cotton fabric. The airship had quarters for 70 passengers and 45 crew members. In 1937, the Hindenburg caught fire and burned while docking at Lakehurst, N.J., with the loss of 35 lives. The Hindenburg was a rigid airship. In a semirigid airship, such as the Norge, flexible gas bays support a keel, engines, and a payload. The Norge went to the North Pole in 1926. A nonrigid airship, such as the U.S. Navy blimp, has a totally flexible envelope. Silhouettes (bottom) indicate sizes of the three craft relative to each other, airship hangers, and mooring mast.

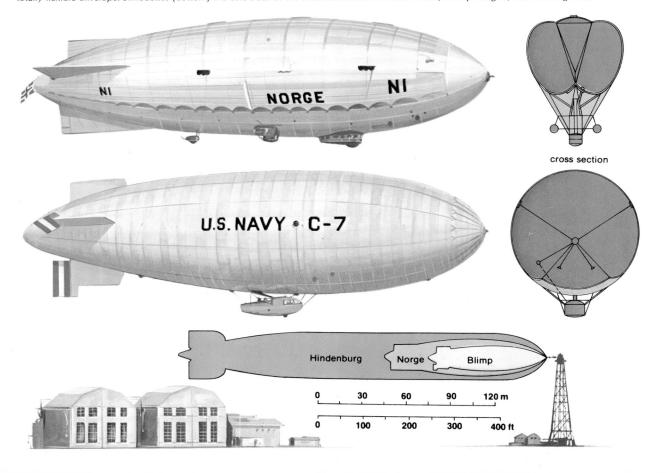

cross section

NI   NORGE   NI

U.S. NAVY · C-7

Hindenburg   Norge   Blimp

| 0 | 30 | 60 | 90 | 120 m |

| 0 | 100 | 200 | 300 | 400 ft |

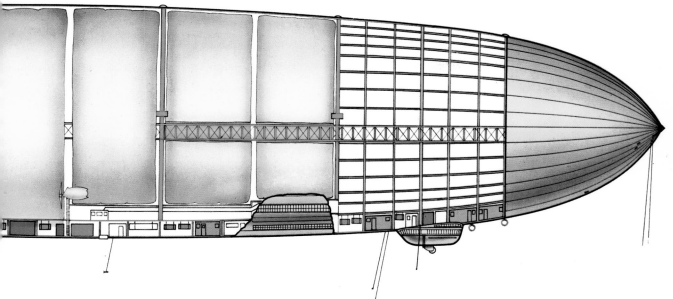

airship

An airship is a type of lighter-than-air AIRCRAFT with propulsion and steering systems; it is used to carry passengers and cargo. It obtains its buoyancy—as does a BALLOON—from the presence of a lighter-than-air gas such as hydrogen or helium (see ARCHIMEDES' PRINCIPLE). The first airship was developed by the French; called a *ballon dirigible* ("steerable balloon"), it could be steered and could also be flown against the wind.

TYPES OF AIRSHIP

Two basic types of airship have been developed: the rigid airship, the shape of which is fixed by its internal structure; and the nonrigid "blimp," which depends on the pressure created by a series of air diaphragms inside its gas space to maintain the shape of its fabric hull. Inventors sought to combine the best features of these models in a semirigid type, but it met with only limited success. Today only the nonrigid airship is used.

Rigid Airship. The rigid airship's structure resembled a cage that enclosed a series of balloons called gas cells. These cells were tailored to fit the cylindrical space and were secured in place by a netting that transmitted the lifting force of their gas to the structure. Each gas cell had two or more valves, which operated automatically to relieve pressure when the gas expanded with altitude; the valves could also be operated manually so that the pilot could release gas whenever desired.

Also on board was a ballast system that used water as ballast. On the ground this ballast served to make the airship heavier than air. When part of it was released, the airship ascended to a cruising altitude where the engines supplied propulsion, and further ballast could be released to gain more altitude. As fuel was consumed, the airship became lighter and tended to climb. This was countered in hydrogen-inflated airships by simply releasing gas into the atmosphere.

The method was uneconomical, however, with helium-inflated airships, and they were therefore equipped with ballast generators, apparatus that condensed moisture out of the engines' exhaust gases to compensate for fuel that was consumed. But this ballast-generating equipment was expensive, complex, heavy, and difficult to maintain and was thus one of the most serious disadvantages of airships filled with the safer but more expensive helium.

Nonrigid Airship. In contrast to the rigid airship, the nonrigid blimp has no internal structure to maintain the shape of its hull envelope, which is made of two or three plies of cotton, nylon, or dacron impregnated with rubber for gas tightness. Inside the gas space of the hull are two or more air dia-phragms called ballonets that are kept under slight pressure, either by blowers or by air that is forced through scoops as a result of the forward motion (ram effect). The ballonets in turn exert pressure upon the gas, which fills the envelope, and this pressure in turn serves to stiffen the shape of the envelope and create a smooth flying surface. On takeoff the ballonets are almost fully inflated, but as the airship gains altitude and the gas expands, air is bled from the ballonets while a constant pressure is maintained throughout the envelope. When the gas contracts upon descent, air is pumped back into the ballonets.

HISTORY OF RIGID AIRSHIPS

The German company Luftschiffbau Zeppelin had the most success in building rigid airships (see ZEPPELIN, FERDINAND, GRAF VON). The first Zeppelin was flown on July 2, 1900; it was 126 m (419 ft) long, 11.4 m (38 ft) in diameter, contained 9,583 m³ (338,410 ft³) of hydrogen gas in 16 cells, and was powered by two 16-hp engines. Its range and payload were negligible. The last Zeppelin was the *Graf Zeppelin II*, which was first flown on Sept. 14, 1938; it was 245 m (803 ft) long, 41 m (135 ft) at maximum diameter, contained 200,000 m³ (7,062,100 ft³) of hydrogen, and was powered by four 1,050-hp Daimler Benz diesel engines. It could carry loads of 30 tons over transoceanic distances. It was scrapped in May 1940.

A total of 119 Zeppelins were built, most of them during World War I, when 103 airships were delivered to the military. The most famous Zeppelin was the original GRAF ZEPPELIN, which during 1928–37 made flights to the United States, the Arctic, the Middle East, and South America; it also made one flight around the world. Another famous Zeppelin was the airliner HINDENBURG, which was destroyed by fire at Lakehurst, N.J., on May 6, 1937.

The British made intermittent efforts to develop the rigid airship; they built eight during World War I and six shortly thereafter. The most noteworthy was the *R-34*, which in July 1919 made the first transatlantic round-trip flight. An effort to develop two airships of 141,000 m³ (5,000,000 ft³) for intercontinental air service came to grief in October 1930 when the *R-101* crashed and burned in France. The *R-100*, which had made a successful flight to Canada earlier in the year, was subsequently scrapped. (See R-34 AND R-101.) In the United States, the development of rigid airships was undertaken by the navy, and only five were operated. The navy-built ZR-1 SHENANDOAH made its first flight on Sept. 4, 1923, and was torn to pieces by a thunderstorm over southern Ohio on Sept. 3, 1925. The ZR-2 (British *R-38*) was procured in England but crashed on Aug. 24, 1921, before it could be delivered to the United States. The ZR-3 *Los Angeles*, built in Germany by Luftschiffbau Zeppelin, made its transatlantic delivery flight during Oct. 11–15, 1924; it was flown successfully until decommissioned in 1931 and was scrapped in early 1940. The ZRS4 and ZRS5 AKRON AND MACON were built by the Goodyear-Zeppelin Co. of Akron, Ohio. These 184,000-m³ (6,500,-000-ft³) sister ships were 239 m (785 ft) long and 40 m (133 ft) at maximum diameter, and were powered by eight 560-hp Maybach engines. Their design was unique in that it provided for an internal space for five airplanes that could be launched and retrieved while the airships were in flight. The *Akron* first flew on Sept. 23, 1931 and was lost in a storm over the Atlantic on Apr. 4, 1933; the *Macon* first flew on Apr. 21, 1933, and crashed in the Pacific on Feb. 12, 1935.

HISTORY OF NONRIGID AIRSHIPS

The first successful nonrigid airships were built by the French. In 1852 Henri Giffard built an airship of 3,200 m³ (113,000 ft³) powered by a steam engine. The brothers Albert and Gaston Tissandier constructed a 1,062-m³ (37,500-ft³) airship propelled by a battery-powered electric motor in 1883, and the following year Charles Renard and Arthur C. Krebs built the 1,869-m³ (66,000-ft³) *La France*, which also used electric power. At the turn of the century the Brazilian aeronaut Alberto SANTOS-DUMONT built and flew a series of small airships in France, all of which used gasoline engines. Blimps were effectively used by the British and French in World War I in maritime reconnaissance against German submarines. The term *blimp*, a British slang expression of unknown origin, came into use about this time.

In World War II, the United States was the only power to use airships; its navy used them for antisubmarine patrols. Its more than 150 blimps operated from bases on the east and west coasts, the Gulf of Mexico, the Caribbean, and as far south as Brazil. The workhorse of these forces was the K-type blimp, 76 m (253 ft) long, 18 m (60 ft) in diameter, containing 12,900 m³ (456,000 ft³) of gas, and powered by two 425-hp engines that gave a top speed of 80 km/h (50 mph). Blimps are not fast, but whereas an airplane can remain airborne for only a few hours, a K-ship could stay aloft for 60 hours. In 1944, six K-ships flew across the Atlantic to Morocco, where they established a low-altitude antisubmarine barrier across the Strait of Gibraltar; later they operated from bases at Cuers, France, and Pisa, Italy.

After 1945 the navy continued to use blimps in antisubmarine warfare, and some were equipped with extraordinarily large airborne radar sets for early offshore warning of bomber attacks against the United States. The largest of these airships was the ZPG-3W; it displaced 43,000 m³ (1,516,000 ft³) and was 121 m (403 ft) long and 22.5 m (75 ft) at maximum diameter—the largest blimp type ever built. On Aug. 31, 1962, the navy terminated its use of blimps.

THE GOODYEAR BLIMPS

The most long-lasting use of airships has been by the Goodyear Tire and Rubber Company. The *Pony* was built in 1919 and the *Pilgrim* in 1923. After 1928 the fleet was expanded with the *Puritan, Volunteer, Mayflower, Vigilant, Defender, Reliance, Resolute, Enterprise, Ranger,* and *Columbia*. During the 1930s these airships were used for advertising, and they barnstormed all over the United States. They were taken over by the navy in World War II; after the war the Goodyear fleet was revived with five airships, but by 1959, only the *Mayflower* was left. Today three Goodyear blimps are in operation—the *Mayflower, Columbia,* and *America*—variously based at Los Angeles, Houston, and Miami. From these home bases they operate over diverse parts of the country. A fourth Goodyear blimp, the *Europa*, is based at Capena, Italy, near Rome, from which it operates over Western Europe.

THE FUTURE OF AIRSHIPS

Proponents of a resurgence in airship use argue that the problems that led to its downfall have now been solved. The use of improved materials for structural parts can help to prevent their failures. Meteorological instrumentation and weather forecasting are now sophisticated enough to give adequate warning of dangerous weather. Safe, nonflammable helium is available and can eliminate airship fires and explosions. Proposals have been advanced for the development of relatively slow-moving airships that can transport cargo and passengers more economically than airplanes. Some research and small-scale tests have already been conducted, and military and commercial interest has been expressed in the revival of the airship.   RICHARD K. SMITH

Bibliography: Deeson, A. F., *An Illustrated History of Airships* (1974); Robinson, Douglas H., *Giants in the Sky* (1973); Ventry, Lord, and Kolesnik, Eugene, eds., *Jane's Pocket Book of Airships* (1977).

airsickness: see MOTION SICKNESS.

Airy, Sir George Biddell   [air'-ee]

The English astronomer George Airy, b. July 27, 1801, d. Jan. 2, 1892, is best known for modernizing the Royal Greenwich Observatory during his 45 years as astronomer royal. A graduate of and professor of astronomy at Cambridge, he exerted a considerable influence on British astronomy and played a controversial role in the famous priority dispute over the discovery of Neptune by delaying action on the prediction of J. C. ADAMS. Although not himself a highly original scientist, Airy was an able organizer who used this talent to substantially improve the Greenwich Observatory. The AIRY DISK diffraction phenomenon is named after him.

Bibliography: Airy, G. B., *Autobiography of Sir George Airy* (1896).

Airy disk   [air'-ee]

The Airy disk, named for the British astronomer Sir George B. AIRY, is a small, disklike image produced by the DIFFRACTION of light when it passes through a telescope. Airy first calculated the size of the disk and found that it depended both on the wavelength of the light and on the diameter of the objective lens or mirror; the larger the aperture (diameter) of the objective, the smaller the Airy disk. A telescope with an aperture of 25 cm (10 in) produces an Airy disk that is 1 arc second in diameter for visible light.   JAMES R. HOUCK

Aisha   [ah'-i-sha]

Aisha, b. 614, d. July 678, was the third and favorite wife of MUHAMMAD and daughter of the caliph ABU BAKR. After the Prophet's death in 632, she opposed the fourth caliph, ALI. When her army was defeated by him in the "Battle of the Camel" (656), she retired to Medina.

Aisne River   [ayn]

The Aisne River is in the northern part of France. It rises in the Meuse department and flows north past Vouziers and then west to Compiègne, where it joins the Oise River. It is about 265 km (165 mi) long, and its main tributaries are the Aire and Vesle rivers. The major city is Soissons. The Aisne marked part of the front lines during much of World War I.

Aitken, Robert Grant

Robert Aitken, b. Dec. 31, 1864, d. Oct. 29, 1951, was an American astronomer who devoted most of his life to the study of double stars. A graduate of Williams College in Massachusetts, Aitken became assistant astronomer (1895) at Lick Observatory in California and eventually rose to director (1930–35). His *New General Catalogue of Double Stars within 120° of the North Pole* (1932), still in use, includes more than 4,400 double stars that he himself discovered.

Aix-en-Provence   [eks-awn-proh-vawns']

Aix-en-Provence is a city in the Bouches-du-Rhône department of Provence in southeastern France. It lies on the principal routes to Italy and the Alps. Aix has a population of 114,014 (1975) and is an agricultural center, producing almonds, olives, and wine. Founded by the Romans in 123 BC near mineral springs, it is the site of Marius's defeat of the Teutons (102 BC). In succession, Visigoths, Franks, Lombards, and Moors invaded and plundered the town. In the Middle

Ages it was a center for the arts and Provençal literature, fostered by rulers such as RENÉ OF ANJOU. After René's death (1480), Aix was annexed (1486) by France. The city has long been a favorite spot for artists, including Paul CÉZANNE, who was born here.

Aix-la-Chapelle: see AACHEN.

Aix-la-Chapelle, Treaties of [eks-lah-shah-pel']

Two important treaties in European history were signed at Aix-la-Chapelle (now Aachen, West Germany). The first, signed on May 2, 1668, concluded the War of DEVOLUTION (1667–68) in which LOUIS XIV of France had overrun the Spanish Netherlands. The treaty returned to Spain much of the territory won by France, including Franche-Comté, but France retained some border towns in the Spanish Netherlands.

The second treaty, signed on Oct. 18, 1748, ended the War of the AUSTRIAN SUCCESSION (1740–48), which had pitted the alliance of Austria, Britain, and the Dutch Republic against the alliance of France, Spain, Bavaria, and Prussia. The treaty essentially restored the prewar situation. In North America, Britain returned Cape Breton Island, including the fortress of Louisbourg, to France, while in India, France returned Madras to Britain. The most important result was that Prussia's right to SILESIA was confirmed, enhancing Prussia's status as a major power in central Europe.

See also: FRENCH AND INDIAN WARS.

Ajaccio [ah-yah'-choh]

Ajaccio (1975 pop., 51,770) is the capital city of the French island of Corsica. It is located on the western coast of the island at the Mediterranean Sea. The main industry is tourism. Napoleon Bonaparte's birthplace in the town is a museum. Ajaccio was the first Corsican town to revolt (1943) against Fascist occupation in World War II.

Ajanta [uh-jahn'-tuh]

Ajanta is a village in Aurangabad district of Maharashtra state in western India. It is the site of famous rock-cut Buddhist sanctuaries dating from the 2d century BC to the 7th century. The Ajanta caves contain extraordinary interior wall paintings from which a survey of early Indian art can be made. The 29 hollowed-out chambers pierce a crescent-shaped granite cliff north of the village. The caves, which served as a Buddhist monastery and a stopping place for pilgrims using the trade route through western India, are of two types: monasteries (*viharas*) and vaulted temple halls (*caityas*) for worship. Intricately carved pillars and niches decorate the facades and interiors of the caves. On the walls and ceilings are frescolike paintings, primarily depicting scenes from the life of the Buddha before his enlightenment. The exuberant paintings, although essentially religious in theme, convey much information about contemporary secular life. The finest date from the 4th to the 7th century, and the style of their sensuously modeled human forms influenced later Buddhist art throughout Asia. With Buddhism's decline in India, the Ajanta caves were abandoned and forgotten until British soldiers rediscovered them in 1819.

Bibliography: Singh, Madanjeet, *India: Paintings from the Ajanta Caves* (1954); Weiner, S. L., *Ajanta* (1977).

Ajax

In Greek mythology, Ajax (or Aias) was the name of two heroes, both of whom fought in the TROJAN WAR. Ajax of Salamis, sometimes called the Greater Ajax, was the son of King Telamon, an old comrade of HERCULES. Although characterized by HOMER as slow-witted, Ajax of Salamis was nevertheless one of the best fighters among the Greeks and was famed for his steadfast courage in the face of adversity. After the death of ACHILLES, whose armor had been claimed by both Ajax and ODYSSEUS and was finally awarded to Odysseus, Ajax's resentment drove him mad, and he eventually killed himself.

Ajax of Locris, or the Lesser Ajax, was also a good fighter, but his ill-mannered and violent behavior is frequently mentioned by Homer. Shipwrecked on his way home to Greece after the war, Ajax of Locris managed to swim ashore with the aid of the sea-god POSEIDON. Later, however, he boasted that he had saved himself without divine assistance, and for this impertinence Poseidon caused him to fall into the sea and drown.

C. SCOTT LITTLETON

Akademie der Wissenschaften der DDR
[ah-kah-dem-ee' dair vis'-en-shaft-en dair day-day-air']

The Akademie der Wissenschaften der DDR (Academy of Sciences of the German Democratic Republic) in East Berlin oversees research and study in the natural and social sciences, technology, and medicine. It comprises 40 institutes and 6 research departments. Twelve scientific societies are among the other branches of the Academy. Publications include proceedings, yearbooks, monthly reports, and a literary journal. Founded in 1700 by Gottfried Wilhelm von LEIBNIZ and reformed many times as a Prussian and national institution, the academy has always enjoyed a reputation as a strong center for science.

JAMES E. MCCLELLAN

Akan [ay'-kuhn]

Akan is a group of AFRICAN LANGUAGES of the Kwa subfamily of the Niger-Congo stock, spoken by several peoples of Ghana and Ivory Coast. The word *Akan* also signifies speakers of these languages having other tribal names, such as the ASHANTI and FANTI.

The Akan are subsistence farmers who produce such cash crops as cacao. They live mostly in compact villages and towns, with well-developed systems of local trade. Descent is matrilineal, and marriage is polygynous. Most Akan societies were traditionally complex states with kings and a hierarchical organization of government, courts, slavery, and, in some tribes, human sacrifice. Akan peoples are also noted for their highly developed art forms, in gold, silver, bronze, wood, and clay.

PHOEBE MILLER

Akbar, Mogul Emperor of India [ak'-bahr]

Akbar (Akbar the Great), b. Oct. 15, 1542, d. Oct. 16, 1605, the third Mogul emperor of India, is considered one of the greatest Indian rulers. The son of Emperor HUMAYON and originally named Jalal ud-Din Muhammad, he ascended the throne of Delhi on Feb. 15, 1556, and ruled under a regency until 1560. His position was immediately confirmed by the defeat of the Afghan claimant to the throne at Panipat on Nov. 5, 1556, which firmly reestablished the Mogul dynasty on the throne of Delhi.

Akbar, the third Mogul emperor of India, was not only a great conqueror but a skillful administrator and a philosopher-king who devised his own religion. Here he is shown seated on a horse as he tames a wild elephant.

Akbar set out to unite all India under Mogul rule. Akbar first set up his court at Agra and then in 1569 built the royal city of FATEHPUR-SIKRI, which was his capital from 1570 to 1585. He began consolidating his power in northern India by annexing Malwa (1562), and by 1595 he had taken Gujarat, Bihar, part of Bengal, Kabul, Kashmir, Sind, and Baluchistan. He moved toward the south in 1596 with the occupation of Berar. He took Khandesh and Ahmadnagar in 1600, but further conquests were thwarted by a rebellion led by his son, Salim.

Akbar moved his court to Lahore in 1585 and returned it to Agra in 1599. In his attempt to unite India, he took Hindu chiefs (particularly the Rajputs) into his administration and otherwise sought to conciliate Hindu interests. He established a fair tax system and a uniform system of weights and measures, developed trade, and practiced religious tolerance. Although illiterate himself, he surrounded himself with scholars and promulgated a new religion, the *Din-i-Ilahi* (Divine Faith), a blend of Islam, Hinduism, and other traditions. He also kept a Jesuit mission at his court.

Bibliography: Smith, Vincent A., *Akbar, the Great Mogul* (1919; repr. 1966); Srivastava, A. L., *Akbar the Great*, 2 vols. (1962–67).

akeake [ah-kee-ah′-kee]

The akeake, *Dodonaea viscosa* in the family Sapindaceae, native to tropical and semitropical regions, is abundant in New Zealand and Australia and is found in the southwestern United States. It ranges in size from a small shrub to a slender tree up to 9 m (30 ft) tall. Leaves and young branches secrete a resinous substance. The wood is extremely tough and durable, and New Zealand's Maoris have used akeake to fashion clubs and other weapons. (The Maori name *akeake* means "forever and ever.")   ROBERT C. ROMANS

Akenside, Mark [ay′-ken-syd]

Mark Akenside, b. Nov. 9, 1721, d. June 23, 1770, an English poet, also studied and practiced medicine. He published many odes and short poems, but his most important work is the blank-verse poem *The Pleasures of Imagination* (1744), which is a didactic mixture of Whig politics, philosophy, and aesthetic theories.   ROBIN BUSS

Akhenaten [ah-kuh-nah′-tuhn]

The Egyptian pharaoh Akhenaten, or Ikhanaton, was one of the earliest monotheists, but his religious reforms did not sur-

The Egyptian pharaoh Akhenaten, who reigned from 1379 to 1362 BC, introduced monotheism in Egypt, although his religious reforms did not survive his death. The art of this period was unusually realistic for ancient Egypt, as shown in this contemporary bust.

vive. He succeeded his father, AMENHOTEP III, in 1379 BC and immediately began building a new type of roofless temple to the Aten ("Sun disk"). He soon forbade the worship of other gods, especially of the state god Amen, or AMON, of THEBES. In 1374 BC he changed his name from Amenhotep ("Amon is satisfied") to Akhenaten ("beneficial to Aten") and left Thebes for a new capital at Tell el-AMARNA. Living there with his queen NEFERTITI, six daughters, and possibly several sons, he fostered new styles in art and literature.

Akhenaten was a complex figure whose historical significance is still debated. His physical abnormalities were exaggerated in contemporary art, and no evidence supports the charge of mental instability that is often leveled against him. He lost Egyptian-held territory in Syria and Palestine but maintained Egypt's status as a great power. Within Egypt he combined religious reform and skillful tactics to strengthen absolute royal power over the bureaucracy and the army, but his monotheism was genuine and innovative. His religious reforms were detested, however, and after his death in 1362 his successors restored traditional religion. The Aten temples were demolished, and Akhenaten came to be called "the Enemy."   DAVID O'CONNOR

Bibliography: Aldred, Cyril, *Akhenaten, Pharaoh of Egypt: A New Study* (1968); Giles, F. J., *Ikhnaton: Legend and History* (1970).

Akhetaten: see AMARNA, TELL EL-.

Akhmatova, Anna [ahk′-muh-toh′-vuh]

Anna Akhmatova is the pseudonym of Anna Andreyevna Gorenko, b. June 23, 1889, d. Mar. 5, 1966. She is considered one of the foremost Russian poets of the 20th century. Together with her first husband, Nikolai Gumilev, and Osip MANDELSTAM, she founded (1910) the ACMEISTS, a Russian literary movement that opposed the mystical vagueness of symbolism. For more than 50 years she wrote polished and elegant yet emotionally charged verse in the manner of PUSHKIN.

Akhmatova's poetry, as shown in her first volumes, *Vecher* (Evening, 1912) and *Chiotki* (The Rosary Beads, 1914), is intensely personal and frequently concerns her favorite themes—love, loneliness, and grief. Her work after the Russian Revolution, published in such volumes as *Belaya staya* (The White Flock, 1917) and *Anno Domini MCMXII* (1922), is more patriotic but retains the basic grace and simplicity of the early poems. Nevertheless, her refusal to write optimistic verse that glorified Soviet accomplishments led to frequent criticism of her work, and she was not allowed to publish again until 1940. In 1946 her poetry was branded as erotic and mystical, and she was expelled from the Soviet Writers' Union. *Requiem* (1935–40; Eng. trans., 1976), a cycle of poems inspired by her son's arrest and exile to a Soviet concentration camp, has appeared only in fragments in the USSR. After Stalin's death (1953), Akhmatova's verse began to appear again, and a collection of it, *The Course of Time*, was published in the USSR a year before her death.

MAURICE FRIEDBERG

Bibliography: Akhmatova, Anna, *Poems of Akhmatova*, selected by Stanley Kunitz and Max Hayward (1973) and *Requiem and a Poem without a Hero*, trans. by D. M. Thomas (1976); Haight, Amanda, *Anna Akhmatova: A Poetic Pilgrimage* (1976).

Akiba ben Joseph [ah-kee′-bah]

Akiba ben Joseph, AD 40–135, was a prominent Palestinian rabbi and master of the TALMUD. In his youth he was an untutored shepherd, but after a period of intensive study he became a man of deep knowledge. He was the first to collect the interpretations of the Hebrew laws, arranging them in what later became known as the MISHNAH. His favorite book of the Bible was the Song of Songs, which he understood to refer, allegorically, to the love between God and Israel. His maxim was "man is created in the image of God." He actively supported the anti-Roman rebellion of BAR KOCHBA and died a martyr.   NAHUM N. GLATZER

Bibliography: Finkelstein, L., *Akiba: Scholar, Saint, and Martyr* (1970).

Akihito   [ah-kee-hee′-toh]

Akihito, b. Dec. 23, 1933, is the oldest son of the Japanese emperor HIROHITO. In November 1952, he was formally declared heir to the throne, the 125th in his dynasty. He was educated at the university for the nobility but studied English with an American, Elizabeth Gray Vining. He married Michiko Shoda, the daughter of a wealthy industrialist, in April 1959. She was the first commoner to marry an heir apparent to the Japanese throne. Their first son, Prince Naruhito Hironomiya, was born on Feb. 23, 1960. As crown prince, Akihito has visited many countries in Asia and the Western Hemisphere, including the United States.

Bibliography: Simon, Charlie May, *The Sun and the Birch: The Story of Crown Prince Akihito and Crown Princess Michiko* (1960).

akita   [ah-kee′-tah]

The akita, a working dog originally from Japan, has a large, sturdy body, a broad head with erect ears, and a curly tail. It measures 61–71 cm (24–28 in) high at the shoulder and weighs 35–55 kg (80–120 lb). The akita has a stiff topcoat of fur and a soft, wooly undercoat, developed to withstand the harsh climate of northern Japan. It hunts large game and retrieves waterfowl by using its keen sight and smell as well as its strength, endurance, and speed. A litter usually contains seven or eight puppies.

For centuries, only Japanese royalty and nobility were permitted to own this breed, but the akita is now used throughout the world as a guard dog. In July 1931, the Japanese government declared the breed a national monument and a national treasure, and in 1972 the akita was recognized by the American Kennel Club.

Bibliography: Delfosse, Edita, *How to Raise and Train an Akita* (1964).

The akita, a large working dog, is the descendant of a smaller dog of ancient Japan whose carved image has been found on tombstones. In 1931 this dog was named a national monument of Japan.

Akkad   [ak′-ahd]

Akkad was an early name for northern BABYLONIA, derived from Agade, capital city of SARGON of Akkad (fl. *c.*2350 BC). For almost a century and a half Sargon and his successors dominated all of MESOPOTAMIA and at times held tributary lands situated to the east and west. The principal ruler after Sargon was Naram Sin, possibly a grandson, who rivaled his ancestor as a conqueror; monuments and inscriptions of his reign have been found over a wide area. Although the Akkadian dynasty finally collapsed as a result of invasions from the north about 2200 BC, the name Akkad continued to be ap-

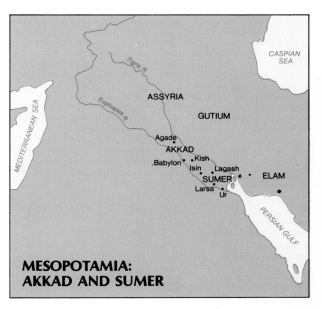

MESOPOTAMIA: AKKAD AND SUMER

plied to the country, and from about 2000 BC rulers of Babylonia often styled themselves kings of SUMER and Akkad.

Sargon and his Akkadians were Semites. Their language (Old Akkadian) is the earliest written Semitic dialect known, and their religious and social institutions clearly set them apart from the people of Sumer to the south. Nevertheless, the Akkadians borrowed and modified numerous cultural elements from the older and more complex civilization of the Sumerians. Among these were the cuneiform system of writing and some aspects of political organization.

TOM B. JONES

Bibliography: Moorgart, Anton, *The Art of Ancient Mesopotamia* (1969); Oppenheim, A. Leo, *Ancient Mesopotamia: Portrait of a Dead Civilization*, 2d rev. ed. (1977); Roux, Georges, *Ancient Iraq* (1976).

See also: MESOPOTAMIAN ART AND ARCHITECTURE.

Akko: see ACRE (Israel).

Akmak   [ahk′-mahk]

Akmak is the name given to an early archaeological assemblage of stone artifacts from the northwest Alaskan site of Onion Portage, located on the Kobuk River about 200 km (125 mi) from its mouth. The site was discovered (1941) by the American archaeologist J. Louis GIDDINGS. Excavations have brought to light one of the longest stratigraphic sequences of prehistoric tool industries yet found in the Americas. The oldest of these industries is the Akmak (from the Alaskan Eskimo word for "hard chert"), estimated to date from 13,000 to 6000 BC.

The Akmak assemblage is composed of large and small tools, including tiny chipped flakes, or microliths. Its closest parallel is found in the Siberian tool types associated with sites in the area of Lake Baikal. Although the artifacts are generally similar, clear differences in details suggest that Akmak culture developed independently after its isolation from Siberian influence. It further appears that certain developments initiated in the Akmak tradition gave rise to the ESKIMO culture.

HANS-GEORG BANDI

Bibliography: Anderson, Douglas D., *Akmak, An Early Archaeological Assemblage from Onion Portage, Northwest Alaska* (1970).

Akron

Akron is a city in Ohio and the seat of Summit County. Known as the rubber capital of the world, it is situated on the Little Cuyahoga River in the northeastern part of the state, 56 km (35 mi) southeast of Cleveland. The city has a population of 237,177 (1980); the metropolitan area has a population of 660,328.

Akron experienced its first growth surge shortly after being founded in 1825; with the completion (1827) of the Ohio and Erie Canal, it became a trading and transportation center. Benjamin F. GOODRICH opened Akron's first rubber factory in 1870, and the city's second period of growth began, accelerating sharply as automobile use grew in the early 20th century.

Today several hundred manufacturing plants are located in Akron, producing rubber, chemicals, plastics, aircraft equipment, and heavy machinery. Akron is also a center of the trucking industry. The University of Akron was founded in 1913, and the city is also host to the Akron Art Institute; the Jonathan Hale Homestead, an authentic Western Reserve home; the home where John Brown lived from 1844 to 1847; and the American Indian Art Hall of Fame.

Akron and Macon

The *Akron* was the second and the *Macon* the third (and last) of the rigid AIRSHIPS built in the United States, the first being the SHENANDOAH. They were the only "flying aircraft-carriers" ever constructed, being able to launch and retrieve planes in midair. Built for the U.S. Navy, they were sister ships, 239 m (785 ft) long and 40 m (133 ft) in maximum diameter. They were rendered airborne by 184,000 m³ (6,500,000 ft³) of helium gas, with a top speed of about 129 km/h (80 mph). The *Akron* cost $4.5 million, the *Macon* $3.5 million, making them the most expensive aircraft built in the United States until after World War II. The *Akron* made its first flight on Sept. 25, 1931, and was wrecked in a storm over the Atlantic on Apr. 4, 1933; only 3 of the 76 men on board survived. The *Macon* made its first flight on Apr. 21, 1933, and was wrecked over the Pacific on Feb. 12, 1935, with 81 of the 83 men on board surviving.

RICHARD K. SMITH

Aksakov, Konstantin Sergeyevich   [ahk-sah'-kawf, kawn-stahn'-teen sir-gay'-e-vich]

Konstantin Sergeyevich Aksakov, b. Apr. 10 (N.S.), 1817, d. Dec. 19 (N.S.), 1860, son of the writer S. T. Aksakov, was a Russian writer and patriot. With his brother Ivan, he was a leader of the so-called Slavophile movement. In his criticism, historical plays, and poetry he emphasized traditional Russian values, Orthodox religion, and the peasant commune. He also wrote extensively about Russian linguistics.

RALPH E. MATLAW

Bibliography: Chmielewski, Edward V., *Tribune of the Slavophiles: Konstantin Aksakov* (1962).

Aksakov, Sergei Timofeyevich   [sir-gay' teem-oh-fay'-e-vich]

Sergei Timofeyevich Aksakov, b. Oct. 1 (N.S.), 1791, d. May 12 (N.S.), 1859, was a prominent Russian writer and literary figure. His early books on fishing and hunting are masterpieces of observation and description. *A Family Chronicle* (1856; Eng. trans., 1917), a fictionalized account of his family and the founding of their estate, was followed by the more overtly autobiographical sequel *Childhood Years* (1858; Eng. trans., 1917). His memoirs (1890) of Nikolai Gogol are basic to the study of that writer.

RALPH E. MATLAW

Aksenov, Vasily Pavlovich   [ahks-yawn'-awf, vuh-see'-lee pahv'-lo-vich]

Vasily Aksenov, b. Aug. 20, 1932, is one of the most important young Soviet prose writers of the 1960s. His stories and novels—*Colleagues* (1961), *Halfway to the Moon* (1961), and *A Ticket to the Stars* (1961)—deal honestly and sympathetically with the postwar generation of Soviet youth. Aksenov's apolitical teenage heroes use colorful slang, copy Western taste in dress and music, and dream of romance and fellowship. He has also written five film scripts and two grotesque dramatic satires, *Always on Sale* and *Your Murderer*.

DANIEL C. GEROULD

Aksenov, Vladimir   [vlahd-ee'-mir]

The Soviet cosmonaut Vladimir Aksenov, b. Feb. 1, 1935, served as flight engineer on an 8-day SOYUZ mission to photograph geological features of the Earth's surface. Aksenov, an engineer in the Soviet space program, became a cosmonaut in 1973. Together with commander Valery BYKOVSKY, he was launched into space on board *Soyuz 22* on Sept. 15, 1976. The Soyuz was the first equipped with a special East German multispectral camera called the MKF-6, later installed on the SALYUT 6 space station. Aksenov and Yuri V. Malyeshev docked with *Salyut 6* during their mission of June 5–9, 1980, in *Soyuz T-2*, a model with an improved propulsion system and solar-cell arrays.

JAMES E. OBERG

Aksum   [ahk'-soom]

Aksum (Axum) is a town in Tigre province of northern Ethiopia, about 135 km (84 mi) south of Asmara. It is an agricultural market center, with a population of 12,800 (1970 est.). As the ancient African commercial town of Axumis, it was the capital of the Axumite kingdom, which during the first two centuries of the Christian Era included much of modern Ethiopia and Sudan. According to Coptic Christians, it is the traditional site of the ark of the covenant, supposedly brought from Jerusalem by the descendants of King Solomon and the Queen of Sheba.

Akutagawa Ryunosuke   [ah'-koo-tah-gah-wah, ryoo'-noh-su'-ke]

Akutagawa Ryunosuke, b. Mar. 1, 1892, d. July 24, 1927, was one of Japan's greatest short-story writers. His mother's insanity and early death and his own poor physical and mental health cast a dark shadow over his work, and he eventually committed suicide. He based his tales on a variety of literary sources and reshaped themes to fit his grotesque, psychological, and often humorous visions. "The Hell Screen" (1916; Eng. trans., 1948), "Rashomon" (1915; Eng. trans., 1930), and the novella *Kappa* (1926–27; Eng. trans., 1947) are among the best illustrations of Akutagawa's preoccupation with madness, social contradictions, and the human search for the courage to live. Akira KUROSAWA's film *Rashomon* (1951) is based on Akutagawa's story of the same title and his "In a Grove" (1921; Eng. trans., 1952).

EDWARD B. FOWLER

Al-Ahram: see AHRAM, AL-.

al-Bayda: see BEIDA.

al-Faiyum   [ahl-fy-oom']

Al-Faiyum (also El Faiyum or El Fayum) is the capital of al-Faiyum governorate in northeastern Egypt. Located about 113 km (70 mi) south of Cairo, it lies below sea level in the Faiyum Depression, the bed of ancient Lake Moeris, between the Nile River and Lake Qarun. It has a population of 166,910 (1976). An irrigated oasis with a hot, dry climate, it is linked to the Nile by canals built in the 17th century BC. The local economy is based on cotton, cereal, and sugarcane, which are processed in the city. Among the many archaeological sites near al-Faiyum are Setje (later Crocodilopolis), the ancient seat of crocodile worship, founded about 2300 BC, and the 4,600-year-old pyramid at Meidum. During the Roman period the city was named Arsinoë for the wife-sister of Ptolemy II.

al-Fatah: see PALESTINE LIBERATION ORGANIZATION.

al-Minya   [ahl-min'-yuh]

Al-Minya (El Minya) is a port and the capital city of the Minya governorate in north central Egypt. It has a population of 146,366 (1976). Al-Minya lies on the left bank of the Nile about 225 km (140 mi) southwest of Cairo, on the Cairo-to-Aswan railroad. The city is a trade center for the cotton and cereal crops grown in the area.

Alabama

Alabama, one of the southern states of the United States, is largely rectangular in shape and is landlocked except for a short coastline along the Gulf of Mexico. It is bordered by Tennessee on the north, by Georgia on the east, by the Florida panhandle on the south, and by Mississippi on the west. The state was visited by Spaniards in the early 16th century, but the first permanent white settlement (present-day MOBILE) was not established until 1711. Alabama became a state in 1819, and during the Civil War it was a member of the Confederacy. The state was profoundly affected by the civil rights movement of the 1950s and '60s. Long a primarily agricultural area, Alabama by the late 1970s had a diversified economy, dominated by manufacturing. The state is named for the Alabama River, whose name was derived from the Alabama Indians, a small Muskogean-speaking group that formerly lived on its banks. The word *Alabama* probably means ''I make a clearing.''

LAND AND RESOURCES

About two-thirds of Alabama is made up of a low-lying coastal plain, which merges, toward the northeast, into regions of medium-altitude hills and mountains. The highest point in the state is Cheaha Mountain (734 m/2,407 ft), in the east, and the lowest elevation is sea level, along the Gulf of Mexico.

Physiographic Regions. Alabama may be divided into four physiographic regions. A vast coastal plain covers the southern half of the state and much of the northwest. The plain includes the famous Black Belt, an area of productive black-clay soils that forms a narrow east-west band across the middle of the state. The southeast also has good farmland, but the soils of the rest of the coastal plain are generally deeply weathered and are of limited agricultural value. A second region, separated from the coastal plain by the FALL LINE, is the PIEDMONT PLATEAU, located in the east central part of the state. It is rolling to hilly, with highly eroded red soils.

The Appalachian Region encompasses much of northeastern Alabama. The eastern portion of this region is an area of sandstone ridges, separated by fertile limestone valleys. The western portion, a continuation of the CUMBERLAND PLATEAU, is a hilly, forested area of poor soils. The fourth region is the Highland Rim, a section of smooth, rolling plains located in the north, astride the TENNESSEE RIVER. Underlain by limestone, the Highland Rim, as well as the eastern Appalachian Region, has formed sinkholes and caverns as a result of the solution of the limestone in the humid climate.

Rivers and Lakes. Alabama has several major rivers. The main rivers flowing north to south are the Alabama River (507 km/315 mi long), formed by the confluence, near Montgomery, of the Coosa and Tallapoosa rivers, and the TOMBIGBEE RIVER, which rises in Mississippi. The Alabama and Tombigbee meet in the southwestern part of the state and then form the Mobile and Tensaw rivers, which continue south to Mobile Bay (an arm of the Gulf of Mexico). Other important rivers are the CHATTAHOOCHEE, which forms part of the eastern border of Alabama, and the Tennessee, which flows west across nearly all of the northern part of the state.

Alabama has no large natural lakes. Dams on rivers, however, have created several extensive artificial lakes, the largest being Guntersville Lake (272 km²/105 mi²), on the Tennessee River.

Climate. Alabama has a humid, subtropical climate. Summers are hot (average July temperature, 27° C/80° F) and humid, with frequent heavy thunderstorms. Winters are cool (average January temperature, 7° C/45° F), with considerable precipitation, including some snow in the north. The amount of annual precipitation generally increases from north to south, ranging from 1,321 mm (52 in) at HUNTSVILLE to 1,600 mm (63 in) at Mobile. Southern Alabama is occasionally affected by hurricanes in the late summer. Tornadoes, which are associated with cold fronts, are most common in the months of March and April.

Vegetation and Animal Life. About two-thirds of Alabama is covered by forests, largely made up of southern yellow pine,

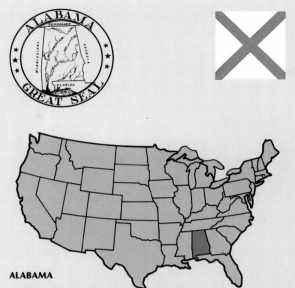

ALABAMA

LAND. Area: 133,915 km² (51,705 mi²); rank: 29th. Capital: Montgomery (1982 est. pop., 182,406). Largest city: Birmingham (1982 est. pop., 283,239). Counties: 67. Elevations: highest—734 m (2,407 ft), at Cheaha Mt.; lowest—sea level, Gulf of Mexico.

PEOPLE. Population (1982 est.): 3,943,000; rank: 22d; density: 30 persons per km² (78 per mi²). Distrib. (1980): 62.0% metro., 38.0% nonmetro. Av. ann. change (1970-80): +1.3%.

EDUCATION. Public enrollment (1982): elem.—509,952; sec.—214,085; higher (1981)—145,000. Nonpublic enrollment (1980): elem.—20,600; sec.—3,900; combined—38,100; higher—20,600. Institutions of higher education (1982): 60.

ECONOMY. State personal income (1982): $34.1 billion; rank: 25th. Median family income (1979): $16,347; rank: 46th. Nonagricultural labor distribution (1982): manufacturing—337,000 persons; wholesale and retail trade—268,000; government—291,000; services—216,000; transportation and utilities—71,000; finance, insurance, and real estate—59,000; construction—57,000. Agriculture: income (1982)—$2.3 billion. Fishing: value (1982)—$46 million. Forestry: sawn timber volume (1977)—69.4 billion board feet. Mining: value (1981)—$2.4 billion. Manufacturing: value added (1977)—$8.4 billion. Services: value (1977)—$1.7 billion.

GOVERNMENT (1985). Governor: George Wallace, Democrat. U.S. Congress: Senate—1 Democrat, 1 Republican; House—5 Democrats, 2 Republicans. Electoral college votes: 9. State legislature: 35 senators, 105 representatives.

STATE SYMBOLS. Statehood: Dec. 14, 1819; the 22d state. Nickname: Heart of Dixie; bird: yellowhammer; flower: camellia; tree: Southern pine; motto: ''We dare defend our rights''; song: ''Alabama.''

red cedar, and other conifers. The most common deciduous trees are hickory, sweet gum, and several species of oak. Alabama has a varied wildlife population with numerous deer, foxes, bobcats, game birds, and other animals. Large numbers of migratory ducks and geese winter in the state.

Mineral Resources. Alabama has significant deposits of several important minerals. Coal, iron ore, and limestone—all used in the production of iron and steel—are found in the north central part of the state, notably around Birmingham. Major crude-petroleum fields are in the southwest, and bauxite deposits are in the southeast.

PEOPLE

Alabama has a population of 3,943,000 (1982 est.), giving the state an average population density of 30 persons per km² (78 per mi²). From 1970 to 1980 the population increased by 13.1% (a rate higher than the national average). In 1980 about 75% of the population were white, and about 25% were black; approximately 7,500 Indians live in Alabama. After several decades of considerable net out-migration (mainly a

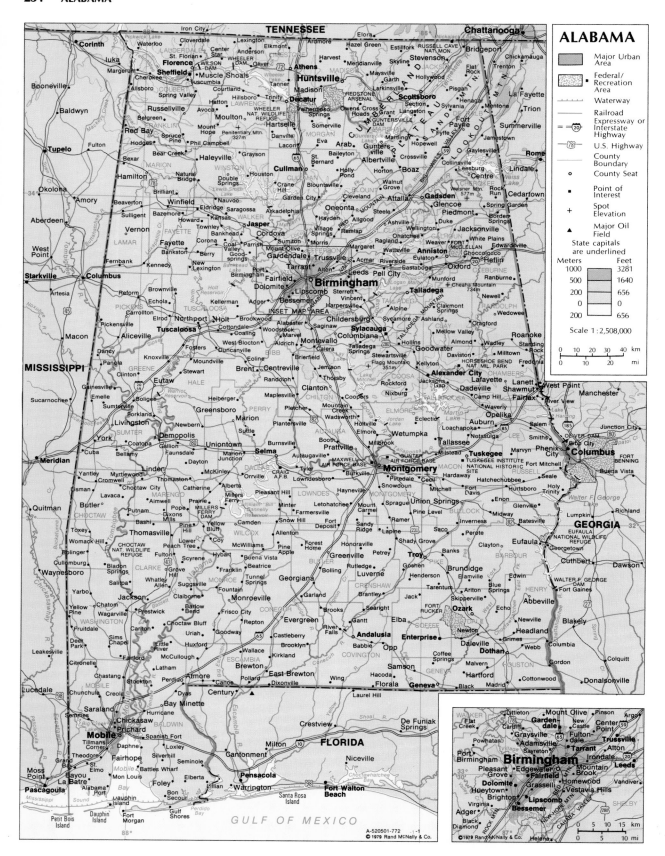

ALABAMA

	Major Urban Area
	Federal/ Recreation Area
	Waterway
	Railroad
	Expressway or Interstate Highway
	U.S. Highway
	County Boundary
o	County Seat
■	Point of Interest
+	Spot Elevation
▲	Major Oil Field

State capitals are underlined

Meters	Feet
1000	3281
500	1640
200	656
0	0
200	656

Scale 1 : 2,508,000

0 10 20 30 40 km
0 10 20 mi

A-520501-772 -1-1
© 1979 Rand McNally & Co.

© 1979 Rand McNally & Co.

result of blacks leaving Alabama for better opportunities elsewhere), the state had a modest net in-migration between 1970 and 1976. About two-thirds of the people live in areas defined as urban; the largest cities are BIRMINGHAM, MONTGOMERY (the capital), TUSCALOOSA, Huntsville, and Mobile. More than 95% of all Alabamians were born in the United States of American parents. The majority of the people are Protestants and are Baptists or Methodists.

Education. Alabama established a statewide public-school system in 1854, but schools received inadequate financial support until the 20th century. Almost all black and white children attended separate public schools until the 1960s. In the late 1970s, 380,000 pupils were enrolled in public elementary schools and 372,500 in public high schools. Alabama has 57 institutions of higher education with 147,000 students. These institutions include Auburn University (founded 1856), main campus at Auburn; Jacksonville State University (1883), at Jacksonville; Samford University (1841), at Birmingham; Troy State University (1887), main campus at Troy; Tuskegee Institute (1881), at Tuskegee Institute; the University of Alabama (1831), campuses at University, Birmingham, and Huntsville; the University of North Alabama (1872), at Florence; and the University of South Alabama (1963), at Mobile.

Cultural Institutions. Among the museums of the state are the Alabama Museum of Natural History, at University; the Alabama Space and Rocket Center, at Huntsville; and the Montgomery Museum of Fine Arts. The decommissioned World War II battleship *Alabama*, now anchored in Mobile Bay, also contains a museum. Large libraries include the University of Alabama Library (1,244,000 volumes), at University, and the Birmingham Public Library (965,000 volumes). Huntsville and Birmingham have professional symphony orchestras, and Birmingham supports a ballet company.

Historical Sites. Russell Cave National Monument (at Bridgeport) contains archaeological records of human habitation dating from at least 7000 BC. At Mound State Monument (near Moundville) are several large mounds of the Indian MOUND BUILDER culture, and Horseshoe Bend National Military Park (near Dadeville) was the site of a decisive defeat (1814) of the Creek Indian Confederacy by Andrew JACKSON. At Tuskegee Institute National Historic Site (Tuskegee Institute) are early buildings of the noted college founded (1881) for blacks. The first capitol (the present state capitol) and the first White House of the Confederacy are both in Montgomery. Alabama has many historic homes, some built before the Civil War.

Communications. In the late 1970s Alabama had 217 radio stations and 26 television stations (including components of the nation's first statewide educational system). Twenty-four English-language daily newspapers were published in the state, with a combined daily circulation of 737,000 copies. Among the more influential dailies were the Birmingham *News*, the Huntsville *Times*, and the Montgomery *Advertiser*. The state's first newspaper was the Mobile *Gazette* (now the Mobile *Register*), founded in 1812.

ECONOMY

Until the late 19th century, when iron and steel mills were established at Birmingham, Alabama's economy was overwhelmingly agricultural, and cotton was the only important cash crop. By the 1930s industrialization was well under way, and by the late 1970s manufacturing was by far the dominant sector of the economy.

Agriculture. In the late 1970s the annual farm output in Alabama was valued at about $1.6 billion. The primary crops were soybeans, groundnuts, maize, and cotton. Large numbers of hogs, cattle, and broiler chickens were raised for market, and many productive dairy farms operated throughout the state.

Foresty and Fishing. Alabama's extensive forests are used to produce much pulpwood and lumber. A small fishing industry operates mainly in the Gulf of Mexico, and the catch includes shrimp, croakers, red snappers, and catfish.

Mining. Alabama's mineral output, valued at slightly more

A plantation home near Mobile, with its Spanish-moss-laden oaks and blooming azaleas, evokes memories of the Old South. The antebellum period produced some of America's most charming regional architecture, particularly in adaptations of the Greek Revival style.

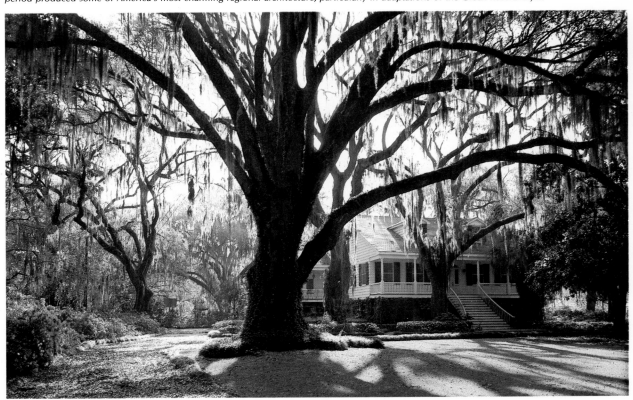

(Right) *Birmingham, the "Pittsburgh of the South," is Alabama's largest city. Although famous as the South's leading producer of iron and steel, Birmingham has become important as a center of commerce and education.*

(Below) *Alabama's State Capitol, overlooking downtown Montgomery, is often called the "Cradle of the Confederacy." The building hosted the convention that founded the government of the Confederate States of America, and Jefferson Davis was inaugurated there in 1861.*

than $2 billion a year, consists mainly of bituminous coal, crude petroleum, natural gas, limestone, stone, sand and gravel, and bauxite. Until the 1960s considerable quantities of iron ore were produced in the state.

Manufacturing. In the early 1980s manufacturing firms in Alabama employed about 350,000 persons, and the value of sales of manufactured goods totaled about $30 billion yearly. The principal manufactures were iron and steel, produced mainly at GADSDEN, Birmingham, Anniston, and Bessemer. Other leading fabricated goods included forest products (chiefly paper), textiles, clothing, chemicals, and processed food. Mobile, Montgomery, and Tuscaloosa also were important manufacturing centers.

Tourism. Alabama has a substantial tourist industry. Many vacationers stay at beach resorts along the Gulf of Mexico, notably on Dauphin Island, at the entrance to Mobile Bay. Hunters and anglers are attracted by the state's ample opportunities for such activity, and many tourists visit Alabama's

historic sites, its 15 state parks, and its 4 national forests.

Transportation. Extensive transportation facilities in Alabama include about 140,000 km (86,940 mi) of all-weather roads and 7,295 km (4,530 mi) of operated railroad track. Mobile is an important seaport, with modern facilities and easy access to the Gulf INTRACOASTAL WATERWAY. The navigable Black Warrior–Tombigbee–Mobile river system links the Birmingham industrial area with the sea, and ships can use the Tennessee River to connect with other parts of the Mississippi River system.

Energy. Alabama's installed electric-generating capacity in the early 1980s was 19.5 million kW, and the annual output of electricity was 75 billion kW h. About 60% of the electricity was generated in thermal plants using coal. Substantial amounts of hydroelectricity were produced on the Tennessee River at Wilson and Wheeler dams (operated by the TENNESSEE VALLEY AUTHORITY) and at installations on several other rivers in the state. Alabama also had five nuclear-powered electric-generating plants.

GOVERNMENT AND POLITICS

Alabama is governed under a 1901 constitution, as amended; previous constitutions had been adopted in 1819, 1861, 1865, 1868, and 1875. The chief executive of the state is a governor, popularly elected to a 4-year term; a governor may not serve more than two consecutive terms. The state has a bicameral legislature, consisting of a 35-member Senate and a 105-member House of Representatives; all legislators are elected to 4-year terms. The state's highest tribunal is the Supreme Court, made up of nine judges elected to 6-year terms. The 67 counties of Alabama are each governed by a board of commissioners. The state is represented in the U.S. Congress by two senators and seven representatives. It has nine electoral votes in national presidential elections.

The Democratic party dominates Alabama politics at the state and local levels. In contests for U.S. president, however, the Democrats after World War II lost their traditional firm hold on the state's electoral vote. Since 1948, the state's presidential electoral votes have often gone either to the Republicans or to minor-party candidates, as in 1968, when Alabama governor George C. WALLACE carried the state as the American Independent party candidate.

HISTORY

Excavations of archaic Indian remains indicate that people lived in the region of Alabama at least as early as 7000 BC. During the Mound Builder, or Mississippian, cultural period (AD 700–1700), large temple mounds were built along the major rivers of the state, notably around Moundville. By the early 16th century this remarkable culture was in a state of decline. At that time, the principal Indian groups in the state

(Left) *The Alabama State Docks in Mobile are an important terminal point for American trade with Latin America. Mobile, the state's only seaport, also supports a thriving oyster and crabbing industry.*

(Below) *Although cotton is no longer Alabama's leading cash crop, mechanization has greatly increased the efficiency of its harvest. Crop failures and a plague of boll weevils at the turn of the century forced the diversification of the state's agriculture.*

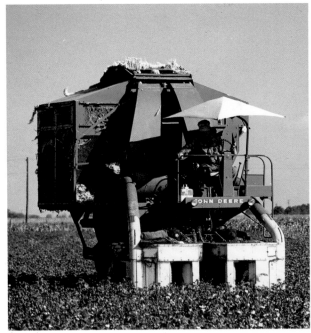

were the CHICKASAW, in the northwest; the CHEROKEE, in the northeast; the CREEK, in the center and southeast; and the CHOCTAW, in the southwest.

European Exploration and Early Settlement. European contact with the Alabama area began when the Spanish navigator Alonso Álvarez de Piñeda explored Mobile Bay in 1519. In 1540 another Spaniard, Hernando DE SOTO, led an army of about 500 men through Alabama; on Oct. 18, 1540, they crushed a large force of Choctaw under Chief Tuscaloosa. The Spanish failed to establish a firm foothold in Alabama, and the French founded (1711) the first permanent white settlement, at present-day Mobile. The French also established large farms, and in 1719 the first black Africans arrived to work as slaves on the farms.

In 1763 France ceded Alabama to Great Britain, and in 1783 most of it became part of the United States. The region around Mobile had been taken by the Spanish during the American Revolution, and it was captured by the United States in 1813, during the War of 1812. Also during that conflict, at the Battle of Horseshoe Bend (Mar. 27, 1814), the power of the Creek Indians was broken by U.S. troops under Andrew Jackson. In the following 25 years nearly all of Alabama's Indians were removed to the western United States.

Statehood. Alabama was organized as a separate territory in 1817, and on Dec. 14, 1819, it was admitted to the Union as the 22d state. Huntsville was the first capital; the capital was moved to Cahaba in 1820, to Tuscaloosa in 1826, and, finally, to Montgomery in 1847. The state's population grew from 127,000 in 1820 to 964,000 (435,000 of whom were slaves) in 1860. The economy was dominated by large plantations (mostly in the Black Belt) that produced cotton for export. The rivers were the prime means of transportation, although the state's first railroad began operations in 1832, and by 1860 about 1,100 km (683 mi) of railroad track had been laid. The state was overwhelmingly rural; Mobile, a growing seaport, was the only sizable city.

The Civil War and Reconstruction. Most white Alabamians viewed slavery as an integral part of their economic and social systems, and they opposed attempts to abolish it. Soon after the election of President Abraham LINCOLN, perceived by Alabamians as a particularly strong opponent of slavery, Alabama seceded (Jan. 11, 1861) from the Union, the fourth state to do so. In February 1861, the Confederate States of America was organized at Montgomery, and Jefferson DAVIS was inaugurated as its president at the Alabama state capitol. Montgomery remained the Confederate capital until May 1861. Alabama contributed about 100,000 troops to the Confederacy, and perhaps 25% of them died during the Civil War. No major land battle was fought in the state, but the Union admiral

David G. FARRAGUT won an important naval engagement at Mobile Bay in August 1864. Union armies captured the Tennessee Valley in 1862 and took Montgomery in early 1865.

The Reconstruction period, which followed the Confederate surrender in April 1865, was one of confusion in Alabama. Because it refused to ratify the 14th Amendment to the U.S. Constitution, Alabama was placed under military rule in 1867. After the amendment was ratified, and blacks were assured citizenship, Alabama reentered (June 1868) the Union. During the next few years black and white Republicans exercised considerable power, but by 1874 white Democrats, including numerous former supporters of the Confederacy, had regained control of the state. In the following years racial segregation was written into many state and local laws.

Economic Recovery. Although Alabama began large-scale industrialization in the late 19th century, the economy continued to be dominated by cotton culture. Cotton was grown mainly by small farmers, largely tenants or sharecroppers,

Booster rockets, guided missiles, and a variety of space hardware are on view at the Space Orientation Center in Huntsville. Called "Rocket City, U.S.A.," Huntsville is also the site of NASA's George C. Marshall Space Flight Center and the Redstone Arsenal.

many of whom became debt-ridden because of the low prices paid for the crop. Alabama was fertile ground for agrarian reformers, and the POPULIST PARTY had numerous adherents in the state during 1890s.

In the early 20th century cotton declined in importance, partly because boll weevil infestations made farming more precarious; many rural Alabamians left the state, especially for cities of the northern United States. The state's economy was rejuvenated by the demands of the American effort during World War I; steelmaking boomed, and Mobile developed an important shipbuilding industry. The state was severely affected by the Depression of the 1930s; many banks failed and unemployment increased drastically. The economy improved again during World War II, and the prosperity carried over into the early postwar years.

Civil Rights. Race relations were a major issue in Alabama in the 1950s and '60s, as civil rights advocates worked to end racial segregation in the state. During 1955–56 Martin Luther KING, Jr., organized a black boycott that ended racially separate seating on municipal buses in Montgomery. In 1954 the U.S. Supreme Court had ruled racial segregation in public schools to be unconstitutional, but white officials in Alabama avoided implementing the decision until 1963, when, after tense confrontations between Gov. George C. Wallace and federal officials, integration was begun.

In 1963 four black children were killed when a bomb destroyed part of their Birmingham church. The incident, widely deplored in the nation, helped create the atmosphere for passage of the landmark federal Civil Rights Act of 1964. In 1965 King led a march from SELMA to Montgomery to protest discrimination in voter registration. The U.S. Congress responded with the Voting Rights Act of 1965, which helped add many blacks to the voting rolls in Alabama and thereby encouraged white politicians in the state to moderate their views in order to attract black votes.

By the early 1970s most of Alabama's schools had been integrated, and blacks had open to them many previously closed opportunities. During the rest of the 1970s public concern shifted from race relations to assuring economic growth in the state and to improving efficiency in government.

DAVID W. ICENOGLE

Bibliography: Abernathy, Thomas P., *The Formative Period in Alabama, 1815–1828*, 2d ed. (1965); Fleming, Walter L., *Civil War and Reconstruction in Alabama*, (1949); Hackney, Sheldon, *Populism to Progressivism in Alabama* (1969); Hamilton, Virginia, *Alabama: A Bicentennial History* (1977); Lineback, Neal G., ed., *Atlas of Alabama* (1973); Peirce, Neal R., *The Deep South States of America* (1974); Richard, Jesse M., and McGraw, E. L., *Geography of Alabama: Her Land and People* (1975); Summersell, Charles G., *Alabama History for Schools* (1975).

Alabama (Indian tribe)

The Alabama, a North American Indian tribe, lived near the junction of the Coosa and Tallapoosa rivers (in present-day Alabama) early in the 18th century. A Muskogean-speaking people, they were members of the CREEK confederacy and lived by hunting, fishing, and farming. They numbered 770 in 1715. From their base at Mobile, Ala., the French established relations with the Alabama early in the 18th century and erected (1714) Fort Toulouse in their midst. After 1763, when French territory in North America was ceded to England, the Alabama began to move west. They first settled (1764) at Bayou Manchac in Louisiana; by 1810 their settlements extended as far west as the Big Thicket region of East Texas. In 1854 the state of Texas granted the tribe 518 ha (1,280 acres) of land in Polk County. Today the Alabama live with the Coushatta Indians on the reservation there. They number about 500. The Alabama-Coushatta filed (1972) for additional land in East Texas with the Indian Claims Commission.

DANIEL JACOBSON

Bibliography: Hudson, Charles, *The Southern Indians* (1976); Jacobson, Daniel, et al., *Alabama-Coushatta (Creek) Indians* (1974).

Alabama, state universities of

Each of ten coeducational state universities in Alabama offers a full range of undergraduate and graduate degrees. The **University of Alabama** at University (1831; enrollment: 16,950; library: 1,250,000 volumes) has schools of liberal arts and sciences and of law, social work, library science, medicine, and dentistry. Branches are at Huntsville (1950; enrollment: 3,900; library: 200,000 volumes) and Birmingham (1936; enrollment: 13,150; library: 500,000 volumes). Other universities are **Alabama Agricultural and Mechanical** (1875; enrollment: 4,650; library: 305,000 volumes), a land-grant school in Huntsville; **Alabama State** (1874; enrollment: 4,750; library: 150,000 volumes) in Montgomery; the **University of Montevallo** (1896; enrollment: 3,100; library: 195,000 volumes) at Montevallo; **Jacksonville State** (1883; enrollment: 7,100; library: 295,000 volumes) at Jacksonville, which has schools of nursing and law enforcement; and **Livingston** (1835; enrollment: 1,400; library: 105,000 volumes) at Livingston. Another land-grant university is **Auburn** (1856; enrollment: 18,000; library: 1,200,000 volumes) at Auburn, with schools of arts and sciences, engineering, pharmacy, veterinary medicine, home economics, and agriculture; a commuter campus is at Montgomery. **Troy State University** (1887; enrollment: 11,250; library: 280,000 volumes) is at Troy; the **University of North Alabama** (1872; enrollment: 5,000; library: 200,000 volumes) is at Florence; and the **University of South Alabama** (1963; enrollment: 6,850; library: 205,000 volumes) is at Mobile.

Alabama Claims

The Alabama Claims were demands made by the United States after the Civil War that Great Britain pay for the wartime damage done to American merchant shipping by Confederate cruisers, notably the *Alabama*, that had been constructed in British shipyards. After a period of bitter dispute, the two countries agreed (1871), in the Treaty of Washington, to submit the question to international arbitration.

The treaty laid down the following principles that subsequently passed into international law. First, a neutral government should endeavor to prevent the outfitting of any vessel that it might believe to be intended to make war against another nation. Second, it should prevent a belligerent from using its ports or waters as a base or supply source for naval operations. Third, it must exercise "due diligence" over all persons within its jurisdiction to prevent violation of these obligations. Acting in accordance with these principles, a panel of American, British, Brazilian, Swiss, and Italian arbitrators met (1872) in Geneva and awarded the United States the sum of $15.5 million.

ROBERT H. FERRELL

Bibliography: Bernath, Stuart L., *Squall Across the Atlantic: Civil War Prize Cases and Diplomacy* (1970); Smith, Goldwin A., *Treaty of Washington* (1941).

Alabama River

The Alabama River is formed in south central Alabama by the junction of the Coosa and Tallapoosa rivers near Montgomery. It drains 58,534 km² (22,600 mi²) of the state, flowing west to Selma and then south to join the Tombigbee River and create the Mobile and Tensaw rivers, which enter the Gulf of Mexico at Mobile. Navigable throughout its length (512 km/318 mi), the river has been an artery for traffic in cotton, lumber, and textiles.

alabaster: see GYPSUM.

Alaca Huyuk   [ahl'-ah-jah hoo-yook']

The archaeological site of Alaca Huyuk, located 160 km (100 mi) east of Ankara, Turkey, was first investigated in the late 19th and early 20th centuries by scholars who concentrated on the still partially visible HITTITE remains. This unidentified center of the second half of the 2d millennium BC is best known for its monumental stone gate with sphinx guardians and lateral reliefs depicting ritual scenes. Excavations begun in 1935 have revealed considerable local wealth and achievement before the time of the Hittites, with the earliest occupation dating from the 4th millennium BC. Tombs of the 3d millennium BC feature metal vessels, jewelry, weapons, and pole finials, or standards, of bulls, stags, and abstract forms often interpreted as solar symbols. Major finds from the site are displayed in the Ankara Archaeological Museum.

LOUISE ALPERS BORDAZ

Aladdin

Aladdin is the idle, good-for-nothing boy hero of one of the most famous tales from *The Thousand and One Nights* (see ARABIAN NIGHTS). He obtains a magic lamp that, when rubbed, has the power to summon a genie who will do his bidding. With the lamp, after many narrow escapes, he gains wealth, power, and the hand of the sultan's daughter.

Alain-Fournier   [ah-lan-foorn-ee-ay']

The French poet, journalist, and novelist Alain-Fournier, b. Oct. 3, 1886, is remembered primarily for his masterful *The Wanderer* (1913; Eng. trans., c.1928), a novel about the innocence of childhood and the awe of first love. Blending memory, dream, and reality, Alain-Fournier creates an idyllic landscape for his adolescent heroes. The novel influenced many 20th-century writers dissatisfied with realism and naturalism. Alain-Fournier's verses and his correspondence with the critic Jacques Rivière are lyric and philosophic. The author was killed in World War I, on Sept. 22, 1914.   JOSEPH A. REITER

Alalakh   [ahl'-ah-lahk]

The ancient city of Alalakh, modern Tell Atchana, is a mound site on the Amuq plain of southeastern Turkey. Sir Leonard WOOLLEY and others excavated the site in 1937–39 and 1946–49. Seventeen building phases were discovered, including a monumental palace complex (level VII) dating from the first half of the 2d millennium BC. On the basis of cuneiform tablets found there, Alalakh has been identified as the center of the ancient kingdom of Yamkhad. Destroyed by the expanding Old Hittite Empire, the site was later absorbed politically and culturally by the New Hittite Empire. Its final destruction (c.1200 BC) is attributed to the invaders referred to in Egyptian texts as the SEA PEOPLES. Artifacts from the site reveal the influence of a variety of southwest Asian and early Aegean cultures.   LOUISE ALPERS BORDAZ

Bibliography: Alkim, U. Bahadir, *Anatolia I* (1968); Wooley, Charles Leonard, *A Forgotten Kingdom* (1953; repr. 1968).

Alamanni, Luigi   [ah-lah-mahn'-ee, loo-ee'-jee]

Luigi Alamanni, b. Oct. 28, 1495, d. Apr. 18, 1556, was an Italian poet and dramatist and a friend of Nicolò Machiavelli. After involvement in an unsuccessful conspiracy against Cardinal Giulio de Medici (later Pope Clement VII) in 1522, Alamanni fled Florence for France, where he became court poet to Francis I. Alamanni's most important work is *La coltivazione* (On Cultivation, 1546), a didactic poem about rustic life. His other works include a comedy, *La Flora*; a tragedy, *Antigone*; and many epigrams.   SERGIO PACIFICI

Alameda

Alameda (1980 pop., 63,852) is a city in west central California, located on an island off the eastern shore of San Francisco Bay. First settled in the 1850s, it is now primarily a residential city, but its waterfront is dominated by ship-service industries and by the Alameda Naval Air Station.

Alamein, El   [al-uh-mayn']

El Alamein was a decisive World War II battle in North Africa between the British Eighth Army under Gen. Bernard MONTGOMERY and German and Italian troops led by Gen. Erwin ROMMEL, the "Desert Fox," from Oct. 23 to Nov. 5, 1942. Rommel's headlong advance had been halted at El Alamein, 112 km (70 mi) west of Alexandria. On Oct. 23, 1942, after a devastating artillery barrage, the British managed to break through the Italian-held center. Rommel was forced to retreat to Tunisia with a loss of 30,000 Axis prisoners, 10,000 of them Germans. El Alamein was a turning point in the war. It saved the Suez Canal for the Allies and facilitated their landings in North Africa.   LOUIS L. SNYDER

Bibliography: Irving, David, *The Trail of the Fox: The Search for the True Field Marshal Rommel* (1978); Montgomery, Bernard L., *Al Alamein to the River Sangro* (1949); Strawson, John, *El Alamein: Desert Victory* (1981).

Alamo, The

The Alamo, site of a heroic battle of the TEXAS REVOLUTION, was founded in 1718 as a Spanish mission during the original settlement of San Antonio, Tex. Secularized in 1792, it fell into decay and was used variously as a hospital and troop garrison.

When the Mexican dictator Antonio López de SANTA ANNA invaded Texas during the Texas Revolution, the Texans withdrew into the crumbling walls of the mission's inner court-

The Alamo, a mission in San Antonio, came to be a symbol of Texas's struggle for independence from Mexico. There, in 1836, fewer than 200 Texans resisted a Mexican siege for almost 2 weeks.

yard. There about 185–190 defenders were besieged by an army of 5,000–6,000, sustaining almost continual cannonades for 12 days. On the 13th day—Mar. 6, 1836—the Mexicans broke through and massacred all the Texan men. A Mrs. Dickenson, her child, and possibly two servants were the only non-Mexican survivors. Although a convention had declared the independence of Texas 4 days earlier, this was unknown to the Alamo martyrs. Thus they died fighting under the Mexican flag and defending the Mexican constitution of 1824, which Santa Anna had abrogated.   SEYMOUR V. CONNOR

Bibliography: Connor, Seymour V., *Texas: A History* (1971); Lord, Walter, *A Time to Stand* (1978); Tinkle, Lon, *Alamo* (1967); Warren, Robert Penn, *Remember the Alamo!* (1958).

Alamogordo   [al-uh-muh-gohr′-doh]

Alamogordo (1980 pop., 24,024), a city in south central New Mexico, is the seat of Otero County. A railroad shipping point for lumber from the Sacramento Mountains, which lie just to the west, Alamogordo was settled in 1898 as a railroad shop center for the Southern Pacific line. The first atomic bomb was exploded (July 16, 1945) 97 km (60 mi) northwest of Alamogordo on what is now the WHITE SANDS MISSILE RANGE. Also nearby are Holloman Air Force Base, Fort Bliss, White Sands National Monument, and Mescalero Indian Reservation.

Alanbrooke, Alan Francis Brooke, 1st Viscount

Alan Francis Brooke, b. July 23, 1883, d. June 17, 1963, was a British general who served (1941–46) as chief of the imperial general staff through most of World War II. At the beginning of the war he commanded the British II Corps in France. As chief of staff he worked closely with Winston Churchill, and his personal records of that experience formed the basis of Sir Arthur Bryant's war history, *The Turn of the Tide* (1957). He was created Viscount Alanbrooke in 1946.

Alarcón, Pedro Antonio de   [ah-lahr-kohn′, pay′-droh ahn-toh′-nee-oh day]

Pedro Antonio de Alarcón, b. Mar. 10, 1833, d. July 19, 1891, a major Spanish novelist, is best known for *The Three-Cornered Hat* (1874; Eng. trans., 1891), a bedroom farce on which Manuel de Falla based his ballet music of the same name. Alarcón published his first novel, a romance in the manner of George Sand, at 18 years of age and then served in the Spanish campaign in Morocco, the setting for his incisive war memoirs, published in 1859. In *Captain Venom* (1881; Eng. trans., 1914) and in a longer novel, *The Scandal* (1875; Eng. trans., 1945), he demonstrated his wit and his skills as an observer. Alarcón was also a newspaper writer and politician.

Alaric I, King of the Visigoths   [al′-uh-rik]

Alaric, c.370–410, was a Visigothic king whose capture of Rome in 410 signaled the final decline of the Roman Empire in the West. The leader of Visigothic mercenaries in the Roman army, he rebelled (395) and was proclaimed king by his troops. He led his army toward Constantinople and then into Greece, where he took increasing advantage of the divisions between the eastern and western halves of the empire. In 397 the emperor in the East, Arcadius, gave Alaric military command of Illyria, from which he staged (401) an invasion of Italy. Twice forced to withdraw (402, 403) by the general Flavius STILICHO, he returned after the execution of Stilicho in 408. His first two sieges of Rome (408, 409) were ended by negotiation, but in 410 he stormed and devastated the city. He died while preparing to invade Africa.

Bibliography: Gordon, Colin D., *The Age of Attila* (1960).

alarm systems

Alarm systems are designed to detect undesirable events—the start of a fire, a burglary, a hazardous change in temperature or pressure—and to issue an alerting signal that will cause corrective action to be taken. Such systems must incorporate a detector, which is designed to sense a particular problem, and an alerting agent, such as a bell or a signal light.

Detectors are sensor mechanisms that respond to changes in such factors as light, sound level, pressure, and temperature. Burglar-alarm systems employ many of the types of detectors in current use. Such systems may utilize electric detectors, circuits whose contacts open when a door or window is opened, triggering an alarm. Electric circuits may also be built into walls to signal if the wall is damaged. Optical detectors use photosensitive elements that are triggered when a light ray or infrared beam is interrupted by an intruder. When the light beam is amplified with mirrors, large areas can be monitored. Acoustic detectors may be highly sensitive microphones that detect the smallest noise in a room, or ultrasonic detectors that constantly transmit an acoustic signal of a frequency that cannot usually be heard by human ears. An intruder's movements disturb the signal and set off an alarm. Other types of detectors utilize electronic, thermal, microwave, or laser devices.

Modern tunnel-alarm systems are equally sophisticated. At low tunnel entrances, for example, a signal cable may be stretched across the road at the maximum permissible height. When the cable is touched by the roof of a truck that is too high, a warning is transmitted to a signal room, and a red light at the tunnel entrance is activated. When tunnel traffic slows down suddenly, an alarm may be triggered by signals emitted from line conductors laid in the road surface. Warnings of excessive carbon monoxide concentrations may be given by a detector that measures the opacity of the light in the tunnel, determining exactly how much smoky exhaust is in the air.

Systems designed for FIRE PREVENTION AND CONTROL use SMOKE DETECTORS or heat detectors—temperature-sensitive devices that sound an alarm or release a shower of water when smoke interrupts a beam of light or when the temperature rises above a preset point. More sophisticated light-sensing devices can instantaneously detect the changes that fire produces in the infrared spectrum.   DAVID B. BROWN

Bibliography: Traister, John E., *Design and Application of Security-Fire-Alarm Systems* (1981).

Alas, Leopoldo   [ah′-lahs]

Leopoldo Alas y Ureña, known as Clarín, b. Apr. 25, 1852, d. June 13, 1901, was a major literary critic and novelist of 19th-century Spain. His most famous novel, *La regenta* (The Professor's Wife, 1884), is a naturalistic treatment of life in his native town of Oviedo. Alas's literary criticism was collected in the volumes *Solos* (1890–98) and *Palique* (Chitchat, 1893).   DANIEL EISENBERG

Alaska

Alaska, the largest in area but the least populated U.S. state, lies astride the Arctic Circle, apart from the "Lower 48" conterminous states. It is bordered on the north by the Arctic Ocean, on the east by the Yukon Territory, on the southeast by British Columbia, on the south by the Gulf of Alaska and the Pacific Ocean, and on the west by the Bering Sea, the Bering Strait, and the Chukchi Sea. Little Diomede Island, in the Bering Strait, is only 4 km (2.5 mi) from the USSR's Big Diomede Island.

Initially inhabited by Eskimos, Aleuts, Athabascans, Tlingit, and Haida, Alaska was first visited by Europeans in the early 18th century. In 1867 the United States purchased Alaska from Russia for only $7.2 million. Alaska's modern economic development was accelerated by World War II, when U.S. military bases were established here. Alaska became a state in 1959, and in 1968 great deposits of petroleum and natural gas were discovered in the Arctic coastal plain, or North Slope; commercial oil production from these fields began in 1977.

The name *Alaska* comes from an Aleut word thought to mean "mainland" or "land that is not an island"; the name originally was restricted to the Alaska Peninsula but by 1800 was used to denote all of present-day Alaska.

LAND AND RESOURCES

Alaska has vast areas of unspoiled natural beauty, including rugged, snowcapped mountains; spectacular glaciers; and vast expanses of rolling tundra. The state's highest peak is Mount McKinley, or Denali (6,194 m/20,320 ft), the loftiest point in North America. The state contains the northernmost land point of the United States—Point Barrow—as well as the country's westernmost point—on western Attu Island (one of the Aleutian Islands). The western tip of the Seward Peninsula of Alaska is only about 80 km (50 mi) from the mainland of the USSR. Alaska has 10,684 km (6,639 mi) of general coastline—or 54,718 km (34,000 mi), if all the small islands and coastal indentations are included. Almost 90% of Alaska's territory is owned by the federal government.

Physiographic Regions. Alaska may be divided into four geographic regions—the Pacific mountain system of the south, the central region of uplands and lowlands, the Brooks Range (the northernmost extension of the Rocky Mountains), and the Arctic coastal plain, or North Slope.

The Pacific mountain system is a complex region of high mountains, broad valleys, and many islands. The Coast Ranges dominate southeastern Alaska, a 644-km-long (400-mi) area known as the Alaska Panhandle. The ranges, many of which have large glaciers, rise to 5,489 m (18,008 ft) at Mount Saint Elias, in the Saint Elias Mountains, and to 4,996 m (16,391 ft) at Mount Blackburn, in the Wrangell Mountains. Just off the southeast coast is the Alexander Archipelago—about 1,100 islands that are the exposed tops of a submerged section of the Coast Ranges. These islands, separated by deep fjords, shelter the Inside Passage. The principal landform of south central Alaska is the Alaska Range, a great mountain arc that contains such lofty peaks as Mount McKinley and Mount Foraker (5,304 m/17,400 ft). In extreme south central Alaska is an extensive area of lowlands, along the lower Susitna River and on the western Kenai Peninsula. Southwestern Alaska is made up of the Alaska Peninsula, the Aleutian Islands, Kodiak Island, the Shumagin Islands, and several other islands. The Alaska Peninsula and the Aleutians are dominated by the volcanically active Aleutian Range.

Central Alaska, between the Alaska Range and the Brooks Range, contains modestly elevated mountains and large lowland regions, especially along the Yukon River and near the Bering Sea, in the west. Higher elevations include West Point (1,788 m/5,865 ft) in the east and Mount Bendeleben (1,137 m/3,730 ft) in the west on the Seward Peninsula.

In the north is the rugged Brooks Range, as well as the De Long, Baird, Schwatka, and Endicott mountains. Lofty points in the Brooks Range include Mount Isto (2,761 m/9,058 ft), Mount Chamberlin (2,749 m/9,019 ft), and Mount Michelson (2,699 m/8,855 ft), all situated in the northeast.

The Arctic coastal plain gradually slopes downward from the Brooks Range to the Arctic Ocean to the north. Permafrost lies under the surface of the plain, as do great deposits of petroleum and natural gas.

Rivers and Lakes. The chief river of Alaska is the Yukon, which flows westward across the central part of the state for 2,036 km (1,265 mi) before emptying into the Bering Sea through a large delta. The Yukon's principal tributaries in Alaska are the Porcupine, Tanana, and Koyukuk rivers. Other major rivers in the state include the Kuskokwim, which flows westward to the Bering Sea; the Kobuk and Noatak, which empty into an arm of Kotzebue Sound; the Kokolik, Meade, and Colville, which flow into the Arctic Ocean; the Copper, which empties into the Gulf of Alaska; and the Susitna and Matanuska, which flow into Cook Inlet. Most of the rivers of the interior and the Arctic coastal plain carry much gravel and silt and display well-developed meander patterns.

Alaska has many lakes, the largest of which is Iliamna Lake (2,675 km²/1,033 mi²) in the south. Several big lakes, such as Becharof Lake, Naknek Lake, and Kukaklek Lake, are on the Alaska Peninsula. Lakes in Alaska have a tendency to fill in with vegetation. Often this leads to freezing of the subsurface material with uplift in the center of the former lake bed, which creates a hill known technically as a pingo.

Climate. Southeastern Alaska and the flanks of the Coast

Ranges in south central Alaska, as well as the Aleutians, are characterized by a maritime climate. Some areas have a mean annual precipitation of more than 5,080 mm (200 in), with 1,651 mm (65 in) being normal for low-lying places. Temperatures are relatively mild in winter and usually are cool in summer. Juneau has average temperatures of −5° C (23° F) in January and 13° C (56° F) in July; the city receives about 1,016 mm (40 in) of moisture each year.

The lowlands along the lower Yukon and Kuskokwim rivers, the Cook Inlet area, the Copper River basin, and the southern Seward Peninsula have a transitional climate, with warm summers, cool winters, and precipitation ranging from 305 to 762 mm (12 to 30 in) a year. Summer temperatures are highest in the Copper River basin and decline to the west because of the moderating influence of the Bering Sea. Anchorage has a mean January temperature of −12° C (11° F) and an average July temperature of 14° C (58° F); its mean annual precipitation is 371 mm (15 in).

The interior of Alaska is shielded from marine influences by the Alaska and Brooks ranges. Thus it receives only 254–610 mm (10–24 in) of precipitation a year and has long winters, with typical temperatures of −40° C (−40° F) and occasional periods of several weeks duration when temperatures drop to as low as −57° C (−70°F). Summers, however, usually are hot—temperatures reach 32° C (90° F), skies are clear, and sunlight lasts for twenty hours a day. Fairbanks has an average

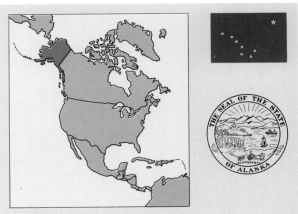

ALASKA

LAND. Area: 1,530,693 km² (591,004 mi²); rank: 1st. Capital: Juneau (1980 pop., 19,528). Largest city: Anchorage (1982 est. pop., 194,675). County equivalents: 23. Elevations: highest—6,194 m (20,320 ft), Mount McKinley; lowest—sea level.

PEOPLE. Population (1982 est.): 438,000; rank: 50th; density: 0.4 persons per km² (1 per mi²). Distrib. (1980): 43.4% metropolitan, 56.6% nonmetro. Av. ann. change (1970-80): +3.3%.

EDUCATION. Public enrollment (1982): elementary—63,211; secondary—26,202; higher (1981)—24,000. Nonpublic enrollment (1980): elementary—1,300; secondary—400; combined—2,100; higher—700. Institutions of higher education (1982): 15.

ECONOMY. State personal income (1982): $7.1 billion; rank: 45th. Median family income (1979): $28,395; rank: 1st. Nonagricultural labor distribution (1982): manufacturing—11,000 persons; wholesale and retail trade—36,000; government—61,000; services—35,000; transportation and utilities—18,000; finance, insurance, and real estate—9,000; construction—15,000. Agriculture: income (1982)—$16 million. Fishing: value (1982)—$576 million. Forestry: sawn timber volume (1977)—188.9 billion board feet. Mining: value (1981)—$14.4 billion. Manufacturing: value added (1977)—$504 million. Services: value (1977)—$514 million.

GOVERNMENT. (1985). Gov.: William Sheffield, Dem. U.S. Congress: Senate—2 Repub.; House—1 Repub. Electoral college votes: 3. State legislature: 20 senators, 40 representatives.

STATE SYMBOLS. Statehood: Jan. 3, 1959; the 49th state. Nickname: The Last Frontier; bird: willow ptarmigan; flower: forget-me-not; tree: Sitka spruce; motto: North to the Future; song: "Alaska's Flag."

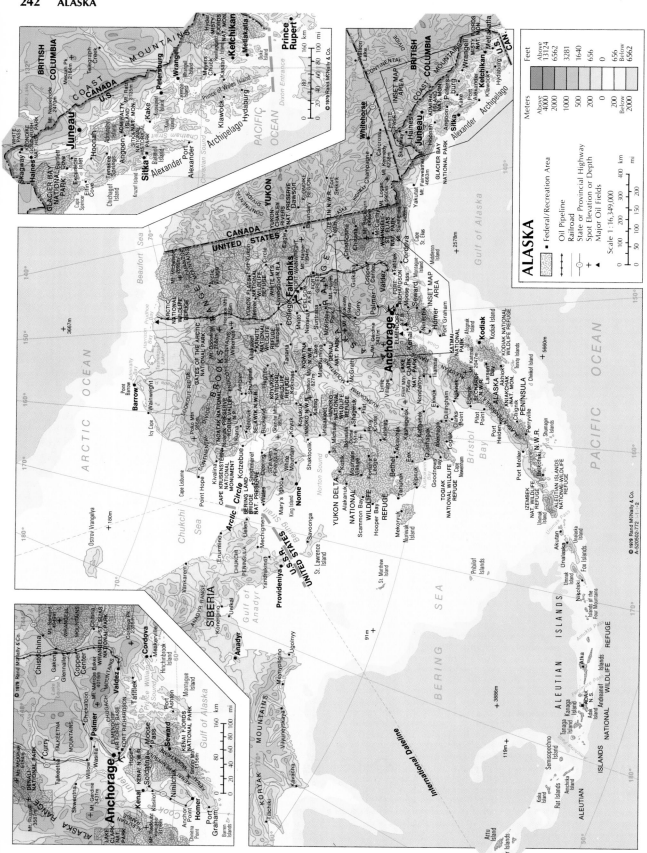

ALASKA

Scale 1:16,349,000

| Federal/Recreation Area
Oil Pipeline
Railroad
State or Provincial Highway
Spot Elevation or Depth
Major Oil Fields

Meters		Feet
Above 4000		Above 13124
2000		6562
1000		3281
500		1640
200		656
0		0
200		656
Below 2000		Below 6562

© 1979 Rand McNally & Co.
A-520500-772-1-2

January temperature of $-25°$ C ($-13°$ F) and a mean July temperature of $16°$ C ($61°$ F); it receives about 287 mm (11 in) of precipitation yearly. Northern and northwestern Alaska has an arctic climate. This is the region of long, dark winters and short, cool summers, with 24 hr of darkness during part of the winter and 24 hr of daylight during part of the summer. Annual precipitation is low, normally between 203 and 533 mm (8 and 21 in). Winter temperatures are not as low as in the interior, but wind speeds are frequently high, causing extreme chill factors. The Beaufort Sea tends to moderate summer temperatures.

Vegetation and Animal Life. About half of Alaska is covered with tundra vegetation, which mainly consists of small plants (such as lichens, mosses, flowering plants, and grasses) and some high brush. Tundra is found on higher mountain slopes and covers most of western Alaska and all of Arctic Alaska. Almost one-third of the state is covered by forest. Southeastern and south central Alaska have large forests composed mainly of hemlock and Sitka spruce, and the interior has extensive forests of black and white spruce, birch, aspen, and larch. About one-sixth of the forest land is within the state's two national forests, Chugach National Forest, in south central Alaska, and Tongass National Forest, in the southeast. Common flowering plants in the state include roses, lilacs, lilies, peonies, and delphiniums.

Alaskan wildlife includes numerous big animals. The southern part of the state has many bears (notably the Alaskan brown bear, or kodiak bear, the world's largest carnivorous land mammal) and deer; large herds of fur seals are found on the PRIBILOF ISLANDS. Alaska has herds of moose, caribou, and reindeer, some domesticated musk-oxen, and mountain goats and sheep. Arctic Alaska has polar bears, caribou, and arctic foxes. The state's numerous streams are well stocked with trout, salmon, grayling, and other fish, and coastal marine waters contain abundant salmon, halibut, cod, herring, pollack, shrimp, clams, and crabs as well as whales.

Mineral Resources. The most valuable mineral deposits in Alaska are petroleum and natural gas, found in great quantities in the Arctic coastal plain (especially around PRUDHOE BAY) and in lesser but significant amounts on the Kenai Peninsula and in Cook Inlet and the Gulf of Alaska. Gold is found in the central Yukon River basin, on the southern Seward Peninsula, and in the Alaska Panhandle. Alaska contains one of North America's largest bituminous coal reserves, located in Cook Inlet, the Nenana area, along the Yukon, and in northwest Alaska. Other minerals include iron ore, copper, molybdenum, antimony, silver, platinum, tin, and mercury.

PEOPLE

Alaska has the fewest inhabitants of any U.S. state, but its population is growing rapidly, increasing more than 32% during the 1970s, or about three times the national increase during that period. Most of the increase resulted from a large net in-migration. During 1970–76, 56% of the growth was made up of net in-migration. Many persons entered the state in the 1970s to work in the petroleum industry or in jobs associated with oil production and transportation.

Alaska has an extremely low average population density— 0.3 persons per km² (0.7 per mi²). Only seven communities are of significant size—ANCHORAGE, FAIRBANKS, JUNEAU (the state capital), Kenai, Ketchikan, SITKA, and Kodiak. Most of these cities are experiencing a rapid pace of growth, partly because most new arrivals settle in them. Some smaller places, such as BARROW, NOME, VALDEZ, Bethel, Petersburg, Seward, and Wrangell (most with fewer than 3,000 inhabitants in 1980), are regional economic centers. The great majority of Alaska's inhabitants are white, and more than 80% were born in the United States of American parents.

The combined population of American Indian, ESKIMO, and ALEUT is 64,047 (1980). The majority of this number are Eskimo (Inuit), most of whom live in the north and east and support themselves in part by catching fish and sea mammals and by herding reindeer. The principal American Indian groups are the Athabascan-speaking Indians of the interior and the HAIDA, TLINGIT, and TSIMSHIAN of the southeast. The Aleut, closely related to the Eskimo, live on the Alaska Peninsula and on the Aleutian and Shumagin islands. Religious groups in Alaska include Roman Catholic, Orthodox, Presbyterian, Baptist, Episcopalian, Methodist, and others.

Education. The first schools in Alaska were established by Russians during the 1820s, but the school system did not expand significantly until the region was organized as a U.S. territory in 1912. In 1979, 61,000 pupils were enrolled in public elementary schools, and 28,000 students were enrolled in public secondary schools. In the early 1980s about 10% of the children attended schools operated by the U.S. Bureau of Indian Affairs.

The University of Alaska (1917) has upper-level campuses at Anchorage, Fairbanks, and Juneau and a network of 10 community colleges (see ALASKA, UNIVERSITY OF). Sheldon Jackson College (1878) was Alaska's first institution of higher learning.

Cultural Institutions. Leading museums reflecting Alaska's native traditions and history are found in Fairbanks (University of Alaska), Juneau (Alaska State Museum), and Sitka (Sheldon Jackson). Anchorage has a museum of fine arts and native

The Alaska Range, which separates the state's southern coastal region from the immense central plateau, includes Mounts McKinley (right), the highest in North America; Hunter (center), and Foraker (left). Mount McKinley National Park was established in 1917 and renamed Denali National Park in 1980; the popular park contains these and other lofty peaks.

(Left) *Juneau, a center of the Alaskan fishing industry and the state capital, occupies a coastal strip bounded by the Gastineau Channel and the steep slopes of Mount Juneau. Through an extension of its municipal limits in 1970, Juneau became, in terms of area, the largest city in the United States.*

(Below) *Anchorage, Alaska's most populous city, lies on a coastal plain bordered by Cook Inlet and the Chugach Mountains. Although the city was devastated by an earthquake in 1964—the most severe ever to strike North America—Anchorage was quickly rebuilt with the assistance of the federal government.*

crafts. Smaller museums are located throughout the state, including at Skagway and Kotzekue. Major libraries include Rasmussen Library at the University of Alaska, Fairbanks; a growing library at the University of Alaska, Anchorage; and the Alaska Historical Library in Juneau. The state has several local drama and music groups, and *Cry of the Wild Ram*, a popular play dealing with the period of Russian control, is presented each August at Kodiak.

Historic Sites. Places of historic interest in Alaska include Klondike Gold Rush National Historical Park, including buildings in Skagway associated with the Klondike gold rush of 1897–98; Sitka National Historical Park, encompassing the site of the 1804 battle in which Tlingit Indians were defeated by Russian colonizers; and several communities in the Aleutian Islands and southern part of the state having Russian Orthodox churches dating from the early 19th century.

Communications. In the late 1970s Alaska had 10 television stations and 41 radio stations. In 1982 the state had 8 English-language daily newspapers, with a combined daily circulation of 130,000 copies. The most influential dailies were the *Anchorage News*, the *Anchorage Daily Times*, the *Fairbanks Daily News-Miner*, and the *Juneau Southeast Alaska Empire*. The state's first commercial newspaper was the *Alaska Times*, initially published at Sitka in 1868.

GOVERNMENT

Alaska is governed under a constitution (as amended) that was adopted in 1956 and became effective in 1959. The capital of Alaska is Juneau; voters in the 1970s approved a plan to move the capital to Willow (near Anchorage), but in 1982 they voted against the expenditure. The state's chief executive is a governor, elected to a 4-year term; a governor may not serve more than two consecutive terms. Alaska has a bicameral legislature made up of a senate (whose 20 members are elected to 4-year terms) and a house of representatives (whose 40 members are elected to 2-year terms). The principal tribunals are the 5-member supreme court and the 16-member superior court; the justices of both are appointed by the governor to terms of approximately 3 years, at the end of which they may be popularly elected to additional longer terms.

Alaska is not divided into counties but rather into organized boroughs and unorganized boroughs. Organized boroughs are similar to counties, however, and each of the 11 such units is supervised by a small assembly. Unorganized boroughs, which together include more than 90% of the state's area but

less than 10% of its population, are administered by the state government. For statistical purposes the state is sometimes divided into 23 census divisions. Alaska is represented in the U.S. Congress by two senators and by one member of the House of Representatives; the state has three electoral votes in national presidential elections. Jay Hammond, a Republican who was governor from 1974 to 1982, was succeeded by Bill Sheffield, a Democrat. The state legislature was controlled by Democrats in the early 1980s. Most local-government elected positions are contested on a nonpartisan basis. In national presidential elections the Republican candidate has usually carried Alaska.

THE ECONOMY

Concerted economic growth in Alaska began only during World War II, when the federal government established several important military bases in the state. Government, especially the armed forces, is now the chief employer in Alaska, but much revenue is derived from the production of petroleum (especially in the Arctic coastal plain), and the state has developed a sizable fishing industry. Alaska has a small farming sector, and it is necessary to import most food.

Agriculture and Forestry. Alaska's annual cash income from farming is lowest among the U.S. states—only $12 million in 1980. The chief farm products are milk, greenhouse crops, hay, and potatoes. The state has only about 290 farms, whose average size is approximately 1,619 ha (4,000 acres); a total of just 8,500 ha (20,000 acres) is used to raise crops. The principal cropland is in the lower Matanuska River valley, near Anchorage. Crops are also raised in the Tanana River valley, near Fairbanks; on the Kenai Peninsula; and in scattered areas of the southeast. The interior has considerable areas of potential farmland including particularly the Delta region of the upper Tanana River. Reindeer are raised on the Seward Peninsula and in the Kotzebue area, producing goods for domestic use and export. Some sheep and cattle are raised, and Alaska has more than 8,000 horses, many used as pack animals. Southeastern Alaska has an important logging and paper-pulp industry centered largely in Ketchikan, Sitka, and Wrangell. Small lumber mills exist elsewhere, including the Fairbanks and Anchorage areas.

Fishing. Alaska has an important fishing industry, and the annual value of its catch—about $560 million—led all other U.S. states in 1980. Salmon account for more than one-half of the annual fishing receipts; also valuable are king crabs, snow crabs, halibut, shrimp, cod, herring, scallops, and clams. The principal fishing grounds are in the southeast, in the Gulf of Alaska, in the Kodiak area, and in Bristol Bay.

Wild-Animal Products. The U.S. government obtains substantial revenues from its monopoly on fur-seal harvesting on the Pribilof Islands. Elsewhere, fur trapping on a small scale provides a significant source of income for some people. Harvesting of moose, caribou, seals, and whales is very important to the economy of native Alaskans.

Mining. Petroleum is the leading mineral produced in Alaska. The principal oil field is on the Arctic coastal plain, around Prudhoe Bay. Petroleum from this field is transported by the 1,287-km-long (800-mi) TRANS-ALASKA PIPELINE to Valdez, where it is transferred to oceangoing tankers. The field began producing in mid-1977, when the pipeline was completed; average daily production in 1980 was about 1.5 million barrels of petroleum.

Other major oil fields are on the Kenai Peninsula and in Cook Inlet; these fields were first exploited in the late 1950s and eventually produced natural gas as well. Natural-gas production totaled about 6.54 billion m³ (231 billion ft³) in 1981, but a projected gas pipeline to Canada and the United States remained unrealized.

Other minerals recovered in Alaska include stone, sand and gravel, gold (mainly in the Yukon and Tanana river valleys, the Seward Peninsula, and the southeast), coal, gemstones, lead, platinum, silver, and barite.

Manufacturing. Alaska has a small manufacturing industry, which in 1980 employed 13,000 persons. The value added by manufacture was more than $500 million a year. The chief products were processed fish, paper, lumber, and refined petroleum. The main manufacturing centers were Anchorage, Fairbanks, Juneau, and Ketchikan.

Tourism. Alaska's splendid scenery, as well as its many opportunities for outdoor recreation, annually attract about 270,000 tourists, who together spend about $100 million in the state each year. National Park Service land—most of it set aside in 1978—totals about 21 million ha (51 million acres) and includes Denali (formerly Mount McKinley), Gates of the Arctic, Glacier Bay, Katmai, Kenai Fjords, Kobuk Valley, Lake Clark, and Wrangell–Saint Elias national parks; Bering Land Bridge, Noatak, and Yukon-Charley Rivers national preserves; Aniachak and Cape Krusenstern national monuments; and Klondike Gold Rush and Sitka national historical parks. The state also operates a system of parks.

Transportation. Alaska has limited land transportation facilities. The road network totals (1979) 20,073 km (12,473 mi). The state has 1,078 km (670 mi) of railroad track, most of it part of the Alaska Railroad, running from Seward (on the Kenai Peninsula) to Fairbanks via Anchorage. Another rail line runs from Skagway to Whitehorse, Yukon Territory. Small airplanes, operated by "bush pilots," carry freight and passengers to remote communities. Major airports are situated at Anchorage, Fairbanks, and Juneau.

An excellent system of ferries links the insular communities of southeast Alaska with nearby mainland communities and with Prince Rupert, British Columbia, and Seattle, Wash. Valdez, a terminus of the Trans-Alaska Pipeline, is a major port for shipping crude petroleum; other important ports in Alaska include Anchorage, Ketchikan, Seward, Sitka, Skagway, Whittier, and Wrangell.

Energy. In 1980, Alaska had an installed electricity-generating capacity of 1.1 million kW, and annual production totaled 3.1 billion kW h. The great bulk of the electricity was produced in thermal plants using coal, natural gas, or refined petroleum.

The state's rivers, notably the Yukon and Susitna, have great potential for producing hydroelectricity, but only a few waterpower facilities had been constructed by the early 1980s; among them is Eklutna Dam, near Anchorage.

HISTORY

The first settlers of present-day Alaska migrated in successive waves from Asia across the BERING LAND BRIDGE; estimates of the date of the earliest such migration range from about 30,000 to 10,000 years ago. When the region was first visited by Europeans, in the early 18th century, it was inhabited by Eskimo in the north, west, and Prince William Sound area; Aleuts in the southeast; Athabascans in the interior and Cook Inlet area; and Tlingit and Tlairda in the southeast.

In 1728 the Danish navigator Vitus BERING, sailing for the Russian government, visited and named St. Lawrence Island, a part of modern Alaska situated in the Bering Sea. In 1741, Ber-

An Eskimo hunter trudges over the icy wastes along the Chukchi Sea with a freshly killed seal. As part of a 1971 claims settlement, the native peoples of Alaska were awarded $962.5 million and 40 million acres (16.2 million ha) of land.

ing undertook a second voyage to Alaska, during which Mount Saint Elias was sighted and a party, under Aleksei Chirikov, landed at Kayak Island. Bering and many of his companions died during the trip, but some survivors returned to Russia with sea-otter furs from Alaska. Soon Russian adventurers were trapping in the Aleutian Islands, and in 1784, Grigory SHELEKHOV founded the first permanent white settlement in Alaska, on Kodiak Island, near modern Kodiak. During the late 18th century Capt. James COOK, the English explorer, as well as Spanish, French, and other English navigators, sailed along the coast of Alaska.

The early Russian trappers were disorganized and rapacious, depleting the stock of fur-bearing animals in many areas and killing or enslaving large numbers of Aleuts. In an attempt to bring order to Russian America, Tsar Paul I in 1799 chartered the RUSSIAN-AMERICAN COMPANY, granting it monopoly trading rights. Under Aleksandr BARANOV, who headed the company during 1800–17, the fur harvest was increased substantially, and several settlements were established. New Archangel (later renamed Sitka), founded in 1799, was destroyed by Tlingit Indians in 1802 but was rebuilt in 1804 as the capital of Russian America. At the same time, many Aleuts were then converted to Russian Orthodoxy, notably by Father Innokenti Veniaminoff.

During the first half of the 19th century, the Hudson's Bay Company and American traders were very active in Alaska. The rights of these traders and most of the current boundaries of Alaska were established by treaties between Russia and Great Britain and the United States (1824–25).

From 1820 onward, the Russian-American Company, managed in large part by famous Russian admirals and scientists, did much to explore Alaska and assess its resources. The Russians built iron foundries and schools; developed coal mining, trading routes, farming, and sheep raising; followed wildlife conservation methods to preserve the fur-seal population; and carried out smallpox inoculations. As a result of the Crimean War and contacts with American businessmen in San Francisco, the Russian government wished to sell Alaska to the United States. The Russians feared losing Alaska to the British in the event of another war and were thus well disposed to the United States.

After the Civil War, the U.S. secretary of state William H. SEWARD, an expansionist who saw the region as having strategic importance, negotiated (1867) the purchase of Alaska. A treaty of cession was signed by Russia and the United States on Mar. 30, 1867, and, after the treaty was ratified by the U.S. Senate, Alaska was formally transferred to the United States on Oct. 18, 1867. The United States paid $7.2 million for Russia's rights in Alaska after a long and bitter debate in Congress. Americans occupied Alaska before the money was paid and moved quickly to take control of the assets of the Russian-American Company, to trade along the Yukon, and to exploit the profitable Pribilof fur-seal trade.

During the early years of U.S. control Alaska was called "Seward's Folly" because it was believed to be useless. Although some economic development was undertaken, the region was generally neglected. It was administered successively by the U.S. War Department, Treasury Department, and Navy before civil government was established by the Organic Act of 1884. The government had little control of Alaska, however, until further laws were enacted in the early 1900s. Fishing grew in importance after 1867, and in 1878 the first salmon cannery was opened. Fur seals were killed in such great numbers that the federal government was obliged in 1910 to take control of the herds to prevent the animal's extermination. (With fur harvesting strictly limited, the number of fur seals increased from about 130,000 in 1910 to more than 2,500,000 in the 1970s.) During the late 19th century, large numbers of whales, sea otters, and walruses were killed. In order to increase the food supply, Sheldon JACKSON, a missionary and educator who established schools in Alaska, in 1891 introduced reindeer (from Siberia) to the region.

The modern economic development of Alaska began in 1897–98 with the rush to the KLONDIKE gold fields in nearby Canada. Southeastern Alaska served as a gateway to the Klondike, and Skagway, Valdez, and other Alaskan communities grew as way stations. In 1899 gold was found on the beach at Nome, and quickly an Alaskan gold rush was under way. By mid-1900 about 10,000 gold seekers were in Nome; they mostly lived in squalid conditions, with no effective government or police force. Important gold discoveries were made around Fairbanks in 1902, in the Yellow and Iditarod river valleys (near the modern town of Flat) in 1906–10, and along the Yukon near Ruby in 1907–10. Much copper ore was recovered in the Copper River basin near McCarthy from 1911 to 1938, when the main mine was exhausted. The number of whites in Alaska increased from about 4,000 in 1890 to 30,500 in 1900 and 36,400 in 1910.

Juneau was made the official capital of Alaska in 1900, but government offices were not moved there from Sitka until

(Below) *The crew of a commercial fishing vessel sorts and unloads a catch of Alaskan king crabs, one of many valuable species taken off the shores of Alaska.*

(Above) *Logs taken from the nearby Tongass National Forest are readied for processing at a pulp mill in Ketchikan. Most of Alaska's usable timber is situated along the state's southern coast. The preparation of lumber for export has become a profitable industry.*

The Trans-Alaska pipeline, one of the most ambitious engineering projects in history, was completed in 1977. The 1,287-km-long (800-mi) pipeline carries petroleum from Prudhoe Bay, on the Arctic Ocean, to the ice-free port of Valdez, on the Gulf of Alaska.

1906, the same year that Alaskans elected their first delegate (nonvoting) to the U.S. House of Representatives. In 1912, Alaska was constituted as a U.S. territory, and Alaskans were able to elect a territorial legislature, whose decisions, however, were subject to veto by the federally appointed governor. In the 1920s and '30s the Alaskan economy grew slowly. In 1923 the Alaska Railroad, running from Seward to Fairbanks, was completed. Also in the 1920s small airplanes, piloted by pioneer commercial aviators, such as Noel Wien, began to link remote areas with the territory's larger towns. An important step in increasing the territory's farm output was taken in 1935, when the federal government set up an experimental agricultural colony in the Matanuska River valley.

World War II brought great changes to Alaska. In 1942 the Japanese bombed Dutch Harbor (on Amaknak Island, near Unalaska Island) and occupied Attu and Kiska islands, in the Aleutians. Recognizing Alaska's strategic location near Asia, the United States countered by building a supply road, the Alaska Highway, in 1942; by retaking Attu and Kiska in 1943; and by establishing several military bases in the territory. The military buildup, which carried over to the postwar period, fostered economic development in Alaska and was largely responsible for the territory's population growth from 72,524 persons in 1939 to 128,643 persons in 1950.

During the 1950s and '60s, Alaska's economy continued to expand as the tourist trade grew. Fishing fleets and canning and timber-processing facilities were enlarged and modernized (partly through an influx of much Japanese capital); an important petroleum industry was established soon after the discovery, in 1957, of major oil fields in the Kenai Peninsula-Cook Inlet region. As the population increased, so did sentiment for statehood. In mid-1958 the U.S. Congress approved statehood for Alaska, and on Jan. 3, 1959, Alaska became the 49th state. Its first governor was William A. Egan, a Democrat, who served until 1966, when he was succeeded by Walter J. Hickel, a Republican. One of Alaska's initial U.S. senators was Ernest H. Gruening, a noted public official and an influential leader in the drive for statehood. In 1964 a powerful earthquake struck south central Alaska; Anchorage suffered extensive damage but was quickly rebuilt.

A new era in Alaska began in 1968 with the discovery of great petroleum and natural-gas deposits in the Arctic coastal plain, or North Slope, around Prudhoe Bay. It was decided to send the oil by pipeline from the north coast through the interior to the ice-free port of Valdez, where it would be transferred to oceangoing tankers. Environmentalists objected to the project, contending, among other things, that the ecological balance in the interior of Alaska would be upset, but after considerable debate the U.S. Congress gave its required approval in 1973. The Trans-Alaska Pipeline was completed in mid-1977 at a cost estimated at more than $10 billion. The government of Alaska gained large new revenues from taxes and other imposts levied on the recovery and transportation of the petroleum. As a result of the state's oil wealth, the Alaska legislature approved (1980) a law eliminating the state income tax and distributing shares of Alaska's oil royalties to its citizens. After passage, however, implementation was stalled until 1982 because of court challenges.

A major issue confronting Alaskans during the 1970s concerned the status of its vast area. At statehood the government of Alaska had been promised eventual control over about 28% of the state, and the U.S. government retained authority over the rest. Under national legislation passed in 1971, an additional 17.8 million ha (44 million acres) of federal holdings in the state were reserved for Alaska's Eskimo, Indians, and Aleuts. In August 1980 the U.S. Senate passed—against strong Alaskan opposition—the controversial Alaska Lands Bill, which protects more than 40 million ha (100 million acres), some from uncontrolled development of resources and some as wilderness areas.

In 1983 the state's inconvenient four time zones became two, with most of Alaska operating within the old Yukon time zone, renamed the Alaskan time zone.   DONALD F. LYNCH

Bibliography: Hulley, Clarence C., *Alaska: Past and Present*, 3d ed. (1970; repr. 1981); Hunt, William R., *Alaska: A Bicentennial History* (1976); McPhee, John, *Coming into the Country* (1977); Oswalt, Wendell H., *Alaskan Eskimos* (1967); Rogers, George W., ed., *Change in Alaska: People, Petroleum, and Politics* (1970).

Alaska, Gulf of

The Gulf of Alaska is a semicircular inlet of the Pacific Ocean on the coast of southern Alaska. It has an area of about 1,533,280 km² (592,000 mi²), and its major ports are Anchorage, Valdez, and Seward. The main current in the gulf is the warm, counterclockwise Alaska Current.

Alaska, University of

The University of Alaska (1917; enrollment: 27,000; library: 510,000 volumes) is a land-grant institution with several campuses. The Arctic Environmental Research Laboratory is among the scientific institutes connected with the university, which has upper-division campuses at Anchorage, Fairbanks, and Juneau and ten community colleges at other locations.

Alaska blackfish

Alaska blackfish (family Umbridae, order Salmoniformes) are small, cylindrical fishes with large pectoral fins. Their dorsal and anal fins are set far back near the tail. Legend has it that they can survive being frozen, swallowed, and regurgitated by husky dogs. Although that is unlikely, this species exhibits remarkable resistance to both extreme cold and low concentrations of oxygen under the ice. The Alaska blackfish is found only in Alaska and Siberia.   A. R. EMERY

Alaska Current

The Alaska Current, an offshoot of the ALEUTIAN CURRENT, is a surface current that is part of the counterclockwise flow in the Gulf of Alaska. Its water at 4° C (30° F) is warmer than the gulf water. Salinity is 32.6 parts/1,000 and average velocity 28 cm/sec (1 km/h/0.6 mph).   JOHN WHEELER

See also: OCEAN CURRENTS.

Alaska Highway

The Alaska (or Alcan) Highway was built by the U.S. Army during World War II to connect military posts in Alaska with the midcontinental United States. Completed in 1942, the highway extends 2,452 km (1,523 mi) from Dawson Creek, British Columbia, to Fairbanks, Alaska. Several connecting highways link it with Alberta and Montana and with other points in Alaska. In 1946 the Canadian section was turned over to Canada, and in the following year the entire highway was opened to the public. It had before that time been maintained as a military supply route.

Bibliography: Remley, David A., *A Crooked Road: A History of the Alaska Highway* (1976).

Alaskan malamute   [mal'-uh-myoot]

The Alaskan malamute, a working dog, originally pulled sleds for the Malamute (Mahlmut) Indians of northwestern Alaska. This dog is known for its endurance as a draft animal and for its affectionate nature: it is especially good with children.

The malamute has a compact, powerfully built body and a broad head. It stands 54–63.5 cm (21.5–25 in) high at the shoulder and weighs about 35 kg (80 lb). The coat is double-layered with wooly underhair and a coarse topcoat. The tail is bushy and loosely curled over the back. The paws are large and well padded with fur, enabling the dog to run over snow. The malamute's brown, almond-shaped eyes and its coat—gray or black and white—give it a wolflike appearance.

Bibliography: Riddle, Maxwell, and Seeley, Eva B., *The Complete Alaskan Malamute* (1976); Ross, Diane, *Your Alaskan Malamute* (1977).

The proud Alaskan malamute traditionally has been used to pull heavily loaded sleds over great snow plains.

Alaskan Pipeline: see TRANS-ALASKA PIPELINE.

Alavi, Bozorg   [ah-la-vee', boh'-zorg]

Bozorg Alavi, b. Feb. 2, 1908, is a radical Persian novelist. Educated in Iran and Berlin, he was imprisoned in 1937 for his leftist politics and in 1941 expelled from Iran. He is professor of Persian at Humboldt University, East Berlin.

Although Alavi is important primarily as a short-story writer, his only novel, *Chashmhayash*, is among the best in contemporary Persian. *Chamadan*, his first collection of short stories, contains masterful studies of character and human relations; like much of his work, these stories are also notable for their social criticism.   MARCIA E. MAGUIRE

Alba, Fernando Álvarez de Toledo y Pimentel, Duque de

The duque de Alba, or Alva, b. Oct. 29, 1507, was a leading Spanish general and statesman under KING PHILIP II. After serving Philip's father, Holy Roman Emperor CHARLES V, in many campaigns, he was named chief of household for Philip and became the leader of a major political faction at his court. From 1555 to 1557 Alba served in Italy, where he distinguished himself for his subtlety and generalship in the war against Pope Paul IV.

Alba helped negotiate the Treaty of CATEAU-CAMBRÉSIS (1559), ending the long war with France, and in 1567 he was dispatched to the Low Countries to quell the DUTCH REVOLT. There, his persecution of the Protestants and his exalted conception of royal authority turned a rebellion into a war of independence. He was recalled in 1573. In 1579 Alba was imprisoned, ostensibly for permitting the marriage of his son without royal consent. He was released in 1580 to lead the Spanish armies in the annexation of Portugal. He died In Portugal on Dec. 6, 1582.   WILLIAM S. MALTBY

Bibliography: Cadoux, Cecil John, *Philip of Spain and the Netherlands* (1969); Grierson, Edward, *The Fatal Inheritance: Philip II and the Spanish Netherlands* (1969).

Alba Longa

Alba Longa was an ancient Latin city about 19 km (12 mi) southeast of Rome, set in the Alban Hills. According to legend, it was founded (*c.*1152 BC) by Aeneas's son, Ascanius, and was the birthplace of ROMULUS AND REMUS. The principal city of the LATINS, it retained its dominance until the 7th century BC, when it was probably destroyed by Rome. Excavations of its necropolis have revealed tombs dating from the 12th century BC. The site of Alba Longa is near the modern Castel Gandolfo, summer residence of the popes.

albacore: see TUNA.

Alban, Saint

Saint Alban, d. 304?, was the first British martyr. According to tradition, he was baptized by a fugitive priest whom he sheltered during DIOCLETIAN's persecution. When the emperor's soldiers came to search his house, Alban, disguised in the priest's cloak, was arrested and then beheaded. Verulamium (present-day Saint Albans, England) was the site of the martyrdom. Feast day: June 17 (Church of England); June 22 (other Western).

Albanel, Charles

Charles Albanel, b. 1616, d. Jan. 11, 1696, was a Jesuit missionary and explorer in Canada. Having come to Quebec from France in 1649, he worked for many years among the Montagnais Indians at Tadoussac. In 1671–72 he traveled overland to Hudson Bay, probably the first European to do so. During a second journey (1673–74) to the bay, Albanel was seized by agents of the English Hudson's Bay Company and sent to England. He later returned (1676) to the Canadian missions, serving at Green Bay and Sault Ste. Marie.

Albanese, Licia   [ahl-bah-nay'-zay, lee'-chah]

Licia Albanese, b. July 22, 1913, is an Italian-American singer who was for 25 years one of the leading sopranos of the Metropolitan Opera. She studied in Italy and made her debut in

Milan in 1934 as Madame Butterfly. After 1940, except for the war years, she sang almost exclusively at the Metropolitan and appeared there more than 1,000 times. She was chosen by Toscanini to record *La Bohème* and *La Traviata* under his leadership.

Albania

Albania, one of Europe's smallest countries, is situated in the western part of the Balkan Peninsula. It has a 360-km (225-mi) coastline on the Adriatic and Ionian seas and is bounded on the north and east by Yugoslavia and on the southeast by Greece. The Albanians' name for their country, *Shqipëri*, which means "eagles' land," aptly suggests Albania's isolated, rugged terrain and its strongly independent people. A Communist country, Albania has engaged in several strong alliances with other Communist countries: Yugoslavia (1945–48), the USSR (1948–61), and China (1961–78). Since the end of World War II, Albania has undergone rapid economic and social change.

LAND

Albania is a predominantly mountainous country; approximately three-fourths of its territory consists of highlands with elevations greater than 300 m (1,000 ft). The mountains, which form a generally north-south backbone, are a southern continuation of the Dinaric Alps. The North Albanian Alps, a glaciated limestone range in the extreme north, are among the most rugged and inaccessible regions in the country. The highest peak, Korab (2,751 m/9,025 ft), is located on the eastern border with Yugoslavia. Much of the population inhabits the elevated basins and plateaus of the central part of the country.

Along the coast is a narrow zone of generally fertile alluvial lowlands (with some marshes) that extend inland along some rivers, especially in the central coastal region.

Most of the rivers in Albania rise in the interior highlands and flow generally eastward, descending rapidly to the coast, many in narrow gorges. The longest river is the Drin, but except for the Buenë none of the rivers is navigable. Most are nearly dry in summer and become torrents in winter. The major lakes (all of which are divided by Albania's borders) are Ohrid, Shkodër, and Prespa.

Climate. The coastal lowlands enjoy a typically Mediterranean climate: hot, dry summers and mild, wet winters. At Durrës, nearly 80% of the annual rainfall occurs between October and March, and the average daily minimum temperature in January is 6° C (42° F). The interior highlands are under the influence of a continental climate and have severely cold winters and warm summers, although at the highest elevations summers are cool. Annual rainfall averages from 760 mm (30 in) in the southeastern highlands to 2,030 mm (80 in) in the northern coastal plain to 1,070 mm (42 in) at Durrës.

Resources. Albania is relatively rich in minerals and is the world's fourth leading producer of chrome. Also present are significant deposits of oil, natural gas, bitumen, copper, iron, nickel, and salt. The country's river systems, especially the Drin, are important sources of hydroelectric power. Forests of oak, chestnut, beech, pine, and fir adequately supply the needs of Albania's woodworking and paper industries.

PEOPLE

For a Balkan state, Albania has an unusually homogeneous ethnic composition, with Albanians comprising 96% of the population. They are believed to be descendants of the ancient Illyrians, who were among the earliest inhabitants of the Balkan Peninsula. Despite centuries of foreign domination, the Albanians managed to preserve their national identity and language. The Albanians comprise two major subgroups: the Ghegs (or Gegs) to the north of the Shkumbi River and the Tosks to the south. The cultural and religious differences between the two groups have been largely eliminated by the current regime. Linguistic differences remain; however, the two dialects are mutually intelligible. The official language since 1944 is based largely on the Tosk dialect, reflecting the fact that Albania's present rulers come from the southern part of the country.

In 1967 all religious institutions were closed by the government, and the country was officially declared an atheist state. At that time, approximately 70% of the population was Muslim (a result of 500 years of Turkish domination), 20% Orthodox, and 10% Roman Catholic.

Demography. Since the 1950s, Albania has had the highest rate of natural population increase (about 3% annually) in Europe. In 1980 the birthrate was 28 per 1,000 inhabitants, a rate resembling that of an undeveloped country and about 50% greater than any other European country. The urban population, although at 35% still minor by European standards, has more than doubled since 1940, when 15% of the people lived in cities. Major cities include Tiranë, the capital, with a population of 220,000 (1981 est.), and Shkodër, Vlorë, and Durrës, none of which has a population greater than 70,000.

Education and Health. Eight years of primary education (from ages 6 to 14) is free and compulsory in Albania. Secondary education consists of four-year technical or professional courses. Since 1976, secondary school students must spend time working on farms or in factories. Higher education is conducted by the State University of Tiranë (1957) and several technical and teacher colleges. In 1975 approximately one-third of the total population was enrolled in the school system.

Illiteracy, widespread before the end of World War II, was virtually eliminated in the population under 40 years of age by the late 1950s but remains at about 30% for the population as a whole.

All medical services are free, and hospitals and clinics now serve all parts of the country.

Cultural Activity. Albanian literature, which first appeared in

PEOPLE'S SOCIALIST REPUBLIC OF ALBANIA

LAND. Area: 28,748 km² (11,100 mi²). Capital and largest city: Tiranë (1981 est. pop., 220,000).

PEOPLE. Population (1982 est.): 2,862,000; density (1982 est.): 100 persons per km² (258 per mi²). Distribution (1979): 35.3% urban, 64.7% rural. Annual growth (1975–80): 2.4%. Official language: Albanian. Major religions: Islam, Orthodoxy, Roman Catholicism.

EDUCATION AND HEALTH. Literacy (1980): 70% of adult population. Universities (1982): 1. Hospital beds (1977): 16,313. Physicians (1980): 4,715. Life expectancy (1979): women—71.4; men—66.8. Infant mortality rate: not available.

ECONOMY. GNP (1981): $2.3 billion; $820 per capita. Labor force (1981): 1,200,000. Foreign trade (1979): imports—$129 million; exports—$143 million; principal trade partners—Czechoslovakia, Yugoslavia, China, Italy, Poland, West Germany. Currency: 1 lek = 100 qintars.

GOVERNMENT. Type: Communist one-party state. Legislature: People's Assembly. Political subdivisions: 26 districts.

COMMUNICATIONS. Railroads (1982): 228 km (142 mi) total. Roads (1971): 5,500 km (3,418 mi) total. Major ports: 4. Airfields (international, 1982): 1.

ALBANIA

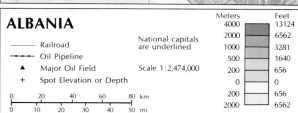

	Meters	Feet
	4000	13124
National capitals are underlined	2000	6562
	1000	3281
	500	1640
Scale 1:2,474,000	200	656
	0	0
	200	656
	2000	6562

——— Railroad

-•-•- Oil Pipeline

▲ Major Oil Field

+ Spot Elevation or Depth

0 20 40 60 80 km
0 10 20 30 40 50 mi

few literary works, Albanian culture has attracted little foreign interest. In the 1960s, Albania experienced a CULTURAL REVOLUTION similar to that of China, and Western works of art were thrown into official disfavor.

ECONOMIC ACTIVITY

Before World War II, Albania was one of the least developed countries in the world. As late as 1938, agriculture produced 92% of the country's national income but did not supply enough food for its population, and imports and foreign aid were necessary to support the economy. Following World War II, capitalism was abandoned, and a highly centralized socialist economic system was introduced. Although Albania's current rulers have sought to transform the country into a modern, self-sufficient, industrial-agricultural state, Albania remains the least economically developed country in Europe.

Agriculture. Albania has relatively little arable land per capita; yet approximately 55% of the labor force is engaged in agriculture. All land is now state owned and operated either as state farms or cooperatives. Yield per acre, although greatly increased since World War II, remains relatively low, and some food products must be imported.

Industry. Industry in Albania, all of which is nationalized, concentrates on the processing of mineral resources. Albania has increased its oil refining capacities and its chemical and engineering industries. By the mid-1970s the nonagricultural sectors of the economy had expanded to account for more than two-thirds of the national income, and industrial products accounted for more than three-quarters of all exports.

GOVERNMENT

Under the 1976 constitution the unicameral People's Assembly, elected every four years by universal suffrage, is the country's highest political authority. However, the assembly meets briefly only twice a year to ratify the actions of the presidium of the assembly, the chairman of which is the head of the state. Actual power is held by the (Communist) Albanian Party of Labor (APL), the only legal political party in the country. Party members hold all key posts in the government, military, and other areas of Albanian life. Enver HOXHA, first secretary of the APL since 1941, was still in the late 1970s the dominant member of the ruling elite.

HISTORY

From the 7th century BC the Greeks colonized the coastal areas of what is now Albania and in the following centuries became a cultural influence on the Illyrians. In about 350 BC an independent kingdom, ILLYRIA, emerged in the region near Shkodër. Illyria and EPIRUS to the south were conquered by Rome in 168 BC. With the division of the Roman Empire in the 4th century AD, Albania came under Byzantine rule. Actual Byzantine power in the area was weak, however, and in the succeeding centuries Albania was overrun by the Goths, Bulgars, Slavs, Serbs, and Normans (see BALKANS).

In the early 15th century the Turks began their conquest of the region. In 1443 Albanian resistance to the Turks was organized under the leadership of SKANDERBEG, who has become glorified as the national hero. Skanderbeg expelled the Turks and kept Albania independent of Turkish rule for more than 20 years. Soon after his death in 1468, however, the Turks reasserted their power, and Albania became part of the OTTOMAN EMPIRE. During the nearly five centuries of Ottoman rule most Albanians converted to Islam, and a substantial number immigrated to other Mediterranean regions. The country remained undeveloped and neglected.

Albanian nationalism revived in the early 19th century and spurred repeated revolts against Turkish domination. In 1912, in the First Balkan War, the Turks were driven from much of the Balkan Peninsula, and Albania declared its independence (see BALKAN WARS).

During World War I, Albania was a battleground for other Balkan powers and Italy. Albania's sovereignty was upheld at the Paris Peace Conference (1919) through the efforts of the American president Woodrow Wilson. After a period of political instability, power was seized (1925) by Ahmed Zogu, a conservative northern tribal chief. In 1928 he proclaimed Albania a monarchy and became King ZOG. During his reign,

the 15th and 16th centuries, remained primarily religious in character until the 19th century. Ottoman political authorities and the Greek Orthodox patriarch collaborated to discourage the use of the Albanian language and the development of Albanian culture. By the 19th century, however, a number of writers had established a secular literature with nationalistic themes.

Albanian literature and culture began to flourish after the achievement of independence in 1912. Since 1945, cultural activity has been subjected to rigid ideological controls; consequently, with the exception of folk music, the folk arts, and a

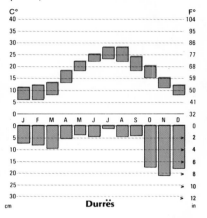

(Left) *The small town of Gjirokastër, an administrative center serving southern Albania, is the birthplace of the nation's Marxist head of state, Enver Hoxha. Despite the rugged terrain, the area is an important producer of olives, tobacco, and wheat.*

The bars indicate monthly ranges of temperatures (red) and precipitation (blue) of Durrës, Albania. Albania has a Mediterranean climate with continental influences that are especially notable in the northeast.

Durrës

Zog began the modernization of the country with Italian aid. Italian financial and military influence increased, and in 1939 Italy invaded Albania, forcing the king into exile.

During World War II a power struggle developed between the Communist (National Liberation Front) and the non-Communist liberation forces. After the Germans withdrew in 1944, a provisional Communist government was established. Between 1944 and 1948 Albania allied itself with Yugoslavia.

In 1948, after the rift in Yugoslav-Soviet relations, Albania allied itself with the USSR. Relations between the two countries grew strained in the late 1950s as Stalinist policies were discredited by Nikita Khrushchev; Hoxha, first secretary of the Albanian Communist party, remained a firm Stalinist. In 1961, Albania and the USSR severed diplomatic relations, and Soviet aid to the country was ended.

Albania turned to China as an economic and ideological ally. China supplied military and economic aid needed to offset Albania's chronic trade deficit. Following Mao Tse-tung's death, however, Albania became increasingly critical of China's "revisionist" leadership. In 1978, China announced an end to all aid to Albania.

In 1981, Prime Minister Mehmet Shehu, Hoxha's longtime second-ranking leader, died under suspicious circumstances.

NICHOLAS C. PANO

Bibliography: Logoreci, Anton, *The Albanians* (1977); Marmullaku, Ramadan, *Albania and the Albanians* (1975); Pano, Nicholas C., *The People's Republic of Albania* (1968); Pollo, Stefanaq, and Puto, Arben, *History of Albania* (1980); Prifti, Peter R., *Socialist Albania Since 1944* (1978).

Albano, Lake

Lake Albano is a crater lake in the Alban Hills, southeast of Rome, Italy. At an altitude of 293 m (961 ft), it is 5 km² (2 mi²) in area and has a maximum depth of 170 m (558 ft). It is fed by underground springs and drained by a tunnel built in the 4th century BC. Among the villas along its rocky shores is Castel Gandolfo, the summer residence of the popes.

Albany (Georgia)

Albany (1980 pop., 74,059) is a city on the Flint River in southwestern Georgia and is the seat of Dougherty County. Crops from the surrounding area, processed in the city, include Spanish peanuts, cotton, and pecans. Aircraft and farm tools are manufactured. Albany State College, Albany Junior College, and Albany Naval Air Station are located there. Founded in 1836, the city was named for Albany, N.Y.

Albany (New York)

Albany, the capital of New York State, is located at the confluence of the HUDSON RIVER and the NEW YORK STATE BARGE CANAL system in the east central part of the state. It is a U.S. port of entry and also serves as the seat of Albany County. It has a population of 101,727 (1980).

Located at the eastern terminal of the Erie Canal, Albany serves as an important port connecting shipping between the Great Lakes and Canada and Atlantic ports. Since the opening (1932) of the Port of Albany, the city has been an important maritime center. Industrial development in the area is extensive and highly diversified, with the manufacture of automotive parts, textiles, chemicals, drugs, plastics, machine tools, felt, and paper. Operation of the state government also adds substantially to the economy.

Although a number of small forts were established in the area from 1540, the first permanent settlement was in 1624, when a group of Walloon families built Fort Orange. A Dutch colony until 1664 when the British assumed control, Albany was renamed in honor of the duke of York and Albany, later James II of England. Albany became the permanent state capital in 1797.

Albany, State University of New York at: see NEW YORK, STATE UNIVERSITY OF.

Albany Congress

The Albany Congress was a meeting held at Albany, N.Y., in June–July 1754, attended by representatives of the colonies of New York, Pennsylvania, Maryland, Massachusetts, Connecticut, Rhode Island, and New Hampshire and of the five Iroquois nations. Although its purpose was to cement ties between the colonies and the Iroquois in preparation for war with the French, it is chiefly remembered as the occasion when Benjamin FRANKLIN presented his Albany Plan of Union. Franklin proposed that the colonies form a self-governing federation under the British crown. Even though the plan was not realized, in many respects it foreshadowed the later union of the American states.

Albategnius: see BATTANI, AL-.

albatross

Albatross is the common name for large web-footed marine birds belonging to the family Diomedeidae, order Procellariiformes. Some of the 13 or 14 species also are known as mollymawks or gooney birds. Albatrosses are concentrated in southern oceans but are also seen in warmer northern waters and may migrate farther north in the summer. Their narrow, graceful wings—wingspan may exceed 3.7 m (12 ft), more than any other living bird—make them superb gliders. Albatrosses often travel great distances. Along with the related PETRELS and SHEARWATERS, albatrosses are the most marine of birds. They sleep on the ocean's surface, drink seawater, and subsist on squid and other small marine life. Some are scavengers, trailing ships for their refuse.

Albatrosses range in length from 50 to 125 cm (20 to 50 in). Plumage varies from white through dark gray or gray-brown, with combinations of all three being common. The large hooked bill, covered with horny plates, has characteristically prominent tubular nostrils. The three front toes are webbed, and the rear toe may be absent or vestigial. Albatrosses live on land only during the breeding season, usually nesting in colonies on the shores of remote oceanic islands. Courtship displays are highly elaborate. Incubation of a single large white egg lasts two to three months.

Because of the albatross theme in Samuel Taylor Coleridge's *Rime of the Ancient Mariner*, the bird's name has become a metaphor for a troublesome burden.   GARY D. SCHNELL

Bibliography: Alexander, Wilfrid B., *Birds of the Ocean*, rev. ed. (1963); Van Tyne, Josselyn, and Berger, Andrew J., *Fundamentals of Ornithology* (1976).

The albatross is one of the largest of all birds. It may remain at sea for months. Some travel entirely around the globe between mating seasons. The black-browed albatross (top), D. melanophrys, has a 2.1-m (7-ft) wingspan. The head of the wandering albatross (bottom), D. exulans, shows the characteristic hooked beak and nostril tubes.

albedo   [al-bee'-doh]

Albedo is a measure of the reflecting power of an object or surface. It is mathematically defined as the ratio of the amount of light reflected from a surface to the amount that is incident upon it, often expressed as a percentage. A surface that reflects half the light it receives has an albedo of 0.5 or 50%. The average value of the Earth's albedo is 39%, largely because of the high reflecting power of clouds, snow cover, and deserts. Planets with cloudy atmospheres have a high value for the albedo: Venus, 76%; Jupiter, 51%; Saturn, 50%; Uranus, 66%; and Neptune, 62%. Rocky surfaces absorb most of the light they receive; hence, the Moon has an albedo of 7%, and Mercury of 6%. The slightly higher albedo of Mars, 15%, is caused by the planet's thin atmosphere.

Bibliography: Mitton, Simon, ed., *Cambridge Encyclopedia of Astronomy* (1977); Pasachoff, Jay M., *Astronomy Now* (1978).

Albee, Edward   [al'-bee]

Edward Franklin Albee, b. Mar. 12, 1928, is one of the most important American playwrights of the 1960s and the one most closely identified with the THEATER OF THE ABSURD. His plays are characterized by sharp dialogue, biting satire, often illogical confrontations between characters, and unconventional theatrical effects.

His first play, ZOO STORY (1958), produced in West Berlin in 1959 and in New York City the next year, is a short, ominous two-character play about how the failure of communication leads to violence. *The Sandbox* (1959) and *The American Dream* (1960) are closely related one-act plays that absurdly parody family life and the American dream of success. *The Death of Bessie Smith* (1960) is a comment on racial prejudice and human cruelty. Albee attained popular and critical success with his first full-length Broadway play, WHO'S AFRAID OF VIRGINIA WOOLF? (1962; film, 1966). Here he shows two couples tensely locked in a painful verbal and psychological duel that strips away all their illusions. It presents in mature form the concerns of Albee's early short plays. *Tiny Alice*

Edward Albee, a contemporary American playwright, amuses audiences with his witty yet biting use of dialogue. His first full-length play, Who's Afraid of Virginia Woolf?, won most of the major dramatic awards of Broadway's 1962 season. He was denied the Pulitzer Prize, perhaps because of the play's explicit sexual references.

(1964) is a complex, puzzling work about sex, morality, and metaphysics, which proved to be less successful than his earlier plays.

Albee's other plays include two Pulitzer Prize winners, *A Delicate Balance* (1966) and *Seascape* (1975); the experimental *Box* and *Quotations from Chairman Mao Tse-tung (Box-Mao-Box,* 1968) and *All Over* (1971); and such adaptations as *Ballad of the Sad Café* (1963) from Carson McCullers's novella.

Bibliography: Bigsby, C. W., ed., *Edward Albee: A Collection of Critical Essays* (1975); Hayman, Ronald, *Edward Albee* (1977); Paolucci, Anne, *From Tension to Tonic: The Plays of Edward Albee* (1972); Stenz, Anita M., *Edward Albee: The Poet of Loss* (1978).

Albéniz, Isaac

Isaac Albéniz, b. May 29, 1860, d. May 18, 1909, was a Spanish composer and piano virtuoso who gave his first public performance at the age of 4. He left home at the age of 13 and traveled as far as Cuba and the United States, supporting himself by concertizing. Like Enrique Granados, Albéniz was a student of Felipe Pedrell, the father of the nationalistic movement in Spanish music. In 1893, Albéniz settled in Paris, where he was influenced by the French composers Paul Dukas and Vincent d'Indy. Although he composed several operas, including *Pepita Jiménez* (1896), Albéniz excelled at writing for the piano. His most important work is *Iberia* (1906–09), a set of 12 piano pieces inspired by the music and dance rhythms of Spain, especially that of Andalusia.

Bibliography: Chase, Gilbert, *The Music of Spain,* 2d ed. (1960).

Alberdi, Juan Bautista

Juan Bautista Alberdi, b. Aug. 29, 1810, d. June 18, 1884, was an Argentinian political philosopher. In his most famous work, *Bases y puntos de partida para la organización política de la república Argentina* (Bases and Starting Points for the Political Organization of the Argentine Republic, 1852), he set forth many of the fundamental principles that were incorporated into the Argentine constitution of 1853. He spent the years 1838–52 in exile as an opponent of the dictator Juan Manuel de Rosas. From 1852 to 1861 he served as a diplomat in Europe and the United States for President Justo José de Urquiza. In his writings Alberdi stressed the need for a strong federal system of government. He also argued that economic development made it necessary to encourage immigration and the influx of foreign capital.

Albers, Josef

The German-born American painter Josef Albers, b. Mar. 19, 1888, d. Mar. 25, 1976, contributed much to modern art through his investigation of color and light perception in nonfigurative painting.

Albers taught design at the BAUHAUS School in Dessau and Berlin from 1923 to 1933; his association with the constructivist movement (see CONSTRUCTIVISM) is derived from this background, although he was not concerned merely with formal abstraction. Albers's experimentation related optics and the natural phenomena of color and light. His first creations at the Bauhaus were composed of glass shards that could not produce subtle gradations of tone, and his later painting demonstrated his proclivity for flat geometry and pure, unmixed color. He is widely considered the father of HARD-EDGE PAINTING.

Albers arrived in the United States in 1933 to teach at Black Mountain College in North Carolina, where he taught (and occasionally dismissed) many of today's avant-garde artists. He subsequently served as a visiting professor at various U.S. universities. From 1950 to 1960 he headed the Department of Design at Yale University. Yale published Albers's major theoretical writings, including his monumental *Interaction of Color* (1963). The culmination of Albers's development is his famous *Homage to the Square* series, on which he worked from 1949 until his death in 1976. Typified by *Homage to the Square: Insert* (1950; The National Collection of Fine Arts,

Homage to the Square: Green Scent *(1963) is an example of Josef Albers's experimentation with the relationships between light and color within a geometric framework. Albers, one of the original teachers in the German Bauhaus, began work on his "Homage to the Square" series of geometric abstractionist paintings in 1949. (Peter Ludwig Collection, Wallraf-Richartz Museum, Cologne.)*

Washington, D.C.), the corpus of his work is concerned not with emotional expression but with the physical fact and psychic effects of seeing.   HARRY RAND

Bibliography: Albers, Josef, *Interaction of Color* (1963) and *Josef Albers: Formulation, Articulation* (1972); Bucher, François, *Josef Albers: Despite Straight Lines* (1961; rev. ed. 1978); Gomringer, Eugen, *Josef Albers, His Work As a Contribution to Visual Articulation in the Twentieth Century* (1969); Wissman, Fronia, et al., *Albers* (1978).

See also: ABSTRACT ART; MODERN ART.

Albert, Carl

Carl Bert Albert, b. McAlester, Okla., May 10, 1908, served as speaker of the U.S. House of Representatives from 1971 to 1977. A Democrat, he represented a rural district of his native Oklahoma in the House from 1947 to 1977, when he retired. He had been a Rhodes scholar and a lawyer before entering politics.

Albert, Eugen d'

Eugen d'Albert, b. Apr. 10, 1864, d. Mar. 3, 1932, was a French-born German pianist who also became a prominent composer, conductor, and editor. He was married six times and was notorious for his fiery temperament. Franz Liszt was among his teachers. In addition to giving concerts, he conducted in Weimar and, from 1907 on, was director of the music conservatory in Berlin. He is remembered for his melodramatic opera *Tiefland* (1903), his performances of Beethoven, and his editions and arrangements of J. S. Bach.   F. E. KIRBY

Bibliography: Schonberg, Harold C., *The Great Pianists* (1963).

Albert, Lake

Lake Albert (Bantu: Albert Nyanza) is located in east central Africa on the border of Zaire and Uganda. Cradled in the western branch of the Great Rift Valley, the shallow, saline lake lies at an altitude of about 610 m (2,000 ft) and is bordered by tall, forested cliffs in the west and east. Lake Albert is 160 km (100 mi) long and 35 km (22 mi) wide. It is fed by the Victoria Nile and the Semliki River and is drained by the Albert Nile into the White Nile. Sir Samuel White BAKER discovered the lake in 1864.

Albert I, King of the Belgians

Albert I, b. Apr. 8, 1875, d. Feb. 17, 1934, king of the Belgians (1909-34), is remembered especially for his strong leadership during World War I. He married (1900) Elizabeth, daughter of the duke of Bavaria, and succeeded LEOPOLD II, his uncle, to the Belgian throne in 1909. In August 1914, when the German armies demanded right of passage through Belgium, Albert refused the ultimatum and assumed personal command of the Belgian armed forces in resisting the German advance. He remained in the small, unoccupied area of Belgium throughout the war, and in September 1918 led Belgian and French troops in the final Allied offensive.

After the war, Albert promoted the economic reconstruction of Belgium and helped introduce (1926) a new monetary system. His death in a mountain-climbing accident (1934) was deeply mourned. He was succeeded by his son, Leopold III.

Bibliography: Cammaerts, Émile, *Albert of Belgium, Defender of Right* (1935).

Albert I, Margrave of Brandenburg (Albert the Bear)

Albert I, or Albert the Bear, b. c.1100, d. Nov. 18, 1170, margrave of Brandenburg, was one of the leaders of the 12th-century German conquests in eastern Europe called the DRANG NACH OSTEN. He inherited the Saxon estates of his father and, after services to Holy Roman Emperor LOTHAIR II, received (1134) the Saxon Nordmark, lying east of the junction of the Elbe and Havel rivers. Although embroiled in rivalry with the WELF dukes of Saxony, Albert campaigned successfully against the Slavic Wends. When their prince Pribislav died childless in 1150, Albert incorporated Pribislav's principality into his domain and took the title of margrave.

Albert, Prince Consort of England

Albert, called the Prince Consort, was the husband of Queen VICTORIA of Britain. The son of the Duke of Saxe-Coburg-Gotha, he was born on Aug. 26, 1819, near Coburg, Bavaria. He married the young Victoria in 1840. As her closest advisor, Albert exercised a restraining influence on the impulsive queen, especially in political matters. Among the political leaders of the period, Albert worked well with Sir Robert PEEL but quarreled frequently with Viscount PALMERSTON. In the TRENT AFFAIR of 1861 the prince actually moderated the hostility of Palmerston's government toward the United States.

Albert was a patron of the arts and sciences and one of the organizers of the Great Exhibition of 1851. His zeal for public improvements, coupled with his industriousness and stern moralism, in many ways set the tone of mid-Victorian England. Albert's death on Dec. 14, 1861, partly the result of overwork, deeply affected Victoria, who went into seclusion for several years.

Bibliography: Bennet, Daphne, *King without a Crown: Albert Prince Consort of England, 1819-1861* (1977); Bolitho, Hector, *Albert, Prince Consort*, rev. ed. (1970); Pound, Reginald, *Albert: A Biography of the Prince Consort* (1973); Richardson, Joanna, *Victoria and Albert: A Study of a Marriage* (1977).

Albert I, King of Germany

Albert I, b. c.1250, king of the Germans (1298-1308), was the son of RUDOLF I, the first HABSBURG to wear the German crown. In 1282 Rudolf granted Albert the duchies of Austria and Styria. When Rudolf died in 1291, however, the German princes, fearful of the growing Habsburg power, denied Albert the crown and instead elected Adolf of Nassau as king. Discontent with Adolf soon enabled Albert to win over the princes, who deposed Adolf in 1298 and elected Albert king. The new king defeated the old at Göllheim (July 1298), where Adolf was slain.

As king, Albert attempted to add Holland and Zealand to the Habsburg domains. This unsuccessful effort, coupled with his alliance with the French king PHILIP IV, provoked a revolt in the Rhineland that was backed by Pope BONIFACE VIII. The

revolt was finally crushed in 1302, and the following year Albert secured papal confirmation of his election in return for an oath of obedience to the pope.

Albert was assassinated on May 1, 1308, by accomplices of his nephew, John Parracide of Swabia. He was succeeded by HENRY VII.

Albert II, King of Germany

Albert II, b. Aug. 10, 1397, d. Oct. 27, 1439, king of Germany (1438-39), succeeded his father-in-law, Holy Roman Emperor SIGISMUND, as king of Hungary and Bohemia as well as Germany. His brief reign was devoted to suppressing a revolt in Bohemia and fighting the Turks in Hungary, where he died from dysentery.

Albert, First Duke of Prussia

Albert, b. May 17, 1490, d. Mar. 20, 1568, was the first duke of PRUSSIA. A member of the HOHENZOLLERN family, he was chosen (1511) grand master of the TEUTONIC KNIGHTS. On becoming a Protestant, however, he secularized (1525) the lands of the knights, converting them into the hereditary duchy of Prussia.

Alberta

Alberta is the westernmost of the Prairie Provinces of Canada. It stretches about 1,215 km (755 mi) north from Montana to the Northwest Territories. Alberta is the fourth largest province of Canada and the fourth most populous, with one of the largest growth rates. Traditionally associated with wheat-growing and cattle ranching, Alberta is today especially important because of its fuel resources, the largest in Canada.

The first European explorer to penetrate the region is thought to have been Anthony Henday, in 1754, and the first European settlement was a fur-trading post established in 1778 on the ATHABASCA RIVER in the northeastern part of today's province. In 1882 Alberta was made a district of the former Northwest Territories and named for a daughter of Queen Victoria who was the wife of the then governor-general of Canada.

THE LAND AND RESOURCES

The eastern three-fourths of Alberta's terrain is made up of plains, which rise from less than 300 m (1,000 ft) in the northeast to more than 1,220 m (4,000 ft) in the southwest. The plains vary locally from very flat and extensive old lake bottoms to rolling landscapes with many lakes and depressions. These landforms reflect the former presence of Pleistocene ice sheets, which, at maximum extent, covered all the province except for a few high pockets. In places, hilly or plateau areas (for example, Cypress Hills and Swan Hills) may rise to 600 m (2,000 ft) above the general surface of the plain.

To the west of the plains, an area of foothill ridges of higher elevation is bordered by the abrupt east-facing rock wall of the ROCKY MOUNTAINS. The Rockies, with several peaks over 3,660 m (12,000 ft), make up the other major physical region of the province.

Geologically the province includes almost a complete range in age, from the ancient Precambrian of the CANADIAN SHIELD in the extreme northeast corner through progressively younger formations in the southwest, including Tertiary deposits.

Soils. Soil types are arranged in concentric arcs from the southeastern part of Alberta and reflect the moisture and natural vegetation patterns. Brown prairie soils are succeeded by rich black soils with a deep humus layer in the central parts of the province. However, more than two-thirds of Alberta, in the northern and western sectors, is marked by podzols, or gray-wooded soils, which are less fertile.

Lakes and Rivers. Most of southern and central Alberta drains eastward into Hudson Bay via the NELSON River system, which in Alberta includes such major rivers as the North Saskatchewan and the South Saskatchewan. West central and northern Alberta is drained into the Arctic Ocean by the MACKENZIE RIVER system, which includes such important rivers as the

PEACE, Athabasca, and Hay. A small sector of the extreme south drains into the Milk River, which is part of the Missouri-Mississippi system. Groundwater aids irrigation, as do diverted mountain-origin rivers in parts of southern Alberta.

Lakes are especially numerous in the central and northern parts of the province. Lake Claire and Lesser Slave Lake are the two largest lakes wholly within Alberta. The western third of Lake ATHABASCA also lies within the province. Lake LOUISE in the Rocky Mountains is known for its beautiful scenery.

Climate. Alberta has a continental climate with long, cold winters and short, cool summers, although summers are longer and warmer in the southeastern quarter. At EDMONTON the average January temperature is−20° C (−4° F) and in July is 23° C (74° F). Precipitation is moderate to light, with the southeast being particularly dry. The average annual precipitation for Edmonton is 440 mm (17 in), much of which falls as snow in the winter. The western foothills and mountains receive more abundant precipitation (more than 500 mm/20 in).

A distinctive local feature that often moderates the winter temperatures of southern Alberta in the foothills and western plains is the CHINOOK, a warm westerly wind that descends the eastern face of the Rockies and raises local temperatures dramatically.

Vegetation and Animal Life. Two-thirds of Alberta is forested. The grasslands of the southeast reflect that region's warmer summers and sparser precipitation. Most of Alberta's forest is a mixture of conifers (white spruce, jack pine) and deciduous trees (aspen, poplar, white birch). However, conifers become dominant in the northeast (the taiga, or boreal coniferous forest) and in the foothills and lower mountains (subalpine forest). In the mountains, TUNDRA occurs above the tree line.

Surviving grassland animals include pronghorn antelope, ground squirrels, and coyotes. Forested areas include a variety of fur-bearing animals (bear, otter, ermine, beaver) and big game animals (moose, caribou, elk, deer), as well as North America's largest surviving herd of wild buffalo.

Resources. Alberta's major natural resources are fuels, forests,

ALBERTA

LAND. Area: 661,185 km² (255,285 mi²); rank: 4th. Capital: Edmonton (1983 est. pop., 560,085). Largest city: Calgary (1983 est. pop., 620,692). Municipalities: 351. Elevations: highest—3,747 m (12,294 ft), at Mount Columbia; lowest—176 m (576 ft).

PEOPLE. Population (1984 est.): 2,345,100; rank: 4th; density: 3.5 persons per km² (9.2 per mi²). Distrib. (1982): 77% metro., 23% nonmetro. Av. ann. change (1976-81): +4.4%.

EDUCATION. Enrollment (1982 est.): elem. and sec.—451,190; higher—49,580. Inst. of higher education (1982): 23.

ECONOMY. Total personal income (1978): $16.4 billion; rank: 4th. Median family income (1980): $18,923. Labor force distribution (1982): agriculture—80,000; manufacturing—96,000 persons; wholesale and retail trade—190,000; government—74,000; services—317,000; transportation and utilities—87,000; finance, insurance, and real estate—71,000; construction—101,000. Agriculture: income (1978)—$649 million. Fishing: value (1977)—$634,000. Forestry: sawn timber volume (1981)—666 million board feet. Mining: value (1979)—$12 billion. Manufacturing: value added (1978)—$2.4 billion.

GOVERNMENT (1984). Lieutenant Governor: Frank Lynch-Stanton. Premier: Peter Lougheed, Progressive Conservative. Parliament: Senate—6 members; House of Commons—21 Progressive Conservatives. Provincial legislature: 79 members. Admitted to Confederation: Sept. 1, 1905, with Saskatchewan, the 8th and 9th provinces.

The Rocky Mountains provide a dramatic background to a freshly harvested field of wheat near Alberta's border with Montana. A very similar scene is depicted on the provincial coat of arms, suggesting the traditional importance of wheat to the economic life of Alberta.

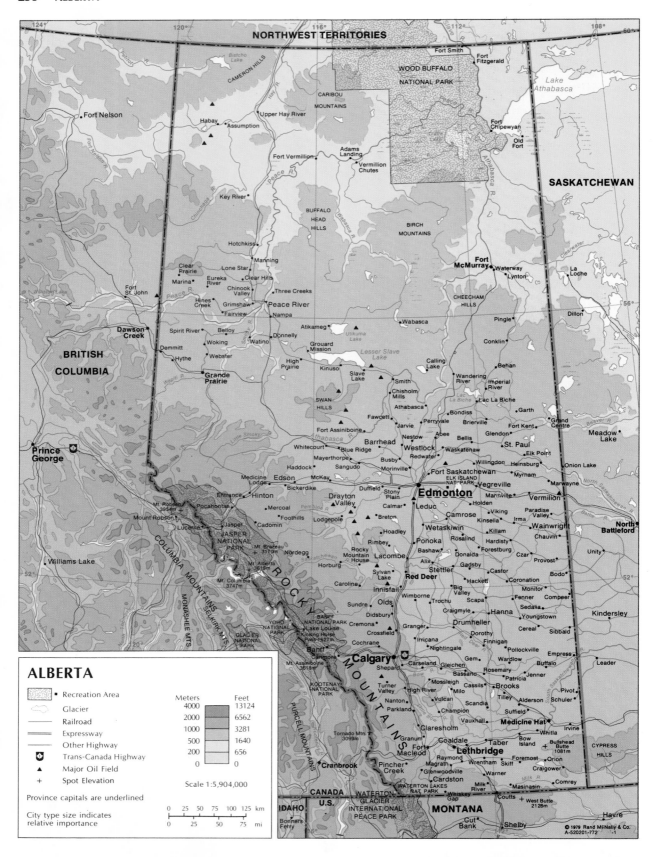

ALBERTA

■ Recreation Area

Glacier

Railroad

Expressway

Other Highway

Trans-Canada Highway

▲ Major Oil Field

+ Spot Elevation

Province capitals are underlined

City type size indicates
relative importance

Meters	Feet
4000	13124
2000	6562
1000	3281
500	1640
200	656
0	0

Scale 1:5,904,000

0 25 50 75 100 125 km

0   25   50   75 mi

© 1979 Rand McNally & Co.
A-520201-772   -1

and productive soils. The province's water resources, which include the source regions for parts of the continent's major river systems, are particularly important, especially to the other provinces to the east. Much of the mountain and foothill zones are included in national or provincial parks and are protected by the government.

ECONOMIC ACTIVITY

Since the early 1950s, when Alberta's economy was dominated by agriculture, mining and manufacturing have grown so rapidly that each now generates a net product value greater than that of agricultural activities.

Manufacturing and Mining. Until recently, Alberta's manufacturing concentrated on processing agricultural products. Food and beverage industries are still the most important manufacturing group (about 36% of the total value). Since the discovery (1947) of the Leduc oil fields near Edmonton, however, both the value and diversity of manufacturing have increased greatly. In the early 1980s about 84% of all Canadian oil production and more than 84% of natural-gas production came from Alberta. Petroleum-product processing is now the second most important industrial group, and it furnishes raw materials for a new petrochemical industry. Preparations to exploit oil-sands resources in the north began in the 1970s.

Alberta contains 48% of Canada's huge minable coal reserves, with this resource underlying most of the southern half of the province. Although production almost ceased after the great petroleum development, it began to prosper again in the 1970s through sales to Japan.

Agriculture and Forestry. Cattle ranching, in the foothills and the drier south, is an important sector of the economy. Wheat and barley are the principal grain crops. Irrigation farming, which is centered in Lethbridge, produces vegetables, sugar beets, and livestock feed. Central Alberta concentrates on mixed farming and dairying, with cash crops and seed production in the Peace River district to the northwest. Sawmills, utilizing both hardwoods and softwoods, operate in the forested areas of the north and west.

Tourism. Three spectacular national parks in the Rocky Mountains—Waterton Lakes, Banff, and Jasper—draw visitors from all over the world. Local attractions, such as the numerous rodeos, Calgary Stampede, and Edmonton Klondike Days, as well as sport fishing and hunting, also contribute to the influx of tourists.

Transportation. In 1976, Alberta had about 11,000 km (7,000 mi) of paved highways. The province is crossed by two transcontinental highway systems (the Trans-Canada Highway and the Yellowhead Highway) and by two transcontinental railroads (the Canadian Pacific Railway and the Canadian National Railways). Alberta is crisscrossed by a network of oil and gas pipelines, the major focus of which is Edmonton. These include the interprovincial Pipe Line to Montreal and the Trans Mountain Pipe Line to Burnaby, Vancouver.

PEOPLE

The population of Alberta has doubled since the end of World War II, when it was about 33% urban; it is now 74% urban. Much of the population increase is a result of the expanded economic opportunities created by the oil boom. The province has received large numbers of immigrants from other parts of Canada and from abroad.

Alberta's population is 94% English speaking; 5% speak English and French. Major ethnic groups include British (46.7%), German (14.2%), Ukrainian (8.3%), Scandinavian (6.3%), and French (5.8%). Native Indians make up 2.7% of the total population and include Plains Indians, such as the BLACKFOOT, and Woodlands Indians, such as the CREE.

Education and Cultural Activity. Much of the provincial income from oil and gas sales has been channeled to education and culture. Alberta has four provincial universities. The oldest and largest is the University of Alberta (1906), in Edmonton. The University of Calgary was established after World War II as an affiliate of the University of Alberta but has been an independent institution since 1966.

Alberta enjoys a variety of cultural institutions. The major collections in the province are housed in the modern Provincial Museum and Archives in Edmonton and the Glenbow-Alberta Institute in CALGARY. Both Edmonton and Calgary have symphony orchestras and professional theater, ballet, and opera companies. The province is well served by communications networks. Special radio-telephone service connects even the remote corners of the province.

Places of Interest. Recreation and sports areas are spread throughout the province and include national parks and provincial parks. Wood Buffalo National Park in northernmost Alberta is, at 44,800 km² (17,300 mi²), Canada's largest national park. Within its wilderness area, besides the buffalo, are the nesting grounds of the near-extinct whooping crane. Resorts are popular in the mountains and the lake areas of central Alberta. The oldest and best known resort is BANFF.

GOVERNMENT

Alberta, like other provinces and Canada as a whole, is a parliamentary democracy, without a formal written constitution. It is governed by a Legislative Assembly of 79 members, with an Executive Council, or cabinet, of 24 members drawn from the Assembly. The Executive Council is headed by the premier, who is the leader of the majority party in the Assembly. The SOCIAL CREDIT PARTY dominated Alberta's government from 1935 to 1971, when the Conservatives—under the premiership of Peter Lougheed—assumed control.

The glacier-fed Athabasca River flows past the Canadian Rockies in Jasper National Park. The scenic preserve, which lies along Alberta's border with British Columbia, is the second largest national park in Canada.

(Right) *Edmonton, Alberta's capital, has expanded rapidly following the discovery of oil nearby. Because it is now Canada's northernmost major city, Edmonton is expected to become a focal point of efforts to develop the natural resources of the Canadian Arctic.*

(Below) *Rodeo events highlight the Calgary Exhibition and Stampede, an annual celebration of international fame that also features livestock shows and a festive parade. Calgary, settled as an outpost of the Royal Canadian Mounted Police, is Alberta's largest city.*

Local government within the province is provided by 30 counties and 18 municipal districts. The sparsely settled areas are included in 22 improvement districts, administered by the provincial department of municipal affairs.

HISTORY

Before European settlement two distinct Indian groups lived in Alberta; each had a culture that corresponded to the natural vegetation patterns of the environment. In the grasslands of the southeast were the Plains Indians, who depended mainly on buffalo hunting. They included the Blackfoot Confederacy—which comprised the Blood, Peigan, and North Blackfoot—and the Sarcee, Stoney, and Plains Cree. In the forested regions, with their more varied hunting patterns, were the Woodland Cree, Beaver, and Chipewyan tribes.

For about 125 years after the visit (1754) of the first European, Alberta was mainly of interest as a fur-producing region. The few European inhabitants were based in trading posts that were established on rivers in forested areas. Most such posts did not last long, although a few survived to become modern cities (for example, Edmonton). The Hudson's Bay Company administered the region during this period.

For a few years after 1870, when the vast area of western Canada was sold by the Hudson's Bay Company to the Canadian government, whiskey traders from the United States moved into the southern parts of Alberta and began selling illegal liquor to the Indians. To stop this practice and establish Canadian authority in the area, the North-West Mounted Police (now the Royal Canadian Mounted Police) was formed and in 1874 marched west to build small forts. Fort Macleod (1874) was the first such fort in Alberta, and Calgary had its origin (1875) in a similar fort. With this security, and after treaties had been signed with the Indians, large ranches were established in the southern grasslands and foothills region.

The arrival of the transcontinental Canadian Pacific Railway at Calgary in 1883, and the rapid construction of other railroad lines soon after, launched the large-scale settlement of Alberta. The settlement process was generally peaceful and orderly. An interruption occurred in 1885 when unrest among Indians and métis (people of Indian and European ancestry) over land ownership flared briefly into the Riel Rebellion (see RIEL, LOUIS). On Sept. 1, 1905, the district of Alberta, with some adjacent territory, was made a province of Canada. It remained a predominantly agricultural province until the development of the petroleum and natural-gas resources in the post–World War II period.

During the early 1980s strains between Alberta and the federal government developed over control of the province's energy resources. In 1980 the federal government announced a new National Energy Program designed to make Canada self-sufficient in energy and to increase the federal share of revenues from exploitation. In protest Alberta reduced its oil production in January 1981, and again in June, necessitating increased foreign oil imports. Although an accord was reached on oil prices in September 1981, the energy dispute and other conflicts had already resulted in a secessionist movement in the province.

WILLIAM C. WONDERS

Bibliography: Frederickson, Olive, and East, Ben, *The Silence of the North* (1972); Hardy, W. G., ed., *Alberta, a Natural History* (1977); Kroetsch, R., *Alberta* (1968); MacGregor, J. G., *A History of Alberta* (1972); Smith, P. J., ed., *The Prairie Provinces* (1972); Warkentin, J., ed., *Canada, a Geographical Interpretation* (1968); Wonders, W. C., et al., *Atlas of Alberta* (1969).

Alberta, University of

Established in 1906, the University of Alberta (enrollment: 23,210; library: 1,790,000 volumes) is a coeducational institution in Edmonton, Alberta, Canada. In 1966 it was reorganized and was separated from its normal school, which became the University of Calgary. The University of Alberta grants undergraduate and graduate degrees and has several professional schools. It administers the Banff School of Fine Arts (1933) in Banff, Alberta, and three theological schools.

Alberti, Leon Battista

Leon Battista Alberti, b. Genoa, Feb. 14, 1404, d. Apr. 25, 1472, was an Italian humanist, architect, painter, sculptor, and musician who contributed greatly to RENAISSANCE ART theory. He is called the father of modern architectural theory, and is probably the first person to whom the term *Renaissance man* can be applied.

Alberti received his humanistic training at the University of Padua and studied law at Bologna. In 1428 he was an aide of the papal legates to Burgundy and Germany. Between 1428 and 1443 Alberti wrote, in Latin and Italian, love poems and dialogues, a Latin comedy, fables, and treatises on virtue, sculpture, agriculture, the care of horses, law, and marriage. One of the finest of these is *Della tranquilità dell' animo* (On Peace of Mind, 1442). In 1431 Alberti became papal secretary in Rome, where he began the study of ancient monuments. Three years later he moved to Florence, becoming a member

The facade of the Palazzo Rucellai in Florence, Italy, was designed by Leon Battista Alberti and built about 1446–51. The palazzo is an example of the Renaissance use of the three classical architectural orders (Doric, Ionic, and Corinthian), which are seen in the three levels of pilasters.

of the inner circle of humanists in Tuscany, among them the sculptor DONATELLO, and was recognized as an authority on art and classical literature. In Florence, Alberti became especially interested in the work of the sculptor-architect Filippo BRUNELLESCHI (1377–1446), to whom he dedicated the Italian edition of *On Painting* (*Della pittura*, 1436), a treatise on the theory and technique of painting. The 1435 Latin edition is dedicated to Gian Francesco GONZAGA of Milan.

Sigismondo MALATESTA, lord of Rimini, commissioned Alberti to redesign the exterior of the medieval church of San Francesco in Rimini as a shrine to the Malatesta court members and family; it is now known as the Temple Malatestiano and bears the date 1450. Alberti did similar reconstruction on the churches of Santa Maria Novella (Florence, 1456) and San Sebastian (Mantua, 1460). His original architectural designs include the Palazzo Rucellai (Florence, 1446–51) and the Church of Sant' Andrea (Mantua, designed 1470).

Alberti returned to Rome in 1452 as a recorder of pagan monuments and papal consultant in remodeling medieval churches, including Old ST. PETER'S BASILICA.

Alberti's primary literary work is *De re aedificatoria*, a 10-book Latin treatise on architecture. To Alberti, beauty was the result of harmonious proportions, simplicity, and the skillful use of classical ornamentation. The treatise was completed about 1452 and published posthumously in 1485, although it was probably known in manuscript to Alberti's contemporaries. The work is considered a major modern contribution to architecture and influenced the development of architectural style in the Renaissance.

Bibliography: Alberti, Leon Battista, *On Painting*, trans. by John R. Spencer, rev. ed. (1966); and *Ten Books on Architecture*, ed. by Joseph Rykwert (1955); Gadol, Joan, *Leon Battista Alberti: Universal Man of the Early Renaissance* (1969); Stokes, Adrian D., *Art and Science: A Study of Alberti, Piero della Francesca, and Giorgione* (1949); Westfall, Carroll W., *In This Most Perfect Paradise: Alberti, Nicholas V, and the Invention of Conscious Urban Planning in Rome, 1447–55* (1974).

See also: ARCHITECTURE; ITALIAN ART AND ARCHITECTURE.

Alberti, Rafael

Rafael Alberti, b. Dec. 16, 1902, is a Spanish poet who abandoned his first career as a painter to write poetry. His first volume, *Marinero en tierra* (Sailor Ashore, 1925), won Spain's National Prize for literature for 1924–25. Other early works include *Cal y canto* (Quicklime and Song, 1927), which was influenced by the baroque poet Luis de GÓNGORA Y ARGOTE, and *Concerning the Angels* (1928; Eng. trans., 1967), an introspective work with elements of SURREALISM. Alberti became a Communist about 1930, and since then his poetry has reflected his strong social and political concerns. He participated in the Spanish Civil War on the loyalist side and after the fall of the Republic in 1939 became an exile. He lived for a while in France and Argentina and since 1964 has lived in Italy. Alberti has published several other volumes of poetry and an autobiography, *The Lost Grove: Autobiography of a Spanish Poet in Exile* (1959; Eng. trans., 1976).

Bibliography: Alberti, Rafael, *Selected Poems*, ed. and trans. by Ben Belitt (1966); Bowra, C. M., *The Creative Experiment* (1949).

Albertina

The Albertina, in Vienna, is the state collection of GRAPHIC ARTS, the largest in the world, named after its founder, Duke Albert of Saxe-Teschen (1738–1822). This extraordinarily rich collection of prints, drawings, and watercolors was amassed through Albert's purchases of a great many private European collections. After the fall of the Austrian monarchy, the archduke's collection was merged with the imperial HABSBURG court collections, to be officially named the Albertina in 1920. Housed in Saxe-Teschen's splendid palace (1804) in the center of Vienna, the Albertina is primarily a huge and growing study collection of more than 40,000 drawings and more than 1 million prints. It encompasses the finest achievements in European graphic arts from the 15th century to the present day. Unusually large holdings in works by DÜRER, MICHELANGELO, RAPHAEL, RUBENS, REMBRANDT, and many later masters of European art (works by American and by Oriental artists were added in the 20th century) are particularly strong features of this famed collection. The Albertina's holdings also include superb miniature paintings and architectural drawings and a large reference library. STEFANIE WINKELBAUER

Bibliography: Koschatzky, Walter, *The Albertina in Vienna* (1969).

Albertus Magnus, Saint

Albert, b. *c.*1200, d. Nov. 15, 1280, was a medieval German (Swabian) theologian, scholastic philosopher, and scientist who is best known as the teacher of Thomas AQUINAS. In his own day, however, Albertus had greater renown than his illustrious pupil. Already called "the Great" (Magnus), Albertus was accepted as an authority equal to ARISTOTLE in philosophy and was known as "the universal doctor" for his work in natural science.

St. Albertus Magnus, medieval philosopher and theologian, was acclaimed for his commentaries on Aristotle. Depicted here in a fresco by Tommasso de Modena, he taught St. Thomas Aquinas at Cologne.

While studying arts at Padua, he was received (1223) into the DOMINICAN Order and spent the next 18 years studying and teaching theology at Cologne and other Rhineland priories. He received his doctorate at the University of Paris in 1245 and taught there for three years. His extraordinary abilities were recognized in 1248 when he was assigned to open the first great center of learning in Germany at Cologne, which eventually became the University of Cologne. Although Albert was provincial of the Dominicans (1254–57), bishop of Regensburg (1260–62), and preacher of the Crusades (1263–64), his main work was the rewriting of all of Aristotle's philosophy. In doing so, he added new areas of investigation. He staunchly advocated the autonomy of human reason and natural experience in defense of the Christian faith. His collected writings on Scripture, philosophy, and natural science fill more than 40 volumes. His work on Aristotle is one of the cornerstones of the REALIST philosophy that constitutes the synthesis of Thomas Aquinas.

Albert was beatified by Gregory XV in 1622. On Dec. 16, 1931, Pope Pius XI declared him a saint and a DOCTOR OF THE CHURCH. Feast day: Nov. 15.   JAMES A. WEISHEIPL

Bibliography: Albert, S. M., *Albert the Great* (1948); Madden, D. H., *A Chapter in Medieval History* (1969); Schwertner, Thomas M., *Saint Albert the Great* (1932).

See also: SCHOLASTICISM.

Albigenses   [al-buh-jen'-seez]

The Albigenses were the members of a religious sect in southern France during the 12th and 13th centuries. Their name is derived from the French town of Albi, where they were centered. Similar groups in other parts of Europe were called Cathari, meaning the pure ones.

Like the ancient Manichaeans (see MANICHAEISM), the Albigenses adhered to a strict DUALISM. They considered the material world as evil; redemption meant the liberation of the soul from flesh. This led them to condemn marriage and sex. Meat, milk, eggs, and other animal products were forbidden. They also rejected the traditional teachings on hell, purgatory, and

the sacraments because of the material elements involved. Their own sacrament, the *consolamentum*, or baptism of the soul, was administered by laying on of hands. Only the "perfect" (*perfecti*) received it, and they were expected to live by a rigorous ethical code. The majority remained in the state of "believers" (*credentes*) and lived less rigorously. The sect's efficient organization, with bishops and clergy supported by the local nobility, helped it to survive even when most of its congregations had been destroyed.

Official countermeasures, such as the preaching efforts of the CISTERCIANS and DOMINICANS, or conciliar decrees of the church (Combers, 1165; Verona, 1184; Fourth Lateran Council, 1215) were only partly effective. When a papal legate was assassinated in the territory of Count Raymond of Toulouse, Pope INNOCENT III called for a crusade that developed into the infamous Albigensian wars (1209–29). Simon of Monfort's massacre (1209) of the inhabitants of Béziers stands out as an example of their cruel conduct. Asked how to separate Christians from heretics, one leader is said to have replied: "Slay them all. God knows his own." The greatest benefit from the enterprise accrued to the French crown. With the taking of Montségur in 1244, the LANGUEDOC province could now be incorporated into the kingdom. Throughout the 13th century the remnants of the Albigenses, together with other Catharist groups and the WALDENSES, were the main target of the organized INQUISITION throughout Europe.   KARLFRIED FROEHLICH

Bibliography: Setton, K. M., ed., *A History of the Crusades,* 2d ed. (1969); Wakefield, Walter L., *Heresy, Crusade, and Inquisition in Southern France, 1100–1250* (1974).

albinism   [al'-buh-nizm]

Albinism is a group of genetic disorders affecting one out of every several thousand humans and other animals. It involves a deficiency of melanin, the dark brown pigment responsible for coloration. Eyes, skin and hair, and other body parts may be affected. A totally albino animal has milky-white skin and white hair or feathers. The iris of the eyes is pink, and reflected light in the retina is red, because no color masks the blood vessels. The eyes are light-sensitive and often astigmatic. Occasionally albinism is associated with mental or physical retardation.

Total albinism is rare in wild animals because few survive to reproductive age. They may lack protective coloration against predators; be driven away by their fellow creatures; or be unable to bear exposure to needed sunlight. Partial albinism is less disabling and is characterized by the appearance of white spots on the skin or white patches in the hair. Vitiligo is the absence of pigment in some body areas only.

Several independent defects can cause albinism: a complete lack of melanocytes, or pigment cells; interference in the migration of the cells to their proper location during embryo development; failure of the cells to produce melanin because of lack of tyrosinase, the stimulating enzyme; or abnormalities within the cells. The gene involved in albinism is recessive and may appear in the offspring of normally pigmented parents who are carriers of the trait. At present, no method for curing albinism is known.   PETER L. PETRAKIS

Albinoni, Tommaso   [ahl-bee-noh'-nee]

Tommaso Albinoni, b. June 8, 1671, d. Jan. 17, 1750, was an Italian composer and violin virtuoso. He is now known mostly because Johann Sebastian Bach used his themes in three popular compositions. A member of a wealthy family, Albinoni had no need to support himself, and his only appointment was as chamber musician to the duke of Mantua. Stylistically, his string music is a transition between that of Arcangelo CORELLI and Antonio VIVALDI and the new courtly style of the classic era. His many operas tend toward the developing opera buffa. The popular "Adagio for Strings" is actually a posthumous concoction based on one of Albinoni's unfinished themes.   FARLEY K. HUTCHINS

Bibliography: Selfridge-Field, Eleanor, *Instrumental Music from Gabrieli to Vivaldi* (1975); Stoeving, Paul, *The Violin: Its Famous Makers and Players* (1970).

albite: see FELDSPAR.

Albizu Campos, Pedro   [ahl-bee'-soo kahm'-pohs]

Pedro Albizu Campos, b. 1891, d. Apr. 21, 1965, was a leader of the Puerto Rican independence movement. Heading the radical Nationalist party from the early 1930s, he was imprisoned (1937–43) in Atlanta, Ga., for his revolutionary activities. In 1950, when Nationalists tried to assassinate President Harry S. Truman, Albizu Campos was charged with inciting the would-be assassins and jailed once again. In 1954 several party members fired shots in the U.S. House of Representatives, wounding five congressmen, and Albizu Campos, who had been pardoned, was sentenced to life imprisonment. He was pardoned a second time in 1964.

albizzia: see MIMOSA.

Ålborg   [awl'-bawr]

Ålborg is the seat of Nordjylands County, in Jutland, Denmark, on the Lim Fjord. It is an important port and commercial center. The population is 154,218 (1982). Industry is diversified and includes shipbuilding, cement, tobacco, and liquor. The city has several parks, and its historical landmarks include St. Botolph's Cathedral (c.1500), Ålborghus Castle (1539), and the Jens Bang Stonehouse (1624). The city's several museums, with Viking artifacts, attract many tourists. Settled about 1000, Ålborg was chartered in 1342. Steady growth followed, and the city was a prosperous commercial center by the 17th century. The Danish surrender during the Thirty Years' War occurred there in 1627.

Albrechtsberger, Johann Georg

Johann Georg Albrechtsberger, b. Feb. 3, 1736, d. Mar. 7, 1809, was a respected Austrian organist, teacher, theorist, and composer. After early training and experience in provincial monasteries and towns, among them Melk, he moved to Vienna, where he eventually became (1792) director of music at St. Stephen's Cathedral. For a time Ludwig van Beethoven was his pupil. He is known for his mastery of the art of COUNTERPOINT and for two treatises on music theory. Most of his numerous compositions remain in manuscript.   F. E. KIRBY

See also: GERMAN AND AUSTRIAN MUSIC.

Albright, Ivan Le Lorraine

Ivan Le Lorraine Albright, b. North Harvey, Ill., Feb. 20, 1897, d. Nov. 18, 1983, was a painter famous for his greatly detailed works reflecting the theme of life's decay. He painted very slowly and produced relatively few works. His paintings include *That Which I Should Have Done I Did Not Do* (1941; Art Institute of Chicago) and the final horrifying portrait for the film *The Picture of Dorian Gray* (1943–44).

Bibliography: Sweet, Frederick A., *Ivan Albright: A Retrospective Exhibition* (1964).

Albright, Jacob

Jacob Albright, b. May 1, 1759, d. May 18, 1808, an American itinerant preacher, became the first bishop of the Evangelical Association. A Pennsylvania German brickmaker, he had no formal education. After converting from Lutheranism to Methodism, he was licensed in 1796 to preach among the German-speaking people of the Shenandoah Valley. His followers, known at first as the Newly Formed Methodist Conference and after his death as the Evangelical Association, gradually formed independent units. They declared Albright their ordained pastor in 1803 and a bishop in 1807. The association came to be known as the Evangelical Church in 1922. In 1946 the Evangelical Church joined with the United Brethren in Christ to form the EVANGELICAL UNITED BRETHREN CHURCH.

Bibliography: Krueger, K. W., ed., *The History of the Evangelical United Brethren Church* (1979); Wilson, Robert, *Jacob Albright* (1940).

albumen print

An albumen print was a positive photographic print made on photographic printing paper coated with egg white, or albumen, which contained the light-sensitive chemical mixture that recorded the image. Developed in 1850 by Louis Désirée BLANQUART-EVRARD, the albumen print had a finish that enhanced image detail by adding brightness to the highlights in the print. Although albumen paper was vulnerable to damp and required careful handling, it remained in general use until about 1900, when more stable emulsions were developed.

Bibliography: Coe, Brian, *The Birth of Photography* (1977); Newhall, Beaumont, *The History of Photography: From 1839 to the Present Day*, 5th ed. (1982).

See also: FILM PROCESSING; PHOTOGRAPHY.

albumin

An albumin is a protein that is soluble in water and in half-saturated salt solutions, in contrast to a GLOBULIN, which is soluble only in dilute salt solutions. Albumins include ovalbumin from egg white, lactalbumin from milk, and serum albumin from BLOOD serum. They make up about half of the protein in human serum, where their main functions are to maintain normal water balance between blood and tissues by osmotic mechanisms and to serve as transport proteins for less soluble substances that can bind to them, such as amino acids. The detection of albumins in the urine is an indication of some types of KIDNEY dysfunction.

Albuquerque   [al'-buh-kur-kee]

Albuquerque, the largest city in New Mexico, has a population of 331,767 (1980) in the city proper and 454,499 in the 2-county metropolitan area. It is located on the Rio Grande in the central part of the state and is the seat of Bernalillo County. Low rainfall (200 mm/8 in) and mild temperatures (average 33° C /91° F in July and 8° C /46° F in January) make the city a health resort. The economy is based on the manufacture of truck trailers, lumber, clothing, gypsum products, and aerospace components, and the city also serves as a center for mining, timber, and ranching operations. Numerous federal agencies have been established since the 1930s. After World War II the development of nuclear and aerospace technology stimulated large population growth.

Founded in 1706 by the Spanish, the city was named for the duque of Alburquerque, then viceroy of New Spain. As the SANTA FE TRAIL achieved importance in the 1800s, more settlers arrived. In 1846 the U.S. Army occupied the area and built a fort here. Although the city was captured by Confederate forces in 1862, it remained loyal to the United States. The arrival of the railroad in 1880 spurred growth. The University of New Mexico (1889) is located in the city.

Albuquerque, Afonso de   [ahl-boo-kair'-kuh]

Afonso de Albuquerque, b. 1453, d. Dec. 16, 1515, founded the Portuguese empire in the Indian Ocean, which lasted for more than a century. First sent to India in 1503, he built a fort at Cochin. In 1506 he explored the coast of East Africa with Tristão da CUNHA and captured Socotra. The following year he took the island of Hormuz, which controlled the Persian Gulf. He arrived in India in 1508 with orders to replace Francisco de ALMEIDA as viceroy, but Almeida did not yield until 1509.

As viceroy, Albuquerque captured (1510) Goa and made it the center of Portuguese power in the east. He then seized (1511) Malacca on the Malay Peninsula, where he built a naval base. In 1515 he completed the capture of Hormuz, while other Portuguese established trading relations with Macao in China. With the acquisition of these bases, the Portuguese not only gained access to the rich SPICE TRADE of the East Indies but were able to destroy their rivals, the Arab seafarers.

DANIEL R. HEADRICK

Bibliography: Boxer, Charles R., *The Portuguese Seaborne Empire, 1415–1825* (1969); Sanceau, Elaine, *Indies Adventure: The Amazing Career of Afonso de Albuquerque* (1936).

Alcaeus   [al-see'-uhs]

Alcaeus of Lesbos, Greek poet, b. c.620 BC, is, along with SAPPHO, the principal writer of archaic Aeolic lyrics. Of more than ten books that he wrote, only fragments survive. War, wine, travel, and the turbulent politics of Lesbos were his main subjects. He once allegorized the shifting fortunes of Lesbos as a ship at sea. Intensely personal, energetic, rich in passion and detail, but sometimes reflective, his poems depict the life-style and the social and political prejudices of a Levantine nobleman in the 7th century BC. He also wrote drinking songs, hymns, and mythological poems. A colloquial stylist, he experimented with various meters; one, the Alcaic stanza, bears his name.   CHARLES SEGAL

Alcatraz

Alcatraz is an island in San Francisco Bay, the site of the famous prison of the same name. The island was discovered by the Spanish in 1545, and named in 1775 for its pelicans (in Spanish, *alcatraces*). Owned by the U.S. government since 1850, it was fortified and used as a military prison until 1933, when it became a federal prison. The prison was considered escape-proof because of its fortresslike structure and the strong, cold currents in the surrounding waters. Closed in

1963, the structure stood empty until it was seized by a group of Indians in November 1969. They held it until June 1971 in an unsuccessful attempt to gain government recognition of their claim to the island. The island was opened (1972) to the public as a part of the Golden Gate National Recreation Area.

Bibliography: De Nevi, Donald P., *Alcatraz '46: The Anatomy of a Classic Prison Tragedy* (1974); Mercer, John D. and Patricia, *Island of the Pelicans: A Photographic Essay of the Island of Alcatraz* (1976).

Alcestis   [al-ses'-tis]

In Greek mythology, Alcestis was the daughter of PELIAS and the devoted wife of Admetus. When Admetus lay dying, Apollo asked the FATES to spare him. It was agreed that he could live if a surrogate were found. Only Alcestis volunteered. In one version of the myth, as Alcestis took her husband's place, Persephone, impressed by her devotion, rescued her from death. In another, HERCULES grappled with Hades for her life and rescued her.

alchemy

Alchemy is an ancient pseudoscience concerned with the transmutation of base metals into gold and with the discovery of both a single cure for all diseases and a way to prolong life

(Left) *A painting of a 16th-century alchemical laboratory is the work of the Flemish artist Jan van der Straet. The alchemist (pointing, lower right) oversees the work of his many assistants. The retort to which he points was called the Philosopher's Egg, in which the magical gold-making liquid known as the Philosopher's Stone was supposed to be formed. Furnaces blaze in the background, while at left a worker extracts liquids.*

(Below) *A 16th-century engraving of the green lion devouring the Sun is an allegorical alchemical schema for a real chemical process in which aqua regia (nitric and hydrochloric acids) dissolved gold (the Sun). Because gold often carried copper impurities, the resulting liquid had a bluish-green tint—the lion's color.*

indefinitely. Alchemy emerged as a pseudoscience in China and in Egypt during the early centuries of this era. In China it was associated with Taoist philosophy and purported to transmute base metals into gold by use of a "medicine." The gold so produced was thought to have the ability to cure diseases and to prolong life. The mystical element was always strong in alchemy and became dominant with time so that alchemy in China degenerated into a complex of superstitions.

In Egypt, the methods of transmutation of metals were kept secret by temple priests. Those recipes became widely known (2d century) at the academy in Alexandria. Alchemy had its basis in the skills of Egyptian artisans, Eastern mysticism, and Aristotelian theory of composition of matter. Aristotle taught that all matter was composed of four elements: water, earth, fire, and air. According to his theory, different materials found in nature had different ratios of these four elements. Therefore, by proper treatment a base metal could be changed into gold. These ideas were further supported by astrological speculations from Mesopotamia.

ASTROLOGY

Astrologers believed that celestial bodies—the Sun, the Moon, and the stars—had a profound influence on the activities of humans. Thus, for alchemists to transmute metals effectively, the heavenly bodies had to be in a favorable configuration. Astrological influence led to ascribing each metal to a heavenly body: for example, gold to the Sun, silver to the Moon, copper to Venus, and iron to Mars. Each metal was represented by the astrological sign of the appropriate celestial body.

As in China and later in Western Europe, the alchemical writing in Alexandria became allegorical and confusing. At the end of the 4th century, the destruction of the academy and its library scattered the alchemists from Alexandria to Byzantium, Syria, and countries of the Near East. There they were persecuted by governments and the church as practitioners of black magic. Their activity thus became limited to writing commentaries on the works of ancient alchemists.

THE ARAB INFLUENCE

In the 5th century, the Nestorians broke away from the official Orthodox church in Byzantium and immigrated to the Near East, where they taught Hellenistic philosophy and science (see NESTORIANISM). They translated Greek treatises, including those on alchemy, into their own language, the Syriac. In the 8th and 9th centuries, the Nestorians came into contact with Arabs, particularly those in the court of the Caliph of Baghdad. As a result, the Alexandrine alchemical manuscripts were translated from Syriac into Arabic.

The Arab alchemists modified the Aristotelian concept of four elements by postulating that all metals were composed of two immediate components: sulfur and mercury. They also adopted the Chinese alchemists' concept of a "philosopher's stone"—a medicine that could turn a "sick" (base) metal into gold and also act as an elixir of life.

A number of alchemical treatises were attributed to Jabir ibn Hayan (721-815), the most notable Arab alchemist and a member of the Ismailiya sect whose present leader is Aga Khan. These manuscripts contained much unintelligible mysticism, but they were popular during the Middle Ages. Other famous Arab alchemists were al-Razi (886-925) and AVICENNA (980-1036), both important Persian physicians. Although their thinking was clouded with mysticism, Arabian alchemists discovered new chemicals such as the alkalies and such processes as distillation.

MEDIEVAL PERIOD

With the fall of Rome, Greek science and philosophy declined in Western Europe. However, close contact with Arabs in Spain and Sicily in the 11th and 12th centuries brought to Europe a new interest in Arabic philosophers, physicians, and scientists. Indirectly through Syriac and Arabic, Greek manuscripts were translated into Latin and European languages. Alchemical explanation of the nature of matter was included in the treatises of such scholars as Arnold of Villanova (1240-1313), Roger Bacon (1214-94), and Albertus Magnus (1193-1280).

The works of Jabir (or GEBER), a practicing Spanish alchemist of the 14th century, became the textbooks of alchemy. They contained not only mystical theory but also important practical recipes. Arnold of Villanova described distillation of wine; Roger BACON gave a recipe for gunpowder and directions for constructing a telescope; ALBERTUS MAGNUS defined a flame as ignited smoke and postulated that "like seeks like." The alchemist became a recognizable figure on the European scene, and kings and nobles often supported alchemists in the hope of increasing their resources. Frequently, however, alchemists who failed in their attempt to produce the promised gold lost their lives.

In time, alchemy fell into disrepute because of the nefarious character of its practitioners. It is said that Frederick of Wurzburg maintained special gallows for hanging alchemists. From the 15th to the 17th century, alchemical symbolism and allegory became increasingly complex. Practical alchemists turned from attempting to make gold toward preparing medicinals. A leader in this movement was Phillippus Aureolus PARACELSUS (1493-1531). He was the first in Europe to mention zinc and to use the word *alcohol* to refer to the spirit of wine.

Classical scholarship in the 16th century shifted attention away from Aristotelian theory and toward Greek atomism. Interest in transmutation was limited to astrologers and numerologists. The chemical facts that had been accumulated by alchemists as a by-product of their search for gold became the basis for modern chemistry.   JOHN TURKEVICH

Bibliography: De Rola, Stanislas K., *Alchemy: The Secret Art* (1974); Doberer, Kurt K., *The Goldmakers: Ten Thousand Years of Alchemy*, trans. by E. W. Dickes (1948; repr. 1972); Grossinger, Richard, ed., *Alchemy*, 4th ed. (1977); Powell, Neil, *Alchemy: The Ancient Science* (1977).

See also: CHEMISTRY, HISTORY OF.

Alcibiades   [al-suh-by'-uh-deez]

Alcibiades, c.450-404 BC, the nephew of PERICLES, was a charismatic Athenian political leader. Although he possessed high intelligence, remarkable physical beauty, and great capacity for leadership, his career ended in disaster to himself and irreparable harm to his city.

Alcibiades felt a strong attraction to SOCRATES, but his energy and ambition found a more natural outlet in politics. By 420 BC he was a leading politician, anti-Spartan and aggressive. In 415 he urged the conquest of SYRACUSE, the most powerful city in Sicily. Over the opposition of NICIAS, his conservative opponent, Athens equipped a mighty expedition with Alcibiades, Nicias, and Lamachus in command. Shortly after it reached Sicily, however, Alcibiades was recalled to stand trial on a charge of impiety. He fled to SPARTA, and while the Syracusan expedition, deprived of his leadership, was ending disastrously, Alcibiades advised the Spartans on how best to wage war against Athens. He changed sides again in 411. After considerable service to Athens, however, he fell under suspicion in 406, when a subordinate was responsible for a naval defeat off Notium. Alcibiades sought seclusion but was murdered in Anatolia at the instigation of his enemies.
CHARLES W. FORNARA

Bibliography: Benson, Edward F., *The Life of Alcibiades* (1928); Bloedow, Edmund F., *Alcibiades Reexamined* (1973); Hammond, N. G. L., *A History of Greece to 322 B.C.*, 2d ed. (1967); Parry, Hugh, *The Individual and His Society; Alcibiades: Greek Patriot or Traitor* (1969).

alcid: see AUK.

Alcmaeon   [alk'-mee-uhn]

In Greek legend, Alcmaeon led the Epigoni, sons of the SEVEN AGAINST THEBES. His father, Amphiaraus, was a part of the expedition. Alcmaeon learned that his mother, Eriphyle, had been bribed to urge the war that brought death to his father, who, as he lay dying, exhorted Alcmaeon to avenge Eriphyle's deceit. Alcmaeon killed his mother, but in punishment he was driven mad by the FURIES. He was worshiped at Thebes after his death.

Alcman [alk'-muhn]

Alcman was a Greek lyric poet active during the middle of the 7th century BC. Although Sardis is mentioned as his birthplace, his life and work are connected exclusively with Sparta. His choral poetry included *parthenia* ("songs for female choirs"). Alcman's lyrics reveal a rare side of Spartan nature in their graceful descriptions of local ceremonies and entertainments.

Alcock, Sir John William

The English aviator J. W. Alcock, b. Nov. 6, 1892, d. Dec. 18, 1919, was the pilot of the first nonstop flight across the Atlantic Ocean. Alcock gained fame as a World War I flying ace. In June 1919 he and his navigator, Lt. Arthur Whidden Brown, made their historic Newfoundland-to-Ireland transatlantic flight—a crossing of 16 hours 27 minutes. Both men were knighted for their accomplishment. Flying to Paris several months afterward, Alcock was killed when his plane crashed on the Normandy coast.

alcohol

The familiar grain alcohol (ethanol), contained in alcoholic beverages, wood alcohol (methanol), and rubbing alcohol (isopropanol) are among the hundreds of organic compounds that form the class known as alcohols. Alcohols are characterized by a hydroxyl group (OH) bonded to a carbon atom. They may contain more than one hydroxyl group per molecule provided each group of hydrogen and oxygen atoms is attached to a different carbon atom. Such alcohols are called polyhydric alcohols, or polyols.

Alcohols that are derived from a simple hydrocarbon are named by adding either *ol* or *yl* plus the word *alcohol* to the name of the parent hydrocarbon. For example, the alcohol derived from ethane (C_2H_6) may be called either ethanol or ethyl alcohol (C_2H_5OH). Dihydric alcohols—those with two hydroxyl groups per molecule—may be named as glycols, as ethylene glycol (CH_2OHCH_2OH), which is the major component of automotive antifreeze solutions. More complex alcohols, such as cholesterol, are not named so systematically.

If the alcohol's chain has three carbon atoms, two ISOMERS (different structures) are possible; the number of isomers increases markedly with the number of carbon atoms. Alcohols may be classified according to the number of hydrogen atoms attached to the carbon with the hydroxyl group. If that carbon has two hydrogen atoms attached, the alcohol is primary; if it

has one, it is secondary; and if it has no hydrogen atoms, it is a tertiary alcohol.

Simple, low-molecular-weight alcohols are colorless, volatile, flammable liquids that are soluble in water. As the molecular weight increases, the boiling point, melting point, and viscosity increase, while solubility in water decreases. Physical properties may be altered by the presence of other functional groups. Adding hydroxyl groups increases the boiling point and solubility in water and often produces sweetness. Branching the carbon chain increases solubility in water and decreases the boiling point.

The important reactions of alcohols are chiefly those of the hydroxyl group. The hydrogen atom of the OH can be replaced by an active metal; dehydration causes the production of unsaturated compounds or ethers; reaction with carboxylic acids forms esters, and the OH may be replaced by other functional groups. The product of oxidation depends on the class of the alcohol. Primary alcohols oxidize to aldehydes, and secondary alcohols oxidize to ketones. Tertiary alcohols do not oxidize readily, and they give products containing fewer carbon atoms than the original compound. It is difficult to reduce alcohols to hydrocarbons.

When ingested in moderate amounts, lower-molecular-weight alcohols act on the central nervous system and higher centers of the brain, lowering inhibitions and affecting judgment. Larger amounts may produce a loss of muscular control, unconsciousness, and even death. Methyl alcohol is extremely toxic, affecting the optic nerve and causing blindness, and as little as 30 ml (1 oz) has caused death. Ethanol is the least toxic, but toxicity increases slowly with molecular weight until the compound is insoluble in water. Most of the lower-molecular-weight alcohols have commercial importance. They are used as solvents and in the preparation of dyes, pharmaceuticals, antifreeze, esters, and other compounds.

ELBERT H. HADLEY

Bibliography: Monick, John A., *Alcohols: Their Chemistry, Properties and Manufacture* (1968); Morrison, Robert T., and Boyd, Robert N., *Organic Chemistry*, 3d ed. (1976); Rodd, E. H., ed., *Chemistry of Carbon Compounds*, vols. 1A–2D, 2d ed. (1965–70); Union Carbide, *Alcohols* (1969).

See also: GLYCOL.

alcohol consumption

Alcohol, probably the oldest drug known, has been used at least since the earliest societies for which records exist. Of the numerous types of alcohol, ethyl alcohol is the type consumed in drinking. In its pure form it is a clear substance with little odor. People drink alcohol in three main kinds of beverages: BEERS, which are made from grain through brewing and fermentation and contain from 3% to 8% alcohol; WINES, which are fermented from fruits such as grapes and contain from 8% to 12% alcohol naturally, and up to 21% when fortified by adding alcohol; and distilled beverages (spirits) such as WHISKEY, GIN, and vodka, which on the average contain from 40% to 50% alcohol. Drinkers may become addicted to any of these beverages.

Physical Effects of Alcohol. The effects of alcohol on the human body depend on the amount of alcohol in the blood (blood-alcohol concentration). This varies with the rate of consumption and with the rate at which the drinker's physical system absorbs and metabolizes alcohol. The higher the alcohol content of the beverage consumed, the more alcohol will enter the bloodstream. The amount and type of food in the stomach also affect the absorption rate. Drinking when the stomach is filled is less intoxicating than when it is empty; the foods in the stomach, which contain fat and protein, delay alcohol absorption. Body weight is also a factor; the heavier the person, the slower the absorption of alcohol.

After alcohol passes through the stomach, it is rapidly absorbed through the walls of the intestines into the bloodstream and carried to the various organ systems of the body, where it is metabolized. Although small amounts of alcohol are processed by the kidneys and secreted in the urine, and other small amounts are processed through the lungs and exhaled in

PROPERTIES OF COMMON ALCOHOLS

Name	Formula	mp° C	bp° C	Sp. Gr.*
Methyl alcohol	CH_3OH	−97	64.7	0.792
Ethyl alcohol	CH_3CH_2OH	−114	78.3	.789
n-Propyl alcohol	$n\text{-}C_3H_7OH$	−126	97.2	.804
Isopropyl alcohol	$i\text{-}C_3H_7OH$	−88.5	82.3	.786
Allyl alcohol	$CH_2{=}CHCH_2OH$	−129	97.0	.855
Crotyl alcohol	$CH_3CH{=}CHCH_2OH$		118	.873
n-Butyl alcohol	$n\text{-}C_4H_9OH$	−90	117.7	.810
Isobutyl alcohol	$(CH_3)_2CHCH_2OH$	−108	107.9	.802
sec-Butyl alcohol	$CH_3CH_2CH(OH)CH_3$		99.5	.808
t-Butyl alcohol	$(CH_3)_3COH$	25	82.5	.789
n-Amyl alcohol	$n\text{-}C_5H_{11}OH$	−78.5	138.0	.817
Isoamyl alcohol	$(CH_3)_2CHCH_2CH_2OH$	−117	131.5	.812
t-Amyl alcohol	$CH_3CH_2C(OH)(CH_3)_2$	−12	101.8	.809
Neopentyl alcohol	$(CH_3)_3CCH_2OH$	50	113	
Cyclopentanol	C_5H_9OH	−19	141	.950
n-Hexyl alcohol	$n\text{-}C_6H_{13}OH$	−52	155.8	.820
Cyclohexanol	$C_6H_{11}OH$	24	161.5	.962
n-Octyl alcohol	$n\text{-}C_8H_{17}OH$	−16	194.0	.827
Capryl alcohol (octanol-2)	$n\text{-}C_6H_{13}CH(OH)CH_3$	−39	179.0	.819
n-Decyl alcohol	$n\text{-}C_{10}H_{21}OH$	6	232.9	.829

SOURCE: Fieser, Louis F. and Mary, *Advanced Organic Chemistry* (1961).
*Specific gravity.

the breath, most of the alcohol is metabolized by the liver. As the alcohol is metabolized, it gives off heat. The body metabolizes alcohol at about the rate of three-fourths of an ounce to one ounce of whiskey an hour. Technically it is possible to drink at the same rate as the alcohol is being oxidized out of the body. Most people, however, drink faster than this, and so the concentration of alcohol in the bloodstream keeps rising.

Alcohol begins to impair the brain's ability to function when the blood-alcohol concentration (BAC) reaches 0.05%, that is, 0.05 grams of alcohol per 100 cubic centimeters of blood. Most state traffic laws in the United States presume that a driver with a BAC of 0.10% is intoxicated. With a concentration of 0.20% (a level obtained from drinking about 10 ounces of whiskey), a person has difficulty controlling the emotions and may cry or laugh extensively. The person will experience a great deal of difficulty in attempting to walk and will want to lie down. When the blood-alcohol content reaches about 0.30%, which can be attained when a person rapidly drinks about a pint of whiskey, the drinker will have trouble comprehending and may become unconscious. At levels from 0.35% to 0.50%, the brain centers that control breathing and heart action are affected; concentrations above 0.50% may cause death, although a person generally becomes unconscious before absorbing a lethal dosage.

Moderate or temperate use of alcohol is not harmful, but excessive or heavy drinking is associated with alcoholism and numerous other health problems. The effects of excessive drinking on major organ systems of the human body are cumulative and become evident after heavy, continuous drinking or after intermittent drinking over a period of time that may range from 5 to 30 years. The parts of the body most affected by heavy drinking are the digestive and nervous systems. Digestive-system disorders that may be related to heavy drinking include cancer of the mouth, throat, and esophagus; gastritis; ulcers; cirrhosis of the liver; and inflammation of the pancreas. Disorders of the nervous system can include neuritis, lapse of memory (blackouts), hallucinations, and extreme tremor as found in delirium tremens. Delirium tremens ("the DTs") may occur when a person stops drinking after a period of heavy, continuous imbibing. Permanent damage to the brain and central nervous system may also result, including Korsakoff psychosis and Wernicke's disease. Recent evidence indicates that pregnant women who drink heavily may give birth to infants with the fetal alcohol syndrome, which is characterized by face and body abnormalities and, in some cases, impaired intellectual facilities. Additionally, the combination of alcohol and drugs, such as commonly used sleeping pills, tranquilizers, antibiotics, and aspirin, can be fatal, even when both are taken in nonlethal doses.

Drinking Patterns. Many studies have been made of attitudes toward drinking in different societies. Every culture has its own general ethos or sense of decorum about the use and role of alcoholic beverages within its social structure.

In some cultures drinking is either forbidden or frowned upon. The Koran contains prohibitions against drinking, and Muslims are forbidden to sell or serve alcoholic beverages. Hindus take a negative view of the use of alcohol; this is reflected in the constitution of India, which requires every state to work toward the prohibition of alcohol except for medicinal purposes. Abstinence from alcohol has also been the goal of temperance movements in Europe and the United States. Some Christian religious groups enjoin abstinence, including the Christian Scientists, Mormons, Seventh-Day Adventists, Pentecostalists, and some Baptists and Methodists.

In some ambivalent cultures, such as the United States and Ireland, the values of those who believe in abstinence conflict with the values of those who regard moderate drinking as a way of being hospitable and sociable. This accounts for the plethora of laws and regulations that restrict the buying of alcoholic beverages. Some psychologists say that this ambivalence in the culture makes it harder for some people to develop a stable attitude toward drinking.

Some cultures have a permissive attitude toward drinking, including those of Spain, Portugal, Italy, Japan, and Israel.

The proportion of Jews and Italians who use alcohol is high, but the rates of alcoholism among them are lower than in Irish and Scandinavian groups.

Some cultures may be said to look too favorably upon drinking, as do the French. In France the heavy consumption of alcohol has been related to the fact that many people are engaged in viticulture and in the production and distribution of alcoholic beverages.

Various surveys indicate that subgroups within a society do not all have the same attitudes toward alcoholic beverages or the same drinking patterns. Drinking behavior differs significantly among groups of different age, sex, social class, racial status, ethnic background, occupational status, religious affiliation, and regional location.   DAVID J. PITTMAN

Bibliography: Birnbaum, I., and Parker, E., *Alcohol and Human Memory* (1977); Hoffman, G., and Adele, D., *A Handbook on Drug and Alcohol Abuse: The Biomedical Aspects* (1975); Walgren, H., *Actions of Alcohol*, 3 vols. (1970).

alcoholism

Alcoholism refers to the drinking of alcoholic beverages to such a degree that major aspects of an individual's life—such as work, school, family relationships, or personal safety and health—are seriously and repeatedly interfered with. Alcoholism is considered a disease, meaning that it follows a characteristic course with known physical, psychological, and social symptoms. The alcoholic continues to consume alcohol despite the destructive consequences. Alcoholism is serious, progressive, and irreversible. If not treated, it can be fatal. It is generally thought that once the disease has developed, the alcoholic will not drink normally again. An alcoholic who abstains from drinking, however, can regain control over the aspects of life with which alcohol interfered. The alcoholic is then said to be "recovering," not "cured" of the disease. It is important to note that the particular symptoms and pattern of drinking problems may vary with the individual. Alcoholism is, therefore, a very complex disorder, and this complexity has led some recent researchers to question the accuracy of the disease concept of alcoholism.

A person does not have to drink every day to be an alcoholic. Moreover, someone who drinks frequently or sometimes gets drunk is not necessarily an alcoholic. It is possible to abuse alcohol for a short or contained period of time without developing alcoholism. For example, some people may drink abusively during a personal crisis and then resume normal drinking. College students tend to drink more heavily than other age groups. It is often difficult to distinguish such heavy and abusive drinking from the early stages of alcoholism. How well the person can tolerate giving up alcohol for an extended time, and the effect of the drinking on family, friends, work, and health, may indicate the extent of the alcohol problem.

More than 10 million Americans are estimated to be alcoholic. Alcoholism is found among all age, sociocultural, and economic groups. An estimated 75 percent of alcoholics are male, 25 percent female. Alcoholism is a worldwide phenomenon, but it is most widespread in France, Ireland, Poland, Scandinavia, the United States, and the USSR.

Symptoms and Causes. Some common signs of alcoholism in the early stages are constant drinking for relief of personal problems, an increase in a person's tolerance for alcohol, onset of memory lapses while drinking ("blackouts"), surreptitious drinking, and an urgent need for the first drink ("craving"). In the middle and late phases, dependence on drinking increases and memory blackouts become more frequent. A physical dependence on alcohol first appears with early morning tremors and agitation that require a drink for relief. In the late stage, drinking bouts are usually very frequent. There is an acute withdrawal syndrome (delirium tremens, or DTs) when drinking ceases. This includes agitation, tremor, hallucination, and possibly seizures.

Most likely, a combination of biological, psychological, and cultural factors contribute to the development of alcoholism in any individual. Alcoholism often seems to run in families. Although there is no conclusive indication of how the alcoholism of family members is associated, studies show that 50 to 80 percent of all alcoholics have had a close alcoholic relative.

Some researchers suggest that some alcoholics have an inherited physical predisposition to alcoholism, making them highly susceptible to alcohol addiction. Some studies of animals and of human twins lend support to this theory. The results of human studies (primarily done in Scandinavia), however, remain inconclusive. Sometimes alcoholism is associated with a family history of manic-depressive illness, and some alcoholics have been known to use alcohol unwittingly to "medicate" a biological depressive disorder.

Alcoholism may be related to underlying emotional problems. Like other drug abusers, alcoholics often drown depressed or anxious feelings by drinking. Conversely, some drink to reduce strong inhibitions or guilt about expressing negative feelings. Psychologists variously suggest that alcoholics have conflicts about dependency, sex roles, and family roles. It is important to note that while many alcoholics share experiences of loneliness, frustration, or anxiety, no one has identified a single personality type who later becomes an alcoholic.

Social and cultural factors may play a role in establishing drinking patterns and alcoholism. Among some cultures there is conflict between values of abstinence and the acceptance of alcohol as a usual way to change moods or to be sociable. These conflicts within the culture may make it difficult for some people to develop their own stable attitudes and moderate patterns of drinking.

Social Effects of Alcoholism. The effects of alcoholism range from the direct physiological impact on the individual (see AL-COHOL CONSUMPTION) to a widespread effect on society. In the United States, one family in three is estimated to be affected in some way by a drinking problem.

Children of alcoholics may be affected by a father's or mother's alcoholism in several ways. Having a problem drinking parent increases the risk of becoming a problem drinker oneself. This may happen because of identification with or imitation of the alcoholic parent, but also because the social and family conditions associated with alcoholism are among those believed to contribute to the development of alcoholism. These include family conflict, divorce, job insecurity, and social stigma.

Other problems reported in children of alcoholic parents in the United States and in Europe include speech disorders, hyperactivity, psychosomatic complaints, school problems, antisocial behavior, and drug use. The type of problem varies with the age and sex of the child.

While having an alcoholic parent may increase the child's risk of developing emotional or drinking problems later in life, it by no means makes becoming an alcoholic inevitable for the child. In fact, some surveys of large communities suggest that two-thirds of adults whose parents were very heavy drinkers drink lightly themselves and have thus turned away from their parents' drinking style.

Alcoholism is an enormous public health problem. The Institute of Medicine of the National Academy of Sciences estimates that alcoholism and alcohol abuse in the United States cost society from $40 to $60 billion annually, due to lost production, health and medical care, motor vehicle accidents, violent crime, and social programs that respond to alcohol problems. One-half of all traffic fatalities and one-third of all traffic injuries are related to the abuse of alcohol. Also, one-third of all suicides and one-third of all mental health disorders are estimated to be associated with serious alcohol abuse. Accidents and suicides associated with alcohol problems are especially prominent among teenagers. It has been estimated that there are over 3 million problem drinkers between the ages of 14 and 17 in the United States.

Treatment. Alcoholism is a complex disorder for which a combination of treatments may be necessary for recovery. If the alcoholic is in the acute phase of alcoholism and is suffering from complications such as delirium tremens or serious health problems, hospitalization may be necessary. Because

alcoholism is a chronic condition, however, hospitalization is only a first step toward recovery. Many alcoholics go through several brief hospitalizations for detoxification before they commit themselves to a program of recovery. A comprehensive treatment plan can incorporate various types of facilities, including hospitals, out-patient clinics, half-way houses, individual or group psychotherapists, social centers, religious organizations, foster homes, and self-help groups. Some large corporations sponsor treatment programs for employees. An assessment of the patient's medical, emotional, and social needs is important in making the proper referral. Not every type of facility is available in every community, but every community probably has access to a state- or city-wide system that provides for alcoholics and can help make appropriate referrals.

The best known and most experienced recovery program is Alcoholics Anonymous (AA). AA was founded in 1935 by Dr. Robert Smith and Bill Wilson as a fellowship organization for those with the common problem of alcoholism. AA defines alcoholism as a disease that is often fatal, as well as a spiritual problem. There are no dues, and members may attend AA meetings as often and wherever they wish. In 1980 there were over 26,000 AA groups in the United States and Canada with an estimated membership of more than 800,000. There are more than 14,000 AA chapters in 90 other countries.

AA's philosophy and program for recovery is stated in the 12 Steps to Recovery. The alcoholic must recognize his or her "powerlessness over alcohol" and seek help from a "higher power" in regaining control of his or her life.

Although alcoholism, according to the AA philosophy, can never be cured—that is, the alcoholic can never safely drink again—the alcoholic can "recover" to lead a productive and normal life as long as he or she remains sober. Since its inception, AA has provided invaluable social and psychological support to many alcoholics. The organization has also reduced popular misconceptions of alcoholics as morally weak or as incurable failures by educating both professionals and the public about the nature of alcoholism. The related organizations Al-Anon and Al-Ateen provide similar support to the families and children of alcoholics.

No one can make an alcoholic commit him- or herself to recovery. Some therapists suggest, however, that family members may influence the alcoholic by not supporting drinking activities, by seeking therapy for themselves, and by not joining in the alcoholic's denial of the problem. Because alcoholism is sometimes thought of as a family disease, the involvement of family members can aid the progress of the alcoholic's recovery. For the approximately 70 percent of alcoholics in the United States who remain married, living with families, and employed, the prognosis with treatment is good. For the fewer than 5 percent who fit the stereotype of the homeless, jobless, skid-row drunk, alcohol worsens the deterioration of family, economic, and social resources.

Perhaps a minute percentage of alcoholics can return to moderate drinking. But no one knows how to identify these few out of some 10 million American alcoholics. For the overwhelming majority, abstinence from alcohol is the one real hope of returning to a normal life. Once drinking has ceased, the alcoholic is free to cope with the psychological, family, social, legal, and medical problems that may be associated with alcoholism.   ROBERTA CAPLAN

Bibliography: *Alcoholics Anonymous*, 3 ed., rev. (1976); Bourne, P., and Fox, R., *Alcoholism: Progress in Research and Treatment* (1973); Cork, Margaret, *The Forgotten Children* (1969); Greenblatt, M., and Schuckit, M., eds., *Alcohol Problems in Women and Children* (1976); Vaillant, George E., *The Natural History of Alcoholism* (1983).

Alcott, Bronson   [awl'-kuht]

Amos Bronson Alcott, b. Nov. 29, 1799, d. Mar. 4, 1888, was an American transcendentalist philosopher and educator. Because his teaching methods were radically egalitarian, the schools he established failed. He and his family were poor until his daughter Louisa May became a literary success. He was a reforming superintendent of the Concord, Mass., public schools from 1859 to 1865 and conducted the Concord School of Philosophy from 1879 until his death. He was a vegetarian, an abolitionist, and an advocate of women's rights.

Bibliography: Shephard, Odell, *Pedlar's Progress: The Life of Bronson Alcott* (1937; repr. 1968).

Alcott, Louisa May

The American children's novelist Louisa May Alcott is best known for LITTLE WOMEN, her popular story of the development of four sisters into young women. She also wrote approximately 270 other works.

Alcott was born Nov. 29, 1832, in Germantown, Pa., the second of four daughters born to Bronson and Abigail Alcott. Her father, a noted educator and transcendentalist, had been involved in a number of financially disastrous utopian schemes, including an ill-fated experimental community called Fruitlands (1843–44) in Harvard, Mass. Although the family was continually in desperate need of money, Alcott's mother firmly believed in her husband's genius and convinced her daughters of it as well. The experiences of the March girls in *Little Women*—Jo, Meg, Beth, and Amy—recall those of the young Alcott sisters. When the family moved to Concord, Mass., their neighbors and friends included Henry David THOREAU, Nathaniel HAWTHORNE, Margaret FULLER, and Ralph Waldo EMERSON. Emerson in particular befriended Louisa and allowed her to use his extensive library. To help her financially burdened family she worked as a seamstress, servant, and schoolteacher, finally turning to writing in hope of earning more money. Alcott sold her first story in 1852, and other salable fiction, mostly sensational thrillers (collected and published in 1975 and 1976), rapidly followed. By 1860 she had published a book of fairy tales, *Flower Fables* (1854), and was a regular contributor to the *Atlantic Monthly*. The poignant letters she wrote as a nurse in Washington, D.C., during the Civil War were published in *Hospital Sketches* (1863) and won her fame. Her first serious novel, *Moods*, appeared the next year.

Alcott became a respected and financially successful novelist with her largely autobiographical *Little Women* (1868). Her work was now in demand, and sequels soon followed: *Little Men* (1871) and her next to last book, *Jo's Boys* (1886). Also successful were *An Old-Fashioned Girl* (1870), *Aunt Jo's Scrap Bag* (6 vols., 1872–82), *Eight Cousins* (1875), and *A Garland for Girls* (1888). Her adult novels *Work* (1873) and *A Modern Mephistopheles* (1877) were less popular. Throughout her life Alcott worked for the abolition of slavery. As her fame grew, she gave her support to the Temperance movement and to women's suffrage. Her last years were spent in sickness, but she continued to write until her death on Mar. 6, 1888, the day of her father's funeral

Bibliography: Alcott, Louisa May, *Louisa May Alcott: Her Life, Letters, and Journals*, ed. by E. D. Cheney (1888; repr. 1928); Anthony, Katharine, *Louisa May Alcott* (1938; repr. 1977); Saxton, Martha, *Louisa May Alcott* (1977).

Louisa May Alcott, a 19th-century American novelist, achieved her life's ambition, financial security, with the publication in 1868 of Little Women, *an autobiographical story about growing up in New England. She remarked that money received from the novel was sweeter than the reviews.*

Alcuin [al'-kwin]

The English scholar Alcuin, b. *c.*735, d. May 19, 804, was the leading figure in the Carolingian Renaissance. While head (from 778) of the cathedral school of York, he was invited by CHARLEMAGNE to establish a palace school at Aachen. He taught there from 782 to 796 and was rewarded with the abbacy of St. Martin of Tours.

Alcuin's task was to introduce English scholastic methods to the Franks. He established the curriculum of the seven liberal arts—grammar, rhetoric, dialectic, arithmetic, geometry, astronomy, and music theory—that became basic to medieval education, and he initiated the large-scale transcription and preservation of ancient texts. Alcuin himself wrote voluminously—letters, school manuals, and theological treatises—and revised the liturgy of the Frankish church.

Bibliography: Allott, Stephen, *Alcuin of York* (1974); Duckett, Eleanor, *Alcuin, Friend of Charlemagne: His World and His Work* (1951; repr. 1965); Wallach, Luitpold, *Alcuin and Charlemagne: Studies in Carolingian History and Literature* (1959).

Aldanov, M. A. [ul-dah'-nawf]

Mark Aleksandrovich Aldanov, b. Oct. 26, 1886, d. Feb. 25, 1957, was a Russian writer who was also known as Landau-Aldanov. He originally studied chemistry, but his true interests were journalism and literature. In 1919 he left Russia and settled in France; then in 1941, fleeing the Nazis, he went to the United States.

While in France, Aldanov wrote historical novels that emphasized the interaction of philosophy and history. His tetralogy *The Thinker* consists of four historical novels—*The Ninth Thermidor* (1923; Eng. trans., 1926), *The Devil's Bridge* (1925; Eng. trans., 1928), *The Conspiracy* (1927), and *St. Helena, Little Island* (1923; Eng. trans., 1924)—and concerns the philosophical problems of the French Revolution. *The Tenth Symphony* (1931) is a novel that draws a brilliant and detailed picture of life and society in Europe after the downfall of Napoleon.

Aldanov viewed the approach of World War II with great anxiety and in *The Fifth Seal* (1939; Eng. trans., 1943) depicted the general disillusionment, pessimism, and feeling of helplessness that characterized prewar Europe.

In *A Night at Ulm* (1956) he further explored the helplessness an individual feels when facing the dark forces of history. Aldanov never hesitated to identify the Soviet Union as one of those dark forces. His animosity toward the Bolshevik Revolution, first expressed in his portrait of Lenin in 1921, is a recurring theme in his novels and many journalistic and literary essays.

LASZLO M. TIKOS

Bibliography: Lee, C. Nicholas, *The Novels of Mark Aleksandrovic Aldanov* (1969).

Aldebaran: see STAR.

aldehyde [al'-duh-hyd]

An aldehyde is an organic compound that contains a carbonyl group (an oxygen atom doubly bonded to a carbon atom) and possesses at least one hydrogen atom covalently bonded to the carbonyl carbon. The structure of aldehydes may be represented as

$$\overset{\displaystyle O}{\underset{\displaystyle R-C-H}{\|}}$$

but is often written as RCHO. R may be hydrogen or any organic group. Aldehydes are close relatives of KETONES, which are carbonyl compounds that possess two carbon groupings linked covalently to the carbonyl carbon.

Aldehydes are so named because they are obtainable by dehydrogenation of primary ALCOHOLS (*alcohol dehydrogen*ated). The common names for specific aldehydes are derived from the CARBOXYLIC ACIDS to which they can be oxidized. Formaldehyde, HCHO, is readily oxidized to formic acid, HCOOH; acetaldehyde, CH_3CHO, to acetic acid, CH_3COOH. The systematic names for aldehydes are derived from the name of the ALKANE having the same number of carbon atoms by appending the suffix *al* in place of the last letter of the hydrocarbon suffix *ane*. Thus HCHO is methanal (from methane), CH_3CHO is ethanal (from ethane), and CH_3CH_2CHO is propanal (from propane).

Aldehydes are prepared in the laboratory by oxidizing primary alcohols with expensive reagents such as potassium permanganate ($KMnO_4$) or potassium dichromate ($K_2Cr_2O_7$). Commercially, aldehydes are made by catalytically removing two hydrogen atoms from a primary alcohol, usually over a copper catalyst at 250° C (520° F) or by air oxidation.

FORMALDEHYDE and acetaldehyde are the two most widely used and industrially important aldehydes. In 1977 about 3 million tons of formaldehyde were produced in the United States, ranking formaldehyde 21st among the industrial chemicals. Most of this formaldehyde was produced as formalin, a 37% solution in water.

Formaldehyde has an irritating odor and is toxic. Industrially it is used for the manufacture of plastics (such as Bakelite and Delrin) and pentaerythritol, from which drying oils and the high explosive penta-erythritol tetranitrate (PETN) are made. Formalin is also used as a disinfectant, as an insecticide, and as a preservative for biological specimens.

Aldehydes are more reactive than ketones because their carbonyl carbon-to-hydrogen bond is easily oxidized. Treatment of an aldehyde with the diammine silver ion produces a silver mirror on the walls of the test tube. This reaction is known as Tollens's test and is used to determine if an unknown substance is an aldehyde.

Another type of reaction characteristic of carbonyl compounds involves addition of a reagent such as cyanide or bisulfite to the carbon-oxygen double bond:

$$R-\overset{\overset{\textstyle O}{\|}}{C}-H \ + \ HCN \longrightarrow R-\overset{\overset{\textstyle H}{|}}{\underset{\underset{\textstyle CN}{|}}{C}}-OH$$

    aldehyde   cyanide   cyanohydrin

Aldehydes undergo this reaction more readily than ketones. Cyanohydrin formation was developed by Heinrich Kiliani and used by Emil Fischer in his classic structure proofs of sugars through synthesis.

HERMAN E. ZIEGER

Bibliography: Allinger, Norman L., et al., *Organic Chemistry*, 2d ed. (1976); Morrison, Robert T., and Boyd, Robert N., *Organic Chemistry*, 3d ed. (1973).

Alden, John

John Alden, d. Sept. 12, 1687, was one of the Pilgrim Fathers who came to America on the MAYFLOWER and founded Plymouth Colony in 1620. He is best known from the story about his wooing of Priscilla Mullins, which is the subject of "The Courtship of Miles Standish," a poem by Henry Wadsworth LONGFELLOW.

alder

The alders, *Alnus*, are deciduous hardwood TREES and SHRUBS that belong to the family Betulaceae. About 30 species of alders are found in north temperate zones.

Alders have smooth to scaly, usually gray bark. The deciduous alternate leaves are short stalked, ovate, usually doubly saw-toothed, and often wavy on the edges. The fruits are small, hard, blackish cones, clustered and persistent, which in summer mature and release many minute, usually winged nutlets.

European alders, *Alnus glutinosa*, were originally introduced into the United States for charcoal manufacture. They now have become naturalized and are planted as landscaping trees. The common streambank alder of the eastern United States and Canada is the speckled alder, *A. incana*.

The red alder, *A. rubra*, is the largest species of the genus and is the most important hardwood of the Pacific Northwest and coastal Alaska. Red alders grow in humid climates and

Alders grow rapidly in a cool, wet climate to a height of more than 20 m (66 ft). The spread of a white alder (top), A. rhombifolia, is half its height, and that of the European, or black, alder (bottom) A. glutinosa, is one-fourth its height. Male and female alder flowers are called catkins. The tassellike male catkin is 5–15 cm (2–6 in) long. In summer, the 2.5-cm (1-in) female catkin becomes a conelike fruit.

are sometimes used as a "nurse crop" to precede more valuable conifer species; nodules on the roots of the tree contain a nitrogen-fixing microorganism that increases the nitrogen content of the surrounding soil.

Sitka alder, *A. sinuata*, is a shrub found mostly in the Pacific Northwest, and only those near Alaska reach tree size.

Thin-leaf alders, *A. tenuifolia*, are thin-leaf trees found at the heads of mountain streams, boggy slopes, and high meadows from Alaska and British Columbia through eastern Washington and Oregon.

CHARLES L. WILSON

Alder, Kurt

The German chemist Kurt Alder, b. July 10, 1902, d. June 20, 1958, was corecipient with Otto DIELS of the Nobel Prize for chemistry in 1950 for his studies of diene reactions and synthesis. The key reaction, first published in 1928 and now called the Diels-Alder reaction, involves the synthesis of complex organic molecules from simpler ones. Specifically, a conjugated diene (a compound with two sets of double bonds separated by a single bond) reacts with an alkene, a hydrocarbon such as ethylene of the form C_nH_{2n}. The new product always contains a six-membered carbon ring with a double bond. The reaction has a wide application in the synthesis of a variety of substances, including STEROIDS and TERPENES.

O. B. RAMSAY

alderfly

Alderflies, family Sialidae, order Neuroptera, are dark-colored, soft-bodied insects, about 25 mm (less than 1 in) in length. They have four membranous wings that are held rooflike over the body at rest. Alderflies are somewhat like LACE-WINGS in appearance. They are primarily found near water; the larvae are aquatic and mostly are found under stones in streams. These insects (especially the larvae) are an important food of fish, and some artificial flies are patterned after them.

DONALD J. BORROR

alderman

An alderman, in the United States, is an elected public official who represents a specific ward or district in the city legislature. In most U.S. cities, aldermen serve 2-year terms.

In England and Ireland, aldermen are officers or magistrates chosen by the members of a city council or municipal corporation. They serve for 6 years. An alderman is called a bailie in Scotland.

Aldington, Richard

Richard Aldington, b. July 8, 1892, d. July 27, 1962, an English author, first established a reputation as an imagist poet with *Images Old and New* (1916). He married the American imagist poet Hilda DOOLITTLE ("H. D.") and contributed to anthologies of the movement. His novels, attacking hypocrisy and pretense, include *The Colonel's Daughter* (1931). He also wrote criticism and controversial biographies of Voltaire, D. H. Lawrence, and T. E. Lawrence ("Lawrence of Arabia").

ROBIN BUSS

Aldiss, Brian W.

Brian W. Aldiss, b. Aug. 18, 1925, is an English writer and critic best known for his apocalyptic and sometimes humorous science fiction. He wrote about the elevation of psychology to a form of religion in *Non-Stop* (1958), the postatomic holocaust world in *Greybeard* (1964), and the worship of science in *Frankenstein Unbound* (1973). The planet Helliconia, whose seasons each last hundreds of years, is the subject of a trilogy of novels. *The Billion Year Spree* (1973), Aldiss's critical history of science fiction, is also highly regarded.

aldosterone   [al-doh'-stuh-rohn]

Aldosterone is a steroid HORMONE that promotes the conservation of sodium ions and water and the excretion of potassium ions by the KIDNEY. It is necessary for the maintenance of a proper balance between these two electrolytes in the body. The secretion of aldosterone by the cortex of the ADRENAL GLAND is regulated by the kidney. When a loss of sodium ions occurs, the kidney produces renin, an enzyme that acts on a plasma protein to manufacture the hormone angiotensin, which stimulates the adrenal cortex to produce aldosterone. Aldosterone then acts on the kidney to increase the excretion of potassium ions in place of sodium ions, with an accompanying retention of water. Excessive production of aldosterone may result in edema and high blood pressure (hyperaldosteronism). Insufficient aldosterone results in dehydration.

PETER L. PETRAKIS

Bibliography: Glaz, Edith, and Vecsei, Paul, *Aldosterone* (1971); Müller, Jürg, *Regulation of Aldosterone Synthesis* (1971); Williams, Robert H., ed., *Textbook of Endocrinology*, 5th ed. (1974).

See also: ENDOCRINE SYSTEM, DISEASES OF THE; HYPERTENSION.

Aldrich, Nelson Wilmarth

Nelson Wilmarth Aldrich, b. Foster, R.I., Nov. 5, 1841, d. Apr. 16, 1915, was an American businessman and politician. Starting in the wholesale grocery business in Providence, R.I., he further invested in sugar, rubber, street railways, and utilities and became a multimillionaire. He served on the Providence city council (1869–74) and in the Rhode Island legislature (1875–76), the U.S. House of Representatives (1879–81), and the U.S. Senate (1881–1911).

In the Senate, Aldrich wielded enormous power—especially after 1897—on behalf of the Republican majority. For a time he was the nemesis of President Theodore Roosevelt, with whom he clashed on foreign policy and railroad legislation. Aldrich advocated a conservative social philosophy on such issues as currency and banking, the tariff, and business regulations. Interested in establishing a central bank in the United States, he became chairman of the National Monetary Commission in 1908. Its report, the so-called Aldrich Plan (1911), served as the basis of the Federal Reserve Act of 1913.

ROBERT F. WESSER

Bibliography: Stephenson, Nathaniel W., *Nelson W. Aldrich, a Leader in American Politics* (1930; repr. 1971).

Aldrich, Robert

Robert Aldrich, b. Cranston, R.I., Aug. 8, 1918, d. Dec. 5, 1983, was one of the most forceful American film directors to emerge in the 1950s. His first popular success was *Vera Cruz* (1954), which was followed by a string of other successes including *What Ever Happened to Baby Jane?* (1962), *The Dirty Dozen* (1967), and *The Longest Yard* (1974). His work's genuine if crude power is perhaps best seen in *Kiss Me Deadly* (1955) and *Ulzana's Raid* (1972). Such later films as *Hustle* (1975) and *The Choirboys* (1977) met increasing critical hostility.

WILLIAM S. PECHTER

Aldrich, Thomas Bailey

The American writer Thomas Bailey Aldrich, b. Portsmouth, N.H., Nov. 11, 1836, d. Mar. 19, 1907, had an illustrious career both as an editor of the *Atlantic Monthly*, where he succeeded William Dean Howells, and as a poet and novelist. He is best remembered for his semiautobiographical novel *The Story of a Bad Boy* (1870), a work that resembles but predates by six years Mark Twain's *Tom Sawyer*.

Bibliography: Aldrich, Mrs. T. B., *Crowding Memories* (1920); Greenslet, Ferris, *The Life of Thomas Bailey Aldrich* (1908; repr. 1965); Samuels, Charles E., *Thomas Bailey Aldrich* (1966).

Aldridge, Ira

Ira Frederick Aldridge, b. New York City, July 24, 1804, d. Aug. 7, 1867, was the first great black American actor. His father was an ex-slave who became a lay preacher. Ira followed an acting company to London, where he made his debut in 1825 as the African prince Oroonoko in *The Revolt of Surinam, or a Slave's Revenge*. Hailed as the "African Roscius," he was considered outstanding as Othello, Macbeth, Lear, and Aaron the Moor. He was especially popular on the German stage. He became a naturalized British citizen in 1863.

ANDREW KELLY

Bibliography: Marshall, Herbert, and Stock, Mildred, *Ira Aldridge, the Negro Tragedian* (1958).

Aldrin, Edwin E.

The American astronaut Edwin E. "Buzz" Aldrin, b. Glen Ridge, N.J., Jan. 20, 1930, was the second man to walk on the Moon. In addition to his achievements as an astronaut, Aldrin's doctoral thesis on orbital mechanics and rendezvous laid the foundation for flight techniques that made the lunar landing possible. Aldrin graduated third in his class from the U.S. Military Academy in 1951 and received his Air Force pilot's wings in 1952. During the Korean War he flew 66 combat missions. He earned a doctorate of science in astronautics from the Massachusetts Institute of Technology in 1963 and later that year was selected as an astronaut.

On his first flight in space (1966), Aldrin piloted GEMINI *12* with commander James LOVELL. During a 5½-hour space walk, Aldrin helped to solve the exhaustion problem that had plagued earlier spacewalkers by using straps on the spacecraft as handholds and by pacing his efforts. He was then assigned as lunar module pilot to what became the first lunar landing mission (APOLLO *11*) in July 1969. His reponsibilities included monitoring the lunar module systems while commander Neil Armstrong concentrated on landing. After Aldrin joined Arm-

Edwin Aldrin, the second man to walk on the surface of the Moon, was photographed by the Apollo 11 mission commander, Neil Armstrong. Aldrin's helmet reflects both Armstrong and the Lunar Module vehicle.

strong on the Moon, they set up basic science experiments and collected samples of the Moon's surface.

After their return to Earth, Aldrin, Armstrong, and command module pilot Michael COLLINS appeared before a joint session of Congress and made a round-the-world goodwill tour. Two years after the Moon landing, Aldrin left NASA to become commander of the Air Force Aerospace Research Pilots School. In 1972 he resigned from the Air Force with the rank of colonel and entered private business. His autobiography, *Return to Earth* (1973), relates the pressures on the Apollo 11 crew and his subsequent nervous breakdown and recovery.

DAVID DOOLING

Aldus Manutius: see Manutius, Aldus.

ale

Ale is brewed from the same basic ingredients as lager BEER; the difference in flavor is caused in part by a different strain of yeast. Ale yeast ferments at higher temperatures than lager and imparts a distinctive tang and a somewhat higher alcohol content. Ale is also generally brewed with more hops than beer. Until lager beer was introduced to the United States in the mid-19th century, ale was the predominant beverage. Today, it is low in popularity in America. English "bitter" refers to a highly hopped pale ale, which is aromatic, rather than bitter, to the taste.   JOHN H. PORTER

aleatory music   [ay'-lee-uh-tor-ee]

Aleatory music is any music that results from the application of chance processes. The term is derived from the Latin word *alea* ("dice"). An aleatory score may include a set of verbal instructions for applying these processes to musical materials. Some typical aleatory devices are the following: dice throwing; random splattering of ink on music paper; drawing of cards; drawing of musical segments out of a hat; playing musical segments printed on a large page in the order that the performer's eye happens to fall on them; improvising music suggested by a graphic design.

Some critics argue that aleatory music represents the composer's rejection of traditional responsibilities. Others see it as an enhancement of the creative process, involving the performer more intimately in the composer's thinking. Contemporary composers who have used aleatory devices include John CAGE, Karl Heinz STOCKHAUSEN, Christian Wolff, Sylvano Bussotti, and Barney Childs. An early example of aleatory music was created by Wolfgang Amadeus MOZART in *Musical Dice Game.*   DIKA NEWLIN

Bibliography: Cage, John, *Silence* (1961); Cope, David, *New Directions in Music*, 2d ed. (1976); Schwartz, Elliott, and Childs, Barney, eds., *Contemporary Composers on Contemporary Music* (1967).

Alechinsky, Pierre

The French abstractionist Pierre Alechinsky, b. Brussels, Oct. 19, 1927, was one of the founders (1949) of the artists' group COBRA, for Copenhagen–Brussels–Amsterdam, which helped pioneer abstract expressionism in Paris. His own painting was influenced by oriental and cartoon styles and took on the appearance of visual commentary and abstract calligraphy. Line is paramount in his work, which often acquires the dripped casualness of Jackson POLLOCK's work. In 1977 Alechinsky won the newly activated Andrew W. Mellon Prize for excellence in contemporary art.   PHIL PATTON

Bibliography: Alechinsky, Pierre, *Paintings and Writings* (1977); Bosquet, Alain, *Alechinsky* (1971).

Alecsandri, Vasile

Vasile Alecsandri, b. *c.*1820, d. Aug. 22, 1890, studied in France and returned to his homeland to become the outstanding Romanian author of the mid-19th century. The Romanian theater depended greatly on his adaptations and original plays. His collection of folk poems strongly influenced the work of other poets. His volume *Pasteluri* (Pastels, 1867–69) shows him at his best as a poet. His finest prose pieces are reminiscences.   ERIC TAPPE

Bibliography: Cioranescu, Alexandre, *Vasile Alecsandri* (1974).

Alegría, Ciro   [ah-lay-gree'-ah]

Ciro Alegría, b. Nov. 4, 1909, d. Feb. 17, 1967, ranks as one of the principal Peruvian contributors to the development of the Indianist novel. His novels, *The Golden Serpent* (1935; Eng. trans., 1943), *Los perros hambrientos* (The Hungry Dogs, 1938), and *Broad and Alien Is the World* (1941; Eng. trans., 1941), reflect his deep concern for the rural population of Peru. These works are presented from the point of view of the many Indian characters who are exploited by authoritarian interests. César VALLEJO was one of his early teachers.   KEITH ELLIS

Aleichem, Sholem   [ah-lay'-kem]

Sholem Aleichem (Hebrew, "Peace be with you") was the pen name of the supreme Yiddish humorist, Solomon Rabinowitz. Along with MENDELE MOKHER SFORIM and I. L. PERETZ, he is a member of Yiddish literature's classical triumvirate.

Sholem Aleichem is best known for his fictional recreations of the world of the Eastern European *shtetl,* or small Jewish town, and for his ragged, quaint characters who remain invincibly optimistic in the face of poverty, persecution, and spiritual anguish. Among the characters exemplifying his "laughter through tears" philosophy are the impetuous, impractical Menachem Mendel; the quintessentially honest dairyman Tevye, whose unquestioning faith in God's design remains unaffected by travails and pogroms; and the cheerful orphan boy Mottel, whose resilience and pranks bring to mind Mark Twain's HUCKLEBERRY FINN.

Born Mar. 3 (Feb. 18, O.S.), 1859, in the Ukraine, Sholem Aleichem received a religious education and served for a time as a rabbi. He began publishing Yiddish sketches and short stories in 1883. Two novels, *Stempenyu* (1889) and *Yosele Solovey* (1890), appeared in *Di Yidische Folksbibliotek,* a literary annual he founded and edited for two years and to which the best Yiddish writers contributed before its demise. For many years he attempted to combine writing and business but, after inheriting wealth, he soon lost it in the stock market. Years of struggle and ill health after 1890 were capped in 1905 by a pogrom in Kiev, which led him to leave Russia. He spent a year in New York and then settled in Switzerland in 1907. From 1914 until his death on May 13, 1916, he lived in New York.

Sholem Aleichem wrote a prodigious number of short stories, novels, and plays. English-language collections of his stories include *Wandering Star* (1952); *Adventures of Mottel, the Cantor's Son* (1953); the autobiographical *Great Fair, Scenes from My Childhood* (1955); *Selected Stories* (1956); *Old Country Tales* (1966); *Tevye Stories* (1966); *Some Laughter, Some Tears* (1968); *Adventures of Menachem-Mendel* (1969); and *Stories and Satires* (1970). His popularity, always great, was further enhanced by the international success that greeted *Fiddler on the Roof*, a musical based on the stories of Tevye and his daughters. It appeared on the stage in 1964 and as a film in 1971.   SOL LIPTZIN

Bibliography: Liptzin, Sol, *History of Yiddish Literature* (1972); Samuel, Maurice, *The World of Sholom Aleichem* (1965).

Aleijadinho   [al-lay-zhah-deen'-yoh]

Antonio Francisco Lisboa, b. 1738, d. 1814, known as "O Aleijadinho" ("Little Cripple"), was the most renowned sculptor and architect of the Brazilian rococo period. He was the illegitimate son of the Portuguese architect Manuel Francisco Lisboa and a black slave called Isabel. At the age of 39 he contracted a disease that crippled him and left him without the use of his hands; thereafter he worked with a hammer and chisel strapped to his arms. His best work was done in his maturity. As an architect he is most noted for the design of the church of São Francisco de Assis in Ouro Preto, for which he also carved most of the interior decoration. His sculptural masterpiece is the series of 12 stone prophets and 6 polychromed wood scenes of the Passion of Christ, which he executed in 1800–05. These are installed in six chapels flanking the approach to the church of Bom Jesus de Matozinhos in Congonhas do Campo (Minas Gerais).   EDWARD J. SULLIVAN

Bibliography: Kelemen, P., *Baroque and Rococo in Latin America* (1951); Mann, G. and H., *The 12 Prophets of Aleijandinho* (1967).

Aleixandre, Vicente   [ah-layks-ahn'-dray]

The Spanish poet Vicente Aleixandre, b. Apr. 28, 1898, won the Nobel Prize for literature in 1977. Born in Seville, he spent his early childhood in Málaga and moved to Madrid in 1909. He first suffered kidney tuberculosis in 1925, which left him an invalid throughout his life. Sickness left its mark on his poetry—desperate songs of his journey from annihilation, evasion, and darkness to an affirmation of life, love, and light. A member of the "generation of 1927" to which Federico GARCÍA LORCA belonged, Aleixandre won Spain's National Prize for literature in 1933 with *La destrucción del amor* (Destruction of Love), picturing a visionary world of erotic love where unchained forces may prove fatal. In later collections Aleixandre portrays man as a being who suffers and dies within a temporal framework but nevertheless remains part of a vast cosmic reality. In *Diálogos del conocimiento* (Dialogues of Knowledge, 1974), he sought to reconcile variety with unity and existential awareness with transcendental intuition.
                                                    KESSEL SCHWARTZ

Bibliography: Morris, C. B., *A Generation of Spanish Poets (1920–1936)* (1969); Schwartz, Kessel, *Vicente Aleixandre* (1970).

Alemán, Mateo   [ah-lay-mahn', mah-tay'-oh]

Mateo Alemán, 1547–c.1614, was a Spanish novelist whose fame rests on his picaresque novel, *The Rogue; or, The Life of Guzmán de Alfarache* (1599; part 2, 1604; Eng. trans., 1622). The work, a narrative interspersed with moralizing digressions, presents a valuable picture of 16th-century Spain. Alemán viewed humankind as universally corrupt but able to achieve salvation through divine grace. After a troubled life—he was twice jailed as a debtor—Alemán migrated (1608) to Mexico, where he spent his last years.

Bibliography: McGrady, Donald, *Mateo Alemán* (1968); Parker, Alexander A., *Literature and the Delinquent: The Picaresque Novel in Spain and Europe, 1599–1753* (1967).

Alemán Valdés, Miguel
[al-lay-mahn' vahl-dayz']

Miguel Alemán Valdés, b. Sept. 29, 1902?, d. May 14, 1983, was the second civilian president of Mexico. A lawyer who represented injured workers, he served as governor of Vera-

cruz and in 1940 became minister of the interior. As president (1946–52), Alemán encouraged U.S. capital investment and stimulated Mexico's industrial development.

Alembert, Jean Le Rond d'   [dah-lahm-bair']

Jean Le Rond d'Alembert, b. Nov. 17, 1717, d. Oct. 29, 1783, was a French mathematician and physicist who developed the early stages of CALCULUS, formalized the new science of mechanics, and was the science editor of Diderot's *Encyclopédie*. With Diderot and Voltaire, he was one of the leading figures of the Enlightenment in France.

D'Alembert grew up in Paris. In 1741 he was admitted to the Paris Academy of Science, where he worked for the rest of his life.

D'Alembert ranks with Daniel Bernoulli, Alexis Clairaut, and Leonhard Euler as one of the leading scientists of his time. He was one of the first to understand the importance of functions and the concept of limits to the calculus, and he pioneered the use of differential equations in physics. He also helped to resolve the controversy in physics over the conservation of kinetic energy by improving Newton's definition of force in his *Traité de dynamique* (1742), which articulates d'Alembert's principle of mechanics. He also studied hydrodynamics, the mechanics of rigid bodies, and the three-body problem in astronomy.   R. CALINGER

Bibliography: Essar, Dennis F., *The Language Theory, Epistemology, and Aesthetics of Jean Lerond d'Alembert* (1976); Grimskey, Ronald, *Jean D'Alembert* (1963); Hankins, Thomas L., *Jean D'Alembert: Science and the Enlightenment* (1970); Pappas, John N., *Voltaire and D'Alembert* (1962); Van Treese, G. J., *D'Alembert and Frederick the Great* (1974).

Aleppo   [uh-lep'-oh]

Aleppo (Arabic: Halab, meaning "milk") is a city of northwestern Syria, the country's second largest, with a population of 919,244 (1979 est.). Abraham is supposed to have milked his flock there, hence the Arabic name. An oasis town on the ancient trade route between Europe and Asia, Aleppo is situated at a height of 390 m (1,280 ft) on a plateau approximately 320 km (200 mi) north-northeast of Damascus. The elevation ensures moderate temperature. January temperatures average 5.5° C (42° F) and July, 28° C (83° F), although extremes of 48° C (118° F) in summer and freezing in winter have been recorded. The average annual precipitation of 400 mm (16 in), most of which falls in the winter, is too little for the city's needs, and water must be piped in from the Euphrates River, some 80 km (50 mi) to the east.

The people of Aleppo are primarily Sunni Muslim Arabs, but there are sizable communities of Armenians and Turks in the newer sections. The city is a trade center where East meets West. Its location made it a stopping point for early caravans, and Aleppo is still famous for its khans (combination warehouse and caravansary) and its suqs, marketplaces where artisans weave fine cloth. Modern Aleppo is Syria's leading industrial center. Manufactures include textiles and garments, cement, vegetable oils, flour, processed foods, leather goods, and articles of gold and silver. Good highways connect Aleppo with Damascus, Baghdad, Mediterranean coastal cities, and Turkish cities to the north. A modern international airport handles both passengers and freight. Railroads connect Aleppo with Damascus, Beirut, and other Middle East cities. Aleppo has a major university, specializing in engineering and science, and a museum with Hittite, Assyrian, and Sumerian collections.

The old city is enclosed by a wall first built during Hellenistic times and reconstructed in the Middle Ages. Among the most important buildings are the noted citadel and the Great Mosque (AD 715), said to contain the tomb of Zacharias, the father of John the Baptist.

In its 4,000-year history Aleppo has witnessed much conflict and has been repeatedly captured by Egyptians, Turks, Arabs, and Mongols. From the 3d century BC to the 6th century, it was known as Beroea, but devastation by the Persians in 540 put an end to its importance. When it again rose to prominence in the 10th century, it reverted to its name of Halab. It saw much action during the Crusades, and under Ottoman rule (1516–1920) it functioned as a provincial seat.

W. A. BLADEN

Alessandri, Arturo

Arturo Alessandri, b. Dec. 20, 1868, d. Aug. 24, 1950, was president of Chile from 1920 to 1925 and again from 1932 to 1938. His first administration was noted for liberal reform. Briefly exiled (1924–25) by the military, he agreed to resume office on the condition that the constitution be changed to provide for a stronger presidency and some political democracy. During his more conservative second term, he concentrated on economic recovery, especially of the nitrate industry, and lost the support of the liberals and workers.

Alessandria

Alessandria is the capital city of Alessandria province in the Piedmont region of northwest Italy and is located southeast of Turin. It has a population of 101,684 (1979 est.) and is an important agricultural and wine market and a railroad center. The city was founded in 1168 by the Lombard League as a part of its defense of Lombardy against Emperor Frederick Barbarossa. First called Civitas Nova, it was renamed for Pope Alexander III. The Visconti dukes of Milan took the free commune in 1348. Remains of the city's fortifications, the cathedral, and the Romanesque-Gothic Church of Sta. Maria di Castello date from the Middle Ages. The city was taken in 1707 by Prince Eugene and ceded to Savoy in 1713. In 1833, as a center of Piedmont's freedom movement, it was the scene of a pro-Giuseppe Mazzini conspiracy.

DANIEL R. LESNICK

Alessi, Galeazzo   [ah-les'-see, gah-lay-ahts'-soh]

Galeazzo Alessi, 1512–72, was an important High Renaissance architect, best known for his work in Genoa and Milan. After receiving (c.1536–42) his training in Rome, probably as a pupil of Michelangelo, Alessi settled (c.1548) in Genoa. His most significant works include the domed church of Santa Maria di Carignano (begun c.1549; Genoa), with a centralized plan based on Donato Bramante's designs for St. Peter's Basilica in Rome, and the Palazzo Marino (1553–58; Milan). Alessi's designs are distinguished by his combination of architectural simplicity with rich decorative detail.

Bibliography: Hartt, Frederick, *History of Italian Renaissance Art* (1969); Keller, Harald, *The Renaissance in Italy* (1969); Murray, Linda, *The High Renaissance* (1967).

Aletsch Glacier   [ah'-lech]

Aletsch Glacier is in the Bernese Alps in Valais canton of south central Switzerland. With an area of 171 km² (66 mi²), it is thought to be the largest alpine glacier. It is composed of three parts: Great Aletsch (the main body) and Upper and Middle Aletsch (branches). Great Aletsch, 16 km (10 mi) long, is fed by streams of ice from the Aletschhorn and other mountains; it flows to the southwest toward the Rhône Valley. Upper Aletsch is at an altitude of 2,643 m (8,672 ft). Alongside are mountain hotels. A small lake, Märjelensee, is to the east. The glacier can be viewed from the train station at Jungfraujoch (3,454 m/11,333 ft).

Aleut   [uh-loot' or al'-ee-oot]

The people known as the Aleuts are the native inhabitants of the islands stretching for about 1,800 km (1,100 mi) southwestward from the Alaskan mainland and now called the Aleutian Islands. They also inhabit part of western Alaska. The Russians first called these maritime hunters "Aleuts," the meaning of which is unknown; their name for themselves is *unangan* ("the people").

Although racially and ethnically related to the ESKIMO, the Aleuts have their own language and culture. Before contact with outsiders in the 18th century, they lived in scattered villages, each consisting of several semisubterranean houses, and had a class system that included nobles and slaves. They

practiced a form of bilateral descent and followed instructions of local shamans regarding hunting taboos and coping with sickness. The Aleuts were adept at harvesting resources of the sea (sea lion, seals, whales, and fish) in their skin-covered boats as well as those of the land (birds, eggs, and plants). Their hunting skills were exploited by Russian fur traders who came to the islands after about 1750 in search of sea otter, fur seals, and foxes. Over the next 100 years the Aleut population severely declined because of sickness and harsh treatment. Today about 1,000 Aleuts remain; before contact with foreigners they had a population estimated at 12,000 to 25,000.

CHARLES C. HUGHES

Bibliography: Jones, Dorothy M., *Aleuts in Transition: A Comparison of Two Villages* (1976); Laughlin, William S., *Aleuts: Survivors of the Bering Land Bridge* (1981).

Aleutian Current   [uh-loo'-shuhn]

The Aleutian, or Subarctic, Current is a surface current that flows eastward between the Aleutian Islands and latitude 42° N. It is formed from the Kuroshio Current and the Oyashio Current. As it approaches the coast of North America, the Aleutian Current divides into the ALASKA CURRENT and the California Current. Surface temperature and salinity are reduced by cooling and heavy precipitation.

JOHN WHEELER

See also: OCEAN CURRENTS.

Aleutian Islands

The Aleutian Islands are a chain of islands stretching west 1,800 km (1,100 mi) from the tip of the Alaska Peninsula and separating the Bering Sea on the north from the Pacific Ocean on the south. Part of the state of Alaska, they include about 70 islands and scores of islets and have an area of 6,821 km² (17,666 mi²). The population is 7,768 (1980). Five major island groups stretch from east to west: the Fox, Islands of the Four Mountains, Andreanof, Rat, and Near. Partially submerged peaks of the volcanic Aleutian range, they rise sharply from the sea. The highest summit is Mount Shishaldin (2,856 m/ 9,387 ft) on Unimak Island. Virtually no trees grow on the islands, and vegetation includes grasses, sedges, and low flowering plants. Cold air and currents of the Bering Sea meet the warmer influences of the Pacific and cause a year-round mixture of fog, rain, high winds, and relatively uniform temperatures (annual average about 3° C/38° F). Discovered in 1741 by Vitus Jonassen BERING and Aleksei Chirikov, the islands were claimed by Russia. The Russians exploited the fur resources (blue foxes, seals) and nearly eliminated the native Aleut population. The islands were purchased along with Alaska from Russia by the United States in 1867. Unalaska (1760–75) is the oldest settlement.

Bibliography: Berkh, Vasilii N., *A Chronological History of the Aleutian Islands*, trans. by Dmitri Krenov (1974); Collins, Henry B., et al., *Aleutian Islands: Their People and Natural History* (1945); Hunt, William R., *Arctic Passage* (1975).

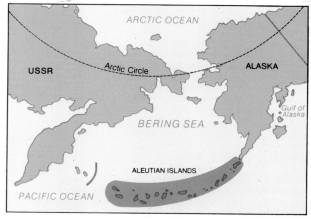

Aleutian Trench: see OCEANIC TRENCHES.

alewife   [ayl'-wyf]

The alewife, A. pseudoharengus, *now of negligible commercial value, was once a mainstay of the U.S fishing industry. About 1900, more than 20,000 metric tons (22,000 U.S. tons) were taken annually.*

The alewife, *Alosa pseudoharengus,* is a fish belonging to the herring family, Clupeidae, in the order Clupeiformes. It is a close relative of the SHAD and leads a similar life. Both the young and adult fish—the latter about 25 cm (10 in)—are found in coastal Atlantic Ocean waters from Canada to Florida. In spring, adults move into the estuaries to spawn. Spawning takes place at night; a pair of rapidly swimming fish rise upward in the water in a tight spiral and release the eggs and sperm in a rush at the surface. The eggs drift for two or three days and then hatch, and by autumn the young move into the sea. First noted in Lake Ontario and then in Lake Erie in the early 1940s, the alewife rapidly spread throughout the Great Lakes by 1954. Lake WHITEFISH populations were on the decline at that time, and it is unclear whether the alewife caused the decline or merely filled an available ecological niche. In the 1960s, SALMON and steelhead were introduced into the Great Lakes, and these fish have thrived by eating the alewife.   CAMM SWIFT

alexander

The alexander is any of several perennial herbs that are members of the parsley family, Umbelliferae. Golden alexander, *Zizia aurea,* with small, golden clusters of flowers in the typical umbel shape of the family, is found in wet meadows and along stream borders in the eastern United States. It blooms in May and June.   ROBERT C. ROMANS

Alexander, Grover Cleveland

The American baseball pitcher Grover Cleveland Alexander, b. Elba, Nebr., Feb. 26, 1887, d. Nov. 4, 1950, was, with Christy Mathewson, one of the two 20th-century major leaguers to win 30 or more games in 3 consecutive years (1915–17). In his 20 big-league seasons (1911–30), all in the National League, "Alexander the Great" won 373 games, tied for 3d on the all-time list. His 1916 season (with Philadelphia) was possibly the greatest ever by a pitcher: a 33–12 record, 38 complete games, 16 shutouts, and a 1.55 ERA.

Alexander, Harold George, 1st Earl Alexander of Tunis

Field Marshal Earl Alexander of Tunis, b. Dec. 10, 1891, d. June 16, 1969, was one of Britain's most successful generals in World War II. Commissioned into the Irish Guards, he was decorated for his service in World War I. In World War II he withdrew (1942) British and Indian forces from Burma and then directed the great Allied offensive to Tunis in North Africa, followed by the invasion of Sicily and Italy. Alexander served as governor-general of Canada (1946–52) and as minister of defense (1952–54) in Sir Winston Churchill's cabinet. He was made a viscount in 1946 and an earl in 1952.

Bibliography: Alexander of Tunis, Earl, *The Alexander Memoirs, 1940–1945* (1962); Nicolson, Nigel, *Alex: The Life of Field Marshal Earl Alexander of Tunis* (1973).

Alexander, Lloyd

Lloyd Alexander, b. Philadelphia, Jan. 30, 1924, is an American writer and translator who wrote the contemporary children's classic *Prydain Chronicles,* which includes *The Book of Three* (1964), *The Black Cauldron* (1965), *The Castle of Llyr* (1966), *Taran Wanderer* (1967), and *The High King* (1968). The last book won the 1969 Newbery Medal. The *Chronicles* were inspired by Arthurian legend and a collection of Welsh myths called the *Mabinogion.* They create a world that contains both humor and the struggle between good and evil. Among Alexander's other works for children are *August Bondi: Border Hawk* (1958) and *The Marvelous Misadventures of Sebastian* (1970), which won a 1971 National Book Award.

Alexander, Samuel

Samuel Alexander, b. Jan. 6, 1859, d. Sept. 9, 1939, was a British philosopher who taught at Manchester University (1893–1924) in England. Influenced by the theory of evolution, he viewed the world as a continuous process of unfolding. In his major work, *Space, Time, and Deity* (1920), he held that everything—including minds and deity—evolved from space and time. Other works include *Spinoza and Time* (1921) and *Beauty and Other Forms of Value* (1933).

Alexander Archipelago

The Alexander Archipelago is a group of about 1,100 islands stretching about 485 km (300 mi) along the southeastern coast of Alaska. Actually the tops of a submerged mountain range, the islands have irregular, steep coasts and dense evergreen forests. The main industry is lumbering; fishing and canning are also important. The largest island is Prince of Wales (225 by 64 km/135 by 45 mi), and the largest towns are Ketchikan (1980 pop., 7,198) on Revillagigedo Island and Sitka (1980 pop., 7,803) on Baranof Island. The islands were discovered by the Russians in 1741.

Alexander the Great, King of Macedonia

Alexander III, king of Macedonia, the first king to be called "the Great," conquered the Persian empire and annexed it to Macedonia. The son of PHILIP II and OLYMPIAS, he was born in 356 BC and brought up as crown prince. Taught for a time by Aristotle, he acquired a love for Homer and an infatuation with the heroic age. When Philip divorced Olympias to marry a younger princess, Alexander fled. Although allowed to return, he remained isolated and insecure until Philip's mysterious assassination about June 336.

Alexander was at once presented to the army as king. Winning its support, he eliminated all potential rivals, gained the allegiance of the Macedonian nobles and of the Greeks (after a rebellion, in which he destroyed THEBES), and defeated the neighboring barbarians. Then he took up Philip's war of aggression against Persia, adopting his slogan of a Hellenic Crusade against the barbarian. He defeated the small force de-

Alexander the Great of Macedonia, one of history's foremost military leaders, established an empire that extended from Greece to India. This detail from a mosaic, found at Pompeii, shows Alexander in the Battle of Issus (333 BC), where he defeated King Darius III of Persia.

fending Anatolia, proclaimed freedom for the Greek cities there while keeping them under tight control, and, after a campaign through the Anatolian highlands (to impress the tribesmen), met and defeated the Persian army under DARIUS III at Issus (near modern İskenderun, Turkey). He occupied Syria and—after a long siege of Tyre—Phoenicia, then entered Egypt, where he was accepted as pharaoh. From there he visited the famous Libyan oracle of Amon (or Ammon, identified by the Greeks with Zeus). The oracle certainly hailed him as Amon's son (two Greek oracles confirmed him as son of Zeus) and probably promised him that he would become a god. His faith in Amon kept increasing, and after his death he was portrayed with the god's horns.

After organizing Egypt and founding Alexandria, Alexander crossed the Eastern Desert and the Euphrates and Tigris rivers, and in the autumn of 331 defeated Darius' grand army at Gaugamela (near modern Irbil, Iraq). Darius fled to the mountain residence of Ecbatana, while Alexander occupied Babylon, the imperial capital Susa, and Persepolis. Henceforth, Alexander acted as legitimate king of Persia, and to win the support of the Iranian aristocracy he appointed mainly Iranians as provincial governors. Yet a major uprising in Greece had him so deeply worried that he delayed at Persepolis until May 330 and then, before leaving, destroyed the great palace complex as a gesture to the Greeks. At Ecbatana, after hearing that the rebellion had failed, he proclaimed the end of the Hellenic Crusade and discharged the Greek forces. He then pursued Darius, who had turned eastward. Darius was at once assassinated by Bessus, the satrap of Bactria, who distrusted his will to keep fighting and proclaimed himself king. As a result, Alexander now faced years of guerrilla war in northeastern Iran and central Asia, which ended only when he married (327) ROXANA, the daughter of a local chieftain. The whole area was fortified by a network of military settlements, some of which later developed into major cities.

During these years, Alexander's increasingly Oriental behavior led to trouble with Macedonian nobles and some Greeks. PARMENION, Philip II's senior general, and his family originally had a stranglehold on the army, but Alexander gradually weakened its grip. Late in 330, Parmenion's oldest

son, Philotas, commander of the cavalry and chief opponent of the king's new policies, was eliminated in a carefully staged coup d'etat, and Parmenion was assassinated. Another old-fashioned noble, Cleitus, was killed by Alexander himself in a drunken brawl. (Heavy drinking was a cherished tradition at the Macedonian court.) Alexander next demanded that Europeans follow the Oriental etiquette of prostrating themselves before the king—which he knew was regarded as an act of worship by Greeks. But resistance by Macedonian officers and by the Greek Callisthenes (a nephew of Aristotle who had joined the expedition as the official historian of the crusade) defeated the attempt. Callisthenes was soon executed on a charge of conspiracy.

With discipline restored, Alexander invaded (327) the Punjab. After conquering most of it, he was stopped from pressing on to the distant Ganges by a mutiny of the soldiers. Turning south, he marched down to the mouth of the Indus, engaging in some of the heaviest fighting and bloodiest massacres of the war. He was nearly killed while assaulting a town. On reaching the Indian Ocean, he sent the Greek officer Nearchus with a fleet to explore the coastal route to Mesopotamia. Part of the army returned by a tolerable land route, while Alexander, with the rest, marched back through the desert of southern Iran, chiefly to emulate various mythical figures said to have done this. He emerged to safety in the winter of 325–24, after the worst sufferings and losses of the entire campaign, to find his personal control over the heart of the empire weakened by years of absence and rumors of his death. On his return, he executed several of his governors and senior officers and replaced others.

He also ordered the governors to dismiss their mercenary armies, originally enrolled at his direction but now a cause of fear. Most of the mercenaries were exiled Greeks. The loss of their livelihood by tens of thousands of these men caused a grave social crisis. Alexander passed the problem on to the Greek cities by arbitrarily commanding them to readmit all their exiles. One side effect was a move to offer him deification (which some Greeks in Anatolia had perhaps already begun to do) in order to obtain concessions. Though the move was not due to his own initiative, this shows what he was

The vast territory conquered by Alexander the Great reached from Greece to India and included Egypt and the Persian Empire. The arrows on the map indicate the route of conquest, beginning in Macedonia in 336 BC and ending with Alexander's death in Babylon in 323 BC.

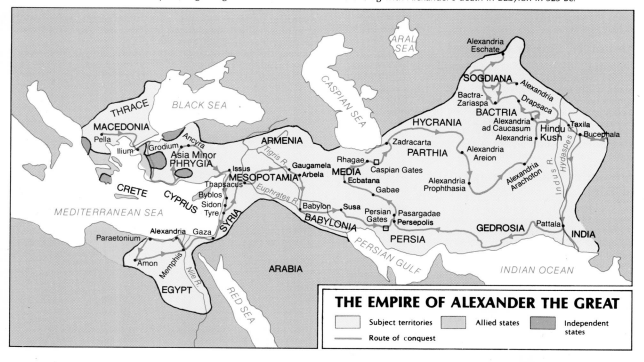

thought to want. In Athens and perhaps elsewhere, the deification was passed after considerable resistance.

In the spring of 324, Alexander held a great victory celebration at Susa. He and 80 close associates married Iranian noblewomen. In addition, he legitimized previous so-called marriages between soldiers and native women and gave them rich wedding gifts, no doubt to encourage such unions. When he discharged the disabled Macedonian veterans a little later, after defeating a mutiny by the estranged and exasperated Macedonian army, they had to leave their wives and children with him. Because national prejudices had prevented the unification of his empire, his aim was apparently to prepare a long-term solution (he was only 32) by breeding a new body of high nobles of mixed blood and also creating the core of a royal army attached only to himself. After his death, nearly all the noble Susa marriages were dissolved.

In the autumn of 324, at Ecbatana, Alexander lost his boyhood friend Hephaestion, by then his grand vizier—probably the only person he had ever genuinely loved. The loss was irreparable. After deep mourning, he embarked on a winter campaign in the mountains, then returned to Babylon, where he prepared an expedition for the conquest of Arabia. He died in June 323 without designating a successor. His death opened the anarchic age of the DIADOCHI.

Alexander at once became a legend to the peoples that had seen him pass like a hurricane. Greek accounts from the start tended to blend almost incredible fact with pure fiction (for example, his meeting with the Queen of the AMAZONS). In the Middle Ages, the *Alexander Romance*, developed from beginnings soon after his death, was favorite light reading. Modern scholars, ever since the German historian Johann Gustav Droysen (1808–84) used Philip II and Alexander to embody his vision of the unification and expansion of Germany, have tended to make him a vehicle for their own dreams and ideals. The truth is difficult to disengage. The only clear features that emerge are Alexander's military genius and his successful opportunism: his unequaled eye for a chance and his sense of timing in both war and politics. The only clear motive is the pursuit of glory: the urge to surpass the heroes of myth and to attain divinity. The success of his ambition, at immense cost in human terms, spread a veneer of Greek culture far into central Asia, and some of it—supported and extended by the Hellenistic dynasties—lasted for a long time. It also led to an expansion of Greek horizons and to the acceptance of the idea of a universal kingdom, which prepared the way for the Roman Empire. Moreover, it opened up the Greek world to new Oriental influences, which prepared the way for Christianity.

E. BADIAN

Bibliography: Borza, Eugene N., ed., *The Impact of Alexander the Great* (1976); Green, Peter, *Alexander the Great* (1970); Griffith, G. T., ed., *Alexander the Great* (1966); Hamilton, J. R., *Alexander the Great* (1973); Milns, R. D., *Alexander the Great* (1968); Tarn, W. W., *Alexander the Great*, 2 vols. (1948); Wilcken, U., *Alexander the Great*, trans. by G. C. Richards, 2d ed., ed. by E. N. Borza (1967).

Alexander Nevsky

Alexander Nevsky, b. c.1220, d. Nov. 14, 1263, was an outstanding Russian prince and military leader who earned his surname by defeating the Swedes at the mouth of the Neva River on July 15, 1240. He also won a famous victory over the German order of Livonian Knights on the ice of Lake Peipus in 1242. Alexander was the son of Yaroslav Vsevolodovich, prince of Novgorod. When his father became prince at Kiev in 1236, Alexander succeeded him as prince of Novgorod. Alexander became grand prince of Vladimir in 1252. He pursued a policy of cooperation with the Mongol suzerains of Russia, who reciprocated by abandoning demands for Russian troops and by withdrawing tax collectors. Alexander was canonized locally in Vladimir in 1380 and generally by the Russian Orthodox church in 1547. In 1942 the Soviet Military Order of Alexander Nevsky was reestablished.

DONALD L. LAYTON

Bibliography: Grunwald, Constantin de, *Saints of Russia* (1960); Vernadsky, George, *A History of Russia*, rev. ed. (1961).

Alexander v. Holmes County (Miss.) Board of Education

In *Alexander* v. *Holmes County (Miss.) Board of Education* (1969) the Supreme Court held for the first time that the BROWN V. BOARD OF EDUCATION OF TOPEKA decision (1954), which invalidated segregation in the public schools, was no longer to be enforced under the enunciated principle of "all deliberate speed." Instead, said the Court, "the obligation of every school district is to terminate dual school systems at once and to operate now and hereafter only unitary schools." The case had reached the Supreme Court after a federal court of appeals had allowed 33 school districts in Mississippi additional time to integrate.

The Supreme Court declared that the lower federal court had erred in granting a motion for additional time, since it had failed to realize that "all deliberate speed" was no longer "constitutionally permissible." The case appeared to emphasize the ruling in *Green* v. *County School Board of New Kent County (Virginia)* in 1968, which had struck down a plan permitting all students to be assigned to the school of their choice. The Court had stated in the *Green* case that the school board must fashion steps that would realistically convert promptly to a "system without a 'white' school and a 'Negro' school but just schools." Under the Court's initial ruling in the *Brown* case, the states had been ordered to abandon legally enforced segregation, but in *Green* and *Alexander* the Court took the advanced position that the Constitution positively requires racially mixed schools.

ROBERT J. STEAMER

Alexander of Hales

Alexander of Hales, b. c.1186, d. Aug. 21, 1245, was an English scholastic philosopher and theologian. He began his formal training in arts, philosophy, and theology at the University of Paris when he was 15 years old and became (c.1220) the first to lecture as a master on the *Sentences* of PETER LOMBARD. After a long and illustrious career, he became a FRANCISCAN friar in 1236 at the age of 50. With him came the right to a chair of theology at the University of Paris, the first and only chair the Franciscans held. Under him the Franciscan John of la Rochelle became master and probably assembled the *Summa Fratris Alexandri*, which influenced the formation of a Franciscan school, notably through St. Bonaventure.

JAMES. A. WEISHEIPL

Alexander III, King of Macedonia:
see ALEXANDER THE GREAT, KING OF MACEDONIA.

Alexander I, Emperor of Russia

Alexander I, b. Dec. 12, 1777, d. Nov. 19, 1825, became emperor of Russia on Mar. 12, 1801, following the murder of his father, PAUL I, by members of a conspiracy in which Alexander was indirectly involved. Alexander had been taken from his parents at birth by his grandmother, CATHERINE II. Some historians see a key to his complex personality in the estrangement between his father and grandmother and in Alexander's feelings of guilt over his father's assassination.

Intelligent and well-educated, Alexander was also vain, suspicious, and pedantic. He hoped to make Russia into a modern, efficient state, but his own uncertainty and irresolution barred the way to comprehensive reform. Nevertheless, for nearly 20 years after coming to the throne, he toyed with one constitutional scheme after another and in 1815 was instrumental in the introduction of constitutions into Poland and the Grand Duchy of Finland.

Alexander tended to rely upon favorites to formulate his reform projects. The earliest example was his Unofficial Committee, composed of four of his youthful companions. Subsequently, he turned to Mikhail Mikhailovich SPERANSKY, perhaps one of the most gifted men of his age, and, following the defeat of NAPOLEON I, Aleksei Andreyevich Arakcheyev (1769–1834) became Alexander's most trusted servant. The re-

Alexander I, emperor of Russia (1801–1825), played a leading role in the defeat of Napoleon I of France and emerged as one of the most powerful rulers in Europe. He was the architect of the Holy Alliance (1815), which was intended to affirm the Christian principles of the European nations but became instead the symbol of the repressive policies followed in Russia, Austria, and Prussia.

sults were few, and Alexander in his frustration turned to religious mysticism, which strongly colored his domestic and foreign policies during the decade following 1812. The most notable example was his proposed HOLY ALLIANCE in 1815.

Alexander had some success, however. Although defeated by Napoleon at Austerlitz (1805) and Friedland (1807) and forced to submit to the humiliating Treaty of Tilsit (1807), Russia endured Napoleon's invasion of 1812 and then played a leading role in the war of liberation and final defeat of the French. Europe's adulation of Alexander as its liberator served to secure for him a place in history. Nevertheless, his failure to solve Russia's basic problems precipitated the DECEMBRIST revolt of 1825 and began the permanent disaffection of much of educated society. FORRESTT A. MILLER

Bibliography: Almedingen, Edith, *The Emperor Alexander I* (1964); McConnell, Allen, *Tsar Alexander I: Paternalistic Reformer* (1970); Palmer, Alan, *Alexander I: Tsar of War and Peace* (1974).

Alexander II, Emperor of Russia

Alexander II, b. Apr. 17, 1818, d. Mar. 1, 1881, emperor of Russia, emancipated the serfs by a proclamation of Feb. 19, 1861, and ushered in an era of reform. The changes included an overhaul of justice and the courts, a tempering of censorship, autonomy for the universities, elected assemblies at the local and provincial levels, and universal military conscription. Alexander succeeded his father, NICHOLAS I, on Feb. 19, 1855, during the dark days of the CRIMEAN WAR. The humiliating loss of that war and the national weaknesses it revealed undoubtedly played some role in Alexander's subsequent reform activity. Even so, a personal conviction that Russia had to modernize may have been at least as important.

As an individual, Alexander II somewhat resembled his uncle, ALEXANDER I. Handsome, charming, and sentimental, he was also irresolute and often was persuaded by the last person to have his ear. Following attempts upon his life, beginning in 1866, he lived in fear and closed himself off to all except a few favorites. Their influence gave a reactionary temper to the latter half of his reign. An assassin—a member of the People's Will, an extremist offshoot of the NARODNIKI (populist movement)—finally succeeded in killing Alexander the same day that he signed a manifesto that would have created a national consultative assembly. The tragedy of Alexander's violent death was compounded by the failure of his successor, ALEXANDER III, to implement this progressive act, thereby ending the moderate reforms that might have helped Russia avoid the revolutions of the 20th century.
FORRESTT A. MILLER

Bibliography: Almedingen, E. M., *The Emperor Alexander II* (1962); Field, Daniel, *The End of Serfdom: Nobility and Bureaucracy in Russia, 1855-1861* (1976); Morse, W. E., *Alexander II and the Modernization of Russia* (1958).

Alexander III, Emperor of Russia

Alexander III, b. Feb. 26, 1845, d. Oct. 20, 1894, emperor of Russia, was an ardent adherent of unfettered autocracy. Coming to the throne on Mar. 1, 1881, following the assassination of his father, ALEXANDER II, he began his reign by repudiating the limited constitution his father had signed on the day of his death and by dismissing the more progressive ministers who had served his father. Blunt and unimaginative, Alexander acted more from instinct than intellect. However, the influence of such persons as his former tutor, K. P. Pobedonostsev, and the publicist M. N. Katkov gave his actions both force and direction.

Much of Alexander's reign was spent in evading or undoing the reforms of his father. A state of emergency, declared in August 1881 but lasting through the reign, circumvented the courts and gave imperial administrators arbitrary powers. Acts promulgated in 1889, 1890, and 1892 sharply circumscribed autonomy at the provincial and municipal levels, and censorship prior to publication was reasserted in 1882. Conformity was enforced by a vigorous program of Russification that included considerable anti-Semitic legislation. Alexander's reign did succeed in muting the voices of change, but the fundamental problems of Russian society remained unresolved and were more pressing than ever when he died.
FORRESTT A. MILLER

Alexander III, King of Scotland

Alexander III, b. Sept. 4, 1241, d. Mar. 18–19, 1286, king of Scotland, succeeded his father, Alexander II, in 1249 while still a young boy. HENRY III of England took advantage of the situation by trying to establish suzerainty (political control) over Scotland, but the bishop of St. Andrews, with help from the papacy, prevented it. In 1263 the Scottish king confronted Haakon IV of Norway concerning the possession of the Hebrides and defeated the Norwegians in the Battle of Largs. Alexander established a united and economically prosperous Scotland. His sudden death, however—followed by that of his heir, Margaret, maid of Norway—opened the way for EDWARD I of England to intervene drastically in Scottish affairs.
CHARLES H. HAWS

Bibliography: Duncan, A. A. M., *Scotland, the Making of the Kingdom* (1975).

Alexander, King of Serbia

Alexander, b. Aug. 14, 1876, d. June 11, 1903, was the son of Milan Obrenović, prince (1868–82) and then king (1882–89) of Serbia. On the abdication of his father, Alexander became king under a regency, but four years later he proclaimed himself sole ruler. His marriage (1900) to Draga Mašin, a widow, was unpopular and even more so was his pro-Austrian foreign policy. Alexander and Draga were assassinated by a group of pro-Russian officers. The Obrenović dynasty was eliminated and that of Karadjordjević restored by PETER I.

Alexander, King of Yugoslavia

Alexander, b. Dec. 16, 1888, first king of Yugoslavia, was the son of King PETER I of Serbia. In June 1914, Peter, being of poor health, appointed Alexander regent of Serbia. During World War I, Alexander was the nominal commander in chief of the Serbian army. On his father's death (Aug. 16, 1921) he became king of the new Kingdom of Serbs, Croats, and Slovenes. Faced with great governmental instability caused mainly by discord between the Serbs and Croats, Alexander abolished (Jan. 6, 1929) the constitution and instituted absolute rule, calling himself king of Yugoslavia. On Oct. 9, 1934, he was assassinated in Marseilles by a terrorist in the pay of a Croatian separatist group. He was succeeded by his son PETER II.

Alexander III, Pope

Alexander III, b. *c.*1105, d. Aug. 30, 1181, was pope from Sept. 7, 1159, until his death. His name was Orlando Bandinelli. One of a continuing line of papal reformers in conflict with the German monarchy, he inherited a war with FREDERICK I and was confronted with antipopes Victor IV, Paschal III, and Callistus III, who were created by Frederick. In these struggles with Frederick he obtained the support of HENRY II of England and Louis VII of France. Nonetheless, he was forced to leave Rome in 1162 and go into exile in France, where the papal court settled at Sens from 1163 to 1165. He finally achieved a reconciliation with Frederick in 1177 owing to Frederick's defeats at the hands of the Italian communes. During his pontificate he also had to moderate the quarrel between Thomas BECKET and Henry II of England.

Alexander III was a recognized scholar. Earlier in his life, he had been a professor at Bologna, where he achieved a reputation for his knowledge of theology and canon law. One of the great medieval popes, he fostered the scholastic revival of the 12th century.　　　　DAVID HARRY MILLER

Bibliography: Baldwin, Marshall W., *Alexander III and the Twelfth Century* (1968); Boso, Cardinal, *Boso's Life of Alexander III,* trans. by G. M. Ellis (1973).

Alexander VI, Pope

Alexander VI, b. *c.*1431, d. Aug. 18, 1503, was pope from 1492 to 1503. A Spaniard, he was named Rodrigo de Borja (Borgia), a member of the famous BORGIA family. He was the nephew of Pope CALLISTUS III, who created him a cardinal in 1456; his election to the papacy was accomplished largely through bribery. Alexander was denounced during his pontificate by the Florentine reformer Girolamo SAVONAROLA, who declared his election to the papacy invalid as a result of simony. This led to Savonarola's excommunication by Alexander in 1497 and to his execution as a heretic in 1498.

Of the Renaissance popes, Alexander is the most notorious for political involvement in favor of his children and for the immorality of his personal life. Some charges made against him are undoubtedly exaggerated, but even the most sympathetic historians have not been able to clear his name, which is almost synonymous with corruption in high ecclesiastical office. Although better educated than Callistus III, Alexander VI contributed comparatively little to the Renaissance as a patron of art and letters.　　　　JOHN W. O'MALLEY

Bibliography: Johnson, Marion, *The Borgias* (1981); Mallett, Michael, *The Borgias* (1975).

Alexandra Fyodorovna, Empress of Russia

[fyaw'-duh-rawv-nuh]

Alexandra Fyodorovna, b. June 6, (N.S.), 1872, was the consort of NICHOLAS II, the last tsar of Russia. She was the daughter of the grand duke of Hesse-Darmstadt and a granddaughter of Queen Victoria of Britain. Her original name, Alix, was changed before her marriage to Nicholas on Nov. 26, 1894. Alexandra was a determined, narrow-minded reactionary, with pretensions to mysticism, and she dominated her irresolute husband. During World War I she became the virtual ruler of Russia, and the debauched monk Grigory Yefimovich RASPUTIN—who claimed healing power over the hemophiliac heir to the throne, Aleksei—was her chief advisor. After the Bolshevik Revolution (1917), Alexandra with Nicholas and all their children were shot on the night of July 16–17, 1918, in Ekaterinburg (now Sverdlovsk).

Bibliography: Bird, Anthony, *Empress Alexandra* (1970); Massie, Robert K., *Nicholas and Alexandra* (1967).

Alexandrescu, Grigore　[ul-ek-suhn-dres'-kue, gree-gor'-eh]

Grigore Alexandrescu, b. *c.*1812, d. Nov. 25 or 26, 1885, pioneered in the modernization of the Romanian language and in the renaissance of Romanian literature. In 1831 he went to Bucharest to study and there he met other students having

progressive ideas. Even though he was arrested for political activities, he later gained posts in the civil service. Much of his poetry is weak. More interesting are his fables satirizing politics and society, published in *Meditatii, elegii, epistole, satire și fabule* (Meditations, Elegies, Letters, Satires, and Fables, 1863).　　　　ERIC TAPPE

Alexandria　(Egypt)

Alexandria (Arabic: al-Iskandariya) is the chief port and second largest city of Egypt. The population is 2,317,705 (1976). Alexandria is located on the west side of the Nile Delta on a strip of land between Lake Maryut and the Mediterranean Sea. An isthmus about 1.5 km (1 mi) wide connects the former island of Pharos with the mainland, separating the East and West harbors. The West Harbor serves as the city's port and has modern facilities. The inner harbor of the West Harbor is protected on three sides (by a breakwater, Pharos, and the isthmus) from Mediterranean storms. The West Harbor was joined to the Nile by a canal early in the 19th century.

Alexandria enjoys a Mediterranean climate. Annual precipitation averages less than 250 mm (10 in), coming mostly during November, December, and January; little or no rain falls in the summer. January is the coolest month, with an average temperature of 18° C (64° F); August is the warmest, with an average of 31° C (87° F). The pleasant climate and sandy beaches make Alexandria a favorite tourist spot.

Contemporary City. Isthmian Alexandria is characteristically Egyptian. The European quarter stands on the mainland south of the East Harbor. The city has numerous mosques, palaces, monuments, parks, and gardens. A suburb, al-Raml, with its fine beaches, is known as the Egyptian Riviera. The West Harbor is the commercial center and has numerous warehouses for cotton, sugar, foodstuffs, grain, and wool. Industries in the city include oil refining, motor-vehicle assembly, food processing, and textile weaving. The bulk of Egypt's foreign trade passes through the port of Alexandria. Excellent railroads and highways connect it with Cairo and other cities.

History. For more than 2,000 years Alexandria was the largest city of Egypt. It was founded in 332 BC by Alexander the Great and was well planned. About 6.5 km (4 mi) in length and 2–3 km (1–2 mi) in width, it had streets crossing at right angles. Two main avenues, the present-day Fuad and Nebi Daniel streets, were then as now the center of the commercial, cultural, and political life of the city. A lighthouse, one of the SEVEN WONDERS OF THE WORLD, was built on the island of Pharos in 280 BC. The island was later connected to the mainland by an isthmus, called the Heptastadium, enclosing the Port of Pharos, now the East Harbor.

Famous buildings in the early city included the Temple of Serapis, the Temple of Poseidon, the Soma (mausoleum of Alexander the Great and the Ptolemies), a museum, a theater, an emporium, and the Alexandrian Library, founded by PTOLEMY I. Under the Ptolemies, the city was the literary and scientific center of the Hellenistic world. Later, under the Romans, its location made it the center of world commerce. Many artifacts from the ancient city are displayed in the Greco-Roman Museum.

Alexandria was captured by the Arabs in AD 642 and nearly destroyed by them. The lighthouse was devastated by an earthquake in 1324. The new lighthouse that took its place stands at Ras el-Tin, overlooking the West Harbor. Napoléon Bonaparte held the city from 1798 to 1801. In 1882, Alexandria was bombarded and occupied by the British, and during World Wars I and II it served as a British naval base. Emigration of the once large foreign community since the 1950s has made Alexandria a more Egyptian city.　　　　W. A. BLADEN

Bibliography: Forster, E. M., *Alexandria: A History and Guide,* 2d ed. (1938; repr. 1974).

Alexandria　(Louisiana)

Alexandria (1980 pop., 51,565), a city in central Louisiana, is the seat of Rapides Parish. Settled in the 1760s, surveyed and named in 1805, and incorporated in 1819, the city became a cotton, sugarcane, and cattle center. It was burned (1864) by Union forces during the Civil War. Recovery came with the arrival of the railroad and the reestablishment of forestry. Today farm products and livestock complement the forestry industry.

Alexandria   (Virginia)

Alexandria is a city in northern Virginia, on the west bank of the Potomac River, 10 km (6 mi) south of Washington, D.C. It has a population of 103,217 (1980). A residential community and commercial center, the city has many old buildings that make it a tourist attraction. The site was first settled in 1695; in 1732 Scottish merchants founded a village, which they named Belhaven. In 1749, by act of the Virginia House of Burgesses, the town was established and renamed Alexandria. Although Alexandria was included in the boundaries of the District of Columbia in 1791, it was returned to Virginia in 1846 as an independent city, free of county affiliations (which it remains). The city was occupied by Union troops throughout the Civil War. The estate of George Washington (who helped lay out Alexandria's streets) is 15 km (9 mi) south.

alexandrine   [al-ig-zan'-drin]

The alexandrine is a 12-syllable line of verse composed of 6 iambic feet. The term is probably derived from the late 12th-century poem *Roman d'Alexandre* and other elevated verse celebrating Alexander the Great. The alexandrine has been a standard meter in French poetry since the 16th century, used in such classical works as the tragedies of Jean Racine. It is also an important feature of Dutch and German poetry. A celebrated example of the alexandrine in English literature, where it is called iambic hexameter, is in Edmund Spenser's THE FAERIE QUEENE (1590–96), where it concludes each stanza.

J. A. CUDDON

See also: VERSIFICATION.

Alexeyev, Vasily   [ah-lek-syay'-ef]

Vasily Alexeyev, b. Jan. 7, 1942, an extraordinary Soviet weight lifter, won the Olympic Games superheavyweight class in 1972 and again in 1976. He also won 8 consecutive world championships (1970–77) and set 80 world records. At the time of his Olympic victory in Montreal (1976), Alexeyev, an engineer, weighed 156 kg (345 lb). He had a 162-cm (60-in) chest, 53-cm (21-in) biceps, and 86-cm (34-in) thighs. He set an Olympic record that year by lifting a combined 440 kg (970 lb)—185.1 kg (408 lb) for the snatch and 254.9 kg (562 lb) for the clean-and-jerk. After a poor performance at the 1980 Moscow Olympics, he virtually retired.

Alexis, Tsar of Russia

Alexis, b. Mar. 10, 1629, d. Jan. 29, 1676, tsar of Russia (1645–76), was a religious and humane but authoritarian ruler. He was the son of Tsar Michael, the first of the Romanov dynasty to rule Russia. Alexis's reign was beset by popular revolts, the most serious being that of the DON COSSACKS under Stenka RAZIN. Alexis harshly suppressed this (1671) and other uprisings. Russian expansion continued under Alexis with the acquisition (1667) from Poland of much territory, part of the later Ukraine. The religious reforms enacted by the patriarch NIKON, which led to the great schism within the Russian church, also occurred during Alexis's reign. Alexis was succeeded by his son Fyodor III, who was in turn succeeded (1682) by his brothers Ivan V and Peter I under the regency of Sophia.

DONALD L. LAYTON

Bibliography: Bergamini, John, *The Tragic Dynasty: The History of Romanovs* (1969).

Alexius I Comnenus, Byzantine Emperor
[kuhm-nee'-nus]

Alexius I Comnenus, b. c.1048, d. Aug. 15, 1118, ruled the Byzantine Empire from 1081 to 1118. With the support of the army and his numerous relatives, he usurped the throne from Nicephorus III. Alexius found the empire beset by foes: Seljuks occupied the Asian provinces, Pechenegs ravaged the Danubian regions, and Normans from southern Italy attacked Epirus. From 1081 to 1092 he was engaged in defeating the Normans and Pechenegs. In 1097–98 he utilized the victories of the First Crusade over the Seljuk Turks at Nicaea and Dorylaeum to regain the coastal regions of Anatolia. From 1099 to 1104 he contended with BOHEMOND I for Antioch; then in 1107–08 he overcame Bohemond's army in Epirus. Internally, Alexius reformed the monetary and taxation systems. Well educated himself, he vigorously repressed the unorthodox philosopher John Italus and the Bogomil heretics. After his death, he was succeeded by his son, John II.   C. M. BRAND

Bibliography: Comnena, Anna, *The Alexiad*, trans. by E. R. A. Sewter (1928; repr. 1969).

alfalfa

Alfalfa, *Medicago sativa*, a legume forage plant belonging to the pea family Leguminosae, has been an animal feed longer than any other forage crop. Alfalfa was planted in hot, dry regions of Mesopotamia before recorded history. The seed was taken to South America by Spanish explorers during the 16th century.

The first attempts to produce alfalfa in North America were made in Georgia in 1736, but the crop did not become important until it was taken from Chile to California, where it flourished in the favorable climate. Alfalfa now is grown throughout the world under extremely varied climatic conditions. The United States produces approximately 68 million metric tons (75 million U.S. tons) of alfalfa hay annually. California, Wisconsin, Iowa, Nebraska, Michigan, and Minnesota lead in production.

The Plant. Alfalfa is a perennial plant and will under normal conditions live for six or more years. Its shoots may grow to stems of more than 1 m (3 ft). The plant produces compound leaves and yellow to purplish-blue flowers, and kidney-shaped seeds develop inside the curled pods. The roots are extraordinarily long, often extending more than 7 m (25 ft) deep, which makes alfalfa an ideal crop for dry climates. It also enriches soil with nitrogen.

Alfalfa will grow in a wide variety of conditions, but it does best in deep, loamy, well-drained soils. It responds well to irrigation and to fertilizers. Alfalfa seed is generally planted with grain drills—in the spring in cooler climates or in the fall if winter temperatures are moderate. Alfalfa can be sown with other grains, such as oats, to reduce weed growth. When sown for pasture, it is sometimes mixed with rye, bromegrass, bluegrass, timothy, or fescue.

Alfalfa, M. sativa, is the most important cattle-fodder crop. The flowers (detail, right) *grow in dense, short, terminal clusters.*

Harvesting. Procedures used to harvest alfalfa depend on the yield, nutritional quality, and physical condition desired. The maximum yield occurs when the plant is cut at full bloom, but other considerations such as stem size, moisture, and vitamin content may alter cutting time. Cuttings range from two to seven or eight a year, depending on the environment.

Harvesting procedures differ throughout the world. Generally, however, alfalfa is cut with a mowing machine and windrowed to permit drying. Modern, self-propelled combine cutters and choppers are used to collect the alfalfa for either silage or dehydration.

Uses. Extremely nutritious, alfalfa is valuable for feeding all kinds of livestock. It is used for pasture, soil building, for dehydration, as meal, or as silage. Dehydrated alfalfa is a common ingredient of feedstuffs and supplies vitamins, protein, lipids, and minerals.   J. A. SHELLENBERGER

Alfieri, Vittorio   [ahl-feeay'-ree]

Vittorio Alfieri, b. Jan. 16, 1749, d. Oct. 8, 1803, a tragic poet, became the prophet of Italian political and cultural resurgence, or RISORGIMENTO. His nationalist sentiments inspired later generations in the arduous task of Italian unification. A member of an aristocratic family in Asti, he achieved early success with a play, *Cleopatra* (1775). In 1777 he fell in love with the Countess of Albany, Louise Stolberg, with whom he lived for the rest of his life after her separation from her husband, Charles Edward Stuart, the pretender to the English throne. Alfieri's works reflect both his reading of French philosophers (Voltaire, Rousseau) and the general tenor of the age. They include classical dramas (*Filippo*, 1783; *Saul*, 1787); prose political works (*Della tirannide*, 1777; On Tyranny, 1961); and poetic political works (*America libera*, 1782–83; *Parigi sbastigliata*, 1789). His themes primarily concern the struggle of heroic individuals for liberty and freedom against tyranny and oppression. In *Il Misogallo* (The French Hater, 1790–99), he inveighed against the French and voiced pro-Italian feelings. The *Vita* (1803; *Memoirs*, 2 vols., 1810; *The Life*, 1949) offers many insights into the events of Alfieri's age and their effect on him.   CHRISTOPHER KLEINHENZ

Bibliography: Megaro, Gaudens, *Vittorio Alfieri, Forerunner of Italian Nationalism* (1930; repr. 1971); Miller, C., *Alfieri, a Biography* (1936).

Alfonsín, Raúl   [al-fohn-seen']

Raúl Ricardo Alfonsín Foulkes, b. Mar. 12, 1927, took office as president of Argentina on Dec. 10, 1983, ending nearly 8 years of military rule. A lawyer, former congressman, and Radical party leader, he quickly moved to prosecute those responsible, including the military, for the disappearance of thousands of persons in the late 1970s. He also worked to alleviate Argentina's severe economic crisis, aspects of which were inflation and a huge foreign debt.

Alfonso V, King of Aragon   (Alfonso the Magnanimous)

Alfonso V, b. 1396, d. June 27, 1458, king of Aragon and Sicily (1416–58), also acquired the kingdom of Naples. Queen Joan II of Naples (r. 1414–35) adopted him as her heir, but she later changed her mind and offered Naples to Louis of Anjou. By 1442, Alfonso V had overcome all opposition and entered Naples in triumph. Thereafter he participated actively in Italian politics. His nickname was bestowed because he was a notable patron of Renaissance humanists. He left Aragon and Sicily to his brother John II and Naples to his illegitimate son FERDINAND I.   JOSEPH F. O'CALLAGHAN

Alfonso I, King of Portugal

Alfonso I, b. *c.*1109, d. 1185, was the first king of Portugal. The son of Henry of Burgundy (d. 1112), count of Portugal, and of Teresa, illegitimate daughter of Alfonso VI of Castile, Alfonso seized control of Portugal from his mother in 1128. He resisted the domination of the neighboring Spanish kingdoms and attacked the Muslim lands south of Coimbra with the help of foreign crusaders. He conquered Santarém and Lisbon in 1147 and Évora in 1165. Though Alfonso had claimed the title of king for 40 years, the papacy did not officially recognize him until 1179.   DANIEL R. HEADRICK

Alfonso II, King of Portugal

Alfonso II, b. *c.*1185, d. Mar. 25, 1223, king of Portugal from 1211, displayed deep concern with legal matters and clashed with the church. Succeeding his father, Sancho I, he helped Castile defeat the Moors in the important victory of Las Navas de Tolosa (1212) and later (1217) captured Alcácer do Sal from the Moors. Alfonso was especially interested in the compilation of Portuguese law regarding personal and property rights. In an attempt to curtail the power of the church, he investigated the legal titles of church properties and attacked various abuses by clergy and aristocrats. As a result he was excommunicated in 1220.   DANIEL R. HEADRICK

Alfonso III, King of Portugal

Alfonso III, b. May 5, 1210, d. Feb. 16, 1279, king of Portugal, completed the reconquest of Portugal by winning the Algarve from the Moors. The younger son of Alfonso II, he assumed powers as regent (1245) when his brother, Sancho II, was deposed by the pope, and became king (1248) on Sancho's death. The conquest of the Algarve in 1249 provoked a quarrel with Alfonso X of Castile, but this was eventually settled by a marriage alliance. Also embroiled in conflict with the church over seizures of church lands, Alfonso broadened support for himself by summoning (1254) representatives of the towns to the Cortes for the first time. He introduced administrative reforms and promoted commercial and cultural development. He was succeeded by his son, DINIS.

Alfonso VI, King of León and Castile

Alfonso VI, d. 1109, Spanish king of León (1065–1109) and Castile (1072–1109), is best known for his capture of Toledo, the ancient Visigothic capital, from the Moors in 1085. With that victory he advanced his frontier to the Tagus River and the center of the Iberian peninsula. French and papal influence were especially marked in his reign. The marriage of his two daughters to French nobles resulted in the establishment of the Burgundian dynasties in León, Castile, and Portugal.   JOSEPH F. O'CALLAGHAN

Alfonso X, King of Castile   (Alfonso the Wise)

Alfonso X, b. Nov. 23, 1221, d. Apr. 4, 1284, Spanish king of Castile and León (1252–84), won distinction as a scholar but failed as a statesman. Known as Alfonso the Wise, he set scholars to work compiling a law code, the *Siete Partidas*, and a *General History of Spain*, as well as translating scientific texts from Arabic to Castilian. He also wrote poems, chiefly in honor of the Virgin Mary. In 1257, Alfonso was elected Holy Roman emperor (in opposition to the English claimant, Richard, earl of Cornwall), and he spent great sums vainly trying to gain recognition. His attempts to impose legal uniformity and his increasing taxation, coupled with a dispute over the succession, caused his son Sancho to rebel against him in 1282. Civil war ensued. At his death his son succeeded him as Sancho IV.   JOSEPH F. O'CALLAGHAN

Alfonso XII, King of Spain

King Alfonso XII, b. Nov. 28, 1857, d. Nov. 25, 1885, is remembered for bringing peace to Spain after years of civil war. Exiled with his mother, Isabella II, in 1868 he returned as king in January 1875. His second wife, María Cristina of Austria, bore him two daughters and a son (later ALFONSO XIII). Alfonso, a weak monarch, left politics to his premiers, especially Antonio Cánovas del Castillo (1828–97). During his reign the constitution of 1876 was enacted, the CARLISTS were defeated, and the TEN YEARS' WAR in Cuba ended (1878) in a truce.   DANIEL R. HEADRICK

Alfonso XIII, King of Spain

Alfonso XIII, king of Spain from 1886 to 1931, lost his throne because he became too involved in politics. Born on May 17, 1886, a few months after his father, ALFONSO XII, had died, he was proclaimed king at birth, with his mother María Cristina of Austria as regent. He grew up amid officers and learned to love the army. In 1906 he married Victoria Eugenia of Battenberg, a granddaughter of Queen Victoria of Britain.

At age 16, Alfonso began to impose his views on his ministers. Because Spanish political life was unstable and corrupt, his influence was often decisive. During World War I he kept Spain strictly neutral. In 1921 he appointed his friend Gen. Fernandez Silvestre to a high command in Morocco. When Silvestre was defeated at Anual (1922) by Moroccan rebels under ABD EL-KRIM, an investigation revealed that the king had encouraged his general to move rashly into the rebels' territory. To hide the scandal, Alfonso supported the 1923 coup d'etat of Gen. Miguel PRIMO DE RIVERA and the dictatorship that followed. After Primo de Rivera left Spain in 1930, Alfonso tried to remain king, but his popularity was damaged by his association with the dictator. A republican landslide in municipal elections in 1931 convinced him that he should leave Spain. Alfonso died on Feb. 28, 1941, having abdicated his rights to his third son, Juan, whose son JUAN CARLOS was restored to the throne in 1975.   DANIEL R. HEADRICK

Bibliography: Petrie, Charles, *King Alfonso XIII and His Age* (1963); Pilapil, Vincente R., *Alfonso XIII* (1969).

Alfred, King of England

Alfred, b. 849, d. Oct. 26, 899, succeeded his brother Æthelred as king of WESSEX in April 871. Both he and his brother were sons of King Æthelwulf. The only English king called "the Great," Alfred is renowned both for his ability as a war leader and for his love of learning. He can be counted, with CHARLEMAGNE, as one of the two most outstanding rulers of the 9th century.

Alfred was the first English monarch to plan systematically for the defense of his realm against the Danes, with whom he was almost constantly at war from 876 until the end of his life. He was also the first monarch of an English kingdom to become a symbol and focus of national unity. Although effective ruler only of Wessex and English MERCIA, he was regarded as the protector of all the English living under Danish rule. His capture of London in 886, which marked the farthest extent of his essentially defensive territorial expansion, led to general English recognition of his leadership. After his death, however, Wessex and Mercia were still unable to expel the Danes from England.

A learned layman, Alfred tried to ensure that his countrymen had the opportunity to become literate. To that end, he relied upon the bishops of the Anglo-Saxon church both to teach and to seek out students. Alfred himself translated into Anglo-Saxon the *Pastoral Care* of Pope Gregory I, Orosius' *Seven Books of History against the Pagans*, Boethius' *Consolation of Philosophy*, (possibly) the *Ecclesiastical History* of the Venerable Bede, and part of Saint Augustine of Hippo's *Soliloquies*. To each of these except the fourth he added his own commentary. Alfred's military victories saved English culture and national identity from destruction, and his intellectual activities began the education of his people in the Latin heritage.   JAMES W. ALEXANDER

Bibliography: Duckett, Eleanor S., *Alfred the Great* (1956); Helm, P. J., *Alfred the Great* (1963); Hughes, Thomas, *Alfred the Great*, 2d ed. (1871); Loyn, Henry R., *Alfred the Great* (1967); Mapp, Alf Johnson, *The Golden Dragon: Alfred the Great and His Time* (1974); Stevenson, W. H., ed., *Asser's Life of King Alfred* (1904; repr. 1959); Woodruff, Douglas, *The Life and Times of Alfred the Great* (1974).

Alfvén, Hannes   [ahl-vayn', hah'-nes]

The Swedish astrophysicist Hannes Olof Alfvén, b. May 30, 1908, shared the 1970 Nobel Prize in physics for his investigation of the properties of diffuse ionized gas, or PLASMA, in interstellar space, and in particular for his discovery of fixed electromagnetic field lines within plasmas. Alfvén received his Ph.D. from Uppsala University in Sweden in 1934, served as a researcher at the Nobel Physics Institute, and from 1940 was professor at the Royal Swedish Institute. Since 1967 he has taught at the University of California at San Diego. At first relegated to little-known journals because of his unorthodox approach, Alfvén's theories are now widely applied in astronomy and thermonuclear reactors.   MICHAEL MEO

Bibliography: Lubkin, G. B., "Nobel Laureates for 1970: Hannes Alfvén and Louis Néel," in *Physics Today* 23 (December 1970).

Alfvén waves: see MAGNETOHYDRODYNAMICS.

algae

Algae are a diverse group of primarily aquatic, mostly plantlike organisms that occur in such dissimilar forms as microscopic single cells, loose, filmy conglomerations, matted or branched colonies, or giant seaweeds with rootlike holdfasts and structures resembling stems and leaves.

Most of the algae have characteristics in common with plants, in that they have cell walls, contain the green pigment CHLOROPHYLL, and manufacture their own food through the process of PHOTOSYNTHESIS. The chlorophyll may be masked by other pigments, giving the various types of algae predominantly different colors. Some types, more animallike, are motile (capable of moving about) and ingest organic food, although they may also contain chlorophyll and conduct photosynthesis. Soft, even gelatinous cell surfaces are usual, but some types form shells or scales, and others produce stony, corallike, or calcareous deposits.

Algae are worldwide in distribution, thriving in all bodies of water, rocky coastlines, and terrestrial environments with ample moisture. Some species are adapted to such extremes of temperature as hot springs or arctic snows. Others survive in sandy soils or deserts. The habitats of marine and coastal algae vary according to degree of wave action, height of tides, and the light intensity required for photosynthesis; the various algal types are found in distinct zones or layers in the oceans and on beaches and cliffs.

REPRODUCTION

Methods of reproduction in algae may be vegetative by division of a single cell or fragmentation of a colony, asexual by production of motile spores (zoospores) or thick-walled nonmotile spores, or sexual by union of gametes (sex cells). The gametes may be identical (isogametes), differentiated into male and female (anisogametes), or markedly differentiated (heterogametes) into small, motile male cells and large, nonmotile female cells. Many species of algae reproduce by an ALTERNATION OF GENERATIONS, requiring separate asexual and sexual organisms to complete a life cycle.

Isogamy is the most common reproductive mode of the green algae and may have been present in the first plants that evolved. The isogametes, that is, sex cells that are not distinguishably male or female, shed their cell walls and slowly fuse their cytoplasm and nuclei, forming a single cell with two sets of genes. The zygote (the first stage of a new organism) develops a thick, protective wall and germinates when conditions are favorable, somewhat like a plant seed. The zygote divides to produce four new haploid cells (one set of genes in each cell), which are released into the surroundings. In some algae, three of the haploid cells fail to develop in the zygote. The haploid stages of the life cycle predominate, because the only diploid stage (two sets of genes in a cell) is the zygote itself. In other algae, notably the complex seaweed, the diploid generation is large with an extended phase, and the haploid generation is microscopic and brief. Many intermediate variations are found.

CLASSIFICATION

Algae are differentiated mainly by cell structure, composition of pigment, nature of the food reserve, and the presence, quantity, and structure of flagella. The following phyla, or divisions, are recognized: blue-green algae (Cyanophyta); euglenids (Euglenophyta); yellow-green and golden-brown algae

(Below) *A colony of Volvox (magnified 336 ×) separates from its parent. Volvox, a genus of green algae, are organized into a hollow, spherical shape.*

(Above) *A stagnant, freshwater pond in the New York Catskill Mountains is covered with a "bloom" of green algae. Like plants, green algae contain chlorophyll, for photosynthesis; like many animals, some green algae can freely propel themselves through water.*

(Chrysophyta); dinoflagellates and similar types (Pyrrophyta); red algae (Rhodophyta); green algae (Chlorophyta); and brown algae (Phaeophyta). A rare class of Pyrrophyta, Cryptophyceae, are sometimes placed in a separate phylum, Cryptophyta.

In systems that divide life into plant and animal kingdoms, algae have been traditionally classified as plants and placed, along with bacteria and fungi, in the subkingdom Thallophyta. A thallophyte is negatively defined by the plant features that the cell or thallus (plant body) lacks: roots, stems, leaves, and embryo formation within a parent plant. Some motile algae that ingest food, such as euglenids, have been placed in the animal kingdom by zoologists. In systems that divide life into several kingdoms, algae are divided among the kingdoms MONERA, PROTISTA, and Plantae according to their complexity of organization and their evolutionary relationships. Blue-green algae are placed with bacteria in the most primitive kingdom, Monera, comprising single-celled organisms that have no cell nucleus. Single-celled free-living and colonial algae (euglenids, yellow-green and golden-brown, dinoflagellates) are placed in the kingdom Protista. Multicellular or multinucleatic algae with characteristics more closely resembling higher plants (red, green, brown, and stoneworts) are placed in the kingdom Plantae in some schemes but are considered protists in others.

Cyanophyta. Members of the BLUE-GREEN ALGAE, Cyanophyta, offer classification difficulties and are placed by some biologists among the bacteria. They are somewhat larger than most bacteria but resemble them in structure and most functions. Unlike true algae they are procaryotes, or one-celled organisms, lacking organelles such as a nucleus (although DNA is present in the cytoplasm) and chloroplasts (although photosynthetic pigments are present in some forms). Unlike bacteria, however, no Cyanophyta exhibit sexual reproduction; nor do any have flagella, although a few forms are motile by unknown means. Cyanophyta also have chlorophyll *a*, which no photosynthetic bacterium possesses, and they produce gaseous oxygen as a waste product just as do all other algae but no bacterium. Fossil masses of simple cells about 3.5 billion years old, called STROMATOLITES, which strongly resemble Cya-

nophyta, are of great significance in having most probably been the major or original contributors to the formation of the oxygen blanket that made possible the evolution of higher life forms. Some Cyanophyta are able to fix atmospheric nitrogen, which is of great ecological importance. Others are thermophiles ("heat-lovers") that represent a large percentage of the life found in hot or boiling springs or pools.

Euglenophyta. The Euglenophyta are free-swimming one-celled organisms of a wormlike shape; they lack cell walls and usually have one or two flagella and a red, light-sensitive eye-spot. Most species are green but contain other pigments besides chlorophyll. Some subsist both by photosynthesis and by ingesting other organisms. Because of their ambiguous form, they have been claimed as animals by some zoologists and as plants by some botanists. Reproduction is by diploid cell division following MITOSIS, in rare instances by sexual means. The best known and the most representative of the phylum is EUGLENA, found in ponds and frequently studied in classrooms and laboratories.

Yellow-green and Golden-brown Algae. The phylum Chrysophyta contains diverse marine and freshwater algae that are free-living, one-celled, or occasionally filamentous. Many form shells composed of silica or lime. Most have one or two flagella. Chrysophyta are grouped mainly by color, ranging from yellowish-green through golden to golden-brown, depending on the proportion of chlorophyll to carotene and xanthophyll, yellow and brownish pigments. Chlorophylls *a* and *e* have been reported, and many forms store oil rather than starch. Modes of reproduction vary. The best known are the biflagellate DIATOMS, the most abundant of the marine plankton. Sometimes called the "grass of the sea," they produce more oxygen than all green land plants combined. Their glasslike, silica-impregnated walls are composed of two pieces that fit together like a box with its lid. Diatoms reproduce by simple cell division as well as by union of gametes. In asexual reproduction the box and the lid separate, and each becomes the top of a new box. In most species the new cells that started as bottoms are always smaller than their parents; if this process continued indefinitely one cell line would finally vanish. Sexual reproduction largely solves this problem

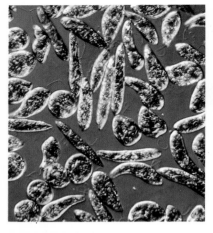

Algae differ widely in size, shape, and color. Euglena (top left, magnified 335 ×) is a genus of unicellular organisms that move through water by beating flagella. They contain chloroplasts, which are photosynthetic cell structures. Kelp (top center), genus Cystoseira, is a multicellular brown algae found in cold coastal waters. Diatoms (top right, magnified 126 ×), class Bacillariophyceae, are known as "jewels of the sea" because of their crystalline shapes. Diatoms largely comprise plankton, the foundation of oceanic food chains. Rockweed (bottom left), genus Fucus, is brown algae that clings to rocks of temperate coasts of the Northern Hemisphere. Red algae (bottom right), phylum Rhodophyta, include beautiful forms of tropical and subtropical seaweed. Many genera of red algae, such as dulse and Irish moss, are important food sources.

by yielding new shells that are full-sized.

Pyrrophyta. The phylum Pyrrophyta, commonly called dino-flagellates, are one-celled free-swimming biflagellates abundant in tropical waters. They contain chlorophyll, carotene, and a large proportion of a golden-brown xanthophyll. One flagellum surrounds the organism and the other trails. Many have a cellulose wall arranged in two interlocking plates; a few resemble AMOEBA and ingest organic food. Dinoflagellates are second in importance to diatoms as providers of oxygen and as a base in the food chain. Many generate light when disturbed (see BIOLUMINESCENCE) and glow at night in tropical seas. Reproduction is usually by cell division.

Rhodophyta. The red algae are multicellular branching filamentous seaweeds, abundant in warm coastal waters. Their color is primarily derived from the pigment phycoerythrin, which enables them to utilize light for photosynthesis at much deeper ocean levels than any other marine algae. Most have gelatinous cell walls. Some species concentrate lime from seawater; their secretions and skeletons contribute to the formation of coral reefs. Reproduction is various and can proceed in elaborate stages. The red algae are the only phylum that produce no motile cells.

Chlorophyta. The green algae variously occur as single cells, as scum or film, as filamentous branching, or matted colonies, or as multicellular marine forms with leaflike fronds. They are diverse in habitat and are the most conspicuous algal type,

forming in ponds and streams, on rocks and trees and almost any damp surfaces, including the hair and claws of certain animals and even the shells of turtles. They are also common in soils. The green algae, typically grass green in color, are characterized by their resemblance to the higher plants in pigment content (the same proportions of chlorophylls *a* and *e* and carotene), in food storage (starch), and in cell walls (true cellulose). This has suggested to scientists that the higher plants are directly descended from the Chlorophyta. Reproduction can be arranged in an evolutionary fashion through the diverse groups, from simple cell fusion to highly differentiated cells functioning as sperm and egg in the *Volvox.* The most common algae found as a mat on rocks and tree trunks is the genus *Protococcus,* which multiplies by cell division and may also combine with fungus as various lichens. The STONEWORTS, which are often covered with lime, differ from all other algae in having a multicellular reproductive structure and are placed by some biologists in a separate division, Charophyta.

Phaeophyta. The brown algae, Phaeophyta, possess the brown pigment fucoxanthin that masks the green color of chlorophyll. All brown algae are multicellular seaweeds with differentiated parts that may superficially resemble true plants. Familiar types are the giant kelps and the genus *Sargassum,* which forms dense mats of surface vegetation in the Sargasso Sea.

ECONOMIC IMPORTANCE

It has been estimated that the marine algae account for more than 90 percent of the world's photosynthetic activity, making them the most important source of oxygen. Algae are also the main source of food for other aquatic life. Seaweeds are used as food by many coastal peoples and are ground into livestock meal. The gelatinous substances carrageenan (from Irish moss, a red alga) and ALGIN (found in kelp and other brown seaweed) are used widely to impart a smooth consistency to ice cream, puddings, processed cheeses, jams, light beers, and other food products. They are also used for finishing leathers. Algin is an ingredient in cosmetics, car polishes, paints, and insecticides. Agar, extracted from red seaweed, is widespread in the Orient as a delicacy and is a familiar laboratory medium for culturing microorganisms. Fertilizers, detergents, polishes, and insulating and soundproofing materials often contain diatomaceous earth, composed primarily of sedimentary shells of diatoms. Now being investigated is the use of unicellular green algae as food for humans and livestock. When grown under suitable conditions, certain types, such as the genus Chlorella, provide a good source of protein, fats, and carbohydrates. Chlorella "farms" have been established on a small scale in various countries. In sewage treatment, green and blue-green algae are a source of oxygen for bacteria that decompose wastes.

HARMFUL EFFECTS

Algae can be harmful to both plants and animals. Parasitic algae are a cause of plant rust. A recurrent "red tide" of certain dinoflagellates produces a potent nerve toxin that may kill millions of fish in temperate and subtropical waters. In lakes and ponds overrich in nutrients, blanketing growths of green and blue-green algae may smother fish and plant life (see NUTRIENT CYCLES). Shellfish feeding on the dinoflagellate *Gonyaulax* absorb large quantities of an alkaloid toxin and may become poisonous. *Lyngbya*, a filamentous Cyanophyta, produces severe skin rashes in some human beings when it is handled.   Reviewed by LAWRENCE J. CROCKETT

Bibliography: Bold, Harold C., and Wynne, Michael J., *Introduction to the Algae* (1978); Chapman, V. J. and D. J., *The Algae*, 2d ed. (1975); Jackson, Daniel F., ed., *Algae and Man* (1964); Lewin, Ralph A., *The Genetics of Algae* (1976).

See also: PLANKTON; PROTOZOA; SEAWEED.

algal mat   [al'-guhl]

Algal mats are composed of various ALGAE and animal-built tubes. Sedimentary particles are trapped in the mat, along with skeletal debris and minute organisms, to form a relatively stable organic film. Because of the presence of these organisms, the mat is a source of food for fish and other animals, especially snails, that browse on the sandy seafloor. Normally the mats are found below water level, but they have been seen on the tops of sandbars exposed to low tide. The algal material is destroyed by organisms or by decaying processes; thus no ancient algal mats have been preserved.

Bibliography: Round, F. E., *The Ecology of Algae* (1982).

Algardi, Alessandro   [ahl-gahr'-dee]

Alessandro Algardi, b. Nov. 27, 1595, d. 1654, was an Italian baroque sculptor who trained in Bologna with Lodovico CARRACCI at the Carracci Academy. Algardi's influence lay in offering a more conservative, academic ideal for patrons who disliked the innovations of his famous contemporary, Giovanni Lorenzo BERNINI. Algardi's early works in Rome include numerous portrait busts, such as that of Cardinal Laudirio Zacchia, for which he was well esteemed. When Bernini temporarily fell from favor on the accession of Pope Innocent X (1644), Algardi received such major commissions as the tomb of Pope Leo XI (1634–52; Saint Peter's Basilica, Rome) and the statue of Saint Philip Neri (1640; Santa Maria in Valicella, Rome). Other important works include the marble relief *The Meeting of Pope Leo I and Attila* (1645–53; Saint Peter's Basilica, Rome) and the *Martyrdom of Saint Paul* (1647; San Paolo, Bologna). Algardi's classicized interpretation of baroque art reached Northern Europe through the paintings of Nicolas

Poussin and the sculptures of François DUQUESNOY, both of whom he befriended during their years of work in Rome.
                                          GIULIA BARTRUM

Bibliography: Pope-Hennessy, John, *Italian High Renaissance and Baroque Sculpture* (1963); Wittkower, Rudolf, *Art and Architecture in Italy, 1600–1750* (1958).

algebra

The word *algebra* relates to procedures for solving EQUATIONS, and the original scope of algebra was confined to this topic. Gradually, however, the subject of algebra has been enlarged to include many more topics. It is an indispensable tool in other branches of mathematics, such as CALCULUS, and in almost every part of applied mathematics.

As long ago as 2000 BC, the Babylonians and the Egyptians posed problems like those found in today's elementary algebra texts. For example, in the Rhind papyrus, dating from about 1650 BC, problem 24 asks for the value of "heap" if heap and a seventh of heap is 19. In modern terminology and notation this problem could be formulated as "What number plus a seventh of that number is 19?" A letter such as x could be used to represent the unknown number, and the equation could be written

$$x + \frac{1}{7}x = 19 \qquad (1)$$

In algebra, $\frac{1}{7}x$ means $\frac{1}{7}$ times x, and a fraction such as $\frac{1}{7}$ is usually written in text in the form 1/7 or $\frac{1}{7}$.

Finding a number x such that $x + \frac{1}{7}x = 19$ is called solving the equation. Learning how to use letters to write equations that describe problems in arithmetic, biology, chemistry, economics, engineering, geometry, and physics, and learning how to solve such equations are the primary concerns of elementary algebra.

Here is an example of a problem that might occur in a chemistry laboratory: How many liters of water must be added to 2 liters of a 30% solution of acid to obtain a 20% solution? The reasoning in solving this problem might be as follows: First, the beginning amount of acid equals the final amount of acid, since only water is to be added. Next, the number of liters of acid at the beginning is 30% of 2 liters, which is $0.30 \times 2 = 0.60$. Now if x is the number of liters of water that need to be added, the total amount of liquid obtained after the water is added will be $x + 2$ liters, and, of this, only 20% is supposed to be acid. Therefore, the number of liters of acid at the end equals 20% of $(x + 2)$, which equals $0.20(x + 2)$. So the equation that needs to be solved is

$$0.60 = 0.20(x + 2) \qquad (2)$$

Equations 1 and 2 are examples of LINEAR EQUATIONS in one variable; ways of solving such equations are an important topic in elementary algebra.

PROPERTIES OF NUMBERS

The procedures for solving equations or systems of equations can become very complicated. All the procedures, however, are based on a fundamental set of properties of numbers. The following properties are needed to solve Equation 1.
(1) For any number x:

$$1 \cdot x = x \text{ (the multiplicative property of 1)}$$

It is customary in algebra to use a centered dot (·) rather than a multiplication sign (×) to indicate multiplication so as not to have × confused with x.
(2) For all numbers x, y, and z:

$$xz + yz = (x + y)z \text{ (the DISTRIBUTIVE LAW)}$$

In algebra xz means x times z, yz means y times z, and $(x + y)z$ means $(x + y)$ times z.
(3) If $x = y$:

$$\text{then } zx = zy \text{ (a property of equality)}$$

(4) For all numbers x, y, and z:

$$x(yz) = (xy)z \text{ (the ASSOCIATIVE LAW of multiplication)}$$

These properties can be applied to solve Equation 1 in the following manner. First, by property 1, the equation $x + \frac{1}{7}x = 19$ can be written as

$$1 \cdot x + \frac{1}{7}x = 19$$

Then, by property 2,

$$\left(1 + \frac{1}{7}\right)x = 19$$

Because $1 + \frac{1}{7} = \frac{8}{7}$,

$$\frac{8}{7} \cdot x = 19$$

so that

$$
\begin{array}{ll}
\frac{7}{8}(\frac{8}{7} \cdot x) = \frac{7}{8} \cdot 19 & \text{[property 3]} \\
(\frac{7}{8} \cdot \frac{8}{7})x = \frac{7}{8} \cdot 19 & \text{[property 4]} \\
1 \cdot x = \frac{133}{8} & \\
x = \frac{133}{8} & \text{[property 1]}
\end{array}
$$

Equation 2 can be solved as follows:

$$
\begin{array}{ll}
0.60 = 0.20(x + 2) & \\
0.60 = 0.20x + (0.20 \cdot 2) & \text{[property 2]} \\
0.60 = 0.20x + 0.40 & \\
0.60 - 0.40 = (0.20x + 0.40) - 0.40 & \text{[property 3} \\
 & \text{for addition]} \\
0.20 = 0.20x + (0.40 - 0.40) & \text{[property 4} \\
 & \text{for addition]} \\
0.20 = 0.20x + 0 & \\
0.20 = 0.20x & \text{[property 1 for addition]} \\
\frac{1}{0.20} \cdot 0.20 = \frac{1}{0.20}(0.20x) & \text{[property 3]} \\
\frac{1}{0.20} \cdot 0.20 = (\frac{1}{0.20} \cdot 0.20)x & \text{[property 4]} \\
1 = 1 \cdot x & \\
1 = x & \text{[property 1]}
\end{array}
$$

Thus 1 liter of water needs to be added to have the 2 liters of a 30% solution of acid become 3 liters of a 20% solution.

KINDS OF NUMBERS

In addition to the numbers of ordinary ARITHMETIC (whole numbers and fractions), algebra deals with negative numbers, IRRATIONAL NUMBERS, and COMPLEX NUMBERS. Negative numbers were first systematically developed by the Hindu mathematician Aryabhata in the 6th century and were used to solve such equations as $x + 3 = 2$ with its solution the negative number -1. Irrational numbers, numbers such as $\sqrt{2}$ and π that are not expressible as fractions, were first discovered by the Greeks in the 5th century BC. They were used extensively by mathematicians from that time on but were not analyzed carefully until the 19th century. Complex numbers were developed in the 16th century but were not generally accepted until late in the 18th century.

Whatever the kind of numbers or the notation used, algebra, until fairly recently, was done on a rather mechanical basis, with rules that worked but without much consideration given as to why they worked. It was not until the early 19th century that such mathematicians as George Peacock (1791-1858) and George BOOLE began to investigate the basic properties of numbers, such as the distributive property, that underlie the subject of algebra.

MATRICES

About the same time, other mathematicians began to investigate other kinds of algebraic systems in which the elements under consideration were no longer numbers and whose properties, although similar to those for numbers, were somewhat different. For example, Arthur CAYLEY developed (mid-1800s) the algebra of matrices (the singular is MATRIX). An example of this algebra is the set of 2 × 2 ("two by two") matrices

$$\begin{pmatrix} a & b \\ c & d \end{pmatrix}$$

where a, b, c, and d are numbers. Addition of matrices is defined by

$$\begin{pmatrix} a & b \\ c & d \end{pmatrix} + \begin{pmatrix} e & f \\ g & h \end{pmatrix} = \begin{pmatrix} a + e & b + f \\ c + g & d + h \end{pmatrix}$$

Thus, for example,

$$\begin{pmatrix} 1 & 2 \\ 4 & 8 \end{pmatrix} + \begin{pmatrix} 3 & 1 \\ 4 & 0 \end{pmatrix} = \begin{pmatrix} 1 + 3 & 2 + 1 \\ 4 + 4 & 8 + 0 \end{pmatrix} = \begin{pmatrix} 4 & 3 \\ 8 & 8 \end{pmatrix}$$

The operation of addition for these matrices has properties similar to the properties of addition of numbers. For example, if A and B are any 2 × 2 matrices, $A + B = B + A$ (COMMUTATIVE LAW of addition for matrices); this corresponds to the equation $a + b = b + a$ when a and b are numbers. If A, B, and C are any 2 × 2 matrices, $A + (B + C) = (A + B) + C$ (associative property of addition for matrices), this corresponds to $a + (b + c) = (a + b) + c$ when a, b, and c are numbers.

Multiplication of 2 × 2 matrices is defined as follows:

$$\begin{pmatrix} a & b \\ c & d \end{pmatrix} \times \begin{pmatrix} e & f \\ g & h \end{pmatrix} = \begin{pmatrix} ae + bg & af + bh \\ ce + dg & cf + dh \end{pmatrix}$$

Thus, for example,

$$\begin{pmatrix} 1 & 2 \\ 4 & 8 \end{pmatrix} \times \begin{pmatrix} 3 & 1 \\ 4 & 0 \end{pmatrix} = \begin{pmatrix} 1 \times 3 + 2 \times 4 & 1 \times 1 + 2 \times 0 \\ 4 \times 3 + 8 \times 4 & 4 \times 1 + 8 \times 0 \end{pmatrix}$$

$$= \begin{pmatrix} 11 & 1 \\ 44 & 4 \end{pmatrix}$$

whereas

$$\begin{pmatrix} 3 & 1 \\ 4 & 0 \end{pmatrix} \times \begin{pmatrix} 1 & 2 \\ 4 & 8 \end{pmatrix} = \begin{pmatrix} 3 \times 1 + 1 \times 4 & 3 \times 2 + 1 \times 8 \\ 4 \times 1 + 0 \times 4 & 4 \times 2 + 0 \times 8 \end{pmatrix}$$

$$= \begin{pmatrix} 7 & 14 \\ 4 & 8 \end{pmatrix}$$

These two examples of matrix multiplication show that matrix multiplication is not commutative. In other words, if A and B are 2 × 2 matrices, then it is not necessarily true that $A \times B = B \times A$; on the other hand, for all numbers a and b, it is true that $a \times b = b \times a$. However, just as it is true that $a \times (b \times c) = (a \times b) \times c$, for all numbers a, b, and c, it is also true that $A \times (B \times C) = (A \times B) \times C$ for all matrices A, B, and C—the associative property of multiplication for matrices.

Matrices were first developed in connection with an abstract concept in mathematics (the theory of linear TRANSFORMATIONS), but they soon became an indispensable aid in many applications of mathematics.

GROUPS

Studying a set on which just one operation is defined led, at about the same time that matrices were developed, to another basic concept of the mathematics of today—a group. Groups, like matrices, were first developed in connection with abstract concepts in mathematics, but GROUP THEORY soon found uses in other parts of mathematics and in such fields of applied mathematics as quantum mechanics.

As an example of a group, consider the five ways in which three letters written in a given order can be rewritten in a different order. There are a total of six PERMUTATIONS, including the original order. The five ways of changing the given order can be denoted by P_1, P_2, P_3, P_4, and P_5, described as follows:

$abc \overset{P_1}{\rightarrow} acb$ (the second and third letters are interchanged)

$abc \overset{P_2}{\rightarrow} bac$ (the first and second letters are interchanged)

$abc \overset{P_3}{\rightarrow} bca$ (the first letter becomes the third; the second letter becomes the first; and the third letter becomes the second)

$abc \overset{P_4}{\rightarrow} cab$ (the first letter becomes the second; the second letter becomes the third; and the third letter becomes the first)

$abc \overset{P_5}{\rightarrow} cba$ (the first and third letters are interchanged).

In addition to the interchanges (permutations) of letters denoted by P_1, P_2, P_3, P_4, and P_5, the identity permutation, P_0, can be defined by $abc \overset{P_0}{\rightarrow} abc$ (no letters are interchanged).

Now the product of transformations $P_1 \times P_2$, $P_2 \times P_1$, $P_2 \times P_3$, and so on can be defined as follows:

$$P_1 \times P_2: abc \overset{P_2}{\rightarrow} bac \overset{P_1}{\rightarrow} bca$$

Since $abc \overset{P_3}{\rightarrow} bca$, it is true that $P_1 \times P_2 = P_3$. Similarly, since

$$abc \overset{P_1}{\rightarrow} acb \overset{P_2}{\rightarrow} cab$$

and $abc \overset{P_4}{\rightarrow} cab$, it is true that $P_2 \times P_1 = P_4$. Since $P_4 \neq P_3$, it is seen that multiplication in this group is not commutative. It can be shown, however, that multiplication here is associative; for example, $P_3 \times (P_1 \times P_2) = P_4 = (P_3 \times P_1) \times P_2$. Furthermore, P_0 acts as 1 does in multiplication of numbers. That is, just as $1 \times a = a \times 1 = a$ for all numbers a, so
$P_0 \times P_0 = P_0$, $P_0 \times P_1 = P_1 \times P_0 = P_1$,
$P_0 \times P_2 = P_2 \times P_0 = P_2, \ldots, P_0 \times P_5 = P_5 \times P_0 = P_5$. Finally, for every P, another or the same P exists such that their product is P_0. For example, $P_0 \times P_0 = P_0$, $P_1 \times P_1 = P_0$, $P_2 \times P_2 = P_0$, $P_3 \times P_4 = P_4 \times P_3 = P_0$, and $P_5 \times P_5 = P_0$.

This system is an example of a group. A group is a set on which there is an operation, $\times$, such that

1. if a is in G and b is in G, then $a \times b$ is in G (closure property);
2. if a, b, and c are in G, then $a \times (b \times c) = (a \times b) \times c$ (associative property);
3. there is an element e in G, such that $e \times a = a \times e = a$ for all a in G (existence of an identity; this is the element P_0 in the above example).
4. for every element a in G, there is an element b in G, such that $a \times b = b \times a = e$ (existence of inverses).

ROY DUBISCH

Bibliography: Barnett, Raymond A., *Elementary Algebra: Structure and Use*, 3d ed. (1980); Birkhoff, Garrett, and MacLane, Saunders, *Survey of Modern Algebra*, 4th ed. (1977).

algebraic geometry

Algebraic geometry is the branch of mathematics that studies the figures, curves, and surfaces that represent equations in algebra. These figures, curves, and surfaces can be considered as sets of points defined by these equations. The numbers involved may be real or complex. One of the main concerns of algebraic geometry is the study of properties that remain invariant, or unchanging, while the equations themselves undergo transformations. Another important aspect is the study of the intersections of two or more algebraic curves. In many of its elementary aspects, algebraic geometry is similar to ANALYTIC GEOMETRY.

Bibliography: Hartshorne, Robin, *Algebraic Geometry* (1977); Kendig, Keith, *Elementary Algebraic Geometry* (1977); Lang, Serge, *Introduction to Algebraic Geometry* (1972).

Algeciras   [ahl-hay-thee'-rahs]

Algeciras, a port city in Cádiz province, Andalusia, is located in southern Spain on the Bay of Algeciras opposite Gibraltar. The port, with a population of 81,662 (1970), handles transatlantic shipping and passengers bound by ferry to and from North Africa. Mild winters and nearby mineral springs combine to make it a resort. Fishing and tourism are the main industries. The town, taken by the Moors in 711, is probably built on the site of the Roman colony of Portus Albus. Although the port was captured in 1344 by Alfonso XI of Castile, it was retaken in 1368 by the Moors, who then razed it. Charles III rebuilt the city in 1760. At a conference of European powers held in its city hall in 1906, France's right to colonize Morocco was recognized.

Algeciras Conference

Early in 1906, European diplomats met at Algeciras, Spain, to settle a dispute arising from the German challenge to the impending partition of Morocco by France and Spain. Although Germany declared its support for Moroccan independence, its primary intention was to break up the Anglo-French Entente of 1904. The effect of the conference was to delay the partition of Morocco (to 1912, after a second international crisis), but Britain stood by France and thus strengthened the entente. (See MOROCCAN CRISES.)

Alger, Horatio

Although he was an ordained Unitarian minister, Horatio Alger, b. Jan. 13, 1834, d. July 19, 1899, is best known as the author of such juvenile novels as *Ragged Dick* (1867), *Luck and Pluck; or, John Oakley's Inheritance* (1869), and *Tattered Tom* (1871). The Alger formula of instant riches accruing to young men because of their goodness and perseverance seems simplistic today. Alger's own success, however, may have convinced him that the formula was accurate; more than 20 million of his books were sold during his lifetime.

Bibliography: Hoyt, Edwin P., *Horatio's Boys: The Life and Works of Horatio Alger, Jr.* (1974); Scharnhorst, G., *Horatio Alger, Jr.* (1980).

Algeria

Located in North Africa, Algeria is Africa's second largest country. From its 1,000-km (620-mi) coastline along the Mediterranean Sea it extends southward into the heart of the SAHARA, bordering six countries. ALGIERS, the capital, is one of the largest cities and leading ports of the continent.

The northern, or Mediterranean, region of Algeria, the Tell, is divided from Saharan Algeria by the ATLAS MOUNTAINS. About 95% of the population live in the relatively humid, fertile north, which constitutes only 12% of the total land area. The desert south is occupied by about 500,000 people.

Algeria won independence from France in 1962 after a long and bitter war. Once claimed as part of France, it had a large French population and an economy geared to wine production. With the establishment of an Arab Muslim government and the massive exodus of Europeans, Algeria faced sudden, disruptive change. A new emphasis on the development of the oil and gas resources of the Sahara, discovered in 1956 before the end of the war, has led to a reorientation of the entire economy. At present, the main source of revenue is oil, but gas may be the major source of revenue in the future. A new socialist agrarian structure is planned by the government, but the focus of development is on heavy industry.

THE LAND AND RESOURCES

Two important mountain ranges, the Tell Atlas and the Saharan Atlas, are the major divide between Mediterranean Algeria and the Sahara. Roughly paralleling the coast, these ranges enclose high plateaus.

Algeria has five main topographic zones, all of which run east to west. The narrow alluvial coastal plains and the Sahel Hills are about 140 km (85 mi) wide. To the south, the Tell Atlas rises to a maximum elevation of 2,308 m (7,572 ft). The intermontane plateaus are semiarid and narrow toward the east, ending in the Hodna Mountains. The plateaus have an average elevation of 1,100 m (3,500 ft). To the south in a rugged, dry region are the Saharan Atlas Mountains, which rise to a maximum elevation of 2,236 m (7,336 ft). The fifth region, the Sahara, is a massive desert area of stony wastes, inland basins, rolling sand dunes, and oases.

Algeria's most fertile soils are found on the coastal plains and are described locally as Tell soils. Elsewhere in the country, except in mountain pockets, soils are mostly infertile.

Climate and Drainage. The pattern of climate is generally analogous to the five main topographic divisions. Coastal plains have a Mediterranean climate with an annual average minimum temperature of 11° C (52° F) and an annual average maximum of 25° C (77° F). The annual average rainfall, concentrated in the winter months, is about 760 mm (30 in).

In the Tell Atlas Mountains temperatures are generally lower, but the extremes are greater. The mean annual range is from 8° to 28° C (46° to 83° F). Annual rainfall ranges from 510 mm (20 in) in the east to as much as 1,015 mm (40 in) in the Kabylia region. The intermontane plateau areas are cool and dry with an annual rainfall of about 305 mm (12 in).

The Saharan Atlas is a sharp climatic divide, and toward the south temperatures rise rapidly; annual rainfall is about 255 mm (10 in). The Sahara is an almost rainless area, with less than 200 mm (8 in) a year. Temperatures range from an average minimum of 11° C (51° F) to an average maximum of well of over 38° C (100° F). Daily extremes are also great.

Only about half the surface area of Algeria drains to the sea. Drainage is characterized by short, irregular streams, except in the coastal plain, through which the only important stream, the Chéliff, flows. The plateau region has many interior basins with shallow salt lakes called *shatts* (or *chotts*). The Sahara is also an inland drainage area, but stream courses are discontinuous; dry water courses are called wadis.

Vegetation and Animal Life. The vegetation pattern is closely associated with climate, except for localized differences due to soil, elevation, and the availability of water. Three major vegetation zones may be distinguished: the Mediterranean, the semiarid, and the desert.

The Mediterranean vegetation cover consists of holm oak, Aleppo pine, cedar, and cork oak, but much of the land is covered with maquis (a scrubby underbrush). The wild olive is characteristic of the drier regions.

The semiarid zone is typified by alfalfa grass, associated with esparto and sagebrush. The date palm is the typical oasis tree. The grapevine and the fig, which were brought to the region from other parts of the world, are now distinctive in the landscape as indigenous species.

The relatively sparse vegetation does not support a large wildlife population. Species include the gazelle, hare, ibex, Barbary ape, and some birds and reptiles.

Resources. Cultivable land in Algeria is almost all in the northern Mediterranean zone. Although only about 18% of the total land area is suitable for agriculture, including pasture, in the coastal areas are rich farming regions. The major natural resources are oil and gas, both found in the Sahara. Oil reserves are about 1% of the world total, but gas reserves

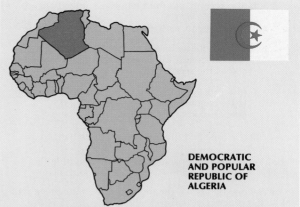

DEMOCRATIC AND POPULAR REPUBLIC OF ALGERIA

LAND. Area: 2,381,741 km² (919,595 mi²). Capital and largest city: Algiers (1978 est. pop., 1,998,000).

PEOPLE. Population (1982 est.): 19,954,000; density (1982 est.): 8.4 persons per km² (21.7 per mi²). Distribution (1977): 40.6% urban, 59.4% rural. Annual growth (1975–79): 3.4%. Official language: Arabic. Major religion: Islam.

EDUCATION AND HEALTH. Literacy (1977): 35% of adult population. Universities (1982): 8. Hospital beds (1977, government establishments only): 45,029. Physicians (1977): 3,203. Life expectancy (1980): women—57.4; men—55.2. Infant mortality (1979): 127.0 per 1,000 live births.

ECONOMY. GNP (1979): $28.7 billion; $1,580 per capita. Labor distribution (1983): agriculture—23%; industry—20%; other—57%. Foreign trade (1980): imports—$10.8 billion; exports—$13.7 billion; principal trade partners—United States, France, West Germany, Italy. Currency: 1 Algerian dinar = 100 centimes.

GOVERNMENT. Type: one-party state. Legislature: National Assembly. Political subdivisions: 31 *wilayaat* (departments).

COMMUNICATIONS. Railroads (1981): 3,912 km (2,431 mi) total. Roads (1981): 18,500 km (11,495 mi) primary; 63,500 km (39,457 mi) secondary. Major ports: 9. Airfields (major international, 1981): 5.

are the third highest in the world. Other resources include iron ore and phosphates.

THE PEOPLE

The majority of people of Algeria are now ARAB, BERBER, or mixed Arab-Berber stock. In the 19th century, French settlements added a large European element to the population. In addition, Italians, Maltese, Greeks, and Spaniards settled in the Oran region. Once 10% of the population, Europeans now account for 1% or less. Most of a small, Arabic-speaking, native Jewish population also left when Algeria achieved independence. Algerians are mainly light skinned. Darker African peoples are found in desert oases, and many of these are descendants of slaves or of *haratins,* an intermediate social group. The TUAREG are a nomadic group in the Sahara.

Annual climate charts for three localities in Algeria illustrate the distinct climate zones in the country. Bars indicate monthly ranges of temperatures (red) *and precipitation* (blue). *Algiers, on the northern coast, has a Mediterranean climate; Mecheria, a livestock market north of the Atlas Mountains, a steppe climate; and Tamanrasset, a town in the Ahaggar Mountains of the Sahara, a desert climate.*

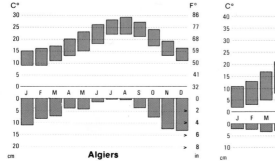

Algiers

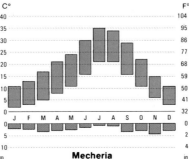

Mecheria

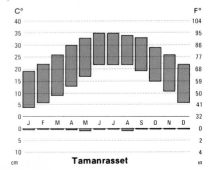

Tamanrasset

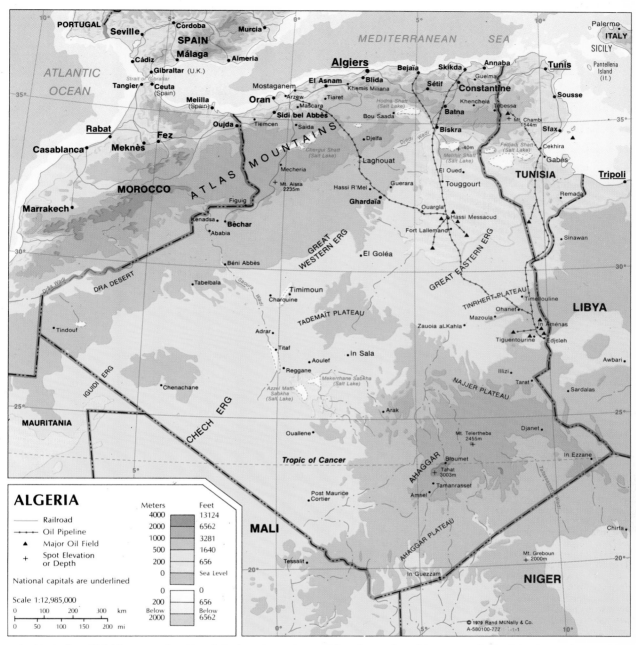

ALGERIA

	Meters	Feet
—— Railroad	4000	13124
·—·—· Oil Pipeline	2000	6562
▲ Major Oil Field	1000	3281
+ Spot Elevation or Depth	500	1640
	200	656
National capitals are underlined	0	Sea Level
	0	0
Scale 1:12,985,000	200	656
0 100 200 300 km	Below 2000	Below 6562
0 50 100 150 200 mi		

© 1979 Rand McNally & Co.
A-580100-772   -1-1

Arabic is the official language, but French is the principal foreign language. There are some minority Berber speakers. Islam is the official religion, and about 99% of all Algerians are Muslims, mostly SUNNITES.

Demography. Population densities are high in the north, and all major cities are located in this region. In addition to Algiers, the most important cities are CONSTANTINE, ORAN, al-Asnam, Tizi-Ouzou, Annaba, Sidi-bel-Abbès, Médéa, and Sétif. The most important towns outside the Mediterranean region are the oases such as Laghouat, Biskra, Colomb-Béchar, Ghardaïa, Touggourt, and El Golea. New settlements on the oil fields, sustained with water from deep boreholes, are Hassi R'Mel, Hassi Messaoud, and Edjeleh. Elsewhere the population densities are low, and the inhabitants are mainly nomadic or seminomadic. The annual rate of natural population increase is among the world's highest, and out-migration (mostly to France) is substantial.

Education and Health. Due to the high birthrate, the number of school-aged children has increased more rapidly than facilities could be expanded. However, the government is devoting about 30% of its annual budget to education. In 1970, 57% of school-aged children attended school, but by 1976 this figure had increased to nearly 80%. Including the University of Algiers, Algeria has four universities, which had a total of about 36,000 students by the mid-1970s.

Free medical attention has been guaranteed to all Algerian citizens since 1974. The number of doctors and hospitals are still, however, inadequate. National health projects have concentrated on the prevention of such diseases as tuberculosis, malaria, and trachoma.

Communications. Press, publishing, radio, and television are under the control of the national government. By the mid-1970s the country had nearly 500,000 television sets. Much of the programming, both from the national noncommercial

Street vendors display their produce in the crowded, narrow alleys of Ghardaïa, a commercial center south of the Atlas Mountains. The scene is typical of Algeria's cities.

television network and the national radio networks, is educational. Algeria has a national press service and four daily newspapers with a total daily circulation of 275,000.

ECONOMIC ACTIVITY

Algeria was once mainly an agricultural country with a commercial sector that produced wine, citrus fruits, and vegetables for the European, and particularly the French, market. Industrial development was minor because most manufactured goods were imported from metropolitan France. The Algerian economy is now almost totally government controlled and is committed to investment in heavy industry based on the revenues from natural gas exports.

Manufacturing and Industry. Algeria has enormous reserves of natural gas (mostly in the Saharan province) and is investing in further exploration and development projects. In 1971 French foreign assets in the oil and natural gas fields were nationalized. A huge industrial "estate" extends along the coast from Oran to Constantine and includes refineries, steel mills, liquefaction plants (for natural gas), and oil pipelines. Other industries include chemical and fertilizer plants; cement works; car, truck, and tractor factories; and paper, textile, and agricultural processing plants.

Agriculture. Agriculture in Algeria is largely confined to the narrow coastal plain. About three-quarters of the labor force is still employed in agriculture, although this sector accounts for less than one-tenth of the gross national product. The government, which spends about 15% of the national budget on agriculture, is restructuring land-holding patterns along socialist lines. The modern government-controlled farms (created largely from former European holdings) account for 60% of the value of production, although they occupy only 28% of all cultivated lands. The traditional peasant farms are gradually being reorganized as cooperatives.

Wine, which is produced on former European estates by worker-management groups, still accounts for nearly two-thirds of agricultural exports. The government is de-emphasizing wine production (strict Muslim teaching forbids the consumption of alcohol) and attempting to achieve self-sufficiency in grains. Some former vineyards have been planted with wheat and barley. Other important commercial crops are citrus fruits, vegetables, olives, figs, and dates.

Transportation and Trade. Good, mostly French-built roads and railroads connect the main cities of the north, but the north-south infrastructure is not yet well developed, and air links remain important. Three main highways extend south into the Sahara. The Trans-Saharan highway was completed from Algiers to Tamanrasset in 1978 and will serve to transport the mineral wealth from the remote Ahaggar region to the north. An international airport is planned for Tamanrasset.

Crude oil and refined products have replaced wine as the major export, earning about 90% of the national income. The USSR now takes two-fifths of the wine production, most of which formerly went to France for blending. France is still the most important trading partner, but is now closely followed by the United States and West Germany. An adverse balance of trade results from the extensive imports of capital goods for the industrialization program.

GOVERNMENT

Algeria is governed under a constitution approved by popular referendum in 1976. The constitution of 1963 had been suspended and the national assembly disbanded since the coup of 1965. Algeria's government is constructed on a one-party system, namely the National Liberation Front (FLN from its French name). All candidates for local or national office must be nominated by the FLN.

The new constitution provides for a president, the head of state, to be elected for a 6-year term by universal suffrage. The unicameral national assembly (members of which are elected to 5-year terms) may be dissolved at any time by the president. The president may also enact legislation when the national assembly is not in session.

Local administration rests in the hands of the 31 provinces (*wilayas*), which are subdivided into 691 communes. Each province and commune has an elected assembly.

HISTORY

The earliest known inhabitants of Algeria were the Berbers, a people that included both settled and nomadic groups. From about the 12th century BC, the Phoenicians began to secure coastal footholds in northwestern Africa. In the 9th century BC they founded Carthage in what is now Tunisia, and eventually

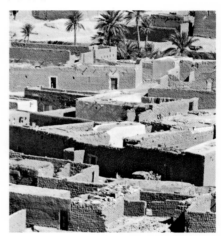

(Left) *Oran, Algeria's vital Mediterranean seaport, is the country's second largest city and a center of the international petroleum trade. The many examples of Spanish and Moorish architecture in the city's older section, the* Casbah, *contrast with modern, high-rise buildings.*

(Below) *The hamlet of El Goléa is one of many Algerian settlements that depend on the water of a Saharan oasis. The homes are constructed of dried clay, one of the few building materials available.*

this city came to dominate much of the coast of North Africa. In 208 BC most of northern Algeria was united in the kingdom of NUMIDIA under the rule of MASINISSA. In 146 BC the Romans destroyed Carthage, and in 106 BC, with the defeat of King JUGURTHA, Numidia became part of the Roman Empire.

A settled, agrarian way of life developed within the Roman frontiers, but the Berbers retained their strongholds in the mountains and the desert to the south. Northern Algeria was divided into Numidia and Mauritania Caesariensis.

Roman rule was brought to an end with the invasion of the VANDALS (AD 430–31). In the early 6th century, under the emperor Justinian, Byzantine influence was extended as far west as present-day Algiers, the rest of North Africa remaining under Berber control.

Arab raids on the region began in the late 7th century, and by the end of the 8th century Byzantine power had been expelled, and the region became part of the UMMAYAD empire. The Arabs established and maintained a flourishing urban and rural life for more than three centuries. The Berbers were rapidly converted to Islam. However, Berber antagonism to Arab dominance grew in the 8th century. For the next several centuries North Africa was controlled by a series of Muslim dynasties that originated in the Maghrib (northwestern Africa), the most important of which were the FATIMIDS (10th century) and the ALMORAVIDS (11th century), a Berber dynasty. The ALMOHADS, also a Muslim Berber dynasty, united North Africa and Spain, bringing great economic prosperity to the region, but their power was not long-lived and had declined by the early 13th century.

By the early 16th century, Spain, having expelled Muslim power from the Iberian Peninsula, captured coastal areas of Algeria. With assistance from the Turks, Spanish power was ended, and northern Algeria came under the rule (1518) of the Ottoman Empire. Piracy flourished, and the Regency of Algiers reached its peak of power and prosperity in the 17th century. (See BARBARY STATES.)

During the Napoleonic Wars in the early 19th century, renewed piracy incurred armed opposition from, among others, the Americans and the British.

Turkish domination was effectively ended in 1830, when

the French occupied Algiers. Beginning in 1834, the French fought a campaign to conquer northern Algeria and were victorious only in 1847 with the defeat of the Algerian leader Abd al-Qadir (c.1807–1883). In 1848, Algeria was declared a French colony, and colonization by Frenchmen and other Europeans proceeded rapidly. In the next few decades French influence was extended into the Sahara, but throughout the 19th century rebellions against French rule were common.

By the 1860s much of the best agricultural land was already in European hands, and the production of wine for export was replacing the traditional grain production for home consumption. By World War I, roads, schools, and hospitals were being built, and the introduction of large-scale agriculture had been implemented. These developments benefited the European population rather than the native Algerians.

Algerian nationalism began to organize after World War I. In 1924, Messali Hadj founded, in Paris, the first Algerian nationalist newspaper. A more moderate group, organized in 1930 under Ferhat Abbas, called for the equality of Algeria within the French Republic.

World War II put a temporary end to nationalist ambitions. Algeria came under the administration of the Vichy government, which was strongly supported by the French settlers. In 1942 the Allies landed in Algeria and used the country as a base of operations for North Africa.

Nationalist riots in Sétif in 1945 provoked harsh French reprisals, in which thousands of Muslims were killed. In 1947, Algerian Muslims were granted French citizenship, but other reform measures were either never fully carried out or thwarted.

In 1954 the FLN began a rebellion in eastern Algeria. The bitter and bloody conflict that followed (see ALGERIAN WAR) lasted ur.til 1962. Independence was granted on July 3, 1962.

The first Algerian government was formed by Prime Minister Ben Yusuf Ben Khedda, but he was replaced in September 1962 by Ahmed BEN BELLA, a leftist. In April 1963, Ben Bella took the post of general secretary of the FLN, thus increasing his powers. In September 1963, a constitution was approved by referendum, and Ben Bella was elected to a 5-year term as president with extensive powers.

The country had been left in dire economic straits by the war. Nearly all the Europeans—that is, most of the professionals and skilled workers—had left the country. Remaining European-owned farms were confiscated, and steps were taken to nationalize the economy.

Discontent over Ben Bella's dictatorial powers and the poor state of the economy led to his ouster on June 19, 1965, in a bloodless coup d'etat led by Col. Houari BOUMEDIENNE. The constitution was suspended, and political authority was put in the hands of a revolutionary council with Boumedienne at its head. Boumedienne announced his intention to make Algeria an "authentic socialist society" and to follow a policy of nonalignment in international relations.

During the Six-Day War in 1967 Algeria declared war on Israel and at the same time severed diplomatic relations with the United States. By the end of 1968, in spite of some continued opposition and an assassination attempt, Boumedienne had strengthened his political position and become more active in foreign policy.

In 1971, French oil and gas interests were nationalized. During the 1970s Boumedienne took a prominent role in Third World affairs; he strongly opposed Morocco's claim to Western Sahara, supporting that country's independence under the Polisario Front. Diplomatic relations with the United States were resumed in 1974.

Boumedienne died in December 1978 and was succeeded as president by Benjedid CHADLI in February 1979. In 1980 and 1981, Algeria was troubled by conflicts between the government and the Berber minority. Under Chadli the official emphasis on heavy industry was modified in favor of agriculture and consumer needs, and a greater role was given to the private sector. In 1984, President Chadli was elected to a second five-year term.

Bibliography: Heggoy, A. A., *Insurgency and Counterinsurgency in Algeria* (1972); Heggoy, A. A., and Crout, Robert R., *Historical Dictionary of Algeria* (1981); Henissart, Paul, *Wolves in the City: The Death of French Algeria* (1970); Julien, Charles-André, *History of North Africa* (1970); Knapp, Wilfred, *North West Africa: A Political and Economic Survey*, 3d ed. (1977); Laroui, Abdallah, *The History of the Maghrib*, trans. by Ralph Mannheim (1977); Ottoway, David and Marina, *Algeria: The Politics of a Socialist Revolution* (1970); Wolf, John B., *The Barbary Coast: Algeria under the Turks* (1979).

Algerian War

The Algerian War, fought from Nov. 1, 1954, until July 1, 1962, was a rebellion by Muslim Algerians against French rule that finally brought the creation of an independent ALGERIA. For France, the war was economically debilitating, socially divisive, and politically disastrous, bringing the collapse of the Fourth Republic. Algeria was the last of the French holdings in North Africa to become independent, Tunisia and Morocco having achieved that status in 1956.

French rule since 1830 had produced an Algeria combining ultramodern and archaic aspects. European-style cities stood alongside centuries-old villages; large-scale agricultural units existed next to hundreds of tiny farms. More than a million European settlers (colons)—a majority of French origin—possessed the principal industrial, commercial, and agricultural enterprises. Most of the 8.5 million Muslims either pursued primitive economic activities or performed menial tasks in the modern sector. Despite reforms over the previous 50 years and despite the fact that Algeria was technically not a colony but comprised three *départements* of France, the Muslim Algerians were politically disadvantaged as well. They had equality before the law but little power to make or administer it.

Nationalist aspirations for liberation heightened Muslim discontent. A National Liberation Front (FLN, from its French name) was formed, and on Nov. 1, 1954, small FLN bands began to raid French army installations and colons' holdings. The FLN also used terroristic and revolutionary war tactics to force adherence by the Muslims or to dissuade them from apathy or sympathy toward the French. Terror begat terror; the French Army responded with traditional and counterrevolutionary military methods.

But the French had little success. Neither the military efforts of the 500,000-man army nor sizable political concessions produced decisive defeat of the rebels or the firm allegiance of the Muslim masses. By 1958 the Fourth Republic was at stalemate—and crisis. The colons and certain factions of the French army were alarmed by the ineffectiveness of the Paris government. On May 13, in Algiers, they rioted, overran the government offices, and established an emergency Committee of Public Safety. In Paris, Premier Pierre Pflimlin's ministry was paralyzed, and Charles DE GAULLE was asked to become premier. He was granted emergency powers and the right to frame a constitution for a Fifth Republic.

As president under the new constitution, de Gaulle moved to pacify the officers and colons, to woo the Muslim population, and finally to negotiate with the FLN, which established a provisional government in 1958. An accord was reached on Mar. 18, 1962, whereby the Algerians were to vote by referendum on their future status. On July 1, 1962, the Algerians adopted independence by a vote of 5,975,581 to 16,534.

DONALD J. HARVEY

Bibliography: Horne, A., *A Savage War of Peace: Algeria, 1954–1962* (1978); Talbott, John, *The War without a Name* (1980).

Algiers

Algiers (French: Alger; Arabic: al-Jazair) is the capital, largest city, and chief port of Algeria, in northern Africa. The city has 29 km (18 mi) of waterfront on the Bay of Algiers, an inlet of the Mediterranean. On the west the Sahel Hills separate Algiers from the surrounding agricultural region, giving the city the appearance of a huge amphitheater facing the bay. The population is 2,200,000 (1981 est.). The climate is mild Mediterranean, with temperatures averaging between 13° C in January and 26° C in July (55° and 79° F). Rainfall is about 762 mm (30 in), falling mostly in the winter months (October–March). Before independence in 1962, Algiers was essentially a French city, and European architectural influences are apparent. However, in recent years thousands of Europeans have left the city, and a large number of immigrants have come to the city from the interior. Suburbs have sprung up, and today less than 2% of the population is non-Arab.

Port activities are the mainstay of the economy. Products from the surrounding agricultural region such as wine, fruits, and vegetables are exported along with iron ore; and the harbor serves as a refueling depot for large vessels. Oil and natural gas deposits being developed in the Sahara are an important source of revenue. Cement, chemicals, and paper products are manufactured in the city. Algiers is the site of the University of Algiers. Notable buildings include the 11th-century Great Mosque and the national library, which is housed in an 18th-century Moorish palace.

Algiers was known to the Romans as Icosium. After being destroyed several times by invaders, the present site was settled in the 10th century by the Berbers. Until the 18th century Algiers was a home base for Barbary pirates, who terrorized ships on the Mediterranean. In 1516, Algiers came under the control of the Turks. The French captured the city in 1830, and it became the colonial headquarters of France until Algeria's independence in 1962. During World War II, Algiers served as a major headquarters for the Allies and for a brief period was the provisional capital of free France.

algin [al'-jin]

Algin is a water-soluble, cream-colored powder, obtained from various kelps (seaweed) that is used as a thickener and emulsion stabilizer. In the manufacture of ice cream, it is added to ensure a creamy texture and prevent the growth of ice crystals. Algin is the sodium salt of alginic acid.

ALGOL [al'-gahl]

ALGOL, which stands for algorithmic language, is a COMPUTER LANGUAGE widely used for scientific PROGRAMMING. It was developed in Europe in the early 1960s and had a profound influence on subsequent programming languages, including

PL/1, Pascal, and Simula 67. ALGOL introduced important control structures, such as the ''if'' statement, ''begin'' and ''end'' blocks for grouping statements into a unit, and more flexible rules for declaring variables. Because of its simplicity, it is often used for communicating or publishing programs.

ELLIOTT ORGANICK AND SUSAN OWICKI

Algol   [al'-gahl]

Algol, also known as β Persei, is a well-known VARIABLE STAR, as well as a BINARY STAR. Its light variations, explained by John Goodricke in 1783, are caused by mutual eclipses of two stars moving in orbits around their common center of gravity, within a period of about 69 hours. When the dimmer star eclipses the brighter star, Algol fades to one-third of its original brightness, from magnitude 2.3 to 3.5, for about 10 hours. Only a slight dimming is apparent when the brighter star eclipses the dimmer star.

The larger star of the Algol system (spectral type B8) has a mass of about 5 solar masses and a radius 3.1 times the solar radius; the other star (spectral type gK0) has a mass about equal to that of the Sun and a radius 3.7 times the solar radius. The two stars are separated by 15 solar radii. A third, more distant star is also part of the Algol system, but it has no effect on the light variations.

Many other eclipsing variables are broadly similar to Algol. In some the two stars appear to be essentially spherical; in others, known as W URSAE MAJORIS STARS, the stars are ellipsoidal, being distorted by their mutual tidal attractions.

R. H. GARSTANG

Algonquin   [al-gahn'-kwin]

The Algonquin (or Algonkin), a North American Indian tribe, inhabited in the 17th century the areas of present-day St. Lawrence and the lower Ottawa River areas of present-day Quebec, Canada. Early French settlers applied the name to a number of independent bands of hunting peoples whom they encountered in that region. These small foraging bands spoke closely related languages of the Algonquian (Algonkian) family and were similar in culture and social organization.

Algonquian-speaking bands allied themselves with the French in their efforts to settle Canada and to block Five Nations IROQUOIS attempts to dominate the fur trade in the eastern interior of North America. Hard pressed by Iroquois raids, however, the Algonquins were eventually forced to abandon their villages and hunting grounds. Some moved west to the Lake Huron region and may be ancestors of the peoples known as the OTTAWA and the Nipissing. Others

moved north and east out of range of Iroquois war parties. Some who later returned to the French colony aided the French in the FRENCH AND INDIAN WARS until the British conquest (1763) of New France. About 2,000 Indians regarded as descendants of the original St. Lawrence-Ottawa River Algonquins today live on small reservations in Canada mainly in Ontario and Quebec.

JAMES A. CLIFTON

Bibliography: Bailey, Alfred G., *The Conflict of European and Eastern Algonkian Cultures, 1504–1700,* 2d ed. (1969); Flannery, Regina, *An Analysis of Coastal Algonquian Culture* (1939); MacNeish, June H., *The Indians of the Subarctic: A Critical Bibliography* (1976); Vastokas, Joan, and Romas, K., *Sacred Art of the Algonkians* (1973).

algorithm

An algorithm is a procedure for solving a usually complicated problem by carrying out a precisely determined sequence of simpler, unambiguous steps. Such procedures were originally used in mathematical calculations (the name is a variant of *algorism*, which originally meant the Arabic numerals and then ''arithmetic'') but are now widely used in computer programs and in PROGRAMMED LEARNING. FLOWCHARTS are frequently used to facilitate understanding of the sequence of steps. Because each step is followed mechanistically, value judgments and complex, nonquantitative situations are usually not susceptible of algorithmic treatment except in the form of greatly simplified models.

See also: PROGRAMMING, COMPUTER.

Algren, Nelson

The American writer Nelson Algren, b. Detroit, Mar. 28, 1909, d. May 9, 1981, became famous as the mythographer of the big city slum, particularly the Chicago slum where he grew up. The work that brought Algren the widest acclaim was his novel *The Man with the Golden Arm* (1949; film, 1955), which won a 1950 National Book Award. Equally impressive, however, was *A Walk on the Wild Side* (1956), a republication of Algren's first novel, *Somebody in Boots* (1935). *The Neon Wilderness* (1947) and *The Last Carousel* (1973) are collections of short stories. Just before his death, Algren was elected to the American Academy and Institute of Arts and Letters.

Bibliography: Cox, Martha H., and Chatterton, Wayne, *Nelson Algren* (1975); Donahue, H. E. F., *Conversations with Nelson Algren* (1964).

Alhambra

The Alhambra is a Moorish fortified palace overlooking the southern Spanish city of Granada. Its name is derived from

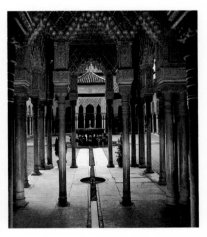

(Left) *The stark exterior of the Alhambra overlooking Granada, Spain, contrasts with its rich interior.* (Right) *The 14th-century Court of the Lions shows Moorish artistry in its slender columns, delicate arches, and intricate ornamentation.*

the Arabic *Kalat-Alhamra*, meaning "red castle." The severe brick walls, punctuated by square towers, extend for more than 1.5 km (almost 1 mi) but give no hint of the rich variety of gardens, courts, and chambers within. In the 13th century the Alhambra became a royal residence of the last great Moorish dynasty in Spain, the Nasrid. Much of the existing structure dates from the reigns of Yusuf I (1334–54) and Muhammad V (1354–91). Yusuf I built the imposing Court of the Myrtles and the lofty domed Hall of the Ambassadors. Muhammad V, in even richer style, created the Court of the Lions, with its arcade set on delicate marble columns, and the Hall of the Two Sisters, which is crowned with intricate honeycomb vaulting.

After the Moors were expelled (1492) from Spain, the Alhambra became a Christian palace, and in the 1520s, King Charles I (Holy Roman Emperor Charles V) began a Renaissance structure (never completed) adjoining the Court of the Myrtles. Spain's political life centered in Castile, and the Alhambra gradually fell into ruin. Now extensively restored, the colorfully decorated palace and surrounding gardens give a vivid impression of the crafts and the artistry of the last flowering of Moorish civilization in Spain.   DAVID W. SCOTT

Bibliography: Bargebuhr, Frederick P., *The Alhambra: A Cycle of Studies on the Eleventh Century in Moorish Spain* (1968); Calvert, A. F., *The Alhambra* (1907); Grasbar, Oleg, *The Alhambra* (1978); Stewart, Desmond S., ed., *The Alhambra* (1974).

Ali

Ali (Ali ibn Abi Talib), b. *c.*600, d. Jan. 24, 661, fourth caliph of the Muslim community, is regarded by SHIITE Muslims as the only legitimate successor of the Prophet Muhammad. The first cousin of Muhammad and husband of the Prophet's daughter FATIMA, Ali was passed over in the caliphal succession until 656, when he received the office after the murder of Uthman, the third caliph. He was immediately challenged by an aristocratic faction led by the prophet's widow, AISHA, whom he defeated. While the caliph was combating a second rebellion, led by MUAWIYAH, governor of Syria, a group of Ali's supporters split away (the so-called Kharijites, or "seceders") and were massacred by Ali's supporters. Ali was then murdered by a Kharijite in retaliation, and Muawiyah seized the caliphate. Ali's partisans, the Shiites, never recognized Muawiyah, claiming that only Ali's sons, Hasan (d. *c.*669) and Husayn (d. 680), could rightfully have succeeded him.

Ali, Muhammad

The American boxer Muhammad Ali, b. Louisville, Ky., Jan. 17, 1942, was perhaps the most celebrated sports figure in the world during most of the 1960s and '70s. He was originally

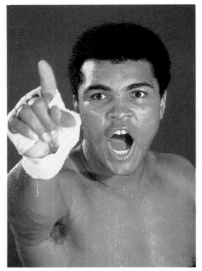

Muhammad Ali, the flamboyant, three-time heavyweight boxing champion, was known for his precise punching and great speed. His most memorable fights were against such hard punchers as Sonny Liston, Joe Frazier, and George Foreman. As age lessened Ali's physical abilities, he maintained his preeminence through his tactical skills.

named Cassius Marcellus Clay, Jr., and fought under that name until after he won his first world heavyweight championship. His rise to prominence may be attributed to a combination of circumstances—his role as a spokesman for, and idol of, blacks; his vivacious personality; his dramatic conversion to the Black Muslim religion; and most important, his staying power as an athlete. Ali first came to world attention in 1960, when he won the Olympic light-heavyweight championship. After his surprising victory over then heavyweight champion Sonny Liston in 1964, he produced a steady stream of headlines. He was the first boxer to benefit from international (satellite) television, making him all the more visible.

Ali, then Clay, won a controversial championship bout from Liston to gain the title. The fight was questioned because Ali seemed to be almost quitting before the bout was over. In his second fight with Liston, more controversy arose over the way Liston went down and stayed down in the initial round. Ali, however, proved to be a "fighting champion," accepting the challenges of every heavyweight with ranking credentials. He was stripped of his title in 1967 for refusing military service on religious grounds during the Vietnam War but was allowed to resume fighting in 1970 and had his appeal of conviction upheld by the U.S. Supreme Court in 1971. Ali regained the championship in a 1974 bout with George Foreman. He lost the crown again in 1978 to Leon Spinks but regained it the same year, thus becoming the first man to win the title three times. Other than Joe Frazier (in 1971) and Spinks, the only boxers to defeat Ali, who had a 55-5 record through 1982, were Ken Norton (1973), who later lost to Ali; Larry Holmes (1980), who foiled Ali's try for a fourth heavyweight championship; and Trevor Berbick (1981), after which Ali announced his retirement.   JIM BENAGH

Bibliography: Ali, Muhammad, *The Greatest: My Own Story* (1975); Mailer, Norman, *The Fight* (1975); Olsen, Jack, *Black Is Best* (1967); Sheed, Wilfred, *Muhammad Ali* (1976).

Ali, Sabahattin   [sah-bah-huh-teen']

Sabahattin Ali, b. Feb. 25, 1907, d. Apr. 2, 1948, a Turkish writer of fiction, is remembered as a forerunner of socialist realism. His work was popular and influential for its crisp narration, colorful dialogue, and concern for impoverished Turkish people. In his last years he wrote for left-wing newspapers and edited *Markopaşa*, a satiric periodical. Ali was jailed several times because of his political views.

          TALAT SAIT HALMAN

Ali Baba

Ali Baba, a woodcutter, is the protagonist of "Ali Baba and the Forty Thieves," one of the most popular tales from the collection known as the ARABIAN NIGHTS. When thieves stash their stolen treasures in a secret cave, Ali Baba accidentally witnesses the act and learns their magic password, "Open Sesame," which he then uses to enter the cave and make off with the gold himself. The robbers' attempts to kill Ali Baba are subsequently foiled by his slave, Morgana, when she finds the band hiding in giant jars.

alias

Alias (Latin, "otherwise") is used in law to connect the names of a person who has been called by a name other than his or her given name. In popular usage it means the name itself, for example, "He took an alias."

Alicante   [ah-lee-kahn'-tay]

Alicante, the capital of Alicante province, is a port city in southeastern Spain. Located on the Mediterranean Sea, 124 km (77 mi) south of Valencia, the city has a population of 226,600 (1976 est.). Industries include textiles, wine, cigars, and tourism. Settled during the 4th century BC, it later became the Roman port of Lucentum (201 BC). The city was captured by Moors in 713 and by James I of Aragon in 1265.

Alice Springs

Alice Springs, with a population of 13,400 (1975 est.), is the chief town of the interior of NORTHERN TERRITORY, Australia. It is the commercial center of the surrounding cattle-raising and mining region. Tourism is important because of the long, warm winter (May to September). The northern terminus of the Central Australia Railway, Alice Springs is also accessible by air and the Stuart Highway. It was settled in 1871.

Alice's Adventures in Wonderland

"The Mad Hatter's Tea Party," from Alice's Adventures in Wonderland, was drawn in 1865 by Sir John Tenniel, an English political cartoonist. Tenniel's illustrations, which have become nearly as famous as the story itself, were specified by the book's author, Lewis Carroll.

Alice's Adventures in Wonderland (1865), by Lewis CARROLL (Charles Lutwidge Dodgson), and its sequel, THROUGH THE LOOKING GLASS (1871), are usually considered the most famous children's books written in English. The story is a dream in which Alice changes size, recites nonsensical parodies of moral verse, encounters such fantastic creatures as the Mad Hatter and the Cheshire Cat, and finally asserts herself against loud but empty threats of trial and execution. Children probably enjoy Alice's triumph and the ingenious invention of the book, while adult readers and critics are engaged by the themes of growing up, death and extinction, and the arbitrariness of moral and social authority. The story was made into an animated film by Walt Disney in 1951 and has been the subject of numerous plays.

DONALD J. GRAY

Bibliography: Carroll, Lewis, *The Annotated Alice*, ed. by Martin Gardner (1960; repr. 1970); Phillips, Robert, ed., *Aspects of Alice* (1971).

alicyclic compounds   [al-ih-sik'-lik]

Alicyclic compounds are members of a class of organic CYCLIC COMPOUNDS, which contain three or more atoms joined to form a closed ring. The ring in alicyclic compounds is composed of only carbon atoms; HETEROCYCLIC COMPOUNDS contain other elements besides carbon in the ring, the most common being oxygen, nitrogen, and sulfur. The more stable alicyclic compounds possess C_5 (5-carbon) and C_6 rings and are called naphthenes. The alicyclic compounds containing only single bonds are named using the prefix *cyclo-* followed by the name of the corresponding open-chain hydrocarbon, for example, CYCLOHEXANE. More-complex molecules are usually given a nonchemical name.

Compounds of commercial importance can be prepared by converting an open-chain ALIPHATIC COMPOUND into a ring structure; for instance, the 6-carbon chain, hexane, can become the ring cyclohexane.

Another way to prepare alicyclic compounds is to add hy-drogen atoms to an AROMATIC COMPOUND, which is a ringed structure having alternate double and single bonds. Three hydrogen atoms added to benzene, for example, yields cyclohexane. The C_3 and C_4 rings are the most difficult to form and are highly reactive; C_5, C_6, and C_7 rings are easy to synthesize and are the most stable. Larger rings are difficult to form but are also stable.

Chemically, the alicyclic compounds resemble the open-chain aliphatic compounds rather than the aromatics, but the cyclic nature of alicyclics confers some special properties that can vary with the size of the ring. The stability and ease of formation of the ring vary with its size. Cyclopropane (C_3) and cyclobutane (C_4) rings are easily broken to form the corresponding open-chain compound, but cyclopentane (C_5) and cyclohexane (C_6) rings, as well as larger rings, are more resistant to such cleavage.

Polycyclic alicyclic hydrocarbons contain two or more rings that share common atoms. A variety of compounds of unusual shapes can be formed, but they are primarily of theoretical interest. Bicyclic alicyclic compounds, those which have only one atom common to two rings, are known as spiranes.

Some alicyclic compounds have commercial application. These include cyclopropane, used as an anesthetic; hexachlorocyclohexane, an insecticide; epoxides to prepare glycols and epoxy resins; cyclohexanol to prepare adipic acid, which, in turn, is used in making nylon; and cyclohexane and dioxane as solvents.

ELBERT H. HADLEY

Bibliography: McQuillin, F. J., *Alicyclic Chemistry* (1972); Morrison, Robert T., and Boyd, Robert N., *Organic Chemistry*, 3d ed. (1976).

alidade   [al'-i-dayd]

An alidade is a sighting device used in optical instruments, such as the SEXTANT, THEODOLITE, and surveying TRANSIT, in order to measure angles. The line of sight is rotated about an axis to point at objects, indicating their direction by the angle between a stationary mark and a mark that follows the line of sight along a calibrated circle.

With a straight edge and an alidade placed on a map and revolved about the observer's position, a line can be drawn on the map representing the straight line from the observer to the object sighted.

CHARLES A. HERUBIN

alien

An alien is a foreign-born person who is not a citizen of the country in which he or she resides. Aliens are not entitled to all the rights of citizens, but in most countries aliens who enter legally are guaranteed the basic protections of the laws. In the United States most aliens are admitted on a temporary basis as visitors or students or for some specific purpose. Resident aliens are admitted permanently; they have the same rights and duties under the law as U.S. citizens except that they cannot vote or run for most public offices. After five years a resident alien becomes eligible for NATURALIZATION. Another category of aliens comprises political refugees who have been allowed to become permanent residents outside the quota provisions of the immigration law.

See also: CITIZENSHIP; IMMIGRATION.

Alien and Sedition Acts

Four acts passed by the U.S. Congress in 1798 came to be known collectively as the Alien and Sedition Acts. By this legislation the dominant Federalist party hoped to cripple its political enemies, the Democratic-Republicans. The latter had attracted the support of many radical immigrants to the United States, especially from Ireland, and were critical of Federalist foreign policy. The Quasi-War with France following the XYZ AFFAIR convinced many Federalists that this criticism was disloyal, and thus the legislation was pushed through Congress, despite the mixed feelings of President John Adams.

The Naturalization Act (June 18, 1798) raised the residence requirement for aliens seeking citizenship from 5 to 14 years. The Alien Act (June 25, 1798), limited to two years' duration, empowered the president to deport any foreigner he regarded as dangerous "to the peace and safety of the United States." The Alien Enemies Act (July 6, 1798), passed with some Republican support, gave the president broad powers to deal with enemy aliens during time of war. The Sedition Act (July 14, 1798), also of two years' duration, made it a crime to publish anything false or scandalous against the government. The last act violated the spirit of the 1st Amendment, although it is notable for revising the concept of seditious libel to accept truth as a defense and to allow juries to rule on questions of law as well as fact—both departures from common law.

As a result of the Republican victory of 1800, the Naturalization Act was repealed in 1802. The others were allowed to expire. With the steady growth of democratic practice in the 19th century, few lingering Federalists publicly defended their wisdom or validity.   MORTON BORDEN

Bibliography: Levy, Leonard W., *Legacy of Suppression: Freedom of Speech and Press in Early American History* (1960); Miller, John C., *Crisis in Freedom: The Alien and Sedition Acts* (1951; repr. 1964); Smith, James M., *Freedom's Fetters: Alien and Sedition Laws* (1956).

Alien Registration Act: see SMITH ACT.

alienation

Alienation is a term widely used to describe and explain a state of estrangement from work, political and social norms, other people, or oneself. It is broadly and sometimes inconsistently used; whereas psychiatrists tend to see alienation as a symptom of an individual's maladjustment to society, some sociologists and philosophers assert that a society can be "sick" or simply foreign and that alienation should not be taken as an indication of an individual's condition. Alienation was a major perspective of 19th-century thought, but its antecedents date from the early Christian Era.

Christian Concept. St. Paul taught that man, by his innately sinful nature, alienates himself from a loving father (God); this concept assumes a particular view of man's nature and of a familial relationship between God and man. St. AUGUSTINE worried about man's reconciliation with God and disputed with the Pelagians (see PELAGIANISM), who denied that man's nature is essentially evil. From the time of Thomas AQUINAS until the present century, God was no longer conceived of as a personal being but as all-powerful and requiring the intercession of others; alienation and reconciliation therefore declined as central theological concerns.

Western intellectual traditions, however, continued to assume a condition of alienation long after theological disputes faded; the romantic movement in philosophy and literature (see ROMANTICISM) viewed civilization as corrupting and alienating man from nature. Certain schools of contemporary psychology still hold this view and maintain that a genuine, integrated person could be discovered if the problems of role and authority did not interfere.

19th-Century Views. Alienation occupies a central place in Georg HEGEL's *Phenomenology* (1807), in which he asserts that man strives to attain actually what he is potentially, but that this realization is mediated by consciousness and will and manifested in physical objects, institutions, and mores. According to Hegel, these impede man's full realization, that is, they are an alienation from self. For Hegel, alienation was exclusively an intellectual construct. One of Hegel's disciples, Bruno Bauer, following this line of argument, popularized the term *self-alienation* when he proposed that religious beliefs cause a separation in man's consciousness between his received idea of the world and the world as he experiences it.

Ludwig FEUERBACH, a contemporary of Bauer and another disciple of Hegel, taught that religion is a projection of man's inner nature and desire and is therefore alienating because it makes man locate his humanity in an external idea and subject himself to the forces and superstitions of traditional organized religion. Feuerbach's concept, like Hegel's, influenced

Karl MARX, who was developing a secular view of alienation.

In Marx's early writings (1846), alienation was discussed as an explicit social phenomenon, empirically verifiable. He used the term to refer to the ways in which man's powers of perception, orientation, and creation become stunted and crippled by the very nature of the industrial organization and by the capitalist economic system. Man is alienated from his work because he plays no role in deciding what to do or how to do it, alienated from the product of his work because he has no control over what he makes or what is done with it, and alienated from other people by economic competition and class hostility. Marx felt that man suffers from alienation to the extent that he does not realize the full potential of his being. This aspect of Marxian thought had little impact on social and economic philosophy until the middle of the 20th century; since then, it has been the focus of intense interest.

Modern Concept. Alienation as a consequence of social organization and culture is a key generative concept of modern sociology; it underlies the analyses of Emile DURKHEIM, Max WEBER, and Georg SIMMEL. Durkheim used the term *anomie* to describe the rootlessness (often resulting in suicide) that resulted from the breakdown of traditional community and religious mores. For Weber, the increasing rationalization of bureaucratic life caused personal relationships and individual values to atrophy. Simmel used the concept to denote the tension within a person seeking to "preserve his autonomy and individuality in the face of overwhelming social forces, of historical heritage, of external culture, and of the techniques of life." Few empirical studies have been done, however, and the term *alienation* is used to explain, among other things, both voter passivity in political elections and student protest movements.

Alienation has been viewed as inherent in human nature by the theologians Martin BUBER and Paul TILLICH and by the EXISTENTIALISTS Jean Paul SARTRE and Albert CAMUS; they have argued that some degree of dissociation of the self in thought and life is inescapable, for man is a stranger in the world.

Bibliography: Arendt, Hannah, *The Human Condition* (1958); Fromm, Erich, *Escape from Freedom* (1941) and *The Sane Society* (1955); Hoffer, Eric, *The True Believer* (1951); Johnson, Frank, ed., *Alienation: Concept, Term, and Meanings* (1973); Josephson, Eric and Mary, *Man Alone: Alienation in Modern Society* (1962); Nisbet, Robert, *The Sociological Tradition* (1966); Ollman, Bertell, *Alienation*, 2d ed. (1977); Slater, Philip, *The Pursuit of Loneliness* (1970; rev. ed., 1976); Sykes, Gerald, *Alienation: The Cultural Climate of Our Time* (1964); Torrance, John, *Estrangement, Alienation, and Exploitation* (1977); Weiskopf, Walter A., *Alienation and Economics* (1973).

alienation of affections

Alienation of affections is the act by a third party of intentionally taking away the affection of a husband or wife for the other marriage partner. A few U.S. states allow a damage suit for interference or alienation of affections against third parties accused of breaking up a marriage or an engagement.

alimentary canal: see DIGESTION, HUMAN; DIGESTIVE SYSTEM.

alimony

Alimony is the money allowance that a court awards to a marriage partner after legal separation or divorce. Temporary alimony may be allowed during litigation. Traditionally, alimony has been paid by the husband to the wife. However, an independently wealthy wife or one whose job gives her a comfortable living may not be awarded alimony. In some cases, well-to-do wives may be ordered to support husbands who are unable to maintain themselves.

Alimony payments may stop if the spouse receiving them remarries. Child-support payments, however, are covered by a separate agreement and usually remain in effect while the children are minors; these payments may include school or college expenses or medical bills. Often a spouse who plans to remarry will accept a low alimony settlement in exchange for a generous child-support agreement.

Alinsky, Saul

Saul David Alinsky, b. Chicago, Jan. 30, 1909, d. June 12, 1972, was a radical activist who organized communities of poor people to help them help themselves. In 1938, after having worked several years as a criminologist, he organized a campaign of picketing, rent strikes, and boycotts among the slum dwellers in Chicago's Back-of-the-Yards district. One year later he founded the Chicago-based Industrial Areas Foundation, through which he did similar work in other communities during the '40s, '50s, and '60s. One of Alinsky's best-known projects was The Woodlawn Organization (TWO), also in Chicago. His books include *Reveille for Radicals* (1946) and *The Professional Radical* (1970).

aliphatic compounds   [al-i-fat'-ik]

An aliphatic compound is any of a major group of organic, or carbon compounds, characterized by a continuous or branched open-chain arrangement of the carbon atoms. The other major groups are the ALICYCLIC COMPOUNDS (carbon atoms arranged in a ring), AROMATIC COMPOUNDS (involving the benzene-ring structure), and HETEROCYCLIC COMPOUNDS (rings incorporating other atoms as well as carbon).

Most organic compounds can be considered as hydrogen-carbon compounds (hydrocarbons), or as compounds in which other elements have substituted for the hydrogen. Aliphatic hydrocarbons comprise three subgroups: ALKANES (paraffin series), characterized by the existence of only single bonds connecting the carbon atoms; ALKENES (olefins), which have at least one double bond; and ALKYNES (acetylenes), which have one or more triple bonds. On any one of these types of compound, one or more hydrogen atoms may be replaced by other elements or groups of elements to produce the entire spectrum of aliphatic compounds.

Alkanes are relatively unreactive. They will burn, producing heat, carbon dioxide, and water; long chains can be pyrolyzed (heated without air), producing either shorter chains or alkenes; and other atoms can substitute for hydrogen, primarily chlorine and bromine atoms. The last-named reactions are catalyzed by ultraviolet light. Alkenes and alkynes are much more reactive. They readily add other molecules or form long chains of repeating molecular units (see POLYMERIZATION).

When a hydrogen atom of an aliphatic compound is removed, an alkyl RADICAL (R) is formed. Radicals often occur as intermediates in reactions but do not exist independently except for short periods of time. The number of radicals that can form generally increases with the complexity of the compound. For example, the gas propane $CH_3CH_2CH_3$ can have a branch-chain radical form by removing a hydrogen from the central carbon, or a straight-chain radical form by removing a hydrogen from the end carbon. Higher molecular weight compounds form an increasing number of radicals.

Functional groups added to the radicals give the other types of aliphatic compounds. When the hydrogen atom of an aliphatic compound is replaced by one or more hydroxyl groups (OH), ALCOHOLS (ROH) are formed. The important reactions of the alcohols are those of the OH group. Either just the H or the entire OH group may be involved. Substitution by a halogen (fluorine, chlorine, bromine, or iodine) produces the alkyl halide (RX); such industrially important compounds do not occur in nature. Two molecules of an alcohol may combine, with the loss of a molecule of water, to form an ETHER (ROR). Ethers are unreactive with most chemicals except at elevated temperatures. Alcohols can be oxidized to form the carbonyl compounds, ALDEHYDES and KETONES.

An amino group (NH_2), containing nitrogen (N), can be attached to the radical, forming an AMINE (RNH_2). Substituted amines can also be formed if the hydrogen atoms on the nitrogen atom are replaced by one or two alkyl groups. The amines are unique in that they are the only common type of basic, or alkaline, organic compounds. They are all reactive and have a distinctive property—a disagreeable odor.

Controlled oxidation of aliphatic compounds, except the saturated hydrocarbons, in which all possible positions are filled by hydrogen atoms, will produce a CARBOXYLIC ACID. Es-

TERS are produced by the reaction of a carboxylic acid with an alcohol. They are characterized by a pleasant odor; many of these compounds occur in nature.

Other aliphatic compounds are the sulfur-containing mercaptan (RSH) and the nitrogen-containing nitrile (RCN) and nitro (RNO_2) compounds. In addition, some derivatives contain two different such groups within the molecule.

ELBERT H. HADLEY

Bibliography: Chapman, N. B., *Aliphatic Compounds* (1975).

alizarin   [ahl-i-zah'-rin]

Alizarin is the principal component in the natural dye MADDER and is obtained from the roots of the madder plant, *Rubia tinctorum*, grown in South India and Sri Lanka. Combined with a mordant, a material that acts as a binder between dye and cloth and determines the end color, alizarin was used to produce shades of red, violet, brown, and black. It was synthesized in 1868 by two German scientists, Karl Graebe and Karl Lieberman. In 1869, Sir William Perkin developed a practical process for manufacturing synthetic alizarin that proved to be less expensive and more consistent in color than the natural material. Today natural alizarin has little importance as a dyestuff, although it is used as a chemical intermediate in the production of more sophisticated dyes and as a coloring material for artists' pigments.

RODERICK H. HORNING

alkadiene: see DIENE.

alkali   [al'-kuh-ly]

In chemistry, alkali refers generally to any strongly basic compound (see ACIDS AND BASES). Alkalies are usually SALTS or hydroxides of sodium, potassium, lithium, or ammonia. Mineral deposits containing large quantities of such compounds are also called alkali.

In a more specific sense, alkali is either potassium hydroxide (KOH) or sodium hydroxide (lye, NaOH). These two strong bases have such similar properties that chemists often specify alkali when either compound may be used.

alkali metals

The alkali metals are the elements CESIUM, FRANCIUM, LITHIUM, POTASSIUM, RUBIDIUM, and SODIUM. These elements form group IA of the periodic table. The alkali metals react violently with water to form strong bases, called alkalies. The alkali metals are monovalent, the outer electron shell consisting of a single electron. This electron is easily shed to form a stable cation— a positively charged ion—that has the electron configuration of an inert gas. The alkali metals readily donate electrons to HALOGEN atoms to form stable salts. The reactivity of the alkali metals increases with atomic weight, or increasing atom radius, because the outer electron is held less strongly. Recent research has shown that atoms of alkali metals can also gain an electron to form highly reactive anions.

Because of their high reactivity, alkali metals are never found in nature as free elements; instead they occur in compounds such as silicates or chlorides. The alkali metals have low density, low melting point, and high ductility.

alkaline earth metals   [al'-kuh-lyn]

The alkaline earth metals are BARIUM, CALCIUM, and STRONTIUM, all of which are members of group IIA of the periodic table. They form strong bases, or alkaline solutions, and are called earths because of the incombustibility and insolubility of their oxides. Sometimes the other members of group IIA—BERYLLIUM, MAGNESIUM, and RADIUM—are included in the class.

Although none of the elements are found in nature in their pure metallic state, compounds containing calcium and magnesium are found throughout nature. Taking these compounds into account, calcium is the fifth most abundant element (3.63%) in the Earth's crust, and magnesium, the eighth (2.09%). Limestone, marble, and chalk are all forms of calcium carbonate, $CaCO_3$. Seashells, pearls, bones, and teeth contain a large amount of $CaCO_3$. Magnesium is found, not only in many minerals, including asbestos, $H_4Mg_3Si_2O_9$, but also in seawater. Compounds of calcium and magnesium are also found in fresh water, where they are responsible for its hardness.

The other alkaline earth metals are less abundant. Radium, a radioactive element, is found in low concentrations in pitchblende, U_3O_8, and is formed during the radioactive disintegration of uranium-238. Alkaline earth metals are found in their +2 oxidation states in the compounds they form. The metals are usually purified by electrolysis of their molten chlorides.   NORMAN V. DUFFY

Bibliography: Cotton, Frank A., and Wilkinson, Geoffrey, *Basic Inorganic Chemistry* (1976); Hampel, C. A., ed., *Encyclopedia of the Chemical Elements* (1968).

alkaloid   [al'-kuh-loyd]

An alkaloid is any of a class of nitrogen-containing natural products of plant origin that have an alkalilike, or basic, chemical nature (see ACIDS AND BASES). Alkaloids are further qualified by some experts as being complex in structure and manifesting some type of biological activity. The term was coined in 1819 by W. Meissner, a pharmacist.
Occurrence. Alkaloids are of many types, and specific types generally are found in certain genera or families. Common alkaloids include morphine (in opium poppy), nicotine (in tobacco), ricinine (in castor bean), strychnine, and quinine.

Although more than 200 alkaloids are known, estimates indicate that they are present in only 10 to 15 percent of all VASCULAR PLANTS. Alkaloids are often found in the dicotyledon group of flowering plants but seldom are found in monocotyledons or gymnosperms. Complex plant alkaloids are usually found in only a few plant species; simpler ones occur in many, including plants that are botanically unrelated.
Function. Why certain plants contain alkaloids remains a mystery, although a number of theories have been formulated: that alkaloids are by-products of plant metabolism; that they are means of defense for plants against animal and insect attacks; or that they are reservoirs for protein synthesis, regulators of growth and reproduction, or detoxifying agents.
Uses. Alkaloids are widely used for the physiological effects that they produce. Socrates was poisoned by conine, the active constituent of hemlock. Other important alkaloids include strychnine, an extremely potent poison that is used as a respiratory stimulant in humans and as a rodenticide; morphine, a powerful addictive painkiller; codeine, a cough repressant and painkiller; atropine, a pupil dilator; and emetine, a powerful emetic used in the treatment of amoebic dysentery. Lysergic acid, an ergot alkaloid, is a starting material in the synthesis of lysergic acid diethylamide (LSD), a powerful hallucinogen.

Recently, medical applications have been discovered for the indole alkaloids of the *Vinca rosea* plant, vinblastine and vincristine; the former is used in the treatment of Hodgkins' disease, the latter in cases of acute leukemia. Other alkaloids of this class are studied experimentally as tumor-repressing agents in various animals. Recent research indicates that alkaloids may have many additional applications.
                                                    RONALD D. JOHNSON

Bibliography: Glasby, John S., *Encyclopedia of the Alkaloids* (1975); McKillop, Alexander, *An Introduction to the Chemistry of the Alkaloids* (1970); Pelletier, S. W., *Chemistry of the Alkaloids* (1970); Wiesner, K. F., ed., *Alkaloids* (1976).

alkalosis   [al-kuh-loh'-sis]

Alkalosis is a disturbed body condition in which the normal balance of acids and bases (alkalies) in body fluids is upset and alkalies predominate. It produces overexcitement of the nervous system and, in severe cases, an onset of muscle spasms known as tetany. The condition can be brought on by hyperventilation (overbreathing), which results in excess loss of carbon dioxide and hence a drop in the carbonic acid content of body fluids; slow, shallow breathing may correct

this. It may also be brought on by loss of gastric acids after severe vomiting or by the ingestion of more alkalies than the kidneys can process. The opposite condition is ACIDOSIS.
                                                    CARL J. PFEIFFER

Bibliography: Hills, Arthur G., *Acid-Base Balance: Chemistry, Physiology, Pathophysiology* (1973).

Alkan, Charles

Charles Alkan, b. Nov. 30, 1813, d. Mar. 19, 1888, a French pianist and composer, was a child prodigy who became a recluse in his 20s and devoted his life to composing. The 24 piano studies in Op. 35 and 39, representing all the major and minor keys, are his best works. The collection includes a concerto, so called because the solo piano takes on the role of both orchestra and solo instrument.

alkane   [al'-kayn]

Alkanes are a class of ALIPHATIC hydrocarbons characterized by open chains of carbon atoms with only single bonds between adjacent carbon atoms. All members of this series have the general chemical formula C_nH_{2n+2} where n is an integer. The related ALICYCLIC COMPOUNDS contain closed chains, or rings.

The carbon atoms may form continuous or branched chains; branching increases the number of possible ISOMERS, or structural differences, for any one empirical formula. There is only one CH_4 (methane) compound but five compounds with the formula C_6H_{14} (hexane), 75 $C_{10}H_{22}$ (decane) compounds, and 366,319 $C_{20}H_{42}$ (eicosane) compounds.

The number of alkane compounds is theoretically endless, but only a relatively few have been characterized. The homologous members, except for the first four, are named using the Greek or Latin prefix for the number of carbon atoms in the chain; all members have the characteristic ending *ane*.

All alkanes are insoluble in water; other physical properties vary with molecular weight. Members C_1 through C_4 are gases at room temperature and pressure; C_5 through C_{17} are liquids. Higher members are solids and are often called the paraffin hydrocarbons. The average increase in boiling point is 20° per CH_2 group.

The primary source of alkanes is natural gas and Pennsylvania and midcontinent crude petroleum. Cracking is an important refinery process in which the long chains are shortened to produce gasoline. The major uses of alkanes are to produce energy by the combustion of gas and gasoline, to lubricate as oil and grease, and to serve as chemicals that form alkenes, polymers, and other derivatives.   ELBERT H. HADLEY

Bibliography: Streitwieser, Andrew, and Heathcock, Clayton, *Introduction to Organic Chemistry* (1976).

alkanet   [al'-kuh-net]

Alkanet, or bugloss, is any of several coarse, hairy, annual, biennial, or perennial PLANTS with freely branching stems. The alkanet belongs to the borage family, Boraginaceae. Often used as an ornamental in perennial beds, it may reach a height of 1.5 m (5 ft). Leaves may be up to 15 cm (6 in) in length. The flowers are pink in the bud stage and bright blue in full bloom. A red dyestuff is obtained from the roots.
                                                    ROBERT C. ROMANS

alkene

An alkene is any of a group of organic compounds that contain a carbon-carbon double bond. The molecules of alkenes are composed only of carbon and hydrogen atoms but contain less hydrogen per carbon atom than the ALKANES, or paraffins, to which they can be converted by the addition of hydrogen. The alkenes (often called olefins) are thus unsaturated hydrocarbons; they have the general formula C_nH_{2n}:

$$C_nH_{2n} + H_2 \xrightarrow{\text{catalyst}} C_nH_{2n+2}$$
$$\text{alkene} \qquad\qquad \text{alkane}$$

Ethene or ethylene, C_2H_4, is the simplest member of the series. Systematic names for alkenes are derived by appending the suffix *ene* to the root name for the alkane with the same carbon content. Thus C_3H_6, commonly called propylene, has the systematic name *propene*, and C_4H_8 is either 1-butene or 2-butene, depending on the position of the double bond:

$$CH_2=CHCH_2CH_3 \qquad CH_3CH=CHCH_3$$
1-butene $\qquad\qquad$ 2-butene

Whereas carbon-carbon single bonds permit rotation of the atoms or groups of atoms linked to the carbons, double bonds between two atoms completely restrict rotation about the double bond. As a result 2-butene can exist in two different configurations of its atoms, called GEOMETRIC ISOMERS; the two forms are *cis*-2-butene and *trans*-2-butene:

cis-2-butene $\qquad\qquad$ *trans*-2-butene

These isomers possess the same number of atoms but have different structures and, therefore, different physical properties such as boiling points.

Alkene hydrocarbons are much more chemically reactive than the alkanes because the double bond is more susceptible to attack by other reagents. The double bond can readily be oxidized or reduced, and a wide variety of reagents can be added to the alkene molecule at the double-bond site.

Ethylene and propylene are the leading industrial organic raw materials. More than 11 billion kg (about 24.6 billion lb) of ethylene are produced annually in the United States, and the consumption of propylene reached 4.5 billion kg (about 10 billion lb) a year in 1977. $\qquad$ HERMAN E. ZIEGER

Bibliography: Allinger, N. L., et al., *Organic Chemistry*, 2d ed. (1976); Morrison, R. T., and Boyd, R. N., *Organic Chemistry*, 3d ed. (1973).

See also: DIENE.

Alkmaar   [ahlk'-mahr]

Alkmaar is a town in the North Holland province of the western Netherlands. Located about 32 km (20 mi) northwest of Amsterdam, it lies on the North Holland Canal, some 10 km (6 mi) inland from the North Sea. Dating from the 12th century, the town has a population of 64,400 (1975 est.); some 99,000 live in the metropolitan area. Alkmaar is famous for a cheese market, now a major tourist attraction, which operates much as it has since it opened in 1571. Alkmaar was the first Dutch town to resist a Spanish siege led by the duque de Alba in 1573, thus paving the way to Dutch independence. Notable buildings include the Gothic-style Town Hall, housing the Municipal Museum; the late 15th-century St. Lawrence's Church; and the 16th-century Weigh House.

alkyl group

An alkyl group is any one of a class of structural units present in the molecules of organic chemical compounds. These groups are composed of carbon and hydrogen atoms and have the general formula C_nH_{2n+1}. When n is 1, the group is methyl; when n is 2, the group is ethyl; and so on.

See also: ARYL GROUP.

alkyne   [al'-kyn]

An alkyne is any of a class of organic compounds similar to the ALKENES but characterized by a triple bond between two carbon atoms. The general formula for alkynes is C_nH_{2n-2}. They are sometimes called the acetylene series because the simplest member of the alkyne family is the colorless gas acetylene, C_2H_2. Names for the other alkynes are derived by adding the suffix *yne* to the root name for the ALKANE of the same carbon content.

Alkynes, like alkenes, undergo addition reactions; that is, substances such as hydrogen, bromine, and water can add to the molecule at the triple bond. Whereas a simple alkene can absorb only one mole of H_2 during reduction to an alkane, an alkyne such as propyne can consume two moles of H_2 during its stepwise conversion to propene and then to propane:

$$CH_3C\equiv CH + H_2 \xrightarrow{Pd-C} CH_3CH=CH_2 + H_2 \xrightarrow{Pd-C} CH_3CH_2CH_3$$
propyne $\qquad\qquad$ propene $\qquad\qquad$ propane

Terminal alkynes, those in which the triple bond is at the end of the carbon chain, are distinguished from other unsaturated hydrocarbons in that the hydrogen atom on the end carbon is weakly acidic and can be removed by reaction with a strongly basic reagent such as sodium amide, $NaNH_2$.

Acetylene is the only member of the alkyne series produced commercially in large amounts. It is made from coal and limestone by the reaction of coke and lime, CaO, in an electric furnace to produce calcium carbide:

$$3C + CaO \xrightarrow{2,000-2,500°C} CO + CaC_2 \xrightarrow{2H_2O}$$
coke $\quad$ lime $\qquad\qquad\qquad$ calcium
$\qquad\qquad\qquad\qquad\qquad$ carbide

$$H-C\equiv C-H + Ca(OH)_2$$
acetylene $\quad$ calcium
$\qquad\qquad\quad$ hydroxide

The calcium carbide reacts with water at room temperature.

In recent years acetylene has been made from natural gas, which is mostly methane. When methane is heated to a high temperature (1,400–1,600°C) and passed over a catalyst, acetylene is one of the products obtained in fairly high yield.

Pure acetylene (bp −83°C) in liquid form decomposes explosively when compressed to several hundred pounds per square inch. Consequently, when acetylene is used for fuel in oxyacetylene torches, it is dissolved in acetone under pressure in a cylinder packed with an inert porous material.

Almost half of the acetylene produced is used for the synthesis of other organic chemicals. The catalytic addition of water to acetylene produces acetaldehyde, which is required for the manufacture of polymerization accelerators. Addition of hydrogen cyanide to acetylene produces acrylonitrile, which is used for the production of synthetic fibers and rubber. Acetylene adds to itself to give vinylacetylene, which serves as a precursor to chloroprene and thence to neoprene, a solvent-resistant synthetic rubber. $\qquad$ HERMAN E. ZIEGER

All Quiet on the Western Front

All Quiet on the Western Front, first published in Germany under the title *Im Westen nichts Neues* in 1929 and translated into English the same year, was not only the finest novel of Erich Maria REMARQUE but also the single most influential piece of fiction to appear in the period between the two world wars. Based on Remarque's firsthand experience of trench warfare in World War I, it realistically and compassionately chronicles the hardships and embittering experiences endured by a group of young German soldiers, the most sensitive of whom is killed shortly before the armistice. By exposing the horror, cruelty, and uselessness of war, the novel quickly won worldwide acclaim and served as a symbol to the post–World War I LOST GENERATION. Banned by the Nazi regime for its antimilitaristic sentiments, the novel remained a focus for the pacifism that played a powerful political role in the Western democracies until the outbreak of World War II. An effective motion-picture version (directed by Lewis Milestone) in 1930 became a film classic.

All Saints' Day

In the Christian church, All Saints' Day is the feast of all known and unknown SAINTS. It is observed on November 1 in the West. During the Middle Ages, the feast was called All Hallows' Day, giving its name to HALLOWEEN (All Hallows' Eve), the preceding day.

All Souls' Day

In Roman Catholicism, All Souls' Day is the feast that commemorates all the dead; special prayers and masses are offered for souls in PURGATORY. It is celebrated on November 2, the day following ALL SAINTS' DAY. In Buddhism, a similar observance is held as an expression of filial piety for deceased family members.

All the King's Men

All the King's Men (1946; film, 1949), a social novel by Robert Penn WARREN, traces the political career of Willie Stark, a Southern backwoods politician who begins by battling the special interests and ends his life totally corrupted, the victim of an assassin's bullet. In general outline, though not in detail, the 1947 Pulitzer Prize–winning novel parallels the life of the Louisiana politician Huey Long, whose career, said Warren, supplied the "line of thinking and feeling" from which the book evolved. The novel is narrated from the point of view of Jack Burden, a young intellectual who wrestles with the moral implications of Stark's career.

All the President's Men

All the President's Men (1974; film, 1976), written almost in the form of a detective story, is an account by two young journalists, Carl Bernstein and Bob Woodward (see BERNSTEIN, CARL, AND WOODWARD, BOB), of how they uncovered the events behind the WATERGATE break-in of June 17, 1972. It tells how the authors, as city reporters for the WASHINGTON POST, pursued their story doggedly for months and, step by step, linked the Nixon Republican administration with the attempted burglary at the Democratic national headquarters. Their fast-paced narrative describes the techniques of investigative journalism. One result was a sharp increase in enrollments in journalism schools in the 1970s as young persons sought careers as reporters dedicated to exposing corruption.

Allah

The Muslim name for God, Allah, in Arabic script and surrounded by an ornamental design, is used as a decorative emblem of Islam. Belief in Allah is the basis of the Muslim faith, and the naming of Allah is an affirmation of absolute submission to the benevolent and just rule of God.

Allah is the proper name of God in ISLAM. He is one, unique and incomparable, and his unlimited sovereignty implies absolute freedom. But there is also a firm relationship between him, the Lord of Mercy, and all human beings, based on his being the creator and sustainer and on his providing in nature and history abundant signs of his goodness, reflected specifically in his sending of messengers and prophets. The interrelated emphases on Allah's uniqueness and on the significance of his revelatory act are expressed in the Islamic witness: "There is no God but Allah, and MUHAMMAD is his messenger."

WILLEM A. BIJLEFELD

Bibliography: Macdonald, D. B., "Allāh," in *Encyclopaedia of Islam* (1913-38); Gardet, L., "Allāh," in *Encyclopaedia of Islam*, new ed. (1960-   ).

Allahabad   [a-lah-huh-bahd']

Allahabad is a north central city of India, situated at the confluence of the Ganges and the Yamuna, two of the most sa-

cred Hindu rivers. Located in Uttar Pradesh state, it is the seat of the Uttar Pradesh High Court. The annual average temperature is 26° C (79° F), and rainfall averages 1,062 mm (40.3 in) annually. Allahabad, whose population is 490,622 (1971), is a center of light industry and food processing. Allahabad University was established in 1887.

The Mogul emperor Akbar erected a fort here in 1583 and designated it Al-Ilahabad ("city of God"). The ancient name of the city was Prayag. The city was ceded to Britain in 1801 and was the scene of extensive violence during the Indian Mutiny (1857). Before 1947 the city was a center for India's nationalist movement and was the headquarters of the All-India Congress Committee until 1948. On Feb. 12, 1948, the ashes of Mahatma Gandhi were placed in the holy waters at Allahabad. Two important religious fairs—the annual Magh Mela and the Kumbha Mela, occurring every 12th year—are held in Allahabad.

ASHOK K. DUTT

Allegheny College   [al-uh-gay'-nee]

Established in 1815 and affiliated with the United Methodist Church, Allegheny College (enrollment: 1,860; library: 252,000 volumes) is a 4-year coeducational liberal arts institution in Meadville, Pa. It shares a program in engineering with Columbia University and Rensselaer Polytechnic Institute.

Allegheny Mountains

The Allegheny Mountains, extending more than 800 km (500 mi) from central Pennsylvania to central West Virginia and southwestern Virginia, mark the eastern edge of the high Allegheny Plateau, which is the western part of the Appalachian mountain system. The highest peak is Spruce Knob in West Virginia (1,481 m/4,860 ft). The ridges are covered with forests of conifers and hardwoods, including oak, maple, and hickory. Huge deposits of coal are mined in West Virginia and Pennsylvania. The barrier of the Alleghenies delayed westward expansion of the early North American coastal settlements, and the region was not occupied until late in the 18th century.

Allegheny River

The Allegheny River rises in north central Pennsylvania, flows north into New York, and then turns south and southwest through Pennsylvania to Pittsburgh. At Pittsburgh it joins the Monongahela River to form the Ohio River.

The Allegheny is 523 km (325 mi) long, and it drains an area of 29,530 km² (11,400 mi²). It traverses a region once rich in petroleum and natural gas reserves that are now largely depleted. Industrial cities on its banks, in addition to Pittsburgh, are Olean, N.Y., and Warren and Oil City, Pa. Before railroads were built, the river was a busy commercial artery. A system of dams on the river and on its main tributaries—the Kiskiminetas, Clarion, and Conemaugh rivers—is important in flood control.

allegiance

Allegiance is the obligation to support and obey a leader or government in return for protection. In medieval times the vassals owed allegiance to their feudal lord, but now citizens owe allegiance to their government.

Traditionally, a national of one country could not change allegiance without that government's consent, but in 1868 the U.S. Congress declared that any U.S. citizen had the right to change allegiance at will. Britain has allowed free choice of allegiance since 1870. Countries in the Soviet bloc require official approval before a citizen can change allegiance.

allegory

An allegory, in poetry or prose, is a narrative in which the characters, events, and setting represent deeper truths or generalizations than those suggested by the surface story. Allegory can thus be understood on more than one level. The more profound meaning, however—religious, moral, political, or personal—is usually of greater importance than the fiction

The frontispiece of The Pilgrim's Progress, written by John Bunyan in 1678, shows the author dreaming of his story's hero, Christian, as he sets out for the Celestial City (heaven). Bunyan's popular religious allegory uses characters, events, and locations to symbolize the forces of good and evil.

itself. The meaning conveyed may be obvious, subtle, or virtually concealed by the writer.

John Bunyan's *Pilgrim's Progress* (1678) is probably the best example of allegory in all literature. In the surface story a hero named Christian travels toward the Celestial City through a landscape marked by the Slough of Despond, the Valley of the Shadow of Death, and Vanity Fair, and he meets characters such as Faithful and Mr. Worldly Wisdom. The deeper story deals with individual salvation.

Like other symbolic literary forms, such as the BESTIARY, FABLE, and PARABLE, allegory is an extended metaphor. It is distinguished from those simpler types chiefly by its greater length and complexity.

Many classical myths may be considered allegorical, and Plato's myth of the cave in the *Republic* is explicitly so. The form became more common in the Hellenistic period, especially as a means of explaining psychological phenomena. The great age of allegory, however, was the medieval period, when it not only characterized much of the didactic literature of the church but also played a fundamental role in the era's whole intellectual approach. Interpretation of Scripture in terms of its allegorical content flourished, inviting explanation of the literally sensuous Song of Solomon as representative of the love of God for his people. Allegory was also central to the popular form of entertainment known as the morality play, which typically featured personages representing abstract concepts such as Everyman, Good Deeds, and Beauty.

Among the more famous allegories are the 13th-century ROMAN DE LA ROSE, parts of Dante's DIVINE COMEDY (1310–14), Langland's PIERS PLOWMAN (1377), Spenser's FAERIE QUEENE (1589, 1596), Dryden's *Absalom and Achitophel* (1681), Jonathan Swift's GULLIVER'S TRAVELS (1726), Samuel Butler's EREWHON (1872), and George Orwell's ANIMAL FARM (1945).

Bibliography: Clifford, Gay, *The Transformations of Allegory* (1974); Fletcher, Angus, *Allegory: The Theory of a Symbolic Mode* (1970); Honig, Edwin, *Dark Conceit: The Making of Allegory* (1959); McClennen, Joshua, *On the Meaning and Function of Allegory in the English Renaissance* (1947; repr. 1974); Tuve, Rosemond, *Allegorical Imagery: Some Medieval Books and Their Posterity* (1966); Wimsatt, James I., *Allegory and Mirror: Tradition and Structure in Middle English Literature* (1970).

Allen, Ethan

Ethan Allen, American Revolutionary soldier and frontiersman, was born in Litchfield, Conn., on Jan. 10, 1738, and moved in 1769 to Vermont—a territory then claimed by both New Hampshire and New York. He became leader of the Green Mountain Boys, a military force of Vermonters who fought against New York to protect their landholdings. When the American Revolution broke out, Allen's Green Mountain Boys helped to capture (May 10, 1775) Fort TICONDEROGA from the British. On Sept. 25, 1775, during the invasion of Canada, he was taken prisoner. After his release (May 6, 1778) Allen received the brevet rank of colonel in the Continental Army, but he did not serve. Upon returning to Vermont, he was giv-

en command of the militia with the rank of major general.

Vermont, although not recognized as independent by the Continental Congress, had declared itself a separate republic in 1777. Allen, along with his brother Ira (1751–1814), entered into negotiations with the British from 1779 on to obtain a guarantee of Vermont's independence. After the Treaty of Paris (1783), which ended the war, he continued to resist New York's claims. He did not live to see Vermont become a state. He died in Burlington on Feb. 12, 1789.

GEORGE ATHAN BILLIAS

Bibliography: Allen, Ethan, *Reason, the Only Oracle of Man* (1784); Jellison, Charles A., *Ethan Allen: Frontier Rebel* (1969).

Allen, Fred

Fred Allen was the stage name of John F. Sullivan, b. May 31, 1894, d. Mar. 17, 1956, known as the "king of the quick quip." Allen, a native of Cambridge, Mass., was an American comedian famous for his topical wit delivered in a dry, sad, sing-song drawl. He first appeared as an inept juggler and then performed in Broadway musicals and in movies before achieving fame in the 1930s with the radio show "Town Hall Tonight." Allen wrote two autobiographies, *Treadmill to Oblivion* (1954) and *Much Ado about Me* (1956).

FRANK MANCHEL

Allen, Frederick Lewis

Frederick Lewis Allen, b. July 5, 1890, d. Feb. 13, 1954, was a contemporary historian and magazine editor. His best-sellers *Only Yesterday* (1931) and *Since Yesterday* (1940) were informal histories of the 1920s and '30s. As associate editor (1931–41) and editor (1941–53) of *Harper's Magazine,* he wrote and edited articles that helped Americans understand contemporary social, political, and economic problems. Allen also wrote *The Lords of Creation* (1935), an economic history of the United States in the 20th century, and a 1949 biography of J. Pierpont Morgan. He collaborated with his wife on several American history picture-and-text volumes.

ERNEST C. HYNDS

Bibliography: Payne, Darwin, *The Man of Only Yesterday: Frederick Lewis Allen* (1975).

Allen, Gracie: see BURNS AND ALLEN.

Allen, Hervey

William Hervey Allen, b. Dec. 8, 1889, d. Dec. 28, 1949, was an American novelist, critic, and poet. He is best known as the author of *Anthony Adverse* (1933), a popular novel set in the Napoleonic era. His critical biography of Edgar Allan Poe, *Israfel* (1926), is still admired. He died in the midst of completing a 5-volume historical saga of western Pennsylvania, *The Disinherited.*

Allen, James Edward, Jr.

As New York State (1955–69) and then U.S. (1969–70) commissioner of education, James E. Allen, b. Apr. 25, 1911, d. Oct. 16, 1971, was a crusader for liberal, city-oriented reforms. He reversed the suspension of six New York City teachers who had refused to inform on associates with past Communist affiliations, solved a dispute about the posting of the Ten Commandments in New Hyde Park schools by ordering their removal, and ordered several school boards to devise racial-balance plans to end de facto segregation. His plan to decentralize New York City schools gave power to 15 locally elected boards, controlled in some cases by minority groups. President Nixon appointed Allen U.S. commissioner of education, but Allen resigned in June 1970 over the administration's policies on school desegregation and the Vietnam War.

Allen, Richard

Richard Allen was the founder and first bishop of the African Methodist Episcopal Church. He was born to slave parents in Philadelphia, Pa., on Feb. 14, 1760. The first General Conference of METHODISM, held in 1784, considered him a promising candidate for the ministry. Asked to preach occasionally at St. George's Methodist Church in Philadelphia, he began prayer meetings among his people. His work attracted large numbers of black people to St. George's, and some white members began to object to their presence. One Sunday in 1787, some of the black worshipers were pulled from their knees during prayer and asked to leave. They withdrew peacefully and under Allen's leadership organized the Free African Society. In 1793 this society became Bethel Church, an independent Methodist church. In 1799, Allen was ordained a deacon, the first black man regularly ordained to the ministry of the Methodist Church. In 1816 representatives of a number of black Methodist churches met in Philadelphia and organized the African Methodist Episcopal Church as the first national black denomination and chose Allen as their bishop. During his ministry he involved the church in various social issues, including the antislavery movement. He died in Philadelphia on Mar. 26, 1831.   JOHN F. PIPER, JR.

Bibliography: Allen, Richard, *The Life Experience and Gospel Labors of the Rt. Rev. Richard Allen* (1793; repr. 1960); George, Carol V. R., *Segregated Sabbaths* (1973).

Allen, Steve

Stephen Valentine Patrick Allen, b. New York City, Dec. 26, 1921, is an American humorist who specializes in low-key, informal comedy. He began as a disc jockey and songwriter and gained national fame as the creator and first host of NBC's "Tonight Show" (1954–56). His other television shows include the award-winning "Meeting of the Minds" (1977–78). Allen starred in the screen biography *The Benny Goodman Story* (1955) and has written several thousand songs and film scores and more than 25 books.   FRANK MANCHEL

Allen, Viola

The American actress Viola Emily Allen, b. Huntsville, Ala., Oct. 27, 1869, d. May 9, 1948, enjoyed a distinguished stage career (1882–1916), becoming famous for her roles in Shakespearean comedies (Viola in *Twelfth Night,* for example) and leading parts in such popular melodramas as *Little Lord Fauntleroy* and *Shenandoah*. Allen formed a Shakespeare company in 1903 and acted in one movie, *The White Sister* (1915).

Allen, Woody

Woody Allen is the stage name of Allen Stewart Konigsberg, b. Brooklyn, N.Y., Dec. 1, 1935. He is considered America's best living film comedian and one of its finest film directors. Allen's highly personal work focuses on contemporary fears and insecurities. On the screen he projects the image of a bespectacled neurotic who rarely measures up to society's standards of proper masculine behavior. While a teenager, Allen worked as a gag writer for a public relations agency. He dropped out of college in 1953 and became a principal writer for such celebrities as Sid Caesar and Garry Moore. His switch to stand-up comedy in the early 1960s led to celebrity status from television appearances and three popular record releases. He made his screen debut as an actor-screenwriter in *What's New, Pussycat?* (1965). Allen's first film project as director-writer-star was *Take the Money and Run* (1969). His other movies include *Bananas* (1971), *Sleeper* (1973), *Love and Death* (1975), *Annie Hall* (1977), which received four Academy Awards, *Interiors* (1978), *Manhattan* (1979), *Stardust Memories* (1980), *A Midsummer Night's Sex Comedy* (1982), and the highly acclaimed *Zelig* (1983). Allen's comic and satirical writings have been collected in three anthologies, and he has also written several Broadway plays, including *Play It Again, Sam* (1969; film, 1972).

Bibliography: Jacobs, Diane, *But We Need the Eggs: The Magic of Woody Allen* (1982).

Allenby, Edmund Henry Hynman, 1st Viscount Allenby of Megiddo

Edmund Henry Hynman Allenby, b. Apr. 23, 1861, d. May 14, 1936, was a British general who commanded the British forces in the Middle East during World War I. A cavalry officer, he served (1899–1902) in the South African War. At the outbreak of World War I he went to France as commander of British cavalry and subsequently led (1915–17) the Third Army. Sent (1917) to Egypt, he began a systematic campaign to expel the Turks from Palestine, capturing Jerusalem in December 1917. His victory at Megiddo (Sept. 18–21, 1918) began the offensive that pushed the Turks back through Syria. Created (1919) a viscount, Allenby was high commissioner for Egypt from 1919 to 1925.

Bibliography: Gardner, Brian, *Allenby of Arabia* (1965); Wavell, Archibald P., *Allenby: A Study in Greatness*, 2 vols. (1941–43), and *Allenby, Soldier and Statesman* (1948).

Allende, Salvador   [ahl-yen'-day]

Salvador Allende Gossens, president of Chile from 1970 to 1973, was the second Marxian socialist (after Cheddi JAGAN in British Guiana) elected to lead a country of the Western Hemisphere. Born July 26, 1908, into an upper-middle-class family, he became involved in radical politics while attending medical school at the University of Chile. Although expelled

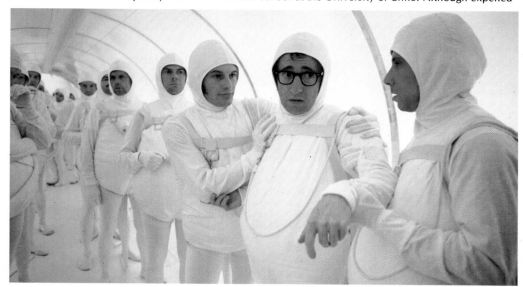

Woody Allen cast himself as a cowardly sperm cell in his cinematic spoof (1972) of the book Everything You Always Wanted to Know about Sex but Were Afraid to Ask. *During his career Allen's sense of humor and of humanity increasingly have become manifested in seriocomic movies that—despite their New York City orientation—zero in effectively on widespread foibles in contemporary American life.*

Salvador Allende (left), the Marxist president of Chile, appears at the entrance of Moneda Palace on Sept. 11, 1973, during the coup that overthrew his government. He either was killed or committed suicide a few hours after the photograph was taken.

from the university and briefly jailed for his revolutionary activities, he completed his medical degree in 1932. In 1933 he helped organize Chile's Socialist party.

After holding several government offices and after three unsuccessful campaigns for the presidency (1952, 1958, 1964), Allende was elected president in 1970. His administration nationalized many industries (including the copper mines, in which U.S. business had a major investment) and accelerated land reform. These measures antagonized right-wing elements, and severe economic problems, aggravated by strikes, resulted in more widespread disaffection, which was encouraged by the U.S. Central Intelligence Agency. Allende died on Sept. 11, 1973, during a military coup that overthrew his government. His successors declared that he had committed suicide; his supporters claimed that he was murdered.

Bibliography: Drake, Paul W., *Socialism and Populism in Chile* (1978); Protopapas, George, *Chile: Allende and After* (1975); Sobel, Lester A., ed., *Chile and Allende* (1975).

Allentown

Located on the Lehigh River in the Pennsylvania Dutch country in eastern Pennsylvania, Allentown is a busy industrial city with a great variety of manufactures. It has a population of 103,758 (1980) and is the seat of Lehigh County. It serves as the marketing, processing, and shipping center for the agricultural products of the fertile Lehigh Valley. Allentown is also an educational center, with Muhlenberg College, Lehigh Community College, and several other colleges located there.

The area was settled in the 1600s by Germans seeking religious freedom. The city itself was founded in 1762 by Pennsylvania Chief Justice William Allen. Originally called Northhamptontown, it was later renamed (1838) in honor of its founder. Allentown's reconstructed Zion Reformed Church contains a replica of the Liberty Bell, which was concealed there in 1777–78 during the British occupation of Philadelphia.

allergy

Allergy is an abnormal reaction of the body to substances normally harmless, such as pollen, dust, certain foods, drugs, and insect stings. The term *allergy* is of Greek origin and means "abnormal response." An estimated 35 million people in the United States suffer from various allergies, some of which are mistaken for the common cold.

The symptoms of allergy vary with the causative agent, which is called an allergen (or ANTIGEN), and with the part of the body affected. The symptoms, or allergic reactions, may include sneezing, watery eyes, and nasal congestion, as in hay fever and allergic rhinitis; a rash, stomach upset, and itchy swellings on the skin (HIVES), as in some food or drug allergies; spasms within the lungs that interfere with breathing, as in ASTHMA; and, in rare cases, anaphylactic SHOCK, which may lead to asphyxiation and death. Anaphylactic shock occasionally follows injections of penicillin or other drugs and may sometimes follow the sting of a bee or wasp.

Common allergens, in addition to those mentioned above, include animal fur, feathers, cosmetics, textile dyes, smoke, bacteria, poison ivy and other plants, molds, chemical pollutants in the atmosphere, animal excretions, and blood serum received by transfusion, which may cause SERUM SICKNESS. Even heat, cold, and light may cause allergy in susceptible people. Allergens may act following inhalation, injection, ingestion, or contact with the skin.

THE ALLERGIC REACTION

An allergic reaction occurs when the immune system, which is the body's normal defense against dangerous foreign substances, "mistakes" a normally harmless substance for an invader, such as a virus. No one knows why this abnormal reaction occurs in some people and not others. People who have this type of unusual immune system are said to be hypersensitive, and medical scientists often use the term *hypersensitivity* instead of *allergy*.

The body's immune system reacts to an allergen in many different ways to cause the discomforting symptoms of an allergy. In many allergies, the process begins when the allergen stimulates the immune system to manufacture certain ANTIBODY molecules called immunoglobulin E (IgE). The antibody molecules then combine with the allergen molecules and bind to certain cells called mast cells and basophils, causing the release of histamine (see ANTIHISTAMINE) and other active compounds. The histamine in turn affects the blood vessels and mucous membranes, leading to swelling, congestion, and leakage. Typically, these physiological changes lead to a runny nose if the allergen is airborne and inhaled. Other cells and other constituents of the blood serum can cause other types of allergies, such as POISON IVY dermatitis and serum sickness.

TYPES OF ALLERGY

Allergies characteristically are not symptomatic with the first exposure to the allergen, and the symptoms occur only upon reexposure to the same agent. A person is said to have been sensitized by the first contact. That is, the immune system somehow "learns" to respond to the agent with an allergic reaction, but it reacts only at contacts that occur later. Sensitization of this type occurs in a variety of infectious diseases, such as BRUCELLOSIS, GLANDERS, SYPHILIS, and coccidioidomycosis, in which allergy develops to the infecting bacteria, fungi, or viruses.

In many persons, heredity is responsible for the tendency to be allergic to a variety of substances. Those persons with such inherited tendencies are called atopic. The common atopies include hay fever; asthma; infantile ECZEMA, which is an itchy skin lesion; contact DERMATITIS, which is a skin inflammation caused by poison ivy or a variety of chemicals that may contact the skin; and perhaps some food or drug allergies. Numerous studies have shown that persons who have one disease in this group are more likely to have other diseases of the group than is the general population. Many people so afflicted have a family history of allergic diseases, usually of the same group.

DIAGNOSIS

Allergic disease is diagnosed from the patient's medical history; symptoms; and so-called skin, or patch, tests, which help to identify the allergen. Small doses of many of the most common allergens are injected just below the skin in separate patches, and substances to which the patient is allergic usually cause redness and swelling at the injection site. Skin tests are often "false positive," however; they may indicate a sensitivity when in fact none exists.

TREATMENT

If the allergens can be identified, treatment of allergy may be merely the avoidance of the offending agents. If they cannot be avoided, as with house dust, pollen, insect stings, and perhaps animal fur, treatment may be of so-called hyposensitization, or desensitization. In desensitization, small amounts of the substance that causes the allergy are injected under the skin during repeated visits to a physician. After many such injections, the body may "learn" not to react to the substance. It is impossible to predict beforehand whether desensitization in a given person will achieve its desired purpose.

The discomforting symptoms of allergy are sometimes relieved by three types of medication: antihistamines, which block release of the histamines that cause swelling and congestion of mucous membranes; anti-inflammatory agents, such as corticosteroids; and decongestants, such as ephedrine, phenylpropanolamine hydrochloride, and phenylephrine hydrochloride.   DAVID S. GORDON, M.D.

Bibliography: Frazier, Claude A., *Coping with Food Allergy* (1974); Gerrard, John, *Understanding Allergies* (1973); Lichtenstein, L. M., and Fauci, A. S., *Current Therapy in Allergy and Immunology* (1983); Middleton, Elliott, Jr., et al., eds., *Allergy: Principles and Practice*, 2 vols. (1983).

See also: IMMUNITY.

Alleyn, Edward   [al'-in]

Edward Alleyn, b. Sept. 1, 1566, d. Nov. 25, 1626, was one of the foremost English actors of his day, rivaling Richard BURBAGE. Chief interpreter of the plays of Christopher MARLOWE, Alleyn probably played the leads in DOCTOR FAUSTUS, TAMBURLAINE THE GREAT, and *The Jew of Malta*. He retired from the stage a wealthy man in 1604 and founded Dulwich College in 1617.   ANDREW KELLY

Bibliography: Hosking, G. L., *Life and Times of Edward Alleyn* (1970).

alliance

In international relations, an alliance is an agreement between two or more states to cooperate for certain political objectives, frequently for mutual defense against a common enemy. Present-day examples are the NORTH ATLANTIC TREATY ORGANIZATION (NATO), comprising the United States, Canada, and 13 European countries, which is designed to defend Europe against attack from the east; and the WARSAW TREATY ORGANIZATION, comprising the USSR and its East European allies, which counterbalances NATO. The United States has also formed alliances with Japan and with countries in Southeast Asia.

Historic alliances have included the QUADRUPLE ALLIANCE of 1814 between Britain, Austria, Russia, and Prussia, which crushed Napoleon; the TRIPLE ALLIANCE between Germany, Austria-Hungary, and Italy before World War I; the TRIPLE ENTENTE between France, Britain, and Russia in the same period; and the alliance between the United States, Britain, and the USSR in World War II.

The first U.S. alliance was that negotiated by Benjamin Franklin with France in 1778, by which the French aided the United States during the Revolutionary War. But Presidents Washington and Jefferson both warned against "permanent" or "entangling" alliances, and the country refrained from entering further alliances until World War II.

Alliance for Progress

The Alliance for Progress was a $100 billion program for the economic and social development of Latin America in the 1960s. First proposed by President John F. KENNEDY, the alliance was formally inaugurated on Aug. 17, 1961, at Punta del Este, Uruguay, by a treaty between the United States and 19 Latin American countries, excluding Cuba. The original 10-year treaty was extended indefinitely in 1965, but operations ceased in 1974, when financial support was discontinued. Although some accomplishments were achieved in health, education, housing, and economic growth, the program generally failed to meet its expectations.   RITA J. IMMERMAN

Bibliography: Levinson, Jerome, and de Onís, Juan, *The Alliance That Lost Its Way: A Critical Report on the Alliance for Progress* (1970).

Allied Powers: see WORLD WAR I; WORLD WAR II.

alligator

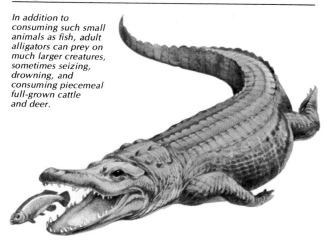

In addition to consuming such small animals as fish, adult alligators can prey on much larger creatures, sometimes seizing, drowning, and consuming piecemeal full-grown cattle and deer.

An alligator is either of two large temperate-zone amphibious reptiles, the Chinese alligator (*Alligator sinensis*) or the American alligator (*A. mississippiensis*). Alligators are related to CROCODILES but have a broad snout and lack the side notch that exposes the long fourth tooth of the lower jaw in crocodiles. In alligators the teeth of the upper jaw overlap those of the lower and hide them from view.

The smaller and less-known species, the Chinese alligator, is now found only in the lower Yangtze River valley of eastern China. It seldom attains a length of more than 1.5 m (5 ft). The American alligator is much larger; an individual specimen 5.8 m (19 ft 2 in) long is on record. Most such alligators have been killed by hunters, however, and a 3.6-m (12-ft) animal is now considered large. American alligators are found in lakes, swamps, and slow-moving streams of the eastern U.S. coastal plain from North Carolina to Texas. For both species of alligators, individuals have been known to live for 50 years.

Alligators eat a wide variety of animals. Small ones feed on insects, crayfish, minnows, and frogs. Adults eat larger fish, water birds, turtles, and various small mammals and occasionally consume larger mammals and such domestic animals as dogs and hogs. They rarely attack humans.

The American alligator's life history is better known than that of any other crocodilian. After mating in the spring, the female prepares, on the bank of a pond, a nest of water plants and mud that may be 1.8 m (6 ft) in diameter and 0.9 m (3 ft) high. The female then digs a hole in the top of the nest, lays 30 to 80 eggs in it, and covers them with wet vegetation and mud. The eggs are incubated by the heat of the Sun and hatch in about 60 days. The young call when hatched, and the mother alligator, who has been nearby during the incubation period, then carries them in her mouth or leads them to the pond, where they remain with her during their first year.

The bellow of male alligators is well known, but only recently has it been recognized that females also call. Alligators call not only during the breeding season but also at other times of year, to announce their presence and perhaps to keep other alligators out of their normal home range. Young alligators call as well, and a distress call by a youngster often brings an immediate response from a nearby adult.

Because the belly skin of alligators lacks the bony plates typical of crocodile and CAIMAN skin, it can be made into an excellent leather for shoes, handbags, and other items. The alligator has therefore been a prime target for hide hunters, who greatly reduced alligator populations in the past. In the 1950s it was recognized that the species was likely to become extinct if the hunting continued. The American alligator was placed under federal protection in 1969, and it now appears to be out of danger.

Alligators belong to the family Crocodylidae, order Crocodylia.   H. G. DOWLING

Bibliography: Coulson, Roland A., and Hernandez, Thomas, *Biochemistry of the Alligator: A Study of Metabolism in Slow Motion* (1964); Hartley, William and Ellen, *The Alligator: King of the Wilderness* (1977); Neill, W. T., *The Last of the Ruling Reptiles: Alligators, Crocodiles, and Their Kin* (1971); Perrero, Laurie, *Alligators and Crocodiles of the World: The Disappearing Dragons* (1975).

Allingham, Margery

Margery Allingham, b. May 20, 1904, d. June 30, 1966, an English writer, produced classics in two genres of the detective novel—the thriller and the problem story. Both feature her series hero, Albert Campion, whose large glasses and indifferent manner mask a first-rate mind and enough physical prowess to deal with the demands of both types of plot. The earlier Campion stories, notably *Mystery Mile* (1929), abounded in hair-raising adventures and criminal conspiracies. In the later novels, beginning with *Death of a Ghost* (1934), the problem to be solved turned on the interaction of the characters, usually sophisticated Londoners. *The Tiger in the Smoke* (1952), a gripping story of a police manhunt, was filmed in 1956.

Allis, Edward Phelps

Edward Phelps Allis, b. May 12, 1824, d. Apr. 1, 1889, founded one of the largest industrial machine plants in the Midwest. He began in the tannery business but in 1854 disposed of his holdings and turned to banking and real estate. In 1861 he bought a small foundry, and in 1869 he gained the job of installing the Milwaukee water system. From then on, the business expanded rapidly. The Allis Company produced machinery for the roller process used in flour mills, made sawmill and mining equipment, and manufactured heavy pumps and Corliss engines.

alliteration: see FIGURES OF SPEECH.

Allosaurus   [al'-oh-sohr-uhs]

The Allosaurus was a typical, meat-eating dinosaur of the Late Jurassic period, about 150 million years ago. It used the huge claws on its forelimbs and powerful jaws to attack its prey.

Allosaurus (Greek: *allos* ["other"]; *saurus*, ["lizard"]), a large, carnivorous DINOSAUR of Late JURASSIC to Early CRETACEOUS PERIOD, ranged in length from 5 to 12 m (16 to 40 ft) and probably weighed 4 metric tons (about 8,800 lb). Like all other theropods, *Allosaurus* walked on only two legs, using its long, heavy tail for balance. The short forelimbs bore three sharp, curved claws adapted for grasping prey. The hindlimbs were powerful, with birdlike feet and less-curved claws. The head was large, nearly 1 m (3 ft) long, with long jaws armed with serrated, bladelike teeth suited to eating flesh.

Allosaurus apparently was the most common of the later Jurassic theropods in North America (others included ORNITHOLESTES, *Ceratosaurus*, and *Coelurus*) and probably was the chief predator of such contemporaneous herbivores as BRONTOSAURUS, CAMPTOSAURUS, DIPLODOCUS, and STEGOSAURUS.

JOHN H. OSTROM

Bibliography: Colbert, E. H., *Dinosaurs, Their Discovery and Their World* (1961); Swinton, W. E., *Dinosaurs*, 5th ed. (1975).

See also: FOSSIL RECORD; MESOZOIC ERA.

allotrope   [al'-oh-trohp]

Allotropes are the individual forms of an element that occur when more than one type of bonding between atoms of the element is possible. Elements that have allotropes include oxygen, carbon, sulfur, phosphorus, iron, and tin, among others. Usually one allotrope is most abundant and indefinitely stable at ordinary temperature and pressure, and the others can be formed only in unusual conditions. No general explanation can be given for the existence of more than one form; each case must be considered individually. Oxygen can exist in two allotropic forms: O_2, a familiar gas constituent of air, and O_3, ozone, which is confined to the upper atmosphere. The allotropes of carbon, which are diamond and graphite, have strikingly different crystal structures and physical properties.   GEORGE GORIN

Allouez, Claude Jean   [ahl-way']

Claude Jean Allouez, b. June 6, 1622, d. Aug. 27, 1689, a French Jesuit missionary in North America, baptized more than 10,000 Indians in the Great Lakes region. Arriving in Canada in 1658, he was appointed vicar general of the Northwest in 1663. He traveled in the territory west and south of the Great Lakes, working among the Potawatomi, the Miami, the Illinois, and other tribes. His reports, published in *The Jesuit Relations* (the Jesuits' record of their activities in North America, 1632–1673), attracted attention to the Great Lakes area.

alloy

An alloy is a mixture or solution of metals that may also include other chemical elements. Well-known alloys are BRASS, an alloy of copper and zinc; BRONZE, an alloy of copper and tin; and steel, an alloy of iron and carbon (see IRON AND STEEL INDUSTRY). Alloys consisting of metals alloyed with semimetals, such as arsenic or antimony, or with nonmetals, such as carbon or silicon, are widely used. Alloys are divided into two basic groups: ferrous alloys, containing iron as the elemental metal, and nonferrous alloys, containing a metal other than iron, such as copper, aluminum, or titanium.

STRUCTURE OF ALLOYS

Most components of alloys are partially miscible (capable of being mixed) or even completely miscible in the liquid state. Different types of alloys can be distinguished, depending on the degree of homogenization in the solid state.

Solid Solutions. These are alloys in which the atoms of the components are randomly mixed throughout the crystals. Since the different kinds of atoms are of different sizes, stresses result in the crystal lattice of the alloy that hinder movement of dislocations, resulting in a harder material.

Intermetallic Compounds. In these alloys the atoms of the different compounds alternate regularly in the crystal lattice. Intermetallic alloys generally have extreme thermal stability, brittleness, and hardness.

Multiphase Alloys. These are alloys in which the solid consists of a disordered mixture (mechanical mixture or mixed phase) of two or more kinds of crystals with different composition. In the simplest case the alloy is made up of two components that mix completely in the molten state. The final structure and properties of the alloy depend markedly on the cooling rate of the molten mass and other circumstances during cooling. If the cooling is very gradual, the heavier phase migrates to the bottom, and the lighter phase moves to the top. Rapid cooling (quenching) may produce a solid solution with no phase separation at all. This is not a stable situation, and eventually separation takes place. If the cooling is somewhere between these two extremes, then partial separation occurs. The final structure of the alloy can be pictured as a granular structure of the most abundant component, with the other component concentrated around the grain boundaries. Structures in which grains of the least abundant component lie embedded in a more or less homogeneous material are often encountered as well. The mechanical properties of the various structures may differ greatly so that, by a judicious selection of cooling techniques, sometimes also followed by other heat treatments, a material with the desired properties can be obtained.

PROPERTIES OF ALLOYS

By alloying metals, a wide range of properties can be achieved. Mechanical strength, resistance to heat and corrosion, and electrical and magnetic characteristics are some of the properties that can be controlled. An example of the change in mechanical properties achieved by alloying materials is the AMALGAM used for dental work. By dissolving metals, such as silver and tin, in liquid mercury, a solid compound is obtained. The first uses of alloys were to improve the mechanical strength of metals. Bronze and brass are well-known examples. The tensile strength of iron can be increased from 275×10^6 to $1,000 \times 10^6$ N/m² (40,000 to 150,000 lb/in²) by adding only a small amount of carbon. Iron alloyed with 0.03 to 1.7 percent carbon forms the important group of steels. STAINLESS STEEL is an alloy of steel with chromium and nickel, with improved resistance to corrosion.

For aircraft and aerospace applications, titanium alloys have been developed with tensile strengths up to $1,400 \times 10^6$ N/m² (200,000 lb/in²), and with a weight of only 60 percent that of steel. Because of their high corrosion resistance and the absence of reactions with living tissues, titanium alloys are used in prosthetic devices and pacemakers. The development of jet engines, with their high internal working temperatures, was made possible by the availability of superalloys. These alloys, based on nickel and cobalt, are used for the manufacture of turbine blades in jet engines, and offer great strength and resistance to corrosion at temperatures as high as 1,100° C (2,000° F).

Alloys with low melting temperatures are used as fusible elements in automatic sprinkler systems. These alloys consist of lead, cadmium, bismuth, and other low-melting-temperature metals, forming a eutectic alloy. Eutectic alloys are mixtures with melting points lower than any of their components; melting points as low as 50° C (120° F) can be achieved. Alloys of columbium and zirconium are used as superconducting materials. Such alloys yield a ductile material used as wire for superconducting magnets.   MERLE C. NUTT

See also: METALLURGY.

Allport, Gordon W.

Gordon Willard Allport, b. Nov. 11, 1897, d. Oct. 9, 1967, was an American psychologist whose theory of PERSONALITY emphasized the uniqueness of the individual. Allport taught at Harvard (1924–26, 1930–67) and also edited the *Journal of Abnormal and Social Psychology* from 1937 to 1949. He maintained that motives were "functionally autonomous" and could not be said to be merely the search for pleasure and the avoidance of pain or derived from an individual's past history. Among his works are *Personality: A Psychological Interpretation* (1937) and *The Nature of Prejudice* (1954).

The allspice tree, P. officinalis, *a tropical tree that has large, simple leaves and tiny flowers, yields fruit that turns a dark purple when it is dried. The unripe berry, used as a seasoning, is named for its flavor, which suggests a combination of nutmeg, cinnamon, and cloves.*

allspice

Allspice is the dried, nearly ripe, berry of the allspice tree, *Pimenta officinalis*, of the MYRTLE family. The name is derived from its flavor, which suggests a mixture of cloves, cinnamon, and nutmeg. Allspice is native to the West Indies and Central America but today is primarily cultivated in Jamaica. It is used whole or ground in pickling spices, mincemeat, roast meats, and baked goods. Its ESSENTIAL OIL is used in meat sauces, catsup, spice blends for pickles, and sausages, as well as for reproducing certain fruit flavors.   ARTHUR O. TUCKER

Allston, Washington

Washington Allston, b. Nov. 5, 1779, d. July 9, 1843, was a pioneer in American landscape painting and the first important American romantic painter. After graduating from Harvard in 1800, Allston studied (1801–03) with Benjamin WEST at the Royal Academy in London, learning the techniques of English painting. He also studied at the LOUVRE and then in Italy, where he became interested in the color techniques of the 16th-century Venetian school and in the serene classicism of

In Moonlit Landscape *(1819) Washington Allston used luminous atmospheric effects to create a feeling of reverie. Allston's romantic paintings greatly influenced the 19th-century American landscape painters, notably Thomas Cole and Asher Durand of the Hudson River school. (Museum of Fine Arts, Boston.)*

Nicolas POUSSIN. While in Italy (1804-08), Allston became a close friend of Samuel Taylor COLERIDGE, whose ideas strongly influenced him.

An important early work is *Rising of a Thunderstorm at Sea* (1804; Museum of Fine Arts, Boston), a dramatic expression of the power of nature. Allston was a subjective artist who used art as a personal statement of the vision in his own mind, as he did in the introspective *Moonlit Landscape* (1819; Museum of Fine Arts, Boston) and the huge *Belshazzar's Feast* (begun 1817, incomplete at the time of his death; Detroit Institute of Arts). Allston's use of color and light to create luminous, atmospheric effects had a great influence on American landscape painting, especially on the HUDSON RIVER SCHOOL.

Bibliography: Flagg, J. B., *The Life and Letters of Washington Allston* (1892; repr. 1969); Richardson, E. P., *Washington Allston: A Study of the Romantic Artist in America* (1948; repr. 1967).

See also: AMERICAN ART AND ARCHITECTURE; NEOCLASSICISM (art); ROMANTICISM (art).

allusion: see NARRATIVE AND DRAMATIC DEVICES.

alluvial fans

An alluvial fan is a flat cone of soil and rock debris deposited by a stream at the mouth of a confining channel as the water spreads out and loses its carrying ability. Although they form under a wide range of climatic conditions, fans are most common in closed desert basins bounded by mountain ranges.

A stream confined to a channel (a canyon, for example) flows rapidly because it is fairly deep and narrow; the cross-sectional perimeter that it drags against is thus minimized. As it leaves its mountain channel, the stream tends to spread out. Its depth decreases and width increases, with a resultant increase in the cross-sectional perimeter along which drag can occur. With increased drag, water flow decelerates, and the stream's ability to carry debris is reduced. The stream adjusts to progressively diminishing capacity and competence by depositing debris along its length.

The caliber of the debris becomes smaller and smaller as the stream breaks up into distributary channels and its flow

Alluvial fans are common landforms that are produced when water-transported debris is swept out of canyons and deposited in valleys as low cones, resembling open Japanese fans. Water flowing down a mountain slope picks up heavy loads of sand and gravel, which are deposited when the stream reaches flatter ground.

velocity slackens. Boulders are dumped at fan heads, but silt and clay may be carried beyond the fan margins. Deposition along any path of a fan decreases the slope along that path. When this happens, adjacent steeper paths begin to draw stream discharge. In this manner, debris is spread evenly and radially away from the fan apex, a process that may take thousands of years to complete.

The surface of a fan is commonly incised by entrenched distributary channels, particularly at the fan head. The shape of a fan depends on the materials and processes that formed it. MUDFLOWS create the steepest fans; boulder-sized debris forms steeper fans than finer debris; and streams with high rates of discharge form flatter fans than streams with low rates. In long profile, the surfaces of most fans slope less than 5° and are straight to slightly concave upward. A series of coalesced fans is referred to as a bajada (pronounced, and sometimes spelled, "bahada").   ROGER S. U. SMITH

Bibliography: Bull, W. B., *Geomorphology of Segmented Alluvial Fans in Western Fresno County, California* (1964).

See also: DESERT; EROSION AND SEDIMENTATION; RIVER AND STREAM.

Allyson, June

June Allyson, b. New York City, Oct. 17, 1923, is an American film actress whose numerous screen appearances projected the wholesome image of the girl next door. She began her career as a dancer on Broadway and became an MGM stock player in such musicals as *Best Foot Forward* (1943) and *Two Girls and a Sailor* (1944). Her dramatic roles include *Little Women* (1949) and *The Glenn Miller Story* (1954).

LESLIE HALLIWELL

Alma-Ata [ahl-mah-ah-tah']

Alma-Ata is the capital of the KAZAKH SSR of the Soviet Union and the administrative center of Alma-Ata oblast, in southeast Kazakhstan. The city has a population of 871,000 (1977 est.). Built along a rectilinear street pattern, it is at the foot of the Trans-Ili Mountains, a range of the TIEN SHAN system. Situated in an area of apple orchards, the city takes its name from the Kazakh *Almaty*, meaning "apple place."

Alma-Ata has a population that is 70% Russian and only 12% Kazakh. It is a diversified manufacturing center (apparel, food products, machinery) and is the site of a university. Founded by the Russians in 1854 as a strongpoint in their advance into Central Asia, it was known as Verny (meaning "loyal") until the present Kazakh name was adopted in 1921.

THEODORE SHABAD

Alma-Tadema, Sir Lawrence [al-muh-tad'-uh-mah]

Sir Lawrence Alma-Tadema, b. Dronrijp, Netherlands, Jan. 8, 1836, d. June 25, 1912, achieved enormous success in his lifetime as a historical painter, specializing in elegant scenes of everyday life in ancient Greece and Rome, as he imagined it. Carefully correct in their archaeological detail, Alma-Tadema's anecdotal canvases exhibit faultless, almost photographic technique and finish. This precision, and his sentimental titles, worked against Alma-Tadema's reputation in the recent past, but the present-day reassessment of 19th-century academicism has rescued his works from oblivion. Such paintings as *A Reading from Homer* (c.1880–1885; Philadelphia Museum of Art) and *Spring* (1894; Getty Museum, Malibu) are now regarded as exemplars of their period and tradition. An esteemed member of the Royal Academy, Alma-Tadema spent most of his career in London and was knighted in 1899.

Bibliography: Swanson, Vern G., *Alma-Tadema* (1977).

See also: ACADEMIES OF ART; ENGLISH ART AND ARCHITECTURE; SALON.

Almagest [al'-muh-jest]

The *Almagest* ("The Greatest Compilation"), the earliest and most important work of the Greek astronomer PTOLEMY

(AD 100–170), was the standard work on astronomy until the time of Copernicus. A compilation of the astronomical knowledge of the past, as well as of Ptolemy's own research, the work is composed of 13 books, or chapters. In each, Ptolemy explains a specific aspect of his GEOCENTRIC WORLD SYSTEM, which places the Earth in the center of the universe. The first two books present the general cosmology, based on ARISTOTLE, of the Sun, Moon, and planets rotating around the Earth and describe the trigonometry of the celestial sphere. Book 3 presents the theory of the motion of the Sun, derived from HIPPARCHUS; books 4 and 5 detail a new and substantially improved lunar theory; book 6 deals with eclipses; and books 7 and 8 catalog the stars. The final books, 9 to 13, contain Ptolemy's most original contribution, a theory of planetary motion.

Ptolemy's explanatory mechanism for all of these models is a system of circles known as epicycles, which were meant to predict the positions of the Sun, Moon, and planets at any given time. In the chapters on planetary motion, Ptolemy introduced the concept of uniform planetary motion around a point eccentric to the Earth, known as the equant point. This device was in part responsible for Copernicus's rejection in the 16th century of the geocentric world system and his proposal of a HELIOCENTRIC WORLD SYSTEM.   STEVEN J. DICK

Bibliography: Taliaferro, R. Catesby, trans., *Almagest* (1952), vol. 16 in *Great Books of the Western World*.

See also: ASTRONOMY, HISTORY OF.

Almagro, Diego de   [ahl-mah'-groh]

Diego de Almagro, b. 1475, was a leader, with Francisco PIZARRO, in the Spanish conquest of Peru. He went to Panama in 1514 and joined Pizarro in the abortive 1524–25 expedition along the west coast of South America. Almagro was also Pizarro's partner in the second expedition of 1526–28 and in the conquest of Peru (1533). Their friendship cooled when Pizarro was awarded a larger fief and Pizarro disputed Almagro's claim to Cuzco.

In 1534 the king of Spain named Almagro leader of the expedition into what is now northern Argentina and Chile. He went as far as the valley of Copiapo (in present-day Chile) and fought intense battles with the Araucanians but found little mineral wealth. In 1537 he returned to Peru, where he put down an Indian insurrection and fought against Pizarro's brothers, who had taken control of Cuzco. He defeated the brothers but was defeated in turn at Las Salinas. He was executed on July 8, 1538, in Cuzco. His son continued the war with the Pizarros until 1542.

Bibliography: Kirkpatrick, Frederick A., *The Spanish Conquistadores*, 2d ed. (1946); Means, Philip A., *Fall of the Inca Empire and Spanish Rule in Peru: 1530–1780* (1932; repr. 1964); Prescott, William H., *History of the Conquest of Peru* (1847; repr. 1931).

almanac

An almanac is a book or table comprising a calendar of the year. Today, almanacs also catalog miscellaneous events that occurred during the previous year and publish selected statistical data. Besides showing the days, weeks, and months, early almanacs registered feast days and saints' days, recorded astronomical phenomena, and sometimes contained meteorologic and agricultural forecasts and miscellaneous advice.

Although almanacs date from ancient times, the term may well be derived from the Spanish-Arabic *almanakh* (*manakh*, "calendar"; *manah*, "sundial"). The term *almanac* was used in Roger Bacon's *Opus majus* (c.1267) to denote permanent tables showing the movements of the stars and planets.

Among the earlier almanacs were the "clog" almanacs of the Danes and Normans. These were blocks of wood on which days of the year were notched. The first printed almanac dates from 1457. Most English almanacs were published by the Stationers Company, the best known being the *Vox stellarum* of Francis Moore, which was first issued about 1699. It survives as *Old Moore's Almanac* and still sells in vast numbers. The first American almanacs were printed in Cambridge, Mass., under the supervision of Harvard University, the earliest being *An Almanac for New England for the Year 1639*. Many followed in the 18th century, including Benjamin Franklin's *Poor Richard's Almanack* (1733) and the *Astronomical Diary and Almanack* (1723). The 18th-century almanac is considered the forerunner of the modern magazine. Between 1700 and 1900 probably more than 2,000 almanacs were issued in the United States. Many, such as Robert Thomas Baily's *The Old Farmer's Almanac*, founded in 1793 and still published, were intended for use by farmers and countrymen.   J. A. CUDDON

Bibliography: Drake, Milton, comp., *Almanacs of the United States*, 2 vols. (1962); Franklin, Benjamin, ed., *Poor Richard, an Almanack* (1732–67; repr. 1976).

almandine: see GARNET.

Almeida, Francisco de   [ahl-may'-thah]

Francisco de Almeida, b. c.1450, was the first viceroy of Portuguese India. He was appointed to that office in 1505 by King MANUEL I. At the time, Portugal had the best ships in the Indian Ocean but lacked the manpower to conquer a land empire, and so Almeida concentrated on dominating the sea lanes. On his way to India in 1505, he captured Kilwa and Sofala and destroyed Mombasa on the East African coast. He then established himself at Cochin in India. In 1508 Almeida's son was defeated and killed in a naval battle against the Arabs, but the following year Almeida destroyed the Arab fleets at Diu. In the meantime he had been replaced as viceroy by Afonso de ALBUQUERQUE, but Almeida refused to accept his dismissal until 1509. On his way back to Europe, he was killed in an encounter with the Khoikhoin in South Africa on Mar. 1, 1510.   DANIEL R. HEADRICK

Bibliography: Whiteway, R. S., *The Rise of Portuguese Power in India, 1497–1550*, 2d ed. (1967).

Almería   [al-mair-ee'-uh]

Almería is the capital of Almería province in the Andalusian region of southeastern Spain. The city has a population of 120,100 (1975 est.). An important Mediterranean seaport at the head of the Gulf of Almería, it is an export point for white grapes, oranges, and other fruits. Almería's Costa del Sol beaches and its pleasant climate make it a tourist center. Landmarks include the cathedral (completed 1543) and the Moorish fort Alcazaba.

Almería was settled by Phoenicians about 238 BC. Subsequently it was the Roman city of Portus Magnus and then a Moorish seaport. The city was captured in 1147 by Alfonso VII of Castile but was retaken by the Moors, who held it until 1489 when it reverted to Spain. It was seriously damaged during the Spanish Civil War (1937).

Almohads   [ahl'-moh-hadz]

The Almohads, an Islamic dynasty, ruled North Africa and Spain from 1130 to 1269. The dynasty originated in a mass movement of BERBER tribesmen initially led by Ibn Tumart, who proclaimed (c.1120) himself the MAHDI, or messiah, come to purify Islam. His successor, Abd al-Mumin (d. 1163), defeated the ALMORAVIDS and made Marrakesh the Almohad capital in 1147. Subsequently, all the Muslim territory in Spain was occupied, and North Africa was conquered as far as Tripoli by 1160.

The Almohad court was a splendid center of art and Arabic learning; yet the empire soon crumbled because of its great size, social divisions, and religious conservatism. Externally, the Almohads were confronted by the Christian reconquest of Spain; their defeat at Las Navas de Tolosa (1212) resulted in their total withdrawal from Spain. In North Africa, the empire divided into local kingdoms, one of which captured Marrakesh in 1269.   MICHAEL W. DOLS

almond   [ah'-muhnd]

The almond tree, *Prunus amygdalus*, which produces the oldest and most widely grown of all NUT crops, is indigenous to

The sweet almond tree, P. amygdalus dulcis, is grown in temperate areas for its fragrant blossoms as well as for its nuts. A leathery hull surrounds the woody shell of a nut and splits open when the kernel is ripe. The milky white kernel, one of the most popular nuts, is consumed raw or processed as almond oil and almond meal.

western Asia and North Africa. Today it is grown in most temperate regions.

A member of the rose family and similar in appearance to the peach tree, the almond tree reaches a height of 3–7 m (9–22 ft) and has pink or white flowers that bloom in early spring. The dry, leathery almond fruit surrounds a seed or kernel—the almond nut—which is harvested when the fruit dries and splits open.

Of the two major types of almonds grown, the sweet almond, *P. amygdalus dulcis*, is cultivated for its edible nut. The bitter almond, *P. amygdalus amara*, is inedible but contains an oil—also present in the sweet almond and in the ripe kernels of the apricot and peach—which, when combined with water, yields hydrocyanic (prussic) acid and benzaldehyde, the ESSENTIAL OIL of bitter almonds. The oil is used in making flavoring extracts and in some sedative medicines.

Almond trees require more than one variety for pollination. Trees are propagated primarily by budding, with bitter almond, almond, or peach seedlings used as rootstocks. Harvests begin the fourth year after planting, and full production is reached by the seventh. In California, the largest American almond-producing state, some 100 varieties are grown.

DONALD K. OURECKY

Almoravids   [al-mor'-uh-vidz]

The Almoravids were an Islamic dynasty that ruled North Africa and Spain from 1056 to 1147. The dynasty originated in the western Sahara among the BERBERS who were united by religious revivalism and reform. From the mouth of the Senegal River, warriors for the faith spread a simple, fundamentalist form of Islam; they moved northward into Morocco and conquered North Africa as far as Algiers. Marrakesh was founded as the capital about 1070.

In 1086 the Almoravids crossed into Spain, defeated the Christian army of reconquest, and annexed the territories of Muslim Spain. These rugged Berber nomads were conquered in turn by the refined civilization of Spain and were unable to defend their empire against the ALMOHADS, another Berber dynasty, who killed the last Almoravid ruler in Marrakesh in 1147.

MICHAEL W. DOLS

Almqvist, Carl Jonas Love   [ahlm'-kvist]

Carl Jonas Love Almqvist, b. Nov. 28, 1793, a Swedish writer, studied at Uppsala University and then, influenced by the mystic Emanuel von SWEDENBORG, briefly attempted life as a

farmer. He later served as principal of an experimental secondary school in Stockholm and also became a clergyman. His novel *Amorina* (1821) is perhaps the foremost fantasy of Swedish romanticism. Between 1832 and 1851 he published *Törnrosens Bok* (The Book of the Briar Rose), a collection of novels and poems of which *Drottningens Juvelsmycke* (The Queen's Diamond Ornament) and "Songes" (Dreams) are today the most interesting. Almqvist moved from romanticism to realism with *Det Går An* (It Will Do), a controversial novella about a common-law marriage. In 1839 he began writing for the liberal press. In 1851, in financial difficulties and suspected of murder, he fled to the United States, where he stayed for 14 years. He died in Germany on Sept. 26, 1866.

aloe   [al'-oh]

Aloe is any of about 200 species and hybrids of perennial succulent PLANTS that belong to the lily family, Liliaceae. They are used as landscape plants in dry, frost-free areas and are sometimes grown as houseplants. Their leaves are fleshy, stiff, and spiny along the edges and are often crowded together into a rosette. The flowers, which are mostly reddish, are produced on showy spikes that may extend 6 m (20 ft) above the ground; some species produce yellow, orange, or whitish-green flowers. Water-aloe is sometimes designated *Stratiotes aloides*, or the water soldier. Juice from the leaves is used to treat burns. The plant is also a source of a purgative drug.

CHARLES L. WILSON

The ox-tongue gasteria, or warty aloe, G. verrucosa, is an easy-to-grow, attractive aloe that has white raised spots covering its leaves.

Alonso, Alicia

Alicia Alonso, born Martinez, in Havana, Cuba, on Dec. 21, 1917, is considered one of the outstanding ballerinas active today. Alonso danced with the AMERICAN BALLET THEATRE intermittently from 1941 to 1960. Her rise was plagued by recurring eye problems, involving several operations and lengthy periods of immobile recuperation. Alonso emerged to become one of the great interpreters of Adolphe ADAM's *Giselle*, as well as the first to dance the demanding ballerina role in George BALANCHINE's *Theme and Variations*. With her husband, Fernando Alonso, she founded the Ballet Alicia Alonso (1948), renamed Ballet de Cuba (1955). After the Cuban revolution (1959), Alonso temporarily gave up performing in the United States to devote her time to her country and the young ballet company. In 1978 she returned to New York with her company for a short but successful engagement.

MICHAEL ROBERTSON

Bibliography: De Gamez, Tana, *Alicia Alonso at Home and Abroad* (1971).

Alonso, Dámaso

Dámaso Alonso, b. Oct. 22, 1898, is a Spanish poet and literary critic whose translated edition of Góngora's *Soledades* in

1927 began a thoroughgoing reinterpretation of the Golden Age of Spanish poetry. In subsequent studies of Góngora, St. John of the Cross, and contemporary poets, Alonso developed a critical method similar to the NEW CRITICISM used in the United Kingdom and the United States. His best poems are included in *Hijos de la ira* (1944; *Children of Wrath*, 1970). Alonso is professor of Romance philology at the University of Madrid.

Alorese [al'-uh-reez]

The Alorese are an Indonesian people who inhabit the mountainous forest interior of Alor, an island located 32 km (20 mi) north of Timor, and the nearby island of Pantar. The present population of Alorese is estimated at 100,000. They speak a language associated with the Malayo-Polynesian linguistic family (see MALAYO-POLYNESIAN LANGUAGES).

The Alorese live in settled villages and raise rice, corn, and various root crops. Their territory is surrounded by narrow coastal lowlands where Indonesian Muslims live, but trade with the coastal villages is rare. The Alorese trace their genealogical descent through the male line. Polygamy is common, and a man's wives often live in separate dwellings. An Alorese achieves social prestige by accumulating wealth in the form of metal kettledrums.

Traditional Alorese religion is animistic (see ANIMISM) and mainly concerned with honoring or appeasing environmental and guardian spirits. In the center of a typical Alorese village is a plaza; its edges are marked by the graves of important deceased village members. On death, part of a person's soul is believed to linger in the village until a final memorial funeral feast marks its departure to an uninhabited island in the afterworld.   DONN V. HART

Bibliography: Du Bois, Cora A., *The People of Alor*, 2 vols. (1944; repr. 1960).

Alouette [al-oo-et']

Alouette (French, "lark") was Canada's first artificial space SATELLITE. Developed to measure variations in the density of electrons in the ionosphere as a function of time of day and latitude, it was a cooperative scientific effort in NASA's Topside Sounder program. Alouette was launched from the Western Test Range (Vandenberg Air Force Base, Calif.) by a Thor-Agena on Sept. 28, 1962. It achieved an orbit with an apogee of 1,027 km (638 mi) and a perigee of 998 km (620 mi) and performed its mission successfully.

The satellite was an oblate spheroid 105 cm (42 in) in diameter, 86 cm (34 in) high, and weighing 144 kg (320 lb). Solar cells and nickel-cadmium batteries supplied power. The primary scientific instrument was a swept-frequency transmitter and receiver. The satellite also had six charged-particle detectors.   MITCHELL R. SHARPE

See also: SPACE EXPLORATION.

alpaca [al-pak'-uh]

The alpaca, L. pacos, grows a lightweight coat of wool that insulates the animal against cold weather of the high Andes plains. The wool is spun and woven into a fine cloth, valued for both its softness and its warmth.

The alpaca is a domesticated LLAMA, *L. pacos*, bred in South America principally for its wool. Because its fleece is longer and more silky than that of other llama species, it was prized by the Incas, who wove its hair into robes reserved for royalty. Today, alpaca is used to make soft, lustrous, pile-weave fabrics for coats. The alpaca requires about two years, spent high in the Andes, to produce a full growth of wool.

Alpha Centauri: see STAR.

alpha particle

The alpha particle is a stable combination of two protons and two neutrons. It is emitted from the nuclei of many heavy radioactive atomic nuclei during decay. The alpha particle is also the nucleus of the atom of helium-4 and can acquire two electrons to become a neutral helium atom.

alpha wave: see BRAIN.

alphabet: see WRITING SYSTEMS, EVOLUTION OF.

Alphonsus Liguori, Saint [lee-gwaw'-ree]

St. Alphonsus Liguori, b. Sept. 27, 1696, d. Aug. 1, 1787, an Italian churchman, founded the Congregation of the Most Holy Redeemer (the Redemptorists) in 1732. His original name was Alfonso Maria de Liguori. He was ordained a priest in 1726 and served as bishop of Sant' Agata dei Goti from 1762 to 1775. In his writings on moral theology he developed a system of CASUISTRY tending toward a stricter interpretation of the law in the application of ethical principles. Canonized May 26, 1839, he was made a Doctor of the Church in 1871 and patron of confessors and moralists in 1950. Feast day: Aug. 1 (formerly Aug. 2).

alphorn

The alphorn is a wooden, tubular instrument best known in its Swiss form, although it is commonly found in many parts of the world. It may be straight or curved and 1.5 to 4 m (3 to 10 ft) in length. The alphorn does not have valves or finger

The alphorn, or alpenhorn, is a wooden horn made without finger holes or valves. Although the alphorn is still used by Swiss herders to call their cattle, the instrument is primarily of interest to tourists.

holes and so can play only the pitches in the natural harmonic series. Swiss mountain herdsmen still use the instrument to summon their cows. Numerous composers have used the characteristic alphorn melodies in orchestral pieces but have given them to traditional orchestral instruments. The German name is *Alpenhorn*.   ELWYN A. WIENANDT

Alps

The Alps constitute Europe's most extensive mountain system, encompassing parts of France, Italy, Switzerland, Germany, Austria, Yugoslavia, and most of Liechtenstein. Beginning along the Mediterranean, at the French-Italian border, as a relatively narrow chain, the mountains gradually widen into a broad arc west of Vienna. More than 965 km (600 mi) long and 200 km (125 mi) wide, they cover an area of more than 207,200 km² (80,000 mi²).

Peaks average 1,800–2,400 m (5,940-7,920 ft), and many rise above 3,050 m (10,000 ft). About 1,200 mountain glaciers cover an area of 3,900 km² (1,500 mi²).

Regional Cultures. Throughout history, this extensive mountain system has acted as a barrier between Mediterranean and northern cultures. Communication between civilizations has been continuous, aided in part by a series of mountain passes and longitudinal valleys. The term *alps* refers to a specific landscape feature, the high mountain pastures. The idea of an alpine way of life is based on the economy and life-style developed within this region.

The cultural diversity of the region is apparent from the variety of languages: French, German, Italian, Slovene, and Romansh. Population density varies with altitude. The Alpine forelands and broader longitudinal valleys are more densely populated than the narrower, more isolated valleys and summit areas.

Topography. Europe's newest folded mountain range, the Alps have not yet been worn down to old mountain stumps but retain instead a distinctly linear configuration. Three zones are recognized: a central zone of crystalline mountain rocks, surrounded by two zones of limestone, one to the north and one to the south. The parallel chains of mountains are separated by longitudinal valleys in many places. Where major rivers have turned and broken through the limestone ranges, transverse valleys have formed. Alpine glaciers of the ICE AGES filled these valleys and portions of the surrounding plains as well. When the glaciers retreated, they left dams

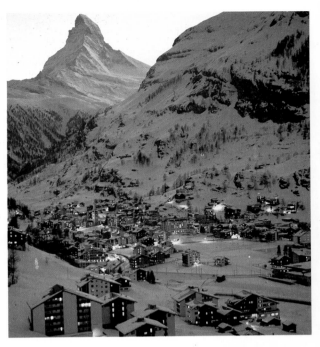

The famed Matterhorn, one of the Perrine Alps, juts dramatically into the skies near the Italo-Swiss border. The alpine village of Zermatt (foreground) is an internationally known ski resort.

of MORAINE, creating finger lakes such as Como, Maggiore, and Geneva.

The Alps can be divided into the western and eastern sections along a line from Lake Como north to the Italo-Swiss border, through Splügen Pass, and down the Rhine Valley to Lake Constance. The western Alps are higher and narrower, with more extensive glaciers and deeply incised valleys. The longitudinal valleys of the eastern Alps are wider, and a number of important cities are located in them. Mont BLANC, (4,634 m/15,203 ft) is the highest peak in the western Alps; Piz

ALPS

+ Glacier
+ Spot Elevation

Capitals are underlined

Meters	Feet
Above 4000	Above 13124
2000	6562
1000	3281
500	1640
200	656
0	0
200	656
Below 2000	Below 6562

Scale 1:7,014,000

0 40 80 120 km
0 20 40 60 80 mi

© 1979 Rand McNally & Co.
A-558900-772

Bernina (4,048 m/13,281 ft) is the highest in the eastern Alps.
Climate and Drainage. Topographic influences such as degree of slope, slope exposure (sun or shade), and altitude give rise to a complex mosaic of microclimates. Major climatic forces, such as the extremes of continentality to the northeast and the moderating influence of the Mediterranean to the south, also play a role. The mountains modify air masses, resulting in anticyclonic activities that become more pronounced toward the east. Precipitation totals range from lows of 580 mm (23 in) for Sion (Rhône Valley) and Briançon (French Alps) to highs of more than 2,300 mm (90 in) in the mountain summit areas of the central Alps. Average temperatures and extremes in temperature decrease with altitude. Innsbruck, at a higher altitude than Klagenfurt, has a January average of −3° C (26° F) and a July average of 18° C (64° F). Klagenfurt, farther east, has a January average of −7° C (20° F) and a July average of 16° C (60° F).

Hydrologically, the Alps affect much of Europe, since runoff from snowmelt within the mountains feeds several major rivers or their tributaries. The Rhine and Rhône rise in the central Alps, as do tributaries of the Po, such as the Ticino and the Oglio, and major Danube tributaries, such as the Inn, the Salzach, and the Enns. The Alps thus form a divide between Atlantic, Mediterranean, and Black Sea drainage.
Vegetation and Animal Life. Natural vegetation is zonal in character. The montaine, or lower level, has deciduous trees extending up to about 1,370 m (4,500 ft). Next is a zone of coniferous forests up to about 1,675 m (5,500 ft), then a zone of bare rocks and grass slopes (alps), followed by the snow line, ranging from 2,440 m (8,000 ft) to 3,050 m (10,000 ft) depending on location. Numerous national parks and nature reserves supply a last refuge for endangered species such as ibex, chamois, golden eagle, rock partridge, and black grouse.   BRUCE L. LA ROSE

Bibliography: Clark, Ronald, *The Alps* (1973); Collet, Leon W., *The Structure of the Alps* (1974); Engel, Claire E., *The History of Mountaineering in the Alps* (1950; repr. 1977).

Alsace-Lorraine   [al-sas'-lohr-rayn']

Alsace and Lorraine (German: Elsass and Lothringen) are two historic provinces in eastern France. Part of the Holy Roman Empire until 1648, Alsace was added to France by the Treaty of Ryswick in 1697. Lorraine was part of the kingdom of LOTHARINGIA, which was divided (959) into the duchies of Lower and Upper Lorraine. The latter, which became modern Lorraine, was an independent but much-fought-over duchy until 1766. Between 1871 and 1918, Alsace (the departments of Bas-Rhin and Haut-Rhin) and the eastern part of Lorraine (now the department of Moselle) were annexed to Germany as a result of France's defeat in the Franco-Prussian War. From 1919 to 1940, the area belonged to France; from 1940 to 1945, to Germany. It was returned to France in 1945. The three departments of Meuse, Meurthe-et-Moselle, and Vosges remained French.

Geologically, western Lorraine is composed of clay vales separated by the north-south trending limestone ridges of the Côtes de Meuse and Côtes de Moselle. The heavy soils of the

The historic French provinces of Alsace and Lorraine lie along the border between the French- and German-speaking areas of Europe. From 1871 to 1918 and from 1940 to 1945, Alsace and part of Lorraine belonged to Germany.

vales support mixed farming—dairying, oats, and wheat. Crop yields are below the French average. The ridges are barriers to communication and invasion. METZ, NANCY, VERDUN, Thionville, and Toul are route centers and fortress cities defending gaps in the ridges. The battle for Verdun was one of the bloodiest of World War I. Nancy (1982 pop., 99,000), the traditional capital and university center of Lorraine, is located on the Rhine-Marne canal, which follows the routeway from Paris to Strasbourg.

The Lorraine iron ore fields, about 110 km (70 mi) long and 20 km (12 mi) wide, run from Nancy northward to the primary iron and steel district around Longwy, Thionville, and Metz. Ore production exceeds 50 million metric tons (55 million U.S. tons) a year, the second highest in Western Europe. The French part of the Saar coalfield lies 64 km (40 mi) to the east. Producing 10 million metric tons (11 million U.S. tons) of coal a year, it now has half the French reserves in easily mechanized, thick seams.

Southeastward, Lorraine rises gradually to the summits of the Vosges. This sandstone massif has a granite core exposed in the south, where elevations exceed 1,200 m (4,000 ft). The political and linguistic divide between French-speaking Lorraine and German-speaking Alsace runs along its crest. At the foot of the steep eastern slope of the Vosges is a famous vineyard region. An adjoining belt of fertile loess soils produces cereals, fruit, tobacco, and vegetables. It also produces hops for Alsatian and German breweries.

STRASBOURG (1982 pop., 252,000), a major port on the Rhine, is the traditional capital of Alsace. Its industries include oil refining, brewing, printing, food processing, and metallurgy. Famous for its university and its *pâté*, Strasbourg is headquarters of the Council of Europe. The Rhine-Rhône canal connects Strasbourg with Mulhouse, the Burgundy Gate, and Lyon. Mulhouse, with a chemical industry based on substantial local potash deposits, and Colmar are centers of the textile industry of Alsace and eastern Lorraine. Temperatures in the region average 0.6° C (33° F) in January and 19° C (60° F) in July. Annual rainfall ranges from 510 to 1,020 mm (20 to 40 in).   TIMOTHY J. RICKARD

Bibliography: Silverman, Dan P., *Reluctant Union: Alsace-Lorraine and Imperial Germany, 1871–1918* (1972).

Alsop, Joseph and Stewart

Joseph and Stewart Alsop, in collaboration and separately, became two of the best-known reporter-columnists in American journalism. In *The Reporter's Trade* (1958) they conveyed their belief that the columnist is primarily a reporter. **Joseph,** b. Avon, Conn., Oct. 11, 1910, was educated at Harvard University, and his brother **Stewart,** b. Avon, Conn., May 17, 1914, d. May 26, 1974, was educated at Yale University. Joseph was co-writer with Robert Kintner of the column "The Capital Parade" from 1937 to 1940. The Alsop brothers later (1945–58) collaborated on the widely syndicated column "Matter of Fact." In tones of approaching doom, they wrote many exclusive stories about ballistic missile developments in the 1950s.   CALDER M. PICKETT

Bibliography: Alsop, Joseph, *FDR: A Centenary Remembrance* (1982); Alsop, Stewart, *Stay of Execution: A Sort of Memoir* (1973).

Alston, Walter

Walter Emmons Alston, b. Butler County, Ohio, Dec. 1, 1911, d. Oct. 1, 1984, was a surprise choice when named to manage the Brooklyn Dodgers starting in 1954, but he stayed 23 years to lead the baseball team (which moved to Los Angeles in 1958) to its greatest successes. "Smokey" Alston made the majors as a player for the St. Louis Cardinals in 1936 but went to bat only one time. As a manager for the Dodgers' minor-league chain in the 1940s, he helped prepare some of the first black players for their historic integration of major-league baseball. As a big-league manager, he won the World Series in 1955 and again in 1959, 1963, and 1965. He led the team to three other National League pennants, was manager of the year three times, and was inducted (1983) into the Hall of Fame.

Altai Mountains [al'-ty]

The Altai Mountains (Mongolian: Altain-ula, "mountains of gold") are an extensive mountain system of Central Asia located at the juncture of the USSR, China, and Mongolia. They cover about 1,600 km (1,000 mi). The range rises to a maximum elevation of 4,653 m (15,266 ft) in the Taban Bogdo Knot. The Altai comprises the SAYAN, the Katun, the Sailyugem, and the Tannu-Ola. The 1,450-km-long (900-mi) Mongolian Altai is the longest range in the system. About 70% of the mountain territory is under dense forest. The range's mean elevation is about 1,500 m (5,000 ft), and steep, deeply eroded mountainsides are typical.

Formed by geological uplift 300 million years ago, the Altai ranges have slowly been worn down to smooth contours. Glaciers, which still cover an area of almost 1,554 km^2 (600 mi^2), deepened their valleys and fed many lakes and rivers. The Altai contain the source of the OB, the IRTYSH, and the tributaries of the YENISEI. The region has a continental climate, with a long, dry winter and a rainy season during the brief summer. Precipitation varies from as much as 2,032 mm (80 in) annually in the west to less than 127 mm (5 in) in the southeast. Silver, copper, lead, zinc, and mercury are mined in eastern Kazakh SSR, where much of the range lies.

Tribal Altaic peoples (KAZAKHS, Mongolikhalks, and Oyrat), who raise cattle, sheep, and horses, were the original inhabitants of the region. Exploitation of hydroelectric and mineral resources and new agricultural methods are drawing immigrants, especially in the USSR.

Altaic languages: see URAL-ALTAIC LANGUAGES.

Altair: see STAR.

Altamira [ahl-tah-mee'-rah]

Altamira is the site of a cave near Santillana del Mar in the province of Santander, northeast Spain. Paleolithic cave paintings discovered here in 1879 by Don Marcelino de Sautuola are acknowledged as one of the summits of PREHISTORIC ART. The painted ceiling near the entrance depicts, in color, large animals, mainly bison. Their vivid impact is enhanced by the artists' apparent incorporation of the natural protrusions and hollows of the surface into the painted and engraved representations. In the rear of the cave are paintings of animals and symbols, outlined in black and red pigment, and many engravings, the finest being that of a group of hinds. The cave art is dated from the late SOLUTREAN to the middle MAGDALENIAN periods.　　　　　　　　　　　　　　LYA DAMS

Bibliography: Breuil, Henri, and Obermaier, Hugo, *The Cave of Altamira at Santillana del Mar, Spain* (1935); Sandars, N. K., *Prehistoric Art in Europe* (1968; repr. 1975).

A reclining bison appears in a painting from the Altamira cave in Spain. The large polychrome work is one of a number of naturalistic animal paintings on the walls and ceiling of the cave.

Altamirano, Ignacio Manuel [ahl-tah-mee-rah'-noh, eeg-nah'-seeoh mah-nwel']

Ignacio Manuel Altamirano, b. Nov. 13, 1834, d. Feb. 13, 1893, was an outstanding Mexican-Indian writer whose fiction and poetry reflected strong nationalistic sentiments. He was a firm ally of the liberal statesman Benito JUÁREZ and rose to literary prominence after 1860. *El Renacimiento*, a journal he established in 1869, contributed to the growth of an indigenous Mexican literature. His best novels are, *Clemencia* (1869), *Christmas in the Mountains* (1870; Eng. trans., 1961), and *El Zarco* (1901).　　　　　　　　　　　　　KEITH ELLIS

Bibliography: Nacci, Chris N., *Ignacio Manuel Altamirano* (1970).

altar

An altar is a table or elevated platform intended for the offering of a religious SACRIFICE. In the religions of ancient times, altars sometimes were composed of the ashes of previous offerings compacted by time. More often, an altar was constructed out of earth or stone. The size of an altar was determined by its specific use. Small altars were used for sacrifices such as the burning of incense; larger altars were required for the offering of animals. Altars were commonly built outdoors, usually in a sacred enclosure in front of a temple.

In the Christian church, the altar is a tablelike structure that serves as the focal point of worship and on which the EUCHARIST is celebrated. Although the table, or mensa, is the only essential part of an altar, other features were added through the centuries: a platform (predella), a canopy, a shelf (retable), a screen (reredos), and a tabernacle (receptacle) for storing the consecrated elements of the Eucharist.

At first, altars were made of wood; later, stone was generally used. The earliest altars were simple in form, consisting of a slab resting on one or more legs. They were frequently adorned with finely embroidered cloths, often of silk, and with gold and silver plate adorned with precious stones.

Traditionally, the altar stood at the east end of the church in the center of the sanctuary, and the position of the altar determined the orientation of the building. The altar was frequently built over a crypt containing the remains of a saint or martyr. Later, additional altars were sometimes installed along the side walls of a church or in chapels dedicated to saints.

During the Middle Ages, altars were lavished with rich decorations by artists and sculptors. For example, the altar of the Capella della Nunziata at the cathedral of Pisa is famous for a cover worked in chased silver. The antique altar in ST. MARK'S CHURCH in Venice is ornamented with carved anchors and dolphins. The high altar of ST. PETER'S BASILICA in the Vatican is highlighted by BERNINI's baldachino, one of the most magnificent altar decorations in Christendom. Many of the best-known examples of Italian and Flemish painting originally formed parts of altarpieces.

The altars in Roman Catholic churches now tend to be simple tablelike structures without decoration and detached from the wall. Many Protestant churches either have no altar or prefer to refer to it as the Communion table.

NORMAN F. JOSAITIS

Bibliography: Pocknee, Cyril E., *The Christian Altar in History and Today* (1962).

Altdorfer, Albrecht [ahlt'-dorf-ur, ahl'-brekt]

Albrecht Altdorfer, b. 1480, d. Feb. 12, 1538, a German Renaissance painter, draftsman, printmaker, and architect is best known as the developer of pure landscape painting. He is generally considered the greatest artist in the Danube School, which also included Lucas CRANACH the Elder, Wolfgang HUBER, Jörg Breu, and Jörg Kölderer.

Except for trips down the Danube to work in Vienna in 1511 and 1535, Altdorfer resided primarily in Regensburg. He was probably born there, became a citizen in 1505, served as the town architect from 1526, and died there. He may have learned his precision in draftsmanship and landscape painting from his father, who was an illuminator, and from his study of DÜRER's and Cranach's paintings and Michael PACHER's *St. Wolfgang* altarpiece.

Albrecht Altdorfer, the foremost artist of the Danube School, was the father of modern landscape painting. His Danube Landscape near Regensburg *(c.1520–25), a finely detailed work, depicts the region surrounding Altdorfer's home town. (Alte Pinakothek, Munich.)*

Although the Emperor MAXIMILIAN I employed Altdorfer, along with such rivals as Dürer and others, to make numerous woodcuts, engravings, and illuminations, Altdorfer's style remained independent and personal. His constant concern with natural growth, his faultless depiction of foliage and trees, and his ability to integrate human moods and action with landscape are evidenced in his St. Florian altarpiece (1509–18), since broken up and dispersed to museums in Nuremberg, Prague, and Florence. Altdorfer's interest in magic, ruins, fantastic landscape, and mysterious light are exemplified in his masterpiece of large spatial organization, *The Battle of Alexander* (1529; Alte Pinakothek, Munich), commissioned by Duke William IV of Bavaria as part of a series of monumental classical battle paintings.   ALAN P. DARR

Bibliography: Benesch, Otto, *The Art of the Renaissance in Northern Europe*, rev. ed. (1965); Burkhard, Arthur, *The St. Florian Altar of Albrecht Altdorfer* (1970); Hollstein, F. W. H., *German Engravings, Etchings, and Woodcuts ca. 1400–1700* (1954); Waldman, Emil, ed., *Albrecht Altdorfer: Catalogue of Engravings and Etchings* (1923).

Alter, David

The American physician, inventor, and physicist David Alter, b. Dec. 3, 1807, d. Sept. 18, 1881, pointed out in 1854 and 1855 that each chemical element has a characteristic SPECTRUM and that the elements present in astronomical bodies could be ascertained through spectral analysis. In this he anticipated the work of Gustav KIRCHHOFF and Robert BUNSEN, who, in 1859, put spectroscopy on a firm scientific foundation.
                                                        RICHARD F. HIRSH

alteration, mineral

Alteration is the geologic process whereby natural chemical solutions react with rocks to form new minerals. The most

common alteration minerals, precipitated from hot aqueous (water-based) solutions reacting with GRANITE and other IGNEOUS ROCKS, are quartz, mica, clay, feldspar, and pyrite. They are usually distributed in regular patterns around ORE DEPOSITS and commonly occupy a larger volume of rock than the ore deposit itself. Modern prospectors use alteration minerals as clues in searching for ore deposits by studying their abundance, type, and distribution. Those produced by the WEATHERING of ores form oxide deposits, or gossans, on or near the earth's surface, and these also serve as guides to subsurface ore.

Alteration reactions may change the chemical characteristics of a mineral-forming solution so that ore minerals will precipitate; they may increase the PERMEABILITY of rock enough to permit ore-forming solutions to gain entry.
                                                        ERIC S. CHENEY

See also: MINERAL.

alternating current

A direct current (DC) always flows through a conductor in one direction, but an alternating current (AC) constantly reverses itself as a result of reversing electromotive force. One complete reversal is a cycle, and the number of cycles per second is the frequency of the alternating current. The standard frequency of alternating current in the United States and the rest of North America is 60 Hz (1 Hz, or hertz, equals 1 cycle per second); in Europe it is 50 Hz. Originally, only direct current was generated for public use. The enormous advantages of alternating current were not realized until George Westinghouse developed the TRANSFORMER in the late 19th century. Buffalo, N.Y., was the first U.S. city to be lighted using alternating current.

The transformer made it possible to change the voltage (and therefore the current) of AC by a simple, static device; this was not possible with DC. When electricity is transmitted, power loss is minimized by stepping up the voltage from the generator, thus transmitting a high voltage, and stepping down the voltage at the user's end. When required, DC is easily obtained from an AC current with a RECTIFIER. Converting DC to AC requires an inverter, which is a more complex device. AC motors and alternators (AC generators) have greater reliability than their DC counterparts, because they do not require commutators (metal slip-rings for picking up current).

If AC voltage is plotted against time, the resulting curve is a sine wave. This characteristic is of interest to physicists and engineers; the physical characteristics of AC can then be deduced from the mathematical properties of a sine wave. The maximum value that the voltage reaches is its peak value, but effective, or root-mean-square (rms), values are nearly always used in practice. The rms value of current or voltage has the same heating effect as an equal, steady-state DC current or voltage. By calculation, it is 0.707 times the peak value. In most countries power is supplied at 240 volts (rms), which means that the voltage rises to a peak of 339 volts. Exceptions are United States and Canada, which supply 110 volts (a peak of 156 volts) of electricity.

AC circuits obey OHM'S LAW, $E = IR$, when R consists of purely resistive elements. When reactive elements (see REACTANCE) are present in the circuit, Ohm's law becomes $E = IZ$, where Z is the IMPEDANCE. The waveforms of current and voltage are usually displaced, reaching their peaks at different times. This difference is denoted by the phase angle ϕ (a

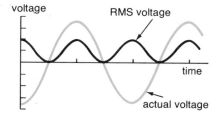

Alternating currents exhibit a definite relation between rms and peak voltages. Maximum voltage (E) of a 110-volt (rms) AC supply is 156 volts.

complete cycle is 360°). Thus the formula for power—which, in DC circuits, is $P = EI$—becomes $P = EI \cos \phi$, and the term $\cos \phi$ is known as the power factor. The value of ϕ depends upon the particular combination of capacitors, inductors, and resistors in the circuit. Numerous, simple electrical devices, such as the light bulb and the heating element, work equally well on AC or DC, although their rates of power consumption may differ slightly.

Bibliography: Dillow, Arthur P., *Alternating Current Fundamentals* (1966); Gibson, W. M., *Basic Electricity*, 2d ed. (1976); Gregory, J. M., *Alternating Currents* (1971).

See also: CIRCUIT, ELECTRIC; ELECTRICITY; POWER GENERATION AND TRANSMISSION.

alternation of generations

Alternation of generations is a biological term referring to the reproductive cycle in which a sexual stage alternates with an asexual stage. This is common in most plant groups, including some algae, ferns, mosses, and seed plants. It is rare in the animal kingdom, coelentrates (jellyfish, sea anemones, hydra) being one notable exception.

The life cycle comprises two structurally distinct organisms, the gametophyte (sexual form) and the sporophyte (asexual form). The gametophyte produces male and female gametes, or sex cells, that fuse to form a zygote, which develops into the embryo of the sporophyte, or asexual generation. The sporophyte gives rise to the gametophyte through spore or somatic-cell production.

The evolutionary trend in vascular plants (those having stems, roots, and leaves) has been toward the reduction in size of the gametophyte stage. Extreme reduction has occurred in flowering plants in which the sexual stage is represented by only a few cells retained in the flower. Thus the sporophyte has become the dominant generation, and the gametophyte is actually dependent on the sporophyte. In mosses, the gametophyte is dominant, and the sporophyte is dependent during its entire existence.

alternative schools

In the United States, the term *alternative schools* commonly refers to nontraditional programs that give educational options to students and parents. Many of the first alternative schools were FREE SCHOOLS established outside the public school system during the 1960s. During that decade, black parents in Boston and other cities set up community schools to escape and confront racism in the public schools. The New York Urban League established street academies for dropouts, and private alternative schools were formed to assist students who had dropped out of public schools. Harlem Prep in New York City and CAM (Christian Action Ministry) Academy in Chicago were notable examples of black alternative schools.

During the late 1960s and '70s some public school districts, especially those in urban areas, began to establish alternatives for their students. Philadelphia set up the Parkway Program to increase students' involvement in settings away from classrooms. Other districts developed alternatives emphasizing the MONTESSORI METHOD, basic skills, informal learning, individualized settings, outdoor study, career exploration, and other approaches. By 1978 at least 500 alternative schools were operating in the United States.   JAMES M. WALLACE

Bibliography: Dropkin, Ruth, and Tobier, Arthur, eds., *Roots of Open Education in America* (1976); Ford Foundation, *Matters of Choice: A Ford Foundation Report on Alternative Schools* (1974); Rich, John Martin, *Innovations in Education: Reformers and Their Critics* (1975); Riordan, Robert C., *Alternative Schools in Action* (1972); Smith, Vernon H., *Alternative Schools: The Development of Options in Public Education* (1974).

Altgeld, John Peter

John Peter Altgeld was a controversial governor (1892–96) of Illinois. Born in Germany on Dec. 30, 1847, he grew up on an Ohio farm. He was a Union soldier in the Civil War, became a teacher, then a lawyer, and first held political office as a Democratic county attorney in Missouri.

Moving to Chicago, he found law unremunerative and became a wealthy builder. He was elected county judge (1886) and then governor of Illinois.

In 1893, Altgeld caused a furor when he pardoned the anarchists convicted as a result of the HAYMARKET RIOT, citing an unfair trial. The next year he protested vehemently when President Grover CLEVELAND sent troops into Chicago during the PULLMAN STRIKE, because the local authorities felt competent to handle the situation. Convinced that Cleveland represented corporate interests, Altgeld led the FREE SILVER forces in the Democratic party, wrested control of the 1896 national convention from Cleveland, and wrote a platform that reshaped the party. Defeated for reelection, his wealth gone, he practiced law until his death on Mar. 12, 1902.

FRED GREENBAUM

Bibliography: Barnard, Harry, *Eagle Forgotten: The Life of John Peter Altgeld* (1938).

Althaea   [al-thee'-uh]

Althaea is a genus of annual or perennial herbs that belong to the MALLOW family, Malvaceae. Marshmallow, *A. officinalis*, is native to northern Asia and Europe and has been naturalized in the eastern United States. It has a fleshy underground stem, lobed leaves, and pale-rose flowers with five petals. Material from the root was once used in making the familiar marshmallows. The leaves are edible, and fiber from the stem is used to make paper. HOLLYHOCK, *A. rosea*, a popular mallow ornamental, is grown worldwide.   ROBERT C. ROMAN

altimeter

An altimeter is an instrument that measures the height above a reference surface such as sea level or the ground surface. This measurement can be based on the variation of atmospheric pressure with changing height above the Earth's surface. In essence, such an altimeter is an aneroid BAROMETER graduated in feet or meters instead of in millibars. This is the type used by mountaineers to ascertain their height above sea level. The instrument is set before climbing commences to correspond with local air pressure, but it is reliable only if the pressure distribution remains constant during the climb.

An altimeter is a necessary part of an aircraft's equipment. A sophisticated radio altimeter, in which a pulse of radio energy is beamed downward and the echo received on the aircraft, enables a pilot to judge the altitude. Signals from a radio altimeter are sometimes incorporated into a control system used for automatic landing.   CHARLES H. COTTER

altitude

In astronomy, navigation, and surveying, the altitude of a celestial object is its angular distance above or below the celestial horizon. The angular distance is measured along the vertical circle—the circle passing through both the celestial object and the ZENITH, an imaginary point directly above the observer. A celestial object's altitude and AZIMUTH—the angular distance of its vertical circle from the north (or south) vertical circle, measuring eastward from that circle—are used to give its position on the CELESTIAL SPHERE, as observed at a specific moment of time from a specific location.

See also: COORDINATE SYSTEMS (astronomy).

Altman, Robert B.

Robert B. Altman, b. Kansas City, Mo., Feb. 20, 1925, won widespread recognition as the trend-setting directorial stylist in American films of the 1970s. He did extensive work in television and directed four little-known features before making *M*A*S*H* (1970), the film that first brought him critical and popular acclaim. *McCabe & Mrs. Miller* (1971), *The Long Goodbye* (1973), and *California Split* (1974) drew increasing attention for their textural richness, multilayered soundtracks, and improvisatory flow. Prominent too was Altman's debunking of the myths of various film genres, from the Western to the private eye. With *Nashville* (1975) Altman had his second

Robert Altman (right), an American film director, confers with the actor Donald Sutherland on the set of M*A*S*H. The film, released in 1970, was a critical success and earned more than $40 million.

commercial success. Critics saw less quality in such films as *Buffalo Bill and the Indians* (1976), *3 Women* (1977), and *Quintet* (1979) but praised *McCabe & Mrs. Miller* (1974), *Thieves Like Us* (1974), and *Health* (1980). Altman also directed the Broadway play "*Come Back to the 5 and Dime Jimmy Dean, Jimmy Dean*" (1982).   WILLIAM S. PECHTER

Bibliography: Kass, Judith, *Robert Altman: American Innovator* (1978).

alto: see CONTRALTO.

Altoona

Surrounded by the rugged Allegheny Mountains in a coal-mining area of south central Pennsylvania, Altoona is an industrial city with a population of 57,078 (1980). It was founded in 1849 by the Pennsylvania Railroad Company, which chose that site to begin the difficult span across the Alleghenies. Altoona is still an important railroad center, with extensive trackage and enormous construction and repair shops. It also has many new diversified manufactures. To the northwest, Wopsononock Mountain, with a height of more than 780 m (2,580 ft), offers a view of six counties. The famous Horseshoe (railroad) Curve, which moves through a central angle of 220 degrees, is 8 km (5 mi) to the west.

altrical animal   [al-trish'-ul]

Mammals and birds that are helpless for a considerable period of time after birth are called altricial. Often blind, they cannot move about independently and in some cases cannot control their body temperature. Marsupial young, sheltered in the mother's pouch for months, are the most altricial of all animals. Other altricial animals are birds, rabbits, carnivores, and most rodents. Human young may be considered altricial because of the long period of care they require. The term *precocial* is applied to animals that are relatively self-sufficient from birth.   EVERETT SENTMAN

altruism   [al'-troo-izm]

Altruism is behavior that benefits others at some cost to the individual. As a philosophical concept, altruism was originally devised by Auguste COMTE as an ethical antithesis to EGOISM. In recent years social scientists and biologists have been especially interested in altruism, although the two groups approach the subject differently.

To most social scientists, altruism occurs when one individual consciously comes to the aid of another, without expecting anything in return. Several things are believed to influ-ence this behavior: empathy, an emotional response that results from being aware of another's emotions; group norms, society's expectation of how people "should" behave toward others; social learning, the personal experiences one has with others; and immediate context, the actual situation at the time an altruistic act is called for (being in a good mood, considering oneself helpful and altruistic, being with others rather than being alone).

Social scientists emphasize the importance of social experiences in producing altruistic behavior. By contrast, biologists, especially sociobiologists, take a different position. They view altruism as any behavior that reduces the Darwinian fitness (reproductive success) of the altruist while increasing the fitness of another. Accordingly, the occurrence of altruism in nature is a biological puzzle, since genes whose effect is to make themselves more rare in future generations should soon disappear altogether. Many examples of animal altruism, however, are known: worker bees, ants, and wasps are themselves sterile while assisting the queen to reproduce. It is common for animals to share food, help provide for another's young, defend others against predators, and give alarm calls when a predator appears. All these acts enhance the fitness of others while often reducing that of the altruist.

Sociobiologists have several explanations for the evolution of altruism. First, a behavior may only seem altruistic. It might actually contribute to one's reproductive success and thus be a selfish act after all. Second, apparent altruism could arise by natural selection if the giver eventually receives comparable benefits from the getter. This reciprocity is actually selfish behavior, although both parties ultimately benefit.

Two mechanisms for the evolution of behavior that actually reduce the personal fitness of the altruist are recognized by sociobiologists: kin selection and group selection. Kin selection is actually genetic selfishness. Altruistic genes can prosper as long as they succeed in making enough copies of themselves in relatives who are fitter because of the altruistic act. Kin selection suggests a biological basis for nepotism.

The notion of group selection is that altruism could theoretically be selected if altruists benefited others within the group so that the group as a whole did better than other groups that lacked altruists. However, individual altruists would be at a disadvantage within each group. Therefore, group selection is considered less likely than kin selection as a mechanism for evolving altruism, although it is theoretically possible.   DAVID P. BARASH

Bibliography: Barash, David P., *Sociobiology and Behavior* (1977); Daly, Martin, and Wilson, Margo, *Sex, Evolution, and Behavior* (1978); Hardin, Garrett, *The Limits of Altruism* (1977); Rushton, J. Phillippe, *Altruism, Socialization and Society* (1980); Sorokin, P. A., *Explorations in Altruistic Love and Behavior* (1950; repr. 1977); Wilson, Edward O., *Sociobiology: The New Synthesis* (1975).

Aluko, Timothy Mofolorunso   [ah-loo'-koh, moh-fohl-oh-run'-soh]

Timothy Mofolorunso Aluko, b. 1918, is a Nigerian novelist who writes satirically about the problems of cultural change in West Africa. Although he began to write when he was in his 20s, he worked for many years as a civil engineer before publishing his first novel, *One Man, One Wife* (1959). Aluko's characters are often stiff and his situations contrived, but at his best he writes with warm understanding of a society trying to reconcile traditional African values and Western values. His other novels include *One Man, One Matchet* (1964), *Kinsman and Foreman* (1966), *Chief, the Honourable Minister* (1970), and *His Worshipful Majesty* (1973).   RICHARD K. PRIEBE

alum

An alum is any of a group of compounds that contain the sulfates of two different metals—aluminum is often one of the metals—and water of hydration. Commercially, the most important alums are aluminum potassium alum, also known as potassium alum, or potash alum; and aluminum ammonium alum. Other double sulfates known as alum include ferric ammonium sulfate (ferric alum), sodium aluminum sulfate (soda alum), and potassium chromium sulfate (chrome alum). The term *alum* is also used for aluminum sulfate, commonly known as "papermaker's alum," or "filter alum." Not a double sulfate, this compound is obtained by treating clay or bauxite with sulfuric acid.

The alums have many uses, particularly in paper manufacture, in textile dyeing, in fireproofing, in water purification, and in medicine—as astringents, styptics, and emetics.

aluminum

Aluminum is the third most abundant element (8%) in the Earth's crust, exceeded by oxygen (47%) and silicon (28%).

Earth scientists generally agree that aluminum, like most other elements, was formed during the birth of our solar system through successive collisions of hydrogen atoms under conditions of high temperatures and pressures. Because of its strong affinity to oxygen, aluminum never occurs as a metal in nature but is found only in the form of its compounds, mostly oxides or silicates. This strong affinity to oxygen also explains why it withstood all attempts to prepare it in its elemental form until well into the 19th century.

The metal's name is derived from *alumen*, the Latin name for alum. In 1761 the French chemist Guyton de Morveau proposed the name *alumine* for the base in ALUM, and in 1787 Antoine LAVOISIER identified alumine as the oxide of a then-undiscovered metal. In 1807, Sir Humphry DAVY assigned the name *alumium* to the metal and later agreed to change it to aluminum. Shortly thereafter, the name *aluminium* was adopted to conform with the *-ium* ending of most elements, and this spelling is now in general use throughout the world, except in the United States (where the second *i* was dropped in 1925) and Italy (where *alluminio* is used).

PROPERTIES OF ALUMINUM (Al)

Atomic number	13
Atomic weight	26.9815
Electron configuration	neon core, $3s^23p^1$
Valency	+3
Isotopes	only one stable, 27
Electronegativity	1.5
Color	silver-white
Melting point	660.24° C
Boiling point	2,450° C
Density	2.699 (20° C)
Heat of vaporization	69.5 kcal/mole
Heat of fusion (enthalpy of fusion)	2.56 kcal/mole
Electron affinity	25.8 joules
	6.2 kcal/g-atom
First ionization potential (25° C)	138.0 kcal/mole
	5.985 eV
$E° = (Al^{3+} + 3e^- \rightarrow Al)$	− 1.66 volts
Atomic volume	9.997 ml/g-atom
Atomic radius	1.431 Å
Interatomic distance (non-bonded)	2.86 Å
Ionic radius	0.50 Å
Non-polar covalent radius	1.43 Å
Crystal structure	FCC

PHYSICAL PROPERTIES

Aluminum, symbol Al, is a silvery white metal in Group IIIA of the periodic table. Its atomic number is 13, its atomic weight 26.9815. It is ductile, nonmagnetic, and an excellent conductor of heat and electricity. The density of aluminum at 20° C is 2.699 g/cm³ (0.1 lb/in³); it melts at 660.24° C and boils at 2,450° C.

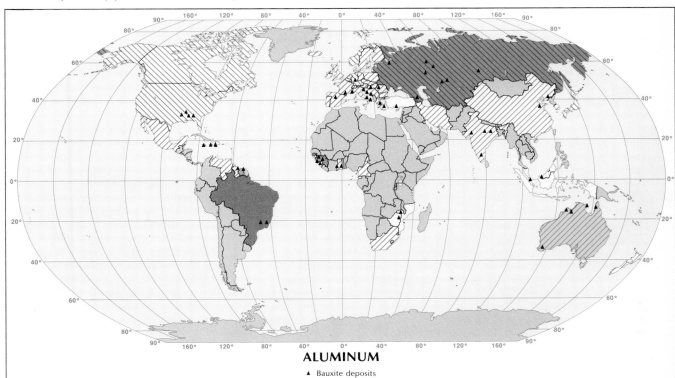

ALUMINUM

▲ Bauxite deposits

BAUXITE: principal producing nations, 1980 (millions of metric tons)   WORLD'S TOTAL 88.57

Australia 27.63	Jamaica 12.05	Guinea 11.76	Suriname 4.89	Soviet Union 4.60	Brazil 4.15	All others 23.49

ALUMINUM: principal producing nations, 1980 (millions of metric tons)   WORLD'S TOTAL 18.69

U.S.A. 6.12	Japan 1.89	Soviet Union 1.79	Canada 1.07	W.Ger-many 0.76	Nor-way 0.66	All others 6.40

Aluminum is widely used in many kinds of products because a combination of properties gives it special advantages over other materials.

Lightness and Strength. Perhaps the best-known quality of aluminum is its light weight. Its specific gravity is only 2.7; it is thus only about one-third as dense as iron, copper, or zinc. Despite its light weight, it can easily be made strong enough to replace heavier and more costly metals in thousands of applications.

Aluminum ALLOYS have the highest strength-to-weight characteristics of any commercial metal. The strength of the various aluminum alloys increases, with little change in ductility, as temperatures drop into the cryogenic range. At temperatures as high as 200° C (392° F), certain alloys remain remarkably strong.

Resistance to Corrosion. Aluminum and its various alloys are highly resistant to corrosion. When exposed to air, the metal develops a thin film of Al_2O_3 almost immediately. The reaction then slows, however, because the film seals off oxygen, preventing further oxidation or chemical reaction. The film is colorless, tough, and nonflaking. Few chemicals can dissolve it. Some aluminum alloys are better suited to certain corrosive environments than others. Many different alloys and claddings are available to meet the requirements of specific corrosive environments.

Electrical and Thermal Conductivity. Aluminum's electrical alloy has the highest conductivity per pound of any commercially sold conductor. Because aluminum is only one-third as dense as copper, it supplies about twice the conductivity per pound. For this reason more than 90% of the transmission and distribution lines in the United States are made from aluminum. Aluminum is an excellent conductor of heat as well. It is about 1.8 times as thermally conductive as copper by weight, depending on the alloy, and about 9 times as conductive as stainless steel. For this reason it is widely used in automobile radiators; cooling coils and fins; heat exchangers in the chemical, petroleum, and other industries; and heater fins in baseboard and other types of heaters.

Reflectivity and Emissivity. Aluminum is an excellent reflector of all forms of radiated energy. This characteristic is commonly put to work in building insulation, including roofing materials. Because it reflects about 90% of radiated heat, aluminum is effective at keeping heat out or in. Aluminum foil can also be used to jam radar by reflecting it.

Aluminum gives off as radiant energy only a small percentage (about 7%) of the heat that it does take on. It gives up most of its heat by conduction and convection. This characteristic, known as low emissivity, is especially valuable in installations where aluminum reflects most of any radiant energy rather than absorbing it and radiating it into the interior.

Workability. Aluminum has a face-centered cubic crystalline structure similar to that of tin and gold. As a consequence, it is very workable. Aluminum is as weldable as steel, at twice the rate of steel. It is also highly amenable to BRAZING, soldering, and cold welding (pressure joining; see WELDING AND SOLDERING).

THE ALUMINUM INDUSTRY

The aluminum industry, founded in 1854, is the newest of the nonferrous metal industries. In the United States, commercial production began in 1859 at a cost of $17 for a pound. Not until the late 1880s was a method found to bring prices down and permit aluminum to be used in a wide range of applications. The aluminum industry is now worldwide.

Bauxite, the Source of Aluminum. Most aluminum produced today is made from BAUXITE. First discovered in 1821 near Les Baux, France (from which its name is derived), bauxite is an ore rich in hydrated aluminum oxides, formed by the weathering of such siliceous aluminous rocks as feldspars, nepheline, and clays. During weathering the silicates are decomposed and leached out, leaving behind a residue of ores rich in alumina, iron oxide, titanium oxide, and some silica. In general, economically attractive ores contain at least 45% alumina and no more than 5% to 6% silica.

Most of the large bauxite deposits are found in tropical and subtropical climates, where heavy rainfall, warm temperatures, and good drainage combine to encourage the weathering process. Because bauxite is always found at or near the surface, it is mined by open-pit methods. It is then crushed if necessary, screened, dried, milled, and shipped for processing. Australia, Jamaica, Guinea, Suriname, the USSR, Guyana, France, Greece, Hungary, and Yugoslavia lead the world in bauxite production.

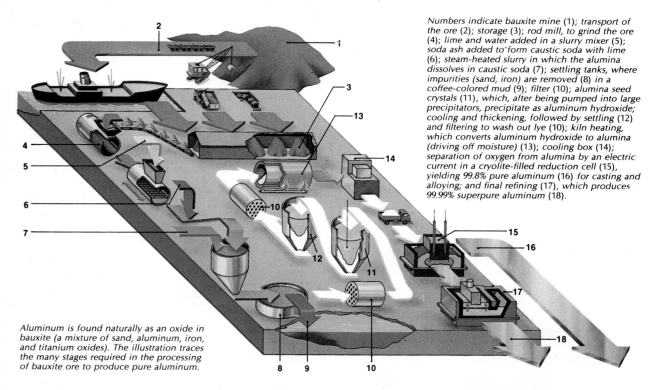

Numbers indicate bauxite mine (1); transport of the ore (2); storage (3); rod mill, to grind the ore (4); lime and water added in a slurry mixer (5); soda ash added to form caustic soda with lime (6); steam-heated slurry in which the alumina dissolves in caustic soda (7); settling tanks, where impurities (sand, iron) are removed (8) in a coffee-colored mud (9); filter (10); alumina seed crystals (11), which, after being pumped into large precipitators, precipitate as aluminum hydroxide; cooling and thickening, followed by settling (12) and filtering to wash out lye (10); kiln heating, which converts aluminum hydroxide to alumina (driving off moisture) (13); cooling box (14); separation of oxygen from alumina by an electric current in a cryolite-filled reduction cell (15), yielding 99.8% pure aluminum (16) for casting and alloying; and final refining (17), which produces 99.99% superpure aluminum (18).

Aluminum is found naturally as an oxide in bauxite (a mixture of sand, aluminum, iron, and titanium oxides). The illustration traces the many stages required in the processing of bauxite ore to produce pure aluminum.

Assuming that 4 tons of bauxite are required to produce 1 ton of aluminum, bauxite reserves known today are large enough to supply the world with aluminum for several hundred years at current production levels. Other ores that might be used when the high-grade bauxite deposits are exhausted include kaolin, anorthosite, and alunite.

Early History of Extraction Processes. Although proof of the existence of aluminum as a metal did not exist until the 1800s, clays containing the metallic element were used in Iraq as long ago as 5300 BC to manufacture high-quality pottery. Certain other aluminum compounds such as the "alums" were used widely by Egyptians and Babylonians as early as 2000 BC. Despite these early uses of the "metal of clay," however, it was almost 4,000 years before the metal was freed from its compounds, which made it a commercially usable metal.

Credit for first separating aluminum metal from its oxide goes to the Danish physicist Hans Christian OERSTED. In 1825 he reported to the Royal Danish Academy that he accomplished this by heating anhydrous aluminum chloride with potassium amalgam and distilling off the mercury. His product was so impure, however, that he did not succeed in determining its physical properties beyond observing a metallic luster.

In 1845, after many years of experimentation, Friedrich WÖHLER succeeded—by substituting potassium for the amalgam—in producing globules of aluminum large enough to allow the determination of some of its properties.

In 1854 Henri Sainte-Claire Deville substituted sodium for the relatively expensive potassium and, by using sodium aluminum chloride instead of aluminum chloride, produced the first commercial quantities of aluminum in a small plant near Paris. Bars and various objects made of this metal were shown at the Paris Exposition in 1855, and the ensuing publicity was in large measure responsible for launching the industry. Several plants using essentially the same process were subsequently built in France and England, but none survived for long, in part because of the lack of an economic source of electricity. The invention of the dynamo in 1866 paved the way for the development of modern aluminum processing.

In 1886 Charles Martin HALL of Oberlin, Ohio, and Paul L. T. HÉROULT of France, both 22 years old at the time, discovered and patented almost simultaneously the process by which alumina is dissolved in molten cryolite and decomposed electrolytically. This reduction process, generally known as the Hall-Héroult process, has survived many attempts to supplant it; it remains the only method by which aluminum is produced in commercial quantities today.

Two years after Hall and Héroult made their discovery, Karl Joseph Bayer, a German chemist, developed a process that improved the method for making alumina from bauxite ores low in silica content, a step necessary before the Hall-Héroult process could be applied. This achievement completed the foundation for a commercially feasible aluminum industry.

Bayer Process: Bauxite to Alumina. The Bayer Process of separating alumina from the bauxite ore was patented in 1888 and is still used today. The process begins when bauxite is pulverized by being mixed with soda ash and lime in a ball mill. Water is added to turn the mixture into a slurry, which is drained from the ball mills into tanks or digesters. In these tanks, which are heated by the injection of live steam, the alumina contained in the slurry is liquefied like sugar in ordinary water, then poured into settling tanks. Solids—largely sand, iron, and other elements that do not dissolve—move downward while a coffee-colored liquor remains on top.

Cleared of all solids, the liquid is pumped into large, open-topped vats, or precipitators, up to six stories high. Here the liquid is agitated, and minuscule alumina crystals begin to form. Agitation causes the crystals to adhere to each other as they slowly sink to the bottom of the precipitators, and they become slightly larger than grains of sugar. They are then pumped into settling tanks and washed again to remove the soda ash and lime solution that was added at the beginning of the process.

The final step is to drive off the remaining moisture by passing the alumina, which now resembles white mud, through kilns that heat it to more than 1,000° C (1,830° F). The sugarlike alumina, now dry and about 99% pure, pours out of the lower end of the tilted kiln and is stored in silos, ready to go into the reduction cells to make the metal.

Hall-Héroult Process: Alumina to Aluminum. Although the original concept of the Hall-Héroult process has not changed, improvements have been made in a continuing effort to lower production costs in both equipment and materials. The ELECTROLYTIC, or smelting, process takes place in reduction cells or pots, of which there may be 1,000 or more in a modern plant. Rectangular in shape, the reduction cells are made of steel with a carbon lining. Generally, two rows of carbon anodes, or electrodes, are suspended overhead from busbars, which carry the electric power.

Cells are filled with molten cryolite maintained at a temperature of about 980° C (1,800° F). Direct electrical current is passed through the cryolite from the suspended carbon anodes to the cathodes, or bottoms of the carbon lining of the cells, and on into the collector bars, or plates, that are embedded in the bottom of the carbon lining. The energy causes a crust to form over the top of the molten cryolite. Alumina is then added to the crust from supply bins above the cells. The electric current passing through the crust drives off the oxygen atoms in the alumina, leaving the aluminum atoms in a molten state. They collect as molten aluminum at the bottoms of the cells. The oxygen atoms adhere to the carbon anodes and gradually erode them. Spent anodes are removed and replaced on a regular schedule.

The process is kept operating continuously by periodically breaking the crusts and adding alumina to the cells. At regular intervals, the molten aluminum is siphoned off from the cells into a crucible lined with high-refractory brick. It is then either transported to a holding furnace, from which are poured the various forms of ingots, or it may be alloyed before being poured into rolling ingots.

Reduction cells are placed on long lines, called potlines, that are connected electrically. The cells operate on from four to six volts; electrical current loads range from 50,000 to 150,000 amperes. Since the process requires direct current, reduction plants located in countries that produce alternating current must include rectifier stations to convert the alternating current to direct current.

A single reduction cell can produce about 900 kg (2,000 lb) of 99.5%-pure metal every 24 hours. The impurities consist of traces of silicon and iron not removed by the reduction process. A 99.99%-pure aluminum can be produced from the basic aluminum. The superpure metal is used in the petroleum, electronics, and jewelry industries; however, most aluminum today is produced in alloy forms. The range of useful alloys is constantly being increased through research.

Alloys: Aluminum to Aluminum Products. Although pure aluminum has good working and forming properties and high ductility, it has low mechanical strength. Before being used in many applications, it must be strengthened by alloying, strain HARDENING (cold working), or precipitation hardening (heat treatment).

Aluminum alloys are generally divided into two basic types, casting alloys and wrought alloys. Aluminum casting alloys most frequently contain silicon, magnesium, copper, zinc, or nickel, alone or in various combinations. Silicon improves the fluidity and castability of molten aluminum; copper and zinc harden the alloy and increase its strength; magnesium improves corrosion resistance, strength, and machinability; and nickel improves dimensional stability and high-temperature strength. The mechanical properties of aluminum casting alloys vary not only with composition but also as a function of casting conditions and subsequent heat treatment, if any. Heat-treated alloys are generally stronger and more ductile than others.

Wrought alloys are alloys that have been mechanically worked after casting. Working operations include FORGING, rolling, drawing, and extruding. Alloying elements (magnesium, silicon, copper, and others) usually make pure aluminum stronger and harder but also render it less ductile and

(Left) *Bauxite from this Jamaican deposit is mined easily and inexpensively by the open-pit, or quarrying, method. The pit extends downward and outward as the bauxite, which is always found near the surface, is loaded onto trucks and taken to docks.*

(Below) *Refined bauxite, or nearly pure alumina, is obtained as a white, crystalline powder after removal of impurities from the raw ore by means of the Bayer process.*

(Above) *Molten aluminum from the reduction cells is poured into molds to form ingots for future processing.*

(Right) *Aluminum plates and thin foils of specified dimensions are fabricated in rolling mills. Ingots are reduced in thickness and increased in width by a series of passages between pairs of hot and cold rolls.*

(Left) *Aluminum is used extensively in aircraft, such as this Boeing 747, because of its good mechanical properties, high corrosion resistance, and light weight.*

(Below) *Pots and pans are among the most useful aluminum products for the household because of the metal's nontoxic nature, compatibility with food, and excellent conductance of heat.*

more difficult to fabricate. Working and heat treatments change these alloys' structure, which in turn determines their corrosion resistance and mechanical properties.

Wrought alloys are divided into two basic classes: non-heat-treatable and heat-treatable alloys. The former rely on the hardening effect of such alloying elements as manganese, silicon, iron, and magnesium for their initial strength. They are further strengthened by various degrees of cold working. Heat-treatable alloys, which contain elements such as copper, magnesium, zinc, and silicon, are strengthened by heat treatment and artificial aging, but they may also be cold worked after an initial heat treatment.

New Uses for Aluminum. Aluminum is increasingly used to conserve energy both in home heating and cooling and in the transportation industry. Aluminum storm doors and windows, insulation backed with aluminum foil, and aluminum siding are excellent insulators. Because vehicle weight is a significant determinant of automobile gas mileage, substituting aluminum for heavier metals in cars saves fuel. Use of aluminum in the manufacture of a car has increased from an average of 38 kg (84 lb) in 1975 to 61 kg (135 lb) in 1983. Drive shafts, suspension parts, and wheels are among the latest car components to be made with aluminum.

The container and packaging industry is by far the largest user of aluminum, consuming about 30% of total U.S. production. Most of the aluminum used by the industry has gone into the production of aluminum cans. Several new packaging concepts, however, have recently shown potential for replacing the standard can and other container forms. Milk and other beverages can now be packaged in "aseptic" containers that are made of a paper-plastic film-aluminum foil lamination. Liquids in aseptic containers need not be refrigerated and can be kept for a considerable time without spoiling. The retort pouch, originally developed for military field rations, is a flexible package made of an aluminum laminate. Food contaminants cannot enter the sealed pouch, and the contents remain edible for years without refrigeration.

Production. World production of primary aluminum was estimated at 13.2 million metric tons (14.6 million U.S. tons) in 1982. The United States is the world's largest aluminum producer, followed by the USSR, Canada, Japan, and West Germany. Together, these five nations manufacture about 55% of the total world production. The United States is also the largest aluminum consumer, having used some 5.4 million metric tons (6 million U.S. tons) in 1982.

The U.S. aluminum industry consumes 1% of the nation's energy, largely in the form of electricity. The amount of electricity used per pound of metal in smelting, which accounts for about two-thirds of the industry's total energy consumption, has decreased steadily, and today the average is about 7 kW h. Aluminum can be recycled for less than 5% of the energy required for producing virgin metal. In 1982, U.S. aluminum-can recycling provided over half the aluminum used in making new cans, and recycling of aluminum scrap equaled over 30% of total aluminum production.   H. D. CHAMBLISS

Bibliography: Altenpohl, D. G., *Aluminum Viewed from Within* (1981); Graham, Ronald, *The Aluminum Industry and the Third World* (1982); Mondolfo, L. F., *Aluminum Alloys: Structure and Properties* (1976); Organization for Economic Cooperation and Development, *Problems and Prospects of the Primary Aluminum Industry* (1973) and *Industrial Adaptation in the Primary Aluminum Industry* (1976); Pampillo, C., and Biloni, H., *Aluminum Transformation Technology and Applications* (1980); Sinia, R. J., *Aluminum in Packaging* (1973); Valeton, I., *Bauxites* (1972); Varley, P. C., *The Technology of Aluminum and Its Alloys* (1970); Woods, Douglas, and Barrows, James D., *World Aluminum-Bauxite Market* (1980).

Alva, Duque de: see ALBA, FERNANDO ÁLVAREZ DE TOLEDO Y PIMENTEL, DUQUE DE.

Alvarado, Juan Bautista

Juan Bautista Alvarado, b. Feb. 14, 1809, d. July 13, 1882, was an important figure in California government and politics during the period of Mexican rule. A participant in governmental affairs from the age of 18, he led a revolt against Mexico in 1836 and served as governor, even after he had made his peace with Mexico, until 1842. He was also a major backer of the revolution in 1844–45 that made Pio Pico governor and reduced Mexico's effective control of California. While Alvarado was governor, the earliest American merchants and settlers, including John A. SUTTER, arrived there.   ELLIOTT WEST

Alvarado, Pedro de

The Spanish explorer Pedro de Alvarado, b. *c*.1485, d. July 4, 1541, was one of the key figures in the Spanish conquest of Central America.

Reaching the New World with an expedition to the Yucatán in 1518, Alvarado joined Hernán CORTÉS in the conquest of Mexico (1519–21), distinguished himself in battle, and became second in command. His harsh rule in TENOCHTITLÁN (Mexico City) led to the Aztec revolt of 1520, which forced the Spanish to evacuate the city temporarily. In 1523, Alvarado was sent on an expedition to conquer El Salvador and Guatemala, an area that then covered much of Central America. Upon the successful completion of this expedition in 1524, he became governor of Guatemala.

In 1534, Alvarado led a force over the Andes to Quito, Ecuador, then held by Francisco PIZARRO. The latter, however, bought him off for a reputed 100,000 gold pesos, and Alvarado returned to Guatemala. There he planned yet another expedition—to the South Sea islands. Before he sailed, however, he stopped off in Mexico and was tempted to join the search for the legendary Seven Golden Cities of CÍBOLA in northern Mexico. En route he participated in the Mixtón War against the Indians of Jalisco and was killed in a fall from his horse.

Bibliography: Kelly, John E., *Pedro de Alvarado, Conquistador* (1932; repr. 1971); Nicholson, Irene, *The Conquest of Mexico* (1968).

Alvarez, A.

Alfred Alvarez, b. Aug. 5, 1929, is an English poet and critic whose major work reflects his concern with extremist perceptions of contemporary life. For example, his study of suicide, *The Savage God* (1971), examines the death of poet Sylvia Plath as a paradigm of modern paranoia. *Life after Marriage* (1982) probes the present state of marriage and divorce in the society Alvarez inhabits. In *The Biggest Game in Town* (1983), the author portrays the poker champions who play in Las Vegas. *Autumn to Autumn and Selected Poems, 1953–1976* (1978) is a collection of Alvarez's poetry.

Alvarez, Luis Walter

The American physicist Luis Walter Alvarez, b. June 13, 1911, is known for his work in high-energy physics, especially for his improvements of Donald Glaser's BUBBLE CHAMBER and his discovery of atomic particles with this device, for which he received the 1968 Nobel Prize for physics. A graduate of the University of Chicago, Alvarez has been professor of physics at the University of California, Berkeley, since 1945.

Using tubular wave guides and resonant cavities, Alvarez developed (1946) the proton linear accelerator, known as LINEAC, in which 4 MeV protons from a VAN DE GRAAFF GENERATOR were ejected into a tank and accelerated to 32 MeV. In 1954 he developed the liquid-hydrogen bubble chamber and used it to identify many atomic particles, including tritium, that occur in high-energy nuclear collisions. He also discovered short-lived (10^{-23} sec) meson and baryon resonance particles, which can be detected only through decay products.   RAYMOND J. SEEGER

Álvarez Quintero, Serafín and Joaquín

The Álvarez Quintero brothers, **Serafín**, b. Mar. 26, 1871, d. Apr. 12, 1938, and **Joaquín**, b. Jan. 20, 1873, d. June 14, 1944, were Spanish dramatists whose lifelong collaboration resulted in more than 200 plays. Most were light romantic farces set in the brothers' native Andalusia. Their warm-hearted and amusing works departed from the realistic drama then popular in Madrid, and they received acclaim for nearly 40 years. Among their best-known works are the comedies *The Flowers*

(1901), *A Sunny Morning* (1905), and *The Merry Heart* (1906), as well as the uncharacteristically serious *Malvaloca* (1912).

Bibliography: Chandler, Richard E., and Schwartz, Kessel, *A New History of Spanish Literature* (1961).

Alvaro, Corrado

Corrado Alvaro, b. Apr. 15, 1895, d. June 11, 1956, was an Italian novelist and poet whose works continued the tradition of Giovanni Verga's *verismo*. His best work, *Revolt in Aspromonte* (1930; Eng. trans., 1962), depicts the hard life of Calabrian peasants. Alvaro's diary, *Quasi una vita* (Almost a Life, 1951), reflects his moral and literary concerns.   LOUIS KIBLER

alveolus: see LUNGS.

Alyssum   [uh-lis'-uhm]

Sweet alyssum, L. maritima, *flowers from late spring until fall in borders or rock crevices of gardens, window boxes, and hanging baskets. It traditionally has a pure white, fragrant flower, but the blossoms may also be clear pink or deep lavender.*

Alyssum is a genus of annual, biennial, and perennial herbs or subshrubs in the mustard family, Cruciferae. Some species of the Cruciferae genera *Lobularia* and *Aurinia* are also called alyssum. All are native to the Mediterranean region. Their foliage is generally grayish and the flowers yellow or, sometimes, white to lavender. Some dwarf forms attain a height of less than 8 cm (about 3 in), but others grow up to 23 cm (9 in) tall. The best-known species, *Aurinia saxatilis,* is commonly called goldentuft alyssum, gold dust, or rock madwort. Sweet alyssum, *L. maritima,* is a perennial.

Alzheimer's disease

First described in 1906 by the German neuropathologist Alois Alzheimer, Alzheimer's disease is a neurological disorder of the brain. Once thought rare because it was believed to be associated with the relatively rare cases of presenile dementia, which strikes persons in their 40s and 50s, it is now considered the largest single cause of senile dementia as well. Senile dementia, a condition of irreversible mental deterioration, always involves memory loss and is almost always accompanied by numerous other difficulties in mental function. Current studies suggest that up to 2 million people in the United States suffer from Alzheimer's disease, or nearly 1% of the population. A comparable percentage is likely in other developed countries with a large proportion of elderly people.

The occurrence of the disease is indicated in the brain by the growth of so-called neuritic plaque, consisting of degenerating nerve terminals and other materials, and by the appearance of fibrous structures, called the neurofibrillary tangle, within nerve cells. Such changes are observable only through autopsy, and no diagnostic test for Alzheimer's disease yet exists. One proposed cause of the growths has been the decline observed, in Alzheimer patients, in the brain's production of ACETYLCHOLINE, an important NEUROTRANSMITTER; abnormal levels of other nerve-signal transmitters are most likely also involved. Recent studies show that diseased brains also metabolize glucose at diminished levels, particularly in the

cortex's posterior parietal lobe, which integrates sensory inputs. Such changes point toward disturbances in brain-stem systems that control cortex functions in ways not yet understood. No theories have yet been confirmed as to the agents that may be involved, although research in California suggests a possible link with the controversial infectious particles called PRIONS, which are much smaller than any known virus and consist entirely of protein. Studies also indicate that susceptibility to the disease might be carried on at least two genes.

At present no cure exists for Alzheimer's disease. Injections of acetylcholine-related chemicals have been tried, but they do not seem to stimulate the brain to produce the neurotransmitter on its own. Attempts to reduce the activity of the enzyme acetylcholinesterase, which breaks down acetylcholine in the brain, have produced relative improvements in some patients but can also have toxic results.

Bibliography: Henig, Robin M., *The Myth of Senility* (1981); Roach, Marion, "Another Name for Madness," *New York Times Magazine,* Jan. 16, 1983.

AM: see AMPLITUDE MODULATION.

AMA: see AMERICAN MEDICAL ASSOCIATION.

Amadi, Elechi   [ah-mah'-dee]

Elechi Amadi, b. May 12, 1934, is a Nigerian novelist with a remarkable talent for re-creating the atmosphere of traditional African life before European colonization. An Ibo, Amadi was commissioned in the Nigerian army and resigned to take a teaching position. *The Great Ponds* (1969), generally regarded as his best work, examines the conflict between two villages in precolonial Nigeria. He has also published *Sunset in Biafra* (1973), a civil war diary, and *The Slave* (1979).

   RICHARD K. PRIEBE

Amado, Jorge   [uh-mah'-thoh, hor'-hay]

Jorge Amado, b. Aug. 10, 1912, is a contemporary Brazilian novelist. He was elected to the Brazilian Academy of Letters in 1961. He depicts life in his native state of Bahia in the early 1900s, when wealthy cacao planters dominated the land, as in *Gabriela, Clove, and Cinnamon* (1958; Eng. trans., 1962). A sympathy for the humble and downtrodden pervades his early writing. In Amado's *Dona Flor and Her Two Husbands* (1966; Eng. trans., 1969; film, 1978) his characters gain greater individuality and evoke subtler social themes. His lyricism, imagination, and humor have given him a worldwide reputation.

   MARIA ISABEL ABREU

Amalekites   [am'-uh-lek-yts]

Constant enemies of Israel in the Bible, the Amalekites were a nomadic tribe finally defeated by David. They are listed among the tribes descended from Esau (Gen. 36:12).

Amalfi   [ah-mahl'-fee]

Amalfi is a town in Salerno province of southern Italy, southeast of Naples, with a population of 6,400 (1974 est.). Built on the Gulf of Salerno and enjoying a mild climate and picturesque scenery, including that of the spectacular Amalfi Drive, the town is a fishing port and one of Italy's most famous tourist areas. Its origins are unclear, but in the 9th century Amalfi became one of the early Italian maritime republics and rivaled the power of Pisa, Genoa, and Venice. Although Amalfi rapidly declined from the 11th century on, its maritime code, the *Tavola Amalfitana,* remained influential in the Mediterranean area until the late 16th century. The town's most impressive monument is the cathedral of Sant' Andrea, begun in the 9th century and subsequently much rebuilt.

amalgam, metallic

An amalgam is an ALLOY of mercury and one or more other metals. An amalgam can also be formed with nonmetals, such as tellurium and ammonium. Silver and gold amalgams occur in nature, but most amalgams are of artificial origin. Amalgams are formed by dissolving metals in mercury. Copper, gold, and silver have to be dissolved in a solution of a mercury salt. Amalgams are used in dental work as fillings; in the manufacture of mirrors, an amalgam of one part tin and three parts mercury is applied to glass.   MERLE C. NUTT

Amalgamated Clothing and Textile Workers Union

The Amalgamated Clothing and Textile Workers Union (ACTWU) is a labor union affiliated with the American Federation of Labor and Congress of Industrial Organizations. The union represents workers who cut, sew, and measure cloth; its members also include laundry workers, dry cleaners, and retail clerks. It has shoe and textile divisions.

The ACTWU was formed in 1976 by a merger of the Amalgamated Clothing Workers of America (founded in 1914 with Sidney HILLMAN as president) and the Textile Workers Union of America (founded 1939). In 1979 the United Shoe Workers of America was absorbed. The Union had approximately 379,000 members in the United States and Canada in 1982.

Bibliography: Hardman, Jacob B. S., *The Amalgamated: Today and Tomorrow* (1939); Zaretz, Charles E., *Amalgamated Clothing Workers of America: A Study in Progressive Trade-Unionism* (1934).

Amalienburg Pavilion   [ah-mahl'-yen-burg]

The Amalienburg is the most famous of three pleasure pavilions in the park of NYMPHENBURG PALACE, on the outskirts of Munich. The pavilion, a sumptuous version of a hunting lodge, was built between 1734 and 1740 by the great rococo architect François CUVILLIÉS for Princess Amalie, wife of Elector Charles Albert of Bavaria (later Holy Roman Emperor Charles VII). Executed with consummate taste and workmanship, the Amalienburg is a brilliant interpretation of rococo architecture; it combines the expected *enfilade* (a suite of ceremonial rooms opening one into the next in a straight line) with the requirements of a hunting retreat. Amalienburg has, in the words of one architectural historian, ''an easy elegance and gossamer delicacy which makes it the supreme secular monument of the rococo.''

Bibliography: Norberg-Schultz, Christian, *Late Baroque and Rococo Architecture* (1974); Sitwell, Sacheverell, *Great Houses of Europe* (1961; repr. 1970).

Amana Society   [uh-man'-uh]

The Amana Society is a religious group in east central Iowa that is conservative in theology and pacifistic; it has a strong communal tradition. Its origins are to be found in German PIETISM of the early 1700s. Some 800 members of the group migrated to the United States in 1842, settling first in Ebenezer, N.Y., but moving later to Iowa. Initially, the members held all property in common, but in 1932 they discarded many communal practices and formed a business corporation to take over the group's farmland and other productive properties. The Amana Society continues as a religious organization, with about 700 members; the corporation engages in farming and makes kitchen appliances.   CONRAD WRIGHT

Bibliography: Perkins, William Rufus, and Wick, Barthinius, *History of the Amana Society* (1891; repr. 1975); Shambaugh, Bertha M., *Amana That Was and Amana That Is* (1932).

amaranth   [am'-uh-ranth]

Amaranth is the common name for members of a family (Amaranthaceae) of warm-region herbs, trees, and vines, especially those of the genus *Amaranthus*, often characterized by reddish pigment in the stems and leaves. Many species, including tumbleweed, *A. alba*, are troublesome weeds. Others are flowering perennials and garden ornamentals, such as love-lies-bleeding, or tasselflower, *A. caudatus*, which has crimson, chenille-textured flower spikes. *A. tricolor*—with bright green, yellow, or scarlet sometimes splotched leaves— serves as a vegetable in parts of Asia. Still other species are being studied as possible grain crops.

Love-lies-bleeding, A. caudatus, *is a species of amaranth that adds an old-fashioned air to gardens. In South Asia it is cultivated for its edible seeds.*

Amaravati   [um-ur-ah-vuh'-tee]

Amaravati, an ancient city in Andhra Pradesh state, southeast India, was the site of an important Buddhist monastery established on the south bank of the Krishna River in the eastern reaches of the Deccan Plateau. The city was a principal center of learning and Buddhist pilgrimage for more than a thousand years. Developed and sustained by generations of Andhra princes and their successors, it was the cultural and spiritual fountainhead for an extensive network of Buddhist establishments in eastern India and Ceylon. Fragmentary sculptural remains of the era of its greatest magnificence, the 2d-3d centuries AD, are now in the Government Museum of Madras, the British Museum in London, and other public collections.

DIRAH KAVORK DOHANIAN

Amarillo

Amarillo (1980 pop., 149,230) is the major metropolis of the windswept Texas Panhandle. Situated both in Randall and Potter counties (the seat of the latter), it is the center of a three-state area where beef and wheat are raised; it is also rich in oil and natural gas. Amarillo is an important producer of helium gas, and although studded with oil refineries, zinc smelters, and heavy manufactures, it is modern and attractive—a glass and concrete oasis rising from desolate plains. Its giant grain elevators and famous cattle auctions give it a Western character. The city was founded when two railroads crossed at that site in 1887. Its name, which is Spanish for ''yellow,'' refers to the color of clay in the area.

Amarna, Tell el-

Tell el-Amarna, on the east bank of the Nile about 306 km (190 mi) south of Cairo, was the capital of Egypt under the heretic king AKHENATEN (Amenhotep IV, r. c.1379–1362 BC). This 18th-dynasty ruler founded the city as the center of his monotheistic religion dedicated to the worship of the sun-god Aten. Tell el-Amarna is a misnomer, combining the name of the village Et-Tell with that of a tribe, the Beni Amran, who settled nearby approximately two centuries ago. Its ancient name was Akhetaten, meaning ''horizon of Aten.''

Akhenaten chose the site for the city and planned its layout, a record of which was carved on 14 stelae marking its boundaries, 3 of them west of the Nile. The administrative offices, the chief palace, and the great temple of Aten stood in the center of the city, flanking the main road. In this region most of the so-called Amarna tablets—diplomatic correspondence in CUNEIFORM script with rulers and vassals in western Asia—were found by chance in 1887. The site was extensively excavated (1891-92) by Sir Flinders PETRIE and by later British and German expeditions. In the crescent-shaped rocks east of the city, the Egyptians constructed tombs of the courtiers, mostly unfinished, and the tomb of the king. The tombs are famous for their lively wall reliefs, the scenes being executed in the so-called Amarna style, which radically departs from the expressive restraint of most EGYPTIAN ART. Early in his reign Tutankhamen (c.1361–1351 BC) abandoned Tell el-Amarna and restored the capital to Thebes.   I. E. S. EDWARDS

Amaryllis

The Amaryllis, H. vittatum, blooms in winter and in spring, displaying trumpet-shaped clusters of flowers. Colors range from white to various shades of pink, orange, and red.

Amaryllis is a genus of South African bulbous plants that bear large, lilylike flowers and belong to the Amaryllidaceae family. The only true species is the belladonna lily, A. belladonna, which is native to South Africa. Plant breeders have produced varieties with white to red flowers, which are grown outdoors in some warm regions of the United States.

The more common Amaryllises of horticulture, however, are species of Hippeastrum. Most are hybrids of the Peruvian H. vittatum. Single large flowers borne on 60-cm (2-ft) stems bloom in a wide variety of colors.   CHARLES L. WILSON

Amasis: see AHMOSE.

Amaterasu   [ah'-mah-tay-rah-soo]

In traditional Japanese mythology, Amaterasu was the sun goddess and the principal deity. According to the 8th-century Kojiki, the oldest Japanese book, she sprang from the left eye of Izanagi, the male of the Heavenly Pair who created Japan. Through her grandson Ninigi, Amaterasu became the ancestor of the Japanese emperors. She created three goddesses who, with the five gods created by her brother, Susa-wo-no, became the ancestors of the highest Japanese nobility.

Amateur Athletic Association

The Amateur Athletic Association (AAA), with headquarters in London, is the official organizer and regulator of amateur track-and-field athletics in England and Wales. It was the first of such national regulatory bodies. The organization sets standards for the training of amateurs, oversees all amateur meets, and conducts annual national and junior-national championships. The AAA represents Great Britain in the management of international competition as a member of the International Amateur Athletic Federation.

The AAA was formed in 1880 when 40 groups were brought together to resolve a dispute regarding separate national athletic meets. The organization was instrumental in rejecting upper-class origins as a condition of amateurism.

Amateur Athletic Union of the United States

The Amateur Athletic Union (AAU) was founded in 1888 to correct widespread problems of amateur athletes in the United States. Since 1889, it has been composed of district associations of clubs and schools, which numbered 58 in the late 1970s. Those associations encompass 300,000 volunteer workers, 372,000 registered athletes, and approximately 15 million participants. A Junior Olympics program for athletes of ages 8 through 18 is one of the AAU's most successful programs, but it also sponsors senior divisions in many sports.

With its national headquarters in Indianapolis, Ind., the AAU is the U.S. governing body for eight Olympic sports: track and field, aquatics (swimming, diving, water polo), bobsled, boxing, judo, luge, weightlifting, and wrestling. The AAU also conducts developmental programs and national and international competition in basketball, baton twirling, gymnastics, handball, horseshoe pitching, karate, powerlifting, physique, synchronized swimming, trampoline and tumbling, and volleyball.

The power of the AAU was somewhat reduced in the 1960s when federations backed by the National Collegiate Athletic Association (NCAA) disputed the AAU's authority over several individual sports. The controversy was carried all the way to the U.S. Senate, and Gen. Douglas MacArthur was named by President John F. Kennedy to mediate the dispute. The result was the lessening of some of the AAU's control, but the organization remains the stronghold and supervisor for millions of American amateur athletes who seek competition.

Since 1930 the AAU has conducted the annual poll for the Sullivan Award, which is presented to the amateur athlete who has done the most to "advance the cause of good sportsmanship." The award is given in memory of James E. Sullivan, a founder of the organization and later its secretary (1889–1906) and president (1906–14). Another prominent figure in AAU history was Dan Ferris, who was an official or a high-ranking executive for more than 70 years until his death in 1977.

Amati   (family)   [ah-mah'-tee]

Amati is the name of a family of violin makers in Cremona, Italy, in the 16th, 17th, and 18th centuries. Together with the STRADIVARI and GUARNERI families, they brought violin making to its highest levels. The Amatis were minor nobility and had long been famous for lutes, viols, and other instruments when they began to make VIOLINS, two generations before Andrea Guarneri and Antonio Stradivari, who learned their craft in the Amati workshop. All members of the Amati family were born and died in Cremona.

Andrea, c.1520–c.1611, began making violins about 1564; a few of his violins and some of his violas and cellos survive. Some sources mention a brother **Nicolo**. It is uncertain that he existed, although some bass viols carry his name. Andrea's sons **Antonio**, 1550–1638, and **Girolamo** (Geronimo), 1551–1635, were partners in the business and advanced the art of violin making to a high state. They are usually called the Amati brothers; their violins are similar but can be distinguished by experts. **Nicolo**, b. Dec. 3, 1596, d. Apr. 12, 1684, the son of Girolamo, is considered the greatest craftsman of the family. His son **Girolamo**, b. Feb. 26, 1649, d. Feb. 27, 1740, carried on the family tradition, but his violins are not equal to those of Guarneri and Stradivari, who were his contemporaries and fellow apprentices.

Virtually all surviving Amati instruments are known and catalogued; so the possibility of finding an unknown example is extremely remote. Thousands of violins by lesser makers bear Amati labels.   FARLEY HUTCHINS

Bibliography: Stoeving, Paul, Violin (1928).

See also: STRINGED INSTRUMENTS.

Amazon Highway: see TRANS-AMAZONIAN HIGHWAY.

Amazon River

The Amazon, approximately 6,450 km (4,000 mi) in length, is, after the Nile, the second longest river in the world. Flowing eastward across Brazil in the broad equatorial part of South America, it has the world's largest drainage basin, more than 7 million km² (2.7 million mi²) or nearly 5% of the world's total land area. It carries nearly 20% of the Earth's total water discharge to the ocean—more than the six next-largest rivers combined. The flow is so powerful that it perceptibly dilutes the ocean water of the Atlantic 160 km (100 mi) beyond the coastline.

The River's Course and Environment. The Amazon's headstreams form in the Peruvian Andes little more than 160 km (100 mi) from the Pacific Ocean. In 1541 the Spanish explorer Francisco de ORELLANA began European exploration here, descending the river to the Atlantic. He is variously reported to have imagined, sighted, or been attacked by female warriors. In any event, he gave the river its name, which refers to the AMAZONS of Greek mythology. Most of the river's drainage basin lies east of the Andes. It is composed of low plains less than 150 m (500 ft) above sea level, strips of floodplain alongside the channels, and broken higher ground in the upper reaches of its many tributaries, to both the north and the south.

The Amazon's mouth is an estuary, 240 km (150 mi) wide at the coast and studded with low muddy islands. These represent the beginnings of a delta formed 5,000 years ago when melting glaciers created an ocean level higher than it is today. A submerged delta built during periods of glacial maximum and low ocean level stands on the continental shelf.

The estuary's tidal range reaches 5.7 m (18.7 ft), and a tidal bore, or wave, occurs from time to time. Ocean tides are felt as far as Obidos, 960 km (600 mi) inland, where the river's discharge is an average 180,000 m³/sec (6,350,000 ft³/sec) and 283,000 m³/sec (about 10 million ft³/sec) at bank-full stage. This enormous volume is a result of the humid tropical climate that characterizes most of the basin: the mean annual temperature is 26° C (79° F); precipitation, 2,000 mm (79 in).

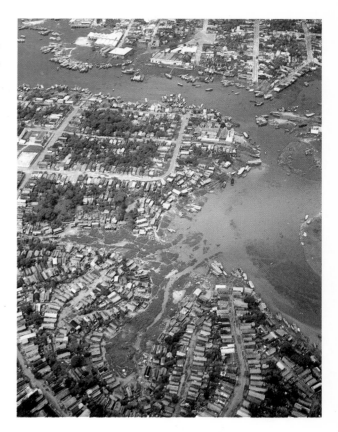

The river port of Manaus, at the Amazon's confluence with the Rio Negro, is the capital and commercial hub of the Brazilian state of Amazonas. Although the city lies more than 1,600 km (1,000 mi) upstream, its harbor is accessible to large, oceangoing vessels.

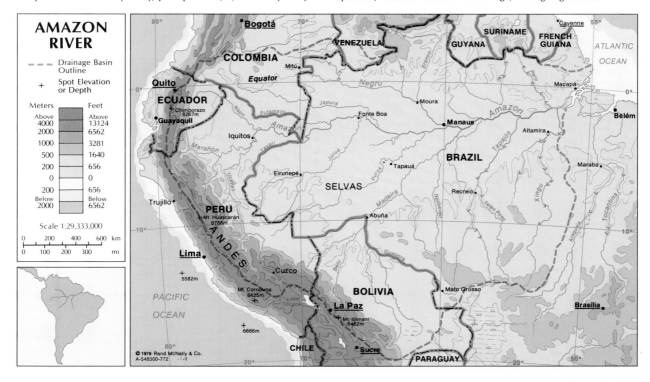

AMAZON RIVER

- - - Drainage Basin Outline

+ Spot Elevation or Depth

Meters	Feet
Above 4000	Above 13124
2000	6562
1000	3281
500	1640
200	656
0	0
200	656
Below 2000	Below 6562

Scale 1:29,333,000

0   200   400   600 km
0 100   200   300 mi

© 1979 Rand McNally & Co.
A-548300-772   -1-1

(Above) *The Amazon River meets the Rio Negro in northwestern Brazil. The Rio Negro, a major tributary, takes its dark color from acids formed by decomposing organic matter.*

(Left) *A Kalapolo Indian displays his catch on the Xingu River, a tributary of the Amazon. The vast Amazon basin covers almost 40 percent of South America.*

The climate sustains the world's largest rain forest, or SELVAS, and promotes intensive land weathering. The suspended load of silt and clay is 350 million metric tons per year (385 million U.S. tons per year) and resembles that of the midlatitude Mississippi River.

The basin's sparse population, estimated at 4 million, is concentrated on the river banks. The rain forest, largely trackless, is difficult to penetrate, and the rivers supply the one reliable means of transportation apart from air travel. The aboriginal groups that inhabit the region include slash-and-burn cultivators and fishing communities. River fish are the leading regional source of protein and number more than 2,000 species, including the flesh-eating piranha.

Economic Development. Channel depths as great as 100 m (330 ft) up to MANAUS, 1,600 km (1,000 mi) inland, permit large ships to enter. The fast midstream currents that result from this great channel size hinder upstream traffic but speed up downstream traffic. Vessels drawing 6 m (18 ft) can reach Iquitos in Peru, 3,700 km (2,300 mi) inland. Of the chief tributary rivers, the NEGRO, Japurá, Putumayo, Napo, Ucayali, Juruá, and Purus are also navigable for long distances, but parts of the Madeira are broken by rapids. Manaus was the central exporter in the main rubber boom (1880–1910), which collapsed with the competition from plantations in Southeast Asia. The region still remains one of low-intensity utilization. Commercial navigation mainly serves minor traders dealing in wild-growing products, but increased traffic is expected as the basin develops economically.   GEORGE DURY

Bibliography: Furneaux, Robin, *The Amazon: The Story of a Great River* (1969); Holland, James R., *The Amazon* (1971); St. Clair, David, *The Mighty, Mighty Amazon* (1968).

amazonite: see FELDSPAR.

Amazons

In Greek mythology, the Amazons were a race of women warriors who lived in Anatolia and fought with the Trojans against the Greeks in the TROJAN WAR. At that time, their queen was Penthesileia, who was eventually killed by the Greek hero ACHILLES. Legend had it that the Amazons dealt with men for only two reasons, procreation and battle, and that they reared only their female young. A number of Greek heroes fought against the Amazons: HERCULES had to obtain the girdle of Queen HIPPOLYTE as one of his Twelve Labors; THESEUS abducted Queen Hippolyte, who bore him a son, HIPPOLYTUS, and who led her tribe in an invasion of Attica; BELLEROPHON had to fight them and escaped with his life, presumably riding PEGASUS; DIONYSUS conquered them as part of his exploits. The Amazons were frequently depicted by artists as being in battle with men.   ROBERT E. WOLVERTON

Ambartsumian, Viktor Amazaspovich   [ahm-bart-soo-myahn', ah-mah-zahs'-poh-vich]

The Armenian astronomer Viktor Amazaspovich Ambartsumian, b. Sept. 18, 1908, is noted for his work on galactic and STELLAR EVOLUTION and for his discovery of STELLAR ASSOCIATIONS. A graduate (1928) of the University of Leningrad, Ambartsumian taught there until 1944, when he left to become professor of astrophysics at Yerevan University. The following year he founded and became director of the BYURAKAN ASTROPHYSICAL OBSERVATORY in Yerevan, Armenia. He advanced a widely accepted theory that the radio waves emitted by certain galaxies are caused by enormous explosions within the galaxies. Since 1964 he has played a major role in the scientific discussion of the possibility of communicating with extraterrestrial life.   STEVEN J. DICK

Bibliography: Ambartsumian, Viktor, *Theoretical Astrophysics*, trans. by J. B. Sykes (1958).

ambassador

An ambassador is the highest-ranking diplomatic representative of one country to another. He or she is entitled to deal directly with the king, president, or other head of state.

The earliest ambassadors were messengers sent by one monarch to another for some specific purpose. In 16th-century Europe the more important monarchs began to establish permanent embassies with one another. In recent times the general practice has been for governments to exchange ambassadors, but ambassadors no longer have the discretionary powers they possessed in earlier times, when the slowness of communications prevented them from consulting with their governments. Today the post is largely ceremonial, and decisions are made in the foreign offices or high councils of government. In the United States, ambassadorships are often given to wealthy supporters of the party in power or as rewards for political service.

After ambassador, the next-ranking diplomatic agent is a minister plenipotentiary or envoy who, like the ambassador, is entitled to communicate directly with the head of state. A third rank consists of charges d'affaires, who are accredited to the foreign minister of their host country. Diplomats of the same rank take precedence according to the length of time they have been in their posts.

Ambassadors, The

The Ambassadors (1903), Henry JAMES's favorite among his own novels, contrasts rigid New England morals with flexible French ones. A Massachusetts dowager orders her fiancé, Lambert Strether, to rescue her son, Chad Newsome, from a Parisian *femme fatale*. But the "ambassador" can only commend the woman for improving Chad's manners, and self-sacrificially he modifies his own philosophy. "Live all you can" becomes his creed, although the aging Strether's pleasures are mostly vicarious ones. *The Ambassadors* illustrates

James's celebrated "major phase" style: restricted point of view, knotty syntax, painterly impressionism, ornate imagery, and dramatic presentation of largely cerebral action.

ROBERT L. GALE

amber

Amber is a fossilized resin from trees that has lost its volatile components after millions of years of burial. One of the first substances used for decoration, it was an object of trade and barter for Baltic peoples. The ancient Greeks saw amber as hardened tears or rays of sunset.

Amber occurs as irregular masses, nodules, or drops that are transparent to translucent and have a yellow color, sometimes tinted red, orange, or brown. It may be clouded by innumerable minuscule air bubbles or contain fossilized insects or plants. Hardness is 2–3, luster resinous, and specific gravity 1.05–1.09. Softening occurs at about 150° C and melting at 250°–350° C. It was called *electrum* or *elektron* by the Greeks, who were aware of its ability to produce a static electrical charge. Of widespread occurrence, amber is particularly

Amber is an organic substance produced by a now-extinct species of coniferous tree. Its warm, golden color and soft, waxy luster obtained after polishing have resulted in its extensive use for thousands of years in elaborate carvings and jewelry. Numerous amber samples have been found that contain entrapped insects and plants.

abundant along the shores of the Baltic Sea where it is mined extensively from TERTIARY glauconite sands that are from 40 million to 60 million years old. Amber is still popular in jewelry and as a decorative material. Sometimes small pieces are fused by compression to form amberoid, which is distinguishable by parallel flow lines.

ambergris [am'-bur-gris]

Ambergris is formed in the intestines of sperm whales. When fresh, it is black, greasy, and malodorous, but after exposure to the air it hardens, turns gray, and develops a pleasant aroma. Ambergris was used in ancient times as a perfume and for its purported medicinal properties. Today it is blended with other fragrances to make perfume.

PETER L. PETRAKIS

Ambler, Eric

The prolific English novelist Eric Ambler, b. June 28, 1909, an acknowledged master of the thriller, popularized the spy story featuring the disenchanted secret agent. The well-known *A Coffin for Dimitrios* (1939) features the typical Ambler hero: a man with no heroic ambitions whose basic motive is survival in a sordid, dangerous world. Ambler has twice won (1964, 1975) the Edgar Allan Poe Award and has written more than 15 screenplays, including that for *Topkapi* (1964), based on his own *The Light of Day* (1962). *The Siege of the Villa Lipp* (1977), *The Care of Time* (1981), and *Dr. Frigo* (1982) are recent novels.

Ambonese [am'-buh-neez]

The Ambonese (Amboinese), also known as South Moluccans, live on the island of Ambon in the Moluccan (Maluku) group that is located east of Sulawesi (Celebes) and north of Timor in Indonesia. Their island is among the fabled Spice Islands that attracted Europeans to Southeast Asia in the 16th century. The Ambonese, who speak a Malayo-Polynesian language, are an ethnic mixture of Southeast Asians and Melanesian peoples of New Guinea. Their skin color is generally a darker shade of brown than is typical of most Indonesians.

The Ambonese are known to have reached Ambon in the 15th century, probably coming from the island of Ceram. A typical Ambonese village includes about 1,500 people who live in houses built on stone foundations with walls made of either woven sago leaves or plastered bamboo. Rice, sago, coconuts, bananas, and other fruits are grown on the steep hillsides. The major cash crops are cloves and nutmeg.

The Ambonese have been heavily influenced by Islam and Christianity, and many indigenous customs have disappeared. Their island population of 114,400 (1971 est.) is almost equally divided between Christians and Muslims.

DONN V. HART

Bibliography: Cooley, Frank L., *Ambonese Adat: A General Description* (1962).

Ambrose, Saint

Saint Ambrose, b. *c.*340, d. Apr. 4, 397, bishop of Milan, was one of the fathers of the Christian church. The son of a high Roman official, Ambrose was trained for government service. About 370 he was appointed Roman governor of Liguria and Aemelia; in that post his firm hand, modest demeanor, and skill as a rhetorician won him enormous popularity. When Auxentius, bishop of Milan, died in 374, a dispute arose between the Arians and Catholics over who should succeed him. While Ambrose, as governor, was trying to calm the people, a cry went up, "Ambrose for bishop!" Although he had not yet been baptized, he reluctantly accepted the office, was received into the church, and was consecrated bishop 8 days later.

Ambrose became a strong opponent of ARIANISM and paganism and vigorously asserted the independence of the church against the Roman state, making Emperor Theodosius I do public penance to atone for a massacre in 390. His greatest gift was his power as a preacher, using allegorical interpretations of Scripture and blending Christian persuasion with Stoic ethics. Among his writings were *De officiis,* a treatise on the duties of the clergy; commentaries on various books of the Bible; and possibly the Athanasian CREED. He also wrote a number of hymns and is regarded as one of the founders of Western church music. His most famous convert, Saint AUGUSTINE, studied Ambrose's preaching style and adopted much of his theology. Feast day: Dec. 7.

WARREN THOMAS SMITH

Bibliography: Dudden, F. H., *The Life and Times of Saint Ambrose,* 2 vols. (1935).

Ambrosian Library

The Ambrosian Library (Biblioteca Ambrosiana) of Milan, the first public library in Italy, was founded by Cardinal Federico Borromeo, bishop of Milan, and named for the patron saint of the city, Saint Ambrose. At its opening on Dec. 8, 1609, it contained 30,000 printed books and 12,000 manuscripts. Its holdings now include 765,000 volumes, 35,000 manuscripts, and 3,000 incunabula.

Perhaps the library's single most famous treasure is the *Codex Atlanticus,* a volume of the works of Leonardo da Vinci, containing 1,700 original drawings and manuscripts. The library is located in the old center of Milan.

COLIN STEELE

ambrotype

An ambrotype is an underexposed glass-negative photograph that appears positive when set against a black background. Glass photo plates with collodion coatings (guncotton dissolved in alcohol or ether) were invented in 1851 by Frederick Scott ARCHER, an Englishman, and were used mainly for portraiture. The FERROTYPE used collodion on varnished metal.

See also: PHOTOGRAPHY.

ambulance

An ambulance is a vehicle designed to transport the critically sick or injured to a hospital or medical center. Originally horse-drawn carts used to evacuate wounded soldiers from the battlefield, ambulances for civilians came into use only in the mid–19th century in New York City. Until the 1960s, they were minimally equipped, and ambulance personnel were trained to handle only relatively simple injuries.

In 1966, Congress created the National Highway Safety Administration, which was charged with issuing guidelines for state emergency medical systems and formulating an emergency medical technician (EMT) training program. Professional requirements for EMTs were established. Today, emergency medical transport is largely the responsibility of community fire departments (more than 7,000 EMT-PARAMEDIC programs are operated by local fire departments), augmented by an increasing number of private ambulance and municipal health department services.

All ambulances are required by federal law to carry certain basic equipment. Ambulances staffed by EMT-paramedics may be provided with the additional technical equipment necessary to render emergency medical treatment to cardiac and accident victims. These cardiac mobile units can maintain communication with an emergency-room physician by means of radio telemetry, and their personnel are trained to start intravenous solutions and administer drugs or cardiopulmonary resuscitation. To become a qualified EMT, a person must complete 81 hours of classroom and clinical instruction and pass written and practical examinations. The EMT-paramedic must complete an additional 400 to 500 hours of advanced training.   THERESA MAROUSEK

Bibliography: Portnoy, William M., *Emergency Medical Care* (1977).

amebiasis   [am-i-by'-uh-suhs]

Amebiasis is a general name for human infections caused by the amoeba *Entamoeba histolytica*. Intestinal infections alone are called amoebic DYSENTERY. Amebiasis occurs worldwide—nearly 3,000 cases were reported in the United States in a recent year—but is most prevalent in tropical regions. In some areas more than half of the population is likely to develop amebiasis at some time. The parasite is usually ingested in encysted form in contaminated food or water. Dysentery symptoms may take a week to a year or more to develop and may recur after long remissions; some people remain symptomless but act as carriers. Untreated amebiasis can lead to stomach ulcers and peritonitis, and the amoeba may be carried in the blood to the liver and cause amebic hepatitis or ulcers. Abscesses may also develop in other organs or, rarely, the brain. Several drugs are effective against amebiasis, but liver and other complications may require surgery.

Bibliography: Hunter, G. W., et al., *Tropical Medicine*, 5th ed. (1976).

Ameling, Elly   [am'-uh-ling]

Elly Ameling, b. Feb. 8, 1938, a Dutch soprano, is world renowned for her recitals of German and French songs and for her superlative interpretive gifts. She is equally at home in chamber music, orchestral concerts, operas, and oratorios. She made her U.S. recital debut at New York's Lincoln Center in 1968 and her opera debut in 1974 as Ilia in Mozart's *Idomeneo* in Washington, D.C. Contemporary works, particularly by her countrymen Bertus van Lier and Robert Heppener, are also part of her large repertoire. Ameling has won many coveted recording prizes. For her services to music the Dutch government made her Ridder in de Orde van Oranje Nassau (Knight in the Order of Orange-Nassau).   ELLA A. MALIN

Amenemhet I, King of Egypt   [ah-men-em'-het]

The Egyptian king Amenemhet I, d. 1962 BC, overthrew the Theban rulers of Egypt to found the 12th dynasty about 1991 BC. He moved his capital from Thebes to central Egypt and built many architectural monuments. A text has been found claiming to record his instructions to his son Sesostris I. The name also appears as Ammenemes.

Bibliography: Hayes, W. C., "The Middle Kingdom in Egypt," in *Cambridge Ancient History*, ed. by J. B. Bury et al., vol. 1, 2d ed. (1961).

Amenhotep I, King of Egypt   [ah-men-hoh'-tep]

Amenhotep I, king of Egypt from 1546 to 1526 BC, was the son of AHMOSE I, founder of the 18th dynasty. Amenhotep undertook military campaigns in Libya and Nubia (now Sudan), extending the boundaries of his empire. The name also appears as Amenophis.

Amenhotep II, King of Egypt

Amenhotep II was king of Egypt from 1450 to 1425 BC. His reign was marked by military exploits, particularly in Syria, where he crushed an uprising and extended Egyptian power by demanding oaths of loyalty from local rulers. His mummy was discovered in the Valley of the Kings.

Amenhotep III, King of Egypt

Amenhotep III, sometimes called "Amenhotep the Magnificent," was an Egyptian king of the 18th dynasty, who ruled from 1417 to 1379 BC. After suppressing a rebellion in Nubia (now Sudan), he reigned peacefully, devoting himself to improving relations with Egypt's neighbors and to construction. He built monuments at LUXOR and KARNAK and created an artificial lake for his wife Tiy. Reports exist of his dispatch of envoys to Babylon, Assyria, and other countries.

Bibliography: Hayes, William C., "Egypt: Internal Affairs from Tuthmosis I to the Death of Amenhotep III," in *The Cambridge Ancient History*, ed. by C. S. Edwards et al., vol. 2, 2d ed. (1962).

Amenhotep IV: see AKHENATEN.

amenorrhea   [ay-men-uh-ree'-uh]

Amenorrhea is the absence of MENSTRUATION in a mature human female. The disorder is referred to as primary in a person who has never menstruated and as secondary in a person who has menstruated. Primary amenorrhea is most often caused by disorders of the endocrine system that result in inadequate stimulation of the ovary by the female hormone estrogen. Other causes include female pseudohermaphroditism (the person has ovaries but possesses both male and female physical characteristics), malnutrition, and emotional trauma.

Secondary amenorrhea is most often caused by pregnancy and its aftermath, puerperium; adrenal-gland disorders; medication with synthetic male hormones called progestigens; malnutrition; emotional trauma; and polycystic ovaries.

The treatment of amenorrhea depends on the cause. Lack of ovulation is treated medically in most cases, but surgery may sometimes be required. Determining the cause and correcting the disorder at an early stage are essential, because in some patients the cause may be a tumor; in a few, prolonged lack of menstruation can lead to cancer of the uterus.

America

The name *America* applies to either continent of the Western Hemisphere (North America or South America), or it may refer to all the land masses in that hemisphere. America is also used as an abbreviated form of the United States of America. The name, derived from that of Italian navigator Amerigo VESPUCCI, was first used on a map in 1507 by Martin Weldseemüller.

American, The

The American (1877), an early novel by Henry JAMES, contrasts rich, unsophisticated Christopher Newman, the American, with aristocratic Madame de Bellegarde and her villainous son. Newman persuades her passive daughter Claire to marry him, but her family finds his money, though tempting, too tainted by commercialism. His Yankee directness and decency are no match for Old World matriarchies, duels, convents, and duplicities. The outcome, a thwarted romance, is hardly tragic, however; James once noted that his hero and heroine "would have made an impossible couple." Because it depicts a clash in cultural values, *The American* is often considered the first "international novel."   ROBERT L. GALE

American Academy of Arts and Letters

The American Academy of Arts and Letters, located in New York City, was created in 1904 as a subdivision of the National Institute of Arts and Letters to further the progress of American literature, music, and the arts. Its membership, limited to 50 persons at any one time, has included such notables as Aaron Copland, Ralph Ellison, Lillian Hellman, and Georgia O'Keeffe. In 1976 the academy, which granted numerous awards and scholarships, merged with its parent organization to become the American Academy and Institute of Arts and Letters.

American Academy of Arts and Sciences

After John ADAMS's suggestion in 1779 that a Boston-based society be formed for the "cultivation and promotion of Arts and Sciences" similar to Philadelphia's AMERICAN PHILOSOPHICAL SOCIETY, the Massachusetts legislature passed an act in 1780 incorporating the American Academy of Arts and Sciences. Today, approximately 2,300 elected fellows grouped in four specialty classes pursue the same broad purposes as their Revolutionary-era predecessors. The academy also conducts interdisciplinary studies of current social and intellectual issues, which are reported in the quarterly journal *Daedalus*.
                                          JEFFREY L. STURCHIO

American Academy of Dramatic Art

Founded in 1884 in New York City by Franklin Sargent as the Lyceum School of Acting, the American Academy of Dramatic Art adopted its name in 1888. The course of study is divided into two 6-month terms—the first devoted to training, the second to public performances.

American art and architecture

Two opposite forces have coexisted in American art since the establishment of the first colonies. On the one hand, American artists have been aware of their European cultural heritage and of continuing innovation in Europe; on the other hand, they have had to adapt European forms to the exigencies of their native situation. This interaction between rival forces is hardly unique to American art—all art grows within a tradition—but what distinguishes the American experience is the ambivalent attitudes brought to that tradition. To many of the early settlers, the ambivalence was clear, since so many of them were religious and political exiles. Yet despite the pressures of conscience and conviction, the European traditions persisted in memory, so that the first American art and architecture were adaptations of European styles and modes, modified to suit the colonists' urgent needs in a new and often hostile world. The conflict, aroused by traditions at once alienating and indispensable, has served as the underlying dynamic for the rise and progress of art and architecture in the United States.

AMERICAN ARCHITECTURE

In a virgin land the art form that developed most rapidly was the one for which the need was most pressing—ARCHITECTURE. The earliest extant buildings are the dwellings, meeting houses, and churches that made up the nuclei of the first colonial settlements in Virginia and Massachusetts. The dwellings, simple in plan and elevation, like the Adam Thoroughgood House, Princess Anne County, Va. (1936–40), resembled English houses of the late medieval or TUDOR STYLE. The most innovative in design were New England meeting houses, because the separatists sought to avoid any associations with the established church in England. These handsome buildings, such as the Old Ship Meeting House, Hingham, Mass. (1681), were either square or rectangular in plan and served as the focal center for northern towns.

Colonial Buildings. As the colonies flourished, more and more elaborate structures were required. By the end of the 17th century, most American public buildings were derived from Sir Christopher WREN's designs for the rebuilding of London after the Great Fire in 1666. The best were the so-called Wren Building (1695–1702) of the College of William and Mary and the Governor's Palace (1706–20), both at WILLIAMSBURG, Va. To stay the random growth of cities, the concept of URBAN PLANNING was introduced, beginning with Thomas Holme's grid plan of 1682 for Philadelphia, then second in population to London within the English-speaking world. By the middle of the 18th century, architects were designing churches, mansions, and public buildings in the current English GEORGIAN STYLE, named for King George I.

Post-Revolutionary Architecture. After the Revolutionary War, the first attempt to create a style expressive of the new republic was made by Thomas JEFFERSON. He based the design of the new capitol building at Richmond, Va., on that of a Roman temple, the MAISON CARRÉE at Nîmes, France. In so doing he laid down an American precedent of modifying an ancient building style for modern use. The Virginia State Capitol (1785–96), both building and symbol, was meant to house the kind of government envisioned by Jefferson, and the Maison Carrée became a paradigm for American public structures.

Jefferson was influential in setting forth the style of monumental NEOCLASSICISM that supplanted Georgian architecture with its taint of monarchy and colonialism. Monumental neoclassicism came to represent the new political and social entity that was the United States of America. Architects committed to neoclassicism designed not only the new CAPITOL OF THE UNITED STATES in Washington, first designed (1792) by William Thornton and Stephen Hallet, and other government buildings, but also factories, schools, banks, railroad stations, and hospitals, modernized by the frequent use of materials such as iron, concrete, and glass. The English-born Benjamin LATROBE, who began his American employment working with Jefferson on the Richmond Capitol, brought American neoclassicism to maturity. Latrobe invented new formal configurations for buildings as varied in function as the Bank of Pennsylvania (1798–1800) and the Centre Square Pump House (1800; both in Philadelphia and both destroyed) and Baltimore's Roman Catholic Cathedral (1806–21). Chosen in 1815 to supervise the rebuilding of the Washington Capitol, gutted by fire during the WAR OF 1812, Latrobe set about producing a

The Capitol at Williamsburg, Va., originally built in 1701–05, is an example of the colonial American style derived from Sir Christopher Wren. This building is a reconstruction (begun in 1927) of the original.

(Above) *The State Capitol (1785-96) at Richmond, Va., was designed by Thomas Jefferson and Charles Louis Clérisseau. It is derived from the form of a Roman temple.* (Left) *Richard Upjohn's Trinity Church (1839-46), New York, was the first Gothic Revival public building in America.*

(Above) *Henry Hobson Richardson's Marshall Field Wholesale Store (1885-87), Chicago, uses the round arches and rusticated masonry construction typical of the Romanesque revival style. Richardson's powerful architecture had a strong influence on members of the Chicago school.*

(Left) *The Wainwright Building (1890-91) was built in St. Louis by the Chicago architects Louis Sullivan and Dankmar Adler. It established the basic style for American skyscraper design through the first decade of the 20th century.*

truly monumental American architecture. In 1817 he procured the assistance of Charles BULFINCH, who had just completed Boston's Massachusetts General Hospital. Together the two men completed plans for the first major building phase of the Capitol.

Revival Styles. Latrobe and Bulfinch were the preeminent architects in the neoclassical mode. The generation following preferred Greek over Roman forms and produced the GREEK REVIVAL. A principal contribution of this style was a modification of the Greek prostyle temple for domestic and public buildings; the style's sphere of influence was rapidly extended north, south, and west. Major surviving examples are William STRICKLAND's Philadelphia Merchants' Exchange (1832-34) and Alexander Jackson DAVIS's La Grange (Lafayette) Terrace (1832-36) in New York. Up to the 1850s classical revival styles led to a homogeneity in American architecture that was never to prevail again.

Yet even before 1810, American architects, following the lead of their English contemporaries, had begun to introduce a rival style of the American scene—the GOTHIC REVIVAL. It is appropriate that this movement, which originated with the rise of ROMANTICISM in England, should have been taken over in a country where romanticism constituted the first intellectual flowering after the nation's founding. Not surprisingly, the style lent itself most naturally to church architecture. Richard UPJOHN, a prolific ecclesiastical architect, made his Trinity Church (1839-46) in New York the prototype for Gothic Revival churches. The style was also widely applied to college buildings, thus identifying those institutions with the prestigious English universities of Oxford and Cambridge.

Before the Civil War other revival styles such as the Romanesque, the Egyptian, and the Italian villa style were introduced, but with less applicability. More widespread was the cottage architecture for the middle class advocated by Andrew Jackson DOWNING. Moderate in price and well constructed, these Downing designs exploited the possibilities of wood both as construction material and as decoration.

Cast-Iron Architecture. An important development was the proliferation of industrial and commercial structures requiring extensive use of iron. At first engineers rather than architects were responsible for buildings that demanded advanced technical planning. Because cast- and wrought-iron columns replaced heavier masonry construction, it became possible to construct a lighter skeleton, use prefabricated modules, and introduce more glass into the facade. James BOGARDUS, an inventor and manufacturer of machinery, is generally credited with the development of CAST-IRON ARCHITECTURE, as demonstrated in his "Cast Iron Building" (Laing Stores; 1848) in New York. In his proposed plan for the Industrial Palace of the

New York World's Fair (1853), also called the New York Crystal Palace, and his Wanamaker Department Store in New York (*c.*1859; destroyed), he pushed this type of engineered building to the limits then possible.

After the financial crash of 1857 and the Civil War, both of which had temporarily halted building construction, Americans gravitated to a style that demonstrably symbolized the nation's rapidly increasing wealth. Mansions and government and civic buildings were designed in the Second Empire style, promoted in France by Napoleon III to bolster his imperial ambitions and exemplified by John McArthur's massive Philadelphia City Hall (1874-1901). Also of great importance was the extension of the Gothic Revival into its Victorian phase. This movement, inspired by the writings of John RUSKIN, emphasized craft and permitted the manipulation of architectural detail to create bold new effects. Two great architects, Frank FURNESS and Henry Hobson RICHARDSON, emerged from Victorian Gothic; Furness created works of idiosyncratic originality, while Richardson created a new vision within a revival style.

Richardson, the most independent and imaginative architect since Latrobe, attained prominence when he gave a new Romanesque form to Boston's Trinity Church (1872-77). Besides churches, Richardson designed numerous residences, libraries, railroad stations, civic and commercial buildings, and

(Above) *The Solomon R. Guggenheim Museum (1956–59) in New York City is one of Frank Lloyd Wright's most original buildings, employing a spiral ramp around a domed court to display the museum's collection.*

even a prison, achieving models of their kind for each type. He favored the Romanesque because he believed it expressed the pervasive energy and dynamism of the American scene. But it was his Marshall Field Wholesale Store (1885-87) in Chicago that was to prove seminal. Its rusticated masonry and multistoried arrangement of arches, reminiscent of Romanesque and expressive of Richardson's sense of ordering masses on a large scale, would be applied by his successors in Chicago to problems of skyscraper design.

Skyscraper Architecture. The skyscraper, defined here as a tall commercial structure, is America's original contribution to the history of architecture. Commercial buildings of several stories, constructed during the 1850s in Philadelphia, anticipated the skyscraper. But before it could become a reality, architects had to incorporate the elevator into the structure. This was done, beginning in the '50s in New York. Chicago, however, was the city where skyscraper design soon attained a kind of canonical perfection.

Since many of the city's commercial buildings needed to be replaced after the great fire of 1871, Chicago served as an excellent testing ground for architects. Preeminent among them was Louis SULLIVAN. He and others working in teams evolved the glass cage that became the hallmark of the CHICAGO SCHOOL OF ARCHITECTURE. William HOLABIRD and Martin Roche's Tacoma Building, Daniel H. BURNHAM and John Wellborn ROOT's Reliance Building, and Sullivan's Gage Building

(Above) *Frank Lloyd Wright's Robie House (1909) in Chicago is a prime example of his "prairie house" style. With its horizontal emphasis, simplicity of materials, and relationship to its setting, the dwelling typifies Wright's early domestic architecture.*

(Right) *The Seagram Building (1956–59), New York City, was designed by Ludwig Mies van der Rohe and Philip Johnson. An example of the glass curtain-wall design for skyscrapers, it displays the clear lines that characterize the International Style of the Bauhaus.*

are outstanding examples of the progressive stages in the sky-scraper's development.

Yet just at the time that an architecture of originality and daring was emerging in Chicago, the New York firm of McKim, Mead, and White successfully introduced a monumental Beaux-Arts style for impressive public buildings such as the Boston Public Library (1887–98). This preference for revival styles continued well into the 20th century, with interesting variations. When, for instance, New York began its campaign to raise the world's tallest buildings, their decorative systems were adapted to revival styles, culminating in the best-known Gothic skyscraper, Cass Gilbert's Woolworth Building (1913) in New York.

Modern Architecture. Far more significant than revival styles to Modern Architecture was, on the one hand, the unfolding of the brilliant indigenous talent of Frank Lloyd Wright and, on the other, the infusion of European modernism through the work of the Bauhaus architects Walter Gropius, Marcel Breuer, and Ludwig Mies van der Rohe, and the independent work of Eric Mendelsohn and Eliel Saarinen. Wright, who early in his career worked for Sullivan in Chicago, believed that the West and Midwest embodied the "real American spirit." Acting on this belief, he designed the houses that were to win him international renown. His "prairie houses" were horizontal, often of one story, with rooms merging in a continuous open space. Wright was a man of fertile imagination; before his long career ended, he designed buildings as various as the Imperial Hotel (1916–22; destroyed) in Tokyo; the Johnson Wax Company Building (1936–39) in Racine, Wis.; and New York's Guggenheim Museum (1956–59).

Wright branded as "un-American" the plans and models of the European International Style of architecture exhibited at New York's Museum of Modern Art in 1932, although European modernists had admired and borrowed from Wright's work. Furthermore, they had studied such American technical achievements as John A. Roebling's Brooklyn Bridge, Ernest Ransome's ferroconcrete cage construction for modern factories, and the midwestern multistory cylindrical grain elevators. Despite some native resistance, from the 1930s on the presence of European modernists was felt in America's urban and industrial culture. After Gropius was appointed chairman of architecture at Harvard University's Graduate School of Design in 1938, many young Americans were trained in the ideas of the German Bauhaus. After the hiatus in building produced by World War II, the influences of Wright and European modernists were balanced.

Postwar Architecture. In architecture the stark, boxy forms of European modernism by way of the Bauhaus dominated American cityscapes in the building boom following World War II. Of special importance was the use of glass curtain-wall construction for the design of large skyscrapers and other buildings, as in the United Nations complex, erected in 1947–53 under the supervision of Le Corbusier and Wallace K. Harrison, and the Seagram Building (1956–59) of Ludwig Mies van der Rohe and Philip Johnson. It was the skyscrapers of the Chicago school, however, that made possible the later use of glass curtain-wall construction. Thus in architecture as in painting, what has come to represent and even symbolize the dynamism of American life—whether it be a skyscraper or an abstract expressionist painting—is born out of both the Old World and the New.

AMERICAN SCULPTURE

Of the three arts, sculpture was the least appreciated in the United States until the 19th century. Expensive to produce because of the materials involved, sculpture seemed a form of conspicuous display and therefore wasteful for a democracy. Also, in attempting the nude in order to follow the outstanding European exemplars, American sculptors tended to run afoul of native Puritan attitudes. Sculptors also employed allegorical symbolism inherited from European humanist tradition, so that their work at first was little understood.

19th-Century Sculptors. The first sculptor of note was the Philadelphian William Rush. He started as a carver of ship figureheads, and his freestanding statues, characterized by an archaic vigor, were also executed in wood. Foreign sculptors,

Horatio Greenough's white marble George Washington *(1840), 3.6 m (12 ft), is based on the statue of the* Olympian Zeus *by Phidias. (Smithsonian Institution, Washington, D.C.)*

however, made a more favorable impression at the time. Foremost among them was Jean Antoine Houdon, who traveled to the United States in 1785 to execute portrait busts of famous Americans, in particular George Washington. Other sculptors, such as the Italians Giuseppe and Carlo Franzoni, Giovanni Andrei, and Luigi Persico, seized the opportunity to provide the marble statues required for the Capitol Building, under construction in Washington in the early 19th century.

Aspiring young Americans, wishing to work in marble and finding no one to train them at home, soon began traveling to Italy. Horatio Greenough was first in a flood tide that, between 1825 and 1875, included Hiram Powers, Thomas Crawford, William Wetmore Story, and Harriet Hosmer, the group Henry James dubbed the "white marmorean flock." Some never returned from Italy; they worked primarily in the neoclassical style and depended on Italian stonecutters to translate their clay models into marble. It was the American-based John Rogers, however—the modeler of statuettes, called Rogers Groups, in realistic, sentimental genre scenes—who first made sculpture appeal to a wide public, primarily through his large mail-order operation.

After 1855 the center of study shifted to Paris, where American sculptors observed that the French, under the Second Empire, received extensive government support. Wishing to create the same situation at home, they trained at the École des Beaux-Arts, then joined forces with those American architects executing the grandiose commissions, both private and governmental, of the day. Augustus Saint-Gaudens and Daniel Chester French were the major practitioners, working in a style infused with the academic eclecticism of the Beaux-Arts tradition. The sculpture and architecture of the World's Columbian Exposition of 1893 in Chicago epitomized the Beaux-Arts phase in the United States and set the style for public monuments for almost 40 years.

Four sculptors forged visions independent of academic eclecticism. Frederic Remington managed to express the raw energy of the American West in his bronze figures of cavalry charges, cowboys, and barroom brawls. Gutzon Borglum, re-

The bronze Trooper of the Plains *is by the American frontier sculptor Frederic Remington. The most gifted artist of the West, Remington also completed a large number of illustrations and paintings that dramatized frontier life. (Gilcrease Institute, Tulsa, Okla.)*

Alexander Calder's mobile Red Petals *(1942) is a sculptural form made of painted organic shapes, connected by wires and carefully balanced. It is kept in constant motion by air currents in the room. (Arts Club, Chicago.)*

alizing a failed dream of Michaelangelo's, took on a mountain when he cut the giant heads of four presidents into Mount Rushmore. To George Gray Barnard, Americans owe a special debt, not only for his sculpture but also for his assembly of a superb collection of medieval sculpture now housed at The Cloisters in New York. Finally, William Rimmer, isolated and unappreciated, nevertheless worked with authority and daring to produce sculpture more like Auguste Rodin's than any American contemporary.

20th-Century Sculptors. The Armory Show, exhibiting sculptures by Constantin Brancusi, Henri Matisse, and Pablo Picasso, brought American sculpture into the 20th century. From the 1920s on, the presence in the United States of such renowned European artists as Elie Nadelman, Max Ernst, Naum Gabo, and Jacques Lipschitz, and the activities of the Museum of Modern Art, further altered the course of American sculpture.

Taking a variety of approaches to both representational and nonrepresentational forms, American sculptors invented new ways to integrate form with space: John Flannagan invested animal and human shapes with a primal, dynamic energy; Joseph Cornell created miniature fantasies by arranging subtly related small objects in boxes; Alexander Calder gave the world a new sculptural form, the mobile; Louise Nevelson's large, freestanding forms restructured the experience of space; and David Smith conceived large metal sculpture for landscape and architectural sites. The visions of these sculptors, although different from one another, combined to create a significant and influential body of works. After World War II, with the emergence of younger sculptors such as Isamu Noguchi, Louise Bourgeois, and Tony Smith, sculpture in the United States became equal to the other arts.

AMERICAN PAINTING

As architecture flourished first because it was needed, so POR-TRAITURE, which was also early in demand, emerged as the first American art of PAINTING. Religious painting was unpopular in a land settled by Protestant sects, and LANDSCAPE, STILL LIFE, and GENRE PAINTING seemed too frivolous to the colonists. But images of the living, ancestor portraits to the next generation, testified to humankind's presence as a civilizing force on a wild continent. The first portraitists, working in a primitive version of the English Tudor style, were called LIMNERS (from the Old French word euminer, "to illuminate"). Limners, largely self-taught, borrowed heavily from English engravings. By 1729, however, when the Scotsman John SMIBERT brought over his casts, copies, and engravings to establish himself as a portraitist and teacher in Boston, American artists were becoming aware that their provincialism required correction.

18th-Century American Painters. The next generation produced the first major native talent in Boston's John Singleton COPLEY. His portraits, stressing surface detail and the solidity of forms, are a vivid record of such important Revolutionary figures as Paul REVERE and other prominent Boston citizens. In 1774 Copley traveled to London for further academic training. His fellow American Benjamin WEST, who had made the pilgrimage 14 years earlier, took Copley into his studio. West and Copley represent American painting coming of age; they also established a precedent for later generations of artists by immigrating to Europe.

West became painter to King George III, president of England's Royal Academy, and host to American artists seeking training and sympathetic support in a foreign city. West's portraits and his historical and religious paintings do not rank with the best of his English contemporaries, but as a catalyst among personalities West was outstanding, and his success enhanced the role of the artist in the eyes of Americans.

The third artist to achieve distinction before the 19th century was Charles Willson Peale. A moving force among artists, he helped launch America's first official painting exhibition in 1795 and was one of the founders of the nation's oldest museum, the PENNSYLVANIA ACADEMY OF THE FINE ARTS (1805) in Philadelphia. In addition, he fathered a dynasty of artists, both men and women, named for artists of the past; two of these outstanding artists were Raphaelle and Rubens Peale.

John Singleton Copley's portrait of Paul Revere *(1768) illustrates the direct painting style of one of America's earliest and most distinguished portrait painters. (Courtesy Museum of Fine Arts, Boston. Gift of Joseph W., William B., and Edward H. R. Revere.)*

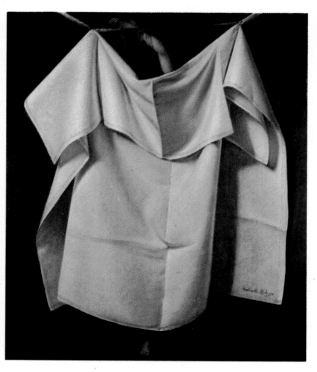

Raphaelle Peale's charming work After the Bath *was painted in 1823. The oldest son of the portraitist Charles Willson Peale, Raphaelle Peale is known best for his consummate still-life paintings. (Nelson Gallery-Atkins Museum of Fine Arts, Kansas City, Mo.)*

American Romantic Painters. After the turn of the century, a greater range of painting types was produced. Copley's and West's success with history paintings executed in England encouraged John TRUMBULL and John VANDERLYN to essay history paintings for an American audience. Neither succeeded in capturing the public's favor, but theirs was an ambitious failure, for they opened the field for other kinds of paintings besides portraiture. Raphaelle Peale, although unrecognized in his lifetime, persisted in the face of economic hardship as a sensitive painter of still life. Back from Europe, Washington ALLSTON executed highly original landscape and figure compositions that revealed a genuinely romantic imagination.

Portraits, however, continued to be the artist's mainstay. Artists of lesser ability fanned out to the edges of the frontier, accepting commissions wherever they could find them. Gilbert STUART and Thomas SULLY returned from England, where they had learned to paint with a lighter, unblended stroke, to become the fashionable portraitists of their day. But the most frequently painted face was that of the *pater patriae,* George WASHINGTON. The demand for his image continued long after his death, with Gilbert Stuart duplicating his Atheneum version (1796; Museum of Fine Arts, Boston) some 70 times and Rembrandt Peale turning out 79 "porthole" portraits of Washington (the head framed by a painted stone "porthole" or oval window).

Not long after the turn of the century the artist-actor-entrepreneur William DUNLAP was sufficiently impressed with the whole artistic enterprise to calculate that the public would welcome a book on the subject. Like Giorgio VASARI in the Renaissance, he collected anecdotes about dead artists, solicited biographies of the living, added his own critical comments, and in 1834 published America's first art history, the *History of the Rise and Progress of the Arts of Design in the United States.*

American Landscape and Genre Paintings. Two significant trends were just beginning when Dunlap's opus appeared, one in landscape painting, the other in genre painting. Land-scape emerged as the subject for expressing themes of symbolic importance in a culture where the land itself was equated with the life of the people. Thomas COLE conceived great multicanvas cycles, *The Course of Empire* (1836; New York Historical Society) and *The Voyage of Life* (1840; Munson-Williams-Proctor Institute, Utica, N.Y.), which served as sermons in paint. By the 1820s a generation of painters was forming whose vision of grandiose scenes untouched by the incursions of civilization remains as a record of a lost past. Asher B. DURAND, Thomas DOUGHTY, Frederic CHURCH, John KENSETT, Sanford Gifford, and Cole all painted in the eastern mountainous regions of the Catskills and along the Hudson River valley—hence their designation as the HUDSON RIVER SCHOOL. Martin HEADE and Fitz Hugh LANE, in works now called Luminist, depicted haunting seascapes and scenes along the coastal waters and marshes. Other artists, notably Karl DODMER and George CATLIN, set out for the West to paint the terrain and the rapidly vanishing world of the Indian.

Genre painting began to grow in popularity and importance by the 1830s. Scenes of Long Island and New England life were portrayed by William Sidney MOUNT and Eastman JOHNSON. The folkways of the Midwest river towns, to which Mark Twain would later give literary form, were charmingly preserved in the paintings of George Caleb BINGHAM.

By the 1940s genre artists such as Johnson and Bingham, as well as those aspiring to history painting, such as Emanuel LEUTZE, were traveling to Düsseldorf for further training. That small Prussian town was the home of the DÜSSELDORF AKADEMIE, where artists received a thorough grounding in figure drawing and composition. It was in Düsseldorf, after the Revolution of 1848, that Leutze posed German friends for what was to become an American national icon, *Washington Crossing the Delaware* (1851; Metropolitan Museum of Art, New York). There too, in 1848, the promising young genre painter Richard Caton WOODVILLE painted *War News from Mexico* (National Academy of Design, New York), a scene concerning America's recent victory over the Mexicans.

Painting at midcentury reflected the life of the people and received broad-based support. Genre and landscape paintings captured the rural, optimistic, and essentially innocent spirit of the times. Still lifes gave evidence of nature's bounty. Portrait commissions continued to abound, although artists had to compete with a new form of portraiture in the DAGUERREO-TYPE, the first form of PHOTOGRAPHY introduced into America in 1839–40. Well-to-do businessmen felt it their patriotic duty to patronize the arts, and the American Art Union distributed paintings by lottery to a wide public.

American Art After the Civil War. The Civil War, in art as in so many other areas of American life, constituted a watershed. At war's end the earlier vision of America as the new Eden had faded. Life in the teeming cities, the struggle to survive in the business world, and the accumulation of wealth in the hands of a few were the overriding realities. From the vulgarity of post-Civil War America, artists chose different avenues of escape. Some determined upon a period of expatriation. Others, principally Thomas EAKINS, Winslow HOMER, and Albert Pinkham RYDER, withdrew from the urban environment. Homer, who had provided illustrations of the Civil War for *Harper's Weekly Magazine*, in the 1870s favored genre scenes of a rural life that was becoming anachronistic, as depicted in *The Country School* (1871; Art Museum, St. Louis, Mo.). In the 1880s he turned to painting scenes of the sea, and until the end of his life he took as his leitmotiv the survival of humans against the elements, as in *The Wreck* (1896; Carnegie Institute, Pittsburg, Pa.). Ryder, an introverted recluse, delved into his imagination to give expression to human isolation when he painted *Moonlight Marine* (1890-99; Metropolitan Museum of Art, New York) and *The Race Track (Death on a Pale Horse)* (1890–1910; Museum of Art, Cleve-

(Above) Kindred Spirits *(1849) is often considered Asher Durand's masterpiece. Durand, a member of the Hudson River school of landscape painting, portrays its founder, Thomas Cole, and the poet William Cullen Bryant in a Catskill mountain glen. (New York Public Library.)*

(Right) *Emanuel Leutze painted the monumental* Washington Crossing the Delaware *in 1851. The work is one of the most familiar American historical paintings. (Metropolitan Museum of Art, New York.)*

(Below) *Winslow Homer's* Northeaster *(1895) captures the power of the sea. One of the most prolific 19th-century American artists, Homer favored marine painting in his later career in Maine. (Metropolitan Museum of Art, New York.)*

land, Ohio). He also found inspiration in Norse mythology. Eakins, following three years of training at the ÉCOLE DES BEAUX-ARTS, returned full of hope to his native Philadelphia. But the work he intended as his masterpiece, *The Gross Clinic* (1875; Jefferson Medical College, Philadelphia, Pa.), shocked Philadelphians; his use of a stripped male model for teaching life drawing to young ladies outraged them and led to his dismissal from the Pennsylvania Academy of the Fine Arts. Following a nervous breakdown, he resumed painting, mostly introspective portraits of friends, usually gratis. Although Homer had the support of collectors, particularly successful businessmen, Eakins and Ryder became typical of the alienated American artist who worked beyond the pale of public sympathy and private patronage.

From the time of Benjamin West, artists had traveled to Europe, but by the 1870s they interacted to a greater extent with the main line of European innovation. The centers of study shifted from London and Düsseldorf to Paris and Munich. In

Siegfried and the Rhine Maidens *(1888–91) by Albert Pinkham Ryder is based on the Wagnerian opera* Götterdämmerung. *The works of Ryder, a 19th-century romantic painter, often relate to mythological themes. (Andrew Mellon Collection, National Gallery of Art, Washington, D.C.)*

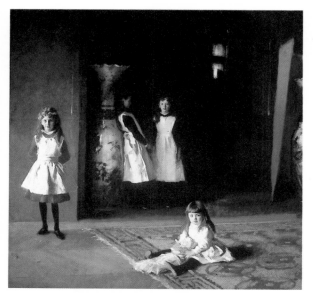

The Daughters of Edward Darley Boit, *painted in 1882 by John Singer Sargent, is one of the elegant and incisive portraits for which the artist is most admired. (Courtesy Museum of Fine Arts, Boston. Gift of the Boit Daughters in memory of their father.)*

Paris, Americans became aware, after a time lag, of *réalisme,* Gustave COURBET's revolutionary departure from the idealizing styles then in vogue. Courbet's REALISM was an attempt to get on canvas a truthful rendition of the commonly observable facts of contemporary life. Courbet and Édouard MANET were the pioneers of realism; of the artists of the past, Diego VELÁZQUEZ was the most admired. William Merritt CHASE and Frank DUVENECK, studying in Munich with the German realists, learned to paint with a loaded brush and a dark palette. John Singer SARGENT, a student of the Parisian society portraitist Émile Auguste Carolus-Durand, achieved his own facile version of realism, sometimes with remarkable success, as in his *Daughters of Edward Darley Boit* (1882; Museum of Fine Arts, Boston). Even so independent a temperament as William HARNETT, the *trompe l'oeil* (illusionist) painter of the oddments of American life, spent four years in Munich, where he refined his realist technique.

American Impressionism. IMPRESSIONISM, which can be understood as the logical end result of realism, also was taken up, after a time lag, by Americans. In 1866, Mary CASSATT arrived in Paris and was invited by Edgar DEGAS to exhibit with the impressionist circle in 1877. She formed a close friendship with Degas, and although she never became his equal as an artist, in her chosen subjects—the mother and child, or women together—she managed subtle observations. Other Americans, in Cassatt's wake, learned to master the new impressionism. Childe HASSAM, John TWACHTMAN, Julian Alden WEIR, and Sargent created works that are distinguished by a lighter palette and unblended strokes. American impressionists differ from the French in their unwillingness to dissolve objects in light so radically.

Of the artists who chose a period of expatriation, James A. McNeil WHISTLER is the most significant. Whistler was the one American cognizant of French avant-grade developments as they were occurring. Courbet befriended the younger artist and introduced him to his creed of realism. Whistler's *The White Girl* (1862; National Gallery of Art, Washington, D.C.) was rejected by the same Paris salon that rejected Manet's *Déjeuner sur l'herbe* (1863; Louvre, Paris) for similiar reasons. In time Whistler regretted the realist influence on his art and, like Sargent, Cassatt, and the French impressionists, turned to the Japanese print as a source of inspiration. By the end of his career Whistler himself constituted an avant-garde, when

he publicly propounded a theory of art for art's sake. The importance of Whistler was not recognized by Americans. Whistler created that American national icon, *Arrangement in Gray and Black No. 1, The Artist's Mother* (*Whistler's Mother;* 1872; Louvre, Paris); the French understood the work's significance and bought it for the Louvre. As a consequence of his neglect, Whistler repudiated his native culture. Asked why he never visited the United States, he explained "It has been suggested many times, but you see I find art so absolutely irritating to the people that really, I hesitate before exasperating another nation."

Whistler's stance toward the public was, of course, exceptional. Most artists painted to please and never more so than when they eschewed innovation to conform to the conservative tastes of the wealthy. Landscape painting continued in popularity, and two artists, Albert BIERSTADT and George INNESS, arrived at highly successful landscape formulas. Bierstadt's preferred subject was the West, which he portrayed on huge canvases concentrating on dramatic effects rendered with careful attention to detail, typified by *Mount Corcoran* (1875–77; Corcoran Gallery of Art, Washington, D.C.). Inness's canvases were smaller and intimate in conception, with romantic, often tree-shrouded scenes painted as though perceived through a veil, as in his *Peace and Plenty* (1865; Metropolitan Museum of Art, New York). William Morris HUNT and John LA FARGE, both members of the upper middle class, achieved styles that romanticized a modified realism. Hunt, who studied with Jean François MILLET, introduced the BARBIZON SCHOOL of painting to Americans; La Farge, after he was commissioned by Richardson to decorate the interior of Boston's Trinity Church, became the premier interior designer of his time, receiving numerous commissions for church interiors, private houses, murals, and stained glass windows.

Development of 20th-Century Painting. By the end of the 19th century, American collectors and a limited segment of the population were catching up with the understanding by some American artists of advanced trends in European painting. Mary Cassatt served the Havemeyer family with prescience when she advised them to buy impressionist works. A few Americans became early and enthusiastic patrons of artists then unappreciated by the French; thus American museums later were bequeathed important holdings of impressionist paintings. This was also the period, however, when

Americans looked nostalgically to the past. Magnates amassed collections of old-master paintings; the moneyed class and the general public were one in admiring the works of French academicians and their American counterparts.

In reaction to an art of and for the middle and upper middle classes, a group of Philadelphia artists arose who chronicled the activities of the masses. Robert HENRI, George LUKS, John SLOAN, and William GLACKENS began as artists trained to provide illustrations for newspapers and magazines. Henri was their leader, and his loosely brushed, dark realist style, as in *Laughing Child* (1907; Whitney Museum of American Art, New York), was emulated by the others. These artists, who became known as the ASHCAN SCHOOL, were the first group in America to make trenchant social comments in their work. But their adherence to a realist style placed them, by the second decade of the 20th century, in the aesthetic rear guard.

The Armory Show. Innovation continued to be a European preserve. In 1913 examples of Europe's most advanced painting and sculpture were introduced to the public by the painter Arthur B. DAVIES, who organized a large exhibition of avant-garde European and American art at the 69th Regiment Armory. This, the epochal ARMORY SHOW, brought the public and the artists abreast of European modernism on native ground. Not suprisingly, some resisted the show. One critic spoke for many when he said at a press dinner, "It was a good show, but don't do it again." Nevertheless, American

ings, for which work of the Mexican muralists José OROZCO and Diego RIVERA often provided inspiration. Another infusion of European culture came about with the appearance of works by the eminent European surrealists André BRETON, Marcel DUCHAMP, and Max ERNST. Finally, European modernism became institutionalized with the founding of the Museum of Modern Art (1929) and the Guggenheim Museum (1937), both in New York.

Abstract Expressionism. The fall of Paris in 1940, the late critic Harold ROSENBERG wrote, shut down the laboratory of the 20th century. When experimentation started up again it was in New York and among a group of artists whose work has come to be known collectively as abstract expressionism: the painters Willem DE KOONING, Adolf GOTTLIEB, Franz KLINE, Robert MOTHERWELL, Jackson POLLOCK, Mark ROTHKO, and Clyfford STILL and the sculptor David SMITH. During the Depression many of these artists had been employed by the WPA to paint in the social realist mode. But coming to maturity in the Depression, they had a sense that their survival as artists was always in doubt. Having nothing to lose, they felt free to make radical departures from previous art. "The situation was so bad that I know I felt free to try anything no matter how absurd it seemed," Gottlieb remembered. The abstract expressionists painted for each other. Some experimented with pure color, and others needed the promptings of their subconscious. Some of their nonobjective, abstract paintings were large enough to become actual environments.

(Left) Young Woman Sewing in the Garden (1886) by Mary Cassatt shows the influence of Edgar Degas. Cassatt, who lived and studied in Europe, is one of America's few impressionist painters. (Louvre, Paris).

(Below) John Sloan's Sixth Avenue and Thirtieth Street was painted in 1907 and is in a private collection. A prominent member of the Ashcan school, Sloan painted realistic scenes of life in New York City.

(Above) *James Abbott McNeill Whistler's* Arrangement in Gray and Black, No. 1: The Artist's Mother *(1872) is also known as* Whistler's Mother. *It is one of the most popular American paintings. (Louvre, Paris.)*

artists, amoung them Arthur DOVE, Marsden HARTLEY, John MARIN, Altred MAURER, Georgia O'KEEFFE, and Max WEBER incorporated modernist innovations in their art. Even before the Armory Show, Alfred STIEGLITZ had exhibited these artists, together with the European modernists, at his Photo-Secession Gallery in New York. Gertrude STEIN and her circle in Paris served as another conduit for the latest European art. Finally, five important European modernist collections, those of Albert Barnes, John Quinn, the sisters Claribel and Etta Cone, Walter Arensberg, and Lillie P. Bliss, were formed. In the 1920s and 1930s the dual currents of SOCIAL REALISM and European modernism continued to flow through American cultural life. After the onset of the Depression, private patronage for artists declined alarmingly, and the federal government assumed that role under the aegis of the WORKS PROGRESS ADMINISTRATION (WPA). Artists frequently depicted subjects of social concern, often in the form of murals for public build-

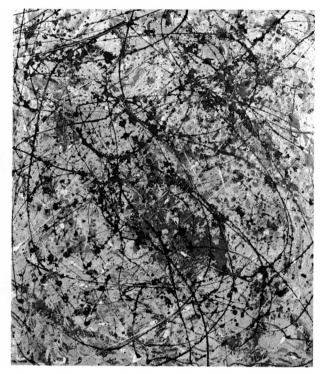

Elements of abstract expressionism had appeared in earlier paintings, and SURREALISM had made the content of the subconscious the content of its art. What made abstract expressionism distinctly American was the emphasis on the energetic large gesture essential to the creative process, and the disdain for conventional notions of beauty. By the 1950s the abstract expressionists had forged a distinctive style; for the first time since Whistler, American artists had international impact. More significantly, they achieved a new order of creation that was neither imitation nor assimilation of European art—it was a new synthesis.

Since World War II, intense interest has been shown in American art, and art historians and critics have made numerous attempts to isolate the American factor. The answer has been sought in the culture, in the lives of the artists, in the topography of the land, in the folkways of the people, in their politics, and in their particular dynamism and energy. It is too early to tell whether the generalizations borne of this search will stand. But it is certain that American artists and architects have attempted to achieve a synthesis of their culture and that of Europe.   PHOEBE LLOYD

Bibliography: Ashton, Dore, *The New York School: A Cultural Reckoning* (1972); Brown, Milton W., *American Art to 1900: Painting, Sculpture, Architecture* (1977) and *American Painting from the Armory Show to the Depression* (1955); Dunlap, William, *A History of the Rise and Progress of the Arts of Design in the United States,* 3 vols., rev. ed. (1965); Fitch, James Marston, *American Building: The Historical Forces That Shaped It,* 2d ed. (1966), rev. and enlarged (1973); Gerdts, William, and Burke, Russell, *American Still-Life Painting* (1971); Green, Samuel M., *American Art: An Historical Survey* (1966); Harris, Neil, *The Artist in American Society: The Formative Years, 1790–1860* (1966); Hitchcock, Henry-Russell, *Architecture, Nineteenth and Twentieth Centuries* (1958); Larkin, Oliver W., *Art and Life in America,* rev. and enlarged ed. (1960); McCoubrey, John W., *American Tradition in Painting* (1963); Mendelowitz, Daniel M., *A History of American Art,* 2d ed. (1970); Nochlin, Linda, *Realism* (1971); Novak, B., *American Painting of the Nineteenth Century* (1969); Wilmerding, John, *American Art* (1976).

See also: ACADEMIES OF ART; ART; ART COLLECTORS AND PATRONS; COLONIAL STYLES IN NORTH AMERICA; FOLK ART; SCULPTURE.

American Association for the Advancement of Science

Today the largest scientific organization representing all fields of science, the American Association for the Advancement of Science was founded in 1848 to further the work of scientists and to foster scientific freedom and responsibility. Its headquarters is in Washington, D.C. In 1978 it had 128,000 members, 290 member societies, 21 sections, and a staff of 135. The association holds annual conventions, publishes the weekly *Science* and the quarterly *AAAS Science Books and Films* and awards several prizes and grants to high school students.

American Association of Community and Junior Colleges

Founded in 1920, the American Association of Community and Junior Colleges coordinates programs for persons interested in the growth, practice, and acceptance of community-college education. Study programs are available in community, paralegal, and occupational education, and educational opportunities are provided for armed-forces personnel and veterans. Its headquarters is in Washington, D.C.

American Association for Higher Education

The American Association for Higher Education was founded in 1870 to sponsor conferences, publications, and research projects about issues concerning higher education. Its headquarters is in Washington, D.C. It publishes several bulletins and occasional reports.

American Association of University Professors

The American Association of University Professors, founded in 1915, is the professional organization of college teachers. Its headquarters is in Washington, D.C. In 1979 it had 2,047

(Above) *Jackson Pollock's* Reflection of the Great Bear *(1947) is a work of the "gestural" wing of Abstract Expressionism. (Stedelijk Museum, Amsterdam)* (Below) *Jasper John's* Flag on an Orange Field *(1957) is an example of pop art, which emerged in the late 1950s in reaction to abstract expressionism. (Wallraf-Richartz Museum, Cologne.)*

chapters and 69,400 members. The AAUP Statement on Academic Freedom and Tenure has served in the United States as the established definition of what is meant by academic freedom. The organization investigates claims of violations of freedom and maintains a list of censured institutions. It has promoted job security, economic welfare, and intellectual freedom for professors. In recent years AAUP chapters have acted as collective bargaining agents.

American Association of University Women

Established in 1882 in Boston, the American Association of University Women (AAUW) is an organization of women graduates of accredited colleges. The AAUW has worked for woman suffrage, equality in pay, the election and appointment of women to public office, and equality and justice for women in all areas. Fellowships are granted for undergraduate and graduate work as well as for dissertation and postdoctoral research. In 1982, about 190,000 women were members in more than 1,950 local branches in the 50 states, the District of Columbia, Guam, and Puerto Rico.

American Astronomical Society

The American Astronomical Society was founded in 1899 by Simon NEWCOMB to encourage the advancement of astronomy and closely related branches of science. Its headquarters is in Washington, D.C. In 1982 it had 3,800 members. The society has specialized divisions in high energy astrophysics, solar physics, planetary sciences, and dynamical astronomy. It publishes the semimonthly *Astrophysical Journal* and the quarterly *Bulletin of the American Astronomical Society*.

American Automobile Association

The American Automobile Association (AAA) was founded in 1902 to coordinate the activities of various local organizations of motorists. It has become a federation of local automobile clubs, with all states represented and a combined membership of about 22 million (1982). Its headquarters is in Falls Church, Va. The AAA promotes highway improvement and supplies travel information and assistance, legal aid, and emergency road service for its members.   JOHN B. RAE

American Ballet Theatre

American Ballet Theatre (ABT) is one of the two classical ballet companies in the United States to have achieved worldwide renown, the other being New York City Ballet. ABT was founded in 1940—as Ballet Theatre, its present name dating only from 1957—by Richard Pleasant and Lucia CHASE. Chase, the company's chief financial support and codirector, with scenic designer Oliver Smith, for more than 25 years, retired in 1980. She was replaced by Mikhail BARYSHNIKOV. From the beginning the company primarily has been a showcase for a succession of visiting artists, including distinguished choreographers as well as star dancers. Although the choreographer Antony TUDOR has been with ABT (with a few interruptions) from the start, and although such star dancers as Nora KAYE and John Kriza spent most of their careers with ABT, Tudor has been an infrequent creator, and the loyalty of Kaye and Kriza has proved exceptional. Consequently, the character of the company has remained both eclectic and unstable. Most of the outstanding original ballets in ABT's repertoire were created between 1942 and 1947: Tudor's *Pillar of Fire* (1942) and *Romeo and Juliet* (1943), Jerome Robbins's *Fancy Free* (1944), and George Balanchine's *Theme and Variations* (1947). Since 1965 the company has specialized in the presentation of evening-length classics: *La Sylphide* (1965), *Swan Lake* (1967), *Giselle* (1968), *Coppélia* (1968), *Raymonda* (1975), and *The Sleeping Beauty* (1976). An exception to this trend is Twyla THARP's brilliant and original *Push Comes to Shove* (1976). Among the notable dancers who have appeared with ABT are Alicia Alonso, Mikhail Baryshnikov, Erik Bruhn, Fernando Bujones, Anton Dolin, Anthony Dowell, André Eglevsky, Carla Fracci, Cynthia Gregory, Gelsey Kirkland, Na-

talia Makarova, Ivan Nagy, Rudolf Nureyev, Lupe Serrano, Maria Tallchief, and Igor Youskevitch. ABT, which has been seen frequently in Europe and has visited the USSR, is the only major ballet company to tour the United States annually.
                                                    DALE HARRIS

Bibliography: Barnes, Clive, *Inside American Ballet Theatre* (1977); Payne, Charles, *The American Ballet Theatre* (1978).

American Bankers Association

The American Bankers Association, founded in 1875, endeavors to promote "the general welfare and usefulness of banks." Through its divisions, corresponding to the division of banks into national, state, mortgage, and savings institutions, the association disseminates to bankers the latest information on activities in their field. It publishes the monthly journal *Banking* and other bulletins, conducts educational and training programs for bankers and bank employees through such schools as the Stonier Graduate School of Banking and the American Institute of Banking, and sponsors symposia and conferences. Its membership includes about 91 percent of U.S. commercial banks.

American Bar Association

The American Bar Association (ABA), founded in 1878, is the largest professional association of U.S. lawyers, with members from all states. Along with promoting social and professional activities, the ABA helps to maintain high standards within the legal profession. The ABA also seeks to advance the practice of law and to promote the administration of justice.

The association has been influential in securing uniform laws and judicial decisions throughout the 50 states, and in approving candidates for judicial posts. Much of its work is accomplished by its more than 25 committees on the legal aspects of a broad range of subjects such as legal education and maritime activity. The ABA has its headquarters in Chicago, where it publishes the *American Bar Association Journal* and the *American Bar News*. Its membership in 1982 was more than 280,000.

American Book Awards: see NATIONAL BOOK AWARDS.

American Broadcasting Company: see RADIO AND TELEVISION BROADCASTING.

American Cancer Society

The American Cancer Society, founded in 1913, is a national voluntary agency of physicians and laymen. It awards grants for cancer research, provides information to the public about detection, treatment, and prevention of cancer, and provides special services to cancer patients. In 1982 its 2,500,000 volunteers raised nearly $180 million through its public fund drives.

American Chemical Society

The American Chemical Society, established in New York City in April 1876, is an educational and professional society for chemists and chemical engineers. With about 122,000 members, the ACS sponsors numerous activities designed to foster the cultivation and diffusion of chemical knowledge in all areas of American society.   JEFFREY L. STURCHIO

American Civil Liberties Union

The American Civil Liberties Union (ACLU) is an organization dedicated to the protection of constitutional rights and liberties in the United States. It was founded in 1920 by a group of civil libertarians including Jane ADDAMS, Helen KELLER, Norman THOMAS, Morris Hillquit, and Roger Baldwin, who served as its executive director for 30 years.

The ACLU operates by providing legal counsel in cases involving civil liberties. It has been active in cases relating to academic freedom, separation of church and state, the right to privacy, due process of law, freedom of speech, other freedoms guaranteed in the Bill of Rights, electoral reapportionment, and desegregation. It has opposed capital punishment, censorship, and loyalty oaths. Nearly every important civil rights or liberties case arising in the United States since 1920 has involved the ACLU, either directly or through the filing of an amicus curiae brief. In addition to engaging in litigation, the ACLU issues public statements, presents testimony before legislative committees, conducts educational programs, and publishes pamphlets and a monthly newspaper.

In 1978 the ACLU was torn with internal conflict when its leadership supported the right of a group of American Nazis to demonstrate in the streets of Skokie, a predominantly Jewish suburb of Chicago. RITA J. IMMERMAN

Bibliography: Habenstreit, Barbara, *Eternal Vigilance: The American Civil Liberties Union in Action* (1971); Johnson, Donald O., *The Challenge to American Freedoms: World War I and the Rise of the American Civil Liberties Union* (1963); Lamson, Peggy, *Roger Baldwin, Founder of the American Civil Liberties Union* (1976); McIlhany, William H., *The ACLU on Trial* (1976); Markmann, Charles L., *The Noblest Cry: A History of the American Civil Liberties Union* (1965).

American Colonization Society

The American Colonization Society, organized on Dec. 28, 1816, sought to settle free American blacks in Africa. In 1822 it established the colony of Liberia, to which 2,638 blacks migrated during the next decade. The society won support from many clergy as well as from some leading free blacks who believed that blacks would never receive just treatment in America. Most free blacks, however, opposed the scheme because they believed that its promoters were primarily interested in removing the threat posed to the institution of slavery by the presence of free blacks. They were also repelled by the society's racist arguments, which characterized them as an inferior, degraded class that should be removed from the United States. The society continued its efforts into the 20th century, although it was never successful in convincing large numbers of blacks to emigrate to Africa. RONALD L. LEWIS

Bibliography: Staudenraus, Philip J., *The African Colonization Movement* (1961).

American Council on Education

The American Council on Education was founded in 1918 to coordinate the activities of U.S. educational associations and institutions. It now has 1,386 institutions and 176 organizations as members. The headquarters is in Washington, D.C. The council publishes a weekly bulletin and quarterly reports and is concerned with the development of leaders for educational institutions, support of education, and international communication among educators.

American Council of Learned Societies

The American Council of Learned Societies was founded in 1919 to promote research in humanistic studies. Its headquarters is in New York City. Comprising 42 national scholarly organizations in the humanities and social sciences, it offers fellowships and grants for study and research and represents American scholars in the humanities at national and international meetings. It also promotes American studies programs in European and western Pacific countries and carries on scholarly exchange with the USSR, the People's Republic of China, and Eastern European countries.

American Dance Festival

The American Dance Festival was founded in 1934 at Bennington College in Vermont as a school, a summer residence for modern-dance choreographers and their companies, and a performing outlet for new dances. Since its inception the festival has presented premieres of more than 200 dances, some of them masterpieces, and its faculty over the years has included almost every important modern dancer. The festival was discontinued in 1942 because of World War II, then rees-

tablished at Connecticut College in 1948. In 1978 it was moved to Duke University in North Carolina.
ROBERT J. PIERCE

Bibliography: Borek, Tom, "The Connecticut College American Dance Festival, 1948-1972," *Dance Perspectives #50* (1972).

American Dental Association

The American Dental Association (ADA) is the major professional society of dentists in the United States. It was founded in 1859 to represent the dental profession, promote the art and science of DENTISTRY, and encourage public health. The association's headquarters is in Chicago. Fully privileged membership is restricted to licensed dentists who hold a doctorate or equivalent degree and who observe the association's principles of ethics. Membership in 1979 was 132,000.

American Dream, An

Norman MAILER's fourth full-length novel, *An American Dream* (1965), is considered a comic masterpiece by some critics; others are repelled by its perverse sexuality and obsession with violence. Through the experiences of the hero, Stephen Rojack, Mailer explores sex, violence, and death in the United States, but any realism is quickly undercut by the author's powerful displays of fantasy and verbal magic. Mailer exploits clichés of a national ideal and archetypes of the American hero in order to create a parodic and highly controversial allegory of contemporary life. ERIC J. SUNDQUIST

American Educational Theatre Association

The American Theatre Association, so named since 1972, was founded in 1936 as the American Educational Theatre Association to promote educational theater programs in the United States. It develops materials for use by children's, school, and community theaters; promotes touring groups, theater for the armed forces, and educational radio and television; and maintains a placement service for teachers and students of drama. The ATA is now based in Washington, D.C.

American English: see ENGLISH LANGUAGE.

American Farm Bureau Federation

The American Farm Bureau Federation is a federation of county farm organizations founded in 1919 to "promote, protect and represent the business, economic, social, and educational interests of the farmers of the nation." It had about 3 million members in 1980. The federation developed from local farm bureaus formed in conjunction with the county agricultural agent plan. Farm Bureau agents, many of whom were employed by the Agricultural Extension Service, had the task of demonstrating improved farming methods to farmers. Their efforts led to the growth of county farm bureaus. The first state federation of county farm bureaus was set up in Missouri in 1915; in 1920 the new national organization opened an office in Washington, D.C., to lobby for the passage of legislation favorable to the federation.

The federation's policies have tended to be conservative. Leaders have favored flexible price supports and a minimum of government interference and control. They have promoted soil and water conservation, rural electrification and roads, and rural education. For many years the federation has been prominent in urging the development of farmer cooperatives. Membership is on a family basis.

Bibliography: Campbell, C., *The Farm Bureau and the New Deal* (1962).

American Federation of Labor and Congress of Industrial Organizations

The American Federation of Labor and Congress of Industrial Organizations (AFL-CIO) is a national federation of labor unions in the United States. It was formed in 1955 by the merger of the AFL, an organization composed primarily of craft unions founded in 1886, and the CIO, a federation of industrial unions founded in 1938. (Craft unions organize workers by trades—bricklayers may form one union, carpenters another. Industrial unions enroll members from an entire industry regardless of trade or level of skill, as in the automobile, steel, or chemical industry.)

The CIO was first formed within the AFL as the Committee for Industrial Organization in 1935; its mission was to organize workers in mass-production industries, which had few unions at that time. In 1938 the CIO was expelled from the AFL and became the Congress of Industrial Organizations. The conflict between the two federations was largely over whether the mass-production industries were to be organized along industrial or along craft lines. The leadership of the CIO included John L. LEWIS of the UNITED MINE WORKERS, David DUBINSKY of the INTERNATIONAL LADIES' GARMENT WORKERS UNION, Sidney HILLMAN of the AMALGAMATED CLOTHING AND TEXTILE WORKERS UNION, and Charles Howard of the INTERNATIONAL TYPOGRAPHICAL UNION.

By 1955, when the two federations merged into the AFL-CIO, the original divisive issue had lost much of its force. A need was felt for unity in the face of antiunion legislation and a slowdown in union growth.

In 1983 the AFL-CIO comprised 98 national and international union affiliates, together with 740 local central bodies, 50 state central bodies (including Puerto Rico, Panama, and Guam), and 8 trade and industrial union departments. The federation membership was 14.2 million in 1983. The state and local bodies are smaller federations made up of locals of the AFL-CIO national unions. The trade and industrial departments are groupings of national unions with interests in a particular industry or field, such as the metal or building trades. They coordinate the activities of affiliates in such matters as organizing, collective bargaining, influencing legislation, and carrying on public relations and various research activities.

The AFL-CIO acts as the political and legislative voice of the trade union movement. It seeks to influence legislation by helping political candidates who are favorable to its aims and by lobbying in Congress and in state legislatures. It maintains a staff of researchers, social insurance experts, lawyers, public relations officers, and specialists in fields ranging from civil rights to veterans' affairs. The AFL-CIO's chief governing body is the executive council, composed of the president, the secretary-treasurer, and 33 vice-presidents. Questions of general policy may be referred to a general board made up of the executive council, one principal official from each of the national and international unions, and one official from each of the trade and industrial union departments.

Major unions not affiliated with the AFL-CIO include the TEAMSTERS, expelled in 1957 on grounds of corruption, and the UNITED MINE WORKERS, which withdrew voluntarily. The UNITED AUTO WORKERS, which had also withdrawn, reaffiliated in 1981. Other unions have never affiliated.

George MEANY, who had served as president of the AFL-CIO since its merger in 1955, stepped down in November 1979. He was succeeded by Lane KIRKLAND, previously the secretary-treasurer.   JACK BARBASH

Bibliography: Barbash, Jack, *American Unions* (1967); Bernstein, Irving, *The Turbulent Years* (1970); Galenson, Walter, *The CIO Challenge to the AFL* (1960); Taft, Philip, *The A. F. of L.*, 2 vols. (1957–59; repr. 1970).

See also: LABOR UNION.

American Federation of Musicians

The American Federation of Musicians (AFM) is a labor union of performing and recording musicians, affiliated with the American Federation of Labor and Congress of Industrial Organizations. It was founded in 1896. Through much of its history the AFM has been faced with competition from other media that threatened its members' livelihood—from military bands and amateur musicians to radio broadcasting and the phonograph. The passing of vaudeville and of silent movies, with their live-music accompaniment, put many theater musicians out of work. Under James C. Petrillo, its president from 1940 to 1958, the union tried to force radio stations to hire standby musicians when they used recorded music, but was unsuccessful. Major strikes in 1944 and 1948 resulted in contracts with the film and record industries that allowed the union to collect royalties on recordings made by its members. In the early 1980s the AFM reported approximately 300,000 members in 600 local unions.

Bibliography: Leiter, Robert D., *The Musicians and Petrillo* (1953; repr. 1975).

American Federation of State, County, and Municipal Employees

The American Federation of State, County, and Municipal Employees (AFSCME) is a labor union representing local and state government workers, as well as clerical workers in some private institutions. Founded in 1936, it is affiliated with the AFL-CIO. Public-employee associations were formed in several states in the early 20th century. The Wisconsin State Administrative Employees Association was a forerunner of the present union. It faced jurisdictional competition, however, from the American Federation of Government Employees. When the AFL granted the AFSCME its charter in 1936, the rivalry ended. The union experienced rapid growth after World War II, in a period when other unions either stopped growing or lost members. It has worked to repeal state laws that restrict collective bargaining and prohibit strikes by government employees. In 1983 the AFSCME had approximately 1,200,000 members in 3,000 local unions.

American Federation of Teachers

The American Federation of Teachers (AFT) is a teachers' union within the AFL-CIO. Founded in 1916 with the aid of the philosopher John Dewey, its headquarters is in Washington, D.C. It grew slowly at first, with only 60,000 members in 1960. Growth accelerated in 1961 after an affiliate became the bargaining agent for New York City public school teachers. In the early 1980s the union had 2,100 locals and approximately 580,000 members. The AFT integrated its southern locals in 1956 and in the late 1960s began organizing among college professors.

American Film Institute

Founded in June 1967 with combined federal and private support, the American Film Institute, located in Washington, D.C., attempts to collect and document, in collaboration with the Library of Congress, every film made in America since 1893. It also supports young filmmakers. The institute's annual Life Achievement Award, established in 1973, has honored such film greats as Bette DAVIS, John FORD, and Orson WELLES.

American foxhound

The American foxhound was developed from English foxhounds imported during the 17th century. The breed is used for the sport of fox hunting.

The American foxhound is a medium-sized, short-coated breed of hound that stands 55–63 cm (21–25 in) at the shoulder and weighs 27–32 kg (60–70 lb). Its coat is usually black and tan on a white body, but any color is permitted in breed contests. The breed is one of the rarest in the United States; only a few dozen are registered annually with the American Kennel Club. However, it is believed that large numbers of unregistered dogs are maintained in fox-hunting packs.

The American breed has a distinguished history and can be traced to packs imported from England, France, and Ireland. The earliest known pack was brought to Maryland in 1650. These early imports were used to hunt the gray fox, but to cope with the faster English red fox—introduced to the colonies in the early 1700s—American foxhounds were interbred with other hound strains imported from France and Ireland. George Washington was among the importers.

JOHN MANDEVILLE

Bibliography: Hart, Ernest H., *How to Raise and Train an American Foxhound* (1967); Moore, Daphne, *Foxhounds* (1981).

American Friends Service Committee

The American Friends Service Committee, a Quaker organization for social service, was formed in 1917 principally to carry out relief programs in war-ravaged areas of Europe and to arrange for its members and other conscientious objectors to replace their required military service with alternative contributions. Since World War I, the committee has participated in national and international humanitarian programs of all kinds and was particularly active during the Korean and Vietnam wars. In 1947 it shared the Nobel Peace Prize with its English counterpart, the Service Council of the British Society of Friends.

Bibliography: Weisbord, Marion, *Some Form of Peace: The Story of the American Friends Service Committee at Home and Abroad* (1966).

American Fur Company

At the peak of its influence in the early 19th century, the American Fur Company was the wealthiest fur-trading firm in the United States. It contributed to the economic development of the West, and the MOUNTAIN MEN it employed made important contributions to western exploration. Formed in 1808 by the German immigrant John Jacob Astor (see ASTOR family), the company founded the trading post of Astoria at the mouth of the Columbia River in 1811, and Astor's employees developed an overland route to the Pacific.

Astor was forced to sell Astoria to the NORTH WEST COMPANY of Canada during the War of 1812. He then concentrated on the upper Mississippi River valley until the 1820s when he bought out competitors, allied himself with the Columbia Fur Company, and directed his immense resources farther west.

Soon after founding Fort McKenzie among the feared Blackfoot Indians on the upper Missouri River, the company dominated the region and then began a bitter competition with the Rocky Mountain Fur Company farther south. Astor sold out his interest in 1834. Within a few years much of the region's furs had been depleted. His successors operated mainly from trading posts on the Great Plains until the American Fur Company sold out to the North Western Fur Company in 1864.

ELLIOTT WEST

Bibliography: Chittenden, Hiram M., *The American Fur Trade of the Far West* (1902; repr. 1954); Franchere, Gabriel, *Adventure at Astoria, Eighteen Ten to Eighteen Fourteen,* trans. by Hoyt C. Franchere (1967); Lavender, David, *The First in the Wilderness* (1964).

American Geophysical Union

The American Geophysical Union (AGU) was established in 1919 by the National Research Council as the U.S. National Committee for the International Union of Geodesy and Geophysics. Today the 14,000-member AGU promotes research in geodesy, geophysics, and related areas through a program of visiting scholars, professional prizes, and research journals such as the *Journal of Geophysical Research.*

JEFFREY L. STURCHIO

American Heart Association

The American Heart Association (AHA) is a charitable organization established in 1924 to combat diseases of the heart and blood vessels, which are the leading causes of death in the United States.

The association supports scientific investigations with research grants, promotes detection programs to identify persons who are at risk, and conducts educational programs for medical professionals and for the general public. The AHA is financed entirely by contributions, obtained mainly through its Heart Fund drives.

American Historical Association

The American Historical Association, founded in 1884, is a society of approximately 14,500 academic historians and others interested in historical studies. The association holds an annual convention and publishes the *American Historical Review,* a journal that contains scholarly articles and reviews.

American history: see UNITED STATES, HISTORY OF THE.

American Independent party

The American Independent party nominated George WALLACE as a third major candidate for president of the United States in 1968. Wallace, nationally known for his racist positions and antiintegration activities as governor of Alabama, had widespread and enthusiastic support from white lower-middle-class voters in his presidential bid.

Wallace ran a populist campaign, proclaiming the superiority of the average man over the experts and intellectuals and stressing states' rights, increased defense spending, Americanism, support for law enforcement agencies at all government levels, and decreased federal expenditures for many domestic programs. The party candidate for vice-president was the retired Air Force general Curtis E. LeMay, who was personally selected by Wallace.

The American Independent party did not expect to win the election. It did hope, however, to get enough votes in the electoral college to require one of the major parties to make concessions to it in return for support. The party polled 9.9 million votes, or about 13.5 percent of the popular vote—the highest vote ever received by a third party—and won 45 electoral votes from Alabama, Arkansas, Georgia, Louisiana, and Mississippi. This was not enough, however, to achieve the hoped-for deadlock in the electoral college.

In 1969, Wallace supporters reorganized as the American party. In 1972, however, after Wallace ruled out a third-party race, John G. Schmitz ran for president, winning 1% of the popular vote. The party split in 1976; in 1980 it presented no national candidates.

RITA J. IMMERMAN

Bibliography: Mazmanian, D. A., *Third Parties in Presidential Elections* (1974); Schlesinger, A., Jr., ed., *A History of U.S. Political Parties,* 4 vols. (1973); White, T. H., *The Making of the President, 1968* (1969).

American Indian Movement

The American Indian Movement (AIM) is an activist Indian group concerned with the civil rights of American Indians. It was formed in 1968 in Minneapolis, Minn. The names of the actual founders of the organization remain unknown, but Dennis Banks, Clyde Bellecourt, and George Miller (Ojibwa Indians) were prominent in its formation. The group was initially organized to deal with discriminatory practices of the police in the arrest of Indians in Minneapolis and Saint Paul. The appeal of the social movement quickly spread to other urban areas in the United States and Canada, where chapters of AIM were formed.

In November 1972, AIM was instrumental in the week-long occupation by Indians of the Bureau of Indian Affairs building in Washington, D.C. Early in 1973 the group's 71-day take-over of WOUNDED KNEE, an Oglala Sioux hamlet on the Pine Ridge reservation in South Dakota, attracted worldwide attention.

Although largely an urban phenomenon that arose in response to racist attitudes in urban ghettos, AIM has also become involved in tribal affairs on Indian reservations, where some chapters now operate. Many tribal peoples disclaim affiliation with the movement, which has been accused of provoking confrontation and of usurping funds from church groups in its demands for reparations.

Recently AIM has established "survival schools" in many urban areas. It has also sponsored international treaty conferences on several Lakota Sioux reservations, resulting in the 1977 International Treaty Conference with the United Nations in Geneva, Switzerland.

In addition to being a social activist movement, the group claims to be oriented toward native religion. Members are not considered bona fide until they have participated in the SUN DANCE ritual on the Pine Ridge reservation, and currently AIM is often cited as a spiritual movement. BEA MEDICINE

American Indian schools: see INDIAN SCHOOLS, AMERICAN.

American Indians: see INDIANS, AMERICAN.

American Institute of Aeronautics and Astronautics

The American Institute of Aeronautics and Astronautics (AIAA) is the main professional organization of aerospace engineers, scientists, and managers in the United States. It is the U.S. representative to the International Astronautical Federation and publishes several technical journals. Formed in 1963 by the merger of the American Rocket Society and the Institute of Aerospace Sciences, the AIAA has 26,000 members. The headquarters is located in New York City.

DAVID DOOLING

American Institute of Architects

The American Institute of Architects (AIA) was founded in New York in 1857 as a club where architects could discuss the profession in a genteel atmosphere. Since 1898 the AIA has had its headquarters in Washington, D.C. For many years it was housed in the Octagon, a historic building (1798-1800) designed by William Thornton, a doctor turned architect. The Octagon had served as a temporary WHITE HOUSE for James and Dolly MADISON in the winter of 1814-15. In 1973 the AIA moved to a new building designed by The Architects Collaborative.

The AIA, as a policy-making body, exists "to serve the needs of, and improve the capability of, the nation's architects and to be of service to the safety and welfare of the public." The institute sponsors educational programs at all levels and presents annual awards for excellence of design and execution. JAMES M. FRANCIS

Bibliography: Saylor, Henry H., *The A.I.A.'s First Hundred Years* (1957).

American Institute of Biological Sciences

The American Institute of Biological Sciences (AIBS), established in 1947, is a federation of scientific societies, professional associations, and science museums with interests in the life sciences. The 10,000 members (1977) of the AIBS are concerned with coordinating efforts among investigators in the biological sciences and with promoting the relationships between biology and other areas of inquiry. The AIBS publishes the monthly *BioScience*, provides advisory services to government agencies, and plays an active role in the improvement of biological science curricula in American educational institutions. JEFFREY L. STURCHIO

American Institute of Chemists

The American Institute of Chemists was founded in 1923 by 33 professional chemists in the New York area to foster the professional interests of chemists and chemical engineers. Headquartered in Washington, D.C., it had 5,200 fellows, members, and associates and a staff of three in 1978. The institute, which has 12 committees, holds annual conventions. It awards a gold medal and publishes a bimonthly journal, *The Chemist*, and a newsletter, *The Chemist News*.

American Institute of Physics

The American Institute of Physics (AIP), founded in 1931, is a federation of nine national physical societies and affiliated organizations interested in physics. From its New York City headquarters, the AIP administers educational and informational programs aimed at advancing and diffusing knowledge of physics and its applications. Among these activities are an active Center for the History of Physics and the publication of many journals, including *Journal of Chemical Physics, Journal of Applied Physics,* and *Physics Today.* JEFFREY L. STURCHIO

American Kennel Club

The American Kennel Club (AKC), founded in 1884, is a nonprofit organization established to aid in developing and maintaining purebred DOG bloodlines. As the principal agency in the United States for the registration of purebred, purebred dogs, the AKC maintains records—some dating from 1878—on the breeding of more than 21 million dogs. It registers more than 1 million dogs annually. In addition, the AKC has established, and enforces, the standards and rules governing dog shows and obedience and field trials. The organization publishes (monthly) *Pure-Bred Dogs* and *Stud Book Register.*

American Labor party

The American Labor party was founded in New York in 1936 to promote liberal, socialistic programs. Created as an alternative to the boss-ridden regular Democratic organization, it had strong backing from organized labor. Its support was often critical to the election of both Democrats and progressive Republicans. By about 1940, the party's influence began to wane as disputes broke out between right- and left-wing factions. In 1944 the anti-Communist wing broke away and formed the Liberal party. The American Labor party declined quickly after that and disbanded in 1956.

American Legion

The American Legion is the largest U.S. veterans' organization; its members are drawn from the veterans of the two world wars and the wars in Korea and Vietnam. The legion was founded in Paris in 1919 and held its first convention in St. Louis that same year. In the 1970s it had about 2.6 million members organized in more than 16,000 local posts. Basically concerned with the social and political interests of veterans, the Legion is also dedicated to community affairs and sponsors patriotic and charitable programs. It has four major fields of activity: rehabilitation of veterans through medical and educational benefits; child welfare; national security; and Americanism. The legion sponsors junior baseball leagues and Boy Scout troops, high school oratorical contests, and the study of government through its Boys' State and Nation groups. On the national level it has been a powerful lobby for military preparedness and veterans' benefits. Its annual conventions are noted for their mammoth parades and for speeches by political leaders.

The legion's headquarters is in Indianapolis, Ind., and it has an office in Washington, D.C. An associated organization is the American Legion Auxiliary, composed of women who are close relatives of Legionnaires or of deceased veterans, and of women who have served in the armed forces. The auxiliary had more than 900,000 members in the 1970s. The Sons of the American Legion, with a membership of about 25,000, includes male descendants, adopted sons, and stepsons of Legionnaires and deceased veterans.

American Library Association

The American Library Association (ALA), founded in 1876, is devoted to the advancement of library science and to the improvement and accessibility of library services. Its annual conference is the major gathering of librarians in North America and attracts colleagues from around the world.

ALA activities cover such issues as library education, library publications, and the establishment of standards for libraries of all kinds. The association encourages public access to library shelves through the use of open stacks; the increase of special services, such as those for children and the blind; the enrichment of rural libraries; and the establishment of national and international interlibrary loan facilities. The organization also seeks to improve professional standards through the accreditation of library schools and through its many publications, the most widely known of which are the monthly *American Libraries* and the book review journals *Booklist* and *Choice*. The many annual ALA awards include the two most prestigious awards for children's books, the Caldecott and the Newbery medals.

The ALA is headquartered in Chicago. It has a membership of over 30,000 and a staff of 200, with an additional voluntary staff serving on its divisions and committees. It sends representatives to international library meetings, promotes the exchange of librarians with other countries, aids in the establishment and support of United States government libraries overseas, and gives advice to federal agencies on domestic library programs.   COLIN STEELE

American literature

From its origins in colonial America to its present status internationally, American literature has stressed the diversity and uniqueness of the American character and experience. The Puritans attempted to demonstrate that God had ordained their emigration and had intended that their communities stand as examples of holiness and right for the rest of the world. In Revolutionary times this idea of specialness came to include unique American types, such as the Yankee, and a belief that the country was destined to produce a new literature. As it matured, American literature followed the major movements of Western literature in the 19th century—romanticism, realism, and naturalism. American writers, however, concentrated on the American scene and sought to affirm a distinct national identity.

COLONIAL LITERATURE

The colonial period extends from the Virginia and Massachusetts settlements of the 17th century through the Great Awakening, a religious revival in the 1740s, and its aftermath. Although dominated by Puritan-Calvinistic doctrine, early American literature was not confined to religious subjects. The religious writings, as well as the more secular chronicles, are the history of exceptional individuals who rose above the physically difficult and spiritually demanding environment of the New World. These early writers set the tone and the rhetoric and foreshadowed the major concerns of later American writing.

The first generation of settlers wrote sermons, religious tracts, diaries, and histories of their undertakings. The leading religious controversialists were John COTTON, Anne HUTCHINSON, Roger WILLIAMS, and John WINTHROP. Winthrop's *Journal*, originally printed as a *History of New England from 1630 to 1649*, remains a major historical source. It was followed by William BRADFORD's *History of Plimouth Plantation* (pub. 1856); Edward Johnson's *History of New England* (1654); and Thomas MORTON's *New English Canaan* (1637), which stands out for its irreverence and hints of bawdiness. Histories of the South with enduring literary qualities were Capt. John SMITH's *The Generall Historie of Virginia* (1624) and, much later, William BYRD's *History of the Dividing Line* (composed and reworked from 1728 but not published until 1841).

Puritan writers stressed religious and didactic themes. The first book published in America was the *Bay Psalm Book: The Whole Book of Psalmes Faithfully Translated into English Metre* (1640). Michael WIGGLESWORTH continued in the Puritan vein, exhorting against sin in his popular poem, *Day of Doom* (1662). Meanwhile, poetry of genuine accomplishment and a less stern, Puritan emphasis was written by Anne BRAD-

Cotton Mather, Boston's leading theologian in the late 17th and early 18th centuries, wrote more than 450 works of literature, many defending the established Puritan religion of the Massachusetts colony. His forward-looking scientific treatises gained him membership in London's Royal Society.

STREET in *The Tenth Muse Lately Sprung Up in America* (1650) and by Edward TAYLOR, whose poems were not discovered until 1939. More in accord with the Puritan temperament are the spiritual autobiographies, which describe the Puritan experience of conversion. Thomas Shepard's *The Sincere Convert* (1640) is one of the first; Jonathan Edwards's "Personal Narrative," first published in 1765 in the *Life of the Rev. J. Edwards* by the theologian Samuel Hopkins, is one of the last.

The memorable works of the colonial period depicted the conditions of life in the New World. The first and best-known narrative of captivity by Indians was Mary ROWLANDSON's *Captivity and Restauration* (1682). Among diarists, Sarah Kemble Knight's account of her journey (1704) from Boston to New York on horseback and Samuel SEWALL's diaries (spanning 1673 to 1729) describe life in the colonies.

The Puritan literary ideal is best summed up in the gargantuan ecclesiastical history by Cotton Mather, the *Magnalia Christi Americana, or the Ecclesiastical History of New England from its First Planting in the New Year 1620, unto the Year of our Lord 1698* (1702). This compendium celebrates America and its religious Puritan leaders in a rhetoric of magnificent extravagance. An equally intense piety pervades the writings of Jonathan EDWARDS early in the 18th century. Besides his spiritual autobiography, Edwards is known for *A Treatise Concerning Religious Affections* (1746) and *Freedom of the Will* (1754), both of which try to incorporate the philosophy of John Locke, and for what is probably the most famous sermon of hellfire and brimstone ever preached, "Sinners in the Hands of an Angry God" (1741). The young Benjamin FRANKLIN wrote during the same period as Edwards. Although his *Poor Richard's Almanack* (1732) anticipated a more rational moralism, it contained much of the proverbial wisdom that Franklin had learned from works such as Cotton Mather's *Bonifacius, or Essays To Do Good* (1710). Similarly, Franklin's *Autobiography* reflected a concern for one's actions that was typical of the Puritan spiritual autobiographers.

REVOLUTIONARY LITERATURE

The American Revolutionary period extends from the first agitations by patriots in the early 1760s through the adoption of the Constitution in 1787. The ardor and disputatiousness characteristic of the Puritans was felt early in this period in the sermons of Jonathan Mayhew and in the political tracts of the patriots. Prominent among the so-called pamphleteers were James OTIS, who wrote five controversial and often intemperate pamphlets; John DICKINSON, the author of a series of letters widely printed in newspapers during 1767 and 1768 and signed "A Farmer in Pennsylvania"; and John ADAMS, the author of *A Dissertation on Canon and Feudal Law* (1765), the first of a long series of works more properly considered philosophical literature than political pamphlets. It was, however, Thomas PAINE's pamphlet *Common Sense,* advocating American independence, that had the greatest revolutionary impact in the colonies and that received the most attention abroad.

The Revolution itself fostered an outpouring of patriotic verse, much of it consisting of satirical attacks on the Loyalists. The most popular of the satires was John Trumbull's *M'Fingal*, a burlesque of Tory politics written in 1775 and expanded in 1782. Trumbull was a leading figure among the Connecticut Wits, who wrote satires similar to his own. A common poetic subject of the Revolutionary period, the coming greatness of America, was expressed in the title of the Princeton college commencement poem of 1771, *On the Rising Glory of America* (1772), written by Philip FRENEAU in collaboration with Hugh Henry Brackenridge.

American literature during this period continued to be expressed largely in histories, journals, personal diaries, letters, and political writing conceived in the revolutionary spirit. An exception was the accomplishment of Phillis WHEATLEY, an African slave, who is now considered America's first important black writer. Her derivative but finely wrought *Poems on Various Subjects, Religious and Moral* was published in London in 1773. The diverse prose of the time included the *Journal* (1774) of John WOOLMAN, a Quaker; the *Letters of an American Farmer* (1782) by the French-born Jean de CRÈVECOEUR; the *Travels* (1791) in the Floridas, Georgia, and the Carolinas of William Bartram; and the Revolutionary-period letters of Abigail ADAMS, the wife of John Adams. Probably the best-remembered works of the period are the state papers, beginning with Thomas JEFFERSON's *Declaration of Independence*. In 1787 and 1788 Alexander HAMILTON, John JAY, and James MADISON collaborated in writing 85 essays defending the new Constitution and collected as *The Federalist*.

The first American play, William Godfrey's *The Prince of Parthia* (1765), appeared during this period despite the moral censure accorded to theater in the colonies. A heroic tragedy in blank verse, it was first performed in 1767. It was followed by the first stage comedy to be produced in the United States, Royall TYLER's *The Contrast* (1787), which introduced Jonathan, the first stage Yankee.

EARLY NATIONAL LITERATURE

The years from the adoption of the Constitution (1787) to the period of Jacksonian nationalism (1828-36) mark the emergence of a self-consciously national literature. The poet Joel BARLOW, who was, like John Trumbull, one of the Connecticut Wits, greeted the new United States with his epic *The Columbiad* (1807), a reworking of his earlier *The Vision of Columbus* (1787). Philip Freneau wrote lyric poetry that fused the native scene and native expression. Other writers strove to develop an American literature but did not concentrate on strictly American subjects, using instead the universal themes of romance, virtue, vice, and seduction that pervaded popular novels in England and on the Continent. William Hill Brown's *The Power of Sympathy* (1789), an imitation of Goethe's *Sorrows of Young Werther*, is regarded by some as the first American novel. Susanna Rowson's sentimental and didactic tale of seduction, *Charlotte Temple*, published (1791) in London as *Charlotte: A Tale of Truth*, was extremly popular. In contrast to the prevailing sentimental novel was Hugh Henry Brackenridge's massive *Modern Chivalry* (1792-1815), a picaresque novel with an underlying satire on bad government. The first professional novelist was Charles Brockden Brown, whose gothic and philosophical romances, beginning with *Wieland* (1798), anticipated Edgar Allan Poe.

Early in the 19th century, Washington IRVING gained European recognition as America's first genuine man of letters. *A History of New York* (1809) is a whimsical satire of pedantic historians and literary classics. His best-known tales, "Rip Van Winkle" and "The Legend of Sleepy Hollow," appeared in *The Sketch Book of Geoffrey Crayon, Gent*, which was published serially in 1819-20. William Cullen BRYANT emerged in the 1820s as a poet of international stature. His "Thanatopsis" (1817), influenced by the English GRAVEYARD POETS, linked American literature to the emerging English ROMANTICISM. Still, despite European influences, American writers attempted to create a distinctive literature during a time of rising literary nationalism. Noah WEBSTER contributed *An American Dictionary of the English Language* (1828), in which he insisted that the country possessed its own language. The nationalist theme was echoed by William Ellery CHANNING, Edward EVERETT, and most memorably by Ralph Waldo EMERSON in his Phi Beta Kappa address at Harvard, "The American Scholar" (1837), which Oliver Wendell HOLMES called "our intellectual Declaration of Independence."

James Fenimore COOPER was the first important American novelist to succeed with subjects and settings that are largely American. Cooper achieved international prominence with his second novel, *The Spy* (1821), a tale of the Revolution. His many novels blending history and romance resulted in his being called "the American [Sir Walter] Scott," a title that put him in the company of one of the period's most popular and respected authors. Cooper became best known for his Leatherstocking Tales, five novels that run from *The Pioneers* (1823) to *The Deerslayer* (1841). Cooper's settings capture the American idea of nature, and his hero, Natty Bumppo, expresses the self-reliant, pioneering spirit of America.

Much of Cooper's sense of America was caught by the Fireside Poets, who celebrated American history and a benign

Washington Irving sits (legs crossed) surrounded by his literary friends at his home, Sunnyside, in Tarrytown, N.Y. The imaginary scene also includes (left to right) Henry T. Tuckerman, Oliver Wendell Holmes, William Gilmore Simms, Fitz-Greene Halleck, Nathaniel Hawthorne, Henry Wadsworth Longfellow, Nathaniel P. Willis, William H. Prescott, James K. Paulding, Ralph Waldo Emerson, William Cullen Bryant, John P. Kennedy, James Fenimore Cooper, and George Bancroft.

Herman Melville (1819–91)

Edgar Allan Poe (1809–49)

Emily Dickinson (1830–86)

American nature. Henry Wadsworth LONGFELLOW displayed his skill at telling a story in verse in *Hiawatha* (1855), *The Courtship of Miles Standish* (1858), and *Evangeline* (1847). But Longfellow and his contemporaries succeeded best in public poetry intended for recitation. Still powerful are Longfellow's *The Midnight Ride of Paul Revere* (1863), John Greenleaf WHITTIER's "Barbara Freitchie" (1863), and Oliver Wendell Holmes's "Old Ironsides" (1830).

Edgar Allan POE stood apart from literary nationalism and represented a gloomier side of romanticism. As a reviewer, he was a harsh critic of second-rate American writing, but he dabbled in many popular sensationalistic forms. His often technically complex poetry uses commonplace romantic themes but gives them a philosophical and mystical application. Many of his short stories remain internationally famous, and he may be said to have invented the detective story. In "The Fall of the House of Usher" and "The Tell-Tale Heart," Poe perfected the tale of gothic horror.

AMERICAN RENAISSANCE

The American renaissance, also known as the American romantic movement, began with the maturing of American literature in the 1830s and 1840s and ended with its flowering in the 1850s. During the 1830s Ralph Waldo Emerson established himself as the spokesman for TRANSCENDENTALISM, first set forth in his essay *Nature* (1836). The group known as the TRANSCENDENTALISTS that gathered around him in Concord, Mass., included Bronson ALCOTT, Margaret FULLER, Theodore PARKER, and William Ellery Channing, who joined with Emerson in the publication of DIAL magazine (1840–44). They subscribed to Emerson's faith that all people are united in their communion with the oversoul, a postreligious equivalent of God. Each individual, Emerson said, finds his or her own way to transcendence through self-knowledge, self-reliance, and the contemplation of nature.

Henry David THOREAU came closest to putting Emerson's ideas into practice. After two intermittent years at Walden Pond in Concord, Mass., he wrote *Walden or Life in the Woods* (1854). In this book, Thoreau observes nature from the viewpoint of a naturalist-philosopher reflecting on the quiet desperation of humanity and the transcendental solace of the natural world. No less consciously indebted to Emerson was Walt WHITMAN, who dedicated the first edition of his poetry, *Leaves of Grass* (1855), to him. Whitman celebrated an untrammeled communion with nature with overtones of sensuality that appeared shocking even though his poetry expressed sound transcendental doctrine. Whitman also took seriously Emerson's appeal for American originality; he devised a loose, "natural" form of versification that seemed unpoetic and jarring to his contemporaries. After the Civil War, Whitman gained wider acceptance with his elegy on the death of Lincoln, "When Lilacs Last in the Dooryard Bloomed" (1865). Whitman's prose works include *Democratic Vistas* (1871), containing his philosophy of American democracy along with prophecies of its future greatness and the coming greatness of its literature, and *Specimen Days* (1882), an autobiographical account of his Civil War experiences as a volunteer nurse.

Unknown to the public, another American innovative poet, Emily DICKINSON, was writing in Amherst, Mass. Her poems, written mostly from the late 1850s through the 1860s, were unconventional and deceptively simple lyrics concerned with death, eternity, and the inner life. Few were published in her lifetime, but when her poems were rediscovered in the 1920s, Dickinson took her place as a major American poet.

Nathaniel HAWTHORNE represents American romanticism with its roots firmly planted in the Puritan past. His stories were collected in *Twice-Told Tales* (1837), which established his importance as an American writer. Some were tales of the Puritans and of early American history; others used a mixture of symbolism and allegory that, together with certain recurrent themes, was carried over into Hawthorne's novels. His masterpiece, the *Scarlet Letter* (1850), is a symbolic romance set in Puritan New England. Hawthorne had been attracted to Emerson's thought but rejected its optimism both here and in *The Blithedale Romance* (1852), a novel based on the transcendentalists' utopian experiment, BROOK FARM. Herman MELVILLE also rejected Emerson's philosophy. His first novel, *Typee: A Peep at Polynesian Life* (1846), based on his own adventures after deserting his ship while on a whaling voyage, challenged the spiritual substance of Christianity. Melville continued to write of the sea and adventure, but now with increasing philosophical complexity and a mixture of allegory and symbolism comparable to Hawthorne's. The culmination of his growth came in *Moby Dick* (1851). This philosophical adventure satisfied the age's aspiration for a great epic of nature and America, yet its greatness was not recognized at the time. Certainly it came nowhere near the success of the great best-seller *Uncle Tom's Cabin* (1852) by Harriet Beecher STOWE. After the failure of Melville's next novel, *Pierre* (1852), Melville continued to write, but he became increasingly discouraged with his inability to reach an audience. At his death in 1891 he was virtually unknown. He left behind poetry on Civil War themes, notably *Battle Pieces and Aspects of the War* (1866) and the short, unfinished novel *Billy Budd*. These and other late manuscripts, neglected for many years, were rediscovered in the 1920s by critics and scholars, whose reassessments established Melville as a superior American writer.

POST-CIVIL WAR LITERATURE

The post-Civil War period is roughly the period from the rise of realism to the advent of naturalism, up to World War I. The Civil War itself affected literature less than did the industrial expansion that came in its aftermath. Nevertheless, the war was the basis for poetry by Melville, Emerson, Lowell, and Whitman, and of significant autobiographical accounts by Thomas Wentworth HIGGINSON, Charles Francis ADAMS Jr., and Ulysses S. GRANT.

Walt Whitman (1819-92)

Mark Twain (1835-1910)

Henry James (1843-1916)

Mark TWAIN led the movement away from the romanticism typical of the American renaissance to a worldly realism that dealt with actual places and situations. In his dialogue he produced equivalents of American speech never before attempted. Twain drew extensively from his personal experiences: on his own travels for *The Innocents Abroad* (1869) and *Roughing It* (1872), on his days as a river boat pilot for *Life on the Mississippi* (1883), and on his youth for his boyhood stories *Tom Sawyer* (1876) and the *Adventures of Huckleberry Finn* (1884). *Huckleberry Finn* is considered by many critics to be the first modern American novel; it is more than likely the best known and is undoubtedly one of the great American literary achievements.

The choice of the pen name Mark Twain by Samuel Clemens followed a practice common among American humorists who wrote during the 19th century. After Augustus B. Longstreet's *Georgia Scenes* (1835), James Russell Lowell wrote as Hosea Bigelow, Joel Chandler HARRIS as Uncle Remus, David Ross Locke as Petroleum V. Nasby, Charles Farrar Browne as Artemas WARD, and Finley Peter DUNNE as Mr. Dooley.

As novelists and critics, William Dean HOWELLS and Henry JAMES contributed to the shift from romance to realism. Howells's *The Rise of Silas Lapham* (1885) concerns an ordinary farmer who becomes wealthy and moves to Boston but whose spiritual rise comes about only when he loses his wealth. Despite a prolific output, Howells's significance rests mostly on his literary criticism and his opposition to provincialism in American literature. James departed even further from the provincial scene. He portrayed expatriate Americans in a European setting in *Daisy Miller* (1879) and in his triumph of psychological realism, *The Portrait of a Lady* (1881). Conversely, James presented the reactions of Europeans to a New England background in *The Europeans* (1878). In *The Bostonians* (1886) he satirized New England reformers and philanthropists. As prolific as Howells, James was also a self-conscious critic and an advocate of realism. In his last novels, notably *The Golden Bowl* (1904), James created a new, complex language and symbolism for the novel that heralded the age of modernism.

Regionalism, the literature of particular sections of the country, flourished, however. Many authors who used this form of realistic local color were women, among them Willa CATHER, Kate CHOPIN, Mary E. Wilkins FREEMAN, Ellen GLASGOW, Sarah Orne JEWETT, and Edith WHARTON. Other writers of the period who are thought of as regionalists are Ambrose BIERCE, Hamlin GARLAND, and Bret HARTE. Much of the literature of black Americans was regional in setting, by force of circumstance. Charles CHESNUTT and William Wells Brown were early black novelists. In *Lyrics of Lowly Life* (1896), the poet and novelist Paul Lawrence DUNBAR used dialect and humble settings in a blend of pathos and humor. Some of the most powerful writing by black Americans has been autobiographical; in the post-Civil War period, works depicting the experi-

ences of black Americans include *The Narrative of the Life of Frederick Douglass, an American Slave* (1845), *Up from Slavery* (1901) by Booker T. WASHINGTON, the *Autobiography of an Ex-Colored Man* (1912) by James Weldon JOHNSON, and *The Souls of Black Folk* (1903) by W. E. B. DU BOIS.

In the 1890s novels emphasizing a harsher view of reality began to appear, marking the beginnings of American naturalism. Stephen CRANE's *Maggie, A Girl of the Streets* (1893) was little noticed, but his *Red Badge of Courage* (1895) was immediately recognized as a classic. Frank NORRIS more nearly exhibited the features of naturalism than did Crane, especially in *McTeague* (1899), *The Octopus* (1901), and *The Pit* (1903). Norris's works, often concerned with the Darwinian struggle for survival, focus upon human greed, depravity, and suffering. Theodore DREISER created the most striking naturalistic works, beginning with *Sister Carrie* (1900) and culminating in *An American Tragedy* (1925). Dreiser's works reflect compassion and an understanding of human motivations. They analyze with dramatic insight the dilemma of the individual in contemporary society.

Social protest and utopianism went hand in hand with naturalism. Upton SINCLAIR exposed the deplorable conditions in the meat industry in *The Jungle* (1906); Jack LONDON rejected society in his autobiographical novel *Martin Eden* (1909); and Jacob RIIS depicted the lives of poor immigrants in photographs and words in *How the Other Half Lives* (1890). Henry Adams, in *The Education of Henry Adams* (1918), critically and ironically explored the quest for meaning in the face of social, historical, and economic change.

American poets in the early part of the 20th century led in developing literary modernism. Vachel LINDSAY and Carl SANDBURG followed in the Whitman tradition of loose versification and the celebration of America, as, to some extent, did Edgar Lee MASTERS in his *Spoon River Anthology* (1915). More traditional in form yet more penetrating in psychology were the works of Edwin Arlington ROBINSON and, particularly, Robert FROST. By the 1930s Frost had become America's best-known and most beloved native poet. Two American expatriates in London, Ezra POUND and T. S. ELIOT, became leading poets of the century. Eliot's *The Waste Land* (1922) represents the extreme of complexity and profundity in modern poetry. Two of Eliot's contemporaries, Wallace STEVENS and William Carlos WILLIAMS, were possibly as influential as Eliot on the rising young poets. Williams, in particular, extended into IMAGISM Whitman's exploration of American themes and rhythms.

POST-WORLD WAR I LITERATURE

American literature of the 1920s was characterized by disillusionment with ideals and even with civilization itself. The writers of the so-called lost generation reacted with disillusionment to the war and adopted the despairing tone of *The Waste Land*. The young poet e e CUMMINGS used his wartime experience as the basis for a novel, *The Enormous Room*

Booker T. Washington (1856–1915)

Stephen Crane (1871–1900)

T. S. Eliot (1888–1965)

Robert Frost (1874–1963)

F. Scott Fitzgerald (1896–1940)

Eugene O'Neill (1888–1953)

(1922), as did John DOS PASSOS and William FAULKNER. Ernest HEMINGWAY, however, captured the experience of war and the sense of loss most lucidly in his first novel, *The Sun Also Rises* (1926), which probes the experience of a group of disillusioned expatriates in Paris, and in *A Farewell to Arms* (1929). American writers gathered in Paris during the 1920s, partly to escape what they regarded as the small-town morality and shallowness of American culture. Among them, F. Scott FITZGERALD had the greatest success in the United States. His masterpiece, *The Great Gatsby* (1925), helped create the image of the Roaring Twenties, the age of the flapper, and the jazz age.

In the United States, a group of writers chronicled their escape from small-town America and exposed its hypocrisies. Sherwood ANDERSON inspired the rest with *Winesburg, Ohio* (1919), based on Anderson's hometown of Clyde, Ohio. Sinclair Lewis attacked provincialism in *Main Street* (1920) and added a word meaning "unthinking conformist" to the language with *Babbitt* (1922). H. L. MENCKEN took up the attack on the "booboisie" in his essays, as did Ring LARDNER in his sports stories and, at the end of the decade, Thomas WOLFE in the autobiographical novel *Look Homeward, Angel* (1929).

The influence of European modernism reached the United States during this period. Gertrude STEIN's experiments with the sounds and speech patterns of the American language, developed earlier in Paris, influenced Hemingway and many others. Marianne MOORE edited the *Dial* magazine and for several decades influenced American poetry with her disciplined, often unconventional verse. Hart CRANE attempted an alternative to Eliot's less vernacular modernism with his American epic, *The Bridge* (1930). William Faulkner assimilated the technique of the STREAM OF CONSCIOUSNESS NOVEL

from James Joyce's *Ulysses* and put it to use in *The Sound and the Fury* (1929). The doctrines of modernism were championed in little magazines such as the *Criterion, Dial,* and *Hound and Horn.* Meanwhile, American literature began to be studied critically. D. H. LAWRENCE's *Studies in Classic American Literature* (1923) was followed by William Carlos Williams's *In the American Grain* (1925) and V. L. PARRINGTON's *Main Currents in American Thought* (1927–30).

During this period the American drama flowered, primarily because of Eugene O'Neill's plays. With such brooding, symbolic, and intensely psychological works as *The Emperor Jones* (1920), *Mourning Becomes Electra* (1931), and his later, poetically autobiographical masterpiece *Long Day's Journey into Night* (1956), O'Neill set a new standard for American playwrights. He was joined by a host of talented dramatists, including Maxwell ANDERSON, Philip BARRY, Lillian HELLMAN, Elmer RICE, Thornton WILDER, and later by Edward ALBEE, Arthur MILLER, and Tennessee WILLIAMS.

THE 1930s

The depression and the rise of fascism in Europe dominated American literature during the 1930s. Proletarian literature consciously aimed at stimulating protest—and, in some cases, revolution—by the working class. John Dos Passos chronicled the age in his trilogy *U.S.A.* (1930; 1932; 1936). James T. FARRELL supplied naturalistic detail in *Studs Lonigan* (1935), as did Meyer LEVIN in *The Old Bunch* (1937). The plays of Clifford ODETS and Sidney KINGSLEY and John STEINBECK's immensely successful *The Grapes of Wrath* (1939) are better remembered today than are the more overtly political works of the time.

Concurrent with socially conscious literature, a detached school of literary criticism emerged. The NEW CRITICISM was

William Faulkner (1897-1962)

Ernest Hemingway (1899-1961)

Photo Jill Krementz © 1975

Robert Lowell (1917-77)

Photo Jill Krementz © 1973

Bernard Malamud (1914-   )

Photo Jill Krementz © 1971

Joyce Carol Oates (1938-   )

Photo Jill Krementz © 1974

Joseph Heller (1923-   )

represented by Yvor WINTERS and Richard P. Blackmur and was dominated by the Southern critics Cleanth BROOKS, John Crowe RANSOM, Allen TATE, and Robert Penn WARREN.

Relatively untouched by the literary or political developments of the period were such innovators as Henry MILLER and Nathanael WEST.

From the 1930s a great many American writers have used the short story as their principal means of expression. Notable exponents of this form were John O'HARA and Katherine Anne PORTER, who were followed in the 1940s and '50s by Carson McCULLERS, Eudora WELTY, and Flannery O'CONNOR. Such writers as Donald BARTHELME, John CHEEVER, and John UPDIKE continue to devote much of their energy to short fiction. The detective short story and novel were also perfected in the 1930s by James M. CAIN, Raymond T. CHANDLER, and Dashiell HAMMETT.

LITERATURE SINCE WORLD WAR II

Many of the new writers of the 1940s and '50s were affected by World War II but did not always express their concern explicitly. James JONES, with *From Here to Eternity* (1951), and Norman MAILER, with *The Naked and the Dead* (1948), made their reputations as war novelists. The poets Randall JARRELL, Robert LOWELL, and Karl SHAPIRO wrote of the war but later, like Delmore SCHWARTZ and Theodore ROETHKE, turned their attention to private events.

American drama began to flourish once again in the years after the war. Tennessee Williams explored the themes of innocence and experience in *The Glass Menagerie* (1944) and *A Streetcar Named Desire* (1947). Arthur Miller's *Death of a Salesman* (1949) is a classic modern tragedy. Edward Albee introduced the tradition of the THEATER OF THE ABSURD in *The Zoo Story* (1958) and *Who's Afraid of Virginia Woolf?* (1962).

The appearance of Saul BELLOW's *The Victim* (1947) and Bernard MALAMUD's *The Assistant* (1957) seem, in retrospect, the first signs of what is loosely described as a "Jewish movement." During the 1950s and '60s many Jewish writers had emerged, including Herbert GOLD, Philip ROTH, and J. D. SALINGER.

The social movements of the 1960s—youth, counterculture, antiwar protest—profoundly affected literature. The Vietnam War gave rise to journalism by Mary McCARTHY, Susan SONTAG, and Frances Fitzgerald; the memoir *Dispatches* (1977), by Michael Herr; and novels by Robert Stone (*Dog Soldiers*, 1974) and Tim O'Brien (*Going after Cacciato*, 1978).

The protest writing of the 1960s and '70s was influenced by earlier experiments in which fictional techniques were used for nonfiction writing. Truman CAPOTE's *In Cold Blood* (1965), an account of a murder, and Norman Mailer's *Armies of the Night* (1968) and *The Executioner's Song* (1980) are examples of this mode. Tom WOLFE's exuberant, rhetorical prose in *The Kandy-Kolored Tangerine-Flake Streamline Baby* (1965) helped establish the "new journalism" (see JOURNALISM).

From the 1960s a great many American writers aligned themselves with ethnic and feminist causes. Ralph ELLISON's *The* INVISIBLE MAN (1952) kept within the mainstream of literary tradition. The poet Gwendolyn BROOKS and the playwright Lorraine HANSBERRY (*A Raisin in the Sun*, 1959) also worked within established conventions, and James BALDWIN began as a writer of traditional prose. In *The Fire Next Time* (1963), however, Baldwin's work grew increasingly committed to the black protest movement of the 1960s and '70s. He was followed by the angry writings of Imamu Amiri BARAKA (LeRoi

Jones), Eldridge CLEAVER, and Ishmael REED, as well as by the less strident work of Toni MORRISON and Nikki GIOVANNI.

Women writers, partly inspired by the example of Betty FRIEDAN's *The Feminine Mystique* (1963), also developed a distinct genre of writing that deals almost exclusively with feminine experience. Sylvia PLATH assumed great importance for reasons that concerned her life as much as her poetry. Tillie OLSEN (*Tell Me a Riddle*, 1961) and Grace PALEY (*The Little Disturbances of Man*, 1959) produced humorous accounts of domestic life. The poets Denise LEVERTOV, Adrienne RICH, and Ann SEXTON also took up feminist concerns in the 1960s. Joan DIDION (*Play It as It Lays*, 1970) described the contemporary situation of women in novels and essays. Joyce Carol OATES, writing in both traditional and experimental forms, was the most prolific novelist of the period whose women writers also include Elizabeth JANEWAY and Kate MILLETT.

Styles of contemporary American literature are as diverse as its subject matter, and whereas several novelists, such as John HAWKES, have experimented radically with technique, others have worked within traditional narrative forms to produce work that draws on several modes of writing. Kurt VONNEGUT has used fantasy and science fiction; Bellow mingled philosophy with the epistolary novel in HERZOG; Gore VIDAL has exploited the historical novel; and John BARTH, Joseph HELLER, and Thomas PYNCHON have written arcane, fantastic, but basically traditional narratives. Wright MORRIS, Walker PERCY, and Peter TAYLOR have maintained the strong tradition of American regional writing, and the novel-of-manners tradition exemplified by Edith Wharton's works is continued in those of Louis AUCHINCLOSS.

Among the most influential innovators of this period was the Russian-born Vladimir NABOKOV, who, after the publication of *Lolita* (1958) and *Pale Fire* (1962), became a best-selling U.S. novelist. The experiments of William S. BURROUGHS and William GADDIS are celebrated but less widely read. John GARDNER, who began his career with ambitious attempts to create ironic, allegorical versions of myths, has recently argued (in *On Moral Fiction*, 1979) in favor of what he calls "moral," or socially responsible, fiction.

Among poets a diversity of style and subject matter prohibits easy summary of the period. The publication of Robert Lowell's *Life Studies* (1959) is often thought to have inaugurated a "confessional" mode in the work of such poets as Plath, Sexton, Levertov, and W. D. SNODGRASS. The work of Charles OLSON and the BLACK MOUNTAIN SCHOOL OF POETRY retained its importance to John ASHBERY, Robert BLY, James MERRILL, and James WRIGHT. W. S. MERWIN, one of the most respected poets of his time, has developed his own distinctive manner from acquaintance with the styles of W. H. Auden, Robert Graves, and Ezra Pound. Allen Ginsberg, developing out of the BEAT GENERATION movement of the late 1950s, and Gary SNYDER emphasized Oriental and American Indian spirituality. Two of the most notable poets of the 1960s and '70s, Elizabeth BISHOP and Richard WILBUR, seem independent of influence or fashion, and they have developed distinct and personal modes of utterance. The number of "little magazines" and small presses increased during the 1970s and '80s, creating an unprecedentedly large number of opportunities for the publication of poetry.

Although American literature in the 1980s stood divided among special-interest groups and opposed aesthetics, its oldest traditions remained recognizable. The major practitioners continued to think of themselves as social critics and harbored a utopian, hopeful attitude even when pessimistic.

PETER SHAW

Bibliography: Chase, Richard, *The American Novel and Its Tradition* (1957); Fiedler, Leslie, *Love and Death in the American Novel*, rev. ed. (1966); Graff, Gerald, *Literature against Itself: Literary Ideas in Modern Society* (1979); Herzberg, Max J., ed., *The Reader's Encyclopedia of American Literature* (1962); Hoffman, Daniel, ed., *Harvard Guide to Contemporary American Writing* (1979); Jones, Howard M., *The Theory of American Literature* (1965; rev. ed. 1966); Leary, Lewis, *American Literature: A Study and Research Guide* (1976); Kazin, Alfred, *Bright Book of Life: American Novelists and Storytellers from Hemingway to Mailer* (1973) and *On Native Grounds, an Interpretation of Modern American Prose Literature* (1956; rev. ed. 1972); Marx, Leo, *Machine in the Garden: Technology and the Pastoral Ideal in America* (1967); Matthiessen, F. O., *American Renaissance* (1941; repr. 1968); Pearce, Roy Harvey, *The Continuity of American Poetry* (1961); Spiller, Robert E., *The Cycle of American Literature* (1955); Spiller, Robert E., et al., *Literary History of the United States*, rev. ed. (1974); Waggoner, Hyatt H., *American Poets from the Puritans to the Present* (1968).

See also: BLACK AMERICAN LITERATURE; INDIANS OF NORTH AMERICA, LITERATURE OF THE; NOVEL; WESTERNS.

American Medical Association

The American Medical Association (AMA) is a national federation of 55 state and territorial medical groups. It was founded in 1847 and is today the largest medical organization in the world, with 224,000 members (1979).

Activities of the AMA include the publication of medical research and review articles in its widely read weekly JOURNAL OF THE AMERICAN MEDICAL ASSOCIATION and in other medical journals; the supervision of standards at medical schools and other institutions in the field of health education; and the sponsoring of scientific councils and committees and more than 1,000 yearly meetings. Its two large annual conventions attract thousands of physicians, who attend the reading of research papers and are shown the latest developments in medical technology.

For the past three decades the AMA has funded a powerful lobby in Washington. Through this group it has attempted to influence the direction of medical legislation. It fought unsuccessfully against paid health care for the aged (Medicare) and against the creation of peer review systems to oversee the quality of publicly funded medical-care programs. Its longest struggle has been against any program of nationalized health care; it has proposed instead legislation for private health insurance to be partly funded by the federal government.

Bibliography: American Medical Association, *Digest of Official Actions, 1959–1968*; Cray, Ed, *In Failing Health: The Medical Crisis and the A.M.A.* (1971); Fishbein, Morris, *History of the American Medical Association, 1847–1947* (1947).

American Museum of Natural History

The American Museum of Natural History, located near Central Park in New York City, was founded by Albert Bickmore, Theodore Roosevelt, and others in 1896. One of the foremost museums of its kind in the world, it is concerned primarily with research, exhibition, and education in the natural sciences. The museum has departments of anthropology, astronomy, entomology, fossil and living invertebrates, herpetology, ichthyology, mineralogy, and ornithology. It maintains public exhibits in all of these areas. It also operates the American Museum–Hayden Planetarium and publishes the *American Museum of Natural History Bulletin* and *Natural History*.

American music

The history of American music may be roughly divided into three periods: (1) the colonial period (the 17th and 18th centuries), dominated by British influence; (2) the period from about 1800 to about 1930, when the United States depended heavily for its musical culture on the importation of music and professional musicians from continental Europe; and (3) the period since about 1930 to the present, during which American music attained an international importance equal to that of European music.

COLONIAL PERIOD

Music had an important place in the life of the Puritan settlers in New England. They used metrical psalms (see HYMN) in their worship, a practice that emphasized text more than music, but they must also have brought with them folk songs that remained unwritten and are therefore unknown today. The first generations to settle in the New World were not skilled in music, and the psalms were perpetuated by "lining out," in which a leader recited or sang each line ahead of the congregation. During the 18th century itinerant singing masters taught the rudiments of music and created a market for the many collections of psalm tunes that reprinted English

(Below) *Lowell Mason, a 19th-century composer and educator, wrote about 1,200 Protestant hymns. He introduced music education into the Boston public school system.*

(Above) *Jenny Lind, known as "the Swedish nightingale," captivated American audiences during her triumphal tour in 1850-51. This contemporary cartoon took a satirical view of her admirers.*

pieces but also contained the music of American composers, including James Lyon's (1735-94) *Urania* in 1761. Except for William BILLINGS, whose ANTHEMS and fuging tunes expressed a rugged individual style, most music of American composers mirrored the styles that were in vogue in England.

Religious vocal music touched all walks of life in the American colonies, but a taste for concerts and more sophisticated music developed early in the cities. Evidence indicates concerts in Boston in 1731, in Charleston in 1732, in New York in 1736, and in Philadelphia in 1757.

The market for concert music attracted foreign musicians, many of them English, who were readily accepted after the Revolutionary War. As business prospered and cities grew, the large number of first-generation urbanites demanded a semblance of the musical life they had known in their homelands.

Even so, the newly arrived musicians found it useful to have another means of livelihood, and from their numbers came the early music-store owners and music publishers. They also taught music, repaired instruments, and organized performing groups. Alexander Reinagle (1756-1809), Benjamin Carr (1768-1831), James Hewitt (1770-1827), and Gottlieb Graupner (1767-1836) were among the early composer-performer-teachers who established a cultured level of musical taste alongside the vernacular idiom.

A high level of musical creativity was reached in the 18th century by the Moravians in Pennsylvania, Ohio, and North Carolina. They composed and performed CHORAL and instrumental music that can be compared to North German works of the late BAROQUE period. The Moravians kept apart from the life outside their communities, and their music failed to influence the development of an American idiom.

THE 19TH CENTURY

During the 19th century American-born composers, performers, critics, conductors, and educators brought the country within a respectable distance of European practices, although for another century the United States was dependent on imported personnel and materials for its highest level of music.

Lowell MASON, an important figure in the early years of the Boston Handel and Haydn Society, and a founder of the Boston Academy of Music (1832), influenced 19th-century musical life in a number of ways. He introduced much European choral music to the United States, pioneered in public-school music education, and sired a musical dynasty that included publishers, organ and piano builders, teachers, and the composer Daniel Gregory Mason (1873-1953). He and his contemporaries, Thomas Hastings (1784-1872), William Bradbury (1816-68), and Isaac B. Woodbury (1819-58), wrote many hymns that continued to be used in the 20th century.

Following the European REVOLUTION of 1848 many German musicians immigrated to the United States. Among them was the Germania Musical Society, an orchestra of about 25 players that toured the country for several years, bringing concert music to places where it had never been known. Numerous teachers and performers, both vocal and instrumental, settled in the cities; concert artists arrived on tour to play in communities of all sizes. The Austrian pianist Henri Herz, the Norwegian violinist Ole BULL, the Swedish soprano Jenny LIND, and the French conductor Louis Jullien attracted large audiences, only some of whom had any experience with musical performances. Performers became show-business properties: P. T. BARNUM promoted the concerts of Jenny Lind; Jullien, engaged by Barnum, beguiled his audiences with stunts and showmanship that often overshadowed his music. The American-born pianist Louis Moreau GOTTSCHALK returned from his European studies in 1853 and undertook concert tours rivaling those of the great European virtuosos. With few exceptions, however, the musical taste of Americans in the 19th century was dominated by German traditions and taste. Only in the music that reached into the unsophisticated levels of life did American musicians find wide acceptance.

Vocal music had the most direct appeal to the majority, and singing families, probably patterned after European folk-singing groups, became popular. The best known was the Hutchinson family, who associated their singing activities with social causes, especially temperance and abolition.

The minstrel shows that arose in the 1820s combined song with the theater. These blackface song, dance, and comedy-skit shows remained popular for a century. At first they were entirely the domain of white performers in costume, but by the mid-1850s blacks also performed in them. The minstrel show was probably begun by T. D. "Daddy" Rice (1808-60) and was popularized by Daniel Decatur Emmett (1815-1904), composer of "Dixie," and E. P. Christy (1815-62). It brought the music of Stephen Collins FOSTER to public attention, and gave him fame if not a sufficient livelihood. His "Jeanie with the Light Brown Hair," "Old Folks at Home," and "Camptown Races" are among the most familiar of his more than 200 songs. Foster outshone all other American composers of the period in popularity, and his works are known for their tunefulness and poetic interest. His contemporaries included the English-born Joseph P. Knight (1812-87) ("Rocked in the Cradle of the Deep") and Henry Russell (1812-1900) ("Woodman, Spare That Tree") and the Americans Septimus Winner (1827-1902) ("Whispering Hope" and "Listen to the Mocking Bird") and John H. Hewitt (1801-90) ("All Quiet Along the Potomac"). The last, along with "Dixie" and "Tenting on the Old Camp Ground," was one of the popular songs spawned by the Civil War.

New York City was the emerging center for the arts, and there the cry for American music by American composers was

Stephen Foster was the best-known composer of American popular music during the 19th century. Many of his simple tunes and lyrical ballads, such as "Old Folks at Home," are familiar songs even in the present day, Foster composed music for the Christy minstrel troupe in the 1850s.

A minstrel band, formed originally by white men in blackface makeup, sat in a half circle. Frequently used instruments were (left to right) bones, banjoes, accordions, and tamborines. Minstrel shows, which originated in the 1820s, toured the country, creating a light, energetic style of music. This popular music eventually evolved into ragtime.

first raised. William Henry Fry's (1813–64) opera *Leonora*, performed in Philadelphia in 1845, was the first by an American composer; George F. Bristow's (1825–98) *Rip Van Winkle*, performed in New York in 1855, was the first on an American suject. Both men wrote instrumental music also, but their work overall is undistinguished.

Music spread westward before the middle of the 19th century, mainly to cities that had a large European-born population. St. Louis, Milwaukee, Cincinnati, and Chicago were early in establishing orchestras, opera companies, and choral groups. Music societies were organized, and some became the nucleus of permanent performing organizations. The NEW YORK PHILHARMONIC was formed in 1842. A number of short-lived groups were organized in New York and elsewhere, and the BOSTON SYMPHONY ORCHESTRA came into existence in 1881; the CHICAGO SYMPHONY ORCHESTRA was formed a decade later. New Orleans had an established opera house (1810) before any of those orchestras were founded.

The rise of performing groups brought the need for competent conductors, and a number of men came forward to guide the course of those organizations. Theodore Thomas (1835–1905), who had played violin in Jullien's orchestra, organized his own group in 1864, and after 1869 toured the entire country with his musicians. He later conducted various established orchestras, including the New York Philharmonic, before organizing the Chicago Symphony in 1891.

BANDS were popular on the American scene; one of the earliest known band concerts was given in Boston in 1771 by Josiah Flagg's (1737–95) 64th Regiment Band. Many 18th-century bands were attached to military units and were little more than small fife and drum corps, but they were heard in public concert, and an enthusiasm for wind music was widespread. By the outbreak of the Civil War, there were more than 3,000 bands in the country; their place in concert life after the war was assured by Patrick Sarsfield Gilmore (1829–92), composer of "When Johnny Comes Marching Home," and by John Philip SOUSA, composer of "The Stars and Stripes Forever," "El Capitan," and "the Washington Post" marches. Gilmore was bandmaster of the Union forces in Louisiana. At the close of the war he remained in New Orleans and gave a concert that featured more than 500 bandsmen and 5,000 voices. Later, he organized his own band and toured widely. Sousa's impact was even stronger. He directed the U.S. Marine Band from 1880 to 1892, then formed his own group, hiring some of Gilmore's best musicians after the latter's death, and toured America and Europe to great acclaim.

Before the Civil War, a serious student of music had to study with European masters, preferably German, since American conservatories were still in the planning stage. The emergence of native musicians and the rise of music schools went hand in hand: the former needed the latter as places to study in their youth and to teach in their maturity. The United States now has a system of private and college-supported music schools, but it has been little more than a century since the teaching of music was first organized. The first conservatory of music was at OBERLIN COLLEGE (1865), followed by the NEW ENGLAND CONSERVATORY OF MUSIC in Boston two years later. Schools were opened in Cincinnati and Chicago in that same year, and the first professor of music at Harvard was appointed in 1875. The country today has hardly an educational institution without a program of music study.

Nevertheless, during the 19th century, music schools and conservatories in the United States served more as preparatory institutions than as finishing ones. Whenever possible, hopeful performers and composers went to Europe to study with the masters at the famous conservatories of Berlin, Leipzig, and Munich. John Knowles PAINE prepared himself in that traditional manner. Arthur Foote (1853–1937), one of the few who studied only in the United States, was Paine's student at Harvard. He, George Chadwick (1854–1931), and Horatio Parker (1863–1919), the so-called Boston Group, taught many composers and teachers of the next generation, including Daniel Gregory Mason, Charles IVES, and Douglas MOORE.

Edward A. Macdowell was an American composer and pianist who won the patronage of Franz Liszt and gained recognition in Europe. He became the first professor of music at Columbia University in 1896.

Louis Armstrong (center) *gained worldwide recognition as the symbol of American jazz. Here he appears with King Oliver's Jazz Band, popular in the 1920s.*

George Gershwin, *a 20th-century composer, wrote scores for musical plays, symphonic jazz such as* Rhapsody in Blue, *and the opera* Porgy and Bess.

A contemporary of the Boston Group, Edward MACDOWELL went directly to the conservatories of France and Germany after private instruction in New York. His work marked one of two main streams in future American composition—imitation of the European practice in the larger forms. The other, the development of an American idiom employing Negro tunes and rhythms, was developed by his pupil, Henry F. Gilbert (1869-1928).

THE 20TH CENTURY

The dependence on German training continued unabated until World War I, during and after which fascination with the German models for music diminished sharply. The postwar center for music study was Paris, but those who remained at home found the American schools prepared to teach them at a high level of competence. Seeking a distinctive American idiom, a number of composers turned to folk sources and the country's unique musical utterance, JAZZ.

Rooted in the RAGTIME of Scott JOPLIN's generation and developing through the addition of the BLUES style, jazz emerged at the close of World War I, spreading northward from the brothels of New Orleans to achieve respectability and wide acceptance in night clubs and cafés. A host of specialized jazz artists, highly skilled in improvisation, developed, and jazz influenced European composers as well as Americans. Jazzmen of the stature of Louis "Satchmo" ARMSTRONG and Edward "Duke" ELLINGTON were world figures. George GERSHWIN brought the jazz idiom to the attention of the concert world with his *Rhapsody in Blue* (1924) and *An American in Paris* (1928). His opera *Porgy and Bess* (1935) combines the Broadway musical and serious art.

The most significant American composer of the early 20th century was Charles IVES. Most of his work was done before his *Concord* Sonata for piano was published in 1920, and he experimented with DISSONANCE, polytonality, assymetrical rhythms, and other advanced techniques before Darius MILHAUD, Igor STRAVINSKY, Arnold SCHOENBERG, and the other Europeans who are usually credited with the break from tradition. Ives was profoundly influenced by the New England transcendentalist writers such as Ralph Waldo Emerson and Henry David Thoreau. In his compositions he frequently quotes traditional American hymns, folk tunes, patriotic songs, and ragtime.

American music of the 20th century is characterized by a wide variety of forms and sounds. Leading experimental composers have been Carl RUGGLES, Edgard VARÈSE, John J. Becker (1886-1961), Henry COWELL, John CAGE, Milton BABBITT (1916-), and George Crumb (1929-). Composers who have sought either a musical Americanism or a cosmopolitanism, or a mix-

ture of both, include Walter PISTON, Virgil THOMSON, Roger SESSIONS, Roy HARRIS, Aaron COPLAND, Elliott CARTER, Samuel BARBER, and William SCHUMAN. Some contemporary American composers have set out along unique paths; many, however, are deeply indebted to the wave of Europeans who went to the United States during the 1930s, among them Arnold SCHOENBERG and Igor STRAVINSKY.

Music for the American theater took a distinctive turn in this century. The European OPERETTA had dominated the light-opera stage, but the shows of GILBERT AND SULLIVAN, Johann STRAUSS, and Franz LEHAR were superseded by those of Reginald De Koven (1859-1920), Victor HERBERT, George M. COHAN, Jerome KERN, Cole PORTER, Irving BERLIN, George Gershwin, Richard RODGERS, Oscar HAMMERSTEIN, and Alan Jay LERNER and Frederick Loewe (1904-). Those successes were exportable, and the American musical found its way to other countries, making a stronger impact than American concert literature. Popular music, once entirely dominated by New York's Tin Pan Alley, was transformed by the needs of Hollywood and, more recently, the new center of the popular music recording industry, Nashville, Tenn. In Nashville, as on Broadway, business rather than artistry has dominated, leading to the creation of expendable entertainment rather than lasting art.

In the United States, only popular music can support itself by means of the box office. Symphony orchestras, opera com-

Aaron Copland is best known for ballet and symphonic scores incorporating folk melodies and jazz. Among his ballet works are Billy the Kid *(1938) and* Appalachian Spring *(1944).*

The long-successful rock-music group Crosby, Stills, and Nash was, into the early 1980s, an extremely influential American band. Stephen Stills (left), David Crosby (center), and the English-born guitarist Graham Nash (right) formed the group in 1969 and in succeeding years were joined occasionally by composer-singer Neil Young. As a quartet, they popularized a soft, melodious folkrock. The trio today composes and plays a harder, louder music that attracts huge audiences to their concerts. They have been outspoken, musically and otherwise, on various social issues, taking, for example, anti-Vietnam War and antinuclear positions.

panies, and radio stations that limit their programs to concert music must obtain outside support to offset their deficits. This financial aid often comes from a few individual donors, foundation and government grants, and small donations by the music-loving public. Since strong financial assistance from national, state, or local governments is not available in the United States, it has become the responsibility of community orchestras and opera companies and state and private colleges and universities (all of which have bands, orchestras, and choruses) to maintain mature musicians and to train new generations of the young. The hundreds of institutions of higher education have produced more professional musicians than there are audiences to hear them. Unless they elect to join the ranks of music teachers, American musicians must once again turn to Europe, not only to study but to find professional positions and the opportunity for public performance. This scarcity of opportunity does not exist, however, for those who work in the field of pop music. Since the advent of ROCK MUSIC in the 1950s, American popular music has become a major industry—capable of employing thousands of talented young musicians—and a significant musical influence around the world.

The easy accessibility of recordings, radio, and television has made music a constant companion to American life. The availability of so much music has not diminished the popularity of live performance; it has, rather, exposed the American public to a wider range of musical styles than can be found elsewhere. Among other unique American musical developments are BARBERSHOP QUARTETS, religious groups that adopt popular musical modes, and popular groups whose musical styles come directly from religion—as in GOSPEL MUSIC. Finally, there are a new group of "serious" composers (Philip GLASS and Steve REICH are the most widely known) who have discovered attractive alternatives to the myriad of "classical" musical styles and whose work may reawaken American enthusiasm for contemporary composition.

ELWYN A. WIENANDT

Bibliography: Cowell, Henry, ed., *American Composers on American Music: A Symposium* (1962); Crawford, Richard, *A Historian's Introduction to Early American Music* (1980); Davis, Ronald L., *A History of Music in American Life*, vol. 3, *The Modern Era: 1920 to the Present* (1981); Ford, Ira W., *Traditional Music in America* (1940; repr. 1978); Jablonski, Edward, *Encyclopedia of American Music* (1981); Marocco, W. Thomas, and Gleason, Harold, *Music in America* (1964); Thomson, Virgil, *American Music since 1910* (1971).

See also: BLUES; COUNTRY AND WESTERN MUSIC; JAZZ; SPIRITUALS.

American National Theater and Academy

The American National Theater and Academy (ANTA) is an organization established in 1935 by an Act of Congress to raise the standards of drama performance in the United States. It has sent American productions, notably *Porgy and Bess*, on foreign tours. ANTA leaders have included Helen Hayes, Peggy Wood, Robert Breen, and Alfred de Liagre. In 1983, ANTA formed the American National Theater Company, a repertory group based at Kennedy Center in Washington, D.C.

American Newspaper Publishers Association

The American Newspaper Publishers Association, formed in 1887, is the trade association of daily newspapers created by their publishers and business managers to represent the industry to the public and in legislative lobbying. Major areas of interest have been technological research, labor union negotiations, newsprint prices, postal rates, and education for journalism. It has a membership of approximately 1,400.

EDWIN EMERY

American Philosophical Society

The American Philosophical Society for Promoting Useful Knowledge is the oldest learned society in the United States. Derived from an earlier group dating from 1743, the society was founded in Philadelphia in 1769. Benjamin FRANKLIN was its first president. Its early fame declined after the American Revolution. A chartered but private association, the society depended largely on members' dues until a bequest in 1931 revived its fortunes. The society, which is still located in Philadelphia, is governed by committee and has a large and distinguished membership. It publishes *Transactions* and *Proceedings*, meets semiannually, and maintains a library and a wide program of grants.

JAMES E. McCLELLAN

American Physical Society

Since its establishment in 1899, the American Physical Society (APS), with 30,000 members in the 1980s, has promoted the advancement and diffusion of knowledge about physics, from cosmic phenomena to the realm of elementary particles. The APS sponsors authoritative, scholarly journals, including *Physical Review, Physical Review Letters,* and *Reviews of Modern Physics*, and awards in such fields as nuclear, solid state, and mathematical physics.

JEFFREY L. STURCHIO

American quarter horse: see QUARTER HORSE.

American Revolution

The American Revolution, the conflict by which the American colonists won their independence from Great Britain and created the United States of America, was an upheaval of profound significance in world history. It occurred in the second half of the 18th century, in an "Age of Democratic Revolution," when philosophers and political theorists in Europe were critically examining the institutions of their own societies and the notions that lay behind them. Yet the American Revolution first put to the test ideas and theories that had seldom if ever been worked out in practice in the Old World—separation of church and state, sovereignty of the people, written constitutions, and effective checks and balances in government.

A struggle to preserve and later to expand the dimensions of human freedom, the American Revolution was also an anticolonial movement, the first in modern history. Before then, countries had usually come into existence through evolutionary processes, the result of tradition and history, geography and circumstance. The United States, on the other hand, had a birth date, 1776; it was "the first new nation," a republic born in revolution and war, a pattern followed by scores of fledgling states since that time, especially in the so-called Third World areas of the globe since 1945.

For many nation-makers the American rebellion has been a relevant revolution, offering insights and parallels that have aided them in their quest for self-determination. The revolutionists of 1776 themselves accurately predicted that the American Revolution would inspire men elsewhere to secure freedom and national identity in their own lands. As Thomas Jefferson assured John Adams, "the Flames kindled on the fourth of July" had spread over too much of the globe ever to be extinguished by the forces of despotism and reaction.

THE COLONIES IN 1763

No revolution, of course, can be fully exported. A vast array of factors that include the political and social backgrounds of a people will shape the precise course of any and all revolutions. So it was in America, where the colonists were not an alien people with a culture very different from that of the motherland. They were for the most part British in origin, English-speaking, Protestant, rural, and agrarian in their principal characteristics. They were proud of their Anglo-Saxon heritage and of the empire of which they were a part—proud, too, of the role they had played in helping to seize Canada and to crush French power in North America in the FRENCH AND INDIAN WAR (known as the SEVEN YEARS' WAR in Europe), which ended in 1763.

At that time the colonists gave little thought to cutting loose from their imperial moorings. They considered the British political system the best in Europe, noted for its equilibrium between King, Lords, and Commons assembled in Parliament. They imported British books, furniture, and clothing; wealthy planters and merchants imitated the manners of the English aristocracy. Even with the restrictions imposed on their external trade by the NAVIGATION ACTS—or perhaps because of them—they had prospered in their direct economic intercourse with Britain, the most industrialized country in Europe. Nor was their trade rigidly confined; they were also permitted to sell an assortment of valuable products such as grain, flour, and rice on non-British markets in the West Indies and in southern Europe.

In 1763 the colonists were an expanding and maturing people; their numbers had reached a million and a half, and they were doubling every quarter of a century—multiplying like rattlesnakes, as Benjamin Franklin said. If most provincials were sons of the soil, Americans could nonetheless boast of five urban centers, "cities in the wilderness"—Philadelphia, Boston, New York, Charleston, and Newport. The cities served as filters through which new ideas of the European Enlightenment entered the colonies, helping to generate an inquisitive spirit about humankind and the total environment. Newspapers and colleges in the cities and towns served as disseminators of the thought and culture of what was truly an Atlantic civilization. A new mobility, together with a receptivity to new ideas, was a hallmark of American society. It came about because of high wages, cheap land, and an absence of legal privilege. Americans were—except for their African slaves—one of the freest people in the world. Another sign of that freedom was their almost complete control over their internal political and domestic affairs, exercised largely through their popularly elected lower houses of assembly, which in turn served as nurturing ground for such future Revolutionary leaders as John ADAMS, John DICKINSON, Thomas JEFFERSON, and George WASHINGTON.

Although the colonists had reached a high level of maturity, there was not at mid-century a meaningful American nationalism. The life and institutions of the parent state continued to provide the central focus of colonial culture. The word *American* appeared infrequently; people were more likely to describe themselves as English or British, or as Virginians or Pennsylvanians. Nor did the provincials display a marked degree of intercolonial cooperation; their own rivalries and jealousies over boundaries, western land claims, and military contributions in the imperial wars all tended to retard American national feeling, as may be seen in the rejection of the Plan of Union presented by Benjamin FRANKLIN to the ALBANY CONGRESS in 1754.

Nothing, however, unites a people like a commonly perceived threat to their way of life; and after 1763 the colonists felt endangered within the empire. There is a real irony in the way the American Revolution began, for the very elements that had wedded the colonists to the mother country—especially their political and economic freedoms—were viewed in London as signs that Britain had lost control of its transatlantic dominions, that the colonists were fast heading down the road to full autonomy or absolute independence. Those sentiments, growing steadily in the 18th century, crystallized during the French and Indian War when British officials complained that Americans cooperated poorly in raising men and supplies and in providing quarters for British troops, to say nothing of trading illegally with the enemy and generating friction with western Indians over land and trade goods.

Whatever the truth of these charges—and they were partly true, if exaggerated—it was not unreasonable after 1763 for Britain to ask more of its prosperous dependencies. Britain's heavy national debt and concurrent tax burdens stemmed partly at least from a series of 18th-century wars that were fought to some extent for the defense of the colonies. Nor was it wrong to argue that a measure of reorganization in American administration would lead to greater economy and efficiency in imperial management. But Britain embarked upon this course with a lack of sensitivity, ignoring the concerns of its maturing subjects, who were scarcely the children they had once been.

In short, Britain's state of mind (meaning that of its rulers and the parliamentary majority) corresponded to its lofty status as the superpower of Europe in 1763. It was said that the *Pax Romana* would pale in comparison with the *Pax Britannica*, which would bring a "prosperity and glory unknown to any former age." Britain no longer felt a need for its former allies in Europe. For what nation could now threaten it? It no longer required the goodwill of its colonies, for France had ceased to be a threat to the thirteen colonies, whose men and other resources—although Britain scarcely admitted it—had in fact aided the British victory in 1763.

Britain's was a mentality unable to appreciate the aims and aspirations of its colonial people. Superpowers, all too often, are not given to introspection, to questioning their values and assumptions. And it had been a long time since the British themselves had felt their liberties threatened, either by a foreign danger or by internal menace from a tyrannical ruler. Thus, when Britain adopted a new imperial program, the colonists were never meaningfully consulted. Furthermore, Britain's tactics could hardly avoid arousing the Americans. Having left the colonies virtually alone for decades with a *de facto* attitude of "salutary neglect," the London government now attempted too much too quickly.

THE GROWING FERMENT

Even before the termination of the French and Indian War,

aflix the STAMP.

This is the Place to

(Above) *A satirical cartoon from a colonial publication suggests this design for the tax stamp intended for use on legal documents, newspapers, and other paper goods, according to the terms of the Stamp Act of 1765. The act enraged the American colonists and stirred up revolutionary sentiments.*

(Right) *The Boston Massacre of Mar. 5, 1770, was provoked by a group of colonists taunting British soldiers. As Paul Revere's engraving depicts, the panic-stricken troops fired into the crowd, killing three colonists and mortally wounding two others. The incident was publicized by rebellious Americans to arouse resentment against British rule. (Courtesy the Metropolitan Museum of Art. Gift of Mrs. Russell Sage, 1910.)*

visible indications had appeared of a new direction in colonial affairs. Beginning in 1759, small-scale disputes broke out between Britain and the colonies over disallowance of measures passed by the popular assemblies, over writs of assistance empowering the royal customs officals to break into homes and stores, and over judicial tenure in the colonial courts. Subsequent decisions made in London forbade "for the time being" western settlement beyond the Appalachian divide (the Proclamation of 1763), eliminated provincial paper currency as legal tender, bolstered the customs department, and enlarged the authority of the vice-admiralty courts in relation to enforcement of the Navigation Acts.

Taxation Without Representation. When these unpopular measures were followed almost immediately by Parliament's placing taxes on Americans for the first time in their history, the result was an explosion that shook the empire to its foundations. George GRENVILLE, chief minister from 1763 to 1765, did not father the idea of American taxation; it had been "in the air" for several years. But it was he who pushed the controversial bills through Parliament in 1764 and 1765. The Sugar Act of 1764, actually a downward revision of an earlier Molasses Act, cut the duty on imported foreign molasses from sixpence to threepence a gallon; but it was to be vigorously enforced, and it was now called a revenue measure rather than a law designed merely to regulate trade. The next year Grenville secured passage of the so-called STAMP ACT, placing taxes on all legal documents and on newspapers, almanacs, and other items. Soon afterward came a third law, the Quartering Act, a form of indirect taxation that required American assem-

blies to provide British troops passing through their colonies with temporary housing and an assortment of provisions.

"Taxation without representation" was the central issue in the imperial rupture. It raised a fundamental question concerning the limits of parliamentary power that was debated throughout the dozen or so years before the declaration of American independence. Although Americans complained about the stream of British acts and regulations after 1759, they now agreed that the constitutional issue of taxation posed the gravest threat of all to their freedom as individuals. If it was legal to take a man's property without his consent, as the philosopher John LOCKE wrote in defense of the GLORIOUS REVOLUTION of 1688 in England, then a man could scarcely have any liberty remaining, since property gave one a stake in society and enabled one to vote. Americans felt confident that Locke would have approved when they wrote in almost countless documents and petitions that Englishmen—in England, in Virginia, or anywhere else—could be taxed only by their own directly elected representatives.

When Parliament retreated in 1766, reducing the Sugar Act to the level of a trade duty and repealing the Stamp Act, it was responding to retaliatory colonial boycotts on British trade goods, not to the justness of American constitutional pronouncements. In 1767, Chancellor of the Exchequer Charles Townshend persuaded a Parliament already antagonistic toward the colonies to pass the TOWNSHEND ACTS. These levied new and different taxes on the American colonists: duties to be collected at the ports on incoming lead, paper, tea, paint, and glass. Besides meeting other imperial expenses such as the upkeep of the army in America, these Townshend duties might go to pay the salaries of royal governors and other crown officials who previously had been paid by the colonial assemblies, which had used this power of the purse to make the king's appointees somewhat responsive to their wishes. A final Townshend scheme reorganized the customs service in America, establishing its headquarters in Boston, where mounting friction between collectors and townspeople led to the dispatch of regular troops to the city to keep order in 1768.

Resistance and Retaliation. The new tensions subsided into a three-year period of calm beginning in 1770, but only because a second round of American reprisals against English trade prompted the removal of all the Townshend duties save the one on tea, which was retained to show symbolically that Parliament had not renounced its right to tax America. Additionally, the British troops, popularly known as "redcoats," had been withdrawn from Boston following the embarrassing and unplanned BOSTON MASSACRE (1770). Unfortunately for the empire, those years were not used to bring about permanent agreements between Americans and Britons on such subjects as the constitutional relationship between the colonies and the mother country and what might be a reasonable way for the provinces to share the costs of imperial administration. In an atmosphere of continuing suspicion and dis-

trust, each side looked for the worst from the other. Instead of rescinding the remaining Townshend tax and exploring inoffensive methods of aiding the financially troubled British East India Company, Parliament enacted the Tea Act of 1773, designed to allow the company to bypass middlemen and sell directly to American retailers. It was hardly a plot to persuade Americans to drink taxed tea at a low price, but the colonists interpreted it in that fashion. Everywhere there was opposition to landing the dutied brew, and in the Massachusetts capital the famous BOSTON TEA PARTY resulted in the destruction by patriots of 340 tea chests on ships in the harbor.

Parliament's retaliation against Massachusetts was swift and severe: the so-called INTOLERABLE ACTS closed the port of Boston, altered town and provincial government, permitted royal officials and functionaries to go to Britain for trial for any alleged crimes, and provided for the quartering of troops once again in Boston. The other colonies rallied to the defense of Massachusetts in a CONTINENTAL CONGRESS that met in Philadelphia in September 1774 and denounced the acts. Already some colonial leaders were arguing that the old federal conception of the empire would no longer protect American rights and liberties, for Britain had demonstrated its unwillingness to let the colonists manage their own internal, domestic affairs. Now, Thomas Jefferson, John Adams, and other writers claimed that the empire should properly be viewed as one in which each colony was the equal of England in all respects, that the only tie with Britain was through the king. Here, in sum, was the COMMONWEALTH idea of the 20th century, which now unites such nations as New Zealand, Canada, and Australia with Britain, an idea then rejected by England.

Lexington and Concord. War clouds were gathering rapidly. The sending of more than 3,000 British army regulars under Maj. Gen. Thomas GAGE to Boston further exacerbated the imperial rift. When a column of these troops under Lt. Col. Francis Smith moved into the countryside to collect arms and munitions gathered by the patriot militia, hostilities erupted at Lexington and Concord on Apr. 19, 1775. Soon afterward militia contingents from places throughout New England took up positions outside Boston, putting the city under siege. Forts TICONDEROGA and CROWN POINT in upstate New York fell to other rebel parties. The misnamed Battle of Bunker Hill was fought on Breed's Hill across from Boston (June 17, 1775). Although Gage's units dislodged the rebels from their advanced positions threatening the city, the British casualties came to 42 percent of the 2,500 redcoats engaged, their heavi-

(Above) *Benjamin Franklin pleaded for unity among the colonies in his cartoon "JOIN, or DIE." By dealing with each colony on an individual basis, Britain had maintained a control over American trade that went virtually unchallenged for nearly a century.*

(Right) *British troops and local colonial militia, the famous "Minutemen," clashed for the first time on Apr. 19, 1775, at Lexington, Mass. The skirmish, an American defeat that cost the lives of eight colonists, marked the opening of hostilities in the American Revolution.*

(Left) *The Battle of Bunker Hill, on June 17, 1775, is depicted in a painting by John Trumbull. After two unsuccessful charges, British troops dislodged the colonists from their defensive positions overlooking Boston Harbor. Despite their victory, the British suffered heavy losses.*

(Below) *Recruitment posters urged volunteers to join the ranks of General Washington's army. Despite the poster's fancy uniforms and assurances that each recruit would "return . . . with his pockets full of money and his head covered with laurels," military service proved neither glamorous nor lucrative for the average colonial soldier.*

est losses of the war. The Second Continental Congress, then meeting at Philadelphia, took control of the New England forces opposing Gage. The lawmakers chose as commander of this "Continental Army" George Washington, a 43-year-old delegate from Virginia, a planter, and a ranking militia officer in the French and Indian Wars.

RESOURCES OF THE OPPONENTS
Britain seemingly had enormous advantages in a war against its colonies. It possessed a well-established government, a sizable treasury, a competent army, the most powerful navy in the world, and a large LOYALIST population in the colonies. By contrast, the American rebels had no chief executive, such as a king, nor a cabinet whose members had assigned responsibilities. In fact, the Americans had no separate or independent departments of government, such as war, treasury, and foreign affairs, until near the end of the conflict. The Continental Congress itself had as its rivals the 13 state legislatures, which often chose not to cooperate with their delegates in Philadelphia. Indeed, Congress was an extralegal body, existing at the pleasure of the states before the Articles of Confederation were ratified in 1781.

American Advantages. The Americans, however, were not without their own advantages. A vast reservoir of manpower could be drawn upon. For the most part, men preferred short-term enlistments—and many who served came out for a few weeks or months—but they did serve: the best estimates are that more than 200,000 participated on the patriot side. General Washington was often short of shoes and powder, but rarely were he and other commanders without men when they needed them most, although at times American leaders had to take into the army slaves, pardoned criminals, British deserters, and prisoners of war. Moreover, Americans owned guns, and they knew how to use them. If the Continental Army won few fixed battles, it normally fought reasonably well; it extracted a heavy toll on the enemy, who usually could not easily obtain reinforcements. Although only Washington and Maj. Gen. Nathanael GREENE were outstanding commanders, many others were steady and reliable, including Henry KNOX, Benjamin LINCOLN, Anthony WAYNE, Daniel MORGAN, Baron von STEUBEN, the marquis de LAFAYETTE, and Benedict ARNOLD, before he defected to the enemy in 1780.

The Americans also were fighting on their own soil and consequently could be more flexible in their military operations than their opponents. Washington and other Continen-

TO ALL BRAVE, HEALTHY, ABLE BODIED, AND WELL DISPOSED YOUNG MEN,
IN THIS NEIGHBOURHOOD, WHO HAVE ANY INCLINATION TO JOIN THE TROOPS, NOW RAISING UNDER
GENERAL WASHINGTON,
FOR THE DEFENCE OF THE
LIBERTIES AND INDEPENDENCE
OF THE UNITED STATES,
Against the hostile designs of foreign enemies,

TAKE NOTICE,

tal Army commanders usually followed the principle of concentration, that is, meeting the enemy in force wherever British armies appeared. In the interior, however, against bands of Loyalists and isolated British outposts and supply trains, the American militia not infrequently employed guerrilla or partisan tactics with striking successes. The major contribution of the militia was to control the home front against the Revolution's internal enemies—whether Indians or Loyalists—while the Continental Army contended with British armies in the eastern or coastal regions in more formalized warfare.

British Disadvantages. British advantages were steadily negated by the vastness of the struggle, by waging war 3,000 miles from Europe against an armed population spread over hundreds of miles, from the Atlantic to the Mississippi, from Maine to Georgia. The land was forested, ravined, swampy, and interlaced by myriad streams and rivers. It was discouraging to win battle after battle and see Britain's armies bled of men and supplies in the process, while the beaten rebels always bounced back. It was equally frustrating to seize at one time or another every American urban center and yet have nothing more to show for it than the mere possession of territory, for the Americans had no single vital strategic center.

(Above) *The Declaration of Independence, which defined colonial grievances against Britain, is presented before the Continental Congress prior to its adoption on July 4, 1776. The painting by John Trumbull portrays that document's drafting committee at center, including (from left to right) John Adams, Roger Sherman, Robert Livingston, Thomas Jefferson, and Benjamin Franklin.*

(Right) *The American naval officer John Paul Jones's* Bonhomme Richard *(center left) battered the larger* Serapis *into submission during a battle in the North Sea on Sept. 23, 1779. This battle, depicted in the painting by Robert Dodd, was the most famous of the duels between individual ships during the naval phase of the Revolution.*

To the British it seemed to take forever—6 to 12 weeks—for word of campaign strategies to pass from London to commanders in the field, for provisions to arrive, and for naval squadrons to appear in time for cooperation with land forces. The scope of the contest also reduced the Royal Navy's effectiveness in blockading the long American coastline. Stores could be landed at too many rivers, bays, and inlets. Nor could the British employ their fast frigates and formidable ships of the line (battleships of the 18th century) against an American fleet. The patriots took to the sea in single ships, either privateers or vessels commissioned by Congress. Consequently, the British-American naval war can be told largely as a story of individual ship duels. The triumph of John Paul JONES in the *Bonhomme Richard* over H.M.S. *Serapis* in the North Sea in 1779 was the most famous of these encounters.

Britain faced a further problem with the nature of its leadership, both civilian and military. King GEORGE III was a conscientious but supremely obstinate monarch whose reluctance to countenance the loss of the colonies probably resulted in a prolongation of the war. However, responsibility for the conduct of the war was not in his hands but in those of his compliant chief minister, Lord NORTH. North, a dull, unimaginative politician, headed a ministry of undistinguished men. Into the leadership vacuum left by North's weakness stepped Lord George GERMAIN, who increasingly assumed the direction of military operations in the colonies. Germain, the colonial secretary, was himself a veteran soldier, intelligent and able; he was also, however, an unappealing man, sharp-tongued and aloof, hardly the minister capable of unifying the country and playing a symbolic role as the popular William PITT the Elder had done in the Seven Years' War.

Unfortunately for Britain, its generals in the field were much like the political leaders at home, possessed of average talents at best. John BURGOYNE, Guy CARLETON, Sir Henry CLINTON, Charles CORNWALLIS, William HOWE, and Thomas Gage were probably reasonably endowed to fight conventional wars on the plains of western Europe, where orthodox linear formations were in order. Eighteenth-century European generals, however, were scarcely professionals in a modern sense. Military education was apprenticeship training in the field rather than schooling at such institutions as the Royal Military Academy at Sandhurst or its U.S. equivalent at West Point, which were created later. Officers lacked a body of strategic doctrine from which to choose between alternatives for practical application. The British generals revealed themselves grossly inept at improvisation in a unique struggle in

Three examples of military dress from the American Revolution are illustrated. (Left) The infantryman from Washington's Continental Army was issued far better equipment than that used by his counterparts in colonial militia units. (Center) The camouflaging dress of a colonial rifleman, by no means a standard uniform, proved its worth in battles contested over forested terrain. (Right) The grenadier of the 2d Foot Guard, an elite force within Britain's colonial army, was among the finest combat soldiers of his time.

America that demanded rapid movement, original tactics, winter campaigning, and—most important—contending with a people in arms. Moreover, some British commanders, notably the Howe brothers, were deliberately slow in prosecuting the war because they favored a political reconciliation with the rebels.

For all these reasons American generals, even with amateurish militia backgrounds, were not at so serious a disadvantage as they might have been in a subsequent period of history. American officers who had fought with the British army in the French and Indian Wars, observing its procedures and reading the standard military treatises, found in the Revolution that the pattern of warfare as practiced by the so-called experts had hardly changed at all. Washington and his comrades lacked experience in directing massive formations and planning campaigns; but, for that matter, British generals—and admirals too—had themselves been subordinate officers in the last war with France.

COURSE OF THE WAR

Britain was slow to take the offensive in the opening rounds of the war because most of its troops in America were at Boston, which continued under siege. Unable to break out of their entrenchments, and threatened by Washington's artillery on Dorchester Heights, British troops evacuated the city by sea in March 1776 and established themselves temporarily at Halifax, Nova Scotia.

Clinton's Southern Expedition. That same spring a small British expedition under Sir Henry Clinton sailed along the coast of the southern colonies in the hope of arousing the Loyalists against the newly established American governments in the Carolinas and Georgia. Reaching the Cape Fear River in North Carolina, Clinton learned that a Loyalist uprising had been smashed by the patriots at the Battle of Moore's Creek Bridge (Feb. 27, 1776) near Wilmington, N.C. Then, continuing southward, Clinton's fleet bombarded the harbor fortifications at Charleston, S.C., perhaps seeking to establish a coastal base for local Loyalists. In any case, the expedition was beaten off (June 28, 1776), terminating important British activity in the South for more than two years.

Invasion of Canada. At best, both sides might consider the first year of conflict a draw. Although the king's regiments

had withdrawn from New England, the colonists in turn had failed to capture the former French province of Quebec. The Americans had hoped to persuade the French inhabitants to join their cause, because they feared that Canada might become a staging area for an invasion of the thirteen colonies. An American army under Brig. Gen. Richard MONTGOMERY advanced from upper New York and seized Montreal (Nov. 13, 1775), while Col. Benedict Arnold led a second force northward through the Maine wilderness. Uniting before the city of Quebec, they attacked the walled capital but were beaten back, and Montgomery was killed (December 31). Although the Americans continued to blockade the city until May 1776, the only serious American threat to Canada in the war had been ended.

Britain's Northern Offensive of 1776. From the summer of 1776 the strategic initiative was taken by the British, who believed that the real core of the insurrection was in the northern tier of colonies, especially in New England. To bring the war to an end in 1776, British planners sent reinforcements to Maj. Gen. Guy Carleton, governor of Quebec, who had already defeated Arnold and Montgomery. Carleton should push the Americans from their remaining toeholds in Canada and pursue them down the Lake Champlain-Hudson River trough, which might be a means of cutting the colonies in half. Simultaneously, a much larger army headed by Maj. Gen. William Howe, who had replaced Gage as supreme commander, should capture New York City and its harbor, a strategic base from which it could advance up the Hudson, unite with Carleton, and overrun New England. But Carleton, after driving his opponents back, was delayed by problems of supply and the difficulties of wilderness campaigning. Then, near Valcour Island on Lake Champlain, his naval complement was checkmated by a tiny American fleet hastily assembled by Benedict Arnold. Time was always of the essence in fall campaigning, and the lateness of the season now prompted Carleton to return to Canada for the winter.

Howe's chances of completing his part of the two-pronged offensive seemed more promising than Carleton's. Howe launched his campaign with the largest force he or any other British general had at his disposal during the war: 32,000 soldiers, together with 400 transports and 73 warships under his brother, Vice Admiral Richard, Earl HOWE, with whom he shared the American supreme command. From a military viewpoint, Washington should not have attempted to retain New York City, with its hard-to-defend islands, rivers, bays, and inlets, although Congress saw strong psychological reasons for holding a major city whose loss might dispirit patriots everywhere. As it was, Washington suffered a defeat on Long Island (Aug. 27, 1776). Fortunately for him, Howe did not attempt to follow up his victory quickly. The explanation may be that the Howe brothers, who were also peace commissioners, hoped to convince the Americans to lay down their arms, apparently in the belief that leniency might encourage the rebels to do so. If that was their theory, it failed. Washington fought a series of rearguard actions with Howe on Manhattan Island, with the result that it took the sluggish Howe from August to November to clear his opponents from New York City and the surrounding area. Howe, like Carleton, never made his move along the Hudson, but contented himself with pursuing the retreating Washington across New Jersey until the Americans managed to escape over the Delaware River into Pennsylvania (Dec. 7, 1776).

Battles of Trenton and Princeton. With the Revolution seemingly at its nadir and desperately in need of a lift, Washington unexpectedly struck back, showing a determination and a persistence that were to be his hallmarks during a war that lasted 8½ years, the longest in American history before Vietnam. Washington noted that Howe, in characteristic European fashion, preferred to avoid winter campaigning and had divided his army between New York City and various New Jersey towns. Collecting scattered regulars and militiamen, the Virginian returned to New Jersey and in a little more than a week of dazzling maneuvers captured the garrison of German mercenaries at Trenton (Dec. 26, 1776) and routed another enemy contingent at Princeton (Jan. 3, 1777).

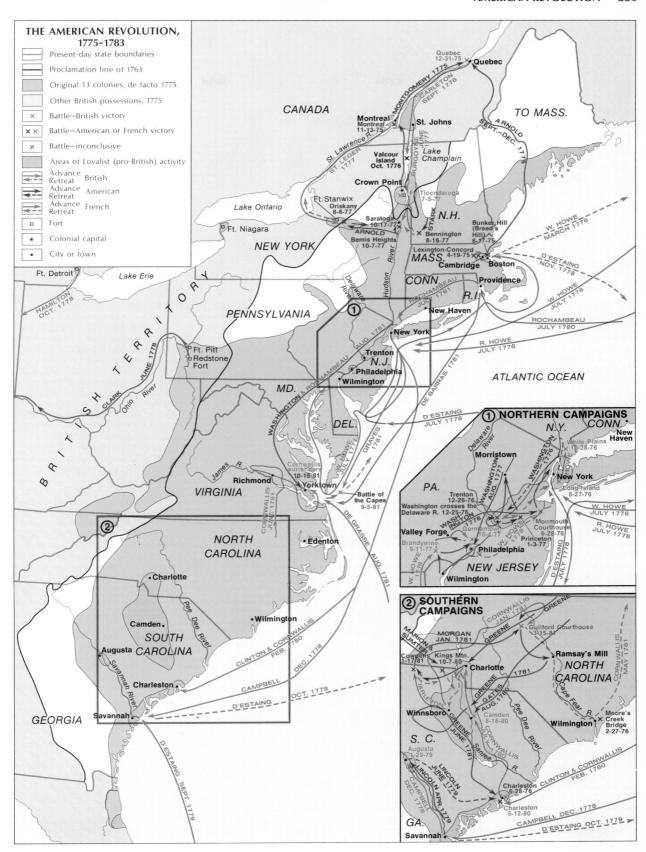

THE AMERICAN REVOLUTION, 1775–1783

- Present-day state boundaries
- Proclamation line of 1763
- Original 13 colonies, de facto 1775
- Other British possessions, 1775
- × Battle—British victory
- × × Battle—American or French victory
- × Battle—inconclusive
- Areas of Loyalist (pro-British) activity
- Advance Retreat British
- Advance Retreat American
- Advance Retreat French
- □ Fort
- ⊙ Colonial capital
- • City or town

CANADA

Quebec 12-31-75 × Quebec

Montreal
Montreal 11-13-75 St. Johns

TO MASS.

MONTGOMERY 1775
CARLETON SEPT. 1776
ARNOLD SEPT.–DEC. 1775

St. Lawrence R.
ST. LEGER 1777

Valcour Island Oct. 1776

Lake Champlain

Crown Point

Ft. Stanwix
Oriskany 8-6-77

Ft. Ticonderoga 7-5-77

N.H.

W. HOWE MARCH 1776

Ft. Niagara

NEW YORK

Lake Ontario

Saratoga 10-17-77
ARNOLD Bemis Heights 10-7-77

STARK
× Bennington 8-16-77

Bunker Hill (Breed's) Hill 6-17-75

Lexington-Concord 4-19-75 × ×
Cambridge MASS. Boston

D'ESTAING NOV. 1778

Ft. Detroit

Lake Erie

HAMILTON OCT. 1778

PENNSYLVANIA

CLARK June 1778
Ohio River

Ft. Pitt
Redstone Fort

CONN
ROCHAMBEAU JULY 1781

R.I.
Providence

New Haven

① AUG. 1781

New York

W. HOWE JULY 1776

ROCHAMBEAU JULY 1780

R. HOWE JULY 1776

ATLANTIC OCEAN

Delaware River
Hudson

Trenton
N.J.
Philadelphia
Wilmington

MD.

WASHINGTON & ROCHAMBEAU 1781

DEL.

D'ESTAING JULY 1778

James R.
Richmond

VIRGINIA

CORNWALLIS JUNE 1781

Cornwallis surrenders 10-19-81
Yorktown

W. HOWE JULY 1777

GRAVES 1781

Battle of the Capes 9-5-81

DE BARRAS 1781

DE GRASSE AUG. 1781

②

NORTH CAROLINA

Edenton

BRITISH TERRITORY

Charlotte

Camden
SOUTH CAROLINA
Augusta

Pee Dee River

Wilmington

CLINTON & CORNWALLIS FEB. 1780

CAMPBELL DEC. 1778

Savannah River
Charleston

GEORGIA

Savannah

D'ESTAING OCT. 1779

D'ESTAING SEPT. 1779

① NORTHERN CAMPAIGNS

N.Y.
CONN
New Haven

White Plains 10-28-76

Delaware River

Morristown

WASHINGTON 1777
WASHINGTON AUG. 1776

New York

Long Island 8-27-76

PA.

Trenton 12-26-76
Washington crosses the Delaware R. 12-25-76

WASHINGTON 1778
Valley Forge

Germantown 10-4-77

Monmouth Courthouse 6-28-78

Princeton 1-3-77

Brandywine 9-11-77

Philadelphia

W. HOWE 1778

NEW JERSEY

Wilmington

W. HOWE JULY 1776

R. HOWE JULY 1776

D'ESTAING JULY 1778

② SOUTHERN CAMPAIGNS

CORNWALLIS JAN. 1781
GREENE
GREENE

MARION & SUMTER

MORGAN JAN. 1781

Guilford Courthouse 3-15-81

GREENE 1781

Cowpens 1-17-81
Kings Mtn. 10-7-80

Charlotte

Ramsay's Mill

NORTH CAROLINA

CORNWALLIS MAY 1781

Cape Fear R.

Winnsboro

GREENE
GATES AUG. 1780

Camden 8-16-80

Pee Dee River

TARLETON 1781

CORNWALLIS 1780

Wilmington

Moore's Creek Bridge 2-27-76

S. C.

Augusta 1-29-79

LINCOLN JUNE 1779

GREENE JUNE 1781
Santee R.

Charleston 6-28-76
LINCOLN APR. 1779

CAMPBELL DEC. 1778

Charleston 5-12-80

CLINTON & CORNWALLIS FEB. 1780

GA.

Savannah

CAMPBELL DEC. 1778

D'ESTAING OCT. 1779

The colored engraving portrays a great fire that swept through New York as the city was being occupied by the British in September 1776. Despite orders from the Continental Congress to hold New York at any cost, General Washington found himself hopelessly outflanked and ordered that the city be abandoned to the British.

The Failure of Negotiation. Just as the Howe brothers had failed in 1776 to crush the rebellion, so also had they failed in their efforts as peace commissioners. They had little with which to negotiate, except the vague assertion that Americans should lay down their arms and trust to the good will of Parliament to remove objectionable laws. Even had they possessed meaningful bargaining powers, the possibility for a reconciliation was probably a thing of the past, since the Americans had already chosen to sever permanently their imperial ties. Fortified by the arguments in the highly influential pamphlet *Common Sense* by Thomas PAINE, the Continental Congress had voted on July 4, 1776, to separate the American colonies from Britain, adopting the immortal words of Thomas Jefferson in the DECLARATION OF INDEPENDENCE.

Saratoga Campaign. Once again in 1777, British campaign planning focused on the northern states. Once again, too, the Canadian–based army and Howe's forces were to mount offensives. This time the Canadian troops, now commanded by Maj. Gen. John Burgoyne, were numerically much stronger, but they had no promise of cooperation from General Howe as they proceeded down the Lake Champlain–Hudson River course. For his part, Howe appeared uncertain for several months about his own course of action. Possibly he still longed for a negotiated peace; perhaps he was becoming doubtful of Britain's ability to win an exhausting land war. Finally, Howe resolved not to march north in support of Burgoyne but rather to leave a garrison under Sir Henry Clinton in New York City and to transport his army by sea for a strike against Philadelphia. Incredibly, neither Howe nor Burgoyne had corresponded with each other about the campaign—each would handle his own affairs. Even so, the greatest fault lay with Lord George Germain, who had approved the campaign but failed to give it a unifying concept.

Burgoyne's operation began well, as was true of most British campaigning during the Revolution. The American Northern army, plagued by shortages and internal divisions, initially offered slight opposition. So confident was Burgoyne that he permitted officers to bring wives and mistresses, sanctioned elaborate dinner parties and heavy drinking bouts, and behaved generally—as did his officers—as if war were romantic and glamorous, as indeed it was for European aristocrats of that age. Events were to show that Burgoyne suffered from overconfidence, which actually increased when he recaptured Fort Ticonderoga (July 5, 1777) at the juncture of Lakes Champlain and George. His leisurely pace allowed the Americans precious time to regroup and to make an ally of the dense wilderness of upper New York. They destroyed his only road south, felling trees to block his progress, and sent out guerrilla bands to harass his flanks and lines of communication.

In mid-August Burgoyne learned that one of his units commanded by Lt. Col. Barry ST. LEGER had been mauled by American militia under Nicholas HERKIMER while laying siege to Fort Stanwix in the Mohawk Valley, and that St. Leger had returned to Canada. More bad news came from Bennington, Vt., where a contingent of his German troops in search of packhorses and provisions had been routed by the militia of Brig. Gen. John STARK. At length, Burgoyne reached the rugged Bemis Heights on the west bank of the Hudson, where he collided with a well-entrenched and much-revitalized Northern army under Gen. Horatio GATES, ably supported by Maj. Gen. Benedict Arnold and Col. Daniel Morgan. Twice—on September 19 and October 7—Burgoyne lunged at the American lines, and both times was driven back with heavy losses. With his southward progress blocked and no help forthcoming from Clinton in New York, he surrendered at Saratoga (Oct. 17, 1777).

British Capture of Philadelphia. Howe, meanwhile, was winning victories in Pennsylvania, although their long-term value was more illusory than real. He was faulted, from the very beginning of the campaign, by Sir Henry Clinton for not advancing up the Hudson to aid Burgoyne or at least marching on Philadelphia by land in order to remain in touch with the Canadian army. Instead of debarking at Delaware Bay near his objective, he landed on upper Chesapeake Bay, 92 km (57 mi) from Philadelphia.

Washington, amazed at Howe's desertion of Burgoyne, hurried south from Morristown, N.J., and positioned his army astride Brandywine Creek to parry his opponent's obvious thrust at Philadelphia. But on September 11, in several hours of furious fighting, Washington's right flank collapsed, and he hastily withdrew.

Soon after the British commander entered the patriot capital, causing Congress to flee, Washington made a night assault on the enemy's advance base at Germantown, Pa., but his plan was probably too complicated for his troops, who nonetheless fought well until they were forced to retire (October 4).

The year 1777 had seen another British failure to crush the rebellion. While one army had been lost, another had occupied Philadelphia. However, the city itself was hardly a staggering loss for the Americans, whose armies were still intact. Howe, too, had paid a heavy price in casualties, whereas the patriots were able to replenish their own depleted ranks.

THE FRENCH ALLIANCE

The new year, 1778, was a time of transition in the Revolutionary War because of Britain's inability to win in the northern colonies and because of the increasing part played by France. The French foreign minister, the Comte de Vergennes,

(Above) *In the Battle of Germantown, Pa., Oct. 4, 1777, Washington's Continental Army enjoyed a rare numerical advantage over its British opponents. The American attack, initially successful, faltered; the battle ended when Washington withdrew to Valley Forge.*

(Right) *The British general Burgoyne offers his sword to Horatio Gates, American commander at Saratoga, in John Trumbull's painting. The surrender (Oct. 17, 1777), which prompted France's entry into the war on the side of the Americans, is regarded as the turning point of the Revolution.*

eager to settle an old score with Britain, convinced his royal master, Louis XVI, to permit France to funnel secret aid to the patriots in 1776 and 1777. That aid took the form of the government's handing over munitions, arms, and clothing to the playwright Caron de BEAUMARCHAIS and his fake "Hortalez and Company," which in turn arranged with Benjamin Franklin and other patriot commissioners in Paris to have them shipped across the Atlantic.

Vergennes, however, was not willing to risk war with Britain until he was sure that the Americans had the ability to continue the fight and the commitment to eschew reconciliation with George III. Gates's victory at Saratoga, combined with rumors that Britain would offer America major concessions in return for peace, finally pushed France over the brink. Formal treaties of commerce and alliance were signed by American and French diplomats on Feb. 6, 1778. France became the first nation to recognize the infant country; it re-

nounced all claims to North America east of the Mississippi River and agreed with the United States that neither would lay down its arms until American independence was guaranteed. Already Spain, a French ally, was giving America modest aid. It declared war on Britain in 1779, without actually joining the United States in a formal alliance.

Valley Forge and the Battle of Monmouth. The winter of the signing of the French alliance was also the Continental Army's time of cruel suffering at VALLEY FORGE, although it was actually not the worst winter of the war. Spring brought Washington not only new recruits but also an army better trained than ever before, due in considerable part to the labors of the Prussian general Baron von Steuben in drilling the troops at Valley Forge.

Spring meant, furthermore, additional pressure on British forces in the New World now that France was entering the struggle. Accordingly, Sir Henry Clinton, who became the new commander in chief when the Howes resigned (May 1778) and returned to England, now received important orders: evacuate his army from Philadelphia, concentrate his forces at New York City, and send men to guard against French threats against British islands in the Caribbean.

Washington, his confidence up, pursued Clinton on his cross-country march through New Jersey, and at Monmouth Courthouse the two armies clashed (June 28, 1778). For the Continentals, who traded volley for volley with the finest soldiers in Europe, it was a moral victory, although the outcome itself was indecisive. In three years of fighting, Britain had little to show for its exertions to regain America, and so it would remain in the northern states, where the heavy campaigning was at an end. Washington, who followed Clinton northward after Monmouth, spent the next three years observing the British from lines outside New York City.

War in the West. In one sense, the struggle on the western frontier paralleled the fighting to the east, in that neither side managed to get the upper hand. To be sure, most Indian tribes that involved themselves in the fray did so in the cause of the "great white father," George III. They had long nourished grievances against the colonists, who had cheated them in land transactions and trade. But it is not clear that the aid of the tribesmen was a positive influence for Britain; their fe-

rocious tactics may well have alienated many colonists who had been neutral or apathetic. Furthermore, because they demanded food in winter and a great variety of other goods and supplies, the Indians were a great financial and administrative burden for British frontier leaders.

Although Kentucky settlers were threatened periodically, in 1778 the young George Rogers CLARK weakened Britain's hold on the interior by overrunning enemy-controlled villages in present-day Illinois and Indiana. He also captured the controversial lieutenant governor of Detroit, Henry Hamilton, the alleged "hair-buyer." Less significant was the role of the Kentuckian Daniel BOONE, a steady if unspectacular leader.

Elsewhere in the West the contest seesawed back and forth. In the lower South the Cherokee proved to be the most formidable of Britain's warrior allies; although the patriot militia handed them a series of stinging defeats in 1776, the Cherokee continued to be troublesome, if not a serious threat. To check the devastating raids of the Iroquois on the New York–Pennsylvania frontier, Washington sent a striking force headed by Maj. Gen. John SULLIVAN into western New York, where the Americans laid waste to many tribal towns.

Even so, Sullivan, Clark, and the American commanders of the Western Department at Fort Pitt (Pittsburgh) could not eliminate all the anchor points of British power in the inte-

(Above) *General Washington reviews the dispirited men of the Continental Army at his winter headquarters in Valley Forge. Washington devoted the harsh winter of 1777 to reorganizing his army and improving morale among his troops.*

(Right) *General Washington, with sword upraised, rallies his troops at the Battle of Monmouth Courthouse, N.J., in June 1778. When an American attack on a British column turned into a disorderly retreat, Washington rode into battle and inspired his men to stand and fight.*

rior. Loyalist and Indian parties based in Detroit and Niagara continued to harass the frontier communities along the Ohio and in the valleys of western New York even after the conclusion of the war, thus contributing to the renewal of war between Britain and the United States in 1812.

War in the South. In the South, a region long neglected by Britain, the war reached its conclusion. Because of the British inability to prevail in the North, London's strategists gradually shifted their attention to the South, beginning in late 1778. They felt that section contained a higher percentage of Loyalists than any other part of America. Then, too, if choices had to be made after France's entry into the war had stretched British resources tissue thin, England preferred to save the South above all other areas. Its raw materials were the most valuable of all American commodities in the mother country's mercantile scheme.

Britain, as usual, opened a new theater of campaigning with a string of triumphs. In December 1778 small British expeditions from New York and Florida subdued Georgia. Fighting in 1779 was inconclusive along the Georgia–South Carolina border, and a combined Franco-American assault on British-held Savannah was beaten off. In February 1780 Britain greatly expanded its southern beachhead when Sir Henry Clinton arrived in South Carolina from New York with 8,700 additional troops. He soon laid siege to Charleston, where on May 12 American Maj. Gen. Benjamin Lincoln surrendered the city and its more than 5,000 defenders. A second, hastily assembled American Southern army under Horatio Gates was crushed at Camden in upper South Carolina (Aug. 16, 1780) by Lord Cornwallis, whom Clinton had left in command when he returned to New York.

These English victories did not extinguish the flames of rebellion. Britain found pacification of the back country difficult. Rebel small-unit operations continued under such local, legendary guerrilla leaders as Francis MARION and Thomas SUMTER. And a body of patriot frontiersmen, mainly from the Watauga settlements in present-day eastern Tennessee, wiped out a 1,000-man contingent of Loyalist troops at King's Mountain on the border of the Carolinas (Oct. 7, 1780).

As the guerrillas tied down Cornwallis, still a third American army formed in the South under Maj. Gen. Nathanael Greene, who then launched the most effective military campaign of the war. Greene's basic plan was to keep his numerically superior antagonist, Cornwallis, off balance by a series of rapid movements and by cooperating with the South Carolina guerrilla leaders. Greene audaciously divided his small

army, sending Brig. Gen. Daniel Morgan into western South Carolina, where he destroyed Lt. Col. Banastre Tarleton's Tory Legion at Cowpens (Jan. 17, 1781). When Cornwallis pursued Morgan, Greene united his army, led Cornwallis on an exhausting chase into North Carolina, and finally fought him to a draw at Guilford Courthouse (Mar. 15, 1781). While the British general limped eastward and then northward to the Virginia coast, the resourceful Greene returned to South Carolina, and between April and July picked off, one by one, every British post save Charleston and Savannah, where the enemy remained isolated and impotent until peace came.

Cornwallis, meanwhile, was sealing his own fate in Virginia, where he united with a raiding expedition under Benedict Arnold (now in British service), already in that state, and erected a base at the port of Yorktown. Both his superior, Clinton, in New York and General Washington recognized that Cornwallis was vulnerable to a land-and-sea blockade on a Virginia peninsula. But Cornwallis refused to leave, arguing the doubtful proposition that Britain would have to capture Virginia in order to have lasting success in the lower South.

At this point, Franco-American army and naval operations, hitherto disappointing in their results, now determined the fate of Cornwallis. Adding to his forces the French troops of the Comte de ROCHAMBEAU in Rhode Island, Washington raced southward and opened siege operations before Yorktown on October 6, while a French fleet under the Comte de GRASSE sealed off a sea escape. Clinton hastened a naval squadron from New York to the Chesapeake, but it was repulsed by de Grasse. After suffering through an intensive artillery bombardment, Cornwallis, on Oct. 19, 1781, surrendered his nearly 8,000 troops to the 17,000-man allied force. The British failed in the South for several reasons, including an exaggerated estimate of Loyalist support, an inadequate program of pacification, and a failure to recognize the significance of sea power.

Conclusion. The war in America rapidly ground to a halt after Yorktown, a war in which neither side had seemingly the energy or the resources to obtain a total victory. Certainly British leaders had lost all enthusiasm for subduing America, although Britain and its European enemies, France and Spain, continued to duel on far-flung battlefronts until the conclusion of peace in 1783.

The struggle had been so unusual that contemporary military thinkers believed that no European nation would ever have to engage in the kind of conflict that Britain had confronted in America between 1775 and 1783. England had dis-

General Washington (center right) presides over the surrender of Charles Cornwallis at Yorktown, Va., on Oct. 19, 1781. The surrender of the British army of 8,000 marked the end of major fighting in the Revolution. Cornwallis does not appear in this painting by John Trumbull. He refused to meet his American conqueror, sending a surrogate with his sword of surrender.

General Washington receives a hero's welcome from grateful citizens of New York as he leads a column of troops into that city. As his triumphal procession marched in on Nov. 25, 1783, British troops were abandoning New York, their last stronghold on the Atlantic seaboard.

patched 60,000 soldiers across an ocean to fight a prolonged war in an alien environment against a people who were numerous and armed. It was a task never paralleled in the past.

As for the Americans, if they won no clear-cut military victory, if they could not drive out the British completely, if Clinton's forces continued after Yorktown to occupy important cities and interior posts, they nonetheless scored a decisive triumph at the peace conference in Paris. Taking advantage of suspicions between the European rivals and sensing England's desire to be generous in order to pry America out of the French orbit, John JAY and Benjamin Franklin secured not only British recognition of American independence but also the entire region from the Appalachians to the Mississippi River as part of the United States. The final Treaty of Paris was signed on Sept. 3, 1783, and ratified by the Continental Congress on Jan. 14, 1784.

POLITICAL, SOCIAL, AND ECONOMIC EFFECTS

The Revolution involved more than battles and diplomacy. If those were the most crucial and immediate objectives, more important long-term goals and purposes were to be met; for this was a constructive, not a negative revolution. If Americans broke a relationship characterized by colonialism and monarchy, that was about the extent of their destructive activity. They still respected British institutions, which they felt had been abused and corrupted by politicians around George III. Consequently, in fashioning their own state institutions—a process that began in the summer of 1776—they usually employed familiar British-American bricks and mortar.

The British constitution was unwritten, but the Americans spelled out the responsibilities and limits of government in written charters. Since their governments rested totally on the consent of the people, they were designated as republican in character. Basic liberties could not be abrogated by government under any pretext. They were defined in bills of rights, which included freedom of the press, right of petition, trial by jury, habeas corpus, and other procedures that came to be known as due process of law.

The direct involvement of the people in government was increased in other ways. Governors were elected, not appointed; both branches of the legislatures were elected directly or indirectly by the citizens. Obviously, special privilege had no place in a republic. Consequently, several states forbade the passage of any office from one man to another by ties of blood. North Carolina's constitution echoed words found in other political parchments when it proclaimed that "no hereditary emoluments, privileges or honors ought to be granted or conferred by this state."

Institutional Changes. The Americans were primarily about a political revolution when they cast off their imperial links and tailored independent governments. Moreover, a revolution coupled with a foreign war is hardly a time for thoughtful social experimentation, especially when—in the case of the Americans—men believed that they already lived in a remarkably free and open society. Some Americans, however—filled with such Enlightenment ideas as that society's institutions should be judged critically in terms of their usefulness to mankind—stirred somewhat uneasily. They acknowledged certain contradictions between their revolutionary theories and their practices.

To be sure, some institutional inequities, such as anachronistic inheritance laws and established churches that received preferential treatment, had been eroded or undermined by the degree of liberty and opportunity that existed everywhere in the twilight years of the colonial era. But during the Revolution, Americans took specific action that resulted in the abolition of primogeniture and entail; in the South the Anglican church lost its already weakened privileged status, as did the Congregational church in New England some years later. Virginia, as was so often true in the Revolution, led the way with its famous Statute of Religious Freedom (1786). An outstanding document of the age, it proclaimed that "no man shall be compelled to frequent or support any religious worship" nor "suffer on account of his religious opinions or belief," nor would his "civil capacities" be affected by any "matters of religion."

The Spirit of Progress. If Americans of the Revolutionary generation did not level the social order, or did not create democracy in its present form, they laid the basic groundwork. Furthermore, the revolutionists elevated the American spirit. They conveyed to their fellow citizens the notion that the country would grow and expand. In opening new lands in the West, they shaped an orderly process by which frontier territories would move from colonial status to statehood; moreover, the infant states would not be inferior to the original states, as had been true of the earlier relationship between the thirteen colonies and Great Britain. Freed from the mercantilism of the old colonial system, Americans found fresh outlets for trade and commerce and devised improved methods of banking and corporate organization. They set up new educational institutions, and they advanced the controversial idea that the state had a responsibility for the education of its citizens, an obligation that had traditionally been the preserve of the church.

From all these accomplishments two additional American

goals developed. First, a sense of mission—of uniqueness and special purpose—was present in the Revolutionary experience. It was to make America a kind of showcase that would enable people everywhere to see what free people were capable of achieving. The sense of mission was later a powerful catalyst for continuing change, for living up to the principles of the Declaration of Independence. The second goal, relating to self-purification and setting one's own house in order, was the appeal for a distinct American culture. Although such a development occurred only in a limited sense—for Americans have always been a part of Western civilization—it did trigger a new and at least partially fruitful quest for attainments in music, the arts, and literature.

Creation of the Constitution. One final accomplishment of the Revolutionary generation was the creation of a viable national government. Without it, all other gains of the period might have amounted to little. Since that achievement had not taken place by 1783, the leaders of the time felt that the Treaty of Paris did not mean the end of the American Revolution. As the poet Joel BARLOW explained, "The revolution is but half completed. Independence and government were the two objects contended for; and but one is yet obtained."

The task of preparing a constitution for the new nation had begun in 1776 in the Continental Congress, when that body worked to define the relations of the states to one another and to the nation. In doing so, Congress found that the old colonial jealousies still existed, as did the suspicions of remote, centralized authority that had led the colonists to criticize and break their ties with the king and Parliament.

Consequently, the first national constitution, the ARTICLES OF CONFEDERATION, was not completed until 1777 and not ratified by all the states until 1781, and it provided for a government of limited national jurisdiction. It was an instrument of one branch, Congress, which now was given legal authority to do what it was already doing in large part in attempting to direct the war effort. Congress was to have exclusive authority over foreign relations, war and peace, weights and measures, admiralty cases, Indian relations outside the boundaries of individual states, and postal services. Congress was crippled in crucial ways, however, especially in obtaining revenues; for it could not tax or levy duties on external commerce, nor did it have legal ways to enforce its legitimate authority if the states chose to disregard its laws.

As the war approached its end, the states displayed less willingness to cooperate with Congress and to support its acts, a trend that grew ominous after the treaty of peace. It was especially depressing to those who had become ardent nationalists through their wartime experiences to see the states ignore the Articles of Confederation by making treaties with the Indians and building state navies, or by failing to send representatives to Congress and neglecting to contribute sums for the support of the Confederation government. To nationalists such as Washington, Alexander Hamilton, James Madison, Henry Knox, and others, a new political system altogether was needed, particularly because all efforts to amend the articles had failed. To that end, the CONSTITUTIONAL CONVENTION, which met at Philadelphia in 1787, decided to try a different form of government—one that would ensure the rights of the states and at the same time provide the country with a central government capable of maintaining domestic tranquillity, preserving individual liberty, providing for the common defense, and raising the status of America in the family of nations.

The result was the federal CONSTITUTION OF THE UNITED STATES, which was approved by the states in ratifying conventions in 1788, despite the cries of opponents that such a powerful government would tyrannize the states and their citizens. The new constitution was federal, in that powers were separated and divided between the national and state governments, both with their own jurisdictions. By turning to federalism the 55 men at Philadelphia solved what had been the central problem of American political history in the quarter century since the end of the French and Indian War, namely, how governmental power should be allocated. First, the question was between Parliament and the colonial assemblies; later, between Congress under the Articles of Confederation and the state legislatures. The American Revolution reached its culmination when the Constitution was adopted in 1788.

DON HIGGINBOTHAM

Bibliography: Alden, John R., *A History of the American Revolution* (1969); Bailyn, Bernard, *Ideological Origins of the American Revolution* (1967); Dupuy, Richard E., *The American Revolution, a Global War* (1977); Higginbotham, Don, *War of American Independence* (1971); Morgan, Edmund S., *Birth of the Republic,* 2d ed. (1977); Morris, Richard B., *The American Revolution Reconsidered* (1967); Shy, John, *A People Numerous and Armed* (1976); Wood, Gordon, *Creation of the American Republic* (1969).

See also: BRANDYWINE, BATTLE OF THE; BUNKER HILL, BATTLE OF; COWPENS, BATTLE OF; LEXINGTON AND CONCORD, BATTLES OF; LONG ISLAND, BATTLE OF; MONMOUTH, BATTLE OF; PARIS, TREATIES OF; SARATOGA, BATTLES OF; TRENTON, BATTLE OF; YORKTOWN CAMPAIGN.

(Left) *The Americans John Jay, John Adams, Benjamin Franklin, Temple Franklin, and Henry Laurens are portrayed at the preliminary peace negotiations in 1782 by Benjamin West.* (Below) *The Constitutional Convention of 1787 formulated the Constitution of the United States to replace the earlier Articles of Confederation.*

The American saddle horse was recognized as a breed of riding horse in 1891. It is known for both its vigor and its beauty.

American saddle horse

The American saddle horse, also called the saddlebred, the saddler, the Kentucky saddle horse, and the gaited horse, is a fashionable light HORSE popular in the show ring. An animal of kingly bearing, it has a well-formed head with a long and arched neck and a short, strong back; the tail is uplifted. The horse stands about 150–160 cm (60–64 in) high and weighs about 450 kg (1,000 lb); the coat is a dark, solid color, often with white markings on head and legs. The breed was developed from the Thoroughbred and the Morgan. Three-gaited American saddle horses do a brisk and lively walk, a showy trot, and a slow, rocking-chair canter. The five-gaited horse also performs a slow (stepping pace) and fast gait (rack) in which only one foot touches the ground at a time.

EVERETT SENTMANN

American Samoa

American Samoa is an island group in the south central Pacific Ocean about 2,576 km (1,600 mi) northeast of New Zealand. An unincorporated territory of the United States, it consists of seven islands: Aunu'u, Ofu, Olosega, Rose, Swain's, Tau (or Ta'u), and Tutuila. The last is the main island. The total area is 199 km² (77 mi²). The population is 32,395 (1980), and the capital and major city is PAGO PAGO (1980 pop., 3,058). American Samoa was created by an 1899 treaty among Great Britain, Germany, and the United States.

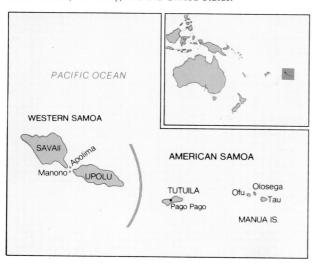

The islands are eroded remnants of volcanic landmasses. The climate is tropical, with temperatures ranging from about 20° C (70° F) to about 30° C (90° F). The rainy season extends from November to April, and hurricanes are prevalent from May to November. Natural resources are limited. The majority of the population is of Polynesian descent, and both Samoan and English are spoken. Village life is communal, based on a complicated social system headed by the matais, or chiefs. Education is compulsory for children 6 to 18 years of age, and the islands have a community college. The main industry is tuna canning. Executive power is held by a governor, elected by popular vote since 1977. The legislature—the Fono—was established by the constitution of 1960. The Samoan islands were first visited by Europeans in the 18th century but were not settled until 1830. The Samoan kingdom, established in 1889, was dissolved by the 1899 treaty. From 1900 to 1951 the territory was administered by the Department of the Navy and since then by the Department of the Interior, under which the islands have received significant aid. A new airport was built, and industry and tourism were stimulated.

See also: SAMOA; WESTERN SAMOA.

American Scholar

The *American Scholar*, founded in 1932 and published quarterly by Phi Beta Kappa, is a magazine edited in Washington, D.C., for the general reader. Although the writers are authorities, the articles, reviews, and opinion pieces are nontechnical and cover many fields. It had approximately 32,000 subscribers in 1982.

WARREN G. BOVEE

American Scholar, The

Ralph Waldo EMERSON's "American Scholar," originally delivered as an address to Harvard's Phi Beta Kappa Society in 1837, the same year of its publication, was called by Oliver Wendell Holmes "America's intellectual Declaration of Independence." In the address Emerson proposed a uniquely American intellectual view drawn from the experience of the New World, one rooted in an understanding of nature as well as of the literary and intellectual achievements of the past. Although he did not totally reject the European experience, Emerson called upon the American academic community to free itself from its strictures and prejudices.

American Scientist

American Scientist, published six times a year in New Haven, Conn., is the official publication of Sigma Xi, a scientific honorary society. It presents recent findings in the earth, physical, life, computer, and behavioral sciences as well as in mathematics and engineering. Established in 1913, it now has a circulation of about 128,000.

WARREN G. BOVEE

American shorthair cat

The American shorthair cat, popularly known as the tabby, was developed as a show breed for generations.

The American shorthair cat, also called the domestic shorthair, was brought to North America from England in early colonial times. An excellent rodent killer and an intelligent, affectionate pet, it has been selectively bred to take top awards at cat shows. It has a large head, well-developed shoulders and chest, and powerful, rippling muscles. The tail is medium long, the coat thick and even. Popular colors include silver tabby, brown tabby, and red tabby.   EVERETT SENTMAN

American Society of Newspaper Editors

The American Society of Newspaper Editors was organized in 1922 to promote professional ideals and provide a forum for debating news and editorial problems at its annual spring meeting. Among its some 800 members are editors in chief, editorial page editors, and managing editors of U.S. dailies with circulations of more than 20,000. The society publishes the monthly *ASNE Bulletin* and the annual *Problems of Journalism.*   EDWIN EMERY

American Staffordshire terrier

The American Staffordshire terrier is a cross between the bulldog and the terrier. A powerfully built dog with strong jaws, it was once used in dogfighting.

The American Staffordshire terrier is a strongly built breed of dog, with a broad head, large cheek muscles, powerful jaws, thick neck, and forelegs set fairly wide apart. It is 43–48 cm (17–19 in) at the shoulder and weighs 15.9–22.7 kg (35–50 lb). The short, stiff coat may be any of the usual dog colors. Uncropped ears are preferable and are held erect; the short tail is carried low. The Staffordshire has been bred in the United States since the mid-19th century but was not recognized by the American Kennel Club until 1935, under the name of Staffordshire terrier. The breed's name was officially changed to American Staffordshire terrier on Jan. 1, 1972, in part to distinguish the breed from the smaller STAFFORDSHIRE BULL TERRIER of England. The two breeds are closely related, both having a common background of cross between bulldog and terrier. They were bred as pit, or fighting, dogs, but today's Staffordshires have stable temperaments and make good household pets.   JOHN MANDEVILLE

American Tragedy, An

Theodore DREISER's massive novel *An American Tragedy* caused a public outcry and was banned in Boston when it was published in 1925. At once satiric and sentimental, the novel is based on an actual murder trial of 1906. Clyde Griffiths, a small-town American youth, dreams of wealth. Although he seduces a young factory worker named Roberta Alden, he hopes to marry the wealthy heiress Sondra Finchly. Unable to free himself from Roberta, he plots to drown her, but at the last moment his nerve fails him. Their boat capsizes accidentally, however, and Clyde makes no attempt to rescue Roberta. Arrested for murder, he becomes the focus of a circus trial. Dreiser felt that the story contained all the elements of American national life: "Politics, society, religion, business,

sex." The novel was twice translated into film, first in 1931 and, under the title *A Place in the Sun*, again in 1951.

American University

Established in 1893 and affiliated with the United Methodist Church, American University (enrollment: 11,200; library: 487,000 volumes) is in Washington, D.C. It has schools of liberal arts, nursing, and education, as well as a college of law.

American University of Beirut

Founded in 1866 as the Syrian Protestant College by the American Board Mission and given its present name in 1920, the American University of Beirut (enrollment: 4,700; library: 425,000 volumes) is a private coeducational school in Beirut, Lebanon. The university has faculties of arts and sciences, medical sciences, engineering and architecture, and agriculture. In 1978 it received an endowment to establish a school of business and management studies. Authority for its degrees is derived from the Board of Regents of the State University of New York. Located in a neutral section of Beirut, the university itself escaped serious damage from the civil strife of the 1970s. In 1982, however, its president, David S. Dodge, was abducted and later released. In January 1984 his successor, Malcolm Kerr, was slain near his office.

American water spaniel

The American water spaniel was bred in the 19th century for the hunting and retrieving of waterfowl.

The American water spaniel is a sporting breed of dog that stands 38–46 cm (15–18 in) at the shoulder and weighs 11.3–20.4 kg (25–45 lb). The dense, tightly curled coat is dark liver or chocolate, and a little white on the chest or toes is accepted in the show ring. The long, drooping ears are wide, and the slightly curved tail is carried a bit below the level of the back.

The dog is one of only a few breeds developed in the United States. Its origins are unknown, but its appearance suggests that the Irish water spaniel, curly coated retriever, and early spaniel types were crossed to develop the breed. Prior to its recognition by the American Kennel Club in 1940, the breed had been used exclusively for hunting, principally in the Midwest. Its qualities in the field are outstanding: it springs rather than points game, is able to note the location of four or five dropped animals and retrieve them all, and is an excellent water retriever, even in rough water. Although mainly popular as a hunting dog, it makes a good household companion.   JOHN MANDEVILLE

Americans for Democratic Action

Americans for Democratic Action (ADA) is a Washington, D.C.-based political action organization dedicated to the advancement of liberal causes. It was created in 1947 by prominent leaders in government, organized labor, academia, politics, and journalism, among whom were Marquis CHILDS, David DUBINSKY, Hubert H. HUMPHREY, Jr., Walter REUTHER,

Eleanor ROOSEVELT, Arthur M. SCHLESINGER, Jr., Leon Henderson, and Joseph L. Rauh, Jr. Its stated objective was to "map a campaign for restoring the influence of liberalism in the national and international policies of the United States," stressing also that the campaign was to be "free of totalitarian influence from either the Left or the Right."

The ADA is formally nonpartisan, but in practice it has mainly endorsed Democratic party candidates, and it is closely identified with the liberal wing of the Democratic party. Its members have held high positions in government.

Besides endorsing candidates, the ADA publishes a yearly appraisal of the performance of members of Congress on important issues. It also formulates comprehensive liberal positions on national issues; publishes books, pamphlets, and a newspaper; and proposes legislation.   RITA J. IMMERMAN

Bibliography: Brock, Clifton, *Americans for Democratic Action* (1962).

America's Cup

The America's Cup is competitive yachting's most prestigious prize. From 1851 to 1980 the best yachtsmen in the world tried unsuccessfully to wrest the trophy from American sailors. Not until 1983 was the American defender of the cup defeated. The competition originated when the New York Yacht Club sent a representative, the schooner *America*, to England to challenge the Royal Yacht Squadron's best. The *America* defeated 17 British opponents in a 93-km (58-mi) race around the Isle of Wight and won the British Royal Yacht Squadron's Hundred Guinea Cup. In 1857 the *America*'s owners presented the cup to the New York Yacht Club, which renamed it America's Cup and began to sponsor challenges for possession. The competition was expanded in 1876 to the best of 3 races, in 1893 to the best of 5, and in 1930 to the best of 7. Since 1930 the races have been held off Newport, R.I. Only three yachts have won twice: *Columbia*, *Intrepid*, and *Courageous*. In 1980 the *Freedom*, skippered by Dennis Conner, defeated the *Australia* in 5 races. In 1983, however, Conner's *Liberty* was beaten in 4 of 7 races by the *Australia II*.

Bibliography: Dunlap, G. D., *America's Cup Defenders* (1970); Hammond, Geoffrey, *Showdown at Newport: The Race for the America's Cup* (1974); Stone, Herbert L., *The America's Cup Races* (1970).

AMERICA'S CUP WINNERS*

1851	*America* defeated *Aurora*, England (1-0)
1870	*Magic* defeated *Cambria*, England (1-0)
1871	*Columbia* (first three races) and *Sappho* (last two races) defeated *Livonia*, England (4-1)
1876	*Madeline* defeated *Countess of Dufferin*, Canada (2-0)
1881	*Mischief* defeated *Atalanta*, Canada (2-0)
1885	*Puritan* defeated *Genesta*, England (2-0)
1886	*Mayflower* defeated *Galatea*, England (2-0)
1887	*Volunteer* defeated *Thistle*, Scotland (2-0)
1893	*Vigilant* defeated *Valkyrie II*, England (3-0)
1895	*Defender* defeated *Valkyrie III*, England (3-0)
1899	*Columbia* defeated *Shamrock*, Ireland (3-0)
1901	*Columbia* defeated *Shamrock II*, Ireland (3-0)
1903	*Reliance* defeated *Shamrock III*, Ireland (3-0)
1920	*Resolute* defeated *Shamrock IV*, Ireland (3-2)
1930	*Enterprise* defeated *Shamrock V*, Ireland (4-0)
1934	*Rainbow* defeated *Endeavour*, England (4-2)
1937	*Ranger* defeated *Endeavour II*, England (4-0)
1958	*Columbia* defeated *Sceptre*, England (4-0)
1962	*Weatherly* defeated *Gretel*, Australia (4-1)
1964	*Constellation* defeated *Sovereign*, England (4-0)
1967	*Intrepid* defeated *Dame Pattie*, Australia (4-0)
1970	*Intrepid* defeated *Gretel II*, Australia (4-1)
1974	*Courageous* defeated *Southern Cross*, Australia (4-0)
1977	*Courageous* defeated *Australia*, Australia (4-0)
1980	*Freedom* defeated *Australia*, Australia (4-1)
1983	*Australia II*, Australia, defeated *Liberty*, U.S.A. (4-3)

*All winners, until 1983, have been from the United States.

americium   [am-uh-ris'-ee-uhm]

Americium is a transuranium element, a radioactive metal of the ACTINIDE SERIES. Its symbol is Am, its atomic number is 95,

and the atomic weight of its stablest isotope is 243. Americium does not occur naturally. It was synthesized for the first time by Glenn Seaborg, A. Ghiorso, R. A. James, and L. O. Morgan in 1944. They bombarded plutonium-239 with helium ions and obtained the isotope ^{241}Am. The known isotopes of americium, whose mass numbers range from 237 to 246, are radioactive. The stablest isotope, ^{243}Am, has a half-life of 7,370 years.

Usable amounts of ^{241}Am are obtained by bombardment of plutonium-241 in nuclear reactors. Americium is fairly reactive: it combines with oxygen when exposed to air. Because it emits strong gamma radiation, ^{241}Am is used in various types of measuring devices and in radiography.

amethyst   [am'-uh-thist]

Hexagonal (6-sided) amethyst crystals often are found lining the interior of a geode, or rock cavity. The outer shell of the geode is usually made of chalcedony, another type of quartz. Colors of amethyst vary from shades of lilac to rich, dark purple, and some stones may be heated slightly to distribute the colors more evenly. Amethysts ranked among the most precious of gems until the 18th century, after the discovery of large deposits in South America.

Amethyst, a violet, crystalline variety of quartz, is the birthstone for February. When transparent and of good color, it is valued as a semiprecious gem and is usually step-cut or intaglio-carved. The color, thought to be caused by impurities of iron, manganese, or hydrocarbons, is changed to citrine yellow by heating the stone; most commercial citrine is heat-treated amethyst. The mineral occurs in cavities in many rock types, and is found in the Ural Mountains, Brazil, Sri Lanka, and the United States.

The ancient Greeks attributed various powers to amethyst, notably that of protecting against drunkenness and passion, but also those of controlling evil thoughts and enhancing shrewdness. The ancients probably applied the name to purple corundum and garnet as well as to true amethyst.

Amhara   [am-hahr'-uh]

The Amhara are a people of the central highlands of Ethiopia. Numbering about 10 million in the early 1980s, they are descended from mixed Hamito-Semitic groups that entered the highlands from southern Arabia between the 6th century BC and the 1st century AD. The Amhara are dark skinned but without Negroid features. Since their establishment of the Solomonid dynasty in the 13th century, they have dominated the history of Ethiopia.

The Amharic language, originally a court language, is the official tongue of Ethiopia. It is a Semitic language closely related to Ge'ez, the sacred literary language of the Ethiopian Orthodox church. Together with the Tigré to the north of them, the Amhara consider themselves the only true Christians. They are identified closely with their church—formerly headed by the Ethiopian emperors—and are still MONOPHY-SITES, believing that Christ has only one nature, which is both perfectly human and perfectly divine.

The Amhara, whose economy is chiefly agricultural, lay great emphasis on land ownership. Although descent, which is traced through the male line, is important among them, their society is organized primarily around a system of patron-client relationships based on landholding. Their traditional dress resembles a toga under which men wear tight-fitting trousers and women wear a gown. Westernization of traditional cultural forms has accelerated, especially among the Western-educated elite, since the military coup d'etat in 1974.

BRIAN SPOONER

Bibliography: Ullendorff, Edward, *The Ethiopians: An Introduction to Country and People*, 3d ed. (1973).

Amherst, Jeffrey, Baron Amherst

Lord Amherst, b. Jan. 29, 1717, d. Aug. 3, 1797, was an able British general who conquered Canada during the FRENCH AND INDIAN WAR (1754–63). After serving in Europe in the War of the Austrian Succession (1740–48), he was ordered to America to command the expedition against the seemingly impregnable French fortress at LOUISBOURG. As a result of his careful planning, the fortress fell on July 26, 1758.

Appointed commander in chief in British North America in 1759, Amherst captured the forts at TICONDEROGA and CROWN POINT. With his forces converging on Montreal from three directions, he captured that city on Sept. 8, 1760, and thus won control of Canada. Amherst was appointed governor-general of British North America and governor of Virginia. Returning to England, he was created a baron in 1776 and made a field marshal in 1796.

GEORGE ATHAN BILLIAS

Bibliography: Long, John C., *Lord Jeffrey Amherst* (1933).

Amherst College

Established in 1821, Amherst College (enrollment: 1,569; library: 530,000 volumes) is a private 4-year liberal arts college in Amherst, Mass. A cooperative program with Hampshire, Mount Holyoke, and Smith colleges and the University of Massachusetts makes libraries and certain courses mutually available. Amherst administers the Folger Shakespeare Library in Washington, D.C.

Amherst   (Massachusetts)

Amherst (1980 pop., 17,773) is a town in the Connecticut River valley of west central Massachusetts. Settled in the 1730s, it developed an economy based on farming. Today Amherst is a college town, the site of the University of Massachusetts, Amherst College, and Hampshire College.

Amherst   (Nova Scotia)

Amherst (1981 pop., 9,684) is located in northern Nova Scotia, near the Cumberland Basin. It overlooks the Tantramar Marshes. Its economic activities include dairy farming and the production of steel, iron, and chemicals. Settled by the French, it was renamed in 1759 after Jeffrey Amherst.

amicus curiae   [uh-mee'-kuhs koo'-ree-y]

The legal term *amicus curiae* (Latin, "friend of the court") means a person who enters a BRIEF in a lawsuit in which he or she is not a party. Organizations and groups often offer arguments or evidence in cases that concern them, particularly in the higher courts, after obtaining permission from the court.

amide   [am'-yd]

Amides are a class of organic compounds related to ammonia and commonly found in nature. PROTEINS and PEPTIDES, compounds fundamental to life, are made up of amides. The chemistry of amides is therefore important to an understanding of many biochemical processes.

Amides have the general structural formula $RCONH_2$, in which R is a hydrocarbon group. Amides may be considered either as substituted ammonia (NH_3) compounds, in which an organic acid radical replaces a hydrogen atom, or as nitrogen derivatives or carboxylic acids (RCOOH). Because of the combination of an acidic group with a basic group, amides in solution are essentially neutral, although they will react with very strong acids or bases. In general, amides have higher melting points and boiling points and are less soluble in water than are their component acids and AMINES. These properties may vary, however, depending on the presence of other groups in the molecule. Amides may be prepared in many ways, and they undergo a range of chemical reactions.

Molecules that have two amide groups are diamides; molecular chains formed from repeating linkages are called polyamides. The simplest naturally occurring amide is UREA, H_2NCONH_2, a diamide that is excreted in the urine of many mammals as a product of protein metabolism. Urea is of some commercial importance as starting material in the manufacture of certain polymers. Proteins are a class of high-molecular-weight polyamides formed by the combination of AMINO ACIDS with each other. Other nonprotenoid amides include penicillin G; niacinamide; piperine, found in black pepper; and other compounds, many with physiological activity. NYLON is a synthetic polyamide made from a dicarboxylic acid and a diamine to form a long-chain polymer.

Some amides exist in ring structure. Among these are riboflavin (vitamin B_2) and some other B vitamins, DNA, RNA, caffeine, uric acid, and barbiturates. Still other amides contain a sulfonyl group, RSO_2NHR. This group, known as sulfonamides, includes sulfonanilamide and other sulfa drugs. A cyclic example is saccharin, having a $-CONHSO_2-$ grouping within a ring.

RONALD F. BROWN

Bibliography: Zabicky, Jacob, and Patai, Saul, eds., *Chemistry of the Amides* (1970).

Amiens   [ah-mee-en']

Amiens is the capital of Somme department, in Picardy in northern France, about 120 km (75 mi) north of Paris. Located on the Somme River, the city is an important rail junction and is known historically for its textile manufacturing. The population is 135,992 (1975). The climate of Amiens is mild, with temperatures averaging 2° C (35° F) in January and 18° C (64° F) in July. Rainfall is about 510 mm (20 in) annually. Other than textiles, manufactured products include chemicals, machinery, and tires. In addition, Amiens is a trade center for the surrounding agricultural region. It is the site of the University of Picardy (1965) and the Picardy Museum. The noted Cathedral of Notre Dame is located there. Begun in 1220, it was finished about 1270, but the transept and rose window were added later (see AMIENS CATHEDRAL).

Amiens was originally the capital of the Ambiani tribe and was under Roman rule when Christianity was introduced in the 4th century. Under French rule from 1185, the city passed to the Burgundians in 1435. It came under French rule again in 1477. The city was the site of the Peace of Amiens (1802) during the Napoleonic Wars. It fell to the Prussians in 1870 and was occupied by the Germans in both world wars, during which it suffered much damage. It has been largely rebuilt.

Amiens, Treaty of

The Treaty of Amiens, signed by Britain and by France, Spain, and the Batavian Republic (Holland) in March 1802, marked the end of the FRENCH REVOLUTIONARY WARS. Britain, which was forced by the treaty to relinquish most of its acquisitions in the preceding conflict, resumed war with France in May 1803. The hostilities between France and coalitions of European powers, including Britain, from 1803 to 1815, are generally called the NAPOLEONIC WARS.

Amiens Cathedral

Amiens, a city 121 km (75 mi) north of Paris, is the site of one of the three most famous High Gothic cathedrals, the others being CHARTRES and REIMS cathedrals. Amiens Cathedral was begun in 1220 at the west or entrance end of the NAVE. The first building campaign, supervised by Robert de Luzarches, lasted until about 1233, producing the nave and TRANSEPT. Thomas de Cormont, successor to de Luzarches, oversaw the construction of the lower parts of the choir and APSE at the east end until 1241. His son Renaud de Cormont completed the east end in the RAYONNANT STYLE (late Gothic) in 1269. The huge church is 145 m (476 ft) long; its vault is 42.3 m (138 ft) high; the building covers 7,700 m² (89,875 ft²), making it the largest French Gothic cathedral ever built. Its plan and design closely follow that of Reims, but in the third building campaign a striking change was made: a glazed triforium (the gallery between the nave arcade and the CLERESTORY), modeled on that of the church of SAINT-DENIS (1130–44) in Paris, was introduced. In stylistic terms, its three west portals, finished in 1236, constitute one of the most stunning and unified High Gothic sculptural groups. RONALD E. MALMSTROM

Bibliography: Braun, Hugh, *Cathedral Architecture* (1962); Frankl, Paul, *Gothic Architecture* (1962).

Amin Dada, Idi [ah-meen' dah-dah, ee'-dee]

Former president and self-appointed field marshal of the Republic of Uganda, Idi Amin Dada, b. Koboko, Uganda, c.1925, was overthrown by Tanzanian regular troops and Ugandan exiles in April, 1979. A Muslim and a member of the Kakwa tribe, Amin joined the British colonial army, serving in World War II and later fighting against the Mau Mau rebellion in Kenya. In February 1966 Amin helped Prime Minister Milton Obote overthrow Kabaka Mutesa II, president of the federation of Uganda. In January 1971 Amin ousted Obote from the presidency, proclaimed himself head of state, and introduced a ruthless dictatorship under which about 300,000 Ugandans have died.

Bibliography: Kyemba, Henry, *A State of Blood: The Inside Story of Idi Amin* (1977); Melady, Thomas, *Idi Amin Dada: Hitler in Africa* (1977).

amine [uh-meen']

Amines are a class of organic compounds that are important in the formation of proteins and are present in great numbers in living organisms. Many have pronounced physiological effects. Among the physiologically active amines are spermine, all of the sulfonamides, most enzymes, serotonin, ephedrine, dopamine, amphetamine, insulin, and adrenaline.

In amines, one, two, or three of the hydrogen atoms of AMMONIA, NH_3, are replaced by hydrocarbon groups, symbolized by R. Thus RNH_2 is called a primary amine, $RR'NH$ or R_2NH a

secondary amine, and $RR'R''N$ or R_3N a tertiary amine (R' and R'' represent different groups). Like ammonia, amines are bases and easily react with an acid to form a SALT, so that NH_3 yields NH_4Cl and RNH_2 yields RNH_3Cl, when they react with hydrochloric acid, HCl. If R has a low molecular weight, the corresponding amines are gaseous (like ammonia) or are low-boiling liquids, and are soluble in water. As the molecular weight of R increases, water solubility declines; even so, the salts remain soluble.

Amines may be synthesized in the laboratory by a variety of methods. Amines undergo many reactions, most of which are initiated by the lone (unbonded) pair of electrons on the nitrogen. One such reaction is the formation of a quarternary salt; a tertiary amine, R_3N, reacts with an alkyl halide, such as methyl iodide, CH_3I, to give $R_3N^+CH_3I^-$. Very similar is the reaction with hydrogen peroxide, H_2O_2, to give an amine oxide, $R_3N^+O^-$. If the nitrogen atom is part of a ring, the characteristic properties still apply.

AROMATIC amines, exemplified by aniline, $C_6H_5NH_2$ (which is present in coal tar), undergo reactions of their own, and have been so widely used in the preparation of synthetic DYES that such dyes are called coal or aniline dyes.

Bibliography: Morrison, Robert T., and Boyd, Robert N., *Organic Chemistry*, 3d ed. (1976).

amino acid [uh-meen'-oh]

Amino acids are organic compounds that are the building blocks of PROTEINS. Hence many of them play an essential role in most animal metabolisms. Each amino acid has at least one carboxyl (COOH) group, which is acidic, and one amino (NH_2) group, which is basic. (The name of the acids comes from the stem word AMINE, meaning "derived from ammonia.") Amino acids join together in long chains, the amino group of one amino acid linking with the carboxyl group of another. The linkage is known as a PEPTIDE bond, and a chain of amino acids is known as a polypeptide. Proteins are large, naturally-occurring polypeptides. Many different amino acids are found, about 20 of which are the main constituents of proteins; only about half of these are classified as essential nutrients, that is, necessary in the human diet.

Although all amino acids have amino and carboxyl groups, they all differ in the rest of the molecule. Some have an additional amino or carboxyl group, and others have water-repelling (hydrophobic) groups. The shape and overall properties of a protein are dependent upon its constituent amino acids. In some proteins, a change in just one amino acid in the

AMINES

Name	Formula	mp° C	bp° C	Sp. Gr.*
Methylamine	CH_3NH_2	−93.5	−6.3	0.699
Dimethylamine	$(CH_3)_2NH$	−96.0	7.4	.680
Trimethylamine	$(CH_3)_3N$	−124.0	3.5	.662
Ethylamine	$CH_3CH_2NH_2$	−80.6	16.6	.689
Diethylamine	$(CH_3CH_2)_2NH$	−38.9	56.0	.711
Triethylamine	$(CH_3CH_2)_3N$	−114.8	89.5	.728
n-Propylamine	$CH_3CH_2CH_2NH_2$	−83.0	48.7	.719
Di-n-propylamine	$(CH_3CH_2CH_2)_2NH$	−39.6	110.7	.738
Tri-n-propylamine	$(CH_3CH_2CH_2)_3N$	−93.5	156	.757
n-Butylamine	$CH_2CH_2CH_2CH_2CH_2NH_2$	−50.5	76	.740
n-Amylamine	$CH_3CH_2CH_2CH_2CH_2NH_2$	−55.0	104	.766
n-Hexylamine	$CH_3(CH_2)_5NH_2$	−19	130^{742mm}	
Laurylamine	$CH_3(CH_2)_{11}NH_2$	28	135^{15mm}	
Ethylenediamine	$H_2NCH_2CH_2NH_2$	8.5	117	.892
Trimethylenediamine	$H_2NCH_2CH_2CH_2NH_2$		135.5	.884
Tetramethylenediamine	$H_2NCH_2CH_2CH_2CH_2NH_2$	27	158	
Pentamethylenediamine	$_2NCH_2CH_2CH_2CH_2NH_2$	9	178	.855
Hexamethylenediamine	$H_2N(CH_2)_6NH_2$	39	196	
Ethanolamine	$HOCH_2CH_2NH_2$		171	1.022
Diethanolamine	$(HOCH_2CH_2)_2NH$	28	270	1.097
Triethanolamine	$(HOCH_2CH_2)_3N$	21	279^{150mm}	1.124
Allylamine	$CH_2=CHCH_2NH_2$		56	0.761
Aniline	$C_6H_5NH_2$	−6	184	1.022

*Specific gravity.

polymer chain, out of a total of perhaps 250 amino acids, or even a change in its position, can cause the protein to become nonfunctional, if it is an ENZYME, or to perform its function differently, if it is not an enzyme. Chemists are currently trying to relate the role of each of these amino acids to the way in which the protein works.

Proteins are an essential substance in the diets of humans and most animals because of their constituent amino acids. Nutritionally, complete proteins are those which contain the right concentrations of the amino acids that humans cannot synthesize from other amino acids or nitrogenous sources. An adequate diet, however, may be achieved by consuming a correct mixture of proteins, some of which might be deficient in one amino acid but rich in another.

A first step in the digestion of proteins is their cleavage by proteolytic (protein-splitting) enzymes into smaller chains of amino acids, or PEPTIDES. These initial peptides are then cleaved into smaller and smaller peptides until free amino acids are available. The amino acids are absorbed from the intestine by a complete biochemical process and are circulated by the blood to the tissues that utilize them. Some of the amino acids are used directly as the building blocks in the synthesis of new proteins unique to the species. Others may be used to supply energy, and still others, particularly when large amounts of proteins are consumed, may be excreted in the urine. Individual amino acids and most small peptides frequently have a bad or even bitter taste, although the same amino acids in a small protein would most likely be tasteless.

In addition to the 20 common amino acids, others occur in proteins. Analysis of many proteins from plant and animal sources has shown that all are made up of about 25 to 30 amino acids. In addition, more than 50 amino acids, not combined in proteins, have been found in plants. Some of these are simple derivatives of the common amino acids; others, usually found in plants and microorganisms, have more complicated structures.

ROBERT E. FEENEY

Bibliography: Chaney, Margaret S., and Ross, Margaret L., *Nutrition*, 9th ed. (1979); Lehninger, Albert L., *Biochemistry*, 2d ed. (1975); Weinstein, Boris, ed., *Chemistry and Biochemistry of Amino Acids, Peptides, and Proteins*, 5 vols. (1974–78).

See also: GENETIC CODE; NUCLEIC ACID.

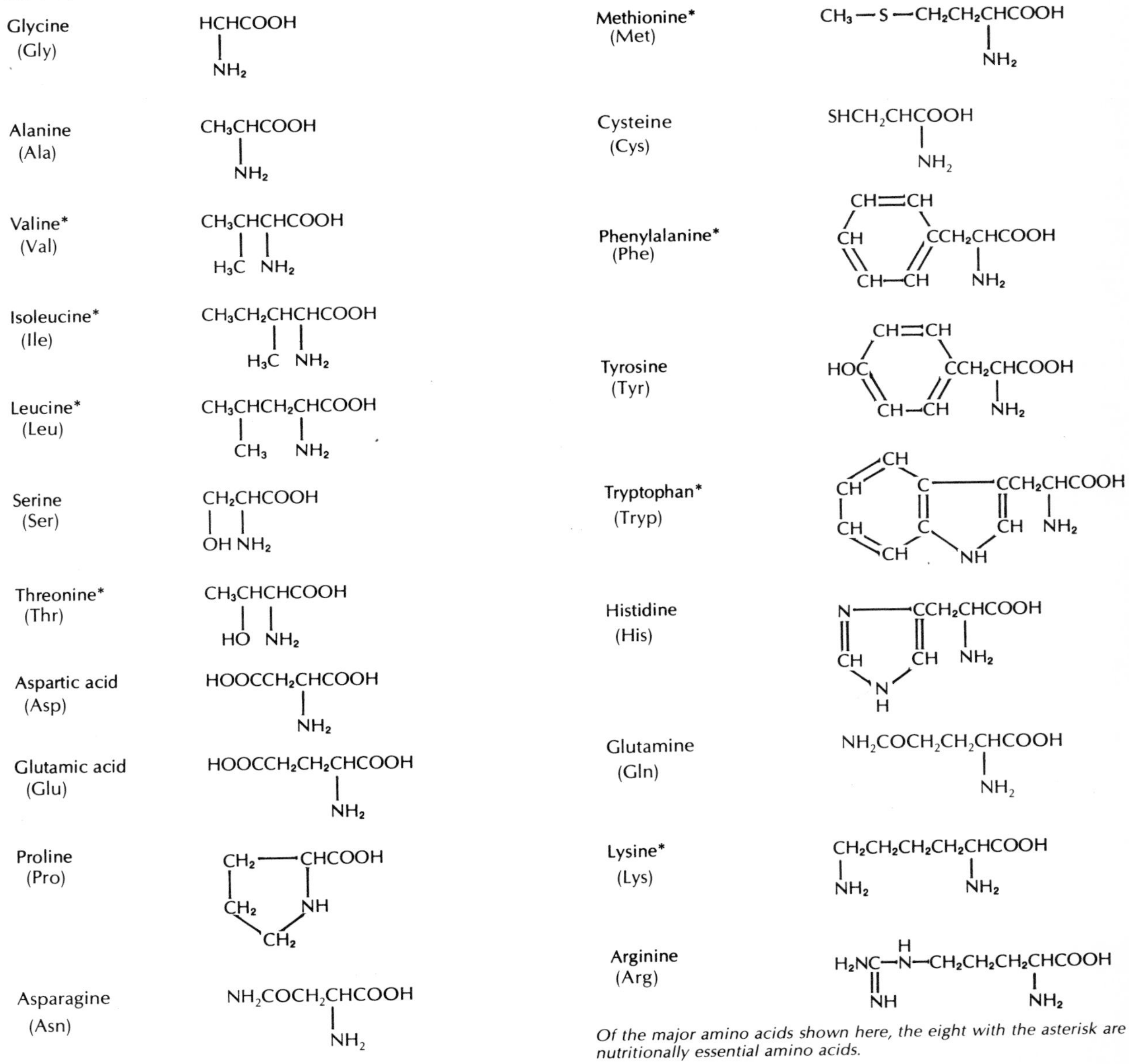

Glycine (Gly)

$$HCHCOOH$$
$$|$$
$$NH_2$$

Alanine (Ala)

$$CH_3CHCOOH$$
$$|$$
$$NH_2$$

Valine* (Val)

$$CH_3CHCHCOOH$$
$$|\quad|$$
$$H_3C\quad NH_2$$

Isoleucine* (Ile)

$$CH_3CH_2CHCHCOOH$$
$$|\quad|$$
$$H_3C\quad NH_2$$

Leucine* (Leu)

$$CH_3CHCH_2CHCOOH$$
$$|\quad\quad|$$
$$CH_3\quad NH_2$$

Serine (Ser)

$$CH_2CHCOOH$$
$$|\quad|$$
$$OH\ NH_2$$

Threonine* (Thr)

$$CH_3CHCHCOOH$$
$$|\quad|$$
$$HO\quad NH_2$$

Aspartic acid (Asp)

$$HOOCCH_2CHCOOH$$
$$|$$
$$NH_2$$

Glutamic acid (Glu)

$$HOOCCH_2CH_2CHCOOH$$
$$|$$
$$NH_2$$

Proline (Pro)

Asparagine (Asn)

$$NH_2COCH_2CHCOOH$$
$$|$$
$$NH_2$$

Methionine* (Met)

$$CH_3-S-CH_2CH_2CHCOOH$$
$$|$$
$$NH_2$$

Cysteine (Cys)

$$SHCH_2CHCOOH$$
$$|$$
$$NH_2$$

Phenylalanine* (Phe)

Tyrosine (Tyr)

Tryptophan* (Tryp)

Histidine (His)

Glutamine (Gln)

$$NH_2COCH_2CH_2CHCOOH$$
$$|$$
$$NH_2$$

Lysine* (Lys)

$$CH_2CH_2CH_2CH_2CHCOOH$$
$$|\quad\quad\quad\quad\quad|$$
$$NH_2\quad\quad\quad\quad NH_2$$

Arginine (Arg)

$$\overset{\displaystyle H}{H_2NC-N-CH_2CH_2CH_2CHCOOH}$$
$$\|\quad\quad\quad\quad\quad\quad|$$
$$NH\quad\quad\quad\quad\quad NH_2$$

Of the major amino acids shown here, the eight with the asterisk are nutritionally essential amino acids.

Amis, Kingsley   [ay'-mis]

An English novelist, poet, critic, and teacher, Kingsley Amis, b. Apr. 16, 1922, came to prominence as one of England's AN-GRY YOUNG MEN with the publication of his first novel, *Lucky Jim* (1954; film, 1957), a sharp satire on education and the establishment. His other novels include *That Uncertain Feeling* (1955; film, 1962), *I Like It Here* (1958), and *Take a Girl Like You* (1960; film, 1970). He has also written volumes of poetry and political and literary criticism. In addition, his detective and science fiction includes *The Anti-Death League* (1966); *Colonel Sun* (1968), a James Bond adventure; and *The Green Man* (1969).

Amish: see MENNONITES.

Amistad Case

In the Amistad Case (1841) the U.S. Supreme Court upheld the principle that people escaping illegal slavery had the right to fight to regain their freedom. The case concerned a group of Africans being illegally shipped as slaves between Havana and another Cuban port aboard the *Amistad;* on July 1, 1839, they seized the ship, killing several crew members. The *Amistad* was captured by a U.S. warship off Long Island in August 1839. A federal court in Connecticut denied extradition claims and acquitted the Africans of murder. This decision was sustained by the Supreme Court, before which the Africans were represented by John Quincy Adams.

Bibliography: Cable, Mary, *Black Odyssey: The Case of the Slave Ship "Amistad"* (1971).

Amman   [ahm-mahn']

Amman, the capital and largest city of Jordan, is located about 40 km (25 mi) northeast of the Dead Sea. A small town until it became the capital of Transjordan in 1921, it now has a population of 648,587 (1979 est.), about one-third of which are Palestinians. Amman is located on a steppe at an altitude of 821 m (2,692 ft). The city itself lies in a narrow valley with the newer sections built on the surrounding slopes to the nearby plateau. A commercial as well as administrative center, Amman exports phosphates mined nearby at El Hasa. Manufactured products include textiles and leather goods. Amman is the site of the Jordan Archaeological Museum and also the University of Jordan (1962).

Amman may have been settled as early as the 17th century BC; it was the biblical city Rabbah (Ammon) and the main city and capital of the Ammonites. As the ancient Greek city Philadelphia, southernmost of the ten cities of the Decapolis, it prospered under the leadership of Ptolemy II Philadelphus (r. 285–246 BC) and later under the Roman Empire. The city assumed its current name in the 7th century.

Ruins of Ammonite tombs, a Roman theater seating 6,000, an odeon (a small, roofed theater), a citadel, and an acropolis remain, although many of the city's ancient buildings have been destroyed by earthquakes. Amman was further damaged during the civil fighting between Palestinian guerrillas and the Jordanian army in 1970 and 1971.

Ammanati, Bartolommeo   [ah-mah-nah'-tee, bahr-toh-loh-may'-oh]

Bartolommeo Ammanati, b. June 18, 1511, d. Apr. 13, 1592, was a leading Florentine sculptor and architect of the Italian Renaissance. He appears to have studied with the sculptor Baccio Bandinelli, after which he worked in Venice with Jacopo Sansovino; in nearby Padua he designed, under Sansovino's influence, the monumental arch (1544) of the Benavides Palace and the Benavides Tomb (1546) in the Church of the Eremitani. Arriving in Rome in 1550, the same year he married the poetess Laura Battiferri, he collaborated with Giacomo Barozzi da Vignola and Giorgio Vasari on the Villa Giulia (1552–55) and executed the Del Monte family tombs (1550–53) in the church of San Pietro in Montorio.

After 1555, Ammanati resided in Florence and was responsible for some of the most important projects of the day: the Santa Trinità Bridge (1567–70; destroyed 1944, rebuilt 1957); the grandiose courtyard (1558–70) of the PITTI PALACE; and the Neptune Fountain (1563–75) in the Piazza della Signoria, with its colossal marble statue of the sea god contrasting with graceful, attenuated bronze figures of other sea deities around the basin.

MARK J. ZUCKER

Ammann, Othmar Hermann   [ahm'-mahn]

The Swiss-born engineer Othmar Hermann Ammann, b. Mar. 26, 1879, d. Sept. 22, 1965, designed many of the most famous bridges in the United States, the Lincoln Tunnel under the Hudson River, Dulles International Airport in Washington, D.C., and other major projects. He was also involved in the design and construction of New York City's Lincoln Center for the Performing Arts. After studying in Zurich, Ammann immigrated to the United States in 1904. Ammann was named chief engineer for the Port of New York Authority in 1927, and in the succeeding years he designed three of the world's longest suspension bridges: the George Washington Bridge in New York (1,067 m/3,500 ft), completed in 1931; San Francisco's Golden Gate Bridge (1,280 m/4,200 ft), completed in 1937; and the Verrazano-Narrows Bridge (1,298 m/4,260 ft), connecting Brooklyn and Staten Island, completed in 1964.

ammeter   [am'-meet-ur]

An ammeter measures the flow of current by converting electrical energy to mechanical energy. Most ammeters measure direct current (DC) and make use of D'Arsonval's classic GALVANOMETER principle, in which the magnetic field of a current-bearing coil opposes that of a fixed magnet. Because a very small current will cause full-scale deflection of the coil, the ammeter must be modified to measure larger currents. If a low-resistant path, or shunt, is attached to the two ends of the coil in a DC ammeter, a part of the current bypasses the meter movement. The true amperage of the current is obtained by multiplying the amperage indicated on the meter by the quantity of one plus the ratio of the coil resistance to the shunt resistance. The introduction of more-sophisticated digital measuring devices has somewhat decreased the wide use of ammeters.

LESLIE W. LEE

ammonia

Ammonia (NH_3), one of the most important nitrogen compounds, is a colorless, poisonous gas that can be distinguished by its characteristic irritating odor. It is extremely soluble in water. The ammonia commonly sold as a household cleanser and disinfectant is a dilute solution of ammonium hydroxide, an alkaline compound that can exist only in aqueous solution.

Ammonia is manufactured directly from its elements, hydrogen and nitrogen, by the Haber-Bosch process (see HABER, FRITZ). The ammonia is then stored either in pressurized cylinders or as an aqueous solution. In the laboratory, ammonia may be prepared by heating an ammonium salt with sodium hydroxide (lye, NaOH). Large quantities are used in manufacturing nitric acid and ammonium salts, and ammonia and its compounds are the principal nitrogen sources for fertilizers, synthetic fibers, and explosives. The SOLVAY PROCESS uses ammonia to manufacture sodium carbonate from common salt.

Ammonia is easily liquefied and thus is widely used as a refrigerant (see REFRIGERATION). It is especially useful for this purpose because it has low density, high stability, low corrosiveness, and a high heat of vaporization. Ammonia salts are used as SMELLING SALTS to relieve faintness.

ammonite   [am'-uh-nyt]

Ammonites are an extinct group of marine mollusks of the CEPHALOPOD class, which includes the OCTOPUS, SQUID, and CUTTLEFISH. Prized as ornaments for the past several hundred years, they are also sought after by geologists, who find them useful for correlating rock strata of one area with those of another. They are found preserved in many different types of SEDIMENTARY ROCK. Because the univalve (one-piece) shells

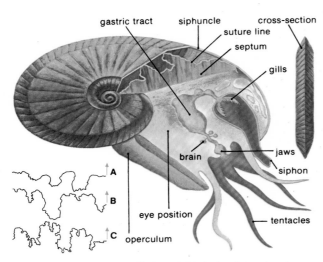

The ammonite, an extinct mollusk, probably had an internal anatomy similar to that of the present-day nautilus. The animal moved by ejecting water rapidly through a siphon tube. The shell was divided into air-filled chambers separated by septa, or walls. The animal lived in the outer open chamber, which it could close with an operculum, or lid. A siphuncle, or tube, connected all the chambers, allowing regulation of air pressure within them. Thus, the animal could sink or swim by altering its buoyancy. The suture line, along which the septa joined the shell, had a characteristic pattern for each species. These patterns became more complex as the ammonites evolved from primitive Ceratites (A), through intermediate Hildoceras (B), to advanced Baculite forms (C). The blue arrows point to the head and siphuncle positions. Various ammonite shell shapes indicate that some were active predators and others were drifters or bottom feeders.

changed rapidly in size and shape throughout the group's 325-million-year history, they are excellent for stratigraphic age determination as well as correlation.

Ammonites were, at least in part, coiled and also chambered. They appear to have formed thin plates, or septa, to wall off the part of the shell that was no longer used, as does the modern NAUTILUS. A thin cord of tissue extending from the living animal to the initial chamber of the shell ran along either the lower (ventral) or upper (dorsal) shell margin. The edges of the septa made a wavy, often intricate pattern on the outer shell surface. This pattern distinguishes ammonite shells from nautilus shells, which have only slightly wavy margins. Shell diameters range from 5 to 15 cm (2 to 6 in) in some species, up to as much as 2.7 m (9 ft) in others.

Ammonites appear to have lived in open ocean, or at least in saline waters. Many were nektic (free-swimming), with some species benthonic (bottom-dwelling) during adulthood; others were planktic (drifting or floating). Ammonites came close to extinction several times. After appearing early in the DEVONIAN PERIOD, they diversified rapidly but then declined markedly in the Late Devonian. They had a marked resurgence during the latter part of the PALEOZOIC ERA but came close to extinction again at its end. Only one group developed in the TRIASSIC PERIOD, and it, too, declined. Again widespread and diverse in the JURASSIC and CRETACEOUS periods, ammonites finally died out as the MESOZOIC ERA ended.

WILLIAM B. N. BERRY

Bibliography: Moore, Raymond, et al., *Invertebrate Fossils* (1952).

Ammons, A. R.   [am'-uhnz]

An American poet and professor, Archie Randolph Ammons, b. Whiteville, N.C., Feb. 18, 1926, moved from short lyric forms to increasingly complex poetic speculations on the nature of perception and language. His first book, *Ommateum*, was published in 1955; he received a National Book Award (1973) for *Collected Poems 1951–1971*.

ammunition

Ammunition includes a variety of devices used to deliver an explosive, chemical, or pyrotechnic charge to a target. Military ammunition includes aerial BOMBS, MINES, TORPEDOS, rockets, and a broad spectrum of EXPLOSIVE and nonexplosive projectiles. Common usage limits the term to devices designed to be ejected from a FIREARM, ARTILLERY piece, or MORTAR.

Ammunition consists of three basic elements: the primer (detonator), the propellant, and the projectile. Most ammunition also has a casing, or cartridge, that encapsulates the primer and propellant and often grips some portion of the projectile.

Primer. Early ammunition was assembled as needed. A fine black powder served as the primer charge to detonate the propellant charge, a coarser powder. Matchlocks, wheel locks, and flintlocks were used to ignite the primer charge. A new method of ignition, the percussion cap, was introduced in the early 19th century. This was a soft copper cup filled with a sensitive explosive and placed over a nipple with a small hole leading to the propellant. A hammer struck the cap and fired the weapon. Percussion caps survive in the form of primers located in the center or the rim of the base of the cartridge.

Propellant. From the late 13th century to the late 19th century, the sole propellant was black powder, or GUNPOWDER. Its composition has varied little in seven centuries, the traditional recipe being 10% sulfur, 15% charcoal, and 75% saltpeter (potassium nitrate). Although it was unchallenged for centuries, black powder has its drawbacks. It produces a large cloud of smoke and fouls the bores of firearms after relatively few shots. Black powder also readily attracts moisture, hence the admonition "keep your powder dry."

Nitrocellulose-base smokeless powders, of which GUNCOTTON was the first, began to replace black powder in the late 1880s; within 20 years, they were being used almost exclusively. The new propellants overcame black powder's deficiencies and were much more powerful.

Small-Arms Projectiles and Cartridge Assemblies. Until the early 19th century, small-arms projectiles consisted of round lead-alloy or iron balls of fractionally smaller diameter than the weapon's smooth bore. Later, spiral-grooved (rifled) bores, designed to make the projectile spin, became prevalent, although smooth-bore shotguns of limited range still exist. Modern projectiles generally have pointed or rounded noses and are clad with copper or brass. The diameter, or caliber, of a projectile is expressed in fractions of an inch or in millimeters. With the advent of the more powerful smokeless powders, the caliber of military shoulder weapons has undergone a drastic reduction. The last U.S. military black-powder rifle round was .45 caliber (0.45 in); a .30 caliber round replaced it; today the caliber is .223, or 5.66 mm.

Paper cartridges, incorporating the powder and projectile into a paper casing, were introduced in Europe during the 16th century. The entire assembly was rammed down the bore. The first successful metallic cartridge to incorporate projectile, propellant, and primer was invented in 1836. Experimentation during the next 50 years resulted in small-arms ammunition as we know it today.

Modern ammunition can be categorized by its degree of preassembly. In fixed ammunition, all the components are held together by a cartridge case. Semifixed ammunition features a projectile that is not firmly held by the cartridge case and is inserted just before firing, allowing adjustments to be made to the propellant. Separated ammunition is similar to semifixed, but the cartridge case comes sealed and is loaded after the projectile. Separate-loading ammunition has no cartridge case, the propellant being packed in combustible bags. Small-arms ammunition is typically fixed, whereas larger types of ammunition are usually separate-loading.

Artillery Projectiles. Artillery projectiles traditionally have been the subject of much research. Exploding, hollow-cast rounds were in use in the 16th century. Bar and chain shot (two balls fastened together) were used against ship's rigging. Grapeshot and canister were used to cut down massed troop formations with large quantities of lead balls.

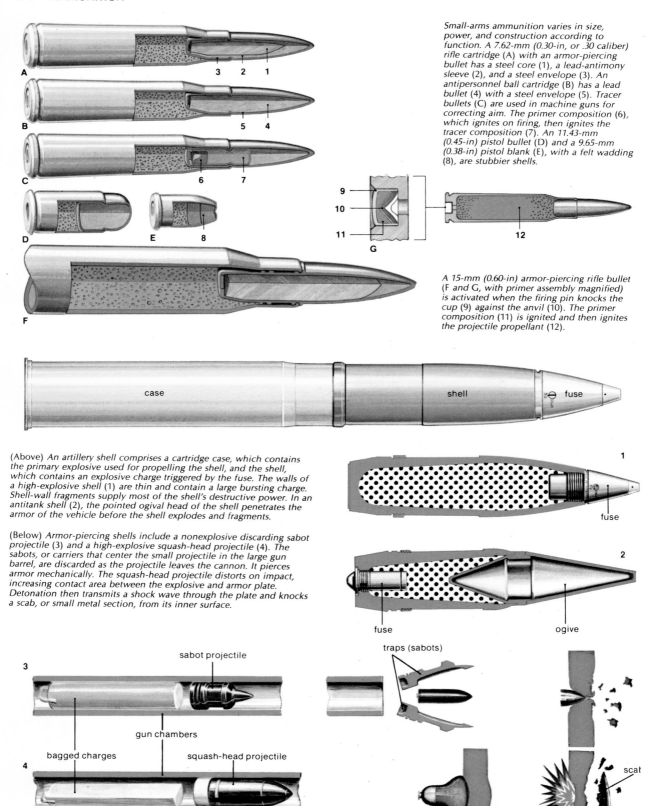

Small-arms ammunition varies in size, power, and construction according to function. A 7.62-mm (0.30-in, or .30 caliber) rifle cartridge (A) with an armor-piercing bullet has a steel core (1), a lead-antimony sleeve (2), and a steel envelope (3). An antipersonnel ball cartridge (B) has a lead bullet (4) with a steel envelope (5). Tracer bullets (C) are used in machine guns for correcting aim. The primer composition (6), which ignites on firing, then ignites the tracer composition (7). An 11.43-mm (0.45-in) pistol bullet (D) and a 9.65-mm (0.38-in) pistol blank (E), with a felt wadding (8), are stubbier shells.

A 15-mm (0.60-in) armor-piercing rifle bullet (F and G, with primer assembly magnified) is activated when the firing pin knocks the cup (9) against the anvil (10). The primer composition (11) is ignited and then ignites the projectile propellant (12).

case **shell** **fuse**

(Above) An artillery shell comprises a cartridge case, which contains the primary explosive used for propelling the shell, and the shell, which contains an explosive charge triggered by the fuse. The walls of a high-explosive shell (1) are thin and contain a large bursting charge. Shell-wall fragments supply most of the shell's destructive power. In an antitank shell (2), the pointed ogival head of the shell penetrates the armor of the vehicle before the shell explodes and fragments.

(Below) Armor-piercing shells include a nonexplosive discarding sabot projectile (3) and a high-explosive squash-head projectile (4). The sabots, or carriers that center the small projectile in the large gun barrel, are discarded as the projectile leaves the cannon. It pierces armor mechanically. The squash-head projectile distorts on impact, increasing contact area between the explosive and armor plate. Detonation then transmits a shock wave through the plate and knocks a scab, or small metal section, from its inner surface.

1
fuse

2
fuse ogive

traps (sabots)

3
sabot projectile
gun chambers
bagged charges

4
squash-head projectile

scat

Modern artillery projectiles are highly specialized to defeat a number of diverse targets. Fuses are available that detonate the projectile when it is a certain selected distance from its target (proximity fuse), at a predetermined point in its trajectory (variable time fuse), upon impact (quick and superquick fuse), and after impact (delay fuse).

Projectiles inflict damage in a variety of ways. Jagged fragments produced by the projectile's bursting charge are effective against troops and lightly armored equipment. Antipersonnel flechette rounds expel thousands of tiny steel darts before reaching the target. Shaped charge rounds are used to defeat armored vehicles and bunkers by burning a small hole with a high-velocity jet of superhot gases. Other artillery projectiles can supply illumination and produce smoke.

During World War I, most belligerents used poison gas rounds. Although they have not been used since, large stockpiles are maintained by several countries. The ultimate artillery projectile, the nuclear round, was developed in the early 1950s. It is currently available in the United States for weapons as small as the 155-mm howitzer.

Latest innovations in artillery ammunition include rocket-assisted projectiles and a laser-guided projectile that homes in on a target that is illuminated, or "painted," by a laser beam.

RUSSELL J. PARKINSON

Bibliography: Guilmartin, John P., *Gunpowder and Galleys: Changing Technology and Mediterranean Warfare at Sea in the 16th Century* (1974); Hackley, F. W., *History of Modern U.S. Military Small Arms and Ammunition* (1967); Johnson, Melvin, and Haven, Charles T., *Ammunition: Its History, Development and Use* (1943); Narramore, Earl, *Principles and Practices of Loading Ammunition* (1954); O'Hart, Theodore, *Elements of Ammunition* (1946).

amnesia

Amnesia is the inability to remember past experiences. It occurs normally during infancy because the brain has not yet developed the myelin needed to wrap and insulate neurons; thus the ability to retain messages in sequence is impaired. Amnesia also may occur as the result of severe head injury, shock, or certain drugs. Retrograde amnesia involves impaired memory of events that occurred before the trauma that caused the condition, whereas anterograde amnesia affects events that follow. Broca's amnesia, or aphasia, is a loss of the ability to use either written or spoken language; verbal amnesia is loss of memory for words; visual amnesia is the inability to recall objects that have been seen; and lacunar amnesia is the inability to remember isolated events rather than a total loss of memory. A. W. DUDLEY, M. D.

amnesty

An amnesty is an exemption from prosecution for criminal acts, usually issued by a government after a time of crisis such as a war or revolution. The amnesty may be for acts such as rebellion, treason, desertion, or draft evasion. It is usually granted to groups of citizens on condition that they abide by the law in the future.

In extending an amnesty, the government does not forgive or approve what was done. It simply says it will not take any action even though it would be within the law to do so. In this respect an amnesty differs from a PARDON, which is normally granted to a person convicted of a crime.

Many amnesties are partial. President Andrew Johnson, after the Civil War, excluded the leaders of the Confederacy when he extended amnesty to former rebels who would support the federal government. The end of the Vietnam conflict in 1973 produced the most controversial amnesty question in U.S. history. Presidents Nixon, Ford, and Carter denied amnesty to deserters and draft evaders of that period, but Ford offered clemency to those who were willing to do public service work, and Carter pardoned most draft evaders.

Amnesty International

Amnesty International, based in London, is an organization devoted to helping people imprisoned for their political or religious beliefs, provided that they have not used or advocated violence. It was awarded the Nobel Peace Prize for 1977 for its contribution to "securing the ground for freedom, for justice, and thereby also for peace in the world." At the time, it had national sections in 35 countries, members in about 70 more, and had been able to obtain the release of 10,600 prisoners.

The organization grew out of an appeal launched in May 1961 by Peter Benenson, a British lawyer, on behalf of prisoners of conscience. Within a month, Benenson had received more than a thousand offers to help by collecting information on prisoners, publicizing cases, and approaching governments to seek their release. Amnesty International opposes the use of torture and the death penalty, and it issues annual reports on prison conditions throughout the world. It urges the observance of the United Nations Universal Declaration of Human Rights and the UN Standard Minimum Rules for the Treatment of Prisoners.

amniocentesis [am-nee-oh-sen'-tuh-sis]

A diagnostic procedure in medical genetics, amniocentesis is a technique in which a sample of the amniotic fluid that bathes the human fetus is removed from the pregnant uterus by suction with a very fine needle. Fetal cells suspended in the fluid can then be grown in the laboratory and studied to detect various genetic disorders in the unborn child.

Diagnostic amniocentesis is usually performed during the 15th week of pregnancy, thus giving ample time to complete the appropriate studies, and, if desired, permit therapeutic abortion by the 20th week of pregnancy, when it is still relatively safe.

Amniocentesis may be advised in several situations:

Chromosome Abnormalities. The risk of DOWN'S SYNDROME (a severe mental deficiency associated with an extra chromosome in the cells) and other chromosomal disorders increases with the age of the mother and with a history of previously affected offspring.

The risk of bearing a child with Down's syndrome is about 1 in 2,000 women in their 20s, 1 in 300 women in their 30s, and 1 in 40 women in their 40s. Therefore, amniocentesis has been advised for women over the age of 35 and for those who previously have been found to have chromosomal abnormalities.

Biochemical Disorders. Frequently, a child of apparently normal parents is born with an inherited biochemical disorder. Genetic testing of the parents may indicate the possibility of a significant recurrent risk in future offspring, and in many cases amniocentesis can then be performed in later pregnancies to determine whether the developing fetus is normal.

Sex-Linked Disorders. Many sex-linked disorders exist, for example hemophilia—a blood-coagulation deficiency that affects males. At present, no specific test can detect this disorder. Thus, a mother who harbors the genetic potential for hemophilia and who wishes to avoid the risk of affected male offspring may want to learn the sex of the developing fetus by amniocentesis. By means of abortion, she can then choose to give birth only to female children thereafter.

Congenital Malformations. Such congenital malformations of the brain and spinal cord as anencephaly and meningomyelocele are associated with increased levels of alpha-fetoprotein, a substance in the amniotic fluid. Since the risk of recurrent congenital malformations is higher in some families than in the general population, a woman who has given birth to an affected child might seek amniocentesis during future pregnancies. LAWRENCE J. SCHNEIDERMAN

Bibliography: Apgar, Virginia, and Beck, Joan, *Is My Baby Alright?* (1973); Davison, B. C., *Genetic Counseling* (1970); Greenblatt, Augusta, *Heredity and You* (1974).

See also: GENETIC COUNSELING; GENETICS; GENETIC DISEASES; PREGNANCY AND BIRTH.

amniotic sac: see DEVELOPMENT; PREGNANCY AND BIRTH.

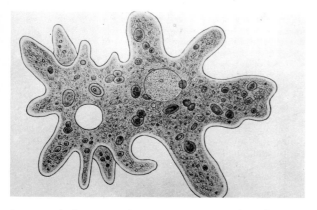

A common freshwater amoeba, A. proteus, *moves and engulfs food by using pseudopods, or false feet, formed by stretching its body.*

amoeba [uh-mee'-buh]

An amoeba is any of several microscopic, one-celled Protozoan organisms commonly found in fresh and salt water, in soil, and as animal parasites; some specialized forms are found in plants.

Amoeba usually refers to members of the order Amoebida in the class Rhizopoda. Amoebas move in a creeping or gliding fashion by extending their protoplasm; the projections are called pseudopodia (false feet). The pseudopod is also extended to surround other organisms or food particles and draw them into the body. The characteristic movement by extension is called amoeboid movement and is a common form of locomotion in other cells.

Despite constantly varying shapes, amoebas are identified by basic form and their distinct type of locomotion. Amoebas vary in size from 0.01 mm (0.0004 in) to 1 mm (0.04 in). They have a contractile vacuole that empties any excess water that has been drawn into the cell. Some amoebas resist unfavorable conditions such as drying or lack of food by secreting a resistant body covering in a process called encystment. Others have permanent shells into which they can withdraw.

The amoeba commonly used in classrooms for demonstrating basic cell function and as a research tool is *Amoeba proteus,* which reproduces by nuclear division followed by binary fission, or splitting into two. Of the six or seven amoebas found in humans, only one, *Entamoeba histolytica,* is harmful. It causes amoebic DYSENTERY, an inflammation of the intestine that if unchecked can lead to abscesses of the liver and brain and to eventual death.   J. F. McCLELLAN

Bibliography: Grell, Karl G., *Protozoology,* 2d rev. ed. (1973).

Amon-Re [ah'-muhn-ray']

Amon-Re (or Amon-Ra), the chief deity and sun god of the Pyramid Age, was believed by the ancient Egyptians to be the creator of all things. In the sun temple at Heliopolis, his image, as Amon, was made of gold lapis lazuli and bore a double crown: red for Lower Egypt, white for Upper Egypt. The symbol of Amon at dawn, the scarab beetle, rolling its dung ball, suggested the sun, which also rolled from east to west. As Re, this god was represented as a man with a falcon's head surmounted by a solar disk and golden cobra. Father of all the pharaohs, Re rode his solar boat across the heavens each day, and under the world each night, past the 12 stations of darkness.   NORMA L. GOODRICH

Amorites [am'-uh-ryts]

The Amorites were a Semitic people of the ancient Near East, mentioned in the Bible as inhabitants of CANAAN at the time the Hebrews settled there. Apparently dominant in Syria and Palestine *c.*2000–1600 BC, they are also known from Babylonian records as the founders of the Amorite, or Old Babylo-

nian, dynasty of MESOPOTAMIA (*c.*1900–*c.*1550 BC). Ezek. 16:3 suggests that they were closely related to the Hebrews.

amortization

Amortization, in finance, is the gradual reduction of a debt over a period of time. A familiar amortization plan is a home mortgage, payable in monthly installments, usually of equal amount, that cover both principal and interest. As the interest on the unpaid balance decreases each month, the payment on the principal increases by a like amount. The longer the amortization period, the larger the total interest on the debt, but the amount of each installment is smaller.

Amortization, in accounting, is the gradual reduction of an amount by periodic accounting entries. When applied to fixed assets such as plant and equipment, it is called *depreciation.* For example, a $10,000 machine with an expected useful life of 10 years may be depreciated at $1,000 a year.

Amos, Book of

Amos, a book of the Old Testament, is the third book of the Minor Prophets. It takes its name from the prophet Amos who lived *c.*750 BC as a shepherd at Tekoa in the southern kingdom of Judah. It was to the northern kingdom of Israel, however, that his prophetic message was addressed. Writing during a time of prosperity, when a sharp contrast existed between the luxurious life of the nation's leaders and the oppression of the poor, Amos preached the urgency of social justice and the threat of impending divine judgment. The structure of the book falls into nine parts, each dominated by a negative message containing threats of darkness, famine, and destruction. Amos is the oldest of the prophetic books of the Bible.
                    GEORGE W. COATS

Bibliography: Mays, J. L., *Amos: A Commentary* (1969).

Amos 'n' Andy

Amos 'n' Andy were the American radio comedy team of Freeman Fisher Gosden (Amos), b. Richmond, Va., May 5, 1899, d. Dec. 10, 1982, and Charles Correll (Andy), b. Peoria, Ill., Feb. 2, 1890, d. Sept. 26, 1972. The "Amos 'n' Andy" show, first aired on Mar. 19, 1928, presented a caricature of two young black men, played by Gosden and Correll, who were both white. The premise was that they came north to make their fortune and went into business as the "Fresh-Air Taxicab Company of America." Until 1943, Gosden and Correll wrote most of the scripts and played all 550 male parts. For a time excerpts were run as a newspaper comic strip. At its peak in the 1930s the show attracted an estimated 40 million listeners among whites and blacks. Over the years it drew increasingly strong criticism from civil-rights organizations. Gosden and Correll retired in 1961.

Bibliography: Correll, Charles, and Gosden, Freeman F., *All About Amos 'n' Andy* (1930); Dunning, John, *Tune In Yesterday: The Ultimate Encyclopedia of Old-Time Radio, 1925–1976* (1976).

Amoy [ah-moy']

Amoy, or Hsia-men (Xiamen), is the major trading port in Fukien (Fujian) province, China. Its harbor, one of the finest along the East China coast, can accommodate medium-sized oceangoing vessels. Part of the city is situated on an island and part on the mainland; the two parts are connected by a causeway on which a railroad has been built. The mainland is surrounded by uplands. Amoy is sometimes called the "Garden in the Sea." It has traditionally been a point of departure for people migrating from southern Fukien to Southeast Asia. As a result, many of its nearly 950,000 inhabitants either have been abroad or are relatives of Chinese living overseas. Amoy has a fishing fleet, fish and fruit canneries, and modern factories for the production of machinery, rubber tires, and mining equipment. It became one of the first treaty ports of China after the Opium War (1839–42) and was an important exporter of tea. In the late 19th century Amoy was the base from which the Chinese settled Taiwan.   JAMES CHAN

Ampère, André Marie   [ahm-pair']

André Ampère, b. Jan. 10, 1775, d. June 10, 1836, was a French physicist who laid the foundations for the science of electrodynamics through his demonstration that electric currents produce magnetic fields, and through his subsequent investigation into the relationship between these two phenomena. The son of a well-to-do merchant, Ampère educated himself through diligent reading in the family library. He survived the French Revolution to become a science teacher, first in Lyons and then in Bourg. He later took a post at the École Polytechnique, and in 1808 became inspector general of the university system in Paris. Beginning in 1824, he also taught physics at the Collège de France and philosophy at the Faculté des Lettres, pursuing diverse scientific interests in the midst of personal tragedy. He was greatly affected by his father's execution by guillotine during the Revolution and, after his first wife's early death, had a catastrophic second marriage.

Ampère's most notable achievements were his independent determination (1814) of Avogadro's law and his work from 1820 to 1827 based on OERSTED's discovery, announced in 1820, that a magnetic needle moves in the vicinity of an electric current. Ampère succeeded in explaining the latter phenomenon by assuming that an electric current is capable of exciting a magnetic field. He further demonstrated that the direction of the magnetic field is determined by the direction of the current. He developed a quantitative relationship for the strength of a magnetic field in relation to an electric current (Ampère's theorem) and propounded a theory as to how iron becomes magnetized. Ampère also devised a rule governing the mutual interaction of current-carrying wires (Ampère's law) and produced a definition of the unit of measurement of current flow, now known as the AMPERE.

Bibliography: Ampère, André, *Correspondence*, 3 vols. (1936–43); Shippen, Katherine B., *The Bright Design* (1949).

ampere   [am'-pir]

The ampere is the unit for measuring electric current. As more accurate procedures have been devised, the definition of the quantity has been changed. The most modern definition is based on the ability of a specified current to deposit a precise amount of a substance on an electrode during ELECTROLYSIS. Formerly, the definition involved the force that was produced between parallel wires carrying a current; still earlier, the ampere was defined as a flow of one COULOMB per second, where the coulomb (a quantity of electrical charge) was taken as the basic unit. The ampere is named for the French physicist and mathematician André AMPÈRE, and its symbol is A.   A. G. ENGLEHARDT AND M. KRISTIANSEN

See also: CURRENT, ELECTRIC; ELECTRICITY.

amphetamine   [am-fet'-uh-meen]

Amphetamines are a class of drugs that are powerful central nervous system STIMULANTS. The drug, usually taken in capsule or tablet form, increases alertness and reduces hunger. Physicians prescribe amphetamines to suppress appetite, for the control of obesity; to treat psychological disorders such as depression; and to calm hyperactive children, although this use of the drug is a subject of some controversy.

Amphetamines are widely misused; large and frequent doses can produce exhilaration. Severe depression often occurs when the drug is discontinued, however, and addiction may be established after only a few days of continuous use. Some misusers of amphetamines dissolve the tablets in water and inject the drug directly into their veins. This may lead to irritable, overactive, or violent behavior. Sporadic users take amphetamine tablets for increased alertness or endurance, for example, in order to be able to drive long hours or to stay awake and cram for an examination. Users commonly refer to amphetamines as pep pills, uppers, or speed.

Amphetamines tend to increase heart rate, raise blood pressure, dilate the pupils, and cause dry mouth and sweating. Addiction to amphetamines can result in psychosis or death from overexhaustion or cardiac arrest. Benzedrine is the trade name for the drug amphetamine. Other trade names for chemical variations of amphetamine are Dexedrine, Methedrine, and Desoxyn, the most rapidly acting of the group.

amphibians

Amphibians are members of the class Amphibia, subphylum Vertebrata, phylum Chordata. The class Amphibia includes frogs, toads, salamanders, newts, and caecilians. Amphibians are characterized by a glandular skin without external scales, by gills during development (and in adulthood in some), and by eggs that may have jelly coats but develop without formation of extra-embryonic membranes such as the amnion. Most amphibians also have four limbs. Limbs and lungs are adaptations for life on land; the limbs evolved from the ancestral fishes' lobed fins. The scales and amniote egg evolved by reptiles, which distinguish them from amphibians, are adaptations for greater terrestriality than amphibians possess.

The class Amphibia comprises three living orders and several extinct ones. The living members of the class include those forms that have been mentioned above. Amphibians are thought to have arisen from lobe-finned crossopterygian fishes. These fish had fins supported by bones, a well-ossified skeleton, lungs, and, in some species, internal openings to nasal passages. Considerable conjecture exists, however, as to whether amphibians actually arose from several lineages. Swedish experts tend to favor separate lineage for each of the modern orders; certain British and American scientists support the idea of two lineages, one giving rise to frogs, the other to salamanders and caecilians. The characteristics of

The relative numbers of amphibians through time, as measured by fossil records, are indicated by the thickness of the black areas. Dotted lines indicate times for which no fossil amphibians have been found. Amphibians evolved during the Devonian Period from a group of crossopterygian, or lobe-finned, fish called rhipidistians (A). Some of the first amphibians were largely aquatic anthracosaurs (B), which included the ancestors of the reptiles; temnospondyls (C), which included flatbodied aquatic forms and well-adapted land animals; and ichthyostegalids (D), the oldest known amphibians, which retained many fish characteristics. Aistopods (E) had snakelike (often limbless) bodies. Some nectrideans (F) had eellike bodies, and some had triangular heads. Microsaurians (G) were tiny animals with weak limbs. Living species are of the order Anura (H) (frogs and toads), Caudata (I) (newts and salamanders), and Gymnophiona (J) (burrowing, wormlike tropical caecilians). The lines indicating evolutionary development are speculative; some scientists would draw them differently.

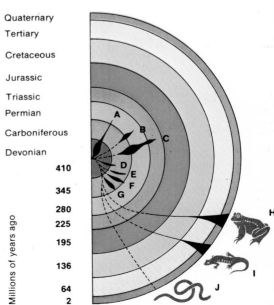

Quaternary
Tertiary
Cretaceous
Jurassic
Triassic
Permian
Carboniferous
Devonian

Millions of years ago

410
345
280
225
195
136
64
2

The American bullfrog, Rana catesbeiana, is the largest frog of North America. Although adapted to breathing air, it prefers to remain underwater. The male bullfrog has a distinctive, loud call, which is heard mostly at night.

The red-backed salamander, Plethodon cinereus, is found throughout the eastern half of North America. Salamanders can be identified by grooves that run down their sides.

Toads, such as the American toad, Bufo americanus, differ from frogs by having a short, stout body and warty skin. Toads secrete a poisonous fluid through the skin that can irritate the eyes or mouth.

The South American caecilian, Siphonops annulatus, of the tropics, is an unusual amphibian. It is blind, lives underground, and probably feeds on earthworms. It measures about 46 cm (18 in) long.

The alpine newt, Triturus alpestris alpestris, found in alpine regions of central Europe, feeds on small insects and worms. The male, about 7.5 cm (3 in) long, develops bright colors during the breeding season.

vertebrae, teeth, and skull bones form the basis for these hypotheses. Further developmental and variational data are necessary to support these ideas.

Two major subclasses of extinct amphibians are found in the fossil record. They are the Labyrinthodontia and the Lepospondyli. The amphibians of the Labyrinthodontia, which lived during the late Devonian through Triassic periods (345 to 190 million years ago), include the most primitive amphib-

ians represented by the genus Ichthyostega. They were freshwater carnivorous animals, with tail fins, small scales, and a fishlike vertebral column. Their skulls had many bones, as did those of their presumed crossopterygian ancestor. The Labyrinthodontia, according to the American paleontologist Alfred S. Romer, include three extinct orders: the Ichthyostegalia, the Temnospondyli, and the Anthracosauria. The Anthracosauria are thought to be the ancestors of reptiles and hence of modern birds and mammals. The Temnospondyli are thought by some scientists to be the ancestors of the modern frogs.

The amphibians of the subclass Lepospondyli, which lived during the Mississippian through lower Permian periods (340 to 270 million years ago), include the extinct orders Nectridea, Aistopoda, and Microsauria. Members of the latter two orders were elongate. Some had limbs, some had reduced limbs, and some had no limbs. Many scientists suggest that the ancestors of modern salamanders and caecilians are among the lepospondyls.

The modern, extant orders of the Amphibia are placed in the subclass Lissamphibia. The superorder Salientia includes extinct froglike forms, and the extant order Anura consists of the frogs and toads. The order Caudata includes the salamanders. The order Gymnophiona includes the limbless caecilians. These three groups are allied to the Lissamphibia by characteristics of tooth, skin, and fat body structure. Vertebral and skull structure, as well as other characteristics, differ markedly among the three groups. This suggests to many scientists separate origins for each of the three modern orders.

HABITAT AND DISTRIBUTION

The distribution of amphibians is worldwide, except in Antarctica and Greenland. They are found on landmasses and in fresh water. Frogs are the most widespread of the three groups, occurring on all major landmasses inhabited by amphibians. They live in a great variety of habitats, ranging from deserts to rain forests, permanent ponds to high mountain meadows. With only a few exceptions, an aquatic situation is required for breeding and tadpole development.

Salamanders are primarily a north temperate group, occurring in North America, Europe, and Asia. Some species are found in Africa north of the Sahara, and one group of some 200 species has had an extensive adaptive radiation in the New World tropics in Central and South America to northern Argentina. Salamanders occupy a variety of terrestrial and aquatic habitats; those found in dry environments, such as the Mexican plateau, usually live in ponds. When on land, they are often found in moist leaf litter and under rocks and logs. In northern areas several species are found in ponds, streams, or rivers. Many species require water for breeding and development, but many other species breed on land and forgo the larval stage.

The caecilians are tropical in distribution. They occur in the New World from southern Mexico to northern Argentina, in tropical Africa, and in Southeast Asia. These limbless animals are usually burrowers. They are found in stream banks, under debris, and along root channels from sea level to 3,000 m (9,840 ft). One family of South America is aquatic and lives in streams, especially in the drainage basin of the Amazon River. The larvae of certain species in Southeast Asia and South America, and probably Africa, also inhabit streams.

CLASSIFICATION

The order Anura or Salientia, the frogs and toads, includes 12 to 18 families, according to the characteristics that are stressed in classification. Familiar species are the leopard and the grass frog (genus Rana), which is used in many biology laboratory excercises; the brown, warty-skinned, drier-adapted toads (genus Bufo); and the aquatic, tongueless African clawed frog (genus Xenopus). This frog was once used in pregnancy tests and is now used in research on genetics and development. Several species are found in the eastern United States. Breeding choruses after the spring rains may include the following: two species of toads; leopard frogs, green frogs, pig frogs, and gopher frogs (Rana); woods tree frogs, green tree frogs, squirrel tree frogs, barking tree frogs, and lit-

The life cycle of the leopard frog, Rana pipiens *(perhaps the most commonly known amphibian in North America), imitates in a few weeks the evolutionary sequence from fish to land animal. Adult frogs live in grassy meadows near marshes and ponds (top). Breeding begins in April when the male and female (right) return to the water. The female lays the eggs while the male clings to her back and fertilizes them. Tadpoles, (lower right), hatch in about 9 days. Breathing is done through three pairs of external gills. Within a few weeks a fold of skin (operculum) covers the external gills, and four pairs of internal gills take over the respiratory function (similar to that of a fish). Eight weeks after hatching, rear legs are present (lower left); part of the ventral surface is cut away to show internal gills. All the limbs have been developed three months after hatching (upper left), and the lungs have become functional. The frog leaves the water to live in the wet meadow grass.*

tle grass frogs (*Hyla*); cricket frogs (*Acris*); and eastern narrow-mouthed toads (*Microhyla*). Among the more bizarre frogs are the following: the giant frog of Africa (*Conraua* or *Giganturana goliath*), which may reach 1 m (39 in) in body length; *Sminthillus*, the smallest frog, at 12 mm (0.5 in) in body length, which lays one egg a year; *Centrolene* of Central America, whose skin is translucent and whose bones are green; and *Pseudis paradoxicus*, whose tadpoles are larger than the adult frogs into which they metamorphose.

Experts usually list from 7 to 10 families in the order Caudata or Urodela, the salamanders and newts. Among the best known genera are the Eastern North American red eft (*Notophthalmus*); the European newts (*Triturus*); and the Spanish *Pleurodeles*, used in developmental studies. Many species are found in the Appalachian Mountains of the southeastern United States, where salamander communities have been analyzed. The largest salamander is the Japanese giant salamander (*Andrias*), which extends up to 135 cm (53 in) in length; the smallest is the tropical genus *Thorius*, at 16 mm (0.6 in).

The order Gymnophiona or Apoda includes the little-known caecilians—the limbless, elongate, tropical amphibians that burrow or swim. These are considered to look wormlike because of their body shape and the presence of many rings, which resemble the segments of worms. The smallest caecilians (*Idiocranium*) are mature at 90 mm (3.6 in); the largest (*Caecilia*) are more than 1,300 mm (52 in).

STRUCTURE AND FUNCTION

The three orders of amphibians are allied by structure of their TEETH and their SKINS particularly. Their teeth have two parts—an upper crown and a pedicel (a thin extension) that is attached to the jaws. The skin is smooth and contains numerous mucous and toxic glands, giving the animals a moist feeling. The outer layer of the skin is keratinized but does not form the epidermal scales seen in reptile skin. In fact, amphibians lack scales except for some species of caecilians that have fishlike scales embedded in the skin. The organ systems of amphibians modify the typical vertebrate plan. They have a relatively straight digestive system with a short intestine, and they have a three-chambered heart; they respire by lungs and sometimes skin as adults and by gills as larvae. Their digestive, excretory, and reproductive systems empty into a common terminal chamber, the cloaca. Their nervous systems are complex and have attributes to facilitate both aquatic and terrestrial life. Larvae and some aquatic adults have multidirectional sensory systems. All amphibians hear. Frogs and sala-manders (except those that live in permanently dark locations) have good vision. Vision is nearly lost in caecilians, whose eyes are covered by skin and sometimes bone. They perceive by chemical cues, using their unique tentacles to conduct stimuli to olfactory centers.

Voice production is largely an attribute of frogs. Salamanders and caecilians produce noises, coughs, and grunts, but apparently not for communication. Frogs have complex sound production and perception systems, with species-specific warning, defensive, and breeding communications.

Amphibians are poikilotherms, cold-blooded organisms; their BODY TEMPERATURE is slightly higher than that of the environment. They are active at optimal temperatures and withdraw from more extreme heat or cold.

Mode of locomotion varies greatly among amphibians. Limbless caecilians burrow, using their heads like shovels and gaining thrust through contraction of muscles to force the body against the soil. The caecilians that swim, and most swimming salamanders, are like eels, using body muscle contraction to propel themselves through the water. Salamanders use their limbs very little in swimming. On land, the limbs give considerable propulsion to the body, and several salamander gaits have been described. The limbs are sprawled out from the body, and the middle of the trunk usually rests on the ground—in contrast to the faster lizards, whose legs are under the body and raise it above the ground. Frogs make use of their long hind-limbs to effect several kinds of loco-motion—jumping, hopping, swimming, burrowing, and climbing.

LIFE CYCLE AND BEHAVIOR
Breeding in most amphibians is seasonal, usually correlated with temperature and moisture optima. Frogs court by using sounds or actions as attractants; salamanders depend primarily on visual and tactile cues. It is not known how male and female caecilians find each other. The modes of FERTILIZATION vary. Almost all frogs practice external fertilization, the females laying eggs in water and the males spraying sperm over them. Primitive salamanders have external fertilization, but most have internal fertilization, with the female taking up the male's spermatophore. All caecilians have internal fertilization, and the male deposits sperm in the cloaca of the female by using the end of his cloaca as an intromittent organ.

Other trends in amphibian reproductive biology include the following: (1) Many frogs lay large numbers of eggs. Few salamanders and fewer caecilians do. (2) Most frog species have tadpoles, a free-living larval stage; few have direct development or retain developing young in the body of the female. (3) Many salamander species have larvae; several have direct development. Only a few retain the young. (4) Few caecilians have larvae; some have direct development. Several have a mode of VIVIPARITY in which the female nourishes her developing young by oviductal secretions, and they are born after metamorphosis. (5) A number of species of salamanders and caecilians brood their egg clutches. Few frogs do, but some carry eggs on their backs, legs, or vocal sacs until hatching or metamorphosis. (6) The species that have direct development, brooding, or maternal retention have reduced litter sizes compared to those that lay eggs and abandon them. The larvae of the three orders are morphologically very different, although all are free-living, foraging animals.

Protective behaviors of amphibians include hiding or staying still in the presence of danger and having coloration matching the environment so that the animal is not obvious. Frogs have warning calls that alert other members of the population. Some salamanders and frogs, when disturbed, arch their backs, stiffen, and rock on their bellies. Other salamanders and frogs have flash colors that warn predators away. Several species of each kind of amphibian have toxic skins; predators learn to avoid them. Some nontoxic species mimic the coloration of toxic species so that they too are not consumed. Some species of salamanders have tails that break off when they are attacked. As the predator pursues the twitching tail, the salamander quietly escapes.

The importance of amphibians is evident throughout the world. They are major components of their ecosystem, both predator and prey. They are food for several human cultures. Interest in them ranges from their aesthetic appeal to their use as a source of arrow poison. They are of considerable importance to science, furnishing material for study of cell function, genetics, and development. Also, they are used as laboratory specimens that can be analyzed in terms of behavior, ecology, and evolution.   MARVALEE H. WAKE

Bibliography: Cochran, D. M., *Living Amphibians of the World* (1961); Goin, C. J., et al., *Introduction to Herpetology*, 3d ed. (1978); Noble, G. K., *Biology of the Amphibia* (1931); Porter, K. R., *Herpetology* (1972).

See also: ANIMAL COURTSHIP AND MATING; AXOLOTL; CLASSIFICATION, BIOLOGICAL; COLORATION, BIOLOGICAL; DEVELOPMENT; FOSSIL RECORD; FROG; MIMICRY; SALAMANDER AND NEWT; TOAD.

amphibious warfare

Amphibious warfare is a military operation that is launched from the sea by naval and landing forces and involves a landing on a hostile shore.

An amphibious assault, the primary form of a combined sea-and-land operation, is conducted to establish a force ashore. A classic reason is to gain a foothold or beachhead as a necessary preliminary to further operations ashore. The Normandy landings in World War II and the Inchon landing in the Korean War are examples of amphibious assaults that made second fronts possible; these fronts, in turn, changed the strategic direction of the wars. Where land masses are more limited or restricted, amphibious assaults tend to be seizures, either for use of the land as an advance base or for denial of such use to the enemy. Tarawa, Peleliu, and Iwo Jima are notable World War II examples of seizures.

Other Operations. Raids, demonstrations, and withdrawals are additional types of amphibious operations, each different from the assault in important ways.

In an amphibious raid the objective area is occupied only briefly, followed by a planned withdrawal. Such raids are conducted to damage the enemy, gain information, or carry out rescues. British commando raids in World War II, culminating in the Dieppe raid, were typical amphibious raids that depended on surprise and stealth for success. The rescue in 1975 of a captured U.S. freighter, the SS *Mayaguez*, and the concurrent landing on Koh Tang Island, had some elements of an amphibious raid.

An amphibious demonstration is a show of force that stops short of an actual landing. Demonstrations are conducted to deceive the enemy or, in situations short of hostilities, to signal presence and intent. During the CUBAN MISSILE CRISIS of 1962, large U.S. amphibious forces were conspicuously moved to the Caribbean, posing the threat of an invasion.

An amphibious withdrawal is essentially an amphibious assault conducted in reverse. The removal of Allied troops from DUNKERQUE, France, in World War II is often cited as the supreme example of an amphibious withdrawal. The evacuation of U.S.–South Korean forces from Hungnam in 1950, however, rivaled Dunkerque in magnitude and was much more successful, probably because the Americans had uncontested control of the air.

Special Vehicles. The most critical period of an amphibious operation has always been the ship-to-shore movement. During World War II, the military developed landing craft and landing ships—including the landing ship/tank, or LST—that could beach and then retract. The problem of moving past the water's edge was partly resolved by the development of amphibian vehicles, like the Alligator, that could cross the beach and move inland on either tracks or wheels. Since World War II, this problem has been further alleviated by the vertical envelopment capabilities of helicopters operating from specialized amphibious ships called helicopter carriers. The evacuations of Phnom Penh and Saigon at the close of the Vietnam War, using helicopters as the principal shore-to-ship vehicle, were successful applications of amphibious techniques.   BRIG. GEN. EDWIN H. SIMMONS, USMC (RET.)

Bibliography: Departments of the Army, Navy, and Air Force, *Doctrine for Amphibious Operations* (1967); Isely, Jeter A., and Crowl, Philip A., *The U.S. Marines and Amphibious War* (1951); Simmons, Edwin H., *The United States Marines, 1775–1975* (1976); Vagts, Alfred, *Landing Operations* (1946).

amphibole [am'-fuh-bohl]

Hornblende, the most common amphibole, has a variable composition, and it may be black, brown, or dark green in color. It is generally opaque to translucent and has a vitreous luster.

Amphibole is the general name of an important group of rock-forming SILICATE MINERALS that are characterized by a particular arrangement of atoms and by similar optical, physical, and chemical properties. Their composition can vary widely, however, which gives them their name—from the Greek word for "ambiguous." They occur as both major and minor constituents of a wide variety of igneous, metamorphic, and sedimentary rocks (see PETROLOGY). Hornblende is the most common amphibole. Fibrous varieties—anthophyllite, actinolite, and riebeckite (crocidolite)—are important sources of ASBESTOS fiber; nephrite JADE, a dense, compact aggregate of actinolite fibers, is used for ornamental carving.

Structure and Chemistry. The basic building unit of the silicate minerals is the SiO_4 tetrahedron, which consists of a silicon (Si) atom bonded to four oxygen (O) atoms in a tetrahedral arrangement. Tetrahedra may share two corners with adjacent tetrahedra to form single, infinite chains of SiO_3 composition that are characteristic of the PYROXENE structure. These chains of tetrahedra sometimes join by sharing corners to form double chains of Si_4O_{11} composition that are characteristic of the amphibole structure.

The complex chemistry of the amphibole group results from the great flexibility of the CRYSTAL structure, which will accommodate a wide range of cations (positively charged atoms). All the major ones—among them aluminum (Al), boron (B), calcium (Ca), iron (Fe), magnesium (Mg), and sodium (Na)—fall within the range of the average composition of the Earth's crust; this accounts for the widespread occurrence of the amphibole minerals. A generalized chemical formula for the most common members of the group is:

$$A_{2-3} B_5 (SiAl)_8 O_{22} (OH)_2, \text{ where } A = Mg,$$

$$Fe^{+2}, Ca, \text{ or } Na, \text{ and } B = Mg, Fe^{+2}, Fe^{+3}, \text{ or } Al.$$

More complex formulas are needed to account for all other amphiboles.

Mineralogy and Occurrence. The similarity in crystal structure throughout the group results in physical properties that are nearly uniform. HARDNESS is 5 to 6, CLEAVAGE is perfect in two directions, and the SPECIFIC GRAVITY is 2.9 to 3.5, depending on iron content. Crystal development varies from stubby prisms to long prismatic needles to silky fibers; irregularly shaped grains are the most common, however. Gedrite and anthophyllite crystallize in the ORTHORHOMBIC SYSTEM; otherwise, virtually all amphiboles belong to the MONOCLINIC SYSTEM. Amphiboles may be colorless, white, gray, violet, blue, green, brown, or black; color is to some extent diagnostic of chemical composition.

The group comprises four main subdivisions: iron-magnesium-manganese, calcic, sodic-calcic, and sodic. Iron-magnesium-manganese amphiboles are generally confined to META-MORPHIC ROCKS. Calcic amphiboles, the most abundant and widespread of the amphiboles, occur in many geologic environments, ranging from metamorphic to IGNEOUS ROCKS. Hornblende, for example, is found in basic and intermediate igneous rocks. The sodic-calcic amphiboles are commonly found in MARBLES, alkalic igneous rocks, and altered GNEISSES.

FRANK HAWTHORNE

Bibliography: Deer, W. A., et al., *Rock-Forming Minerals*, vol. 2 (1962); Ernst, W. G., *Amphiboles* (1968); Papike, J. J., *Pyroxenes and Amphiboles: Crystal Chemistry and Phase Petrology* (1969).

amphidromic point [am-fi-drahm'-ik]

An amphidromic point is a place near the center of an ocean basin where the range of TIDES is zero. The tidal range increases from this point outward toward the perimeter of the basin. The reason is that astronomical tides in ocean basins and in partially enclosed seas tend to propagate as waves around such basins—counterclockwise in the Northern Hemisphere, clockwise in the Southern Hemisphere—under the influence of the CORIOLIS EFFECT and the constraint of the enclosing landmasses.

ROBERT E. WILSON

Bibliography: Defant, A., *Ebb and Flow* (1958).

See also: OCEAN AND SEAS.

amphioxus [am-fee-ahk'-suhs]

An amphioxus, or lancelet, is any of about 30 species of primitive CHORDATES that live in coastal waters of temperate and tropical oceans. The name *lancelet* refers to the animal's lance-shaped tail on a semitransparent, streamlined body that is usually 4–7 cm (1.5–3 in) long. It is eyeless and earless and has no distinct head, but below the pointed front end is an oral cavity ringed with long, slender cilia. A low fin runs down the back, around the tail, and partly up the lower surface. The flattened body sides are marked with forward-pointing, V-shaped muscle segments. The lancelet swims strongly at night and in the breeding season but spends its days buried in sand or fine gravel with only the mouth free. It draws in water, which is filtered for organic fragments and plankton before it passes out through the many gill slits that line the large pharynx. Mucus carries food into the intestine.

An inconspicuous animal, the lancelet is of little economic importance but of considerable scientific interest. It is conjectured to be a descendant of the kind of primitive chordate from which all vertebrates began to evolve about 500 million years ago. The lancelet retains its simple, rodlike backbone, or notochord, throughout its life, and a hollow nerve cord extends the length of the body above the notochord. These structures develop embryonically in the same way that they do in vertebrates. Lancelets are classified in the single genus, *Branchiostoma* (formerly *Amphioxus*), that constitutes the subphylum Cephalochordata, phylum Chordata.

J. H. BUSHNELL

The amphioxus is a primitive chordate that retains a simple backbone, or notochord (A), throughout its life. It eats food by allowing water to filter through oral hairs (B) to the gills (C), where food is trapped in mucus and then is digested by the animal.

amphipod [am'-fuh-pahd]

The beach flea scud, an amphipod, is a small marine animal with movable plates that cover its body and allow the scud to curl into a ball.

Amphipods are tiny animals, usually no more than 12 mm (0.47 in) long, that belong to the order Amphipoda of crustaceans. The order encompasses about 3,800 species of mostly marine, shrimplike creatures, including the common sand or beach flea family, Talitridae; a sand flea can hurl itself many times its own length with its taillike telson. Amphipods usually are flattened laterally, they lack a carapace, and their long legs are unsuited for walking. Numerous species that scavenge in the Antarctic are a primary source of food for many fish. The largest and most important group of amphipods is the suborder Gammaridea, which includes about 300 species in Siberia's Lake Baikal alone, the blind "well shrimps" (Niphargus) that live in caves and in wells, and about 600 species that live in fresh water or moist land environments. All members of the family Cyamidae are parasites of whales and dolphins, clinging to the skin of their hosts and eating the surface layers. Members of the suborder Caprellidea are known as skeleton shrimp because of their extremely slender bodies.

Bibliography: Bousfield, E. L., *Shallow-Water Gammaridean Amphipoda of New England* (1973).

amphisbaena: see WORM LIZARD.

Amphitryon [am-fi'-tree-ahn]

In Greek mythology, Amphitryon was the son of Alcaeus, king of Tiryns. His wife, Alcmene, asked him to avenge the death of her eight brothers. While Amphitryon was away on this mission, ZEUS, disguised as Amphitryon, visited Alcmene and made her pregnant. When Amphitryon returned, he also made Alcmene pregnant. She gave birth to twin sons—Iphicles, the son of Amphitryon, and HERCULES, the son of Zeus. PLAUTUS based the comedy *Amphitruo* on this theme.

amphoteric compounds [am-fuh-tair'-ik]

In chemistry, an amphoteric compound is a compound that is capable of reacting in solution, either as an acid or a base, by donating hydrogen ions to a stronger base or by accepting hydrogen ions from a stronger acid.

The oxides and hydroxides of a number of metallic elements are amphoteric. They can react with acids (act as bases) to produce normal salts, or with bases (act as acids) to produce salts in which the metal ion is incorporated into a negatively charged complex ion.

An example of an amphoteric salt is di-sodium acid phosphate, Na_2HPO_4, which dissolves to give the ions Na^+ and HPO_4^-. Depending on the acidity (pH) of the solution, the latter ion can dissociate to H^+ and PO_4^{3-} and hence act as an acid, or it can combine with an additional H^+ ion to form $H_2PO_4^-$ and act as a base.   CHARLES F. BAES, JR.

See also: ACIDS AND BASES; ION.

amphotericin B: see ANTIBIOTICS.

ampicillin: see ANTIBIOTICS.

amplifier

Any device or circuit that receives a signal, amplifies it—that is, makes it stronger, ideally without changing the signal in any other way—and sends the signal out again may be called an amplifier. The term usually refers to amplifiers of electronic signals, used in such familiar systems as radios, televi-

sion sets, tape recorders, record players, and other electronic equipment; such amplifiers are the subject of this article. There are also magnetic amplifiers, used in computers and other devices; amplifiers of mechanical motions, such as the PANTOGRAPH; and hydraulic amplifiers, such as the power brakes in a car.

Electronic amplifiers can be based on ELECTRON TUBES or SEMICONDUCTOR devices. The simplest electron tube that can perform amplification is the TRIODE. However, in most modern devices, electron tubes have been replaced by semiconducting circuit elements, such as the TRANSISTOR. This article, therefore, emphasizes amplifiers having transistor circuitry.

Operation of Amplifiers. In a basic transistor amplifier, the transistors act as sources of current or voltage whose output value is larger than but controlled by a current or voltage related to the signal. When the smaller current flows, so does the larger one, in proportion to the power of the smaller current. As the input modulates, so does the output. The ratio of the output voltage to the input voltage is called the voltage gain of the amplifier. In general, this gain is made greater than unity. Other gains that are sometimes considered are the current gain, which is the ratio of output current to input current, and the power gain, the ratio of power output to power input.

In order to increase the amplification, amplifiers are often designed by connecting several stages in cascade. This means that the output of the first stage supplies the input signal to a second stage; the output of the second stage is connected to the input of a third stage, and so on. The overall gain of such a multistage amplifier can be determined from the basic definition of gain, or it can be found as the product of the gains of the individual stages. In modern equipment, such amplifiers are usually manufactured on a tiny square silicon wafer, about 2 mm (0.08 in) along each edge, and can have gains of 10,000 to 100,000.

Transistors, whether bipolar or field-effect, have three internal elements. Since external input and output circuits have two pairs of connections, it is necessary to choose one internal element to be connected in common to an input and output terminal. Thus three basic circuits are possible for each form of transistor; the choice of the common element determines the performance of the amplifier.

In order to obtain the required gain and to improve the matching of the input and output impedances, two circuits may be combined in cascade. It is also possible to use three-stage connections. This is especially advantageous when the circuit is in monolithic form on a single silicon chip, since all circuits and connections are fabricated in the same operation, and increased complexity of the circuit does not appreciably raise the manufacturing cost.

Kinds of Amplifiers. Amplifiers can be classified according to the frequency range that they are designed to handle. For example, an audio amplifier is for the range from zero to about 100,000 cycles per second, or hertz; an intermediate-frequency (IF) amplifier is for 400 kilohertz (kHz) to 5 megahertz (MHz); a radio-frequency (RF) amplifier handles signal frequencies up to several hundred MHz; and an ultrahigh-frequency (UHF) amplifier employs specialized electronic devices that enable it to operate above 100 MHz.

The response or gain of an amplifier varies with the signal frequency. The gain may be held constant down to zero frequency or that of a steady input, but inevitably, at some high frequency, the gain will start to drop. This is because it takes a finite time for internal storage elements to become fully charged. At very high frequencies, this time becomes comparable to the period (time for a complete cycle) of the signal wave. It is possible to design circuitry so that uniform, or flat, response is obtained over most of the frequency range of the signal.

Amplifiers can also be distinguished by the fraction of the cycle during which there is an output current. Some amplifiers are designed to handle large power outputs; they can be provided with means of cooling—such as cooling fins, forced air, and liquid cooling—to remove the heat that is generated. Another approach, however, is to reduce such heat losses by reducing the time of current conduction per signal cycle. In Class A amplifiers, the current conduction is continuous and distortion is low. Power efficiency is about 25 to 45%. In Class B amplifiers there is an output current for about half the input cycle. Efficiency can exceed 60%, but distortion is higher. The distortion can be decreased, however, by having push-pull connections with a pair of transistors. Class C amplifiers have current conduction in pulses that last for less than half the input cycle. Efficiency can reach 85%, but distortion is very high; such amplifiers are used only for radio-frequency signals. Class D amplifiers employ constant-amplitude current pulses; here it is the duration of the pulse that varies with the modulating signal. The signal is recovered by averaging the pulses. Efficiency approaches 100%.

A special, monolithic form of amplifier has positive and negative inputs, giving an output controlled by the difference of the input signals, and is called a differential amplifier. This amplifier discriminates against noise and other inputs common to the two terminals. It is often used with various feedback circuits and is then called an OPERATIONAL AMPLIFIER (op-amp), because it was originally used for mathematical operations on signals, such as summation, differentiation, and integration.　　　　J. D. RYDER

Bibliography: Kahn, Michael, *The Versatile Op-Amp* (1970); Morrison, Ralph, *DC Amplifiers in Instrumentation* (1970); Schwartz, Martin, *Radio Electronics Made Simple* (1982).

amplitude

In physics, the maximum displacement of a particle executing a periodic motion from the equilibrium position is known as the amplitude of the motion. For example, the farthest distance a pendulum swings away from the vertical position is its amplitude. For a ripple in water, the maximum height of the wave above the surface is the amplitude of the water wave. The amplitude of a periodic motion is related to its energy, which is proportional to the square of the amplitude. When the system in motion loses energy, the amplitude decreases; as long as the system gains energy, the amplitude increases, becoming extremely large during the phenomenon of resonance.　　　　S. BHATTACHARYA

See also: RESONANCE (physics).

amplitude modulation

Amplitude modulation is a technique for varying the height, or amplitude, of a wave in order to transmit information. Much of radio broadcasting uses amplitude modulation (AM), although other types of MODULATION are possible. A convenient and efficient means of transmitting information is by the propagation of waves of ELECTROMAGNETIC RADIATION (see WAVES AND WAVE MOTION). Sound waves in the audible range, such as speech and music, have a frequency that is too low for efficient transmission through the air for significant distances. By the process of modulation, however, this low-frequency audio information—the signal—can be impressed on a carrier wave that has a much higher frequency and can propagate through space for great distances. The transmitter at a radio station generates a carrier wave having constant characteristics, such as amplitude and frequency. The signal containing the desired information is then used to modulate the carrier; that is, the signal produces a variation in the form of a certain characteristic of the carrier wave. This new wave, called the modulated wave, will contain the information of the signal.

In AM, it is the amplitude of the carrier wave that is made to vary so that it will contain the information of the signal. When the modulated wave reaches a radio receiver tuned to the proper frequency, it is demodulated, "revealing" the wave that was carried. (Demodulation is the process of reconstructing the original signal from the modulated wave; it is essentially the opposite of modulation.) The signal can then reproduce the desired sound by using a loudspeaker. AM radio is still a popular form of radio broadcasting, but it does have a number of shortcomings. The quality of reproduction is relatively poor because of inherent limitations in the technique

and because of interference from other stations and other electrical signals, such as those produced by lightning or by electronic devices. When the frequency, rather than the amplitude, of the carrier wave is modulated, the process is called FREQUENCY MODULATION or FM.　　FORREST M. MIMS III

Bibliography: Math, Irwin, *Morse, Marconi, and You* (1979).

amputation

Amputation is the surgical removal of part or all of an appendage, such as a limb or a breast. It is usually done for life-saving reasons when gangrene infection, massive injury, cancer, or impaired blood flow occurs. Many amputations are performed on older people, mainly because of the higher incidence of vascular diseases that restrict blood circulation in the limbs. The most common reason for amputations among younger people is massive injury to limbs from automobile and motorcycle accidents.　　PETER L. PETRAKIS

Amritsar　[um-rit'-sur]

Amritsar, district headquarters for Punjab state, is a city in northwestern India with a population of 589,229 (1981). It is located about 48 km (30 mi) from the Pakistan border in a semiarid region. The city is an important regional market center for agricultural goods and the center for border security in the northwest. Manufactured products include textiles, particularly carpets, silks, and brocades.

Amritsar is the most important religious center of the SIKHS, who make up about one-third of the city's inhabitants. The city was founded in 1577 by Ram Das, the fourth Sikh guru, on land furnished by the Mogul emperor Akbar. Ram Das also began construction of the *Amrita Saras* ("Pool of Immortality"), an artificial lake from which the city takes its name. On an island in the lake is the most important Sikh shrine, the Golden Temple, so called because of its copper roof covered with gold foil. In its present form the temple, which contains the most sacred text of the Sikhs, the Granth Sahib, dates from the reign (1792–1839) of the Sikh ruler Ranjit Singh.

In the Amritsar Massacre (Apr. 13, 1919) troops commanded by the British general Reginald Dyer fired on an Indian crowd peacefully demonstrating against the Rowlatt Acts, by which the British administration had recently given itself emergency powers. Casualties were officially estimated at 379 deaths and some 1,200 wounded. The site of the massacre, an open area called the Jallianwallah Bagh, is now a national shrine.

In 1982, Sikh extremists launched a terrorist campaign to force the Indian government to grant Sikhs greater autonomy. They used the Golden Temple as a sanctuary, turning it into a fortified base. As a result the temple was stormed by Indian troops in 1984. Restoration work began almost immediately.　　ASHOK K. DUTT

Amsterdam

Amsterdam is the chief city and nominal capital of the Kingdom of the Netherlands (The Hague is the seat of government). It lies where the little IJ River flows into the IJSSELMEER (formerly the Zuiderzee). Its name is derived from a dam once built on the Amstel, which flows into the IJ at this point. Amsterdam has 687,397 (1983 est.) inhabitants, making it the largest city in the country. Its urban agglomeration population is 955,515 (1981 est.).

The city lies below sea level and is built on piles into the soft alluvial clay. By the late 16th century Amsterdam had become the chief Dutch port; for a century it was Europe's most important port and commercial center. Much of the building in the inner city dates from this period. The Old City consists of a series of concentric roads and canals on each side of the Amstel near its junction with the IJ. The docks, which lie along the IJ River, were formerly approached from the Zuiderzee, but in 1876 the NORTH SEA CANAL was opened from the city westward to the coast at IJmuiden.

The Contemporary City. The population is mainly Dutch, the majority of whom belong to the Dutch Reformed or Calvinist

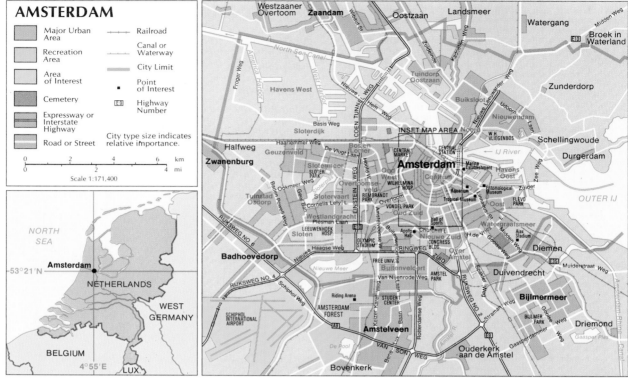

AMSTERDAM

	Major Urban Area		Railroad
	Recreation Area		Canal or Waterway
	Area of Interest		City Limit
	Cemetery	▪	Point of Interest
	Expressway or Interstate Highway	E9	Highway Number
	Road or Street		City type size indicates relative importance.

Scale 1:171,400

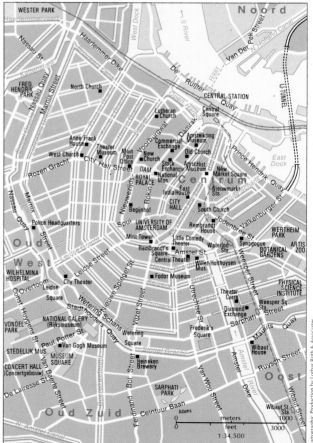

church. The city also has a large Jewish community and a significant Indonesian minority.

Amsterdam is primarily a commercial and financial center. Its industries have developed from its role as a port trading with the East. The processing of oil seeds, tobacco, coffee, tea, and other imported goods is important, as are engineering and shipbuilding. Diamond cutting and polishing is a major industry, and there is a large trade in timber. The port of Amsterdam tends to concentrate on light cargoes, leaving the handling of bulk cargoes to its neighbor to the south, Rotterdam.

Waterborne communications are important, and a network of canals links the city with the rest of the Netherlands and with the Rhine River. Even within the city, water transportation continues to be much used. Amsterdam has an excellent railroad service with the rest of the Netherlands as well as with Western and Central Europe, and it is served by Schiphol Airport, 8 km (5 mi) to the southwest, one of the most modern in Europe.

Amsterdam is the chief educational and cultural center in the Netherlands. It has two universities and is noted for its museums, including the RIJKSMUSEUM (State Museum; 1876–85). This contains a large collection of paintings by the Dutch masters, including Rembrandt, whose house is also preserved as a museum. The Concert Hall is the home of the famous CONCERTGEBOUW ORCHESTRA. The architecture of the Old City, made up mainly of merchants' houses of the 16th and 17th centuries, helps attract visitors and has made Amsterdam a center of tourism. Near the city center are the Royal Palace (1648–65), the Oude Kerk ("Old Church"; early 14th century), and fragments of the city's medieval defenses.

History. Amsterdam developed in the Middle Ages as a small fishing port and commercial center. It was greatly expanded during the 14th century by the counts of Holland; joining the HANSEATIC LEAGUE in 1369, its merchants opened up trade with the Baltic. In the late 16th century, with the decline of Antwerp, Amsterdam became the chief port of northwestern Europe. The city experienced rapid growth and extensive rebuilding, and its defensive canals were successively extended to enclose an ever greater area. Amsterdam welcomed politi-

Amsterdam's extensive system of canals, totaling more than 80 km (50 mi), has earned the city its reputation as the "Venice of the North." Although The Hague, to the southwest, serves as the Netherlands' administrative center, Amsterdam is the official capital and the nation's largest city in population and the second largest in metropolitan area.

cal and religious refugees, including Flemings from the Spanish Netherlands, Jews from the Iberian Peninsula, and Huguenots from France. This was the city's golden age. In the 18th century a gradual silting of the Zuiderzee occurred and Amsterdam suffered a decline. The larger ships of the day had difficulty reaching the city, and much of the Rhineland trade passed to Rotterdam. The city was revitalized by the opening of the North Sea Canal in 1876, and in the late 19th century it again developed as the chief port for the domestic trade of the Netherlands. During World War II Amsterdam's port was largely destroyed by the occupying Germans. It has since been rebuilt.   NORMAN J. G. POUNDS

Bibliography: Kroon, Ben, and Van Der Heyden, A. A., *The Glory of Amsterdam* (1975); Regin, Deric, *Traders, Artists, Burghers: A Cultural History of Amsterdam in the 17th Century* (1976).

Amsterdam, University of: see EUROPEAN
UNIVERSITIES.

Amtrak

Amtrak is the semipublic corporation, created by the Rail Passenger Service Act of 1970, that has provided most of the intercity rail passenger service in the United States since May 1, 1971. The legislation instructed the secretary of transportation to establish a reduced but basic rail passenger service for the United States, financed by payments made by the participating RAILROADS and by federal grants and guaranteed loans.

Postwar Decline in Rail Service. The establishment of Amtrak followed several years of public concern over the continuing decrease in the number of passenger trains and a long period of ever-increasing deficits for passenger service.

During World War II, passenger rail traffic was profitable. In 1944 more than 75% of all commercial intercity travel was by rail. In the postwar years, however, rail travel rapidly declined. Annual passenger kilometers of rail travel dropped from 157.7 billion (98 billion mi) in 1944 to only 17.7 billion (11 billion mi) in 1970. As rail travel declined, that by air and private automobile boomed, and by 1970 only 7% of all inter-

city passenger travel was accomplished by rail. Railroad companies, which had been losing up to $600 million yearly on passenger service, dropped so many routes that passenger trains used only about one-quarter of the national rail network.

Amtrak Service. When Amtrak went into operation in 1971, 18 of the 22 large passenger railroads joined the corporation. Amtrak reduced routes and service by roughly half, to a total of 21 routes serving 340 U.S. cities on about 32,000 km (20,000 mi) of track. The 4 remaining passenger lines came into the system later—the last, the Denver and Rio Grande Western Railroad, only in 1983. With the exception of commuter lines connecting major cities with their suburbs, all intercity passenger rail service today is supplied by Amtrak, which now serves almost 500 stations. At the same time, the corporation has eliminated routes it judges to be uneconomic. In 1983, for example, a route across southern Wyoming was dropped—it averaged only 150 passengers per day—in favor of a more scenic and tourist-attractive route through the Colorado Rockies. The route elimination left Wyoming without passenger rail service. Also without Amtrak service are Maine, New Hampshire, South Dakota, Hawaii, and Alaska.

Greater operating efficiencies and a rise in passenger use have reduced Amtrak's dependence on federal funding to about 50% of its total expenditures. In 1982 the government supplied Amtrak with $558 million.   JOHN F. STOVER

Bibliography: Dorin, Patrick C., *Amtrak Trains and Travel* (1980); Thomas, William E., *Reprieve for the Iron Horse: Amtrak* (1974).

Amu Darya   [ah-moo dahr'-yah]

The Amu Darya is the longest river in the Central Asian region of the USSR. Formed by the joining of the Pyandzh and Vakhsh rivers, which originate in the Pamirs, the Amu Darya flows for 2,540 km (1,578 mi), emptying into the Aral Sea where it forms a marshy delta. The river carries little traffic but supplies much of the area's hydroelectric power. The Amu's drainage basin extends about 965 km (600 mi) from north to south, and more than 1,450 km (900 mi) from east to west. Much of the river's water is drawn off for desert irrigation (Kara Kum Canal system) or is lost to drainage or evaporation before reaching the sea. A complex dam and reservoir system is being enlarged. The river was called the Oxus in ancient times, and it played a role in the campaigns of Alexander the Great.

amulet

An amulet is an object used as a charm, either to protect against harm or to promote good fortune. It is usually worn or carried on the person but may be attached to animals, houses, automobiles, or other property. Examples of amulets include the scarab of ancient Egypt, the horseshoe and other iron objects used against WITCHCRAFT in early European tradition, the blue beads used in some Islamic countries to guard against the EVIL EYE, and charms for good luck, such as the rabbit's foot. Stones, horns, bones, figurines, coins and medallions, and many other objects are used as amulets in a great range of cultures. Persons especially vulnerable, such as children or the sick, are often thought to need amulets. Some amulets bear religious images or texts; others have astrological significance. The source of power attributed to amulets may be defined within a particular belief system or may remain an obscure supernatural influence.   CHRISTIAN CLERK

Bibliography: Bonner, Campbell, *Studies in Magical Amulets* (1950); Budge, E. A. Wallis, *Amulets and Superstitions* (1930; repr. 1978 as *Amulets and Talismans*).

Amundsen, Roald   (ah'-mun-suhn, roh'-ahl]

Roald Amundsen, the Norwegian explorer, led the first successful expedition to the South Pole. Racing against another team of explorers, Amundsen reached his destination on Dec. 14, 1911.

Roald Engelbregt Grauning Amundsen, a Norwegian, explored the Arctic ice cap and Antarctica and led the expedition that first reached the SOUTH POLE. Born near Oslo on July 16, 1872, he left medical school in 1897 to go to the Antarctic with a Belgian expedition, the first group to spend a winter there. Between 1903 and 1906 he passed from east to west across the Arctic Ocean above North America, the so-called NORTHWEST PASSAGE. He was mounting an expedition to the North Pole when he learned that an American, Robert PEARY, had already reached the pole (1909).

In June 1910 he sailed from Norway, intending to be the first to reach the South Pole. He knew of a similar expedition being launched by the British under the direction of Robert Falcon SCOTT. The race of the two expeditions captured the imagination of Europe.

Amundsen, with a shorter overland route and a disciplined plan involving the use of dogs to pull the sleds and provide food for the return journey, arrived at the pole with four men on Dec. 14, 1911, one month ahead of the British. Amundsen left a sympathetic note to Scott at the pole. It was found with the frozen bodies of Scott and his men, who died on the way back to their base camp. Amundsen's victory failed to win the fame and money he thought it deserved. Instead, Scott was remembered as the hero. Amundsen died on June 18, 1928, while flying to the Arctic to rescue an Italian explorer, Umberto Nobile, from a dirigible crash.

Bibliography: Amundsen, Roald, *My Life as an Explorer* (1927); Turley, Charles, *Roald Amundsen, Explorer* (1935).

Amur River   [uh-moor']

The Amur River is located in eastern Asia and forms part of the Soviet-Chinese border. It flows 2,825 km (1,755 mi) from the confluence of the Shilka and Argun rivers, north of Inner Mongolia, eastward to its mouth at the Tatar Strait, which separates Siberia from the Sakhalin Islands. The Amur is the longest river in the eastern Soviet Union, and from May to November, when it is navigable, it is an important trade route. It also supplies water for irrigation and supports a large fish population.

The river is divided into three parts. The upper Amur is the portion in the mountains, the middle part flows through the Zeya-Bureya Depression and plains, and the lower part flows through marshes, where it is joined by numerous other streams. The principal city along the river is Khabarovsk. The population of the surrounding region is composed of Russians as well as the original tribal population (including the YAKUT and the BURYAT) in the north and Chinese, Mongolians, and Manchurians in the south. The Amur is rain-fed, and its basin has a monsoon climate. As a result, flooding is common along much of its course from May to October; water may rise 7.5 m (25 ft) above normal.

amusement park

An amusement park is a recreational area devoted to such entertainments as the FERRIS WHEEL and roller coaster, shooting galleries, fun houses, sideshows, and dance bands. Amusement parks are an outgrowth of CARNIVALS AND FAIRS. In the United States, these parks were first built at popular beaches in the 1800s. Usually a roller coaster, originally called the "sliding hill," was the major attraction.

Walt DISNEY created the first "theme" park, DISNEYLAND, in Anaheim, Calif., in 1955. Elaborate fantasy realizations were constructed around such themes as the world of the future, the Old West, and a small-town main street. Its phenomenal success prompted the building of other theme parks throughout the United States and Europe. Walt Disney World, opened in Buena Vista, Fla., in 1971, is the largest and most popular. Others are Six Flags over Texas in Arlington, Tex., which has an American history theme; Opryland, USA, in Nashville, Tenn., which has a country music theme; and Astroworld in Houston, Tex. Great Adventure in Jackson, N.J., and the many Lion Country Safari parks combine traditional amusements with spacious open zoos, where animals roam while people, confined to cars, drive through the park to see them. In the United States amusement parks attract 170 million visitors a year.

Bibliography: Hunter, Susan, *A Family Guide to Amusement Centers* (1975); Kyriazi, Gary, *The Great American Amusement Parks* (1976); McCullough, Edo, *World's Fair Midways* (1966; repr. 1976).

Amvets

Amvets, or American Veterans of World War II, Korea, and Vietnam, was founded in 1944 by veterans of World War II. Membership is open to anyone who has served in the armed forces of the United States or any U.S. citizen who has served in the forces of an allied nation during these wars. Amvets is active in veterans' rehabilitation, legislative affairs, employment of the handicapped, and visiting hospitalized veterans. In 1978 the organization had 150,000 members in 1,100 local groups. It publishes a bimonthly magazine, the *National AMVET.*

amyl nitrite   [am'-ul ny'-tryt]

Amyl nitrite is a volatile drug used to relax spasms of arteries, control convulsions, and relieve asthmatic paroxysms. Administered by inhalation in 3- to 5-drop doses, it furnishes immediate relief by widening constricted blood vessels. Popularly known as "poppers," amyl nitrite is also reputed by illicit users to be an effective mood elevator or stimulant.

An: see ANU.

An-shan [ahn'-shahn']

An-shan, a city in Liaoning province, southern Manchuria, China, is the leading iron- and steel-producing center in China and is surrounded by a fertile agricultural area. Located about 90 km (55 mi) southwest of Shen-yang (Mukden), it has a population of 1,100,000 (1980 est.). The city was first settled in 1387. After extensive destruction during the Boxer Rebellion, it was rebuilt in 1909 as an industrial city. In 1917–18 the Japanese established steelworks there. In 1945 invading Soviet forces dismantled the factories, but they were rebuilt after 1949 and played a major role in the First Five-Year Plan (1953–58). The blast furnaces were damaged again in 1967 during the Cultural Revolution but have since been rebuilt.

Bibliography: Wu, Yuan-li, *China: A Handbook* (1973).

Anabaena [an-uh-bee'-nuh]

Anabaena is a genus of BLUE-GREEN ALGAE usually found on moist soil or floating on shallow water as solitary forms or gelatinous colonies, sometimes producing flowerlike blooms during the summer in northern regions. The algae produce a toxin fatal to animals that ingest sufficient amounts in drinking water.

Anabaptists

Anabaptists, or rebaptizers, were members of a variety of 16th-century religious groups that rejected infant BAPTISM. Since they believed that only after an adult had come to faith in Christ should he or she be baptized, they taught that converts who had been baptized in infancy must be rebaptized.

Anabaptists held the church to be the congregation of true saints who should separate themselves from the sinful world. Their theology was highly eschatological (see ESCHATOLOGY), and they claimed direct inspiration by the Holy Spirit. The Anabaptists refused to take oaths, opposed capital punishment, and rejected military service. Their beliefs made them appear subversive and provoked persecution. Many of the Reformers disclaimed them, regarding them as fundamentally opposed to the ideas of the REFORMATION.

In Zurich, Conrad Grebel performed the first adult baptism on Jan. 21, 1525, when he rebaptized Georg Blaurock in the house of Felix Manz. Anabaptism spread to southwest Germany, Austria, Moravia, along the Danube, and down the Rhine to the Netherlands. Numbering less than 1 percent of the population, the Anabaptists were for the most part of humble social origin. Among their leaders were Balthasar Hubmaier, Hans Denck, Jacob Hütter, and Hans Hut.

In 1534, militant Anabaptists, inspired by radical Melchior Hofmann, seized control of the city of Münster. Led by Bernt Knipperdollinck, Jan Mathijs, and Jan Beuckelson, better known as John of Leiden (c.1509–36), they drove out all Protestants and Roman Catholics. John set up a theocracy, became king, and established polygamy and communal property. After a 16-month siege, the bishop of Münster recaptured the city and executed the rebels. MENNO SIMONS, a Dutchman, restored the reputation of the Anabaptists through his moderate and inspired leadership. His followers have survived and are known as MENNONITES. The HUTTERIAN BRETHREN are descendants of the group led by Hutter.

LEWIS W. SPITZ

Bibliography: Clasen, Claus P., *Anabaptism: A Social History, 1525–1618* (1972); Estep, William, *The Anabaptist Story* (1975); Hershberger, Guy F., ed., *The Recovery of the Anabaptist Vision* (1957); Littell, Franklin H., *Origins of Sectarian Protestantism* (1964); Williams, George H., *The Radical Reformation* (1962); Williams, George H., and Mergal, Angel, eds., *Spiritual and Anabaptist Writers* (1957).

anabatic wind: see MOUNTAIN AND VALLEY WINDS.

Anaconda

Anaconda (1980 pop., 12,518) is a city in southwestern Montana. Formerly the county seat of Deer Lodge County, in 1977 it was consolidated with that county to form a single administrative unit. The city was founded in 1883 by Marcus DALY as a smelting center for ores from his copper mine. Originally named Copperopolis, it was incorporated in 1888 and renamed Anaconda after Daly's mine. Anaconda's smelter, which had been one of the world's largest, was closed in 1980.

anaconda

The giant anaconda or water boa, E. murinus, *throttles a collared peccary before swallowing it whole. The largest of all nonpoisonous constricting snakes, the giant anaconda may reach 7.6 m (25 ft) in length and 90 cm (3 ft) in girth and may live 50 years.*

The anaconda, *Eunectes murinus,* a semiaquatic snake of the BOA family, Boidae, is found in Central America and tropical South America. The largest boa in the Western Hemisphere, it can reach a length of 7.6 m (25 ft). Both the young, which are born alive in large broods, and the adults are dark green with round black markings. A smaller species, *E. notaeus,* the yellow anaconda, is found in rivers of southern South America. It is yellowish green in color with irregular dark blotches. Although not venomous, anacondas can defend themselves by inflicting severe bites. They are strong constrictors and feed on birds and small animals.

PETER L. PETRAKIS

Anacreon [uh-nak'-ree-ahn]

Anacreon, c.570–478 BC, was a notable Greek lyric poet. He composed imaginative verses for solo voice about love, friendship, and wine. Although a number of serious epigrams and hymns are also attributed to him, he gained fame for the graceful style of his verse. The *Anacreontea,* a collection of poems written in imitation of Anacreon's style and metrics, influenced writers for centuries.

anaerobe [an'-uh-rohb]

An anaerobe is an organism that obtains all the energy it needs from food without the use of oxygen by a method called FERMENTATION. Certain bacteria that cannot use oxygen and are even poisoned by it are called obligate anaerobes; they produce gases such as methane or hydrogen sulfide from organic compounds that do not contain oxygen. Other bacteria and YEAST are facultative anaerobes; they may or may not use oxygen and can survive either way. Plants and animals can also obtain energy by fermentation, but they are obligate aerobes in that they must always have oxygen to survive—with the exception of some internal parasites. The anaerobe METHANOGEN is believed to be related to the earliest life forms.

See also: METABOLISM.

anagram

A word or phrase formed by rearranging the letters of another word or phrase is an anagram (*shape: phase; revolution: love to ruin*). The making of anagrams as a game dates back to ancient times, and such letter rearrangements have also been used to disguise names or messages and to coin pseudonyms. *Erewhon,* for example, the title of Samuel Butler's utopian novel, is an anagram of *nowhere.*

Bibliography: Borgman, Dmitri A., *Language on Vacation* (1965); Espy, Willard R., *The Game of Words* (1972).

Anaheim   [an'-uh-hym]

Anaheim, a suburban city in the Santa Ana River valley in southern California, lies 40 km (25 mi) southeast of Los Angeles. Its growth has been extremely rapid as industries and housing replaced the citrus groves and vineyards planted by the early settlers. Since 1950, when the population was less than 15,000, Anaheim has grown to a city of 221,847 (1980); metropolitan Orange County, which also includes Santa Ana and Garden Grove, has a population of 1,931,570.

Anaheim is the site of DISNEYLAND amusement park, Anaheim Stadium (home of the California Angels baseball team), and the Anaheim Convention Center. Industries produce aerospace systems, electronic equipment, paper converters, greeting cards, and processed foods. The city was founded by German immigrants in 1857 as an experiment in communal living. Its name means "home on the Ana."

analgesic   [an-ul-jee'-zik]

Analgesic drugs and techniques diminish the perception of pain while causing minimal loss of sensibility to other stimuli. Analgesic drugs include ASPIRIN, ACETAMINOPHEN, IBUPROFEN, MORPHINE and other narcotics, general anesthetics in low doses, and local anesthetics (see ANESTHESIA). Analgesic techniques include ACUPUNCTURE, BIOFEEDBACK, HYPNOSIS, electrical stimulation, and surgical separation of nerve fibers.

Treatment of acute pain is necessary after surgery, dental procedures, muscular strains and sprains, or trauma. Chronic pain requiring therapy may arise following infection, with malignancies, or with nerve irritation or compression, for example, a pinched nerve. Pain may be a symptom of an underlying problem that needs further treatment.

Some of the drugs most often used as analgesics are acetylsalicylic acid (aspirin), the drug most commonly taken for the relief of mild pain; phenacetin and acetaminophen (Tylenol), which are comparable to aspirin in reducing pain and fever but are much less effective in alleviating inflammation; and ibuprofen (Advil), which is less irritating to the stomach than aspirin and also acts to reduce inflammation. All of the above drugs achieve their analgesic effect through inhibition of the synthesis of PROSTAGLANDINS in the body. Propoxyphene (DARVON), which is effective in relieving mild pain, has been used in the treatment of narcotic addiction. Narcotic analgesics are used only for the treatment of severe pain. OPIUM, derived from the juice of the poppyseed capsule, has been in use for centuries; CODEINE, HEROIN, and morphine are derivatives of this drug.

Small amounts of general anesthetics can be used for pain relief without producing unconsciousness. Topical local anesthetics, such as benzocaine (ethylaminobenzoate), are widely used for blocking the transmission of pain signals to the brain from the affected area. A local anesthetic can be injected near nerve fibers to block pain sensation in an entire area of the body. This procedure is useful for analgesia in treatment of chronic pain and during localized surgery.

Electrical stimulation of large fibers by the replacement of electrodes on the skin, in specific nerves, or within the spinal cord has produced analgesia. Hypnosis is a proven method for achieving pain relief in both acute and chronic disorders in susceptible patients. This technique requires a conducive atmosphere and a cooperative patient. Acupuncture, a technique derived from Chinese medicine and involving the insertion of needles into the skin at certain points on the body, is

also sometimes successful in producing adequate analgesia for major surgical procedures and for the relief of chronic pain. Biofeedback control has been useful in relieving some forms of chronic pain; the patient learns to modify his or her response to stress through concentration and relaxation.

The PLACEBO effect—by which patients given a sugar pill experience the same lessening in pain as when given an analgesic—must be considered whenever analgesics are compared. Studies have shown that up to 30 percent of a group of patients will experience some relief of pain when only a dummy pill has been administered.

In the early 1970s it was discovered that opiates bind to specific receptors in the brain. Subsequently, naturally occurring compounds called encephalins and endorphins, which bind to the OPIATE RECEPTORS, were isolated from animal brain tissue. As more is learned about these compounds, artificial regulation of their levels may produce effective analgesia.

GERALD F. LEFEVER AND HARRY WOLLMAN

Bibliography: Goodman, L. S., and Gilman, A., *The Pharmacological Basis of Therapeutics* (1975); Mimes, Samuel, *The Conquest of Pain* (1974); Toure, Halima, *Pain* (1981); Williams, N. E., and Wilson, H., eds., *Pain and Its Management* (1983).

analog computer

An analog computer is an apparatus that employs continuously variable physical phenomena, such as mechanical motions, flows of fluids, or currents of electricity, to make computations. It may be contrasted with the DIGITAL COMPUTER, which makes use of digital, or discrete, elements to make computations. A primitive example of an analog computer is the immersion of an object of irregular shape in water contained in a graduated vessel to determine displaced volume. This example uses continuously variable magnitudes as input data, as well as throughout the computational process and even to convey the outcome, since final conversion to numerical form by comparison with discrete graduations is optional. Although the calculation seems quite simple and immediate because the apparatus directly embodies level-seeking and volume-conserving laws of fluids that appear familiar and obvious, this is deceptive, because details of what occurs are very complicated to describe exactly, or, in modern parlance, to "program." Such examples, found in early science, mensuration, and commerce, are recognized today as analog computations predating the advent of mathematical tools such as calculus, capable of analyzing them in terms of the elementary operations of addition, subtraction, multiplication, and division, with differentiation and integration.

Each instance of a direct-embodiment analog computer such as the one described above is suited only for computations built into its structure and can be viewed as a convenient model accurate enough for quantitative representation. Prior to the scientific revolution brought about by Sir Isaac Newton, such apparatus evolved through physical insight into particular problems, and its application to other uses resulted from trial and error to establish analogical validity. Since Newton, it has become understood that phenomena are properly analogous when mathematical analysis reveals similar underlying formulas. This now defines the range of applicability of an analog computer. During the last three centuries the sciences of mechanics, electrodynamics, and heat and light were found frequently to involve similar formulas, indicating wide applicability. Apparatus and instrument construction skills in these sciences were greatly expanded and refined, and analog computing devices were evolved to perform basic operations, then combined in multistage assemblies to solve more complex problems.

Addition and subtraction of continuously variable magnitudes may easily be done using sliding mechanical displacements, either rotational or straight-line. The logarithmic SLIDE RULE, invented about 1620 and still used, adds or subtracts two input lengths by straight-line sliding of one part relative to another so that the output length equals their sum or difference. The two inputs are set in according to logarithmic scales, and the output read from a logarithmic scale, so that what is read is equivalent to multiplication or division of numbers. Modern slide rules often have other scales so that a wide variety of trigonometric, exponential, and complex vector operations can be done. Moreover, simple displacements and measurements, referred to more complicated scales and graphed curves, brought about an extensive branch of calculational mathematics known as nomography (see NOMOGRAM). In mechanical form, these techniques gave rise to a class of analog computing devices known as computing linkages.

The two basic operations of calculus (differentiation and integration) can be viewed as finding the tangent to a curve at each point, and as finding the area under a curve $y=f(x)$ from x_1 to x_2. Integration can be performed by a simple and elegant mechanism, known since about 1800, called a disk-and-wheel integrator, which acts like a transmission having a continuously variable ratio. The independent variable x turns a shaft carrying a disk much like a phonograph turntable. A small follower wheel is maintained at disk radius equal to the variable y and is turned by friction contact with the disk at that radius. A wheel of unit radius turns y times as much as the x shaft and thus turns in proportion to the area.

Many varieties of the disk-and-wheel integrator have been developed, the simplest being manually operable on graphed curves; they are called planimeters. Apparatuses involving several such devices in combination with other mechanisms were developed to perform harmonic (Fourier) analysis and also to solve differential equations automatically. These are called DIFFERENTIAL ANALYZERS of the Kelvin and Bush types and were used during World War II to calculate ballistic trajectories; disk integrators were also used in gunfire directors and in airborne bombsights. Electric, and most recently electronic, analog computers have supplanted the earlier mechanical machines. The most widely used analog computer, the domestic electric watt-hour meter, computes the sum over time of the product of two continuously variable vectors—current and voltage; this quantity, which is the definite integral of power, is the energy consumed.

Because the fundamental electrical components—resistors, inductors, and capacitors—can be produced far more cheaply and to much greater accuracy than their mechanical equivalents and also can readily be connected and rearranged, they are both convenient and economical. They respond far more quickly than mechanical apparatuses and do not wear or develop unwanted friction. Analog computers based on electrical networks are useful in the simulative study of many physical phenomena. With the introduction of electronic (feedback) amplifiers to facilitate coupling, they can effectively perform a wide variety of mathematical calculations. The outputs of analog computers can also be used to control the operation of other equipment.   JULIAN BIGELOW

Bibliography: Adams, J. M., *Computers* (1973); Dodd, K. N., *Teach Yourself Analogue Computers* (1969); Dorf, Richard C., *Computers and Man* (1974); Fenichel, R. R., and Weizenbaum, J., eds., *Computers and Computation: Readings from Scientific American* (1971); Fields, Craig, *About Computers* (1973); Rekoff, Michael G., *Analog Computer Programming* (1967); Roden, Martin, *Analog and Digital Systems* (1979); Tomovic, Rajko, and Karplus, Walter J., *High-Speed Analog Computers* (1970).

See also: COMPUTER.

analog-to-digital converter

The analog-to-digital, or A/D, converter is a device that converts analog signals to numerically equivalent form for input to a DIGITAL COMPUTER. The analog signals are electrical voltage levels derived from transducers that measure such continually varying physical properties as temperature and pressure. A digital computer handles discrete bits of information rather than continually changing values, so the A/D converter breaks down such values into discrete bits.

A typical A/D converter is made from a register that can hold a digital value, an operational amplifier, and a voltage comparator. The register outputs are electrically summed to produce an electric current proportional to the digital value of the register. This current causes a proportional voltage gain at the amplifier output. The amplified voltage is compared to the unknown input analog signal. As long as there is a discernible difference, the comparator allows the register value to change one step at a time until there is no difference. The register holds the digital value equivalent to the analog input.

Analog-to-digital converters are common computer INPUT-OUTPUT DEVICES for control applications. Computer-produced control signals may require the complementary conversion to analog by using DIGITAL-TO-ANALOG CONVERTERS.

EDWARD W. DAVIS

Bibliography: Clayton, G. B., *Data Converters* (1982).

analytic and linguistic philosophy

The analytic and linguistic movements, which have strongly influenced 20th-century British and American philosophy, have focused on the logical clarification of various kinds of statement.

The analytic movement began about the turn of the century with Bertrand RUSSELL and G. E. MOORE, both of Cambridge University, as its cofounders. At first, Russell and Moore seemed to be working along the same lines, for both reacted against the neo-Hegelian idealism of F. H. BRADLEY, which held that the world one experiences is only appearance, not reality. But whereas Russell rejected idealist metaphysics in favor of a metaphysics of his own, which he came to call "logical atomism," Moore abandoned metaphysical speculation altogether. Moore embodied the respect for common sense that became characteristic of much subsequent analytic and linguistic philosophy, a respect that Russell never shared.

In "On Denoting," a paper of 1905, Russell first put forward his theory of descriptions, suggesting that philosophical analysis should investigate the underlying logical forms of propositions, which might be quite different from their surface grammatical forms. Such analysis would reveal exactly what is affirmed by the proposition. The theory of descriptions shows, for example, that making a meaningful statement about "the greatest prime number" does not by itself commit one to belief in the existence of such a number. The fewer different kinds of things one admits exist, the more systematic and secure knowledge becomes. So analysis, and its converse, logical construction, seemed to promise a new, more scientific approach to metaphysical and epistemological questions: what things ultimately exist, and how secure is knowledge of them?

Russell's greatest analytic achievement was his reduction of mathematics to logic by the development of a new system of symbolic LOGIC, far more powerful than the traditional Aristotelian theory of the syllogism. Russell and Alfred North WHITEHEAD's monumental *Principia Mathematica* came out in three volumes from 1910 to 1913. By accounting for the distinctive character of mathematical truths without recourse to problematic metaphysical assumptions, Russell opened the way for a new, logically sophisticated version of EMPIRICISM, for which he was a leading spokesperson.

Russell thought of the new logic as the bare bones of an ideal language, a language in which the wording of all propositions would reveal their true logical forms. One of Russell's pupils, the Austrian Ludwig WITTGENSTEIN, argued that language's capacity to represent the world depended on their sharing a common structure, the structure of logic. Thus what Russell saw as an ideal, Wittgenstein saw as already hidden in language, waiting to be uncovered by analysis. According to Wittgenstein, any meaningful statement not belonging to logic or pure mathematics was a statement of fact. Moreover, all statements of fact had to be analyzable into "elementary propositions," which were, in a technical sense, "logical pictures" of possible facts.

The adherents of LOGICAL POSITIVISM, who were strongly influenced by Wittgenstein's ideas, held that any significant proposition that was not a tautology had to be observationally verifiable. They argued that propositions that did not meet this condition—for example, those belonging to ethics, religion, and, above all, traditional metaphysics—might have a certain emotional significance, but were literal nonsense. For the logical positivists, philosophical analysis became the clarification of statements belonging to science: in particular, making clear the relation between various kinds of theoretical claims and the observational evidence by which they could be verified or refuted.

Beginning in the 1930s and coming to fruition in the 1940s and '50s, however, there was a reaction against the Russellian and positivist conceptions of analysis; this reaction led eventually to the emergence of ordinary-language philosophy. The leading figures in this movement were Wittgenstein and John WISDOM at Cambridge and Gilbert RYLE and J. L. AUSTIN at Oxford.

Russell and the early Wittgenstein had a general program for reforming or uncovering the logical structure of language. The positivists had a general program for relating scientific statements to their observational bases. The ordinary-language philosophers, however, saw no need for a general program of analysis. Rather, propositions needed to be clarified only if they were already a source of philosophical perplexity. Moreover, clarification came to be seen, most notably in the work of Austin and the later Wittgenstein, as showing how statements that have generated philosophical conundrums function in ordinary concrete contexts and not as revealing some hidden logical structure. Philosophy came to be seen as descriptive more than theoretical, its aim being the elimination or "dissolving" of problems by diagnosing the misuses of language that generate them. This "linguistic philosophy" should not be confused with philosophy of language—a branch of philosophic inquiry dealing with problems about language itself.

Russell's heir in analytic philosophy is the American philosopher Willard Van Orman QUINE. Like Russell, Quine attempts to clarify and reduce the ontological commitments of language, or at least that fragment of it adequate for mathematics and natural science, though he calls his procedure "regimentation," not analysis. And although Quine sees himself as an empiricist of sorts, he is a trenchant critic of the kind of empiricism espoused by Russell and the logical positivists. Indeed, ironically, his epistemological holism, according to which beliefs are tested against experience as a body, not one at a time, is reminiscent of some of the idealist views Russell reacted against when the analytic movement first began.

Although the philosophy taught and practiced in major British and American universities today is by and large the outgrowth of the analytic and linguistic movements, it must be recognized that even philosophers willing to be described as analytic question or reject outright most of the theoretical presuppositions of analytic and linguistic philosophy as it was originally formulated. In calling themselves analytic philosophers, they mean to indicate their continuing interest in the problems that the analytic tradition addressed and their respect for the standards of clarity and rigor in argument that are its legacy.   MICHAEL WILLIAMS

Bibliography: Ayer, A. J., *Russell and Moore: The Analytical Heritage* (1971); Hacking, Ian, *Why Does Language Matter to Philosophy?* (1975); Mehta, Ved, *The Fly in the Fly Bottle* (1968); Passmore, John, *A Hundred Years of Philosophy* (1957); Pears, David, *Wittgenstein* (1969); Urmson, J. O., *Philosophical Analysis* (1956).

analytic geometry

Analytic geometry, also known as coordinate geometry, is a branch of mathematics in which geometric investigations are carried out by algebraic procedures. Although originally designed to investigate problems in plane geometry (geometry in a two-dimensional plane), analytic geometry can also be used to explore spaces of higher dimensions. *Plane analytic geometry* includes the systematic study of CONIC SECTIONS. Analytic geometry of three dimensions is called solid analytic geometry and includes the study of quadric surfaces.

In analytic geometry, positions of points are specified by means of suitable sets of numbers (coordinates) so that geometrical relationships between the points are equivalent to algebraic relationships between their coordinates. Because of this correspondence between algebra and geometry, it is often possible to prove propositions concerning geometric relationships by means of algebraic calculations. Such algebraic techniques have proved so effective that they have practically eliminated purely synthetic geometric methods.

HISTORY

The invention of analytic geometry is generally credited to the 17th-century French philosopher and mathematician René DESCARTES. Descartes enunciated the fundamental principles of analytic geometry in his *Discours de la méthode* (1637), a significant work on the history of philosophy that was published anonymously to avoid a dispute with the church. Pierre de FERMAT had also worked out the methods of analytic geometry at the same time, but his treatise on the subject was not published until 1679. The subject in its present form was developed later by Leonhard EULER. The birth of the methods of coordinate geometry and the consequent growth of the methods of the CALCULUS characterize the transition from classical mathematics to a new era in the history of mathematics (see MATHEMATICS, HISTORY OF). Thus, the creation of analytic geometry was an important step toward the generalization of the classical geometry of the Greeks, which was based on the use of axioms.

PLANE ANALYTIC GEOMETRY

Two perpendicular lines—the coordinate axes—are needed to fix the position of a point in a plane. The point of intersection of these axes is called the origin and is denoted by O. Usually the x-axis is a horizontal line, and the y-axis is the vertical line at the origin. The positive x-axis is the part to the right of the origin, and the positive y-axis is the part above the origin. The axes divide the plane into four quarters, called quadrants, from the upper right as the first quadrant, counterclockwise to the lower right as the fourth quadrant.

The x-coordinate of any point P on the plane is the perpendicular distance of P from the y-axis; it is taken to be positive if P is to the right of the y-axis (in the first or fourth quadrant), zero if P is on the y-axis, and negative if P is to the left of the y-axis. Similarly, the y-coordinate of P is the perpendicular distance of P from the x-axis and can also be positive, zero, or negative. If the x-coordinate of P is x and the y-coordinate of P is y, then the ordered pair (x, y) represents the Cartesian coordinates (named in honor of Descartes) of P with respect to the fixed coordinate axes. For example, $(3, -5)$ represents the Cartesian coordinates of a point P in the fourth quadrant situated 3 units to the right of the y-axis and 5 units below the x-axis. Every ordered pair (x, y) of real numbers represents a unique point on the plane and vice versa. The origin is the point $(0, 0)$. The point P with coordinates (x, y) is symbolically represented as $P(x, y)$.

The COORDINATE SYSTEM thus described is known as a rectangular Cartesian coordinate system. Oblique coordinate systems are not considered in this article.

A polar coordinate system is determined by a fixed point O, called the origin, or pole, and a fixed axis through the point, called the polar axis or polar line. A point P on the plane can be located by specifying two quantities: (1) the angle θ through which the polar axis must be rotated counterclockwise so that it will pass through P, and (2) the positive distance r of the point P from the origin. The angle determines a line by specifying its rotation about the fixed axis, and the distance r indicates how far along the line to proceed from the origin to reach P. The point P in polar coordinates is represented as $P(r, \theta)$. It is always possible to convert from one Cartesian coordinate system into another and also from one Cartesian system to a polar system and vice versa (see TRANSFORMATION and TRANSLATION).

The path traced by a moving point $P(x, y)$ in the plane is a CURVE. An EQUATION in two variables x and y that is satisfied by those points on the curve and by no other points is called the equation of the curve. Once the coordinate system has been fixed, a curve has a unique equation, and each equation represents a unique curve—once again bringing out the connection between algebra and geometry that is supplied by analytic geometry. Any first-degree equation of the form $ax + by + c = 0$ (where a, b, and c are constants) is the equation of a straight LINE, sometimes called simply a line. The equation of a CIRCLE with its center at the origin and radius r is $x^2 + y^2 = r^2$. A conic section can be represented by a second-degree equation in x and y; the general equation is $ax^2 + bxy + cy^2 + dx + ey + f = 0$, where a, b, c, d, e, and f are constants. Basic conics are the ELLIPSE, HYPERBOLA, PARABOLA, and circle.

Two lines $ax + by + c = 0$ and $a'x + b'y + c = 0$ are parallel if and only if $ab' - a'b = 0$, and they are perpendicular if and only if $aa' + bb' = 0$. Elimination of either x or y between the equations of a line and a conic produces a quadratic equation whose two ROOTS will be equal if and only if the line is a tangent to the conic.

SOLID ANALYTIC GEOMETRY

The concepts outlined above can be easily generalized to a space of three dimensions. Through an arbitrary point O (the origin), three mutually perpendicular coordinate axes are drawn (the x-axis, the y-axis, and the z-axis), dividing the space into eight parts, or octants. The plane determined by the x-axis and the y-axis is known as the xy-plane; the xz-plane and yz-plane are similarly defined. These three planes are called the coordinate planes. The x-coordinate of a point P is the perpendicular distance from P to the yz-plane. The other two coordinates are defined similarly. The ordered triple (x,y,z) represents the point P with coordinates x, y, and z. If P is in the first octant, all the coordinates of P are nonnegative (positive or zero). Such a coordinate system is a rectangular Cartesian system. For every point there corresponds uniquely a triple of real numbers, and to every triple of real numbers there corresponds a unique point of space.

In solid analytic geometry there are two kinds of extensions of plane polar coordinates: those called spherical coordinates and those called cylindrical coordinates. It is possible to convert from one system to another by making a transformation of coordinates.

The equation of a plane is a first-degree equation in the three variables: $ax + by + cz + d = 0$. If $d = 0$ this plane passes through the origin. In particular, the equations of the coordinate planes are $x = 0$ (the yz-plane), $y = 0$ (the xz-plane), and $z = 0$ (the xy-plane). A line may be specified as the line of intersection of two planes or as the line drawn through two points. The line joining $P_1(x_1, y_1, z_1)$ and $P_2(x_2, y_2, z_2)$ has the equation

$$\frac{x - z_1}{x_2 - x_1} = \frac{y - y_1}{y_2 - y_1} = \frac{z - z_1}{z_2 - z_1}$$

The set of all points whose rectangular coordinates satisfy an equation of the form $f(x,y,z) = 0$ is called a surface. A surface represented by an algebraic equation of the second degree is called a quadric surface, or quadric. The general equation of a quadric has 10 coefficients.   V. K. BALAKRISHNAN

Bibliography: Leithold, Louis, *The Calculus with Analytic Geometry*, 3d ed. (1976).

analytical chemistry

Analytical CHEMISTRY is a branch of chemistry principally concerned with determining the chemical composition of materials. Those materials may be solids, liquids, or gases; pure elements or compounds; or complex mixtures. Chemical analysis can also determine their molecular structures and measure such physical properties as pH, color, and solubility.

Wet analysis involves substances that have been put into solution, and microanalysis simply means that extremely small amounts of the substances being analyzed are all that are needed for accurate determinations. QUALITATIVE CHEMICAL ANALYSIS is used to detect and identify one or more constituents of a sample, and QUANTITATIVE CHEMICAL ANALYSIS is used to determine the amounts of those constituents. The greater part of work in analytical chemistry, and usually the more difficult, is quantitative.

Methods of chemical analysis are frequently classified as classical and instrumental, depending on the techniques and equipment used. Many of the methods currently used are of relatively recent origin (since 1950) and employ sophisticated instruments to measure physical properties of molecules, atoms, and ions. Such instruments have been made possible by spectacular advances in electronics, including computer

and microprocessor development. Instrumental measurements can sometimes be carried out without separating the constituent of interest from the rest of the sample, but often the instrumental measurement is the final step following separation of the sample's components, frequently by means of one or another type of CHROMATOGRAPHY. Some of the instrumental methods used are various types of SPECTROSCOPY; decomposition, in the case of hydrocarbons, with extremely high temperatures and subsequent computerized analysis; and observation through an ELECTRON MICROSCOPE. Despite these techniques, such classical chemical procedures as gravimetric analysis—determination of components by their weight—and volumetric analysis—determination by volume as in TITRATIONS—are still practical and reliable means of analyzing or characterizing many samples.

Analytical chemistry has widespread useful applications. For example, the problem of ascertaining the extent of pollution in the air or water involves qualitative and quantitative chemical analysis to identify contaminants and to determine their concentrations. Diagnosing human health problems in a clinical chemistry laboratory is facilitated by quantitative analyses carried out on samples of the patient's blood and other fluids. Modern industrial chemical plants rely heavily on quantitative analyses of raw materials, intermediates, and final products to ensure product quality and provide information for process control. In addition, chemical analyses are essential to research in all areas of chemistry as well as such related sciences as biology and geology.

LAURANCE A. KNECHT

Bibliography: Christian, Gary D., *Analytical Chemistry*, 2d ed. (1977); Laitinen, Herbert A., and Harris, Walter E., *Chemical Analysis*, 2d ed. (1975); Lee, Leslie W., *Elementary Principles of Laboratory Instruments*, 4th ed. (1978); Schenk, G. M., Hahn, R. B., and Hartkopf, A. V., *Introduction to Analytical Chemistry*, 2d ed. (1981).

analytical psychology: see JUNG, CARL.

anamorphosis   [an-uh-mor'-fuh-sis]

Anamorphosis, an optical illusion, is a curiosity or game in art that began in the Renaissance, with the rediscovery of perspective. The term itself appeared in the 17th century. By distorting perspective a drawing or painting could be made that would appear meaningless until viewed from a particular angle, when the image would appear normal. Leonardo da Vinci made anamorphic drawings in the 1470s, although he was probably not the first to experiment with anamorphosis. The most famous example of an anamorphic object in a painting is in Hans Holbein the Younger's *The Ambassadors* (1533; National Gallery, London). Between the two men in this double portrait is what seems to be a blurred image that, when viewed from close up and to one side of the painting, appears to be a skull. This is probably a pictorial pun, for the name *Holbein* translates into English as ''hollow bone.'' The only known practical application of anamorphosis is in baroque architecture and stage scenery, in which anamorphic distortion creates the illusion of depth within a small space.

E. M. PLUNKETT

Bibliography: Baltrusaitis, Jurgis, *Anamorphic Art* (1977); Leeman, Fred, *Hidden Images* (1976).

See also: BAROQUE ART AND ARCHITECTURE; GALLI DA BIBIENA (family); ILLUSION; perspective (art); SERLIO, SEBASTIANO; THEATER ARCHITECTURE AND STAGING.

anapest: see VERSIFICATION.

anaphylaxis   [an-uh-fuh-lak'-sis]

Anaphylaxis is an extreme allergic reaction to a foreign substance. Subsequent exposure can produce an overwhelming body reaction called anaphylactic shock. Symptoms of an anaphylactic reaction include severe itching, muscle spasms, facial swelling, obstruction of respiration from swelling in the larynx, and a drastic fall in BLOOD PRESSURE caused by widespread dilation of blood capillaries. The drop in pressure can lead to circulatory collapse and death.

In some individuals hypersensitive to bee or wasp venom, death from anaphylaxis can occur within an hour of a sting. Anaphylaxis can also occur in patients receiving serum therapy, which is still administered for such diseases as botulism and tetanus and for the prevention of rabies after exposure to an infected animal. Such serums are prepared by injecting animals with a specific antigen to produce antibodies in the serum. The animal serum is then injected into a patient to neutralize the same antigen. Because the injected serum is foreign, however, patients can produce antibodies against it. Repeated injections may then cause an allergic reaction called SERUM SICKNESS, which can range from a mild reaction to anaphylaxis. Serum therapy has been discontinued for most infectious diseases since the development of antimicrobial drugs, but these drugs can also produce anaphylaxis in some individuals.

Anaphylaxis is treated by injecting powerful stimulants to restore blood circulation and using ANTIHISTAMINES to combat the allergic reaction.   PETER L. PETRAKIS

Bibliography: Amos, Harry, *Allergic Drug Reactions* (1976); Belanti, Joseph, *Immunology* (1971); Graedon, Joe, *The People's Pharmacy* (1976); Sell, Stewart, *Immunology, Immunopathology, and Immunity* (1972); Thompson, William, *Black's Medical Dictionary*, 31st ed. (1976); Wilson, David, *Body and Antibody* (1971).

See also: ALLERGY.

anarchism

Anarchism (from the Greek, "without government") is a political ideology based on the belief that government is bad and unnecessary. Anarchists advocate a society organized by free association, in which cooperation would take the place of compulsion and competition.

A few anarchists have committed violent acts in the belief that terror would help to prepare the way for the revolution; most, however, have opposed violence.

Early Writings. The English writer William GODWIN (1756–1836) was one of the first to put forward anarchist ideas. He wrote that the state corrupts the life of the individual and creates an unjust distribution of property and power. He believed that the best form of government would be a decentralized democracy in which as many tasks as possible would be left to the citizens themselves.

A much more influential anarchist was the French writer Pierre Joseph PROUDHON (1809–65). He wrote, "Property is theft," a contention that land and any other possessions not acquired as a product of one's own labor in effect have been stolen. One of his key principles was mutualism, by which he meant cooperation on a basis of equality. He wanted the centralized state to be replaced by a federation of communities and associations that would work out their own problems. Proudhon called this direct democracy.

Political Movement. The history of anarchism as a political movement began with Mikhail BAKUNIN (1814–76), a Russian aristocrat who was converted to anarchism by Proudhon. He spent much of his life in Italy, Spain, and Switzerland organizing secret revolutionary groups. He believed that a revolution would be necessary in order to destroy the old system.

Another Russian aristocrat who turned to anarchism was Prince Pyotr KROPOTKIN (1842–1921), who wrote influential books. In his *Mutual Aid* (1902) he argued that cooperation rather than conflict is the main factor in biological evolution. He called his system anarchist communism.

Assassinations. In the latter part of the 19th century a movement called "anarchism of the deed" arose. Individuals or small groups calling themselves anarchists set out to assassinate government officials in the belief that their deeds would arouse the masses. Their victims included the Russian tsar ALEXANDER II, the French president Sadi CARNOT, the Austrian empress ELIZABETH, and the U.S. president William McKINLEY. The main result of their activities was to associate anarchism with violence in the public mind.

20th-Century Activities. An important 20th-century movement

An engraving depicts the assassination of President William McKinley on Sept. 6, 1901, at the Pan-American Exposition in Buffalo, N.Y. His assassin, an avowed anarchist named Leon F. Czolgsoz, defended the murder, claiming, "I don't believe we should have any rulers."

was anarcho–syndicalism, a movement among anarchists in the trade unions of France, Spain, and Italy. Their ultimate aim was a general strike that would overthrow capitalism and the state and leave the means of production in the hands of revolutionary unions, or syndicates.

Anarchists were denied entry to the United States after the HAYMARKET RIOT of 1886 and the assassination of President McKinley in 1901. Public concern about anarchism was still apparent during the 1920s, in the controversy over the SACCO AND VANZETTI CASE involving two Italian radicals accused of murder. Since World War II there has been no strong anarchist movement in any country.

Bibliography: Hoffman, Robert, *Anarchism* (1970); Krimerman, Leonard, and Lewis, Perry, eds., *Problems of Anarchist Tradition* (1966); Woodcock, George, *Anarchism: A History of Libertarian Ideas and Movements* (1962).

See also: NIHILISM; SYNDICALISM.

Anasazi   [ahn-uh-sah'-zee]

Anasazi (from a NAVAJO Indian word meaning "the ancient ones") is the term archaeologists use to denote the cultures of the prehistoric Basket Makers and the PUEBLO Indians of North America. Anasazi culture has been divided into eight periods, as follows: (1) Basket Maker I (prior to Christian Era), (2) Basket Maker II (beginning of Christian Era–450), (3) Basket Maker III (450–750), (4) Pueblo I (750–900), (5) Pueblo II (900–1100), (6) Pueblo III (1100–1300), (7) Pueblo IV (1300–1600), and (8) Pueblo V (1600 to present).

The Anasazi built the numerous communal dwellings, or pueblos, many now in ruins, on the high plateau of the Southwestern United States. The oldest remains are in the Four Corners region, where the states of Arizona, Colorado, New Mexico, and Utah adjoin. At the time of its greatest extent, the Anasazi culture was spread over most of New Mexico, northern Arizona, southwestern Colorado, southern Nevada, and much of Utah. This is a region comparable in size to modern France, but great stretches of uninhabited land lay between the villages, which were located where water was available.

Origins. The Anasazi culture is believed to have gradually evolved out of the nonagricultural base of the Desert culture, once widespread in western North America, although precise evidence of the transition has not yet been discovered. It may have been in part derived from the Mogollon culture, an older tradition of settled agriculturalists and ceramics producers who flourished from c.100 BC to AD 1400 in the mountain areas of east central Arizona and west central New Mexico. There are many evidences of trade and cultural interchange between the Mogollon and the Anasazi.

The Basket Makers. Although direct evidence is as yet lacking, archaeologists have postulated an initial phase of Anasazi culture, designated as Basket Maker I. This would have been a preagricultural, nonceramic stage during which the Basket Makers were nomadic hunter-gatherers.

Although Basket Maker I remains hypothetical, Basket Maker II is fairly well known. The Basket Makers were given their name because of the profusion of skillfully woven baskets discovered in sites associated with their culture. Many of the baskets have been well preserved by the exceedingly dry conditions in the shallow caves where the Basket Makers stored their belongings. Numerous other perishable items have also withstood the ravages of time, including bags, sandals, and nets of yucca fiber. Clothing was scanty, consisting of woven G-strings for the men and short skirts of fiber for the women. The seminomadic Basket Makers of this period had no bows and arrows, but in hunting deer and small game relied upon light spears and darts, propelled by spear-throwers—flexible sticks that give additional force to the throw. Animals were also caught by the Basket Makers with a variety of ingenious nets and snares.

The Basket Makers had begun by this time to cultivate squash and a primitive type of maize. They lived in unpretentious shelters of perishable materials or in shallow caves or rock shelters. At least some of them made more substantial houses of logs and mud over saucer-shaped depressions. To supplement their meager harvests of farm crops, they roamed over the country periodically on hunting and gathering expe-

ditions. During their absence, treasured articles and reserve supplies of food were cached in storage pits or cists, excavated in the dry floors of caves. The cists were used not only for storage, but also as sepulchers, in which the dead were buried with accompanying mortuary offerings. In some of the cists the unintentionally mummified bodies of Basket Makers have been found, with hair and dehydrated flesh adhering to the bones.

Basket Maker III (AD 450–750) witnessed the expansion of Basket Maker territory and the introduction of several new and important cultural items, including pit houses, erected over shallow excavations, and pottery. With the addition of beans and new varieties of maize, agriculture became more important to Basket Maker subsistence. The greater reliance on farming made it possible for the Basket Makers to begin a sedentary mode of life in villages. Toward the end of the period, the spear was replaced by the bow and arrow.

The Pueblo People. Pueblo culture developed directly out of that of the Basket Makers and continued the same basic mode of life, elaborated with inventions and innovations, and enriched also by diffusion from alien cultures. The Pueblo I and II periods (750–1100) represented a time of territorial expansion and transition to the later cultural climax of the Anasazi tradition. Among the important developments were the introduction of cotton cloth, the building of above-ground houses of stone and adobe masonry, and the improvement of pottery. The Pueblo people were experimenting at this time in the building of houses, but the trend was toward single-story, multiroom pueblos of stone and adobe masonry. The old pit houses persisted in some districts, and in other places they survived as ceremonial chambers called KIVAS. Villages were usually located on the tops of mesas or at the edges of canyons. Pottery was of two general types: culinary wares in

The Cliff Palace of Mesa Verde, in Colorado, was an Anasazi center of trade and religion, reconstructed here in an artist's rendering. The pueblo, which was built in the sheltered recess of a cliff, contains more than 200 rooms and 23 kivas, or ceremonial chambers. To maintain a reliable food supply, the Anasazi cultivated maize and are thought to have domesticated the wild turkey.

Baskets woven of coiled fabrics (left) *and pottery decorated with geometric designs* (right) *are artistic hallmarks of Anasazi civilization. Prior to the importation of pottery-making techniques in the 8th century, baskets were daubed with mud to create watertight containers.*

ANASAZI RUINS IN NATIONAL PARKS AND MONUMENTS

Aztec Ruins National Monument. In northwest New Mexico, near the town of Aztec. Established 1923; 11 ha (27 acres). An excavated pueblo, built in AD 1100–25 (Pueblo III period), and a completely restored kiva.

Bandelier National Monument. In northern Mexico, near Los Alamos. Established 1916; 11,864 ha (29,661 acres). Cliff dwellings and open sites of the Pueblo III period (1100–1300), located in Frijoles Canyon.

Canyon de Chelly National Monument. In northeast Arizona on the Navajo Indian Reservation, near the town of Chinle. Established 1931; 33,140 ha (83,849 acres). Several Anasazi ruins, ranging from Basket Maker II (1st century AD–450) to the Pueblo III period (1100–1300), including the White House cliff dwelling.

Chaco Canyon National Monument. In northwest New Mexico, 101 km (64 mi) north of Thoreau and 101 km (64 mi) south of Aztec. Established in 1907; 8,604 ha (21,509 acres). A major center of Anasazi culture, ranging from Basket Maker sites through huge communal buildings of the Pueblo III period (1100–1300), which include the Pueblo Bonito and Chetro Ketl.

Gila Cliff Dwellings National Monument. In western New Mexico, north of Silver City. Established 1907; 215 ha (533 acres). Cliff dwellings of mixed Anasazi-Mogollon derivation.

Gran Quivira National Monument. In central New Mexico, 40 km (25 mi) south of Mountainair. Established 1909; 247 ha (611 acres). Ruins of a pueblo of Pueblo IV period (1300–1600) and a Spanish mission.

Kinishba National Historic Landmark. In east central Arizona on the Fort Apache Indian Reservation. An excavated and partially restored pueblo of the period 1000–1400.

Mesa Verde National Park. In southwest Colorado, near Cortez. Established 1906; 20,830 ha (52,074 acres). Numerous, massive cliff dwellings and open pueblos of the Pueblo III period (1100–1300).

Navajo National Monument. In northeastern Arizona, 217 km (135 mi) north of Flagstaff. Established 1909; 146 ha (360 acres). Large cliff dwellings of the 13th century (Pueblo III).

Pecos National Monument. In northern New Mexico, 16 km (25 mi) southeast of Santa Fe. Established 1965; 138 ha (341 acres). Ruins of a great pueblo of the Pueblo IV period (1300–1600), which was occupied as late as 1838, and of a Spanish mission.

Walnut Canyon National Monument. In northern Arizona, near Flagstaff. Established 1915; 761 ha (1,879 acres). Anasazi and Sinagua ruins, including pit houses and pueblos of the period 1100–1300.

which the coils were pinched to produce a corrugated effect, and decorated wares with black designs in elaborate patterns on a white background.

The climax of Pueblo development was reached during the Pueblo III period (1100–1300). Anasazi achievements in art and architecture were then at their height. The finest styles of black-on-white and corrugated pottery date from Pueblo III, and polychrome wares appeared with black-and-white designs on orange or red backgrounds. During this period were constructed the spectacular cliff dwellings at Mesa Verde in southwest Colorado, huge apartment houses of stone and adobe masonry built on ledges in the cliffs.

Despite the cultural culmination achieved during Pueblo III, the ultimate decline of the Anasazi was forecast. Toward the end of the period, and continuing into Pueblo IV (1300–1600), there was marked contraction of Pueblo territory, with a gradual abandonment of the outlying areas. This may have been due in part to raids by marauding nomads, in part to factional quarrels among the Pueblo, and in part to a prolonged drought between 1276 and 1299 that caused famine. The people were obliged to migrate to places with a better water supply to the south and east, particularly to the drainage area of the Rio Grande in New Mexico, to the HOPI country in northeastern Arizona, and to the ZUÑI country of western New Mexico. Pueblo V (c.1600 on) marks the start of the historic period, which dates from the time of the arrival of the first Spanish colonists in the Southwest. The Hopi, Zuñi, and Rio Grande Pueblo peoples of today are the direct descendants of the prehistoric Anasazi, although the Zuñi have merged with the Mogollon descendants.

KENNETH M. STEWART

Bibliography: Longacre, W. A., ed., *Reconstructing Prehistoric Pueblo Societies* (1970); Pike, Donald G., *Anasazi: Ancient People of the Rock* (1974); Terrell, J. V., *Pueblos, Gods, and Spaniards* (1973); Watson, Don, *Indians of the Mesa Verde* (1961); Wormington, H. M., *Prehistoric Indians of the Southwest* (1964).

See also: CLIFF DWELLERS; HOHOKAM CULTURE; INDIANS, AMERICAN; NORTH AMERICAN ARCHAEOLOGY.

Anatolia   [an-uh-toh'-lee-uh]

Anatolia, also called Asia Minor, is a peninsula of Asia coextensive with the greater part of modern Turkey. The peninsula, 756,954 km² (292,260 mi²), is separated from Europe by the narrow straits of the Bosporus and the Dardanelles and by the Sea of Marmara. It is bounded on the north by the Black Sea, on the south by the Mediterranean Sea, and on the west by the Aegean Sea. Anatolia has a population of 40,200,000 (1975 est.). ANKARA, the capital of Turkey, is the major city. The name *Anatolia* comes from the Greek *anatolē* ("rising of the sun" or "east"). As a part of the land bridge between Europe, Asia, and Africa, the region has played an important role in world history.

Much of the area is occupied by a central plateau—elevations range from 610 to 1,200 m (2,000 to 4,000 ft)—and is sur-

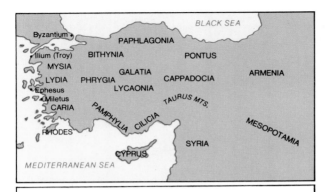

ANATOLIA IN ANCIENT TIMES

The map shows the provinces of Anatolia, or Asia Minor (now Turkey), under Roman rule at the beginning of the Christian era.

rounded by coastal mountains and a narrow coastal plain. On the central plateau July temperatures average above 20° C (68° F); January temperatures average below 0° C (32° F). Temperatures are more moderate along the coasts. The central plateau is arid; precipitation increases toward the coasts.

Most of the people are Turkish, although small Kurdish and Arab minorities also live here. The predominant religious affiliation is Sunni Islam. More than 40 percent of the population is urban. In addition to Ankara, major cities include ADANA, BURSA, and IZMIR. Cereals, silk, tobacco, grapes, and other fruits are the principal agricultural products. Iron and steel and food processing are major industries. Copper and chrome are mined in the region.

Early rulers of Anatolia included the Hittites, Phrygians, Cimmerians, Persians, Greeks, and Romans. The Arabs occasionally raided the area in the 7th century. The Seljuk Turks took control in the 11th century, the Crusaders in the 12th, the Mongols in the 13th, and the Ottoman Turks in the 13th to the 15th centuries. The region formed the heart of the OTTOMAN EMPIRE until 1919.   IRA M. SHESKIN

Anatolian languages: see LANGUAGES, ANCIENT.

anatomy

Anatomy is the branch of biology involving the structure of plants, animals, and other forms of biological organisms. It is related to morphology, which is concerned with the description of organisms, and MORPHOGENESIS, concerned with their development. COMPARATIVE ANATOMY is concerned with the difference in structure of animal forms.

Anatomy is divided into several subdisciplines. Gross anatomy involves studies on structures that can be seen with the naked eye. HISTOLOGY is the study of tissue structure and CYTOLOGY that of cell structure; because histological and cytological studies require the use of a microscope, they are known together as microscopic anatomy. When the word *functional* is placed before any of these words, as in "functional anatomy," reference is being made to the subject of PHYSIOLOGY. Often anatomy cannot be discussed properly without introducing some physiology, and physiology can almost never be discussed properly without an anatomical background.

Two other divisions of anatomy are EMBRYOLOGY and paleoanatomy. Embryology is commonly called developmental anatomy because it is concerned with the genesis and development of a fully differentiated tissue, organ, or organism. Paleoanatomy is the study of the structure of extinct organisms.

EARLY HISTORY OF ANATOMY

Aristotle. The first recorded attempts to study anatomy were made by ARISTOTLE (384–22 BC), although hieroglyphics and papyruses produced from 3000 to 1600 BC indicate that some interest was taken in certain anatomical aspects, or appear-

ances, in mummies. Aristotle, the founder of biological science, dissected plants and animals, although neither he nor HIPPOCRATES (460–374 BC), the father of MEDICINE, dissected the human body. Both believed that the HEART is the seat of thought and of the soul.

Herophilus and Erasistratus. Soon after the death of Aristotle the Ptolemies, kings of Egypt, encouraged dissections. Herophilus (335–280 BC) and his contemporary ERASISTRATUS (310–250 BC) were perhaps the most active practitioners.

Herophilus dissected about 600 human bodies and wrote more than one treatise on anatomy, another on the eyes, and a handbook for midwives. His greatest contribution was to dispel the earlier erroneous notions of Aristotle and Hippocrates about the mind, proving that the BRAIN is the center of the NERVOUS SYSTEM and the seat of intelligence by tracing nerves from the brain to the spinal cord and classifying them as voluntary and involuntary.

Erasistratus observed lymph carrying fat toward the heart, described the function of the epiglottis in closing the larynx, identified the tricuspid valve of the heart, and was able to distinguish sensory nerves from motor nerves. He studied the CIRCULATORY SYSTEM intensively, but, like his predecessors, he held that the arteries contain air. This was a common belief, since the veins normally contain about 60 percent of the total BLOOD, and on death the arteries empty out into the capillary beds and veins.

Galen. Despite many incorrect observations by the ancients, perhaps as many principles were known by the end of Cleopatra's reign (around 30 BC) as were to be discovered during the next 1,000 years. Shortly after Cleopatra's death, Alexandria became a Roman city and one of the main centers of the Christian church. Its leaders then began to discourage dissections. Leaders in other parts of the world, except Arabia, also denounced them. The fervor for achievement of anatomical knowledge did not die immediately, however, in spite of these difficulties.

Most notable among those who strove to advance anatomical understanding was Claudius GALEN (AD 131–200), physician to the Roman emperor Marcus Aurelius. Known historically as the founder of experimental physiology, Galen showed that urine is formed in the KIDNEYS, not in the bladder, and that sectioning of the spinal cord results in paralysis to that part of the body below the cut. His monumental work, *On the Use of the Parts of the Human Body,* served as the standard medical text for 1,400 years.

Despite some excellent contributions to experimental medicine, however, Galen may have delayed anatomical progress. Because of religious prejudice and superstition, he was not permitted to dissect human bodies, and many of his conclusions were based on dissections of oxen, dogs, swine, and apes. More important, he perpetuated false beliefs established by his predecessors and contemporaries—that cosmic life is taken into the body with each breath (pneuma) and that three separate spirits dwell in the body: a "natural" spirit in the LIVER, a "vital" spirit in the heart, and an "animal" spirit in the brain. The first of these gained further credence in that it was established on Galen's experimental approaches. Although Galen's beliefs suited and pleased the leaders of both church and state, they served to misinform the concerned portion of the populace who, although wishing to know the truth, had to accept a fallacious presentation until William HARVEY would prove it wrong in the 17th century.

Galen's view of the circulatory system was also incorrect. Like his predecessors, and despite numerous studies on his own, Galen traced the passage of blood from the liver—where, he maintained, it was formed—to the heart, where supposedly a breath of air was injected into it as a gaseous material from the LUNGS. One important contribution of his is that the arteries carry blood, not air. According to Galen, the blood then travels to the rest of the body rather than first going to the lungs and back into the heart. This view of the circulatory passage as one-way was also maintained as scientific thought until the 17th century.

Avicenna and the Arabs. Meanwhile, faced with increasing religious antipathy, anatomical pursuit was virtually aban-

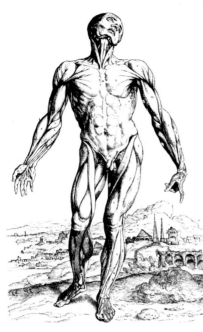

(Left) *Andreas Vesalius, a 16th-century anatomist, changed the concepts of internal human anatomy with his accurate, detailed illustrations of muscles, blood vessels, and organs. Prior to Vesalius, medical lecturers taught anatomy according to the ideas of Galen, an ancient Roman physician.*

(Right) *William Harvey, an English physician, used anatomical illustrations such as this to describe the circulation of blood in the body. By applying fingertip pressure on blood vessels of an arm, Harvey demonstrated how valves regulate blood flow to and from the heart.*

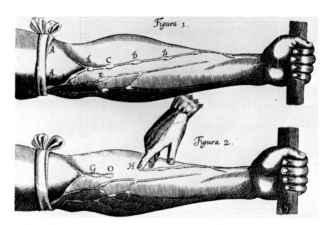

doned, except for what work was done by the Arabs. Unfortunately, their studies were based on Aristotle's and Galen's works, which the Arabs had translated into their language. AVICENNA (AD 980–1037) was perhaps the most famous of the Arab anatomists. His *Canon of Medicine*, published in AD 1000, contained information based on observations derived from studies on humans, apes, dogs, and other animals. Neither he nor his peers, however, carried out systematic studies. Dissections were sometimes performed, mainly in an attempt to learn the causes of death, and occasionally public authorities permitted physicians to dissect executed criminals.

Vesalius. Gradually, as the Renaissance became established, some individuals began to circumvent authoritarian restrictions, and the number of anatomists increased rapidly. Perhaps the most important of these was Andreas VESALIUS (1514–64), who ushered in the modern era of anatomy. Rather than accept many of the incorrect observations of Galen and pursue the study of the topic through metaphysical dialectic, he took a straightforward scientific experimental approach. He compared the anatomy of various animals with humans and noted the fallacy of extrapolating from one to the other. His work culminated in *On the Structure of the Human Body*, which was published the same year (1543) as Copernicus's *On the Revolution of Celestial Bodies*. Vesalius's work was most significant in that it was the first to contain accurate depictions of the inner structure of the human body. Successors and contemporaries of Vesalius added important details to the basework he had created, and in less than a century they had completed much of the basic studies on gross anatomy.

Harvey. This basic work culminated in the accomplishments of William Harvey (1578–1657), an English physician who was the first to postulate that the blood moves in a circle from left heart to arteries to veins to right heart. He also postulated the existence of thousands of miles of microscopic blood capillaries, a theory that was proved correct after microscopes became available. At about this time anatomy began to become established as a full-fledged science. Scientific societies were formed, textbooks and atlases began to appear, schools were established, and laws were enacted regulating the acquisition of human bodies for dissection and study.

HISTORY OF MICROSCOPIC ANATOMY

Rapid strides were made as microscopic anatomy began to be established and, together with gross anatomy, merged with comparative and developmental anatomy. Marcello·MALPIGHI

(1628–94), a young contemporary of the elderly William Harvey, demonstrated that blood went through capillaries in the lungs before reaching the left heart. He described many other important histological features, such as the germinal layer at the base of the outer layer (epidermis) of SKIN and the structure of the functional units of the kidney (nephrons) through which blood is filtered in producing urine.

Robert HOOKE (1635–1703) also was an outstanding physicist. In 1665 he reported in *Micrographia* his observations on plant anatomy. Based on his microscopic observations of cork, he coined the word *cell*. His observations later helped other investigators advance the concept that cells are the unit structures of tissues. In particular, about a century later, Caspar Friedrich WOLFF (1733–94), as a result of intensive study in embryology, hinted that cells are the building blocks of organs. Later, Robert Brown (1773–1858) discovered the cell nucleus, probably because staining techniques became available. Still later, M. J. Schleiden (1804–81) and Theodor SCHWANN (1810–82) in 1840 advanced the theory that all tissues, including bone, tendon, and ligament, are composed of cells. In doing so, they brought cytology into existence as a separate, although interrelated, field of inquiry. This field now comprises the subspecialties of cytochemistry and cytogenetics.

Two other investigators figured prominently as contemporaries of Malpighi and Hooke. Anton van LEEUWENHOEK (1632–1723) was the first to observe and describe bacteria, protozoa, and other microorganisms, as well as sperm and the cross striations of skeletal and cardiac MUSCLE. In addition, he provided visual proof that William Harvey's theory on blood circulation was indeed correct. The other notable microanatomist, Jan SWAMMERDAM (1637–80), is famous for his remarkable work on the developmental anatomy of various insects and is considered the first person to observe and describe (1658) red blood cells.

Near the end of the 17th century, histology emerged as a distinct discipline of study. Its development went hand in hand with advances in the microscope itself, the invention of instruments (microtomes) for cutting thin sections of plant and animal tissues, and the introduction of staining procedures. The major advances in each of these technological fields were especially prominent in the 19th century. Long before this, however, Xavier Bichat (1771–1802) distinguished himself as an animal histologist by pointing out the similarities that exist between certain tissues widespread in the body and by classifying these tissues as muscle, nerve, and connective. Today, these tissues, together with epithelial tissues, are recognized as the four principal tissues of animals.

HISTORY OF COMPARATIVE ANATOMY

Comparative anatomy is the science that concerns evolutionary advances in animal structure and the anatomical and physiological adaptations animals have made in response to environmental demands. As a discipline with these objectives, it may be said to have begun with Aristotle, who dissected numerous animals in an attempt to develop theories on animal classification and evolution. Galen also involved himself with comparative anatomy, although his objective was to ob-

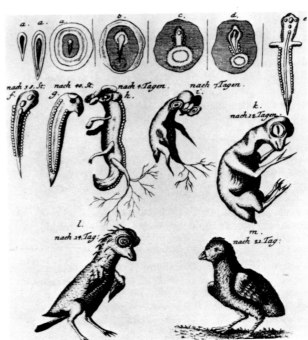

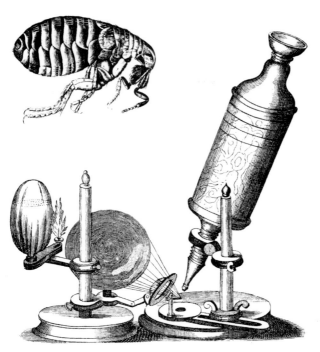

(Above) *A detailed drawing of the external anatomy of a flea is one of many illustrations in Robert Hooke's book* Micrographia *(1665). He used the microscope (bottom) to study plants and animals and coined the word* cell *after observing the fine structure of cork.*

(Below) *Jan Swammerdam, a Dutch microscopist, studied the anatomy of invertebrates by performing minute dissections. This mayfly larva measures only 6.4 mm (0.25 in).*

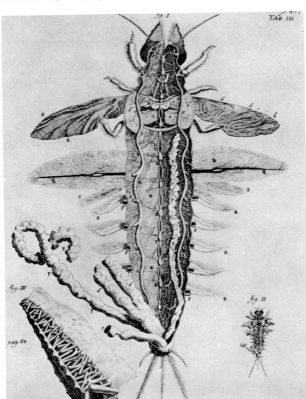

Marcello Malpighi, known as the founder of embryology, made detailed observations in 1672 on the development and growth of a chick embryo. In addition to his anatomical studies, he completed the work on blood circulation begun by William Harvey.

tain a better understanding of human anatomy. Other anatomists, beginning especially in the Renaissance, dissected and described certain anatomical aspects of fish and other animals, but Georges BUFFON (1707–88) was the first to attempt a major compilation of data. The results were published in the first 15 volumes of his 44-volume *Natural History, General and Particular* (1749–1804; Eng. trans., 20 vol., 1781–1812), a monumental work that took 53 years to complete.

Buffon's accomplishments paved the way for Georges Baron CUVIER (1769–1832), the first to attempt the synthesis of comparative anatomy into a framework of principles. Instead of trying to fit fact to preconceived theory, as was commonly done, Cuvier attempted to establish new theories based on the available facts. In his 9-volume work *Le Règne animal distribué d'après son organisation* (The Animal Kingdom Distributed According to Its Organization, 1817–30), he included the results of all his research on the structure of extant and fossil animals.

Many anatomists followed Cuvier's lead, but none contributed as much as Richard Owen (1804–92), who originated the concept of homology. This concept concerns the anatomical structures in terms of their embryology and evolutionary origin. The wings of a bat, for example, are homologous to the arms of a man, since each pair of these structures is derived from the same germinal centers in the embryo.

HISTORY OF DEVELOPMENTAL ANATOMY

In the 17th century, embryological studies were conducted by Swammerdam (on invertebrates) and Malpighi (on chicks), but it was not until the 19th century that this science gained considerable momentum. Among the most famous embryologists are E. R. Lankester (1847–1929), Oscar Hertwig (1849–1922), and Richard Hertwig (1850–1937), all of whom worked on the development of body cavities. Equally important were F. M. Balfour (1851–82), who published a 2-volume *Treatise of Comparative Embryology* (1880–81), the first volume on invertebrates and the second on vertebrates; and Ernest HAECKEL (1834–1919), who advanced the useful concept that in the development of an advanced organism, such as a mammal, the embryo proceeds progressively through the stages of its forebears, including fishes and amphibians. This concept is usually summarized as "ontogeny recapitulates phylogeny." It is not strictly correct, although some embryonic developments relate closely to it, such as the events associated with the acquisition of the mammalian jaws, eardrum, thymus, and parathyroid glands.

MODERN WORK

Anatomical studies today are characterized by their interdisciplinary nature and their emphasis on function, or physiology. At the whole-body level, anatomists with training in physics are attempting to learn the anatomical bases of speed in the locomotion of such animals as cheetahs and horses; of power in digging animals, such as moles; of flight in such diverse animals as bats and birds; and of swimming in animals as different from each other as whales and salmon. In the study of specific organs, neurobiologists are attempting to map out brains in order to correlate complex functions, such as behavior, with networks of neuronal circuitry. Histologists are exploring problems relating to the origin of hormones, the occurrence of enzymes, and the storage depots of trace elements; histochemical procedures, combined with immunoradiography, are commonly employed. Cytologists use a wide variety of approaches, including electron microscopy, ultracentrifugal separation of subcellular organs (organelles), cytochemistry, and biochemistry. Anatomy as a whole has advanced in the course of two millennia from an area of absolute ignorance to a sound science that is integrated with all other biological sciences.   ROY HARTENSTEIN

Bibliography: Dowban, Robert, *Cell Biology* (1971); Goss, Charles, ed., *Gray's Anatomy,* 35th ed. (1973); Green, John, *Medical History for Students* (1968); Keen, Harry, ed., *Triumphs of Medicine* (1976); Long, Esmond, *A History of Pathology* (1928); Lund, Fred, *Greek Medicine* (1936); Singer, Charles, *Short History of Anatomy and Physiology* (1957); Stenn, Frederick, ed., *The Growth of Medicine* (1967); Thorwald, Jurgen, *Science and Secrets of Early Medicine* (1962).

Anatomy of Melancholy, The

The Anatomy of Melancholy by Robert BURTON, first published in 1621 under the pseudonym Democritus Junior and often revised and expanded, is a learned and highly idiosyncratic study of the symptomatology of emotional illness as it was understood in the late Renaissance. In the humors theory of physiology, melancholy is produced by an excess of black bile (one of the four bodily fluids or humors). There are elaborate and sympathetic discussions of scholars' and nuns' melancholy, with many playful explorations, such as the celebrated "Digression on Air." Burton's work is a good example of the then-new copious style, bursting with odd bits of scientific knowledge and lore and extensive quotation of authorities, often in Latin.   MAURICE CHARNEY

Bibliography: Babb, Lawrence, *Sanity in Bedlam: A Study of Robert Burton's Anatomy of Melancholy* (1960); Mueller, William R., *Anatomy of Robert Burton's England* (1952).

Anawratha   [an-uh-rath'-uh]

Anawratha, d. 1077, was a Burmese ruler who united Burma politically for the first time in history. Becoming king of Pagan in 1044, he merged into his realm most of Burma proper, including northern Arakan and Lower Burma, home of the Mon people. Mon culture thereafter became predominant at the court of Pagan. Theravada Buddhism, which came to be a powerful unifying factor in Burmese national life, attained its position because Anawratha obtained copies of the Pali canon, with its Buddhist ethics, from the conquered Mon capital of Thaton. Anawratha's conquest of the Mon gave Burma control of the Irrawaddy delta and an outlet to the sea.

Bibliography: Aung, Maung Htin, *Burmese History before 1287* (1970) and *A History of Burma* (1967).

Anaxagoras   [an-ak-sag'-uh-ruhs]

Anaxagoras of Clazomenae, *c.*500–428 BC, was a pre-Socratic Greek philosopher (see PRE-SOCRATIC PHILOSOPHY). A native of Ionia, he spent much of his life in Athens, where he was associated with the Athenian leader Pericles. Only fragments of

his writings survive.

Anaxagoras was influenced by Parmenides, another of the pre-Socratics, who argued that all change is impossible and that reality is one and indivisible. Anaxagoras tried to find a way to allow for change and a plurality of existing things. He posited a world composed entirely of an indefinite number of unchanging everlasting substances whose parts have the same nature as their whole. No matter how finely divided, these substances do not change into something else: splitting a nugget of gold or a piece of wood always yields gold or wood. Change is possible because each everlasting substance contains smaller portions of all other substances. Thus, in Anaxagoras' view, when a child drinks milk, there are portions of bone in the milk that aggregate to the child's bones and increase their size.

Complex organisms, he believed, are not everlasting. They come about by the mingling of everlasting substances and cease when those substances remingle in a different way. He seems to have tried to explain this structural and dynamic complexity by invoking the activity of Mind (*Noûs*), a force he described as unlimited and independent. This concept, which probably originated with Anaxagoras, was of major significance in later Greek philosophy.   WILLIAM E. MANN

Bibliography: Allen, R. E., and Furley, David J., eds., *Studies in Pre-socratic Philosophy,* vol. 2 (1975); Schofield, Malcolm, *An Essay on Anaxagoras* (1980).

Anaximander   [an-ak'-suh-man-dur]

Anaximander of Miletus, *c.*610–545 BC, is the earliest Greek thinker about whom much is known. Called a pupil of THALES, he wrote a comprehensive history of the universe. His bold use of nonmythological explanatory hypotheses radically distinguishes his work from the earlier literary cosmologies.

Anaximander challenged Thales' view that a single element can be the origin of all. He argued that known elements are constantly opposing and changing into one another, and that therefore something different from these elements must underlie and cause changes. He postulated the *apeiron* ("boundless," or "indefinite") as the originative and sustaining substance. The one surviving quotation from his book uses a legal metaphor to describe the balanced reciprocal changes of the elements: they perish into the things from which they came, "as is fitting and due: for they pay penalty and make retribution to each other for their injustice, according to the ordering of time."

Anaximander believed that the universe is symmetrical, the Earth remaining stable at the center because it has no reason to move one way rather than another. He was apparently the first philosopher to use an argument from sufficient reason. He also drew the first Greek world map and boldly speculated about the marine origins of animal life. He is sometimes called the founder of astronomy.   MARTHA C. NUSSBAUM

Bibliography: Furley, D. J., and Allen, R. E., eds., *Studies in Pre-socratic Philosophy,* vol. 1 (1970); Kahn, C. H., *Anaximander and the Origins of Greek Cosmology* (1960); Kirk, G. S., and Raven, J. E., *The Presocratic Philosophers* (1957).

Anaximenes   [an-ak-sim'-uh-neez]

The Greek philosopher Anaximenes flourished in Miletus *c.*545 BC and was the last of the MILESIAN SCHOOL founded by THALES. Anaximenes' primary concern was the origin and structure of the universe. He maintained that the primary substance is air (Greek, *aer*); everything else in the world, including the gods, is no more than rarefied or condensed air. He believed that by rarefaction air grew hot and became fire; this formed the Sun and heavenly bodies. By condensation air grew cold and became wind, water, and earth. Anaximenes' writings, except for a few fragments, are lost.

ancestor worship

Ancestor worship refers to the rites conducted in honor of deceased relatives by their descendants. Related to ANIMISM, such worship is based on the idea that the dead continue to influence the world of the living. Ancestor worship has been the most popular ritual in China and is also widespread in Korea, Japan, India, and sub-Saharan Africa. In China it began as a practice of a fertility cult, which used the phallus as an ancestral symbol. In the Shang dynasty (*c.*1600–*c.*1027 BC) and the Chou dynasty (*c.*1027–256 BC), only royal ancestors were worshiped. But beginning with the Han dynasty (202 BC–AD 220), the preceding four generations of ancestors of all classes were honored. Chinese villages and towns had ancestral halls where ancestors of the same paternal lineages were worshiped.   DAVID C. YU

Bibliography: Ahern, Emily M., *Cult of the Dead in a Chinese Village* (1973); Frazer, J. G., *The Belief in Immortality and the Worship of the Dead,* 3 vols. (1913–14; repr. 1968); Newell, William H., ed., *Ancestors* (1976); Smith, Robert J., *Ancestor Worship in Contemporary Japan* (1974); Wolf, Arthur P., ed., *Religion and Ritual in Chinese Society* (1974).

See also: PHALLIC WORSHIP.

Anchieta, José de   [ahn-shee-ay'-tah]

José de Anchieta, b. Mar. 19, 1534, d. June 9, 1597, was a Portuguese Jesuit writer who spent his life in Brazil as a missionary. His writings reveal religious devotion and include autos sacramentalis (sacramental verse plays), poems, descriptive prose, and the first Iupí Indian grammar (1595).
                                          MARIA ISABEL ABREU

Bibliography: Dominian, H. C., *Apostle of Brazil* (1958).

Anchisaurus   [ang'-ki-sohr'-uhs]

Anchisaurus (Greek for "near lizard"), a DINOSAUR of Early Jurassic time, was among the first of the dinosaurs recognized (1885) in North America. Most of what is known about it comes from skeletons found in Connecticut and South Africa. Of modest proportions (length about 270 cm/106 in) and relatively slender build, the body was intermediate in form between the distantly related carnivorous saurischian dinosaurs, such as TYRANNOSAURUS and *Antrodemus,* and the huge Jurassic and Cretaceous sauropod dinosaurs, such as DIPLODOCUS and *Camarasaurus*—descendants of the prosauropods. The animal was herbivorous, and although basically quadrupedal, it could also stand on its hind feet.
                                          WANN LANGSTON, JR.

Bibliography: Colbert, E. H., *The Dinosaur World* (1977).

See also: FOSSIL RECORD; MESOZOIC ERA.

Anchises   [an-ky'-seez]

In Greek mythology, Anchises was the father of AENEAS, whose descendants founded Rome. A handsome young man, Anchises was seduced by Aphrodite who, disguised as a shepherdess, bore his son Aeneas. During the Trojan War, Aeneas carried the aged Anchises to safety; they were refugees first in Carthage, then in Italy. Their adventures are described in Virgil's *Aeneid.*

anchor

An anchor is a device designed to hold a buoy, boat, or ship in a stationary position by digging into the seabed or by its own weight. It is attached with a heavy cable or chain and is usually in the shape of a double or triple hook.
    Early anchors were relatively simple in design. They were sometimes simply baskets of rocks or lead-weighted logs, or they were made of three or four long poles lashed together with wooden hooks secured at the bottom end. The poles formed the shank, and the hooks were called the crown. At the top of the shank was a fixed crosspiece, the stock, which served to tilt the anchor against the sea bottom so that one of the hooks would catch and hold.
    Later iron anchors had U-shaped hooks, or flukes, and removable stocks. Modern anchors for large ships are generally stockless, so that they may be drawn up into the opening for the anchor cable, called a hawsehole. Stockless anchors have pivoting crowns that tilt to dig into the bottom when the anchor shaft lies flat. A large ship may use several anchors, both fore and aft.

Grapnels—light anchors with four or five flukes—are used to anchor small boats. A sea anchor, a floating metal and cloth device, is used when the ship is under way in order to slow it or to keep it pointing into the waves.

A stockless anchor (left) has heavy, pronglike flukes for digging into the sea bottom and is generally used on large ships to hold them in place. An admiralty (right), used on small boats, has an unwieldy crosspiece stock, which has been eliminated in most other types.

Anchorage

Anchorage is the most populous city in Alaska, with a population of 173,017 (1980), and one of the country's largest in terms of area. Located at the head of Cook Inlet, a bay of the Pacific Ocean, it was founded in 1914 as a construction base for the Alaska Railroad. It developed as a railroad town, vital to the coal, gold, and fishing industries. Construction of the immense Fort Richardson and Elmendorf Air Force Base during World War II made the city an important transportation and defense center. The international airport services domestic, European, and Far Eastern flights. Discoveries of oil nearby made Anchorage a focus of the state's rapidly expanding oil, coal, and natural-gas industries. The seaport is equipped to handle oil shipments year round. In 1964 a severe earthquake damaged much of the city, necessitating a major urban-renewal program. Alaska Pacific University and the University of Alaska at Anchorage are there.

anchorman

In radio or television, an anchorman is a person who presides over or narrates a news broadcast in which correspondents give their reports. The term became widely used after CBS-TV adopted it to describe the role of Walter CRONKITE as the central figure in its coverage of the 1952 national political conventions.   S. KUCZUN

Bibliography: Gates, Gary Paul, *Air Time: The Inside Story of CBS News* (1978).

anchovy   [an'-choh-vee]

The anchovy is a herringlike member of the fish family Engraulidae. Many of the 20 genera and more than 100 species are distributed throughout the temperate and tropical seas of the world. A few species of anchovy are confined to

The European anchovy, Engraulis encrasicholus, *is valuable to the European fishing industry, which catches tons of anchovies for canning, salting, or conversion into fish pastes.*

400 ANCIENT MARINER

fresh waters. The common anchovy, *Anchoa mitchilli*, also called white bait, is a small, almost translucent fish, with a silvery stripe on the side of its body and a large mouth. It grows to a maximum length of about 10 cm (4 in) and runs in extensive schools in inshore waters from Cape Cod to Yucatán. Spawning takes place from May to August. The principal food of the common anchovy is small, shrimplike animals. The fish themselves are the prey of seabirds.

A Mediterranean species of anchovy is used as human food. Others are processed into fish meal, fertilizer, or oil. Peru's important anchovy industry is periodically affected by changes in offshore current patterns that deplete the anchovy population (see EL NIÑO).   ALFRED PERLMUTTER

Ancient Mariner: see RIME OF THE ANCIENT MARINER.

Ancona [ang-koh'-nah]

Ancona, situated on a promontory in the Adriatic Sea in central Italy, is the capital of Ancona province and Marche administrative region. Its population is 107,800 (1976 est.). A rail and sea transportation hub and market center, Ancona is active in trade with Yugoslavia across the Adriatic. The city has a petroleum refinery, and its industries manufacture chemicals, ships, foodstuffs, furniture, and musical instruments. Fishing is also important to the local economy. Ancona has been the seat of an archbishopric since the Middle Ages.

Settled about 390 BC by Greeks from Syracuse, Ancona was taken by Rome during the 2d century BC and became a flourishing port after the harbor was enlarged under Emperor Trajan. Ancona was under papal rule from 1532 until 1860, except for a relatively brief period of French control (1797–1816). In 1860 it became part of Italy. The city was severely damaged by Allied bombing during World War II. Notable landmarks that have been restored are the marble Arch of Trajan (AD 115) and the 12th-century Cathedral of St. Ciriaco.

Andalusia [an-duh-loo'-zhuh]

Andalusia (Spanish: Andalucía) is a historic region of Spain lying in the extreme south of the country. It is generally considered the area south of the Sierra Morena, which roughly coincides with Spain's eight southernmost provinces. Andalusia covers approximately 87,000 km² (33,500 mi²) and has a population of 6,230,100 (1974 est.) Its name is derived from al-Andalus, the Moorish name for the Iberian Peninsula.

The chief topographical feature of Andalusia is the wide, fertile plain of the GUADALQUIVIR RIVER, which flows west across the region. In the extreme south, the SIERRA NEVADA, the highest mountain range in Spain, reaches 3,482 m (11,423 ft) at the Mulhacen. Andalusia has both an Atlantic and a Mediterranean coast. Summers are hot and dry, and winters are mild. At SEVILLE, the average temperature in July is 28° C (82° F) and in January, 10° C (50° F). Annual rainfall averages 560 mm (22 in) but is greater in the mountains.

Andalusia is primarily an agricultural region. Grapes and other fruits, olives, tomatoes, wheat, and barley are grown. With extensive pasture land, Anadalusia is famous for its horses, bulls (for bullfighting), and sheep. The region is also highly urbanized, and manufacturing has recently been expanded in the cities. Sherry, textiles, leather, and cork are leading manufactures. Fishing, especially for sardines and tunny, is important along the coast. Seville, the chief city of Andalusia, has a busy inland port; ALGECIRAS, CADIZ, and MALAGA are ocean ports. The population is Spanish, but Moorish influence is strong, and Andalusia has a vigorous movement for local autonomy.

Andalusia was settled in turn by Phoenicians, Greeks, Carthaginians, Romans, and Visigoths. It was conquered by the Moors in 711. The independent Moorish caliphate of Andalusia, with its capital at CORDOBA, was the center of culture and learning in Europe. Three successive dynasties, the UMAYYADS, ALMORAVIDS, and ALMOHADS, ruled until Christian Spaniards finished conquering Andalusia in 1492.
                                         NORMAN J. G. POUNDS

Bibliography: Epton, Nina C., *Andalusia* (1968); Naylor, John, *Andalusia* (1975); Sordo, Enrique, *Moorish Spain: Cordoba, Seville, Granada* (1963; repr. 1971).

andalusite [an-duh-loo'-syt]

Andalusite is an aluminum SILICATE MINERAL (Al_2SiO_5) used in the manufacture of spark-plug porcelain and other refractories. Specimens of the variety chiastolite, when cut in cross section and polished, display a cross of black, carbonaceous impurities against a grayish ground. Andalusite commonly forms elongated, red to reddish-brown, prismatic crystals (ORTHORHOMBIC SYSTEM), some displaying pleochroism, and granular or columnar masses. HARDNESS is 7½, LUSTER vitreous, and SPECIFIC GRAVITY 3.2. Small amounts occur in many contact METAMORPHIC ROCKS, particularly altered sediments, and pebbles of the mineral are found in some gem gravels.

Andaman Islands [an'-duh-muhn]

The Andaman Islands are more than 200 islands in the eastern Bay of Bengal, about 480 km (300 mi) southwest of Rangoon; together with the Nicobar Islands, the Andamans form one of the territories of India. The area of the Andamans is 6,374 km² (2,461 mi²), and the population is 115,000 (1971 est.). Most of the islands are hilly and forested. At 732 m (2,402 ft), Saddle Peak on North Andaman Island is the highest point. The Andamans are separated from the Nicobars to the south by the Ten Degree Channel. Port Blair, the territorial capital, is the only sizable town (1971 pop., 26,212). Temperatures are moderate (18°–38° C/65°–100° F), and rainfall is heavy (about 3,050 mm/120 in per year). The first British settlement was in 1789. From 1858 to 1945 the Andamans served as a British penal colony, and many Indian and Burmese inhabitants are descended from guards or convicts. Indigenous Andamanese, originally of a Stone Age culture, number in the hundreds. Rice, coconuts, and especially timber are economic staples.

Andaman Sea

The Andaman Sea is an extension of the Indian Ocean bounded on the west by the Andaman and Nicobar islands; on the north and east by Burma, Thailand, and the Malay Peninsula; and on the south by the Strait of Malacca and Sumatra. About 1,200 km (750 mi) long and 650 km (400 mi) wide, it covers an area of 798,000 km² (308,000 mi²).

Andamanese

The Andamanese are the indigenous inhabitants of several of the more than 200 islands known as the Andamans, located in the Bay of Bengal. Their name may have come from Angaman, first used by Marco Polo in 1292 to refer to the islands. Ethnically related to the NEGRITO peoples of Malaysia and the Philippines, the Andamanese have dark-brown skin and tightly curled black hair. They speak a language not identified as related to any linguistic family.

Before the arrival of the Europeans from the mid-19th century onward, the Andamanese reportedly had no knowledge of agriculture or fire, used tools made of stone, and lacked domesticated animals. The dog was introduced in the 19th century. As food gatherers and hunters, the Andamanese collect wild fruits, roots, and nuts, hunt wild pigs with the bow and arrow, and, in outrigger canoes, obtain turtles, fish, and shellfish with nets and harpoons.

The Andamanese are believed to trace genealogical descent through both parents. The nuclear family is the most important social and economic group, and divorce is rare. The powers of the leaders rarely extend beyond their communities. Andamanese religion is animistic and includes ceremonies held to honor or placate environmental and ancestral spirits. The noted social anthropologist Alfred R. RADCLIFFE-BROWN conducted field work among the Andamanese in 1906–08.   DONN V. HART

Bibliography: Cipriani, Lidio, *The Andaman Islanders*, ed. and trans. by D. Tayler Cox (1966); Radcliffe-Brown, Alfred R., *The Andaman Islanders*, 2d ed. (1948; repr. 1964).

Anders, William Alison

The American astronaut William A. Anders, b. Hong Kong, Oct. 17, 1933, flew on the first manned mission around the Moon. Anders was a U.S. Air Force interceptor pilot and, after receiving a master's degree in nuclear engineering, served at the Air Force Weapons Laboratory. He was selected as an astronaut in 1963.

His only flight in space was as the LUNAR EXCURSION MODULE pilot of Apollo 8, the first manned mission around the Moon, with Frank BORMAN and James LOVELL. (See APOLLO PROGRAM.) He, Lovell, and Borman read from Genesis as part of a Christmas greeting to the world from the Moon. During 1969–73 he served as executive secretary of the National Aeronautics and Space Council. He later served as commissioner of the Atomic Energy Commission and U.S. ambassador to Norway before becoming general manager of General Electric's Nuclear Energy Products Division.   DAVID DOOLING

Andersen, Hans Christian

Hans Christian Andersen, a 19th-century Danish novelist, dramatist, and poet, is remembered chiefly as a creator of fairy tales. Andersen's 168 stories, the first of which were published in 1835, have been translated into more than 80 languages.

The Danish writer Hans Christian Andersen, b. Apr. 2, 1805, d. Aug. 4, 1875, is renowned for his fairy tales that combine childlike fantasy with a penetrating wisdom. Between 1835 and 1872 he wrote 168 such tales, as well as poetry, novels, plays, travel sketches, and memoirs.

Andersen was the son of a poor cobbler and a superstitious, illiterate mother. At the age of 14 he left his home in Odense for Copenhagen, where he worked for a time as an actor with the Royal Theater with little success. Largely through the help of Jonas Collin, a director of the theater, Andersen entered grammar school at Slagelse, where he endured harsh treatment from a malicious schoolmaster. Again with Collin's help, he attended Copenhagen University in 1827–28. His poetry and prose, which began to appear soon afterward, exhibited the romantic influence of Sir Walter SCOTT and of such German writers of fantasy as E. T. A. HOFFMANN. During the 1830s Andersen traveled throughout Europe and the Mediterranean, briefly settling in Italy. He described these travels in *A Poet's Bazaar* (1842; Eng. trans. 1846) and other travel books.

In 1835 Andersen published *The Improvisatore* (1835; Eng. trans., 1845), the first and most successful of his six autobiographical novels. During that year he also published *Tales Told for Children*, which contained his first four fairy tales: "The Tinderbox," "Little Claus and Big Claus," "The Princess and the Pea," and "Little Ida's Flowers." Most of Andersen's subsequent tales, which were translated into other languages during his lifetime, appeared in sets of four. They include the memorable classics "The Emperor's New Clothes," "The Ugly Duckling," "The Snow Queen," "The Nightingale," "The Red Shoes," "The Little Fir Tree," "The Little Match Girl," and "The Constant Tin Soldier." Now translated into more than 100 languages, his tales rely heavily on elements of fantasy and folklore. Yet they also reveal a deep, often pessimistic insight into human nature. Andersen used his own difficult life as the basis for many of his tales. In 1855 he published the autobiographical *Fairy Tale of My Life* (Eng. trans., 1954). Several English-language editions of his collected tales have appeared since the first in 1869–71.

Bibliography: Böök, Fredrik, *Hans Christian Andersen* (1938; Eng. trans., 1962); Dahl, Svend, and Topsøe-Jensen, H. G., eds., *A Book on the Danish Writer Hans Christian Andersen: His Life and Work* (Eng. trans., 1955); Godden, Rumer, *Hans Christian Andersen* (1955); Stirling, Monica, *The Wild Swan* (1965).

Andersen Nexø, Martin: see NEXØ, MARTIN ANDERSEN.

Anderson, Carl David

The American physicist Carl David Anderson, b. New York City, Sept. 3, 1905, won the 1936 Nobel Prize for physics for his work on COSMIC RAYS. In his CLOUD CHAMBER studies, Anderson found decisive proof of the existence of the POSITRON, a positively charged electron. In 1938 he and Seth H. Neddermeyer announced the discovery of the MESON, a type of subatomic particle whose existence had earlier been predicted by Hideki YUKAWA. In 1948, Cecil POWELL found that in reality another meson, called the pi-meson, or pion, had the properties of Yukawa's model and decayed to the known meson discovered by Anderson.   JAMES A. BOOTH

Anderson, Dame Judith

Judith Anderson, b. Adelaide, Australia, Feb. 10, 1898, is an actress noted for her powerful portrayals of tragic characters. She made her debut in Sydney in 1915 and went to the United States three years later. Her first major New York success was in *Cobra* (1924), but she is equally remembered for her parts in Luigi PIRANDELLO's *As You Desire Me* (1930–31) and Eugene O'NEILL's *Mourning Becomes Electra* (1932). In 1936 Anderson appeared in *Hamlet* opposite John GIELGUD and in 1937 as Lady Macbeth opposite Laurence OLIVIER. Her riveting portrayal of Medea in 1947 is often considered her best performance. She has also appeared in films, notably as the formidable Mrs. Danvers in *Rebecca* (1940).

Anderson, Jack

Jack Northman Anderson, b. Long Beach, Calif., Oct. 19, 1922, is an American newspaper columnist and investigative reporter. He was a Mormon missionary in the South (1941–44),

Jack Anderson, an American newspaper columnist, developed his journalistic style as a war correspondent and later as an assistant to the columnist Drew Pearson. Anderson's syndicated column on current political affairs enjoys a wide circulation.

briefly worked as a war correspondent (1945), and in 1947 joined the staff of Drew Pearson's influential muckraking column "Washington Merry-Go-Round." The two journalists collaborated on *The Case Against Congress* (1968). Anderson took over the column after Pearson's death in 1969 and won a 1972 Pulitzer Prize for national reporting after exposing U.S. political intervention in the India-Pakistan War. Anderson's reports on the Watergate affair were lauded, but his treatment of incidents in the personal life of Sen. Thomas Eagleton, the initial choice of Sen. George McGovern as a candidate for the vice-presidency in 1972, drew criticism. His own books include *The Anderson Papers* (1973).

CALDER M. PICKETT

Anderson, John

John Bayard Anderson, b. Rockford, Ill., Feb. 15, 1922, represented Illinois in the U.S. House of Representatives from 1961 to 1981 and ran unsuccessfully for U.S. president in 1980. Trained in law at the University of Illinois and Harvard University, Anderson entered the foreign service in 1952 and state politics in 1956. Elected to Congress in 1960, he served as chairman of the House Republican Conference from 1968 until 1979, when he declared his presidential candidacy and withdrew from reelection to the House. Defeated by Ronald Reagan for the Republican nomination, Anderson campaigned as an independent, winning about 7 percent of the popular vote. His published writings include *Between Two Worlds: A Congressman's Choice* (1970) and *Vision and Betrayal in America* (1975).

Anderson, Margaret

The American publisher Margaret Anderson, b. Indianapolis, Ind., c.1890, d. Oct. 18, 1973, introduced works by such important literary figures as T. S. Eliot, Ernest Hemingway, and James Joyce in *The Little Review,* which she founded in Chicago in 1914 and edited with Jane Heap. Anderson, with the encouragement of Ezra Pound, foreign editor from 1917 to 1919, supported all modernist literary movements. She became involved in a celebrated obscenity case when she published Joyce's novel *Ulysses* in installments, beginning in 1918. The book was held to be obscene and was ruled legally inadmissible to the United States. Anderson described her life and literary acquaintances in a 3-volume autobiography—*My Thirty Years' War* (1930), *The Fiery Fountains* (1951), and *The Strange Necessity* (1969). All three volumes were published as a set in 1970 along with the anthology *The Little Review.*

ERNEST C. HYNDS

Anderson, Marian

Marian Anderson, b. Philadelphia, Feb. 17, 1902, was the first black singer to perform at the Metropolitan Opera House in New York City. Anderson, who was a contralto, made her de-

The contralto Marian Anderson, known for her rich voice and wide range, was the first black to sing at the Metropolitan Opera. She was named to the National Arts Hall of Fame in 1972, and she was cited for her contribution to the American performing arts at the first annual Kennedy Center Honors in 1978.

but (1955) as Ulrica in Giuseppe Verdi's *Un Ballo in Maschera.* She was, however, primarily a concert artist and was particularly acclaimed for her singing of spirituals. Anderson first sang in church choirs. Because of her race she had to overcome great difficulties to obtain the training necessary for a career. In 1935 she sang for Arturo Toscanini, who said she had "a voice that comes once in a hundred years." In 1939 the Daughters of the American Revolution denied her access to Washington's Constitution Hall for a concert; Eleanor Roosevelt then arranged her concert outdoors on the steps of the Lincoln Memorial before an audience of 75,000 people. Anderson was named by the government as an alternate delegate to the United Nations in 1958. She sang at the inaugural balls of Presidents Eisenhower (1957) and Kennedy (1961). Anderson made many recordings and was noted for the warm, deep timbre and for the style of her oratorio singing. She retired after a successful concert tour in 1965. In 1978 she was one of five recipients of the first Kennedy Center Honors.

Bibliography: Anderson, Marian, *My Lord, What a Morning: An Autobiography* (1956); Vehanen, Kosti, *Marian Anderson: A Portrait* (1941; repr. 1970).

Anderson, Maxwell

James Maxwell Anderson, b. Atlantic, Pa., Dec. 15, 1888, d. Feb. 28, 1959, was one of the most admired American playwrights of his time. His reputation reached its peak when he wrote such colorful historical verse plays as *Elizabeth the Queen* (1930), *Mary of Scotland* (1933), *Valley Forge* (1934), and *Winterset* (1935), a tragedy set in modern times. Today, however, these and Anderson's many other verse plays have fallen from favor as critics have come to complain about their unrealistic plots and clumsy poetry. His most durable work is the prose play *What Price Glory?* (1924), a collaboration with Laurence Stallings (1895–1968), about American soldiers in France during World War I. The comedy *Both Your Houses* (1933), a satire on congressional corruption, won Anderson the Pulitzer Prize. Other works include *Key Largo* (1939) and the musicals on which he collaborated with composer Kurt Weill, *Knickerbocker Holiday* (1938) and *Lost in the Stars* (1949), which was based on Alan Paton's novel *Cry, the Beloved Country.*

MALCOLM GOLDSTEIN

Bibliography: Anderson, Maxwell, *Dramatist in America: Letters of Maxwell Anderson, 1912-1958,* ed. by Laurence G. Avery (1977); Shivers, Alfred S., *Maxwell Anderson* (1976).

Anderson, Philip Warren

The American physicist Philip Warren Anderson, b. Indianapolis, Ind., Dec. 13, 1923, shared with Sir Nevill Mott and J. H. Van Vleck the 1977 Nobel Prize for physics for their development of basic theories of magnetism and conduction as applied to electronic solid-state circuitry. This work made possible the use of economical materials, such as silicon, in computers. Anderson was a visiting professor of theoretical physics at Cambridge University from 1967 to 1975 and has served as assistant director of physics research at Bell Laboratories since 1974 and professor of physics at Princeton University since 1975.

Anderson, Sherwood

The prolific American novelist, short-story writer, and critic Sherwood Anderson, b. Sept. 13, 1876, d. Mar. 8, 1941, is best known for his sensitive portrayals of the lives of small-town midwesterners. Born in Camden, Ohio, and raised in nearby Clyde, Anderson served in the Spanish-American War, became a copywriter in Chicago, then managed a paint plant in Elyria, Ohio, before taking up writing as a career in 1913.

Anderson's first novel, set in a small town in Iowa, was *Windy McPherson's Son* (1916); this was followed the next year by *Marching Men.* He achieved fame with WINESBURG, OHIO (1919), a group of interconnected stories about small-town people whose frustrations and shattered dreams turn them into what he called "grotesques." This remained a primary focus in Anderson's work, the means by which he illustrated the effects of industrialization on the life of the individual. The theme found further expression in the novels *Poor White* (1920), *Many Marriages* (1923), and *Dark Laughter* (1925).

Anderson permanently influenced the short story, concentrating on mood and psychological insight rather than on plot. Three collections, *The Triumph of the Egg* (1921), *Horses and Men* (1923), and *Death in the Woods* (1933), show his mastery of the genre. Some of his finest writing appears in his autobiographical works: *A Story Teller's Story* (1924); *Tar: A Midwest Childhood* (1926); and *Sherwood Anderson's Memoirs* (1942).

Bibliography: Anderson, David, *Sherwood Anderson: An Introduction and Interpretation* (1967); Burbank, Rex, *Sherwood Anderson* (1964); Howe, Irving, *Sherwood Anderson: A Biographical and Critical Study* (1951; repr. 1966); Rogers, Douglas, *Sherwood Anderson: A Selective, Annotated Bibliography* (1976); Taylor, Welford D., *Sherwood Anderson* (1977); Sutton, William A., *The Road to Winesburg* (1972); White, Ray L., ed., *The Achievement of Sherwood Anderson: Essays in Criticism* (1966).

Andersonville Prison

Andersonville Prison, near Americus, Ga., was a Confederate stockade for Union prisoners during the Civil War. The inmates suffered from overcrowding, starvation, and the cruelty of the superintendent; about 13,000 died. The prison is now a historic site that includes Andersonville National Cemetery.

Andersson, Dan

Dan Andersson, b. Apr. 6, 1888, d. Sept. 16, 1920, was one of the earliest Swedish working-class authors and is still the most popular. In *Kolarhistorier* (Charcoal Burners' Tales, 1914) and *Charcoal Burner's Ballad and Other Poems* (1915; Eng. trans., 1943) he described men's lonely toil in the Swedish wilderness in musical prose and poetry, skillfully blending mysticism and naturalism. A number of Andersson's poems have been set to music. He died accidentally from gas poisoning in a Stockholm hotel.   VIRPI ZUCK

Andersson, Johan Gunnar

Johan Gunnar Andersson, b. July 3, 1874, d. Oct. 29, 1960, was a Swedish geologist and archaeologist who laid the foundations of Chinese prehistoric studies in the 1920s. Employed by the Chinese government in 1914 as a geological advisor, he became increasingly interested in paleontology and prehistory. In 1921, through his discovery of an occupation site at Yang-shao T'sun in Honan, he showed the existence of Chinese Neolithic culture. This site gave its name to the Yang-shao culture. He was also responsible for the first excavations at CHOU-K'OU-TIEN, where skeletal evidence of PEKING MAN, a variety of *Homo erectus*, was subsequently found. He published an account of his own career in *Children of the Yellow Earth: Studies in Prehistoric China* (1934).

Andes

The Andes (Spanish: Los Andes, or Cordillera de los Andes, the latter for "Andes Mountain Range") constitute one of the world's major mountain systems and form the backbone of South America. Paralleling the Pacific coast of the continent, they extend north about 7,250 km (4,500 mi) from Cape Horn at the tip of Tierra del Fuego to the Caribbean coast of Colombia and Venezuela. Although the Andes have a relatively narrow width—generally less than 325 km (200 mi) except in Bolivia, where this figure doubles—they form one of the longest uninterrupted high barriers of the world. More than 40 peaks exceed 6,100 m (20,000 ft). The Andes are not a single high range, however, but a complex series of ranges (cordilleras) separated by plateaus and elevated basins.

The geological evolution of the Andes began with the folding and uplift that took place in the Cretaceous Period (140 to 65 million years ago). The development of the modern Andes, however, stems from mountain-building activity that began in the Pliocene Epoch (6 to 2 million years ago). Disturbances of the Earth's crust continue in the form of volcanic activity and

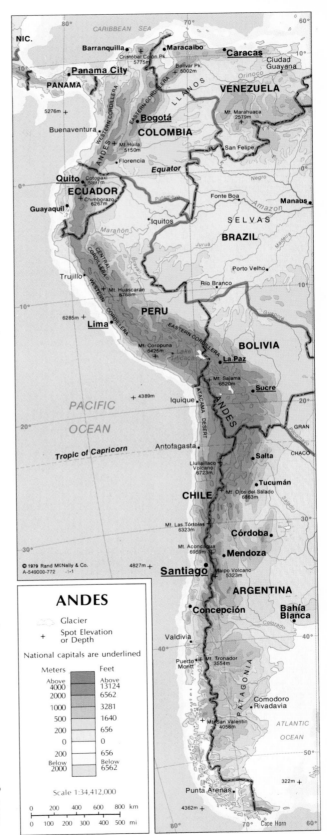

ANDES

⌇⌇⌇⌇ Glacier

+ Spot Elevation
   or Depth

National capitals are underlined

Meters	Feet
Above 4000	Above 13124
2000	6562
1000	3281
500	1640
200	656
0	0
200	656
Below 2000	Below 6562

Scale 1:34,412,000

0   200   400   600   800 km

0   100   200   300   400   500 mi

Bowler-type hats and finely woven blankets insulate the Indian women of Copacabana, Bolivia, against the crisp Andean climate. Despite the hardships associated with the area's high altitude, the Andes have been a major center of Indian cultures since ancient times.

earthquakes. These are especially prevalent in the western ranges from southern Colombia to northern Chile.

TOPOGRAPHY

From Tierra del Fuego north to 40° south latitude, the Andes form a single dominant range, with a mean elevation less than 2,000 m (6,600 ft) but with occasional higher peaks. Extensive glaciation has left many glacier-fed lakes, including Argentino, Buenos Aires, and Llanquihue on the eastern flanks, and many islands and fjords on the western. North to 27° south latitude, the single range, with a mean elevation of 3,960 m (13,000 ft), contains ACONCAGUA (6,960 m/22,840 ft), the highest peak in the Western Hemisphere. It then splits into three ranges. Two of these continue north into Bolivia as the Cordilleras Occidental (western) and Oriental (eastern). Between them is the Altiplano, a string of high intermontane basins. Lake TITICACA, the largest South American lake and the highest large lake in the world, occupies the northernmost basin. Major peaks include Ollagüe (5,875 m/19,250 ft), Sajama (6,520 m/21,390 ft), Illimani (6,460 m/21,200 ft), and Illampu (6,400 m/21,000 ft). The Cordillera Oriental veers northwest, as the Cordillera Real, at 17° south latitude, the point at which the Andes is the widest.

In Peru the Andes extend northwest to Ecuador (lat. 5° S) as a high plateau with a mean elevation that declines from 4,575 to 3,050 m (15,000 to 10,000 ft). Above this surface rise mountains to heights exceeding 6,400 m (21,000 ft), including HUASCARÁN (6,775 m/22,200 ft). Tributaries of the Amazon have cut deep gorges into this surface. In Ecuador, where the Andes narrow to less than 115 km (70 mi), the Cordilleras Oriental and Occidental overlook an intercordilleran depression divided into 15 distinct basins. This two-cordillera pattern continues northward into Colombia, where the Andes fan out into three major northeast-trending ranges: the Occidental, Central, and Oriental, separated by the Cauca and Madalena river valleys. Major peaks include Cristóbal Colón (5,775 m/18,950 ft), Huila (5,150 m/16,900 ft), and Tolima (5,600 m/18,425 ft). The Cordillera Oriental forks north of Bogotá. One branch continues north as the Sierra de Perijá to form the west edge of the Maracaibo Basin. The other extends northeast to Barquisimeto as the Sierra de Mérida. It continues east as the Central Highlands, a double row of lower ranges, the Sierra de Cumana and the Paria Peninsula.

CLIMATE, VEGETATION, AND FAUNA

The wide latitudinal range of the Andes results in a series of climates resembling those along the western edge of North America from Panama to southern Alaska. Annual precipitation exceeds 2,540 mm (100 in) on the Pacific slopes of Colombia and southern Chile and on those facing the Amazon Basin, but it drops below 250 mm (10 in) in the zone that extends from southern Ecuador to central Chile and includes highland Bolivia.

About two-thirds of the Andes lie within the tropics. More significant, however, is the vertical zonation of climates caused by changes in elevation. The *tierra caliente* ("hot land"), extending from sea level to 900 m (3,000 ft), has a mean temperature of 26° C (79° F), abundant rainfall, and tropical rain forest vegetation. The *tierra templada* ("temperate land"), extending to 1,800 m (6,000 ft), is cooler and humid, with a mean temperature of 21° C (70° F) and subtropical forest vegetation. The *tierra fría* ("cold land"), extending to 3,000 m (10,000 ft), has a mean temperature of 15° C (59° F). Above the *tierra fría*, the *páramo* extends to the snow line. The *páramo* is humid, cloudy, and too cold for trees, which are replaced by bunch grass and tundralike vegetation. The snow line is at about 4,500 m (15,000 ft) on mountains near the equator.

The distribution of animal life is also determined by elevation. At low and intermediate elevations, Andean bird life is rich, and mammals include the cougar, ocelot, opossum, and coatimundi. The llama, alpaca, guanaco, and vicuña are found in the Altiplano. The now rare condor inhabits higher elevations.

PEOPLE AND ECONOMY

Spanish invaders settled the intermontane basins within the *tierra templada* and *tierra fría*, which had long been occupied by Indians, including the INCAS in Peru and the CHIBCHAS in Colombia. About 60% of the Andean inhabitants reside in these basins. The Pan American Highway extends through the highlands from Venezuela to Peru and then along the coast to southern Chile.

Subsistence agriculture based on corn, wheat, potatoes, and grazing predominates in the *tierra fría*, and subtropical crops—sugar, rice, and, in Colombia especially, coffee—in the *tierra templada*. Industry, although of increasing importance, focuses primarily on supplying basic manufactures for local consumption. The heavily mineralized Andes, long mined for gold and silver, are now more valued for copper and tin, along with smaller amounts of lead, zinc, and antimony. Colombia and Peru produce small amounts of coal for local use. Snow-capped peaks are an additional source of irrigation water and are scenic attractions for a growing tourist industry.

DAVID G. BASILE

Bibliography: Kazami, Takehide, *The Andes* (1972).

andesine: see FELDSPAR.

andesite   [an'-duh-zyt]

Andesite is a fine-grained, gray-to-black, volcanic IGNEOUS ROCK. Andesite PORPHYRY contains PHENOCRYSTS of plagioclase FELDSPAR and other SILICATE MINERALS (olivine, pyroxene, hornblende, or biotite) in a matrix of plagioclase, dark minerals, and natural glass. Magnetite, apatite, and ilmenite occur in lesser amounts. Glass predominates in andesitic OBSIDIAN. Andesite is often difficult to distinguish from BASALT, but petrographic analysis of feldspar in the matrix reveals a higher albite content than in basalt, while chemical analysis reveals more SiO_2 (50–65%), Na_2O, and K_2O, and less total iron, MgO, and CaO than in basalt.

Andesite commonly occurs as LAVA flows and DIKES in zones of continental plate convergence (the Pacific RING OF FIRE, including VOLCANOES of the Andes—from where the name "andesite" is derived—and the Cascades, Aleutians, Siberia, Japan, Southeast Asia; the Caribbean; and the north edge of the Mediterranean). Some andesite may form by differentiation of basaltic MAGMA, but much probably results from partial melting of deeply buried crustal rocks.

WILLIAM D. ROMEY

See also: PETROGRAPHY; PLATE TECTONICS.

Andhra Pradesh [an'-druh pruh-daysh']

Andhra Pradesh is a state in southeast India, bounded by the Bay of Bengal on the east and Tamil Nadu (formerly Madras) on the south. It covers 275,068 km² (106,204 mi²) and has a population of 53,592,605 (1981). The state capital and largest city is HYDERABAD (1981 pop., 2,142,087). The region is bisected by the Eastern Ghats, which divide the coastal plain from the arid Deccan Plateau to the west. The major economic activity is agriculture; cotton, rice, corn, wheat, tobacco, and sugarcane are the main crops. Light industry is concentrated in Hyderabad, Vishkapatnam, and Vijayawada.

The Buddhist Andhra dynasty, from which the state derives its name, ruled there from c.230 BC to AD 230. In the 14th to the 16th century the Vijayanagar empire ruled, but by the early 19th century most of the area was under British colonial rule. Formed in 1956 from the Telugu-speaking districts of Madras and Hyderabad states, Andhra Pradesh was the first Indian state organized for a linguistic group.

Ando Hiroshige: see HIROSHIGE.

Andorra [an-dohr'-uh]

Andorra is a tiny state of 453 km² (175 mi²), located on the border of France and Spain and surrounded by them. It has a population of 38,050 (1982), with the capital city of Andorra-la-Vella accounting for 14,783.

THE LAND AND PEOPLE
Set in the eastern PYRENEES, Andorra is a contrast of high mountains and deep valleys. The Valira River drains the area. Temperatures in the valleys can reach 32° C (90° F) in the summer, but the winters are cold (average January temperature is about 0° C/32° F), with an abundance of snow. One major highway connects Andorra with France and Spain, and other roads make the whole area accessible by automobile. The country has no railroad and no airline.

Approximately 60% of Andorra's citizens are of Spanish origin; 6% are French. One-third are descendants of an ancient tribe known in Roman times as Andosians, from whom the country got its name. The main language is Catalan, and Spanish and French are spoken widely. Roman Catholicism is the official religion.

ECONOMY
Only 4% of Andorra's land is arable, so the country must import food from France and Spain. Tobacco, potatoes, rye, and buckwheat are grown in the lower valleys, where a few vineyards and olive groves are also located. Large flocks of sheep are brought from France and Spain each summer to graze on the abundant mountain pastures. Small quantities of iron, lead, silver, and alum are mined. Three major hydroelectric plants enable Andorra to export electricity to Spain.

For many centuries Andorra's most profitable, although unofficial, industry was smuggling between Spain and France. This remains a profitable sideline for some, but in recent years tourism has become by far the nation's largest industry. Tourism and rapid growth were spurred in the 1960s when Andorra established itself as a duty-free area. Excellent skiing in the winter, hunting and fishing, and the many folk festivals in the summer, as well as the mineral baths at Les Escaldes, have generated a tourist flow of more than 6 million visitors a year. Andorra has no sales tax, and both French and Spanish currency are recognized as legal tender (the country has none of its own). Its postal system is free, being totally supported by the sale of Andorran stamps to collectors around the world.

GOVERNMENT AND HISTORY
In 1278 the feudal state of Andorra was placed under the joint rule of the Spanish bishop of Urgel and the French count of Foix. The system remains technically the same today, though the count has been replaced by France's president. In actual practice the country, which is governed by a general council of 24 elected representatives, is independent and pays token homage to Spain and France. Women obtained the right to vote in 1970. Only men, however, may hold public

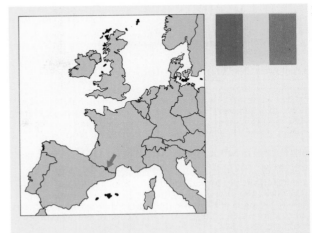

PRINCIPALITY OF ANDORRA

LAND. Area: 453 km² (175 mi²). Capital and largest city: Andorra-la-Vella (1982 pop., 14,783).

PEOPLE. Population (1982): 38,050; density (1982): 84 persons per km² (217 per mi²). Distribution (1982): 66.8% urban, 33.2% rural. Annual growth (1975–80): 4.8%. Official language: Catalan. Major religion: Roman Catholicism.

EDUCATION AND HEALTH. Literacy (1979): 100% of adult population. Universities (1982): none. Infant mortality rate: not available.

ECONOMY. Foreign trade (1977, with France and Spain only): imports—$208 million; exports—$6 million; other principal trade partners—West Germany, Japan. Currency: 1 Spanish peseta=100 céntimos; 1 French franc = 100 centimes.

GOVERNMENT. Type: limited rule by co-princes. Legislature: General Council of the Valleys of Andorra. Political subdivisions: 7 parishes.

COMMUNICATIONS. Railroads (1982): none. Roads (1978): 124 km (77 mi) paved. Major ports: none. Airfields (international, 1982): none.

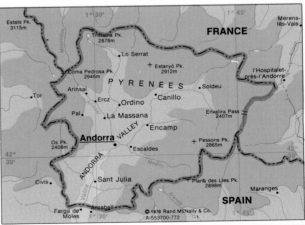

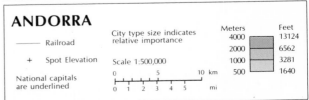

ANDORRA

——— Railroad

+ Spot Elevation

National capitals are underlined

City type size indicates relative importance

Scale 1:500,000

Meters	Feet
4000	13124
2000	6562
1000	3281
500	1640

office. Andorra, like Switzerland, maintains a policy of strict neutrality in international affairs.   PAUL C. HELMREICH

Bibliography: Carter, Youngman, *On to Andorra* (1964); Deane, Shirley, *The Road to Andorra* (1964); Morgan, Bryan, *Andorra: The Country in Between* (1964).

Andover Newton Theological School

Founded in 1807, Andover Newton (enrollment: 835; library: 194,000 volumes) is a private, interdenominational Protestant theological seminary for men and women in Newton Centre, Mass. It grants graduate divinity degrees and, in cooperation with Boston College, the Ph.D. in Theological Studies.

Andrada e Silva, José Bonifácio de   [ahn-drah'-thah ay sil'-vah, hoh-say' boh-nee-fah'-see-oh day]

José Bonifácio de Andrada e Silva, b. June 13, 1763, d. Apr. 6, 1838, was a Brazilian political leader and an internationally known geologist. He led the movement that persuaded PEDRO I to declare Brazil an empire independent of Portugal in 1822. Bonifácio served as prime minister until Pedro dismissed him in 1823 for seeking a liberal constitution. Vindicated by the adoption of the 1824 constitution, which incorporated many of his ideas, he later tutored PEDRO II.

Andrade, Mário de   [ahn-drah'-day]

A novelist, poet, literary and art critic, musicologist, and teacher, Mário Raul de Morais Andrade, b. Sept. 9, 1893, d. Feb. 25, 1945, was a leading cultural figure in the modernist movement in Brazil. His book of poetry, *Hallucinated City* (1922; Eng. trans., 1968), can be considered a manifesto of a literary trend toward popularizing art. His dynamic leadership and his enormous influence led Andrade to be called the "Pope of Modernism." Several of his short stories and *Macunaíma* (1928), his most famous prose work, are considered masterpieces.   MARIA ISABEL ABREU

andradite: see GARNET.

Andrássy, Gyula, Count   [awn'-drah-shee, dyu'-luh]

The Hungarian statesman Count Andrássy, b. Mar. 3, 1823, d. Feb. 18, 1890, played a key role in European diplomacy in the late 19th century. He took part in the unsuccessful Revolution of 1848 in Hungary and afterward lived in exile until 1857. Andrássy worked with Ferenc DEÁK to arrange the Compromise of 1867, which created the Dual Monarchy of AUSTRIA-HUNGARY. He then served (1867–71) as prime minister of Hungary before becoming foreign minister (1871–79) of the Dual Monarchy.

As foreign minister Andrássy sought closer alignment with Germany. He first agreed (1872) to alliance with both Russia and Germany, the so-called Three Emperors' League; but distrusting Russia's ambitions in the Balkans, he concluded (1879) the Dual Alliance with Germany. This was expanded into the TRIPLE ALLIANCE when Italy joined in 1882. In 1878, Andrássy represented his country at the Congress of Berlin (see BERLIN, CONGRESS OF), where he secured for Austria-Hungary the right to occupy BOSNIA AND HERCEGOVINA.

His son, also named **Count Gyula Andrássy**, b. June 30, 1860, d. June 11, 1929, was foreign minister of the Dual Monarchy at the end of World War I (1918).

Andre, Carl

The artist Carl Andre, b. Quincy, Mass., Sept. 16, 1935, is one of the chief proponents of the MINIMAL ART movement that developed in New York during the early 1960s. Influenced by the sculpture of Constantin BRANCUSI, Andre began his career in the late 1950s by making objects composed of notched, weathered wood. He experimented with new forms and techniques in 1960–64, during which time he earned a living by working as a freight brakeman and conductor for the Pennsylvania Railroad. In 1965 he began to produce his best-known

works, composed of a variety of preexisting standardized materials, such as unrelated, repetitive blocks, usually placed in a line on a floor. Defining sculpture as "form-structure-place," Andre attempts to make the space for which his structures are designed a component in what he terms his "primary objects."   BARBARA CAVALIERE

Bibliography: Battcock, Gregory, ed., *Minimal Art: A Critical Anthology* (1968); Waldman, Diane, *Carl Andre* (1970).

André, John

John André, b. May 2, 1750, was a British officer involved in the treason of the American revolutionary general Benedict ARNOLD. In the summer of 1780, Arnold, commander of West Point, contacted Major André in New York City and offered to surrender his post to the British. André met Arnold secretly near West Point on September 21 but was captured by the Americans while on his way back to New York. Because he was in civilian clothes and was carrying incriminating papers, he was condemned to death as a spy and hanged on Oct. 2, 1780, at Tappan, N.Y.

Andrea del Castagno   [ahn-dray'-ah del kahs-tahn'-yoh]

Andrea del Castagno, b. c.1421, d. Aug. 19, 1457, one of the most forceful painters of the Early Renaissance, was recognized even in his own time as a master of DRAWING and PERSPECTIVE, startling his contemporaries with vivid images that seemed to jut out of his paintings. The jealousy of lesser talents also spawned the rumor that he had murdered his fellow artist Domenico Veneziano. Giorgio VASARI, in his biographies of artists, perpetuated these slanders for centuries, and it remained for 20th-century scholars to restore Castagno's good name.

The earliest record of his artistic activity refers to frescoes he painted with Francesco de Faenza in Venice in 1442. Before that, however, he had achieved recognition in Florence for a representation on the facade of the Palazzo del Podestà (Bargello) of hanged men who had been traitors to Florence during the Battle of Anghiari in 1440. For this work he earned the sobriquet *Andreino degli Impicatti* ("Little Andrew of the Hanged Men"). Upon his return from Venice, Castagno worked at the Florence Duomo (cathedral), where he supplied the cartoon for the stained-glass window depicting the deposition of Christ. The full scope of his genius and his masterly technique are best seen in his many mural paintings. Many of his frescoes were detached from their original locations, revealing Castagno's superb *sinopia*, or preparatory drawings, on the plaster beneath them. The frescoes and their *sinopia* are displayed in the refectory of the Monastery of Sant'Apollonia, Florence. This refectory, now the Castagno Museum, is also the site of one of Castagno's largest and most important frescoes, *Last Supper* (1447).

Little is known of Castagno's earliest training. His figure drawing indicates that he was strongly affected by the works of MASACCIO. DOMENICO VENEZIANO, DONATELLO, GHIBERTI, and PIERO DELLA FRANCESCA were also influential in his development. Even in his earliest works, however, the figures are stamped with an unmistakable personal quality, monumental and strong, with a sculptural grandeur.

Castagno frequently manipulated perspective to underscore the expression and content of a painting, as in the extreme foreshortening of the image of the Holy Trinity in the fresco *Trinity with St. Jerome and Two Holy Women* (c.1453; Santissima Annunziata, Florence). In his later works the elements of movement and vigorous action are increasingly accentuated.

Castagno's paintings and drawings exerted a powerful influence on such artists as the young MICHELANGELO, Antonio and Piero POLLAIUOLO, and Andrea del VERROCCHIO. His early Venetian works (recently cleaned) were important models for the development of 15th-century Venetian painting.   JULIA KEYDEL

Bibliography: Borsook, Eve, *The Mural Painters of Tuscany* (1960); Richter, George, *Andrea del Castagno* (1943).

See also: ITALIAN ART AND ARCHITECTURE; PAINTING, HISTORY OF.

Andrea del Sarto's Madonna of the Harpies *(1517) depicts the Virgin and Child with St. Francis and St. John the Evangelist. One of Andrea's most famous works, the painting uses rich color and achieves expressiveness and compositional unity. (Uffizi Gallery, Florence.)*

Andrea del Sarto   [ahn-dray'-ah del sahr'-toh]

Andrea del Sarto, b. July 14, 1486, was a major painter in the classical tradition during the Florentine High Renaissance and Mannerist periods. Even so, he was overshadowed by LEONARDO DA VINCI, MICHELANGELO, and RAPHAEL before they left Florence in 1508–09.

Giorgio VASARI, who studied in Sarto's studio, characterized Sarto's paintings as "faultless" but called his personality "weak," since he usually deferred to his domineering wife, Lucrezia del Fede. Essays, operas, a poem by Robert BROWNING, and a psychoanalytic discussion by Ernest Jones have suggested that the lack of excitement in Sarto's personal life led him to depict figures lacking emotional depth. Two recent monographs, however, one by Sydney Freedberg and the other by John Shearman, have purged these romantic biographical theories from Sarto studies and have supplied the necessary positive reassessment of his career.

At the age of seven Sarto was apprenticed to a goldsmith. Between 1498 and 1508 he was apprenticed to the painter PIERO DI COSIMO and possibly also to Raffaellino del Garbo. By 1508 he shared a workshop with Franciabigio. Sarto's early (1510) S. Filippo Benizzi fresco series in the atrium of Santissima Annunziata in Florence owe their fantastic landscapes to the conservative style of Piero di Cosimo.

After 1511 Sarto developed new classical interests, made greater use of *sfumato* (extremely subtle shading), and painted psychologically animated portraits such as the *Annunciation* (1512; Pitti Palace), his *grisaille* (monochromatic) frescoes in the Chiostro dello Scalzo (1511–26), and his fresco cycle for the cloisters of Santissima Annunziata, as in *Birth of the Virgin* (1514).

Sarto established this mature style through his contact with Leonardo, Fra BARTOLOMMEO, Raphael's paintings, contempo-

rary sculpture (especially that of Jacopo SANSOVINO, with whom he collaborated), and the prints of DÜRER. The *Madonna of the Harpies* altarpiece (1517; Uffizi, Florence) is the most famous of his popular dark-eyed madonnas. It does not evoke the Mannerist forebodings of contemporary Raphael altarpieces but displays instead Sarto's characteristic classical formal harmony, deep colors, and noble sweetness. These features characterized all his subsequent works. He died on Sept. 28 or 29, 1530, during one of the frequent Florentine plagues.

Although Sarto traveled briefly to France in 1518, the crucial influences on his last 12 years were Raphael and the Roman High Renaissance. Sarto's late style became more heroic and controlled, as in the *Last Supper* (1522–27; San Salvi refectory). Some of his late compositions, such as *The Sacrifice of Isaac* (1529; Dresden), either seem protobaroque or else suggest the Mannerist experiments that his famous pupils—PONTORMO, ROSSO FIORENTINO, and Vasari—were then undertaking.

ALAN P. DARR

Bibliography: Freedberg, Sydney, *Andrea del Sarto,* 2 vols. (1963); Shearman, John, *Andrea del Sarto,* 2 vols. (1965).

See also: ITALIAN ART AND ARCHITECTURE; MANNERISM; RENAISSANCE ART AND ARCHITECTURE.

Andretti, Mario

Mario Andretti, b. Montona, Trieste, Italy, Feb. 28, 1940, is an American auto racer known for a hard-driving style that enabled him to win the championship on the international Formula One Grand Prix circuit in 1978. He was only the second American, and the first since 1961, to win racing's most prestigious title. He went to the United States with his family at the age of 15, but only after he had begun to idolize the great Italian drivers. One of the most versatile drivers ever, Andretti won with stock, Indy, and Grand Prix cars. He was U.S. Auto Club champion three times (1965, 1966, 1969). He won the Daytona 500 stock-car title in 1967, the Indianapolis 500 title in 1969, and the Grand Prix in 1978, becoming the only driver ever to win all three events.

Bibliography: Andretti, Mario, *What's It Like Out There* (1970).

Andrew, Saint

St. Andrew was a fisherman whom Jesus called to be an APOSTLE (Matt. 4:19). He was also the brother of Simon Peter. According to a popular but mistaken tradition, Andrew was crucified on an X-shaped cross. The crossed bars of the Scottish flag are derived from this belief. St. Andrew is the patron saint of Scotland and Russia. Feast day: Nov. 30.

Andrew II, King of Hungary

Andrew II, b. 1176?, d. Sept. 21, 1235, was one of the better-known, although not highly regarded, kings of Hungary (1205–35). He was the son of Bela III (r. 1173–96) and brother of Imre (r. 1196–1204), whose son Ladislas III Andrew deposed (1205). Andrew's reign was characterized by a series of foreign misadventures (including a costly crusade to the Holy Land in 1217) and by a growing conflict between the king and the powerful magnates, as well as by a struggle between the latter and the emerging lower nobility. To protect their social and economic position, the lower nobility forced the king to issue a Golden Bull (1222)—the Hungarian Magna Carta—which became the foundation stone of Hungarian constitutionalism.

S. B. VARDY

Andrewes, Lancelot

Lancelot Andrewes, b. 1555, d. Sept. 26, 1626, was the leading theologian of the High Church party in the Church of England during the 17th century. Educated at Cambridge, he had a command of biblical languages and early church history. He was bishop successively of Chichester, Ely, and Winchester.

As a result of his participation in the Hampton Court Conference of 1604, convened to consider English church reforms requested by the Puritans, Andrewes helped prepare the King

James Version of the Bible. His sermons were always finely done; after his death they were edited by William Laud. Andrewes's *Private Devotions* (1648) became known as a spiritual classic. He was firmly in the Anglican tradition of the church, midway between Catholicism and Puritanism. This position led him into controversy with Robert BELLARMINE during Andrewes's defense of the Stuart Oath of Allegiance, which Bellarmine had attacked.   FREDERICK A. NORWOOD

Bibliography: Welsby, Paul A., *Lancelot Andrewes, 1555–1626* (1958).

Andrews, Charles McLean

Charles McLean Andrews, b. Wethersfield, Conn., Feb. 22, 1863, d. Sept. 9, 1943, Farnam professor of American history (1910–31) at Yale University, was a leader of the school of historians who maintained that the American colonies should be studied not in isolation but as dependent components of the British Empire. He introduced his "imperial" viewpoint in *The Colonial Period* (1912). Andrews took the same approach in his *Colonial Background to the American Revolution* (1924). He won a 1935 Pulitzer Prize for the first volume of his 4-volume *Colonial Period of American History* (1934–38), largely a study of political institutions.

Bibliography: Eisenstadt, A. S., *Charles McLean Andrews* (1956).

Andrews, Julie

Julie Andrews is the stage name of Julia Elizabeth Wells, b. Walton-on-Thames, England, Oct. 1, 1935, an actress and singer who created the Broadway roles of Eliza Doolittle in *My Fair Lady* (1956) and Guinevere in *Camelot* (1960). She is best remembered for her performances in the films *Mary Poppins* (1964), for which she won an Academy Award, and *The Sound of Music* (1965). Among the successful attempts to change her saccharine image are the Hollywood farce *S.O.B.* (1981) and *Victor/Victoria* (1982), in which she plays a woman masquerading as a homosexual female impersonator. Both films were directed by her husband, Blake Edwards.

Andrews, Roy Chapman

Roy Chapman Andrews, b. Beloit, Wis., Jan 26, 1884, d. Mar. 11, 1960, was an American explorer and naturalist who made many important contributions to paleontology and zoology. Andrews joined the staff of the American Museum of Natural History in 1906 and later, from 1935 to 1941, served as its director. Traveling on whaling expeditions to Alaska and the waters off Korea, he helped build the museum's collection of aquatic mammals into one of the world's foremost. From 1917 to 1930 Andrews led expeditions to Central Asia, where he discovered the first dinosaur eggs known to science; found the first traces of dinosaurs north of the Himalayas; made important finds about now-extinct mammals, including the largest known land mammal, *Baluchitherium*; and found evidence of early Stone Age humans in Central Asia. A prolific author, he detailed the scientific reports of his Asian travels in the multivolume *Natural History of Central Asia*. He also wrote *On the Trail of Ancient Man* (1926), *The New Conquest of Central Asia* (1932), *Heart of Asia* (1951), and an autobiography, *Under a Lucky Star* (1943).

Bibliography: Archer, Jules, *From Whales to Dinosaurs: The Story of Roy Chapman Andrews* (1976); Green, Fitzhugh, *Roy Chapman Andrews, Dragon Hunter* (1930).

Andrews, Thomas

The Irish chemist and physicist Thomas Andrews, b. Dec. 19, 1813, d. Nov. 26, 1885, studied the liquefaction of gases and established the concepts of critical temperature and critical pressure. He was vice-president of Queens College, Belfast, from 1845 and served as professor of chemistry from 1849 until his retirement in 1879.   RALPH GABLE

Andreyev, Leonid Nikolayevich [ahn-dray'-yef, lee-uh-neet' nik-uh-ly'-uh-vich]

The Russian writer Leonid Andreyev, b. June 18 (N.S.), 1871, d. Sept. 12, 1919, became famous for his short stories and

novels, many of which dealt in an exaggerated fashion with sex, crime, and death. He consciously imitated Leo Tolstoi, especially Tolstoi's moralistic tales, and was also influenced by Fyodor Dostoyevsky and Arthur Schopenhauer. Andreyev is best remembered for his stories *The Red Laughter* (1904), *King Hunger* (1908), and *The Seven That Were Hanged* (1908) and for his plays *Life of a Man* (1906) and the more important *He Who Gets Slapped* (1916). These allegorical and satirical dramas are now being regarded with renewed interest. An agnostic and pessimist, Andreyev saw death and sex as the only realities of life and denounced everything else as idealistic illusions. His nihilistic attitude was taken by many as the best expression of the mood of intellectuals after Russia's defeat in the Russo-Japanese War of 1905 and the failure of the revolution that followed. His close friendship with Maksim Gorky ended when Andreyev refused to accept the Bolshevik Revolution. In 1919 he appealed to the Western powers to intervene in the Russian Civil War. He immigrated to Finland, where he died.   LASZLO M. TIKOS

Bibliography: Newcombe, Josephine, *Leonid Andreyev* (1973).

Andrić, Ivo [ahn'-drich, ee'-voh]

Ivo Andrić, b. Oct. 10, 1892, d. Mar. 13, 1975, was a Yugoslavian writer who won the 1961 Nobel Prize for literature. In his novels, short stories, poems, and essays he portrayed the various nationalities, religions, and creeds of his native Bosnia. He often used local color while dealing with universal concerns and themes. His major novel, *The Bridge on the Drina* (1945; Eng. trans., 1959), is set at the crossroads of the East and the West, symbolically connected by a stone bridge; in it he depicts the centuries-old struggle of his people against various invaders. *Bosnian Story* (1945; Eng. trans., 1959) concerns the Turkish occupation, and *The Devil's Yard* (1954; Eng. trans., 1962) extols the victory of human dignity over the lust for power. Andrić's style is characterized by a lyrical realism and a fine psychological insight.   VASA D. MIHAILOVICH

Androcles [an'-droh-kleez]

Androcles was a 1st-century AD Roman slave who, according to a story by Aulus Gellius, once helped a lion by removing a thorn from its paw. Later, when he was thrown to the wild beasts in the arena, the lion recognized him and refused to harm him. The story was the subject of George Bernard Shaw's play *Androcles and the Lion* (publ. 1916).

androgen: see SEX HORMONES; STEROID.

Andromache [an-drahm'-uh-kee]

In Greek legend, Andromache was the wife of HECTOR, the Trojan hero killed during the Trojan War. When Andromache learned that Hector was dead, she tried to throw herself down from the city walls in grief. She was taken captive, however, and made the concubine of NEOPTOLEMUS, one of the victorious Greek warriors. Andromache is one of the great tragic figures of literature and art. She is the subject of plays by Euripides and Jean Racine; the farewell scene between Andromache and Hector in the Iliad has been frequently depicted in paintings.

Andromeda (astronomy) [an-drahm'-uh-duh]

Andromeda, named for a princess in Greek mythology, is a constellation most prominent during autumn in the Northern Hemisphere. Situated between the constellations Cassiopeia and Pegasus, Andromeda's brightest star, Alpheratz, forms one corner of the square of Pegasus. Andromeda contains the ANDROMEDA GALAXY, M 31, located more than 2.2 million light years from the Earth, and the planetary nebula NGC 7662, located within our galaxy about 5,000 light years distant.

Bibliography: Burnham, Robert, *Burnham's Celestial Handbook*, 3 vols., rev. ed. (1980); Menzel, Donald, *A Field Guide to the Stars and Planets* (1975).

Andromeda (mythology) [an-drahm'-uh-duh]

In Greek mythology, Andromeda was an Ethiopian princess, daughter of King Cepheus and Queen Cassiopeia. When Cassiopeia boasted that Andromeda was more beautiful than the sea-goddesses called Nereids, POSEIDON, god of the sea and father of the Nereids, sent a sea monster to ravage Ethiopia. Only the sacrifice of Andromeda could persuade Poseidon to call off the monster, so Andromeda was chained naked to a sea cliff. The hero PERSEUS saw her plight, rescued her, and killed the monster. Thereupon, Poseidon turned the dead monster into the sea's first coral. Perseus married Andromeda, and they eventually became king and queen of the Greek city of Tiryns.   ROBERT E. WOLVERTON

Andromeda galaxy

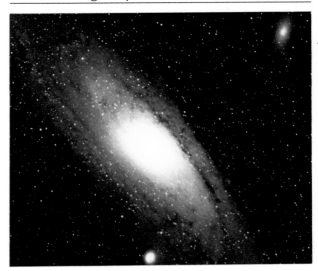

The Andromeda spiral galaxy and its dwarf elliptical companions M 32 (bottom) and NGC 205 (upper right) are members of our local group of galaxies. The points of light are all stars in our Milky Way system.

The Andromeda galaxy is the nearest spiral galaxy beyond the Milky Way, but, at a distance of 2.2 million light years, it is also the most distant celestial object visible to the naked eye. It is listed in astronomical catalogs as M 31 or NGC 224. The Andromeda galaxy has an estimated mass of 300 billion solar masses and a diameter of 130,000 light years, about 1.3 times that of our galaxy. Like our galaxy, it has globular CLUSTERS, open clusters, and NEBULAE of gas and dust. It is sometimes erroneously referred to as the Andromeda Nebula because it was believed to be a nebula when first discovered.

Bibliography: Abell, George, *Drama of the Universe* (1978).

Andropov, Yuri V. [an-draw'-pawf]

Yuri Vladimirovich Andropov, b. June 15 (N.S.), 1914, d. Feb. 9, 1984, succeeded Leonid Brezhnev as general secretary of the Soviet Communist party and thus leader of the USSR in November 1982. A native of the Stavropol region of the northern Caucasus, where his father was employed as a railroad worker, Andropov graduated from a water transport technical institute and began service on the Volga River system in 1936. Active in the Communist Youth League (Komsomol), he rose in 1938 to be first secretary of the Yaroslavl region group and soon became a full-time party activist.

Andropov distinguished himself organizing guerrilla activity against the Germans during World War II. Intelligent and hardworking, he advanced rapidly. In 1947 he became second secretary of the regional party committee in the Karelo-Finnish SSR, and in 1951 he was transferred to the central committee apparatus in Moscow. Appointed ambassador to Hungary

As leader of the Soviet Communist party and president of the USSR, ex-KGB chief Yuri Andropov began an effort to improve efficiency and productivity in the Soviet system during the early 1980s.

in 1953, he impressed his superiors with his handling of the anti-Soviet Hungarian Revolution of 1956 and was brought back to Moscow to help coordinate diplomatic affairs for the central committee. He became a member of that important body in 1961 and a secretary in late 1962.

In May 1967, Andropov was named head of the KGB, the political police and intelligence agency. Tough, shrewd, and a skillful administrator, he made serious efforts to understand the nature of Soviet dissidence, even while overseeing its repression. In 1973 he became a full member of the politburo, the party's chief executive organ.

Assuming power on the death of Brezhnev, Andropov made it his principal task to revitalize the Soviet economy. Surprise visits to factories and tough-minded speeches heralded a campaign against inefficiency and waste. These efforts were soon slowed, however, by his own bad health and the USSR's intractable economic problems. In foreign affairs, he generally continued the policies of his predecessor. In June 1983, Andropov became president of the USSR.   WILLIAM G. ROSENBERG

Andros, Sir Edmund

Sir Edmund Andros, b. Dec. 6, 1637, d. Feb. 27, 1714, was a colonial governor in the expanding British empire in America. As deputy of the duke of York (later King James II), Andros accepted the final Dutch surrender of New York (1674) and became governor of the province. He had frequent disputes with the colonists and with neighboring colonies over his aggressive assertion of the duke's rights as proprietor and was recalled (1681) when charged with profiteering.

When James became king, he appointed (1686) Andros governor of the Dominion of New England, which consolidated the New England colonies and, subsequently, New York and New Jersey into one viceroyalty. Andros and his council were given enormous powers, and his unpopular measures convinced the New England Puritans that his regime subverted their institutions and way of life. When Boston learned of the overthrow of James in England (the GLORIOUS REVOLUTION), it rebelled in April 1689. The Dominion government collapsed, and Andros was sent back to England.

Andros later served as governor of Virginia, where his administration (1692–97) was regarded as more successful and popular. His last governorship was of his native island of Guernsey (1704–06). Andros was an able, efficient, but abrasive administrator.   OSCAR ZEICHNER

Bibliography: Barnes, V. F., *Dominion of New England* (1923); Lovejoy, D. S., *The Glorious Revolution in America* (1972).

anemia [uh-nee'-mee-uh]

Anemia is the loss of the oxygen-carrying capacity of the blood resulting from a deficiency in quantity or quality of red blood cells or the hemoglobin in the blood. Symptoms of anemia include pale skin, weakness, fatigue, and dizziness. Severe anemia may result in difficulty in breathing and heart abnormalities.

The most common type of anemia is iron deficiency anemia, which most often results from chronic blood loss and also from lack of iron in the diet, impaired absorption of iron from the intestine, or increased need for iron, as in pregnancy. Iron is an essential component of the hemoglobin, which carries oxygen to the tissues in chemical combination with its iron atoms. Pernicious anemia is a chronic inherited disease of middle-aged and older people in which the stomach fails to produce a factor needed for the absorption of vitamin B_{12}, which is essential for mature red blood cells. The disease can be treated by lifelong injections of the vitamin. Aplastic anemia is the result of the failure of bone marrow cells to manufacture mature red cells. It is usually caused by toxic chemicals (for example, benzene) or by radiation. Treatment includes preventing further exposure to the causative agent, eliminating any remaining toxic substance from the body, stimulating the proliferation of remaining bone-marrow cells, and preventing infection, while keeping the patient alive withblood transfusions. SICKLE-CELL ANEMIA, inherited as a recessive trait, is found mainly in blacks.

Bibliography: Galton, Lawrence, *The Disguised Disease: Anemia* (1975); Thompson, William, *Black's Medical Dictionary*, 31st ed. (1976); Whitby, Sir Lionel, *Disorders of the Blood* (1953).

anemometer   [an-uh-mah'-muh-tur]

The anemometer is an instrument designed to measure wind speed. The earliest wind-speed indicator was the pressure anemometer, in which a plate hung perpendicular to a wind vane, which measures wind direction; the stronger the wind, the larger the displacement of the plate. A modern version measures the displacement of a standing column of water in a FLOWMETER known as a Pitot tube. The rotation anemometer may consist of a windmill or propeller or, more often, of three semiconical cups rotating on a pivot attached to an electric generator. The hot-wire anemometer measures the amount of electric current required to keep a hot wire at a constant temperature as the wind blows past. The acoustic anemometer, which dates from about 1950, works on the principle that wind affects the speed of a sound signal.

Pressure anemometers are no longer widely used, with the exception of the Pitot tube. Rotation anemometers are standard in most weather stations, and the hot-wire and acoustic types are mainly used for research.   WILLEM VAN DER BIJL

anemone   [uh-nem'-uh-nee]

Anemone, or windflower, is any of the perennial flowering herbaceous plants belonging to the genus *Anemone* in the buttercup family. They produce cup-shaped yellowish, white, purple, violet, or red flowers that make attractive additions to perennial flower gardens. Among the most popular are the au-

The Japanese anemone, A. japonica, as well as other species of anemone, has large, colorful sepals instead of petals. Sepals in other plants are generally small, green leaves that surround the petals of a flower.

tumn-flowering Japanese anemone, *A. hupehensis*, and the spring-flowering, tuberous-rooted poppy anemone, *A. coronaria*, with its red, white, and blue range of color.

anesthetics   [an-es-thet'-iks]

An anesthetic is a substance or procedure that produces a state of insensibility to pain, usually administered for performance of SURGERY. Anesthesia, the state of being insensible to pain, may or may not be associated with loss of consciousness. Anesthesiology is the medical specialty concerning anesthesia and anesthetics. Anesthetics may be administered by anesthesiologists—physicians specializing in anesthesiology—or by anesthetists—certified registered nurses—working under the supervision of a physician.

HISTORY

Prior to the availability of anesthetics, surgery was infrequent. Operations were completed in minutes because of the pain and shock accompanying operation on unanesthetized body parts. For centuries physicians sought agents that would permit painless surgery. Alcohol and opium compounds were used. The Chinese used hashish, while the Incas used the coca extract, cocaine, on the skin. Direct pressure and cold on nerve trunks were occasionally used. Each of these was only partially effective. A dramatic breakthrough occurred in 1846 at the Massachusetts General Hospital in Boston, when William Morton, a dentist, administered diethyl ETHER to a patient, and Dr. John C. Warren painlessly removed a tumor from the patient's jaw. The news of this event spread rapidly, and within two years general anesthesia was widely used throughout the United States and Europe.

GENERAL ANESTHESIA

During general anesthesia, DRUGS primarily affecting the brain render the patient unconscious and insensible to pain and surgical stimulation. The patient awakens only when the administration of the drug is discontinued. A patient has no memory of events that occur during anesthesia. General anesthesia may produce side effects and complications but, carefully administered, is remarkably safe.

Inhalants. Some general anesthetics are inhaled by the patient. They are known as inhalational agents and can be either gases or volatile liquids. The anesthetic gases are mixed with oxygen in measured concentrations just before delivery to the patient. The anesthetic liquids are placed in vaporizers. Of all the known inhalational agents, only three—nitrous oxide, halothane, and enflurane—are in widespread use. Nitrous oxide, sometimes termed laughing gas, was discovered in 1799 by the British chemist Sir Humphrey Davy. In most patients it will not produce anesthesia when used alone, but it makes it possible for decreased amounts of other drugs to be used. The side effects are minimal and include asphyxia and diffusion anoxia (lack of oxygen). Halothane (Fluothane), introduced in 1956, is a more potent anesthetic than nitrous oxide and can be used alone for anesthesia. It is more likely than nitrous oxide to produce the side effects typical of general anesthesia. Halothane has been associated with liver toxicity (halothane hepatitis), which can be fatal. Enflurane (Ethrane), released for clinical use in 1972, is similar to halothane in its properties and side effects, although liver toxicity has not been established. With enflurane, however, increased electrical activity occurs in the brain at deep levels of anesthesia, and recordings of the electroencephalogram have revealed seizure activity in some patients. Isoflurane (Forane) has properties similar to those of halothane and enflurane.

Drugs. Some general anesthetics are administered intravenously. Thiopental (Pentothal), thiamylal (Surital), and methohexital (Brevital) are intravenous anesthetics belonging to the BARBITURATE group of drugs. They are characterized by rapid onset of anesthesia (30–90 seconds); the duration of action is short (5–10 minutes). Although consciousness is lost quickly, patients tend to respond to surgical stimulation unless high doses are used. The barbiturates are particularly useful in beginning an anesthetic. Anesthesia is then maintained with such agents as halothane or enflurane. Barbiturates used with nitrous oxide, narcotics, and muscle relaxants can often produce anesthesia sufficient for many types of surgery.

Diazepam (VALIUM), a TRANQUILIZER, can produce anesthesia when given intravenously. It has less effect on the heart and respiration than the barbiturates, and the dose of diazepam needed to produce loss of consciousness is variable. Ketamine, while not a general anesthetic, is an intravenous drug with many anesthetic properties and is useful for short procedures. A drawback is that 10 to 15 percent of adult patients have vivid, often unpleasant dreams during emergence.

Two other groups of drugs are important in modern anesthetic practice. The first is such narcotics as morphine, meperidine (DEMEROL), and fentanyl. These drugs are ANALGESICS (pain relievers), not anesthetics. Their analgesic properties, however, add to the effects of anesthetic agents. The second group of agents comprises such muscle relaxants as succinylcholine, d-tubocurarine, gallamine, and pancuronium. These agents interfere with the transmission of impulses from nerve to muscle and consequently relax the muscle.

Anesthetic Action. The exact mode of action of general anesthetics is difficult to explain because of the many effects of anesthetic drugs and the complexity of the central NERVOUS SYSTEM. Consequently, many theories of anesthetic action exist. The site of action is the brain, the basic unit of which is the neuron, or nerve cell. Proponents of neurophysiological theories hold that anesthetics work by decreasing transmission across the neural synapse, the gap between nerve cells. Others have formulated biochemical theories, which hypothesize that anesthetics decrease energy production within the nerve cell, thus decreasing the ability to produce nerve impulses. A recent combination of these two theories states that the decrease in energy production shifts metabolic pathways and allows an increase in the production of certain compounds, such as gamma-amino butyric acid, which decrease synaptic transmission. Several theories have been proposed to explain the effect of anesthetic molecules on the nerve-cell membrane. Anesthetic molecules dissolved in the cell membrane are believed to alter the arrangement of membrane lipids or proteins. This will disrupt the flow of ions across the membrane and interfere with nerve impulse conduction.

LOCAL ANESTHESIA
In contrast to general anesthesia, regional anesthesia affects only the part of the body on which surgery is to be performed. In general, the patient is awake and remembers the operating room, but no pain occurs during surgery. The anesthetic drugs used to produce regional anesthesia are called local anesthetics. Commonly used local anesthetics such as COCAINE, procaine, and tetracaine are metabolized in the blood, and their duration of action is therefore shorter than other local anesthetics, such as lidocaine, bupivacaine, and etidocaine, which are metabolized in the liver. Cocaine and lidocaine are absorbed through mucous membranes and can be used to anesthetize the inner surface of the mouth, pharynx, nose, or other mucous membranes.

Four major types of local anesthesia are in use. In infiltration anesthesia, the anesthetic is injected into the area upon which surgery is to be performed. In nerve-block anesthesia, the local anesthetic is injected near specific nerves that innervate the area of operation. In general, the local anesthetic is applied at some distance from the actual site of operation. In spinal anesthesia, a small needle is introduced into the subarachnoid space of the vertebral canal, and a small amount of local anesthetic is injected. The local anesthetic spreads into the cerebrospinal fluid and anesthetizes the nerve roots coming out of the spinal cord. This technique can be used for surgery on the entire lower half of the body. Epidural and caudal anesthesia involve depositing anesthetic into the epidural space of the vertebral canal. These techniques are popular for labor and delivery.

Complications can occur with the use of local anesthetics. By blocking normal regulation of blood vessels, spinal and epidural anesthesia can decrease the blood pressure. High blood levels of local anesthetic, obtained by inadvertent intravenous injection or excessive drug dosage, produce distinct effects on the brain. At first, lightheadedness and dizziness occur, and this can be followed by disorientation or drowsiness. With still higher blood levels, seizures can occur.

HYPNOTISM
Anesthesia can also be produced by some nonchemical means. HYPNOSIS is used, but preoperative training of the patient is required, and only a low percentage of patients achieve a trance profound enough for major surgery. Hypnosis, however, can be useful for minor procedures and in the preoperative preparation of patients for surgery.

ACUPUNCTURE
ACUPUNCTURE is a traditional Chinese medical art that can be used to produce anesthesia. Like hypnosis, its success as the sole anesthetic agent is unpredictable, and it requires careful patient selection and preparation. Electric current administered through electrodes on the head can also produce anesthesia. This procedure is still experimental.

Modern anesthetic techniques permit complex surgical procedures to be performed without pain and with minimal complications. Postanesthetic complications can still occur, however.   DAVID S. SMITH AND HARRY WOLLMAN

Bibliography: Dripps, Robert D., Eckenhoff, J. E., and Vandam, L. D., *Introduction to Anesthesia* (1977); Goodman, Louis S., and Gilman, Alfred, *The Pharmacological Basis of Therapeutics* (1975); Keys, Thomas E., *The History of Surgical Anesthesia* (1945); Wilie, W. D., and Churchill-Davidson, H. C., eds., *A Practice of Anesthesia* (1972).

aneurysm [an'-yur-izm]

An aneurysm is a widening or dilation of a blood vessel caused by thinning of the vessel wall. A potentially lethal complication is the rupture of the vessel with resultant massive hemorrhage. Aneurysms usually occur in arteries but may also be seen in the heart after local damage, or in veins.

Arterial aneurysms are more common than venous, occurring most often in elderly, diabetic, or hypertensive persons. They may be caused by congenital thinning of the muscular portions of the artery; during atherosclerotic degeneration of the aorta or of the carotid or basilar arteries; by trauma to a vessel wall; by infectious injury; or by degeneration from other causes. The likelihood of rupture is increased by high blood pressure. Defects in arteries of the eye may result in miliary (small, multiple) aneurysms of the retina.

Myocardial infarction (death of heart cells) provokes a reaction by white blood cells that secrete digestive enzymes in an effort to clean up dead tissue. This begins about three days after the damage and continues for several weeks. Scar tissue forms a patch for the weak tissue but does not begin to be significantly protective until the 10th to 14th day. Hence, spontaneous rupture of a ventricular aneurysm tends to occur between the 5th and 10th days of a person's recovery.

Treatment of a person with a ruptured aneurysm may include reduction of blood pressure, bed rest for two weeks, replacement of the weakened vessel by a graft or encasement in plastic, or mechanically stopping blood flow to or through the aneurysm.   ALDEN W. DUDLEY

Bibliography: Friedberg, C. K., *Diseases of the Heart*, 3d ed. (1966).

Anfinsen, Christian Boehmer [an'-fin-sen]

The American biochemist Christian Boehmer Anfinsen, b. Monessen, Pa., Mar. 26, 1916, shared the 1972 Nobel Prize for chemistry with Stanford MOORE and William H. STEIN for fundamental contributions to the chemistry of enzymes. Anfinsen was cited for his research into the way in which the enzyme ribonuclease is produced in cells.

Angara River [an-gar'-uh]

The Angara River in Siberia flows generally northwest from Lake BAIKAL to join the Yenisei River at Strelka. Most of its 1,779 km (1,105 mi) are navigable. Irkutsk is a major port.

angel

An angel (Greek: *angelos*, "messenger") is a celestial being believed to function as a messenger or agent of God in CHRIS-

TIANITY, ISLAM, JUDAISM, and ZOROASTRIANISM. In the Near Eastern antecedents to Judaism, angels were often understood to be gods or lesser divinities. Their existence was taken for granted by the biblical authors. The use of the word *angel* may have been a way of describing what was believed to be an appearance of God himself in human form.

In the Old Testament, angels are called "messengers," "men," "powers," "princes," "sons of God," and the "heavenly host." They either have no body or one that is only apparent. They come as God's messengers to aid or punish, are assigned to individual persons or nations, and often have a name (Michael, Gabriel, Raphael, Uriel). New Testament statements about angels reflect Jewish views of these beings. Angels, for example, announced Christ's birth (Luke 2) and resurrection (Matt. 28).

Ancient and medieval peoples widely accepted the influence of good spirits, or angels, and evil spirits, or fallen angels (see DEMON; SATAN). During the Middle Ages, theologians developed a hierarchy of angels. They were classified in the following nine ranks (beginning with the lowest): angels, archangels, principalities, powers, virtues, dominations, thrones, cherubim, and seraphim. Angels are a popular subject in folklore, literature, and art.   ANTHONY J. SALDARINI

Bibliography: Davidson, Gustav, *A Dictionary of Angels* (1967); Field, M. J., *Angels and Ministers of Grace* (1972); Heidt, W. G., *Angelology of the Old Testament* (1949); Regamey, Raymond, *What Is an Angel?*, trans. by Mark Pontifex (1960).

angel dust

Angel dust is the common name for a dangerous drug whose illicit use has been spreading rapidly among teenagers since 1975. Known also as PCP (phencyclidine hydrochloride), the substance was developed in the 1950s as a potential anesthetic for human use, but tests showed that it caused hallucinations, convulsions, and violent behavior. Controlled dosages, however, have been found useful in limited circumstances to tranquilize or stupefy animals. The National Institute of Drug Abuse issued warnings that when angel dust is smoked or ingested in various ways by humans it has unpre-

dictable psychic effects. Psychoses, deaths, and even murders have been reported.

Angel Falls

Angel Falls (Spanish: Salto Angel) is the highest waterfall in the world. It is located within Canaima National Park, in Bolívar state in southeastern Venezuela, about 258 km (160 mi) southeast of Ciudad Bolívar, where the Río Churún falls from the flat mountain plateau of Auyán-Tepuí in the Guiana Highlands. The greatest uninterrupted drop is 800 m (2,640 ft). James Angel, a U.S. explorer and aviator, discovered the falls in 1935.

angelfish

The angelfish, in the family Chaetodontidae, are among the showiest denizens of the sea. Most species exhibit brilliant colors, some with irregular patterns that serve as camouflage. Often the young are differently colored than the adults. At night when these diurnal fish enter a state of torpor, their colors may change. The angelfish inhabit warm seas and are abundant in coral reefs. They usually swim singly or in pairs. The five Atlantic species are the blue angel, *Holacanthus isabelita*; the rock beauty, *H. tricolor*; the queen, *H. ciliaris*; the gray, *Pomacanthus arcuatus*; and the French, *P. paru.*

Angelfish have deep, thinly compressed bodies and a strong, backwardly directed spine on the corner of each preopercle, the lower part of the cheekbone. The mouth is small and protractile with fine bristlelike teeth in narrow bands in the jaws. They feed primarily on sponges, tunicates, zoantherians, and algae. Some species act as cleaners, picking external parasites and necrotic tissue from the surface of other fish. Most individuals are less than 43 cm (17 in) long. Fish of the genus *Pterophyllum*, family Cichlidae, also called angelfish, are popular in home aquariums.   C. P. IDYLL

Bibliography: Migdalski, Edward C., and Fichter, George S., *Fresh and Salt Water Fishes of the World* (1976).

Angelfish are among the most colorful of all fish. Their exotic coloration facilitates territoriality by warning off intruders. (Clockwise, starting at upper left): emperor angelfish, Pomacanthus imperator; French angelfish, P. paru; blue-faced angelfish, Euxiphipops xanthometapon; blue angelfish, P. semicirculatus; and majestic angelfish, E. navarachus.

Lamentation over the Dead Christ *is one of a series of frescoes executed about 1437–45 by Fra Angelico and his assistants for the convent of San Marco in Florence. Highly spiritual in expression, the work reflects Angelico's purity of form and spatial clarity.*

angelica tree

The angelica tree, *Aralia spinosa*, also commonly known as devil's-walking-stick, prickly ash, or Hercules'-club, is a shrubby plant belonging to the aralia, or GINSENG, family, Araliaceae. The angelica tree sometimes grows to a height of 13.7 m (45 ft). The trunk and twigs are spiny, and the prickly leaf stalks bear compound leaves. An ornamental that produces large clusters of small, white flowers, it grows from western New York to Iowa and south to the Gulf Coast. The fruit was once used as a hair dye; both bark and roots may cause a rash when handled.

The plant species known simply as angelica, genus *Angelica,* belong to the carrot family, Umbelliferae, and are native to the Northern Hemisphere and New Zealand.

ROBERT C. ROMAN

Angelico, Fra

Fra Angelico was one of the most prolific and beloved painters of the Italian Renaissance. In a letter written in 1438, DOMENICO VENEZIANO called Fra Angelico and Fra Filippo LIPPI the two most important Italian painters of the day. Each continued, in parallel directions, the heritage of MASACCIO, generally considered the father of Florentine Renaissance painting. Together with Veneziano, ANDREA DEL CASTAGNO, PIERO DELLA FRANCESCA, and Paolo UCCELLO, they developed a second Florentine painting style that flourished from the 1430s through the 1450s.

It has been determined recently that Fra Angelico was born about 1400 (not 1387, as Giorgio VASARI records) and given the name Guido di Pietro. Documents prove that he received payment as a layman for an altarpiece in 1418. In June 1423 he was mentioned as Fra Giovanni da Fiesole, the name by which he was known to his contemporaries. His nickname *Angelico* first appeared in 1469, 14 years after his death, and he is also known in Italian as *Beato* ("Blessed One").

The chronology of his early life is controversial; yet he seems to have been trained as an illuminator and, between 1418 and 1421, to have become a member of the Dominican order. Angelico became the artistic spokesman for the Dominicans, as Masaccio was for the Carmelites, and always remained a professional artist in touch with contemporary advancements in Florentine painting.

Although a large number of paintings are associated with his early period, one of the finest, and one that has had great influence, is the Cortona *Annunciation* panel (1432–38; Diocesan Museum). The monumental figures on the *Linaiuoli Triptych* (Museum of San Marco, Florence), commissioned in 1433 for the Linen Drapers Guild, reflect Angelico's awareness of contemporary sculpture by DONATELLO and Lorenzo GHIBERTI for Or San Michele, the Florentine grain market.

In 1436, Cosimo de' Medici and Pope Eugene IV requisitioned the decaying convent of San Marco and invited the Dominicans to build and decorate a new monastery. In collaboration with the architect MICHELOZZO, Angelico and his assistants frescoed various scenes from the life of Christ in the 44 monks' dormitory cells and connecting corridors. Each of these clearly-drawn frescoes, such as the San Marco *Annunciation,* embellishes the contemplative, religious setting. Angelico's San Marco altarpiece, *Madonna and Saints in a Sacred Conversation* (1438–39; Museum of San Marco)—he created the form called *Sacra Conversazione*—although now overcleaned, is a masterpiece remarkable for its rendering of the human figure and its use of natural light and Leon Battista ALBERTI's systematic perspective.

About 1445, Angelico was called to Rome, where he continued to paint. All the buildings he worked on there have been destroyed, except for the private chapel of Pope Nicholas V in the Vatican, which contains Angelico's frescoes of scenes from the lives of St. Stephen and St. Lawrence.

When Angelico died in Rome on Feb. 18, 1455, he was considered the most influential of all contemporary Florentine painters. Although his art was sentimentalized by the 19th-century NAZARENES and PRE-RAPHAELITES, it has always been admired, imitated, and widely reproduced.   ALAN P. DARR

Bibliography: Argan, Giulio Carlo, *Fra Angelico,* trans. by James Emmons (1955); Pope-Hennessy, J. W., *Fra Angelico,* 2d ed. (1974).

See also: ITALIAN ART AND ARCHITECTURE; RENAISSANCE ART AND ARCHITECTURE.

Angell   (family)

James Burrill Angell, b. Jan. 7, 1829, d. Apr. 1, 1916, and James Rowland Angell, b. May 8, 1869, d. Mar. 4, 1949, father and son, were innovative American university presidents. **James Burrill Angell** was a professor of modern languages and literature at Brown University from 1853 to 1860. He was president of the University of Vermont from 1866 to 1871 and president of the University of Michigan for the next 38 years. At Michigan he introduced the nation's first medical school requirements and the first chair in the art and science of teaching. Angell edited the *Providence Journal* during the Civil War, and he also interrupted his academic career to serve as U.S. minister to China (1880–81) and to Turkey (1897–98).

James Rowland Angell taught psychology at the University of Chicago for 25 years and was a leader of the functionalist school of psychology, which seeks to study the mind as it functions to fit the organism to its environment. From 1921 to 1937 he was president of Yale University, where he established new departments and directed new construction.

Bibliography: Angell, James Burrill, *Reminiscences and Selected Addresses* (1912; repr. 1971).

Angelou, Maya   [an'-juh-loo, mah'-yah]

Maya Angelou, b. Apr. 4, 1928, is an American writer, stage performer, and composer. Her widely acclaimed autobiography, *I Know Why the Caged Bird Sings* (1970), is a moving and often humorous account of her childhood in segregated Arkansas. In addition to her autobiographical sequels *Gather Together in My Name* (1974) and *Singin' & Swingin' & Makin' Merry Like Christmas* (1976), she has written plays, books of poetry, and screenplays.

anger: see EMOTION.

Angers   [ahn-zhay']

Angers, the capital of Maine-et-Loire department in western France, is situated on the Maine River about 560 km (160 mi) southwest of Paris. The population is 137,437 (1975). The city is known for its black slate quarries. Other industries include electronics, textiles, and paper products. Tourists are attracted by the 12th-century Cathedral of Saint-Maurice and the Museum of Tapestry housed in the walled chateau, built 1230–40. The University of Angers dates from 1875. First a Gaulic settlement and then the Roman city of Juliomagus, Angers became the seat of the counts of Anjou in 870. It was taken by the Huguenots in 1585.

Angevins   (dynasties)   [an'-juh-vinz]

The two Angevin dynasties in medieval Europe originated from the French countship of ANJOU. In 1131, Fulk V, count of Anjou, became king of the Latin Kingdom of Jerusalem, which his descendants ruled until 1186. Fulk's eldest son, Geoffrey Plantagenet, married (1128) MATILDA, queen of England, and their son HENRY II became (1154) the first Angevin, or Plantagenet, king of England. This house ruled England until Richard II was overthrown (1399) by Henry IV of Lancaster.

A second Angevin dynasty came into being after King Louis IX of France gave (1246) Anjou to his brother, who became (1266) CHARLES I of Naples. The latter's son, CHARLES II of Naples, had seven children. They, with their descendants, created a tangled dynastic situation for Naples, involving the

royal houses of both France and Aragon. One grandson became (1308) king of Hungary as CHARLES I, but the Angevin line in eastern Europe ended on the death (1382) of his son, LOUIS I, king of Hungary and Poland.

See also: JERUSALEM, LATIN KINGDOM OF; NAPLES, KINGDOM OF.

angina: see HEART DISEASE.

angiosperm   [an'-jee-oh-spurm]

Angiosperms are the most highly evolved plants, constituting diverse flowering species, from garden-variety flowers and such grains as corn and wheat to flowering trees, shrubs, and vines. They inhabit almost all regions except the open ocean.

Angiosperms constitute the class Angiospermae in the plant phylum TRACHEOPHYTA (vascular plants). The seeds of these plants are developed and retained within an ovary, which, after seed formation, expands into a fruit. The two distinct subclasses of Angiospermae are Dictyledonae (dicots) and Monocotyledonae (monocots). Dicots are more abundant and include most of the flowering trees and shrubs (apple, peach, cherry, elm, rubber, oak, and others), as well as strawberry, bean, cabbage, cotton, cacao, coffee, goldenrod, tomato, and hundreds more. Monocots include, for example, wheat, corn, rice, bamboo, palms, lilies, orchids, sugarcane, and grasses.

The flower, and the fruit that develops from it, most readily distinguish angiosperms from other vascular plants. Four types of floral whorls exist: *calyx,* consisting of sepals; *corolla,* the petals; *androecium,* composed of stamens; and *gynoecium,* or pistil, consisting of stigma, style, and ovary. The showy petals or sepals and sweet-scented nectaries are not the most important floral components. Of most biological importance to the plant are the stamens and pistil. One or both of these structures constitute a flower. Each floral whorl has evolved from leaves, which are the most recognizable of the sepals.

Pollination occurs by introduction of the male gametophyte—pollen from anthers of stamens—to the stigma of the pistil by wind, water currents, animal bodies, or the mechanics of the flower itself. If chemically compatible, the male gametophyte germinates and grows a pollen tube down the style, through the ovary to the ovule, and into the embryo sac (female gametophyte), where it releases its two sperms to fuse with two endosperm nuclei and the egg nucleus. Following these fusions (see FERTILIZATION), one nuclear pair becomes the zygote, and the trinuclear association becomes endosperm. Various developments follow pollination and fertilization: the zygote becomes the embryonic plant; endosperm becomes stored food for the embryo; the ovule, containing endosperm and embryo, becomes the seed, and its integuments become seed coat; and the ovary, stimulated by the hormonal effects of the germinated male gametophyte, matures into the fruit.

Fruits take many different forms and textures. Some are fleshy, like the berry of tomato and orange; some are spiny (burdock); others have stony outer coverings (nuts such as the acorn, and drupes); and still others are aggregates of achenes (strawberries) and multiple fruits (pineapples). In some angiosperms the form of the fruit is the typical characteristic of an entire taxonomic plant family—such as the winged seed (schizocarp) of maples, the bean of the legume family, and the grain (caryopsis) of grasses.   CARL D. FINSTAD

Bibliography: Eames, A. J., *Morphology of the Angiosperms* (1961); Hutchinson, J., *The Families of Flowering Plants* (1973); Porter, T. L., *Taxonomy of Flowering Plants,* 2d ed. (1967).

See also: FLOWER; FRUIT, CLASSIFICATION OF; GYMNOSPERM; PLANT.

Angkor   [ang'-kor]

Angkor, north of Tonlé Sap in northwest Cambodia, was the great capital city of the KHMER empire from the city's founding in about AD 880 until about 1225. Lost in the jungle for centuries, it was discovered by French missionaries in the 1860s. Its immense temple complexes, which are larger in scale than the Egyptian pyramids, are ranked among the masterpieces of world architecture.

Temple City. Angkor was both a sacred temple city and the center of a vast irrigation system. Its Hindu temple architecture, inspired perhaps by the monuments at BOROBUDUR, was built by successive kings and their families on an increasingly vast scale. Standing amid a grid of reservoirs and canals, the temples symbolized the royal function of metaphysical mediation between the divine source of life-giving water and the human population.

The early temples were built of brick; the later, beginning with the Ta Keo (c.1020), of stone. All these so-called temple mountains were elaborately ornamented and filled with stonecut images. The central icon represented the monarch in the guise of his patron deity. The two earliest surviving structures, built during the reign of Yasovarman I (889–900), are the Bakong (881) and the Bakheng (893), which had 108 tower-shrines around its central sanctuary. The Pre Rup (961) was the first temple intended as a dwelling for the deified spirit of a dead king.

Angkor Wat. The greatest temple designed for this purpose is the huge Angkor Wat ("Angkor Temple") of the early 12th century. Built under Suryavarman II (r. 1113–50), the compound at Angkor Wat covers an area of 1,500 by 1,300 m (4,920 by 4,265 ft) and is surrounded by a vast moat 180 m (590 ft) wide. Along the causeway leading to the enormous entrance gate are balustrades shaped as giant serpents, emblems of cosmic fertility.

The temple proper consists of a towering complex of terraces and cloisters arranged in a series of three diminishing stories and surmounted by five towers, in which were contained the principal icons. The roofed and unroofed enclosures are superbly articulated with bands of finely carved foliage. Rows of shrines line the galleries, the walls of which are covered with elaborate carved reliefs that illustrate Hindu mythology, principally scenes relating to the god VISHNU, to whom the temple was dedicated.

Angkor Thom. Following the sack of Angkor by the Chams in 1177, Angkor Wat was abandoned. In the early 13th century Jayavarman VII (1181-c.1281) established a new capital and sacred precinct, Angkor Thom ("Great Angkor"). The four gateways into the city bear huge masks of its new patron, the Buddhist deity Lokesvara, Lord of the Universe. Avenues leading to the central temple, Bayon, were lined by rows of over 50 colossal towers, some 45 m (150 ft) high, decorated with multiple heads generally thought to represent the king. After the destruction of Angkor by Thai forces in 1431, the Khmer capital was moved to Phnom Penh, and the site fell into ruin.

PHILIP RAWSON

Bibliography: Audric, John, *Angkor and the Khmer Empire* (1972); Giteau, Madeleine, *Khmer Sculpture and the Angkor Civilization* (1965); Groslier, Bernard, and Arthaud, Jacques, *The Arts and Civilization of Angkor*, rev. ed. (1966).

See also: SOUTHEAST ASIAN ART AND ARCHITECTURE.

angle

A plane angle is the measure of the amount of rotation when a line segment rotates in a plane about a fixed point. By convention, a counterclockwise rotation is positive, and a clockwise rotation is negative. The Babylonians divided a complete rotation using units of 60 (a sexagesimal system) in the following manner:

1 revolution = 360 degrees (360°)
1 degree = 60 minutes (60′)
1 minute = 60 seconds (60″)

An angle equal to the angle between the horizontal (horizon) and vertical (upright) directions is equal to 90° and is called a right angle. In advanced mathematics the usual unit is the radian (1 revolution = 2π radians).

A solid angle is generated by an infinite set of line segments having a common vertex and passing through a simple closed curve. In the accompanying diagram, the solid angle subtended at P by the surface S is measured by the area U, which is the portion of the spherical surface with center P,

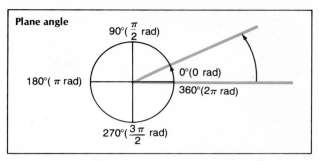

Plane angle

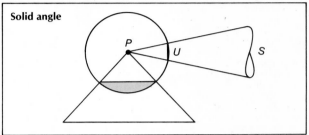

Solid angle

and radius 1, lying within the solid angle. The unit solid angle is the steradian, the largest solid angle being 4 π steradians. If the steradian is defined by the solid angle at the vertex of a right circular cone, opposite generating lines of the cone will make an angle of approximately 65° 32′.

ALARIC MILLINGTON

anglerfish

Anglerfish is the common name for more than 200 species of marine fish families Lophiidae (anglerfish), Antennariidae (frogfish), and Ogcocephalidae (batfish) in the order Lophiiformes. Anglerfish are named for their method of fishing for prey, using a specialized spiny ray above the snout that serves as rod and lure. The ray is a modified portion of the dorsal fin and is tipped with a baitlike plug of flesh. The old name for anglerfish is Pediculati, or "small foot," which refers to the footlike pectoral fins. The frogfish are camouflaged for seabed life with a variety of bumps, knobs, and flaps of skin, so that the fish resemble surrounding seaweed. Anglerfish are found at all depths of tropical and temperate seas and are classified in two broad groups, anglerfish and deep-sea anglers.

The frogfish has the habit of lying among rocks or seaweed or moving slowly across the bottom. When lying motionless on the bottom, the angler dangles and wiggles its lure until prey is attracted. When the lure is touched, the enormous mouth gapes, creating a vacuum that sucks the prey within range of its back-pointing teeth; these stoke the food into the belly.

The goosefish, or fishing frog, *Lophius piscatorius*, is a bizarre, short-bodied fish with a large flattened head, an enormous mouth, dorsally situated jaws, and eyes on the top of its head. Its large mouth and expandable stomach allow it to swallow fish as big as itself.

The goosefish is common in cold, shallow waters of Europe and North America. It is often 1 m (3 ft) long and can be as long as 1.5 m (5 ft) and weigh up to 23 kg (51 lb). The transparent eggs are laid in masses of jelly 60–90 cm (24–35 in) broad and up to 10 m (33 ft) long.

Deep-sea anglers, family Ceratiidae, are small inhabitants of the middle depths of the ocean (500–2,000 m/1,640–6,560 ft). The females rarely grow larger than a man's fist; the males are much smaller. Most of them are jet black or dark brown. These anglers cruise slowly in the dark, cold waters, glowing with lighted lures in front of them. The light in the lure is supplied by luminous bacteria shining through skin that has lost its pigment. In some species the lure is complexly branched and filamented.

A particularly ugly species of anglerfish, L. piscatorius, or goosefish, is shown catching its meal. It lies in wait, camouflaged against the ocean floor, and attracts a fish by dangling a fleshy appendage that looks like a fishing bait and line. As the victim touches the lure, the anglerfish opens its huge jaws and gulps down its prey.

Shortly after hatching, the male seeks out a female anglerfish and clamps onto her body with his teeth. He retains this hold for the remainder of his life, his mouth becoming surrounded by the tissue of the female. His sustenance is supplied by his mate through vascular connections. The parasitic male is commonly one-tenth as long as the female.

C. P. IDYLL

Anglesey: see GWYNEDD.

anglesite   [ang'-gul-syt]

Anglesite, a lead SULFATE MINERAL (PbSO$_4$), is a minor ore of lead. It forms prismatic, tabular, or pyramidal crystals (ORTHORHOMBIC SYSTEM), as well as granular to compact masses that are white to grayish or yellowish and have an adamantine to vitreous luster. HARDNESS is 2½–3, STREAK white, and SPECIFIC GRAVITY 6.2–6.4. A common WEATHERING product of GALENA, anglesite is found with CERUSSITE and other secondary minerals in the oxidized zone of sulfide ORE DEPOSITS; galena crystals often have an earthy concentric coating of anglesite.

See also: SULFIDE MINERALS.

Anglican Communion

The Anglican Communion is a worldwide fellowship of independent churches derived from the Church of England. The communion has 40 provinces, located on every continent, with 393 dioceses, and approximately 47 million members. Although independent, the member churches acknowledge a common heritage including the BOOK OF COMMON PRAYER, the THIRTY-NINE ARTICLES, and the threefold ministry of BISHOPS, PRIESTS, and DEACONS. The bishops meet every ten years, at the invitation of the archbishop of Canterbury, in the Lambeth Conference. Cooperation between the member churches is facilitated by the Anglican Consultative Council, with its secretary general and with the archbishop of Canterbury as president. Regional councils link provinces within specific geographical regions.

The Anglican Communion is committed to the reunion of all Christian churches. In 1888 the Lambeth Conference adopted as its basis for reunion a Quadrilateral, by which it defined those things essential to any church: (1) "The Holy Scriptures of the Old and New Testaments, as 'containing all things necessary to salvation,' and as being the rule and ultimate standard of faith"; (2) "The Apostles' Creed, as the Bap-

tismal Symbol; and the Nicene Creed, as the sufficient statement of the Christian faith"; (3) "The two Sacraments ordained by Christ Himself—Baptism and the Supper of the Lord—ministered with unfailing use of Christ's words of Institution, and of the elements ordained by Him"; (4) "The Historic Episcopate, locally adapted in the methods of its administration to the varying needs of the nations and peoples called of God into the Unity of His Church."

JOHN E. BOOTY

Churches of the Anglican Communion

Church of England
Church of Ireland
Episcopal Church in Scotland
The Church in Wales
Anglican Church of Canada
Episcopal Church (United States)
Church of India, Pakistan, Burma and Sri Lanka
Church of the Province of South Africa
Church of England in Australia and Tasmania
Church of the Province of New Zealand
Church of the Province of the West Indies
Chung Hua Sheng Kung Hui (China)
Nippon Sei Kwai (Japan)
Church of the Province of West Africa
Church of the Province of Central Africa
Church of the Province of East Africa
Church of the Province of Uganda and Rwanda and Burundi
    Episcopal Church of Brazil

Bibliography: McAdoo, H. R., *The Spirit of Anglicanism* (1965); Neill, Stephen, *Anglicanism* (1958).

See also: ENGLAND, THE CHURCH OF

Anglo-Australian Telescope

The Anglo-Australian Telescope, a reflecting telescope with a mirror 3.9 m (153 in) in diameter, is located with other Australian and British instruments at Siding Spring Observatory in the Warrumbungle Range near Coonabarabran, New South Wales, 400 km (250 mi) northwest of Sydney. The observatory, which opened in 1974, is a major astronomical research center in the Southern Hemisphere. It sits at an altitude of 1,160 m (3,800 ft). The United Kingdom Schmidt telescope is a near-twin of the 48-in (122-cm) Schmidt at Palomar Mountain, Calif., and has been used to complete an important reference survey by photographing all the sky that is too far south to be seen from Palomar.

NORMAN SPERLING